Lecture Notes in Computer Science 8514

Commenced Publication in 1973
Founding and Former Series Editors:
Gerhard Goos, Juris Hartmanis, and Jan van Leeuwen

Constantine Stephanidis Margherita Antona (Eds.)

Universal Access in Human-Computer Interaction

Universal Access to Information and Knowledge

8th International Conference, UAHCI 2014
Held as Part of HCI International 2014
Heraklion, Crete, Greece, June 22-27, 2014
Proceedings, Part II

Volume Editors

Constantine Stephanidis
Foundation for Research and Technology - Hellas (FORTH)
Institute of Computer Science
N. Plastira 100, Vassilika Vouton, 70013 Heraklion, Crete, Greece
and University of Crete, Department of Computer Science
Heraklion, Crete, Greece
E-mail: cs@ics.forth.gr

Margherita Antona
Foundation for Research and Technology - Hellas (FORTH)
Institute of Computer Science
N. Plastira 100, Vassilika Vouton, 70013 Heraklion, Crete, Greece
E-mail: antona@ics.forth.gr

ISSN 0302-9743
e-ISSN 1611-3349
ISBN 978-3-319-07439-9
e-ISBN 978-3-319-07440-5
DOI 10.1007/978-3-319-07440-5
Springer Cham Heidelberg New York Dordrecht London

Library of Congress Control Number: 2014939292

LNCS Sublibrary: SL 3 – Information Systems and Application, incl. Internet/Web and HCI

Typesetting: Camera-ready by author, data conversion by Scientific Publishing Services, Chennai, India

Printed on acid-free paper

Springer is part of Springer Science+Business Media (www.springer.com)

Foreword

The 16th International Conference on Human–Computer Interaction, HCI International 2014, was held in Heraklion, Crete, Greece, during June 22–27, 2014, incorporating 14 conferences/thematic areas:

Thematic areas:

- Human–Computer Interaction
- Human Interface and the Management of Information

Affiliated conferences:

- 11th International Conference on Engineering Psychology and Cognitive Ergonomics
- 8th International Conference on Universal Access in Human–Computer Interaction
- 6th International Conference on Virtual, Augmented and Mixed Reality
- 6th International Conference on Cross-Cultural Design
- 6th International Conference on Social Computing and Social Media
- 8th International Conference on Augmented Cognition
- 5th International Conference on Digital Human Modeling and Applications in Health, Safety, Ergonomics and Risk Management
- Third International Conference on Design, User Experience and Usability
- Second International Conference on Distributed, Ambient and Pervasive Interactions
- Second International Conference on Human Aspects of Information Security, Privacy and Trust
- First International Conference on HCI in Business
- First International Conference on Learning and Collaboration Technologies

A total of 4,766 individuals from academia, research institutes, industry, and governmental agencies from 78 countries submitted contributions, and 1,476 papers and 225 posters were included in the proceedings. These papers address the latest research and development efforts and highlight the human aspects of design and use of computing systems. The papers thoroughly cover the entire field of human–computer interaction, addressing major advances in knowledge and effective use of computers in a variety of application areas.

This volume, edited by Constantine Stephanidis and Margherita Antona, contains papers focusing on the thematic area of Universal Access in Human-Computer Interaction, addressing the following major topics:

- Access to mobile interaction
- Access to text, documents, and media

- Access to education and learning
- Access to games and ludic engagement
- Access to culture

The remaining volumes of the HCI International 2014 proceedings are:

- Volume 1, LNCS 8510, Human–Computer Interaction: HCI Theories, Methods and Tools (Part I), edited by Masaaki Kurosu
- Volume 2, LNCS 8511, Human–Computer Interaction: Advanced Interaction Modalities and Techniques (Part II), edited by Masaaki Kurosu
- Volume 3, LNCS 8512, Human–Computer Interaction: Applications and Services (Part III), edited by Masaaki Kurosu
- Volume 4, LNCS 8513, Universal Access in Human–Computer Interaction: Design and Development Methods for Universal Access (Part I), edited by Constantine Stephanidis and Margherita Antona
- Volume 6, LNCS 8515, Universal Access in Human–Computer Interaction: Aging and Assistive Environments (Part III), edited by Constantine Stephanidis and Margherita Antona
- Volume 7, LNCS 8516, Universal Access in Human–Computer Interaction: Design for All and Accessibility Practice (Part IV), edited by Constantine Stephanidis and Margherita Antona
- Volume 8, LNCS 8517, Design, User Experience, and Usability: Theories, Methods and Tools for Designing the User Experience (Part I), edited by Aaron Marcus
- Volume 9, LNCS 8518, Design, User Experience, and Usability: User Experience Design for Diverse Interaction Platforms and Environments (Part II), edited by Aaron Marcus
- Volume 10, LNCS 8519, Design, User Experience, and Usability: User Experience Design for Everyday Life Applications and Services (Part III), edited by Aaron Marcus
- Volume 11, LNCS 8520, Design, User Experience, and Usability: User Experience Design Practice (Part IV), edited by Aaron Marcus
- Volume 12, LNCS 8521, Human Interface and the Management of Information: Information and Knowledge Design and Evaluation (Part I), edited by Sakae Yamamoto
- Volume 13, LNCS 8522, Human Interface and the Management of Information: Information and Knowledge in Applications and Services (Part II), edited by Sakae Yamamoto
- Volume 14, LNCS 8523, Learning and Collaboration Technologies: Designing and Developing Novel Learning Experiences (Part I), edited by Panayiotis Zaphiris and Andri Ioannou
- Volume 15, LNCS 8524, Learning and Collaboration Technologies: Technology-rich Environments for Learning and Collaboration (Part II), edited by Panayiotis Zaphiris and Andri Ioannou
- Volume 16, LNCS 8525, Virtual, Augmented and Mixed Reality: Designing and Developing Virtual and Augmented Environments (Part I), edited by Randall Shumaker and Stephanie Lackey

- Volume 17, LNCS 8526, Virtual, Augmented and Mixed Reality: Applications of Virtual and Augmented Reality (Part II), edited by Randall Shumaker and Stephanie Lackey
- Volume 18, LNCS 8527, HCI in Business, edited by Fiona Fui-Hoon Nah
- Volume 19, LNCS 8528, Cross-Cultural Design, edited by P.L. Patrick Rau
- Volume 20, LNCS 8529, Digital Human Modeling and Applications in Health, Safety, Ergonomics and Risk Management, edited by Vincent G. Duffy
- Volume 21, LNCS 8530, Distributed, Ambient, and Pervasive Interactions, edited by Norbert Streitz and Panos Markopoulos
- Volume 22, LNCS 8531, Social Computing and Social Media, edited by Gabriele Meiselwitz
- Volume 23, LNAI 8532, Engineering Psychology and Cognitive Ergonomics, edited by Don Harris
- Volume 24, LNCS 8533, Human Aspects of Information Security, Privacy and Trust, edited by Theo Tryfonas and Ioannis Askoxylakis
- Volume 25, LNAI 8534, Foundations of Augmented Cognition, edited by Dylan D. Schmorrow and Cali M. Fidopiastis
- Volume 26, CCIS 434, HCI International 2014 Posters Proceedings (Part I), edited by Constantine Stephanidis
- Volume 27, CCIS 435, HCI International 2014 Posters Proceedings (Part II), edited by Constantine Stephanidis

I would like to thank the Program Chairs and the members of the Program Boards of all affiliated conferences and thematic areas, listed below, for their contribution to the highest scientific quality and the overall success of the HCI International 2014 Conference.

This conference could not have been possible without the continuous support and advice of the founding chair and conference scientific advisor, Prof. Gavriel Salvendy, as well as the dedicated work and outstanding efforts of the communications chair and editor of *HCI International News*, Dr. Abbas Moallem.

I would also like to thank for their contribution towards the smooth organization of the HCI International 2014 Conference the members of the Human–Computer Interaction Laboratory of ICS-FORTH, and in particular George Paparoulis, Maria Pitsoulaki, Maria Bouhli, and George Kapnas.

April 2014

Constantine Stephanidis
General Chair, HCI International 2014

Organization

Human–Computer Interaction

Program Chair: Masaaki Kurosu, Japan

Jose Abdelnour-Nocera, UK
Sebastiano Bagnara, Italy
Simone Barbosa, Brazil
Adriana Betiol, Brazil
Simone Borsci, UK
Henry Duh, Australia
Xiaowen Fang, USA
Vicki Hanson, UK
Wonil Hwang, Korea
Minna Isomursu, Finland
Yong Gu Ji, Korea
Anirudha Joshi, India
Esther Jun, USA
Kyungdoh Kim, Korea
Heidi Krömker, Germany
Chen Ling, USA
Chang S. Nam, USA
Naoko Okuizumi, Japan
Philippe Palanque, France
Ling Rothrock, USA
Naoki Sakakibara, Japan
Dominique Scapin, France
Guangfeng Song, USA
Sanjay Tripathi, India
Chui Yin Wong, Malaysia
Toshiki Yamaoka, Japan
Kazuhiko Yamazaki, Japan
Ryoji Yoshitake, Japan

Human Interface and the Management of Information

Program Chair: Sakae Yamamoto, Japan

Alan Chan, Hong Kong
Denis A. Coelho, Portugal
Linda Elliott, USA
Shin'ichi Fukuzumi, Japan
Michitaka Hirose, Japan
Makoto Itoh, Japan
Yen-Yu Kang, Taiwan
Koji Kimita, Japan
Daiji Kobayashi, Japan
Hiroyuki Miki, Japan
Shogo Nishida, Japan
Robert Proctor, USA
Youngho Rhee, Korea
Ryosuke Saga, Japan
Katsunori Shimohara, Japan
Kim-Phuong Vu, USA
Tomio Watanabe, Japan

Engineering Psychology and Cognitive Ergonomics

Program Chair: Don Harris, UK

Guy Andre Boy, USA
Shan Fu, P.R. China
Hung-Sying Jing, Taiwan
Wen-Chin Li, Taiwan
Mark Neerincx, The Netherlands
Jan Noyes, UK
Paul Salmon, Australia
Axel Schulte, Germany
Siraj Shaikh, UK
Sarah Sharples, UK
Anthony Smoker, UK
Neville Stanton, UK
Alex Stedmon, UK
Andrew Thatcher, South Africa

Universal Access in Human–Computer Interaction

Program Chairs: Constantine Stephanidis, Greece, and Margherita Antona, Greece

Julio Abascal, Spain
Gisela Susanne Bahr, USA
João Barroso, Portugal
Margrit Betke, USA
Anthony Brooks, Denmark
Christian Bühler, Germany
Stefan Carmien, Spain
Hua Dong, P.R. China
Carlos Duarte, Portugal
Pier Luigi Emiliani, Italy
Qin Gao, P.R. China
Andrina Granić, Croatia
Andreas Holzinger, Austria
Josette Jones, USA
Simeon Keates, UK
Georgios Kouroupetroglou, Greece
Patrick Langdon, UK
Barbara Leporini, Italy
Eugene Loos, The Netherlands
Ana Isabel Paraguay, Brazil
Helen Petrie, UK
Michael Pieper, Germany
Enrico Pontelli, USA
Jaime Sanchez, Chile
Alberto Sanna, Italy
Anthony Savidis, Greece
Christian Stary, Austria
Hirotada Ueda, Japan
Gerhard Weber, Germany
Harald Weber, Germany

Virtual, Augmented and Mixed Reality

Program Chairs: Randall Shumaker, USA, and Stephanie Lackey, USA

Roland Blach, Germany
Sheryl Brahnam, USA
Juan Cendan, USA
Jessie Chen, USA
Panagiotis D. Kaklis, UK
Hirokazu Kato, Japan
Denis Laurendeau, Canada
Fotis Liarokapis, UK
Michael Macedonia, USA
Gordon Mair, UK

Jose San Martin, Spain
Tabitha Peck, USA
Christian Sandor, Australia
Christopher Stapleton, USA
Gregory Welch, USA

Cross-Cultural Design

Program Chair: P.L. Patrick Rau, P.R. China

Yee-Yin Choong, USA
Paul Fu, USA
Zhiyong Fu, P.R. China
Pin-Chao Liao, P.R. China
Dyi-Yih Michael Lin, Taiwan
Rungtai Lin, Taiwan
Ta-Ping (Robert) Lu, Taiwan
Liang Ma, P.R. China
Alexander Mädche, Germany
Sheau-Farn Max Liang, Taiwan
Katsuhiko Ogawa, Japan
Tom Plocher, USA
Huatong Sun, USA
Emil Tso, P.R. China
Hsiu-Ping Yueh, Taiwan
Liang (Leon) Zeng, USA
Jia Zhou, P.R. China

Online Communities and Social Media

Program Chair: Gabriele Meiselwitz, USA

Leonelo Almeida, Brazil
Chee Siang Ang, UK
Aneesha Bakharia, Australia
Ania Bobrowicz, UK
James Braman, USA
Farzin Deravi, UK
Carsten Kleiner, Germany
Niki Lambropoulos, Greece
Soo Ling Lim, UK
Anthony Norcio, USA
Portia Pusey, USA
Panote Siriaraya, UK
Stefan Stieglitz, Germany
Giovanni Vincenti, USA
Yuanqiong (Kathy) Wang, USA
June Wei, USA
Brian Wentz, USA

Augmented Cognition

Program Chairs: Dylan D. Schmorrow, USA, and Cali M. Fidopiastis, USA

Ahmed Abdelkhalek, USA
Robert Atkinson, USA
Monique Beaudoin, USA
John Blitch, USA
Alenka Brown, USA
Rosario Cannavò, Italy
Joseph Cohn, USA
Andrew J. Cowell, USA
Martha Crosby, USA
Wai-Tat Fu, USA

Rodolphe Gentili, USA
Frederick Gregory, USA
Michael W. Hail, USA
Monte Hancock, USA
Fei Hu, USA
Ion Juvina, USA
Joe Keebler, USA
Philip Mangos, USA
Rao Mannepalli, USA
David Martinez, USA
Yvonne R. Masakowski, USA
Santosh Mathan, USA
Ranjeev Mittu, USA
Keith Niall, USA
Tatana Olson, USA
Debra Patton, USA
June Pilcher, USA
Robinson Pino, USA
Tiffany Poeppelman, USA
Victoria Romero, USA
Amela Sadagic, USA
Anna Skinner, USA
Ann Speed, USA
Robert Sottilare, USA
Peter Walker, USA

Digital Human Modeling and Applications in Health, Safety, Ergonomics and Risk Management

Program Chair: Vincent G. Duffy, USA

Giuseppe Andreoni, Italy
Daniel Carruth, USA
Elsbeth De Korte, The Netherlands
Afzal A. Godil, USA
Ravindra Goonetilleke, Hong Kong
Noriaki Kuwahara, Japan
Kang Li, USA
Zhizhong Li, P.R. China
Tim Marler, USA
Jianwei Niu, P.R. China
Michelle Robertson, USA
Matthias Rötting, Germany
Mao-Jiun Wang, Taiwan
Xuguang Wang, France
James Yang, USA

Design, User Experience, and Usability

Program Chair: Aaron Marcus, USA

Sisira Adikari, Australia
Claire Ancient, USA
Arne Berger, Germany
Jamie Blustein, Canada
Ana Boa-Ventura, USA
Jan Brejcha, Czech Republic
Lorenzo Cantoni, Switzerland
Marc Fabri, UK
Luciane Maria Fadel, Brazil
Tricia Flanagan, Hong Kong
Jorge Frascara, Mexico
Federico Gobbo, Italy
Emilie Gould, USA
Rüdiger Heimgärtner, Germany
Brigitte Herrmann, Germany
Steffen Hess, Germany
Nouf Khashman, Canada
Fabiola Guillermina Noël, Mexico
Francisco Rebelo, Portugal
Kerem Rızvanoğlu, Turkey
Marcelo Soares, Brazil
Carla Spinillo, Brazil

Distributed, Ambient and Pervasive Interactions

Program Chairs: Norbert Streitz, Germany, and Panos Markopoulos, The Netherlands

Juan Carlos Augusto, UK
Jose Bravo, Spain
Adrian Cheok, UK
Boris de Ruyter, The Netherlands
Anind Dey, USA
Dimitris Grammenos, Greece
Nuno Guimaraes, Portugal
Achilles Kameas, Greece
Javed Vassilis Khan, The Netherlands
Shin'ichi Konomi, Japan
Carsten Magerkurth, Switzerland
Ingrid Mulder, The Netherlands
Anton Nijholt, The Netherlands
Fabio Paternó, Italy
Carsten Röcker, Germany
Teresa Romao, Portugal
Albert Ali Salah, Turkey
Manfred Tscheligi, Austria
Reiner Wichert, Germany
Woontack Woo, Korea
Xenophon Zabulis, Greece

Human Aspects of Information Security, Privacy and Trust

Program Chairs: Theo Tryfonas, UK, and Ioannis Askoxylakis, Greece

Claudio Agostino Ardagna, Italy
Zinaida Benenson, Germany
Daniele Catteddu, Italy
Raoul Chiesa, Italy
Bryan Cline, USA
Sadie Creese, UK
Jorge Cuellar, Germany
Marc Dacier, USA
Dieter Gollmann, Germany
Kirstie Hawkey, Canada
Jaap-Henk Hoepman, The Netherlands
Cagatay Karabat, Turkey
Angelos Keromytis, USA
Ayako Komatsu, Japan
Ronald Leenes, The Netherlands
Javier Lopez, Spain
Steve Marsh, Canada
Gregorio Martinez, Spain
Emilio Mordini, Italy
Yuko Murayama, Japan
Masakatsu Nishigaki, Japan
Aljosa Pasic, Spain
Milan Petković, The Netherlands
Joachim Posegga, Germany
Jean-Jacques Quisquater, Belgium
Damien Sauveron, France
George Spanoudakis, UK
Kerry-Lynn Thomson, South Africa
Julien Touzeau, France
Theo Tryfonas, UK
João Vilela, Portugal
Claire Vishik, UK
Melanie Volkamer, Germany

HCI in Business

Program Chair: Fiona Fui-Hoon Nah, USA

Andreas Auinger, Austria
Michel Avital, Denmark
Traci Carte, USA
Hock Chuan Chan, Singapore
Constantinos Coursaris, USA
Soussan Djamasbi, USA
Brenda Eschenbrenner, USA
Nobuyuki Fukawa, USA
Khaled Hassanein, Canada
Milena Head, Canada
Susanna (Shuk Ying) Ho, Australia
Jack Zhenhui Jiang, Singapore
Jinwoo Kim, Korea
Zoonky Lee, Korea
Honglei Li, UK
Nicholas Lockwood, USA
Eleanor T. Loiacono, USA
Mei Lu, USA
Scott McCoy, USA
Brian Mennecke, USA
Robin Poston, USA
Lingyun Qiu, P.R. China
Rene Riedl, Austria
Matti Rossi, Finland
April Savoy, USA
Shu Schiller, USA
Hong Sheng, USA
Choon Ling Sia, Hong Kong
Chee-Wee Tan, Denmark
Chuan Hoo Tan, Hong Kong
Noam Tractinsky, Israel
Horst Treiblmaier, Austria
Virpi Tuunainen, Finland
Dezhi Wu, USA
I-Chin Wu, Taiwan

Learning and Collaboration Technologies

Program Chairs: Panayiotis Zaphiris, Cyprus, and Andri Ioannou, Cyprus

Ruthi Aladjem, Israel
Abdulaziz Aldaej, UK
John M. Carroll, USA
Maka Eradze, Estonia
Mikhail Fominykh, Norway
Denis Gillet, Switzerland
Mustafa Murat Inceoglu, Turkey
Pernilla Josefsson, Sweden
Marie Joubert, UK
Sauli Kiviranta, Finland
Tomaž Klobučar, Slovenia
Elena Kyza, Cyprus
Maarten de Laat, The Netherlands
David Lamas, Estonia
Edmund Laugasson, Estonia
Ana Loureiro, Portugal
Katherine Maillet, France
Nadia Pantidi, UK
Antigoni Parmaxi, Cyprus
Borzoo Pourabdollahian, Italy
Janet C. Read, UK
Christophe Reffay, France
Nicos Souleles, Cyprus
Ana Luísa Torres, Portugal
Stefan Trausan-Matu, Romania
Aimilia Tzanavari, Cyprus
Johnny Yuen, Hong Kong
Carmen Zahn, Switzerland

External Reviewers

Ilia Adami, Greece
Iosif Klironomos, Greece
Maria Korozi, Greece
Vassilis Kouroumalis, Greece
Asterios Leonidis, Greece
George Margetis, Greece
Stavroula Ntoa, Greece
Nikolaos Partarakis, Greece

HCI International 2015

The 15th International Conference on Human–Computer Interaction, HCI International 2015, will be held jointly with the affiliated conferences in Los Angeles, CA, USA, in the Westin Bonaventure Hotel, August 2–7, 2015. It will cover a broad spectrum of themes related to HCI, including theoretical issues, methods, tools, processes, and case studies in HCI design, as well as novel interaction techniques, interfaces, and applications. The proceedings will be published by Springer. More information will be available on the conference website: http://www.hcii2015.org/

General Chair
Professor Constantine Stephanidis
University of Crete and ICS-FORTH
Heraklion, Crete, Greece
E-mail: cs@ics.forth.gr

Table of Contents – Part II

Access to Mobile Interaction

Access to Text, Documents and Media

Access to Education and Learning

Access to Games and Ludic Engagement

Access to Culture

Access to Mobile Interaction

Effects of User Age on Smartphone and Tablet Use, Measured with an Eye-Tracker via Fixation Duration, Scan-Path Duration, and Saccades Proportion

Suleyman Al-Showarah, Naseer AL-Jawad, and Harin Sellahewa

Applied Computing Department, The University of Buckingham, Buckingham, UK
{suleyman.al-showarah, naseer.al-jawad,harin.sellahewa}@buckingham.ac.uk

Abstract. The design of user interfaces plays an important role in human computer interaction, especially for smartphones and tablet devices. It is very important to consider the interface design of smartphones for elderly people in order for them to benefit from the variety applications on such devices. The aim of this study is to investigate the effects of user age as well as screen size on smartphone/tablet use. We evaluated the usability of smartphone interfaces for three different age groups: elderly age group (60+ years), middle age group (40-59 years) and younger age group (20-39 years). The evaluation is performed using three different screen sizes of smartphone and tablet devices: 3.2", 7", and 10.1" respectively. An eye-tracker device was employed to obtain three metrics: fixation duration, scan-path duration, and saccades amplitude. Two hypothesis were considered. First, elderly users will have both local and global processing diffieculties on smartphone/tablet use than other age groups. Second, all user age groups will be influnced by screen sizes; small screen size will have smaller saccades proportion indicating uneasy interface broswing compared to large screen size. All these results have been statistically evaluated using 2-way ANOVA.

Keywords: Smartphone interfaces, elderly people, eye tracking, mobile computing, human computer interaction, interfaces evaluation, and usability of smart phone.

1 Introduction

Smartphones and tablets increasingly play an important role in many aspects of our daily lives. These devices, together with the hundreds of thousands of 'apps' that are available to download onto these devices, are widely used in educational, social, cultural, communication, entertainment, and health related activities. Whilst these devices are commonly owned and used by relatively young users, they could be an integral part of managing the ever increasing ageing population. Therefore, it is important to understand the usability issues of smartphones faced by elderly people and design devices and software applications that are easily accessible and useable by elderly people [4]. The importance of research in this area has been highlighted in previous studies such as in [6], [15]. This paper investigates effects of age on smartphone usability.

C. Stephanidis and M. Antona (Eds.): UAHCI/HCII 2014, Part II, LNCS 8514, pp. 3–14, 2014.

Few studies have investigated the effects of age on the usability of cell phones [9]. However much has changed in both hardware and applications since these works; changes are introduced at a rapid pace and there is a variety of device manufactures and operating system providers. In order to evaluate user interfaces of smartphones, we need to look at the way the participants interact with these devices. Aspects of interactions to consider includes the way in which users interprets screen components (e.g., icons, widgets, shortcuts, etc.); the way users interact with screen components by gestures (e.g., finger based touch) and by conversational speech [14].

Eye movement analysis has been used in different fields and applications such as in marketing, advertising and user-interface evaluation [3], [19]. Eye movement metrics such as fixation points, durations and scan paths are used widely in studies of Human Computer Interaction (HCI). These metrics give indications related to search efficiency/inefficiency and cognitive processing ease/difficulty [8].

In this paper, we investigated the effects of age and screen size on the usability of smartphones and tablet devices. Essentially, we will examine – based on a number of eye movement metrics -- two hypotheses on the effects of age on smartphone usability. First, previous works have shown that elderly people have difficulties in using technologies [11]. This leads us to predict that elderly users of smartphones and tablet devices will exhibit longer fixation durations (FD) for local processing tasks, and longer scan path durations (SPD) for global processing tasks than users of other age groups (e.g., middle and younger ages). This reflects the cognitive ability of elderly users in browsing content on smartphone interfaces/applications. Second: as the performance task of all age groups will be influnced by screen sizes [7]. Small screen size will have smaller saccades proportion than other screen sizes for complex design of interfaces, especially for elderly users.

We used an eye-tracker to record participants' eye movements and fixations during a number of search tasks on three different smartphone/tablet sizes. We will demonstrate that there are significant differences between all age groups in browsing smartphone interfaces. Elderly users will be shown to have less cognitive ability in browsing smartphones interfaces compared to younger age groups.

Also, experiments will show that small screen size will have significantly smaller saccades proportion compared to larger screen sizes of tabelts indicating that the usability in browsing smartphone/tablet interfaces and applications difficult for all age groups, more so for elderly users.

The rest of the paper is organized as follows. Related studies on the effects age on technology are discussed in section 2. Section 3 explains the methodology and procedures relevant to this study, followed by a discussion of experimental results in section 4. Our conclusions and future work are presented in section 5.

2 Related Work

Most existing studies have evaluated the effect of age on PCs. Fukuda et al. conducted a study using an eye tracker to establish the difficulties between elderly people and younger people when browsing web pages on PCs. The results revealed that elderly people have difficulties in using online timetables using PC compared with younger people. The visual perception of elderly people was less efficient than younger age group when web browsing. Moreover elderly participants required longer time than the younger ones to accomplish the given tasks [11].

Iwase et al. studied the ability of elderly users to use and accept new designs [13]. They conducted the study using a PC mouse for 49 participants that included participants from three different age groups. The results revealed that the mouse pointing time was relatively longer for the elderly group compared with other two age groups, and the error rate increased when distance to the target increases and also when the target size is decreased.

Findlater et al. [10] conducted a study on 20 elderly participants (ages between 61 and 86 years) and 20 adult participants (ages from 19 to 51 years). They used Apple iPads and Apple laptops (Mac OS X 10.7) to examine five tasks: pointing, dragging, crossing, and steering. On the touch screen, they also examined pinch-to-zoom gestures. Results showed that elderly people were slower in using both touch screen and mouse movements in general. Also, the error rate decreased on the touch screen for both age groups. In addition steering was the most difficult task when using a mouse, while dragging was the slowest gesture on the touch screen.

Few studies have evaluated the effect of age on usability of smart/mobile devices. Rogers et al. in [21] conducted a study to evaluate how task demands and user age influenced task performance on touch screen devices and non-touch screen devices (rotary encoder). Their study involved 40 younger (18–28 years) and 40 middle-aged to older adults (i.e. 51–65 years). They used control tasks such as sliders (scrolling), up/down buttons, list boxes, and text boxes. They found that older adults were slower than younger adults on pointing and sliding tasks on a touch screen. Moreover, they found small button sizes were particularly problematic for the older adults. Al-Showarah et al. [1] conducted study to examine eye movements of elderly and young participants to find dissimilarities in browsing on different smartphone/tablet applications. Their results found that elderly participants have high dissimilarity than younger ages. In other words, elderly participants were less efficient in browsing smartphone applications/interfaces than younger participants. They also reported that scan paths are stimulus-driven than smartphone screen size driven. Christian et al. [7] conducted a study on three different smartphone display sizes (small: 1.8 inch, medium: 3.6 inch display, large: 7.2 inch) for 36 participants (average age of younger participants were 26 years, and the average age of elderly participants were: 63 years). The experiment was based on finger gestures on touch screens. The results revealed a clear effect of display size on task performance, where the performance was better on the larger display size. Moreover elderly participants were slower in performing tasks than younger participants.

3 The Study Methodology and Procedure

This section describes apparatuses, experiment procedures, stimuli, participants, and dependent variables.

3.1 Apparatuses

Eye-tracker. Eyelink-1000 desktop device amounted with IR illuminator was used to track and record eye movements. The illuminator is used to generate reflection patterns on the user's cornea [17], [22]. A chinrest was used to fix both the chin and forehead of participants at a distance of 50-55 cm. A distance as recommended from where the participant's eyes will typically is, to the illuminator and eye camera facing the participant. Experiment interfaces (i.e., Smartphone screenshots) were prepared and displayed on the eye-tracker device using Experiment Builder Software. The results of metrics were obtained using Data Viewer [22].

Smartphones. Three mobile devices were used to conduct the experiments: 1) HTC wildfire smartphone, dimensions 106.8 x 60.4 x 12 mm, screen resolution: 240 x 320 pixels, with screen size of 3.2 inches; 2) Samsung Galaxy Tab 2, dimensions 193.7 x 122.4 x 10.5 mm, screen resolution 1024 x 600 pixels, with screen size 7 inches; and 3) Samsung Galaxy Note 10.1 inches, dimensions 262 x 180 x 8.9 mm with a screen resolution of 1280 x 800 pixels.

The smartphones/tablets were selected to represent three screen sizes. Small size represents typical smart phones, which have screen sizes between 3 and 5.5 inches. Medium size represents mini tablets, which are typically 7 inches. Large size represents full-size tablet devices which are typically around 10 inches. We chose 3.2 inches to represent small screen sizes, 7 inches to represent medium screen sizes, and 10.1 inches to represent large screen sizes.

3.2 Participants

The participants of the experiment were selected from different age groups and they include university students, university staff, and people from the local community. A total of 104 participants participated in the study and they were grouped into three age groups: the elderly group (EG), which consists of 22 participants aged 60 and over; the middle-age group (MG) consisting 31 participants aged 40-59; and the young group (YG), which consists of the remaining 51 participants aged 20-39. In terms of selecting the elderly age group, there are no agreed definitions on the age range in the literature. However, the United Nations considers elderly population to be those 60+ years of age [18].

3.3 Experiments Structure

Each smartphone size has two experiments: EXP1 and EXP2. Each experiment is conducted using participants from three age groups. A participant will be involved in only one smartphone size and in one experiment to avoid any influence on the participant's performance. Fig. 1 illustrates how experiments and different groups of participants are organized.

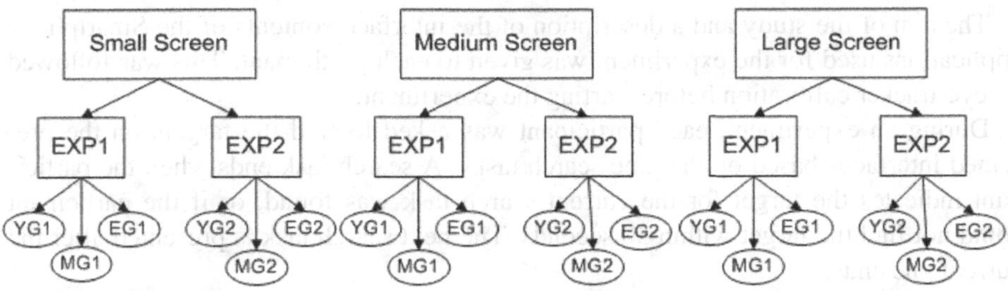

Fig. 1. Organization of smartphone experiments and age groups

3.4 Stimuli

The experiment is composed of nine smartphone applications; each of these applications has two search tasks as shown in Table 1, which forms the two experiment groups (i.e., EXP1 and EXP2) described earlier in Fig. 1. A screenshot of the smartphone application relevant to the search task is displayed on a computer screen that is connected to the eye-tracker.

Table 1. Smartphone applications and questions for experiment one and experiment two

App no	Apps	EXP1	EXP2
1	Skype contact list	Locate the user who is not online.	Locate the image of David Albert.
2	Skype Calling screen	Locate the Backspace button.	Locate the Numbers Field.
3	Skype Profile screen	Locate the button used to change your current status to be visible	Locate the account holder's Picture.
4	Facebook account holder profile	Locate the number of incoming messages	Locate the account holder's name?
5	Yahoo Email folder list	Locate the number of deleted messages.	Locate the number of new messages?
6	Gallery screen	Locate the delete image button?	Locate the Share photo button?
7	Alarm screen	Locate the active alarm?	Locate the button to add a new alarm?
8	Skype Main Screen	Locate the button that will show a list of contacts?	Locate the 'exit' button?
9	Settings screen	Locate the button to view Wireless and networks settings?	Locate the button that lets you change Sound settings.

3.5 Experimental Procedure

Participants were asked to perform the search tasks described in either EXP1 or EXP2 based on the Smartphone application interfaces of a selected screen-size. Each search task was designed carefully and has a specific answer; this is based on Broder's recommendation in terms of finding specific information on a web page [5]. Each participant was tested individually in a lab environment set for conducting the experiment.

The aim of the study and a description of the interface contents of the Smartphone applications used for the experiment was given to each participant. This was followed by eye-tracker calibration before starting the experiment.

During an experiment, each participant was asked to find the targets on the presented interfaces based on the nine search tasks. A search task ends when the participant indicates the target for the current search task was found, or if the participant could not find the target within 30 seconds. The next search task is presented after the current one ends.

3.6 Eye-Tracking Metrics

We used the following four eye-tracking metrics as dependent variables to explore the determinants of visual behavior on smart device interface: 1) Fixation Duration; 2) Saccade Amplitude; 3) Scan-Path Duration; and 4) Saccades Proportion.

Fixation Duration (FD): measures the amount of time the eyes are focused on a particular point on the screen (i.e., local process) [8]. A longer fixation duration reflects the participant's difficulties in locating a given target in the local process [2], [11-12] [20]. FD is measured in milliseconds.

Saccade Amplitude (SA): saccades occur when the eye moves from one fixation to the next fixation [8], [20]. Large length of saccade amplitude gives more meaningful cues and less task difficulty [12]. SA is measured in terms of visual angle degree.

Scan-Path Duration (SPD): a scan-path is a sequence of all fixations and saccades across a visual display [8], [20]. SPD measures global processing of interfaces, where longer SPD indicates less efficient scanning and browsing [2], [12], [17]. SPD is measured in milliseconds.

Fig. 2. Visual output of eye-tracking metrics. The circles are tagged by its fixation time in milliseconds, saccades amplitude is represented by the arrows between fixations.

Saccades Proportion (SP): is a measurement derived from the metrics above - SP is the total length of SA divided by SPD. A larger SP indicates more meaningful search and efficient browsing. Saccades proportion is used to test the effects of screen sizes on browsing efficiency and application usability for all age groups.

Fig. 2 displays an example of FD, SPD, and SA metrics as produced by the eye-tracker software tool.

We calculated the average FD, SPA, SPD and SA of each participant (based on non-erroneous search tasks of the 9 search tasks) [7]. A two-way ANOVA test was used to provide us with the average metrics for each age group with a Standard Deviation (STD), and Alpha (α). In ANOVA, we used $\alpha < 0.05$, which indicates the confidence level between the tested means, and gives strong evidence against null hypotheses.

4 Experimental Results and Discussions

We evaluated age groups' effect on each of the three screen sizes using fixation duration and scan-path duration data. Moreover, saccades proportion data were used to find the influence of screen size on all three age groups.

4.1 Fixation Duration (FD) Results

Average fixation durations for all three screen sizes are shown in Table 2 and Table 3. The elderly age group took 2922.47 ms on average (across all screen sizes) to complete an experiment, whilst it took 2375.94 ms and 1686.45 ms respectively for the medium and young age groups. The results show a significantly longer fixation duration for elderly participants when compared to younger participants (i.e. $\alpha = 0.000$), and middle age participants (i.e. $\alpha = 0.019$). Moreover, FD of the middle-age group is significantly longer than that of the younger-age group. These results support our first hypothesis; elderly users will exhibit difficulties in using smartphones. Also, longer FDs of the EG indicates their difficulties in local processing.

Fig. 3, Fig. 4, and Fig. 5 show the results of the two experiments for small, medium and large screen sizes respectively and they demonstrate effects of age on smartphone usability measured in terms of FD. Our findings are in line with previous works on the effects of age on technology where it has been shown that in general, elderly people are less efficient when using technology [7], [10], [11], [13], and [21].

4.2 Scan-Path Duration (SPD) Results

Scan-path duration results for all three screen sizes are shown in Table 2, and Table 3. Fig. 3, Fig. 4, and Fig. 5 show results for each screen size. As expected, the elderly group have significantly longer SPD compared to the younger age group for experiments on each of all three screen sizes. Moreover, the middle-age group has a significantly longer SPD than the younger age group. However, there is no significant difference between SPDs of elderly and middle age groups (i.e. $\alpha = 0.182$).

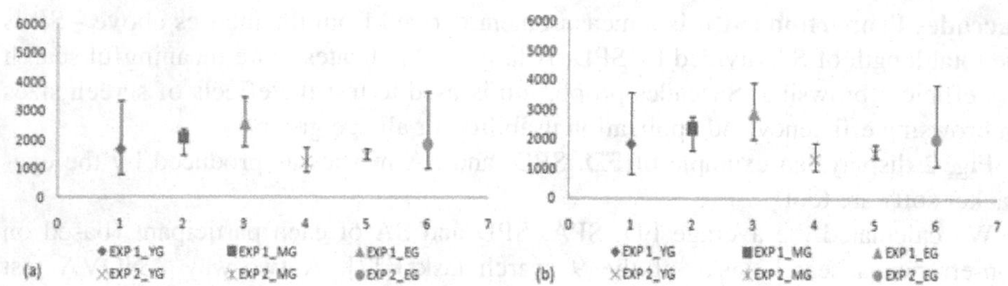

Fig. 3. Eye-tracking metrics for small screen size. (a) Mean FD, and (b) Mean SPD, in millisecond.

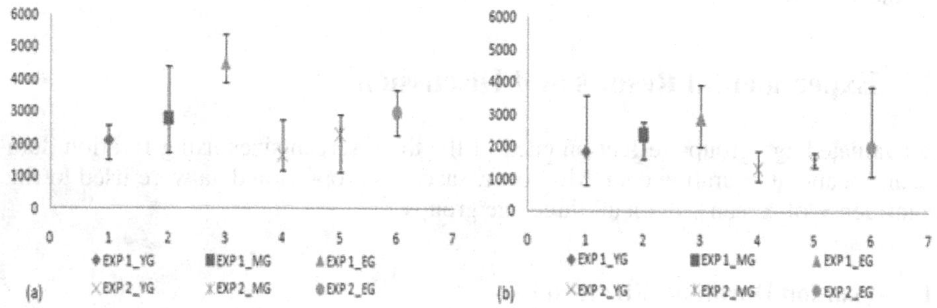

Fig. 4. Eye-tracking metrics for medium screen size. (a) Mean FD, and (b) Mean SPD, in millisecond.

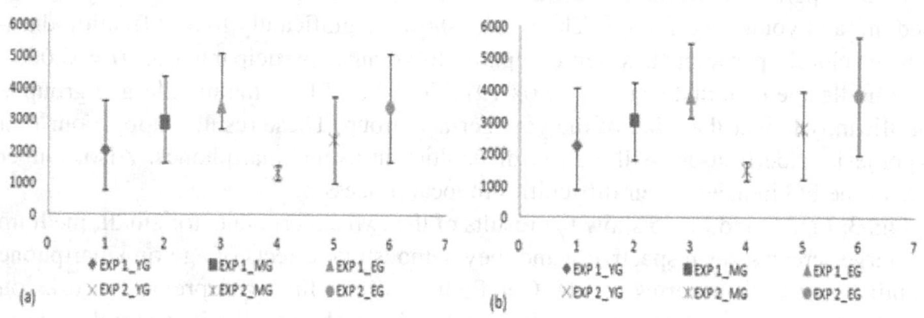

Fig. 5. Eye-tracking metrics for large screen size. (a) Mean FD, and (b) Mean SPD, in millisecond.

Table 2. Mean and STD of FDs and SPDs across all three screen sizes for each age group when $\alpha < 0.05$

Age Group/ Metrics	YG mean	YG STD	MG mean	MG STD	EG mean	EG STD
FD	1686 ↓	701.47	2376	857.84	2922 ↑	1267.19
SPD	1884 ↓	774.04	2810	973.34	3172 ↑	1428.21

Table 3. Means all metrics: Fixation Durations, Scan-Path Durations

Age Group	Small Screen				Medium Screen				Large Screen			
	FD		SPD		FD		SPD		FD		SPD	
	mean	STD	mean	STD	mean	STD	Mean	STD	mean	STD	mean	STD
EG	2067 ↑	922	2152	1020	3615 ↑	1009	3401 ↑	1404	3397 ↑	1380	3812 ↑	1460
MG	1825	458	2325	768	2542	770	3142	937	2607	1096	2927	1097
YG	1467 ↓	701	1604	710	1891 ↓	569	2167 ↓	686	1738 ↓	777	1949 ↓	851

Scan-path duration is used as a metric to discover if elderly users find difficulties in processing global information. The results of small, medium and large screen sizes demonstrate that elderly users find it difficult to process global information on smartphone interfaces.

These results support our first hypothesis; elderly users will exhibit difficulties in processing local and global information on smartphone applications. These results concur with previous works as highlighted in Sec. 4.1.

4.3 Effect of Screen Size on Smartphone Usability

The results in Table 4 and Table 5 show the effect of smartphone screen size, measured by saccades proportion, on three age groups. Note that larger values of SPs indicates better usability of smartphone interfaces, easier browsing and more meaningful cues [12]. As expected in our second hypothesis, screen size has had an effect on the usability of smartphones by users of all age groups, especially elderly users.

The average SP on small screens is smaller than medium and large screen sizes. There is no significant difference between the SPs of small and medium screen sizes (i.e., $\alpha = 0.981$). But there is a significant difference between the SPs of small and large screen sizes, and between medium and large screen sizes (i.e., $\alpha = 0.000$). These observations indicate that large screen size has had a better effect on the usability of smartphones.

However the average experience of participant in using smartphones who were involved in small screen size was larger than middle and large screen sizes; the small screen size still has smaller saccades proportion for difficult use. The average experience in small, medium, and large screen sizes are: (1.14 years), (0.82 years) and (0.76 years) respectively as shown in Fig. 6.

To the best of our knowledge, we have not come across a research study conducted to analyze the effects of smartphone screen size on elderly users based on saccades proportion captured using an eye tracker.

The average SP for elderly (across all screen sizes) is smaller than middle and younger age groups. There is a significant difference between the SPs of younger and middle ages (i.e., $\alpha = 0.000$). Similarly, there is a significant difference between the SPs of younger ages and elderly ages, and between middle ages and elderly ages (i.e., $\alpha = 0.008$). This further indicates that users in the elderly age group find smartphones/tablets less useable than their counterparts in younger age groups.

When compared with other studies that used different tools and metrics, our findings are in line with works such as in [7] that elderly users were influnced in their performance to be less on small screen size than larger screen sizes

Table 4. Mean saccades propotions of three screen sizes. significants differences for means of screen sizes when (α< 0.05).

Metrics/Screen Sizes	Small Mean	STD	Medium Mean	STD	Large mean	STD
Saccades Proportion	1.219 ↓	0.303	1.221	0.395	1.584 ↑	0.669

Table 5. Mean of saccades proportion for three age groups. Significant differences between means of age groups are (α < 0.05).

Age Group	YG mean	STD	MG mean	STD	EG mean	STD
Saccades Proportion	1.65 ↑	0.493	1.15	0.217	0.893 ↓	0.305

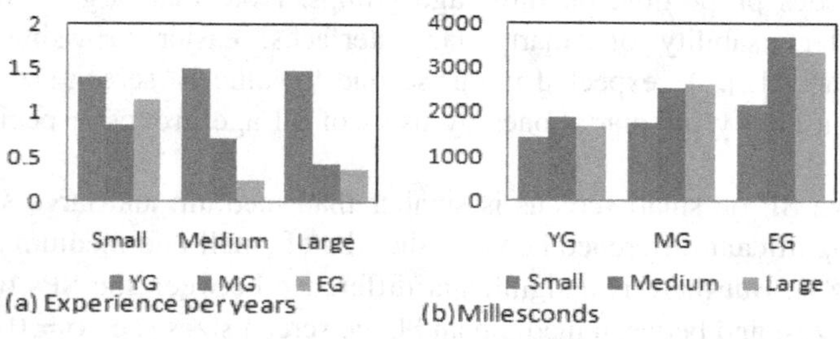

Fig. 6. (a) Participants' experience in using smartphone/tablets (b) Mean FD for three age groups and three smartphone screen sizes

5 Conclusions and Future Work

In this study we analyzed the effects of age on smartphone and tablet use. Also, we investigated if screen size has an effect on smartphone/tablet usability. Experiments were conducted on three screen sizes using participants of three different age groups. An eye-tracker was used to measure fixation, scan paths and saccades.

Elderly people were less efficient and have less cognitive ability in browsing smartphone interfaces. They exhibited more difficulties in processing information at both local and global level on smartphones across all screen sizes than middle and younger age groups. The results of saccades proportion indicated that the usability in browsing smartphone/tablet interfaces and applications on a small screen size is difficult for all age groups – more so for elderly user group – compared to larger (i.e., tablet size) screen sizes.

In general, the results revealed a possible relationship between getting older with less experience in using smartphones and the complexity of interface design with smaller screen sizes of smartphone for elderly users.

In future work, we will analyze the influence of age and screen size on the accuracy and efficiency of gestures on smartphones.

Acknowledgments. The authors would like to thank Dr David Windridge from University of Surrey, UK, for lending the eye tracker machine to collect data for this study, and all participants of the experiments. Also, they would like to thank the University of Buckingham's PGRCF grant for part sponsoring this research.

References

1. Al-Showarah, S., Al-Jawad, N., Sellahewa, H.: Examining eye-tracker scan paths for elderly people using smart phones, York Doctoral Symbosium (YDS), the paper has been published as a York Computer Science technical report. University of York, UK (2013)
2. Al-Wabil, A.: The Effect of Dyslexia on Web Navigation, City University London, UK (2009)
3. Andrienko, G., Andrienko, N., Burch, M., Weiskopf, D.: Visual Analytics Methodology for Eye Movement Studies. IEEE Transactions on Visualization and Computer Graphics 18(12), 2889–2898 (2012)
4. Balakrishnan, S., Salim, S., Hong, J.L.: User Centered Design Approach for Elderly People in Using Website, pp. 382–387 (2012)
5. Broder, A.: A taxonomy of web search, pp. 3–10 (2002)
6. Caprani, N., O'Connor, N.E., Gurrin, C.: Touch screens for the older user (2012)
7. Stößel, C., Wandke, H., Blessing, L.: Gestural interfaces for elderly users: Help or hindrance? In: Kopp, S., Wachsmuth, I. (eds.) GW 2009. LNCS, vol. 5934, pp. 269–280. Springer, Heidelberg (2010)
8. Cooke, L.: Is Eye Tracking the Next Step in Usability Testing? p. 7. IEEE (2006) 0-7803-9778-9/06/$20.00
9. Dongfang, Z., Qiang, S.: A discussion based on a design of cell phones usability by the elderly in China, pp. 1385–1389 (2009)
10. Findlater, L., et al.: Age-related differences in performance with touchscreens compared to traditional mouse input, pp. 343–346 (2013)
11. Fukuda, R., Bubb, H.: Eye tracking study on Web-use: Comparison between younger and elderly users in case of search task with electronic timetable service, p. 27 (December 2010)
12. Goldberg, J.H., et al.: Eye tracking in web search tasks: design implications, pp. 51–58 (2002)

13. Iwase, H., Murata, A.: Comparison of mouse performance between young and elderly - basic study for designing mouse proper for elderly, pp. 246–251 (2002)
14. Jacob, R.J.: Eye Tracking in Advanced Interface Design, p. 53 (2006)
15. Kim, H.-J., Heo, J., Shim, J., Kim, M.-Y., Park, S., Park, S.-H.: Contextual Research on Elderly Users' Needs for Developing Universal Design Mobile Phone. In: Stephanidis, C. (ed.) HCI 2007. LNCS, vol. 4554, pp. 950–959. Springer, Heidelberg (2007)
16. Miyoshi, T., Murata, A.: Usability of input device using eye tracker on button size, distance between targets and direction of movement, vol.1, pp. 227–232 (2001)
17. Nettleton, D., Gonzalez-Caro, C.: Analysis of User Behavior for Web Search Success Using Eye Tracker Data, pp. 57–63 (2012)
18. Organization, W.H., et al.: Definition of an older or elderly person. Health statistics and health information systems (2010), `http://www.who.int/healthinfo/survey/ageingdefnolder/en/index.html` (accessed June 21, 2012)
19. Poole, A., Ball, L.J.: Eye Tracking in Human-Computer Interaction and Usability Research: Current Status and Future Prospects (2004)
20. Rayner, K.: Eye movements in reading and information processing: 20 years of research. Psychological bulletin 124(3), 372 (1998)
21. Rogers, W.A., Fisk, A.D., McLaughlin, A.C., Pak, R.: Touch a screen or turn a knob: Choosing the best device for the job. Human Factors: The Journal of the Human Factors and Ergonomics Society 47(2), 271–288 (2005)
22. SR_Research.Ltd., EyeLink? 1000 Installation Guide Tower, Desktop, LCD Arm, Primate, and Long Range Mounts Remote, Hz and Fiber Optic Camera Upgrades (2010)

LifeSpeeder
A Web and Mobile Platform for Events Location

Pedro J.S. Cardoso[1], Jânio Monteiro[1,2], José dos Santos[1], Natália Baeza[1], and Sérgio Tarazona[1]

[1] Institute of Engineering (ISE), University of Algarve, 8005-139 Faro, Portugal
{jmmontei,pcardoso}@ualg.pt
[2] INOV, Lisbon, Portugal

Abstract The use of smartphones and tablets as become almost banal in these days. Smartphones, besides serving their main purpose of making and receiving calls, come to be one of the main equipments to obtain information from the Internet, using the commonly installed browsers or through the use of dedicated applications. Furthermore, several other devices are also very frequent to the majority of the modern smartphones and tablets in the market (e.g., GPS – Global Positioning System). This devices give the current systems a very high potential of usage.

One example of applicability, comes from the wish to find and navigate to events or activities which are or will soon be occurring near the user. The LifeSpeeder platform is one of the first applications in the mobile equipment market of applications which take into consideration exactly what we have just outlined, i.e., a mobile and desktop application which allows the users to locate events according with their preferences and to get help navigating to them. In this paper we briefly describe the LifeSpeeder's front and back-end.

Keywords: Geographic and Temporal Location of Events, Android, NoSQL Databases.

1 Introduction

The growing usage of Information and Communication Technologies has recently been followed by a significant increment on the number of heterogeneous terminals that are used to access the Internet. Such terminals are currently being used in a personalized and mobile way, integrating sensors and global positioning receivers with an ubiquitous Internet access. In this field, there is a shift from location agnostic web content retrieve, to a new type of applications that take into consideration users preferences and their location to identify which data is more relevant to them.

Such shift in Internet usage gains a particular relevance in the case of events location. Information about events, like concerts or sport competitions, is by its nature associated with one or more sites and occur in one or more moments in time, after which it tends to be irrelevant. The importance of the information is

C. Stephanidis and M. Antona (Eds.): UAHCI/HCII 2014, Part II, LNCS 8514, pp. 15–25, 2014.

also very much dependent on the users preferences. In this field while numerous sites are specialized in some set of event types, the information they have tend to be sparsely distributed and do not automatically associated with user preferences and location. Also users tend to search and select which events to attend within hours or days before its occurrence, which requires a solution on time for their requests.

For this purpose, some applications are already available in the market. For example, the *Scoutmob* Android app [1] is a mobile guide to local deals, events, restaurants in some US cities. The *Eventbrite* Android app [2] allows to create, promote and manage events. Some cities or regions have also dedicated applications [3, 4]. The *Where To Go? GPS POI Finder* [5] provides turn-by-turn directions to the chosen destination, which include a dozen of categories. However, as far as we know none of them includes in a single application all the mentioned features, location and navigation to events with multilingual support and responding to the users preferences.

In response to the above mentioned requirements (e.g., spatially and temporally locate events according with the users preferences and navigation to them), in this paper we present the LifeSpeeder platform which combines into a web and a mobile application interfaces an event driven computational core to the localization of events. In other words, using a mobile device with an Internet connection, users are able to quickly and easily obtain lists of events that are going to happen near them or at some other temporal and spacial location. Then the mobile application calls an external application to navigate to the events. In the back-end a MongoDB database stores the data providing the support for an efficient and relatively easy implementation of the multilingual and the geolocation mechanisms [6].

The remaining document is structured as follows. The second section describes the front-end of the LifeSpeeder platform. Section 3 presents resumed details about the LifeSpeeder back-end, namely some of the used technologies. Conclusions and future work are presented in the fourth and final section.

2 Lifespeeder's Frontend

The LifeSpeeder project consists on the development of a platform to manage, monitor and locate events in a simple and fast way. The motivations behind the developed work starts at the fact that we are located in one of the touristic regions of Portugal. Mostly during the summer season, the Algarve's region is replete with many events and tourists that do not know well the regions, but want to get the best experience possible. Furthermore, many people decide to spend a few days in the region on the off-peak time, tacking advantage of the weather conditions and lower prices of the flights, hotels, golf courses and other infrastructures.

Although the initial idea was explored taking into consideration specially the touristic case, we came to the conclusion that most of the times the majority of the residents also don't have knowledge about the region events, since the corresponding ads do not exist, have a small regional spread, or are scattered in different locations.

Unquestionably, the described problems are common to the large majority of the touristic regions and to day-to-day situations where dedicated platforms do not exist, where the information is scattered or where the information is relatively limited.

Taking advantage of various information technologies currently available, the LifeSpeeder platform presents a tool that can assist the users in the search for such events. The LifeSpeeder platform consists of: (a) a web application, where in addition to the search for events, the registered users can post their own events; and (b) A mobile application, implemented for the Android operating system devices, which implements the search for near (geographically and temporally speaking) events and the GPS navigation to them (using an external application).

The events/activities information, with all the necessary details, are gathered in one information system, facilitating the location according with the interest of the user, avoiding trials at multiple sites on the Web. Further details about the information system are presented in Section 3.

Furthermore, the platform offers multilingual supports and advanced search options. In other words, searches on the platform goes beyond the more classic searches since it allows the user to set its preferences, filtering and customizing the results of those queries. For example, user preferences can be based on a particular type of event (e.g., sports) or in a specific subcategory of event (e.g., football), can include parameters related to distance between the user and the event, date/time, place and language, among others.

Figure 1 sketches a global vision of the LifeSpeeder platform, where multiple devices (PC, tablets, smartphones, etc) connect to the LifeSpeeder information system, retrieving and sharing information from it. The next sections will describe in more detail the mobile and the web application.

2.1 Mobile Application

The growth of the mobile technologies has provided a wide variety of options and therefore its selection is of great importance. Among them, and in terms of mobile operating systems, Android OS is currently the most common operating system for smartphones, surpassing 80% market share in the third quarter of 2013 (see Table 1) [7]. It was therefore natural that the Lifespeeder's first mobile application implementation was for Android devices.

As depicted in Figure 1 the mobile application gets the information from the back-end (see Section 3). The communication steps between the mobile application and the back-end, from the first moment that the application makes a request until it receives a response, are the following:

Step 1. The mobile application uses the HTTP protocol to make a request to the LifeSpeeder Web Service (LSWS). The LSWS in turn interprets this request and verifies if the mobile device has sent its ID. If that was the

Fig. 1. Global vision of the LifeSpeeder platform

case, then it goes directly to step 2. If no ID was sent then the device will be registered in the system with a new generated ID, which is then sent to the device in step 4, along with the response of the request.

Step 2. The LSWS interprets the request, and builds and executes the necessary queries to reply to the requisition made by the mobile application.

Step 3. The database management system returns the result to the Web Service, which in turn uses thes results to build a JSON document with the information.

Step 4. With the query results formated in JSON, the LSWS sends the document to the mobile application, thus closing the communication loop.

For example, a request with the form `URL:/webservice?UID=NULL&lat=37.027996&lng=-7.922763&events=ALL&lan=pt` corresponds to a query where a not registered or an anonymous user wants to view events of any type (`events=ALL`), that are near the location with latitude equal to 37.027996N and longitude equal to 7.922763W (`lat= 37.027996&lng=-7.922763`) and preferably in Portuguese (`lang=pt`).

As already mentioned, the answer returned to the mobile application consists of a JSON document with the events found in the vicinity of the user, plus the user ID (`UID`) designed to identify him. The `UID`, in addition of being an identifier of the device, also serves to record the actions of the user, keeping them even if he changes or uses other devices.

Regarding the localization of the users, it can be almost precisely obtained using the Global Positioning System (GPS) or approximated using IP address

Table 1. Worldwide smartphone sales to end users by operating system in the 3rd quarters of 2012 and 2013 (Source: Gartner, November 2013)

Operating System	3Q13 Market Share (%)	3Q12 Market Share (%)
Android	81.9	72.6
iOS	12.1	14.3
Microsoft	3.6	2.3
BlackBerry	1.8	5.2
Bada	0.3	2.6
Symbian	0.2	2.6
Others	0.2	0.4

geo-location [8]. The former solution is appropriate for a large percentage of mobile devices which already incorporate GPS, however it tends to require longer synchronization times. The latter one is quicker and works as a fallback to devices which do not have GPS. Furthermore, in Android devices, the access to the GPS is not possible using a browser, leaving in this case the single alternative of using the available APIs to get an approximated location.

Figure 2 shows six screen captures of the mobile application, namely: (a) the login form, (b) the main menu; (c) the setting menu; (d) a list of event grouped by category; (e) a list of events sorted by date; and (f) the geolocation of an event on a map. Regarding the location on the map screen capture we must refer that selecting the "Guide me" button (on the right upper corner of Figure 2 (f)) will open the default navigation application which is used to navigate to the selected event location using the Google maps and the GPS device.

2.2 Web Application

The web application can be considered as the main entrance to the LifeSpeeder platform. It is from it that the events are loaded into the database, and are then provided to both applications, i.e., to the mobile applications as it has already been addressed and to the web application itself. The interface of this web application has a multilingual (currently Portuguese, Spanish and English) support, which allows to extend the horizon of usability of the platform.

As in the previous case, the web application provides the following types of searches:

Normal search (default) - the Geolocation API [9] approximates the location of the user based on the user's machine IP[1]. The approximated location of the user and the current date is then used to search the database for spatially and temporally near events.

[1] For location more accurate, it is necessary that the user agrees to share its location.

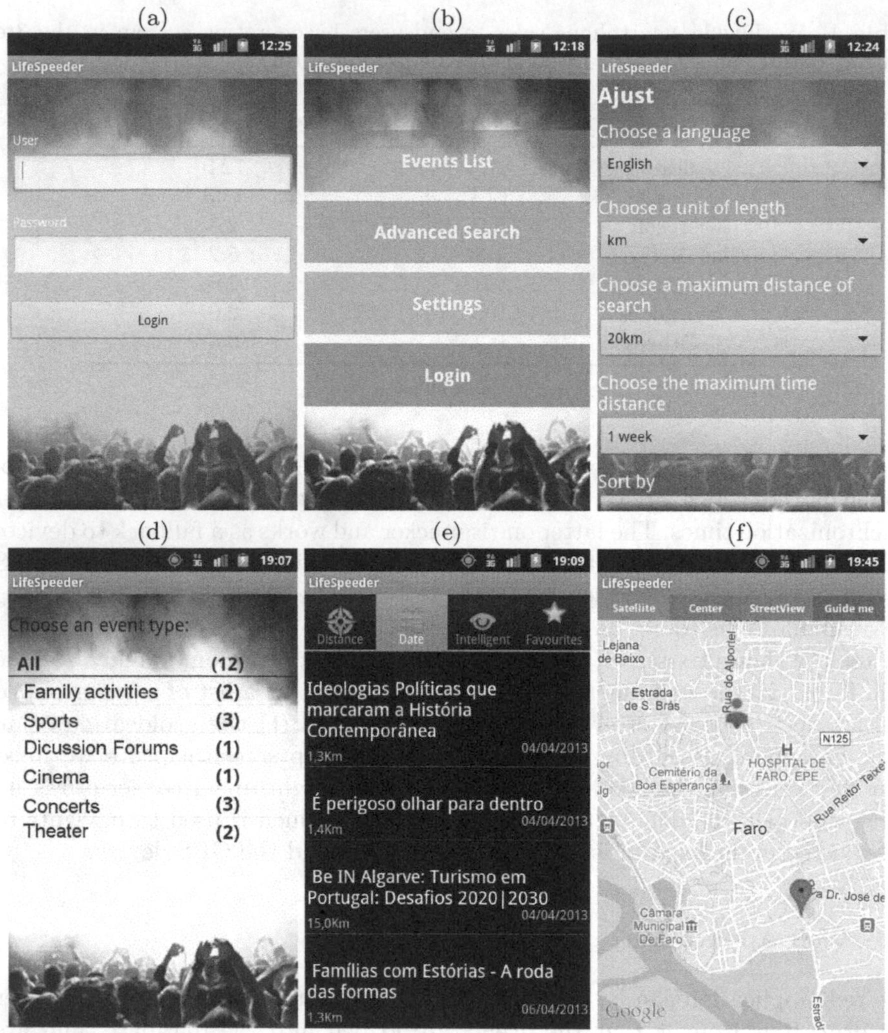

Fig. 2. Screen captures of the LifeSpeeder mobile app: (a) Login form; (b) Main menu; (c) Setting menu; (d) List of event grouped by category; (e) List of events sorted by date; and (f) Geolocation of an event on a map

Advanced search - just as in the mobile application the user has the option to choose the types of events and places that he prefers. If he chooses the type and/or subtype of event but does not specifies the location, the returned list of events reflects the estimated location of the terminal. When the user chooses a location (e.g., Lisbon, Portugal), the geographical coordinates of the selected location will be obtained via the Google Maps API [10] and the events satisfying the search conditions are returned.

Free search - apart from the two aforementioned forms of search, you can make free query, consisting in the introduction of a string which will be looked up in the events names and descriptions.

Figure 3 shows two screen captures of the web application, namely: (a) the home page, and (b) the grouped results from a search made to the system. In the latter case, the page with the search results is divided into three sections: (i) the events grouped in different time intervals are displayed in the left side section; (ii) the events grouped in different categories are displayed in the central section, and (iii) classified and feature events on the right section.

The next section will give an overview of the Lifespeeder's back-end.

3 Lifespeeder's Back-end

In terms of the Lifespeeder back-end, preliminary studies have shown a relatively large complexity of the data to be stored (e.g., events with distinct characteristics, events with multiple activities, events translations, multilingual support, etc). Besides, since new ideas for the application where constantly appearing, it was decided to use an iterative and incremental agile software development framework for managing the software implementation [11, 12].

An appropriate way to deal with the above mentioned conditions was to use a document oriented database solution in detriment of a relational database. In that sense, the MongoDB database was selected as the Lifespeeder datastorage [6, 13, 14]. MongoDB is an open source database, written in C++ with document oriented storage, that uses the JSON documents style, although the documents are stored in BSON. The MongoDB allows dynamic schema, since it is a schema-less database, which was a serious advantage due to the diversity of situations found in the problem. However, there are also some disadvantages such as the tendency to grow the number of fields to accommodate the variety of scenarios. This fact suggests that a modeling and analysis phase similar to the ones made for the relational schema designs is also important to avoid future drawbacks. Contrary to the modeling and analysis of the relational data bases, more centered on the data, a proper analysis for the documents structure should take into consideration the type of queries that will be done to the data and the limitation of the MongoDB's query framework. This is particularly important due to the fact that MongoDB does not support joins, and therefore it recommended to place in the same collection the data that is commonly requested together. In resume, MongoDB offers full index support, mirroring across LANs and WANs for scaling, autosharding, rich document based queries, map/reduce, and GridFS [15, 16].

Figure 4 presents a simplified example of a JSON document relative to an event. The document contains informations in three languages, the date, users comments, and the geolocation of the event.

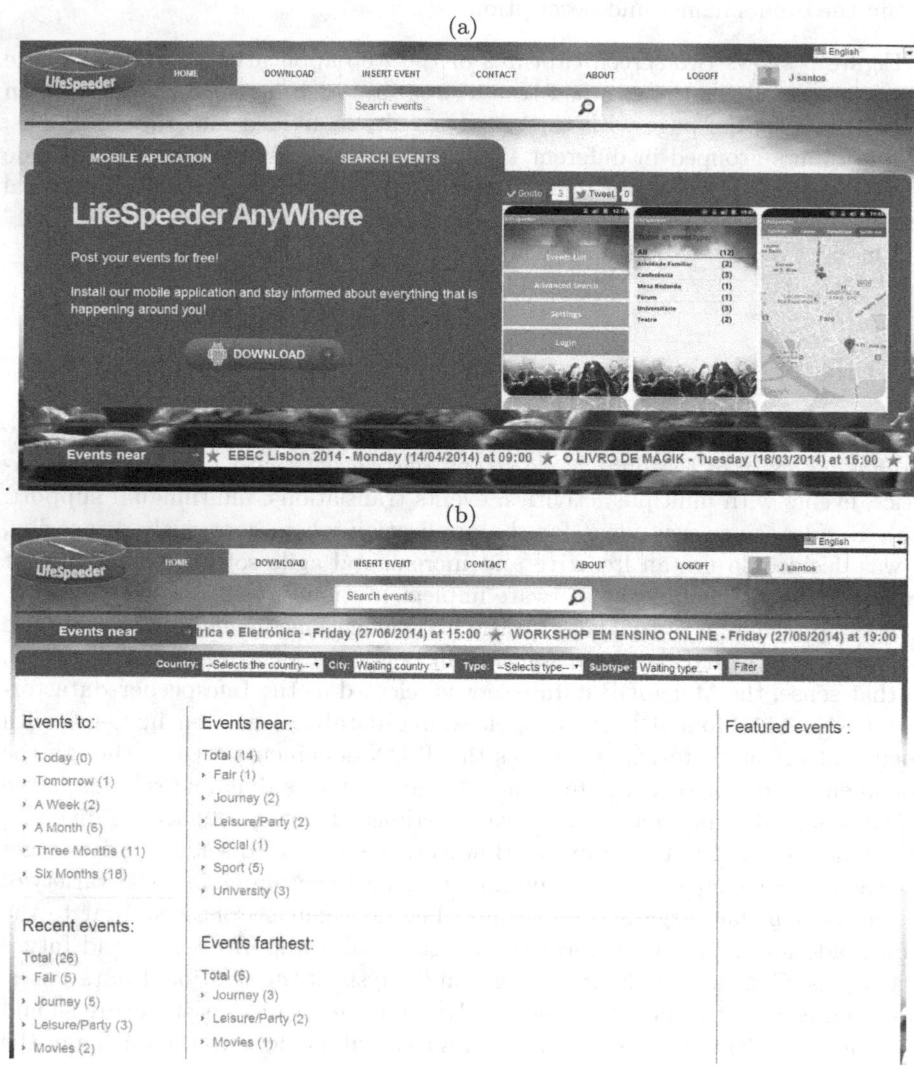

Fig. 3. Screen captures of the LifeSpeeder web application: (a) Home page; (b) Grouped results from a search;

```
{
  Id_Event : 1,
  Translations : [ // array with 3 languages
    { Lang : "Portuguese",
      Title : "A UNIVERSIDADE E O MUNDO",
      Description : "'A Universidade e o Mundo' e' o tema da
          exposicao ..."
    },
    {
      Lang : "English",
      Title : "THE UNIVERSITY AND THE WORLD",
      Description : "'The University and the World' is the
        theme of the exhibition ..."
      },
      {
      Lang : "Spanish",
      Title : "LA UNIVERSIDAD Y EL MUNDO",
      Description : "'La Universidad y el mundo' es el tema
        de la exposicion ..."
      },
  ],
  Date_time : { Data : "27/09/2013", Hora : "17h30" },
  Locations:[
    {
      Location : "Biblioteca de Gambelas ",
      City : "Faro",
      Country : "Portugal",
      loc: { lat : 37.044362, lon : -7.971557}
    }
  ],
  Comments : [
    {
      User : "Marli Silva ",
      Comment : "Boa iniciativa, gosto..."
    },
    {
       User : "Beto Gomes",
       Comment : "Vou participar no evento..."
    }
  ]
}
```


Fig. 4. Example of a single JSON document containing information about an event

As a final word, the remaining technologies are common in this type of projects. PHP was elected as the server-side general-purpose scripting language for the web development. On the client side it was used HTML, CSS and javascript.

4 Conclusions and Future Work

Taking advantage of the various features and technologies currently available, it was possible to implement a tool that can assists the users to get information about events simply using a computer or some Android device.

After analyzing several storage solutions, it was concluded that a solution based on a document oriented database would be a good option. Since the events need to contain sufficient information, including geographical position, the choice of a database that natively supports these data types proved to be an asset, allowing to obtain good performances especially in queries involving research with latitude and longitude information.

On the other hand, the platform developed can be easily adapted to different situations, which opens the possibility to the creation of rebrandings. In other words, this platform can easily be adapted and customized by a company that organizes events and want to keep their customers informed about the dates and locations of the same. Another example can go through a company or agency that works with promotions, to inform customers what are the regions as well as the dates and products covered by a particular promotion.

Acknowledgments. This work was partly supported by the Portuguese Foundation for Science and Technology (FCT), project LARSyS PEst-OE/EEI/LA0009 /2013 and project i3FR – QREN I&DT, n. 34130.

References

[1] Scoutmob: Scoutmob. (2014), `https://play.google.com/store/apps/details?id=com.scoutmob.ile` (retrived: October 24, 2014)
[2] Eventbrite: Eventbrite (2014), `https://play.google.com/store/apps/details?id=com.eventbrite.attendee` (retrived: October 24, 2014)
[3] Bordeaux Agenda: Bordeaux Agenda (2014), `https://play.google.com/store/apps/details?id=fr.bordeaux.agenda2` (retrived: October 24, 2014)
[4] Hamburg Events: Hamburg Events (2014), `https://play.google.com/store/apps/details?id=com04131.android.hamburg` (retrived: October 24, 2014)
[5] Where To Go?: Where To Go? GPS POI Finder (2014), `https://play.google.com/store/apps/details?id=com.ondemandworld.android.wheretogo` (retrived: October 24, 2014)
[6] MongoDB: MongoDB (2014), `http://www.mongodb.org/` (retrived: October 24, 2014)

[7] Butler, M.: Android: Changing the mobile landscape. IEEE Pervasive Computing 10(1), 4–7 (2011)
[8] Poese, I., Uhlig, S., Kaafar, M.A., Donnet, B., Gueye, B.: Ip geolocation databases: unreliable? ACM SIGCOMM Computer Communication Review 41(2), 53–56 (2011)
[9] W3C: Geolocation API specification (2012), `http://dev.w3.org/geo/api/spec-source.html` (retrived: October 24, 2014)
[10] Google Maps API: Google Maps API (2014), `https://developers.google.com/maps/` (retrived: October 24, 2014)
[11] Shore, J., et al.: The art of agile development. O'Reilly (2008)
[12] Blankenship, J., Bussa, M., Millett, S.: Pro Agile.NET Development with Scrum. Apress (2011)
[13] Han, J., Haihong, E., Le, G., Du, J.: Survey on NoSQL database. In: 2011 6th International Conference on Pervasive Computing and Applications (ICPCA), pp. 363–366. IEEE (2011)
[14] Chodorow, K.: MongoDB: The Definitive Guide. 2nd edn. O'Reilly Media (2013)
[15] Leavitt, N.: Will NoSQL databases live up to their promise? Computer 43(2), 12–14 (2010)
[16] Wei-ping, Z., Ming-xin, L., Huan, C.: Using MongoDB to implement textbook management system instead of MySQL. In: 2011 IEEE 3rd International Conference on Communication Software and Networks (ICCSN), pp. 303–305. IEEE (2011)

Elders Using Smartphones – A Set of Research Based Heuristic Guidelines for Designers

Stefan Carmien and Ainara Garzo Manzanares

TECNALIA Research & Innovation
Paseo Mikeletegi, 1
20009 Donostia - San Sebastian, Spain
{stefan.carmien,ainara.garzo}@tecnalia.com

Abstract. Smartphones and an increasingly aged population are two highly visible emergent attributes in the last decade. Smartphones are becoming the canonical front end for the cloud, web, and applications from email to social media - especially so if you include pads in the same category. In Europe, the Americas and Asia the ratio of over those over 65 compared to the total population that is becoming increasingly skewed. This paper is about the intersection of these two socio-technical vectors, or more to the point about the mismatch between them: a mismatch which can lead to an increase in the digital divide rather than the decline that the more affordable smartphones could promise. We present a study of literature and results of a design process in the form of heuristics to support smartphone/tablet designers making useable and useful products for elder end-users.

Keywords: Smartphone, Small touch screens, Older adults, Hueristics, GUI design guidelines.

1 Introduction

Smartphones and an increasingly aged population are two highly visible emergent attributes in the last decade. Smartphones are becoming the canonical front end for the cloud, web, and applications from email to social media - especially so if you include pads in the same category (see Fig. 1).

In Europe, the Americas and Asia the ratio of over 65 population is producing a now common inverted triangle graph (see Fig. 2). This paper is about the intersection of these two socio-technical vectors, or more to the point about the mismatch between them; a mismatch which can lead to an increase in the digital divide [1] rather than the decline that the more affordable smartphones could promise.

The current population of elders (65-70 and above) were too old to be raised with home computers, beyond calculators; as a result the level of computer literacy of this segment of the population is considerably lower than the generation below them and far below the current generation of software/hardware designers and early-adopters [2]. This is compounded by the inevitable sensory and possible cognitive decline by

C. Stephanidis and M. Antona (Eds.): UAHCI/HCII 2014, Part II, LNCS 8514, pp. 26–37, 2014.

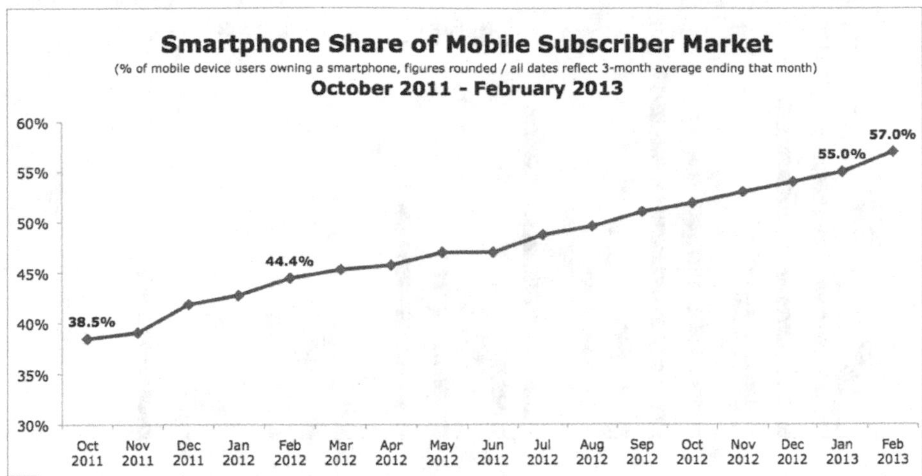

Fig. 1. Smartphones Share of Market

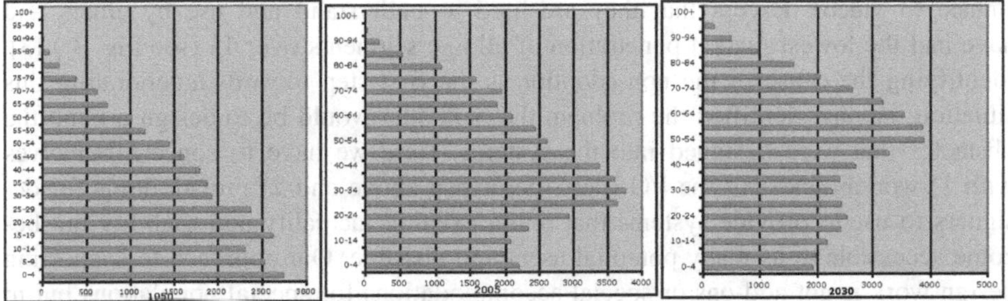

Fig. 2. Age Spread in Spain 1950-2030

Smartphones are the epitome of economy of scale and mores law. Their rapid ride in popularity has driven costs down faster than previous hardware advances (modulo iPhones). The confluence of so many technologies into the smartphone means that in one small package you often find Wi-Fi, Bluetooth, NFC, GPS, 3-D accelerometers, compass, microphones, cameras (still and video), gyroscope, and proximity sensors; and the explosion of information that can be gained by sensor fusion. These phones can currently connect with others and the Internet by phone service, Wi-Fi, GRPS and new evolving wireless technologies. Combining the two advances listed previously the phones enable the sorts of context awareness and ambient intelligence that provide abilities and information only accessible to the very few previously. As the form factor of smartphone became capable of being smaller and smaller, the affordances for I/O become similarly constrained. Input becomes based on touch screens, on screen keyboards, on gesture and finger input; the output is delivered by small low-powered speakers and tiny high definition screens.

Elders with smartphones are a great way to facilitate the lowering of the digital di-vide – low cost, portable, able to access every application and information type

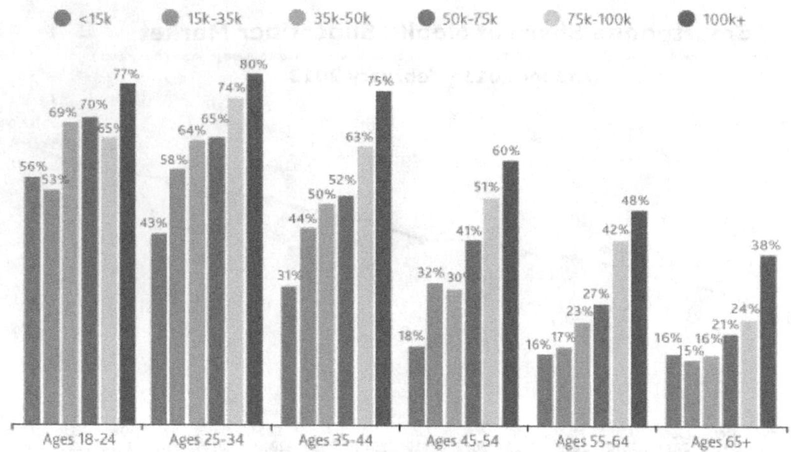

Fig. 3. Smartphone Penetration by Age and Income (Jan. 2012)

(music to video). Except that they are hard to understand and use by elders and have had the lowest market penetration of all age segments over 15 (see Fig. 3) [3]. Identifying the cause of the non-adoption is the first step towards ameliorating this situation; having identified the problem the next step would be to design around the obstacles that were designed into the systems. Here we have to concern ourselves with 1) workarounds for the I/O issues described above and 2) provide tools for designers to use to provide systems that retain existing factuality and usability but become accessible to as many potential users and possible. Our approach to supporting design work is not add-ons or special accommodations for special populations but to provide guides that maximise broad use while increasing the quality of fundamental design styles and approaches.

2 Gathering Heuristics

Our approach to producing a set of heuristics followed the typical path of literature research and user studies. Works on elders and design include general approaches [4-8] and several approaches to systemic guidance [9, 10]. Also included were more specific works on elders and small factored portable devices like smartphones and tablets [11-14].

With this perspective we performed two sets of user interviews and focus groups. The population was drawn from the cities that would be evaluating the ASSISTANT smartphone application [15]: Paris (France), Vienna (Austria), and San Sebastian (Spain).

Initially, interviews were used to identify user needs and requirements and to know better the use of this kind of systems and public transportation by elderly. From these first sessions we discovered that in recent years the use of mobile phones by elderly has become common. Most of them have a mobile phone especially for emergencies.

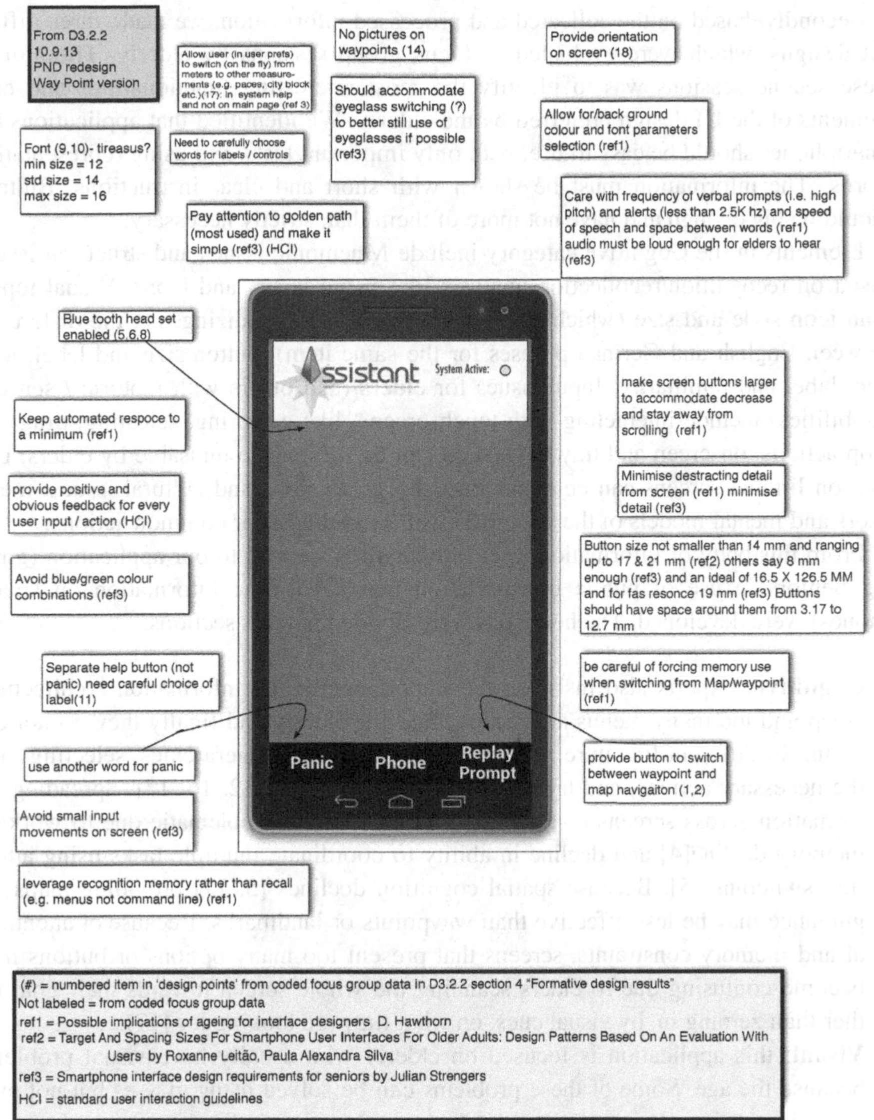

Fig. 4. ASSISTANT Smartphone initial design guidelines

We conducted interviews in different countries, and learned that the use of mobile phones is different in different locales. For example, in Spain it is not common to see an elderly using a smartphone and they usually have a mobile phone only for making or receiving calls. In the cases of France and Austria more elders have smartphones and they access more functionalities such as Internet navigation. Those that who use few of the available functionalities said that the menus are very complicated to learn to use them.

Secondly, based on the collected and processed information, we made three different designs, which were evaluated in focus group sessions by elderly. The aim of these second sessions was to identify the most interesting functionalities and also elements of the UI design preferred by the elderly. We identified that applications for smartphones should be easy to use, with only important tasks and using representative words. The information must be shown with short and clear instructions. Buttons should be big enough and have not more of them than strictly necessary.

Elements in the Cognitive category include Mnemonic issues and structural issues based on recognition/recollection analysis like menu layers and icons. Visual topics span icon style and size (which may vary by language localizing, i.e. the difference between English and German phrases for the same item), button size and label, icon size, label and familiarity. Input issues for elders (and others with motoric / sensory disabilities) include interacting with touchscreens, like gesturing, selecting, drag and drop actions; onscreen and tiny keyboards can be difficult to unusable by elders. Design on limited screens can be constrained by generations and cultural issues, metaphors and mental models of the system as well as verbiage for common actions.

From this body of information a set of heuristics specific to our application (guiding Seniors in use of public transportation using real-time information on smartphones) were developed. The heuristics were divided into six sections:

- **Cognitive:** Experts also insist on the importance of the information architecture. Deep and too many menus are complicated for elderly and finally they do not use them. So different literature recommend avoiding deep hierarchies, selecting only the necessary actions, and trying to group information [12, 16, 17]. Spreading information across screens or forcing scrolling may be problematic due to working memory decline[4] and decline in ability to coordinate multiple tasks using attention switching [5]. Because spatial cognition declines [5, 17] providing maps for guidance may be less effective than waypoints or landmarks. Because of attentional and memory constraints, screens that present too many options or buttons may become confusing due to elders scanning the whole screen towards their goal rather than zeroing in, by visual cues, on what they are looking for [17].
- **Visual**: this application is focused on elderly who usually have visual problems because the age. Some of these problems can be solved using glasses but not everyone is wearing glasses all the time (because they are reading glasses) so for using the phone this can be a problem. This is the reason because most of elderly prefer to have haptic (vibratory) or sound alarms, or in some cases spoken instructions. With the aim of solving some visual problems, according to the literature it is recommended to use only colours and graphics[11], of course these must have the alt text attribute filled in to enable screen readers. If written text is needed it should be in 12-14 point size [4, 7, 10, 16, 17]. Font type is also important to help people reading text easily. The experts recommend not using decorative fonts [16] and

using serif or sans-serif types such as Helvetia, Times New Roman or Arial [5, 9, 16]. The text should be left justified in countries using left writing, with spacing between lines, and important information must be highlighted and in the middle of the screen [16]. Main body must be written in lower cases and with short sentences [16] because capital letters must be used to draw attention to something important [5, 7]. Colours are also important to make readable the texts. For people blind to colours the important information should not be signalled by colours, or not only by colours. The contrast ration between background and text must be 50:1 [5, 7, 16] and ideally background must be in white and text in black [5, 7, 10] because elderly people have problems with background colours[11]. Blue and green tones and the brightness changes between screens should be avoided.

- **Input:** elderly people, because the age, usually have dexterity problems, which evokes difficulties to work with a touch screen. This application is based on a smartphone, so most input should be done by a touch screen. Buttons of touch screens react too fast and this is a problem for the elderly [11], so it is recommended to add a small delay and feedback (auditory or haptic) when a button is pressed [5]. Only basic actions (go back or close the application) will be done by hardware buttons. There is some evidence about that the elderly use back button more than young people because they understand it such as undo actions [17] so this function is very important to be implemented. According to the literature, scrolling and double click is difficult for elderly because it is not intuitive, it should be learned [16, 17]. Smartphones usual keypad is not good for elderly and the physical buttons from mobile phones are too small [18] so text input should be avoided and replaced by speech-to-text [11]. To solve the identified problems with touch buttons the main actions of an application for a smartphone should have big buttons [5] no smaller than 16.5x16.5mm (for faster responses 19.05x19.05mm) [11, 19, 20]. Some experts conclude that there is no evidence about the spacing between buttons for elderly, but they recommend 3.17 mm [13]. Others recommend at least 6.35mm [5, 17, 19], which is preferred by adults[11].
- **Audio:** according to Fisk et al. [5] 10% of middle-aged adults suffer hearing losses, but in the case of people over 65 years old, the half of men (50%) and the 30% of women has hearing problems. Hawthorn [10] also says that the 75% of the people over 75-79 have audio impairments. So it is clear that the hearing problems appear with the age. Because of this, when some instructions of a UI want to be given by voice, some recommendations must be taken into account. Some experts recommend using frequencies between 500-2,000Hz [7, 10] and avoiding frequencies over 4,000Hz [5, 7, 10, 21]. In the case of warning signals they should be lower than 2,000Hz, most preferable is 500Hz if they are fast (less than 0.5sg of sound and 0.5sg of silence) [21] or more than 2,000Hz but longer than 0.5sg [7]. About the intensity experts agree that it should be 60 dB, and 50dB for conversional speech. Regarding the speech speed for texts, Fisk et al. [5] recommend a

rate of 140 words per minute or less. Female's or kid's voice have higher frequencies, and because of that they are not recommended except on cases where it is needed to pay attention [5, 7]. Artificial voices (synthesized) must be avoided also [5, 7]. The volume adjustment must be configurable according to each user's needs, and it is recommended to use redundant information for any audio signal (light or haptic signals, text…)

- **Haptic:** with the age also the sense of touch changes and the thresholds for temperature and vibration perception increase [5, 7]. For UI design, if we are using vibration signals for warning the user, in the case of elderly some issues should be taken into account:
  - Every people are more sensitive to vibration in upper body sites than lower ones [5].So in the case of elderly, to ensure that they are noticing the warning they should have the phone next to upper side. In this case, the designers cannot control it. It is also recommended to use low frequencies for vibration in the case of elderly. Fisk et al. [5] recommend 25 Hz for warnings.
  - Because elderly has problems to identify haptic signals, it is recommended to use other kind of identification to help with sensitive problems. For example, Farage, Ajayi and Hutchins [7] recommend using colour contrast in hardware buttons because the elderly has problems to differentiate them by touching.
- **Generational/ cultural:** Elders may have problems with mental models of the application and the computer itself. Things that are familiar, like check boxes and menu systems may be incomprehensible to new, older users ("where is the 'any' key?") [4]. Icons that may be 'standard' but have lost the original meaning due to technology changes (i.e. the printer icon) may be mystifying to the elder [17]. Verbiage also may have this property as well as require an understanding of computer basics to make sense [17]. Buttons may be seen as decorative (especially decorative buttons) and not functional. Presenting 'common sense' choices "save the file to this folder?" may cause problems with retrieval.

3 Heuristics

The list of heuristics for UI designers focusing on small touch screens (smartphones) for the elderly:

Area	Heuristic	Comment
Cognitive	Shallow menus	Spread functionality across menu bar and pages.
	All information for a given need on one page	Don't force leafing back and forth between pages, or scrolling up and down – hiding information causes mnemonic problems.

Area	Heuristic	Comment
Cognitive (continued)	Avoid deep hierarchies, group information	Spread across pages – avoid one page does it all approach.
	Select important actions and make them easiest	Determine what are the most frequent acts that the user wants to do and make them easy. Less frequently used ones can require more effort.
	Be consistent with details of interface	Using different designs between screens can cause frustration and confusion.
	Don't force use of multiple tasks	Allow tasks to be accomplished serially, don't force them to be done at the same time requiring cognitive switching.
	Support easy paths	Always provide a 'home' button, and let users know 'where' they are.
Visual	Use colours, icons and graphics	Often better than using text.
	Font size: 12-14 point	It could be a problem when same text has to be written in different languages and resultant phrase has different length.
	Font type: serif or sans-serif (Helvetia, Arial, Times New Roman…)	Avoid decorative fonts. Recommended: Helvetia, Arial, Times New Roman…
	Text left justified for left writers	Important text should be centre justified to highlight it.
	Spacing between text lines	Try using short sentences. If they are longer than one line, use at least usual spacing.
	Lower cases	Capital letters must be used for highlight important text.
	Colours: don't use to convey critical information (for people blind to colours)	They can be used if they are combined with other signalling (icons, symbols …)
	Contrast ratio: 50:1.	Best: text in black, background in white.
Input	Delay and feedback when pressing a button	The touch screen buttons react too fast.
	Back button provided	It can be implemented by hardware buttons.
	Avoid scrolling and requiring double click	It is not intuitive, it should be learned.
	Avoid use of keypad in smartphones	Replace with drop down menus, choices or speech-to-text.

Area	Heuristic	Comment
Input (continued)	Buttons size: 16.5x16.5 mm	This can be designed for a size of screen, but it is difficult to define a concrete size if the application can be used in smartphones with different screen sizes. For faster responses use 19.05x19.05mm.
	Buttons spacing: 3.17-6.35mm	There is no evidence about the appropriated spacing, but older adults prefer 6.35mm spacing.
Audio	Frequencies: 500-2,000Hz	Warning signals >2,000Hz with duration of 0,5sg. or <2,000Hz.
	Intensity: 60dB	50dB for conversational speech.
	Speech speed: 140 wpm	No faster than 140wpm.
	Male voice	Female/child voice only to draw attention.
	Use redundant information: light or haptic signals as well as audio.	The combination of several signals is recommended for elderly, i.e. haptic feedback when clicking in buttons.
Haptic	Best warning frequency: 25Hz.	Always use lower frequencies.
Generational / cultural	Avoid 'technical terminology	Be aware that words the designer may find commonplace may be arcane to an elder.
	Avoid assuming that the elder has a usable mental model of the smartphone	Asking the elder to perform acts like 'scroll down' to expose the status/notification screen may be incomprehensible and lead to frustration and abandonment.
	Avoid relying on gestures that may be novel	Better to give a virtual button than force the user to do 'invisible' actions.
	Find representative words and icons	Use common words or icons or check with final users if they mean what you expect.
	Carefully use icons	'Standard' icons may be unfamiliar –use with care or better reinforce with words
	Always provide an exit	Small problems may escalate to abandonment when use is backed into a screen that apparently has no way to exit.

In Figures 5 and 6 you can see examples of the above heuristics. Cognitive concerns include keeping all information on one page and easy paths between screens. According to the visual heuristics we can say that the text size and type has been respected. The instructions are short (in one sentence) in the middle of the screen but they are centre justified, not left justified, with the aim of highlighting the instructions such as main text. The colours and the contrast ration are also the same as in the heuristics.

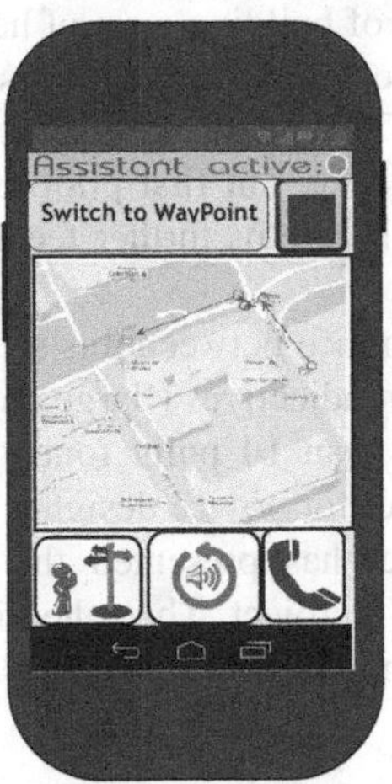

Fig. 5. ASSISTANT project Personal Navigation Device (PND) interface

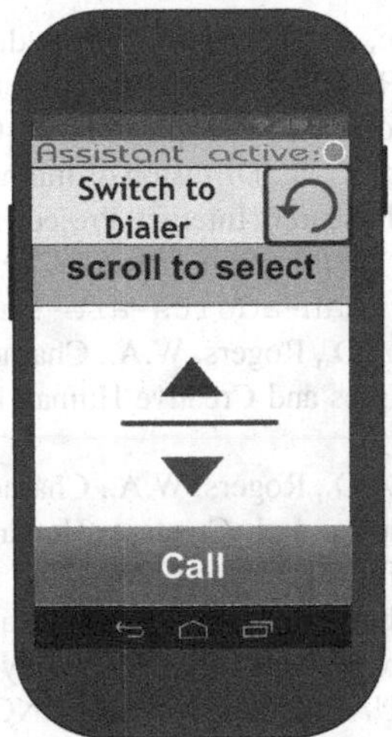

Fig. 6. ASSISTANT PND Auxiliary Interfaces

The input is done with touch screen buttons which has the proposed size in the literature. Because there is no evidence about the minimum spacing, it has not been respected, but with the aim of avoiding wrong clicks, the buttons have been delimited by a clear black line which visually helps the user differentiate the space of each button. Scrolling and double clicking have been avoided; also the design keeps all the important elements in one screen.

In figure 6, to avoid the need to scroll, arrows had been added to go ahead or back in contact list. While not visible in the figures, the audio and haptic alert are in the right frequency range and with signal modality redundancy. The wording is carefully chosen and checked with elderly in Focus Groups and many functions are represented by easy to understand icons.

The start of building a set of heuristics consisted of compiling these lists into a design document for the mobile user interface for the personal navigation device for ASSISTANT, implemented on a Samsung Galaxy 3 android smart phone. With a pilot type system out first pilot tests will be performed in April 2014 and we expect that they will give us further feedback to clarify and extend the heuristics we have so far codified.

The difference between this set of heuristics and the anticipated final set are the replacement of adjectives ('large enough', 'high contrast') with quantifiable goals ('san serif, larger than 14 point font', contrast levels following WCAG 2.0 conventions) that are easier for novice designer to follow.

The paper has presented the initial heuristics derived in the first half of the ASSISTANT project. These heuristics and data derived from use studies will be examined in the ASSISTANT pilot study with a goal of expanding and clarifying these guidelines.

References

1. Clarke, A., Concejero, P.: The digital divide–services for the elderly and disabled in 2010– the PRISMA project. In: 18th International Symposium on Human Factors in Telecommunication, vol. 2991, pp. 1–8 (2010)
2. Rogers, E.M.: Diffusion of Innovations, 4th edn. The Free Press, New York (1995)
3. Pew Research Internet Project Nearly half of American adults are smartphone owners (2013), http://www.pewinternet.org/2012/03/01/nearly-half-of-american-adults-are-smartphone-owners/ (accessed on: Febuary 2014)
4. Fisk, A.D., Rogers, W.A., Charness, N., Czaja, S.J., Sharit, J.: Designing for Older Adults: Principles and Creative Human Factors Approaches. CRC Press J Taylor&.Francis Croup (2004)
5. Fisk, A.D., Rogers, W.A., Charness, N., Czaja, S.J., Sharit, J.: Designing for Older Adults: Principles and Creative Human Factors Approaches, 2nd edn. CRC Press J Taylor&.Francis Croup (2009)
6. Kleinberger, T., Becker, M., Ras, E., Holzinger, A., Müller, P.: Ambient Intelligence in Assisted Living: Enable Elderly People to Handle Future Interfaces. In: Stephanidis, C. (ed.) UAHCI 2007 (Part II). LNCS, vol. 4555, pp. 103–112. Springer, Heidelberg (2007)
7. Farage, M.A., Miller, K., Ajayi, F., Hutchins, D.: Design Principles to Accommodate Older Adults. Global Journal of Health Science 4(2), 2–25 (2012)
8. Hawthorn, D.: How universal is good design for older users? In: CUU 2003 Proceedings of the 2003 Conference on Universal Usability, pp. 38–45 (2003)
9. Zajicek, M.: Successful and available: interface design exemplars for older users. Interacting with Computers 16(3), 411–430 (2004)
10. Hawthorn, D.: Possible implications of aging for interface designers. Interacting with Computers 12, 507–528 (2000)
11. Strengers, J.: Smartphone interface design requirements for seniors. In: Information Studies. University of Amsterdam, Amsterdam (2012)
12. Kurniawan, S.: Older people and mobile phones: A multi-method investigation. Int. J. Human-Computer Studies (66), 889–901 (2008)

13. Leitão, R.: Target and Spacing Sizes for Smartphone User Interfaces for Older Adults: Design Patterns Based on an Evaluation with Users. In: Pattern Languages of Programs, Tucson, Arizona (2012)
14. Darroch, I., Goodman, J., Brewster, S., Gray, P.: The Effect of Age and Font Size on Reading Text on Handheld Computers. In: Costabile, M.F., Paternó, F. (eds.) INTERACT 2005. LNCS, vol. 3585, pp. 253–266. Springer, Heidelberg (2005)
15. ASSISTANT. ASSISTANT Website (2012), http://www.aal-assistant.eu/ (January 2013)
16. Kurniawan, S., Zaphiris, P.: Research-derived web design guidelines for older people. In: Proceedings of the 7th International ACM SIGACCESS Conference on Computers and Accessibility, pp. 129–135. ACM, Baltimore (2005)
17. Chisnell, D., Redish, J.: Designing web sites for older adults: a review of recent research. AARP.org/olderwiserwired (2004), http://assets.aarp.org/www.aarp.org_/articles/research/oww/AARP-50Sites.pdf (accessed on: February 2014)
18. Häikiö, J., Isomursu, M., Matinmikko, T., Wallin, A., Ailisto, H., Huomo, T.: Touch-based user interface for elderly users. In: MobileHCI, Singapore (2007)
19. Jin, Z.X., Plocher, T., Kiff, L.: Touch Screen User Interfaces for Older Adults: Button Size and Spacing. In: Stephanidis, C. (ed.) HCI 2007. LNCS, vol. 4554, pp. 933–941. Springer, Heidelberg (2007)
20. Murata, A., Iwase, H.: Usability of Touch-Panel Interfaces for Older Adults. Human Factors: The Journal of the Human Factors and Ergonomics Society 47(4), 767–776 (2005)
21. Huey, R.W., Buckley, D.S., Lerner, N.D.: Audible Performance of Smoke Alarm Sounds (1994)

VIC – An Interactive Video System for Dynamic Visualization in Web and Mobile Platforms

Benjamim Fonseca[1,2], Hugo Paredes[1,2], Paulo Martins[1,2], André Alberto[1], José Rego[1], Leonel Morgado[2,3], and Arnaldo Santos[4]

[1] Universidade de Trás-os-Montes e Alto Douro (UTAD), Vila Real, Portugal
{benjaf,hparedes,pmartins}@utad.pt,
{andrealbertto,zerego.utad}@gmail.com
[2] INESC TEC - INESC Technology and Science, Porto, Portugal
[3] Universidade Aberta, Lisbon, Portugal
leonel.morgado@uab.pt
[4] Portugal Telecom Inovação, Aveiro, Portugal
arnaldo@ptinovacao.pt

Abstract. This paper presents an interactive video system that enables users to change the flow of video playback by interacting with hotspots that were predefined throughout the video streams. These hotspots are synchronized with the underlying video streams and the interactions result in smooth transitions between the preloaded targets. This approach allows the dynamic visualization of content by interacting with the hotspots and producing the consequent changes in the flow of the story. The system includes web-based and mobile video players specifically developed to deal with the interactive features, as well as a configuration tool that allows content managers to choose which pre-produced interaction possibilities will be used for a specific target audience. The interactive video solution presented herein has potential to be used as a powerful communication tool, in commercial, e-learning, accessibility and entertainment contexts.

1 Introduction

Video is often a key element in the communication strategy of many organizations, but it is frequently convenient to have distinct content directed to different target audiences, which in turn tend to consume it differently, depending on several factors such as visualization equipment, time constraints or even the mood.

The way users access and consume information has changed significantly over the last decade, namely with the emergence of social networks. Indeed, Facebook and YouTube provided users with great freedom in choosing which content they want to visualize and when they want to do it. This growing demand for personalized content challenges efficiency in producing content that is able to suit as much people as possible. One possibility to cope with this issue is to put in the same monolithic media file all the information required to satisfy the majority of people, but this will probably lead to cognitive overload or can make it too boring for many users. Alternatively, content

C. Stephanidis and M. Antona (Eds.): UAHCI/HCII 2014, Part II, LNCS 8514, pp. 38–49, 2014.

providers can produce a lot of smaller and distinct media files, but this can make it harder for users to choose the information they want. These two approaches seem to be inadequate to be used isolated, but its combination can provide a suitable solution. Indeed, the combination of all the information in one master stream, from which the user can interactively select the appropriate sub-streams corresponding to the desired content, can allow a great degree of personalization, reaching a large audience, providing multilevel information (e.g., allowing incremental learning). This solution poses challenges related with the technologies required to provide the interactivity features, but also in the narratives, which can be quite different from the traditional ones.

Some technologies have emerged in the last decade, which facilitate the development of interactive applications and the combination of media in increasingly sophisticated multimedia content. However, there are not yet known solutions for the production of interactive video as envisaged above.

In this paper we present an interactive video solution, which main principle is the interaction with hotspots marked in a video, resulting in a change to another video or other content that presents additional information about the underlying subject. This approach, named VIC (Portuguese-language acronym for Interactive Video for Communication), required the development of solutions for coping with the interaction, the media synchronization and the smooth transitions between sub-streams, as well as the players required to visualize this new kind of media in desktop computers, laptops and mobile devices. It was also necessary to specify some video pre-production procedures and to develop a management tool that allows media managers to configure interaction, selecting the appropriate hotspots and actions from the ones specified in the pre-production stage.

This paper is organized as follows: in section 2 we present some previous work related with the solution and technologies used for our approach; section 3 describes the solutions adopted in the VIC project, presenting its requirements, model of interaction and the video production stages; section 4 shows the VIC prototypes, presenting the technologies used for the presentation and interaction with the video streams, platforms and formats supported, screenshots of the web and mobile players, as well as a tool for configuring interaction options for each video and the results obtained with these prototypes; finally, section 5 presents some concluding remarks.

2 Related Work

In the last decades a series of technologies emerged that allow developing and manipulating multimedia products. Some of these technologies, such as MPEG-21 [1], have been researched partially, but there are no commercial products available that explore the whole potential. There are a few players available, such as QuickTime [2] and AXMEDIS [3] that are able to play MPEG-21 files, but access to content and its production is still difficult.

Back in the 1980s, an early approach to interactive video used videotape recorders, audio track tones to control it and light flashes as a feedback mechanism, introducing a basic interactive experience for learning activities [4]. In 1992, Tani *et al.* [5] presented an interactive video technique that allowed interacting with a graphics layer that interfaces physical objects being displayed in live video, allowing users to remotely control the movement of those objects.

The "Featured Media" prototype [6] implemented the ability to interact with objects in metadata enriched video streams being transmitted through IPTV. The user interacts with the system using the TV remote control and interactive objects are highlighted under pause of the video playing.

Wang *et al.* presented an interactive system that allows extracting foreground objects from a video sequence and its use with another different video [7]. A model for linking and describing interactive TV programs was presented in a work by Goularte *et al.* [8], in which MPEG-7 was used to describe media and to segment objects in a video frame. In [9] the authors present an object tracking system for videos streams, using a sprite layer for implementing interactivity.

3 The VIC Solution

VIC's aim is to enable interaction with video objects without the cumbersome pauses caused by pre-buffering alternative streams, which results in the provision of several playing flows in the same video stream, allowing for content personalization. To achieve this, a technological solution was designed and implemented, as well as an interaction model and application scenarios. The technological solution and the interaction model will be presented further in this section, but regarding the scenarios, VIC was initially targeted to support the following corporate business activities:

- Commercial presentation, presenting functional and commercial features of a product, to be used in corporate websites but also by the product manager at the client premises, as well as by the client to support buying decisions.
- Technical presentation, describing the product's technical characteristics (product datasheet), to be used by the product manager to clarify technical questions at the client premises, and by the client as a basic technical support tool.
- Step-by-step wizard, working as an installation or user manual.

However, VIC's characteristics make it potentially attractive for other scenarios, such as e-learning, advertising, and entertainment.

3.1 Requirements

The VIC solution requires the use of technologies that enable the creation of multimedia content in a format that allows the inclusion of interaction objects (hotspots) and several presentation flows. The interaction with these interactive objects shall result in a change in the flow of visualization, either by showing a different video stream (sub-flow), or by showing additional information, such as text, photos, graphics or web pages. At the end of a sub-flow, playback must return automatically to the point of interruption in the parent stream. It is also convenient to have the possibility to interrupt sub-flow payback earlier and return to the point of interruption in the parent stream. The interactive video players shall also enable VCR-like commands (play, pause, fast forward, rewind), as well as zooming a region of the video or repositioning additional content windows, using drag-and-drop capabilities provided by mice or touchscreens.

The interactive video content is intended to be visualized in a web page, but also in mobile devices such as smartphones and tablets.

From this set of main characteristics, a number of functional (Table 1), nonfunctional (Table 2) and interface requirements (Table 3) were specified.

Table 1. Functional requirements

ID	Requirement
F01	Change video presentation flow (reproduction of sub-flows) by interacting with hotspots
F02	Control video playback with VCR-like commands
F03	Allow return to normal flow interruption point, after completion of sub-flow
F04	Allow digital zoom in a video region
F05	Show additional information by interacting with hotspots
F06	Follow hyperlink by interacting with hotspots
F07	Allow high level interaction editing. trhough a configuration tool, allowing product manager to select which interactive functionalities to enable
F08	Reposition video and additional information windows
F09	Explicitly change playing video, without interaction with hotspots
F10	Allow the automatic change of the organization of a mobile interface, through orientation change (using device sensors)

Table 2. Nonfunctional requirements

ID	Requirement
N01	To have a data model supporting the functionalities related with the additional information and the editing tool
N02	To use visualization formats suitable for wen and mobile distribution
N03	To use mechanisms of synchronize between visualization flows and sub-flows that allow smooth transitions
N04	To use common editing tools in the early stages of video editing (prior the configuration tool)

Table 3. Interface requirements

ID	Requirement
I01	To have easily identifiable and nonintrusive video interaction regions (hotspots)
I02	To have additional information viewing areas (text, photo, graphics, hyperlinks, auxiliary videos)
I03	To provide VCR-like controls
I04	Configuration tool must provide activation and deactivation buttons for the interactive features
I05	Provide web and mobile interfaces with equivalent interaction features

3.2 Interaction Model

To cope with the scenarios envisaged for VIC, it is desirable to have solutions for diverse computational environments, from desktop and laptop computers, to smartphones and tablets. This diversity requires mainly two types of interaction devices: the mouse, for desktops and laptops, and the touchscreen, for smartphones and tablets. Based on these interaction devices and on the functional requirements identified in Table 1, the interactive functionalities were specified, which can be seen in Table , with its relationship with the corresponding functional requirements shown in Table 5.

Table 4. Interactive functionalities

ID	Requirement
X01	Mouse click
X02	Touch interaction
X03	Mouse double click
X04	Multitouch interaction
X05	Drag-and-drop
X06	Touch with drag-and-drop
X07	Device rotation

3.3 Production Stages

Traditional video production is usually a complex work, requiring careful planning (pre-production), capturing the several video sequences and editing them trough an often long and skilled process of cutting, dubbing, subtitling, adding special effects or exporting to distribution formats (post-production).

Beyond the traditional production chain, interactive video requires the addition of the interactive functionalities, which depend much on a careful definition of all the interactions that can take place. This requires the development of a storyboard that takes into consideration the interaction and the possibility of multiple stories, in a combination of traditional screenplay with interaction design skills.

Table 5. Relation between functional requirements and interactive functionalities

ID	Requirement	Functionality ID
F01	Change video presentation flow (reproduction of sub-flows) by interacting with hotspots	X01, X02
F02	Control video playback with VCR-like commands	X01, X02
F03	Allow return to normal flow interruption point, after completion of sub-flow	X01, X02
F04	Allow digital zoom in a video region	X03, X04
F05	Show additional information by interacting with hotspots	X01, X02
F06	Follow hyperlink by interacting with hotspots	X01, X02
F07	Allow high level interaction editing. trhough a configuration tool, allowing product manager to select which interactive functionalities to enable	X01, X02
F08	Reposition video and additional information windows	X05, X06
F09	Explicitly change playing video, without interaction with hotspots	X01, X02
F10	Allow the automatic change of the organization of a mobile interface, through orientation change (using device sensors)	X07

Taking these new issues into consideration, after the prior definition of the interactive storyboard, the interactive video production chain can be divided in three stages:

- Stage 1: basic editing of digital content – this corresponds to the traditional video editing, resulting in the video sequences that can be manipulated and combined to form the interactive video.
- Stage 2: interaction editing – definition of all the possible hotspots, without making it correspond to any specific action. The result is an XML file that contains a list of editing decisions that identify potential hotspots, as well as synchronization information. The definition of the hotspots requires that the corresponding region can be delimited spatially but also in time. This is achieved using a tracking mechanism of well-known commercial editing software.
- Stage 3: interaction configuration – from the XML file produced in stage 2, the user can enable or disable any of the hotspots, define its shape and specify its targets.

Stages 1 and 2 are carried out by video editors while stage 3 is performed typically by product managers (at least in the corporate scenarios considered).

4 VIC Prototypes

The project which originated VIC has produced 3 completely functional prototypes:

- A web player – web application that allows visualization and interaction with the interactive video, requiring only a common web browser.

- A mobile player – mobile application developed for the Windows 8 platform, that allows visualization and interaction with the interactive video.
- An interaction configuration tool – web application that allows configuring the interactive video from the possibilities created during stage 2 of the production chain.

Interaction in the VIC players is achieved through the use of interaction layers that are overlapped to the video stream and synchronized with it. This allows to define the hotspots in this overlay layer and trigger the corresponding actions. The hotspot is thus a mask that defines the interactive area while keeping the video visible to the user.

All the content to be presented is formatted with HTML5 and CSS3 is used to implement the interaction layer, both technologies widely supported by current browsers. The choice of the CSS3 technology was also due to the ability to animate the interaction objects, which enabled us to have dynamic hotspots that track video objects.

The prototype of the web player is compatible with all common browsers, operating systems and video formats. A similar situation occurs with the mobile player but the prototype was built only for the Windows 8 platform, due to organizational constraints and for the sake of interface homogeneity.

In the case of the web player, the video content is delivered via streaming, using double buffering to achieve the N03 nonfunctional requirement (quick transition between flows, upon hotspot interaction). However, for the mobile player video can be delivered with the application installation, through app update or in the first time the video is requested, keeping it in the device's memory and thus achieving N03 and keeping synchronization of video with other content.

4.1 Web Player

When a user selects a video from the list the player starts its visualization. Fig. 1 shows a message that is shown at this time, alerting for the interactive possibilities, while Fig. 2 shows the reproduction of an interactive video that has an active hotspot (double dot on the upper left corner) and Fig. 3 shows the result of interactions with hotpots.

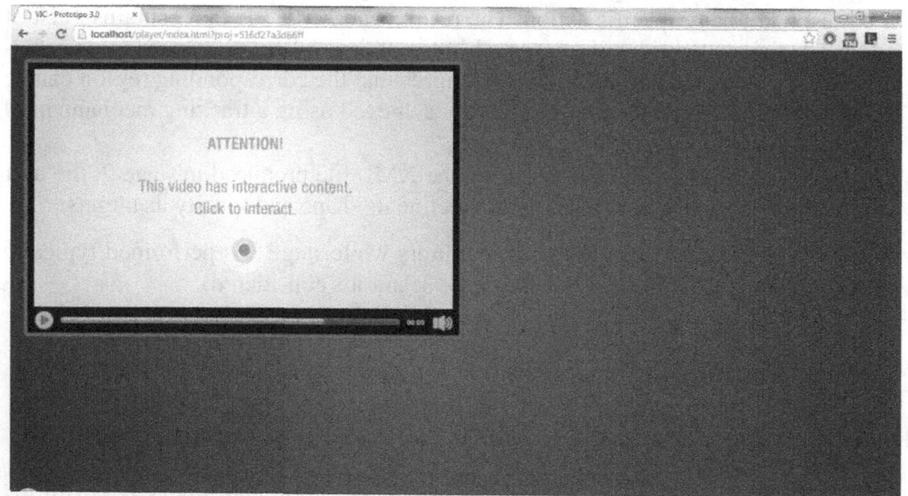

Fig. 1. Web player – starting visualization of an interactive video on a web page

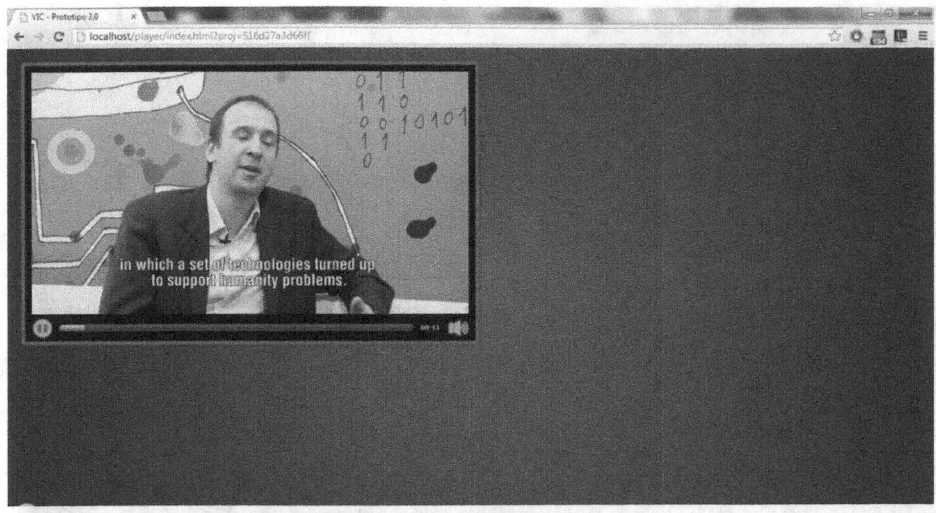

Fig. 2. Web player –an active hotspot (concentric circles on the left) visible during video play

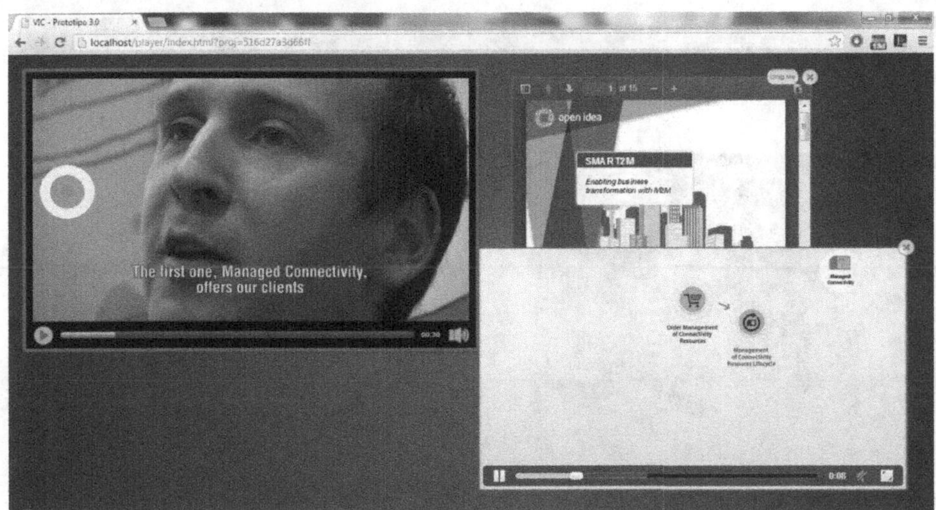

Fig. 3. Web player – showing additional content after interaction with hotspots

4.2 Mobile Player

The mobile player has the same capabilities as the web player, being the main difference the interaction with the touchscreen – for the web player the mouse is used for interacting with the hotspots). Fig. 4 shows the interactive video selection panel that is shown in the mobile player prototype, in this case running in a Windows 8 tablet. Fig. 5 shows an example of text information shown upon interaction with a hotspot.

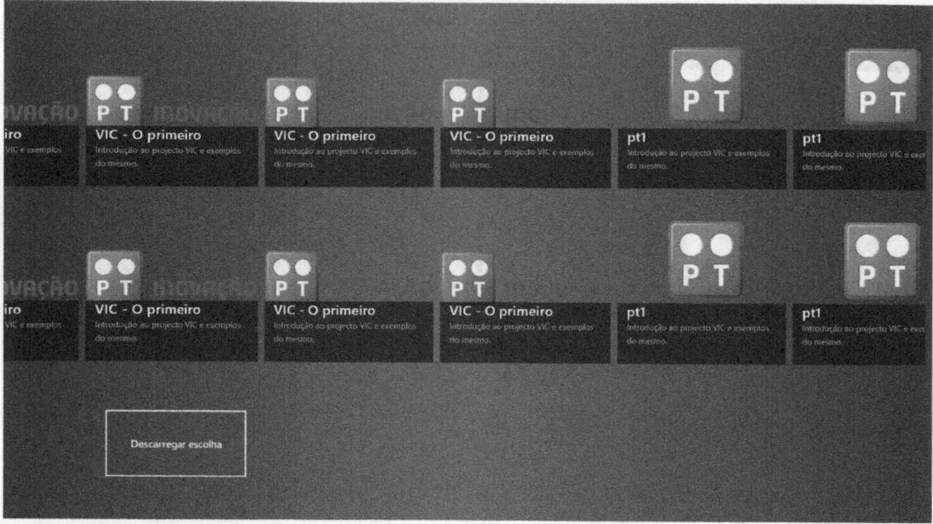

Fig. 4. Mobile player – interactive videos selection panel

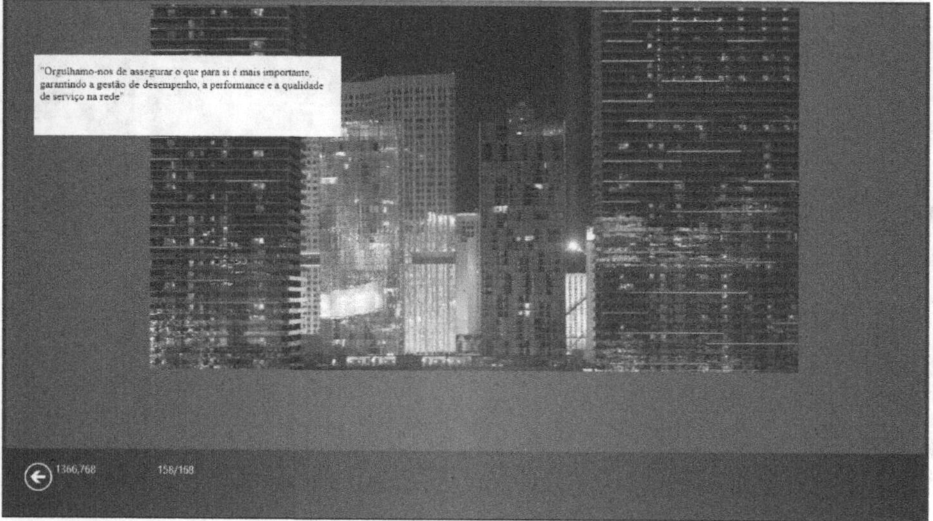

Fig. 5. Mobile player – text box shown upon interaction with hotspot

4.3 Interaction Configuration Tool

The configuration tool is a web application that allows product managers to build the interactive video to be shown to the audience, choosing the hotspots and resulting actions from a list of possible ones, built during stage 2 of the production chain, and according to a storyboard where interaction is crucial. Fig. 6 shows an example of the page that allows configuring several properties of the hotspot, such as shape, size, position, type of content that is shown upon interaction or the "Draggable" property.

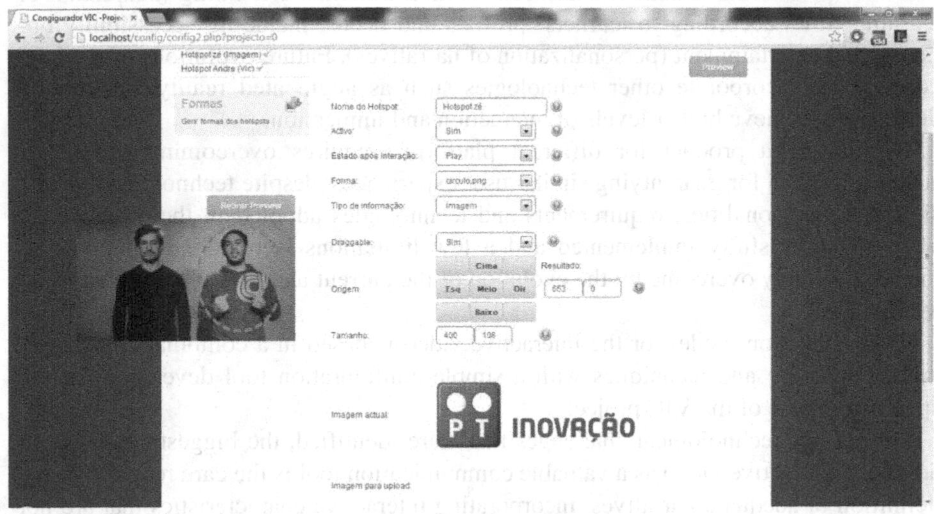

Fig. 6. Configuring the hotspot

4.4 Results

The implementation of the prototypes fulfilled all the requirements defined for the VIC project. However, a few problems were found and considered for further developments. For the web player, the following limitations were identified:

- Synchronization problems occur when the visualization flow is changed manually (for example, clicking in the time bar to return to a specific moment).
- Browser processing capabilities affect synchronization and response to events.
- Bandwidth, browser processing capabilities and target video duration affect transition between videos.
- Necessity to have the videos available in 3 formats (Ogg, MPEG4 and Webm) because browsers do not support all the same formats.

The mobile player has an additional set of problems that are essentially due to the option for the platform and also to usual performance limitations of mobile devices:

- There's no possibility to play 2 videos simultaneously.
- Transitions between videos are slower than in the web version and sometimes the delay is sensible.
- The visualization of a PDF file requires an external application which implies leaving the player application.

5 Concluding Remarks

The development of VIC has shown the viability of the interactive video concept and allowed envisaging its potential as a powerful communication tool, in commercial contexts (product information, datasheets, demonstrations), e-learning (adaptation of learning flows according to learners' profiles and needs, including accessibility options), and entertainment (personalization of narratives). Future evolutions of the VIC concept can incorporate other technologies such as augmented reality and motion detection to achieve higher levels of interaction and immersion.

Developing a product for different platforms requires overcoming challenges such as the need for guarantying similar user experiences, despite technological diversity. The functionalities, requirements and technologies adopted in the VIC project were all successfully implemented and a few limitations were identified, most of them predictably overcome by the evolution of the current and future mobile and web technologies.

The production model for the interactive video is based in a combination of well-known software and techniques with a simple configuration tool developed for the specific purpose of the VIC project.

Despite the technological challenges that were identified, the biggest challenge in adopting interactive video as a valuable communication tool is the care required in the definition of adequate narratives, incorporating interactive characteristics that are not familiar to storyboarding professionals. For interactive video production, video capture and basic editing have to be carefully planned and executed in order to achieve a coherent set of stories and not just a unordered sequence of information, which could avoid users from keeping a notion of the sequence or main narrative. It is also important that interaction points are envisaged and several aspects like its duration planned from the very beginning, because it can impact video production and direction.

Acknowledgements. This work is funded by Portugal Telecom Inovação under the Innovation Plan of the PT Group, and by FEDER funds through the Programa Operacional Fatores de Competitividade – COMPETE and National Funds through FCT - Foundation for Science and Technology under the project «FCOMP - 01-0124-FEDER-022701».

References

1. The Moving Picture Experts Group, http://mpeg.chiariglione.org/standards/mpeg-21 (accessed in February 20, 2014)
2. Apple Inc., http://www.apple.com/quicktime/what-is/ (accessed in February 20, 2014)
3. AXMEDIS, http://www.axmedis.org/com/ (accessed in February 20, 2014)
4. Emmens, C.A.: slj/Video Watch. SLJ School Journal, 40–41 (February 1981)
5. Tani, M., Yamaashi, K., Tanikoshi, K., Futukawa, M., Tanifuji, S.: Object-oriented video: interaction with real-world objects through live video. In: CHI 1992 Proceedings, pp. 593–598. ACM (1992)
6. Rack, C., Seeliger, R., Arbanowski, S.: Featured Media Nonlinear, clickable multimedia content for an interactive video experience. In: Proceedings of the 2010 Second International Conferences in Advances in Multimedia, pp. 39–43. IEEE Computer Society (2010)

7. Wang, J., Bhat, P., Colburn, R.A., Agrawala, M., Cohen, M.F.: Interactive Video Cutout. In: ACM Transactions on Graphics (TOG) – Proceedings of ACM SIGGRAPH 2005, vol. 24(3), pp. 585–594. ACM (2005)
8. Goularte, R., Moreira, E.S., Pimentel, M.G.: Structuring Interactive TV Documents. In: Proceedings of DocEng 2003, pp. 42–51. ACM (2003)
9. Smith, J.C., Stotts, D.: An extensible Object Tracking Architecture for Hyperlinking in Real-time and Stored Video Streams. In: Technical Report TR02-017. Department of Computer Science, University of North Carolina at Chapel Hill (2002)

Implementing GPII/Cloud4All Support for Mobile Accessibility for Android

Ferran Gállego

Code Factory S.L., Terrassa, Spain
ferran.gallego@codefactory.es

Abstract. Mobile Accessibility for Android is a combination of a suite of accessible apps and a screen reader which provide accessibility on Android devices for blind and visually impaired users. Main functionality of Android devices is made available to the user through Mobile Accessibility's voice and Braille based UI. This paper describes the process of integrating this commercial product with GPII/Cloud4All online architecture, providing auto-configuration based on user's online profile and NFC user identification.

Keywords: Access to mobile interaction, Cloud4All, GPII.

1 Introduction

Mobile Accessibility (MA) for Android is a suite of 12 accessible apps with a simplified User Interface (UI) that has been specially designed for blind and visually impaired users [1], it also implements an Android Accessibility Service that offers screen reading functionality, allowing the blind user to interact with the native Android UI similarly as the native Android Screen Reader (TalkBack) does.

Mobile Accessibility Input/Output interface is voice based. The product also offers Braille support for different grades and languages, compatible with the most popular Bluetooth Braille devices.

Assistive Technologies like Mobile Accessibility are highly configurable, offering a number of settings that allow the user to adjust the interface behavior based on his preferences, experience and other factors. Adjusting settings based on the needs and preferences of a given user is not an inmediate task, it requires the user to navigate several menus and configuration options related to voice settings, text processing, Braille input/output preferences, screen reader options and more. Moreover, modern mobile devices are 100% touch based, so this configuration process is still more complicated because adapted touch interfaces for blind users are not as productive as keyboard based UIs.

Auto configuration functionality is definitely a huge step in order to allow users to set up new phones, share devices with other members of the family that have different needs and lots of situations where there's no time enough to manually configure the tool to fit the needs and preferences of the user.

C. Stephanidis and M. Antona (Eds.): UAHCI/HCII 2014, Part II, LNCS 8514, pp. 50–57, 2014.

Moreover, since the Near Field Communication (NFC) technology has been widely adopted by phone manufacturers, this features offer the opportunity to develop user identification by touching the device with easily wearable NFC tags integrated on cards, rings, etc.

2 Mobile Accessibility Role in Cloud4All Project

Cloud4All/GPII offer a cloud infrastructure where needs and preferences of users are stored. When a user is identified in a Cloud4All compatible technology, it requests the cloud infrastructure for the preferences of the new person and applies it automatically.

This integration can be done at platform level, where the Operating System (OS) is responsible of the interaction with Cloud4All/GPII infrastructure, providing APIs that would allow third party developers for this platform to take benefit of auto-configuration features supported by the OS.

When Cloud4All/GPII integration is not present at platform level, individual applications could individually integrate Cloud4All/GPII, implementing the communication with online infrastructure and offering auto-configuration as a feature implemented inside the app. This is the case covered by Mobile Accessibility in Cloud4All project (A304.2: Auto-configuration of assistive solutions in mobile phones), so the implementation of Cloud4All/GPII for this solution doesn't assume any platform level integration on Android. Other parts of the project take care of the integration of Cloud4All/GPII at OS level.

3 Mobile Accessibility Settings and Cloud4All/GPII Common Terms

Mobile Accessibility offers a high number of settings that allow the user to adjust the behavior of the app on different aspects: Text-To-Speech (TTS), text input preferences, details about interaction with external Bluetooth Braille devices, screen reader configuration, call management options and more.

A subset of configuration options available on Mobile Accessibility has been selected in order to implement auto-configuration features offered by Cloud4All/GPII:

- *Access_commonprefs_speechrate*: TTS speech rate. Type: Numeric values from 0 to 10.
- *Access_commonprefs_speechpitch*: voice pitch. Type: Numeric values from 0 to 10.
- *Settings_phone_usesystemcallscreens*: this setting allows the user to determine how to manage incoming calls, this can be done through a specific call screen offered by Mobile Accessibility or the default Android call screen. Type: Boolean.

- *Access_commonprefs_turnofflistnumbering*: allows the user to activate/deactivate list numbering information (current item number and total number of items) when navigating lists. Type: Boolean.
- *Access_commonprefs_editingspeakdelchar*: through this setting the user can decide if he wants to get voice output announcing the deleted character while typing text. Type: Boolean.
- *Access_commonprefs_srspeaksystemnotifications*: this setting determines if system notifications should be spoken aloud by the TTS when they arrive. Type: Boolean.
- *Access_commonprefs_numberprocessing*: indicates how long numbers are spoken by the TTS. Type: Numeric from 0 to 3. Values can be: none(0): read the entire number, single(1): read the number by digits, pairs(2): read the number by pairs of digits, triplets(3): read the number by triplets of digits.
- *Access_commonprefs_editingkeyboardecho*: keyboard echo while typing text. Type: numeric from 0 to 3. Values can be: none(0), characters(1), words(2), characters and words (3).
- *Access_commonprefs_editingsecretmode*: allows to determine what keyboard echo to get while typing text in password fields. Type: numeric from 0 to 2. Values can be: say star(0: the TTS says "star" for each character), speak characters (1: the TTS speaks the introduced character -the field will still look like a password field visually, this only affects text output-), silent (2: no speech output while typing on password fields).
- *Settings_phone_usevolumekeysforcalls*: for incoming calls and also while in a call, volume keys can keep its default behavior and allow to adjust the volume or, if the user prefers, it can be used to accept the call (volume up), reject the call or hang up the current one (volume down). This setting allows the user to choose how he wants to use volume keys in this scenario. Type: Boolean.
- *Access_commonprefs_spellphonetically*: how the characters of a word will be spelled. Type: Boolean. Values can be true: character names: a, b, c, d...; false: use NATO phonetic alphabet: Alpha, Bravo, Charlie, Delta...
- *Access_commonprefs_punctuation*: indicates how many punctuation symbols will be spoken when reading text. This is very common between different screen reader solutions. Punctuation characters will take effect on the spoken text, so commas, dots etcetera will produce pauses and so. Anyway, some users will prefer to hear the name of the punctuation symbol when it appears. This is commonly needed for non-advanced users or when they need to read carefully. Type: Numeric from 0 to 3. Possible values are: none(0: no punctuation symbols are spoken), some(1: only some non common punctuation symbols are spoken), most (2: most of punctuation symbols are spoken but not the most common ones such as dot, comma, etc.), all (3: all punctuation symbols are spoken).
- *Access_commonprefs_capitalization*: allows the user to determine whether or not capitalization should be announced when reading text by characters. Type: Boolean. Values can be true (capitalization should be spoken), false (ignore capitalization, just speak character names regardless its upper or lower case condition).

4 Common Terms

Mobile Accessibility application-specific terms (settings described in point 3) have correspondences with Cloud4All/GPII common terms, which define stable definitions of settings or preferences that would apply across many applications or devices. For example, some common terms that match Mobile Accessibility specific terms are:

- *speechRate*: defined as number of words per minute.
- *pitch*: floating point value from 0.0 to 1.0.
- *keyEcho*: type of speech output to get when typing characters. Type: Boolean (true: provide TTS output on key presses, false: no TTS output for characters).
- *wordEcho*: type of speech output to provide after completing each word while typing text. Type: Boolean (true: read the entire word after typing it, false: no TTS output for words).
- *announceCapitals*: same as *access_commonprefs_capitalization* Mobile Accessibility specific setting.
- *punctuationVerbosity*: same as *access_commonprefs_punctuation* Mobile Accessibility specific setting.

5 Transformations

Needs and preferences sets stored in the online Cloud4All/GPII architecture are defined using common terms which will be applied across different technologies and solutions. In order to translate this common terms in application specific terms we need to define transformation rules.

Several transformation functions are available for this puposes. They are documented in the entry Architecture - Available transformation functions from Cloud4All/GPII Wiki site [2].

To do this, we need to add a solution entry for Mobile Accessibility so the architecture knows about our application. This entry will also describe the transformations that need to be perfomed by the online architecture, so the preferences sets sent to Mobile Accessibility are defined in app-specific terms.

Solution entries with transformation definitions are stored in the Cloud4All/GPII online architecture and they are implemented in JSON language. Transformations for Mobile Accessibility's specific terms are defined with the following structure:

```
<MA_specific_term>:{
   "transform": {
      "type": <type_of_transformation>,
      <transformation_parameter_1>: <value_1>,
      ...
      <transformation_parameter_n>: <value_n>
   }
}
```

The following transformation examples show how to transform the common terms described in point 4 to convert it in the corresponding Mobile Accessibility application-specific terms.

5.1 Speech Rate

Speech rate common term defines it as words per minute, while Mobile Accessibility specific terms needs values from 0 to 10. A good approach for this transformation is defining

```
  MA_speech_rate = speechRate_common_term / 40
This transformation can be implemented as follows:
"access_commonprefs_speechrate": {
        "transform": {
            "type": "fluid.transforms.binaryOp",
            "leftPath": "display.screenReader.speechRate",
            "operator": "/",
            "right": 40
        }
    }
```

Here the transformation is of type flu-id.transforms.binaryOp, that means a simple binary operation that needs 3 parameters to define the left operand (speechRate common term in this case), operator and right operand for the transformation: leftPath, operator, rightPath.

5.2 Speech Pitch

Same as for the speech rate, speech pitch common term can be converted to Mobile Accessibility's specific term for pitch with a simple arithmetic operation

```
  MA_speech_pitch = 10 * pitch_common_term
```

This transformation is a binary operation same as 5.1 and can be implemented as follows:

```
"access_commonprefs_speechpitch": {
        "transform": {
            "type": "fluid.transforms.binaryOp",
            "leftPath":
"diplay.textReadingHighlight.pitch",
            "operator": "*",
            "right": 10
        }
    }
```

5.3 Keyboard Echo

This case needs more attention. Mobile Accessibility specific term for this is defined as a numeric value between 0 and 3, where each value means

- 0: no keyboard echo.
- 1: character echo.
- 2: words echo.
- 3: characters and words echo.

There's no exact common term correspondence for this definition. Instead, there are 2 different common terms that combine this user preferences:

- keyEcho: boolean that defines if the user wants characters echo or not.
- wordEcho: boolean that defines if the user wants words echo or not.

So the transformation here must combine both keyEcho and wordEcho common terms in a single Mobile Accessibility specific terms.

This can be implemented by nesting some conditional transformations:

```
"access_commonprefs_editingkeyboardecho": {
   "transform": {
      "type": "fluid.transforms.condition",
      "conditionPath":
"display.screenReader.-provisional-keyEcho",
      "true": {
         "transform": {
            "type": "flu-id.transforms.condition",
            "conditionPath":
"display.screenReader.-provisional-wordEcho",
            "true": "3",
            "false": "1"
         }
      },
      "false": {
         "transform": {
            "type": "flu-id.transforms.condition",
            "conditionPath":
"display.screenReader.-provisional-wordEcho",
            "true": "2",
            "false": "0"
         }
      }
   }
}
```

Conditional transformations accept 3 parameters: conditionPath (path the boolean value to be evaluated, in this case it'll be keyEcho and wordEcho common terms), true (value to return when the condition is true), false (value to return when the condition is false).

The combined Mobile Accessibility specific setting is obtained by first checking wordEcho common term, then we evaluate keyEcho common term for each possible value of wordEcho, returning the combined value that Mobile Accessibility needs in each case.

The previous JSON fragment represents what in pseudo-code would be

```
if keyEcho_common_term then
    if wordEcho_common_term then
       MA_keyboard_echo_setting = 3
    else
       MA_keyboard_echo_setting = 1
else
    if  wordEcho_common_term then
       MA_keyboard_echo_setting = 2
    else
       MA_keyboard_echo_setting = 0
    end if
end if
```

5.4 Punctuation Verbosity and Capitalization

Mobile Accessibility specific terms for this preferences exactly coincide with the definition of its corresponding common terms. This makes trivial its transformations, that can be implemented like this:

```
"access_commonprefs_punctuation":
"display.screenReader.-provisional-punctuationVerbosity",

"access_commonprefs_capitalization":
"display.screenReader.-provisional-announceCapitals"
```

In both cases we're simply indicating that the Mobile Accessibility specific term can take the exact value coming from its corresponding common term.

6 Online Flow Manager

Once the online servers of Cloud4All/GPII architecture have the information about Mobile Accessibility and how to transform common terms in specific terms for our app, we can request the Online Flow Manager (part of the architecture in charge of receiving requests for preferences sets for a given user ID, communicate with other architecture components and provide the preferences back to the caller according to user's needs and preferences and transformations defined for each solution) for a set of preferences for a given user. The requested preference set will be retrieved by the Flow Manager and translated to Mobile Accessibility specific terms.

This call to the online Flow Manager can be done via HTTP GET request in the form defined in Flow Manager documentation from GPII wiki page[3].

Preferences sets from the online Flow Manager are provided also in JSON format, which can be easily parsed using org.json components natively available on Android.

7 NFC User Listener

User identification for Mobile Accessibility has been based on NFC, so the user can request Mobile Accessibility to be auto configured according to his needs and preferences by simply touching the back side of the device with a NFC token. This token has to provide the userID in plain text format, future implementations could change according to security requirements, for example.

NFC support natively provided by Android API through android.nfc library.

References

1. Code Factory website, `http://www.codefactory.es`
2. Architecture - Available Transformation Functions documentation, GPII Wiki site: `http://wiki.gpii.net/index.php/Architecture_-_Available_transformation_functions`
3. Flow Manager API - Cloud based deployment, GPII Wiki site: `http://wiki.gpii.net/index.php/Flow_Manager_API#Cloud_Based_Deployment`

The GPII on Smart Phones: Android

Javier Hernández Antúnez

Emergya, Sevilla, Spain
jhernandez@emergya.com

Abstract. The focus of this presentation is to go through all the aspects that are being covered during the works on the implementation of the Global Public Inclusive Infrastructure (GPII) [1] on Smart Phones, the scope, the status of the current implementation and upcoming developments where the Cloud4all [2] project is working on.

Since The Global Public Inclusive Infrastructure aims to become an international standard, one of the biggest challenges of the GPII project is to support all those devices that are using, and will use in the future, the technologies around the Smart Phones. This initial implementation is coming from the Cloud4all project, which has bet on the Android platform to demonstrate the features that the GPII will offer to us on every device that could run Android on it, either a Smart Phone, or Tablet, or DigitialTV, etc, and will serve as inspiration for future implementations on other Smart Phone platforms such as the popular iOS and Windows Phone, or the emerging Firefox OS, Tizen or Ubuntu Touch.

Keywords: Accessibility, Internet Access, Health, Social inclusion, Cloud, Mobility.

1 Background

The concept of Smart Phone was first used when Ericsson described its GS 88 "Penelope" concept as a Smart Phone, but nowadays, by Smart Phone we usually understand the technology who has brought the digital era of the Internet to our hands, as a tiny and lightweight, but a powerful device which can fit into our pockets.

For a long time now, several platforms that conceptually matched the definition of Smart Phone has existed such as Symbian, PalmOS, Windows CE, etc, and these triggered the competition between many companies for building the most successful one. As a result of this, today, around 1.5 billion of Smart Phones are being used around the world, where Android from Google, IOS from Apple, Windows Phone from Microsoft and BlackBerry, are the most relevant mobile platforms in the world.

2 Motivations

2.1 About Android

Although Android was developed early in 2005, it wasn't unveiled as a product until November 5, 2007, when a consortium of technology companies including Google,

C. Stephanidis and M. Antona (Eds.): UAHCI/HCII 2014, Part II, LNCS 8514, pp. 58–67, 2014.

device manufacturers such as HTC, Sony and Samsung, announced the creation of the Open Handset Alliance [3], with a goal to develop open standards for mobile devices. The first device running Android was announced the next year. Right now, Android represents more than the eighty percent of Smart Phones platforms on the market around the world.

As of the end of 2013, Android was the most popular operating system, with a 81.9% market share, followed by iOS with 12.1%, Windows Phone with 3.6% and BlackBerry with 1.8%. These numbers are reflected in the following table extracted from *Worldwide Smartphone Sales to End Users by Operating System* [4]

Table 1. Comparison table of Smartphone platforms and its Market Share

Operating System	2013 Market Share (%)
Android	81.9
iOS	12.1
Microsoft	3.6
BlackBerry	1.8
Bada	0.3
Symbian	0.2
Others	0.2

2.2 Online Software

Another concept which became popular at the same time we started using Smart Phones massively, was the ability to install software into a Smart Phone immediately, and this concept has impacted on the software business dramatically. And nowadays, we could call them:

- Google Play
- App Store
- Windows Phone Marketplace

By using these application markets, the people now have a huge amount of software available to them, and ready to be immediately installed on their Smart Phone devices.

Nowadays, the companies around the most successful application markets are making a profit of them, and talking in numbers, around 25$ billion in sales as we can read in this article [5]:

App stores run by Apple and Google Inc. now offer more than 700,000 apps each. With so many apps to choose from, consumers are estimated to spend on average about two hours a day with apps. Global revenue from app stores is expected to rise 62% this year to $25 billion, according to Gartner Inc,

2.3 Accessibility on Android

The Android community, and by having Google included into it, are working together to address the most common problems that people with disabilities find out when trying to use the system.

To illustrate the state of the art of the accessibility on Android, there is a detailed article about it from Darren Burton and Matthew Enigk called *Android Ice Cream Sandwich: Evaluating the Accessibility of Android 4.0* [6]. In this article, Darren Burton and Matthew Enigk go through the built-in features that Android 4 offers to address the problems of people with disabilities, taking special attention to low-vision and blind users. And as a resume of the most relevant features:

- A user who is blind or visually impaired does not need any sighted assistance to turn on the screen reader, so they can start using the device by their own
- Android comes with *Explore by Touch*, which allows to the user the ability to explore the content of the screen just by moving their fingers around the screen
- An accessible tutorial comes on screen when the screen reader starts, and the *Talk Back* speech synthesizer talks you through practicing how to use *Explore by Touch*
- The *Haptic Feedback* is a must have feature for the people who are blind or visually impaired and Android comes with it
- *Touch gestures* are well supported so users can use built-in, or define their own, gestures to handle the environment
- The *On Screen Keyboard* is accessible and usable within the screen reader
- Most of the basic but required tasks that we make on our Android device is accessible for people who are blind or visually impaired
  - Making a call
  - Messaging
  - Web browsing
  - E-mailing
  - Unlocking and answering an incoming call are easy

3 Goals

One relevant goal of the Cloud4all project is to create a real demonstration about how to cover the personal needs and preferences of a user who is using an Android device, either if it's a phone, a tablet, a DigitalTV, or a Kiosk running Android on it, and by using the benefits from the GPII personalization framework. But to specifically, cover all those needs and preferences that people with disabilities have when using an Android device, and solve their problems by automatically running ATs or any built-in feature.

From the Description of Work of the Cloud4all project we can extract the objectives to be addressed during the project, they are:

- To identify the built-in accessibility features of smartphones that can be auto configured based on the user profile. These accessibility features may include screen/graphical characteristics, user input and/or sound speech capabilities
- To design the accessibility solutions for mobile devices that will enable the auto-personalization from profile" (APfP) capability
- To build "auto-personalization from profile" (APfP) capability into prototype mobile devices. This solution provides an adaptative accessibility solution for smartphones that is based on the user profile and needs
- To test whether these disparate mobile environments can provide the same user experience for a common user profile. This will ensure the interoperability of the solutions and will allow users to change from one mobile device to another with minor effort

4 Implementation

The implementation of the GPII on Android is taking place on the Cloud4all european project, which is putting a lot of efforts on creating the mechanisms to take advantage of the GPII's "Auto-personalization from users' needs and preferences" features and capabilities.

4.1 Technical Solution

The implementation of the GPII on Android is being built on top of the GPII core architecture, and since the GPII core architecture is based on Node.js [7], this implementation makes use of a port of Node.js for Android, called Anode [8]. By using Anode, all the components from the GPII architecture can run locally into an Android device.

And like in the rest of the local implementations of the GPII (Windows and GNU/Linux), only a few platform specific parts were required to be implemented. All these platform specific developments are living together into GPII's Android repository on Github [9], and there are a lot of literature about the works on Android:

- An Overview of the details and information about the implementation in the wiki of the GPII project [10]
- A useful FAQ about this implementation [11]

To mention about the platform specific developments, the source code includes platform-specific modules that are required to communicate with Android's built-in features such as:

- Activity Manager, to deal with Android's activity manager and allow us to start or stop applications.

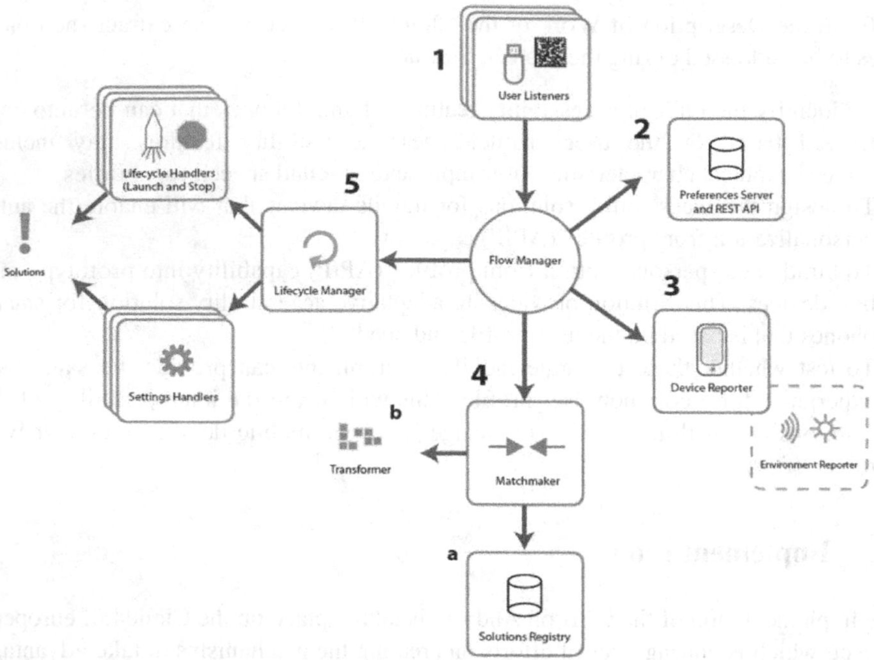

Fig. 1. GPII Architecture overview

- Android Settings, to deal with some settings that are accessed through a concrete API
- Audio Manager, to deal with system's volume levels
- Persistent Configuration, to deal with some settings that are accessed through a concrete API

All these components are loaded by the start script of the GPII on Android, and the work on this implementation ends up by registering the well-known Android's platform specific solutions into the GPII's universal source code repository. These well known solutions include:

- A description of a solution
- The settings handlers that the GPII uses to automatically configure this solution
- The available mechanisms to move specific settings from a platform or application into common terms [12]
- The lifecycle managers of each solution, describing how a solution has to be configured, started and stopped after logging out from the GPII.

Another platform specific work was in relation to the User Listeners. The User Listeners are the user's entry point to the GPII, and nowadays we support many ways to use the GPII on Android:

- By using an NFC tag
- By using a QR code

There are two different and working User Listeners, and they're available to download.

The first one [13] was developed by Tony Atkins and it includes support for NFC. The second one [14] was developed from some of the Cloud4all project partners, and includes the following features:

- Support for reading NDEF and GPII-specific mime-type NFC tags to log into the GPII
- Support for writing GPII-specific mime-type NFC tags
- Support for reading QR codes to log into the GPII
- Support for creating QR codes with a given user token

4.2 Developmental Issues

Since the beginning of the Cloud4all project, the Android team has been putting its effort on giving to Android (as a platform) the possibility to run the GPII core framework by itself, and this goal was successfully achieved by using Anode.

Despite all the restrictions regarding the access to the system's internals on Android, the implementation of the GPII on Android has the ability to take advantage of the auto-personalization from users' needs and preferences feature of the GPII, which has been addressed in the most recent versions of Android.

These problems and restrictions can be summarized in the following list:

- Root access are required to deal with some Android's internal components and APIs.
- Different versions of Android can provide a different set of settings that can be accessed through its APIs
- Debugging Node.js applications running on Android is hard
- Despite of the fact that Anode works, it still needs some improvements to make this implementation more rock-solid

Although these problems and restrictions are more or less under control, the Android team is continuously improving the system to address or at least, minimize the impact of having them.

4.3 Results

At this moment, the current implementation of the GPII on Android is a full-featured one, with the abilities to:

- Run their own instances of the GPII Architecture Framework by itself
- Intercommunicate with the system, configure its settings, and take advantage of the built-in features that Android has on it
- Intercommunicate with any Android's accessibility native service such as Talkback, the Android's built-in screen reader for visually impaired people

- Providing to third-party applications installed on the system the ability to take advantage of the GPII's "Auto-personalization from users' needs and preferences" features and capabilities, and being launched and automatically configured by the GPII
- Automatically translate settings from any other platform and or any application, into Android, and vice versa

5 Delivering the GPII to the End-Users

As part of Cloud4all, the implementation of the GPII on Android will be tested during the second pilots iteration of the project, where a lot of users with many different disabilities will have the opportunity to test this implementation, and to enrich the future developments on Android.

This second pilots iteration will take place this year again in three different pilot sites, in Germany, Greece and Spain.

As we can extract from the Cloud4all's deliverable *Pilots evaluation framework, experimental plan and logistics V2*, [15]

The scope of this second iteration phase is to evaluate with real user or demonstrate and capture the opinion of the users for the Cloud4all prototypes that are ready to be tested. The prototypes to be tested at this iteration phase are either tested for first time, or they are updated and extended prototypes of tools that have already been tested during the first iteration phase. In this iteration phase, the plan is to go one step forward from the previous phase and try to test a scenario much closer to the final Cloud4all/GPII vision, including additional integrated components of the holistic approach of Cloud4all.

The auto-configuration scenario where this implementation will take part of can be summarized as follows:

1. The user sets his/her needs and preferences for using any application or device. This can be done using a web-based Preference Management Tool (PMT) [16] or snapshot the current settings of the current system.
2. The user can store a token in NFC tag or USB key.
3. The needs and preferences of the user are stored in the N&P server in a safe and secure way.
4. Whenever a user encounters a GPII-compatible device (a PC, a mobile device, an ATM, etc.), he/she can key in using the NFC card or the USB key where he/she has stored his/her personal token.
5. The device sends the token and info about its accessibility features to the Cloud4all/GPII infrastructure.
6. The architecture takes the needs and preferences of the user from the N&P server.
7. The matchmakers get information about the needs and preferences of the user, the device and the environment, and will calculate the most appropriate device settings for this user and this situation.
8. Now the user can use the new device without having to tweak any settings. If the device has not all the accessibility features needed, the GPII will recommend

solutions available in the Cloud. When the user keys back, the system will get back to its default setting.

People that will take part of this pilot iteration will test this auto-configuration scenario on many different devices and situations:

9. Using a PC operating system (either GNU/Linux or Microsoft Windows) with built-in ATs, platform specific features, and/or third party ATs.
10. Using a PC operating system (either GNU/Linux or Microsoft Windows) without any built-in ATs, platform specific features, or third party ATs. These will make use of cloud-based ATs or browser-specific extensions.
11. Using an Android device with the GPII running locally, making use of Android's built-in features and ATs, and third-party applications that are supported by the GPII.
12. Using an Android device without the GPII running locally, making use of third-party applications that make use of the GPII's Cloud-based Flow Manager.
13. Using a simple phone (JME-based phone platforms) with a third-party application that makes use of the GPII's Cloud-based Flow Manager.

Note that all the scenario can not be run in every device/situation but when applicable.

The following picture resumes very well the scenario and how the user will make use of the system:

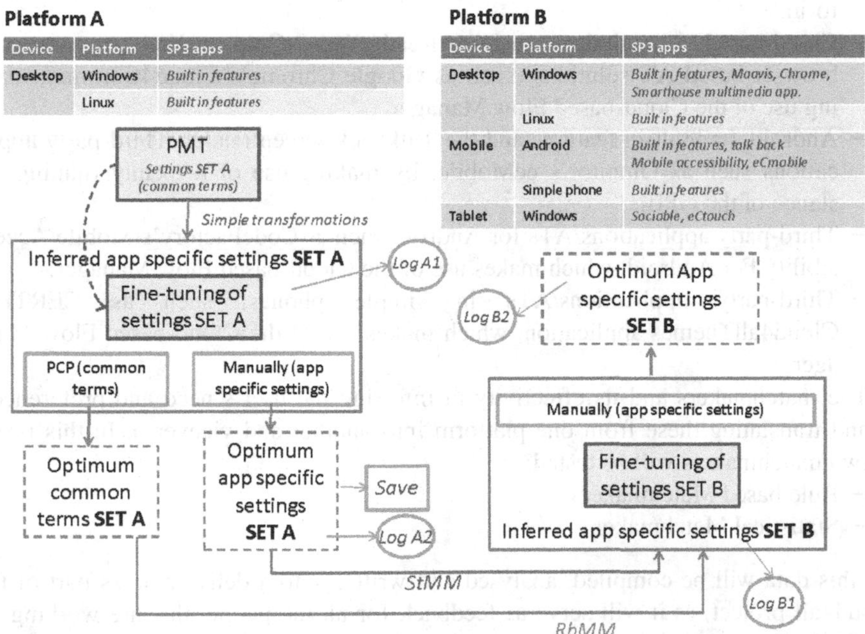

Fig. 2. Cloud4all second pilots scenario

In this scenario, the user will be asked to perform the following tasks:

14. To create an account (NP set). The user is asked to create an initial set of needs and preferences using the PMT, in a familiar desktop environment (Windows or Linux)
15. To edit inferred settings. The user is asked to edit/optimize the settings in this first platform, using the PCP [16].
16. To change platform. When the user keys in into a different platform, the auto-configured interface appears.
17. Edit inferred settings. The user is asked to edit/optimize the settings presented to his/her in the second platform.

With every step, a lot of sub-tasks will be performed by the facilitators of the pilots, and these will be the resulting data that will be used to evaluate the many different components of the system.

- The whole architecture itself.
- The PCP and the PMT as the available user interfaces to interact with the GPII.
- The implementations on many different platforms, applications, etc. ie:
  - GNU/Linux and the GNOME desktop, its built-in features, including the Orca screen reader.
  - Microsoft Windows, its built-in features, including the NVDA screen reader.
  - Maavis, as a standalone AT running on a locally running GPII windows platform.
  - Cloud-based AT solutions such as Read&Write Gold or Web Anywhere or browser-based AT solutions (such as Google Chrome's Cloud4Chrome), making use of the Cloud-based Flow Manager.
  - Android, its built-in features and the Talkback screen reader. Third-party applications such as Omnitor's ecMobile, by making use of a locally running instance of the GPII.
  - Third-party applications/ATs for Android such as CodeFactory's Mobile Accessibility For Android, which makes use of the Cloud-based Flow Manager.
  - Third-party applications/ATs in simple phones, such as CERTH's Cloud4allThemes application, which makes use of the Cloud-based Flow Manager.
- The matchmakers and its effectivity in inferring the user's need and preferences, and translating these from one platform into another and viceversa. In this phase two matchmakers will be tested:
  - Rule based Matchmaker
  - Statistical Matchmaker

All this data will be compiled, analysed and written into a deliverable as part of the Cloud4all project, as it will serve as feedback for all the people that are working on the GPII.

Acknowledgements. The research leading to these results has received funding from the European Union's Seventh Framework Programme (FP7/2007-2013) under grant agreement 289016. The present work benefited form the input of the architecture team from the GPII project, and specially from Steven Githens, architect at the GPII, who provided the initial work of this implementation.

References

1. http://gpii.net
2. http://cloud4all.info
3. http://www.openhandsetalliance.com/
4. http://www.gartner.com/newsroom/id/2623415
5. http://online.wsj.com/news/articles/SB10001424127887323293704578334401534217878
6. http://www.afb.org/afbpress/pub.asp?DocID=aw130302
7. http://nodejs.org/
8. https://github.com/paddybyers/anode/wiki
9. https://github.com/GPII/android
10. http://wiki.gpii.net/index.php/Android_Overview
11. http://wiki.gpii.net/index.php/GPII_Android_FAQ
12. http://wiki.gpii.net/index.php/Common_Terms_Registry
13. https://github.com/duhrer/gpii-android-listener
14. https://github.com/javihernandez/android-user-listeners
15. Sainzet, F., et al.: Pilots evaluation framework, experimental plan and logistics, Cloud4all project deliverable D402.2.2
16. http://wiki.gpii.net/index.php/PCPs,_PMTs,_etc

Effects of Interaction Style and Screen Size on Touchscreen Text Entry Performance: An Empirical Research

Sandi Ljubic[1], Vlado Glavinic[2], and Mihael Kukec[3]

[1] Faculty of Engineering, University of Rijeka, Vukovarska 58, 51000 Rijeka, Croatia
[2] Faculty of Electrical Engineering and Computing, University of Zagreb, Unska 3, 10000 Zagreb, Croatia
[3] Medimurje University of Applied Sciences in Cakovec, Bana Josipa Jelacica 22a, 40000 Cakovec, Croatia
sandi.ljubic@riteh.hr, vlado.glavinic@fer.hr, mihael.kukec@mev.hr

Abstract. In this paper we investigate text entry performance for mobile touchscreen devices with emulated QWERTY keyboards, with special emphasis on interaction style and screen size. When addressing interaction style, we are referring to the five most common combinations of hands postures and device orientations while executing text entry tasks. Both single-finger and two-thumb methods for typing in portrait and/or landscape layout are considered. As for screen sizes, several classes of popular mobile devices are examined, specifically smartphones and tablets with smaller and larger form factor. In addition, the mobile device emulator is included in the study, in order to report the comparative analysis of text entry with an actual device and its emulation-based counterpart. The touchscreen desktop monitor was used so as to provide touch input for the device emulator. Results obtained from experimental testing, supported by thorough data analysis, provide a valuable insight into the user behavior when typing on touchscreens.

Keywords: text entry, interaction style, screen size, touchscreens, mobile devices.

1 Introduction

Following the commercial success of touchscreen mobile devices, virtual keyboards (soft/touchscreen/on-screen keyboards) turned into dominant tools for typing "on the move". However, when compared with typing on physical keyboards, text entry on popular touchscreen smartphones and tablets is considered slow, uncomfortable, and inaccurate [1]. These usability issues, derived mainly from limited screen size and "fat finger syndrome", are usually addressed by making use of virtual keyboards' software based characteristics. Soft keyboards can be easily programmed to accommodate different layouts, screen sizes, device orientations, and languages, as well as to provide dictionary support and auto-correction features. Furthermore, innovative

C. Stephanidis and M. Antona (Eds.): UAHCI/HCII 2014, Part II, LNCS 8514, pp. 68–79, 2014.

interaction methods can be utilized, such as in gestural text input [2, 3], and in tilt-based text entry [4, 5]. Although multimodal text entry represents a valuable benefit in the area of universal access, users are in general resistant to waste their time in order to learn new text-input techniques [1]. This could be the actual reason why QWERTY still stands as the default keyboard layout in contemporary mobile touchscreen devices.

In studying text entry performance for mobile touchscreens, screen size is definitely the factor worth to consider. Larger devices naturally offer layouts with more convenient key button sizes, thus ensuring lower probability of making pointing errors. On the other hand, wider layouts come with increased distance between buttons, implying longer path that has to be covered by finger movements. Consequently, screen size can have a certain impact on both text entry speed and accuracy. The way of holding a mobile device can also play a significant role in touch typing scenarios. Users may interact with the mobile device in ways that are detrimental to performance, as the grip on a device determines several performance-affecting factors: the degrees of freedom in joint movement, the controlling muscles, and the orientation of the fingers' joints in relation to the display [6].

Owing to above mentioned remarks, we decided to carry out an empirical research of touchscreen text entry performance with two factors being in the main focus: (i) mobile device screen size, and (ii) interaction style – a combination of hands posture and device orientation used in text entry tasks.

2 Related Work and Motivation

In the context of touchscreen text entry study, HCI-based research is commonly called in to provide for trouble-free and more efficient touch typing. This includes dealing with typical problems such as the "fat-finger syndrome", optimal character layout, and appropriate size of key buttons. A huge amount of work has already been done by introducing many alternative keyboard designs and new input modalities, investigating typing behavior, and providing new metrics for text entry performance measurement.

The effect of soft button size on touch pointing and typing performance is already well documented [7, 8, 9]; however, there is a lack of focused studies related to present-day mobile devices' native keyboards. Recent research on touchscreen based text entry that addresses the way of holding mobile devices can be found in [10] and [11]. Nicolau and Jorge [10] focused their research exclusively on thumb typing, while considering three possible hand postures under three mobility settings. For an HTC Desire smartphone device, the two-thumbs landscape method was reported as the fastest one, followed by two-thumbs portrait and one-thumb portrait. Interaction based on forefinger usage was not included in this study. Azenkot and Zhai [11] explored touch behavior on soft keyboards when used with two thumbs, a forefinger, and one thumb. The Samsung Galaxy S smartphone was the only testing device used, and the corresponding results confirmed the two-thumbs text entry method as the

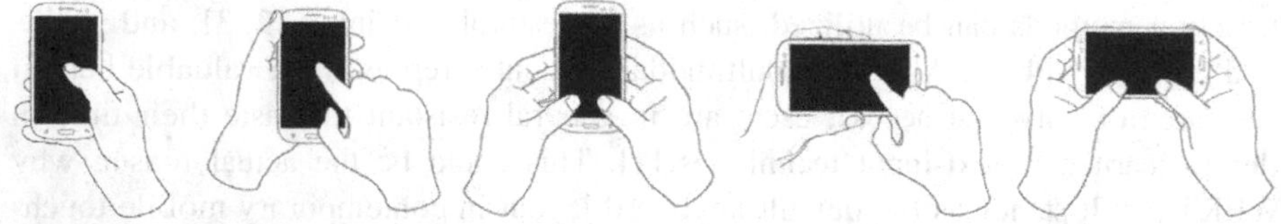

Fig. 1. Examples of well-suited interaction styles for smartphone text-entry. From left to right: one-thumb/portrait, forefinger/portrait, two-thumbs/portrait, forefinger/landscape, two-thumbs/landscape.

fastest one, followed by forefinger usage and the one-thumb technique. The error rates among postures reflected a speed-accuracy trade-off, since classification regarding erroneous input was the same as with the typing speed. Although both thumb usage and forefinger usage were considered, device orientation (portrait/landscape) was not addressed in the mentioned research.

Regarding the above reported related work, the motivation for our research stems from the need to strengthen the understanding of touchscreen text entry performance by providing a comparative analysis of all convenient interaction styles, as defined on Fig. 1.

Forefinger-based interaction styles correspond to use cases wherein one hand is holding the device, while the other – usually the dominant one – performs the text entry. In his field study regarding mobile device grip, Hoober [12] terms this interaction style as *cradling*, mentioning that either forefinger or thumb can play the role of the pointing tool. While both cradling and two-thumbs techniques are also fully eligible for text entry on touchscreen tablets, single-handed usage is not appropriate due to the tablets' form factor. Apart from smartphone and tablet classes, we additionally want to tackle text entry on a mobile device emulator. To the best of our knowledge, there is no study reporting the comparative analysis of interacting with an actual touchscreen smartphone/tablet and its emulator counterpart. For that reason, we make use of a touchscreen desktop monitor, and assume forefinger-based interaction style as the only option for text entry. The complete set of device classes, corresponding screen sizes, and interaction styles targeted by our research is presented in Table 1.

Table 1. Terget device classes, corresponding screen sizes, and interaction styles within our text entry research

Device class	Touchscreen size	Text entry interaction style				
		one-thumb portrait	cradling portrait	two-thumbs portrait	cradling landscape	two-thumbs landscape
Smaller smartphones	< 4"	✓	✓	✓	✓	✓
Larger smartphones	[4" - 5"]	✓	✓	✓	✓	✓
Smaller tablets	~ 7"		✓	✓	✓	✓
Larger tablets	~ 10"		✓	✓	✓	✓
Emulator	4.3" emulation		✓		✓	

3 Empirical Evaluation: Materials, Methods, and Metrics

For testing purposes, we implemented a simple Android application for gathering text entry events and the corresponding timing data. The application stores measurement results, along with the information about user ID and utilized interaction style, in CSV format on the device's internal SD card. Built-in text entry tasks are transcription-based, meaning that each trial requires rewriting a displayed text phrase randomly selected from a 500 instances set developed by MacKenzie and Soukoreff [13]. We consider a single task to be done when a particular phrase is fully and correctly transcribed, so a distinct cognitive load for error checking is assumed. Since input verification can impact the text entry speed, we try to decrease this cognitive demand by providing visual feedback about (in)correct letters (see Fig. 2.).

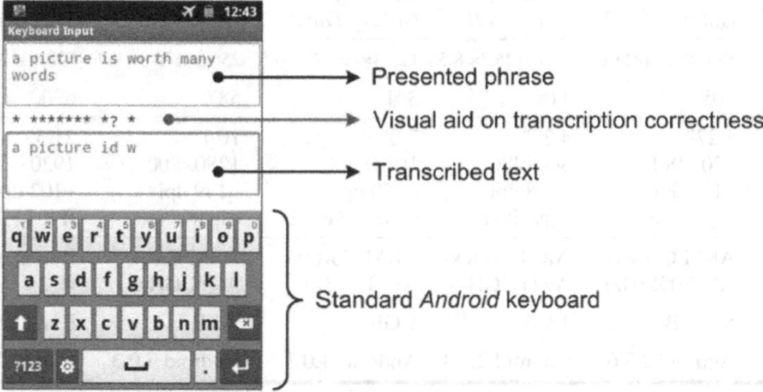

Fig. 2. Testing application: mistaken letters in the input stream are indicated with a question mark. Snapshot taken on *Samsung Galaxy Mini 2* (GT-S6500D).

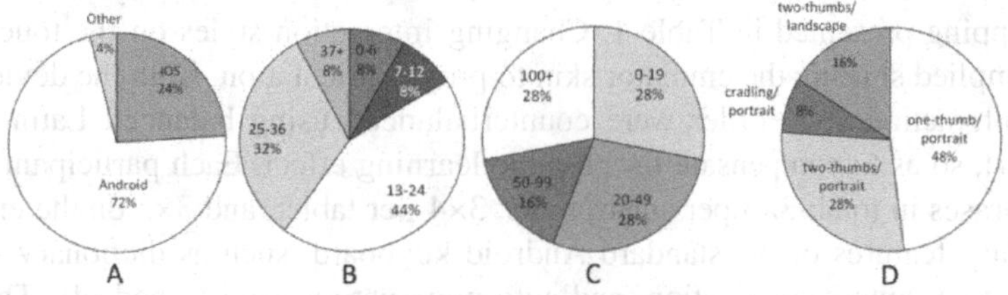

Fig. 3. A – operating systems of mobile devices owned by test users; B – users' experience with touchscreen mobile devices (in months); C – approximate number of touchscreen text entry tasks made per day; D – preferred interaction style when texting with smartphone

Twenty-five users were involved in our empirical research (20 males, 5 females), their age ranging from 21 to 35 with an average of 24 years. The statistics about their touchscreen usage is depicted in Fig. 3.

In the experiment we used four different mobile devices (D1–D4) running the Android OS, two from the smartphone class (D1, D2), and two from the tablet one (D3, D4). A default emulator from the Android SDK, with a 4.3" target skin, was tested on a touchscreen desktop monitor (D5), thus providing the basis for comparison with the larger smartphone (D2). Details about all used devices are presented in Table 2.

Table 2. Devices used in text entry empirical research. In order to minimize possible bias caused by devices' different technical specifications, a single manufacturer's products were selected. Also, testing application was developed targeting minimal CPU and RAM requirements.

Device	D1	D2	D3	D4	D5
Class	Smaller smartphone	Larger smartphone	Smaller tablet	Larger tablet	Touchscreen desktop monitor
Model	*Samsung Galaxy Mini 2*	*Samsung Galaxy S II*	*Samsung Galaxy Tab 2*	*Samsung Galaxy Tab 2*	*Dell Multitouch ST2220T*
W/H/D [mm]	58.6×109.4×11.6	66.1×125.3× 8.5	122.4×193.7× 10.5	256.6×175.3× 9.7	528.1 × 380.1 × 58.5
Weight [g]	105	116	341	587	6300
Display	3.27" 320×480 ~176 dpi capacitive	4.27" 800×480 ~218 dpi capacitive	7.0" 1024×600 ~170 dpi capacitive	10.1" 1280×800 ~149 dpi capacitive	21.5" 1920×1080 ~102 dpi IPS TFT optical
CPU	ARM Cortex-A5 (800MHz)	ARM Cortex-A9 (1.2GHz)	ARM Cortex-A9 (1 GHz)	ARM Cortex-A9 (1 GHz)	Run under: i5-2400 (3.1GHz)
RAM	512MB	1 GB	1 GB	1 GB	Run under: 4 GB
OS	Android 2.3.6	Android 2.3.4	Android 4.0.3	Android 4.0.3	Run under: Win 7

At the beginning of the testing session, users were involved in a short practice session (about 30 minutes) in order to familiarize with available devices, standard keyboard layouts, and testing application features. In the actual experiment, for each device D1–D5, participants were instructed to enter three different text phrases "as quickly as possible, as accurately as possible", using all interaction styles – according to the mapping presented in Table 1. Changing interaction styles on the touchscreen monitor implied shifting the emulator skin to proper orientation. Both the device order and the interaction style order were counterbalanced using balanced Latin squares design [14], so as to compensate for possible learning effect. Each participant entered 60 text phrases in total: 3×5 per smartphone, 3×4 per tablet, and 3×2 on the emulator. All auxiliary features of the standard Android keyboard, such as dictionary support, predictive text, auto-capitalization, and auto-punctuation were turned off. The backspace key was the only option allowed for deletion. Text entry tasks could have been accomplished while sitting or standing in a laboratory environment, so each participant had to make a choice of respective position in regard to her/his own preference.

Text entry performance was evaluated using data obtained from the devices' CSV files. Text entry speed was measured in words per minute (WPM). Three error rate types, as provided in the work by Soukoreff nad MacKenzie [15, 16], were used as accuracy metrics: T_{ER} (*Total Error Rate*), CAW_{ER} (*Corrected-And-Wrong Error*

Rate), and CBR_{ER} (*Corrected-But-Right Error Rate*). CAW_{ER} and CBR_{ER} represent corrections made on letters that were actually in error, and on letters that were correct, respectively.

Altogether 1500 text phrases were entered using five different touchscreens and five different hand postures, thus making a good basis for studying effects of interaction style and screen size on touchscreen text entry performance.

4 Results and Discussion

Mean values and standard deviations for text entry speed and accuracy metrics are presented in Table 3. As opposed to WPM, T_{ER} standard deviation values indicate that the error rate data deviates from a bell shaped curve. This assumption was later confirmed as Shapiro-Wilk tests of the observed values for T_{ER} showed no fit with normal distribution.

Table 3. Results: descriptive statistics summary for WPM and T_{ER} metrics

Device (D)	Text entry interaction style (S)									
	S1: one-thumb portrait		S2: cradling portrait		S3: two-thumbs portrait		S4: cradling landscape		S5: two-thumbs landscape	
	WPM	T_{ER} [%]	WPM	T_{ER} [%]	WPM	T_{ER} [%]	WPM	T_{ER} [%]	WPM	T_{ER} [%]
D1	28.80 ±6.67	5.38 ±6.07	27.97 ±7.07	6.80 ±6.52	32.41 ±9.16	5.55 ±4.88	32.43 ±8.04	3.00 ±5.94	37.21 ±7.93	2.59 ±3.65
D2	30.23 ±5.29	3.12 ±4.69	29.24 ±5.30	3.69 ±5.04	32.11 ±6.79	5.42 ±6.13	33.27 ±6.57	1.51 ±3.67	37.41 ±8.31	3.70 ±5.42
D3	not appropriate		31.71 ±6.11	2.66 ±4.90	36.80 ±8.23	2.97 ±3.59	32.05 ±7.51	2.59 ±5.65	33.43 ±6.99	2.83 ±6.08
D4	not appropriate		34.85 ±6.06	0.78 ±1.19	36.78 ±7.87	2.15 ±3.51	33.01 ±5.82	1.32 ±2.27	32.12 ±6.23	3.06 ±4.45
D5	not appropriate		16.36 ±5.64	6.62 ±7.35	not appropriate		16.47 ±4.90	6.44 ±7.24	not appropriate	

Since WPM data normality was verified on majority of conditions, a two-way repeated-measures ANOVA was selected for further WPM-related analysis. The goal of statistical analysis is to check whether the null hypothesis, stating "there is no difference in text entry speed with respect to the screen size and interaction style used", can be rejected. However, given that our experiment design is rather complex, single two-way RM ANOVA run would not be appropriate. Not all interaction styles (5 levels of factor S) are appropriate for every screen size (5 levels of factor D), so there is no complete data set for all D×S combinations. Consequently, our data analysis consists of three separate RM ANOVA runs that encompass all valid conditions, as illustrated in Fig. 4.

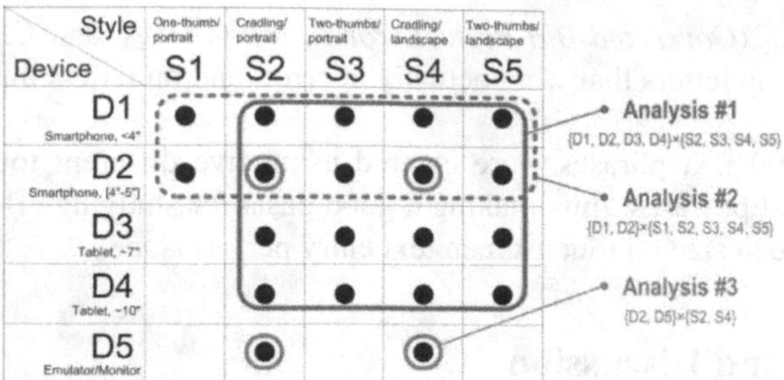

Fig. 4. WPM data analysis strategy

The first analysis (Analysis #1) deals with a complete set of mobile devices (D1–D4), and corresponding interaction styles suitable for every mobile device (S2–S5). Since one-thumb interaction is considered appropriate for smartphone class exclusively, the related analysis that covers all interaction styles, here including S1 also, applies only to D1–D2 set (Analysis #2). Indeed, there is no justification in comparing one-thumb/portrait with any other style used with devices D3–D5, because neither emulator nor tablets support equivalent interaction. Finally, the last stage of data analysis (Analysis #3) refers to text entry speed achieved using emulator and its mobile device counterpart. The larger smartphone (D2) is selected as the target device for comparison, because its screen size matches the emulator's skin dimensions.

4.1 Interaction Styles Common for All Mobile Devices

The outcome of the first analysis revealed a significant effect of interaction style (factor S) on WPM: $F_{3,72}$=12.225, p<0.001. Post-hoc pairwise comparisons with Bonferroni adjustment showed that:

- text entry using S5 is significantly faster with respect to using S4 (p<0.05) and S2 (p<0.001)
- text entry using S3 is significantly faster with respect to using S2 (p=0.001)
- text entry using S4 is significantly faster with respect to using S2 (p<0.05).

As expected, two-thumbs interaction generally results with faster text input, while cradling in portrait mode produces by far the slowest typing. The influence of screen size cannot be completely neglected in this analysis, as significant interaction between factors D and S was also found: $F_{9,216}$=9.495, p<0.001. The effect of D*S interaction is presented in Fig. 5, where several different "trends" can be observed. For example, it can be seen that cradling in portrait mode (S2) becomes more efficient when used with larger touchscreens. This can be explained by the increased key button sizes which allow easier targeting and, consequently, faster typing. However, text entry with two-thumbs in landscape orientation (S5) shows a completely different tendency, as typing performance declines with larger touchscreens. Once again we can address the role of keyboard dimensions, with the main difference being that larger button size is not a decisive factor in the related case, as the longer distance that fingers have to cross for button activation becomes critical instead.

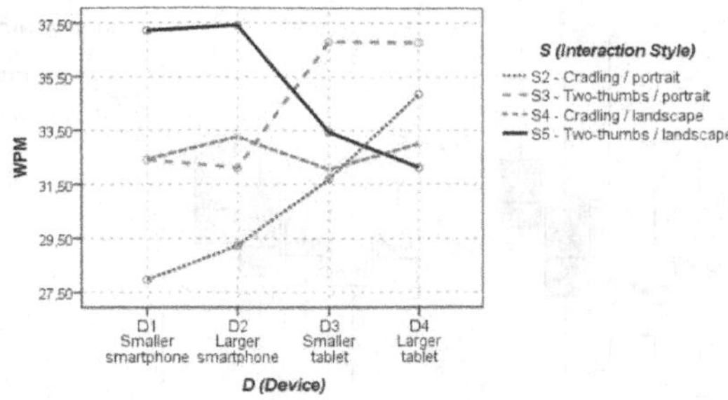

Fig. 5. Estimated marginal means of WPM

Afore mentioned observations can also support explaining the difference in two-thumbs typing between landscape (S5) and portrait (S3) orientation on different mobile devices. While two-thumbs interaction in portrait mode is clearly more efficient when used on tablets, landscape mode implies faster two-thumbs typing on smartphones. Using two hands for typing on portrait-oriented smartphones can be cumbersome because of diminutive high-density keyboard layouts, hence it is understandable that a tablet represents a faster texting device in the two-thumbs/portrait context. Regarding two-thumbs usage in landscape orientation, smartphone keyboards happen to be well-suited considering appropriately larger buttons and reasonable fingers workload, as opposed to tablets that become less efficient because thumbs are required to travel more from one key to another.

The same effect can be seen in cradling-based interaction styles S2 and S4. Concerning these cradling styles, WPM mean values for device D3 represent an especially interesting case since they approximately form a point of equal performance ($WPM_{D3,S2}$=31.71, $WPM_{D3,S4}$=32.05). Apparently, keyboard layouts displayed on smaller tablets, although with different geometry in landscape and portrait orientation, define almost equal conditions for typing with the dominant hand while the non-dominant one provides stability.

4.2 Smartphone Class

The second two-way RM ANOVA was applied to the smartphone class exclusively, and the involved complete set of interaction styles (S1–S5). This is where one-thumb text entry was also being considered. A significant effect of interaction style on WPM was found again: $F_{3.044,\ 73.049}=21.722$, $p<0.001$. Greenhouse-Geisser correction was applied, as Mauchly's test showed violation of sphericity (W=0.457, p=0.041). Post-hoc pairwise comparisons with Bonferroni adjustment showed that:

- text entry using S5 is significantly faster with respect to using S4 ($p<0.05$), S3 ($p<0.001$), S2 ($p<0.001$), and S1 ($p<0.001$)
- text entry using S3 is significantly faster with respect to using S2 ($p<0.05$)
- text entry using S4 is significantly faster with respect to using S2 ($p<0.001$).

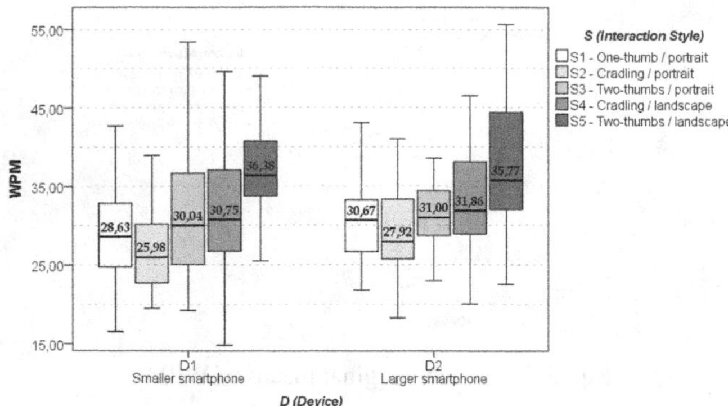

Fig. 6. Text entry speed (WPM metrics) for smartphone class. For every observed D×S combination, the corresponding box plot shows minimum and maximum, 25 percentile (Q1), 75 percentile (Q3), and median value. Outliers are excluded.

Two-thumbs text entry in landscape orientation is by far the fastest for smartphone devices. While cradling in landscape mode and two-thumbs typing in portrait mode are somewhat equally leveled, portrait-oriented cradling once again showed to be the least efficient interaction style for text input. When it comes to one-thumb typing (S1), its usage produced the second worst performance, although comparison with the best interaction style (S5) is the only one statistically significant. It is interesting to find out that S2 does not outperform S1, meaning that forefinger-based targeting with provided device stability does not help in gaining better text entry results.

In this stage of data analysis, significant effects of screen size and D*S interaction were not found. Descriptive statistics summary (in boxplot form) for text entry speed in smartphone class is presented in Fig. 6

4.3 Emulator Case

The third two-way RM ANOVA provided a special case investigation by addressing difference in text entry speed between emulator and actual mobile device. Cradling-based interaction styles were tackled only, as they represent valid methods for providing touch input on desktop monitor. The outcome of the analysis showed significant effect of both the screen size ($F_{1,24}$=156.6, $p<0.001$) and the interaction style ($F_{1,24}$=10.755, $p<0.05$), as well as significant D*S interaction ($F_{1,24}$=6.66, $p<0.05$). Although such a type of outcome is less frequent in data analysis, it makes sense in the observed context. Text entry using emulator (D5) is significantly slower with respect to using its device counterpart (D2), with WPM mean values being nearly two times larger for the actual smartphone device. As for the interaction style factor, text entry with cradling in landscape mode (S4) is significantly faster with respect to cradling in portrait orientation (S2), what is an expected outcome in line with previously derived conclusions. The significant effect of D*S interaction can be explained by the fact that interaction style does not make such a difference when using an emulator, as opposed to using a smartphone. In fact, while landscape-oriented cradling with smartphone benefits with 20 more letters in a minute (4 wpm) with respect to portrait orientation, text entry speed on the touchscreen desktop monitor is equal regardless of the emulator's display orientation. Due to the monitor's native resolution, key buttons within the emulator skin are somewhat larger than the ones on the real device, so changing orientation doesn't really play a critical role. However, the emulation mechanism does matter, as it imposes a latency that drastically decreases overall performance. Accordingly, for smartphone-emulator comparison, we can address screen size as the factor with essential influence on WPM, although *device* would be a better name for this factor in the observed context.

4.4 Errors

For text entry accuracy, we report descriptive statistics only. Table 4 includes mean values for total error rate (T_{ER}), as well as mean values for both CAW_{ER} and CBR_{ER} corresponding fractions.

Table 4. CAWER and CBR_{ER} contributions to the T_{ER} metrics (mean values)

Device (D)	Text entry interaction style (S)									
	S1: one-thumb portrait		S2: cradling portrait		S3: two-thumbs portrait		S4: cradling landscape		S5: two-thumbs landscape	
	T_{ER} [%]	CAW_{ER} / CBR_{ER}	T_{ER} [%]	CAW_{ER} / CBR_{ER}	T_{ER} [%]	CAW_{ER} / CBR_{ER}	T_{ER} [%]	CAW_{ER} / CBR_{ER}	T_{ER} [%]	CAW_{ER} / CBR_{ER}
D1	5.38	61.01% / 38.99%	6.80	58.98% / 41.02%	5.55	62.12% / 37.88%	3.00	73.20% / 26.80%	2.59	73.19% / 26.81%
D2	3.12	71.98% / 28.02%	3.69	68.78% / 31.22%	5.42	67.70% / 32.30%	1.51	93.37% / 6.63%	3.70	51.51% / 48.49%
D3	not appropriate		2.66	37.73% / 62.27%	2.97	57.38% / 42.62%	2.59	38.03% / 61.97%	2.83	94.44% / 5.56%
D4	not appropriate		0.78	84.19% / 15.81%	2.15	80.43% / 19.57%	1.32	94.41% / 5.59%	3.06	86.06% / 13.94%
D5	not appropriate		6.62	86.71% / 13.29%	not appropriate		6.44	86.43% / 13.57%	not appropriate	

When generally addressing mobile devices, we can say that text entry is more erroneous on touchscreen smartphones in portrait orientation. Other conditions involve more appropriate keyboard layouts wherein higher level of target precision is easier to achieve. Emulator-based text entry is highly error-prone, contributing to its overall low-level performance. Obtained CAW_{ER} and CBR_{ER} values are quite interesting to examine. In 18 out of 20 observed conditions CAW_{ER} is larger than CBR_{ER}, indicating that users in general made majority of corrections on letters that were actually in error. In other words, users were able to notice their errors quickly after misspell, what could be the result of built-in visual aids for enhancing transcription correctness.

5 Conclusion

Touchscreen text entry performance has been examined on several classes of mobile devices, including an AVD (*Android Virtual Device*) – mobile device emulator. All convenient interaction styles were included in the study, meaning that all valid combinations of hand postures and device orientations have been tested. As expected, it was confirmed that different conditions induce diverse text entry speed and accuracy.

Interaction style showed to have a decisive impact on touchscreen text entry performance, however screen size have to be taken into account as well. In fact, certain interaction styles are more appropriate for typing on tablets, while others are better fitted for smartphones. In general, two-thumbs text entry in landscape orientation allows higher input rates, as opposed to low efficiency when typing is performed with one finger in portrait mode. It is worth noting here that only 16% of participants reported two-thumbs/landscape as their preferred interaction style, opposing to 56% that favor one-finger portrait-oriented typing. In many cases text entry speed demonstrates a tradeoff between size of key buttons and their mutual distance, thus being dependant on keyboard layout geometry.

Mobile device emulators are often used for testing user interfaces and look-and-feel of related mobile applications. Unfortunately, even the most popular emulators are in general considered slow and frustrating. We were able to quantify emulator shortcomings, at least from the text entry standpoint. Poor typing performance has been confirmed on standard Android SDK emulator, with obtained WPM values being twice as lower as the ones achieved on the equivalent smartphone device. Future research could investigate whether text entry performance differs in the case when the emulator is operated by mouse instead of a touch.

The results described in this paper may provide a baseline for future text entry studies that would address all well-suited interaction styles, various touchscreen mobile devices, and different types of soft keyboards. The described empirical research is limited in scope since the related experiment took place in laboratory settings, and only tapping modality was considered valid for text input. Further work need to be done in order to investigate the observed effects in a real-life mobile context, as well as their impact on gesture-based text entry performance.

Acknowledgments. This paper describes the results of research being carried out within the project 036-0361994-1995 *Universal Middleware Platform for e-Learning Systems*, as well as within the program 036-1994 *Intelligent Support to Omnipresence of e-Learning Systems*, both funded by the Ministry of Science, Education and Sports of the Republic of Croatia. The authors wish to thank Susanne Bahr for valuable help in providing comments on several data analysis strategies.

References

1. Findlater, L., Wobbrock, J.O.: From Plastic to Pixels: In Search of Touch-Typing Touchscreen Keyboards. ACM Interactions XIX 3, 44–49 (2012)

2. Zhai, S., et al.: ShapeWriter on the iPhone – From the Laboratory to the Real World. In: Proc. Extended Abstracts on Human Factors in Computing Systems (CHI EA 2009), pp. 2667–2670. ACM Press, New York (2009)
3. Swype, `http://www.swype.com/`
4. Fitton, D., MacKenzie, I.S., Read, J.C., Horton, M.: Exploring Tilt-Based Text Input for Mobile Devices With Teenagers. In: Proc. 27th Int'l British Computer Society HCI Conference (HCI 2013), British Computer Society, London (2013)
5. Ljubic, S., Kukec, M., Glavinic, V.: Tilt-Based Support for Multimodal Text Entry on Touchscreen Smartphones: Using Pitch and Roll. In: Stephanidis, C., Antona, M. (eds.) UAHCI 2013, Part III. LNCS, vol. 8011, pp. 651–660. Springer, Heidelberg (2013)
6. Oulasvirta, A., et al.: Improving Two-Thumb Text Entry on Touchscreen Devices. In: Proc. SIGCHI Conf. Human Factors in Computing Systems (CHI 2013), pp. 2765–2774. ACM Press, New York (2013)
7. Lee, S., Zhai, S.: The Performance of Touch Screen Soft Buttons. In: Proc. SIGCHI Conf. Human Factors in Computing Systems (CHI 2009), pp. 309–318. ACM Press, New York (2009)
8. Parhi, P., Karlson, A.K., Bederson, B.B.: Target Size Study for One-Handed Thumb Use on Small Touchscreen Devices. In: Proc. 8th Int'l Conf. HCI with Mobile Devices and Services (MobileHCI 2006), pp. 203–210. ACM Press, New York (2012)
9. Sears, A., Zha, Y.: Data Entry for Mobile Devices Using Soft Keyboards: Understanding the Effects of Keyboard Size and User Tasks. Int. J. Hum. Comput. Interaction 16(2), 163–184 (2003)
10. Nicolau, H., Jorge, J.: Touch Typing using Thumbs: Understanding the Effect of Mobility and Hand Posture. In: Proc. SIGCHI Conf. Human Factors in Computing Systems (CHI 2012), pp. 2683–2686. ACM Press, New York (2012)
11. Azenkot, S., Zhai, S.: Touch Behavior with Different Postures on Soft Smartphone Keyboards. In: Proc. 14th Int'l Conf. HCI with Mobile Devices and Services (MobileHCI 2012), pp. 251–260. ACM Press, New York (2012)
12. Hoober, S.: How Do Users Really Hold Mobile Devices? In: UXmatters, `http://www.uxmatters.com/mt/archives/2013/02/how-do-users-really-hold-mobile-devices.php`
13. MacKenzie, I.S., Soukoreff, R.W.: Phrase Sets for Evaluating Text Entry Techniques. In: Proc. Extended Abstracts on Human Factors in Computing Systems (CHI EA 2003), pp. 754–755. ACM Press, New York (2003)
14. MacKenzie, I.S.: Human-Computer Interaction: An Empirical Research Perspective. Morgan Kaufmann, San Francisco (2013)
15. Soukoreff, R.W., MacKenzie, I.S.: Metrics for Text Entry Research: An Evaluation of MSD and KSPC, and a New Unified Error Metric. In: Proc. SIGCHI Conf. Human Factors in Computing Systems (CHI 2003), pp. 113–120. ACM Press, New York (2003)
16. Soukoreff, R.W., MacKenzie, I.S.: Recent Developments in Text-Entry Error Rate Measurement. In: Proc. Extended Abstracts on Human Factors in Computing Systems (CHI EA 2004), pp. 1425–1428. ACM Press, New York (2004)

Access to Text, Documents and Media

An Experimental Approach in Conceptualizing Typographic Signals of Documents by Eight-Dot and Six-Dot Braille Code

Vassilios Argyropoulos[1], Aineias Martos[1,2], Georgios Kouroupetroglou[2], Sofia Chamonikolaou[1], and Magda Nikolaraizi[1]

[1] University of Thessaly, Department of Special Education, Volos, Greece
vassargi@uth.gr
[2] National and Kapodistrian University of Athens, Department of Informatics and Telecommunications, Athens, Greece
koupe@di.uoa.gr

Abstract. The main research aim of the present study focuses on issues of reading comprehension, when users with blindness receive typographic meta-data by touch through a braille display. Levels of reading comprehension are investigated by the use of 6-dot and 8-dot braille code in matched texts for the cases of bold and italic meta-data. The results indicated a slight superiority of the 8-dot braille code in reading time and scorings. The discussion considered the practical implications of the findings such as issues regarding education as well as the development of suitable design of tactile rendition of typographic signals through 6-dot or 8-dot braille code in favor of better perception and comprehension.

Keywords: typographic signals, 6-dot braille, 8-dot braille, braille display, blindness, document accessibility, assistive technology.

1 Introduction

This paper reports on the results from a series of experiments in the field of haptic representation of typographic meta-information or meta-data embedded in rich texts or documents. Similar attempts are emerging for incorporating typographic knowledge of documents into Text-to-Speech [1]. Typographic signals [2] is the information that readers get from the documents at the typographic layer which includes font (type, size, color, background color, etc.) and font style such as bold, italics, underline [3-4]. These attributes play a crucial role in comprehension. It seems that there is a plethora of semantics in applying the typographic layer. For example, in contrast to the tags introduced by the W3C for the bold and italic font styles [5], we have identified [6] the following eight different "labels" that the readers seem to use most frequently in order to semantically characterize text in "bold" and "italics (a total of 2,927 entities, of which 1,866 were occurrences of "bold" and 1,061 of "italics" were manually labelled in a

C. Stephanidis and M. Antona (Eds.): UAHCI/HCII 2014, Part II, LNCS 8514, pp. 83–92, 2014.

corpus of 2,000 articles of a Greek newspaper): emphasis, important / salient, basic block, quotation, note, title, list / numeration category and interview / dialogue.

The scope of this study is to investigate the rendition of typographic signaling in a haptic interface. This specific haptic representation relies on braille. In order to describe better the approach of this study it is important to distinguish some basic peculiarities between the embossed braille and the braille produced by a braille display. In embossed braille, titles, subtitles, headings and indentation are used almost in the same way as in print [2]. On the other hand, when braille is rendered by electronic devices such as braille displays, then readers normally use their working memory to store the words, text attributes and ideas [7]. Usually only underlined text is tagged in embossed braille [8], whereas braille displays use dots 7 and 8 to highlight a various number of points in the document. The lack of rendering typographic signals in embossed braille as well as the limited rendering of meta-information of documents through a braille display might have a negative impact on blind individuals' education and on their reading abilities as well [9].

Thus, the main research aim of the present study focuses on issues of reading comprehension, when blind users receive typographic meta-data (bold and italic) by touch through a braille display, i.e. an electro-mechanical device for displaying braille characters [10]. Levels of reading comprehension are investigated by the use of 6-dot braille and 8-dot braille code in matched texts. In essence, the research objectives of the present study are the following:

a. To compare the Overall Reading Time (ORT) required for each participant to read matched texts in 8-dot and 6-dot braille code,
b. To compare the average time required for each participant to answer comprehension questions in 8-dot and 6-dot braille code through matched texts, and
c. To compare the participants' Overall Scoring (OS) in answering comprehension questions in matched texts in 8-dot and 6-dot braille code respectively.

2 Method

2.1 Participants

In the present study, eight individuals (A, B… H) with blindness participated in a series of experiments using braille displays. All participants were good braillists, had no other additional disabilities and their age range was from 20 to 40 years (mean= 31.25, SD= 6.07).

2.2 The Experimental Design

The experimental design comprised two parts: the preliminary phase and the main research.

Preliminary Phase. The main prerequisite for this study was to determine the rendition of the typographic signals "bold" and "italic" in the 8-dot and 6-dot braille code respectively through a braille display.

Regarding the 6-dot braille code there are indicators (tags) in the Nemeth code which specify the presence of the typographic signals, i.e. bold letters are tagged by dots 4 and 6 and italics are tagged by dots 4, 5 and 6. Yet, the rendition of these specific typographic signals in the 8-dot braille code is not well established [11]. What is common so far in braille displays is the use of the dots 7 or 8 in the braille character cell, to indicate additional information, which is embedded in the document (e.g. a typographic signal of the text in use) [11]. Thus, in this preliminary phase, a number of tests were conducted by two blind users with a series of texts to choose the appropriate combination for the rendition of the typographic signals "bold" and "italic" in the 8-dot braille code through a braille display. Two rendition versions were tested in order to conclude which one was the best to apply (see Table 1). Also, there was a thought of a 3rd version of shifting the braille characters in the lower part of the 8-dot braille cell, indicating in this way either the bold or the italic typographic attribute, but at the end it was considered very complicated and eventually was excluded from the tests. The criterion for the best suited version in our case was the participants' subjective evaluations regarding the element of familiarization, in conjunction with the time needed to go through the texts.

Table 1. Renditions of the typographic signals "bold" and "italic" in the 8-dot braille code

Version	Bold (word or phrase)	Italic (word or phrase)
1	rendition by raising constantly pins 7 and 8	rendition by raising pins 7 and 8 intermittently (i.e. at the first, middle and last letters of the word/phrase)
2	rendition by raising pin 8 only for the consonants in the word/phrase (the vowels were excluded as Greek the accent of the vowels is rendered by raising pin 8 in the 8-dot braille code [12]	rendition by raising pin 8 intermittently (i.e. at the first, middle and last letters of the word/phrase)

It was conjectured that Version 1 enabled the blind users to recognize faster and more accurately the typographic signals of bold and italic within the texts in 8-dot braille code. They highlighted the facilitating character of the bold rendition by the constant raised pins 7 and 8 throughout the whole word or phrase.

Moreover, all participants' reading performances were timed. Version 1 occupied the best reading rate with the least errors. For the rendition of the typographic signals bold and italic in the 6-dot braille code, the researchers used the tags which are specified by Nemeth code (as mentioned in the Introduction section) with a slight modification.

They replaced dots 4 and 6 by dots 5 and 6, because the former constitutes the indicator for capitals in the 6 dot Greek Braille code.

Main Research. During the main research, each of the eight participants was invited to read through a braille display four expository texts and then asked to answer five comprehension questions for each text. All participants were given appropriate time to familiarize themselves with the use of a braille display.

There are two strands of texts; narrative and expository. Narrative texts facilitate students' reading comprehension because they have a structured schema and contain sequences that are easier to follow. On the other hand, expository texts contain information that may be unknown to the students or may require the activation of their prior knowledge while they have a more abstract structure [13-14]. Since the age range of the participants was from 20 years to 40 years, it was decided that expository texts would best fit to the needs of the present study.

As mentioned above, the participants' ability to comprehend a text was assessed through four expository texts. The number of words in each text ranged from 115 to 179 words. In specific, two pairs of texts were selected which were matched on three factors: a) grade, b) number of typographic signals (each text included three words/phrases in bold and three words/phrases in italic), and c) content. Thus, we have selected two texts with general informative content without any technical terms (179 words and 165 words respectively) and two texts with scientific content and mathematical terminology (115 words and 119 words respectively). The first text of the first pair was rendered by 6-dot braille code and the second text of the same pair was rendered by 8-dot braille code. The rendition of the typographic signals "bold" and "italic" in the 8-dot braille code followed Version 1 (Table 1), whereas regarding the 6-dot braille code, the researchers adopted the indicators of the Nemeth code with a slight modification as mentioned in the preliminary phase [i.e. dots (4, 5) for bold and dots (4, 5, 6) for italic]. Finally, all the selected texts were in fact extracts from textbooks used in Greek public high schools.

Five comprehension questions corresponded to each text. Participants were instructed to read each text aloud or silently through a braille display and, when finished, the researchers asked the participant each question orally. Participants were allowed to go back to the passage in order to search for the right answer when needed. The questions corresponded to the three types of the reading comprehension question taxonomy of Pearson and Johnson [15]: textually explicit, textually implicit and scriptually implicit. Textually explicit questions require no inference and the answer is literally mentioned in the passage [15]. Textually implicit questions require inference and the activation of background knowledge. Scriptually implicit questions are based on the background knowledge of the reader who is asked to make inferences about the general meaning of the text and rely on his background knowledge in order to grasp the meaning [16].

The researchers constructed five questions for each text which corresponded to the three types of reading comprehension questions. Specifically, the first three were textually explicit questions, the fourth question was textually implicit, and the fifth question was scriptually implicit. All correct responses were scored with 1 while all incorrect responses were scored with 0. The scores that participants could achieve for all texts were from 0 up to 20.

3 Results

3.1 First Research Objective: The Overall Reading Time

Figure 1 provides a description of the ORT that the participants' dedicated while reading the general informative text (G) by the 8-dot and the 6-dot braille code. Initial examination of the data in the graph shows that all participants dedicated more time to read the text by the 8-dot (8D) braille code (min.ORT8DG=7.2 minutes & max.ORT8DG=13.57 minutes) rather than by the 6-dot (6D) braille code (min.ORT6DG=4.08 minutes & max.ORT6DG=11.23minutes). Only participant F seemed to spend more time when reading by the 6-dot braille (9.28 minutes) compared to the 8-dot braille code (8.1 minutes).

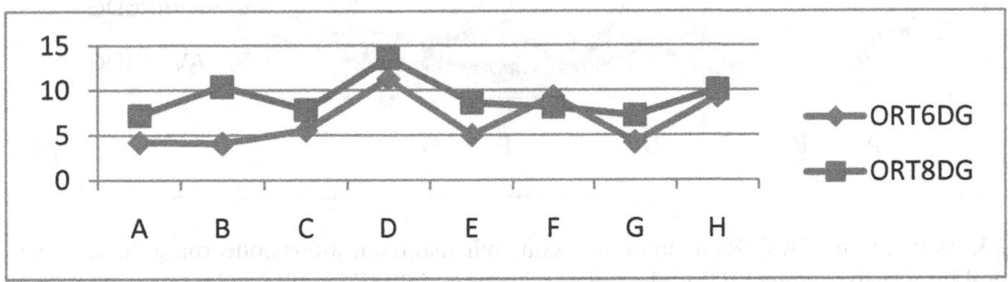

Fig. 1. Overall reading time (ORT) for general informative text (G) in the 8-dot (8D) and the 6-dot braille code (6D)

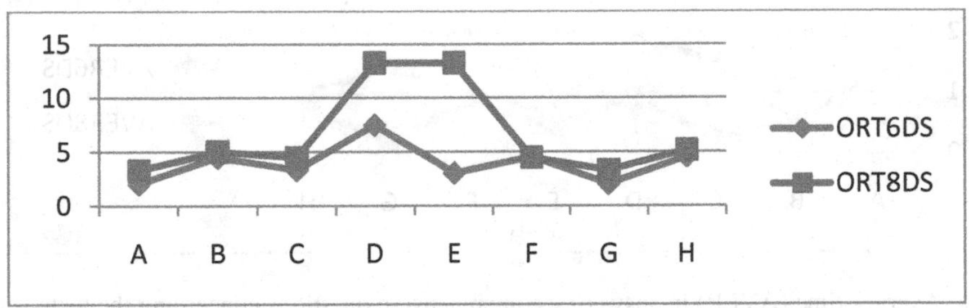

Fig. 2. Overall reading time (ORT) for scientific text (S) in the 8-dot (8D) and the 6-dot braille code (6D)

The same analysis took place regarding the texts with the scientific content. In particular, all participants seemed to spend more time to read the scientific text (S) by the 8-dot (8D) braille code (min.ORT8DS=3.3minutes & max.ORT8DS= 13.25minutes) rather than by the 6-dot (6D) braille code (min.ORT6DS=2.01minutes & max.ORT6DS=4.54 minutes) (Figure 2).

3.2 Second Research Objective: The Average Answering Time

In contrast to the above figures (1 & 2) which provide a "whole picture" of the participants' reading time through the texts by both braille codes, the second measure actually focuses on the participants' average amount of time dedicated to listening the comprehension questions, searching the answers in the text through the braille display as well as answering them. Figure 3 shows that the situation here is the other way round. In specific, the average time (AVER) that the participants spent to answer the comprehension questions concerning the texts with the general informative content (G) in the 8-dot (8D) braille code was less than that in the 6-dot (6D) braille code (min.AVER8DG=0.63 minutes & max.AVER8DG =1.63 minutes vs min.AVER6DG= 0.83minutes & max.AVER 6DG=3.93 minutes) (Figure 3).

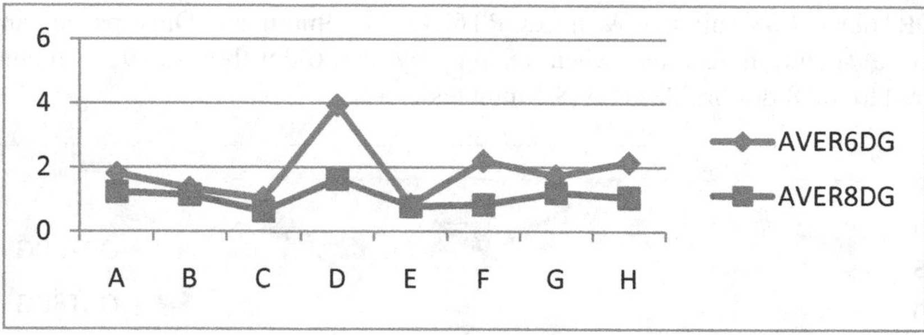

Fig. 3. Average time (AVER) in answering comprehension questions concerning the texts with general informative content (G) in the 6-dot (6D) and 8-dot (8D) braille code

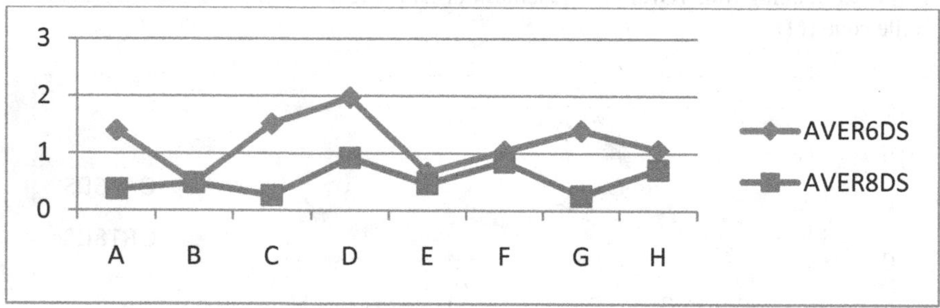

Fig. 4. Average time (AVER) in answering comprehension questions concerning the texts with scientific content (S) in the 8-dot (8D) braille code

The same picture came up regarding the texts with scientific content. The average time (AVER) for the participants to answer the comprehension questions regarding the texts with the scientific content (S) in the 8-dot (8D) braille code was less than that in the 6-dot (6D) braille code (min.AVER8DS=0.26 minutes & max.AVER8DS =0.92 minutes vs min.AVER6DS=0.49 minutes & max.AVER6DS=1.97 minutes) (Figure 4).

3.3 Third Research Objective: The Overall Scoring

The third measure was based on the overall scoring (OS) in answering the comprehension questions. Figure 5 shows the participants' overall scorings in the general informative (G) texts. It seems that they got similar results with almost equivalent values in averages (AVEROS8DG=3.63 & AVEROS6DG=3) and standard deviations (STDOS8DG=2 & STDOS6DG=1.69). It is worth mentioning the slight superiority of the 8-dot braille code in answering the 4th question (4Q) which was textually implicit (4Q8DG=5 vs 4Q6DG=2) and the 5th question (5Q) which was scriptually implicit (5Q8DG=6 vs 5Q6DG=4).

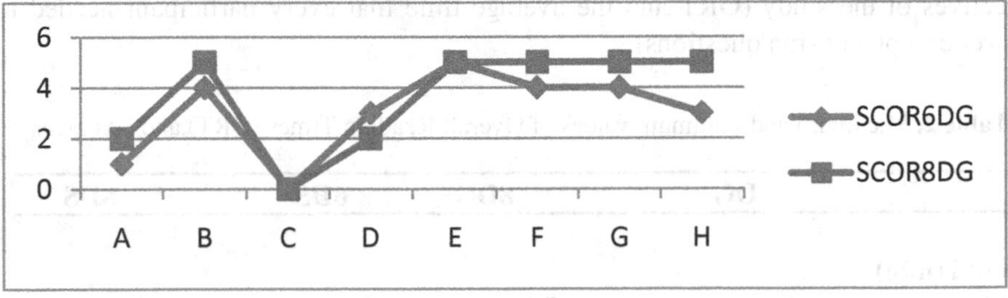

Fig. 5. Overall scorings (OS) in answering comprehension questions concerning the texts with general informative content (G) in the 6-dot (6D) and 8-dot (8D) braille code

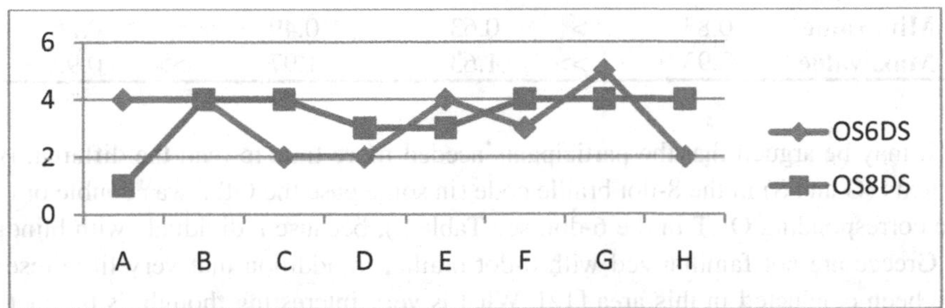

Fig. 6. Overall scorings (OS) in answering comprehension questions concerning the texts with scientific content (S) in the 6-dot (6D) and 8-dot (8D) braille code

Figure 6 provides information about the participants' overall scorings in the scientific (S) texts. It could be argued that the participants' OSs when using 8-dot (8D) and 6-dot braille code (6D) were equivalent since they had the same average (AVEROS8DS=3.38 & AVEROS6DS=3.25) and the same standard deviations (STDOS8DS=1.06 & STDOS6DS=1.16). It is worth mentioning that the participants' biggest convergence in scoring was in the 1st comprehension question (1Q), which was textually explicit (1Q8DS=8 & 1Q6DS=7), whereas the biggest divergence took place on the 4th comprehension question (4Q) which was textually implicit (4Q8DS=7 & 4Q6DS=3).

4 Discussion and Conclusions

This paper addresses issues of reading comprehension, when blind users receive typographic meta-data (bold and italic) by touch through a braille display in 6-dot braille and 8-dot braille code in matched texts (general content and scientific content).

Based on the results, it was found that participants needed more time to read the texts (general and scientific) in the 8-dot braille code compared to the 6-dot braille; on the contrary, the participants spent, on average, less time to detect and answer the comprehension questions in the 8-dot braille code compared to the 6-dot braille. A "snapshot" of the above is provided in Table 2 and refers to the first two research objectives of the study (ORT and the average time that every participant needed to answer comprehension questions).

Table 2. Maximum and minimum values of Overall Reading Times (ORT) and Averages

	6DG		8DG	6DS		8DS
ORT(min)						
Min. value	4.08	<	7.2	2.01	<	3.3
Max. value	11.23	<	13.57	4.54	<<	13.25
AVER(min)						
Min. value	0.83	>	0.63	0.49	>	0.26
Max. value	3.93	>>	1.63	1.97	>>	0.92

It may be argued that the participants needed more time to read the different types of texts (G and S) in the 8-dot braille code (in some case the ORT was double or triple the corresponding ORT in the 6-dot, see Table 2), because individuals with blindness in Greece are not familiarized with 8-dot braille, in addition that very little research has been conducted in this area [12]. What is very interesting though, is the fact that the participants needed less time to answer the comprehension questions in 8-dot braille. This finding might be attributed to the fact that the participants' tactile movements on the 8-dot cell was more sophisticated compared to the 6-dot braille and as a result their attention was more intense in the first case. In turn, this elaborating process – when using the 8-dot braille code - might enhance the participants' cognitive operations of reading which take place in "working memory". "Working memory" describes the cognitive work called for by thinking tasks at the same time that it keeps information fresh in current memory [7]. Hence, it may be argued that the participants' working memory functioned more effectively when they were dealing with the 8-dot braille code and for this they spent less time - on average - to answer the comprehension questions.

The third research objective dealt with the participants' overall scoring (OS). It seems that the participants' performances in both braille codes were equivalent. Nevertheless, it is worth mentioning that they managed to get slightly better scores in the implicit questions (textually and scriptually implicit questions require an inferential answer, a response that is not literally or explicitly mentioned in the text) when they were reading through the 8-dot braille code in both general and scientific texts (also see Figures 5 & 6). It may be argued that this finding empowers the above reasoning about working memory.

Finally, further investigation is needed to choose the most appropriate braille indicators in order to represent typographic signals. Based on the results of this study, although marking with dots 7 and 8 was perceived as a good representation method in the 8-dot braille code for bold and italic, it remains quite limited since no other typographic signal can be rendered. The focus of relevant studies should put emphasis a. on the educational implications of the results, and b. on the development of a suitable design of tactile rendition of typographic signals through six or eight-dot braille code in favor of blind users' better perception and comprehension.

Acknowledgements. This research has been co-financed by the European Union (European Social Fund – ESF) and Greek national funds through the Operational Program "Education and Lifelong Learning" of the National Strategic Reference Framework (NSRF) under the Research Funding Project: "THALIS-University of Macedonia- KAIKOS: Audio and Tactile Access to Knowledge for Individuals with Visual Impairments", MIS 380442

References

1. Kouroupetroglou, G.: Incorporating Typographic, Logical and Layout Knowledge of Documents into Text-to-Speech. In: Proc. of the 12th European Conference on Assistive Technologies (AAATE), Vilamoura, Portugal, September 19-22, pp. 708–713. IOS Press (2013), doi:10.3233/978-1-61499-304-9-708
2. Lorch, R.F.: Text-Signaling Devices and Their Effects on Reading and Memory Processes. Educational Psychology Review 1, 209–234 (1989)
3. Kouroupetroglou, G., Tsonos, D.: Multimodal Accessibility of Documents. In: Pinder, S. (ed.) Advances in Human-Computer Interaction, I-Tech Education and Publishing, Vienna, pp. 451–470 (2008)
4. Tsonos, D., Kouroupetroglou, G.: Modeling Reader's Emotional State Response on Document's Typographic Elements. In: Advances in Human-Computer Interaction 2011, Article ID 206983, pp. 1–18 (2011), doi:10.1155/2011/2069832011
5. `http://www.w3.org/International/questions/qa-b-and-i-tags`
6. Fourli-Kartsouni, F., Slavakis, K., Kouroupetroglou, G., Theodoridis, S.: A Bayesian Network Approach to Semantic Labelling of Text Formatting in XML Corpora of Documents. In: Stephanidis, C. (ed.) HCI 2007. LNCS, vol. 4556, pp. 299–308. Springer, Heidelberg (2007)
7. Cohen, H., Scherzer, P., Viau, R., Voss, P., Lepore, F.: Working memory for braille is shaped by experience. Communicative & Integrative Biology 4(2), 227–229 (2011)

8. Braille Formats, Principles of Print-to-Braille Transcription, The Braille Authority of North America (2011)
9. Cheryl-Kamei, H.: Creative typesets require innovative solutions: A study of differences in braille indicators. PhD thesis, Department of Special Education, Rehabilitation and School Psychology, The University of Arizona (2008)
10. Cook, A., Polgar, J.M.: Essentials of Assistive Technologies. Elsevier, St. Louis (2012)
11. Dixon, J.: Eight-dot Braille. A Position Statement of the Braille Authority of North America (2007), `http://www.brailleauthority.org/eightdot/eightdot.html`
12. Kacorri, H., Kouroupetroglou, G.: Design and Developing Methodology for 8-dot Braille Code Systems. In: Stephanidis, C., Antona, M. (eds.) UAHCI 2013, Part III. LNCS, vol. 8011, pp. 331–340. Springer, Heidelberg (2013)
13. Diakidou, I.-A., Stylianou, P., Karefillidou, C., Papageorgiou, P.: The relationship between listening and reading comprehension of different types of text at increasing grade levels. Reading Psychology 26, 55–80 (2005)
14. Horiba, Y.: Reader control in reading: Effects of language competence, text type and task. Discourse Processes 29, 223–267 (2000)
15. Pearson, P.D., Johnson, D.: Teaching reading comprehension. Rinehart & Winston, New York (1978)
16. DuBravec, S., Dale, M.: Reader question formation as a tool for measuring comprehension: narrative and expository textual inferences in a second language. Journal of Research in Reading 25, 217–231 (2002)

Document Transformation Infrastructure

Lars Ballieu Christensen[1] and Amrish Chourasia[2]

[1] Sensus ApS, Denmark
lbc@sensus.dk
[2] Trace Center, UW Madison, USA
amrish@trace.wisc.edu

Abstract. Many people face barriers to accessing textual information due to visual, reading or language limitations. They need alternative formats to text such as Braille or audio. However, producing accessible formats is often expensive, time consuming, and requires special expertise and training. RoboBraille offers a cost-effective and timely manner to accessible material production. It provides fully automated conversion of text into a number of alternative formats, including mp3 files, Daisy full text/full audio, e-books or Braille books. As part of Prosperity4all project, RoboBraille will be adapted to fit into the overall technical architecture of the Global Public Inclusive Infrastructure (GPII), and interfaces for new conversion capabilities such as semantic structure recognition, text-to-sign language and language-to-language translation will be added.

Keywords: Accessibility, Document Transformation, Braille, e-books.

1 Introduction

Many people face barriers to accessing textual information due to visual, reading or language limitations. They need alternative formats to text such as Braille or audio. However, producing accessible formats is often expensive, time consuming, and requires special expertise and training [2]. For example, a Braille translator need to not only have a good knowledge of various document types, character sets and formats, but also know details about the device on which the text is to be displayed. In addition, readily available accessible materials are limited given that print-disabled people may need a diverse range of alternative formats.

RoboBraille offers a cost-effective and timely manner to accessible material production [2-4]. RoboBraille is developed jointly by Synscenter Refsnæs (the National Centre for Visually Impaired Children and Youth in Denmark) and Sensus ApS. It provides fully automated conversion of text into a number of alternative formats, including mp3 files, Daisy full text/full audio, e-books or Braille books. RoboBraille is a web and email based service. Through its website, users can upload a file for conversion such as a document, an image, or an image-only PDF. Based on the type of original file, the user can select an output format from a list of supported formats. RoboBraille will automatically process the file and convert it into the accessible

C. Stephanidis and M. Antona (Eds.): UAHCI/HCII 2014, Part II, LNCS 8514, pp. 93–100, 2014.

format the user selected. In a short while, the final document will be sent to the user's email. RoboBraille is currently available free of charge, and users need not register to use the service.

RoboBraille offers four main categories of services [5]:

1. Braille services: Translation to and from Braille (contracted, un-contracted) in Danish, British English, American English, Italian, French, Greek, German, Icelandic, Norwegian, Polish, Portuguese and Spanish. Supported document types include text files (DOS and Windows), Microsoft Word documents (doc, docx, Word xml), html documents, rtf files, tiff, gif, jpg, bmp, pcx, dcx, j2k, jp2, jpx, djv and all types of pdf documents. Before the Braille document is returned to the user, it may be converted to a particular Braille character set based on user settings. Documents can also be returned in Unicode Braille or formatted in either text format or PEF (Portable Embosser Format).
2. Audio services: All document types listed in the previous section may be converted into mp3 files. Furthermore, RoboBraille is capable of converting well-structured Word documents (doc, docx, xml) into Daisy Talking Books complete with audio. Similarly, RoboBraille can convert docx documents containing math (written in MathType) into Daisy books witg spoken math. The audio conversion services currently include high-quality voices for the following languages: Arabic, Arabic/English bilingual, Bulgarian, Danish, Dutch (male, female), English/American, English/British, French, German, Hungarian, Italian, Lithuanian, Polish, Portuguese, Romanian, Slovenian Spanish/Castilian and Spanish/Latin American.
3. E-Book services: Most document types listed above may be converted into the popular EPUB and Mobi Pocket (Amazon Kindle) e-book formats. The service also supports conversion of documents into the EPUB3 format. Furthermore, EPUB may be converted to Mobi Pocket and vice versa. To accommodate users with low vision, the base line of the body text in an e-book may be raised to allow for more appropriate text scaling in mainstream e-book readers.
4. Accessibility services: Otherwise inaccessible documents such as image files in gif, tiff, jpg, bmp, pcx, dcx, j2k, jp2, jpx, djv and image-only pdf, as well as all types of pdf files can be converted to more accessible formats including tagged pdf, doc, docx, Word xml, xls, xlsx, csv, text, rtf and html. Word and rtf files are converted into text or tagged pdf files subject to the format specified by the user in the subject line, e.g., txt or pdf. PowerPoint files are converted into tagged pdf, web projects or rtf files.

RoboBraille also offers several auxiliary services:

5. Visual Braille services: To support the requirements of pharmaceutical companies, RoboBraille can create graphical Braille artwork based on the Braille codes of many European countries. Pharmaceuticals, printers and designers submit control files with the product name and strength, Braille number encoding regime and language codes. A subscription is required for these services.
6. RoboBraille Tools: A number of utility accounts support functions such as file partitioning; file conversion and file export to particular Braille character sets.

2 RoboBraille Interfaces and Formatting

2.1 Web Interface

The RoboBraille web form is the main interface to the RoboBraille service [5]. A location where it can be found is: www.RoboBraille .org. The form complies with the W3C WCAG2 guidelines and can be used by screen reader users and others with special needs. To convert a document, the user goes through a four-step process:

- Step 1: Select the file and upload it to the RoboBraille server. Alternatively, an URL or plain text can also be used as input.
- Step 2: Select output format of the document.
- Step 3: Provide options for conversion. These options are specific to the target format selected, e.g., contraction level and Braille code for Braille conversion, TTS language and speed for mp3 audio conversions and e-book format and base line font text size for e-book conversions.
- Step 4: Provide a valid email address. The result of the document conversion will be mailed to the email address provided.

Convert a File
Follow the four easy steps below to have your document converted into an alternative, accessible format. The result is delivered in your email inbox. You may upload a file, enter a URL to a file or simply type in the text you wish to have converted. The form expands as you make your selections.
Source
File
URL
Text
Step 1 - Upload the file
Select your file and upload it to the server (max 32 mb). Supported file types are .doc, .docx, .pdf, .ppt, .pptx, .txt, .xml, .html, .htm, .rtf, .epub, .mobi, .tiff, .tif, .gif, .jpg, .bmp, .pcx, .dcx, .j2k, .jp2, .jpx, .djv and .asc
File name: Choose File no file selected
Upload
The file Introduction.docx has been successfully uploaded to the server (130 kb).
Step 2 - Select output format
Specify the target format of your document. For this document type, the following formats are available:
Target format
mp3 audio
Daisy full text and audio
Daisy Math full text and audio
Braille
e-Book
Document conversion
Step 3 - Specify audio options
Specify the natural language of your document and how fast you want the speech.
Options
Language: British English
Speed: Normal
Step 4 - Enter email address and submit request
Email address: 123456@gmail.com
Submit

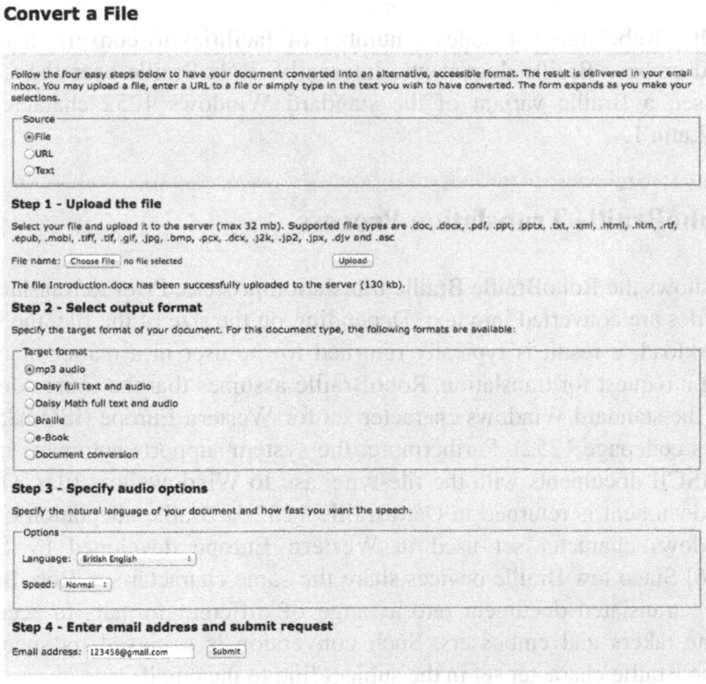

Fig. 1. The Robobraille Web Interface

2.2 RoboBraille Email Interface

The email interface was the original interface to RoboBraille. Users submit their documents to various email accounts in order to have the documents converted into alternate formats. Options are provided through the subject field of the email. In fact, the RoboBraille Web Form merely composes and submits an email to match the requested document conversion. Thus, all functions available through the web interface are available through email. The email interface even supports functions and options that are not made available through the web interface. The categories of email accounts available are:

- Braille
- MP3
- Daisy
- Daisy Math
- Accessibility
- e-book
- EPUB3
- RoboBraille tools

2.3 Formatting and Embossing Documents

Additionally, RoboBraille includes a number of facilities to convert character sets, format and emboss Braille documents. Internally, RoboBraille uses the OctoBraille character set, a Braille variant of the standard Windows 1252 character set also known as Latin 1.

3 RoboBraille Translation Process

Fogure 2 shows the RoboBraille Braille translation process. Prior to translation, Word and RTF files are converted into text. Depending on the size of the file, the traffic and server workload, a result is typically returned to the user in a matter of minutes of submitting a request for translation. RoboBraille assumes that the source document is written in the standard Windows character set for Western Europe (ISO 8859-1/Latin 1/Windows codepage 1252). Furthermore, the system supports automatic conversion of older ASCII documents with the file-type .asc to Windows text files. Once translated, the document is returned in OctoBraille 1252, a Braille adaptation of the standard Windows character set used in Western Europe developed by Synscenter Refsnæs [6] Since few Braille devices share the same character set, RoboBraille can convert the translated document into a range of different formats to accommodate Braille note takers and embossers. Such conversion is achieved by specifying the name of the Braille character set in the subject line to the email.

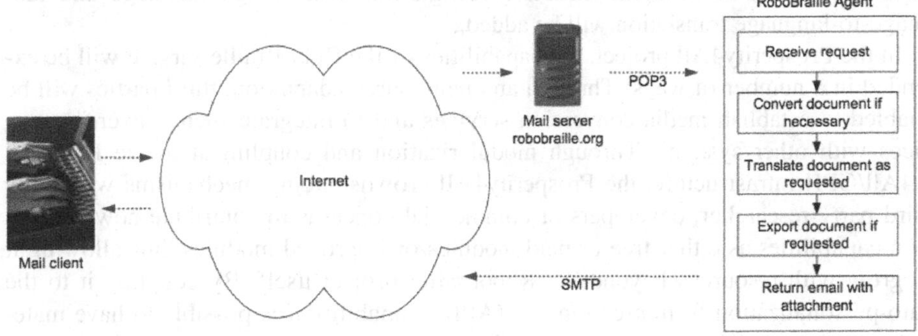

Fig. 2. RoboBraille Braille Translation Process. From [1].

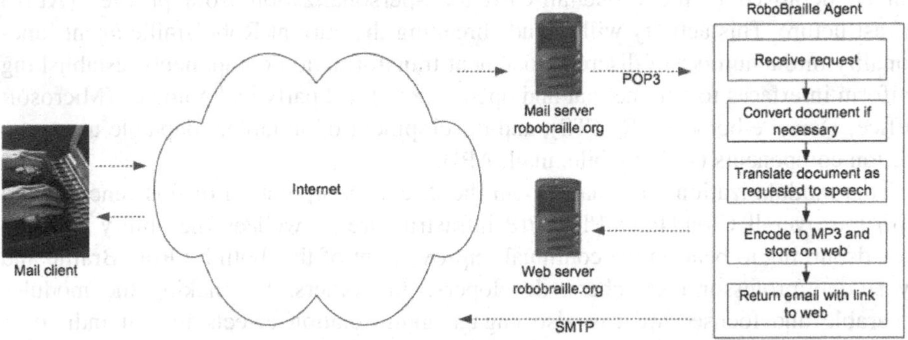

Fig. 3. RoboBraille text-to-speech translation process. From [1].

Likewise, the user may request a document be translated into synthetic speech. The process is similar to that of Braille translation, although some of the steps are different. The illustration below illustrates how a user may use the RoboBraille service to translate a document into synthetic speech:

First, RoboBraille translates an attached document into a WAVE file. WAVE files are rather large and unsuitable for transmission via the Internet. Therefore, the WAVE file is subsequently encoded and compressed into an MP3 file. The resulting audio file is copied with a unique name to the web server using FTP, and a link to the file is returned to the user.

4 RoboBraille and the GPII

Prosperity4All is a four year project funded by the European Commission under the 7th Framework Programme (FP7) that seeks to build the Global Public Inclusive Infrastructure (GPII) [7]. During the project, RoboBraille will be adapted to fit into the overall technical architecture of the project, and interfaces for new conversion capabilities such as semantic structure recognition, text-to-sign language and language-to-language translation will be added.

In the Prosperity4All project, the capabilities of the RoboBraille service will be extended in a number of ways: Through an open-source adaptation, third parties will be enabled to establish media conversion services and to integrate such conversion services with other systems. Through modularization and coupling it to the Prosperity4All/GPII infrastructure, the Prosperity4All crowdsourcing mechanisms will allow third party researcher, developers or commercial concerns to contribute new conversion capabilities as either free or paid modules or improved modules thus allowing it to grow with resources beyond the Robobraille project itself. By coupling it to the auto-personalization from preferences" (APfP) capability it is possible to have materials sent to an individual be automatically transformed before delivery.

The RoboBraille agent will be reimplmented in a set of modules that support crowdsourcingX2 (support for crowdsourcing by both developers and users) and that can be deployed in the Cloud4all/GPII auto-personalization from profile" (APfP) infrastructure. This activity will include breaking the current RoboBraille agent functionality into a number of discreet document transformation components, establishing uniform interfaces to commercial and open source third party technologies (Microsoft Office, Daisy, e-book, OCR, TTS), and development of suitable, adaptable user interaction components (web, mobile, mail, API).

This modularization will enable both the direct incorporation of this functionality with the overall Cloud4all/GPII APfP infrastructure as well as the ability to bring crowdsourcing to bear on the continual improvement of this both by RoboBraille and by student/professor researchers, developers, and others. By making the modules separable and focused we can also engage gamificiation effects in that individual modules (new or better) can be tackled by an individual or group that could not hope to even learn the system as a whole. For example, a Ph.D. student working on machine vision might create a new module for OSR that would allow the system to handle pages with more complicated layout – advancing the usefulness of the whole infrastructure which could then transform those materials into accessible formats that the machine vision student doesn't even know exist.

At the same time – the new engine will be developed so that it can be replicated so that it can stand alone behind firewalls. The activity will be based experienced from the implementation of bespoke versions of RoboBraille at academic institutions [2], and well as in the financial and pharmaceutical sectors.

This activity will include specification and implementation of a stand-alone version of the document transformation engine as well as a specification and implementation of a set of interface components This activity will be based on experiences from the implementation of bespoke versions of RoboBraille at academic institutions [2] , as well as in the financial and pharmaceutical sectors.

This activity will include specification and implementation of a stand-alone version of the document transformation engine as well as a specification and implementation of a set of interface components to allow third parties to integrate existing systems with the document conversion service. This ability has proven to be essential not only for companies wishing to make internal documents available freely to employees with disabilities while maintaining their confidentially and security behind corporate firewalls, but also for government agencies who face the same problem with social benefit information which they need to make accessible both to consumers and to employees while maintaining strict control of the information. The implementation will be designed to handle these and similar situations. to allow third parties to integrate existing systems with the document conversion service.

Currently, even highest quality commercial OSR (optical structure recognition) engines have trouble dealing with some types of tabular, math and science Materials. One particular problem is sparsely populated tables that do not have lines and that span across pages with headers and footers. Such tables can be common in materials sent to consumers. However it is impossible for them to make sense of them if they cannot see them. They're also hard to decipher if highly enlarged. Part of the Prosperity4All project will be to explore machine vision techniques to see if this can be resolved. We will also collaborate with external researchers and to see if a means for better processing of math and science materials can be identified and coupled with the system using its new (to be implemented) modular approach.

This project will also couple, for the first time, language translation capability with the accessible format transformation engines. This will allow individuals to not only get materials accessible form, but also in a language that may be easier for them to understand. As part of this, RoboBraille will develop the capability to attach text to sign language translation engines so that materials can be presented in sign language for those who would find the material easier to understand that form as soon as sign language translation modules are available and for the languages in which they are available. (Note: This project is not proposing to create a text to sign language translator.)

This project also seeks to, for the first time, combine document transformation technologies with media access technologies to create a combined system/process that could be used to make next-generation books with embedded video accessible.

5 Conclusion

RoboBraille was initially developed in an attempt to make Braille easily available to anyone with a need. It now offers audio, e-book, and accessibility services as well. It has been successfully used in educational and commercial environments. RoboBraille is widely used within Europe and is now being adapted to fit in to the GPII. Interfaces for new conversion capabilities such as semantic structure recognition, text-to-sign language and language-to-language translation are to be added.

Acknowledgements. Different components of the body of work described in this paper was, and/or is being, funded by the European Union's Seventh Framework Programme (FP7/2007-2013) grant agreement n° 289016 (Cloud4all) and 610510 (Prosperity4All), by the National Institute on Disability and Rehabilitation Research, US Dept of Education under Grants H133E080022 (RERC-IT) and H133E130028 (UIITA-RERC) and contract ED-OSE-12-D-0013 (Preferences for Global Access), by the Flora Hewlett Foundation, the Ontario Ministry of Research and Innovation, and the Canadian Foundation for Innovation. The opinions and results herein are those of the authors and not necessarily those of the funding agencies.

References

1. Christensen, L.B., Refsnæs, S.: RoboBraille–Braille Unlimited. The Educator, ICEVI 21(2), 32–37 (2009)
2. Christensen, L.B., Keegan, S.J., Stevns, T.: SCRIBE: A model for implementing robobraille in a higher education institution. In: Miesenberger, K., Karshmer, A., Penaz, P., Zagler, W. (eds.) ICCHP 2012, Part I. LNCS, vol. 7382, pp. 77–83. Springer, Heidelberg (2012)
3. Christensen, L.B.: RoboBraille – automated braille translation by means of an E-mail robot. In: Miesenberger, K., Klaus, J., Zagler, W.L., Karshmer, A.I. (eds.) ICCHP 2006. LNCS, vol. 4061, pp. 1102–1109. Springer, Heidelberg (2006)
4. Christensen, L.B., Stevns, T.: Biblus – A digital library to support integration of visually impaired in mainstream education. In: Miesenberger, K., Karshmer, A., Penaz, P., Zagler, W. (eds.) ICCHP 2012, Part I. LNCS, vol. 7382, pp. 36–42. Springer, Heidelberg (2012)
5. Robobraille Service Summary (March 17, 2014), `http://www.robobraille.org/sites/default/files/resourcefiles/RoboBrailleServiceSummaryversion1-23en.pdf`
6. The OctoBraille character set (March 17, 2014), `http://www.sensus.dk/sb4/OctoBraille1252.pdf`
7. Prosperity4All (March 17 (2014), `http://www.raisingthefloor.org/prosperity4all/`

Accessible Metadata Generation

Anastasia Cheetham, Dana Ayotte, Jonathan Hung, Joanna Vass, Colin Clark*, Jess Mitchell, and Jutta Treviranus

Inclusive Design Research Centre, OCAD University, Toronto, ON, Canada
{acheetham,dayotte,jhung,jvass,cclark,jmitchell}@ocadu.ca

Abstract. This paper outlines a strategy and suite of tools for creating more accessible and personalizable web content by supporting the creation of accessibility metadata. The tools showcased below allow content creators to easily generate metadata at the point of creation, reducing the cost and complexity of producing and delivering content that can be tailored to a user's needs and preferences.

This work follows the AccessForAll approach, which focuses on meeting individual user's needs by matching those needs to appropriate content [1]. This level of personalization depends upon both the availability of infrastructure that can deliver alternative and adapted versions, and on the availability of content with accessibility metadata that can be used in the matchmaking process.

Keywords: Metadata, personalization, user needs and preferences, authoring, matching, AccessForAll.

1 Introduction

Users should be able to choose the type of content they consume, and they should make this choice without having to justify it, explain it, or sift through piles of content that don't match that choice. Work is being done in projects like Cloud4All [2] and Floe [3] to create tools that empower users to declare their needs and preferences. These expressions can then be mapped to content that meets those needs and preferences, thereby delivering a personalized web experience. Metadata is essential to this effort.

In order to match users' preferences to the content, that content must come with metadata that describes its features and alternatives. By meaningfully tagging online content with the appropriate metadata (particularly metadata about the accessibility features, capabilities, and adaptability of a resource) significant barriers to access can be broken down as a user's needs are matched to content that best meets those needs.

Everyone is a content creator. We take pictures with our phones and share them online instantly, we have blogs, we Tweet, we create videos, etc. But how much of that content has meaningful metadata associated with it? Few authoring or publishing applications make metadata tagging easy or compelling, and few users know what

---

* Corresponding author.

C. Stephanidis and M. Antona (Eds.): UAHCI/HCII 2014, Part II, LNCS 8514, pp. 101–110, 2014.

metadata is or how to create it. Yet metadata is a powerful and essential piece in the larger vision of delivering personalized content to meet the needs of individuals.

The Global Public Inclusive Infrastructure (GPII) and within it, the Cloud4All Project [4, 2] are developing reusable components that can be embedded in a variety of applications and authoring tools, which provide the ability to:

- Automatically generate metadata where possible
- Easily create, edit, and maintain accessibility metadata for digital content.

Designers and developers at the Inclusive Design Research Centre (IDRC) [4], in collaboration with GPII partners within the Cloud4All [2] and Floe Projects [3], are building tools that will automatically derive or detect metadata information regarding digital resources in various formats and media, primarily on the web.

In cases where metadata cannot be automatically derived or detected, we have built easy-to-use web components for metadata creating, editing, and viewing. Because these tools can be integrated into common authoring applications, accessibility metadata will be integrated into the authoring process from the beginning rather than being neglected or left as an afterthought. As a result, more metadata will exist alongside content, enabling the GPII infrastructure to make matches between user needs and content that addresses those needs, delivering an experience tailored to the individual.

2 Background

Over the past decade, the IDRC has helped to establish and evolve a collection of interrelated standards that support the personalized delivery of user interfaces and content. These standards, as a whole, are based on an approach we have dubbed Access For All. Below, we describe the history and evolution of the Access For All approach and its relationship to various standards organizations

2.1 Access For All

The Access For All approach to accessibility is based on the idea of matching and adapting content to the individual needs and preferences of a user. This approach includes two key components:

1. A statement of the user's needs and preferences, and
2. Metadata describing the content

With these two components, content can be automatically selected to meets the needs of the user, or adaptations can be carried out on the content to adjust it to meet the user's needs.

Access For All was first developed as part of the Web-4-All project, which was an early precedent for the GPII initiative [6, 7]. Web-4-All provided users of public access facilities with the ability to log onto a Windows-based computer using a smart-card that contained their personal assistive technology needs. The taxonomy of user needs and preferences that was defined as part of the Web-4-All project became the basis for the initial specification of Access For All.

The IMS Global Learning Consortium (IMS) published the first Access For All specification in 2003. The specification defined a common vocabulary for declaring preferences and for creating metadata. The IDRC was the initiator of the Access For All approach, and continues to be an active partner in developing the specification. A public draft of version 3 of the specification is now available [1].

In 2008, ISO/IEC JTC 1/SC 36 adopted the Access For All specification into a multi-part international standard known as ISO/IEC 24751:2008 Individualized Adaptability and Accessibility in E-learning, Education and Training. The IDRC also participated and continues to participate in the development of the ISO standard. In 2011, they began the process of updating the standard to a 2nd edition.

2.2 Schema.org

Schema.org [8] is a collaboration among Google, Bing, Yandex and Yahoo! to define common microdata formats to improve the findability of content on the Internet. In 2013, the IDRC participated in the development of a proposal to Schema.org to add accessibility metadata based on the Access For All IMS specification. In January of 2014, the proposal was accepted, and Schema.org adopted the accessibility metadata fields [9].

The adoption of the proposal by Schema.org, in conjunction with the development of metadata tools, and paired with an architecture capable of matching users with content has created an opportunity for a powerful and transformative workflow that can deliver personalized content to users.

3 Metadata Generation

3.1 Automatically Derived Metadata

To develop metadata generation tools, the team began by analyzing the properties in the Schema.org accessibility metadata set to determine what information is required and to decide how much of this information could be deduced automatically based on the media in question, the context, etc. For example, if an author is adding a video, it can reasonably be assumed that the video has both visual and auditory content. If an image is added that is known to be a math lesson, it might be reasonably assumed that the image contains math in visual format.

By comparing the schema.org metadata properties to possible media types, Table 1 was produced. This table was created using knowledge of accessibility experts, including the people who created the schema.org metadata fields, and represents the best possible "educated guess" at what metadata would be appropriate based on the content. The metadata generation tools automatically create the appropriate fields as the author edits the content.

Table 1. Metadata fields potentially auto-generated

Content Type	Metadata properties																
	auditory	**tactile**	**textual**	**visual**	**Colour-dependent**	**Text-on-visual**	**Math-on-visual**	**Chart-on-visual**	**Alt text**	**captions**	**transcripts**	**Flashing**	**No flashing**	**Motion simulation**	**No motion simulation**	**Sound hazard**	**No sound hazard**
video	S		A	S	A	A	A	A	A	R	R	A	A	A	A	A	A
audio	S										A		S		S	A	A
image				S	A				R			A	A	A	A		S
Image with text				S	A	S			R			A	A	A	A		S
Image with math				S	A		S		R			A	A	A	A		S
Image with chart				S	A			S	R			A	A	A	A		S
transcript			S										S		S		S
caption			S		A								S		S		S
sign language				S									S		S		S
audio description	S										R		S		S	A	A
music/ dialog	S								R	R	R		S		S	A	A
braille		S											S		S		S

Legend: S: Set by default R: Recommend that authors provide A: Available for authors to edit

3.2 For Content Authors

Because the automatically generated metadata is an algorithmically-determined "educated guess," there is no guarantee that it will be correct or complete. For example, an automated process can't tell if a video contains flashing lights (which might cause seizures in some viewers), or if an image has text embedded in it (which wouldn't be available to a screen reader). There will be details that the author knows about the content that cannot be deduced or inferred; the author must provide some information. To that end, the tools we have designed also present a summary of the metadata that was generated along with features for updating, improving and adding to that metadata.

3.2.1 Authoring User Interface

This section presents the designs for the metadata editing interface, developed for the Cloud4All and Floe projects by inclusive designers at the IDRC.

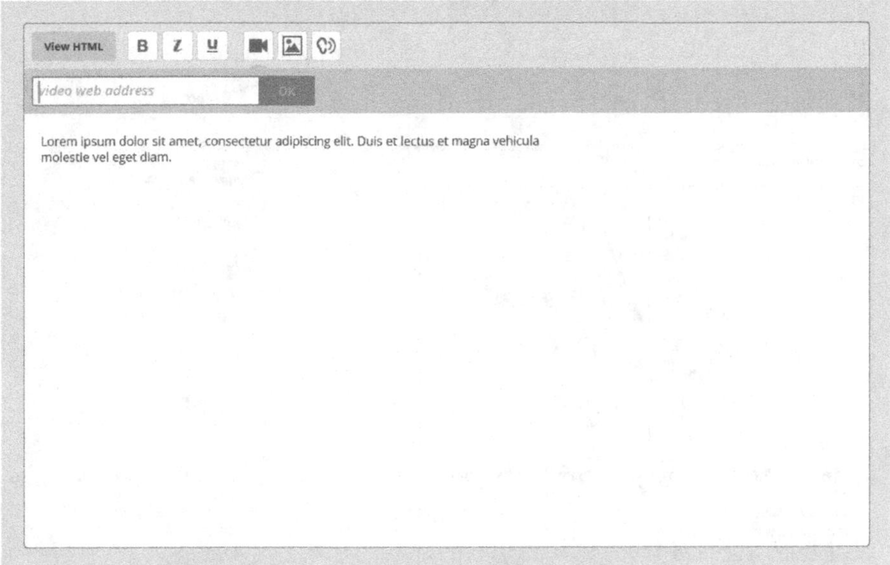

Fig. 1. Typical authoring interface

Fig. 1 shows a typical authoring interface. The metadata editor is introduced in an author's regular workflow of adding media, such as video, images, or audio to a resource.

Fig. 2 shows, on the right, the interface that will be presented when the author has added content to the authoring tool – in this case a video. After media is added, all potential features of the media are listed. The availability of a feature is visually indicated through different icon states to encourage the author to add more features. Textual descriptions are also available on hover. When a feature is selected a panel opens to the side. In the case of the 'Video' feature, the author answers a few questions for relevant metadata to be generated.

Fig. 3 show, on the right, the interface that will be presented to the author when "captions" has been selected. In this case, the author is prompted to add captions and specify the language or indicate that the video already has captions embedded. Relevant metadata is generated from the author's additions.

Fig. 4 shows, on the right, the summary of the metadata that has been generated plus "recommended" features for updating, improving and adding metadata and alternatives. The intention is that authors will be curious about other "adaptations" that the interface suggests, and could feel encouraged to create missing alternatives to see a "completed" metadata summary.

The metadata editor component is modular and designed to be embeddable in a wide range of authoring environments. Fig. 5 illustrates the metadata component floating on top of the editor. When a video feature is selected, an overlay appears on top of the page (Fig. 5). Metadata icons have different states to encourage authors to add features and to inform consumers of the availability of features.

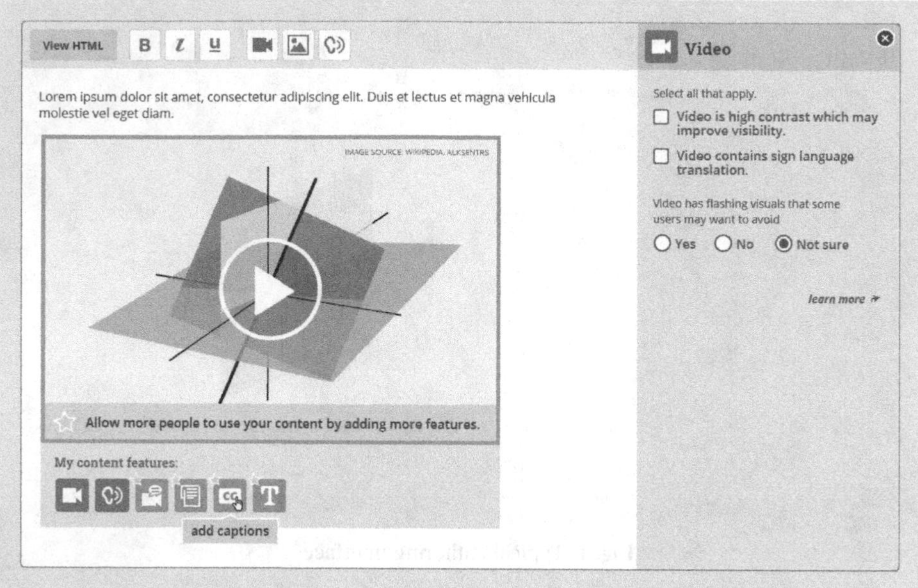

Fig. 2. Interface after a video has been added to the content

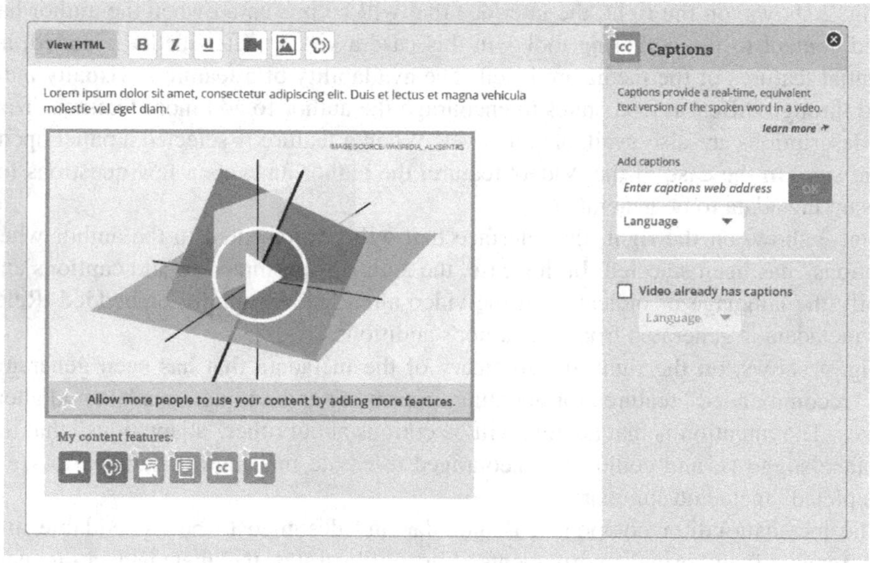

Fig. 3. Interface after author has selected "captions"

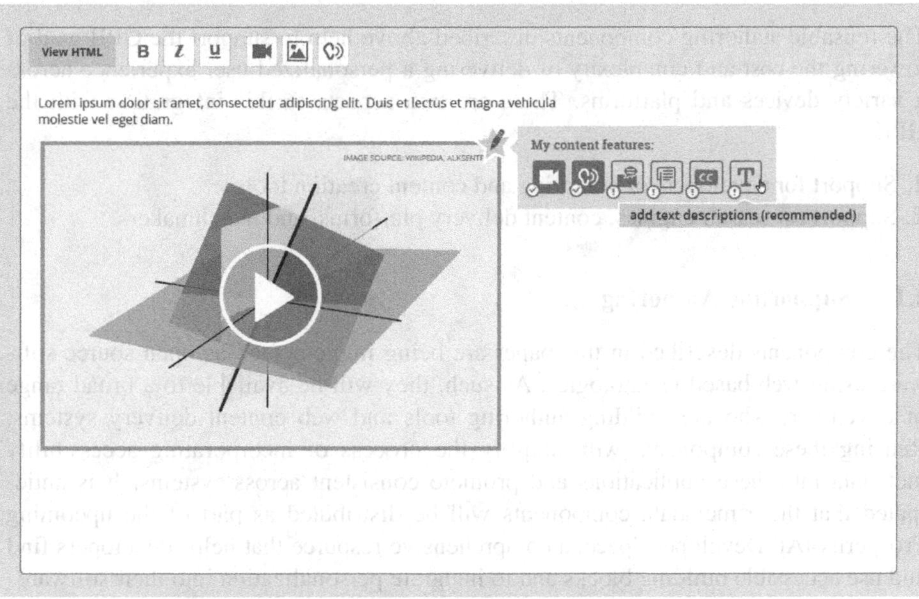

Fig. 4. Alternative interface, presented as a floating widget

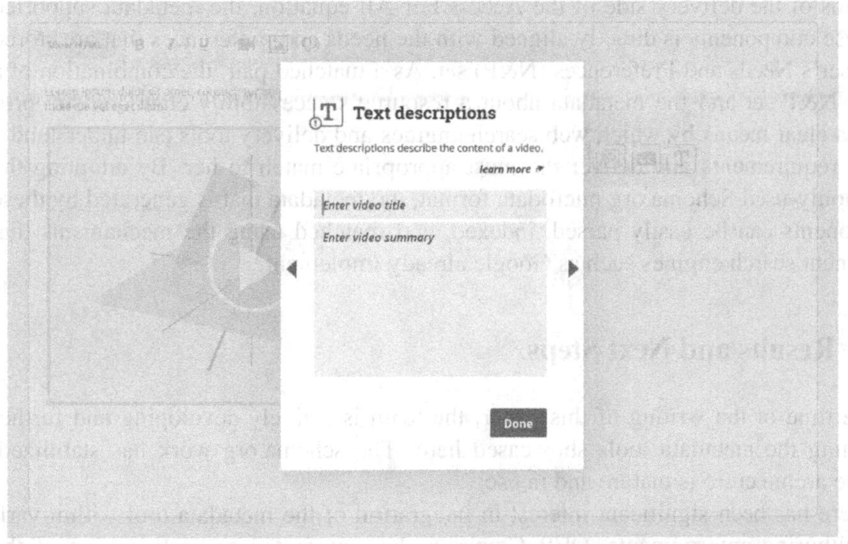

Fig. 5. Overlay presentation of dialog for text description input

4 Integration with the GPII

The reusable authoring components described above help to support the GPII goal of lowering the cost and complexity of delivering a personalized user experience across a variety devices and platforms. There are two aspects to this integration with the GPII:

1. Support for developers of authoring and content creation tools
2. Support for search engines, content delivery platforms, and matchmakers

4.1 Supporting Authoring

The components described in this paper are being implemented as open source software using web-based technologies. As such, they will be available to a broad range of developers who are building authoring tools and web content delivery systems. Reusing these components will simplify the process of incorporating accessibility metadata into these applications and promote consistent across systems. It is anticipated that these metadata components will be distributed as part of the upcoming Prosperity4All Developer Space, a comprehensive resource that helps developers find and use accessible building blocks and to integrate personalization into their software.

4.2 Supporting Delivery

In terms of the delivery side of the Access For All equation, the metadata supported by these components is directly aligned with the needs and preferences that are stored in a user's Needs and Preferences (N&P) set. As a matched pair, the combination of a user's N&P set and the metadata about a resource's accessibility characteristic provides a clear means by which web search engines and delivery tools can understand a user's requirements and deliver the most appropriate match to her. By adopting the commonly-used Schema.org microdata format, the metadata that is generated by these components can be easily parsed, indexed, and matched using the mechanisms that prominent search engines such as Google already implement.

5 Results and Next Steps

At the time of the writing of this paper, the team is actively developing and further designing the metadata tools showcased here. The schema.org work has stabilized, and the architecture is mature and in use.

There has been significant interest in integration of the metadata tool within various authoring environments. OER Commons has integrated an early design of the authoring tool that empowers content authors to include metadata into a large repository of Open Education Resources [10]. OER Pub has expressed interest in also integrating the tool for a new authoring tool currently under development [11]. And the Floe Project has been disseminating the components that contribute to the workflow of metadata creation and increased accessibility of content where educational content is being created.

The code for the Cloud4All (and Floe Project) metadata components is available within the Fluid Project [12] Github space (a space that also contains the Fluid Infusion suite of reusable, web-based components): https://github.com/fluid-project/metadata

For the latest work, visit a (sometimes unstable) nightly build of a demo online: http://metadata.floeproject.org/demos/html/metadata.html

5.1 Next Steps

Forthcoming features for the metadata authoring tools include ways to refine and improve the accuracy and usefulness of the metadata claims through use. Users will be able to inform and affect metadata based on whether it met their needs or not, further refining matching accuracy. Means of both

a) automatically deriving usage metrics in a way that supports privacy and of

b) enlisting users and their support team to provide feedback on the utility of the resource component for specific user needs will be developed and integrated into the overall metadata processes.

Planning has begun for the interfaces that will enable end-users to easily contribute metadata back to the resource. That metadata can include information about the efficacy of the supplied resource in meeting their particular need or preference. User feedback regarding the efficacy of the supplied resource once captured can be used to rank and refine resources and services. This 'paradata' about the use and efficacy of a resource can be used to capture feedback regarding the inclusive design or accessibility of resources and then be used as a trigger for improving the resource or its alternative. This can serve as a means for users to request an alternative that doesn't yet exist, for example. There are many opportunities to match service providers with user needs once this information can be collected and shared.

6 Conclusion

The work showcased here represents a long history of conceiving of and creating a personalized approach to accessibility: from Web4All to AccessForAll to the IMS accessibility specification to Schema.org integration and now culminating in the work on the Global Public Inclusive Infrastructure.

To ensure the most accurate metadata is created and propagated, the metadata approach outlined here takes a hybrid model where the tools automate as much as possible while still allowing for human intervention. By creating easy-to-use interfaces that allow authors and users to ultimately intervene and correct and refine the gathered metadata, the GPII team is ensuring a mechanism for creating the best, personalized results. By supporting authors and end-users, the metadata tools will have a profound impact on metadata creation, propagation, and ultimately matching and delivery.

Acknowledgments. The authors would like to thank the larger community of designers, developers, volunteers, testers, and users for their contributions to this work. In particular thanks to the GPII User Experience team and the team from the Preferences for Global Access project.

References

1. IMS Global Learning Consortium, `http://www.imsglobal.org/accessibility/`
2. Cloud4All Project: `http://wiki.gpii.net`
3. FLOE Project: `http://floeproject.org`
4. Global Public Inclusive Infrastructure: `http://gpii.net`
5. Inclusive Design Research Centre: `http://idrc.ocadu.ca`
6. Web4All: `http://web4all.ca`
7. Treviranus, J.: Making yourself at home - portable personal access preferences. In: Miesenberger, K., Klaus, J., Zagler, W.L. (eds.) ICCHP 2002. LNCS, vol. 2398, pp. 643–648. Springer, Heidelberg (2002), `http://link.springer.com/chapter/10.1007/3-540-45491-8_123`
8. Schema.org: `http://schema.org`
9. Accessibility Metadata Project: `http://www.a11ymetadata.org`
10. OER Commons: `http://oercommons.org`
11. OER Pub: `http://oerpub.org`
12. Fluid Project: `http://fluidproject.org`

EAR-Math: Evaluation of Audio Rendered Mathematics

Hernisa Kacorri[1,2], Paraskevi Riga[1], and Georgios Kouroupetroglou[1]

[1] National and Kapodistrian University of Athens
Department of Informatics and Telecommunications,
Panepistimiopolis, Ilisia, 15784 Athens, Greece
[2] City University of New York (CUNY)
Doctoral Program in Computer Science, The Graduate Center,
365 Fifth Ave, New York, NY 10016 USA
{c.katsori,p.riga,koupe}@di.uoa.gr,
hkacorri@gc.cuny.edu

Abstract. Audio rendering of mathematical expressions has accessibility benefits for people with visual impairment. Seeking a systematic way to measure participants' perception of the rendered formulae with audio cues, we investigate the design of performance metrics to capture the distance between reference and perceived math expressions. We propose EAR-Math, a methodological approach for user-based evaluation of math rendering against a baseline. EAR-Math measures systems' performance using three fine-grained error rates based on the structural elements, arithmetic operators, numbers and identifiers in a formula. The proposed methodology and metrics were successfully applied in a pilot study, where 5 sighted and 2 blind participants evaluated 39 stimuli rendered by MathPlayer in Greek. In the obtained results, we observed that structural elements had the highest mean and variance of errors, which improved from 18% in the first attempt to 10% and 7% in two following attempts.

Keywords: mathematics, audio rendering, visually impaired, blind, evaluation, user study.

1 Introduction

The World Health Organization estimates a total of 285 million people with visual impairment of which 39 million are blind [1]. One considerable accessibility barrier is the comprehension of mathematical concepts and formulae through audio or haptic modality, which require significant additional cognitive processing [2]. Braille, linear in nature, faces difficulties in keeping up with complex mathematical expressions represented in two dimensions. Moreover, as 6-dot braille is limited to 64 characters, it results in complex notations to represent the vast number of mathematical structures and symbols. Usually this is performed through escape sequences, which map more than one meaning to the same braille character depending on the context.

Audio, a popular output medium for the visually impaired, is one approach favored by researchers to create an accessible platform for mathematics [3]. Similar to braille, audio rendering of a mathematical formula, either by a trained reader following a

C. Stephanidis and M. Antona (Eds.): UAHCI/HCII 2014, Part II, LNCS 8514, pp. 111–120, 2014.

spoken structure (e.g. [4-5]) or by synthetic speech driven by a rule-based system such as [6-10], [24], communicates the expression using lexical and prosodic cues in a linear way. Researchers have investigated the possibility of alternating between multiple audio views such as summarization and detailed description [7], user customization of the rendering rules [7-8][10], and the use of non-speech audio cues or spatial audio to indicate structural delimiters within the formula [11-13].

Blind students may avoid adopting approaches for accessing mathematics that require the use of a language or representation of mathematics which differs from the one used by their teachers or peers. An adaptation of lexical cues, which indicate the structural information in the student's native language, is often required.

In the past few years, the Speech and Accessibility Lab, University of Athens, has focused on accessible mathematics [14-15] and the support of the Greek language for MathPlayer [8]. To construct the audio rendering rules we typically consult blind students during the initial design and the development phase. The challenges during these phases are: achieving a delicate balance between resolving ambiguity and reducing verbosity, and fine-tuning other non-lexical parameters such as pauses, pitch, and volume. When selecting between differently parameterized rendering styles, we are interested in quantitative results obtained from the users to measure the performance of our system. Despite advances in the audio rendering of mathematics, there are no widely accepted methodologies or benchmarks.

In this paper, we propose EAR-Math, a methodological approach along with a set of metrics, designed to evaluate and compare audio rendering systems for math expressions. Furthermore, we present results from an application of the proposed methodology in a pilot study evaluating the Greek audio rendering rules of MathPlayer.

2 Related Work

Relatively few researchers have evaluated the performance of math audio-access approaches. We reviewed prior studies evaluating math audio rendering systems based on perception by visually impaired and sighted participants. We present in Table 1 the relative methodologies based on the groups of participants recruited, selected stimuli, and the type of feedback obtained from the participants.

MathTalk [9] incorporates a set of rules to insert prosodic cues into spoken expressions. In a user study, participants wrote their recall of the formulae once the rendering was over using either question marks or ellipses to denote any missing objects. Responses were graded for comprehension of the structure and retention of content. A correct answer required over 75% of an expression's content and the major structural features.

TechRead's [16] used prosody to indicate nested structure. Sighted participants were asked to choose among 4 answers matching the audio stimuli. Of 16 rendered math expressions, 3 were in training while the remaining were played in 3 speech modes.

Gellenbeck et al. [17] conducted a study to assess whether insertion of pauses inside spoken mathematical expressions reduces ambiguity between similar algebraic expressions. Participants heard stimuli and rated side-by-side formulae, using a 0-10 Likert-scale, on how well they thought the visual expression matched the audio. Before the study, participants gained familiarity through four ungraded example tasks.

Murphy et al. [13] used a mixture of non-speech auditory cues, modified speech, and binaural spatialization for disambiguation. To evaluate initial cues, the authors conducted a four-part accessible online survey with no training phase. The first part tested word recognition and lexical language of spoken mathematics, the second measured understanding of spoken equations with non-speech sound elements, the third assessed intuitiveness of spatial attributes, while the fourth was purely qualitative. The listeners chose among 3 alternatives rendered both graphically and acoustically.

I-Math [18] was evaluated by participants with varying visual ability. Audio stimuli were graded on speech quality, comprehension effort, and transcription. Transcriptions were compared to original textual expressions and correct, missing, and incorrect words were counted. The number of correct words and positions were evaluated using precision, recall, and F-score.

Table 1. User studies evaluating approaches for audio rendering of mathematics

	MathTalk	TechRead	Gellenbeck et al [10]	Murphy et al [14]	I-Math
# Participants	24 (sighted)	20 (sighted)	16 (sighted)	35 (sighted) 21 (blind)	35 (sighted) 6 (blind), 4 (v.i.)
Participants' Age	university students	university students	university students ~22,7	~38	students and teachers
Knowledge/ Use of Math	daily-infrequent use (qualification > 'O' Level)	good knowledge of math constructs in stimuli	N/A	10 years since last exam (mean)	N/A
# Stimuli	2 matched sets of 12 and 3 samples	16 (3 samples)	30 min. session	13 (6 partial)	35
Stimuli Categories	fractions, parenthesised subexpressions, superscript	simple fractions, radicals, sum, limits, integrals, trigonometry	selected from the general area of algebra	N/A	fractions, vectors, superscripts, log, radicals, lim, sum., trigonometry, integrals
Training	explanation and synthetic speech familiarization	explanation and examples	description and examples	-	N/A
Language	English	English	English	N/A	Thai (tonal)
Participants' Answers	written math expression	4 multiple-choice solutions	rating of 2 alternatives	3 multiple-choice solutions	transcribed text
Baseline/ Comparison	lexical vs. prosodic cues, lexical vs. neither lexical nor prosodic cues	natural vs. enhanced vs. unenhanced speech	pauses vs. no pauses	sighted vs. blind participants	-
Quantitative	accuracy	accuracy	average rating	accuracy intuitiveness, confusion	intelligibility, speech quality, understanding effort
Qualitative	-	-	-	Alternatives, comments	usefulness, ease of use

3 Evaluation Methodology

Evaluation of Audio Rendered Math (EAR-Math) is proposed as an experimental methodology for user-based performance evaluation of mathematical expressions described by a rule-based system with audio output. The accuracy scores achieved over the stimuli in a user study depend not only on the system output, but also on the difficulty of the mathematical expressions chosen and on the group of participants. Thus, EAR includes a baseline in the studies to make the results more meaningful. This baseline may typically be a trained reader following a spoken structure to read mathematical expressions aloud. The baseline could be a previous version of the system for researchers who wish to evaluate improvements within their system. Similarly, EAR-Math allows for direct comparison between two or more alternative systems.

3.1 Experiment Design

Since it is not feasible to exhaustively examine the mathematical expressions likely to be rendered by a system, the design of a smaller representative subset is required. Stimuli should cover an extended number of mathematical structures (e.g. fractions, integrals, roots, subscripts, and arrays). They should be engineered to reveal potential ambiguity in the system output and have a realistic length. The number of stimuli should also allow incorporation in an experimental session lasting less than 2 hours. We considered the publicly available set of formulae for ASTeR demonstration [19] as a potential candidate.

The EAR-Math user study consists of three phases. As a preliminary phase, participants are introduced to the system's rules with sample examples to gain familiarity with the generated output. Symbols naming, a list that can extend over 2.000 Unicode characters, is mentioned only for a small number of characters, which are included in the stimuli and are assigned a non-familiar name.

In phase 2, participants listen to the description of the math formula (rendered either by the system being evaluated or the baseline) and are prompted in parallel to keep notes of the formula. Notes may be taken on paper for sighted participants in Braille for blind participants, in LaTeX, or in any other format and means the participant is familiar with. Stimuli are played upon request two more times and the participants are allowed to correct their initial guess.

In phase 3 of the study, participants hear two sequential versions of the same mathematical expression rendered by the system and baseline (with alternating sequence). The participants can hear any of the outputs as many times as they wish. They are then asked to respond on a 1-to-10 Likert-scale question about how sure they are that the expressions are identical. For each of the two versions, participants were asked two 1-to-10 Likert-scale questions about the understandability and naturalness of the rendered formula.

3.2 Performance Metrics

EAR-Math proposes a performance metric to measure the distance between the intended math expression and the actual one delivered by the system as perceived by sighted or blind users. Our metric is tailored to account for both content and structure. Specifically, the performance of a math audio rendering system is defined as a triplet of fine-grained error rates on the structural elements, arithmetic operators, and numbers and identifiers of the math formula:

$$Structure\ Error\ Rate\ (SER) = \frac{\#ins + \#del + \#sub}{\#structuralElem}$$

$$Operator\ Error\ Rate\ (OER) = \frac{\#ins + \#del + \#sub}{\#operators}$$

$$Identifier/Number\ Error\ Rate\ (INER) = \frac{\#ins + \#del + \#sub}{\#identifiers + \#numericalValues}$$

The proposed metrics are derived by first aligning the perceived mathematical expression with the original expression to be rendered by the system. Alignment is performed between the syntax trees of both expressions. Figure 1 illustrates an example demonstrating the process. Our metrics can then be computed as error rates; number of insertions, deletions, and substitutions in the perceived expression compared to the reference over the total number of elements in the reference expression for each of the three categories of elements. Structure Error Rate (SER) involves structural components of a math formula such as fractions, roots, and arrays. Operator Error Rate (OER) is focused on mathematical operators e.g. plus, minus, and times. And last, Identifier and Number Error Rate (INER) represent the number of errors for identifiers and numerical values within the expression. For example, given a reference and the perceived expression pair, we get the syntax trees and alignment of Fig. 1.

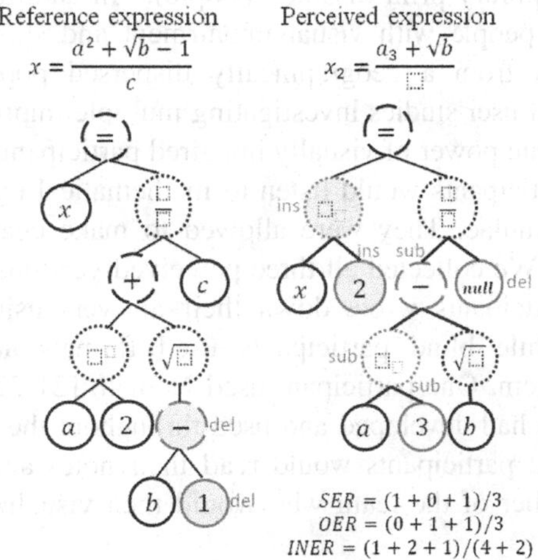

Fig. 1. An example of alignment and SER, OER, and INER calculation

Word Error Rate (WER), commonly used in the field of speech recognition, was adopted for the design of the proposed performance metrics. To group the components that comprise a mathematical formula, we were inspired by the token and layout elements in Presentation MathML, such as <mo> for operators, <mi> for identifiers, and <mn> for numbers. This grouping simplified incorporating user's feedback towards the improvement of our Greek audio rendering rules for MathML expressions in MathPlayer.

4 Pilot User Study

To assess feasibility, time, and statistical variability required for evaluating MathPlayer's Greek audio rendering rules, we conducted a pilot user study. This helped to test, adjust and obtain valuable insights in the design of EAR-Math and particularly its metrics and is shown as an applied example of the proposed methodology.

For the purposes of this study, the system was not evaluated against a baseline. Therefore, only the first two phases of EAR-Math were employed. Stimuli were based on the set of formulae for ASTeR demonstration [19] rendered through the Dimitris of Acapela Text-to-Speech [20] driven by MathPlayer with lexical and prosodic cues. The voice, volume, and speed for all stimuli were identical. Mathematical expressions were prerecorded, thus there was no navigation and no control over the speech velocity.

Of the 7 participants recruited for the study: 2 were congenitally blind and 5 were sighted. Participant attended a Greek university whose entrance required a high level of mathematics according to the Greek educational system (6 were majoring in computer science and 1 in law). Thus, all participants had been exposed to more complex mathematical expressions than the stimuli. There were 5 men and 2 women of ages 20-34 (average age 25.9). While using a sighted comparison group wouldn't be either fair or appropriate, we included people both with and without visual impairment. The rationale behind this decision is that audio rendering of mathematics has universal benefits (e.g. to temporary print disabled people). In addition, recruitment of a homogeneous group of people with visual impairment and similar performance in mathematic assessments from a geographically dispersed population is difficult. These challenges may set user studies investigating multiple improvements within the same system with adequate power of visually impaired participants impossible.

During the study, participants would listen to mathematical expressions and write down the perceived formulae. They were allowed to make changes to their initial guess two more times. We collected all three perceived versions for each of the expressions. Sighted participants wrote down their answers using a pen-and-paper experimental packet while blind participants used formats and technology that were most familiar to them. One participant used Nemeth [21-22]. The other used a variant math notation he had developed and used throughout the years. After the experimental session, blind participants would read their notes and describe their answers to a sighted member of the team who would then visualize the expression in two-dimensions.

Short mathematical expressions described in the design of Greek audio rendering rules for math [23] served as sample expressions to familiarize the participants with the experiment and the output of the system.

5 Results

In our study, MathPlayer's Greek audio rendering of math is evaluated with a set of 49 stimuli with 190 structural elements, 113 operators, and 295 identifiers or numbers. While not compared against a baseline, this evaluation demonstrates the EAR-Math performance metrics within the proposed experimental setup.

In our calculations, all reference expressions from the stimuli and perceived expressions were drawn as syntax trees. A computer science PhD student 'manually' aligned the perceived formulae syntax tree to the reference tree and recorded the errors. While identifying the operator, identifier, and number errors were a straightforward process, structural elements errors were more challenging, especially when the correct structure was improperly positioned in the tree. An improper position of the structural element was calculated as a delete and re-insert.

The number of mathematical elements for each stimuli varied by context: 0-13 structural (mean 5), 1-10 operators (mean 2.97), and 3-18 identifiers and numbers (mean 7.76). Therefore the error rates were calculated for the aggregated elements among all stimuli, as shown in Table 2.

Table 2. Overall error rates in the stimuli set

	SER	OER	INER
1st Attempt	18%	12%	11%
2nd Attempt	10%	6%	4%
3rd Attempt	7%	4%	2%

Figure 2 shows the distribution of the SER, OER, and INER in the perceived mathematical expressions from the participants as boxplots with whiskers at the 1.5 IQR (inter-quartile range). To aid the comparison, mean values, illustrated with a star, are added as labels at the top of each plot. For the first attempt, we observe that both the structural error rate (SER) and the error rate for identifiers and numbers (INER) have higher variance than the operators' error rate (OER). We speculate this is due to the inherent dependence of the INER on SER. For example, when participants do not understand a structure and omit it, they often omit the identifiers and numbers within the structure. We also observe that participants tend to improve their errors the second and the third time they hear the mathematical expression. This suggests that the audio rendering might have been accurate, but other factors (such as audio memory and familiarity with the system) may have an effect on the results and should be taken into account when designing the experiment.

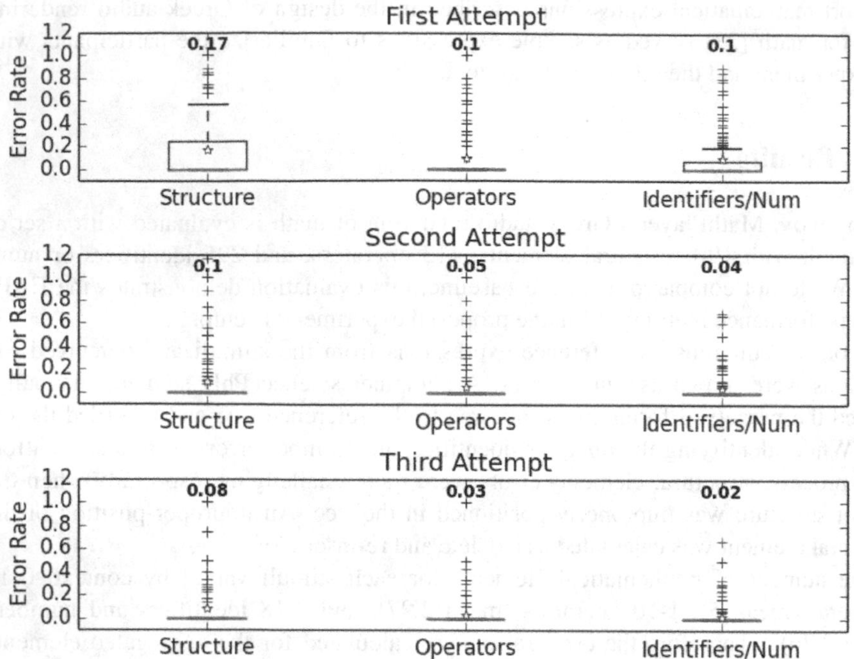

Fig. 2. Error rate distribution in each of the three attempts

$$(12)\quad 1+\cfrac{\chi}{1+\cfrac{\chi}{1+\cfrac{\chi}{1+\cfrac{\chi}{1+\cfrac{\chi}{\ddots}}}}} \qquad (39)\quad e^{(e^{e^{\chi}}+e^{\chi}+\chi)}$$

Fig. 3. Stimuli with the Highest Structure Error Rate in the User Study

We analyzed the data and found that the two most misperceived stimuli at a structural level (12 and 39) had SER improving in each of the attempts from 93% to 69% and 38% for expression (12) and from 14% to 3% and 3% for expression (39).

6 Discussion and Future Work

This paper has described EAR-Math, a methodological approach for the evaluation of math audio rendering systems with users and a set of performance metrics that capture the distance between the reference and the perceived math expressions. In particular, EAR-Math metrics are defined as error rates (Structure Error Rate, Operator Error Rate, and Identifier and Number Error Rate) calculated by comparing the syntax trees of the reference and perceived mathematical expressions. Our methodology and metrics are demonstrated in a pilot user study evaluating the Greek audio rendering rules of MathPlayer with 7 participants and 39 stimuli. Obtained results, show that Structure Error Rate had higher mean and variance than the other two metrics, which was improved the second and third time participants heard the stimuli.

This research has two key contributions. First, it provides guidance for researchers conducting user-based evaluation studies to measure the performance of math audio rendering systems against a baseline, compare alternative systems, or iteratively evaluate improvements/styles. Second, it provides results from a pilot study to assess feasibility, time, and statistical variability required for a case study.

In future work we want to explore alternative ways to automate the calculation of the proposed metrics without human intervention. This would allow for more robust results with less human errors during the data processing steps.

Acknowledgments. We would like to thank Neil Soffer from DesignScience for his support during the development of the Greek rules in MathPlayer. This research has been co-financed by the European Union (European Social Fund – ESF) and Greek national funds through the Operational Program "Education and Lifelong Learning" of the National Strategic Reference Framework (NSRF) under the Research Funding Project: "THALIS-University of Macedonia-KAIKOS: Audio and Tactile Access to Knowledge for Individuals with Visual Impairments", MIS 380442.

References

1. World Health Organization. Fact Sheet 282: Visual Impairment and Blindness (2013), `http://www.who.int/mediacentre/factsheets/fs282/en/index.html`
2. Dick, T., Kubiak, E.: Issues and aids for teaching mathematics to the blind. The Mathematics Teacher 90(5), 344–349 (1997)
3. Freitas, D., Kouroupetroglou, G.: Speech Technologies for Blind and Low Vision Persons. Technology and Disability 20, 135–156 (2008)
4. Chang, L.A., White, C.M., Abrahamson, L.: Handbook for spoken mathematics. Lawrence Livermore National Laboratory (1983)
5. Nemeth, A.: Tips for Reading Math Out loud to Blind Students, `http://www.rit.edu/easi/easisem/talkmath.htm`
6. Edwards, A.D., McCartney, H., Fogarolo, F.: Lambda: a multimodal approach to making mathematics accessible to blind students. In: Proceedings of the 8th International ACM SIGACCESS Conference on Computers and Accessibility, pp. 48–54 (2006)
7. Raman, T.V.: ASTER-Towards modality-independent electronic documents. In: Electronic Multimedia Publishing, pp. 53-63, Springer US (1998)
8. Soiffer, N.: A flexible design for accessible spoken math. In: Stephanidis, C. (ed.) UAHCI 2009, Part III. LNCS, vol. 5616, pp. 130–139. Springer, Heidelberg (2009)
9. Stevens, R.D.: Principles for the design of auditory interfaces to present complex information to blind people. Doctoral dissertation, University of York (1996)
10. Yamaguchi, K., Komada, T., Kawane, F., Suzuki, M.: New features in math accessibility with infty software. In: Miesenberger, K., Klaus, J., Zagler, W.L., Karshmer, A.I. (eds.) ICCHP 2008. LNCS, vol. 5105, pp. 892–899. Springer, Heidelberg (2008)

11. Bates, E., Fitzpatrick, D.: Spoken mathematics using prosody, earcons and spearcons. In: Miesenberger, K., Klaus, J., Zagler, W., Karshmer, A. (eds.) ICCHP 2010, Part II. LNCS, vol. 6180, pp. 407–414. Springer, Heidelberg (2010)
12. Brewster, S.A.: Using non-speech sound to overcome information overload. Displays 17(3), 179–189 (1997)
13. Murphy, E., Bates, E., Fitzpatrick, D.: Designing auditory cues to enhance spoken mathematics for visually impaired users. In: Proceedings of the 12th International ACM SIGACCESS Conference on Computers and Accessibility, pp. 75–82 (2010)
14. Kouroupetroglou, G., Kacorri, H.: Deriving Accessible Science Books for the Blind Students of Physics. Proceedings of the American Institute of Physics 1203, 1308–1313 (2010)
15. Tsonos, D., Kacorri, H., Kouroupetroglou, G.: A design-for-all approach towards multimodal accessibility of mathematics. Assistive Technology Research Series 25, 393–397 (2009)
16. Fitzpatrick, D.: Towards Accessible Technical Documents: Production of Speech and Braille Output from Formatted Documents. Doctoral dissertation, Dublin City University (1999)
17. Gellenbeck, E., Stefik, A.: Evaluating prosodic cues as a means to disambiguate algebraic expressions: an empirical study. In: Proceedings of the 11th International ACM SIGACCESS Conference on Computers and Accessibility, pp. 139–146 (2009)
18. Wongkia, W., Naruedomkul, K., Cercone, N.: I-Math: an Intelligent Accessible Mathematics system for People with Visual Impairment. Computational Approaches to Assistive Technologies for People with Disabilities 253, 83–108 (2013)
19. Raman, T.V.: Mathematics for computer generated spoken documents - ASTeR Demonstration, http://www.cs.cornell.edu/home/raman/aster/demo.html
20. Acapela text-to-speech, http://www.acapela-group.com/
21. Kouroupetroglou, G., Florias, E.: Greek Braille Scientific Notation – Application in Information Systems for the Blind. Education and Rehabilitation Center for the Blind, Athens (2003) ISBN 960-87918-0-4
22. Nemeth, A.: The Nemeth Braille code for mathematics and science notation: 1972 revision. Produced in braille for the Library of Congress, National Library Service for the Blind and Physically Handicapped by the American Printing House for the Blind (1972)
23. Kacorri, H.: Audio Rendering Rules for Mathematical MathML Expressions in Greek, Diploma Thesis, University of Athens (2006)
24. Ferreira, H., Freitas, D.: Audio rendering of mathematical formulae using MathML and AudioMath. In: Stary, C., Stephanidis, C. (eds.) UI4ALL 2004. LNCS, vol. 3196, pp. 391–399. Springer, Heidelberg (2004)

Riemann Geometric Color-Weak Compensation for Individual Observers

Takanori Kojima[1], Rika Mochizuki[2], Reiner Lenz[3], and Jinhui Chao[1]

[1] Chuo University, 1-13-27, Kasuga, Bunkyo-ku, Tokyo, Japan
jchao@ise.chuo-u.ac.jp
[2] NTT Cyber Solutions Laboratories, Japan
[3] Linköping University, Bredgatan, 60174 Norrköping, Sweden

Abstract. We extend a method for color weak compensation based on the criterion of preservation of subjective color differences between color normal and color weak observers presented in [2]. We introduce a new algorithm for color weak compensation using local affine maps between color spaces of color normal and color weak observers. We show how to estimate the local affine map and how to determine correspondences between the origins of local coordinates in color spaces of color normal and color weak observers. We also describe a new database of measured color discrimination threshold data. The new measurements are obtained at different lightness levels in CIELUV space. They are measured for color normal and color weak observers. The algorithms are implemented and evaluated using the Semantic Differential method.

Keywords: Universal Design, Color-barrier-free Technology, Color-weak Compensation, Riemann geometry.

1 Introduction

Presenting a color image to observers so that their perception of the image is as similar as possible is a difficult problem. Methods to achieve this goal are important in human computer interface and have received a lot of interest due to recent rapid developments of visual media and wearable display technology. One cause for the problems encountered is the wide variation among observers from those with normal color vision over color-weak to near color blind observers. A second problem is the fact that perception is not directly measurable and there is therefore no objective criterion to measure the differences between the color perception of different observers.

A fundamental information used to characterize color vision properties is color discrimination thresholds and it is thus natural to compensate color-weak vision based on these data. This was described in [2] and [4]. This method characterizes color vision by using the fact that color spaces have a structure that can be described with the help of Riemann geometry [3]. This is used to construct a criterion for color-weak compensation that aims at the preservation of subjective color differences between color-normal and color-weak observers. A map preserving color-differences or Riemannian distance between color spaces is called an

C. Stephanidis and M. Antona (Eds.): UAHCI/HCII 2014, Part II, LNCS 8514, pp. 121–131, 2014.

isometry. Therefore the task to compensate color-weak vision becomes to built a color difference preserving map or an isometry[2].

There are two ways to build an isometry between two color spaces when the Riemann metric tensor in both spaces are available. One is shown in [2][4] to build a set of local isometry maps at neighborhoods of sampling points in the color spaces. The other is shown in [6][5] to build a Riemann normal coordinate system using geodesics in both color spaces. The first one is easier to implement since it only needs linear algebra manipulations at each neighborhood, while the second requires to solve the second order ordinary differential equation to draw geodesics. It also needs a smooth interpolation of the Riemann metric tensor.

However, two problems remained unsolved for the first method. Firstly, estimation of local isometries from observed data could result in ill-conditioned linear equations. One also needs to establish the correspondence between neighborhoods or the origins of local coordinates before estimating the local isometries between them. Both problems are not trivial, in fact, as shown below, the first estimation problem is underdetermined or there is no unique solution to find a local isometry based on Riemann metric tensor information alone. The second problem is directly related with unobservability of color perception. Besides, previously used discrimination threshold data were measured on the chromaticity plane, so only 2D compensation was possible.

In this paper we build on these results and extend them in two directions:

1. The compensation is based on a function that maps the color spaces of the color-weak and the color-normal observer in a way that preserves the color differences as represented by the discrimination ellipsoids. We introduce a new algorithm to determine such a local ellipsoid preserving function f. The construction requires the solution of a nonlinear equation or a singular-value-decomposition of a restricted form of f.
2. The constructed functions f are local and defined on patches. It is therefore necessary to paste these patches together in order to construct a global mapping. We do this by introducing a new algorithm to find correspondences between the origins of local coordinates [1].

All these methods are based on the characterization of the color perception properties in the form of color discrimination data. We also present a new database of threshold data measured at lightness levels $L = 30, 40, 50, 60, 70$ (CIELUV). Previously such data was only available for one lightness level.

We will evaluate the proposed color-weak compensation methods based on the new measurement database in experiments where the performance is evaluated by the Semantic Differential (SD) method [9].

2 Geometry of Color Spaces and Color-Weak Compensation

Color spaces can be modeled as Riemann spaces in which the Riemann metric tensor is defined by the color discrimination threshold (MacAdam ellipsoids).

At a point x in a Riemann space C, the length of the deviation Δx from x is computed as

$$\|\Delta x\|^2 = \Delta x^T G(x) \Delta x. \quad (1)$$

$G(x)$ is a smoothly-varying positive-definite matrix, the Riemann metric tensor. Color differences are distances in the color space and the color discrimination threshold at x is the unit sphere at x. $G(x)$ is determined by color matching psychophysical experiments. The distance between color vectors x_1, x_2 is defined as the length of the shortest curve connecting the two points.

$$d(x_1, x_2) = \int_{\gamma_{12}} \|\Delta x\| = \int_{\gamma_{12}} \sqrt{\Delta x^T G(x) \Delta x} \quad (2)$$

For color spaces C_k with Riemann metric $G_k(x), (k = 1, 2)$ a map f from C_1 to C_2 is a local isometry if it preserves local distance and map discrimination ellipsoid at every x onto ellipsoid at $y = f(x)$:

$$G_1(x) = (D_f(x))^T G_2(y) D_f(x) \quad (3)$$

with D_f the Jacobian of f [3].

A map preserving large color-differences is called a global isometry, which means that the distance between any pair of points in one space is equal to the distance between the corresponding pair of points or their images in the other space. In fact a global isometry is also local isometry and vice versa[1].

If C_n, C_w are the color spaces of a color-normal observer and a color-weak observer, and if we can match the thresholds at every corresponding pair of points in the color spaces, such that the small color differences are adjusted to be always the same everywhere, then the large color difference between any corresponding pair of colors is also identical. The criterion of color-weak compensation is therefore proposed to transform the color space of the color-weak observer by an isometry so that it has the same geometry and therefore the same color differences everywhere as in the color space of color-normal observers[2].

Until now, two ways are proposed to construct an isometry either as a local isometry by discrimination threshold matching at every point [2] or as a global isometry by construct the Riemann normal coordinates at each color spaces[3][6][5]. In the following we will use only the first approach.

3 Compensation Algorithms

3.1 Compensation in 1D Spaces

The colorweak compensation algorithms [2,4] work in the 1D lightness compensation case as follows.

Denote the color spaces of a color-weak and a color-normal observer by C_w, C_n, and the isometry $y = f(x)$ with $f : C_w \longrightarrow C_n$. The discrimination thresholds at $x \in C_w$ and $y \in C_n$ are $\alpha_w(x)$, $\alpha_n(y)$. Denote the common reference point in both C_w and C_n as Q' .

In this case we have: $G_1(x) = 1/\alpha_w^2(x), G_2(y) = 1/\alpha_n^2(y)$ and then we find from the local isometry condition (3) that $1/\alpha_w^2(x) = D_f^2(x)/\alpha_n^2(y)$. Therefore, the isometry f from C_w to C_n has Jacobian

$$D_f(x) = \frac{\alpha_n(y)}{\alpha_w(x)} =: 1 - \omega(x) \quad (0 \leq \omega < 1) \tag{4}$$

Here ω describes the degree of color-weakness: e.g. $\omega = 1$ is color-blind, $\omega = 0$ is color-normal.

Then the color-weak simulation map f can be uniquely obtained from the integral of its Jacobian in C_w:

$$Q'' = f(Q) = \int_{Q'}^{Q} (1 - \omega(x))dx \tag{5}$$

On the other hand, the inverse f^{-1} of f, or the color-weak compensation map, can be obtained from the integral in C_n:

$$P = f^{-1}(Q) = \int_{Q'}^{Q} \frac{1}{(1 - \omega(y))} dy \tag{6}$$

Assuming piecewise constant thresholds or $\alpha_w(x)$, x in the k-th interval $[x_{k-1}, x_k]$ of C_w is a constant equal to $\alpha_w^{(k)} := \alpha_w(x_k)$ on the right end of the interval (and $\alpha_n(y)$ is a constant in k-th interval in C_n equal to $\alpha_n^{(k)} := \alpha_n(y_k)$), the color-weak map (and the compensation map) can be realized by a sum of the discrimination thresholds on direction of lightness:

$$Q'' = \sum_{i=0}^{I} (1 - \omega_i)(x_{i+1} - x_i) = \sum_{i=0}^{I} \alpha_n^{(i)} \tag{7}$$

$$P = \sum_{j=0}^{J} \frac{1}{1 - \omega_j}(y_{j+1} - y_j) = \sum_{j=0}^{J} \alpha_w^{(j)} \tag{8}$$

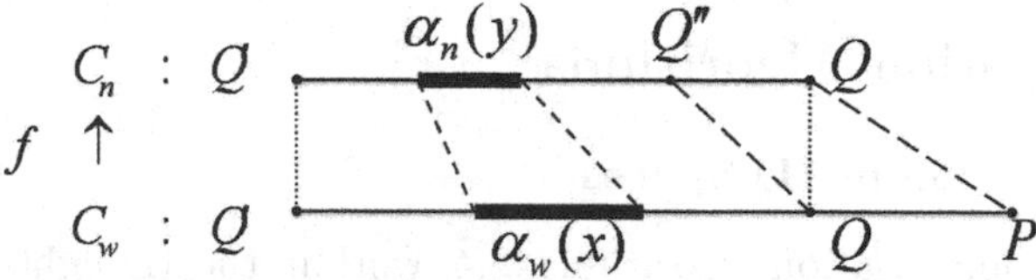

Fig. 1. Local isometry: 1D colorweak map

3.2 Color Weak Compensation in Higher Dimensions

Below, we show how to build the local isometry between color spaces. Such a map from the color space of a color-weak observer to that of color-normal observers is called the color-weak map w in the sense that it shows to color normal observers what the color-weak observer actually sees, which therefore will serve as color-weak simulation map. The inverse map of w, also an isometry, will serve as the compensation map which shows to the color weak observer what the color-normal observers see.

Assume we have a set of sampling points in the, three-dimensional, color space C_w of a color-weak observer: $\{x_i = (x_1^i, x_2^i, x_3^i)^T\}, i = 1, 2, \ldots$. They correspond to the set of the images of the sampling points in the, three-dimensional, color space C_n of a color-normal observers: $y = (x_2, y_2, z_2)^T = w(x) \in C_n$, $\{y_i = (y_1^i, y_2^i, y_3^i)^T\}, i = 1, ..., N$.

The colorweak map $w : C_w \longmapsto C_n$ is linearly approximated by the Jacobian matrix $D_w^{(k)} = D_w(x_k)$ in the neighborhood of each sampling point and its image neighborhood.

This defines the local affine map between the neighborhood of x_k and the neighborhood of its image $y_k = w(x_k)$ given by

$$y - y_k = D_w^{(k)}(x - x_k) \tag{9}$$

The Jacobian matrix $D_w^{(k)}$ of w is determined again by the local isometry or threshold matching condition (3):

$$G_n^{(k)} = (D_w^{(k)})^T G_w^{(k)} D_w^{(k)} \tag{10}$$

and we will combine the above 1D algorithm in the direction of L with a 2D isometry which compensates chromaticity differences.

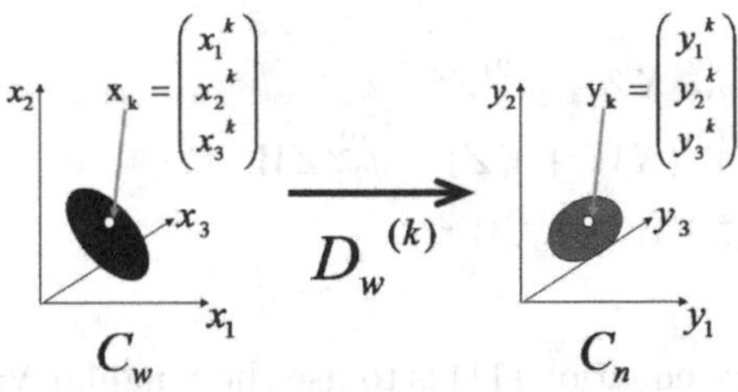

Fig. 2. Local isometry: 3D colorweak map

4 Estimation of the Local Affine Isometry

4.1 Local Linear Isometry

We assume first that a pair of color stimuli x, y of two color spaces C_1 and C_2 corresponding to each other under a (global) isometry is given. The metric tensors at these two points are $G_1(x)$ and $G_2(y)$. We show a method to determine a local linear isometry which maps $x \in C_1$ to $y \in C_2$ which preserves the local geometry or local color difference between the neighborhoods of $x \in C_1$ and $y \in C_2$.

The local linear isometry is the Jacobian of the global isometry at x or a matrix D_f which preserves the Riemann metric $G_1(x), G_2(y)$. It is given as a solution of the following equation:

$$G_2(y) = D_f^T G_1(x) D_f \tag{11}$$

This local linear isometry is not unique as can be easily seen. In the 2D case, this equation involves symmetric matrices of size 2×2 which gives three independent scalar equations. The matrix of the local isometry has however four entries and thus multiple solutions. In 3D case one has six equations and a local isometry defined by nine entries.

In the following we consider a restricted form of f which consists of scalings of the long and short axes of the ellipsoids and a rotation.

$$D_f = R\Lambda = \begin{pmatrix} \cos\theta & \sin\theta \\ -\sin\theta & \cos\theta \end{pmatrix} \begin{pmatrix} a & 0 \\ 0 & b \end{pmatrix} = \begin{pmatrix} a\cos\theta & b\sin\theta \\ -a\sin\theta & b\cos\theta \end{pmatrix}$$

Now we denote $X = a\cos\theta, Y = b\sin\theta, Z = -a\sin\theta, W = b\cos\theta$ to obtain a nonlinear equations in X, Y, Z, W as

$$XY + ZW = 0. \tag{12}$$

Further by choice of the local coordinates as the eigen vectors of $G_1(x)$ one can assume that $G_1(x)$ is a diagonal matrix

$$G_1(x) := \begin{pmatrix} \lambda_1 & 0 \\ 0 & \lambda_2 \end{pmatrix}, G_2(y) := \begin{pmatrix} g_{11}^{(2)} & g_{12}^{(2)} \\ g_{12}^{(2)} & g_{22}^{(2)} \end{pmatrix}.$$

Therefore the following nonlinear equation can be solved to obtain the entries of D_f.

$$\begin{aligned} \lambda_1 &= g_{11}^{(2)} X^{(2)} + 2g_{12}^{(2)} XZ + g_{22}^{(2)} Z^2 \\ 0 &= g_{11}^{(2)} XY + 2g_{12}^{(2)} (XW + YZ) + g_{22}^{(2)} ZW \\ \lambda_2 &= g_{11}^{(2)} Y^2 + 2g_{12}^{(2)} YW + g_{22}^{(2)} W^2 \\ 0 &= XY + ZW \end{aligned}$$

Another way to solve equation (11) is to use the Singular Value Decomposition (SVD) of a matrix. The SVD provides a decomposition of a matrix M as a product $M = UAV$ where U and V are rotation matrices and A is diagonal. We apply this decomposition to the symmetric matrices $G_1 = V_1' A_1 V_1$ and $G_2 = V_2' A_2 V_2$ and the Jacobian $D_f = U_f A_f V_f$ and get

$$V_2' A_2 V_2 = V_f' A_f U_f' V_1' A_1 V_1 U_f A_f V_f \tag{13}$$

We see that we find a solution by first setting $V_2 = V_f, U_f = V_1'$. Using the fact that these matrices are orthogonal we find $A_2 = A_f A_1 A_f = A_1 A_f^2$ and therefore $A_f = \sqrt{A_2 A_1^{-1}}$.

4.2 Estimation of Affine Shifts in the Local Isometries

Now we build the global isometry by stitching local affine isometries. These local isometries are defined in the neighborhoods of every corresponding pair of points in C_w and C_n. Therefore they can be described as linear maps D_i between tangent spaces at $x_i \in C_w$ and $y_i \in C_n$ for $i = 1, ..., N$. So the D_i is defined with x and y as the origins in $T_x C_w$ and $T_y C_n$. However, the determination of the correspondence between x and y is not trivial.

Here we use a method we call neighborhood expansion to estimate the correspondence. We start with a known corresponding pair $O_w \in C_w$ and $O_n \in C_n$ and the Riemann metric $G(O_w)$ and $G(O_n)$ are also given. Such a pair can be chosen as e.g. D65. The two points are used as the origins in the local coordinates given above.

We then build a local linear isometry D between two linear spaces $T_{O_w} C_w$ and $T_{O_n} C_n$ in the way presented in the previous section.

Next we choose the points $x_i, i = 1, .., I$ inside the neighborhood N_{O_w} of O_w which are going to be used as the origins of local coordinates of the second generation in C_w. These neighborhoods then expand from the first neighborhood of O_w. Their images in C_n under the local isometry D can be found as

$$y_i = O_n + D(x_i - O_w) \in T_{O_n} C_n$$

which are used as the origins of the local coordinates in C_n corresponding to the neighborhoods of x_i.

Now for the second generation of these origins one builds local isometries $D_i : C_w \supset N_{x_i} \longrightarrow N_{y_i} \subset C_n, i = 1, .., I$ based on the Riemann metric $G_w(x_i)$ and $G_n(y_i)$. This process is repeated to expand the neighborhoods and for every new generation of origins to build $D_{ji} : C_1 \supset N_{x_{ji}} \longrightarrow N_{y_{ji}} \subset C_2, i = 1, .., N_j$ based on the Riemann metric $G_1(x_{ji})$ and $G_2(y_{ji})$. These local isometries will then eventually define a global isometry from C_w to C_n.

5 Color Discrimination Threshold Data

We used pair comparison experiments to determine the color discrimination thresholds. Measurement methods in psychophysical experiments vary from totally random ordering to adjustments by the observers themselves. While the totally random measurement is precise but time consuming, one wishes to avoid bias due to anticipation and adaptation or learning effects of observers. Therefore, we have chosen a randomized adjustment method as follows.

The observers include a D-type color weak observer and a color-normal observer. The illumination is Panasonic Hf premiere fluorescent light and a SyncMaster XL24 by Samsung is used for display. The Background is neutral grey of N 5.5. The observing distance is 80cm, the two frames on the display are 14×14 cm squares, with the left one as the test color and the right one is compared with the test color.

A session of color-matching starts with the display of a comparison color on the right frame. The observer is asked to use either the mouse wheel or a key touch to adjust the comparison color to the test color as close as possible. An accepted match finishes the session. The comparison color of the test color is randomly chosen on straight lines in 14 directions centered at the test color, with a random distance. The speed of the comparison color changes, responding to the movement of the mouse wheel or the number of key touches are also random. After 4 sessions, neutral gray is shown on the whole display for 7 seconds.

The sampling points in the CIELUV space are arranged on five planes of $L = 30, 40, 50, 60, 70$. On each plane, a uniform grid of sampling points is selected using the following number of gridpoints within the gamut of the lightness : 9 points in $L = 30$, 13 points in $L = 40$, 19 points in $L = 50$, 20 points in $L = 60$, 16 points in $L = 70$, therefore 77 points in the whole space.

The ellipsoids are then estimated from the observation data using the methods in [2][7][8].

Example threshold ellipsoids measured in 3D and $L = 60$ are shown in Fig. 3 to Fig. 6.

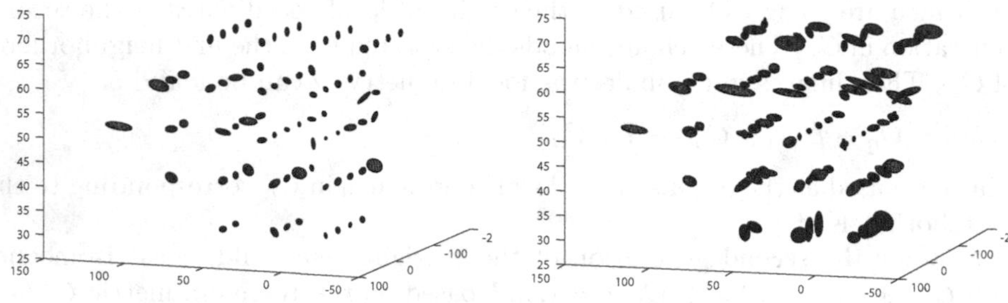

Fig. 3. Ellipsoids of color normal observer

Fig. 4. Ellipsoids of color weak observer

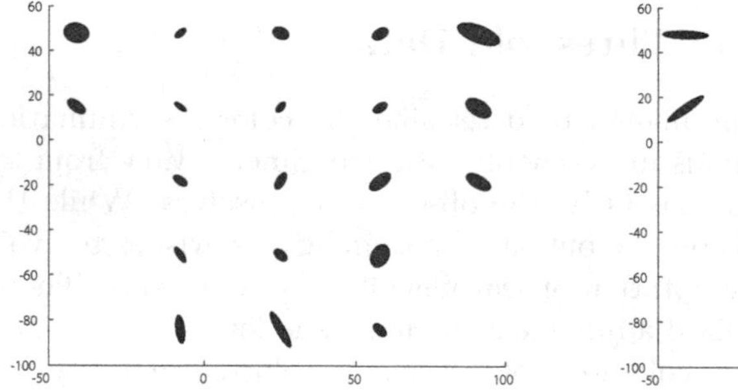

Fig. 5. Color normal discrimination threshold ellipses in L=60

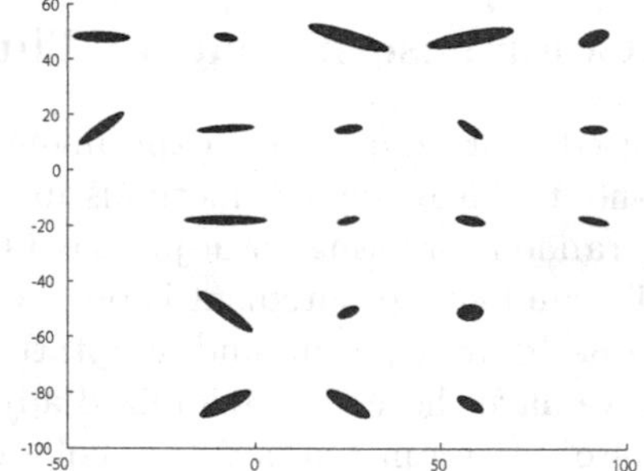

Fig. 6. Color weak discrimination threshold ellipses in L=60

6 Experiments and Evaluation

Compensation and color-weak simulation of an image using the proposed algorithms applied to the new data are shown in Fig.7,8,9.

Fig. 7. "Mountain": Original

Fig. 8. "Mountain": Color-weak simulation

Fig. 9. "Mountain": Compensation

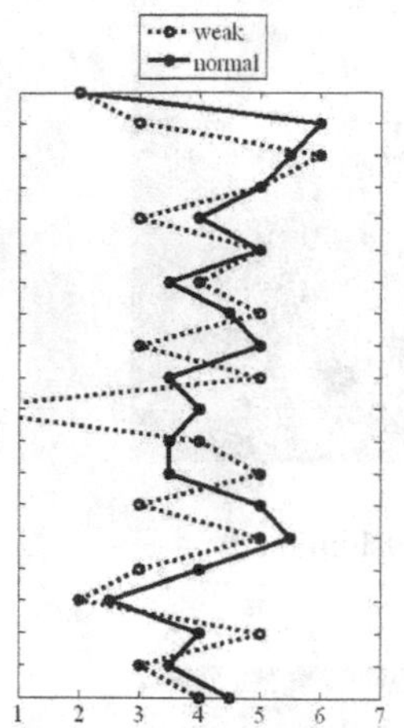

Fig. 10. Color-normal and color-weak view the original "Mountain"

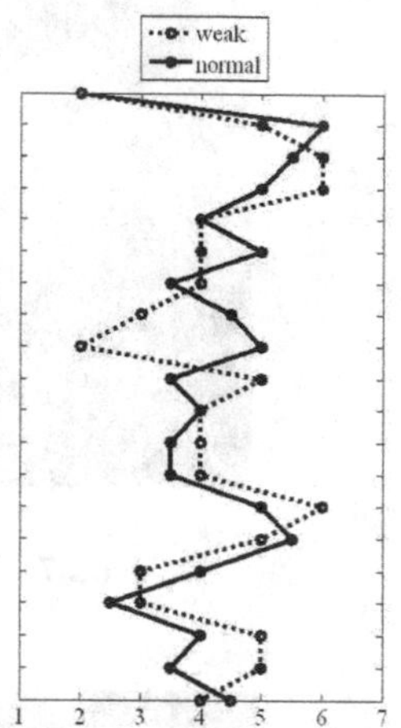

Fig. 11. Color-normal views the original, color-weak views the compensation of "Mountain"

Table 1. "Moutain": SD score

	Correlation	Distance
Before compensation	-0.721866	0.558297
After compensation	0.238643	0.380957

The performance of the color-weak compensation is difficult to evaluate directly. Below we apply the Semantic Differential (SD) method [9] to evaluate the results of the proposed method.

We choose 20 adjective pairs from the 76 pairs used in [9]. Objectives are marked for every question in a seven score scale.

7 Summary and Conclusions

We used approaches from the theory of Riemannian manifolds to develop a new method to construct mappings between color spaces of color weak and color normal observers. We showed how the linear approximation of the local mapping between the color spaces can be found by solving non-linear equations or Singular Value Decomposition. We also presented a method that allows us to stitch together these local solutions. Furthermore we described a new, extended database containing the color discrimination data of color normal and color weak observers. We illustrated the results obtained with the new method and evaluated it with the help of SD-evaluation.

References

1. Chao, J., Osugi, I., Suzuki, M.: On definitions and construction of uniform color space. In: Proceedings of The Second European Conference on Colour in Graphics, Imaging and Vision (CGIV 2004), pp. 55–60 (2004)
2. Mochizuki, R., Nakamura, T., Chao, J., Lenz, R.: Color-weak correction by discrimination threshold matching. In: Proceedings of CGIV 2008, 4th European Conference on Color in Graphics, Imaging, and Vision, pp. 208–213 (2008)
3. Chao, J., Lenz, R., Matsumoto, D., Nakamura, T.: Riemann geometry for color characterization and mapping. In: Proceedings of CGIV 2008, Proceedings of 4th European Conference on Color in Graphics, Imaging, and Vision, pp. 277–282 (2008)
4. Mochizuki, R., Oshima, S., Lenz, R., Chao, J.: Exact compensation of color-weakness with discrimination threshold matching. In: Stephanidis, C. (ed.) Universal Access in HCI, Part IV, HCII 2011. LNCS, vol. 6768, pp. 155–164. Springer, Heidelberg (2011)
5. Oshima, S., Mochizuki, R., Lenz, R., Chao, J.: Color-Weakness Compensation using Riemann Normal Coordinates. In: Proc. of ISM 2012, IEEE Int. Symp. on Multimedia, pp. 175–178 (2012)
6. Ohshima, S., Mochizuki, R., Chao, J., Lenz, R.: Color Reproduction Using Riemann Normal Coordinates. In: Trémeau, A., Schettini, R., Tominaga, S. (eds.) CCIW 2009. LNCS, vol. 5646, pp. 140–149. Springer, Heidelberg (2009)
7. Lenz, R., Mochizuki, R., Chao, J.: Iwasawa Decomposition and Computational Riemannian Geometry. In: Proceedings of ICPR 2010, 2010 International Conference on Pattern Recognition, pp. 4472–4475 (2010)
8. Lenz, R., Oshima, S., Mochizuki, R., Chao, J.: An Invariant Metric on the Manifold of Second Order Moments. In: Proceedings ICCV2009, IEEE International Conference on Computer Vision, IEEE Color and Reflectance in Imaging and Computer Vision Workshop 2009 - CRICV, pp. 1923–1930 (2009)
9. Osgood, C.E.: The Measurement of Meaning (1957)

Effect of the Color Tablet Computer's Polarity and Character Size on Legibility

Hsuan Lin[1,*], Wei Lin[2], Wang-Chin Tsai[3], Yune-Yu Cheng[4], and Fong-Gong Wu[4]

[1] Department of Product Design, Tainan University of Technology, Tainan, Taiwan
te0038@mail.tut.edu.tw

[2] Department of Interior Design, Hwa Hsia Institute of Technology, Taipei, Taiwan
D9313001@mail.ntust.edu.tw

[3] Department of Product and Meida Design, Fo Guang University,Yilan, Taiwan
forwangwang@gmail.com

[4] Department of Industrial Design, National Cheng Kung University, Tainan, Taiwan
{c280643,fonggong}@mail.ncku.edu.tw

Abstract. This study aimed to explore how different polarities and character sizes on tablet e-readers affect users' legibility and visual fatigue. Following the experimental method, 30 participants were required to search for the target words in pseudo-texts; meanwhile, the experimental data were connected to an exclusive database through the Internet. Thus, the participants' search times, accuracy rates, and visual fatigue levels could be analyzed. As indicated by the analytic result, all the four kinds of character size affected search time. Specifically, the 8-pt target words on a 10.1-inch screen had the slowest search speed. As character size increased to 12 pt, search speed became significantly faster. Besides, the interaction between polarity and character size had a significant effect on the accuracy rate of searched target words. This study showed that as a character size increased, polarity produced a higher accuracy rate, and that negative polarity had a more significant effect than positive polarity. Under positive polarity, 8 pt had the lowest accuracy rate, and 10 pt had the next lowest accuracy rate. However, after the character size was increased to 12 pt or above, the accuracy rate was not promoted. Moreover, a larger character size produced a higher accuracy rate. Therefore, 12 pt and 14 pt got the best performance. As for visual fatigue, a small character size was the main factor. The findings of this study can be used in the design of tablet e-readers.

Keywords: tablet computer, legibility, visual fatigue, character size.

1 Introduction

Mobile devices have been around in our daily lives. While on the move, users depend on portable mobile devices to access real-time information and read texts conveniently. By using mobile devices, users can not only surf the Internet but also read real-time messages, e-mail, and data files. Different text contents and character sizes presented on the screens may affect a user's working efficiency and satisfaction level

* Corresponding author.

C. Stephanidis and M. Antona (Eds.): UAHCI/HCII 2014, Part II, LNCS 8514, pp. 132–143, 2014.

[1]. Poorly-designed display layouts easily cause fatigue to the user and reduce his/her efficiency in reading texts and browsing pages [2]. On the contrary, well-designed reading devices contribute to the legibility of texts.

The polarity and character size of any tablet computer have a great influence on a user's search efficiency. With the color LCD employed as the display medium, this study investigated how different polarities and character sizes affected the search efficiency and visual fatigue of those users who read Chinese texts. As the experimental tool, the tablet computer was connected to an online database. Afterwards, the relevant trials were conducted and analyzed; also, the levels of subjective visual fatigue were measured. This study was intended to probe into the current status and limitations of the tablet computer used for reading Chinese texts. In addition, further analyses and discussions herein are expected to be referred to when tablet computers are designed and developed in the future.

There are two types of polar display on the screen: positive polarity and negative polarity. Positive polarity refers to black characters on white background while negative polarity refers to white characters on black background [3]. Wang and Chen suggested that polarity had no significant effect on visual performance or subjective preference [4]. Cushman discovered that words displayed under positive polarity tended to be read faster, but comprehension shower no difference at all [5]. Saito et al. and Nishiyama also argued that positive polarity was better than negative polarity [6, 7]. Contrarily, Mills and Weldon maintained that negative polarity is more suitable for computer screens, for users feel less sensitive to the flashing of the screen with negative polarity display than with positive polarity display [8]. Chan and Lee investigated reading on a 15-inch CRT computer screen, employing different fonts and character sizes [3]. They discovered that the 14-pt Ming-style font, double line height and positive polarity showed a higher reading rate and legibility than the 10-pt Li-style font, single line height and negative polarity. Shen et al. explored two different display media i.e., electronic paper made of cholesteric liquid crystal (Ch-LC) and electrophoretic electronic ink (E-ink), discovering that positive polarity produced a higher accuracy rate than negative polarity [9]. There are a lot of factors that influence positive polarity and negative polarity, and it is still not determined which kind of polarity is superior. Unlike previous e-readers which focused on black-and-white displays, this study employed a tablet computer as the experimental tool.

Various fonts and character sizes on the display significantly affect a user's reading performance. Boyarski et al. investigated textual readability on the desktop computer [10]. The researchers discovered that character size had a significant effect on the recognition rate and that different fonts affected reading performance. As for the effect of different character sizes on reading performance, Bernard et al. studied children aged from 9 to 11, comparing 12-pt with 14-pt characters [11]. It was determined that the 14-pt sans serif font was more appealing, readable, and recognizable. I. Darroch et al. made a similar study, focusing on mobile devices with a pocket-sized screen [1]. It was learned that the character sizes from 8 pt to 12 pt were more suitable for the user.

Huang et al. studied Chinese characters, employing a PDA as the experimental tool [12]. The researchers discovered that the 1.0-mm character whose resolution was below 250 dpi was the most illigible. By contrast, the 3.0-mm character showed the highest reading speed. Chai et al. made another study to compare the recognition rates of different Chinese typefaces [13]. According to the above study, the Ming typeface performed better than Kai typeface and that the standard typeface performed better than the Li typeface. Huang et al. also compared the performances of different character sizes on PDA screens with different resolutions; besides, the researchers recommended the character size compatible with small screens [12]. However, some other studies suggested that a larger character size did not always produce a better reading performance [3, 8] . In some cases, a smaller character size performed better than a larger one in terms of reading speed. To exolre the relationships between polarity and character size, this study experimented with the character sizes from 8 pt to 14 pt presented under different polarities, with the legibility compared in various conditions. And the findings can be refered to by those engaged in designing Chinese-reading interfaces.

2 Methods

2.1 Experimental Design

With a tablet e-reader employed as the experimental tool, this study aimed to explore the effect of polarity and character size on visual performance. Following the experimental method, the 30 participants were required to locate the target words in pseudo-texts. Thus, the effects of the two variables on the search time, accuracy rate, and subjective fatigue level were determined. Formerly, the relevant experiments primarily counted the correct words found by the participants [9, 14-16]. Unlike those previous studies, this study established an online database to increase experimental accuracy. By utilizing WiFi technology embedded in the tablet computer, the participant was connected to the Internet, logged onto the exclusive website, and then started the trial. Recorded in the website automatically, the experimental results were analyzed as objective information.

With a tablet computer serving as the experimental tool, this study was intended to evaluate how legibility and visual fatigue are affected by two independent variables, i.e., polarity and character size. The new Ming typeface was used in Chinese pseudo-texts, which were presented under two different kinds of polarity, namely, positive polarity and negative polarity. Meanwhile, there were four different character sizes used: 8 pt, 10 pt, 12 pt, and 14 pt. Consequently, the independent variables consisted of two polarities and four character sizes. In other words, there were 8 (2×4) trials in total, with 30 participants undertaking the within-subjects trials. Also, in compliance with the principle of counterbalance, the order in which each participant operated the experimental interface varied with his/her experimental sequence. Through built-in WiFi technology in the tablet computer, the participant was connected to the exclusive website for legibility and visual fatigue. After entering his/her personal information in the website, the participant started to perform the 8 trials in the predetermined sequence. As soon as each of the trials was completed, its experimental results were automatically stored in the system.

During each trial, the participant had to read the meaningless pseudo-text appearing on the tablet computer. Once a target word in the pseudo-text was found, the participant had to be touch it with his/her finger, and then it turned red in color, which meant a successful search. When the participant misjudged the target word and touched it by mistake, the false one also turned red and was recorded in the system. But it was excluded from the evaluation of the accuracy rate.

2.2 Participants

30 participants (15 males and 15 females) were involved in the trials. They were all ninth-graders aged from 18 to 23 (M = 20.30, SD = 1.39). None of them was color-blind or suffered from other eye diseases. Their natural or corrected eyesight was above 0.8. The experimental sequence of each participant was randomly arranged through permutation and combination. Additionally, each participant was rewarded with NT$200 after all the trials came to an end.

2.3 Measurements of Legibility

Reading Speed and Accuracy. In previous studies, reading speed and accuracy rate were regarded as the chief indicators of reading performance. With pseudo-texts searched, how fast the target words were found by the participant was effectively measured [9, 14-16]. Besides, the measurement of accuracy revealed whether the participant recognized the text typeface clearly. In that way, the effect of character size on reading accuracy was determined [14]. The pseudo-texts used in this study are explained below.

1. The pseudo texts consisted of randomly selected traditional Chinese characters, all of which were selected from the first 198 frequently-used characters in the standard Chinese typeface list [13]. Each pseudo-text appeared to be a normal Chinese passage, but it was meaningless to read. This study was meant to evaluate word recognition in various experimental situations rather than passage comprehension. Any meaningful text would have interfered with the evaluation of word recognition [17].
2. Each pseudo-text contained 2500 traditional Chinese characters. Moreover, each of the target words was arranged in such a way that it appeared at an interval of 100 to 150 characters. For instance, if 六 (six in Chinese) was chosen as a target word, it appeared randomly in the pseudo-text, but never at the beginning or end. There were 25 target words in each pseudo-text. To eliminate any anticipatory behavior, the participant was not told the total number of the target words before a trial.
3. Throughout the trials, every participant was required to locate the target words as fast as possible. Furthermore, the search time and the number of the correct words were automatically recorded in the computer system. To prevent fatigue from disturbing the experimental operations, the participant had to rest for 5 minutes after each trial.

4. The tablet computer was employed as the experimental tool. By means of its built-in WiFi capability, the participant was connected to the website, with the personal information entered in the website. Each participant is required to complete the trials in the predetermined sequence, and the results are automatically recorded in the system. The pseudo-texts read by each participant are selected randomly, and the order in which they are read by the 30 participants differs from one to another. Since all the experimental procedures are recorded and executed on the website, the errors arising from artificial interpretation are reduced. In this way, the experimental results are more objective and accurate.

Measurements of Visual Fatigue. After the legibility test is conducted by the participant, his/her visual fatigue is measured mentally. Generally, the change in the scores from the subjective questionnaire are taken as the criteria of visual fatigue [9, 14-17]. As for measuring the subjective fatigue, the participant is required to answer a subjective measurement questionnaire [18]. There are six questions in the questionnaire as set forth below: 1) I have difficulties in seeing; 2) I have a strange feeling around the eyes; 3) My eyes feel tired; 4) I feel numb; 5) I have a headache; 6) I feel dizzy looking at the screen. Each question is given a score ranging from 1 to 10. While 1 stands for "not at all", 10 stands for "very much". Based on the responses to the 6 questions, the participant's fatigue level after the legibility test is identified.

2.4 Apparatus and Workplace Condition

As is explained below, the experimental tool is composed of software and hardware. (1) Software: Microsoft ASP.NET 2.0 is used to establish the legibility and visual fatigue website. After logging in, the participant can start to conduct the trials, with the experimental results automatically recorded on the website. (2) Hardware: the tablet PC, acer ICONIA W510, is employed. Its dimensions are 167.5 (W) x 258.5 (L) x 8.8 (H) mm, its screen size is 10.1", and its resolution is 1366 × 768 px.

The screen is put on a table which is 73 cm in height, with its center being 18 cm away from the table surface. The screen center is 36 cm away from the edge of the table. The distance between the participant's eyes and the screen is 50 cm. Besides, the participant's chin is upheld by a chin support. The screen inclines at an angle of 105 degrees [9, 14-16, 19]. The above parameters remain unchanged throughout the experiment. As for the chair, it can be adjusted to match the individual requirement for comfort. The ambient luminance is 700 lux and the light source is DL65[9].

2.5 Data Collection and Analysis

The information collected during this research includes the participant's personal information, the time spent in locating the target words, accuracy, and the subjective visual fatigue questionnaire. The ways these kinds of information are processed are explained below.

1. Search time and accuracy: immediately after each trial, the participant's search time and accuracy rate will be automatically recorded in the system. The search

time refers to the total time spent by the participant in finding the 25 target words during the legibility test. Accuracy means the total number of the correct target words divided by the total number of clicks (touches).

2. Subjective visual fatigue questionnaire: the scores for the six questions on the subjective questionnaire are added up to get the measurement of subjective visual fatigue. The original data is processed with Microsoft Excel and then analyzed with the statistical software SPSS to get the variable values. The adopted significant level is $\alpha < 0.05$.

3 Result

3.1 Search Time

With the tablet computer adopted as the experimental tool, this research is aimed to compare the effects of polarity and character size on the search time, accuracy, and subjective satisfaction.

As is shown in Table 1, polarity has no significant effect on search time. By contrast, character size has a significant effect on search time ($F_{(3, 87)} = 4.508$, $p< 0.01$). The mean search time of 8 pt is 288.367s, that of 10 pt is 280.317s, that of 12 pt is 251.000s, and that of 14 pt is 282.200s. After the LSD multiple range test is used to analyze the result, it is discovered that 12 pt takes a shorter time than 10 pt, 14 pt, and 8 pt (Table 2.).

3.2 Accuracy

As shown by the ANOVA of accuracy rate in Table 3., polarity has a significant effect on accuracy rate ($F_{(1, 29)}$ =4.213, p <0.05). The accuracy rate resulting from positive polarity is 91.8%, which is significantly higher than that of negative polarity, or 88.5%. Moreover, character size has a significant effect on accuracy rate of searched target words ($F_{(3,87)}$ = 10.921, p< 0.001). Through the LSD multiple range test (Table 4.), it is discovered that the mean accuracy rate of positive polarity and negative polarity is 91.8% and88.5% respectively. In other words, the accuracy rate resulting from positive polarity is higher than that resulting from negative polarity. As shown in Table 3., character size exerts a significant effect on the accuracy rate of the searched target words ($F_{(3,87)}$ = 0.069, p< 0.001), while screen size makes no significant difference. Through the LSD multiple range test (Table 4.), it is discovered that the accuracy rate of 8 pt is 85.5% , that of 10 pt is 89.9%, that of 12 pt is 92.2%, and that of 14 pt is 93.1%. That is to say, 12 pt and 14 pt show the highest accuracy, 10 pt ranks third, and 8 pt has the poorest accuracy.

As is shown in Fig. 1., the interaction between polarity and character size has a significant effect on the accuracy rate of searched target words ($F_{(3, 87)}$ = 4.027, p< 0.01). As polarity increases in this study, all the four character sizes showed a higher accuracy rate of searched target words, especially the character size presented in negative polarity. Under negative polarity, 8 pt has the lowest accuracy. However, after the character is enlarged, a higher accuracy rate is produced.

Table 1. ANOVA result of search time

Source	*df*	SS	MS	*F*
Within subjects	29	908532.671	31328.713	
Polarity (P)	1	6773.437	6773.437	.658
P × Subject within group	29	298303.438	10286.325	
Character size (C)	3	50033.279	16677.760	4.508**
C × Subject within group	87	321877.346	3699.740	
P × C	3	1555.246	518.415	.167
Subject within group	87	270468.379	3108.832	

Significant at * ≦0.05 ; **≦0.01; ***≦0.001 level.

Table 2. Mean values of search time under each level of the independent variables and LSD's multiple range tests on significant factors

Source	n	Search time (s)	Std. Error	LSD
Polarity				
Positive (P)	30	270.158	14.637	
Negative (N)	30	280.783	11.513	
Character size				
8 pt	30	288.367	12.119	8, 10, 14 > 12
10 pt	30	280.317	11.369	
12 pt	30	251.000	11.907	
14 pt	30	282.200	17.006	

Table 3. ANOVA result of accuracy

Source	*df*	SS	MS	*F*
Within subjects	29	2.258	.078	
Polarity (P)	1	.067	.067	4.213*
P × Subject within group	29	.459	.016	
Character size (C)	3	.208	.069	10.921***
C × Subject within group	87	.553	.006	
P × C	3	.062	.021	4.027**
Subject within group	87	.447	.005	

Significant at * ≦0.05 ; **≦0.01; ***≦0.001 level.

Table 4. Mean values of accuracy under each level of the independent variables and LSD's multiple range tests on significant factors

Source	n	accuracy (%)	Std. Error	LSD
Polarity				P>N
Positive (P)	30	91.8	.021	
Negative (N)	30	88.5	.019	
Character size				
8 pt	30	85.5	.027	14, 12>10>8
10 pt	30	89.9	.017	
12 pt	30	92.2	.017	
14 pt	30	93.1	.017	

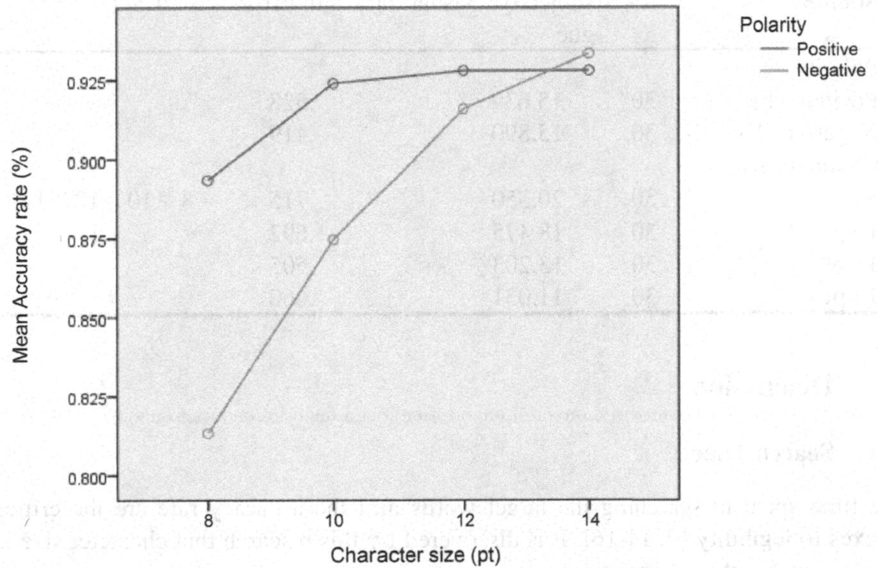

Fig. 1. Polarity × Character size interaction for accuracy rate

3.3 Subjective Visual Fatigue

As shown by ANOVA of subjective visual fatigue in Table 5., polarity has no significant effect on subjective visual fatigue. On the other hand, character size has a significant effect on subjective visual fatigue ($F_{(3,87)} = 56.891$, $p< 0.001$). It is discovered that a smaller character size causes more subjective visual fatigue. Through the LSD multiple range test (Table 6.), it is discovered that the mean subjective visual fatigue score of 8 pt is 20.350 points, that of 10 pt is 18.475 points, that of 12 pt is 13.203 points, and that of 14 pt is 11.031 points. The above results indicate that, in terms of subjective visual fatigue, 8 pt gets the highest level, 10 pt ranks second, 12 pt ranks third, and 14 pt gets the lowest level.

Table 5. ANOVA result of subjective visual fatigue

Source	*df*	SS	MS	*F*
Within subjects	29	1170.334	40.356	
Polarity (P)	1	3.792	3.792	.269
P × Subject within group	29	408.385	14.082	
Character size (C)	3	3440.776	1146.925	56.891***
C × Subject within group	87	1753.936	20.160	
P × C	3	50.247	16.749	1.284
Subject within group	87	1134.646	13.042	

Table 6. Mean values of subjective visual fatigue under each level of the independent variables and LSD's multiple range tests on significant factors

Source	n	subjective visual fatigue	Std. Error	LSD
Polarity				
Positive (P)	30	15.639	.528	
Negative (N)	30	15.890	.419	
Character size				
8 pt	30	20.350	.715	8>10>12>14
10 pt	30	18.475	.692	
12 pt	30	13.203	.505	
14 pt	30	11.031	.660	

4 Discussion

4.1 Search Time

The time spent in searching the target words and the accuracy rate are the critical indexes to legibility [9, 14-16]. It is discovered by this research that character size all have a significant on search time.

Character size also has an effect on the user's searching speed. The smallest character size, namely, 8 pt, takes the longest search time. When the character size is increased from 8 pt and 10 pt to 12 pt, its searching speed is improved. However, when the character size reaches 14 pt, it takes a longer time than 12 pt but a shorter time than 10 pt. The result agrees with the conclusion reached by other researchers, who compared the Chinese legibility on the 15" screen [3]. Besides, the conclusion of this research that the smaller character size causes slower reading speed agrees with the findings of other researchers [11, 20]. Generally speaking, the larger character size accelerates reading speed. Moreover, when it reaches the critical point, the maximum reading speed is achieved. Nevertheless, if the critical value is exceeded, reading speed will decline [16, 21]. However, there is some limit on searching speed, which does not increase endlessly as the screen size and the number of words in a line increase. A study was made to compare the reading performance shown by 25 cpl (characters per line), 55 cpl, and 100 cpl [22]. It was discovered that 55 cpl performed best, 100 cpl ranked second, and 25 cpl performed worst.The Ch-LC display, E-ink display and conventional paper were used by other researchers to compare the effect of different character sizes on the search time spent in reading English texts [14]. It was discovered that the 3.3-mm font got the highest reading speed. But if the font exceeded 3.3 mm, the reading speed could not be enhanced any more. On the other hand, too small a font also caused reading difficulty, especially the 1.4-mm font.

4.2 Accuracy

Polarity and character sizes are the major factors influencing the accuracy rate of searched articles. This study shows that, in terms of searching with e-readers, the accuracy rate of positive polarity is clearly higher than that of negative polarity. Although the LCD colour display employed in this study is different from a CRT display or VDT electronic paper, positive polarity is significantly superior to negative polarity in terms of accuracy rate. The findings of this study are similar to those obtained by Bauer & Cavonius [23] and Shen et al. [9]. Bauer & Cavonius investigated the effects of polarity on reading performance, discovering that the accuracy rate of positive polarity was clearly higher than that of negative polarity. Shen et al. analyzed how different dispalys affected visual perfromance and fatigue by comaring liquid crystal displays (Ch-LC), electrophoretic electronic ink display (E-Ink), and paper. The above researchers discovered that the accuracy rate of negative polarity was significantly lower than that of positive polarity.

Besides, as a character size becomes bigger, the accuracy rate of Chinese text-reading is higher. However, it is discovered by this study that the character size above 12 pt does not enhance accuracy anymore. The above conclusion is similar to the findings of Lee et al. (2008) [14], who discovered that too small a character size led to reading difficulty and the declining accuracy of text recognition. On the contrary, as the character size became larger, accuracy was improved. Yet, when the character size exceeded a particular value, the accuracy rate of reading did not improve anymore.

The interaction between polarity and character size has a significant effect on the accuracy rate of searched target words. As shown by this study, as a character size increases, polarity produces a higher accuracy rate, and negative polarity has a more significant effect than positive polarity. Under positive polarity, 8 pt has the lowest accuracy, and 10 pt has the next lowest accuracy. However, after the character size is increased to 12 pt or above, the accuracy rate is not promoted. As a character size increases, negative polarity produces a significantly higher accuracy rate. Under negative polarity, 8 pt has the lowest accuracy. After the character size is increased from10 or12 pt to 14 pt, negative polarity shows a significantly higher accuracy rate of searched target words. As for 8 pt and 10 pt, positive polarity has a significantly higher accuracy rate than negative polarity. However, when the character size is increased to 12 or 14 pt, positive polarity and negative polarity show no significant difference in accuracy rate.

4.3 Subjective Visual Fatigue

As for the measurements of subjective visual fatigue, it is discovered by this research that character size is largely responsible for visual fatigue. It is discovered that, when searching the 8-pt words, the participant is most likely to feel tired. Besides, the 10-pt words rank second in terms of visual fatigue, 12-pt ranks third, while the 14-pt words are least likely to cause visual fatigue. Another study was made to compare different sizes of English typefaces which were read on the 17" screen [24]. It was discovered that the 12-pt font combined with any typeface got the highest level of readability. Moreover, the 10-pt font caused more difficulty in reading than the 12-pt font. The main reason was that the larger character size generated better readability. Still another study was made to compare the comprehension score for the 10-pt and 14-pt Chinese characters which were read on the 15" screen [3]. It was discovered that the 14-pt font performed better than the 10-pt font in terms of reading comfort, reading ease, reading fatigue and overall performance. Furthermore, the result was statistically significant.

References

1. Darroch, I., Goodman, J., Brewster, S., Gray, P.: The effect of age and font size on reading text on handheld computers. In: Costabile, M.F., Paternó, F. (eds.) INTERACT 2005. LNCS, vol. 3585, pp. 253–266. Springer, Heidelberg (2005)
2. Streveler, D.J., Wasserman, A.I.: Quantitative measures of the spatial properties of screen designs. pp. 81–89 (1984)
3. Chan, A., Lee, P.: Effect of display factors on Chinese reading times, comprehension scores and preferences. Behaviour & Information Technology 24(2), 81–91 (2005)
4. Wang, A.H., Chen, M.T.: Effects of polarity and luminance contrast on visual performance and VDT display quality. International Journal of Industrial Ergonomics 25(4), 415–421 (2000)
5. Cushman, W.H.: Reading from microfiche, a VDT, and the printed page: subjective fatigue and performance. Human Factors: The Journal of the Human Factors and Ergonomics Society 28(1), 63–73 (1986)
6. Saito, S., Taptagaporn, S., Salvendy, G.: Visual comfort in using different VDT screens. International Journal of Human-Computer Interaction 5(4), 313–323 (1993)
7. Nishiyama, K.: Ergonomic aspects of the health and safety of VDT work in Japan: A review. Ergonomics 33(6), 659–685 (1990)
8. Mills, C.B., Weldon, L.J.: Reading text from computer screens. ACM Computing Surveys (CSUR) 19(4), 329–357 (1987)
9. Shen, I., Shieh, K.K., Chao, C.Y.: Lighting, font style, and polarity on visual performance and visual fatigue with electronic paper displays. Displays 30(2), 53–58 (2009)
10. Boyarski, D., Neuwirth, C., Forlizzi, J.: A study of fonts designed for screen display. pp. 87-94 (1998)
11. Bernard, M.L., Chaparro, B.S., Mills, M.M.: Examining children's reading performance and preference for different computer-displayed text. Behaviour & Information Technology 21(2), 87–96 (2002)

12. Huang, D.L., Patrick Rau, P.L., Liu, Y.: Effects of font size, display resolution and task type on reading Chinese fonts from mobile devices. International Journal of Industrial Ergonomics 39(1), 81–89 (2009)
13. Cai, D., Chi, C.F., You, M.: The legibility threshold of Chinese characters in three-type styles. International Journal of Industrial Ergonomics 27(1), 9–17 (2001)
14. Lee, D.S., Shieh, K.K., Jeng, S.C.: Effect of character size and lighting on legibility of electronic papers. Displays 29(1), 10–17 (2008)
15. Lin, Y.T., Lin, P.H., Hwang, S.L.: Investigation of legibility and visual fatigue for simulated flexible electronic paper under various surface treatments and ambient illumination conditions. Applied Ergonomics 40(5), 922–928 (2009)
16. Lin, H., Wu, F.G., Cheng, Y.Y.: Legibility and visual fatigue affected by text direction, screen size and character size on color LCD e-reader. Displays (2012)
17. Boschman, M.C., Roufs, J.A.: Text quality metrics for visual display units:: II. An experimental survey. Displays 18(1), 45–64 (1997)
18. Heuer, H., Hollendiek, G., Kröger, H.: Die Ruhelage der Augen und ihr Einfluß auf Beobachtungsabstand und visuelle Ermüdung bei Bildschirmarbeit. Zeitschrift für Experimentelle und Angewandte Psychologie 36(4), 538–566 (1989)
19. Turville, K.L., Psihogios, J.P., Ulmer, T.R.: The effects of video display terminal height on the operator: a comparison of the 15 and 40 recommendations. Applied Ergonomics 29(4), 239–246 (1998)
20. Tullis, T.S., Boynton, J.L., Hersh, H.: Readability of fonts in the windows environment. pp. 127-128 (1995)
21. Legge, G.E., Pelli, D.G., Rubin, G.S.: Psychophysics of reading—I. Normal vision. Vision Research 25(2), 239–252 (1985)
22. Dyson, M.C., Haselgrove, M.: The influence of reading speed and line length on the effectiveness of reading from screen. International Journal of Human-Computer Studies 54(4), 585–612 (2001)
23. Bauer, D., Cavonius, C.: Improving the legibility of visual display units through contrast reversal. Ergonomic aspects of visual display terminals, pp. 137–142. Taylor and Francis, London (1980)
24. Bernard, M.L., Chaparro, B.S., Mills, M.M.: Comparing the effects of text size and format on the readibility of computer-displayed Times New Roman and Arial text. International Journal of Human-Computer Studies 59(6), 823–835 (2003)

A Proposal for an Automated Method to Produce Embossed Graphics for Blind Persons

Kazunori Minatani

National Center for University Entrance Examinations
Komaba 2-19-23, Meguro-ku, Tokyo, 153-8501 Japan
minatani@rd.dnc.ac.jp

Abstract. The aim of this paper is to provide examples illustrating the conditions for effectively functionalizing the "method of converting graphics into a form that can be perceived using senses other than sight" in the field of HCI. Specifically, it is shown that advantages that method are fully achieved with the implementation of a prototype embossed graphics output function for the statistical analysis software R. In attempting to generate automated tactile graphics from the output of any kind of graphics software, the strategy described below will be useful: a. To investigate whether the intermediate graphics format used in the relevant software consists of primitive vector format drawing commands and character printing commands that handle characters as codes, and b. If the latter conditions are fulfilled, to perform conversion to tactile graphics at the stage of graphics data expressed as that intermediate format.

Keywords: blind person, embossed graphics, vector format.

1 The State of the Art

Among sighted persons, communicative expressions are often performed using graphical representations as well as by using words. There are significant constraints on making good use of such graphical representations for blind persons. For expressions using words, there are established methods for expressing the words themselves as a braille transcription or by having them read out by voice. Effective methods of communication are being explored on the basis of such methods. On the other hand, standard methods have not been established for graphical representations, and there are limitations on the ability to make use of such representations. In what follows, methods of presenting graphical representations for blind persons that have a particularly notable relationship to Human-Computer Interaction (HCI) are described, and their advantages and disadvantages are summarized.

1.1 The Method of Translating Graphics to Explanatory Sentences

As a substitute for graphics, sentence-based explanations are generated that interpret the content depicted by the graphics. This method has been widely used both for

C. Stephanidis and M. Antona (Eds.): UAHCI/HCII 2014, Part II, LNCS 8514, pp. 144–153, 2014.

braille transcriptions and for reading out by voice. Particularly for reading books [1], this method is almost only one available. A typical example within the HCI context is to provide explanatory sentences to a graphics object using the ALT attribute in the HTML specification [2]. To provide an audio description to a movie also falls under this method [3].

An advantage of this method is in using the same media to convert graphics to a medium used for presentation by words (braille or voice). In addition, the mental workload imposed on the user (the blind person) is sufficiently low if appropriate explanations are provided.

A first disadvantage is that human intervention is necessary to generate the explanatory sentences. Primarily, this is a limitation that results from only humans being able to judge what is intended by a picture (recent developments in image recognition are mitigating this limitation). A more basic problem is that the function graphics perform in a document cannot be recognized without understanding the context in which they are used. For example, when a picture of a national flag appears in a document, whether the flag's design is being discussed or if it is used as an icon to represent the country that uses the flag can be grasped after understanding the context in which the picture is used.

The disadvantage of human intervention necessarily results in a second disadvantage: the impossibility of providing on-the-fly accessibility to graphical representations. This problem may be not severe in a classical form of assistance for blind persons involving the provision of previously prepared static content as material transcribed in braille or read by voice. However, it is a critical limitation in HCI, which is characterized by the dynamic generation of content. Recent services that use cloud sourcing [4] are showing hints of how to solve this problem, but this does not eliminate this limitation.

A third disadvantage with this method is that it is difficult to convey an object that is effectively represented to the user graphically. Typical examples are details of trends represented by line graphs and complex topography represented by maps.

1.2 The Method of Transcribing Values Represented in Graphics into Characters

For graphics that are intended to show values intuitively (e.g., graphs and charts) there is a method for transcribing the values (numerical values) represented in the graphics into characters using a tabular format.

A first advantage of this method is that it can show values exactly (in some cases it will be more exact than the source graphics). Therefore, it is often used for content with strict requirements (e.g., an examination questionnaire transcribed into braille).

Next, a second advantage is that, if sufficient numerical data values are supplied, this method can be applied to dynamically generating content on-the-fly. This means that the human intervention necessary for the method of translating graphics to explanatory sentences is not required.

A first disadvantage of this method is its lack of the intuitive understandability of the visual presentation of graphics (which is often a reason to use graphical representation). With supplied numerical data, the user must reconstruct the information intended in the graphics, so the mental workload is relatively heavy.

A second disadvantage is that, as in Method 1 (the method of translating graphics to explanatory sentences), it is difficult to convey an object that is effectively represented to the user graphically.

A third disadvantage is that it is not applicable to graphical representations that cannot be shown by the extraction of numerical values (such as pictures and nearly all maps).

1.3 The Method of Converting Graphics into a Form that can be Perceived Using Senses other than Sight

This is a method involving converting a two-dimensional representation shown as graphics into another form (generally tactile graphics) that can be perceived using senses other than sight (practically the sense of touch) with a one-to-one conversion. It is generally used for graphics for which the two-dimensional layout is critically significant (e.g., maps). For output, braille embossers that have a function of embossing graphics and swellpaper are widely used. There have also been attempts to implement and apply presentation using a refreshable two-dimensional braille display. In addition to using the sense of touch, there have been attempts to represent curved lines on graphs using audible tones [5-6].

A first advantage of this method is that it can represent an object that is effectively represented graphically as-is. Although it cannot be assumed that presentation via the sense of touch has the same intuitive perceptibility as that of the sense of sight, there is a high value in representing an object represented as graphics as-is. Compared to the former two methods, being able to reproduce the details of a trend represented by a line graph and complicated topography represented by a map is a critical advantage.

A second advantage is that on-the-fly generation of tactile graphics is possible if machine-understandable data used to render the source graphics is supplied. As an attempt to make good use of this advantage, there have been studies and developments to realize automated tactile map creation systems [7-8] intended to be equal to online map viewing services (e.g., Google Maps [9]).

A third advantage results from the two above advantages: namely that a blind person can take direct part in activities which require the use of graphics. Such activities are innumerable. One typical example is exploratory study using statistical methods: that is, to investigate relationships among data plotted as various forms of charts.

A disadvantage of this method is that it is difficult to realize the same intuitiveness and lucidity for the sense of touch as well as for the sense of sight. For example, to convert a national flag icon used to represent a country into a tactile graphic would only degrade the speed of understanding: the name of the country should be written instead of the tactile graphic. Color representation such as that used in normal graphical representation is not available in tactile graphics. Therefore, this method should be applied for uses in which a one-to-one conversion can derive high utility (e.g. graphs and maps).

A second disadvantage is that the requirement for the second advantage, the supply of machine-understandable data that is used to render the source graphics, is severely limited at present. Thus, many studies [10] and developments that aim to realize this method (the method of converting graphics into a form that is perceptible using senses other than sight) are being implemented that attempt to recognize rendered graphics (bitmap data) then convert them to tactile graphics. In such approach using machine recognition, it is difficult to ensure the practical utility of the fully automated conversion.

In particular, it is difficult to recognize characters contained in graphics as a string rather than an image: in tactile graphics, characters contained in the source graphics must not appear as glyphs but as transcribed braille characters. Therefore, these studies have concentrated on the development of authoring software for sighted persons that furnishes tactile graphics [11].

As a result, the third advantage of this method, that a blind person can take direct part in activities that require the use of graphics, is not being sufficiently realized.

2 Scope of this Work

The aim of this paper is to provide examples illustrating the conditions for effectively functionalizing the third method, which has a high affinity with HCI from among the three methods described above. Specifically, it will be shown that the three advantages of the third method are fully achieved with the implementation of a prototype tactile graphics output function for the statistical analysis software R's graphics output. R [12] is widely recognized and utilized as advanced statistical analysis software. Thus, to achieve access to its graphics output function would be very useful to realize an environment in which a blind person can take on an active role in exploratory study using statistical methods.

The BrailleR project, conducted by Jonathan R. Godfrey, is a case of research and development focusing on such potential of R. This project can be summarized as an attempt to provide textual information to a blind user in conjunction with a graph, [13] and therefore it falls under Method 2 (the method of transcribing values represented in graphics into characters). With respect to the BrailleR project, the present research has the merits of being able to represent an object which is effectively represented as graphics as-is (e.g., trends of line graphs and distributions of boxplots), and of being able to comprehensively support R's graphics output. Moreover, with respect to the research aim of generating tactile graphs from raw numeric data, the present research is useful in making good use of the various graphical representations that are supported by R (e.g., line graphs, boxplots, candle charts and so on).

3 Implementation of the Prototype

R outputs various plots to computer monitors and files in many image formats using a mechanism called GRdevice. Graphics data is first rendered within R by many graphics functions using a common intermediate format. The production of final output data is handled by drivers that support the respective output formats after reading this intermediate format data. The list of supported image formats includes not only bitmap formats such as PNG and JPEG but also vector formats such as PostScript and SVG. Therefore, a vector format is used at the stage of the intermediate format. Letters in a graphic are expressed not by sets of vector data that represent glyphs but by character codes.

There are differences in the supported drawing commands among the various vector image formats. Therefore, at the stage of the intermediate format, only primitive drawing commands which are supported by all vector image formats must be used. The principal commands used in R's intermediate format are limited to a command to draw any straight line and a command to draw any arc of a circle. To implement automated tactile graphics output for R's graphics output, major tasks are to create line drawing functions that correspond to these two drawing commands and to print characters appropriately.

The present research is currently being carried out to develop software to generate tactile graphics from data described using the PicTeX format [14].

The PicTeX format is one of R's supported vector image formats. This approach was chosen for the following reasons: the drawing commands used in the PicTeX format have nothing in addition to R's intermediate format, so they are substantially the same; the set of drawing commands in the PicTeX format is highly human-readable, and debugging in the software development is easily done; and because it would be troublesome to maintain consistency with all of R's program code in the case of integration in R as one of the drivers that supports all the output formats.

The Ruby programming language was used to develop the software. Using Ruby enables it to run on a multi-platform basis similar to R. Tactile graphics are output by the ESA721 (Ver'95) [15] braille embosser, which is widely used in Japan. Therefore, this software produces tactile graphics as embossed graphics.

Special care is needed to transcribe characters in graphics generated by R into braille in tactile graphics. There are often problems in simply transcribing characters in graphics into braille, such as a set of braille characters lying on top of another object or running over the edge of the paper. This reasons for this are because: in general, a braille character occupies a larger space than a character in the source graphics; and braille is specifically used as horizontal writing, so the method of rotating a character string vertically or obliquely (such methods are often used in graphics) cannot be used.

Therefore, in the present research, a labeling approach was adopted. Strings of characters in graphics are assigned labels from "a" to "z" according to their order of appearance. In the tactile graphics, only these one-character labels are printed on the respective points where the original strings would be positioned. A list showing pairs of the respective labels and strings is printed on another sheet of paper. Referring to this list, users can understand what string is represented by the label in the tactile graphic.

4 Results

Examples of embossed graphics output are shown in the next figures. Fig. 1 is a line graph plotted by R, showing monthly average temperatures in Tokyo in 2012. The same data output as an embossed graphic is shown in Fig. 2. Braille labels are marked with corresponding block letters.

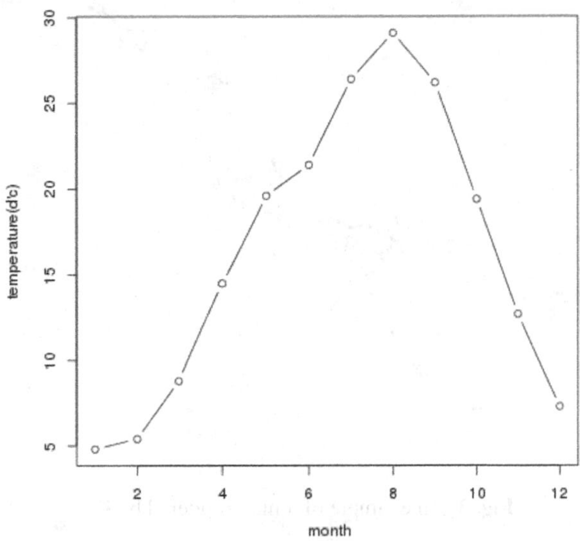

Fig. 1. An example of a line graph plotted by R

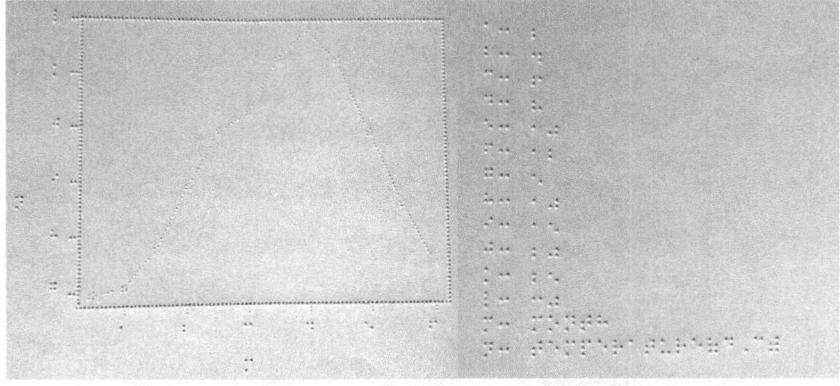

Fig. 2. An embossed graphic of Fig. 1. (left) and its listing sheet (right) produced by the developed software.

As discussed above, the present research focuses not only on graphs, but also on any graphics that would be effective when converted to tactile graphics, and thus aims to realize a comprehensive conversion system for R's graphics output. An enhanced GIS data processing package has been developed for R, so it is often used to process map data. Fig. 3 is a map of Japan rendered by R using GIS data. The same data output as an embossed graphic is shown in Fig. 4.

Fig. 3. An example of a map rendered by R

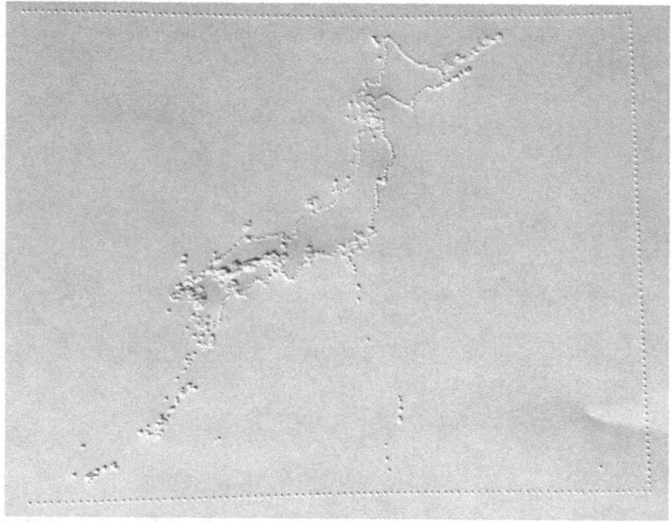

Fig. 4. An embossed graphic of Fig. 3's bitmap data converted by Tenka

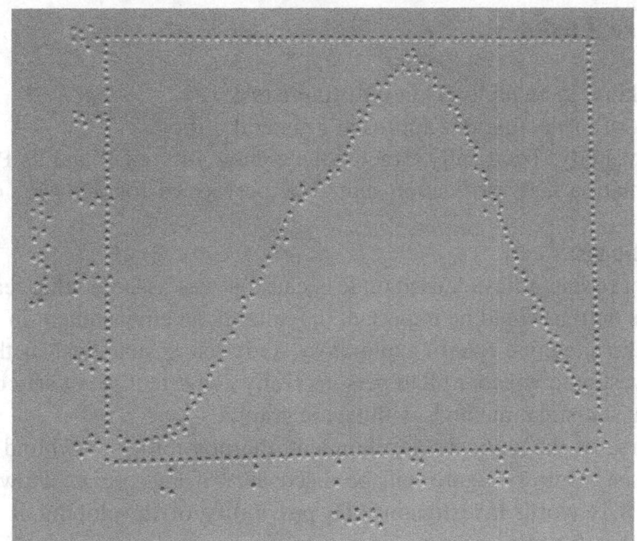

Fig. 5. An embossed graphic of Fig. 1's bitmap data converted by Tenka

Fig. 5 is an embossed graphic of Fig. 1's bitmap data (png format) using the software called Tenka [16] which is aimed to convert bitmap files for ESA721's drawing software Edel.

It is remarkable that not only pointing circles are collapsed but also letters are degraded unrecognizable.

5 Conclusion

A prototype system for generating tactile graphics output that can be applied in practical use has been developed targeting R's graphics output. It is anticipated that this method can realize the three advantages of Method 3 to a high level.

Such a result can be obtained because the second disadvantage of Method 3 can be avoided using R's intermediate graphics format. For instance, it can be anticipated that the results would be unsuccessful if an approach were adopted involving conversion from a bitmap that is the final output of one of R's drivers. The lines appearing in the graphics would become obscure and, in particular, there would be a severe limitation on processing text strings such as Fig. 5.

The results of the present research indicate that, in attempting to generate automated tactile graphics from the output of any kind of graphics software, the strategy described below will be useful.

1. To investigate whether the intermediate graphics format used in the relevant software consists of primitive vector format drawing commands and character printing commands that handle characters as codes.
2. If the latter conditions are fulfilled, to perform conversion to tactile graphics at the stage of graphics data expressed as that intermediate format.

6 Future Tasks

Broadly speaking, there are two kinds of future tasks:

1. The task of inspecting this approach's general utility

The present study specifically targeted the combination of R and its PicTex output, but implementation and verification should be performed for other R's output format or software.

2. R-specific tasks

The present research has focused on R because it was assumed that realizing access to its graphics output would be important in realizing an environment in which a blind person can take an active role in exploratory study using statistical methods. It is necessary to investigate whether blind persons really can effectively carry out exploratory study using statistical methods with tactile graphics.

In the course of the software development, the possibility of a blind person being able to draw an arbitrary figure will be discovered if appropriate drawing functions are defined. It is worth investigating the possibility of developing R as a form of drawing software for blind persons.

References

1. National Braille Association: NBA Tape Recording Manual, Third Edition. National Braille Association, Rochester (1979)
2. G82: Providing a text alternative that identifies the purpose of the non-text content, `http://www.w3.org/TR/WCAG20-TECHS/G82`
3. Snyder, J.: Audio Description: The Visual Made Verbal. International Journal of The Arts in Society 2(2), 99–104 (2007)
4. TapTapSee - Blind and Visually Impaired Camera, `http://www.taptapseeapp.com/`
5. Brown, L., Brewster, S., Ramboll, R., Burton, M., Riedel, B.: Design Guidelines for Audio Presentation of Graphs and Tables. In: Proceedings of the 2003 International Conference on Auditory Display (2003)
6. Accessible Math Audio Graphing Calculator, `http://www.viewplus.com/products/software/math/`
7. Miele, J., Marston, J.: Tactile Map Automated Production (TMAP): Project Update and Research Summary. In: CSUN, 2005 Proceedings (2005)
8. Minatani, K., Watanabe, T., Yamaguchi, T., Watanabe, K., Akiyama, J., Miyagi, M., Oouchi, S.: Tactile Map Automated Creation System to Enhance the Mobility of Blind Persons—Its Design Concept and Evaluation through Experiment. In: Miesenberger, K., Klaus, J., Zagler, W., Karshmer, A. (eds.) ICCHP 2010, Part II. LNCS, vol. 6180, pp. 534–540. Springer, Heidelberg (2010)
9. Google Maps, `http://maps.google.com`
10. Way, T.P., Barner, K.E.: Automatic Visual to Tactile Translation–Part II: Evaluation of The Tactile Image Creation System. IEEE Transactions on Rehabilitation Engineering 5(1), 95–105 (1997)

11. Jayant, C., Renzelmann, M., Wen, D., Krisnandi, S., Ladner, R., Comden, D.: Automated Tactile Graphics Translation: In the Field. In: Proceedings of 9th International ACM SIGACCESS Conference Computers and Accessibility, Tempe, pp. 75–82 (2007)
12. Core Team, R.: R: A language and environment for statistical computing. R Foundation for Statistical Computing, Vienna (2012)
13. Godfrey, A.J.R.: BrailleR: The BrailleR Project. In: Digitization and E-Inclusion in Mathematics and Science 2012 (2012)
14. PICTEX command summary, ftp://ftp.riken.go.jp/pub/tex-archive/info/pictex/summary/pictexsum.pdf
15. ESA721 Ver 1995, http://www.jtr-tenji.co.jp/products/ESA721_Ver95/ (in Japanese)
16. Edel and its related software, http://www7a.biglobe.ne.jp/~EDEL-plus/EdelDownLoad.html (in Japanese, English version of these software are also hosted)

Usability Evaluation of a Web System for Spatially Oriented Audio Descriptions of Images Addressed to Visually Impaired People

José Monserrat Neto, André P. Freire, Sabrina S. Souto, and Ramon S. Abílio

Universidade Federal de Lavras (UFLA) - Departamento de Ciência da Computação
Caixa Postal 3037 – 37200-000 – Lavras – MG – Brasil
{monserrat,apfreire}@dcc.ufla.br, sabrina@comp.ufla.br,
ramon@posgrad.ufla.br

Abstract. This paper describes a web system designed to provide spatially oriented audio descriptions of an image for visually impaired users. The system uses a hardware-independent platform of the technique of multimodal presentation of images. Visually impaired users interact with an image displayed on the screen while moving the cursor – with a mouse or a tablet (pen or finger touch) – and listening to the audio description of previously marked areas within the image. The paper also describes the usability evaluation performed with five participants and its main results. Generally, the five participants accomplished the usability test tasks and could better understand the image displayed. The paper also describes the main findings and discusses some implications for design, suggesting some improvements.

Keywords: Spacial orientation, audio descriptions.

1 Introduction

There are 285 million visually impaired people worldwide of which 39 million are blind [1]. In Brazil, there are 6.5 million visually impaired, of which 582 thousand are blind [2]. In the last 20 years screen reader software have been increasingly improved and become more accessible, rendering broader educational and social inclusion.

However, visually impaired people face serious problems with images when using screen readers. Generally, they cannot "read" digital images such as gif, jpg or png files of a web page, as often it lacks alternative text. And even when this is available, it is usually insufficient for visually impaired users to comprehend the image [3].

Therefore, we need an alternative that allows visually impaired people interact with an image and understand what is represented in it. This paper presents a proposal of software to address this issue, along with this alternative and, in order to test it, also a task-based usability test with five participants that aimed at verifying the usefulness and validity of the implemented solution.

Initially in Section 2, the educational, scientific and technological context of the image information problem for visually impaired people is briefly discussed. It is then

C. Stephanidis and M. Antona (Eds.): UAHCI/HCII 2014, Part II, LNCS 8514, pp. 154–165, 2014.

presented a simpler and cheaper solution for the technique of multimodal presentation of images, implemented with web technologies. Using such solution, in Section 3 a prototype of a web system called AudioImagem for spatially oriented audio descriptions of images addressed to visually impaired people is described. Next, in Section 4 the usability evaluation of the prototype in order to verify its usefulness and validity is presented, seeking to make a proof-of-concept of the technology implemented; and in Section 5 results of evaluation are presented. At last, in Section 6 the findings and implications for design are presented, and in Section 7 the conclusion and future works.

2 Educational, Scientific and Technological Context

For didactic-pedagogic purposes, a student is regarded as visually impaired when he or she cannot grasp regular classes using traditional materials and teaching methods which require visual skills.

To overcome this situation, many visually impaired people use *screen reader* software that works through electronic voice. Through keyboard (or eventually with a mouse) users can select a text of a file, screen element, or web page, hence resulting in an electronic voice audio that reads the text by means of the computer loud speaker, or an ear headset. Visually impaired users can listen to the texts of files, screen selected items and web pages. There are several screen readers on the market, such as JAWS, Virtual Vision, DOSVOX, Orca, WindowEyes, among others.

However, the presence of inaccessible images still emerges as a great challenge for screen readers. Any digital image such as jpg, gif or png file does not keep in itself information in text format about the image, to be read by a screen reader. Usually, images such as photos, drawings, charts, diagrams and so on are in the middle of texts about any subject matter, and their information are often essential for a clear understanding of those texts. In education in general but particularly in higher education, that fact is sheer apparent. Any student learns the several concepts of sciences with numerous figures and diagrams such as those of an eukaryotic cell, a block on inclined plane, a helium atom and so on. As screen reader is unable to "read images" visually impaired people are usually excluded from full understanding of usual digital didactic texts.

Fortunately in web pages it is possible to write an 'alt text' in place of an image in case this cannot be loaded or accessed for any technical reason, or cannot be seen in the case of visually impaired users.

There are two problems with using alternative text in web pages. Firstly, alternative text are seldom properly placed and written to describe the image. Strictly few web pages follow the recommendations of the Web Content Accessibility Guidelines 2.0 [4], which propose to always place alternative text for visually impaired users.

Secondly, even when there is such a text description of the image, it is usually insufficient for the visually impaired person to understand the image [3]. It is difficult to write an image description that can cover various types of information that a visually impaired user could ever possibly need to understand a certain image in a particular context of a web page. Besides, the text description is insufficient to make users understanding clearly the spatial arrangement of elements in the image.

An alternative to face the problem of image understanding by visually impaired people is the use of technology with tactile interaction [5]. The basic idea is to develop a screen-like device capable of creating shapes in high relief to be felt by the user's fingers with visual disability. For instance, in the contest winner work of the Mobile Design Competition 2012, organized by the LG Company, proposed a device that has a "membrane of a touch sensitive polymer that changes constantly to give user a tactile feedback according to what is displayed on the screen" [6]. Another similar alternative, though older, is to use micro-pins on the screen device surface which dynamically creates the relief of a figure and can be felt by a visually impaired user's touch. Such alternatives are very promising, however involve developing specific hardware, which ends rendering these solutions more expensive.

Power & Jürgensen [5] analyzed several options available to render information available to people with visual disabilities, and conducted an extensive review of presentation tools and techniques of textual documents and graphics for visually impaired people, using audio and tactile modalities.

One trend is the combination of techniques based on touching with audio feedback in tactile interaction with a special haptic device developed for such, being this technique called "multimodal presentation of charts" [5, p107). The technology presented in this paper (AudioImagem) follows that technique. In this case, unlike the special screen devices with pins or sensitive polymer membranes, the technique simply uses the positional information of the finger or a pen on a tablet to activate the audio feedback. Many devices were created with this technique [7, 8, 9, 10].

In common, all these devices are based on specific hardware system, that is, each system has its own tablet device. For instance, Touch Graphics Company [11] sells a product called "Talking Tactile Tablet 2" which allows a visually impaired user to interact by touch with an image displayed on the tablet and listen audibly the information about the image displayed.

Again, such tablets have specific hardware and are generally more expensive. Furthermore, the material created to be accessible by people with visual disabilities can only be created and accessed through the system itself, generating dependence on the company that produces the system, and making it difficult to share the material created via internet, for instance.

A different solution would be a combination of technique of the audio feedback with that of the positional interaction on the image by touch of the visually impaired user. And fortunately, unlike the alternatives above, this solution does not need to employ any specific hardware, making it a platform independent alternative. User interaction on the image may be accomplished with a mouse, tablet (that one used for drawing), hand held tablet for general use, such as Ipad and Android tablets, touchscreen monitor, and any interface that is able to control the cursor movement (the little arrow) on the screen monitor.

Thus, a simple and cheap but no less promising solution is to implement the multimodal presentation technique with web technologies, generating web pages with images that contain audio information about themselves which may be accessible to impaired visual people in a broader way through the internet using a regular web browser.

3 Description of AudioImagem

Based on the works of Freitas [12] and De Sousa [13], the Polaris Company [14] has developed a software prototype of a web technology – called AudioImagem – through which a sighted person is able to delimit areas within an image and associate audio descriptions to them. The system can then yield spatial references of the marked areas on the image and describe them audibly whenever a visually impaired user "walks over" the image using a mouse or a tablet.

There are two modes for the visually impaired user to interact with the image and listen to its audio descriptions: the static mode and the navigational mode. The first mode does not depend on the cursor position, that is, does not depend on the interaction of visually impaired users with the image.

There are two static audio descriptions: the short and the long one, which are activated by the keys 'C' and 'L' in the keyboard, respectively. The short description is envisaged to describe briefly the image; and the long description to describe it with more details. The short one is also envisaged to describe the kind of image, like photo, drawing, diagram, graphic, table, chart, formula, etc. The long description may describe the image elements with more details, specially their disposition on the image providing the first spatial orientations to visually impaired users before navigating on the image.

The second mode of the user interaction with the image is the navigational one. Visually impaired users may interact with the image using a mouse or tablet (pen or finger touch), so that they may "walk over" the image. When the cursor is over an image area – which was previously marked and described – the user immediately listens to its audio description. So the user may listen to all demarcated and described areas of the image, when "walking over" and "exploring" the image.

However this way of the navigational mode over the image may be not enough for the user to be spatially oriented on the image in that she or he may leave the image inadvertently and stay out of it. That is, the cursor may go out or be out of the figure and the user may not find it and come back to the image easily. To face this problem the navigational mode also adopted two solutions: (a) at the moment the cursor goes out of the image, it provides an audio message describing to which side it left the image (1 to left, 2 to above, 3 to right or 4 to below); and (b) it provides the 'N' key that activates an audio message of the cursor position both outside the image and within it, as shown in Figure 1.

When the 'N' key is pressed in the computer keyboard and the cursor is out of the image the system yields an audio description that says in which of eight positions the cursor is placed at the moment (1 above left, 2 above, 3 above right, 4 left, 5 right, 6 below left, 7 below, 8 below right).

And when the key 'N' is pressed and the cursor is within the image the system provides an audio description that speaks in which of nine positions the cursor is placed within the image (1 above left, 2 center above, 3 above right, 4 center left, 5 center, 6 center right, 7 below left, 8 center below, 9 below right).

Fig. 1. Audio feedback of the cursor position in the navigational mode

To sum up, the navigational mode depends on the cursor position and yields audibly both its position on the screen – out and within the image – and the description of a marked area of the image. It also yields to which side the cursor moved when leaving the image.

Yet, it is not well known what the actual usefulness of such technology would be for visually impaired users. Among other questions, we investigate whether such a model of interaction between the visually impaired user and the image is enough for her or him to understand the image. Thus, it is necessary to carry out a proof-of-concept test of the "spatial audio description" technology by means of a usability test of the prototype developed.

4 Usability Test

The usability test comprised a task-based user evaluation by participants and employed a think-aloud protocol while the users performed their tasks. Audio and video recording were taken.

The test set consisted of a desktop computer with: a) a tablet controlled by pen and finger touch; b) two webcams, one addressed to the participant's face and another to the keyboard and tablet; c) a microphone embedded in one of the webcams, that was over the keyboard and tablet; d) a loud speaker set; e) Linux operation system; f) Guvcview to capture video in two windows in the screen, for each webcam (user face and keyboard-tablet) to be shown on the screen during test; and (e) SimpleScreenRecorder for recording the screen and the audio. The Figure 2 exhibits a test set photo.

Five visually impaired persons have participated in the usability evaluation which was composed of twelve tasks. Each task was elaborated as a web page presenting the image information audibly described and a specific question associated to the image, which could only be answered by the user by "wandering" on the image and listening to its spatial audio descriptions.

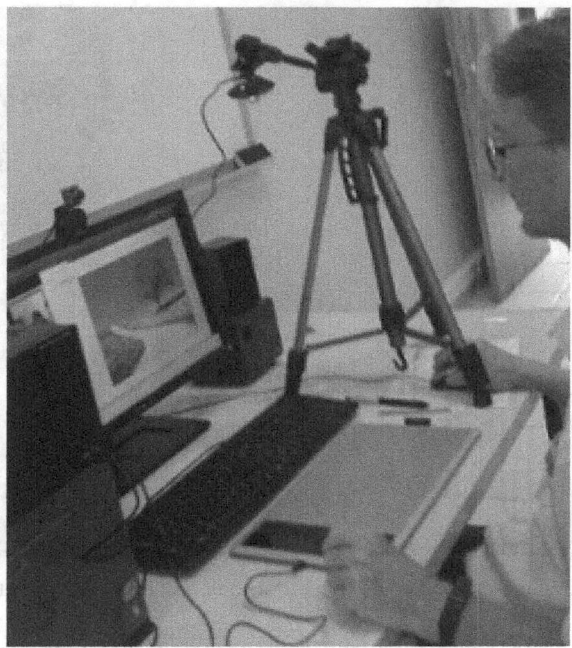

Fig. 2. Photo of the test set showing the first task

The log of the tasks was accomplished through three tools: a) a screen recorder that recorded cursor movements, made by the user on the system during the tasks; b) a voice recorder which recorded all user comments and the system audio descriptions; and c) two webcams which recorded user movements over the keyboard and tablet and the user face during task performance.

In each task the system presented two descriptions of the respective image, a short and a long one, explaining statically the image for the visually impaired user. She or he could always listen to an audible help about the navigation commands on the page and on the image. Besides the short and long descriptions, the system provided also the audio description of the task to be accomplished by the user. So, the keys 'C', 'L' and 'T', when pressed, activated the three audio descriptions, respectively short, long and task one. For instance, in the second task (Figure 3) its image was presented audibly with the following descriptions:

- Short description: “Photo of an autumn landscape”.
- Long description: “This is a photo of a bleak autumn day landscape. There is a street crossing the photo on the left and a leafy tree with orange leaves on the right side”.
- Task: “Observe the photo and describe as you understand it”.

Various types of image were selected for each task such as photo, plan drawing, graph, flowchart, diagram and table.

Fig. 3. Landscape photo used in the second task of the usability test

Briefly, tasks 1 and 2 displayed landscape photos, task 3 a drawing of the world globe, task 4 a geographical map of Brazil, task 5 an ecosystem flowchart, task 6 a trigonometric table, task 7 an algorithm flowchart, task 8 a drawing of the kinds of cow meat, task 9 a phase graph diagram of chemical substance, task 10 a plan drawing of chessboard with all pieces, task 11 a diagram of Daniel chemical cell, and task 12 a figure of the periodic chemical table.

The objective of performing several tasks with so many images was to test different types of images usually employed in the sciences that may be potentially useful in education and described audibly, listened to and comprehended by visually impaired students.

Figure 4 shows the graph image used in the ninth task, that was to find out the triple and critical points.

Each task was designed to be accomplished in between 5 and 10 minutes. The user could choose to employ the tablet with pen or finger touch that was configured to function in absolute mode. After some time becoming familiarized with the system, the five users attempted the tasks taking in average 2 hours and 20 minutes in total.

The usability test script followed by participants was: 1) reading the presentation of the usability test and explaining the basics of AudioImagem system navigation; 2) starting screen and audio recording; 3) answering the pretest questionnaire; 4) familiarizing with the system in doing the first task; 5) choosing between pen or finger touch on tablet; 6) performing the other 11 tasks; 7) answering the task questionnaire after each task; and 8) answering the posttest questionnaire.

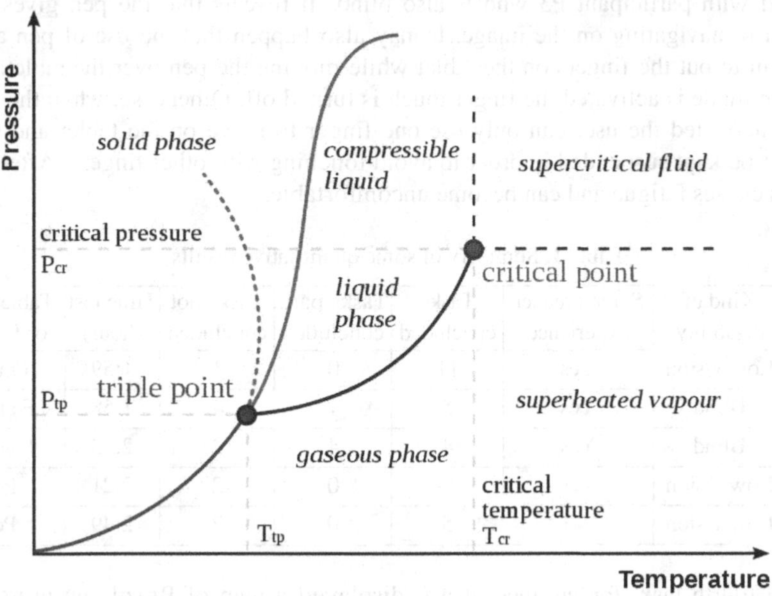

Fig. 4. Image of a phase graph of a chemical substance

The pretest questionnaire asked information about the participant, such as name, age, gender, education level, motivation to participate in the test, kind of visual disability, origin of disability, proficiency in reading Braille, other disabilities, and kinds of assistive technology used – type, model, version and use time of each technology.

The task questionnaire asked the final answer to the respective task, the degree of difficulty of each task done (very easy, easy, more or less, difficult, very difficult) and its reason, the system helpfulness to perform the task (essential, helpful, more or less, little helpful, not at all helpful) and its reason, and the degree of trust in the answer given.

The post-test questionnaire presented questions about the difficulties faced by users, their suggestions to make the system more helpful for them, about what they liked most in using it, and also asked whether the system could be helpful in education, receiving the unanimous answer: yes. In participants' words: "Of course it is" and "For sure".

5 Results

A brief summary of some quantitative results of the usability test is presented in the Table 1. For example, participant P2 is blind and has experience using screen reader. In the study, this user concluded 5 tasks, partially concluded 1 task, and did not succeed to conclude 4 tasks, and took 1 hour and 58 minutes using the finger (F) and pen (P) on the tablet. This user first chose to use finger touch, but when faced problem in finding out smaller marked areas in the image the user changed to pen.The same happened with participant P3 who is also blind. It reveals that the pen gives more precision in navigating on the image. It may also happen that the use of pen allows her or him to put the fingers on the tablet while moving the pen over the tablet, since when pen mode is activated the finger touch is turned off. Otherwise, when the finger touch is activated the user can only use one finger to move on the tablet and so the arm must be kept suspended in order to avoid touching with other fingers. After some time this causes fatigue and can become uncomfortable.

Table 1. Summary of some quantitative results

Users	Kind of disability	Screen reader experience	Tasks concluded	Tasks part. concluded	Tasks not concluded	Time test (hour)	Tablet (Pen or Finger)
P1	Low vision	Yes	11	0	1	1:59	Finger
P2	Blind	Yes	5	1	4	1:58	F and P
P3	Blind	Yes	4	4	2	2:43	F and P
P4	Low vision	Yes	9	0	2	2:21	Pen
P5	Low vision	No	5	0	7	2:49	Pen

In the fourth task, for instance, it was displayed a map of Brazil and users were asked about the number of states that compose the northeast region of Brazil. This region has nine states and many of them are small areas in the map. So all users found very difficult to navigate on that image and figure out where all states are.

6 Findings and Implications for Design

The usability evaluation has brought important findings and implications for design which are discussed around four themes: 1) the interface for interacting with the image; 2) audio descriptions and previous knowledge; 3) the borders or limits of delimitated areas within an image; and 4) modes and strategies of navigation on the image.

Although five users are indeed a very small sample of visually impaired people, clearly the two blind users had more difficulty in navigating on the task images. Any visual hint such as shadows, blurry spots, colored blots on the image displayed in the screen ends helping low vision user to navigate on the image. Blind users cannot count on such hints, only on the audio feedbacks while wandering out spatially on the image. For this reason the two blind users did not accomplished the twelve tasks designed avoiding getting too tired.

6.1 Mouse, Tablet and Other Interface Devices

In the usability test, the mouse was regarded as inappropriate to visually impaired users since it provides less control over the cursor localization on the image. This conclusion was based on preliminary tests. However, this is not always true. Participant P1 showed that low vision users may opt to use a mouse. Specifically, this user had great difficulty in using the finger on the tablet in absolute mode, and preferred finger touch in relative mode since the participant was used to the notebook mousepad, which is by default always in relative mode. This user said that colored blots helped very much to find out the small areas on the image as in the ninth task, displayed in Figure 4.

The comparison between pen and finger touch is not conclusive yet. While touching with the finger seems to provide more freedom to navigate on the tablet, at the same time it is not as precise as the pen, especially on small image areas. It also seems to be somehow stressing since finger touch obliges the user to keep her or his arm suspended over the tablet, since absolute mode is the only way to use finger touch on tablet, as the cursor on the screen cannot be controlled by two fingers at the same time.

6.2 Audio Descriptions and Previous Knowledge

The usability test revealed that describing an image properly for visually impaired students is not as trivial as it seems to be at first. First, the long audio description is very important to orient users spatially before they try "walking over" the image. Some task images were not suitably described with the long audio description, such as in the autumn landscape photo of the second task, as shown in Figure 2.

It also revealed the need of knowing more precisely the previous knowledge of users about any given image. The deeper is the user's knowledge, the less need there is to extend the description in the long audio description option, before the user navigates on the image. For instance, participant P4 knew the periodic chemical element table and remembered roughly the position of metals, semimetals, non metal and noble gases in the table. So this user had an advantage over the other users. Thus, for people who already know, even roughly, the elements of an image the long audio description must be different from those who are newbie in a given subject matter that is shown in the image.

6.3 Image Marked Areas and Their Borders

A problem of AudioImagem system readily identified by all users was the response speed of the audio feedback that is slightly slow and needs to be faster as users usually pass on an area at a higher speed and miss the audio description of the respective area. This was especially true in relation to small image areas.

Another problem was that as the user moved to a marked area and listened to its audio description, the user could not know where that marked area finished. Only when the user reached another marked area and listened to its associated audio description, could the user know that the previous marked area had finished. So they moved many times from one side to the other within a given marked area in order to know its extension within the image. There should be a way, perhaps an audio feedback or another key, to warn that the user is still in the same marked area.

A closed related problem was to find out the borders of the marked areas. One strategy of some users was to travel in zigzags between two areas to localize spatially the contours of the given marked areas.

This findings show clearly the need of a feedback of the border of marked areas. One suggestion is to create an "audio line" – an audibly feedback to reveal the contours of an area within the image for the visually impaired user. The same could be done regarding the contours of the whole image, as one participant suggested. So, instead of seeing the borders of the image and its marked areas, the user could listen to such contours.

6.4 Navigation Modes and Strategies

Two participants adopted the following strategy to scan the images while performing the tasks: they traveled with finger or pen in horizontal lines over the tablet, changing at each time only the height the user traversed the image, so that the user could avoid missing small areas and ensure they were finding out all marked areas of the image. The same strategy was also performed in vertical lines.

This finding reveals the need for a sort of directed navigation to a given delimited image area. The present navigational mode of audio description is a sort of free navigation on the image. The user must wander over the image to find out the marked areas. The only help is the long audio description option in the static mode of navigation. Another suggestion is to create another alternative to the navigational mode, a "directed navigation" that directs the user to a selected marked area. So the user could choose in a list of areas that one he or she wants to find on the image. The system could then direct the user to that area giving an audio feedback. The closer the user is to the area the louder is the audio feedback, and so the user could find smaller areas of the image more easily.

7 Conclusion

We discussed and described a platform independent alternative of the technique of multimodal presentation of images, implemented as a prototype of a web system called AudioImagem and designed for visually impaired people. Also we presented the usability test of the AudioImagem, performed with 5 participants, and its main results. The videos recorded have still much information to be more in depth examined. Generally the prototype fulfilled its purpose to allow visually impaired people to interact with an image and understand what is displayed in it, as revealed by the number of tasks concluded, 70% in average. Nevertheless it revealed some weaknesses, such as the speed of audio feedback and the problem of border in marked areas. However it also suggested some solutions to them, such as the "audio line" to allow visually impaired users to listen the contours of the area of an image, and the "directed navigation" to direct users to an area of the image. Future works include the improvements of AudioImagem, creation of didactic material using audio described images, and new usability tests with this assistive technology and the didactic materials created.

Acknowledgements. We thank all the participants for their most valuable contributions to this work. We also thank CNPq for the financial support to this research via Grant 458795/2013-5.

References

1. WHO – World Health Organization, In: Visual Impairment and Blindness, Fact Sheet No 282 (June 2012)
2. IBGE, In: IBGE Census, General characteristics of the population, religion and people with disabilities (2010)
3. Petrie, H., Harrison, C., Dev, S.: Describing images on the web: a survey of current practice and prospects for the future. In: 3rd International Conference on Universal Access in Human-Computer Interaction, part of HCI International 2005 (2005)
4. Caldwell, B., Cooper, M., Guarino Reid, L., Vanderheiden, G.: "Web Content Accessibility Guidelines 2.0", In: W3C Recommendation. (2013), `http://www.w3.org/TR/WCAG20` (accessed in November 2013)
5. Power, JüRgensen: "Accessible presentation of information for people with visual disabilities". Universal Access in the Information Society 9.2, 97–119 (2009, 2010)
6. Techtudo: "Smartphone conceitual premiado em concurso da LG investe em telas táteis" In: Techtudo Curiosidades, reportagem de dezembro de 2012 (2012), `http://www.techtudo.com.br/curiosidades/noticia/2012/12/smartphone-conceitual-premiado-em-concurso-da-lg-investe-em-telas-tateis.html` (accessed in October 2013)
7. Poh, S.P.: Talking diagrams., Master's Thesis, The University of Western Ontario (1995)
8. Landau, S.: "Tactile graphics: strategies for non-visual seeing", In: Thresholds. MIT School of Architecture (1999)
9. Landau, S., Gourgey, K.: Development of a talking tactile tablet. Information Technology Disability 7(2) (2001), `http://www.rit.edu/~easi/itd/itdv07.htm`
10. Xu, H.: "A Support System for Graphics for Visually Impaired People", Master's Thesis in Computer Science, The University of Western Ontario, Canada (2013)
11. Touch Graphics Inc., "Talking Tactile Tablet 2", tablet para pessoas com deficiência visual (2013), `http://touchgraphics.com/OnlineStore/index.php/featured-products/talking-tactile-tablet-2-ttt.html` (accessed in November 2013)
12. Freitas, A.C.F.: Study and proposal of an assistive technology of audio description of images for visually impaired persons. Undergraduate final year dissertation, Amanda Cristina Ferreira de Freitas, Computer Science, UFLA (2010)
13. Da Silva, R.C.: Study and proposal of a spatial navigability model for a software of audio description of images addressed to visually impaired people. Undergraduate final year dissertation, Renato Corcovia da Silva, Computer Science, UFLA (2011)
14. Polaris, Polaris Inovações em Soluções Web (2011), `http://www.polarisweb.com.br/`

Emotional Prosodic Model Evaluation for Greek Expressive Text-to-Speech Synthesis

Dimitrios Tsonos[1], Pepi Stavropoulou[1], Georgios Kouroupetroglou[1], Despina Deligiorgi[2], and Nikolaos Papatheodorou[1]

[1] National and Kapodistrian University of Athens, Department of Informatics and Telecommunications, Athens, Greece
{dtsonos,pepis,koupe}@di.uoa.gr

[2] National and Kapodistrian University of Athens, Department of Physics, Athens, Greece
despo@phys.uoa.gr

Abstract. In this study we introduce a novel experimental approach towards the evaluation of emotional prosodic models in Expressive Speech Synthesis. It is based on the dimensional emotion expressivity and adopts the Self-Assessment Manikin Test. We applied this experimental approach to evaluate an emotional prosodic model for Greek expressive Text-to-Speech synthesis. We used two pseudo-sentences for each of the Greek and English HMM-based synthetic voices, implemented in the MARY TtS platform. Fifteen native Greek participants were asked to assess eleven emotional states for each sentence. The results show that the "Arousal" dimension is perceived as intended, followed by the "Pleasure" and "Dominance" dimensions' ratings. These preliminary findings are consistent with the results in previous studies.

Keywords: Expressive Speech Synthesis, prosody evaluation, Text-to-Speech, emotional state.

1 Introduction

Expressive Speech is "the speech which gives us information, other than the plain message, about the speaker and triggers a response to the listener" [1]. Accordingly, Expressive Speech Synthesis (ESS) [2] is a method for conveying emotions (and other paralinguistic information) through speech, using the variations and differences of speech characteristics. There is a plethora of studies towards the creation of expressive speech synthesis in order to achieve a more natural result during Human-Computer Interaction. Furthermore, in the domain of document accessibility, emotional-based mapping has been recently proposed [3] for rendering document signals to the auditory modality through Document to Audio systems [4, 5] that incorporate ESS. This approach aims to overcome the limitation of the current Text-to-Speech (TtS) systems [6] towards an effective acoustic provision of the semantics and the cognitive aspects of the visual (such as the typographic signals) and non-visual (such as the logical structure) knowledge embedded in rich text documents [7].

C. Stephanidis and M. Antona (Eds.): UAHCI/HCII 2014, Part II, LNCS 8514, pp. 166–174, 2014.

Several works [8-11] suggest that there is a certain universal character behind the vocal expression of emotions. The approach followed by Schröder [11] for speech rule-base synthesis builds on the hypothesis that vocal emotion expression is very similar across languages. More specifically, he presents a model for expressive speech synthesis in MARY TtS [12] using the dimensional "Pleasure", "Arousal" and "Dominance" (PAD) approach of emotions. PAD methodology has the advantage of using continuous values of the emotional expression. PAD values can be mapped to a specific emotion or variations of the emotion. For example, the emotion "happy" can have variations like "quite happy", "very happy", "less happy". Schröder [11] uses several equations to describe how the prosodic elements vary while changing the emotional states. The parameters are distinguished as: a) "Standard" global parameters: "pitch", "range", "speech rate" and "volume", b) "Non-standard" global parameters: "pitch-dynamics" and "range-dynamics" and c) specific entities like ToBI accents and boundaries.

The MARY (Modular Architecture for Research on speech sYnthesis) Text-to-Speech system [12] is an open-source, Java implemented platform. The system follows the Client-Server (CS) model. Server side executes text preprocessing / normalization, natural language processing, calculation of acoustic parameters and speech synthesis. The client sends to server the requests, including the text to be processed and the parameters for the text handling by the server side. The system is multi-threaded, due to CS implementation, flexible (modular architecture) and XML-based, adding support for DOM and XSLT [12]. MARY TtS includes a number of tools, in order to easily add a new language and build Unit Selection and HMM-based synthetic voices [13-14].

In the present study, we first introduce a novel experimental approach towards the evaluation of emotional prosodic models in Expressive Speech Synthesis. Then we investigate how emotions are communicated through speech/prosodic channel excluding any emotion from content's semantics. The results can be incorporated into TtS systems for the acoustic rendition of document's typographic signals. Our study also builds on the universal character of emotions hypothesis according to which emotion is similarly expressed across languages. It ultimately aims to evaluate this hypothesis by testing an existing, language-agnostic / universal prosodic model for conveying emotions through TtS. In contrast, previous approaches (e.g. [15-17]) to developing a prosodic model for the Greek language are based on the creation of an emotional speech database, along with feature extraction and analysis.

2 The Experimental Approach

We adopted the Self-Assessment Manikin Test (SAM) [18] which measures the emotional response, based on the dimensional approach of emotions [19-20]. SAM test provides to evaluators the ability to avoid the verbal expression of emotions in the assessment. It introduces a quick and easy procedure. This tool has been designed to replace the course of self-assessment of the emotions. In the context of the current study, we have designed and developed a web-based version of the SAM experimental procedure, similar to the one described in [21].

2.1 Stimulus Design

In order to eliminate any expression of emotions through the verbal/semantic channel, the selection of meaningless pseudo-sentences that resemble normal speech (in both Greek and English TtS) is mandatory. In the Greek version of synthesized stimuli, the selection of the pseudo-sentences was done according to the methodology proposed in [22]. A set of random short sentences was selected and phonemes of the content words of the sentences were replaced, such that pseudo-words were formed. Vowels were replaced by vowels and consonants by consonants, and the syllabic structure and stress of the original word were maintained.

The pseudo-sentences were converted into synthetic speech, using MARY TtS [12]. A number of languages are currently supported by MARY TtS, such as English, German, Russian, Italian, Turkish and Telugu. But the Greek language is not included. Following the basic and necessary steps for the baseline support of a new language in the MARY TtS framework [13] we have developed a HMM-based Greek voice. The dimensional description of emotional states and the prosodic model [11] [23] for *pitch*, *rate* and *volume* has been applied, in order to acoustically render "Pleasure", "Arousal" and "Dominance".

Participants first hear each pseudo-sentence two times and then they assess the emotional state they perceive using manikins. The stimulus presentation sequence (frame) is presented in Fig. 1. The audio cue begins with a short pause (2 seconds), followed by the synthesized pseudo-sentence, a short pause, repetition of the pseudo-sentence and an ending pause.

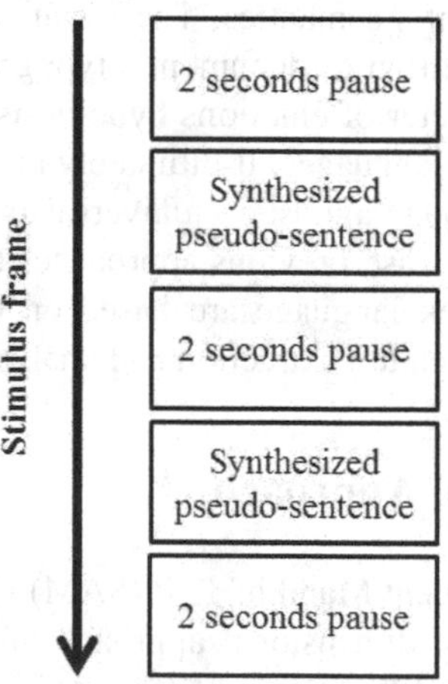

Fig. 1. The stimulus audio sequence (frame) during the experimental procedure

2.2 Stimuli Implementation

We selected the dimensional representation (Table 1) of 10 emotions provided by [24] and the "neutral" emotional state. Fig. 2 presents the scatter graph of the ten emotional states on the "Pleasure - Arousal" grid. Finally, we selected two sentences that can be optimally processed by the TtS system. The sentence "Ήταν όμως λίγο απότομος" was transformed into "Ήταν ένως τίγο αφόθονος" and the second pseudo-sentence was "Η αφιστροπή της σάστες είναι γογεμός". For the English stimuli we selected two pseudo-sentences "Hat sundig pron you venzy" and "Fee got laish jankill gosterr" [9] [25]. The total stimuli were 44 (we implemented 11 emotional states X 2 pseudo-sentences for each version of the TtS language).

Table 1. The 10 emotional states and their corresponding values on the "Pleasure", "Arousal" and "Dominance" dimensions in scale [-1, 1]

Emotional State	Pleasure	Arousal	Dominance
A	-0.51	0.59	0.25
B	-0.60	0.35	0.11
C	-0.64	0.60	-0.43
D	0.81	0.51	0.46
E	-0.63	-0.27	-0.33
F	0.40	0.67	-0.13
G	0.74	-0.13	0.03
H	0.87	0.54	-0.18
I	0.68	-0.46	0.06
J	-0.65	-0.62	-0.33

2.3 Participants and Procedure

In total 15 students (9 male and 6 female) participated in the experiment with an average age of 24.4 year-old (SD=3.5). They were graduate and post-graduate students of the Department of Informatics, University of Athens. Their native language was Greek (with excellent or good proficiency in English). They did not report any hearing problem, and they had none or a little familiarization with synthetic speech or Text-to-Speech systems.

The participants were asked to hear and estimate the emotional state that is communicated by the synthesized speech. They were introduced in the experimental procedure and they had to complete a form about their demographic data (age, occupation, educational level, frequency of computer usage) and that they consent to participate in the experimental test. Then, they were familiarized with the experiment by participating in a short demo session. They had to assess 4 demo stimuli (2 in Greek and 2 in English version). They could repeat the demo session if they believed that they were not familiarized with the procedure. After the demo version of the experiment, they participated in the main procedure, where they assessed the 44 stimuli. The stimuli playback was provided in a random order for each participant, through a high performance headset (AKG K271). The average assessment time was 18.1 minutes (SD=3.3).

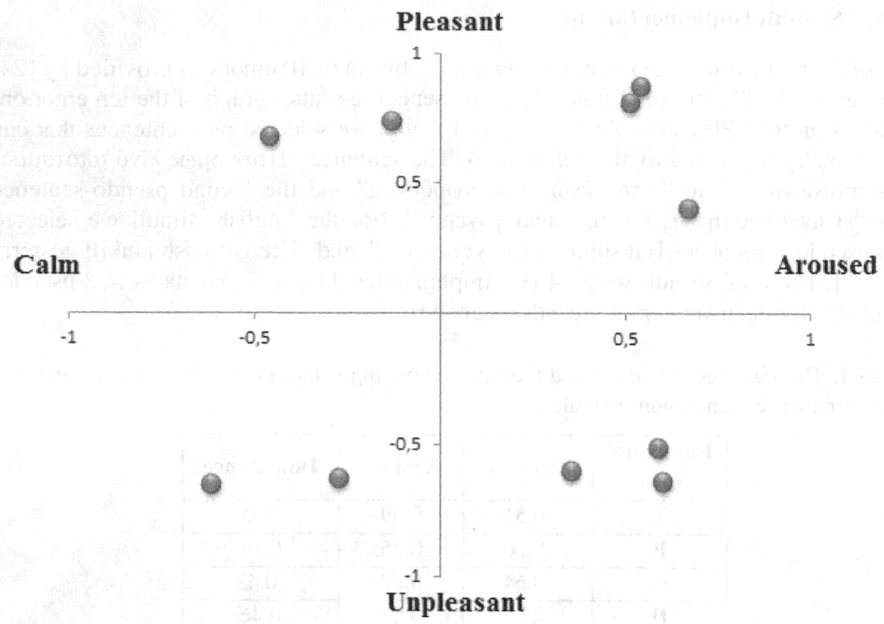

Fig. 2. Scatter graph of the 10 emotional states on the "Pleasure - Arousal" grid

3 Results

Tables 2 and 3 present the results for the Greek pseudo-sentences and Tables 4 and 5 the corresponding English ones. Each table includes the average responses for

Table 2. Average values with their corresponding standard deviation for each emotional state on the Pleasure, Arousal and Dominance dimensions for the Greek pseudo-sentence #1

	Greek pseudo-sentence #1					
Emotional State	**Pleasure (SD)**	**Target Value**	**Arousal (SD)**	**Target Value**	**Dominance (SD)**	**Target Value**
A	-0.10 (0.43)	*-0.51*	0.57 (0.26)	*0.59*	0.23 (0.80)	*0.25*
B	-0.17 (0.31)	*-0.60*	-0.33 (0.41)	*0.35*	0.43 (0.50)	*0.11*
C	-0.10 (0.43)	*-0.64*	0.47 (0.30)	*0.60*	0.40 (0.63)	*-0.43*
D	-0.30 (0.41)	*0.81*	0.83 (0.24)	*0.51*	-0.27 (0.62)	*0.46*
E	-0.40 (0.47)	*-0.63*	-0.60 (0.34)	*-0.27*	0.03 (0.52)	*-0.33*
F	0.00 (0.53)	*0.40*	0.90 (0.21)	*0.67*	-0.13 (0.81)	*-0.13*
G	-0.13 (0.23)	*0.74*	-0.20 (0.37)	*-0.13*	0.33 (0.62)	*0.03*
H	0.03 (0.44)	*0.87*	0.67 (0.24)	*0.54*	0.07 (0.59)	*-0.18*
I	-0.10 (0.34)	*0.68*	-0.47 (0.40)	*-0.46*	0.33 (0.72)	*0.06*
J	-0.53 (0.44)	*-0.65*	-0.87 (0.30)	*-0.62*	0.10 (0.71)	*-0.33*
Neutral	0.00 (0.19)	*0.00*	0.00 (0.33)	*0.00*	0.13 (0.61)	*0.00*

Table 3. Average values with their corresponding standard deviation for each emotional state on Pleasure, Arousal and Dominance dimensions for the Greek pseudo-sentence #2

Greek pseudo-sentence #2						
Emotional State	**Pleasure (SD)**	**Target Value**	**Arousal (SD)**	**Target Value**	**Dominance (SD)**	**Target Value**
A	0.07 (0.46)	*-0.51*	0.33 (0.49)	*0.59*	-0.10 (0.57)	*0.25*
B	0.07 (0.37)	*-0.60*	0.10 (0.34)	*0.35*	0.10 (0.57)	*0.11*
C	0.03 (0.48)	*-0.64*	0.43 (0.37)	*0.60*	-0.17 (0.67)	*-0.43*
D	-0.13 (0.55)	*0.81*	0.90 (0.21)	*0.51*	-0.27 (0.80)	*0.46*
E	-0.60 (0.34)	*-0.63*	-0.53 (0.40)	*-0.27*	0.10 (0.60)	*-0.33*
F	0.10 (0.51)	*0.40*	0.77 (0.32)	*0.67*	0.00 (0.76)	*-0.13*
G	-0.20 (0.32)	*0.74*	-0.20 (0.53)	*-0.13*	0.30 (0.49)	*0.03*
H	0.00 (0.57)	*0.87*	0.83 (0.31)	*0.54*	-0.13 (0.88)	*-0.18*
I	-0.17 (0.45)	*0.68*	-0.20 (0.37)	*-0.46*	0.20 (0.41)	*0.06*
J	-0.53 (0.40)	*-0.65*	-0.67 (0.45)	*-0.62*	0.27 (0.56)	*-0.33*
Neutral	-0.07 (0.32)	*0.00*	-0.07 (0.42)	*0.00*	0.23 (0.50)	*0.00*

"Pleasure", "Arousal" and "Dominance" with their standard deviation (in brackets). Also, the initial values of the emotional states used during the speech synthesis procedure for the stimuli implementation is presented (Tables 2-5, named as "Target Value").

We observe that "Arousal" dimension was perceived as intended in both pseudo-sentences (Greek stimuli). The only exception was noticed in Table 2, emotional state B. In the "Pleasure" dimension, the positive valued states were not perceived as intended contrary to negative ones. The "Dominance" dimension did not have the desired results. It is worth noting that for both "Pleasure" and "Arousal' dimensions, neutral state was correctly perceived.

The results for the English pseudo-sentences were slightly worse than those presented for the Greek language. There is a consistency; that "Arousal" dimension was better perceived than "Pleasure" and "Dominance".

Table 4. Average values with their corresponding standard deviation for each emotional state on the Pleasure, Arousal and Dominance dimensions for the English pseudo-sentence #1

English pseudo-sentence #1						
Emotional State	**Pleasure (SD)**	**Target Value**	**Arousal (SD)**	**Target Value**	**Dominance (SD)**	**Target Value**
A	0.10 (0.28)	*-0.51*	-0.07 (0.37)	*0.59*	0.37 (0.58)	*0.25*
B	-0.10 (0.39)	*-0.60*	-0.30 (0.49)	*0.35*	0.23 (0.50)	*0.11*
C	0.20 (0.32)	*-0.64*	0.23 (0.46)	*0.60*	0.33 (0.62)	*-0.43*
D	-0.10 (0.47)	*0.81*	0.67 (0.31)	*0.51*	-0.13 (0.69)	*0.46*
E	-0.53 (0.35)	*-0.63*	-0.67 (0.56)	*-0.27*	0.10 (0.66)	*-0.33*
F	0.00 (0.46)	*0.40*	0.70 (0.37)	*0.67*	-0.20 (0.59)	*-0.13*
G	0.03 (0.35)	*0.74*	-0.33 (0.41)	*-0.13*	0.23 (0.59)	*0.03*
H	0.20 (0.53)	*0.87*	0.57 (0.37)	*0.54*	0.00 (0.82)	*-0.18*
I	0.00 (0.27)	*0.68*	-0.30 (0.49)	*-0.46*	0.13 (0.64)	*0.06*
J	-0.83 (0.31)	*-0.65*	-0.57 (0.56)	*-0.62*	-0.20 (0.80)	*-0.33*
Neutral	-0.10 (0.21)	*0.00*	-0.13 (0.40)	*0.00*	0.20 (0.59)	*0.00*

Table 5. Average values with their corresponding standard deviation for each emotional state on the Pleasure, Arousal and Dominance dimensions for the English pseudo-sentence #2

English pseudo-sentence #2						
Emotional State	**Pleasure (SD)**	**Target Value**	**Arousal (SD)**	**Target Value**	**Dominance (SD)**	**Target Value**
A	-0.10 (0.28)	*-0.51*	-0.03 (0.48)	*0.59*	0.17 (0.52)	*0.25*
B	-0.17 (0.41)	*-0.60*	-0.37 (0.55)	*0.35*	0.27 (0.62)	*0.11*
C	0.07 (0.46)	*-0.64*	0.17 (0.59)	*0.60*	0.23 (0.53)	*-0.43*
D	0.17 (0.56)	*0.81*	0.70 (0.32)	*0.51*	0.00 (0.82)	*0.46*
E	-0.50 (0.46)	*-0.63*	-0.67 (0.36)	*-0.27*	0.03 (0.69)	*-0.33*
F	-0.17 (0.56)	*0.40*	0.53 (0.40)	*0.67*	-0.03 (0.72)	*-0.13*
G	-0.23 (0.37)	*0.74*	-0.37 (0.44)	*-0.13*	0.13 (0.58)	*0.03*
H	0.00 (0.42)	*0.87*	0.67 (0.41)	*0.54*	0.00 (0.73)	*-0.18*
I	-0.33 (0.45)	*0.68*	-0.40 (0.43)	*-0.46*	0.20 (0.41)	*0.06*
J	-0.70 (0.37)	*-0.65*	-0.87 (0.23)	*-0.62*	-0.10 (0.74)	*-0.33*
Neutral	-0.37 (0.40)	*0.00*	-0.30 (0.49)	*0.00*	0.30 (0.59)	*0.00*

4 Conclusions

In this study, we introduce a novel experimental approach towards the evaluation of emotional prosodic models in Expressive Speech Synthesis. This approach is based on the dimensional emotion expressivity and adopts the Self-Assessment Manikin Test. We apply this experimental approach to evaluate the emotional prosodic model, proposed by Schröder [11], for the Greek expressive Text-to-Speech synthesis. We used two pseudo-sentences for each of the Greek and English HMM-based synthetic voices, implemented in the MARY TtS platform. Fifteen native Greek participants were asked to assess eleven emotional states for each sentence.

According to Schröder's results [11] we expected that the best perceived dimension is "Arousal" followed by "Pleasure". In the same study the "Dominance" dimension was not investigated. The preliminary results indicated that "Arousal" dimension was perceived as intended by the participants for both Greek and English pseudo-sentences. "Pleasure" and "Dominance" dimensions were not perceived as accurately as "Arousal". A noticeable result was that Greek pseudo-sentences in the "Pleasure" dimension with positive values were perceived as negative. In contrast, the neutral state for both "Pleasure" and "Arousal" in the Greek version was perceived correctly (especially the first pseudo-sentence).

The proposed experimental approach can also be applied to the study of the degree of speaker's emotional state perception, combining the semantic channel (emotions deriving from text's content) and expressive speech synthesis (ESS). Furthermore, a future implementation would be the adaptation of interaction during the experiment e.g. blind and/or low-vision participants using the haptic modality. This would facilitate to investigate how participants with visual impairment, including blindness, perceive the emotional states through the acoustic channel, using prosodic variations and/or content's semantic information.

Acknowledgements. This research has been co-financed by the European Union (European Social Fund – ESF) and Greek national funds through the Operational Program "Education and Lifelong Learning" of the National Strategic Reference Framework (NSRF) under the Research Funding Project: "THALIS-University of Macedonia- KAIKOS: Audio and Tactile Access to Knowledge for Individuals with Visual Impairments", MIS 380442.

References

1. Tatham, M., Morton, K.: Expression in Speech: Analysis and Synthesis. Oxford Linguistics, Oxford University Press (2006)
2. Campbell, N., Hamza, W., Hoge, H., Tao, J., Bailly, G.: Editorial Special Section on Expressive Speech Synthesis. IEEE Transactions on Audio, Speech, and Language Processing 14(4), 1097–1098 (2006)
3. Kouroupetroglou, G.: Incorporating Typographic, Logical and Layout Knowledge of Documents into Text-to-Speech. In: Encarnacao, P., Azevedo, L., Gelderblom, G.-J., Newell, A., Mathieassen, N.-E. (eds.) Assistive Technology: From Research to Practice, Proceedings of the 12th European AAATE Conference, Vilamoura, Portugal, September 19-22, pp. 708–713. IOS Press (2013), doi:10.3233/978-1-61499-304-9-708
4. Kouroupetroglou, G., Tsonos, D.: Multimodal Accessibility of Documents. In: Advances in Human-Computer Interaction, pp. 451–470. I-Tech Education and Publishing, Vienna (2008)
5. Kouroupetroglou, G., Tsonos, D., Vlahos, E.: DocEmoX: A System for the Typography-Derived Emotional Annotation of Documents. In: Stephanidis, C. (ed.) UAHCI 2009, Part III. LNCS, vol. 5616, pp. 550–558. Springer, Heidelberg (2009)
6. Freitas, D., Kouroupetroglou, G.: Speech Technologies for Blind and Low Vision Persons. Technology and Disability 20, 135–156 (2008)
7. Tsonos, D., Kouroupetroglou, G., Deligiorgi, D.: Regression Modeling of Reader's Emotions Induced by Font Based Text Signals. In: Stephanidis, C., Antona, M. (eds.) UAHCI 2013, Part II. LNCS, vol. 8010, pp. 434–443. Springer, Heidelberg (2013)
8. Abelin, A., Allwood, J.: Cross Linguistic Interpretation of Expressions of Emotions. In: Proceedings of the 8th Simposio Internactional de Communicacion Social, pp. 387–393 (2003)
9. Scherer, K.R., Banse, R., Wallbott, H.G.: Emotion Inferences from Vocal Expression Correlate Across Languages and Cultures. Journal of Cross-Cultural Psychology 32(1), 76–92 (2001)
10. Pell, M., Paulmann, S., Dara, C., Alasseri, A., Kotz, S.: Factors in the Recognition of Vocally Expressed Emotions: A comparison of Four Languages. Journal of Phonetics 37(4), 417–435 (2009)
11. Schröder, M.: Expressing degree of activation in synthetic speech. IEEE Transactions on Audio, Speech and Language Processing 14(4), 1128–1136 (2006)
12. Schröder, M., Trouvain, J.: The German Text-to-Speech Synthesis System MARY: A Tool for Research, Development and Teaching. International Journal of Speech Technology 6, 365–377 (2003)
13. Pammi, S., Charfuelan, M., Schröder, M.: Multilingual Voice Creation Toolkit for the MARY TTS Platform. In: Proceedings of the International Conference on language Resources and Evaluation (LREC), pp. 3750–3756 (2010)

14. Schröder, M., Charfuelan, M., Pammi, S., Steiner, I.: Open source voice creation toolkit for the MARY TTS Platform. In: Proc. of the 12th Conference of the International Speech Communication Association (INTERSPEECH), pp. 3253–3256 (2011)
15. Fakotakis, N.: Corpus Design, Recording and Phonetic Analysis of Greek Emotional Database. In: Proceedings of the International Conference on language Resources and Evaluation (LREC), pp. 1391–1394 (2004)
16. Kostoulas, T., Ganchev, T., Mporas, I., Fakotakis, N.: A real-world emotional speech corpus for modern Greek. In: Proceedings of the International Conference on language Resources and Evaluation (LREC), pp. 2676–2680 (2008)
17. Lazaridis, A., Mporas, I.: Evaluation of Hidden Semi-Markov Models Training Methods for Greek Emotional Text-to-Speech Synthesis. International Journal of Information Technology and Computer Science 05(04), 23–29 (2013)
18. Bradley, M.M., Lang, P.J.: Measuring emotion: The self-assessment manikin and the semantic differential. Journal of Behavior Therapy and Experimental Psychiatry 25(1), 49–59 (1994)
19. Scherer, K.R.: What are emotions? And how can they be measured? Social Science Information 44(4), 695–729 (2005)
20. Russell, J.A., Mehrabian, A.: Evidence for a three-factor theory of emotions. Journal of Research in Personality 11(3), 273–294 (1977)
21. Kouroupetroglou, G., Papatheodorou, N., Tsonos, D.: Design and Development Methodology for the Emotional State Estimation of Verbs. In: Holzinger, A., Ziefle, M., Hitz, M., Debevc, M. (eds.) SouthCHI 2013. LNCS, vol. 7946, pp. 1–15. Springer, Heidelberg (2013)
22. Castro, S., Lima, L., Recognizing, C.F.: emotions in spoken language: A validated set of Portuguese sentences and pseudosentences for research on emotional prosody. Behavior Research Methods 42(1), 74–81 (2010)
23. OpenMARY, Emotion-to-Mary XSL, `http://mary.dfki.de/lib/emotion-to-mary.xsl/view`
24. James, A., Russell, J.A., Mehrabian, A.: Evidence for a three-factor theory of emotions. Journal of Research in Personality 11(3), 273–294 (1977)
25. Banse, R., Scherer, K.R.: Acoustic profiles in vocal emotion expression. Journal of Personality and Social Psychology 70(3), 614–636 (1996)

Eye Tracking on a Paper Survey: Implications for Design

Lauren Walton[1], Jennifer C. Romano Bergstrom[2], David Charles Hawkins[2], and Christine Pierce[1]

[1] The Nielsen Company, Tampa, FL, USA
{lauren.walton,christine.pierce}@nielsen.com
[2] Fors Marsh Group, Arlington, VA, USA
{jbergstrom,dhawkins}@forsmarshgroup.com

Abstract. Asking respondents to record their activity in a diary can be a difficult task due to retrospective reporting and cognitive burden as well as the complexity of the data collection tool. Diary questionnaires typically require multiple pieces of information including demographics, activities, and duration over a data collection period. Like other questionnaire types, visual design principles can be used to help people perceive and understand what is being asked of them during diary measurement. Eye tracking, a technology that allows us to passively study people's eye movements, has been used mostly for questionnaire testing within the survey research field. This study focuses on using eye tracking and other user experience measures to analyze how respondents perceive, understand and experience different designs of the paper Nielsen TV Diary. We used eye tracking to gain insights into visual elements that draw attention, the amount of text that respondents read (e.g., terms/instructions), and how respondents complete the survey. This paper centers on the collecting and analyzing of qualitative and quantitative measures of the user experience, including eye-tracking data (e.g., fixation count, time to fixate), participants' verbalizations, self-reported satisfaction, and performance data (e.g., accuracy, steps to complete). We also provide recommendations about the design of the paper diary based on the user experience and eye-tracking results.

Keywords: Eye tracking, survey, diary, visual design, usability.

1 Introduction

1.1 Diary Research

Survey researchers are continuously trying to understand how design decisions impact data quality and with it, total survey error [1]. Changes to a survey's design may affect the representativeness of the data collected because design may encourage or discourage people from responding. Each survey is unique, as are the visual stimuli given to respondents. The survey response process for self-administered surveys begins with the respondent's perception of the survey materials. Traditional pretesting methods like cognitive interviews, think-aloud interviews, and focus groups are

C. Stephanidis and M. Antona (Eds.): UAHCI/HCII 2014, Part II, LNCS 8514, pp. 175–182, 2014.

dependent on the participant being able to tell the researcher what they are thinking or feeling. Passive methods present data and allow researchers to make inferences without the data suffering from social desirability or recall bias.

Eye tracking is a passive technology used to study people's eye movements. Recording eye movements allows researchers to infer where and for how long a participant's attention is directed. In market research, eye tracking has been used to study products that participants are drawn to while looking at grocery store shelves as well as what parts of websites people examine the most. Because people have difficulties recalling everything they look at or the order in which they examine objects, collecting eye-tracking data removes the measurement error associated with asking respondents directly. Instead, eye-tracking data can show objectively what was looked at first and how long the eyes fixated a given element.

Within the survey research literature, the library of eye-tracking research is relatively small. Eye tracking has been used to study how respondents perceive question stems, response options, and images within self-administered surveys. Current eye-tracking research mostly focuses on internet surveys and is limited to a few key papers (see [2], [3], and [4]). Redline and Lankford [2] found that participants did not read linearly, and they skipped around looking at the survey. Galesic, Tourangeau, Couper, and Conrad [4] used eye tracking as a method to understand how respondents perceive survey questions and found that participants spend more time looking at options on the top of a list of responses, and participants who took the time to read the entire response list also took the time to read the instructions and other parts of the questionnaire. Lenzner, Kaczmirek, and Galesic [5] examined if respondent comprehension is impacted by text features going beyond response time as an indicator and found that longer fixation time on question stems equate to comprehension issues. Libman and Smyth [6] looked at smiley faces as symbolic language and found that participants with low literacy levels moved faster to look at the smiley faces in the web survey. No research to date, to our knowledge, has used eye tracking to understand how respondents process and work through a paper diary survey and how much attention is given to various visual elements. This study aims to fill this gap. We used eye tracking to understand how participants perceived, processed and used various versions of a paper diary.

1.2 The Nielsen Company

The Nielsen Company is the world's leading provider of global marketing information, consumer insights, business media products, and services. The mission of Nielsen is to provide clients with the most complete understanding of consumers and markets worldwide. Nielsen has measured the television audience of the United States for over 60 years producing the Nielsen TV Ratings.

Nielsen uses both electronic and paper measurement techniques to collect viewing data. The focus of this paper is the Nielsen TV Diary (shown in Figure 1), which is a week-long survey sent to randomly selected households across the United States, using an address based sampling approach, during data collection windows known as "TV sweeps."

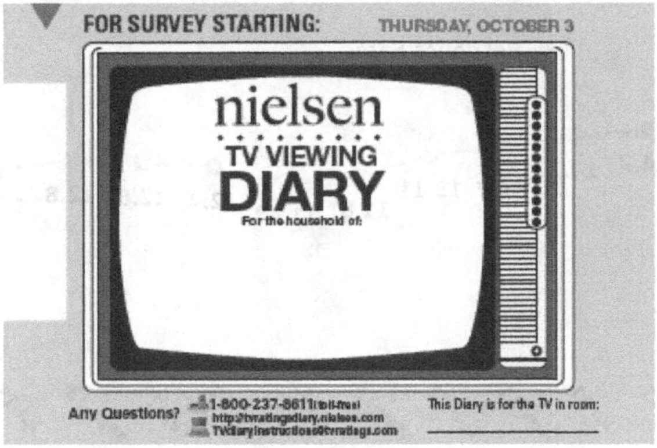

Fig. 1. Nielsen TV Diary Cover

Nielsen strives to improve the diary product through, including but not limited to, testing the optimization of household incentives, advanced sampling techniques, and improvements to survey visual design. In February 2012, Nielsen tested newly designed diary materials (Figure 2) that did not perform as well as anticipated. The new household communications utilized motivational messaging for hard to reach groups following best practices of organizations including the Hispanic / Latino Advisory Council, African American Advisory Council, U.S. Census Bureau, Scarborough Research, internal diary data analysis, and Nielsen internal best practices on recruitment and compliance for long-term panels. The communications were vetted via focus groups for confirmation with these demographic groups that the approach/messaging was appropriate, and for "red flags" with the non-targeted demographics. There was a high level of due diligence in the development of the new communications, but a significant decrease in cooperation was seen for these "New" household communications materials (16.7% vs. 18.4%, $p \leq .001$).

These new materials were used by Nielsen during February, May, and July, and were retested in November 2012. Figure 3 presents Nielsen Diary response rates over time showing a decline in response when these "New" materials were used. In order to understand these Diary materials further, Nielsen partnered with Fors Marsh Group to design an innovative study to examine these paper diaries using eye tracking. Results of this usability study are presented in this paper.

Fig. 2. Example of "Old" (left), "Bilingual New" (middle), and "English New" (right) household communication diary

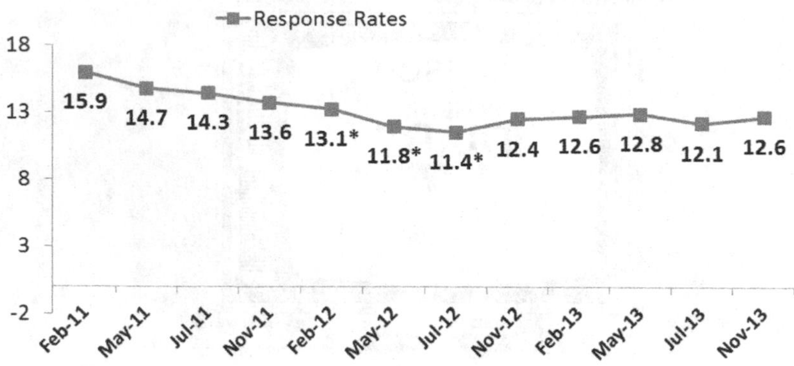

Fig. 3. Nielsen TV Diary Response Rates

*Diary measurements where "New" household communications materials were used.

2 Eye-Tracking Usability Study

Researchers used a combination of metrics to understand users' experiences while working on the diary. To assess the behavioral impact of additional changes to the diary, a fourth "Prototype" diary was also tested. The Prototype had the same cover as the Old diary (Fig. 2), did not have any motivational language, and contained some alterations to the TV recording grid.

2.1 Participants and Procedure

Seventy-four participants (29 male, 45 female) with an average age of 37 were recruited from the greater Washington DC area to take part in the usability study. Sessions took place in the Fors Marsh Group User Experience Laboratory, and each session lasted approximately one hour, during which time participants were randomly assigned to work with the "Old" diary being mailed to households, the "New" February 2012 household communications test paper diary, or the redesigned "Prototype" diary. Participants were instructed to work on the diary "as if they were at home" and to think aloud as they worked. The diary was mounted on a stand above a Tobii X2-60 eye tracker.

Upon completion of the sessions, researchers identified Areas of Interest (AOIs) and examined eye-tracking patterns for these AOIs. AOIs included various visual components of the diary that were hypothesized to increase user engagement (e.g., logo on cover, motivational language). In addition, we examined the order in which participants interacted with various components, such as reading the instructions and entering TV viewing.

Attention to the Cover Images

We used Tobii Studio to create mean fixation count heat maps to examine attention to the covers of the different diaries (shown in Figure 4). We found that the Nielsen logo was fixated less often on the cover of the "Bilingual New" and "English New" diaries than on the "Old" diary. The logo on the "Old" diary is located in the middle of the page, while on the "New" diaries it is on the bottom left. Additionally, participants' statements during debriefing interviews indicated that the television set on the "New" diaries was hard to identify – specifically, many participants said they thought the modern flat screen TV on the cover was a picture frame. When shown the "Old" diary cover, participants said it was easier to see that the "Old" cover had a TV. Thus, possible explanations for the drop in response rates for the new diary are a loss of brand recognition and lack of recognition of the TV image. Both of these issues may have led to people being less inclined to respond.

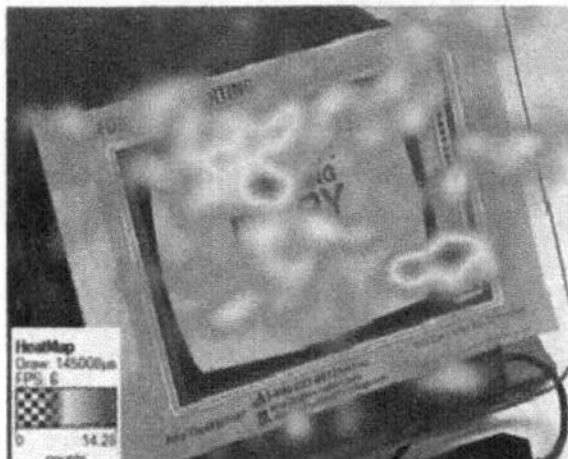
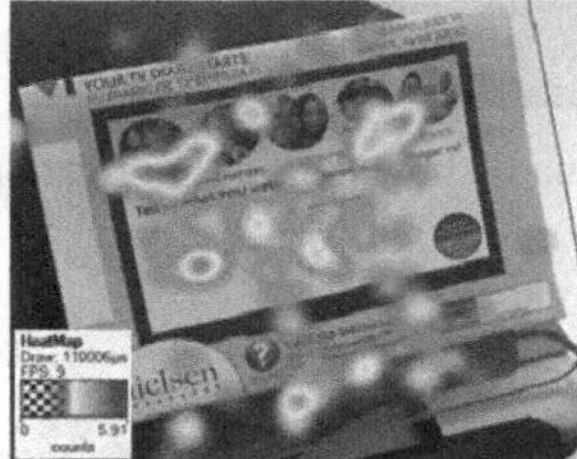

Fig. 4. Left to right: "Old," "Bilingual New," "English New" diaries. Mean fixation count heat maps show that fixations to the logo on the "New" covers were less frequent than on the "Old" cover.

Motivational Language

Much time and effort was spent making sure that motivational language was relevant for targeted demographics. However, eye-tracking data of the "New" diaries showed that the motivational language was not regularly attended to. Figure 5 shows that the motivation language (in blue circles) was not fixated as participants completed various sections. These results suggest that the messages may have been overlooked in the fielded survey, and thus, the motivational language may not have had its intended effect because it was not seen or read.

Processing the Diary Grid

It is important to test proposed design changes to evaluate whether or not the alterations will have a positive impact on performance. In this study, a redesigned "Prototype" diary (in addition to the "Old" and "New") was tested to examine a new layout of the viewing grid pages. We found that participants viewed and used the "Prototype" grid in a left-to-right progression, while attention to the "Old" Diary and "New" diary grids was less uniform and more scattered, as shown in the gaze plots in Figure 6. Eye-tracking data provided insight into the user experience of the column ordering. The first column in the "Prototype" grid asks for the name of the program; the first column in the "New" and "Old" diary grids asks for the channel number. Participants'

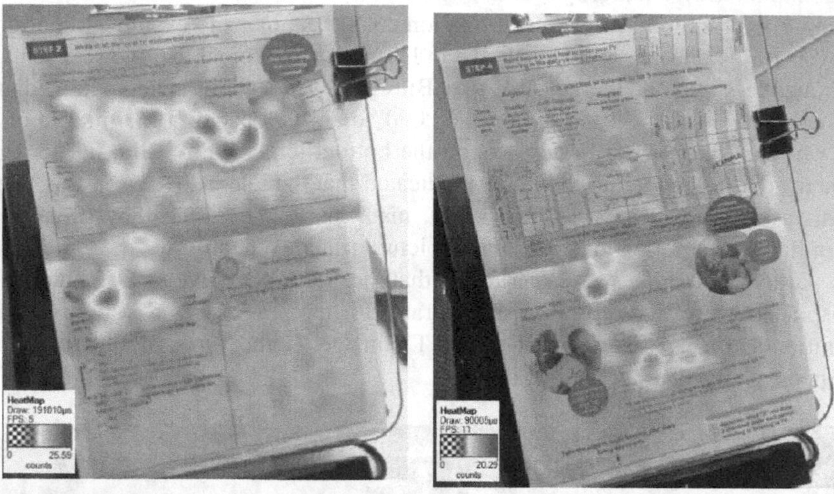

Fig. 5. Mean fixation count heat maps show that the motivational language in the blue circles was not fixated

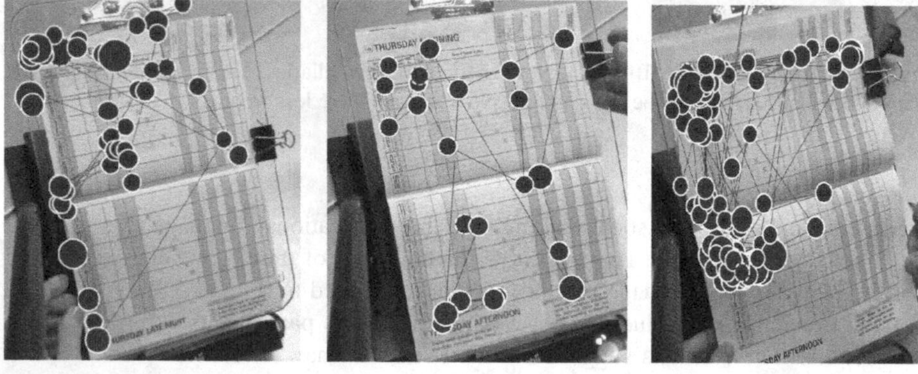

Fig. 6. Participant gaze plots for the "Old" diary grid (left) and "New" diary grid (middle) are more scattered and do not follow a left-to-right pattern like in the "Prototype" diary grid (right)

Examples are Overlooked

In Step 3 of the diary, the directions instruct respondents to report the people living in their household. An example is provided to aid in the proper and thorough reporting of all household members and any potential guests. Participants reported that the example was helpful; however, because the example is located below the form, 45% of participants did not notice the example until after they had recorded (often incorrectly) all household members (see example gaze plots in Figure 7). Results from eye tracking informed researchers that on average, 55 fixations were made on the Step 3 pages before participants noticed the example. Part of the reason why it was so

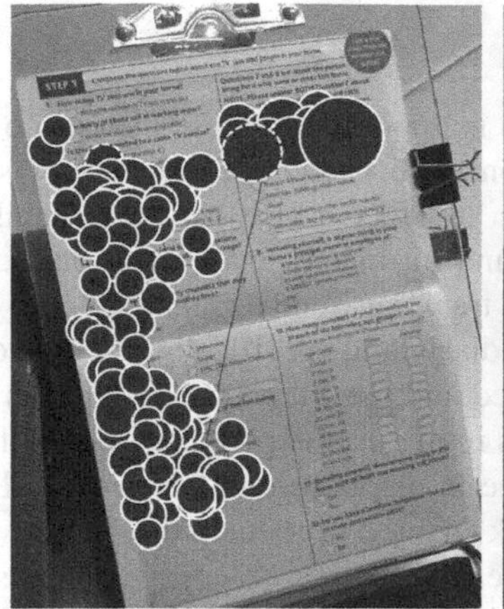
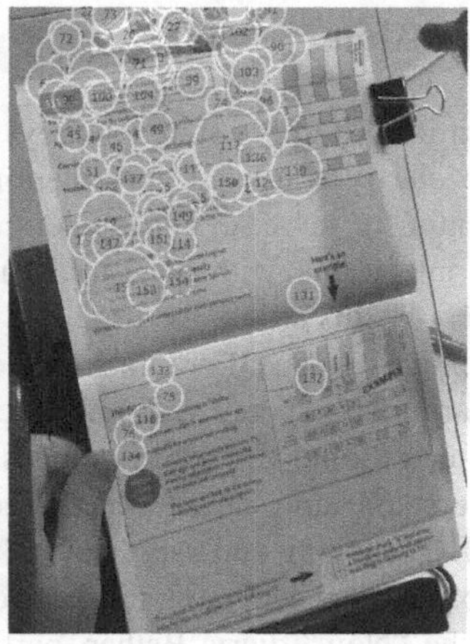

Fig. 7. Example gaze plots demonstrating the linear progression in Step 1 (left image) and the lack of linear progression in Step 3 (right image) in which the participant did not see the example at the bottom of the page until after recording housemates at the top of the page.

common for participants to miss the Step 3 example was because Steps 1 and 2 followed a linear progression. For example, in Steps 1 and 2, survey items were located on top of each other. Participants worked their way down the page as they responded to various demographic questions. The layout of instructions in Step 3 did not meet their expectations. Participants became used to the line-by-line progression and had no reason to suspect that for Step 3 they needed to examine the entire page before getting started.

Satisfaction

Each participant only worked with one version of the diary. After working with the diary and recording up to three previously viewed TV shows, participants completed a seven-item satisfaction questionnaire. We conducted paired t-tests comparing satisfaction among the diaries and found no difference in satisfaction between the "Old" and "New" diaries and between the "Old" and "Prototype" diaries. However, two differences in satisfaction were discovered when comparing the "New" diary to the "Prototype" diary. Users of the "Prototype" diary (N = 24) rated the instructions as significantly more clear than users of the "New" diary (N = 28) ($\mu = 3.45$, $\mu = 2.96$, respectively on a scale of 1 – 5; $p = .007$). Additionally, the organization and location of instructions in the "Prototype" diary (N = 24) were rated as significantly more clear than in the "New" diary (N = 28) ($\mu = 3.3$, $\mu = 3.03$, respectively; $p = .025$). The participants' perceptions of instruction clarity and organization may be related to the organization of the grid – as mentioned, the "Prototype" diary grid promoted a greater degree of left-to-right processing and visual search than the other grids.

3 Conclusion

Visual design in self-administered surveys is important because there is no interviewer present to clarify confusing information or to encourage response. Visual design has the potential to increase engagement; however it also has the capability of distracting and interfering with the survey and ultimately may affect data quality and response rates. In this study, we used eye tracking to understand the user experience of several versions of a self-administered diary, and specifically, we aimed to understand how participants perceived, processed and used the various versions of a paper diary. We aimed to understand differences in the user experience of the different versions to understand more about the decline in response rate that previously occurred in the field. Eye tracking and user feedback enabled us to learn that images (e.g., logo, TV) and motivational language did not lead to increased engagement, as had been intended in the "New" diary. Rather, participants did not pay attention to these elements and/or did not recognize them (e.g., the TV). These findings suggest that graphics and images should only be used when they supply meaning, and that including them to encourage motivation and engagement [7] is not always successful. We learned that participants process TV viewing information in a very specific way, and the "Prototype" diary TV viewing grid that was organized in a way that matched users' mental models was processed more efficiently. Based on these findings, Nielsen is testing the "Prototype" diary grid design, mailing it to thousands of homes during the February 2014 diary sweep in the hopes of minimizing respondent burden while optimizing respondent reporting. We are looking forward to results in Spring 2014.

References

1. Groves, R.M., Lyberg, L.: Total survey error: Past, present, and future. Public Opinion Quarterly 74(5), 849–879 (2010)
2. Redline, C.D., Lankford, C.P.: Eye-movement analysis: A new tool for evaluating the design of visually administered instruments (paper and web). In: Proceedings of the Section on Survey Research Methods, American Statistical Association. Paper presented at 2001 AAPOR Annual Conference, Montreal, Quebec, Canada (2001)
3. Graesser, A.C., Cai, Z., Louwerse, M.M., Daniel, F.: Question understanding aid (quaid) a web facility that tests question comprehensibility. Public Opinion Quarterly 70(1), 3–22 (2006)
4. Galesic, M., Tourangeau, R., Couper, M.P., Conrad, F.G.: Eye-tracking data new insights on response order effects and other cognitive shortcuts in survey responding. Public Opinion Quarterly 72(5), 892–913 (2008)
5. Lenzner, T., Kaczmirek, L., Galesic, M.: Seeing through the eyes of the respondent: An eye-tracking study on survey question comprehension. International Journal of Public Opinion Research 23(3), 361–373 (2011)
6. Libman, A., Smyth, J.: Turn that frown up-side down: The use of smiley faces as symbolic language in self-administered surveys. Paper presented at 2012 AAPOR Annual Conference, Orlando, Florida (May 2012)
7. Manfreda, K.L., Batagelj, Z., Vehovar, V.: Design of web survey questionnaires: Three basic experiments. Journal of Computer-Mediated Communications 7(3) (2002)

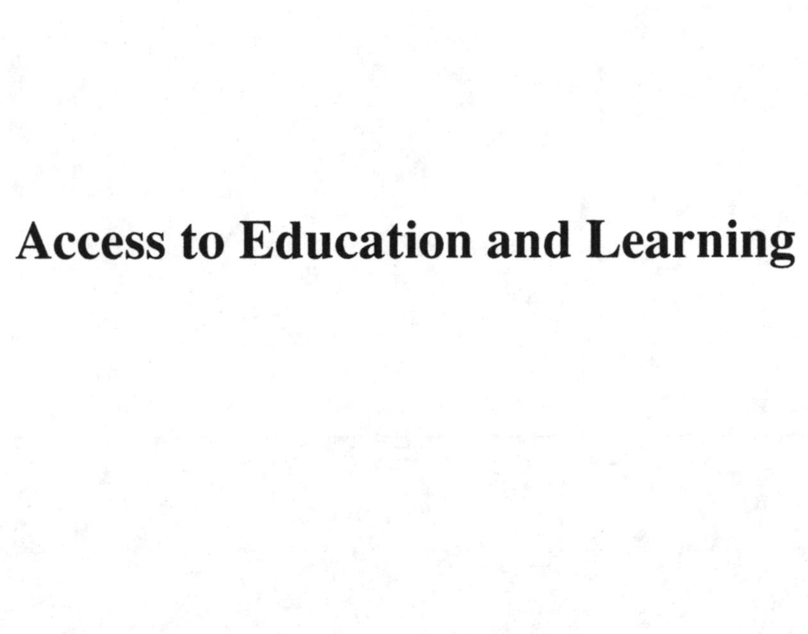

Access to Education and Learning

Can Evaluation Patterns Enable End Users to Evaluate the Quality of an e-learning System? An Exploratory Study

Carmelo Ardito[1], Rosa Lanzilotti[1], Marcin Sikorski[2], and Igor Garnik[2]

[1] Computer Science Department, University of Bari Aldo Moro, Italy
{carmelo.ardito,rosa.lanzilotti}@uniba.it
[2] Faculty of Management and Economics, Gdansk University of Technology, Poland
{msik,igar}@zie.pg.gda.pl

Abstract. This paper presents the results of an exploratory study whose main aim is to verify if the Pattern-Based (PB) inspection technique enables end users to perform reliable evaluation of e-learning systems in real work-related settings. The study involved 13 Polish and Italian participants, who did not have an HCI background, but used e-learning platforms for didactic and/or administrative purposes. The study revealed that the participants were able to effectively and efficiently apply the PB inspection technique with minimum effort. However, in some cases, participants complained that, in some cases, the technique appeared time demanding. This work provides some valuable suggestions to redesign the evaluation tools of the PB technique, in order to improve the focus on specific elements of the e-learning system and to streamline better the evaluation process.

Keywords: usability, inspection technique, exploratory study.

1 Introduction

Internet and the recent developments in information technology have provided huge opportunities for education making *e-learning* one of the most used means for long-term personal and business education. Thus, practitioners working to the development of e-learning systems are required to create software tools that are both able to engage learners and to support their learning. This means that, as for any interactive system, usability is a primary requirement.

Evaluation of e-learning systems deserves special attention and usability inspectors need effective evaluation methods, which can be easily applied with delivering reliable outcomes. Literature reports various studies comparing analytical approach with usability testing in order to establish which approach is better. The results are contradictory, especially related to the relative power of different evaluation techniques in terms of problem count, severity rating and time requirements. They suggest that different techniques have strengths and weaknesses, and therefore should be used in combination [1, 2, 3].

C. Stephanidis and M. Antona (Eds.): UAHCI/HCII 2014, Part II, LNCS 8514, pp. 185–196, 2014.

In e-learning domain, analytical methods have been proved to be the most adopted evaluation approach [4, 5, 6, 7]. This is due to the fact that such methods are cost-saving: 1) they do not require the involvement of final users and special equipment or lab facilities; 2) experts can detect a wide range of problems of complex systems in a limited amount of time [8]. On the other hand, analytical approach highly depends on the inspectors' skills and experience, as heuristics are often generic and underspecified [9, 10].

To counteract this problem, there is a need to provide tools able to guide inspectors, even not expert in usability engineering, in performing evaluations with objective and reliable outcomes. An inspection technique, named *Pattern-Based Inspection* (PB inspection) has been proposed; it exploits a set of *Evaluation Patterns* (EPs) to systematically drive inspectors in their evaluation activities [11]. Studies carried out to demonstrate the validity of a such inspection technique confirmed the effectiveness of the patterns to evaluate interactive systems in different domains (e.g. multimedia [12], e-learning [11]). In particular, Lanzilotti et al. in [11] present the results of comparative study aimed at investigating whether patterns can help "novice" inspectors. The study demonstrated that patterns improved evaluation on a number of measurement qualities, including reliability, validity, effective range, design impact and cost. An important result was that patterns have the potential to reduce the dependency on the inspector's skills and experience, thus simplifying the inspection process for newcomers. The authors in [11] wrote: "An obvious limitation [of the study] regards the nature of the sample and the evaluation context. More research is needed to understand how these findings extend to real work-related settings."

This paper reports the results of an exploratory study performed in a real context in order to verify if and how the EPs help end users, who use e-learning platforms in their work but do not have an HCI background, in assessing the quality of such educational tools. The participants discovered the more serious usability problems of the platform. They were able to apply the method and to perform the inspection with minimum effort. They found the PB inspection easy to learn, efficient, pleasant and reliable, even if in some extent time demanding. Despite it was a small-scale study, it delivered a set of valuable improvement suggestions, useful for further refinement of the PB inspection technique.

The paper has the following organization. Section 2 illustrates the role of usability processes and methods within the software life cycle. Section 3 briefly illustrates the PB inspection. Section 4 reports the exploratory study and Section 5 closes the paper.

2 Usability in the Software Lifecycle

Nowadays, Information and Communication Technology is providing everybody with the possibility of interacting with software systems for accomplishing tasks of their daily working activities and/or for pure entertaining. As a consequence, current software systems must provide enhanced user interfaces that support users to achieve their goals with *effectiveness, efficiency* and *satisfaction* in their context of use. In other words, an interactive system should be *usable*. Thus, practitioners are required to develop user interfaces, whose quality is primarily evaluated from the users' point of view. Usability Engineering Methods (UEMs) have to be applied in order to allow practitioners to understand who will be the users of the software system, the tasks they need to accomplish, the context in which they work.

Although documented benefits of UEMs exist [3], practitioners devote scarce attention to it with the result that most software systems are very hard to use. Traditionally, practitioners are trained to judge software system by criteria, such as efficiency of code or flexibility of the programs, which have little to do with the users' needs. UEMs are applied only to a limited extent by practitioners, as shown in [14, 15, 16, 17, 18]. In particular, the results of a study we have carried out to understand how UEMs are addressed in current practices showed that still today too many companies neglect these important quality factors. Once again, the study confirmed that many companies complained that UEMs are very much resource demanding and that no methods suitable to companies' needs exist.

The gap between theory and practice has been studied by several researchers and several solutions have been suggested. In particular, Höök and Löwgren in [19] proposed a middle territory, called *intermediate-level knowledge,* in which the knowledge constructed through the interaction design practices exists. It is more abstracted than particular instances, yet does not aspire to the generality of a theory. This knowledge assumes different forms, such as guidelines, patterns, annotated portfolios, etc. The EPs, as they have been defined, can be considered a specific type of the intermediate-level knowledge, since they capture the knowledge of skilled inspectors and express it in a precise and understandable form so that this knowledge can be reproduced, communicated and exploited by other people.

With the aim to define a usability method enabling novice and not professional evaluators to perform reliable evaluation, the PB inspection has been proposed. Lanzilotti et al. in [11] presented a study whose results showed that EPs provide a systematic framework, which has the potential to reduce the dependency on the evaluator's skills and experience, increases inter-rater reliability and output standardization, permits discovering a larger set of different problems and decreases evaluation cost.

3 An Inspection Technique to Evaluate e-learning Systems

The Pattern-based inspection (or PB inspection) was defined with the aim to identify an inspection technique able to exploit the advantages of the inspection techniques (i.e. they are cost-saving, do not require any special equipment, nor lab facilities) and overcome their major drawbacks (i.e. dependence on the inspectors' skills and experience, heuristics driving the evaluation are often too generic and not adequate to inform the activities of less experienced evaluators). The EPs provide a structured guidance to the evaluators performing the inspection of an interactive application. As demonstrated in [11], EPs are able to provide support to novice inspectors. Furthermore, using the precise terminology suggested by the patterns, the resulting evaluation reports are more consistent and easier to compare.

Table 1. An example of evaluation pattern of quality in use category

QU_27: Availability of course evaluation tools

Focus of action: course evaluation tools (e.g. evaluation test, exercises, etc.)

Intent: verify the availability of course evaluation tools

Activity prompts: Using the evaluation tools:

- Change an answer, after you entered an answer
- Do not answer to some questions
- Repeat the same test several times
- Check if the evaluation tool considers all the theoretical aspects presented in the course
- Use again the evaluation tool to determine if the test result is updated
- Verify if the obtained results are explicative

Output: a description reporting if:

- The evaluation tools are not available
- It is difficult to identify and use an evaluation tool, that is:
  - It is not possible to modify an answer
  - It is not possible to not give an answer to some questions
  - It is not possible to use the evaluation tool again and again
- The evaluation tool does not consider all the theoretical aspects presented in the course
- The student's improvements are not updated
- The evaluation tool is not explicative

Table 2. An example of evaluation pattern of the educational quality category

EQ_05: Quality of the authoring tools

Focus of action: authoring tools that allow lecturers to provide didactic material

Intent: evaluating the authoring tools

Activity prompts: choose an authoring tool:

- Modify/update a document already available
- Create a new document, also testing all the available functions
- Check if an appropriate feedback about the procedure is provided
- When the document has been created, verify if the result complies with the expectations

Output: a description reporting:

- If the authoring tool is not available
- If important functions are not available
- If modifying/updating a document is not easy
- Which are the difficulties in inserting new documents

The PB inspection is a general method, applicable to the evaluation of any interactive system, provided that a proper set of EPs is defined. Different sets of EPs have been defined, i.e. for hypermedia system [12], for virtual reality systems [20], and e-learning system [11]. EPs are formulated by an iterative approach that consists of the following four phases: a) Observations of evaluators at work, focusing on their main activities; b) Observations of end users using the system; c) Reviews of literature in the domain of the system; d) Executions of brainstorming sessions with professional evaluators and domain experts. During such sessions, an initial set of EPs is identified by considering all the gathered information. This set is then tested through pilot studies asking novice evaluators to use them and provide comments about their clarity, utility, guidance, etc. Based on these comments, the patterns were refined iteratively.

Each pattern is formulated by means of a common template composed of 5 items: 1) the *Classification Code and Title* that identify the pattern; 2) the *Focus of Action,* that indicates the application components to be evaluated by it; 3) the *Intent,* which clarifies the specific goals to be achieved through the pattern application; 4) the *Activity Prompts,* which prompts the activities to be performed by evaluators; 5) the *Output,* which suggests a standardized terminology that inspectors has to use for reporting the inspection results. Evaluators choose the set of EPs to be used during the inspection by reading the first three elements of the pattern template, i.e. *title, focus of action* and *intent.* The patterns were carried out one at a time. Inspectors perform the activities suggested by the *activity prompts* and report their finding according to the *output.*

The set of EPs considered in this study has been defined to evaluate e-learning systems. It consists of 69 EPs, divided in two broad categories: *quality in use*, consisting of 33 patterns, deals with technological and interaction characteristics of the system (an example is in Table 1); *educational quality*, consisting of 36 patterns, refers to the degree to which a system supports effective teaching and learning (an example is in Table 2).

4 The Exploratory Study

In the following sub-sections we illustrate the method adopted to verify if and how the EPs can help people, who use e-learning platforms in their work but do not have an HCI background, in assessing the quality of such educational tools. The method follows the one of the study reported in [11].

4.1 Participants and Design

A total of 13 participants evaluated the EDUX platform described in Section 4.3. They were university lecturers, who used e-learning platforms in their courses, and university administrative staff members, whose role was to manage through the e-learning platform students' profiles and learning material provided by professors. They never had any previous experience in evaluating any software systems. 9 out of 13 participants performed the evaluation in a quiet research laboratory of the Faculty of Management and Economics of the Gdansk University of Technology. The remaining 4 participants were Italian participants, having the same role as their Polish counterparts; they performed the evaluation of EDUX in a laboratory of the Department of the Computer Science of the University of Bari.

4.2 Procedure

A couple of days before the study session, a training session of about thirty minutes introduced participants with the EPs to be used for evaluating EDUX platform. Then, they participated in a thirty-minute demonstration of the platform. A few summary indications about the platform content and its main functions were introduced, without providing too many details. Data were collected in a group setting, but every participant worked individually. The study consisted of two experimental sessions lasting three hours each. During the first session, participants evaluated the EDUX platform applying eight EPs that, in our previous studies, had been demonstrated an adequate number for an experimental session lasting three hours (see Table 3). The selected EPs mainly addressed the operational activities permitted by the platform that are the significant aspects to which academics are interested for evaluating if a platform is adequate to their needs. The EPs were essential to guide inspectors in the analysis of the main application elements of the e-learning platform.

Table 3. The eight evaluation patterns tested in the study

Code	*Title*
QU_01	Availability of communication tools
QU_02	Quality of the graphical interface elements
QU_27	Availability of course evaluation tools
QU_06	Ease of use of the system
QU_08	Errors management
QU_20	Availability and quality of the help
EQ_24	Topic prerequisites[1]
EQ_05	Quality of the authoring tools

Participants had to find usability problems and to record them on a booklet. The booklet was composed of 8 evaluation forms, each one for an EP, where the participant had to indicate the start time and end time of execution of the EP, the number of the discovered and a description of the problems detected through the specific EP, where they occurred, and a proposal of design solution to the problem. Only after the participants had applied all the EPs, they had to assign a rating from 1 to 5 to each problem (1 = Slight, 5 = Catastrophic). A day after, each evaluator was asked to type their discovered problems in an electronic form. This was required in order to avoid readability problems during data analysis. At the end of the second session, participants were invited to fill in the evaluator-satisfaction questionnaire also proposed in the other studies in which the PB inspection was tested [11, 12]. Differently from the other study, in this case, the participants participated in additional focus group aimed at gathering subjective feedback from the evaluators on the PB inspection technique.

[1] Topic prerequisites: compulsory topics for understanding the course content.

4.3 The e-learning Platform

The EDUX e-learning platform has been used for a few years in the Polish-Japanese Institute of Information Technology in Warsaw, Poland. It was developed as an internal project by the IT staff of the Institute and it was intended to support both distance learning and regular courses.

The EDUX platform is now quite expanded, covering many modules typical for this type of systems (e.g. uploading lectures and exercises, executing evaluation tests, assessment of students' progress, etc.). Assigning students to specific courses is the duty of system administrators, while other activities - as configuring specific course modules and updating the content - belong to the teachers. Unfortunately, only a small part of the EDUX's capabilities is used in practice. The lecturers usually use EDUX only as a repository of teaching materials, therefore communication functions of the system have been used to a very small extent.

In order to discover reasons of such a situation (and to evaluate user experience of EDUX considered as an internal on-line service [21]) a questionnaire survey was conducted among faculty and students of the Institute in the mid-2013, well before this PB study was started. The survey revealed that in addition to complaints about usability problems, in fact very few teachers used this platform, as it was not compulsory, moreover no training was provided and on-line help was very limited. The survey also showed that the graphical user interface of EDUX is unclear and the interaction is not intuitive. Respondents indicated that the purpose of some modules was unclear, there was ambiguous and inconsistent labelling of icons, names, etc., as well as many modules had rather similar functionality, so they seemed to be redundant.

The results of the survey were forwarded to EDUX's developers, but they have not yet implemented the changes. Therefore, because the EDUX system has still many visible usability flaws, it was considered as a suitable object for testing the PB inspection technique. Moreover, some additional factors supported this choice:

- Experiment participants (both from Gdansk and from Bari) had no previous contact with the evaluated system, hence no prior experience bias had to be considered;
- The user interface of EDUX at the first glance seems transparent and appealing, and its basic functions seemingly are easy to use and encouraging for novice users;
- Formerly identified usability problems are easily perceptible even by non-experienced users in very simple operations, and – most importantly - are not critical for completing evaluators' task scenarios, what supports the idea of using EDUX for PB inspection experiment;
- Serious usability problems arise only in more complex operations, which were not included in the scope of this study.

It was also very important that due to rather easy start provided for novices in EDUX, the participants were able to perform their testing tasks within the PB inspection experiment without any previous training.

As a result, the EDUX system was found as a very convenient object to be evaluated by novice experts with PB inspection technique, whose verification was the primary main objective of this experiment.

4.4 Data Coding

Two expert usability evaluators independently examined all the electronic forms in order to identify single and unique usability problems. The inter-rater reliability was .75 and all differences were solved by discussion.

4.5 Results and Discussion

The analysis of the data collected during the study identified 115 unique problems and 31 non problems, i.e. statements reported in the evaluator's booklet containing not understandable content or unverifiable information.

Usability problems were classified into 4 categories: 1) *graphical design*, i.e. adverse comments on aesthetic aspects of the interface; 2) *feedback*, i.e. problems in the dialogue, mediated by the interface, between the user and the platform; 3) *navigation*, i.e. problems referred to the appropriateness of mechanisms for accessing information and for getting oriented in the system; 4) *functionality*, i.e. problems related to functions need to support the fruition of online courses but are not present. Table 4 reports frequencies and percentages of these categories.

Table 4. Frequency and percentage of usability problems classified by category

Category	*F*	*%*
Graphical design	40	35%
Feedback	22	19%
Navigation	17	15%
Functionality	36	31%
Total	115	100%

Participants frequently addressed the poor graphical design of the platform; they complained about confusing field names, too intense colors, inconsistent icons, etc. The platform often does not give any feedback during critical tasks, for example, at the end of the authoring of a quiz. The lack of tooltips makes it impossible to interpret the meaning of inappropriate icons. Navigation is hampered by a confusing navigational menu.

Table 5 reports the distribution of the problems in the five severity categories that were based on the coding of the two experts that coded the data. The most serious problems reported by the evaluators where related to the difficulties experienced using tools which are fundamental in a e-learning platform. For example, they reported that the authoring tool for creating and managing online tests had severe problems: adding or removing questions, limited types of questions, previewing authored tests, results management.

Table 5. Distribution of problems in the five severity categories

Severity 1 ***Not serious at all***	***Severity 2***	***Severity 3***	***Severity 4***	***Severity 5*** ***Very severe***
13	27	43	30	2

A thoroughness index was analysed to verify the completeness of the evaluation results with respect to the total number of real usability problems affecting the system [22]. This value was computed by the following formula:

$$Thoroughness = Mean\frac{P_i}{P_t}$$

where P_i is the number of problems found by the i-th inspector, and P_t is the total number of problems existing in the application (n = 115). The thoroughness index was 0.12 (std dev = 0.04) was very low. This is due to the high variability of the problems discovered by each participant and the many problems present in the platform. However, it can be considered a good result if it is compared to the PB inspection thoroughness index reported in [11], i.e. 0.09. This showed that even if evaluators are non expert in HCI discipline, they are able to perform reliable usability evaluation through the use of EPs, as novice evaluators could do.

Participants carried out the 8 EPs worked on average 73 minutes. This result is very different from that reported in [23], i.e. 177 minutes. In our opinion, this difference can be explained by two reasons. The first one is related to the *motivation* that stimulated people in participating in the study. Participants of the study reported in [23] were students of an HCI course who participated in the experiment as part of their course-work for an advanced HCI course. During that study we observed a sort of competition among the three groups involved. Each group used a specific usability evaluation technique, i.e. PB inspection, heuristic inspection, and user testing, to evaluate an e-learning platform. Thus, each group wanted to do right. Furthermore, during that study we observed a sort of competition among the three groups: they wanted to discover as many problems as possible to demonstrate the primacy of the technique they were adopting. In the current study, the participants' final goal was to decide if the platform was adequate or not to their needs and they stopped applying each EP when they believed that they had enough information about a specific aspect.

However, the efficiency index, which reflected the average number of problems each participant found in 10 minutes, was 1.43 (std dev = 0.47). Again, this can be considered a good result, since the efficiency index reported in [23] was 1.19. Thus, even if participants spent on average less time, the results of their evaluation are considerable. The efficiency was measured also through the cost-benefit curve, proposed by Nielsen and Landauer [24], which analyzes the minimal number of evaluators for a reliable evaluation. In our study, 5 evaluators were able to find the 30% of the problems (see Fig. 1). In [11], 5 evaluators applying heuristics specific for

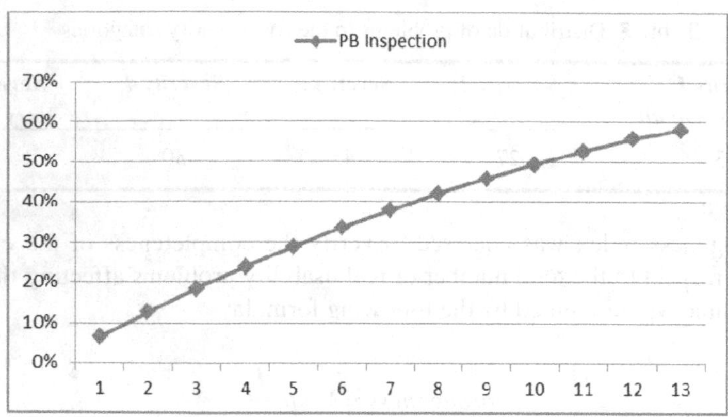

Fig. 1. The cost-benefit curve for the PB inspection

e-learning systems, discovered about the 22% of the problems. This demonstrates that EPs reduced the dependency on the evaluators' skills and experience which affects all the inspection methods.

The participants' satisfaction was assessed by both the data collected with the questionnaire administered at the end of the evaluation session and their comments during the focus group. The perceived satisfaction of the use of the PB inspection was assessed by using a semantic differential scale requiring users to judge the method on 11 items (e.g. easy to use, usual, efficient, reliable, etc.). The participants could modulate their judgment on each item through a 7-point scale (1 = negative, 7 = positive). A satisfaction index, computed as the mean value of the scores across all the 11 items, was 3.25 (std dev = 0.76). Participants' dissatisfaction was confirmed during the focus group: they complained that, in some extent, the technique made more complicate their task of assessing the EDUX platform. They felt tired applying the EPs requiring long explorations of the platform.

The participants were asked to judge their performance as evaluators on a 5-point scale (1 = negative, 5 = positive). The participants were slightly satisfied by their work (mean = 3.75, std dev = 1.58). This was confirmed by the answers to the question asking participants to indicate the percentage of the problems they thought to have discovered respect to the total number of problems the e-learning platform really had. On average, the participants stated they were able to discover 51% of the problems.

5 Conclusion

Since 2002 one of our main research goals is to identify an inspection technique able to support inspectors in performing reliable usability evaluation. To reach this goal, the Pattern-Based inspection was defined and in 2011 a comparison study has demonstrated that the technique is able to support novice evaluators in performing reliable, valid and economic evaluations. The study reported in this paper investigated how the PB inspection works in a real work-related setting. The results provided some answers about the question we posed in the title of the paper. EPs enable end users to evaluate the quality of an e-learning system. However, the study also demonstrated that the current definition of the EPs makes the technique difficult to be applied in some extent by people with no experience in usability evaluations. In the focus group, the participants reported that, even if they felt guided in the exploration of the system, they judged the execution of an EP time demanding since a variety of platform elements have to be considered. They would have preferred a larger set of patterns, but focused on a restricted number of elements. Another difficulty they experienced was related to problem reporting: they were not familiar with usability reports and they would have appreciated a more schematic and faster output layout. Some of them proposed a checklist. As future steps of our research, we are redesigning the EP template to improve the focus on specific elements of the e-learning system and to streamline the evaluation process.

Acknowledgments. This work was partly supported by the Polish National Science Centre under the contract No. 2011/01/M/HS4/04995.

References

1. Hornbæk, K., Frøkjær, E.: Comparing usability problems and redesign proposals as input to practical systems development. In: Proc. of CHI 2005, pp. 391–400. ACM (2005)
2. Steves, M.P., Morse, E., Gutwin, C., Greenberg, S.: A comparison of usage evaluation and inspection methods for assessing groupware usability. In: Proc. of ACM SIGGROUP Conference on Supporting Group Work, pp. 125–134. ACM (2001)
3. Tan, W., Dahai, L., Bishu, R.: Web evaluation: heuristic evaluation vs. usability testing. International Journal of Industrial Ergonomics 39(4), 621–627 (2009)
4. Gerdt, P., Miraftabi, R., Tukiainen, M.: Evaluating educational software environments. In: Proc. of Computers in Education, pp. 675–676. IEEE Computer Society (2002)
5. Mendes, E., Hall, W., Harrison, R.: Applying metrics to the evaluation of educational hypermedia application. Journal of Universal Computer Science 4(4), 382–403 (1998)
6. Quinn, C.N., Alem, L., Eklund, J.A.: Pragmatic evaluation methodology for an assessment of learning effectiveness in instructional systems. In: Bewster, S., Cawsey, A., Cockton, G. (eds.) Human–Computer Interaction, vol. II, pp. 55–56. British Computer Society (1997)
7. Squires, D., Preece, J.: Predicting quality in educational software: evaluating for learning, usability, and the synergy between them. Interact. with Computers 11(5), 467–483 (1999)
8. Jeffries, R., Desurvire, H.W.: Usability testing vs heuristic evaluation: was there a context? ACM SIGCHI Bulletin 24(4), 39–41 (1992)
9. Doubleday, A., Ryan, M., Springett, M., Sutcliffe, A.: A comparison of usability techniques for evaluating design. In: Proc. of DIS 1997, pp. 101–110. Springer, Heidelberg (1997)
10. Law, E.: Heuristic Evaluation. In: Proceedings of COST294-MAUSE International Workshop “Review, Report and Refine Usability Evaluation Methods (R3-UEM)”, pp. 61–63 (2007)
11. Lanzilotti, R., De Angeli, A., Ardito, C., Costabile, M.F.: Do patterns help novice evaluators? A comparative study. Intern. Journal of Human-Computer Studies 69, 52-69 (2011)

12. Matera, M., Costabile, M.F., Garzotto, F., Paolini, P.: SUE Inspection: an effective method for systematic usability evaluation of hypermedia. IEEE Transactions on Systems, Man and Cybernetics – Part A 32(1), 93–103 (2002)
13. Bias, R.G., Mayhew, D.J.: Cost-justifying usability: An update for the Internet age, 2nd edn. Morgan Kaufmann Publishers, San Francisco (2005)
14. Hudson, J.: Beyond Usability to User Experience. In: Workshop UXEM at CHI 2008 (2008), http://www.cs.tut.fi/ihte/CHI08_workshop/papers.shtml (last access on January 31, 2012)
15. Lallemand, C.: Toward a closer integration of usability in software development: a study of usability inputs in a model-driven engineering process. In: Proc. of EICS 2011, pp. 299–302. ACM (2011)
16. Rosenbaum, S., Rohn, J.A., Humburg, J.: A toolkit for strategic usability: Results from workshops, panels, and surveys. In: Proc. of CHI 2000, pp. 337–344. ACM (2000)
17. Seffah, A., Donyaee, M., Kline, R.B., Padda, H.K.: Usability measurement and metrics: A consolidated model. Software Quality Journal 14(2), 159–178 (2006)
18. Venturi, G.: Troost. J. 2004. Survey on the UCD integration in the industry. In: Proc. of NordiCHI 2004, pp. 449–452. ACM (2004)
19. Höök, K., Löwgren, J.: Strong concepts: Intermediate-level knowledge in interaction design research. ACM TOCHI 19(3), Article 23 (2012)
20. Ardito, C.: Usability of virtual reality systems. Thesis. University of Bari Aldo Moro, Italy (2002)
21. Sikorski, M., Garnik, I.: Towards Methodology for User Experience Measurement in online Services. In: Korczak, J., Dudycz, H., Dyczkowski, M. (eds.) Advanced Information Technologies for Management - AITM 2010, Research Papers of Wroclaw University of Economics, vol. (147) (2011)
22. Hertzum, M., Jacobsen, N.E.: The evaluator effect: a chilling fact about usability evaluation methods. Intern. Journal of Human–Computer Interaction 15(1), 183–204 (2003)
23. Ardito, C., Costabile, M.F., De Angeli, A., Lanzilotti, R.: Systematic evaluation of e-learning systems: an experimental validation. In: Proc. of NordiCHI 2006, pp. 195–202. ACM (2006)
24. Nielsen, J., Landauer, T.K.: A mathematical model of the finding of usability problems. In: Proc. of INTERCHI 1993, pp. 296–313. ACM (1993)
25. Vredenburg, K., Mao, J.Y., Smith, P.W., Carey, T.: A survey of user-centered design practice. In: Proc. of CHI 2002, pp. 471–478. ACM (2002)

Computer-Based Cognitive Training in Adults with Down's Syndrome

Stefania Bargagna[1], Margherita Bozza[1], Maria Claudia Buzzi[2], Marina Buzzi[2], Elena Doccini[1], and Erico Perrone[2]

[1] IRCCS Stella Maris, viale del Tirreno 331, 56128 Calambrone (PI), Italy
{sbargagna,mbozza}@fsm.unipi.it, elenadoccini@virgilio.it
[2] IIT-CNR, via Moruzzi 1, 56124 Pisa, Italy
{Claudia.Buzzi,Marina.Buzzi,Erico.Perrone}@iit.cnr.it

Abstract. Adults with Down Syndrome show a clear genetic susceptibility to developing Alzheimer's Disease, the most common cause of dementia worldwide. In this paper we describe a set of computer-based exercises designed for cognitive training of adults with Down Syndrome. The aim is to provide telerehabilitation via a Web application that can be used at home to create an enriched environment. Each exercise is presented as a game with images, text and vocal communication. The user moves forward at increasing levels of difficulty according to previous positive percentage thresholds. Performance data is centrally collected and available to the tutor to check progress and better define the training. Several categories of exercises are needed to train different abilities: attention, memory, visual-spatial orientation, temporal orientation, prelogical and logical operations, perception, visual analysis, language, and data relevance. At this time, two modules have been implemented for exercising attention and memory.

Keywords: Training software, tele-rehabilitation, Down Syndrome, dementia, accessibility, learning games.

1 Introduction

Down Syndrome (DS) is the most common form of mental retardation of genetic origin. In the last few decades, life expectancy in people affected by DS has increased greatly, from an average of 25 years of age in the 1980s to an average age of 60 years [1, 2]. In Italy, about 60% of all subjects with DS are adults [3].

Adults with DS show a clear genetic susceptibility to developing Alzheimer's Disease (AD), the most common cause of dementia worldwide. Neuropathology of AD can be observed virtually in all subjects with DS older than 40 years of age, while the onset of the clinical signs of dementia is on average observed around 50 years of age [4].

Strong evidence supports the beneficial effects of enriched environment (EE) on several aspects of brain development and brain plasticity in the mouse model of DS [5]. Preliminary results of a randomized controlled ongoing trial at IRCCS Stella Maris have assessed the effect of EE intervention based on psycho-physical training for the prevention of functional and cognitive decline in adults with DS.

C. Stephanidis and M. Antona (Eds.): UAHCI/HCII 2014, Part II, LNCS 8514, pp. 197–208, 2014.

In this paper we describe a set of computer-based exercises designed for cognitive training of adults with DS, called "STELLA DS" - Software To Exercise Learning and Language in Adults with Down Syndrome. The aim is to provide tele-rehabilitation through a Web application that users with DS can utilize at home to create an enriched environment to train the brain and prevent dementia.

Each exercise is presented as a game with images, text and vocal communication, e.g., statements, cues, and reinforcers. The user moves forward in increasing levels of difficulty according to positive results, assessed by percentage thresholds; otherwise he/she remains at the same level or goes back. Tutors can personalize the training depending on the skills and preferences of each subject. Performance data for each subject and exercise is centrally collected and available to the tutor for checking progress and issues, and to better define the training.

Several categories of exercises are needed to train different abilities: attention, memory, visual-spatial orientation, temporal orientation, pre-logical and logical operations, perception, visual analysis, language and data relevance. At this time, the first two modules have been implemented for exercising attention and memory. The effects of the use of the cognitive training through STELLA DS will be tested following a neuropsychological protocol that will check the degree of the enrolled subject's abilities before and after the training.

2 Related Work

Tele-rehabilitation offers cost-effective services that can improve access to care for patients with neurological disorders. The techniques of tele-rehabilitation are now widely used internationally, and are based on online rehabilitative exercise monitoring by specialized medical personnel. The Internet offers new methods of intervention and a greater and more effective clinical supply. Tele-rehabilitation maximizes the potential of rehabilitation, allowing the clinician to assign specific tasks to be carried out daily at a distance, while maintaining full control and constant monitoring of the rehabilitation.

Nouchi et al. (2012) investigated the impact of playing brain training games for 4 weeks, in elderly subjects. Results showed improvement in cognitive function (executive function and processing speed). Results indicated that the elderly can improve both executive functions and processing speed in short-term training [6].

Using computerized versions of training programs has allowed the implementation of adaptive algorithms that ensure that the level of task difficulty is always challenging for the individual, something shown to be crucial for the training to be effective [7].

Computerized training has been shown to improve working memory performance in healthy children and adults [8-11], in adults recovering from strokes and other acquired brain injuries [12, 13], and in children born preterm [14], in children with attention-deficit hyperactivity disorder (ADHD) [15], and in children with intellectual disabilities [16].

Previous research in children with DS has indicated that rehearsal training can improve working memory [17, 18].

A recent study by Bennet et al. 2013 [17] evaluated the impact of a computerized visual-spatial memory training intervention on memory and behavioral skills in 21 children with DS, aged 7-12. Following training, performance on trained and non-trained visual-spatial short-term memory tasks was significantly enhanced for children in the intervention group. This study was carried out in school. A previous study [18], not based on computerized training, suggested that parents can be good trainers and auditory working memory can improve with parents as trainers.

There are no studies with computerized training in adults with DS to prevent the development of Alzheimer's Disease (AD). Strong evidence supports the beneficial effects of enriched environment (EE) on several aspects of brain development and brain plasticity. We aimed to study the improvement of cognitive abilities also in older DS subjects, with computerized training that can also be used at home with clinical monitoring.

Our application, unlike other software in use (such as Cogmed JM), is open source and free, relieving families and rehabilitation centers of the burden of license costs. Furthermore, STELLA DS do not require the user to install any software: it is a Web application, thus usable through a browser on any device connected to the Internet.

3 Designing the Software

As previously mentioned, there is evidence that supports the beneficial effects of EE on several aspects of brain development and brain plasticity in a mouse model of DS [5]. Preliminary results of a randomized controlled trial in IRCCS Stella Maris has assessed the effects of EE intervention based on psycho-physical training for the prevention of functional and cognitive decline in adults with DS. Based on this observation, it is crucial to maximize the time that the subject devotes to the rehabilitation. Moving from the classic face-to-face approach to a technology-enhanced therapy (i.e. executed interacting with a computer or a tablet) is a natural evolution today. Removing the constraint of physically obliging the DS subject to go to medical labs for therapy alleviates the burden on families, allowing subjects to exercise their brain more comfortably at home, independently and at their own pace. In fact, independence may encourage the subject to increase training time, while the electronic tool may provide more agreeable stimuli, both leading to better results. Tele-rehabilitation is conceived as a tool that enables the individual's independence in performing the training and thus empowers the DS person, taking full advantage of her/his residual abilities.

The STELLA DS software has been designed following participatory design principles, involving psychologists and doctors from the earliest steps of the projects, to guarantee the creation of a flexible and usable product that is pleasant for the users. Specifically, face-to-face meetings, Skype sessions, and interaction via email have been adopted as collaboration mechanisms, to collect user requirements and collaboratively design the software and its function. In order to achieve targeted features we defined main software design constraints:

- To propose the exercises as a serious game, with increasing/decreasing levels of difficulty, in order to dynamically adapt the trial flow to the subject's responses and interactions. This adapts the proposed trial to the pace of the student, decreasing stress and favoring the independence of the subject in carrying out the rehabilitation.
- To provide psychologists and doctors with a tool for easily assessing the learning trend of their patients and refining the training program.

The W3C Web Accessibility Guidelines (WCAG 2.0) and usability criteria drove the design of the software STELLA DS. The software exploits all the user's sensorial channels in order to provide an enriched environment that favors the subject's comprehension and stimulates attention, providing visual, audio and vocal information. For instance, to keep the subjects' attention, textual commands are shown on the screen and vocally announced. To sustain learning, a short demo video is shown before the game starts for teaching by visual examples. Furthermore, the touchscreen device allows one to use pointing, which may be more natural, intuitive and easy to use than the mouse and touch pad.

The system is accessible after a log-in phase. For DS people who may have difficulty remembering passwords, the log-in phase is simplified, requiring only a nickname. No time constraints are applied when the tasks are assigned to the student and (s)he can stop and resume the game anytime. Feedback and reinforcers appear on the screen during the exercise, and are also announced, to increase the probability that the subject manifests positive behaviors in the future. Pre-recorded audio files, instead of a speech synthesis engine, have been used to make interaction more comfortable for the user. After the development of the prototype, a pilot test with two users was carried out, to better understand the needs of subjects with DS.

3.1 The Architecture

The architecture consists of a web server integrated with a PHP interpreter and a MySql database. The classic LAMP Server -- Linux, Apache, MySql and PHP has been adopted. The database is used for data gathering, for adaptation, keeping the functional parameters, and for user management. It also enables multilinguism: depending on the selected language, a corresponding set of labels is visualized in the user interfaces (UIs) of the application.

To make the software (SW) fully flexible and configurable, each training exercise is implemented as a finite-state machine, defined through two database tables. One describes the states associated with the implemented page, the other the transactions from one state to another, based on the results of the previous state execution. In this way it is simple to modify the behavior of each module by only changing its description tables; no changes are required to the code.

The UIs are implemented with HTML 5, style sheets (CSS) and Javascript (specifically jQuery). Each user interface is controlled by a routine Javascript with Ajax calls, both for the content processing and their presentation. Through Javascript, the user input is controlled both for users interacting via keyboard, mouse/touchpad and touchscreen devices. The global architecture of the STELLA DS application is synthesized in Fig. 1.

Three kinds of users can interact with the system in different places and times, as shown in Fig. 1: a) Tutors (psychologists, doctors, parents and caregivers); b) Students/patients (adults with DS), and c) Administrator, the person in charge of changing system configurations and updating the software. The application is able to execute three main functions:

- Enable tutors/teachers/caregivers to assign one or more educational training modules
- Enable patients to carry out their assigned exercises/games. The exercise can be stopped and resumed at the next login, without losing data and maintaining the last state (ensuring the consistency of the intervention)
- Gather and process data related to the exercises executed (learning data analytics). Data is collected during the execution of Modules to assess the level of performance achieved. For each learning module a success rate has been defined in order to make the student progress through the levels. The tutor can monitor the performance data and decide to suspend the execution of a module when the level seems to be too difficult.

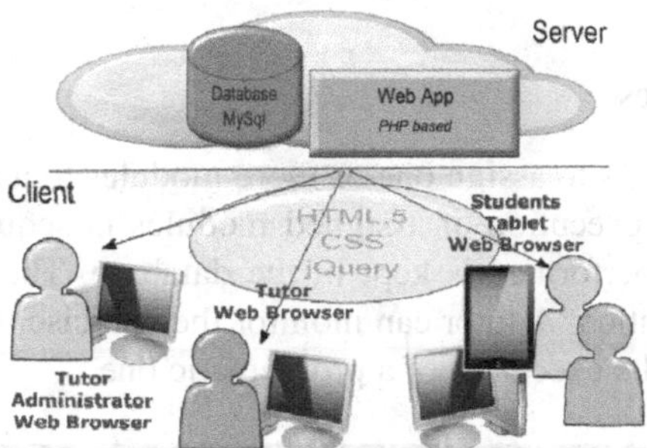

Fig. 1. Software Architecture

4 Software Components

4.1 Access Component

The access page represents the entry point of the application and requires a log-in. Depending on the user -- Administrator, Tutor or Student, the access component visualizes the appropriate user interface (UI) as defined in the database. In the following the different UIs are described.

4.2 Administration Tools

With the administration tools it is possible to create, modify and delete users, and set up values of the application parameters. Tutors and administrators can create "student" users by personalizing the profile according to several attributes, such as the speaker voice -- male or female -- and the language. This allows tutors to have more flexibility in profiling the user, adapting the exercises to their preference. After the creation of a student, the tutor may assign him/her a sequence of training modules to do at home, monitoring their execution and the performance data at any time. It is possible to cancel a student – a logical and not a physical cancellation -- to assure the integrity of the historical data stored in the database.

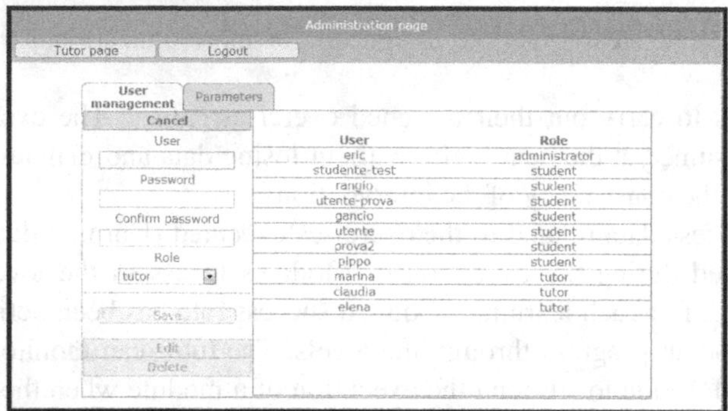

Fig. 2. Administration Tools

4.3 Tutor Interfaces

The tutor interface allows to assign one or more modules to a student. After login, the student will begin the execution of assigned modules in sequence (Fig. 3). Information on the exercises performed is kept in the database. The tutor interface collects and shows this information. A tutor can monitor the exercise the student is engaged in and possibly suspend the execution of a problematic one.

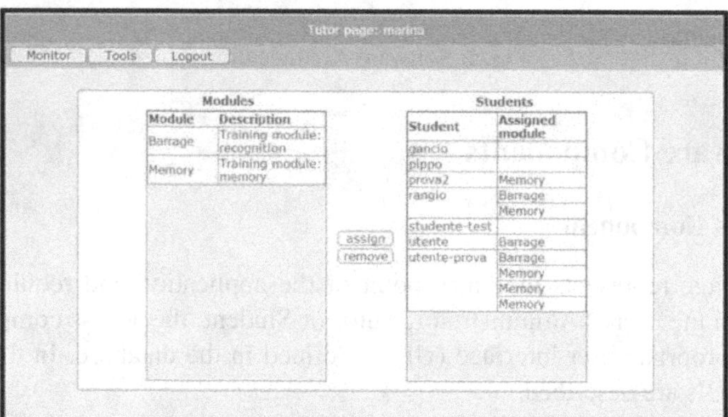

Fig. 3. Tutor Interface

4.4 Data & Statistics

During the execution of training modules, the data collected is used in assessing the level of performance achieved. This data is processed and shown with the details of each session and the possibility of obtaining a broader or in-depth view. For each learning module a simple statistical index has been defined that is referred to as the success rate characteristic of that specific module. An example of statistics is shown in Fig. 4:

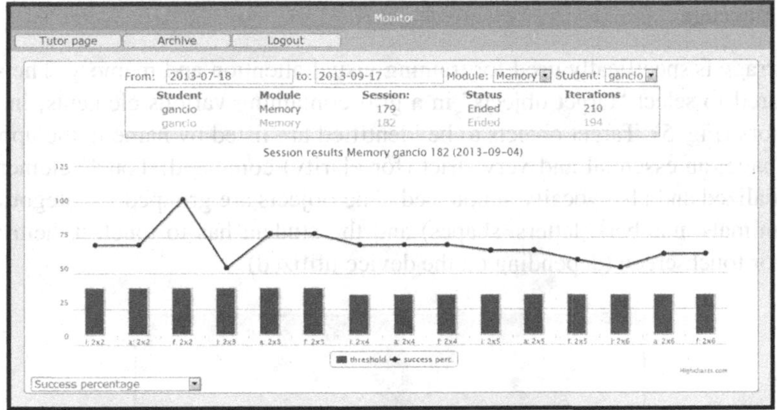

Fig. 4. Data & Statistics

4.5 The Student User Interfaces: The Learning Modules

This component implements the training exercises assigned to the students. The UI that implements the exercises is presented as a gaming session where student interaction occurs via mouse or touchscreen. JavaScript features have been used for the interactivity such as: animations based on the visibility and size of html page portions, use of timers to put the correct chronological sequence the actions, the control of user input, etc. The pages are scalable as much as possible to the size of the browser window, recalculating at each event 'window resizing' the optimal page view, in accordance with its specific geometry.

The task to be executed by the student is written in the upper part of the interface and also announced. In order to make interaction more comfortable for the user with a voice that is "warmer" and less "robotic" than the speech synthesis one, we used recorded voices. There are two possible voices: a male and a female have recorded all the words and phrases used in the UI and all data is memorized in the database. Javascript procedures reconstruct the phrase in the correct sequence, by combining, through the use of HTML 5 Audio objects, the pre-recorded vocal files. There can be multiple speakers for each supported language. The training exercises (learning modules) are the core of the application; thus, in the following we will describe them in detail.

5 Training Exercises

At this time, the first two learning modules have been implemented: 1) barrage and 2) memory. Each exercise starts with a demo that visually presents the assigned task, in order to better allow the student to understand the task and imitate the actions. The execution of each module can be suspended by the student, i.e., interrupted and resumed later at the same point where the user was working at the time of the stop.

5.1 Barrage

The barrage is specifically used for training visual attention and memory. The student is required to select "target objects" in a grid containing various elements, including distractors (Fig. 5). Target objects to be identified are listed by name in the upper part of the page; an essential and very strict (for clarity) command: Touch 'element lists' are visualized and also vocally announced. The objects are grouped in categories (objects, animals, numbers, letters, shapes) and the student has to touch it/them via the mouse or touchscreen (depending on the device utilized).

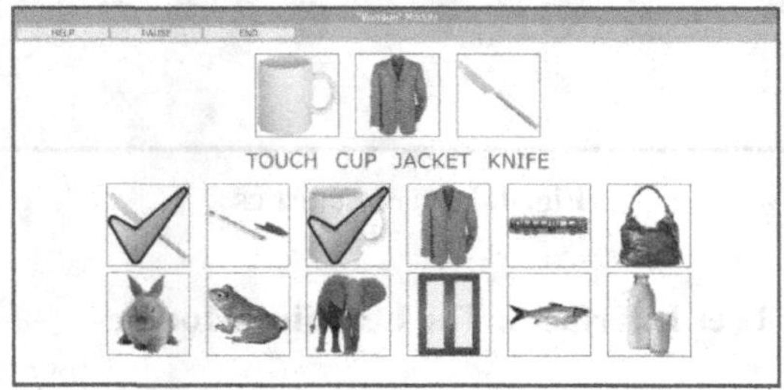

Fig. 5. Barrage UI

The number of target objects varies from 1 to 3, while the grids are composed of 3, 6 or 12 elements. The level of difficulty increases from the simplest (touch 1 target in a grid of 3 items), the less simple (touch 1 target in a grid of 6 items, and then touch 1 target in a grid of 12 items), to the hardest (touch 3 targets in a grid of 12 items).

This sequence of exercises is applied to all four identified categories, which are also of increasing difficulty themselves: 1. objects/animals, 2. numbers, 3. letters and 4. shapes. The whole schema of levels above described is first proposed on the first category, and then on the second and so on.

Every click of the mouse or finger pressure (click) on the touchscreen has an immediate feedback: a green tick, if the touch is correct, i.e., a target has been identified, or red "X" in case of error. The success rate for a level is considered the percentage of the number of correct answers provided by the subject compared to the total number of possible correct answers (< = 1). There is a tolerance threshold of the number of possible errors (we set 20%, but this parameter is configurable). If the number of errors goes above this threshold, there is a repetition of the trial in the same configuration. Two consecutive errors make the game return to the previous level of difficulty.

The user can explicitly ask for help (by pressing an icon), or otherwise help is automatically provided if, after a fixed time (configurable as system parameter by the tutors) the user has failed to solve the trial. A request for help leads to repeating the exercise, if the student does not provide the correct answers with a percentage of at least 60%. The help functionality automatically runs after a fixed (configured in the application's parameters) amount of time if no actions in the Barrage module are performed. Progressing one level is highlighted by a successful message vocally announced. Furthermore, the completion of a scheme of difficulty levels in a category receives a reinforcement provided by a short animation in addition to the sound message. The execution of one of the modules can be halted when the user wishes. The next time the user accesses the software, it will resume from the point where it had been interrupted.

5.2 Memory

The second module is an electronic version of the classic Memory game: the screen displays a grid containing "covered" cards. The user is invited by a pre-recorded voice to find the matching pair of cards. Next, the user can begin to uncover a pair of cards. When two matching cards are identified, a confirmation tone (trumpet) is played and the two cards disappear. Conversely, if the two cards are different, they are again covered and an audible failure sound is played. At the bottom of the interface there is a progress bar to show the percentage of correct matches performed. At the end of the game, when all the card pairs are found, the whole schema is shown and a success message is vocally announced.

Cards are grouped in categories: objects, animals and shapes. The game starts with the first category, progressing through the others, passing from the simplest scheme (two pairs of objects) to the most complex (six pairs of objects). When the user finishes a schema, a visual and audible feedback is provided, as in the Barrage module.

Each schema is associated with a threshold value, which takes into account the maximum number of attempts to solve a schema. If a student goes over this error threshold, the same pattern is repeated automatically.

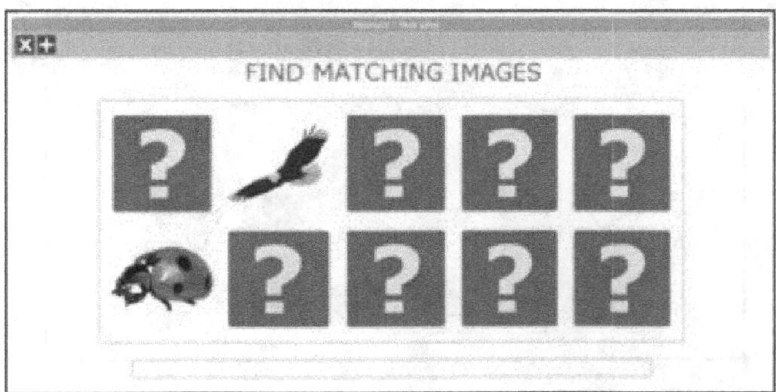

Fig. 6. Memory User Interface

5.3 Pilot Test

A pilot test has been performed with two adults with DS to refine the software functionalities and improve the user interfaces. In order to be able to generalize our results to wider clinical samples of adults with intellectual disabilities, we included subjects with DS with additional co-morbid diagnoses and/or who are taking prescribed medication. Exclusion criteria were a diagnosis of autism and severe motor and sensory problems, as these were considered to affect pre- or post- assessment (and hence reliability of assessment) or training ability.

The software was described to the participants showing the demo and all the functions. Then each of the two subjects, G. and O., performed the assigned Barrage and Memory modules using a laptop. Each subject executed the modules separately under the supervision of the tutor and the STELLA DS engineer.

Two subjects with different abilities were chosen, in order to cover more functioning levels. Results were quite different and reflected their abilities: one subject executed the trials autonomously; the other performed very slowly, requiring many tutor prompts.

The pilot test highlighted very positive features of the application, and the STELLA DS application was enthusiastically accepted by the testers. Positive points are the attractive images and the vocal feedback: the application "speaks" to the users. One of the users was charmed by the new words, and he repeated them to himself after they were announced. Both students appreciated the vocal reinforcement during the execution of the exercises. Some critical points emerging from the pilot test:

- In some points the demos were not effective and clear as we supposed. We are planning to substitute them with short videos showing the correct interaction with the game.
- During the execution of the Barrage module, images used as stimulus (to indicate the targets) can be confused with the images to be searched. These prompts are important since they offer a visual model when the word is unfamiliar. To clarify the exercise, we have modified the UI, miniaturizing these images, removing their surrounding boxes and creating a visual separation between the discriminative stimulus and the area where user interaction is required; see Fig. 7.

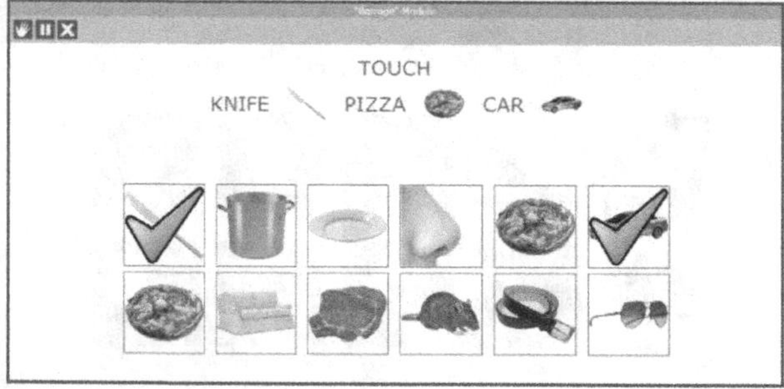

Fig. 7. Barrage UI: the revised interface

Currently the application allows tuning the game's level of difficulty based on student responses. Due to the large variability of users in terms of aptitude and skills, it would be appropriate to plan to diversify the trials depending on user abilities. For example, particularly able subjects may avoid too-simple levels of difficulty, which bore them.

6 Discussion

Preliminary results of a randomized controlled trial ongoing at IRCCS Stella Maris assessed the effect of an intervention of EE (psycho-physical training regarding functional and cognitive skills) in adults with DS. The good success of previous training experience realized in IRCCS Stella Maris Institute suggests enlarging the number of the trainable people with STELLA DS. Tele-rehabilitation offers cost-effective services that can improve access to care for patients with cognitive disorders.

Tele-rehabilitation through a Web application can be utilized at home to create an Enriched Environment to train the brain and prevent dementia in subjects with DS. Specific rehabilitative content (memory, attention, cognition, reasoning, visual-constructive and spatial abilities) will be trained and the effects of treatment will be tested by a neuropsychological protocol before and after training. We speculate that our software will support the rehabilitation of cognitive function at home, at low cost and with the possibility of increasing the number of involved people with the collaboration of family associations.

The STELLA DS arose from a collaboration of the Institute of Informatics and Telematics of CNR in Pisa and the Stella Maris, a National Biomedical Research Institute for neurological and psychiatric disorders in children and adolescents. The aims of the two groups are dissemination of the importance of a tele-rehabilitative training to a large community of disabled people.

7 Future Work

This paper describes the design and development of software for combating the mental decline of people with DS. The software is a web application usable anytime, anyplace, with any device supporting a web browser. The application is partly customizable and is currently available in Italian and English. Two training exercises have been implemented to verify the feasibility of the proposed approach. A pilot test with two users has shown the interest of participants in using the software, confirming the opportunity to investigate the efficacy of the tool for tele-rehabilitation.

For future studies we will develop more training games, and will carry out a user test recruiting a large sample of participants in order to investigate long-term effects of the use of the software and to evaluate its relevance in preserving cognitive ability and individual autonomy in everyday functions.

The effects of cognitive training via STELLA DS will be tested following a neuropsychological protocol that will evaluate the enrolled subject's abilities before and after the training.

References

1. Yang, Q., Rasmussen, S.A., Friedman, J.M.: Mortality associated with Down's syndrome in the USA from 1983 to 1997: a population-based study. Lancet. 359(9311), 1019–1025 (2002)
2. Bittles, A.H., Bower, C., Hussain, R., Glasson, E.J.: The four ages of Down syndrome. Eur. J. Public Health 17(2), 221–225 (2007)
3. Vicari, S.: La sindrome di Down. Il Mulino (2007)
4. Zigman, W.B., Devenny, D.A., Krinsky-McHale, S.J., Jenkins, E.C., Urv, T.K., Wegiel, J., Schupf, N., Silverman, W.: Alzheimer's Disease in Adults with Down Syndrome. Int. Rev. Res. Ment. Retard. 36, 103–145 (2008)
5. Bartesaghi, R., Guidi, S., Ciani, E.: Is it possible to improve neurodevelopmental abnormalities in DS? Rev. Neurosci. 22(4), 419–455 (2011)
6. Nouchi, R., Taki, Y., Takeuchi, H., Hashizume, H., Akitsuki, Y., Shigemune, Y., Kawashima, R.: Brain training game improves executive functions and processing speed in the elderly: a randomized controlled trial. PloS one 7(1), e29676 (2012)
7. Klingberg, T.: Training and plasticity of working memory. Trends Cogn. Sci. 14, 317–324 (2010)
8. Olesen, P.J., Westerberg, H., Klingberg, T.: Increased prefrontal and parietal activity after training of working memory. Nat. Neurosci. 7, 75–79 (2004)
9. Jaeggi, S.M., Buschkuehl, M., Jonides, J., Perrig, W.J.: Improving fluid intelligence with training on working memory. Proc. Natl. Acad. Sci. U.S.A. 105, 6829–6833 (2008)
10. Thorell, L.B., Lindqvist, S., Bergman Nutley, S., Bohlin, G., Klingberg, T.: Training and transfer effects of executive functions in preschool children. Dev. Sci. 12, 106–113 (2009)
11. Bergman Nutley, S., Soderqvist, S., Bryde, S., Thorell, L.B., Humphreys, K., Klingberg, T.: Gains in fluid intelligence after training non-verbal reasoning in 4-year-old children: a controlled, randomized study. Dev. Sci. 14, 591–601 (2011)
12. Westerberg, H., Jacobaeus, H., Hirvikoski, T., Clevberger, P., Östensson, M.L., Bartfai, A., Klingberg, T.: Computerized working memory training after stroke–A pilot study. BrainInj. 21(1), 21–29 (2007)
13. Lundqvist, A., Grundstrom, K., Samuelsson, K., Ronnberg, J.: Computerized training of working memory in a group of patients suffering from acquired brain injury. BrainInj. 24, 1173–1183 (2010)
14. Lohaugen, G.C., Antonsen, I., Haberg, A., Gramstad, A., Vik, T., Brubakk, A.M., Skranes, J.: Computerized working memory training improves function in adolescents born at extremely low birth weight. J. Pediatr. 158, 555–561 (2011)
15. Beck, S.J., Hanson, C.A., Puffenberger, S.S., Benninger, K.L., Benninger, W.B.: A controlled trial of working memory training for children and adolescents with ADHD. J. Clin. Child Adolesc. Psychol. 39, 825–836 (2010)
16. Söderqvist, S., Nutley, S.B., Ottersen, J., Grill, K.M., Klingberg, T.: Computerized training of non-verbal reasoning and working memory in children with intellectual disability. Front. Hum. Neurosci. 6, 271 (2012)
17. Bennett, S.J., Holmes, J., Buckley, S.: Computerized Memory Training Leads to Sustained Improvement in Visuospatial Short-Term Memory Skills in Children with Down Syndrome. American Journal on Intellectual and Developmental Disabilities 118(3), 179–192 (2013)
18. Conners, F.A., Rosenquist, C.J., Taylor, L.A.: Memory training for children with Down syndrome. Down Syndrome Research and Practice 7(1), 25–33 (2001)

An Analytic Tool for Assessing Learning in Children with Autism

Valentina Bartalesi[1], Maria Claudia Buzzi[2], Marina Buzzi[2], Barbara Leporini[1], and Caterina Senette[2]

[1] CNR-ISTI, via Moruzzi 1, 56124 Pisa, Italy
{Valentina.Bartalesi, Barbara.Leporini}@isti.cnr.it
[2] CNR-IIT, via Moruzzi 1, 56124 Pisa, Italy
{Claudia.Buzzi,Marina.Buzzi,Caterina.Senette}@iit.cnr.it

Abstract. One approach for teaching subjects with autism is Applied Behavior Analysis (ABA). ABA intervention aims to model human behavior by observing, analyzing and modifying antecedents and/or consequences of a target behavior in the environment. To achieve this, many data are recorded during each trial, such as subject response (correct/incorrect, level of prompt, inappropriate behavior, etc.). In this paper we present a web application that aggregates and visualizes data collected during technology-enhanced educational sessions, in order to monitor learning in children with autism. In a previous study we developed a free open source web application called ABCD SW, to support educators in administering ABA programs. In this study we present a learning analytic tool that retrieves, aggregates and shows -- in graphical and table form -- data gathered by ABCD SW. This software offers accurate real-time monitoring of children's learning, allowing teachers to analyze the collected data more rapidly, and to accurately tune and personalize the intervention for each child.

Keywords: Learning Analytic tool, Data Analysis, web application, Autism, ABA.

1 Introduction

Autism Spectrum Disorder (ASD) is a type of Pervasive Developmental Disorder that affects individuals with varying degrees of impairment. In general, it concerns three areas of disability: (a) communication, (b) socialization, (c) repetitive and stereotyped patterns of behavior, play and interests [1]. Early and intensive educational approaches are needed to minimize the disability's impact and better exploit the subject's abilities. One method specifically applied to teaching subjects with autism is Applied Behavior Analysis (ABA), a scientific approach that has proved to be very effective in this field ([2], [3]). ABA models human behavior by observing, analyzing and modifying antecedent and/or consequence behaviors, focusing on objectivity and systematic measures. The main criterion is to observe the environment that provides the stimuli to which a person responds, and the environment in past experiences that caused the same stimulus-response association [4]. Children are more likely to repeat

C. Stephanidis and M. Antona (Eds.): UAHCI/HCII 2014, Part II, LNCS 8514, pp. 209–220, 2014.

or maintain behaviors and responses that are rewarded or reinforced by giving them something they like very much. The reinforcement is progressively reduced so that the child can learn without constant rewards.

Usually, software and technology can be used in a worthwhile way by autistic persons, keeping in mind any potential disturbance caused by colors, lights, animations, automatic behaviors implemented on the screen, etc. Nearly all children are attracted to computers, and when interacting with them feel free from expectations and social behavioral rules. Several studies have shown the effectiveness of computer-based training for teaching a variety of skills to children with autism ([5], [6], [7]).

We have developed a free open source web application (ABCD software) to help educators administer basic ABA programs facilitating early teaching of children with autism [8]. This software allows the child to become familiar with categories -- such as food, animals, colors -- and their articles -- such as apple, dog, and yellow (discriminative training). Usually, the ABA educators propose certain exercises of increasing levels of difficulty to a child, using cardboard pictures or real objects. Decreasing the time needed for the trial set-up, the ABCD SW automates the execution of three basic exercises: 1. matching programs, with combinations of images and words; 2. receptive programs, with the recognition of an article among others; 3. expressive programs, for labeling an article with verbal expression or -- for non-verbal children -- with text labels. The didactic software allows the educator to just press a key to quickly insert subjective data such as the type and level of prompt provided to the child, crucial for monitoring and evaluating learning progress. All data produced during the session -- article, category, execution time, success/error, prompt, etc., are automatically recorded and stored by the software.

In order to efficiently analyze the enormous amount of data collected by this software, we developed a learning analytic tool, described in this paper. This tool automatically extracts, aggregates and visualizes the children's performance data related to the ABA programs performed with the ABCD SW. The learning process is more effective when educators perform systematic data collection and analysis [9]. The analytic tool provides the teachers with easy real-time monitoring of learning progress, extracting data to assess a variety of skills and behaviors, and thus enabling the continuous evaluation and personalized tuning of the didactic intervention.

In the following, we first introduce basic ABA principles with special focus on data collection, as well as other studies in the field. Next, we describe the proposed learning analytic tool.

2 Data in ABA Intervention

For simplicity's sake, in the following the term "tutor" will refer to all members of the ABA team, with various levels of experience, including (special needs) teachers, educators, communication assistants, parents and caregivers.

ABA intervention requires collecting data about learning activities (e.g., subject's behaviors and skills acquired) in order to evaluate the effectiveness of intervention procedures. The aim of ABA methodology is to improve the abilities (communication, socialization, etc.) of a subject and increase his/her frequency of appropriate behaviors, while discouraging and extinguishing problem behaviors. For this, different types of data must be recorded, such as correct/incorrect responses and occurrence of inappropriate behaviors (problem behaviors/self stimulation/no collaboration), to analyze the subject's progress and better refine the intervention. According to several studies, early intervention in children affected by autism disorder is more effective for learning and developing social abilities ([10], [11], [12]).

The creator of ABA intervention, Loovas [2] recommended recording data for each trial proposed to a child. Today, some studies suggest considering accurate data collection since recording large amounts of data can interfere with performing the ABA session itself, and thus with learning, especially if data are recorded manually. In this context, professionals have provided recommendations for building data collection related to the child's daily activities, using efficient data collection techniques and when possible, selecting procedures that can be executed during other tasks [13]. In order to understand the type of data to collect, a more detailed look at how ABA intervention works is provided in the following.

The ABA approach to autism utilizes several strategies and tools. Usually it relies on Augmentative and Alternative Communication (AAC) and Discrete Trial Training (DTT). DTT can help autistic children who often do not learn spontaneously as typically developing children do naturally, through imitation [14]. According to [15], DTT learning procedures improve attention, motivation, discrimination between relevant stimuli (stimulus control), generalization, cause-effect relationships, observational learning and communication. Each discrete trial has five components [16]:

1. Antecedent: a discriminative stimulus, for soliciting the behavior (a request by the tutor or an element in the environment that is highlighted)
2. Prompt: a cue or suggestion provided by the tutor to facilitate the child's answers
3. Response of the subject
4. Consequence for a correct response (reinforcement) or for an incorrect response
5. Inter-trial interval: a brief pause between consecutive trials when the tutor records the trial data.

The skill to be learned is broken down into small units for easy learning; there is a systematic repetition of each small unit (trial) according to the subject's needs. The ABA errorless principle requires that during the learning phase, each response of the child can be prompted to prevent the subject from providing an incorrect answer, since it is very difficult to correct the error later. The prompt is gradually removed ("prompt fading") when the child becomes more familiar with the trial.

In the ABA method, performance data related to each trial are: (i) correct, (ii) incorrect, (iii) non-response, (iv) correct but prompted, (v) incorrect but prompted responses [17]. Then, when the educational aims increase, a simpler correct/incorrect data collection scheme can be used to measure the child's answers, focusing on the amount of prompt used by the tutors in each trial.

Data collection is crucial for analyzing whether and how educational programs for subjects with autism are evolving. ABA programs take into account considerable data regarding the child's progress, such as the frequency of challenging behavior and the percentage of correct behaviors. Recording the entire educational process is an important aspect of an educational program. Data collection helps measure the effects of the intervention, thus allowing the tutors to better refine it. Every change in the learning process can be observed from stored data. Monitoring a child's learning progress through the analysis of collected data also allows replacing interventions that do not seem to be beneficial for a child. In other words, data collection allows making more effective personalized changes to the program, based on children's abilities and real evidence.

According to [18] two types of behavior sampling can be identified:

- Event sampling: the count of the frequency or occurrence of a defined behavior in a period of time. This sampling indicates how many times the behavior occurs in a period of time (minutes, hours, days, months, etc.). Event sampling is useful in counting discrete behaviors with clear beginnings and endings.
- Time sampling: whether a behavior is present or absent at certain time point. This is useful for investigating behaviors that are continuous or difficult to count.

Usually, there are few software tools available to help tutors in recording data from ABA sessions, so recording data on paper is widespread, limiting the possibility of quick and powerful analysis.

3 Related Work

In recent years, various data collection systems for monitoring children with autism have been proposed. However, they mainly rely on systems specifically designed to observe behaviors and not to monitor learning trends. Leroy [16] presented a digital library of data related to appropriate and inappropriate behavior of children with autism in different social settings during the therapy, which includes video recordings. Decision trees and association rules provided more detailed insight into high and low levels of appropriate and inappropriate behavior.

DDtrac is software for educational programs of children with autism, and supports the collection and analysis of data for documenting the progress of children with autism [19]. DDtrac supports both quantitative (numeric) and qualitative autism data collection. The quantitative data that can be collected include instructional data, social data and behavior data.

The Kellar Instructional Handheld data (KIHd) System [20] is a real-time data collection tool for gathering instructional data about students diagnosed with autism. The software presents a database-driven handheld-based data collection and analysis system.

Both software programs, DDtrac and KIHd, require manual input of data from the therapists in order to analyze them. By contrast, our software automatically records and stores most of the data, such as programs, levels, categories, articles, progressive number of trials, errors and time elapsed between the trials as well as the child's response. Tutors complete the evaluation of the exercise by simply pressing a key on the keyboard (to insert the type, full or partial -- and percentage of prompt provided, i.e., 100, 80, 50, 20 or 0). In this way, data can be homogeneously analyzed through the data analysis tool presented here.

Another tool is ABPathfinder (http://www.abpathfinder.com/) a cloud-based software program that improves the efficiency and effectiveness of ABA therapy by reducing paperwork and improving data outcomes. All the complex processes of ABA therapy, including data collection and charts, are specifically created for this therapy. Unfortunately, ABPathfinder is a commercial product representing additional expenses for the family of an autistic child, already burdened with the cost of the behavioral intervention.

Recently Tarbox et al. have compared the use of a PDA (Personal Digital Assistant) for collecting behavior data with traditional pen-and-paper data recording. Their conclusions were that data accuracy are equal for both formats, but traditional data collection was faster [21]. However, we claim that rapidity mainly relies on the software features and the usability of user interfaces (UIs) as well as on the subjective user's ability to insert data. The use of gestures would make the process more natural. In addition, having electronic data enhances the evaluation and assessment phases.

Lastly, scientists have applied data mining techniques in order to analyze large sets of stored ABA data. In Freeman [22] the relation between physiological events, environmental factors, and the occurrence of problem behaviors are analyzed using the data mining system LERS (Learning from Examples based on Rough Sets).

4 Data Gathering/Collection

The proposed learning analytic tool is a web-based application that allows ABA tutors and parents to visualize information about the learning trends of children executing the ABA intervention with a specific software. In this section we briefly describe the didactic software used for data collection to better understand the kind of data.

The ABA-based didactic software implements matching, receptive and expressive programs. Each program is executed according to DTT (Discrete Trial Training) levels and each trial can be repeated several times. For each trial, the percentage of prompt provided, the occurrence and type of errors, the independent trials, and the use of reinforcement are recorded. A didactic session of about 2.5 h can produce a large amount of data since the trials are very short. Data automatically collected during each session are stored in a database and available real-time in statistical format during the exercise. This provides the tutors with a summary of data taken at different times or places from different educators, very helpful for monitoring the performance trend at any time.

The behavioral data types used in our analysis mainly refer to an event sampling, as previously defined, i.e., how many times the behavior occurs in a defined range of time. The possible behaviors are related to the learning: articles and categories mastered, successful trials, errors and prompts. The learning analytic tool elaborates data gathered by the didactic software and shows it through graphs and charts to make monitoring and evaluating a child's progress quick and easy for tutors so they can modify the objectives of the ABA programs if needed, to improve learning or behavior outcomes.

5 The Learning Analytic Tool

The tool supports tutors in data analysis, aggregating and extracting data automatically according to the preferred view and displaying it in a more intuitive rendering. The tool is a web-based application implemented in PHP and JavaScript that relies on an SQL database for extracting session data. The implementation makes use of the jQuery framework.

The application is embedded in the didactic software environment for the tutor's benefit, making it easy to analyze a particular section of data before starting a didactic session, offering a quick look at the child's learning progress or difficulties. This possibility is also helpful for assessing the materials before the session starts. The learning analytic tool can also help the consultant who coordinates the ABA intervention, to prepare reports before team meetings and assess future refinements. To efficiently analyze the large amount of data collected, different functions could be developed to provide data views for the educators, according to their expertise as well as needs. Thus we decided to base the functions' design on what tutors usually look for when analyzing the child's data of the ABA sessions, traditionally recorded on paper.

During the learning activities, tutors are mainly interested in collecting data that could reveal a positive/negative learning trend and increased/decreased occurrence of problematic behaviors. Periodically tutors need to assess the intervention based on the current status of the child. For this they need to analyze data related to learning: 1) period of time it took to acquire a certain article, thus knowing the dates of its introduction and mastery; 2) number of articles mastered in a certain period; 3) occurrence of problem behaviors and 4) quantitative/qualitative evaluation of use of tutor's prompt during the exercises. All this data related to the children's trials are recorded by the ABA-based didactic software.

Therefore, the proposed learning analytic tool integrated in the didactic software provides a basic set of queries that tutors usually need in order to monitor the child's learning progress and that are arduous to implement manually. However, if the predefined queries implemented are insufficient, it is possible to save raw data to refine the view and the analysis as preferred.

The tool supports multiple types of charts in order to show the child's progress. Stacked bar, multi-line and single-line charts are used to show the results of different queries. To implement these charts we used Highcharts[1], a library written in JavaScript, which offers intuitive and interactive charts to web sites or web applications. Highcharts library is supported by the most recent versions of browsers, including Safari. This library allows users to interact with charts providing access to the information according to levels of increasing/decreasing complexity, i.e., obtaining detailed or overall information. For example, if there is more than one data series, the user can click on one of them to hide or unhide it, selecting what to highlight. Indeed, when 'on mouse over' events above the charts occur, a tooltip text is shown with information on each point and series following the movement of the mouse over the

[1] http://www.highcharts.com/

graph. Another interesting feature is that by zooming in (in the X or Y dimensions) on a chart, it is possible to closely examine a particular portion of the data.

Two buttons on the upper right of each chart allow the user to manage data shown by the tool, for instance to produce reports. One button automatically provides a print version of the chart, the other button handles data saving in various formats: PDF file, image PNG or JPEG, or SVG representation.

Finally, we implemented an additional Javascript function that allows users to automatically export and download all the data extracted by the learning analytic tool into CSV format. This feature is particularly important since it allows the tutors to obtain and manage raw data on the children's learning, to permit further elaboration processes not provided by the tool.

To access the learning analytic tool, the tutor typically logs in to start an ABA session via the didactic software, selecting a child to work with. After login, s/he can decide to access the didactic software or the learning analytic tool by pressing a button on the UI. In this way the data analysis tool shows only data related to the selected child. The first page of the tool allows the tutor to choose from among six different predefined queries. For each query the user can set a time interval by specifying the start and the end date of interest. The queries are described in detail in the following:

1. **Articles:** Shows a table with the list of the articles used in the didactic software sessions executed in the selected time interval, detailed in a monthly resolution. For each article, the table reports the number of trials performed on each article and the ABA programs in which the article has been totally or partially mastered. Clicking one of the articles opens a pop-up with more detailed information, such as the date of the first and last use. A button allows downloading data selected in a CSV file.
2. **Categories:** Shows a table with the list of categories used in the didactic software sessions executed in the selected time interval, detailed in a monthly resolution. Clicking one of the categories produces a pop-up with more detailed information, such as the date of the first and last use of the category and the list of the articles used. A button allows downloading the data selected in a CSV file.
3. **Articles Mastered:** This query reports the number of articles mastered by the child, the number of sessions performed and their ratio. The query results are created in tabular and graphic formats. In Fig. 1 the upper line (blue) shows the number of articles mastered vs time, and the lower one (red) represents the number of articles mastered compared to the number of sessions completed. The number of sessions is an important parameter in such an analysis since it can highlight a child's greater or lesser need in terms of frequency of work (session hours) in order to obtain good results. The chart can be dynamically modified to highlight specific information, selecting only the line of interest.

   As previously mentioned, for all the graphs on the upper right side of the chart two buttons are available (see Fig. 1): one for the print version of the chart, and the second for exporting/downloading it as a PDF file, a PNG or JPEG image or an SVG vector image. It is also possible to download all the data extracted by the query into CSV format.

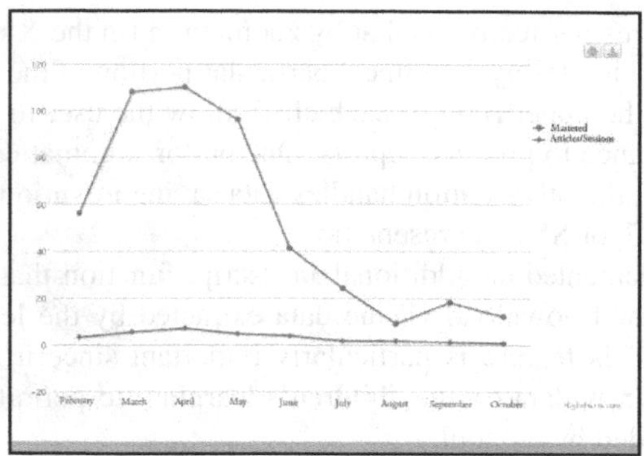

Fig. 1. Graph of number of articles mastered vs time

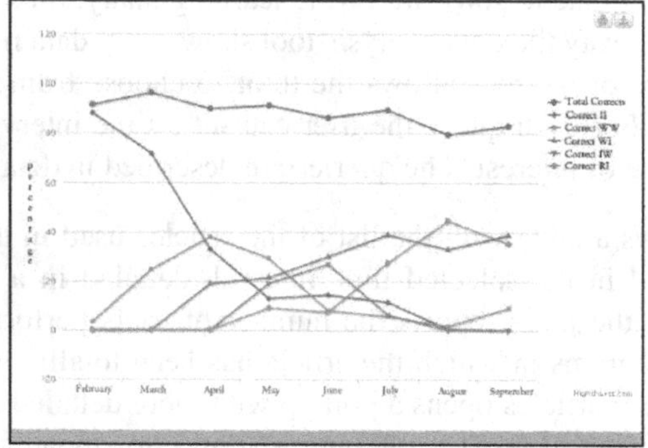

Fig. 2. Graph of correct trials vs time

4. Successful trials: The query returns the percentage of correct independent trials performed by the child (without prompt) through the ABCD software. If necessary, the tutor can access an additional table available through a pop-up menu with the list of the articles used in each trial. Information is shown as a textual table and as a chart. An example of the chart produced by this type of query is shown in Fig. 2: the acronyms refer to matching (M) and receptive (R) programs indicating whether combinations of Images (I) and Words (W) are used, as described in the Introduction of this paper. It is possible to print or download the chart in different format, and to download raw data in CSV format. The chart can be dynamically modified to highlight specific information selecting only the line of interest.

5. Error types: The query provides the percentage of different kinds of errors (i.e., error performing the exercise, auto-stimulation, no collaboration). It is possible to have information on which article was under acquisition when the child made a specific error, at which level, and so on (Fig. 3). The chart is interactive and allows highlighting specific information. It is possible to print or download the chart in different format, and to download raw data through a CSV file.

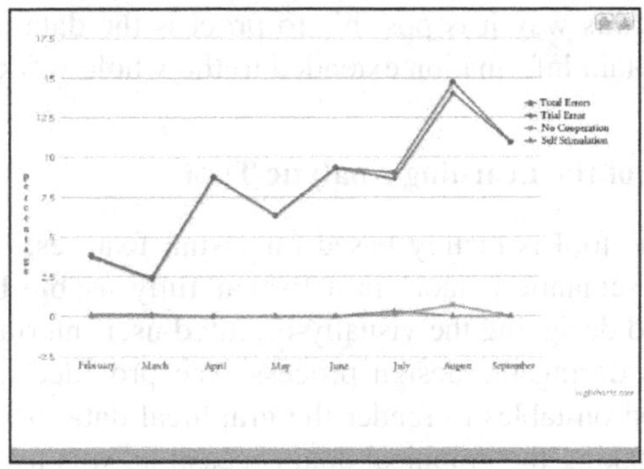

Fig. 3. Graph of error types vs time

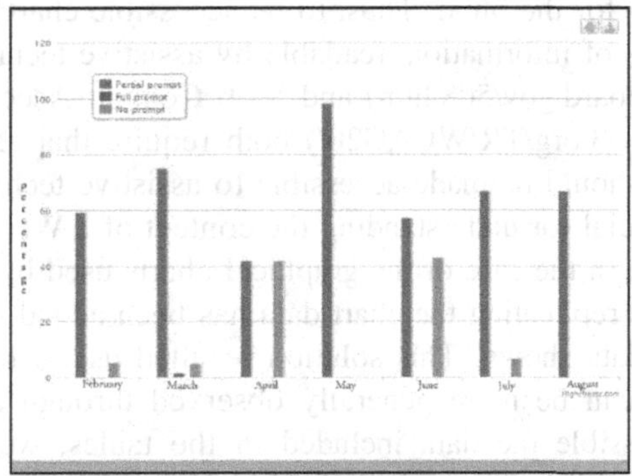

Fig. 4. Graph of prompts provided vs time

6. Prompts provided to the child: The query returns the percentage of occurrence of different levels of prompts, aggregated by relevance, i.e., Full prompt, Partial prompt and No prompt. The didactic software allows easy recording of prompt levels by pressing a key on the keyboard; keys from 1 to 5 are associated with percentages from 0% to 100%. All the data information is shown as a textual table and as a chart; an example of outcome is shown in Fig. 4. The chart is the result of grouping the prompts by the three abovementioned classes. If a more detailed view is desired, this query provides information (in table format) about the articles for which one or more prompts have been needed. For this type of query, a daily view of the use of prompts is also available, if required. As for the previous queries, it is possible to dynamically modify the chart to highlight specific information, print or download it in different format, and to download raw data in CSV format.

The tool can also be used outside the didactic software environment, although the database exploited is certainly the one collected by that software. This can be useful for offering an overview of the learning results to different subjects involved -- also indirectly -- in the intervention. In this case, after the log-in phase, it offers a look at the data of all the children associated with the logged-in tutor, since a specific child was not selected. In this way it is possible to process the data of all the children together, in order to obtain information extended to the whole working group.

5.1 Accessibility of the Learning Analytic Tool

The learning analytic tool is mainly based on visual features, but we focused especially on providing semantic content in a format fully usable by everyone. In fact, while developing and designing the visually-oriented user interfaces, we kept in mind accessibility aspects during the design process. We provided an alternative way to present content based on tables to render the graphical data in a textual format. This solution, aimed at making the graphical data accessible, was useful for observing the data from another point of view, enriching the analysis.

Due to their visual nature, charts present a real problem for people with visual impairments, especially for the blind. Thus, to be accessible charts should be presented with additional kinds of information, readable by assistive technologies. Section 508 (http://www.access-board.gov/508.htm) and Web Content Accessibility Guidelines - WCAG (http://www.w3.org/TR/WCAG20/) both require that all non-decorative and non-textual content should be made accessible to assistive technologies. Thus, if the data in a chart is crucial for understanding the content of a Web page, a text description has to be added. In the case of the graphical charts used by the learning analytic tool, a numeric table replicating the chart data has been added to provide an alternative version of the data shown. This solution resulted useful for providing granular information, which can be more generally observed through a graphical show. In order to make accessible the data included in the tables, we used the traditional HTML tags such as TH, TD and SUMMARY, which provide valuable meta-information about the table. We tested interface accessibility using the screen reader Jaws (http://www.freedomscientific.com/), which was able to correctly read the entire content of the tables.

6 Conclusions

The work presented herein is a learning analytic tool, web-based and implemented in conjunction with a didactic software program that enables technology-enhanced ABA intervention for children with autism. ABA intervention relies on the systematic collection of data in which the environmental variables involved in a specific behaviour are carefully annotated. Its efficacy is steadily monitored by analyzing this data. The learning analytic tool favors this monitoring by automatically extracting, aggregating and visualizing the children's progress, based on data from the didactic software sessions. Data are visualized in a different way, through charts and graphs, allowing the user to further explore them in an interactive modality. In this way, the application provides tutors with accurate real-time monitoring of children's learning and behavior, allowing them to more accurately tune and personalize the intervention for each child.

The learning analytic tool is open source and freely available. It was designed involving all members of an ABA team in order to better respond to their needs when performing data extraction and processing from the large amount of automatically collected data. A set of predefined queries has been implemented for retrieving the most relevant information on a child's performance over time, presented in an intuitive and interactive way, using tables and charts.

The ABA tutors were involved in the design and test phases of the tool to better understand the type of analysis needed as well as to improve the UI usability. Results from an online questionnaire showed that this tool is well-appreciated by 12 ABA professionals using the software since it reduced the effort of manually retrieving the large amount of data produced in ABA sessions: each tutor is able to view the child's performance in real time, useful both at the beginning of each intervention (to rapidly see previous progress) and for child assessment..

As future work, a larger set of users would be recruited to collect more feedback and suggestions, to further enrich the monitoring tool.

Acknowledgments. We thank the Regione Toscana, which funded this project within the framework of the "FAS 2007 2013 Delibera CIPE 166/2007 PAR FAS Regione Toscana Action Line 1.1.a.3" (14 Feb 2011-14 Ago 2013).

References

1. Sicile-Kira, C.: Autism Spectrum Disorders: A Complete Guide to Understanding Autism, Asperger Syndrome. Pervasive Developmental Disorder and Other ASDs. The Berkley Publishing Group, New York (2004)
2. Lovaas, O.I., Smith, T.: Intensive behavioral treatment for young autistic children. Advances in Clinical Child Psychology 11, 285–324 (1988)
3. Rogers, S., Vismara, L.: Evidence-based comprehensive treatments for early autism. Journal of Clinical Child & Adolescent Psychology 37, 8–38 (2008)
4. Leaf, R., Baker, D., McEachin, J.: Sense and Nonsense in the Behavioral Treatment of Autism: It has To be Said. Chapter 1: What is ABA? DRL Books Inc., New York (2008)
5. Bernard-Opitz, V., Ross, K., Nakhoda-Sapuan, S.: Enhancing social problem solving in children with autism and normal children with computer-assisted instruction. Journal of Autism and Developmental Disorder 31(4), 377–384 (2004)
6. Bosseler, A., Massaro, D.W.: Development and evaluation of computer-animated tutor for vocabulary and language learning in children with autism. Journal of Autism and Developmental Disorders 33(6), 553–567 (2003)
7. Moore, M., Calvert, S.: Brief report: Vocabulary acquisition for children with autism: Teacher or computer instruction. Journal of Autism and Developmental Disorders 30(4), 359–362 (2000)
8. Buzzi, M.C., Buzzi, M., Rapisarda, B., Senette, C., Tesconi, M.: Teaching Low-Functioning Autistic Children: ABCD SW. In: Hernández-Leo, D., Ley, T., Klamma, R., Harrer, A. (eds.) EC-TEL 2013. LNCS, vol. 8095, pp. 43–56. Springer, Heidelberg (2013)
9. Deno, S.L.: Developments in Curriculum-Based Measurement. The Journal of Special Education 37(3), 184–192 (2003)

10. Anderson, S.R., Romanczyk, R.G.: Early Intervention for Young Children with Autism: Continuum-Based Behavioral Models. The Journal of The Association for Persons with Severe Handicaps 24(3), 162–173 (1999)
11. Corsello, C.M.: Early intervention in autism. In: Infants & Young Children, vol. 18(2), pp. 74–85. Lippincott Williams & Wilkins, Inc. (2005)
12. Dawson, G., Zanolli, K.: Early intervention and brain plasticity in autism. Novartis Found Symp. 251, 266–274 (2003); discussion 274–280, 28–97
13. Evidence based practice and Autism in the school. A guide to providing appropriate interventions to students with autism spectrum disorders. NAC-National Autism Center. Massachusetts (2009) ISBN 978-0-9836494-1
14. Klin, A.: Listening preferences in regard to speech in four children with developmental disabilities. J. Child Psychol. Psychiat. 33, 763–769 (1992)
15. Leroy, G., Irmscher, A., Charlop-Christy, H.M., Kuriakose, S., Pishori, A., Zurzman, L., Ash-Rafzadeh, A., Seffrood, M., Buxton, S.: Data mining techniques to study therapy success with autistic children. In: DMIN, pp. 253–259 (2006)
16. Moderato, P., Copelli, C.: L'analisi comportamentale applicata Seconda parte: metodi e procedure. Autismo e Disturbi Dello Sviluppo 8(2), 191–233 (2010)
17. Calouri, K., Hamblen, A., Drill Book, E.: Project Pace, Inc. (1996)
18. Kearney, A.J.: Understanding applied behavior analysis: an introduction to ABA for parents, teachers, and other professionals. JKP essentials. Jessica Kingsley (2008)
19. Gregg, D.G.: Using Data Collection and Analysis to Improve Outcomes for Children with Autism. The Voices and Choices of Autism 1(3) (2009)
20. Shi, L., Graff, H., Wang, S.: Design and Development of KIHd System: A Data Collection and Analysis System for Teachers and Parents Working with Children with Autism and Other Disabilities. In: Society for Information Technology & Teacher Education Int. Conference, pp. 4231–4236 (2006)
21. Tarbox, J., Wilke, A.E., Findel-Pyles, R.S., Bergstrom, R.M., Granpeesheh, D.: A comparison of electronic to traditional pen-and-paper data collection in discrete trial training for children with autism. Research in Autism Spectrum Disorders, Elsevier 4(1), 65–75 (2010)
22. Freeman, R., Grzymala-Busse, J., Harvey, M.: Functional behavioral assessment using the data mining system-strategies for understanding complex physiological and behavioral patterns. J. Intell. Inf. Syst. 21(2), 173–181 (2003)

Towards Improving the e-learning Experience for Deaf Students: e-LUX

Fabrizio Borgia[1,2], Claudia S. Bianchini[3], and Maria De Marsico[2]

[1] Université Toulouse III - Paul Sabatier,
18 Route de Narbonne 31062 Toulouse CEDEX 9, France
[2] Sapienza Università di Roma, Dip. Informatica,
Via Salaria 113, 00198 Rome, Italy
{borgia,demarsico}@di.uniroma1.it
[3] Université de Poitiers,
1 Rue Raymond Cantel (Bat A3 - UFR L&L), 86073 Poitiers CEDEX 9, France
claudia.bianchini@univ-poitiers.fr

Abstract. Deaf people are more heavily affected by the digital divide than many would expect. Moreover, most accessibility guidelines addressing their needs just deal with captioning and audio-content transcription. However, this approach to the problem does not consider that deaf people have big troubles with vocal languages, even in their written form. At present, only a few organizations, like W3C, produced guidelines dealing with one of their most distinctive expressions: Sign Language (SL). SL is, in fact, the visual-gestural language used by many deaf people to communicate with each other. The present work aims at supporting e-learning user experience (e-LUX) for these specific users by enhancing the accessibility of content and container services. In particular, we propose preliminary solutions to tailor activities which can be more fruitful when performed in one's own "native" language, which for most deaf people, especially younger ones, is represented by national SL.

Keywords: Deaf needs, Sign Language, SignWriting, User Experience, e-learning.

1 Introduction

Just like any other software, e-learning applications need to be understood by their users in order to be effectively exploited. In particular, they require an even more careful design, during which many issues must be addressed. Most of all, they must be so easy to use to become "transparent" and let the user focus on the true goal of their use, i.e. learning. A first point to take in consideration is the difference between the container, i.e. the software platform or framework to deploy the e-learning content, and the content itself, i.e. the learning material [1]. The former might be designed once and for all, while the latter undergoes continuous development and update. It is often the case that attention merely focuses on features available on the container, and this is also true when addressing accessibility issues. However, content, and particularly the way it is

C. Stephanidis and M. Antona (Eds.): UAHCI/HCII 2014, Part II, LNCS 8514, pp. 221–232, 2014.

conceived and structured, is even more important when addressing users with special needs. This calls for devising ways to transmit the information through the best suited (sensory) channels for each category of users. Moreover, in many cases not only the transmission medium, but also the structure of the content must be adapted and deeply revised [2] [3].

Deaf people are among those groups of individuals with special needs who are most heavily affected by the digital divide. Despite the increasing attention towards accessibility issues, inclusion design for deaf people is often carried out using solutions on the edge of the workaround. In fact, most accessibility guidelines that should address their needs just deal with textual captioning and audio-content transcription [4]. However, this way of approaching the problem reveals an old misunderstanding: the cognitive structures underlying the language processing of deaf people are deeply different from those exploited by people experiencing Vocal Languages (VL) since infancy. As a consequence, most deaf people have big troubles with VLs, even in their written form, so that the solution is many times not better than the problem.

While captioning-based accessibility design may support the needs of people who become deaf after the acquisition of speech and language (post-lingual deafness), issues related to pre-lingual deafness are seldom and poorly addressed. Moreover, all deaf people generally experience major difficulties with the written form of Vocal Languages (VLs), making their level of proficiency with it comparable to that of foreign students [5]. Among the possible reasons for this peculiarity, deaf people base their perception and cognitive structuring of information from exterior world mostly on the sense of sight. Therefore, they tend to reflect their visual organization of the world over the organization of language. For this reason, despite some deaf people can use VL, dealing with the issues of deaf-oriented accessibility using written VL is quite unrealistic, especially within the e-learning context.

Only a few organizations produced guidelines dealing with one of the most distinctive expressions of deaf people: Sign Languages (SLs), i.e. the languages used by most deaf people in the world to communicate inside their community. Such languages are natural historical languages, based on the visual-gestural channel. The whole body (non just the hands, but even the arms, shoulders, torso, facial expression, and especially the look) is involved simultaneously and multimodally in the expression of the meaning (see the work of Pizzuto and Cuxac, such as [6] and [7]). The World Wide Web Consortium (W3C) has been one of the first organizations to require SL support in deaf-oriented accessibility design, through the Web Content Accessibility Guidelines (WCAG) 2.0 [8]. The WCAG 2.0 covers a wide range of recommendations for making Web content more accessible to a wide range of people with disabilities. Criterion 1.2.6, for instance, which is necessary to achieve the highest level of compliance (Level AAA), requires SL interpretation to be provided for all prerecorded audio content in synchronized media [8].

It is of paramount importance, for every group of individuals, to benefit from content written in one's own native language. Along this line, this work aims towards promoting e-learning accessibility for deaf people. In particular, we propose blueprints and preliminary solutions to support e-learning-tailored activities for deaf people, exploiting written SL.

2 Improving e-learning Experience for Deaf People

It is worth starting from the deep meaning that must be associated to the term "User Experience Design". It is quite easy to associate it to User Interaction Design, Information Architecture, Human-Computer Interaction, Human Factors Engineering, Usability and User Interface Design. As a matter of fact, according to [9], elements from each of these fields contribute to devising and implementing a positive user experience, and these field overlap themselves. It is important to underline that accessibility has always been considered as one of the constituent facets of user experience [10]. "It is not just an additional feature, it is a core component that makes modern interfaces complete. If designers fail to pay attention to the design needs for a small percentage of the population, they ultimately fail on a global scale" [11]. In this context, issues related to e-learning are especially ticklish. Given the problems often faced by people with special needs when interacting with ICT, the risk is that the kind of divide experienced in everyday life can also reflect on a kind of even more critical digital divide. As a matter of fact, unique occasions for accessing information and services otherwise hindered may be definitively lost. And if it is accepted that usability of e-learning applications is especially important [1], it is crucial to recognize that designing effective e-learning containers and contents for users with special needs requires a wider group of competences [2]. In this scenario, experts and subjects possibly belonging to the target categories of users play a special role. This is long put in practice for some disabilities, especially blindness. Internet offers plenty of research, tools and services supporting blind or partially-sighted students, which, though not always effective, reveal a good understanding of their problems at least. The situation is dramatically different for deaf users, and more critically for their access to e-learning applications. Textual captioning and subtitling of videos, as well as audio-content transcription have been long considered as viable strategies to support these users [4]. However, this approach is grounded on a serious misunderstanding, based on the assumption that sight was able to play for deaf a symmetrical role to hearing for blind: "writing" an audio content to the former should have been as much effective as "speaking" a written text to the latter. While it is often the case even for blindness that changing the channel might not be sufficient in itself [2], it is further to consider that cognitive structures underlying the language processing of born deaf people are deeply different from those exploited by people experiencing VLs since infancy. As a consequence, most deaf people hardly handle VLs, even in their written form. Since the solution is many times not better than the problem, the quality of e-Learning User Experience (e-LUX) dramatically degrades. Both containers and contents must be carefully (re)designed

3 Written SL and the Digital World

A necessary condition to achieve the goal of full access for deaf learners to the digital world is integrating SL resources and tools within e-learning applications, since the benefits of this methodology cannot be matched by any other accessibility solution [4]. As a matter of fact, SL can be considered as a native language for a wider and wider part of the deaf community, especially younger ones, who did not experience the ostracism exercised by oralism supporters towards SLs. Oralism is based on the belief that full integration of deaf students requires their education to oral languages using among others tricks like lip reading, or mimicking mouth shape and breathing patterns of spoken speech. The decline of oralism is marked by the work by Stokoe [12], but not before the 1970s.

In deaf-oriented accessibility design, SL is primarily supported by including videos within digital artifacts. SL videos are usually employed to make a digital resource available to deaf people, but, in most cases, they are included into VL-featuring artifacts [4].

A few technologies have been developed to produce artifacts exclusively oriented to deaf-people, in order to provide both SL-based navigation and content fruition. Sign Language Scent [4] and SignLinking [13], are among those technologies. They all implement the Hypervideo pattern, which provides navigation and content fruition solutions by embedding one or more hyperlinks in SL videos, thus allowing the user to navigate and retrieve further information if interested in the concept conveyed by a particular sequence (i.e. at a particular time interval) in a SL video.

Though effective when exploitable, videos cannot completely substitute written text, most of all in tasks requiring continuous interaction with the system. While textual chat can be nowadays easily substituted by a video one, and annotation and tagging can be achieved by attaching short clips to the relevant contents, search for relevant information using SL is much harder to design and implement. This is a crucial task. Image processing and pattern recognition techniques applied to videos are computationally (more) demanding and may lack the required accuracy. A viable solution seems to be the adoption of a writing system able to transcribe SLs in an intuitive way.

Like most languages in the world, SLs have not developed, during the course of their long history, a writing system achieving a wide recognition within its community. However, unlike VLs without a written form, SLs cannot be represented through the adaptation of a pre-existing notation (e.g. the International Phonetic Alphabet) because of their nature and their visual-gestural multilinearity and simultaneity [14][15]. Designing a writing system from scratch has therefore proven necessary to solve the problem of the graphical representation of SLs.

Different writing systems have been devised for SL over time: Stokoe's notation [12], in 1960, was the first one to achieve an international dissemination, followed, in the late 1970s, by SignWriting (SW) [16] and by Hamburg Sign Language Notation System (HamNoSys) [17], during the 1980s, see Fig.1 for a

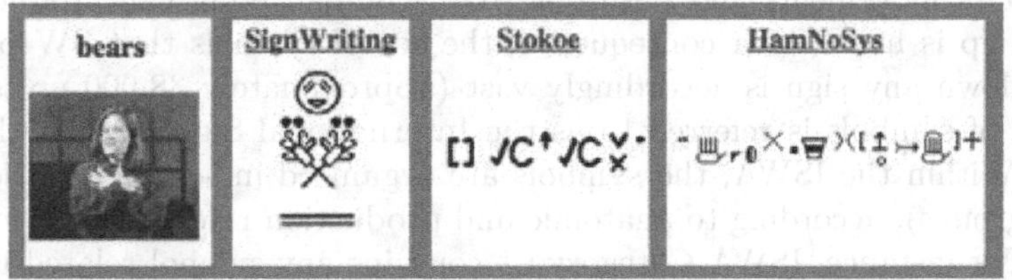

Fig. 1. ASL sign for "Bear", comparison between three different writing systems, extracted from [19]. From left to right: SW, Stokoe, HamNoSys.

Fig. 2. LIS sign for "Fun", written in SW. Extracted from [21].

visual comparison between the three systems[1]. Each of the aforementioned writing systems has its strengths and weaknesses, among them, SW proved more compatible with our goals, for reasons that are explained later in this section. According to Sutton [20], SignWriting is a writing system which uses visual symbols to represent the hand shapes, movements, and facial expressions of SLs. It is an "alphabet", a list of symbols used to write any SL in the world. Fig. 2 represents the Italian Sign Language (LIS) sign for "Fun", written in SW. Our reasons to adopt SW as the preferred SL writing system for our work are basically two: SW is a very iconic system, and it actually represents the physical production of the signs.

The high iconicity of the system is due to the shapes of the symbols themselves, which are 2-dimensional abstract images depicting positions or movements of hands, face, and body. The spatial arrangement of the symbols on the page also plays a core role since it does not follow a sequential order (like the letters that make up written English words) but it follows the natural arrangement suggested by the human body.

As mentioned before, SW preserves the actual physical formation of the signs, using an analogy-based representation, but no information is conveyed about their meaning; no phonemic or semantic analysis of a language is required to write it. "A person who has learned the system can "feel out" an unfamiliar sign in the same way an English speaking person can "sound out" an unfamiliar word written in the Latin alphabet, without even needing to know what the sign means" [19].

[1] For a comparison between the three writing system, which is beyond the scope of this paper, please refer to [18].

The set of movements and positions that a human body can produce from the waist up is huge. As a consequence, the set of symbols that SW provides to write down any sign is accordingly vast (approximately 38.000 units). The whole set of symbols is referred to as the International SignWriting Alphabet (ISWA). Within the ISWA, the symbols are organized in sets (categories) and subsets (groups), according to anatomic and production rules (see [22] for more details). For instance, ISWA Category 01 contains any symbol related to hand configurations. Category 01 includes different groups, one of them being ISWA Group 01, which contains any hand configuration featuring a single extended index finger. The organization introduced with the ISWA also allows to identify a unique 13-digit code for each symbol, each code provides information about which category and group its associated symbol belongs to.

The 2010 version of the ISWA (ISWA 2010) [22] is the most recent official one, and it has been adopted as the current standard by many research teams. In practice, we preferred to adopt the revised version of the ISWA by Bianchini [14].

Just like any other writing system, a SW text can be produced simply using pencil and paper. Despite this, SW has been oriented to digital production since its early years. The first digital editor for SW, named "SignWriter" was developed in 1986 by Richard Gleaves [23]. Since then, many applications have been produced by different teams, delivered in different ways, ranging from desktop to web applications. These applications can be considered as a class of software which basically provides the same functionalities, which are:

- Pick or type a symbol in order to insert it on the sign composition area.
- Manage the symbols on the sign composition area.
- Save the sign in one or more formats.

In the last years, SW has also been exploited to narrow the effects of the digital divide on deaf people, in fact, a fair number of SW-based resources is emerging on the Internet, to provide SL deaf-accessible content. The produced artifacts include websites, blogs, online SW editors and mobile applications. A notable example is "The SignWriting Website" [19], which is the main SW research and dissemination portal providing content both in VL and SL (through video and SW). Another ambitious project is the ASL Wikipedia Project [24], whose goal is to provide a American Sign Language (ASL) Wikipedia written in SW. Finally, Adam Frost's "The Frost Village" [25] represents an example of bilingual blog, since it can be accessed both in VL (American) and SL (ASL). Witnessing the expressive capacity and the relative ease to learn of SW [14], our work focused on making it effectively exploitable as a communication mean, and as a suitable learning support for deaf people. To this aim, we designed, developed and tested a new SW digital editor, the SignWriting improved fast transcriber (SWift)[2] [26] [3]. SWift allows users to compose single signs or signed stories in a simple interface-assisted way, and save them in multiple formats. In order to produce an editor specifically tailored to the needs of its target users, we worked with the

[2] SWift is available at `http://visel.di.uniroma1.it/SWift`.

advice of experts and deaf researchers from the Institute of Cognitive Sciences and Technologies of the Italian National Research Council (ISTC-CNR), following the principles of contextual design [27]. The software has been developed as a self-containing web application, therefore it can be easily included within a Document Object Model (DOM) element, thus allowing SWift to be included within any web-based learning platform, in order to provide a prompt SL support for e-learning. Actually, the editor has already been successfully integrated within a deaf-centered e-learning environment, (DELE) [28]. Once embedded within DELE, SWift has been employed to provide language support both to authoring and to communication tools for learners, such as chat, and forums.

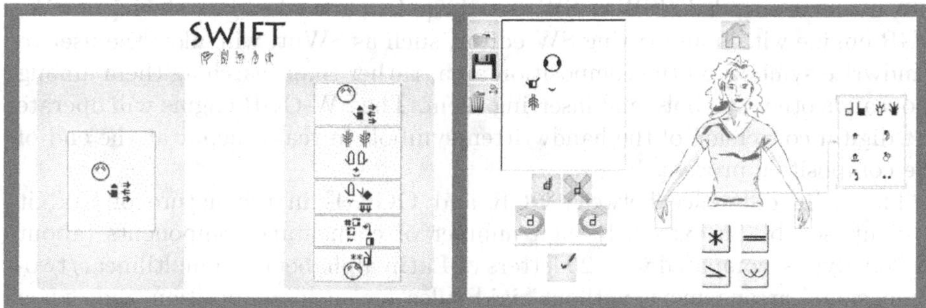

Fig. 3. Two screenshots taken from SWift. The home screen (left side) allows the user to choose between two modalities, depending on whether he wants to compose a single sign, or a whole signed story. The composition interface (right side) allows the user to actually enter a sign, in this case, the composition of the LIS sign for "Fun", shown in Fig. 2) is underway.

4 SignWriting Optical Glyph Recognition (SW-OGR)

Despite their increasing capabilities in terms of speed, usability, and reliability, SW digital editors are still far from granting the user a sign composition interface capable of challenging the simplicity of the non-digital handwritten approach. Actually, any software solution developed to support this need relies heavily on "Windows, Icons, Menus, Pointer" (WIMP) interfaces, both for accessing the application features and for the SW production process itself. The problem is all but a theoretical one, since in fact, during years of work along the ISTC-CNR team, which includes SW-proficient deaf researchers, we grew aware of a trend. We observed that SW users are far more accurate, fast and comfortable when using the traditional paper-pencil approach, than when dealing with the (more or less) complex interaction style of a digital editor.

Observing the intrinsic shortcomings of the present digital SW editors, we evaluated the possibility to design a new generation of SW editing applications, able to partially overcome the concept of the WIMP interface and to move along the line of the so called "natural interfaces" [29]. The new tools are intended to lift the user of any burden related to clicking, dragging, searching, browsing on the UI during the SW production process, and to provide him an interaction style which is as similar as possible the paper-pencil approach that humans normally use when writing or drawing. Of course, since WIMP is currently the easiest, most common interface style in the world, it cannot be totally left behind, because it is necessary to access the features of most applications. Nevertheless, our aim is to limit or dismiss the WIMP style during the SW production process, which is the core part of any SW editor.

To achieve this goal, we produced a SignWriting Optical Glyph Recognition (SW-OGR) engine, designed to operate the electronic conversion (recognition) of user-produced images containing handwritten (or printed) SignWriting symbols into machine-encoded (ISWA) SW text [30]. In particular. introducing a SW-OGR engine within an existing SW editor, such as SWift, will allow the user to handwrite symbols on the composition area, rather than searching them among thousands other symbols, and inserting them. The SW-OGR engine will operate the digital conversion of the handwritten symbols in real-time, or at the end of the composition process.

The main difference between OCR and OGR is in the nature of SW: it is composed by an extremely high number of elementary components (about 38.000 glyphs, compared with 26 letters of Latin alphabet) in a multilinear/two-dimensional arrangement, without rigid rules for such composition and, when handwritten, with a complex segmentation. OGR must be able to process such data, which is much more complex than alphabetic writing. Due to the huge amount of patterns to recognize, and consequently to the overwhelming training required, it is not feasible to exploit traditional pattern matching or machine learning approaches. We rather devised a software procedure driven by geometric as well as perceptual features of glyphs to recognize.

Our idea for the new generation of SW digital editors is illustrated by the diagram in Fig. 4. Our OGR-powered SW-editor is composed by the following modules:

- The **Data Acquisition Module**, included within the **User Interface**, whose purpose is to provide the user with a simple interaction style for SW composition, focusing on intuitiveness (or, better, invisibility) and accuracy. An ideal setting to provide a paper-pencil-like tangible interaction style requires the usage of an additional hardware component: the graphic tablet. However, a feasible alternative, though not always providing the sufficient stroke accuracy, is represented by touch screens. This module must also collect the data produced by the user (typically an image) and hand it to the SW-OGR module.
- The **SW-OGR Engine**, which globally handles and controls the recognition process. Two modules belong within the SW-OGR Engine:
  - The **OGR Module**, whose purpose is to provide a fast and as accurate as possible recognition of all (or most) symbols composed by the user.
  - The **OGR Data Embedding Module**, which is responsible for the creation of a result image embedded with the data produced by the

OGR Module (it will most likely produce an image and an associated OGR data file, typically a SWML-encoded file).

- The data from the SW-OGR Engine are sent back to the **User Interface**, and are shown within the **Review Module**, which also allows the user to make corrections and/or add other data. The work done to produce SWift could prove very useful during the development of this module, since their functionalities (symbol search and editing) are very similar.
- The **Data Finalization Module** which receives the user-reviewed OGR data from the User Interface. The purpose of this module is to save in the proper form (file, DB, etc.) the data it receives.

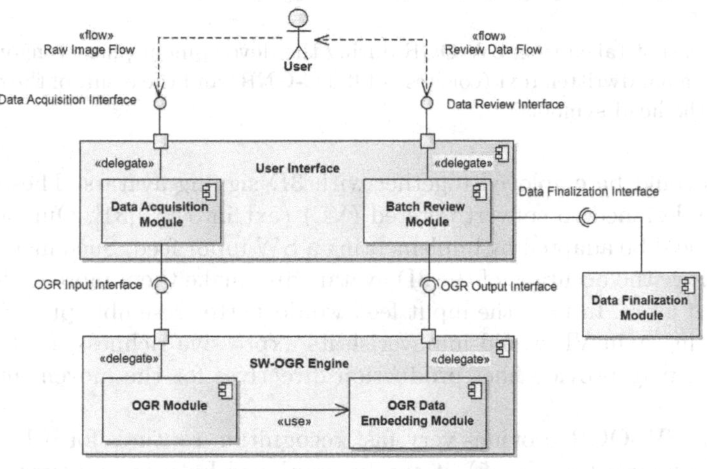

Fig. 4. Component diagram for a new generation of SW editors featuring a SW-OGR engine

The achievement of such an editor is the main reason why we decided to work on a SW-OGR engine[3], since we think that it is bound to be the core component of a future SW digital editor (as illustrated in Fig. 4).

Another motivation fueled our efforts while working on SW-OGR. Since the beginning of our work, we were aware of the presence (and of the considerable size) of a number of handwritten SW corpora, produced from different communities around the world. In [14], for instance, Bianchini gathered every story written using SW by the deaf community of ISTC-CNR. Such corpora are an invaluable asset, and they could become even more useful if digitalized. Besides allowing a wider and faster diffusion of the information carried by the corpora themselves, we expect such resources to have several fields of application. They could, for instance, provide whole new SW datasets for the linguistic research community to perform any kind of analysis. Moreover, the produced digital SW

[3] For further information about SW-OGR, please refer to [30].

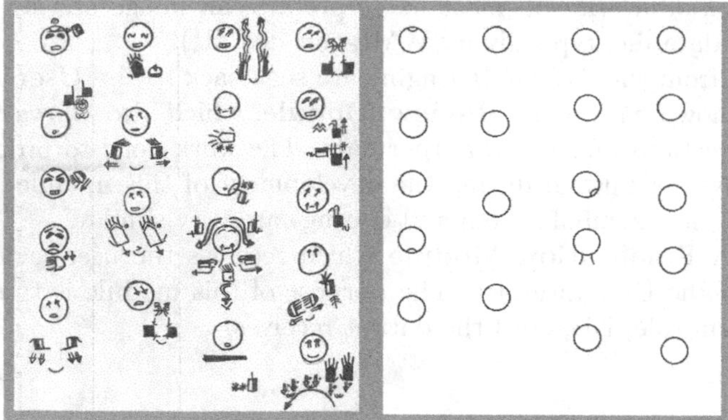

Fig. 5. Screenshot taken from SW-OGR during the development phase (ongoing). The image shows a handwritten text (courtesy of ISTC-CNR) and the result of the detection routine for the head symbols.

documents could be employed together with 3D signing avatars. These kind of avatars are designed to convert entered (VL) text into SL [31]. Our opinion is that they could be adapted by implementing a SW input feed. Such methodology would improve the accuracy of the 3D avatars and make them more understandable by deaf users. In fact, the input feed would better resemble pure SL, while pre-converting it in VL would impoverish its expressive richness. Furthermore, ISWA codes may provide finer production directives for the movements of the avatars.

Since the SW-OGR provides very fast recognition routines for a large number of SW symbols (see Fig. 5), it can be employed both in real-time (e.g. SW editing) and batch (e.g. mass SW corpora digitalization) processing. In the second case, the diagram in Fig. 4 can be easily adapted to forbear the constant presence of a human actor (see [30]).

5 Conclusion and Future

The inclusion of deaf people in the context of the best e-LUX achievements requires to carefully rethink the formulation and design of appropriate frameworks for ICT deployment. While SLs represent a widely spread form of expression for deaf people, their inclusion in electronic services and contents is still limited, when available, to videos. However, interactive tasks and search may take great advantage from exploiting a written system to translate SL expressions and contents in an intuitive way. This work is a brick in the creation of an overall framework targeting at supporting deaf people through their most natural form of expression. The final result, namely SWORD (SignWriting Oriented Resources for the Deaf) will represent a step towards full integration of deaf people in digital society.

References

1. Ardito, C., Costabile, M., De Marsico, M., Lanzilotti, R., Levialdi, S., Roselli, T., Rossano, V.: An approach to usability evaluation of e-learning applications. Universal Access in the Information Society 4(3), 270–283 (2006)
2. De Marsico, M., Kimani, S., Mirabella, V., Norman, K.L., Catarci, T.: A proposal toward the development of accessible e-learning content by human involvement. Universal Access in the Information Society 5(2), 150–169 (2006)
3. Bianchini, C.S., Borgia, F., Bottoni, P., De Marsico, M.: SWift: a SignWriting improved fast transcriber. In: Tortora, G., Levialdi, S., Tucci, M. (eds.) Proceedings of the International Working Conference on Advanced Visual Interfaces, pp. 390–393. ACM, New York (2012)
4. Fajardo, I., Vigo, M., Salmerón, L.: Technology for supporting web information search and learning in Sign Language. Interacting with Computers 21(4), 243–256 (2009)
5. Perini, M.: Les conditions de l'appropriation du français (écrit) langue seconde par les Sourds profonds locuteurs de la LSF: Analyse des difficultés et propositions méthodologiques. PhD thesis, Université de Paris 8, Paris, France (2013)
6. Antinoro Pizzuto, E., Chiari, I., Rossini, P.: Representing signed languages: theoretical, methodological and practical issues. In: Pettorino, M., Giannini, F.A., Chiari, I., Dovetto, F. (eds.) Spoken communication, Cambridge Scholars Publishing, Newcastle upon Tyne (2010)
7. Cuxac, C.: La Langue des Signes Française (LSF): les voies de l'iconicité. In: Cuxac, C. (ed.) Faits de langues, vol. (15-16). Ophrys, Paris (2000)
8. Caldwell, B., Cooper, M., Guarino Reid, L., Vanderheiden, G.: Web Content Accessibility Guidelines 2.0, WCAG 2.0 (December 11, 2008), `http://www.w3.org/TR/WCAG` (retrieved November 11, 2013)
9. Paluch, K.: What is User Experience Design (October 10, 2006), `http://www.montparnas.com/articles/what-is-user-experience-design/` (retrieved December 29, 2013)
10. Morville, P.: User Experience Design (June 21, 2004), `http://semanticstudios.com/publications/semantics/000029.php` (retrieved December 29, 2013)
11. So, Y., Veneziano, L.: Designing for Everyone: The Role of Accessibility in Service Design. UX Magazine (July 26, 2012), `http://uxmag.com/articles/designing-for-everyone` (retrieved December 29, 2013)
12. Stokoe, W.C.: Sign Language structure: an outline of the visual communication systems of the American deaf. Studies in Linguistics 8 (1960); occasional papers
13. Fels, D.I., Richards, J., Hardman, J., Lee, D.G.: Sign language Web pages. American Annals of the Deaf 151(4), 423–433 (2006)
14. Bianchini, C.S.: Analyse métalinguistique de l'émergence d'un système d'écriture des Langues des Signes: SignWriting et son application à la Langue des Signes Italienne (LIS). PhD thesis, Université de Paris 8, Paris, France (2012)
15. Garcia, B.: Sourds, surdité, Langue(s) des Signes et épistmiologie des sciences du langage: problématiques de la scripturisation et modélisation des bas niveaux en Langue des Signe Franaise (LSF). Mémoire de HDR, Université de Paris 8 (2010)
16. Sutton, V.: Sutton Movement Shorthand: Writing Tool for Research. In: Stokoe, W.C. (ed.) Proceedings of the First National Symposium on Sign Language Research & Teaching, pp. 267–296. Department of Health, Education and Welfare, Chicago (1977)

17. Prillwitz, S., Leven, R., Zienert, H., Hanke, H., Henning, J.: Hamburg Notation System for Sign Languages: an introductory guide, HamNoSys version 2.0. Signum, Seedorf, Germany (1989)
18. Channon, R., van der Hulst, H.: Notation Sytems. In: Brentari, D. (ed.) Sign Languages. Cambridge University Press, Cambridge (2010)
19. Sutton, V.: SignWriting For Sign Languages, `http://www.signwriting.org/` (retrieved from November 13, 2013)
20. Sutton, V.: Lessons in SignWriting. Deaf Action Commitee for SignWriting, La Jolla (1995)
21. Di Renzo, A., Gianfreda, G., Lamano, L., Lucioli, T., Pennacchi, B., Rossini, P., Bianchini, C.S., Petitta, G., Antinoro Pizzuto, E.: Scrivere la LIS con il SignWriting: manuale introduttivo. ISTC-CNR, Rome, Italy (2012)
22. Slevinski Jr., S.E.: International SignWriting Alphabet 2010 - HTML Reference, `http://www.signbank.org/iswa` (retrieved from November 10, 2013)
23. Sutton, V.: SignWriter-At-A-Glance Instruction Manual, SignWriter Computer Program Notebook. Deaf Action Commitee for SignWriting, La Jolla (1993)
24. Sutton, V.: ASL Wikipedia Project, `http://ase.wikipedia.wmflabs.org/wiki/Main_Page` (retrieved from November 10, 2013)
25. Frost, A.: The Frost Village, `http://www.frostvillage.com/lang/ase` (retrieved from December 27, 2013)
26. Borgia, F., Marsico, M., Panizzi, E., Pietrangeli, L.: ARMob - Augmented reality for Urban Mobility in RMob. Paper presented at the International Working Conference on Advanced Visual Interfaces (May 2012)
27. Beyer, H., Holtzblatt, K.: Contextual Design: Defining Customer-centered Systems. Interactive Technologies Series. Morgan Kaufmann, San Francisco (1998)
28. Bottoni, P., Borgia, F., Buccarella, D., Capuano, D., De Marsico, M., Labella, A.: Stories and signs in an e-learning environment for deaf people. Universal Access in the Information Society 12(4), 369–386 (2013)
29. van Dam, A.: Post-WIMP User Interfaces. Commun. ACM 40(2), 63–67 (1997)
30. Borgia, F.: Informatisation de forme graphique des Langues des Signes: application l'ècriture de SignWriting. PhD thesis, Université Toulouse III - Paul Sabatier, Toulouse, France (Exp. 2014)
31. Efthimiou, E., Fotinea, S.E., Hanke, T., Glauert, J., Bowden, R., Braffort, A., Collet, C., Maragos, P., Lefebvre-Albaret, F.: Sign Language technologies and resources of the Dicta-Sign project. In: Proceedings of the 5th Workshop on the Representation and Processing of Sign Languages, Istanbul, Turkey, pp. 37–44 (2012)

Medium for Children's Creativity: A Case Study of Artifact's Influence

Nanna Borum, Kasper Kristensen,
Eva Petersson Brooks, and Anthony Lewis Brooks

Department for Architecture, Design and Media Technology, Aalborg University, Denmark
(nb,ep,tb)@create.aau.dk,
kkrist87@gmail.com

Abstract. This paper reports on an exploratory study that investigates 16 elementary school children's interaction with two different mediums for creativity, LEGO® bricks and paper collages, drawing on the previous creativity assessment test carried out by Amabile [1]. The study is based in a playful learning theoretical framework that is reflected in the means for analyzing the video material inspired by Price, Rogers, Scaife, Stanton and Neale [2]. The findings showed that the children explored the two mediums to the same degree, but that they were more structured in their planning and division on labor when working with LEGO bricks. It was also evident that the children assigned preconceived affordances to the two mediums. The results from this study should feed into to a technology enhanced playful learning environment and these are the initial steps in the design process.

Keywords: Creativity, Playful Learning, Play, Artifacts, Technology Enhanced Learning.

1 Introduction

Children are increasingly relying on interactive technology for learning and such technologies were believed to revolutionize learning. Schools have however in general, remained to a traditional instructional model of the teacher, written material and the textbook as primary sources of knowledge primarily conveyed through lecturing, discussion and reading. In line with this, the current development of intuitive technologies has enabled children to interact with contemporary technology as the most natural act in the world. This widespread "digital adoption" offers new opportunities for playful learning, which can be individual, together with parents, or in supervised peer-groups, and embedded education potentials to foster development of creative and innovative competencies.

Creativity has become a vital and highly valued aspect of science, technology, education, as well as everyday life by the end of the 20th century due to economic, social as well as technological drivers [3]. While there have been great expectations about the use of interactive technology to support learning and creativity in educational [4]

C. Stephanidis and M. Antona (Eds.): UAHCI/HCII 2014, Part II, LNCS 8514, pp. 233–244, 2014.

as well as professional settings [5], the creative and multimodal workflow of children provides a major obstacle to current use of technology-based systems and resources. Yet, while being an inherently knowledge-based process, creativity from this perspective is more than mere information processing but a direct involvement with artifacts aimed at transformation.

In this way, creativity links to play and, in particular, to the way the play activity is perceived by the player [6]. Accordingly, children's tendency towards play, or playfulness, has been linked to creative thinking skills [8], [9]. In line with Howard et al. [7], this paper suggests a distinction between the act of play and the sense of playfulness, which implies that the experience of playfulness is applicable to play as well as work. It is this sense of playfulness that can contribute to creativity, particularly in an educational context. "Whilst certain activities may appear more play-like, we can never be sure whether the individual is feeling playful." ([7] p. 5). If playfulness in this way constitutes an internal state that a child brings to an activity, it is important to understand the influence of the context and the way objects may foster playfulness. Price, Rogers, Scaife, Stanton and Neale [2] have defined a range of elements that are essential for playful learning, e.g. exploration through interaction, engagement, reflection, imagination, creativity and thinking at different levels of abstraction, and collaboration. These elements can be related to how children in their everyday life naturally, and often playfully, explore the world [10],[11]. It is envisioned that such playful explorations, based on children's own interests and desires, elicit creativity through their involvement with the world.

Building on this and on recent work in the field of creativity (e.g. [5], [12], [13], [14]), this study starts from a notion of creativity as a materially mediated practice. In line with this perspective, the focus is on the particular qualities of such practices rather than on particular methods or techniques. Hence, this paper addresses the question of how artifacts can evoke creativity and how this might afford a material linking between playful learning and creativity. In particular, this study examines how creativity turns into playful and productive activities through actual manipulation of two types of medium: Paper collage and LEGO®. In line with van Leeuwen [15] this approach includes an explorative investigation of how a specific medium is used and how the children talk about them, justify them, and critique them. In addition and based on this investigation, our intention is to discover and design a new digital playful learning medium fostering creativity in educational settings. This study focuses on the first step, which is to say how a specific medium is used, talked about and negotiated and how this gives input to the initial conceptual framework and design requirements.

2 Related Work

In this paper, we investigate the potential link between play and creativity suggested by a range of researchers ([16], [9]) and more specifically the potential link between perceived level of mastery of a medium and how it affects the level of creativity in a given task [2]. This build on a pragmatist notion of action (and interaction) as developed by Dewey [17] and offers an understanding of creativity as an emergent, situated and reciprocal process comprising action and reflection as well as an interplay between the subject and the environment [18]. The pragmatist notion also shares basic premises with play theories. For example, play is commonly used as a motivator in learning situations where the adding of play elements to an activity targets an increased situational engagement and, thereby, motivation to participate in the specific activity [19]. This is in line with Chally [20] who states that such an engagement enhances self-agency through creative and playful assignments. Furthermore, Wood [21] underlines that play activities create affordance for learning. This is in line with what Resnick [22] describes as playful learning; situations where play is fully integrated in the learning activity and, consequently, an integral part of the learning experience. Still, though, many schools approach playful learning activities with resistance and skepticism considering them as 'just play' [22].

Bringing a playful learning perspective to creativity, involve that actions, objects as well as events must be understood in the context of the situation of which they are involved. In this regard, Dewey [23] emphasizes the notion of inquiry, acknowledged as a mode of action. This resonates with Beardon, Ehn & Malmborg ([24] p. 503) who argue that creativity constitutes a mode of interaction with the world rather than being a property of a person, process, product, or environment. Sullivan [25] states that play is an important mode of inquiry when the learning targets creativity. Howard et al.[6] and Broadhead and Burt [26] emphasize that a child initiated environment and its possibilities promotes less separation of play and learning resulting in playful learning. Petersson and Brooks [27] describe how toys contributed to an increased motivation to learn and had a potential to aid learning in a playful way; this perspective has substantial implications for the classroom habitus [28]. In line with this, we investigate how media in the form of LEGO® and paper collage, might elicit creativity through exploration and mastery. In doing so, we further the related work on creativity, play, and learning by emphasizing that playfulness in learning situations are not only connected to individual interests and desires, but also to the material affordances involved in such situations. In this sense, the affordances refer to the potential uses of a given medium, based on the perceivable features of this medium [29] and how these affordances are actualized in concrete social practices [15].

Conceptualizing creativity as a playful learning practice entails, among others, the following propositions:

- Creativity and playful learning is mediated by artifacts and results in a transformation of the physical world. Artifacts provide essential resources for agents to communicate, store, catalyze, evaluate and reflect on ideas while trying to overcome the indeterminate situation. Artifacts, from this perspective, are not mere carriers of information, but enable and constrain an actor's moves ([27], [18]).
- Creativity and playful learning goes along with the generation of new knowledge. As creative practices attempt to act upon a hitherto undetermined situation, the outcomes of this attempt necessarily add to the actors' body of knowledge either in that assumptions about the situation are contested or supported. Creative practice hence can be understood as a form of inquiry ([23], [30], [25]).

The focus of this study, how media creatively can be used in playful learning situations, hence is based on the assumption that in these situations are deliberately cultivated. This knowledge creates a basis for the design of a new digital playful learning medium fostering creativity in educational settings.

The aim of playful learning is to allow children to learn and apply learned knowledge to playful situations. Thus by applying and constructing new knowledge iteratively in play the child, in line with Gee [31], attains a deep practical knowledge of the subject at hand.

3 Method

The exploratory study took place in a private Danish elementary school (16 children, 11 boys, 5 girls, age 10-11 years) and it was carried out during a Danish class with the teacher of the class present in the room. It consisted of two sessions a) a collage test, and b) a LEGO®-building test. In each session, 20 minutes each, the 16 children were divided into 4 groups with 4 children in each. 2 groups were to work together and 2 groups worked individually. All groups had the same introduction to the activities on the day. They were instructed that they should have fun and be as creative as possible, and that they should try to produce something really silly and something that would be for the researchers to keep. In line with Amabile [1], the intention with silliness was to establish a fairly high baseline for creativity and also in an effort to reduce extraneous variables in the children's choice of theme.

In the collage test each table was provided with approx. 500 pieces of paper of different shapes and sizes that they were instructed to share, and also to be nice to each other and not hoard any specific piece or color of paper. In the LEGO-building test, the procedure was similar. Each table was provided with approx. 1600 pieces of LEGO of different size and shapes and again instructed to share as in the collage session. The children immediately started to investigate the materials, playing with them, touching them and talking about them. In general the children expressed a high level of interest in the materials. The sessions were video recorded with 5 cameras in total, having one camera at each table and one camera filming the whole scene.

After each session the children were asked to fill out 13 questions that were read aloud enabling them to ask questions on the wording to ensure understanding. The questions were partially from Amabile [32], [1], and Conti et al. [33] since no full questionnaire from Amabile [1] was accessible. Questions covered areas on intrinsic and extrinsic motivation, and their joy of the medium and had wordings such as "Was the activity more like play than work?", "Were you motivated more by your own interest in the collage/ LEGO or the instructions from the experimenter?", and "How much did you want to make a design that was better than the other kids' designs?".

3.1 Data Treatment

As a means to investigate the children's interactions with the artifacts and with each other an 'Interaction Analysis' of the video material was carried out [34]. The data was transcribed, coded and analyzed by two researchers independently. The analysis focused on 5 topics related to playful learning developed by Price et al. [2]: (a) Exploration through interaction, (b) engagement, (c) reflection, (d) imagination, creativity and thinking at different levels of abstraction, and (e) collaboration, discussed below.

Still images of the creative contributions of the children were uploaded to an online questionnaire that was distributed to a group of experienced artists to assess the level of creativity through 16 artistic dimensions in accordance with Amabile [32] such as expression of meaning, degree of representationalism, and silliness. The results from the assessments together with the self-report data from the tests were examined to search for emerging trends and patterns. The results from this analysis will be presented in the findings when relevant.

4 Findings and Discussion

The findings from the data treatment, shows distinct differences between the creative products made from each artifacts as well as differences in the process of making them. The individual findings are discussed in the next sessions. The names of the participating children are anonymized for ethical reasons.

4.1 Exploration through Interaction

The two artifacts used for the sessions were familiar to all participants, as such there was not much basic functionality for the participants to discover and interpret, leaving room for more playful interaction.

Brooks and Petersson [35] make a distinction between exploration and play. Where exploration gave way to play the emphasis changes from the question of "what does this object do?" to "what can I do with this object?". Both mediums allowed for instances of peer learning. In the LEGO® session the children would instruct each other building patterns as exemplified:

- GL: Do it like this, build in this pattern, then it will hold better.
- BE: Can I see how you do it?

The two artifacts facilitated the assignment in different ways, each evidently pushing towards certain themes, of which the children chose to pursue. In the paper collage sessions all but one participant chose to create representations of creatures (often people) with a hint of fairytale such as a pirate or a strong man. This is interestingly compared to the LEGO session where the most common theme was houses, which half of all participants decided to do, and that all but one of the participants chose to create inanimate objects. One individual choose to create a human face that he however stated to be a mask and not a human (see figure 1).

As such each artifact seems to come with a preconceived framework of possibilities that are available within that medium. This could be a result of the perceived qualities of each artifact. LEGO bricks do not allow soft curves, and seemed associated with masonry, architecture and defined structures.

Fig. 1. Example of LEGO

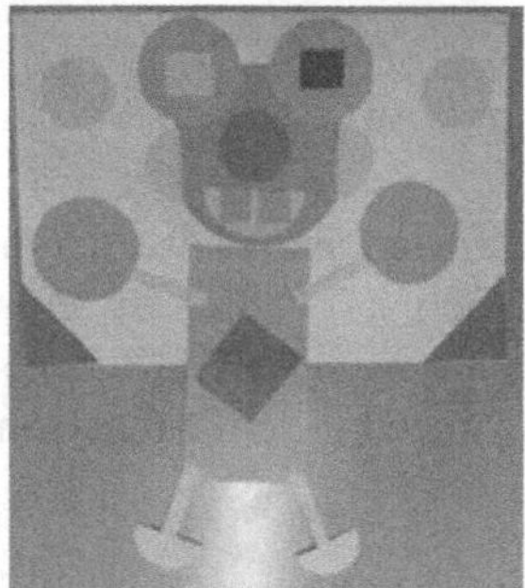

Fig. 2. Example of paper collage

Similarly in the paper collage session the children had assigned preconceived assets to the mediums. They were handed a white paper to function as background for their creations. This paper constituted and functioned as a frame for many of the children. Most of the children chose to stay inside this frame, but two of them pushed the boundaries of the frame and let their creations move outside the frame (see figure 2).

Another preconceived asset the children seemed to have assigned to the mediums were the dimensions they supported. When the children constructed with LEGO they mainly build 3D constructions, except a single child (see figure 1). When constructing with paper none of the children tried to explore the medium and construct in more dimensions than two. They could easily have folded and glued the paper to construct 3D object but that did not appeal to any of them.

4.2 Reflection

Throughout the test the participants would communicate with each other and when needed with the researchers. These conversations serve as the primary report for the children's reflections and understanding of the assignment. When the children asked questions to the researchers the subjects showed what the participants perceived as normal use of each artifact. In the LEGO® session the children would ask if the creative product should be solidly build. While in the paper collage session the questions related to tearing and writing on the paper e.g.:

– TO: Can we tear them apart, we have tools for it (raises his hands in the air)
– AN: We tear a bunch of small ones.
– TO: They should be yellow so that they look like teeth.

Interestingly the children had strong opinion about LEGO; how good they were, and if they liked it. In the paper collage such opinion were absent. Also for the paper collage session there was a greater focus on detail; which shape to use for what, whereas in the LEGO session focus was on the look of the finished construction.

4.3 Imagination and Creativity

Each of the participants' concepts of creativity was most evident at the start of each collaboratory session. This was where participants had short conversations related to what they should create together. In these discussions the children often argued against the ideas that they did not consider creative:

– SA: We could build a bridge?
– VI: We could build a bridge!
– AU: Build a bridge, yes!.
– LA: No, it needs to be something new.
– VI: we could build a statue?
– LA: It should be something new!
– VI: A statue, a big beautiful statue.
– LA: That's not new.
– SA: A statue is actually a really good idea, we just need to put lots of stuff on it.

Here we see the children trying to align their concepts of a creative contribution, using the idea of newness as their primary criteria, and arguing that more detail is what makes a concept new.

The artists rated the collaboratory groups higher than their individual counterparts at average. Interestingly, the LEGO® session scored higher compared to the paper collage in the collaboratory groups, but the relationship was reversed for the individual groups. From the collaboratory LEGO sessions, where both groups made a house, it was apparent that the participants came to the decision through a compromise. They were however, able construct something unique, due to the fact that they were more people. This was not the case for the individual LEGO participants, who most often only had time for a basic construction. This could explain the difference between the individual LEGO group and collage paper. Collage paper is not as time intensive to use as LEGO bricks, allowing for multiple iterations and added detail.

4.4 Excitement

In line with Price et al. [2] excitement was assessed on the children's' verbal accounts on their expressed involvement and participation desire. In both the LEGO® session and the paper collage sessions the children generally showed interest in the tasks and were enthusiastic towards the medium. In the LEGO task one or two children at each table expressed that they did not how to build with LEGO or that they did not feel skilled in building with LEGO bricks and their overall enthusiasm towards the task seemed to reflect this feeling, they would spend longer time on deciding a motive and would verbalize more negatively about their construction in process. It should be noted that this did not reflect in their self-report data on motivation afterwards. In the paper collage session the children did not have any similar statements regarding their skills. The children seemed to consider each other equally skilled in constructing with paper, and throughout the session they had positive exclamations towards both own work and the work of others e.g.:

— TO: It needs a jaw.
— ST: These will work. (ST hands TO a pile of triangularly shaped cut outs
— ST: Wow, this actually looks really good
— AN: It does not only look good, it looks superpower cool..

4.5 Collaboration

The focus when analyzing for collaboration between the children was on sharing of artifacts, the children's skills in receiving and giving instructions; their skills in turn taking and sharing roles, their skills in encouraging each other, and on their ability to scaffold on other children's' ideas.

In the LEGO® session there was generally more communication between the children. They discussed what to build and elaborated on each other's ideas and gave space to all having a say in the ideation process. In both sessions it however gave rise to a level of autonomy in the group members whose ideas were voted down. In some cases they constructed models that reflected bits of their own idea and in other cases they stayed out of the construction for a period of time as to show their disapproval. The other children seemed to accept the behavior and tried to encourage the disgruntled child by including him/her in specific tasks or including his/her construction in the shared construction. This is exemplified below:

(After LA have worked alone silently for a while):

— LA: I 've made a thing.
— VI: We could really use that in our house (places it in their shared construction). It could be a small bookshelf.
— LA smiles: I don't even know what it was supposed to be.
— VI: It looks like a bookshelf. Could you build some more interiors for the house?
– LA: smiles and starts finding more LEGO bricks.

In the building process the LEGO bricks allowed the children to construct in a parallel fashion, which means that often they built next to each other and then combined the different sections in the end. The children communicated on their design decisions along the way but seemed to feel ownership of the specific section and sought encouragement at each other but did not necessarily follow the instructions

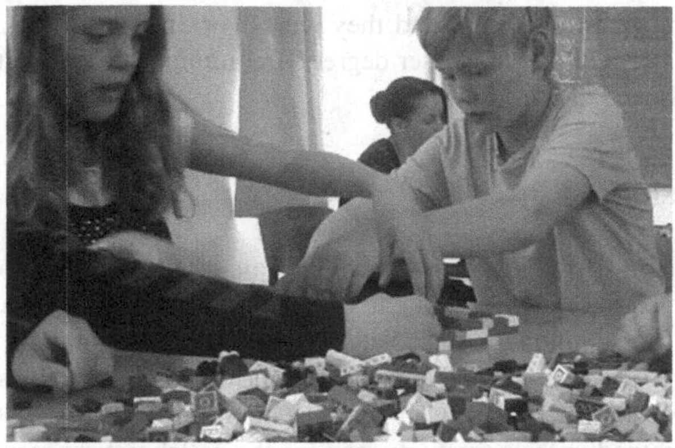

Fig. 3. Example of three children working together

and recommendations from their peers. In another group in the LEGO session all the children were involved in not only the design decisions but also the assembling of LEGO bricks, resulting in situations where up to five hands were working on the same model simultaneously (see figure 3).

It is evident that when working with LEGO the children share the different roles easily and show excellent turn taking skills. The roles that emerge in the session include designer/ coordinator, brick finder, and construction worker. In the paper collage task the division of work and the roles the children differ between are similar to the LEGO session, however, the work seems more open-ended and less planned for giving the designer/ coordinator a weaker role in the creative work. On some occasions the group tended to work without a fixed goal and to allow the construction evolve along the way. This is evident in the conversation below between three of the children about the almost finished construction. The tone of the conversation is friendly:

— AN: Wow now it really looks like a lion!
— TO: yeah any animal will do.
— AN: perhaps we are done then?!
— TO: It looks cool. Wait a second; we could also… (ST cuts in)
— ST: Are we making a lion?
— AN: Now we are.
— TO: A MOUSE! It's a mouse.
— AN: No it isn't. It's a lion.
— TO: A lion with short teeth that is.

In general the children in the paper collage task communicated well with each other. Compared to the LEGO session they did it to a lesser degree and the conversations were more focused towards the task. There was only minimal small talk around the table as the paper collage affordance a more closed interaction. The children were bent over the pieces of paper gluing them together while in the LEGO task, the children had a more open posture and they were working with the LEGO bricks in front of them. It seemed that the lesser degree of communication affected the level of collaboration between the children.

5 Conclusion

In the paper collage it was apparent the children made the creative contribution they immediately wanted to create, with little to no consideration of their own ability to carry out the work. As a result of these immediate decisions the most common depicted theme were characters, such as people and animals as opposed to constructions or landscapes. It was evident that the participants were more challenged in the LEGO® session. They were more constrained in their creativity, and for the collaboratory groups had a strong need for a coherent goal, and to delegate the tasks efficiently in order to finish within the assigned time. As a result there was generally more communication between participants in the LEGO sessions. In the collaboratory groups the participants in the LEGO session were observed to change their theme during construction. In both cases they went from a character design to a building, as such it is likely that if the children had been better supplied with a diverse allotment of bricks in the LEGO session, they would likely have preferred more animated designs.

In relation to the proposition that the perceived level of mastery with a media affects the creative process [2], the participants needs to be aware of what an artifact is able to do, before realizing what they are personally able to accomplish with the artifact [35]. The subjective judgments by the two experienced artists showed a decrease in creativity when the participants worked alone using LEGO compared to the group working alone using paper collage. This paired with the finding that the collaboratory LEGO groups changed their goal as a result of their own lacking mastery, suggesting that the individual participants had similar difficulty, and as a result defaulted to an output they felt able within, in this case creating houses. Interestingly the collaboratory LEGO groups scored relatively higher than their paper collage counterparts while still adapting their design to a house. This could indicate the participants were able to come up with a even better idea as a result of the initial challenge, or that LEGO being more time consuming simply benefits more from the extra hands present in the collaboratory groups.

In sum, the paper collage sessions showed more playful behavior. There was less dissent, and critical discussion between participants, but also less communication overall. The participants in the LEGO session were more critical in their decision-making, but shared the work more efficiently between them, which resulted in more communication.

References

1. Amabile, T.M.: Children's Artistic Creativity: Detrimental Effects of Competition in a Field Setting. Personality and Social Psychology Bulletin 8, 573–578 (1982)

2. Price, S., Rogers, Y., Scaife, M., Stanton, D., Neale, H.: Using 'Tangibles' to Promote Novel Forms of Playful Learning. Interacting with Computers 15, 169–185 (2003)
3. Craft, A.: Creativity and Education Futures: Learning in a Digital Age. Trentham Books Ltd., Westview (2010)
4. Loveless, A.M.: Creativity, Technology and Learning – a review of recent literature, Futurelab Series, No. 4 update (2007)
5. Shneiderman, B.: Creativity Support Tools – Accelerating Discovery and Innovation. Communications of the ACM 50(12), 20–32 (2007)
6. Howard, J.: Eliciting Young Children's Perceptions of Play, Work and Learning Using the Activity Apperception Story Procedure. Early Child Development and Care 172, 489–502 (2002)
7. Howard, J., Bellin, W., Rees, V.: Eliciting Children's Perception of Play and Exploiting Playfulness to Maximise Learning in the Early Years Classroom. In: Proceedings from BERA (British Educational Research Association) Annual Conference, University of Exeter, September 11-12, pp. 1–15 (2002)
8. Liebermann, J.N.: Playfulness and Divergent Thinking: An Investigation of Their Relationship at the Kindergarten Level. Journal of Genetic Psychology 107, 219–224 (1965)
9. Liebermann, J.: Playfulness: Its Relationship to Imagination and Creativity. Academic Press, New York (1977)
10. Vygotsky, L.S.: Mind in Society: The Development of Higher Psychological Processes. Harvard University Press, Cambridge (1978)
11. Bruner, J.S.: Nature and Uses of Immaturity. In: Bruner, J.S., Jolly, A., Sylva, K. (eds.) Play: Its Role in Development and Evolution, Penguin, New York (1972)
12. Fischer, G., Giaccardi, E., Eden, H., Sugimoto, M., Ye, Y.: Beyond binary choices: integrating individual and social creativity. International Journal of Human-Computer Studies 63(4-5), 482–512 (2005)
13. Brereton, M., McGarry, B.: An observational study of how objects support engineering design thinking and communication: implications for the design of tangible media. In: Proceedings of the SIGCHI Conference on Human Factors in Computing Systems, pp. 217–224. ACM (2000)
14. Brooks, E.P.: Ludic Engagement Designs: Creating Spaces for Playful Learning. In: Stephanidis, C., Antona, M. (eds.) UAHCI 2013, Part III. LNCS, vol. 8011, pp. 241–249. Springer, Heidelberg (2013)
15. Van Leeuwen, T.: Introducing Social Semiotics, pp. 219–247. Routledge, London (2005)
16. Dansky, J.L., Silverman, I.W.: Effects of Play on the Associative Fluency in Preschool-Aged Children. Developmental Psychology 9 (1973)
17. Dewey, J.: Democracy and Education: an Introduction to the Philosophy of Education. Cosimo Classics, New York (2005)
18. Biskjaer, M.M., Dalsgaard, P.: Toward a Constrating Oriented Pragmatism Understanding of Design Creativity. In: Proceedings of The 2nd International Conference on Design Creativity (ICDC 2012), Glasgow, UK, September 18-20, pp. 65–74 (2012)
19. Norman, D.: Emotional Design: Why we Love (or Hate) Everyday Things. Basic Books, New York (2004)
20. Chally, P.S.: Empowerment Through Teaching. Journal of Nursing Education 31, 117–120 (1992)
21. Wood, E.: Developing a Pedagogy of Play. In: Anning, A., Cullen, J., Fleer, M. (eds.) Early Childhood Education: Society and Culture, SAGE Publications Ltd., London (2004)
22. Resnick, M.: Edutainment? No Thanks. I Prefer Playful Learning. Associazione Civita Report on Edutainment (2004)

23. Dewey, J.: Democracy and Education. The Free Press, New York (1966)
24. Beardon, C., Ehn, P., Malmborg, L.: Design of Augmented Creative Environments. In: Proceedings of CSCL 2002, Boulder, Boulder, Colorado, January 7-11, pp. 503–504. Lawrence Erlbaum Associates, Hillsdale (2002)
25. Sullivan, F.R.: Serious and Playful Inquiry: Epistemological Aspects of Collaborative Creativity. Educational Technology & Society 14, 55–65 (2011)
26. Broadhead, P., Burt, A.: Understanding Young Children's Learning Through Play: Building Playful Pedagogies. Routledge, London (2012)
27. Petersson, E., Brooks, A.: Virtual and Physical Toys: Open-ended features for non-formal learning. Cyber Psychology & Behavior 9(2), 196–199 (2006)
28. Bordieu, P.: The Forms of Capital. In: Richardson, J. (ed.) Handbook of Theory and Research for the Sociology of Education, pp. 241–258. Greenwood, Westport (1986)
29. Gibson, J.J.: The Theory of Affordances. In: Shaw, R.E., Bransford, J. (eds.) Perceiving, Acting, and Knowing: Toward an Ecological Psychology, pp. 67–82. Lawrence Erlbaum Associates, Inc., Hillsdale (1977)
30. Schön, D.A.: The Theory of Inquiry: Dewey's Legacy to Education. Curriculum Inquiry 22(2), 119–139 (1992)
31. Gee, J.P.: What Video Games Have to Teach us About Learning and Literacy. Palgrave Macmillan, New York (2007)
32. Amabile, T.M.: Effects of External Evaluation on Artistic Creativity. Journal of Personality and Social Psychology 37, 221–233 (1979)
33. Conti, R., Collins, M.A., Picariello, M.: The role of gender in mediating the effects of competition on children's creativity. Personality and Individual Difference 30, 1273–1289 (2001)
34. Jordan, B., Henderson, A.: Interaction Analysis: Foundations and Practice. The Journal of the Learning Sciences 4, 39–103 (1995)
35. Brooks, A., Petersson, E.: Raw Emotional Signalling, via Expressive Behaviour. In: Proceedings of the 15th International Conference on Artificial Reality and Telexistence, Christchurch, New Zealand, pp. 133–141 (2005)

Action Research to Generate Requirements for a Computational Environment Supporting Bilingual Literacy of Deaf Children

Juliana Bueno and Laura Sánchez García

Informatics Department, Federal University of Paraná, Centro Politécnico, Jardim das Américas, Curitiba - PR - Brazil
{juliana,laura}@inf.ufpr.br

Abstract. Having as premises the user-centered design and the necessity for a greater knowledge about the real context of teaching and learning a second language to Deaf children, this study makes use of action research to get requirements for the conceptual model of a computational environment supporting bilingual literacy of Deaf children. This paper describes the activities of a particular action research process, together with its stages, performed with four Deaf children within a Brazilian public bilingual school. The process lasted three months and achieved the following results: a significant improvement in the interest of participating children in written Portuguese – qualitative, measured by their motivation in not stopping their learning process - and a set of functional and non functional requirements for the conceptual model to be developed.

Keywords: Action-research, user-centered design, deaf children, requirements.

1 Introduction

New contexts and paradigms about accessibility and design artifacts to support social inclusion require investigations, which in an inter- and transdisciplinary perspective, contribute significantly in building knowledge for Deaf children users of sign language. "The design should make use of the inherent characteristics of people and the natural world, to explore the natural relationships and natural constraints [...]" [14:222]. And Human-Computer Interaction (HCI) should be held accountable to better understand the needs of the Deaf to inform design [19].

This study is founded in the User- Centered Design Principles (UCD) since it seeks the effective participation of Deaf children during the whole process of a technological artifact developing.

Additionally, the Deaf are situated and are part of an oral culture – one that uses an oral language. So, this study agrees that is very important to Deaf learn reading and writing the oral language of their country, but it is known that there isn't use of the written text for the Deaf child, if words have no meaning and are not interesting to her.

C. Stephanidis and M. Antona (Eds.): UAHCI/HCII 2014, Part II, LNCS 8514, pp. 245–253, 2014.

Nobody cares to read something that does not understand [6:296]. The genuine path for reading and writing by Deaf is through bilingual literacy.

Literacy is understood in this study as a product of social participation in practices that use writing as a symbolic system and technology. Discursive practices are in need of writing to make them significant, although sometimes do not involve the specific activities of reading or writing. And "writing brings social consequences, cultural, political, economic, cognitive, linguistic, for the social group in which it is introduced, and also, for the individual to learn to use it" [16:17]. "Therefore, literacy as effective appropriation is pleasurable, is leisure, is access to information, is communication, is a way to exercise citizenship in different social practices" [2:131].

Bilingual literacy consists in the use of, at least, two languages: SL, as a first language (so called L1), and a second language (L2). In our case, the L1 is the "Brazilian Sign Language" (Libras) and L2 is Portuguese, the official oral language of Brazil.

Unfortunately, there is a lack of research not only on effective tools for literacy of the Deaf audience, but on effective methodological strategies for Deaf teachers as well. Guimarães et al. [7] surveyed some related work on existing tools for literacy: existing technologies are inadequate to the Deaf specificities (e.g. they are not in SL); they lack usability for the target audience; they do not allow for multiple and full collaboration; they are not designed for literacy as per the needs of the Deaf.

The challenge is: how to produce a computational environment supporting the bilingual literacy of Deaf children, if the designer is not aware of the social practices and interactions that occur in a real classroom?

Searching for answers, this study took advantage of the Action Research that emerged from the need to fill-in the gap between theory and practice [10, 11]. It is an empirically based type of social research, designed and carried out in close association with an action or problem solving within an activity in which researchers and participants are involved in cooperative or participatory way [18: 14]. The central idea was to take advantage of Action Research results to design a conceptual model of a computational environment supporting bilingual literacy of Deaf children.

The practice activity resulting from Action Research had qualitative results, causing an increase of interest of Deaf children on written Portuguese together with a more consistent process of learning observed by the teacher. As for the researcher, the practice activity resulted in a set of computational requirements for interaction to feed the desired environment's conceptual model creation.

2 Theoretical Background

This section explores some considerations that will provide scientific basis to the study in question.

Literacy is the resulting process of social practices using the written form of the oral language as a symbolic system in specific contexts, for specific goals where the language assumes a character of real meaning. An interactive system to support reading ability acquisition of the oral language by the Deaf should present verbal and nonverbal elements, leading to encourage the association of SL and the oral language to form a single concept [4].

The proposed study started from User-Centered Design (UCD), which is "[...] concerned with the incorporation of user perspective in the software development process in order to achieve a usable system" [12:1].

The UCD entails: think about what people want to do instead of what technology can do; designing new ways to connect people, engage people in the design process, designing for diversity [1: 28]. The same author also emphasizes that to ensure a usable system it is necessary to adopt an approach in which the evaluation is critical.

UCD approach facilitates requirements elicitation. A requirement is something that a product must do or a quality he must have [15]. Requirements can be divided into functional and non-functional. Functional requirements refer to those capacities that the system should offer and non-functional ones are associated to features or qualities that the system should have [1].

As a strategy for a better understanding of stakeholders and of the teaching-learning process within a real bilingual school context, this study used as a basis the Action Research principles. AR is a type of research participant engaged, in opposed to traditional research, which is considered "independent", "non-reactive" and "objective". It is not necessary a method but instead "a series of commitments to observe and problematize through practice a series of principles for conducting social enquiry" [13:248].

"AR is explicitly democratic, collaborative and interdisciplinary" [8:3]. It can be used in many general fields of inquiry such as bilingual education, clinical psychology, sociology, and information systems [9]. AR has the features stated in the following six paragraphs [3:184].

The research process must become a learning process for all participants and the separation between subject and object of research must be overcome.

The strategies and products will be useful for those involved if they are able to grasp your situation and modify it. The researcher looks in this context to a practitioner involved in a social situation in order to check whether a new procedure is effective or not.

In education, action research has as its research object human actions in situations that are perceived by the teacher as being unacceptable in certain ways, which are susceptible to change and therefore require a practice response. Problematic situations are interpreted from the point of view of the people involved, thus relying on the representations that different stakeholders (teachers, students, directors, etc.) have in the particular situation.

Action Research is situational: the investigation diagnoses a specific problem in a specific situation too, in order to achieve practice relevance of the results. It is not therefore, primarily interested in obtaining generalizable scientific statements (global relevance). There are, however, situations in which one can claim some degree or generality of the results of action research. Provided that several studies in different situations lead to similar results, they can determine some general statement.

Action research is self-evaluative, in that the changes in practice are constantly evaluated during the intervention process and the feedback obtained from monitoring practice is transformed into modifications, changes of direction and resets as needed, bringing benefits to the process itself.

Action Research is cyclical: the final stages are used to enhance the results of previous ones.

According to Kock [9], "one of the key characteristics that distinguishes Action Research from most other research approaches, is that "AR aims at both improving the subject of the study (often called the research "client"), and generating knowledge, achieving both at the same time". The most widely referred version of the "Action Research cycle" has been proposed by Gerald Susman and Roger Evered (Figure 1). It comprises five stages [17]:

- **The diagnosing stage** is where the cycle begins, involves the identification of an improvement opportunity or a general problem to be solved at the client organization;
- **The action planning stage** involves the consideration of alternative courses of action to reach the improvement or to solve the identified problem;
- **The action taking stage** involves the selection and the implementation of one of the courses of action considered in the previous stage;
- **The evaluating stage** involves the study of the outcomes of the selected course of action;
- **The learning specifying stage** involves reviewing the outcomes of the evaluating stage and, based on this, the knowledge building in the form of a model describing the situation under study.

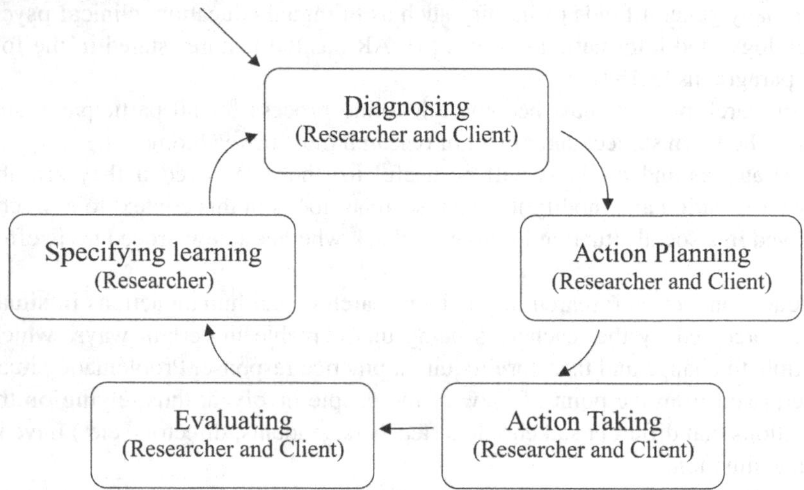

Fig. 1. Action Research cycle based in Susman and Evered's (1978)

3 Applying Action Research

This study is part of a thesis situated in the area of Human Computer Interaction in which the researcher felt herself at a crucial moment when the theoretical basis did not supply her needs of understanding of how the pedagogical practices of bilingual literacy of Deaf children occurred in a real and practice context.

This moment lead naturally to action research, which could bring substantial contributions to the thesis in question, together with a testified improvement in the teaching-learning process within the target school. The AR cycle followed (Gerald Susman and Roger Evered, 1978) is described below.

3.1 The Diagnosing Stage

The researcher choose an elementary bilingual Deaf school located in the metropolitan region of Curitiba (south of Brazil) where she had easy entrance and she accompanied and observed weekly bilingual literacy classes to Deaf children during the years of 2011, 2012 and 2013.

The external perspective provided a better understanding of the problems found apart from a contraposition between what the literature indicates as effective strategies for bilingual literacy of Deaf children and the way in which the school applies them, sometimes with unnecessary actions and sometimes in wrong ones. The teachers claims were also heard.

The exposure of children to Libras always associated with images as a teaching resource creates in the Deaf the hypothesis that written Portuguese is unnecessary for their learning. The written code did not instigate the pupils and become meaningless during class, leading to their irritation when they were asked to write. This merged as one critical research result.

3.2 The Action Planning Stage

In early 2013, there was an opportunity for dialogue with one of the teachers about the problems observed during the classes. The researcher and the teacher proposed jointly a practice activity of bilingual literacy with focus on the context and the meaning of written Portuguese. Such practice activity was systematized and well-founded mainly on contributions from Foucambert [5], on practice experiences of the French Association for Reading, and on the assumption that literacy by direct route works independently of the child's mother tongue. The several guidelines extracted from literature for the practice activity were the following:

- *Recall previous knowledge of the subject*;
- *First* show *the text and then the illustration (*the smaller the *child*, the more it *does not focus on detail at all*);
- *Stimulate the collective* learning;
- *See how the writing is organized (*title, paragraphs, *paragraphs), in other words, explore the graphical* reason of the *text;*
- *Explore the linguistic construction of the text*;
- *Build various kinds of texts from a central text*;
- *Knowledge of writing and* World *knowledge*. Not the way in which they *are combined.*

The activity planning was conducted jointly by the researcher and the teacher, as well as the search for materials and other resources to carry out the literacy classes.

3.3 The Action Taking Stage

The activity occurred with a group of the 3rd year of elementary school and had four Deaf and proficient in Libras participant children (two boys and two girls) aged 8-9 years. It is worth mentioning that none of the children had oral capacity, or practiced lip reading.

For three months, this activity was duly recorded by report, images and videos. It is also relevant mentioning that such documentary material was elaborated with the permission of the school and the participating children parents.

At the beginning, the teacher started with a fable, which was told in Libras. Then, the teacher made a series of questions about the story to instigate the children imagination. Afterwards the children were asked to draw the sequence of the fable (Figure 2).

From the fable, the activity moved to other genres (magazines, brochures, travel booklets, etc.) that had related vocabulary and/or subjects.

Fig. 2. Illustration made by one of the children from the fable narrated in Libras

Always from the genre worked, in the following class the teacher asked the children to give her keywords in sign language, which were written on the blackboard by her. From these keywords, the teacher wrote a collective text, which was copied by the children in their notebooks. Then, they highlighted the keywords with crayons, each word in a different color. The copy in the notebook served as support.

After that, the children received the paragraphs of the text in different pieces and were asked to rearrange them, sometimes on their own and others collectively (Figure 3). Once the children had organized the original text several times, a few parts of the text were modified purposely.

Several textual genres (correlated with the thematic vocabulary) were treated during this activity, up to the stage where the children could recognize various words in written Portuguese (which, at that time, had meaning for them) and had reached autonomy trying to read a written text themselves, without the support of imaging resources or sign language. To reinforce the content learned, the text was read in Libras and the children were asked to dramatize it (Figure 4).

Fig. 3. A child trying to organize paragraphs of text and a finished collective organization on the blackboard

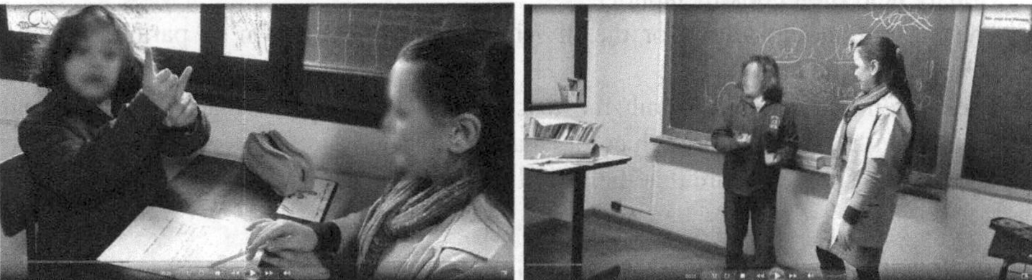

Fig. 4. A child reading and doing the dramatization of the text read

3.4 The Evaluating Stage

For the class teacher, it was satisfactory for the children autonomy them reading the text, showing that, from the information signified through keywords, they had gained the ability to make connections between the pieces of information. Thereby, they acquired an effective experience of reading, without requiring any imaging resources and demonstrated interest in Portuguese written language, which had not happened before the reading learning by the direct route.

Due to the positive feedback of the activity, the school also gained prominence within the city and even internationally. As an additional result one can quote the teacher's engagement to continue the research with other teachers and develop similar activities in other school levels.

For the researcher, the activity was very important for her gaining a better understanding of the way in which such activity occurred in the classroom and in getting insights related to the manners in which it could be transformed into a process, who would be the stakeholders and the way in which computing artifacts could mediate effectively bilingual teaching and learning of Deaf children.

3.5 The Learning Specifying Stage

This stage seeked the transposition of the literacy activities such as the one developed in this research action instance to a computational environment to enable the teacher to plan her lessons and the Deaf children to do their tasks making use of computer. Some requirements were raised to make this possible:

Main General Requirements (Functional).

- The system must take into account two profiles of users, the teacher and the student (the child);
- The instructions for activities for the child profile should be all in sign language;
- The interface should be arranged to associate text, sign language and images;
- The system should allow the children to see other literacy activities they had previously held (notebook metaphor);
- The system should allow for the division and reorganization of paragraphs and sentences of the text;
- The system should allow both the teacher and the child to mark-up words and phrases within the text through color, shape and size;
- The system should ensure that the activities can be printed.

Main Specific Requirements (Non Functional).

- The system should allow for importation of texts, images and videos;
- The system should allow for access to storaged photos;
- The system should allow for access to storaged videos;
- There must be a tool for editing text;
- There must be a tool for video editing;
- There must be a tool for scanning files;
- There must be a tool for drawing.

4 Conclusions and Future Work

The Deaf demand further investigation of pedagogical strategies and studies in the field of HCI that support their plain bilingual literacy. In this context, the present work research was based in UCD and used the principles of Action Research as a way to generate requirements to a conceptual model for an environment supporting bilingual literacy of Deaf children.

After two and a half previous years of systematic observations, action research was carried on naturally; practice activity was developed collaboratively by the researcher and the target school teacher and was applied for three months within the classroom with four Deaf children of a public school with bilingual learning purposes.

The Action Research followed the five stages proposed in the basic cycle (the diagnosing stage, the following action stage, the action taking stage, the evaluating stage and the specifying the learning one). The process brought qualitative positive results for both the target school and the researcher, who generated as the end product the primary set of requirements that will feed substantially the application conceptual model under construction.

References

1. Benyon, D.: Interação Humano-Computador, 2nd edn. Pearson Prentice Hall, São Paulo (2011)
2. Chomsky, N.: Language and Problems of Knowledge. The Managua Lectures. The MIT Press, Cambridge (1998)
3. Engel, G. I. Pesquisa-Ação. Educar. UFPR, Curitiba 16, 181-191 (2000)
4. Fernandes, S.F.: Educação bilíngue para surdos: identidades, diferenças, contradições e mistérios. Tese de doutorado. UFPR, Curitiba (2003)
5. Foucambert, J.: Modos de ser leitor: Aprendizagem e ensino da leitura no ensino fundamental. UFPR, Curitiba (2008)
6. Groht, M.: Some thoughts on reading. Volta Review 57, 294–296 (1955)
7. Guimarães, C., Antunes, D.R., Garcia, L.S., Peres, L.M., Fernandes, S.F.: Pedagogical Architecture – Internet Artifacts for Bilingualism of the Deaf (Sign Language Portuguese). In: 46th HICSS, vol. 46, pp. 40–49. IEEE CPS (2013)
8. Hayes, G.R.: The relationship of action research to human-computer interaction. ACM Trans. Comput. -Hum. Interact. 18(3), Article 15 (2011)
9. Kock, N.: Action Research: Its Nature and Relationship to Human-Computer Interaction. In: Soegaard, M., Dam, R. (eds.) The Encyclopedia of Human-Computer Interaction, 2nd edn. The Interaction Design Foundation, Aarhus (2013), `http://www.interactiondesign.org/encyclopedia/action_research.html`
10. Lewin, K.: Action research and minority problems. J. Soc. 4(2), 34–46 (1946)
11. Lewin, K.: Resolving Social Conflicts. Harper (1948)
12. Maguire, M.: Methods to support human-centered design. International Journal of Human-Computer Studies 55(4), 587–634 (2001)
13. Mctaggart, R.: Issues for participatory action researchers. In: New Directions in Action Research. Falmer Press (1996)
14. Norman, D.: The design of everyday things. MIT Press, London (1998)
15. Robertson, S., Robetson, J.: Mastering the requirements process. Addiison-Wesley, Harlow (1999)
16. Soares, M.: Letramento: um tema em três gêneros, 3rd edn. Autêntica Editora, Belo Horizonte (2009)
17. Susman, G.I., Evered, R.D.: An Assessment of the Scientific Merits of Action Research. Administrative Science Quarterly 23(4), 582–603 (1978)
18. Thiollent, M.: Metodologia da pesquisa-ação. Cortez Editora, São Paulo (2002)
19. Winchester III, W.W.: Realizing our messy future: Towards culturally responsive design tools in engaging our deeper dives. ACM Interactions V.XVII (6), 12–19 (2010)

Early Interaction Experiences of Deaf Children and Teachers with the OLPC Educational Laptop

Maíra Codo Canal[1], Juliana Bueno[1], Laura Sánchez García[1], Leonelo D.A. Almeida[2], and Alessio Miranda Jr.[1]

[1] Department of Informatics, Federal University of Paraná, Centro Politécnico, Jardim das Américas, Curitiba - PR - Brazil
{mccanal,juliana,laura}@inf.ufpr.br, alessio@timoteo.cefetmg.br

[2] Department of Informatics, Federal University of Technology, Paraná, Av. Sete de Setembro, Curitiba -PR- Brazil
leoneloalmeida@utfpr.edu.br

Abstract. The adoption of computing technologies in the schools has the potential for supporting the digital and social inclusion. However, whether such technologies are not accessible they can deepen the exclusion of students with disabilities, and other minorities. This work investigated questions regarding the use of the laptops from OLPC by deaf children between 7 and 12 years old and by teachers from a bilingual school. The results indicate that children were excited due the use of the device; even they behaved reticent during the interaction. The study also identified interaction problems regarding both hardware and software in the use of the laptop.

Keywords: Accessibility, XO laptop, computer-based learning, deaf children, OLPC.

1 Introduction

The preliminary ideas of introducing computer technologies in educational context emerged in the 60s. In 1968, Kay and Papert introduced the concept of Dynabook (*i.e.* similar to computer laptops today) and believed that the laptop would play a key role in education and also in other aspects of contemporary society [16]. In 2001, the One Laptop Per Child (OLPC), a non-profit organization, inspired by the concept of the Dynabook and constructionist learning theory [14], designed and developed the low-cost educational laptop XO to be used by children in developing countries [13].

Considering the use of computer technologies in Brazilian schools and the XO laptop as an important instrument of access to knowledge, it is necessary to ensure that these technologies can be used by all students, independent of their cultural, physical or intellectual diversities. As noted by the challenge umber 4 of the Brazilian Computer Society [1] it is necessary to research ways to reduce barriers of access to knowledge. Thus, it is expected that, when introduced in the classroom and in the students' homes, laptops could be relevant instruments to digital and social inclusion

C. Stephanidis and M. Antona (Eds.): UAHCI/HCII 2014, Part II, LNCS 8514, pp. 254–264, 2014.

of minorities. Also Schneider et al. [19], who conducted studies on the use of educational laptops in Brazilian classrooms, concluded that changes may occur in the social dimensions of people with disabilities when mediated by educational laptops in schools. In this sense, there is room for fruitful investigations on the interaction of deaf public with these educational laptops.

Studies on the use of technologies for deaf children indicate that they are visual learners and mainly use pictures to illustrate the meaning of words [18]. Thus, the computing technologies that use pictures, sign language, graphics and animations for their interaction are more effective for learning of deaf children [6]. Moreover, some studies involving deaf children point to difficulties in reading and writing texts, since they are not their primary language. Sign language (SL), that is visual, consequently affects the level of lexical, morphological and inferential comprehension [21].

This work investigates the first contacts of deaf children and teachers with the XO laptop. The research was conducted through 4 tasks involving the contact of users with the laptop's hardware, the Sugar environment, the applications Record and Drawing.

During the experience users were enthusiastic on and, also, showed interaction problems that may interfere with student learning. Some of these problems have also been previously reported by other investigators, who researched for different publics.

It is noteworthy that this work does not address political and pedagogical issues about the relationship between inclusive and specialized schools. But it is relevant informing that the tests were conducted along with children and teachers who study and work in an institution of bilingual education. Bilingualism, considered the most suitable approach for the education of deaf people; it is the movement that claims the use of at least two languages: SL as the first language (L1) and as the second language the writing mode (L2) [4]. In the Brazilian context, the L1 is the Brazilian Sign Language (LIBRAS) and the Portuguese, the official language of Brazil orally, is L2.

This article is organized as follows: Section 2 presents the research related to the use of the XO laptop, Section 3 describes the method used in this work, Section 4 summarizes the results of the activities; Section 5 presents a discussion of the work and finally, Section 6 presents our conclusions.

2 XO in School and Beyond

The XO laptop has an operating system that presents a graphical environment called Sugar, which runs on the Fedora Linux distribution. The Sugar environment was designed by researchers at the Massachusetts Institute of Technology (MIT) to be used by children [13]. Applications built-in the Sugar are designed with the aim to contribute to student learning.

The distribution project of the XO laptop has reached many countries, among them: Uruguay, Peru, Argentina, Mexico, Ethiopia and Rwanda. In these countries, pilot projects reported positive changes in the socio-educational context, as enrollment increases, the decrease of absences in classes, greater student participation in activities in the classroom and more disciplined students [9]. The projects reported that students and teachers have demonstrated great enthusiasm about using the XO, however, students and teachers were confused and found difficulties in using the educational applications of the laptop.

Hansen *et al.* [7] conducted tests with children in Ethiopia and concluded that the use of XO in schools and in their homes, contributed to the academic performance and the development of abstract reasoning of students. In underserved schools in China, Yang *et al.* [22] found that the use of the XO laptop was an effective means of improving student learning. In Uruguay, Hourcade *et al.* [8] reported the first experiences of using the XO by children in the classroom and the difficulties regarding the use of touchpad and user file manager called Everyday interface. Still in Uruguay, Flores & Hourcade [5] conducted tests with adults and identified difficulties in opening the laptop and using the touchpad.

In Brazil, some studies were conducted in order to explore the use of the XO laptop. Martinazzo *et al.* [10] conducted usability tests of the application Drawing with children and found some problems, such as difficulties of users in exiting the application and handling the touchpad. Canal *et al.* [2] analyzed the simplicity of the OLPC laptop and some problems related to its interaction design of both hardware and software.

Miranda *et al.* [12] identified usability problems and accessibility barriers on the laptop. Canal *et al.* [3] evaluated the accessibility applications of the XO laptop and some problems were found, such as the use of the Sugar environment and the applications to take pictures. Venâncio *et al.* [20] reported experiences of using the XO in school and concluded that the use of the laptop had significant influence on student learning. However, the authors reported that some students had difficulty using the laptop and that students experienced more difficult to use it were those with problems in reading and writing, or students who have problems in learning

3 Method

Based on the investigations already made with other different publics, the method adopted in this study consists of an initial exploration into the use of hardware and software for the XO laptop by deaf children in a bilingual school. The method was based on the recommended guidelines for conducting software review proposals involving deaf children by Mitch [11] .The author points out that software testing with deaf children are best conducted in public spaces, such as schools, with duration of no more than 30 minutes of testing, and that the instructions are better passed to children orally and sign language. As this study addressed the initial contact of deaf children with the XO laptop, the exploration was conducted individually, point that differs from the adopted guidelines. The method also relied on guidelines for conducting user testing proposed by Preece *et al.* [15]; like explaining to participants the purpose of the study and how should be their participation, as well as direct observation of user interaction during the tests .

3.1 Study Participants

The activity involved 6 deaf children between 7-12 years of a bilingual school in the city of São José dos Pinhais, in the metropolitan region of Curitiba. Two teachers of the school (one of them is deaf) also participated. There was agreement of participation and the use of images from the parents or guardians through an statement of Informed Consent Form (ICF). Two researchers in human-computer interaction conducted the activities.

3.2 Materials

The environment for performing the activities was the computer room of the school. One researcher acted as a direct observer, taking notes and observing the interaction between users, the other researcher acted as interpreter, since she is fluent in LIBRAS. The experiment was also recorded with images.

Two dolls of cartoon characters were used in one of the tasks of the activity. Each participant used an XO laptop version 1.0, with the installed version of Sugar 0.98.2, build 36.

3.3 Procedure

For each activity session in the computer room were present only one participant and the researchers. Immediately upon entering the room, the researchers presented the XO laptop and objectives of the activity. Following the explanation, we applied a pretest interview (in a playful way and LIBRAS) in order to obtain some information about the participants, such as age, school year (grade), how long the student attends the school, whether the participant have computer at home and who uses it.

After the completion of the tasks a post-test interview was applied to determine whether the children and the teachers enjoyed to use the XO, what else do the XO liked and what they did not like regarding the laptop.

The activities involved performing simple tasks (because it was a first contact with the device) that are relevant to the process of teaching and learning supported by the XO laptop. Furthermore, it is noteworthy that the choice of the applications involved in the tasks is related to activities that may be attractive not only to deaf children, as well as other children, such as the use of images and the ability to paint and draw.

The tasks are identified by labels: open the XO laptop (T1), turn on the laptop (T2), take pictures of the doll (T3), and open the drawing application and insert the photo taken in the previous activity and draw on it (T4). The activities T3 and T4 are also related to the use of the hardware, such as the action of handling the laptop's touchpad. In addition, the tasks in this sequence were prepared by the understanding that, in this way, the complexity increases gradually.

4 Results

This section first presents the results of the pre-test interviews, followed by the findings from the participants' interaction with the XO laptop and, finally, the results of the post-test interviews.

4.1 Pre-test Interviews

The responses for the pre-test interview questions were obtained primarily by participants mediated by the interpreter. Table 1 shows the responses of the pre-test interviews about the students.

Table 1. Students´ responses for the pre-test interviews

Student	Age	Gender	School year
1	7	Male	First Year
2	7	Male	First Year
3	8	Female	First Year
4	8	Female	Third Year
5	12	Male	Fourth Year
6	8	Male	Third Year

It was also noted during the pre-test interviews that all students have computers at home. The Student 2 said that despite of having a computer at home, he does not use it. All the students have weekly activities at school and involving the use of computers for word processing, Internet research, paintings, drawings, and games. The school's computers use Microsoft Windows® operating system.

The Teacher 1 is 28 years old and is deaf. She is fluent in LIBRAS and is a professor of early childhood education until the fifth year of school for 4 years. On the use of computer, the teacher said that at home she uses it to plan lessons, record videos and access the Facebook®. The Teacher 2 is 40 years old and is not deaf and teaches classes for childhood education until the fifth year and, at the time of the activity, he has been also the principal. The Teacher 2 said they use the computer at home to write texts, view photos, and access the Internet and Facebook®.

4.2 Interaction with the Laptop

The average length of the interaction was 25 minutes. Figure 1 shows some relevant moments during the execution of this activity, which will be detailed in the following paragraphs of this section.

Open the Laptop (T1). All the students experienced difficulties in opening the device. Except for Student 6, all other participants (including teachers) were able to open the laptop only after the intervention of the researchers. Some of them tried clicking on the hinge between the body of the laptop and the monitor (see Figure 1a, arrow 1 and the rightmost photo), others tried clicking on the green circle of the XO logo (see Figure 1a, arrow 2). Student 3 came to employ certain strength in trying to open the laptop, however, as the locks were still closed, he could not open it. The Student 4 (see Figure 1.a, leftmost photo) came to get unlock the laptop, but could not open it. The two teachers tried to open it by clicking the green circle of the XO logo (see Figure 1a, arrow 2).

Turn on the Laptop (T2). Students 1, 5, and 6 turned on the laptop without difficulties. However the students 2, 3 and 4 attempted to press other buttons that are next of the screen and are intended for games; however they also succeed in turning on the device. Teacher 1 turned on the laptop, but she initially tried pressing the right button of the touchpad. Teacher 2 was able turn on it without difficulty. Both teachers commented that the device was slow at startup.

Take a Picture of the Doll (T3). In this activity, participants were first invited to open the application to take pictures, and then they were given the option to choose between two dolls to take a picture and, finally, close the application (see Figure 1.d). Not all the students were able to find the application to take pictures and for these cases the interpreter signaled an eye, which is the icon of taking pictures in order to facilitate the identification of the application by the students.

In the moment of taking the picture, students 1 and 4 clicked repeatedly in the icon that has an image of a photo that is located in the top bar of the application (indeed, it is the selector of media to be recorded). The button for taking pictures is a circle at the bottom of the screen. The Student 2 was excited by the activity and took several pictures. Student 4 chose to take pictures of herself, because she found it difficult to hold the doll and use the touchpad at the same time.

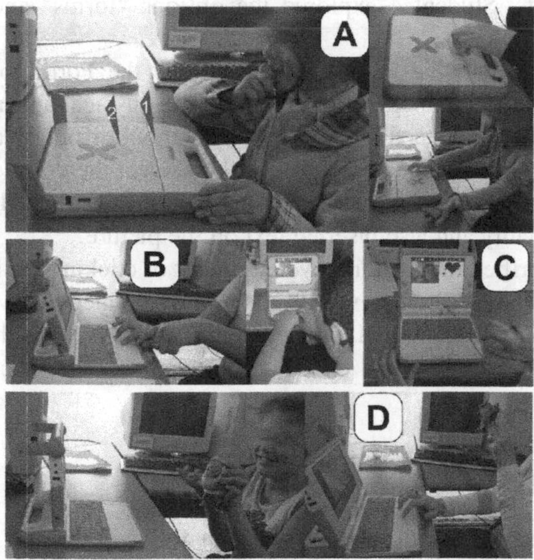

Fig. 1. Interaction with the laptop: (a) opening the laptop, (b) using the touchpad, (c) using the taken picture in the application Paint and (d) student (left) and teacher (right) taking pictures

Teacher 1 initially thought the application to take pictures was Fototoon, because of its name. Entering in the correct application, she did not found problems to take pictures. Teacher 2 easily found the application to take pictures, but she confused, as students 1 and 4, the button to take a picture with the media selector.

None of the participants were able to close the application. Student 5 tried to press a button that resembles the icon for closing applications of traditional operating systems (*i.e.* letter X) that is located in the upper left corner of the laptop keyboard. Teacher 2 clicked on the text "stop", which is the text hint of the icon for this function. However the visual appearance of such hint is very close to a sub-menu.

One difficulty faced during the interaction with the hardware was the use of the touchpad because it does not have the click function by tapping. Consequently, clicks must be made only by buttons located just below the touch area. This resulted in unsuccessful and frequent attempts, by all the participants who tried to access the functions by touchpad (see Figure 1b).

Import the Taken Picture into the Paint Application and Draw on it (T4). In this activity the interpreter invited the participants to open the Paint application. After opening the application, the interpreter signaled to participants the task of "insert the taken pictures". Then the participants were invited to draw on the picture. Except for Student 5, all the participants opened the Paint application without difficulties. Student 2 took the opportunity to play with the dolls while waiting for the application to load. Student 5 initially opened the application Writing.

Students 2 and 3 found the option to "insert picture" without difficulty. However the students 1, 4 and 5 failed to identify it without the intervention of the researchers. After selecting the button for inserting picture, students found it difficult to select the desired picture, because the browsing window (*i.e.* Journal) does not show thumbnails of picture's contents. Student 4 explored the options "forms" and chose the form "heart" (see Figure 1.c).

Teacher 1 thought that the Paint application was the Portfolio application. The teacher argued that the icon application looks like the physical apparatus that she uses in her classes. Teacher 2 opened the application without difficulty and also imported the picture. Both teachers encountered problems to select the desired picture. Teacher 2 was the participant who most explored the application; she clicked in all the icons to verify their functionality and also inserted text on the picture.

In general, we verified that children were reticent of clicking the buttons. They frequently questioned the researchers whether icon they pointed out was the correct before trying it. Student 4 was excited by the activity and, even after the researchers had informed him that the activity had ended, the student wanted to continue using the device.

4.3 Post-test Interviews

The post-test interview aimed to identify whether the children and the teachers liked to use the XO laptop, what they liked to do and they did not like.

Except by the Student 6, the other participants affirmed they enjoyed interacting with the XO laptop. Student 6 considered the laptop is too hard to use. The researchers noted, in some moments of the activity, when he was not able to complete a task, he was nervous. The teachers reported that this student had some behavioral disorders previously diagnosed at the school.

When asked what they had most liked to do on the XO laptop, two of them answered to draw, a student answered to paint, the other answered to take pictures and the last said he liked everything. Next, when asked about what they had not liked, two of them said the delay in loading applications.

Both teachers said they enjoyed interacting with the XO laptop. Teacher 1 positively highlighted the physical aesthetics of the laptop and she said that would like to use the laptop in his classes. Teacher 2 said she most like the Drawing application, the possibility of coloring, drawing, and writing. In contrast, Teacher 1 put the Paint application as one of the items that she did not like in the XO laptop. The main criticism is the need to drag using the touchpad to draw. The Teacher 1 also pointed that the colors of icons, both the Sugar and the others applications do not facilitate viewing. Both teachers said the application icons are not very significant (*e.g.* an icon of an eye for the take pictures application). Teacher 2 indicated that it is difficult to see when an icon is selected in the Paint. Finally, Teacher 2 also said that she would include the XO laptop in the classroom.

5 Discussion

This work investigated the initial contact of deaf children and teachers (one deaf) with the XO laptop. While being expected that children be guided during the use of this device in the classroom, one of the expectations is that the OLPC laptops could be taken home by students. Therefore, autonomy in using the device is an important feature to the learning process.

Influence of Deafness in the Interaction. Although this is an occasional activity and of short duration, it is possible to verify that a significant part of the results obtained are consistent with those obtained in research with children without this disabilities (*i.e.* [8]). However, it is worth emphasizing that the choice for activities that are primarily not dependent of text, influence positively the results of the interaction of deaf children. An interesting fact is that the only participant who used text in the Drawing application was just the teacher who does not have hearing loss. It is still necessary to investigate what are the reactions when interacting with applications containing more texts.

Reticence During the Interaction. A fact that caught our attention during the activity was the children's reticence during the activity. During a considerable part of the activity the children consulted the interpreter and/or researcher before performing actions. As the activity reported here had an average duration of 25 minutes is not possible to say that this reticence would be persistent when in longer interaction scenarios. However, we should emphasize the initial insecurity and also is necessary future researchs to verify this behavior in situations of prolonged use of the device.

Physical Aspects of the XO Laptop. During the execution of the tasks T1 and T2 it was evident the initial difficulty of use of the hardware device. As already identified by [12], [5] and [2], the opening mechanism with two locks is not intuitive and difficult the initial contact with the device. Despite the button to turn on the laptop uses a common sign to electronic devices, some of the participants did not identify it initially.

The tasks T3 and T4 involved the use of the touchpad and most participants reported difficulty in using the device, especially because it does not offer the option of click by tapping the touch area. Problems with the touchpad had been pointed by [5] although those authors did not have provided information about the specific problem with the touchpad.

XO Laptop Software. Two of the main characteristics of Sugar are the focus on iconic representation and in the children audience. However, in this activity was noted that some of the icons in the Sugar environment do not have the expected representation. In the task T3, some of the children did not relate the icon of the Record application, which is an eye, with the function of taking pictures. Still in the Record application, the metaphor of the circle button, referring to the "record" of the electronic devices to recording audio and video did not make sense to some of the participants, for the function of taking photos. The Stop button's icon used to close applications also did not make sense to the participants.

Another identified issue is in the task T4, while using the Journal application for the inclusion of the taken picture on the Record applications. As already reported in [8] the lack of thumbnail images makes the selection of the required resource more difficult. Still about the task T4, in contrast to the results reported by [10] – in which participants reported usability problems resulting from the extensive use of the Paint application – in this activity the children just used few resources of the application. Although, in the post-test interview, some participants have mentioned the application as the activity they most liked.

Early Impressions. In general, the reaction was very positive of practically all participants (except for Student 6), which motivates future researches about this theme. And the school also demonstrated interest for the inclusion of XO laptops within the context of the school classroom.

6 Final Considerations

The use of computer technology for educational purposes is a reality. However, the design of technologies to support the use by children and adolescents still has many barriers of use that are currently being studied by several researches. This work presented an activity of evaluation of the XO laptop for six deaf children and two teachers (one being deaf) in a Brazilian school that focuses on bilingual education. The evaluation involved aspects of hardware and software, considering the initial contact with the XO laptop. Therefore, this work was based on the guidelines for evaluating applications for deaf children [11] and the guidelines to user testing proposed by [15].

The activity results indicate a consistent scenario with the problems already identified by earlier works with children without this disability. Therefore, we conclude that such problems are faced during the interaction by different user profiles, what makes these users (in all their diversity) face interaction barriers that may impair their social inclusion, digital inclusion and even interfere with the learning process of students. Furthermore, we consider that the proposed design solutions for the problems here reported can potentially solve the barriers of interaction of different user profiles, including deaf and not deaf children or adults. However, the reticent behavior during the interaction and the use of applications that are dependent on textual resources still require further investigation. Possible future works involve the use of the XO laptop in the classroom for an extended period of time, aiming at observing the changes in the interaction behavior, and its possible effects on children's learning as in the didactic techniques used by the teachers of the school.

Acknowledgments. We would like to thank the students and teachers that collaborated to this research. This work is partially funded by Conselho Nacional de Desenvolvimento Científico e Tecnológico - CNPq (process #134218/2013-2).

References

1. Baranauskas, M.C.C., Souza, C.S.: Desafio n º 4: Acesso Participativo e Universal do Cidadão Brasileiro ao Conhecimento. Computação Brasil, ano VII(23), 7 (2006)
2. Canal, M.C., Miranda, L.C., de, A.L.D.A., Baranauskas, M.C.C.: Analisando a Simplicidade do Laptop da OLPC: Desafios e Propostas de Soluções de Design. In: Anais do XXXI Congresso da Sociedade Brasileira de Computação, pp. 1250–1264. SBC (2011)
3. Canal, M.C., Almeida, L.D.A., Baranauskas, M.C.C.: Uma avaliação de acessibilidade no laptop educacional da OLPC na perspectiva de pessoas com dislexia. In: Anais do 23º Simpósio Brasileiro de Informática na Educação, Sociedade Brasileira de Computação, Porto Alegre (2012)
4. Chomsky, N.: Language and Problems of Knowledge. The MIT Press, Cambridge (1998)
5. Flores, P., Hourcade, J.P.: Under Development: One year of experiences with XO laptops in Uruguay. Interactions 16(4), 52–55 (2009)
6. Gentry, M., Chinn, K., Moulton, R.: Effectiveness of multimedia reading materials when used with children who are deaf. American Annals of the Deaf 149(5), 394–403 (2005)
7. Hansen, N., Koudenburg, N., Hiersemann, R., Tellegen, P.J., Kocsev, M., Postmes, T.: Laptop usage affects abstract reasoning of children in the developing world. Comput. Educ. 59(3), 989–1000 (2012)
8. Hourcade, J.P., Beitler, D., Cormenzana, F., Flores, P.: Early olpc experiences in a rural uruguayan school". In: CHI 2008 Extended Abstracts on Human Factors in Computing Systems, pp. 2503–2512. ACM (2008)
9. Kraemer, K.L., Dedrick, J.: e Sharma, P.: One Laptop per Child: Vision vs. Reality. Communications of the ACM 52(6), 66–73 (2009)
10. Martinazzo, A.A.G., Patrício, N.S., Biazon, L.C., Ficheman, I.K., Lopes, R.D.: Testing the OLPC Drawing Activity: An Usability Report. In: 8th IEEE International Conference on Advanced Learning Technologies, pp. 844–846 (2008)

11. Mich, O.: Evaluation of software tools with deaf children. In: Proc. 11th ASSETS, pp. 235–236. ACM (2009)
12. Miranda, L.C., Hornung, H.H., Solarte, D.S.M., Romani, R., Weinfurter, M.R., Neris, V.P.A., Baranauskas, M.C.C.: Laptops Educacionais de Baixo Custo: Prospectos e Desafios. In: XVIII SBIE, pp. 358–367 (2007)
13. One Laptop per Child, `http://www.laptop.org`
14. Papert, S.: Mindstorms: Children, Computers and Powerful Ideas. Basic Books (1980)
15. Preece, J., Rogers, Y., Sharp, E.: Interaction Design: Beyond Human-Computer Interaction. John Wiley & Sons, New York (2002)
16. Press, L.: Dynabook Revisited - Portable Computers Past, Present and Future. Communications of the ACM 35(3), 25–32 (1992)
17. Programa Um Computador por Aluno, `http://www.uca.gov.br`
18. Roccaforte, M., DeMonte, M., Groves, K., Tomasuolo, E., Capuano, D.: Strategies for Italian deaf learners. In: Editore, S. (ed.) Proc. 4th International conference on ICT for language learning (2011)
19. Schneider, F.C., Santarosa, L.M.C., Conforto, D.: Cidade Um Computador por Aluno - UCA Total A identificação de situações inclusivas na totalidade. In: Anais do XXII SBIE - XVII WIE, pp. 568–577 (2011)
20. Venâncio, V., Telles, E.O., Franco, J.F., Aquino, E., Ficheman, I.K., Lopes, R.D.: UCA – Um computador por Aluno: um relato dos protagonistas do Piloto de São Paulo. In: XIX SBIE, Workshop IV (2008)
21. Vettori, C., Mich, O.: Supporting deaf children's reading skills: the many challenges of text simplification". In: 13th ASSETS, pp. 283–284. ACM (2011)
22. Yang, Y., Zhang, L., Zeng, J., Pang, X., Lai, F., Rozelle, S.: Computers and the academic performance of elementary school-aged girls in China's poor communities. Computers & Education 60(1), 335–346 (2013)

Research on Accessibility of Question Modalities Used in Computer-Based Assessment (CBA) for Deaf Education

Maíra Codo Canal and Laura Sánchez García

Department of Informatics, Federal University of Paraná,
Centro Politécnico, Jardim das Américas, Curitiba - PR - Brazil
{mccanal,laura}@inf.ufpr.br

Abstract. Virtual learning environments (VLEs) are increasingly being used for several purposes and audiences worldwide. VLEs are often used for communication with peers and with teachers, for sharing and collaborating on assignments and for assessments. Although the ultimate goal of distance learning is to make education available to anyone anywhere and at anytime, this goal cannot be accomplished unless VLEs are designed to be accessible to all potential students, including those with disabilities. In this paper, we investigated the accessibility of some question types (*e.g.* multiple choice, essay) used in Computer-based Assessment (CBA) in the Moodle platform, focusing on deaf students. Evaluation results indicate problems related to the use of videos, images, texts and customization for users. We also propose some design solutions for those problems.

Keywords: Computer- based assessment, deaf students, virtual learning environments.

1 Introduction

Assessment is recognized as a key element in learning, as it empowers, directs and motivates students and provides success criteria against which to measure their progress. The computer resources for the assessment process have the potential of becoming an essential educational advancement; they automate and facilitate the lengthy and tedious procedures involved in the design, delivery, scoring and analysis of assessment [Sim *et al.* 2004]. In many studies, teachers and students seemed to embrace this view and were positive towards Computer-Based Assessment (CBA). Some of the main advantages of this approach are the reduction of testing and marking time, the speed of results, administration of assessments, monitoring of students, the increased objectivity and security, less difficult or stressful [Thelwall 2000; Croft *et al.* 2001].

CBA offers opportunities for innovations in testing and assessing. Also, it can be used in many different fields [Chatzopoulou and Economides 2010]. Formative and summative assessments are the two major categories of CBA. Summative assessments help students to evaluate their effectiveness in learning. On the other hand, formative assessment helps students in reaching their targets through appropriate feedbacks

C. Stephanidis and M. Antona (Eds.): UAHCI/HCII 2014, Part II, LNCS 8514, pp. 265–276, 2014.

[Turner and Gibbs 2010]. CBA used in the context of e-learning or in classroom education may help in assessing the learning. Currently, CBA is employed in both higher and secondary education [Kaklauskas et al. 2010]. CBA may be composed of different question types (or modalities), such as true/false, multiple choice, fill-in-the blank questions, assertion-reason multiple choice items, drag-and-drop items, problem solving simulations, and others. Also the level of complexity can vary according to the educational objectives as represented in the Bloom's Taxonomy that involves since questions that demand just remembering to analyzing, evaluating and creating solutions [Krathwohl 2002].

As CBA is increasingly being used in the educational practice, it is necessary to ensure that this type of assessment could be used for all, including persons with disabilities. Studies report accessibility problems in certain types of CBA questions, such as multiple choice and true/false that need to be solved. Luephattanasuk et al. (2011) investigated the accessibility of CBA questions in the context of blind students and interaction problems were reported. The authors also claim that more specific guidelines are needed to identify accessibility problems in the context of users with disabilities for interacting with CBA. In the context of deaf people whose main communication channel is the sign language, Bueno et al. (2007) claim that e-learning environments can be an appropriate way for supporting learning of deaf students. However such potential can only be explored if the courses are properly adapted since, among other differences, deaf students process images more easily and efficiently than words.

In this study we investigated the accessibility of question modalities used in CBA in the context of deaf students. We present the results of an accessibility evaluation conducted by experts in the field of Human-Computer Interaction (HCI) based on a set accessibility guidelines for interface designers of projects involving literacy of deaf people, proposed by Abreu et al. (2010). The evaluation involved some types of questions used in CBA by the e-learning management system Moodle as multiple choice, true/false, embedded answers (cloze), essay and matching. The guidelines used in this evaluation are based on W3C/WAI but are detailed in the context of deaf education. Evaluation results indicate problems related to the use of videos, images, texts and customization for end-users.

This work is organized as follows: Section 2 presents related works, Section 3 describes the evaluation methodology used in this work, Section 4 presents the results of the evaluation and Section 5 presents conclusions and future works.

2 Related Works

Virtual learning environments are used to refer the several kinds of on-line interactions that take place between students and teachers. VLEs have many features and capabilities such as forums, content management, real-time chat communication, electronic mail, quizzes with different types of questions, and a number of activity modules. There are several software systems available that provide VLE systems. Moodle is one of the most popular systems worldwide for e-learning system [Kumar *et al.* 2011].

Moodle is now used not only in universities, but also in high schools, primary schools, non-profit organizations, private companies, by independent teachers and even home-schooling parents [Martin *et al.* 2004; Koh 2006]. Moodle supports any types of questions used for CBA such as multiple choice, calculated, description, essay, matching, short answer, numerical, true/false embedded answers (cloze), and others [Sokolova 2007].

According to Burgstahler *et al.* (2004), VLEs offer opportunities for education and career enhancement for those who have access to a computer and the Internet. However, some potential students and instructors who have access to these technologies cannot fully participate because of the inaccessible design of courses. These individuals include those with visual and hearing impairments. Online courses can inadvertently impose barriers for students and instructors with disabilities. Web pages with complex navigation mechanisms can be difficult to use for people with mobility impairments. Content within graphic images may be meaningless to someone who is blind. Words spoken in an audio clip are potentially unavailable to someone who is deaf. Furthermore, according to Burgstahler *et al.* (2004), avoiding some access barriers can be simple. For example, text alternatives such as <alt> tags can be provided for graphics images for blind students and instructors be able of making sense of their the content. Likewise, captions on video and other multimedia products make content accessible to students who are deaf.

Potential students of an online course may have mobility, visual, hearing, speech, and other types of disabilities that could impact their participation. Today, most programs only deal with accessibility issues when a student with a disability enrolls in the course; they usually provide sticky solutions. Planning accessibility along with the courses is easier and therefore less expensive than quickly developing accommodation strategies, once a student with a disability enrolls in a course.

Seale (2006) conducted studies on accessibility in VLEs and concluded that the lack of knowledge about how to make e-learning accessible was evident, given the large number of external tools that had been developed to supposedly help teachers in this endeavor. Consequently, Seale argues that current VLEs are not appropriate to fit accessibility needs.

Power *et al.* (2010) evaluated the accessibility of the Moodle environment and found problems with text equivalents for non-text element, color contrasts between background and foreground colors; language appropriateness, and the size of large blocks of content that could be divided into manageable chunks. The evaluations presented in that study demonstrate that there are some relevant accessibility issues regarding the use of VLEs in the current practice. Those results demonstrate a need for training individuals responsible for developing, deploying and selecting VLEs to the adopted in institutions, regarding the accessibility lenses.

Hashim *et al.* (2013) argue that the use of e-learning environments for deaf students should help them in boosting their motivation level and at the same time, enhancing their performance in learning any subjects or courses available in schools or learning institutions.

In literature there are works related to the accessibility of VLEs in the context of deaf. Debevc *et al.* (2003) highlight there are also important guidelines for subtitles:

text in the subtitle should be equivalent to the spoken text; the subtitles should present sound information (*e.g.* phone ringing); subtitles should be presented inside the video frame in its lower part which is useful to deaf students. Khwaldeh *et al.* (2007) say that when designing and implementing an e-learning system for deaf students, one should consider offering all audio information in a visual way; subtitles for each video, picture, and text; a dictionary and glossary of terms; attractive and effective graphical user interface (GUI); an effective approach to navigate inside the learning material; several difficulty levels for assessments; and presenting e-learning material in a structured, understandable, and logical way. Drigas *et al.* (2005) proposed an e-learning environment for deaf students and emphasize the importance of presentation of bilingual information (text and sign language), high level of visualization, interactive and explorative learning, and the possibility of learning in peer groups via video conferencing.

Straetz *et al.* (2004) conducted studies on virtual learning environments for deaf students and concluded that for each block of text information should have an option to display the video information and this information presented immediately next to that information in text. That approach allows independent learning and gives the deaf learners the feeling that they are being taken seriously in their cultural and linguistic identity. The accessibility of e-learning was also improved when spoken text and other sound information are presented together inside the video. Besides its potential in improving the reading skills among deaf students, it will also enable them to learn independently [Debevc *et al.* 2012].

The literature review indicated that some studies already investigated the accessibility of deaf students in the context of VLEs. Some of them propose environments to be exclusively used by deaf students. In our work, we focus on the types of questions VLEs provide for being used by all students. For that purpose, the proposed design solutions discussed in this paper refer to adaptations in the Moodle environment, instead of proposing specialized VLEs, so that we expect the question types be able to support the learning process of students, including those who are deaf. We were not able to find literature approaching accessibility of question types used in CBA, in the context of deaf students.

3 Evaluation Methodology

The accessibility evaluation of the questions types used in CBA present in the Moodle platform is based on predictive assessment conducted by 2 experts and supported by a set of guidelines. The evaluation process consisted of: (1) Selection of a subset of guidelines that better fits the goals of this work; (2) Preparation of the evaluation activity; (3) Conducting the evaluation and data collection; (4) Analysis of the collected data; and (5) Reporting of results.

There are studies that provide general accessibility guidelines for web systems, *e.g.* W3C/WAI[1]. The W3C´s accessibility guidelines are useful for web content regardless

[1] W3C´s Web Accessibility Initiative. `http://www.w3.org/WAI/`.

context. However they do not provide detailed information on specific needs of deaf people or in specific domains such as education.

The work of Abreu *et al.* (2010) presents some guidelines geared specifically to deaf people accessibility and literacy. The set of recommendations were made based on a pair of investigative works. The first consisted of an analysis of the guidelines from W3C/WAI that took into consideration the culture and the needs of deaf people. Based on that analysis, Abreu *et al.* proposed a compilation of guidelines directly related to the accessibility of deaf users accompanied by a detailed explanation of their impact for this community. The second investigation was a qualitative research using the Method for Explicit Underlying Discourse (MEDS)[2] for identifying relevant issues to literacy of deaf children. In addition to the recommendations for the design of systems, the interviews allowed the identification of deaf children's literacy activities that teachers consider efficient for the learning process. This set can be useful to anyone interested in the process of literacy of deaf children, including the designers of systems for supporting the literacy.

In this work we selected some guidelines from Abreu *et al.* (2010) that best fit the context of use of question types of CBA for deaf students. For means of identification, the guidelines from the W3C/WAI begin with 'W', the guidelines generated by interviews with teachers of deaf students by 'I', and the guidelines related to activities related to the literacy process will be represented by 'A'. Next we present the selected set of guidelines for this work (free translation):

W1 – Use Transcription for Podcasts. Providing a transcript makes the audio information accessible for deaf or hearing impaired. Do not just make a literal transcription of the content. It must be considered how to present expressions and figures of language that are not easily understood by the deaf. For example, in the case of metaphors it must present the metaphor and a possible explanation associated to it. Moreover, if there is sound on the podcast along with the speeches, (*i.e.* thematic background music), they must be also identified.

W2 – Provide Alternative Texts Equivalent to Visual Content. Designers must provide text equivalents of non-textual content (*i.e.* images, video). Despite deaf people are able to see image or video, the transcript can be critical to facilitate their understanding of the meaning of visual content and/or its relationship with the text (if any).

W3 – Provide Several Ways for Document Reading. When a document with some important information is presented in the system, the content should be presented in text, video with information in sign language, or an avatar for translating the information for sign language, which is the first language of the deaf.

W4 – Adapt-the Interface Features for the Deaf. Designers can do whatever he/she want in the interface since he/she ensures that the contents, pictures and banners

[2] This is a qualitative research method through which the semi-structured interviews are guided in Humanities and Social Sciences. The main objective of MEDS in HCI, is making visible internal aspects of human nature important for the development of interactive systems as their preferences, difficulties, wishes, desires, etc. Its relevance for the field of HCI is the possibility to capture what is not tangible by other methods [Nicolaci-da-Costa *et al.* 2004].

are adapted to the reality of the deaf, which means that, when possible, the designer must use the sign language (video or avatar) to explain it.

W5 – Provide a Video Description of the Audio Information that is Relevant in a Multimedia Presentation. Supplement the text with graphic presentations or visual whenever they can facilitate the page/interface understanding. Designers must adapt all the information that is available in audio in the website or computer program, by providing it also in text. For any type of multimedia presentation (*e.g.* a movie or animation), equivalent alternatives should be synchronized (*e.g.* captions or text descriptions of audio clips, preferably in videos with the information in sign language). The deaf, due to its auditory limitation, need graphical or visual interfaces to facilitate understanding of presented information, since audio information and complex texts hinders the access of deaf people to the system.

W7 – Provide Information so that Users May Receive Documents According to their Preferences (e.g. language, content type). Designers must develop systems that provide information to the user according to their preferences. In the case of the deaf user, it should be able choose the language (verbal or sign language).

I3 – Provide Feedback to the Child about His/Her Activities, this Feedback Should Be in a Language that the Deaf Child Understands. The developed system, as any system, shall provide feedback to the child in relation to his/her activity and this feedback should be in a language the child understands (*e.g.* an image) or can even approach aspects related to the purpose of the system (*e.g.* associate images and words). This is important so that the child can use the system autonomously.

A1 – Consider Proposing Situations where it is Possible to Perform Activities in Groups or in Pairs. Deaf children learn a lot from the pair. Therefore, proposing exercises in pairs facilitates interaction and learning of deaf children since they have the opportunity of interacting with the system autonomously and also learn from his colleague.

The preparation of the assessment activity involved the configuration of the computing environment, the definition of the tasks and also the definition of procedure to be followed by the evaluators. The computing environment involved the virtual learning environment Moodle version 2.5. The tasks involved the questions repository in Moodle environment and the types of questions: multiple choice, essay, true/ false, embedded answers and matching. The procedure of the evaluation consisted of using the questions repository of the Moodle for instantiating each question type approached in this work. The evaluators took notes according the set of selected guidelines, by registering issues and possible design solution for them.

The data analysis is organized according to the 9 selected guidelines. We adopted a qualitative approach. For each problem found it was expected that the evaluators make suggestions for solutions whenever possible and necessary.

4 Results of Evaluation

This section initially provides information about the setup and conduction of the evaluation and follows witch presentation and the analysis of the collected data.

4.1 Scenario and Tasks of the Study

The evaluation was conducted by 2 evaluators that work in the area of Human-Computer Interaction. Both the evaluators are experts on accessibility in computer systems. One of them focuses on accessibility in the context of deaf people.

The questions repository of Moodle provides several types of questions that can be used to compose questionnaires. In this work we focus in 5 types of questions: multiple choice, true/false, essay, matching and embedded answers (cloze). In Moodle, for each type of question there are fields to fill in order to formulate the questions, the answers and the respective feedbacks.

Questions of the type multiple choice provides a field for formulate of the question (question text), fields to formulate possible alternatives of answer, and fields for general feedback and feedback for each alternative. For all these fields, Moodle provides an enhanced HTML editor called TinyMCE[3], henceforth called "HTML editor". Using this editor it is possible to insert text, images, videos, audios and others HTML elements. Table 1 summarizes the fields that provide the HTML editor for formulating questions.

Table 1. HTML editor availability by question type and field

Field	Types of question				
	Embedded Answer (Cloze)	**Essay**	**Matching**	**Multiple Choice**	**True/False**
Question	Yes	Yes	Yes	Yes	Yes
Answer	No	Yes	No	No	No
Feedback	Yes	Yes	Yes	Yes	Yes
Option Question	Yes	N/A	Yes	N/A	N/A
Option Answer	No	N/A	No	Yes	N/A

Essay questions provide the fields: question text, general feedback and the field for the answer. In all these fields, it is possible to use the HTML editor.

Matching questions have the field for the question text, general feedback and fields that must be attached to their respective correct answers. For the answers of this type question, it is necessary to select the correct answer using a "combo box" widget.

True/False question is composed of a field for the question text, general feedback and feedback for the possible answers. When answering this question type students must select an option in a pair of "radio button" widgets (*i.e.* selecting true or false).

Embedded answers (Cloze) questions are composed of a passage of text (in a Moodle's specific set of tags) that provide means for embedding several answers within it, including multiple choice and short answers. This question type has only one field with the HTML editor. That field is used for formulate questions, answers, and feedback. However, the answers can only be presented in text format *i.e.* it is not

[3] `http://www.tinymce.com/`

possible to insert video and images in the answer. The general feedback also can be formulated using the options of the HTML editor. Additionally, it is possible to provide feedback for the answers using HTML editor.

4.2 Collected Data

This section presents and analyses the collected data according to the selected guidelines, and are reported by indicating the question type and the situation in which the item was observed.

W1 – Use Transcription for Podcasts. In all types of questions analyzed in this work, there is no specific feature for transcription of audio and video. There is not any guidance for the creator of the question regarding how he/she could do it. Using the HTML editor it is possible to insert text transcriptions right below the media, however there is neither synchronism nor semantic relation (*e.g.* one specific HTML tag) between them.

In embedded answers questions in which the answers are composed only of textual information, an example of the use of the podcast or any other multimedia content to this type of question can be observed in Figure 1. In our proposed design solution, the selection of the answer could be implemented by an "radio button" widget followed by additional/redundant media, as for example and podcast or a video, so that teachers could provide different media for both questions and answers.

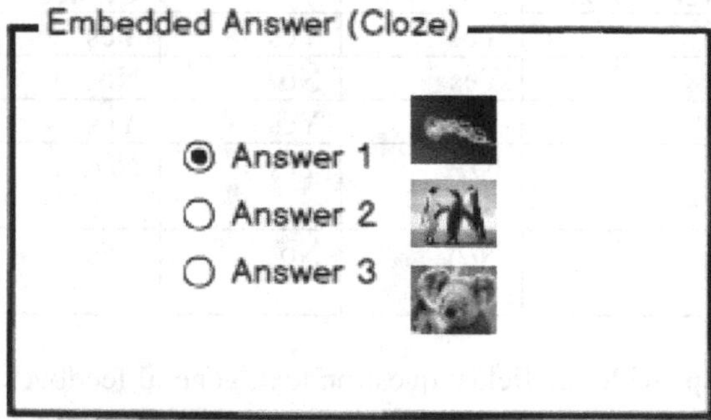

Fig. 1. Possible solution for multimedia use in the answers in question type embedded answers

W2 – Provide Alternative Texts Equivalent to Visual Content. In the types of questions that have fields with HTML editor, it is possible to insert the image description. This description is useful for screen readers or for using text-only mode. However, it is not possible to insert semantic markup for linking captions to pictures. A workaround could be inserting a text below the picture and use it as a caption. It is also possible to insert videos, but there is no option to insert synchronized text transcription for media. One alternative is to insert the video with embedded subtitles. For audio, a palliative solution could be inserting the text equivalent right below the audio. Another possible solution could be to provide an option to choose the default media for presenting questions. Such option could be placed at the user profile.

In the essay questions, the student can answer using the HTML editor, therefore it is possible to answer with media. However, the limitation is that it is not possible to record the answer lively. The user is supposed to use only prerecorded media. A possible solution could be to provide a media (audio e video) recorder for users so that they can answer essay questions using this resource for the answer.

The answers of matching questions are only text-based. A possible solution could be using a numbered index for each question and changing the answers to accept the HTML editor. Also it would be necessary to change the "combo box" widget in order to keep only the indexes from the questions, so that the constraint for answers with text only could be eliminated, since they would not need to be presented in the "combo box". Figure 2 shows an example of our proposed design solution for the question of type Matching.

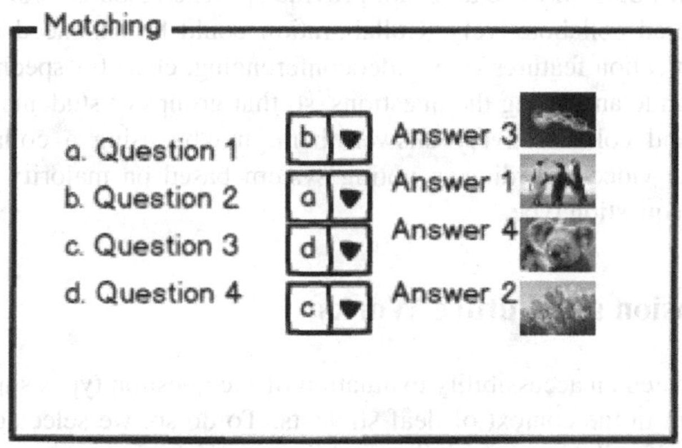

Fig. 2. Possible design solution for matching questions

Questions of the type true/false could be improved by inserting representative images for the texts of true or false in the selection of the appropriate answer. This resource would be redundant to the text already available.

W3 – Provide Several Ways for Document Reading. For all types of questions related in this work, there is no specific option in Moodle platform for inserting alternative media. In the HTML editor it is possible to insert several types of media (text, graphic, audio, video). However, there is no semantic link between one media and another. Also, there is not an avatar for translation of information for sign language, which is the first language of the deaf people

W4 – Adapt-the Interface Features for the Deaf. Moodle does not provide specific resources for the use of sign language or simplified text. Instructors could possibly insert some resource through the HTML editor, however there are no resources directed to this purpose.

W5 – Provide a Video Description of the Audio Information that is Relevant in a Multimedia Presentation. Supplement the text with graphic presentations or visual whenever they can facilitate the page/interface understanding. Again, it is possible to insert alternative media through the HTML editor, but it does not offer any specific resource to bind the media.

W7 – Provide Information so that Users may Receive Documents According to their Preferences (*e.g.* language, content type). Moodle not provide resources for this purpose. A possible solution could be inserting this option at the user profile so that user would be able to select the default media for presentation. However, regardless this option it is important to allow user to select media at any time.

I3 – Provide Feedback to the Child about his/her Activities, this Feedback should be in a Language that the Deaf Child Understands. All fields' feedbacks of all question types related in this work have the HTML editor; therefore the teacher can choose using text, image, or video to formulate the feedback. Assuming that the first language of the deaf is sign language [Chomsky 1998], it is possible to insert feedback information in sign language by inserting a prerecorded video.

A1 – Consider Proposing Situations where it is Possible to Perform Activities in Groups or in Pairs. Moodle does not provide specific resources for questions that could be answered collaboratively. Collaboration could be enhanced in Moodle by adding communication features (*e.g.* videoconferencing, chat) for specific students (a pair, a group) while answering the questions, so that groups of students could discuss the questions and collaboratively answer them, maybe using a collaborative text editor, an online video recording, a voting system based on majority or consensus, according to the question type.

5 Conclusion and Future Works

This work presented an accessibility evaluation of the question types supported by the Moodle platform in the context of deaf students. To do so, we selected some guidelines geared specifically for accessibility and literacy of deaf users.

The predictive evaluation was conducted by experts using the selected guidelines to perform selected tasks that involved the preparation of questions and answers for the set of questions types: multiple choices, essay, matching, embedded answers (cloze) and true/false; all of them supported by the Moodle platform.

The evaluation results indicate using the selected guidelines in this work has supported and allowed the evaluators to realize that some of these issues could receive less attention without this support. About the evaluated content (question types), we can conclude that there are some accessibility problems with those types of questions in the Moodle environment, most of them involving the use of images, texts, videos, audios, and user customization.

Further works include the involvement of users in the process of evaluation, in order to validate the results identified in this review and also validate the proposed design solutions. Lastly, we expect in a future be able to propose a consolidated set of guidelines for the development of accessible question types in the context of deaf students, for use in VLEs or other systems that could support question and answers features.

Acknowledgments. This work is funded by Conselho Nacional de Desenvolvimento Científico e Tecnológico - CNPq (process #134218/2013-2).

References

1. Abreu, P.M., Prates, R.O., Bernardino, E.L.: Recomendações de acessibilidade para projetos de TICs para alfabetização de crianças surdas. In: Anais do XXXVII Seminário Integrado de Software e Hardware (SEMISH), pp. 1–7. Congresso da Sociedade Brasileira de Computação (2010)
2. Bueno, J.F., Castilho, D.F.R.J., Garcia, S., Borrego, R.: E-learning content adaptation for deaf students. In: Proc. 12th annual SIGCSE conference on Innovation and technology in computer science education (ITiCSE 2007), pp. 271–275. ACM, New York (2007)
3. Burgstahler, S., Corrigan, B., McCarter, J.: Making distance learning courses accessible to students and instructors with disabilities: A case study. The Internet and Higher Education 7(3), 233–246 (2004)
4. Chatzopoulou, D.I., Economides, A.A.: Adaptive assessment of student's knowledge in programming courses. Journal of Computer Assisted Learning 26(4), 258–269 (2010)
5. Chomsky, N.: Language and Problems of Knowledge. The Managua Lectures. The MIT Press, Cambridge (1998)
6. Croft, A.C., Danson, M., Dawson, B.R., Ward, J.P.: Experiences of using computer assisted assessment in engineering mathematics. Computers & Education 27, 53–66 (2001)
7. Debevc, M., Stjepanovič, Z., Holzinger, A.: Development and evaluation of an e-learning course for deaf and hard of hearing based on the advanced Adapted Pedagogical Index method. Interactive Learning Environments, 1–16 (2012)
8. Debevc, M., Zoric-Venuti, M., Peljha, Z.: E-Iearning material planning and preparation. Report of the European project BITEMA (Bilingual Teaching Material For The Deaf by Means of ICT) (2003)
9. Drigas, A.S., Kouremenos, D., Kouremenos, S., Vrettaros, J.: An e-learning system for the deaf people. In: 6th International Conference on Information Technology Based Higher Education and Training, ITHET, pp. T2C/17–T2C/21 (2005)
10. Hashim, H., Tasir, Z., Mohamad, K.S.: E-learning Environment for Hearing Impaired Students. TOJET: The Turkish Online Journal of Educational Technology (2013)
11. Kaklauskas, A., Zavadskas, E.K., Pruskus, V., Vlasenko, A., Seniut, M., Kaklauskas, G., Matuliauskaite, A., Gribniak, V.: Biometric and intelligent self-assessment of student progress system. Computers & Education 55(2), 821–833 (2010)
12. Khwaldeh, S., Matar, N., Hunaiti, Z.: Interactivity in deaf classroom using centralised E-learning system in Jordan. PGNet (2007) ISBN, 1-9025
13. Koh, K.: Moodle as a Course Management System. eslweb.org (2006)
14. Kumar, S., Gankotiya, A.K., Dutta, K.: A comparative study of moodle with other e-learning systems. In: 3rd International Conference on Electronics Computer Technology (ICECT), vol. 5, pp. 8–10, 414–418 (2011)
15. Krathwohl, D.R.: A revision of bloom's taxonomy: An overview. Theory into Practice 41(4), 212–218 (2002)
16. Luephattanasuk, N., Suchato, A., Punyabukkana, P.: Accessible QTI presentation for web-based e-learning. In: Proc. of the International Cross-Disciplinary Conference on Web Accessibility (W4A 2011), Article 26. ACM, New York (2011)
17. Martin, C., Morris-Cotterill, N., Smith, M.: Open source software for the education market. Eduforge (2004)
18. Nicolaci-da-Costa, A.M., Leitão, C.F., Dias, D.R.: Como conhecer usuários através do Método de Explicitação do Discurso Subjacente (MEDS). In: Anais do VI Simpósio Sobre Fatores Humanos em Sistemas Computacionais, IHC, pp. 49–59 (2004)

19. Power, C., Petrie, H., Sakharov, V., Swallow, D.: Virtual learning environments: Another barrier to blended and E-learning. In: Miesenberger, K., Klaus, J., Zagler, W., Karshmer, A. (eds.) ICCHP 2010, Part 1. LNCS, vol. 6179, pp. 519–526. Springer, Heidelberg (2010)
20. Seale, J.K.: E-Learning and Disability in Higher Education: Accessibility Research and Practice. Routledge, Oxford (2006)
21. Sim, G., Holifield, P., Brown, M.: Implementation of computer assisted assessment: Lessons from the literature. Association for Learning Technology Journal (ALT-J) 12(3), 215–229 (2004)
22. Sokolova, M., Totkov, G.: Accumulative question types in e-learning environment. In: Rachev, B., Smrikarov, A., Dimov, D. (eds.), Article 90 , 6 pages. ACM, New York (2007)
23. Straetz, K., Kaibel, A., Raithel, V., Specht, M., Grote, K., Kramer, F.: An e-learning environment for deaf adults. In: 8th ERCIM Workshop (2005)
24. Thelwall, M.: Computer-based assessment: A versatile educational tool. Computers & Education 34(1), 37–49 (2000)
25. Turner, G., Gibbs, G.: Are assessment environments gendered? An analysis of the learning responses of male and female students to different assessment Environments. Assessment & Evaluation in Higher Education 35(6), 687–698 (2010)

Assessing Group Composition in e-learning According to Vygotskij's Zone of Proximal Development

Maria De Marsico[1], Andrea Sterbini[1], and Marco Temperini[2]

[1] Dept. of Computer Science, Sapienza University of Rome, Italy
{demarsico,sterbini}@di.uniroma1.it

[2] Dept. of Computer, Control, and Management Engineering
Sapienza University of Rome, Italy
marte@dis.uniroma1.it

Abstract. In this paper we build on previous work exploring a formal way to assess the composition of learning groups. We start from our existing framework, designed to provide support to personalization in e-learning environments, comprising an implementation of the Vygotskij Theory of proximal development. In such theory, effective individual learning achievements can be only obtained within the boundaries of a cognitive zone where the learner can proceed without frustration, though with support from teacher and peers. In this endeavor, the individual development cannot disregard social-collaborative educational activities. Previously we gave operative definitions of the Zone of Proximal Development for both single learners and groups; here we aim at assessing the viability of a partition of students in groups over a common task.

Keywords: Individual Zone of Proximal Development, Group Zone of Proximal development, Personalized learning path, Social collaborative e-learning.

1 Introduction and Motivations

Recent research on e-learning has especially focused on personalization and adaptivity. Several investigations mainly addressed tailoring the learning experience to personal-individual characteristics (such as learning styles and achievements) [1-5]. However, also planning and coordination of work in groups has deserved attention from recent related research [6-10], due to the increasing interest in investigating effective strategies to motivate and enhance study activity through social-collaborative learning [11,12]. The present work introduces a first attempt to formally define a "viability" measure for the composition of learning groups. It is a further step along our research line aiming at the concrete implementation of the principles underlying the concept of Zone of Proximal Development (ZPD) from Vygotskij theory [13] in a platform for adaptive e-learning.

The present discussion stems from two previous achievements. In [14] we presented a framework for the dynamic configuration of personalized learning paths for both individual students and groups, in a way adaptive to a continuous assessment and

C. Stephanidis and M. Antona (Eds.): UAHCI/HCII 2014, Part II, LNCS 8514, pp. 277–288, 2014.

student model updating. Such framework can be integrated in present state-of-the-art e-learning platforms, such as Moodle [15], to avoid much of the cumbersomeness of the implementation of an entirely new system. Later [16], we focused on refinements related to individual profiling. The quality of personal achievements (skill acquisition) can vary according to features which are not presently accounted for in widespread learning environments, such as the time required to acquire a skill, or the linearity (rate of success/failure results) of the acquisition. Moreover, the difficulty of an activity is determined both by the skills required to tackle it, and by the quality/firmness of their possession by the student. Those factors too may vary from student to student (or between different phases in the development of the learner, as mirrored by the evolution of the individual student model). Quite straightforwardly, all this changes the level of "difficulty" which each single student is subjected to.

If considering these aspects may be of paramount importance in individual personalization, it deserves even more attention when composing working groups. From one side, we can "exploit" the definition of the group ZPD, and from the other side we can include into it a group-bounded version of the formal definitions of "difficulty" which might be actually encountered in tackling a learning activity. In many cases the group composition follows personal preferences of students with respect to their mates. However, from a pedagogical point of view such choices might not be the most appropriate ones. Members that are too "strong" may be demotivated by having to adapt to "weakest" ones, and, symmetrically, less bright members of the group may be frustrated by having to forcedly follow the smarter colleagues. And of course grouping and separating "brighter" students from "weaker" may be detrimental for the class as a whole and leave too many students behind.

While in face-to-face activities the experience and sensibility of the teacher might guide the choice of group partition, a similar guidance is very hard to achieve automatically in distance settings. We argue that a suitable extension to groups of the formal strategies applied to individual students in our previous work can help "measuring" the appropriateness of a given partition in groups of a class of students. Rather than exploiting any "viability" measure for group composition in order to determine from scratch the best partition of the class (as it might be computationally heavy), we try to define such an analysis on already stated class subdivision. We intend to tackle this problem in a formal way, within our e-learning framework. In this endeavor, the value of such framework is twofold: it is detached by any present concrete e-learning platform, in particular from the Moodle prototype presented in [9], and provides a ground layer to realize the pedagogical principles of the theory of Vygotskij, by extending the formal bases for the practical implementation of concepts such as the Zone of Proximal Development in an e-learning setting.

2 Framework Core Definitions

We report here for reader's convenience only the most basic concepts that make up the formal definition of our framework. Further details can be found in [14].

2.1 The Learner and the Learning Activities

A learner *l* is represented in the system by a student model, that in this barebones description is constituted by a set of his/her achieved *skills* (Student Knowledge – *SK(l)*). A skill [14] represents knowledge possessed by the learner, and is qualified by a measure of *certainty* (about its possession by *l*) $c \in [0...1]$):

$$SK(l) = \{<s_1, c_1>, \ldots, <s_{nl}, c_{nl}>\}$$

A learning activity *la* is defined by: *la.Content* (learning material); *la.A* (Acquisition: skills provided by *la*); *la.P* (Prerequisites: skills "needed" to tackle *la*); *la.Effort* (an estimate of the cognitive load associated to *la*).

The completion of a *la* by learner *l* will trigger the insertion of *la.A* into the set of skills in *SK(l)*, with an assigned *certainty* depending on the student's performance in, say, a final test. In this way, *SK(l)*, is continuously updated during course. The updates reflect the evolution of *l* following the tackled learning activities.

In particular C_{ENTRY} is the default value assigned to a newly acquired skill. Further successful assessments for *s* increase its certainty, *c*, while unsuccessful ones decrease it. When *c* in *<s, c>* decreases below a level C_{DEMOTE} *<s, c>* is removed, and further activities will be needed to acquire it back; a value of *c* exceeding $C_{PROMOTE}$, states that the skill is firmly acquired, and no further assessment will be required. As for C_{ENTRY}, C_{DEMOTE}, $C_{PROMOTE}$ the teacher can confirm platform defaults, or assign them differently.

A *learning path* can be defined as a set $LP=\{la_i\}_{i \in \{1...n\}}$. A certain *LP* entails an overall set of acquired skills *LP.A*, and an overall set of requirements *LP.P* such that

$$LP.A = \cup_{i\in \{1...n\}}\, la_i.A \qquad LP.P = \cup_{i\in \{1...n\}}\, la_i.P \setminus LP.A$$

and an overall effort $\quad LP.Effort = \sum_{i \in \{1...n\}} la_i.effort$

A personalized course delivery for a learner *l*, is a learning path built basing on the initial $SK(l)_{INIT}$ and adaptively updated basing on *SK(l)* evolution. In particular a student *l* is able to access a certain activity iff all skills in *la.P* are in *SK(l)*.
For $SK(l) = \{<s_1, c_1>, \ldots, <s_{nl}, c_{nl}>\}$, its *s-projection* is its set of skills:

$$s\text{-}proj(SK(l)) = \{s_i, \text{ with } <s_i, c_i> \in SK(l)\} = \{s_1, \ldots, s_{nl}\}$$

The relations between Prerequisite and Acquired sets induce a partial order on the learning activities: if $la.A \cap \underline{la}.P \neq \emptyset$, some skills needed by <u>la</u> are acquired through *la,* so that *la* has to precede <u>la in any learning path</u>. The framework lets the learner choose the "next learning activity" in the course as freely as possible. To be educationally feasible, this must take into account both the present learner's knowledge and the partial order among activities. To allow this, we attempt a formalization of the concept of Zone of Proximal Development (ZPD) from Vygotskij theory [13].

2.2 A Formal Definition of ZPD

Given a learner *l*, working on a configured course $\underline{LP} = \{la_1, \ldots, la_{tl}\}$, some significant cognitive areas related to student's learning state, and defined by Vygotskij, have been formalized in our framework. The area of Autonomous Problem Solving (*APS*) is the area of firm knowledge in the present state of knowledge *SK(l)*:

$APS(l) = \{s, \langle s, C_{PROMOTE}\rangle \in SK(l)\}$. Of course, $APS(l) \subseteq s\text{-}proj(SK(l))$.

The *ZPD* for the learner is a zone where (s)he has no firm achievements yet, but that can be explored with some help from the teacher or from peers. On the contrary, the zone of Unreachable Problem Solving (UPS) is the area (of the course) where it is not pedagogically safe for the learner to enter, given the present level of skills:

$$UPS(l) = \underline{LP}.A \setminus (APS(l) \cup ZPD(l))$$

Given a learning path $\underline{LP}$, its knowledge domain is $KD(\underline{LP}) = \underline{LP}.A \cup \underline{LP}.P$. In particular the set difference, $KD(\underline{LP}) \setminus s\text{-}proj(SK(l))$ is the set of all skills in the course knowledge domain, that are not yet acquired in *SK(l)*. A subset of these skills constitutes the ZPD of the student *l*, denoted as *ZPD(l)*. We are interested in identifying such subset, as composed by those skills that are at an "affordable" cognitive distance from the present *SK(l)*. In doing this, our aim is not to pack an additional bag of skills which can possibly be acquired, but rather to take into account the genuine interpretation of ZPD as a region of cognitive *development* [17].

Firstly, for each skill *s* outside *SK(l)*, we define the set of possible learning (sub)paths *LP'* in $\underline{LP}$, that can eventually allow to acquire *s*, and that can start from the current state of skills:

$$Reach(s, SK(l), \underline{LP}) =$$
$$= \{G=\{la_i\}_{i \in \{1...nG\}} \subseteq \underline{LP} \mid s \in la_{nG}.A \wedge G.P \subseteq s\text{-}proj(SK(l)) \cup G.A\}$$

where the last condition relating G.P to G.A expresses the possibility that the prerequisites of some $la_i \in G$ might be acquired through a previous $la_j \in G$. We define the distance of *s* from the present *SK(l)* as

$$D(s, s\text{-}proj(SK(l)), \underline{LP}) =$$
$\underline{G}.Effort$, where $\underline{G}$ is an element of minimal overall effort in *Reach*(s, SK(*l*), $\underline{LP}$).

The set $Support(s, SK(l), \underline{LP}) = \underline{G}.P \cap s\text{-}proj(SK(l))$ denotes the skills already possessed by the learner that are necessary to reach *s* along a minimal-effort path in $\underline{LP}$. We designate such a set as the *support set* to reach *s*.

We assume that a higher certainty for the skills in the support set can facilitate the learner in reaching *s*. Furthermore, certainty in the support set can affect the distance from the *SK(l)* that we can span, and yet still consider *s* in the *ZPD(l)*. In other words, supposing that $D(s, s\text{-}proj(SK(l)), \underline{LP}) \geq D(s', s\text{-}proj(SK(l)), \underline{LP})$ while the overall certainty of the $Support(s, SK(l), \underline{LP})$ is higher of $Support(s', SK(l), \underline{LP})$, *s* might be reachable while *s'* might not, despite the closer distance. The effort required along the way to the target has a further role in determining the maximum reasonable distance. According to these preliminary considerations, we attempted to define such distance in a reasonable yet challenging way, which may stimulate the student without causing frustration, being dynamically tuned to his/her evolving cognitive state. To take into account both average certainty of the support set and expected average effort along the path towards a certain skill, in [14] we introduced functions *AvgCertainty()* and *AvgEffort()*. In the initial definition we considered only the pure level of certainty of a skill, and the level of effort estimated by the teacher. However, in the follow-up of the creation of our framework we realized that it is not pedagogically realistic to assign to each effort (or resp. certainty) a constant weight, as the effort in acquiring a skill may depend on the firmness of required knowledge, and the certainty of a skill may be weighted by the variable paths through which it has been secured. Therefore, in [16] we refined both *AvgCertainty()* and *AvgEffort()*. A kind of more realistic "average certainty" is obtained by a weighed sum through a backward computation starting from a skill to be possibly included in *ZPD*, and going back towards its support set. Skills with different certainty may contribute differently, and different skills presenting the same certainty might contribute differently too, depending on both the consolidation of a skill in time and the ways that certainty has been reached by the learner. For a given learner l and a given skill s_i, with certainty c_i in $SK(l)$ the weight for s_i is:

$$w_i = \frac{age(s_i) * age(cert(s_i))}{\big(age(s_i) - age(cert(s_i))\big) * (ntests/npostests)}$$

$age(s_i)$ being the age of the skill, $age(cert(s_i))$ the age of the present value of certainty, $(age(s_i)\text{-}\ age(cert(s_i)))$ an estimate of the time to reach $cert(s_i)$ and $ntests/npostests$ the ratio between the number of tests and the number of positive increments of certainty, i.e., an estimate of the linearity of the learning process. *AvgCertainty()* is then:

$$AvgCertainty(Support(s, SK(l), \underline{LP})) = (\textstyle\sum_{<si,ci> \in Support(s,\ SK(l),\ \underline{LP})} w_i \cdot c_i) \,/\, Card(Support(s, SK(l), \underline{LP}))$$

Notice that this is not a true weighted average, since the sum of weights is not 1. In a similar way, "average effort" can be obtained by a forward computation starting from a support set towards any reachable skill to be possibly included in the ZPD. Each activity has an effort value in its definition, however each student may experience a different one. We can assume that, for each *la* in *G*, a subset of skills in both *la.P* and *la.A* are already in *SK(l)* with its certainty level. Skills already possessed, both in *la.P* and *la.A* sets, can decrease the effort actually experienced, and symmetrically a poor performance in pre-requisites may increase it. As for skills in *la.A*,

$$wa(la.A) = Card(la.A) \cdot C_{ENTRY}, / \textstyle\sum_{s\ in\ la.A} f(s, SK(l))$$

where

$$f(s, SK(l)) = \begin{cases} c & if < s, c > \in SK(l) \\ C_{ENTRY} & otherwise. \end{cases}$$

Reminding that the expected level of certainty for a newly acquired skill is C_{ENTRY}, notice that if no skill is already possessed, $w(la) = 1$ and originally defined effort is still valid. On the other hand, a level of certainty already achieved, or a low value, are able to respectively decrease or increase the effort to acquire that skill. A symmetric argument holds for prerequisite skills in *la.P*:

$$wp(la.P) = Card(la.P) \cdot C_{promote} / \textstyle\sum_{s\ in\ la.P} f(s, SK(l))$$

where *f(s, SK(l))* is defined in the same way as above. Reminding that he best supportive level of certainty for a prerequisite skill is $C_{PROMOTE}$, if all the skills are already possessed with certainty $C_{PROMOTE}$ (as it should preferably be) then $wp(la.P) = 1$ and effort is not affected. Values better than $C_{PROMOTE}$ means a firmer achievement and decreases effort, and the contrary. For a certain student *l* and a given activity *la*, the weight of the activity in computing the "average effort" on a learning path will be

$$w(la) = \frac{wa(la.A)+wp(la.P)}{2}$$

We can now define :

$$A1 = AvgCertainty(Support(\mathrm{s}, \mathrm{SK}(l), \underline{\mathrm{LP}})) =$$

$$\left(\sum_{<si,ci>\in Support(s,\ SK(l),\ \underline{LP})} w_i \cdot c_i\right) / \mathrm{Card}(Support(\mathrm{s}, \mathrm{SK}(l), \underline{\mathrm{LP}}))$$

$$A2 = AvgEffort(\mathrm{G}^{\min}, Support(\mathrm{s}, \mathrm{SK}(l), \underline{\mathrm{LP}})) =$$

$$\sum_{la\in G^{min}} w(la)\cdot la.effort\ /\ Card(\mathrm{G}^{\min})$$

and finally

$$DTreshold(\mathrm{s}, \mathrm{SK}(l)) = (\mathrm{A1/A2}) \cdot Eff(R) \cdot dF.$$

The term *A1/A2* can be considered as the amount of certainty per unit of effort which is currently available to the student, so that the higher this ratio, the farther the student can explore; *Eff(R)* is the average effort over the learning activities in the learning domain; *dF* is a daring factor that can be configured by the teacher. Finally:

$$\mathrm{ZPD(l)} = \{\mathrm{s} \in KD(\underline{LP}) \setminus \mathrm{APS}(l), \text{ such that}$$
$$\mathrm{D}(\mathrm{s}, s\text{-}proj(\mathrm{SK}(l)), \underline{\mathrm{LP}}) \leq DTreshold(\mathrm{s}, \mathrm{SK}(l))\}$$

The final result is a *ZPD()* with a variable radius, i.e., a radius which is not the same for all students but depends on their present state of knowledge. We think that this operational definition of an individually tuned *ZPD* can support a true implementation of a zone of development, coherently with the concept originally portrayed by Vygotskij, although in a framework where the word "development" is intended as acquisition of techniques and knowledge skills from previously possessed ones.

2.3 ZPD for Groups

When we have to select an appropriate *LP* for a given group of students, we have to first determine the overall group's state of skills (Group Knowledge - *GK*), and *ZPD*, starting from the individual ones. If we identify the group *ZPD* with the pedagogically admissible set of learning activities that the group can tackle, such set should be defined so as to maximize members' gain from the collaborative activities.

We first compute the group's *GK* as the union of the members' *SK*, where each skill has group-certainty equal to its average certainty in the members' *SK*:

$$GK(ST) = \{<s,c> \ /\ \forall l\in ST\ (<s,c_l>\in SK(l) \wedge c=((\textstyle\sum_{l\in ST,\ <s,cl>\in SK(l)} c_l)\ /\ Card(ST))\}$$

In order to take into consideration the possible reciprocal support in a *group-autonomous* achievement, we also modify the definition of the *APS* of the group, by considering a "pseudo-intersection": skills that are not firmly possessed by *all* members are included in the *APS(ST)* iff they are in *APS(l')* for *some* $l' \in ST$ and they are in *SK(l)* for all the other members $l \in ST$ with a minimum certainty τ_C, chosen as:

$$\tau_C = C_{PROMOTE} - C_{ENTRY}/2$$

Since the *l'* students above will support the *l ones*, they have to be sufficiently many in the group (according to teacher's advice), say one for each *g* members:

$$\mathrm{APS(ST)} = \{s \in \cup_{l \in ST} APS(l) \mid$$
$$\forall l \in ST(\langle s,c\rangle \in SK(l) \wedge c \geq \tau_C) \wedge Card(\{l' \in ST \mid$$
$$\langle s,c\rangle \in SK(l') \wedge c = C_{PROMOTE}\}) \geq Card(ST)/g$$

We use a reverse strategy and define implicitly the group *ZPD*, through criteria of *admissibility* of activities. Two conditions are defined, by working on the *APS(l)*s, the *ZPD(l)*s, and the SKs of the group members. As for the first one, given a group of students ST and a learning path LP, 1) *the group members must share a common portion of APS, and 2) each activity prerequisites is firmly possessed by at least one of the members*:

$$\cap_{l \in ST} APS(l) \neq \emptyset \quad \wedge \quad LP.P \subseteq \cup_{l \in ST} APS(l)$$

The second condition states that students in a group ST must share some common proximal development, and that an activity $la \in LP$ is admissible for ST iff, though possibly being off the *ZPD*s of some members, it is *not too distant* from them, and it is comprised in the *ZPD* of at least a number of members sufficient to support the others - τ is a threshold to establish admissibility, for learner *l*, of an la not in *ZPD(l)*:

$$\cap_{l \in ST} ZPD(l) \neq \emptyset \quad \wedge \forall la \in LP \; \forall s \in la.A \; \forall l \in ST \quad \mathrm{D(s, ZPD(}l\mathrm{), LP)} < \tau$$
$$\wedge \; \forall la \in LP \; Card(\{l \in ST \mid la.A \subseteq ZPD(l)\}) \geq Card(ST/g)$$

As above, *g* represents the number of students which can be supported by a peer. Being τ a threshold beyond individual ZPDs, i.e. beyond the daring zone for the individual learner, we set it as the minimum daring threshold for the skills in *la.A* [14]:

$$\tau = \min_{l \in ST} p(\textstyle\sum_{s \in la.A} AvgCertainty(Support(\mathrm{s, SK(}l\mathrm{), LP}) / Card(la.A))$$
$$ZPD(ST) = \{s \in KD(\underline{LP}) \mid D(s, GK(ST), LP) \leq \tau$$

3 Assessment of Group Composition

In Sec. 2, we assumed to already have groups, and to identify their *ZPD*s in order to deploy appropriate paths. Here we tackle the symmetric problem. We assume that we have a group activity (*la*) to submit to the class. This translates in assuming that the *la.A* is within the reach of each one of the group (i.e. in their *ZPD*s). Whatever is the chosen strategy to create groups, it is to consider that two different and complementary aspects play a role in their assessment: the different groups may have different degrees of *intra-group compatibility* and/or *inter-group balance*.

Compatibility among the members inside a group (intra-group) could be considered with respect to several aspects. Here we consider only the aspects related to the knowledge possessed by the students, i.e., the information stored and updated in the personal *SK()* of the group members. In other words, we account for the degree of sharing of cognitive resources and potentialities, which can affect the way the members interact and help each other, and acquire new (firm) knowledge as a results of such collaboration. On the other hand, inter-group balance is the most difficult to achieve, since it entails an attempt for global optimization. Grouping the "smartest" and the "weakest" students separately should be avoided, despite the obviousness of this criterion with respect to intra-group compatibility. It is trivial to consider that the most preforming students may take the greatest learning advantage from interacting with each other. However, if we consider the performance of the overall class, this "segregating" choice may result in leaving behind the students with greatest difficulties. Moreover, supporting and being supported is part of a global social training and improves meta-cognitive abilities. It is often observed that the best way to check one's knowledge about a topic is to let her/him try to explain the core concepts to another person. As it often happens, in the attempt to formalize the activity of group creation we realize how much it is difficult, and how valuable is the experience of a teacher able to do this according to a deep pedagogical sensitiveness. We want to devise viable strategies to identify (a-priori, very hard) or assess (a-posteriori) the intra-group compatibility and inter-group balance.

As above mentioned the most trivial approach would be to create homogeneous groups, but this would exclude weakest students. Therefore the idea is to get the maximum possible *ZPD* for each group, yes minimizing the variance of *ZPD* extension among different groups. Though attractive, this solution is not feasible, since the cognitive span of *ZPD* is not a scalar value. In other words it is not reliable to measure *ZPD* by, e.g., the number of included activities, since this would disregard the most important qualitative element which is the actual content of the activities. Moreover computing a variance would imply to figure out how to compute the difference between a given *ZPD* and an "average" one. Last but not least, computing the complete individual as well as group *ZPD*s constitutes a very demanding task. As a matter of fact we have so far bypassed this problem, in favor of a plainer verification of the possible inclusion of single activities in the *ZPD*. Of course we must assume that it contains at least the skills in *la.A* (with *la* the activity assigned to the group). So we must investigate on a more feasible measure, capable to capture *ZPD* quantitative as well as qualitative span.

3.1 Preliminaries

First of all, given the activity *la* to perform by the groups, we compute for each learner in the class, and for each skill *s* in *la.A*, its inclusion in the individual *ZPD*, according to Sec.2. For some skill this inclusion might not be verified, yet, as discussed above, this can be balanced by the inclusion of the learner in a suitable group, where the condition holds for a sufficient number of members. From this computation, in particular, we retain the value of the *AvgEffort()* to endure reaching the skill. In the following we discuss two possible approaches to group assessment procedure. In both cases we assume a distribution of students in a class in groups $D=\{g_i\}$ *for i=1,...,n.*

3.2 First Approach

We firstly define the *TargetWorkload(l, la)* required to the members of $g \in D$ by the activity, as the sum of the *AvgEffort()* for each $s \in la.A$. Then we can consider:

– *IntraGroupTotEff(g)* as the sum of the *TargetWorkload(l, la)* of all members;
– *IntraGroupAvgEff(g)* as the average *TargetWorkload(l, la)* over all members;
– *InterGroupAvgEff(D)* as the average of the *IntraGroupAvgEff(g) for g in D*
– *InterGroupVarEff(D)* as the variance of the *IntraGroupAvgEff(g) for g in D*

A possible way to optimize the distribution of students in groups, is to minimize both *InterGroupAvgEff(D)* and *InterGroupVarEff(D)* at once.

Additionally, a possible measure of the quality of the distribution can be provided by the comparison between *InterGroupAvgEff(D)* and the sum of *TargetWorkload(l, la)* for all *l* in the class, divided by the *Card(D)*. This might be relevant when a better distribution among the possible ones is sought.

3.3 Second Approach

A second approach entails considering the daring threshold, *DTreshold(s,SK(l))*, used in the definition of the individual ZPD. We remind that it depends on the firmness of the skills owned by the learner *l* in the *Support* subset of the *SK(l)* (cfr Sec. 2.2). It is conceivable that for some learners in the group the distance *D(s, ZPD(l))* will be zero (i.e. $s \in ZPD(l)$), while for the others it will be a positive value. Notice that the distance between *ZPD(l)* and s can be measured in the same way as for *SK(l)*.

A quality of the group (meaning a characteristics helpful in order for the group members to reach *s* after a collaborative learning experience) is in the couple $\langle m_g, \sigma_g \rangle$, where

– m_g = average(*D(s, ZPD(l))*) for $l \in g$
– σ_g is the variance of the *D(s, ZPD(l))* for $l \in g$

A lower σ_g tells us that the group is homogeneous. A higher m_g might point out that the skill is hard to reach for the group members, or that there is a very limited subset of members that could pull the rest towards the skill.

Regarding the distribution, also in this approach a better quality is reached when m_g and σ_g are minimized at once throughout the groups.

3.4 Third Approach

A further approach takes into consideration the definition of individual *ZPD(l)*, given in Sec. 2, and in particular the daring factor *dF*, configured by the teacher. We define a partition of a group *g* as

- $F(g, s) = \{l \in g$ such that $s \notin ZPD(l)\}$
- $H(g, s) = \{l \in g$ such that $s \in ZPD(l)\}$

It is reasonable to think that by modifying dF we could enlarge or shrink a given *ZPD(l)*, so we consider the following measures:

- for each *l* in *F(g, s)* the minimal value $\Delta^{+}dF(l)$ such that computing the *ZPD(l)* using $(dF+\Delta^{+}dF(l))$ causes $s \in ZPD(l)$
- for each *l* in *H(g, s)* the minimal value $\Delta^{-}dF$ such that computing the ZPD(l) using $(dF\text{-}\Delta^{-}dF)$ causes $s \notin ZPD(l)$

So a characteristics of the group is in the balance between the measures of affordability of the skill by the two group partitions, defined as the subtraction

$$Avg(\Delta dF(l)\ for\ l \in H(g, s)) - Avg(\Delta' dF(l)\ for\ l \in F(g, s))$$

The bigger this value, the less the difficulties of the learners whose *ZPD* has been stretched, because their difficulties can be eased by the potential support of the learners in *H(g, s)*. The lower this value, the closer (more homogeneous) are the learners in *H(g, s)* and *F(g, s)*.

Even in this case the variance of this value over the groups of a distribution gives an estimate of their inter-homogeneity.

4 Conclusions and Future Work

In this paper we described a stage in our effort to implement the concept of Zone of Proximal Development (*ZPD*), originated in the educational theories of L.V. Vygotskij, within a framework of web based technology enhanced learning. In particular our framework tries to join the more traditionally individualized activities of a system for personalized e-learning with the learning experience allowed in an environment supporting social and collaborative e-learning. This is done also by "using" the concept of *ZPD* to support an as free as possible navigation of the personal learning path, under the sole constraints given by the needs to take *ZPD* into consideration while navigating. The first requirement is a suitable definition of individual *ZPD* in terms of feasible activities. A further extension to groups can be a valuable help in the task of partitioning a class in a pedagogically effective way.

In our framework we attempted to define the *ZPD* in a reasonable yet challenging way, which may stimulate the student without causing frustration, and for this reason we defined it so that its radius is not the same for all students but depends on their present state of knowledge. As a matter of fact, it is often the case that the *ZPD* is merely considered as an additional bag of skills which is possible to acquire, disregarding its genuine interpretation as a region of cognitive *development*. On the contrary, we think that our definition of an individually tuned *ZPD* can support a pedagogically meaningful implementation of a zone of development, spurring the acquisition of techniques and knowledge skills from previously possessed ones.

We also attempted the definition of group *ZPD* starting from a given group and including from time to time "pedagogically sound" activities. Here we have extended our (still theoretical) work to support the symmetric operation, i.e. to start from a given activity and partition a class in the most effective set of groups. It was soon clear to us the difficulty of both automatically creating a class partition as well as of assessing the validity of a given one. Teachers are smart in this task, while automatic processing of students' data requires a complex double optimization procedure. In fact, the final aim is to both maximize intra-group compatibility and/or inter-group balance. The first should ensure fair collaboration within the group, and the second should avoid creating "best" and "worst" groups by enforcing the sense of collaboration and of general belonging to a same super-group (the class). Given this double goal, the most obvious solutions soon appeared unfeasible. This work presented a first attempt to mark a line along which to continue investigating appropriate alternatives.

In the future, besides assessing starting group adequacy, it would be also beneficial to assess the positive/negative dynamics within the groups, according to the amount of growth of individual *APS*s and *ZPD*s.

References

1. Martens, A.: Modeling of Adaptive Tutoring Processes. In: Ma, Z. (ed.) Web-Based Intelligent e-Learning Systems, pp. 193–215. IGI-Global (2005)
2. Limongelli, C., Sciarrone, F., Vaste, G.: LS-PLAN: An effective combination of dynamic courseware generation and learning styles in web-based education. In: Nejdl, W., Kay, J., Pu, P., Herder, E. (eds.) AH 2008. LNCS, vol. 5149, pp. 133–142. Springer, Heidelberg (2008)
3. Limongelli, C., Sciarrone, F., Vaste, G.: Personalized e-learning in moodle: The moodle-LS system. J. of E-Learning and Knowledge Society 7(1), 49–58
4. Limongelli, C., Lombardi, M., Marani, A., Sciarrone, F.: A Teacher Model to Speed Up the Process of Building Courses. In: Kurosu, M. (ed.) HCII/HCI 2013, Part II. LNCS, vol. 8005, pp. 434–443. Springer, Heidelberg (2013)
5. Limongelli, C., Sciarrone, F., Temperini, M., Vaste, G.: The Lecomps5 Framework for Personalized Web-Based Learning: a Teacher's Satisfaction Perspective. Computers in Human Behavior 27(4) (2011)
6. Ivanova, M., Popova, A.: Formal and Informal Learning Flows Cohesion in Web 2.0 Environment. Int. J. of Information Systems and Social Change, IJISSC 2(1), 1–15 (2011)
7. Sterbini, A., Temperini, M.: Learning from Peers: Motivating Students through Reputation Systems. In: Proc. Int. Symp. on Applications and the Internet, SAINT, pp. 305–308. IEEE (2008)
8. Cheng, Y., Ku, H.: An investigation of the effects of reciprocal peer tutoring. Computers in Human Behavior 25 (2009)

9. De Marsico, M., Sterbini, A., Temperini, M.: A strategy to join adaptive and reputation-based social-collaborative e-learning, through the Zone of Proximal Development. Int. Journal of Distance Education Technology, IJDET 11(3), 12–31 (2013)
10. De Marsico, M., Sterbini, A., Temperini, M.: The Definition of a Tunneling Strategy between Adaptive Learning and Reputation-based Group Activities. In: Proc. 11th IEEE Int. Conf. on Advanced Learning Technologies, ICALT, pp. 498–500 (2011)
11. Kreijns, K., Kirschner, P.A., Jochems, W.: Identifying the pitfalls for social interaction in computer supported collaborative learning environments: a review of the research. Computers in Human Behavior 19, 335–353 (2003)
12. Limongelli, C., Lombardi, M., Marani, A., Sciarrone, F.: A Teaching-Style Based Social Network for Didactic Building and Sharing. In: Lane, H.C., Yacef, K., Mostow, J., Pavlik, P. (eds.) AIED 2013. LNCS, vol. 7926, pp. 774–777. Springer, Heidelberg (2013)
13. Vygotskij, L.S.: The development of higher forms of attention in childhood. In: Wertsch, J.V. (ed.) The Concept of Activity in Soviet Psychology, Sharpe, Armonk (1981)
14. De Marsico, M., Sterbini, A., Temperini, M.: A Framework to Support Social-Collaborative Personalized e-Learning. In: Kurosu, M. (ed.) HCII/HCI 2013, Part II. LNCS, vol. 8005, pp. 351–360. Springer, Heidelberg (2013)
15. Dougiamas, M., Taylor, P.: Moodle: Using learning communities to create an open source course management system. In: Proc. World Conference on Educational Multimedia, Hypermedia and Telecommunications, vol. 1, pp. 171–178
16. De Marsico, M., Temperini, M.: Average effort and average mastery in the identification of the Zone of Proximal Development. In: Proc. 17th IEEE Int. Conf. on System Theory, Control and Computing, ICSTCC, 6th Int. Workshop on Social and Personal Computing for Web-Supported Learning Communities, SPeL, pp. 651–656 (2013)
17. Chaiklin, S.: The zone of proximal development in Vygotsky's analysis of learning and instruction. In: Kozulin, A., Gindis, B., Ageyev, V., Miller, S. (eds.) Vygotsky's Educational Theory in Cultural Context, pp. 39–64. Cambridge University Press (2003)

A Data Mining Approach to the Analysis of Students' Learning Styles in an e-Learning Community: A Case Study

Valentina Efrati[2], Carla Limongelli[1], and Filippo Sciarrone[1]

[1] Roma Tre University - Engineering Department
Via della Vasca Navale, 76
00146 Rome, Italy
{limongel,sciarro}@dia.uniroma3.it

[2] Roma Tre University - Fil.Co.Spe Department - Filosofia,
Comunicazione e Spettacolo Via Ostiense, 234, 00144 Rome, Italy
valentina.efrati@uniroma3.it

Abstract. In recent years, there has been a radical change in the world of education and training that is causing that many schools, universities and companies are adopting the most modern technologies, mainly based on Web architectures and Web 2.0 instruments and tools, for learning, managing and sharing of knowledge. In this context, an e-Learning system can reach its maximum potential and effectiveness if it could take advantage of the information in its possession and process it in an intelligent and personalized way. The Educational Data Mining is an emergent field of research where the approach to personalization makes use of the log data generated by learners during their training process, to dynamically update users learning profiles such as skills and learning styles and identify students behavioral patterns. In this paper we present a case study of a data mining approach, based on cluster analysis, in order to support the detection of learning styles in a community of learners, following the Grasha-Riechmann learning styles model. As an e-learning framework we used the Moodle LMS platform and studied the log files generated by a course taken by a community of learners. The first experimental results suggest a connection between clusters and learning styles, reinforcing the use of this approach.

1 Introduction

Nowadays with the exponential growth of the Internet and the use of the Web 2.0 instruments and tools, distance education is more and more adopted by educational institutions and companies, producing a lot of data concerning learners behavioral patterns. Educational Data Mining (EDM) is an emerging discipline, concerned with the developments of methods for exploring the unique types of data that come from educational settings, and using those methods to better understand students, and the settings which they learn in[1] [24]. In particular,

[1] `http://www.educationaldatamining.org/`

C. Stephanidis and M. Antona (Eds.): UAHCI/HCII 2014, Part II, LNCS 8514, pp. 289–300, 2014.

this approach is useful for personalized educational environments where one can use the data generated by learners during their training process to dynamically update their learning profiles, such as skills and learning styles. In this paper we present a case study of a data mining approach to the detection of the learning styles in a community of learners, following the Grasha-Riechmann Model (GRM) [11]. To this aim we based our study on an e-learning course delivered in by a Governative Italian institution [2] for training teachers to teach in high schools. The course was delivered using the Moodle e-learning environment [3], which is one of the most used open source e-learning platforms. We studied the navigational behaviors of learners through the analysis of the log files generated by their actions during the learning process, with the specific goal to predict the learning styles of each student, using a data-driven approach by means of the use of clustering algorithms. The goal of our work aimed to find a matching between the groups of students, i.e., the clusters, and the three dimensions of the GRM. A classic data mining process has been performed, using the Weka machine learning framework[4] while the log data files contained almost 1, 500.000 record of actions. Firstly we obtained 6 clusters of students and secondly we performed a mapping between the average values obtained for each attribute of each cluster and the values proposed by Grasha and Riechmann The experiment was conducted through the application of the clustering algorithms known as *Expectation Maximization* [12] (EM) applied to all the attributes identified in the Feature Selection phase. The mapping between the clusters and the learning styles was built taking into account, for each analyzed attribute, its average value in the cluster, as calculated by the EM algorithm. The effect of this experiment is that the learning characteristics that students belonging to the same cluster seem to possess, fit well with learning styles. The paper is structured as follows. In Section 2 some related literature and state of the art is shown while in Section 3 the pedagogical background is reported. In Section 4 we show the framework and the context of the work while in Section 5 the evaluation of the approach is reported and finally in Section 6 conclusions are drawn.

2 Related Work

One of the aims of EDM is to create user profiles automatically in order to improve the design of a course and its customization to be more responsive to the needs of the learner. On the other hand, learning environments can take advantage of the knowledge management techniques such as data mining [13], to collect and process disseminated information from exchanged e-mails and documents, from discussion forums and so on. EDM is the field of research of this work, where we address in a suitable case study the detection of learners learning styles. In the literature there are already many attempts of using data mining techniques in the e-learning field. In fact, most of e-learning platforms have a

[2] SSIS Lazio `http://www.ssis-lazio.it`
[3] `http://www.moodle.org`
[4] `http://www.cs.waikato.ac.nz/ml/weka/`

tracing mechanism storing the interactions between the learner and the learning environment in log files that subsequently can be analyzed to study the learners behaviors [23]. In [10], the authors use the Felder and Silvermann learning styles model [5] and do not use a data mining approach. Moreover they compare their results vs. the ILS questionnaire. In the work of Gaudioso and Tavalera [8], the application of data mining techniques to the virtual learning community aims to provide support for the evaluation of the course through the characterization of patterns concerning the performance of learners who then help to determine the profiles of weak learners and to identify and improve this type of behavior for future courses. In addition, they provide support to the identification and characterization of patterns of behaviors that can help to determine the different roles among learners and to manage groups in collaborative activities. An interesting framework has been developed by Mor et al. [22]. The purpose of the framework is the study of the navigational behavior of the students of an e-learning environment integrated in a virtual campus through the extraction of information that can be used to validate several aspects related to the design and usability of a virtual campus and also to determine the optimal scheduling for each course based on the profile of the student. To all the students of the *Foundations of programming 1* and *Compilers 1* was strongly advised to carry out certain activities. In the work of Wang are presented some models and methods to analyze log files in order to build a model of user behavior when browsing, that support the applications of e- Learning [28]. The teachers can investigate the model to identify some interesting or even more unexpected learning patterns in the navigational behavior of the learners and use this information to revise and reorganize the structure of content more effectively. To do this have been developed a set of tools based on data mining techniques such as clustering and association rules combined with collaborative filtering. Tang and McCalla [27] presented a system capable of suggesting to learners interested in a specific research area of scientific papers. Such a system in the domain of e-Learning requires special requirements that are not necessary in other domains. The most important requirement is the need to consider the pedagogical aspects of the learner and the need to organize the concepts actually taking into account these pedagogical issues; the result should be to maximize the utility that the learner obtains from the system gaining maximum knowledge keeping highly motivated. Other works aim to help teachers to produce and to deliver suitable didactic material to students [19,17,9,6], to propose personalization engines embedded into the Moodle platform [21,7,20,1] and also into real-work e-learning systems [18,15,14,16]. In a perspective of technology enhanced learning, there is research work [4,3,2] aiming to integrate more traditional individualized e-learning [26].

3 The Grasha-Riechmann Learning Styles Model

The GRM defines learning as a process of social nature, so also influenced by the different individual approaches to the environment class, by the relationship with peers and with the teacher. The GRM proposes the following three dimensions, each of which based on a three values scale: low, moderate and high:

- *Intra-subjectivity Vs. Inter-subjectivity*: the categories are related to the self-perception in relation to the environment and to the culture of belonging. In the context of learning, a intra-subjective personality prefers self-analysis, self-evaluation and also in cooperative contexts tends to bring out her own personal contribution vs. the group and to search for the contribution that the group can give to her personal growth. An inter-subjective student prefers socialization, knowledge of and learn through social mediation and knowledge sharing;
- *Competitive Vs. Collaborative*: the motivation for learning can be of a competitive nature and therefore connected to the need to stand out in the class, to receive awards, and to work individually, or collaborative character, and therefore related to the need to work with others, to share experiences, knowledge and tasks;
- *Independence Vs. Dependence*: a student may express a desire for autonomy and independence in relation to the rest of the class, the teacher and the task, preferring to work alone; on the contrary a dependent student feels the teacher as an authority, so strictly following her instructions and has a few perception of her educational autonomy.

Grasha and Riechmann have reviewed and evaluated the learning styles of college students through a social perspective in order to identify the different approaches to the environment of the classroom [11]. This learning style can be seen as a scale of social interactions because it is the way of interaction of the student with teachers and peers in a learning environment rather than the way they perceive and organize the information. Although these categories are not readily translated into learning strategies, are defined by three dimensions of class: the student's attitude towards learning, vision teacher and/or peer reactions to procedures performed in the classroom. Most individuals do not put themselves at the extremes of these bipolar styles, but indicate some degree of preference for each of these three categories, i.e., low, moderate and high. The scale intra-subjectivity Vs. inter-subjectivity measures how much an individual wants to be involved in the class, as it reacts with the procedures of the class and its attitudes towards learning. The scale collaborative/competitive measures the basic motivation of an individual's interaction with others while the third, independent/dependent, measures the attitude of the student towards teachers and how much she prefers freedom or control in the learning environment.

4 The Framework

In this Section we describe the framework used for analyzing the behavior of the learner in an environment of e-Learning to try to predict a profile for her learning styles. We used the Moodle LMS e-learning environment to log data form several learners actions and activities. After we used the Weka machine learning environment to run some clustering algorithms by which to support the inference of the learner's learning styles.

4.1 The E-learning Environment

The e-Learning environment used as a data source is the Moodle platform, the most used open source e-learning environment. Moodle is a software package for producing Internet-based courses and web sites. It is a global development project designed to support a social constructionist framework of education. In particular it is a web application, using MySql as the database where all the learners actions are stored in log files. We used a course delivered to teacher trainees by S.S.I.S. Lazio, a public training organization for teachers. In Fig. 1 the home page of the course is shown. Learners can participate to many didactic activities such as read lessons, interact with the tutor or exchange knowledge with peers in forums, chat, wiki pages and so on. All these actions are stored in some log data.

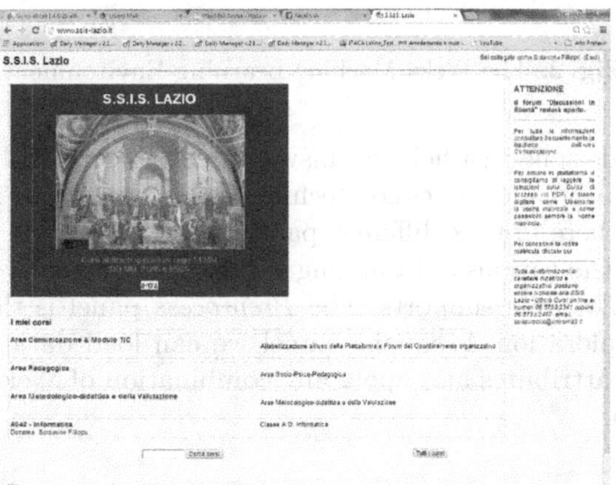

Fig. 1. The Home Page of the Moodle Environment

4.2 The Weka Platform

As a data mining environment, we selected the Weka platform, the most used open source machine learning environment. It is a collection of machine learning algorithms for data mining tasks where the algorithms can either be applied directly to a data set or launched from our own Java code. This platform contains tools for data pre-processing, classification, regression, clustering, association rules and visualization. It is also well suited for developing new machine learning schemas and comprises many state-of-the-art algorithms for supervised and unsupervised learning, providing an easy-to-use framework for performing experimental comparisons among different machine learning outcomes. The easiest way to use Weka is through a graphical interface called *the Explorer*. There are two other graphical user interfaces in Weka: *The Knowledge Flow* interface allows for designing configurations for streamed data processing while *The*

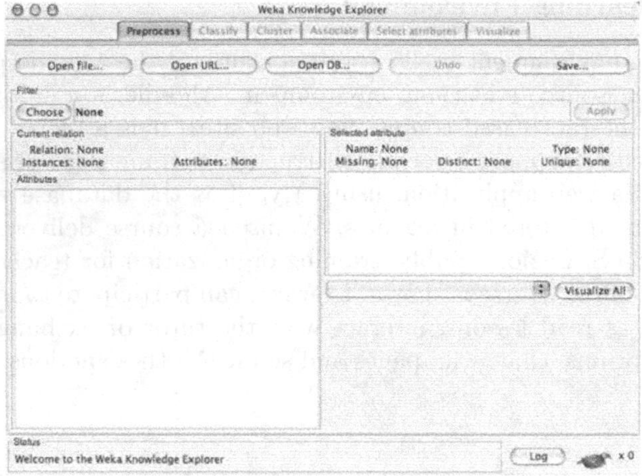

Fig. 2. The Weka Machine Learning Environment

Experimenter is designed to help to answer to basic practical questions when applying classification and regression techniques, as shown in Fig. 2. In *The Explorer* interface, there are six different panels, selected by the tabs at the top, corresponding to the various data mining tasks: the six tabs are the basic operations that *The Explorer* supports. The *Preprocess* panel is the starting point for knowledge exploration. From this panel we can load data sets, browse the characteristics of attributes and apply any combination of Weka's unsupervised filters to the data.

5 Evaluation

In this Section we show the evaluation of a data mining approach to the building of learners learning styles, according to the Grasha-Riemann learning styles model. More specifically, the research question to validate is if clustering the huge amount of source data according to some relevant features, we obtain groups of similar learners according to the Grasha-Riemann learning styles model.

5.1 The Overall Data Mining Process

When students navigate through the services provided by the Moodle environment, they leave traces that can be analyzed a posteriori with the purpose of building or integrating a student model. Most of this information is stored by the server in the form of web server log files and the analysis of these files may be of interest to obtain information about significative learning patterns. For every student action, accomplished in the learning environment a row is added to the system log file. This log file must first be pre-processed to remove all those log lines that are definitely not hits produced by the student. This step greatly reduces the amount of lines of log. Consequently, we used a classic data mining process, according to the following schema [12,25]:

1. *Problem Definition.* Clear definition of the problem and of the goals one wants to achieve;
2. *Feature selection.* What are the relevant dimensions to select for the study?
3. *Data Gathering and Preparation.* In this phase all data are gathered and transformed in order to be elaborated by the data mining algorithms selected;
4. *Model Building and Evaluation.* Here the bottom-up models produced by the data mining algorithms are evaluated in order to asses their validity with respect to the main goals;
5. *Discussion.* Here the results of the mapping between the clusters and the GRM is discussed.

5.2 Problem Definition

One of the greatest problems related to the design of online learning environments is to extract meaningful information about the actions of the students, their behavior, their way of navigating, that is about their use of the system. It is hard to monitor what the student actually does and what it is expected to be able to do and above all to represent this in the form of behavioral and navigational patterns. Often these models are used and are very useful to determine the degree of quality of the design of the learning environment and to measure the degree of association between the requirements of usability and the navigational behavior of the students. However, finding a correlation between behavioral patterns and pedagogical issues like learning styles is a very important step to understand learner's personality. It is clear that the extraction of patterns of behavior and learning must not be used in any way with the purpose of spying the student to obtain data used for other purposes but only to ensure a satisfactory process of learning and training.

5.3 Feature Selection

The log data files generated by the learners activities contain a large set of instances and one needs to select a subset of them in order to reduce the space dimensionality from a very large set, and consequently intractable, to a reasonable tractable set. In literature this is the classic *curse of dimensionality* problem. After a deep heuristic analysis of the variables stored by Moodle in the log data, we selected the following features, as relevant for Grasha-Riemann model:

- *allresourceview.* It indicates the total number of accesses for each student to all resources both theoretical and practical. In the Moodle environment, a resource can be defined as every didactic material accessible to learners;
- *resourcetheoryview.* This feature indicates the total number of accesses of each student to theoretical didactic materials.

- *totmoveforum*. It indicates the total number of accesses for each student carried out to all kinds of forums in both reading and posting;
- *visiteforum*. It indicates the total number of accesses for each student carried out to all kinds of forum in reading only modality;
- *useforum*. It indicates the total number of messages posted by each student to all kinds of forum;
- *totmoveforumdiscipl*. It indicates the total number of accesses for each student to all disciplinary forum;
- *totmoveforumgeneral*. It indicates the total number of accesses for each student to organizational or administrative forum.
- *extra*. It indicates the total number of accesses of learners to complementary didactic resources.

Basically, the various clusters computed basing on the above features should represent different groups of students with different ways of approaching the study, i.e., learning styles. From the log data, we produced a text file containing all those user records extracted from the original log data.

5.4 Data Gathering and Preparation

Our data source was composed by 1.500.000 records. In Fig. 3 a screenshot of it is shown. The learners that took the course were 1854 over one year. Starting from this large file, we preprocessed it, forming a text file containing features instances only. It was obtained through a multiple join among all the tables created for each feature of interest, and stored using a vector of student objects.

Fig. 3. A Screenshot of an Excerpt of the Log File

5.5 Model Building and Evaluation

As data mining model, we used the clustering unsupervised learning, a very useful technique to find out the distribution of the input data, allowing for a meaningful partitioning of the input data set. To perform such an analysis we

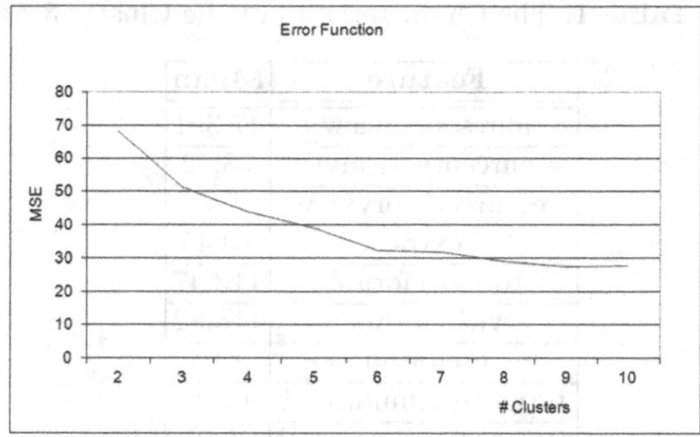

Fig. 4. The Clustering Process

used the Weka open source tool which has been fully reported in section 4. The experiment was conducted through the application of the EM algorithm of clustering applied to all the attributes identified in the previous preparation phase and stored in the user records. To estimate the right number of clusters, we used the Cross Validation technique, which consists in partitioning the training data into K distinct sub-sets, the training is done using $K-1$ subset and the network test on the remaining subsets, i.e., K-fold cross-validation. The process of training and test is repeated for each of the K possible choices of the subsets omitted from the training. The average performance on the K subsets is omitted in the estimation of the generalization performance. This procedure has the advantage of using a large portion of the data available for training and all data to estimate the error of generalization. The disadvantage is the need to train the network K times. In fact, the processing time of the EM algorithm with large data sets is quitc high. From Fig. 4 we see the MSE error in the training phase. We stopped the algorithm at six clusters because this number corresponds to the six Grasha-Riemann dimensions and also because the error trend after six clusters did not present relevant changes.

5.6 Results and Discussion

In Tab. 2 the results are shown. In particular, the first three columns report, for each cluster C_i the number of students both in absolute values and in percentage with respect to the overall sample. The last three columns report the correspondent Grasha-Riechmann learning styles. This mapping has been performed at hand, reasoning on the characteristics of the features belonging to a cluster compared with those belonging to the GRM. For the sake of brevity we report here the mapping process for cluster C_3, i.e., for the cluster with the great number of learners. The characteristics of this cluster are shown in Tab. 1. This is the case of a student that has visited general forums (totmoveforum and visiteforum) moderately, has visited moderately practical and theoretical resources (allresourceview, resourcepracticalview, resourcetheoryview), has used very few times the administrative forum (useforum) and moderately disciplinary

Table 1. The Characteristics of the Cluster 3

Feature	Mean
allresourceview	47,391
resourcepracticalview	78,52
resourcetheoryview	29,35
extra	19,45
totmoveforum	113,47
visiteforum	118,82
useforum	1,64
totmoveforumdiscipl	15,08
totmoveforumgeneral	35,95

Table 2. The Results of the Clustering EM Algorithm

Cluster	# learners	%	Independent	Competitive	Intra-subjective
C0	218	11,76%	Low	Moderate	Low
C1	185	9,98%	Moderate	Moderate	Moderate
C2	377	20,33%	Low	Low	Low
C3	811	43,74%	Moderate	Moderate	Moderate
C4	176	9,49%	High	High	High
C5	87	4,69%	High	High	High

and general forums (totmoveforumdiscipl and totmoveforumgeneral). Finally she did some visits to extra materials. So this student is a classic moderate student, according to the GR model because she prefers a moderate social activity, a moderate competition among peers, i.e., she visits all resources and finally she prefers practical aspects.

6 Conclusions

In this paper we presented a case study of the use of a data mining approach to the detection of the learning styles of a community of learners, according to the GR model, to explore the effectiveness of such an approach. We addressed a classic unsupervised learning classification problem performed through the Weka data mining platform, running the EM clustering algorithms on our data set. After we verified a mapping among each cluster and the learning styles. Reasoning on the characteristic of each cluster, represented by its own centroid, we performed such a mapping at hand, with encouraging results. The overall process can be completely automatized in the future, e.g. giving some threshold ranges to all the means of each cluster. As a result the student model can be dynamically and automatically enriched over time. As a future work we plan first to completely automatize the overall process and second to test the method with other learning styles models.

References

1. Biancalana, C., Micarelli, A.: Social tagging in query expansion: A new way for personalized web search. CSE (4), 1060–1065 (2009)
2. De Marsico, M., Sterbini, A., Temperini, M.: The definition of a tunneling strategy between adaptive learning and reputation-based group activities. In: Proc. 11th IEEE Int. Conf. on Advanced Learning Technologies, ICALT, pp. 498–500 (2011)
3. De Marsico, M., Sterbini, A., Temperini, M.: A strategy to join adaptive and reputation-based social-collaborative e-learning, through the zone of proximal development. Int. Journal of Distance Education Technologies 19(2), 105–121 (2012)
4. De Marsico, M., Sterbini, A., Temperini, M.: A framework to support social-collaborative personalized e-learning. In: Kurosu, M. (ed.) HCII/HCI 2013, Part II. LNCS, vol. 8005, pp. 351–360. Springer, Heidelberg (2013)
5. Felder, R.M., Silverman, L.K.: Learning and teaching styles in engineering education. Engineering Education 78(7), 674–681 (1988)
6. Gasparetti, F., Micarelli, A., Sansonetti, G.: Exploiting web browsing activities for user needs identification. In: Proceedings of the 2014 International Conference on Computational Science and Computational Intelligence (CSCI 2014), IEEE Computer Society, Conference Publishing Services (March 2014)
7. Gasparetti, F., Micarelli, A., Sciarrone, F.: A web-based training system for business letter writing. Knowledgel-Based Systems 22(4), 287–291 (2009)
8. Gaudioso, E., Talavera, L.: Data mining to support tutoring in virtual learning communities: experiences and challenges. In: Romero, C., Ventura, S. (eds.) Data Mining in E-Learning. ch.12, pp. 207–225. WIT Press (2006)
9. Gentili, G., Micarelli, A., Sciarrone, F.: Infoweb: An adaptive information filtering system for the cultural heritage domain. Applied Artificial Intelligence 17(8-9), 715–744 (2003)
10. Graf, S., Kinshuk, Liu, T.: Supporting teachers in identifying students' learning styles in learning management systems: An automatic student modelling approach. Educational Technology & Society 12(4), 3–14 (2009)
11. Grasha, A.: Observations on relating teaching goals to student response styles and classroom methods. American Psychologist 27, 144–147 (1972)
12. Hand, D., Manila, H., Smith, P.: Principles of Data Mining. MIT Press (2001)
13. Hanna, M.: Data mining in the e-learning domain. Campus-Wide Information Systems 21(1), 29–34 (2004)
14. Limongelli, C., Lombardi, M., Marani, A., Sciarrone, F.: A teacher model to speed up the process of building courses. In: Human-Computer Interaction. Applications and Services - 15th International Conference, HCI International 2013, Proceedings, Part II, Las Vegas, NV, USA, July 21-26, pp. 434–443 (2013)
15. Limongelli, C., Lombardi, M., Marani, A., Sciarrone, F.: A teaching-style based social network for didactic building and sharing. In: Lane, H.C., Yacef, K., Mostow, J., Pavlik, P. (eds.) AIED 2013. LNCS, vol. 7926, pp. 774–777. Springer, Heidelberg (2013)
16. Limongelli, C., Mosiello, G., Panzieri, S., Sciarrone, F.: Virtual industrial training: Joining innovative interfaces with plant modeling. In: ITHET, pp. 1–6. IEEE (2012)
17. Limongelli, C., Sciarrone, F., Starace, P., Temperini, M.: An ontology-driven olap system to help teachers in the analysis of web learning object repositories. Information System Management 27(3), 198–206 (2010)

18. Limongelli, C., Sciarrone, F., Temperini, M., Vaste, G.: Lecomps5: A web-based learning system for course personalization and adaptation. In: Proceedings of IADIS 2008, Proceedings, Amsterdam, The Netherlands, July 22-25, pp. 325–332 (2008)
19. Limongelli, C., Sciarrone, F., Temperini, M., Vaste, G.: The lecomps5 framework for personalized web-based learning: A teacher's satisfaction perspective. Computers in Human Behavior 27(4), 1310–1320 (2011)
20. Limongelli, C., Sciarrone, F., Vaste, G.: LS-PLAN: An effective combination of dynamic courseware generation and learning styles in web-based education. In: Nejdl, W., Kay, J., Pu, P., Herder, E. (eds.) AH 2008. LNCS, vol. 5149, pp. 133–142. Springer, Heidelberg (2008)
21. Limongelli, C., Sciarrone, F., Vaste, G.: Personalized e-learning in moodle: The moodle-ls system. Journal of E-Learning and Knowledge Society 7(1), 49–58 (2011)
22. More, E., Minguillón, J., Carbó, J.M.: Analysis of user navigational behavior for e-learning personalization. In: Romero, C., Ventura, S. (eds.) Data Mining in E-Learning. ch.13, pp. 227–243. WIT Press (2006)
23. Pahl, C.: Data mining for the analysis of content interaction in web-based learning and training systems. In: Romero, C., Ventura, S. (eds.) Data Mining in E-Learning. ch. 3, pp. 41–56. WIT Press (2006)
24. Romero, C., Ventura, S.: Educational data mining: A survey from 1995 to 2005. Expert Syst. Appl. 33(1), 135–146 (2007)
25. Sciarrone, F.: An extension of the q diversity metric for information processing in multiple classifier systems: a field evaluation. International Journal of Wavelets, Multiresolution and Information Processing IJWMIP 11(6) (2013)
26. Sterbini, A., Temperini, M.: Selection and sequencing constraints for personalized courses. In: Proc. IEEE Frontiers in Education, FIE, pp. T2C1–T2C6 (2010)
27. Tang, T.Y., McCalla, G.: Active, context-dependent, data centered techniques for e-learning: a case study of a research paper recommender system. In: Romero, C., Ventura, S. (eds.) Data Mining in E-Learning. ch. 5, pp. 207–225. WIT Press (2006)
28. Wang, F.: On using data mining for browsing log analysis in learning environments. In: Romero, C., Ventura, S. (eds.) Data Mining in E-Learning. ch. 4, pp. 57–73. WIT Press (2006)

Augmented Reality Tools and Learning Practice in Mobile-Learning

Mauro Figueiredo[1,2,3], José Gomes[2,4], Cristina Gomes[2,4], and João Lopes[3]

[1] Centro de Investigação Marinha e Ambiental, Portugal
[2] Centro de Investigação em Artes e Comunicação, Portugal
[3] Institute of Engineering (ISE), University of Algarve, Faro, Portugal
{mfiguei,jlopes}@ualg.pt
[4] Universidade Aberta, Portugal
{jdgomes65,ccardosogomes}@gmail.com

Abstract. There are many augmented reality (AR) applications available that can be used to create educational contents for these mobile devices. This paper surveys the most popular augmented reality applications and we select AR eco-systems to be used in daily teaching activities which are user friendly, do not require programming skills and are free. Different augmented reality technologies are explored in this paper to create teaching activities with animations, videos and other information to be shown on top of interactive documents. It is presented the creation of a novel augmented reality book that was developed with teachers and students. Several examples are also presented that are used in educational activities, from kindergarten to elementary and secondary schools, to improve reading, comprehension and learning of music.

Keywords: Augmented reality, e-learning, m-learning.

1 Introduction

Mobile computing devices allow an exponential expansion of social and participative web technologies, since they represent an increase in the ease of data access and the creation of textual and audiovisual content, even implying a situation to link at anytime and anywhere, where ubiquity is the keyword [1].

These devices have increased processing power and usability, and are accessible on a large scale, which has significantly contributed to their ease of use and at implementing innovative educational processes [2], [3] in numerous educational institutions and universities.

Many augmented reality applications are currently available. The most popular augmented-reality eco-systems are explored in this paper. We present Augmented Reality systems that can be used in daily learning activities. Such AR eco-systems must be *user friendly*, since they are going to be used by teachers that in general do not have programming knowledge; and *open source* or *free for non-commercial*, without any type of water marks.

C. Stephanidis and M. Antona (Eds.): UAHCI/HCII 2014, Part II, LNCS 8514, pp. 301–312, 2014.

This paper presents several educational activities and a novel Augmented Reality book created using free augmented reality tools that do not require programming knowledge to be used by any teacher. We discuss different AR eco-systems and show the most appropriate for each particular educational activity presented in this paper covering K-12 teaching. Marker-based and marker less augmented reality technologies are presented to show how we can create learning activities to visualize augmented information that help students understand the educational content.

This paper is organized as follows. Section 2 surveys the most common augmented reality eco-systems. In section 3 we present activities supported on marker based augmented reality for teaching music and improve reading and comprehension. Section 4 describes activities that can be used in a kindergarten and the creation of an AR book, based on marker less AR technology. Finally conclusions are presented in Section 5.

2 Augmented Reality

Augmented Reality applications combine images, 2-D or 3-D virtual objects with a 3-D real environment in real time. Virtual computer generated and real objects appear together in a real time system in a way that the user sees the real world and the virtual objects superimposed with the real objects. The user's perception of the real world is enhanced and the user interacts in a more natural way. The virtual objects can be used to display additional information about the real world that are not directly perceived.

Ronald Azuma [4] defines augmented reality systems as those that have three characteristics: 1) combines real and virtual; 2) interactive in real time; 3) registered in 3-D.

In general, augmented reality applications fall in two categories: *geo*-base and *computer vision* based.

Geo-based applications use the mobile's GPS, accelerometer, gyroscope, and other technology to determine the location, heading, and direction of the mobile device. The user can see overlapping computer-generated images onto a real world in the direction he is looking at. However, this technology has some problems. The major problem is imprecise location which makes difficult for example the creation of photo overlays.

Computer vision based applications use image recognition capabilities to recognize images and overlay information on top of this image. These can be based on *markers*, such as QR (Quick Response), Microsoft tags or LLA (latitude/longitude/altitude), or *marker less* that recognize an image that triggers the overlay data.

There are currently many augmented reality applications and development systems for Android and iOS (iPhone Operating System) smartphones and tablets.

We explored the following Augmented Reality systems: Wikitude[1], Layar[2], Metaio[3] and Aurasma[4]. These are the most popular and enable the visualization of text, pictures or videos as an augmented layer.

Wikitude delivers the Wikitude World Browser for free, which is an augmented reality web browser application, and the Wikitude SDK (software development kit) for developers which is free for educational projects. However, the educational version of the wikitude SDK always displays a splash screen and the wikitude logo.

The wikitude browser presents users with data about their points of interest, which can be the surroundings, nearby landmarks or target images, and overlays information on the real-time camera view of a mobile device.

Augmented reality learning activities can be realized with the wikitude SDK. The wikitude SDK can be used to display a simple radar that shows radar-points related to the location based objects. It is also possible to recognize target images and superimpose 2D or 3D information on top of them. The developer can also combines image recognition and geo-base augmented reality. However, the building of these capabilities using the wikitude SDK requires programming knowledge.

Layar has the Layar App, an augmented reality web browser, and the Layar Creator, which is a tool for creating interactive printing documents. With the Layar Creator it is easy to make an interactive document for a teaching activity. There is no need to do any programming and, in this way, it does not require any developers with programming skills. The teacher can easily upload the trigger page to which he wants to associate augmented information. Marker less image recognition techniques are used and with the Layar Creator interface the teacher can easily associate a video, for example. Later, with the Layar App, the student can view, on the camera of his mobile device, the overlaied information associated to the page. These applications are both free. However, every trigger image published within the Layar's publishing environment is paid. For this reason, it is not affordable for developing interactive printing documents for teaching. Geo-location based augmented reality information is free of charge.

Metaio delivers the junaio, metaio Creator and a development SDK. Junaio is the metaio's free augmented reality browser and is free. The metaio Creator is an augmented reality tool to create and publish augmented reality scenarios and experiences within minutes. With the metaio Creator the teacher can connect 3-D content, videos, audio, and webpages to any form of printed medium or 3D map (object-based or environment-based). However this tool is paid. If a user wants to develop augmented reality applications for iOS or Android, the developer can use the metaio SDK. However, this development SDK is also paid.

Aurasma delivers the Aurasma App and the Aurasma Studio.

---

[1] `http://www.wikitude.com/`

[2] `http://www.layar.com/`

[3] `http://www.metaio.com/`

[4] `http://www.aurasma.com/`

The Aurasma App is available for Android and iOS and uses advanced image recognition techniques to augment the real-world with interactive content such as videos, 3D objects or animations associated to trigger images or geo-based information.

The Aurasma Studio is an online platform that lets the teacher create and publish their own augmented reality information in an intuitive and user friendly environment. It is not required any programming knowledge and the teacher can upload trigger images that can be associated to videos, images, 3D objects or other information. The Aurasma eco-system delivers these application free for non-commercial use.

In this way, as our concern is to find augmented reality eco-systems that do not require programming, that are free and easy to use for learning activities. For this reason, in the following sections of this paper we present several examples of teaching activities using the right augmented reality application that teachers can use in the classroom.

3 Creating Learning Activities Using Marker-Based AR Technologies

Marker based augmented reality technologies recognize a pattern/code when a camera points at it that is used to trigger the AR content. The most common marker-based Augmented Reality implementations use Quick Response (QR) codes. There are other markers that can be used such as the Microsoft tags or the LLA (latitude, longitude and altitude).

In this section, we present several examples of using marker based augmented reality technologies to create teaching activities.

Using marker based codes for presenting additional information in a mobile device. The teacher can use QR two dimensional codes for associating information such as text, URL or any other data. Quick response codes are much more popular than the other code formats. Its main advantages is that they use open source technology and in this way they are free and always will be. There are several sites where the teacher can easily create such codes. One that can be used and is free is `http://keremerkan.net/qr-code-and-2d-code-generator/`.

This Website links the QR code to text, to make a phone call, to send an email, to tweet, to open google maps and many other possibilities. In practice, there is no limit, since the QR code can link to an *url*. In this way, using for example dropbox[5] the QR code can open sound, images or movies files that can be stored in the cloud.

Figure 1 shows an example of using QR codes to study the Portuguese author *Fernando Pessoa* by students of the 12th grade. With this sheet the students can explore in the class, or at home, other materials that teachers consider to be important for them.

[5] `http://www.dropbox.com/`

Fig. 1. Study of the Portuguese author Fernando Pessoa using QR codes to access additional materials

A disadvantage of the QR codes is that they are in general large and can take too much space, specially if they have to store too much information. When we want to use smaller codes that become less intrusive we can use the Microsoft tags. Reading smaller Microsoft tags are more reliable then the equivalent QR codes. The example presented in figure 2 uses Microsoft tags.

Microsoft tags are also very easy to create, requiring only the registration at the site `http://tag.microsoft.com`.

The example of figure 2 uses the Microsoft tags to show the answers to the different questions. We created other augmented reality documents with music sheets and we noted that the students were more interactive in the classroom, improving the learning process [5].

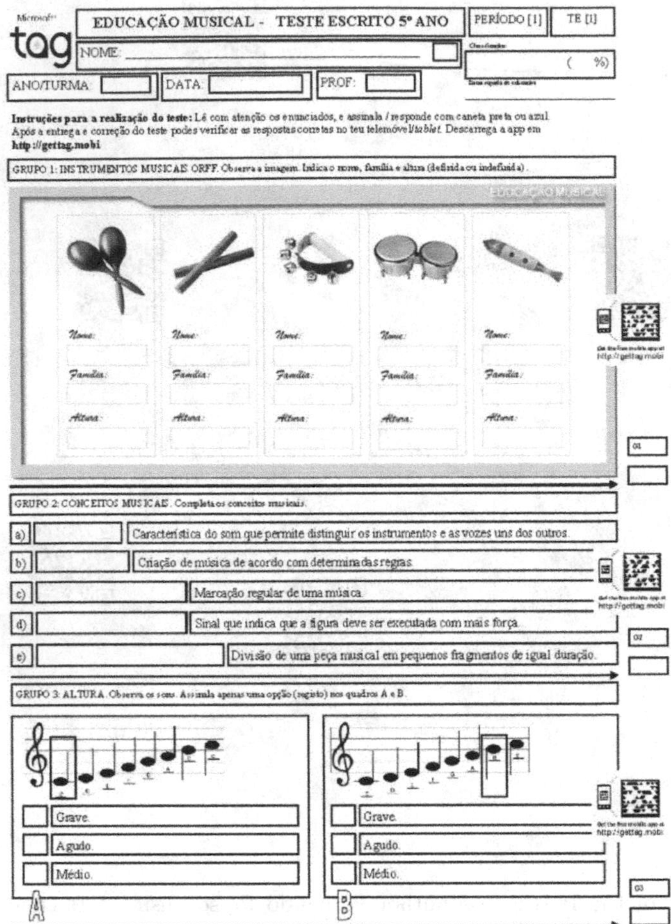

Microsoft tag

EDUCAÇÃO MUSICAL - TESTE ESCRITO 5º ANO | PERÍODO [1] | TE [1]

NOME: ______________________ (%)

ANO/TURMA: | DATA: | PROF:

Instruções para a realização do teste: Lê com atenção os enunciados, e assinala / responde com caneta preta ou azul. Após a entrega e correção do teste podes verificar as respostas corretas no teu telemóvel/*tablet*. Descarrega a app em **http://gettag.mobi**

GRUPO 1: INSTRUMENTOS MUSICAIS ORFF. Observa a imagem. Indica o nome, família e altura (definida ou indefinida).

Nome: | Família: | Altura: (×5)

GRUPO 2: CONCEITOS MUSICAIS. Completa os conceitos musicais.

a) ______ Característica do som que permite distinguir os instrumentos e as vozes uns dos outros.

b) ______ Criação de música de acordo com determinadas regras.

c) ______ Marcação regular de uma música.

d) ______ Sinal que indica que a figura deve ser executada com mais força.

e) ______ Divisão de uma peça musical em pequenos fragmentos de igual duração.

GRUPO 3: ALTURA. Observa os sons. Assinala apenas uma opção (registo) nos quadros A e B.

A: Grave. / Agudo. / Médio.

B: Grave. / Agudo. / Médio.

Fig. 2. Music test with Microsoft tags codes

4 Creating Learning Activity Using Marker Less AR Technologies

In this section, we introduce the augmented reality technologies that we found more appropriate to create learning activities based on an image that triggers an animation that can be used for teaching activities in a kindergarten (subsection 4.1) or for creating an Augmented Reality book (subsection 4.2).

4.1 Activities for Kindergarten

In a kindergarten a childhood educator frequently reads a story to children and then make an activity about it. In this section, it is shown a form of a puzzle (fig. 3) that is shown to children after the childhood educator reads to them

Fig. 3. Puzzle

Fig. 4. Two of the possible characters that children have to choose

the story of the "Frog and Duck". The children have to choose the appropriate character (fig. 4) to the question formulated by the childhood educator to place in the puzzle (fig. 3). Once they choose the right character, the trigger image (fig. 5) activates the associated animation that was generated with Microsoft Power Point.

The images presented in figures 3 to 5 were created from an original image from the story and edited using GIMP[6] (GNU Image Manipulation Program). Although GIMP is an advanced application, it was easy to use and very useful

[6] `http://www.gimp.org/`

Fig. 5. Trigger image that is used to start the animation

for: i) extracting the characters with transparency from the original image and to ii) fulfill the background after removing the duck. For this purpose, we used the GIMP *Foreground Select Tool* and *Heal Selection* which are very easy to use and yet very powerful.

After making the trigger image and the animation, it is time to use an augmented reality eco-system so that when using a mobile device it can recognize the trigger image and activate the animation.

For the recognition of marker less images we used the Aurasma eco-system which is free, does not require programming knowledge and is easy to use.

After registering to Aurasma we can access to the Aurasma Studio that begins with the step by step tutorial.

The teacher setups his augmented reality contents with the following steps.

First, the teacher creates a *channel*. It is like a YouTube Channel or TV Channel, except that this is the teacher augmented reality channel and, there is no limit, the teacher can create multiple channels. In this case, we created an *education* channel that can be followed using the following link to subscribe `http://auras.ma/s/tBkQ0`. This is created once and the teacher can add multiple augmented reality contents into the same channel.

The second step is to upload the *trigger* image of figure 5. The trigger image is a still image that will trigger the augmented reality contents. It is a JPEG or PNG file that in the Aurasma Studio has less than 500,000 pixels. The one used in this example has 720 x 540 pixels which makes the total of 388,800 pixels. The teacher only has to give a name to the trigger image, select the file to upload and save it.

The third step is to upload the *overlay* content that will replace the trigger image. Overlays can include videos, images, 3D scenes or web pages. The teacher gives a name to the overlay content, select the file to upload and save it. It is recommended the use of MP4 video format files up to 100MB.

The final step is the *aura* creation. Auras are augmented reality actions - images, videos or 3D animations that appear when the mobile device is pointed to a real world image or object. The auras associate the trigger image to the overlay animation and stores it to the channel created before. This information is stored in Aurasma Central. Whenever the Aurasma application is running on a mobile device it connects to Aurasma Central to download auras that the user is subscribing in a channel.

4.2 Creating an Augmented Reality Book

At the grouping of schools of Padrão da Légua we started a project, which aimed at the integration of AR technology with the mobile-learning concept. The establishment of collaborative work between different disciplinary areas, teachers and students, were one of the main project objectives, focusing to develop an artifact with potential use in the process of teaching and learning within educational contexts. The work took the form of a book to which audiovisual elements (multimedia) were added using AR supported by the Aurasma platform that can be explored in the Aurasma Chanel:`http://auras.ma/s/30BNz`.

Development of Interdisciplinary Cooperative Work The project had the support of teachers and students in the subject areas of Music Education, Visual Education, Visual Arts, Educational Resource Center and Special Education students from the school of Leça do Balio. The unifying theme chosen was the sea. The project was selected from more than sixty schools and presented in the national fourth contest Sea Kit, at the Pavilion of Knowledge in Lisbon on May 17th, 2013. The coordination of the project consisted in the allocation of tasks and work proposals for teachers and students, with the following contributions:

- Musical Education teachers and students focused their research efforts in finding songs that included ocean related elements in their lyrics or theme. That research returned a set of songs suited to play on the fipple flute. These songs were adapted to the flute tessiture and complemented with orchestral accompaniment. Finally the songs were recorded onto video to support students live play, known as *play-along* (fig. 6). Information about the composers, interpreters or the song itself was gathered and present in video format.
- Visual Education teachers and students researched the marine fauna and flora of the Portuguese coast, from which they produced a collection of drawings and art, using different techniques, from textured materials suited to the tactile experience to colored pencil or china ink contour.
- The Visual Arts teachers and students produced two short movie sequences, animated according to the stop-motion technique. One was created using sequential drawings. Students draw the aquarium and the fishes to generate the animation (fig. 7). The second, the movie 'The Little Girl and The Sea

b)

Fig. 6. With a mobile device the student can follow the (a) high-lighted guitar chords; and (b) and the high-lighted play-along

Star" (fig. 8), was created using moldable plastic figures and received a sound track fully elaborated by a special education student. The movie sound track involved environment sounds recollection and audio manipulation in Audacity by the student itself, using different techniques and resources. The final video file, was produced in Movie Maker according to a storyboard depicting the scenes, planes and the audio soundtrack.

– The Educational Resources Center, contributed with a photo sequence depicting scenes from the life of Matosinho's fishermen from the past to the present day. This contribution took the form of a video with a popular sea theme related sound track.

Fig. 7. Augmented Reality aquarium example

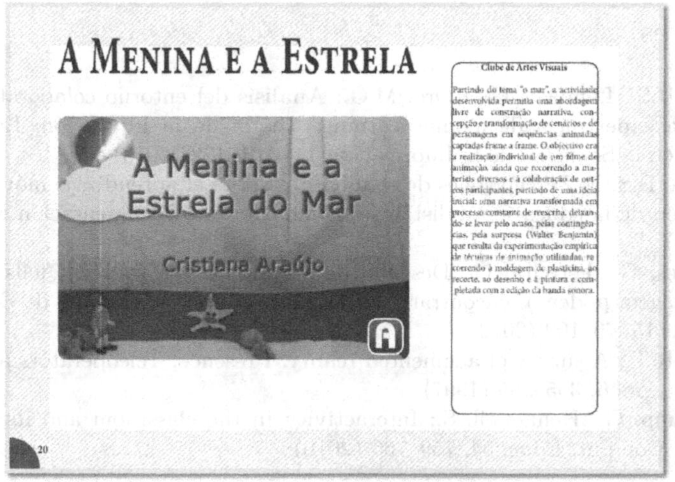

Fig. 8. Short animation movie "The Little Girl and the Sea Star"

Along the first and second period of the school year a large amount of works took shape. From these, a few were chosen according to higher quality patterns or those that meant greater effort and involvement from the students. The cooperative work established between teachers and students around a common project contributed significantly to greater involvement and motivation of everyone, extending it to the school management, the parents and the educational community.

5 Conclusions

The dissemination of low cost smartphones and tablets of increasing processing power makes it possible the use of mobile platforms in the classroom. In recent years surged many augmented reality applications that are available in mobile platforms.

In this paper we explored the most popular augmented reality applications. We find out the most appropriate for teaching and learning. We selected those that can be used by teachers which do not require programming knowledge and are free for educational purposes. This paper also presents several examples of augmented reality activities for the classroom.

We explored AR marker based codes using Quick Response codes and Microsoft tags in activities to study a portuguese author and for music evaluation. We prefer the smaller Microsoft tags that are better recognized than the Quick Response codes.

We created educational activities based on marker less images for kindergarten and it is presented an augmented reality book that was developed with students and teachers from the school of Leça do Balio.

References

[1] Gómez, R.S., Lanna, L.C., i Oro, M.G.: Análisis del entorno colaborativo creado para una experiencia de mobile learning. Teoría de la Educación: Educación y Cultura en la Sociedad de la Información 14, 101–122 (2013)

[2] Espinosa, R.S.C.: Percepciones de estudiantes sobre el aprendizaje móvil; la nueva generación de la educación a distancia. Cuadernos de Documentación Multimedia 21 (2010)

[3] Fernandes, G., Ferreira, C.: Desenho de conteúdos e-learning: Quais teorias de aprendizagem podemos encontrar? RIED: Revista Iberoamericana de Educación a Distancia 15, 79–102 (2012)

[4] Azuma, R.T.: A survey of augmented reality. Presence: Teleoperators and Virtual Environments 6, 355–385 (1997)

[5] Beauchamp, G., Kennewell, S.: Interactivity in the classroom and its impact on learning. Comput. Educ. 54, 759–766 (2010)

e-Testing with Interactive Images - Opportunities and Challenges

Marjan Gusev*, Sasko Ristov, and Goce Armenski

University Ss Cyril and Methodius, Faculty of Computer Science and Engineering, Rugjer Boshkovic, 16, 1000 Skopje, Macedonia
{marjan.gushev,sashko.ristov,goce.armenski}@finki.ukim.mk

Abstract. Modern e-Education systems lack some basic functionalities the e-Testing systems have, such as reuse of question database, random positioning of answer options in multiple choice questions, generation of different tests with the same complexity for students, prevention of cheating by guessing and memorizing etc.

Multimedia is essential in the delivery of e-Learning and e-Testing. However, most of the existing systems include multimedia only as delivery of static pictures and animations without any interaction with images. In this paper we refer to opportunities and challenges the interactive image might have for e-Testing.

We present features of a new human computer interface and discuss the basic architecture of interactive images to be applied in the delivery of interactive e-Testing. At the end we discuss the benefit of this approach and present proof of a concept by analyzing the application domain.

Keywords: Google maps engine, interactive image, e-testing.

1 Introduction

E-Education and particularly e-Learning are modern disciplines that support education and learning processes by sophisticated use of ICT technologies. A very comprehensive overview of methodologies and various interfaces are given by Clark and Mayer [4]. They define e-Learning to be an instruction delivered on a computer by way of CD-ROM, Internet, or intranet with features, such as content relevant to the learning objective, instructional methods including examples and practice, media elements including words and pictures to deliver content and methods etc.

E-Testing is the provision of testing via electronic means. Here we refer to it as a technology delivered mostly via Internet and we are especially interested in cloud solutions as advanced technology for the delivery of massively open online courses (MOOC). A nice overview of existing e-testing systems and their application for e-Learning is given by Gusev and Armenski [8].

Udacity [16] is an example of a MOOC delivery that includes a lot of multimedia elements organized in micro lectures that last approximately 1-2 minutes,

* Corresponding author.

C. Stephanidis and M. Antona (Eds.): UAHCI/HCII 2014, Part II, LNCS 8514, pp. 313–324, 2014.

as kind of explanation of essential knowledge items (learning objectives). Each learning objective is followed by a quiz to assess the student's knowledge. The Cisco NetSpace online learning environment combines several applications for teaching, learning, and collaboration in order to enable an interactive and engaging learning experience [3].

Most of the existing systems include multimedia in the delivery of e-Learning and e-Testing only as static pictures and animations. They lack interaction with images, which includes navigation of the visible part within the image, navigation of details (zooming) or interacting with graphical objects. We refer to this kind of defined navigation and interaction as a technology to deliver *interactive images.*

Application of interactive images in web technology is mostly used in GIS systems, particularly by Google and other providers of web enabled navigation maps. We refer to opportunities and challenges of using this technology for e-Testing in this paper by defining the human computer interface for interactive images.

The rest of the paper is organized as follows. Section 2 analyzes the features of existing e-Testing systems and their graphical user interface. In Section 3, we propose interactive image, a part of the human computer interface, as a technology for e-Testing systems, which includes navigation, zooming and interaction with graphical objects. Google Maps Engine technology, which is a baseline for this system is briefly described in Section 4. Discussion about new developed question types is presented in Section 5. Section 6 discusses the challenges and opportunities of such interactive image system and Section 7 concludes our work.

2 Analysis of Existing Technology

In this section we analyze features of existing e-Testing systems and their graphical user interfaces.

Standard e-Testing Systems are part of e-Assessment, which includes more sophisticated assessment than conventional e-Testing. The main e-testing engine consists of module for user management, including authentication, authorization and accounting; question database module; test generation module; test engine module: assessment module and reporting module. We have presented a highly sophisticated scalable and elastic architecture of an e-Assessment system [14], along with analysis of features and functional descriptions. In the next section we will discuss only those features that give advantage of our e-Testing with interactive images into e-Education systems.

2.1 State of the Art

Most of the existing e-Learning systems only partially realize the e-Testing and do not cover all relevant functionalities presented in the next paragraph.

Question Database is a database with questions and answers capable to be exchanged among different systems and reused in several courses.

Coordinated Test Generation is a feature that enables generation of different tests for each student with same complexity of questions.

Scrambled Options is a technique that presents options of multiple choice questions in random order, so no two repetitive occurrence of the same question will have the same order of offered options.

Negative Score Schema is a method that enables negative grading of incorrect answers to prevent guessing as a method of answering.

Question types have been analyzed by several authors. For example, Crisp presents a taxonomy of question types based on the level of constraint in the item/task response format [5]. A taxonomy or categorization of 28 innovative item types that may be useful in computer-based assessment is defined by Scalize and Gifford [17].

Recently, we have analyzed the multiple choice questions and determined additional deficiencies with the guessing method, despite the negative grading scheme [15]. For example, if a question has three offered answers and two of them are correct, then by answering two questions randomly, a student will achieve at least 0.5 points in the worst case (+1 point for 1 correct and -0.5 for incorrect answer), that is, an always win situation without showing any knowledge. Therefore, we defined a correlation among these two parameters: the number of offered answers should be limited between 4 and 6, while the number of correct answers must be at least 2 and maximum half of the number of the questions.

The classical Graphical User Interface (GUI) for realization of the e-Testing systems is analyzed in the following section.

2.2 Graphical User Interface

Most of the existing e-Testing systems include GUI based on both the mouse and keyboard entry, as presented in Fig. 1. The classical pointing and clicking device is mouse and the device for data entry and navigation is keyboard. In this context we can add that modern graphical user interfaces use touch pads instead of classical mouse devices, either by realization of a special touchpad entry device, or by a screen available on mobile phones, tablets, laptops and emerging new computers. Therefore in the following sections we will use mouse/touchpad as a pointing and clicking device.

Our experience showed that the students prefer the *click test* based only on mouse/touchpad clicks avoiding switch of the input between the keyboard and mouse/touchpad, which initiates lack of concentration while testing. This leads to a situation when the questions are mostly realized as multiple choice questions.

Images are also a constituent element of all existing realizations of e-Testing systems. However, they are mostly used as a static presentation element, which enhances the multimedia presentation only.

So far, the existing e-Testing systems do not use interactive technologies with images, where one can interact with image objects and customize image presentation according to preferred parameters.

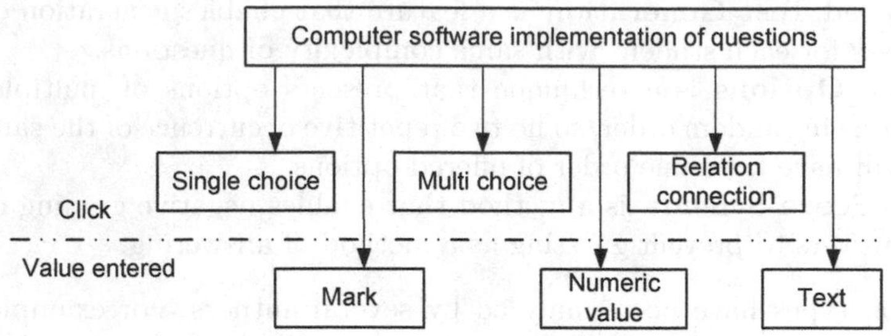

Fig. 1. Classification of question types according to the input device interface

3 A New GUI Model of e-Testing with Interactive Images

In this paper we propose *interactive image* as a technology to realize e-Testing systems. An interactive image is a part of the human computer interface, that includes navigation, zooming and interaction with graphical objects.

3.1 Navigation and Zooming

Navigation and zooming as GUI is mostly understood as an environment where the human sets various parameters for a given image and the system adopts the presentation according to the given parameters. Let the system present only a small image part, called visible image part. These parameters can be at least:

XY position of the visible image part are the parameters that enable navigation by moving the visible part in left/right or up/down position within the complete image.

Size of the visible image part is a parameter that defines the zoom level in the navigation.

The mechanism of defining these parameters can be realized by clicking on specifically defined buttons; by mouse/touchpad drag and drop actions; or by clicking Ctrl (Cmd) button and sliding up/down on the mouse/touchpad. One can also use sliders as an old-fashioned interface to define the position of the visible image part.

3.2 Interaction with Graphical Objects

Besides definition of essential parameters for navigation and zooming, the user can interact with the computer by the following actions:

Object selection is an action realized by mouse/touchpad clicking on the object.

Region marking action is defined by drawing a multiple point polygon, by a series of clicks on consecutive points that define the edges of the polygon.

Setting a pin and commenting is an action defined by mouse/touchpad clicking on a given object and entering a text (comment) for the pin via a conventional keyboard.

Selecting multiple objects action is defined by a combination of pressed Ctrl (Cmd) keyboard button and by mouse/touchpad clicking on several graphical objects.

The left part of Fig. 2 shows an example used in the Computer Network course. The question is to analyze the network and identify the type (router, switch, or bridge) of a certain networking device. Navigation and zooming can lead to present an image portion as in the right part of the Fig. 2. In this case the information in the image portion can be used to make a proper decision and apply relevant knowledge to identify the requested object.

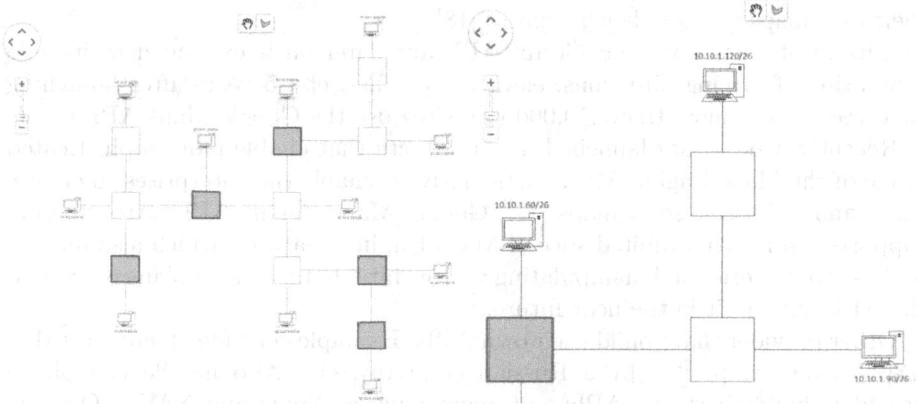

Fig. 2. An example of a question from Computer Network course about networking devices using the eTii system and its image portion obtained by zooming

3.3 Obstacles for Web Enabled GUI

Navigation, zooming and interaction with graphical objects as a human computer interface are integrated in modern existing operating systems. However, we can witness that the web technology enabling navigation, zooming and interaction is only available by small number of providers.

A good example of web enabling interactive images is the Google map engine technology for big high resolution images. The problem that has been solved by Google for realization of Google maps and Google Earth is in the web mapping service, which enables only a small part of a huge image to be transferred to the web browser. This is accompanied by a special preprocessing that defines small images by cutting the huge image into small pieces on different zoom levels and saving them in predefined resolution that will fit for optimized throughput by existing Internet links and presentation on a web browser. The final part is the engine that invokes those small image parts and present a continuous picture environment to the user.

4 Enabling Interactive Image Technology

This section briefly describes the Maps Engine technology and its applications.

4.1 Providers of Maps Engine Technology

Google has used this technology for creation of maps, based on extremely huge satellite images, and enabling a system that defines coordinates and size of a predefined visible image part. Besides the technology, they have been working on marking street maps, by providing a tool to calculate optimized route or business locator.

One of the probably best decisions Google has made is to enable an interface to third party service providers by launching Google Maps Application Program Interface (API) in June 2005, which will increase a possibility for business to use their own maps and for their purposes [18].

Initially it was only a JavaScript API, and later on it expanded to include generation of driving directions, elevation profiles, etc. 5 years after launching as a free service, more than 350,000 web sites use the Google Maps API [6].

Recently, Google has launched new products that enable more sophisticated usage of the Maps Engine API , particularly to enable the enterprises to create, share and publish custom maps [11]. Google Maps Engine API currently only supports a somewhat limited slice of Maps Engines features, which also include basic spatial queries and manipulating vector data, but the team plans to expand the API quite a bit in the near future.

Other providers have build their own APIs. Examples include OpenStreetMap [13], Yandex Maps [21] by a Russian company, etc. Also mobile cell phone providers build their own APIs and maps, such as Nokia and NAVTEQ's [9]. Other big players in the Internet search and e-Business area have also build their own APIs and maps, including Bing Maps by Microsoft [1], Yahoo Maps [20]. Main purpose of these APIs is realization of a geographic information system (GIS) service providing maps of major cities and lands.

4.2 Applications of Maps Engine Technology

Most of the users also see this technology as a tool for GIS enabled systems. Various services have been created using maps, such as the geographical epidemiology mapping [22]. There are examples of using the system even in education [2]. It is considered to be a very successful productivity tool [12]. Juntunen et al. have used Google Maps as a web tool for traffic engineers, helping them for direct manipulation and visualization of vehicular traffic [10].

Although maps are the essential target by Google Earth and similar maps delivering companies, we find that this technology can be efficiently used for other applications, such as education or analysis of medical images. Virtual microscopes use the same approach for interactive images, mainly intended for medicine and biology to enable a tool for individual or collaborative education [19].

In this paper we propose a novel human computer interface for an e-Testing system using interactive images. In addition, this technology also enables tools to organize large datasets and make decisions based on analysis of a given part.

We developed an open-source VM system based on the Google Maps engine to transform our histology education and introduce new teaching methods. The eTii model is based on the architecture model presented in our earlier paper [7].

5 Discussion

Recently, we have developed three new question types, identified as SGC (Single Graphic Choice), OM (Opinion Map) and MGC (Multiple Graphic Choice) [7]. They enable the user to click on a graphical object or point in the interactive image, mark a region where the answer domain is found, enter a textual answer (explanation) on appropriate marked graphical pin, etc. Coordinates of clicked pins, regions and entered texts are sent as answers to the system and further on evaluated by the system automatically or with the support of the instructor.

These results can be efficiently used for e-Testing with interactive Images. In the meantime we have developed a prototype of the eTii system and are in the process of assessing the student knowledge using this system, exploiting the challenges and benefits of the application domain explained in this paper. We have started to create a question database for realization of the course Computer Networks for computer science students.

The process of developing content realized as defining questions is more complex when interactive images are used in comparison to textual multiple choice questions. Besides the developing of a concept for the question, one has to draw a picture, which usually takes a lot more time than just typing a textual question and possible answer options.

Another disadvantage is that not all concepts can be visualized and not any questions be developed. For example, one might rather easily develop multiple choice questions for a definition of a certain knowledge item or learning objective, such as asking "Which option gives the definition of a certain concept?". However, this is not convenient for questions with interactive images.

A typical example of a question with an interactive image is the following "Where can you find an occurrence of a typical object or a concept on the figure?". These question types that include interactive images are application oriented and demonstrate perform skills, when the student is expected to perform according to the obtained knowledge, not just to correlate concepts. They show that the student has deeper understanding of the concept and its application in various context. The main accent is on the application of obtained knowledge and presenting analytical skills to find a typical pattern or concept occurrence, instead of just defining a concept. It is a step forward compared to simply understanding a definition, since the student will not just memorize the concept, but apply its essence in practice, presenting knowledge and skills of applying the concept in various situations and environments.

The classical multiple choice questions are presenting mostly memorizing skills, asking the student to memorize concept names and descriptions. They fit into inform goals that build on learning methods that communicate information.

E-Testing with interactive images evaluate skills, which apply knowledge with perform procedure goals. These goals are based on learning methods that build procedural skills how to realize a certain procedure or perform a task by following steps, such as how to log on or complete a form, etc. The final goal is to achieve a system with perform principle goals based on learning methods that build strategic skills, such as how to design a computer network, how to analyze a communication problem, etc. These questions require the student to to adapt strategies and knowledge to various environments and situations, by applying learned objectives.

6 Opportunities and Challenges

This section gives an overview of benefits, disadvantages, opportunities and challenges this system has in comparison to the classical e-Testing systems.

The main benefits of the new model are summarized as follows.

- The expected image sizes are enormous in comparison to the existing technology to transfer and process these images. The alternative offered by the discussed GUI is promising in terms of being used by a single web browser that loads only small predefined image portions and enables responses in real time by a conventional computer communication network.
- The ability to interact with images enables added value to express application of concepts and not just memorizing of concepts written by textual

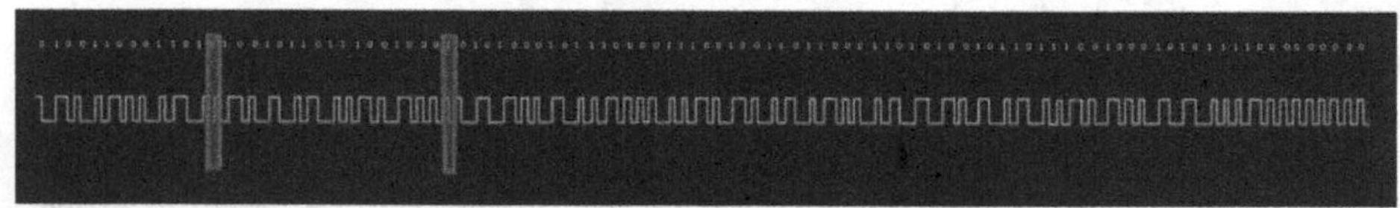

Fig. 3. An example of a question from Computer Network course about signals and coding algorithms using the eTii system

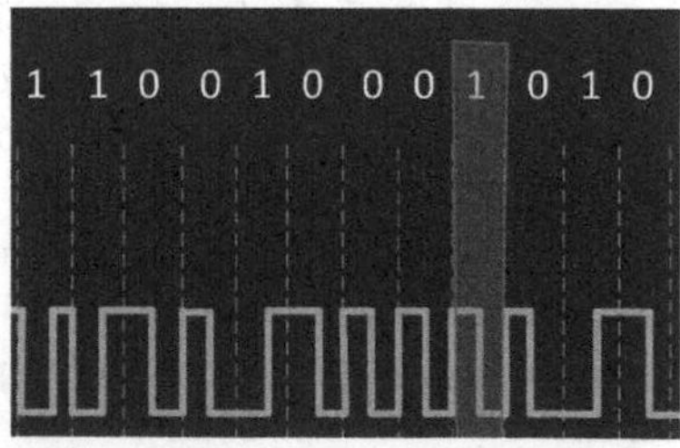

Fig. 4. A zoomed image portion of Fig. 3 displays sufficient information

paragraphs. It goes into the essence of understanding and practical application of knowledge concepts, avoiding just correlating of textual paragraphs.

6.1 Opportunities

So far we have concluded the following add-on values of interactive images to the e-Testing:

Extended domain of options is a feature that extends the domain of offered answer options, by using a possibility to choose enormous amount of positions for possible answers in a huge image. Usually the domain of options in a multiple choice questions is limited by the length of the visible textual part, while the image can offer a lot more positions as answer options. Although Fig. 2 shows only five objects, where one can provide an answer, the example presented in Fig. 3 uses a lot more options where one can provide an answer.

Extended answering possibilities is a feature that offers a possibility to express different answers for selected image objects. In a classical multiple choice questions, the user can select correct answer options for a given question. By using an interactive image with a possibility to set placeholders and comments for each placeholders, one can provide different answer options for each placeholder, meaning that it realizes several multiple choice questions in one occurrence of the image. The example in Fig. 2 enables setting a different answer for each of the five possible objects, as setting a comment in a different placeholder.

Decreased cheating Several features determine decreased ability to cheat. The first one is to avoid using memorization as method for answering, as is done by learning combinations of textual questions and textual correct answers, instead of the essence and context of the questions. In case of images, it is harder to memorize the position of a particular graphical pattern as a correct answer, especially if the image is huge and the visible part can be navigated with its position and size. The second feature is to prevent the ability to use search engines while answering the test. For example, if the question and answer options are textual, one might rather easily find the correct combination, while in the image it is quite difficult to tell the search engines to find the occurrence of this pattern within the huge set of images. For example, it is not possible to memorize the type of the device in the example in Fig. 2, since the IP addresses can be changed in the same image, and the student is expected to apply procedures or principles and analyze the given image.

Favoring creativity and solution discovery instead of memorizing is an add-on obtained by applying the concept to apply knowledge and find an occurrence pattern in an image as an constructive method, instead of matching concept names and descriptions in multiple choice questions, which is reflecting memorizing features of instructional methods. The example in Fig. 3 shows that the student has to apply the coding algorithm and analyze the signals to interpret if the algorithm is applied correctly.

6.2 Challenges

For us, the process of developing content is a really motivating challenge, since not all concepts can have a visual presentation and application. We found that constructive methods that express perform goals and perform procedures, rather than instructional methods can be applied for engineering and natural sciences, as well as in medicine. The application domain in medicine is well known for MRI or cell analysis, but was never been used for e-Testing. The application domain in engineering and natural sciences is rather new and challenging, especially for technology application domains.

There are several challenges that motivate further research.

The first challenge concerns the performance issues. Although the images are stored as small resolution image portions, we expect to face huge data transfers and delays. Especially if a user is anxious and navigates and zooms fast. In these cases, the user can demand a series of image portions to be downloaded from the server.

Elasticity and scalability are challenges to implement a cloud solution and migrate all the functions in an environment that performs as a service. Solving the elasticity problem is not a trivial action. It is not enough to only analyze the transactions and dedicate them to a separate thread, followed by scheduling those threads in a set of virtual machines. A careful analysis and design of an efficient cloud solution would organize the building blocks into static and dynamic modules and map static parts into a static VM, and dynamic parts into a set of dynamic VMs. The development of this solution will enable an environment for a system with more faster response than the conventional thread based approach.

Availability and quality assurance are features expected from any system, especially this one that is going to be used as assessment tool in educational process. Enabling these features depends on third party solutions and services.

Data itself becomes a challenge if it is analyzed by a perspective of a growing database and establishing interoperability of the question database, testing and users information. There are no commonly agreed upon standards among various producers, although several recommendations exist for learning systems.

Security management is always a challenge when building such systems. Managing the firewall and avoiding environments that enable cheating is a top demand of the users.

7 Conclusion

In this paper we propose a new model of human computer interaction for e-Testing that includes interactive images. The model includes features for navigation of the position and size of the visible image part, and also several interaction functionalities, such as, pointing a graphical object in the image, marking a region, setting placeholders in the image, and typing messages in placeholders. This human computer interface for e-Testing with interactive images enables the development of questions that have nature to express constructive skills of the student.

The technology of interactive images is not new, rather it has been in use for delivery of geographical maps by Google and other providers. In this paper we present opportunities and challenges of offering this technology in the e-Testing concept. It allows an extended domain of options in comparison to the limited multiple choice options in conventional systems. In addition it allows more possibilities to provide and answer using placeholders and setting a different answer for each placeholder. The overall system enables less cheating, avoiding memorization, search support and guessing methods as inappropriate.Finally, the system favors creativity and practical application of obtained knowledge towards solution discovery, instead of concept correlation only found in conventional multiple choice questions.

Therefore this technology allows an added value to the classical e-Testing systems, enabling a possibility to test procedural and principle skills rather than just the information concept correlations with multiple choice questions.

Several questions are still open and motivate further research as engineering and scientific challenges. We have analyzed briefly the problems of performance issues as increased traffic, enabling elasticity and scalability of the solution, database organization, interoperability, availability, security etc. Most of these challenges are planned for future work, including experimental research and design of new solutions and models.

The main benefit this system offers in comparison to the conventional one is the add-on value in the pedagogical method of delivery of e-Learning. We have discussed that two approaches used in e-Education as instructivism and constructivism can also have two implementations in e-Testing. The conclusion is that classical textual multiple choice questions are mainly addressing questions applying the instruct learning methods, where a concept is to be associated with some offered answer options. E-Testing using interactive images and described human computer interface can better address procedural skills and constructive methods, where one can apply knowledge in the context of reality.

References

[1] Bing Maps: Home page, `http://www.bing.com/maps/`

[2] Byrne, R.: How to Use Google Maps Engine Lite (September 2013), `http://www.freetech4teachers.com/2013/09/how-to-use-google-maps-engine-lite.html`

[3] CISCO: Cisco networking academy, `https://cisco.netacad.com/`, (retrieved: November 2013)

[4] Clark, R., Mayer, R.: E-learning and the science of instruction: Proven guidelines for consumers and designers of multimedia learning. Pfeiffer (2011)

[5] Crisp, G.: Teachers handbook on e-assessment (2012), `http://www.sblinteractive.org/Portals/4/docs/Publications/Crisp_Handbook_2012.pdf`

[6] Google: Big Birthday.. Google Maps API Turns 5! (June 2010), `http://googlegeodevelopers.blogspot.com/2010/06/`

[7] Gusev, M., Ristov, S., Armenski, G., Gushev, P., Velkoski, G.: E-assessment with interactive images. In: 2014 IEEE Global Engineering Education Conference (EDUCON), Iistanbul, Turkey, pp. 484–491 (2014) (in Press)

[8] Gusev, M., Armenski, G.: E-Assessment Systems and Online Learning with Adaptive Testing. In: Ivanovic, M., Jain, L.C. (eds.) E-Learning Paradigms and Applications. SCI, vol. 528, pp. 229–249. Springer, Heidelberg (2014)
[9] HERE Maps: Home page, `http://here.com/`
[10] Juntunen, T., Kostakos, V., Perttunen, M., Ferreira, D.: Web tool for traffic engineers: direct manipulation and visualization of vehicular traffic using google maps. In: MindTrek, pp. 209–210 (2012)
[11] Lardinois, F.: Google Launches Maps Engine API To Allow Enterprise Developers To More Easily Create, Share And Publish Custom Maps (June 2013), `http://techcrunch.com/2013/06/05/`
[12] Lev-Ram, M.: Are Google Maps the new productivity tool? (October 2013), `http://tech.fortune.cnn.com/tag/google-map-engine-pro`
[13] OpenStreetMap: Home page, `http://www.openstreetmap.org`
[14] Ristov, S., Gusev, M., Armenski, G., Bozinoski, K., Velkoski, G.: Architecture and organization of e-assessment cloud solution. In: 2013 IEEE Global Engineering Education Conference (EDUCON), pp. 736–743. IEEE, Berlin (2013); best Paper Award
[15] Ristov, S., Gusev, M., Armenski, G., Velkoski, G.: Scalable and elastic e-assessment cloud solution. In: 2014 IEEE Global Engineering Education Conference (EDUCON), Istanbul, Turkey, pp. 762–769 (2014) (in Press)
[16] Salmon, F.: Udacity and the future of online universities (January 23, 2012)
[17] Scalise, K., Gifford, B.: Computer-based assessment in e-learning: A framework for constructing intermediate constraint questions and tasks for technology platforms. The Journal of Technology, Learning and Assessment 4(6) (2006)
[18] Taylor, B.: The world is your JavaScript-enabled oyster (June 2005), `http://googleblog.blogspot.com/2005/06/world-is-your-javascript-enabled_29.html`
[19] Triola, M.M., Holloway, W.J.: Enhanced virtual microscopy for collaborative education. BMC Med. Education 11(1), 4 (2011)
[20] Yahoo! Maps: Home page, `http://maps.yahoo.com/`
[21] YandexMap: Home page, `http://maps.yandex.com/`
[22] Zhang, J., Shi, H., Zhang, Y.: Self-organizing map methodology and google maps services for geographical epidemiology mapping. In: Digital Image Computing: Techniques and Applications, DICTA 2009, pp. 229–235. IEEE (2009)

On Enhancing Disabled Students' Accessibility in Environmental Education Using ICT: The *MusicPaint* Case

Sofia J. Hadjileontiadou[1], Erasmia Plastra[2], Kostantinos Toumpas[3], Katerina Kyprioti[3], Dimitrios Mandiliotis[3], João Barroso[4], and Leontios J. Hadjileontiadis[3,*]

[1] Tutor at Hellenic Open University, Katakouzinou 58A 68100 Alexandroupolis, Greece
shadjileontiadou@gmail.com
[2] MEd EEEK Komotini Vrioulon 8, 69100 Komotini, Greece
isminie.p@gmail.com
[3] Department of Electrical and Computer Engineering, Aristotle University of Thessaloniki, 54124 Thessaloniki, Greece
{ktoumpas,kiaikate,leontios}@auth.gr, dimandili@gmail.com
[4] Dept. of Electrical Engineering, Universidade de Trás-os-Montes e Alto Douro (UTAD), 5001-801 Vila Real, Portugal
jbarroso@utad.pt

Abstract. This work draws upon the theoretical foundations of Special Education for People with Disability, Environmental Education and the Human Computer Interaction (HCI), from the Activity Theory perspective, to propose the *MusicPaint* software. Initially, the design considerations of *MusicPaint* are presented. Then, its pilot use by seven students with disability is described. From the qualitative and quantitative evidence of performance that was gathered, the key findings are presented and discussed. Despite the limited number of participants in the experimental validation scenarios, the findings reveal the potentiality of the *MusicPaint* to enhance the accessibility of students with disability to Environmental Education opportunities, contributing to the HCI-based enhancement of accessibility in the educational settings.

Keywords: Students with Disability, Special Education, Environmental Education, ICT, MusicPaint, Human-Computer Interaction, Didactical Instruction, Activity Theory.

1 Introduction

The evolution of society and change attitudes towards disability has led to the transition from the medical model, where the concept of disability is identical with that of the illness and interventions implemented are intended to provide the individual skills for restoration [1], to the social model created in Great Britain in the '70s with the

* Corresponding author.

C. Stephanidis and M. Antona (Eds.): UAHCI/HCII 2014, Part II, LNCS 8514, pp. 325–336, 2014.

establishment of the Association of Physically Disabled against segregation (Union of the Physically Impaired against Segregation, UPIAS). In this vein, the environmental education gains its ground as it aims at the reconciliation of society with nature and between man and man for a sustainable development. A development that would destroy the balance of natural systems on the planet, covering the needs of the present, but not at the expense of future generations and ensuring ecological sustainability and social justice [2]. In recent years, developments both on the rights of persons with disabilities and in the field of environmental education is great. The marginalization of the disabled has been replaced by the principles of inclusion and inclusive education. In the context of integrating both the environmental education and education for students with disability (SwD) can be the means to achieve the cooperation of the people, the exemption from prejudice and changing attitudes that consider human master of nature and the "different" threat [3]. One of the basic problem in the environmental education is linking theory with practice. This is even worse in the cases of SwD, such as those with Moderate mental retardation. The latter have difficulty in abstract ability and symbolism; hence, they need specific examples, detailed descriptions and images to understand the symbolic meanings [4].

The conjunction of the technological evolution with the struggle of people with disabilities for autonomous and socially integrated educational experiences, set the horizon of new technological challenges and new research endeavors. Within this framework, theoretical insights to the Human-Computer Interaction (HCI) issue evolve through time, moving from the "first-wave HCI" (i.e., employing a perspective of cognitivist, information processing psychology) to the "second-wave HCI" (i.e., employing a perspective of context that includes motivation, meanings, culture, and social interactions) [5]. Among "second-wave HCI" theories, such as phenomenology [6] and distributed cognition [7], the Activity Theory (AT) was introduced to HCI [8]. It provided a theoretical insight to the analysis of the interaction with technology by considering the computer as a mediating artefact rather than an object and relating the operational aspects of the interaction with technology to meaningful goals and, ultimately, needs and motives of technology users [9].

The current paper places efforts upon the combination of the educational areas of Environmental and Special Education by employing a HCI design, influenced by AT basic principles and materialized in the form of a specially designed software, namely MusicPaint. Empirical uses of the latter provide evidence of the potentiality of the proposed design, as presented in the next sections.

2 Background

2.1 Special Education of Students with Mild and Moderate Mental Retardation and Disabilities

According to [10], disability is defined as any restriction or lack (resulting from an impairment) of ability to perform an activity in the manner, or within the range, considered to be normal for human being. The term disability reflects the consequences of impairment in terms of functional performance and activity by the individual. Disabilities thus represent disturbances at the level of the person.

The Procedure for determining the level of retardation, as proposed by the [11], includes the following steps:

1. Recognize that a problem exists (e.g., delay in developmental milestones),
2. Determine that an adaptive behavior deficit exists,
3. Determine measured general intellectual functioning,
4. 'Make decision about whether or not there is retardation of intellectual functioning,
5. Make decision about level of retardation as indicated by level of measured intellectual functioning ([11], p.13). More specifically, a classification of the levels of retardation indicated by IQ range obtained on measure of general intellectual functioning, includes
   (a) Mild mental retardation (50-55 to approx. 70),
   (b) Moderate mental retardation (35-40 to 50-55),
   (c) Severe mental retardation (20-25 to 35-40), and
   (d) Profound mental retardation (below 20 or 25) [11].

Students with mental retardation problems face difficulties to include deficiencies in academic achievement, information-processing problems, attentional deficits, hyperactivity, uneven patterns of learning performance, and difficulties in social relationships. Since the latter have been noted especially in interactions with peers and teachers, these difficulties could stem from reactions to academic frustration and failure [11]. However, students with Mild mental retardation can understand elementary school level knowledge, perform social adaptation that enables them to perform autonomously and can be trained in a profession. Students with Moderate mental retardation are able to achieve basic school skills, some level of social responsibility, adaptation to the housework, collaboration and respect to the human rights. Moreover, they may be able to work in a protected, simple workplace after receiving training, e.g., in Special Vocational Schools, where they receive specially designed intensive instruction referring to adaptations of content, methodology, or delivery to meet students' needs. It must ensure effective learning through goal-directed instruction, achieve maximum benefits with individualization and validation, and set special education apart through intensive, explicit support [12]. More specifically, the work of [13] provided highlights of research on explicit (direct) instruction, which leaves nothing to chance; all skills are taught directly. A typical direct instruction lesson includes:

(a) explicit and carefully sequenced instruction provided by the teacher (a model of what students will do),
(b) scaffolding to provide students the assistance they need before being able to complete the task on their own (guided practice),
(c) frequent opportunities for students to practice skills (independent practice), and
(d) repeated practice over time (review).

2.2 The Concept of 'the Water Cycle'

Although 'the water cycle' is a subject matter that is contained in most curricula around the world, perceptions of students about it are fragmented [14] and students do not realize its important role in life [15]. Research on perceptions of 1.000 students from 13 to 15 years old, revealed that most students find it difficult to understand the change of matter (water), to link school-knowledge concerning 'the water cycle' with their daily lives and to realize the connection of atmospheric and underground water [15]. Moreover, their finding that students consider the underground water as a static one is verified by [16]. Through empirical research with students of 8-17 years old, researchers of [17] concluded that students generally do not understand the phase changes of water, with older children being able to understand evaporation, but no liquefaction. Research with students of 10 to 15 years revealed that [18]:

(a) students 5-7 years old believe that clouds are made of tobacco or cotton and the rain falls when someone, maybe God, opens the water supply. Some students believe that clouds are bags of water and when it rains they collide or are being torn,
(b) students 8-10 years old thought clouds like sponges with water and when they swing or get cool or warm the drops fall and so it is raining, and
(c) students 11 to 15 years old believe that clouds are created when the steam cools and the rain falls when the drops become large and heavy.

Students with Mild and Moderate mental retardation, are considered students of the above age range. Environmental education from the broad perspective of the equality of students, foresees Special education as intensive, motivated, individually planned, specialized, goal-directed instruction to meet students' needs and to ensure their access in the general curriculum. Moreover, it focuses on a systemic perception of the nature's function through cycles (e.g., 'the water cycle') towards a holistic approach to nature, through multiple educational stimuli, activity-based and close to everyday life learning [2]. The effective Information and Communication Technology (ICT) integration within a didactical approach towards the realization of the 'the water cycle' as a cycle *per se* (with an empirical approach to the change of matter issues involved) by students with Mild and Moderate mental retardation, motivated the following design considerations.

2.3 The *MusicPaint* Software within the Activity Theory Context

The *MusicPaint* software, developed by the authors of the Dept. of ECE (Thessaloniki, Greece), proposes effective ICT integration to a goal-directed instruction for students with Mild and Moderate mental retardation. Figure 1 depicts the *MusicPaint* workspace, which makes explicit the simple functions that it provides. The empty workspace provides room for the user to express his/her creativity, by choosing color and simultaneously instrument, line type and drawing object.

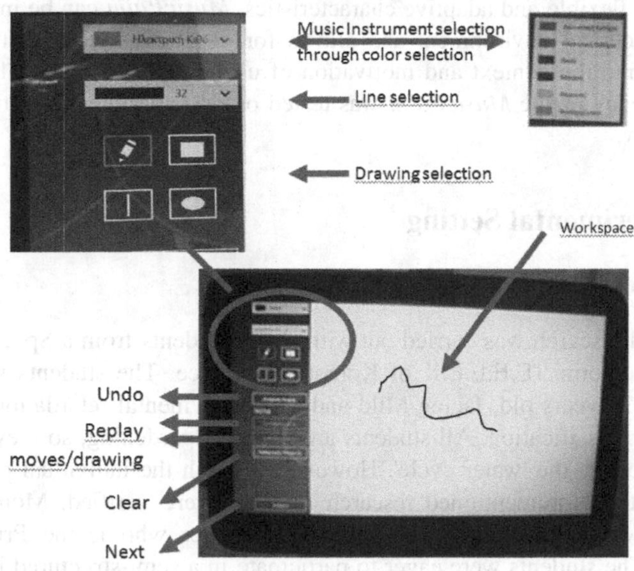

Fig. 1. Depiction of the *MusicPaint* workspace

Extra buttons of the workspace support simple undo, clear, and self-reflection actions. The next button materializes a route through three scenarios, IMAGINE, SEE and HEAR, respectively, with five experiments (#) per scenario. In every scenario, the user is asked to draw upon a stimulus that s/he receives as follows. In the IMAGINE scenario, the stimulus are five keywords, in the SEE scenario five depictions and in the HEAR scenario, five pieces of music of the domain of interest. By the end of (#5) of each scenario, the next button asks the user to fill a Likert-scaled questionnaire concerning the experience of the completed scenario. Finally, the user is asked to complete an open-ended questionnaire concerning his/her experience of the Music Paint.

MusicPaint runs at `Microsoft Windows 8` on tablets and was developed using the `C#`, `XAML` and `ASP.NET` programming languages. Automated logging of the interactions of the user allows for later raw data analysis. From the Special education perspective, the design of the *MusicPaint*, materializes a looping process (3 scenarios with #1-5 experiments per scenario), yet involving different levels of attention at each loop, according to the stimulations of the especially designed, dedicated software. Moreover, due to its simplicity in use and the open character of the design, *MusicPaint* provides the students with Mild and Moderate mental retardation a working environment that complies with basic instructional design considerations in Special education, i.e., systematic, purposeful, well-organized, hierarchical explicit direct instruction supported through feedback and iterations.

On the other hand, from the AT perspective, *MusicPaint* materializes a "second-wave HCI", as it is not designed upon a pre-conceived idea about what the users might do, but with its context-based design it focuses on what the users actually do.

Due to its flexible and adaptive characteristics, *MusicPaint* can be integrated within the instructional environment and allows for depending the investigation of the researchers into the context and motivation of user's behavior [19]. The verification of the efficiency of the *MusicPaint* was tested on an experimental setting that is described below.

3 Experimental Setting

3.1 Sampling and Pre-testing

An empirical research was carried out with seven students from a Special Vocational School in Komotini (E.E.E.E.K of Komotini), Greece. The students were aged between 17 to 23 years old, facing Mild and Moderate mental retardation according to their official classification. All students are studying gardening, so they are expected to roughly realize the 'water cycle'. However, through the individual pre-testing that took place, the aforementioned research findings were verified. More specifically, pre-testing was conducted by the second researcher who is the Principal of the E.E.E.E.K. The students were eager to participate in a semi-structured interview with open-ended questions. During the interview, the students were asked to solve a five-piece puzzle depicting the 'water cycle'. None of the students was able to realize the 'water cycle' and solve the puzzle.

3.2 The Experimental Setup of the *MusicPaint*

Upon the pre-test findings, an experimental instructional intervention was prepared that integrated *MusicPaint*, as it is depicted in Table 1. IN the latter, the selection of the Keywords, the Pictures (pieces of the puzzle) and the Sounds/music were combined with the 'water cycle'. The repetitive nature of the design that aligns with the Special education needs, along with the direct instruction, was foreseen through repetitive circular, iterative processing of the phases of water designs, i.e., of the 'water cycle', the implementation of each scenario both in the classroom (preparation through direct instruction) and in the MusicPaint environment (autonomy in practical implementation) and the specific circular nature of the *MusicPaint*.

The aims of this design were:

1. *In terms of knowledge*: to recognize and name the water phases and describe the water cycle,
2. *In terms of skills*: to paint the phases and eventually the whole water cycle, assuming different stimuli (words, images, environmental sounds/audio) using tablets and the *MusicPaint* software, and
3. *In terms of attitudes*: to appreciate the natural environment, discover a new use of technology through tablets and boost their self-esteem through the whole process.

Table 1. The proposed instructional design

MusicPaint Scenario 1: IMAGINE				
Preparation in the classroom. Experimental-realistic representations of the 'water cycle'				
Text Input (Keywords)				
Cloud	Snow	Water	Plants	Cycle
Outcome paintings using the *MusicPaint*				
(#1)	(#2)	(#3)	(#4)	(#5)
***MusicPaint* Scenario 2: SEE**				
Preparation in the classroom. Representing the 'water cycle' in the classroom schematically				
Visual Input (Images)				
Sea-Sun	Snow	River	Forest	The 'water cycle'
Outcome paintings using the *MusicPaint*				
(#1)	(#2)	(#3)	(#4)	(#5)
***MusicPaint* Scenario 3: HEAR**				
Scenario 3-preparation in the classroom. Listen to music pieces with lyrics concerning the sea, the sun, the cloud, the rain, the snow, the river, the 'water cycle'				
Audio Input (Sound/music files)				
Sound of boiling water	Song concerning the snow	Song concerning the river	Sound of irrigation	Song concerning the 'water cycle'
Outcome paintings using the *MusicPaint*				
(#1)	(#2)	(#3)	(#4)	(#5)

3.3 Implementation Steps

Before the implementation of the scenarios shown in Table 1, two tablets were used for the acquaintance of the students with the *MusicPaint* environment. Due to the flexibility and user friendliness of the latter, the SwD were, quite quickly, autonomous in its use.

The intervention initiated on the April 2, 2013, with the scenario 1-preparation of the students in the classroom. This step included experiments with the phases of the water (drink it as liquid, see it as a gas after boiling, experiencing ice cubes), PowerPoint and video presentations with realistic representations of the 'water cycle' and discussion on the role of the plants. Another teacher of the school was the external observer of all the discussion that took place. At the end of this step, the *MusicPaint* Scenario 1: IMAGINE was conducted individually by all the students. After a week, the second implementation step took place and the aforementioned PowerPoint was projected again (repetitive mode) and the picture of the puzzle was used during the discussion, moving the representation of the 'water cycle' from the realistic to a more abstract depiction. At the end of this step, the *MusicPaint* Scenario 2: SEE, was individually performed by all the students. The last step was realized on the April 23, 2013, where the scenario 3-preparation was conducted. A repetitive projection of the above PowerPoint and the picture of the puzzle were again presented to the SwD. The students listened to songs from different singers and music trends yet upon the predefined lyrics. At the end of this step, he use of the MusicPaint Scenario 3: HEAR, upon sounds and songs, was individually performed by all the students.

The duration of the preparation scenarios 1 and 2 was 45 minutes, whereas of scenario 3 was 60 minutes. All the SwD were enthusiastic with the *MusicPaint.* They enjoyed the use of a new artefact within the classroom and the freedom and ability to use it. On May 15, 2013, the researcher invited each student in a semi-structured interview. She asked each student to explain the content of each piece of the puzzle. Most of the questions were the ones addressed to them during the pre-test. Finally, she asked each student to solve the puzzle.

4 Results and Discussion

4.1 Qualitative Approach

The implementation of the above experiment provided triangulated evidence of the performance of each student, mainly of qualitative nature (i.e., the observations, the semi-structured interviews, the *MusicPaint* outcome paintings), revealing in depth information of the context and the outcome of the learning procedure.

In Figs. 2 and 3, the initial and final solution of the puzzle and the drawings of #5 from the three *MusicPaint* scenarios (see Table 1) from the third student are presented, respectively, documenting effective results.

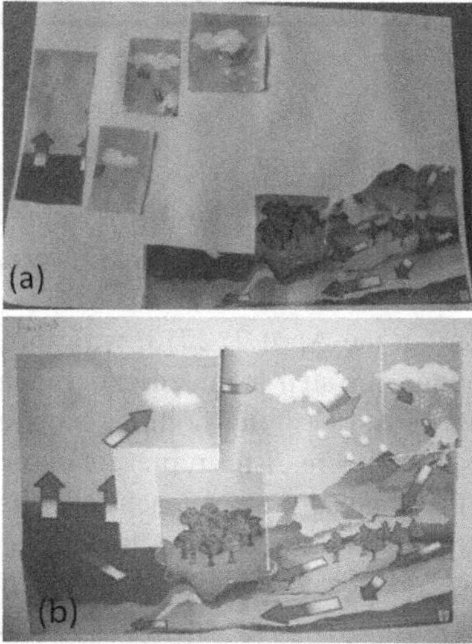

Fig. 2. (a) Initial and (b) final solution of the puzzle by the third student

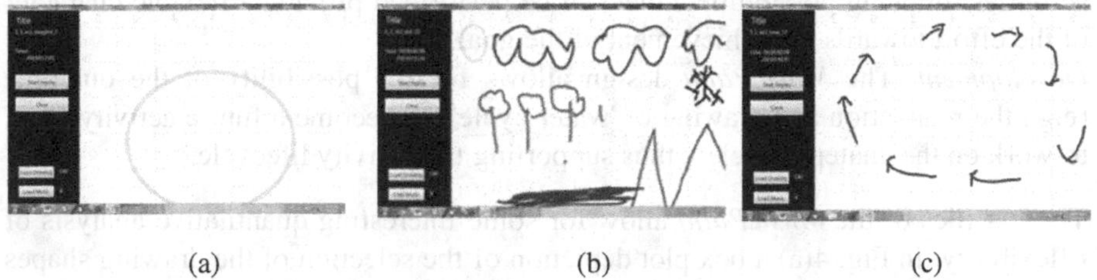

(a) (b) (c)

Fig. 3. The *MusicPaint* drawings during the fifth (#5) experiment of the scenarios: (a) IMAGINE, (b) SEE and (c) HEAR, by the third student.

The qualitative analysis of the drawings like the ones shown in Fig. 3 verifies the contribution of the *MusicPaint* to the perception of the circular character of the water, through the adaption of necessary skills and knowledge to the students under consideration. This was notice in the drawing outcomes from all SwD participated in the experimental phase, and all of them managed correctly to solve the puzzle at the end, like in Fig. 2(b). This explains the liaison of the students' HCI expression and knowledge conquer, stimulating further the introduction of ICT-based activities in the corresponding educational curriculum.

4.2 Quantitative Approach

In parallel to the qualitative analysis, a quantitative analysis of the *MusicPaint* log files was conducted, contributing to its evaluation as an HCI that implements the AT perspective. In this vein, aspects that derive from the Activity Checklist [20] are discussed.

- *Means and ends*: The *MusicPaint* deals with human activity through the simple design of its interface that allowed the SwD to perform actions (use of buttons) that are part of an activity (# drawing), that holds many sub-activities (choices of instruments, line types, objects) in order to achieve the goal (realize the 'water cycle'). All the above were performed easily as derived from the relatively small duration of time that was on average 8 mins (±std 2 mins) per scenario. The distinct resources at the right hand side of the workspace provide a clear understanding of their parallel function, e.g., the distribution of the drawing within the workspace is related to the instruments frequency (higher values at the edges).
- *Social and physical aspects of the environment*: The MusicPaint was integrated with the Microsoft Windows 8 and combined with the merits of a tablet to provide touch-screen possibilities. This was proved to address effectively the social and physical aspects of the context of the specific students. Moreover, it can load the drawings from all the scenarios and replay them through a *MusicPaint Viewer*.
- *Learning, Cognition and Articulation*: The students materialized a series of repetitions along the five experiments per scenario of the *MusicPaint*, which highly contributed to realize their goal and work for it. Towards this direction, it is interesting that there were not any missing drawings from all the scenarios. The infinite

activities (drawing possibilities) that can be performed provide a flexible character of the effort towards the achievement of the goal.

- *Development*: The *MusicPaint* design allows for the possibility of the outcome (e.g., the realization and drawing of 'water cycle') to become a future activity (e.g., to work on the 'material cycle'), thus supporting the activity lifecycle.

The log files of the *MusicPaint* allow for some interesting quantitative analysis of this flexibility. In Fig. 4(a) a box plot depiction of the selection of the drawing shapes from all the students for the experimental scenario HEAR is presented. It is interesting to notice that the predominant choice is the 'Free Line' selection across the experiments (#1-3). This flexible tool yet is eliminated up to the experiment #5, where the Circle/ Ellipse tool is also preferred. This trend is depicted also in the previous two scenarios, underlining a move to a more formal and abstract (i.e., scientific) representation of the 'water cycle'. In Fig. 4(b) the box plot of the music instrument selection across all students and scenarios is presented. It is interesting to notice that acoustic guitar (i.e., the blue color) is the first choice of the students, followed by the piano (black) and harmonica (with more symmetrical ±std). It is noteworthy to realize that all the provided choices were tested, a trend that exists along each scenario. Finally, the sound characteristics (duration and volume) are influenced by the width of the line selection. In Fig.4(c), the box plot of the drawing line width selection across all scenarios and students, is presented. It can be noticed that the width selection has values that show distribution among low and high durations and volumes, a pattern that exists in all the scenarios.

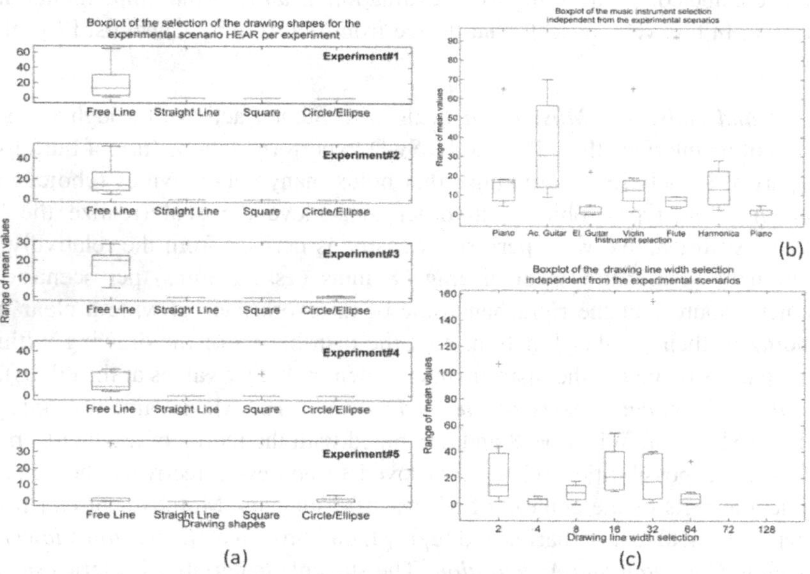

Fig. 4. Boxplots of: (a) selection of drawing shapes, (b) music instrument selection and (c) drawing line width selection

The above findings provide evidence that the students were fully engaged with the *MusicPaint*. This was also verified by their answers to the *MusicPaint* questionnaires. Moreover, they imagine its future uses, as it is seen in their responses to the general open question: "What else do you wish to do with the Music Paint", including "Music and songs", "Games", "Painting with houses", "Internet". From the latter it seems that they imagine the MusicPaint as an integrated educational framework. Furthermore, the new knowledge gained from the ICT-based teaching intervention remained in their memory, as it is shown by the confidence in the final interview and the accuracy in the students' questionnaire responses. Moreover, they developed a positive attitude to participate in the educational scenarios, mainly because a stage of familiarity with tablets initially took place. Apparently, due to the limited number of participants, the results from the above quantitative analysis cannot be generalized. The latter serves, however, as a means to the realization of the creativity of the students. Moreover, it reveals possibilities of self-monitoring feedback along with the *MusicPaint Viewer*. Following the pathway of [15], noting that it is important to stimulate students' interest first and then make the teaching of abstract concepts, *MusicPaint* was used by the students without any interference of the researcher-teacher and this filled them with joy and boosted their confidence. At the end, the students knew the 'water cycle' and what elements were set during the teaching intervention. In the approach followed here and by taking into account the methodological tools, the semi-structured interviews and the follow-up discussions, an opportunity was given to discover students' views and beliefs towards the issue of the 'water cycle'.

5 Conclusions

In this paper, the design considerations of the *MusicPaint* software were discussed within the Special Education, the Environmental Education and the Activity Theory perspectives. Synergies of instructional directions of the aforementioned perspectives, resulted in a design, which through an empirical study, was initially verified as to the potentiality to enhance students with disabilities accessibility in Environmental Education using ICT. However, due to the small number of the participants, the current study serves as a pilot one and certainly more large-scale experiments should take place to achieve generalization; it provides, however, a real-life example of an HCI-based accessibility instance in action.

Acknowledgements. The authors would like to express their gratitude to the seven students participated in the study.

References

1. Silvers, A., Wasserman, D., Mahowald, M.B.: Disability, Difference, Discrimination: Perspectives on Justice in Biothecs and Public Policy. Rowman & Littlefield, New York (1998)

2. Flogaiti, E.: Environmental education-Contemporary approaches. In: Dimitriou, A., Flogaiti, E. (eds.) Introduction at the Natural and Human Environment-Environmental Education, Hellenic Open University, Patra, pp. 13–41 (2008) (in Greek)
3. Dimitriou, A.: Views of primary school teachers in environmental issues. In: Kaila, M., Theodoropoulou, E., Dimitriou, A., Xanthakou, J., Anastasatos, N. (eds.) Environmental Education. Research Data & Instructional Design, Atrapos, Athens (2005) (in Greek)
4. Erez, G., Peled, I.: Cognition and metacognition evidence of higher thinking in problems solving of adolescents with mental retardation. Educational Training in Mental Retardation and Developmental Disabilities 36(1), 83–93 (2001)
5. Cooper, G., Bowers, J.: Representing the user: notes on the disciplinary rhetoric of human-computer interaction. In: Thomas, P.J. (ed.) The Social and Interactional Dimensions of Human-Computer Interfaces (Cambridge Series on Human-Computer Interaction), Cambridge University Press (1995)
6. Dourish, P.: Where the Action Is: The Foundations of Embodied Interaction. MIT Press (2001)
7. Rogers, Y.: New Theoretical Approaches for HCI. Annual Review of Information Science and Technology 38, 1–43 (2004)
8. Bødker, S.: Through the Interface - A Human Activity Approach to User Interface Design. Lawrence Erlbaum Associates, Hillsdale (1991)
9. Kaptelinin, V.: Activity Theory. In: Soegaard, M., Dam, R.F. (eds.) The Encyclopedia of Human-Computer Interaction, 2nd edn., The Interaction Design Foundation, Aarhus (2013), http://www.interaction-design.org/encyclopedia/activity_theory.html
10. WHO: A glossary of terms for community health care and services for older persons centre for health development. Ageing and Health Technical Report, 5 (2004)
11. (AAMD) American Association on Mental Deficiency: Classification I, In Mental Retardation, 1719 Kalorama Road, NW Washington, DC 20009 (1983)
12. Marchand-Martella, N., Kinder, D., Kubina, R. (n.d.).: Special Education and Direct Instruction: An Effective Combination. Making the difference. McGraw Hill (2014), http://www.mheresearch.com/assets/products/1679091c5a880faf/di_special_ed_results.pdf (retrieved February 6, 2014)
13. Rosenshine, B.V.: Synthesis of research on explicit teaching. Educational Leadership 43(7), 60–69 (1986)
14. Havu-Nuutinen, S., Karkkainen, S., Keinonen, T.: Primary school pupils' perceptions of water in the context of STS study approach. International Journal of Environmental & Science Education 6(4), 321–339 (2011)
15. Ben-Zvi-Assarf, O., Orion, N.: A study of junior high students' perceptions of the water cycle. Journal of Geoscience Education 53(4), 366–373 (2005)
16. Cardak, O.: Science students' misconceptions of the Water cycle According to their Drawings. Journal of Applied Sciences 9(5), 865–873 (2009)
17. Osborne, R.J., Cosgrove, M.M.: Children's conception of the changes of state of water. Journal of Research in Science Teaching 20(9), 825–838 (1983)
18. Driver, R., Squires, A., Rushworth, P., Wood-Robinson, V.: Building on the concepts of Natural Sciences. In: Kokkotas, P. (ed.), Typothito, Athens (1998)
19. Gay, G., Hembrooke, H.: Activity-Centered Design: An Ecological Approach to Designing Smart Tools and Usable Systems (Acting with Technology). MIT Press (2004)
20. Kaptelinin, V., Nardi, A.B., Macaulay, C.: Methods & tools: The activity checklist: a tool for representing the space of context. Magazine Interactions 6(4), 27–39 (1999)

Accessibility in Multimodal Digital Learning Materials

Bolette Willemann Jensen and Simon Moe

Nota, The National Library for People with Reading Difficulties, Copenhagen, Denmark
{bwj, sme}@nota.nu

Abstract. This review is based on research-based guidelines and principles for accessibility in multimodal digital learning materials and educational texts. It also includes research on the use of the body and interaction as a kind of modality. In the context of the review a number of recommendations is themed, based on findings in the literature, from a didactic-pedagogical perspective. These themes relate to: the structure and content of learning materials; software and formats; the correlation between modalities; and kinesthetics. We conclude with a presentation of general principles for the idea of broad accessibility.

Keywords: Accessibility, Multimodality, Digitalisation, Learning materials, Reading.

1 Introduction

Accessibility is a continuously changing concept, which depends on the context, in which the concept is discussed. It is often presented in the form of a statement of intent, backed up in varying degrees by concise requirements for the form and content in a particular context. In The United Nations Convention on the Rights of Persons with Disabilities accessibility is defined as follows: "Recognizing the importance of accessibility to the physical, social, economic and cultural environment, to health and education and to information and communication, in enabling persons with disabilities to fully enjoy all human rights and fundamental freedoms".[1]

More specifically this article examines new conditions surrounding accessibility, which are relevant vis à vis the fact that materials are increasingly digitised, which enables them to express themselves in multiple modalities. Accessibility relates to: access, readability, correlation, motivation, recognition and interaction (Carlsen et al. 2009, Hansen 2012, Hansen and Bundsgaard 2013).[2]

Multimodality is also a concept on the move and can contain different meanings. In this article we define modality as "a culturally and socially fashioned resource for representation and communication" (Kress 2003:45). That is to say, modality refers to

1 http://www.un.org/disabilities/convention/conventionfull.shtml, retrieved 22.01.2014.

2 http://www.laeremiddeltjek.dk/, retrieved 01.02.2014.

C. Stephanidis and M. Antona (Eds.): UAHCI/HCII 2014, Part II, LNCS 8514, pp. 337–348, 2014.

the way, in which a representation (a picture or a text, for example) relates to the content it represents (Hansen 2010:1). The use of multiple modalities is thus a combination of forms of representation (ibid:2). For example, a combination of modalities can be used to assist the understanding and creation of meaning in relation to a material. Løvland, D.A., underlines: "Multimodal texts combine units, which create meaning in a variety of ways. This might involve the combination of words, which we understand, because we know the verbal language system; and photography, which we understand, because we think it resembles something real." (Løvland 2010:1). This article looks at the combination of text, sound and visual forms and the significance of kinesthetics and interaction.

Nota is The Danish National Library for People with Reading Difficulties. Nota has approximately 58,000 members, most of whom are young dyslexics in education. In addition, the library has a large group of older blind or visually impaired members and people with other disabilities. However, Nota's membership represents only a section of the Danes, who have a great need for accessibility in texts. PISA (Programme for International Student Assessment) 2012 shows that 15% of Danish pupils in lower secondary education do not possess functional reading skills (Egelund 2013:7), so a lack of literacy can be considered as an obstacle to further education for a very large group of students in society as a whole.

The research in this article is not directed at specific disabilities, but at a broader approach to the concept of accessibility as a tool to enable as many people as possible to understand and make use of texts. Thus, while the motivation for investigating the concept of accessibility is of particular relevance for Nota, the findings of this article concern anyone involved in the design and accessibility of digital materials.

Within the area of research on the subject of accessibility and multimodal digital books, there is a tendency to concentrate on learning materials, perhaps due to the fact that textbook systems are particularly representative of the use of multimodal devices (Hansen 2010:5). It may also relate to a growing political focus on reading difficulties as a serious barrier to the ambition of getting more people through the education system.[3] On the basis of the issues mentioned, the article concentrates specifically on accessibility in books for school and study.

2 Review of the Literature

In what follows, the way in which the literature is methodically selected is outlined. The review is illustrated in a summary, before expanding upon relevant aspects of accessibility in multimodal learning materials.

---

[3] Research has shown a direct correlation between poor literacy skills and lack of education (Andersen 2005). The current Danish government have set an objective that 95% of young people should complete a secondary education, 60% higher education and 25% a further education (Woller 2013).

2.1 Method

The literature for this review was not found via specific databases, but from search/inclusion criteria: that the literature is in English, Danish, Norwegian or Swedish; and that the research is less than 10 years old. The review is based on articles, reports, books and a single website.

2.2 Structured Review Summary

Table 1. Summary of the literature used for the review

Author	Published	Chosen purpose	Selected findings
Arnbak	2005	To give teachers the tools to assess whether academic texts are accessible and readable for the students on vocational education.	Use of language, correlation between text elements, and layout and organisation of content are vital for accessibility.
Carlsen and Krog	2012	Presentation of an e-learning concept, which focuses on multimodal forms of expression.	Design framework which connects various didactic spaces with the use of mobile phones, QR-codes, videos, and the body.
Carlsen et al.	2009	User manuals for teachers and for publishers. How a learning material should be organised and used in order to be accessible to pupils.	There should be meta text; the learning material should include tasks, which support access to, and the learning of content; technical terms should be explained; and the link between modalities should be explicit.
Hansen	2010	Development of structure for analysis of learning materials and planning of multimodal teaching	Forms of representation, whether in terms of body, object, picture, diagram, language and symbol, are important parameters in relation to making knowledge accessible. Multimodality can be divided into: conventional and unambiguous; and creative and ambiguous. Learning materials do not make a particularly conscious use of multimodality
Hansen	2012	Create a summary of important didactic and usability parameters in relation to evaluations of accessibility of digital educational material	Didactics and usability in learning materials should be evaluated from a macro, medium and micro perspective, where micro involves didactic elements: accessibility and flexibility

Table 1. *(continued.)*

Hansen and Bundsgaard	2013	Recommendations, benchmarks and criteria in relation to digital learning materials and pedagogical practices using them	A typology of digital learning materials. The selection criterion involves open standards. Design principles relating to the learning material is focused, supports and challenges
Kirkeby et al.	2009	Create knowledge of how schools' physical contexts and IT can support teaching and work processes	Teaching and teaching environment should have a clarified structure of expectations. Examples of these include: the instructive, the dialogue-based, the nomadic, the physically active and the multifaceted environment
Kress	2003	Discussion of what literacy and multimodality is in an age with many new types of media	A modality is a socially and culturally contingent resource for representation and communication. Multimodality can support understanding and learning The importance of a clear reading path
Læremiddeltjek.dk		Didactic guidelines and criteria for analysing readability in multimodal digital learning materials (web-based)	Development of the Læremiddeltjek.dk model, which is based on expression, content, and activities in relation to the following parameters: accessibility, progression, differentiation, teacher support, correlation and legitimacy
Løvland	2010	Define multimodality on the basis of social semiotics and multimodal theory	A multimodal text creates meaning by combining different modalities. Taking into account the interaction between culture, situation and multimodal expression

2.3 The Architectural Structure of the Learning Material

Although the design and structure of multimodal digital learning materials vary, the layout, organisation and outline of materials are all important, if the reader is to know exactly where s/he is and create an overview (Arnbak 2005:57,64).

Specifically, elements such as typography, layout and logical structure play a vital role in the actual accessibility of the content of learning material (ibid.:53). We will now briefly consider these three elements.

Typography. Fonts with serifs and a point size of minimum 12 is appropriate to support the visual accessibility of a text (ibid.:53).

It is therefore recommended to use upper case letters and clear typography, such as fonts, that are specially designed for reading on a screen, including Verdana Font, Georgia Font, Font Tahoma and Trebuchet MS (cf. Rainger 2003:6). It is also recommended that the user should be able to change the style of lettering and size as required.

THIS HEADLINE HAS BEEN WRITTEN FOR DYSLEXICS

Fig. 1. 'Dyslexia', which the Dutch graphic designer Christian Boer has developed for people with reading difficulties, concentrates on the distinction between letters and comes across clearly on a screen.[4]

Layout. Layout contributes to clarity and directs the reader's attention to the relevant elements in the correct order.

It is useful to have a minimalist design (Hansen 2012:2), which cuts out superfluous information, so that the reader's attention is drawn towards relevant factors (Hansen and Bundsgaard 2013:30).[5] "Layout in an item of digital learning material helps to guide both the direction and way of reading" (Hansen 2010:3).

Associate professor in audiologopedics Arnbak denotes texts with many modalities as mixed-mode texts (Arnbak 2005:48-49). In contrast to highly text-heavy, classic "black-and-white" books, the challenges of recent tests are: "There are far too many different text elements, models, illustrations, colours and fonts on the same page. All these sources of information compete for the reader's attention." (ibid.:53).

The lack of a clear reading order of the elements in the learning material hampers the reader's assimilation of the content, thus reducing accessibility, because the reader has to work cognitively to find a meaningful reading path (cf. Kress 2003). So, even though multimodal learning materials may contain substantial learning potential, given that the many modalities provide more opportunities for understanding and making use of the content (Carlsen and Krog 2012), research also indicates that it may be an advantage, in terms of layout, to limit the amount of different expressions and forms.

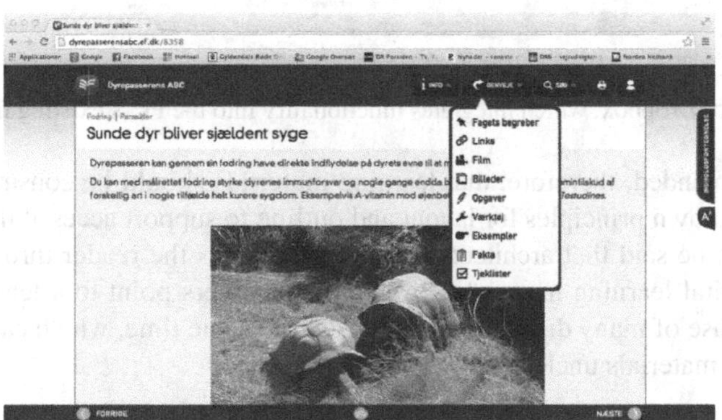

Fig. 2. Example from the publisher EF Digital's iBooks, which acts as a web page, and which has shortcut headlines for expressions, links, tasks, checklists etc. in the book.

---

4 `http://www.studiostudio.nl/en/the-designer/`, retrieved 01.02.2014.

5 Neurological research substantiates this point. As neurobiologist Mikkelsen, MD and From-Poulsen MA (Literature) say: "One recalls simply better by only reading the text than by reading it in conjunction with other audio-visual information, whether they are related to the text or not."(Mikkelsen and From-Poulsen 2011:3).

Navigation. Navigation options also constitute an important parameter, when it comes to accessibility. In this context, Hansen presents some important options: "Does it [the learning material] have a good navigation structure? Do you know where you are and where you can go?" (Hansen 2012).

It is essential that the learning material has a clear navigation structure, so that the reader is always aware of his/her place in the book. Therefore, it is recommended that the text be laid out with a thorough overview of content, and that navigation in the text be organised flexibly with good keyboard shortcuts.

Repetition. Another important parameter is familiarity, which can be used to create coherence in a text (Løvland 2010:4). Hansen and Bundsgaard use the word repetition in the sense that a learning material should both include something of the same, thus creating recognition, and expand with something different, thus creating awareness (Hansen and Bundsgaard 2013:30). Hansen uses the web service Dropbox as a good example of a system which, by reason of a recognisable construction with folders as an archive system, in conjunction with the functionality, which the system provides, is often used in the context of teaching and digital learning materials (Hansen 2012).

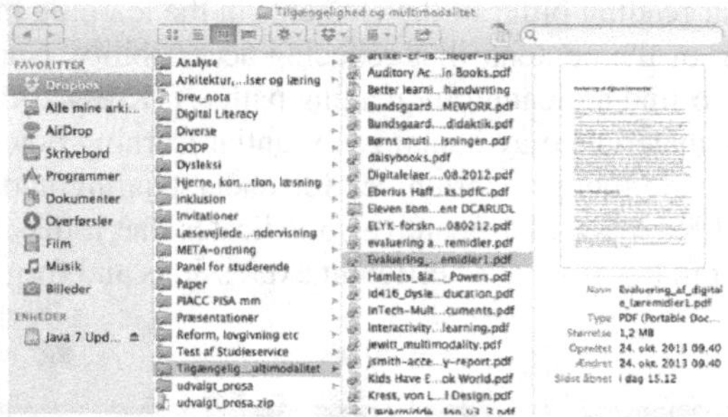

Fig. 3. Photo of Dropbox, which integrates functionality into the PC's existing filing system

It is recommended, therefore, that learning materials should be constructed on the basis of well-known principles for layout and outline to support accessibility.

Thus, it can be said that architectural structure guides the reader through the content of the digital learning material. However, researchers point to a tendency for an unconsidered use of many different modalities at the same time, which can sometimes make learning materials unclear.

2.4 Content

The extent to which the content of a book is actually accessible for the reader is closely related to its linguistic composition and complexity. The readability index LIX, introduced by the educationalist Björnsson, aims to measure a text's readability. Despite its extensive use, it is far from sufficient to assess linguistic accessibility, since it only evaluates the complexity of a text's content (cf. Arnbak 2005:51).

Textual Content. Arnbak focuses specifically on the text, including the complexity of the subjects, the text's organisation of the information, and the outline of the subjects and calls this "The text's linguistic accessibility" (ibid.: 50-52,54). In relation to this, she mentions partly the outline of text in headlines and clear paragraphs, and partly support for difficult words and concepts in relation to the placement of figures, tables and illustrations (ibid.:52). The text should be readable without excessive effort.

Scaffolding and Personalisation. Hansen introduces the concept of "scaffolding", which suggests that the text's content should be flexible, so that it can constantly be adapted to the development of the pupil (cf. Hansen 2012). In this context, scaffolding should also be understood as processual assistance and support, the building up of a ladder over time, via technology. For example, this can be done by applying some options, which the printed book does not have, such as making the book clickable, so the reader can use links for quick and easy access to glossaries etc.

Digitisation facilitates the processing of content and differentiation in relation to the individual's need for support. Hansen and Bundgaard go on to discuss "the personalisation principle" (Hansen and Bundsgaard 2013:32): "The form of inquiry and user interface of the digital learning material should be personalised or personalisable in relation to the target group." (ibid.). In addition to customising learning materials to suit the level and needs of the reader, a personalisation can motivate and create attention via the interaction between material and user. Examples of this could be: options for creating bookmarks or jotting down notes in a text.

Readability, organisation, scaffolding and personalisation are all factors to be taken into consideration and incorporated into multimodal digital learning materials in order to increase accessibility.

2.5 Software and Formats

According to research, when dealing with digital learning materials, it is essential that they can be implemented in many different browsers, operating systems and formats, which meet certain standard requirements, such as those defined by W3C.[6]

Standards and Text-To-Speech Programmes. Hansen and Bundsgaard emphasise "openness" as a key word (Hansen and Bundsgaard 2013: 28-29). Software and formats must also be open, in terms of time. This means that the latest knowledge within a given topic should be available in the digital learning material via constant updating. This is hampered, if programmes are not open to information updates.

In this context, Hansen and Bundsgaard make use of the concept of "universal text-to-speech programmes" and emphasise how important it is that material should be made compatible with these so-called universal programmes (ibid: 18.30). Here, "universal" means that programmes can read any text out loud from the user interface, regardless of the software, which is displaying it. However, there is no

6 Word Wide Web Consortium, `http://www.w3.org/Translations/WCAG20-da/`, retrieved 03.02.2014.

universal standard for how this goal can be achieved. Researchers are careful about providing specific criteria or guidelines in this area, since text-processing and text-to-speech programmes are constantly developing, thus changing the premise for decent accessibility. An important principle is, however, that the software used to implement a learning material should work, regardless of which platform one uses, and that it should be compatible with the text-to-speech software used by the user.

Intuitive Software. In line with the recommendation for a single minimalist design (cf. Hansen 2012), this is significant for accessibility, to the extent that the reader will intuitively find out how to use of the digital multimodal learning material (ibid.). According to Hansen, everything, which appears intuitive, is based on tradition, thus one can instead speak of familiarity with the technology (Raskin in Hansen 2012). Therefore, for the purpose of accessibility, it is an advantage, when software is based on widely familiar icons, design and interaction structure.

Fig. 4. On their website Apple refer to "Accessible to the core" and stress that their accessibility functions work in the same way across Apple's products and apps.[7] However, Apple is also well known for not being compatible with non-Apple products. For example, their screen reader, VoiceOver, can only be used on Apple products, and thus does not comply with Hansen and Bundsgaard's principle of universal programmes (Hansen & Bundsgaard 2013:30).

So far the article has looked at the fact that accessibility is to do with the form and organisation of the learning material, and with how the outline and support of the content increase not only access to learning, but also accessibility. Independent software also has an important role to play. In what follows the article looks at how the correlation between various modalities is important for access and assimilation of the content in a learning material. It also considers the body as a resource for learning.

2.6 Correlation between Modalities in Context

Correlation in the use of different modalities is related to accessibility (Løvland 2010:4). It is important, therefore, that the modalities such as text, graphics and sound is linked, and that the combination makes sense in relation to both purpose and user.

---

[7] https://www.apple.com/accessibility/, retrieved 01.02.2014.

Interaction. Different modalities have different potentials of meaning. For example, writing is a good modality for conveying a person's name or a road sign, whereas a piece of music is a modality, which works well, when expressing a mood or emotion. Therefore, the use of multiple modalities can increase the understanding and anchoring of the content of a learning material, thus improving accessibility. "A good multimodal text combines modalities in a way, which makes the text function optimally in relation to the various objectives, which the creator of the text may intend for the text in different contexts" (ibid.:3).

When different forms of representation, for example, image and text, are combined in a way, in which they both embody something of the same, but also elaborate upon each other and create variety, there is positive redundancy (Hansen and Bundsgaard: 30-31). Such redundancy makes pupils perform more successfully, which suggests that accessibility to the content is increased.

Fig. 5. Nota's comic strips combine sound, images and text, in an attempt to provide the reader with a coherent multimodal experience

As Løvland also stresses, it is important that one gives very careful consideration to the use of different modalities and develops a certain sensitivity in relation to the many idioms (Løvland 2010:5).

The Reader's Context. Accessibility is not just about how the modalities are combined, but also about being able to understand and interpret the use of different modalities (ibid.:5). The reader's prerequisites for identifying or assessing, when and how something is a modality depend on culture and tradition (ibid.:2-3) : "A mode of expression, which creates meaning in one context might not in another. Deliberate use of a religious colour will for example not be meaningful in a culture that does not know or take into account the conventions of this use of colour" (ibid.:1). It is precisely for this reason that Kress describes a modality as socially and culturally shaped (Kress 2003). As Hansen argues, the accessibility of the expression and content of a learning material also depends on the extent, to which the structure and complexity reflect the reader's social, cognitive and emotional skills (Hansen 2012).

When modalities are put together, it is important to reflect on how the interaction strengthens the reader's access to content. In addition, the reader's reception of the modalities depends on culture and tradition as well as on personal skills.

2.7 Kinaesthetic Dimension

Digitisation has given rise to new opportunities for linking physical activity to learning. As Hansen says, this means that the pupil's "body acts as a medium for an academic representation." (ibid.:3). This dimension can refer to both small and large physical forms of interaction, as well as the possibility of co-creating and designing a learning material by adding content oneself.

Physical Kinaesthetic Dimension. Physical kinaesthetic dimension refers to the sensation of physical movement. Such a sensation and consciousness can be important in the assimilation of new knowledge. Architect and D.Tech Kirkeby et al. use the so-called physically active playing space as an example, where an interactive IT-based glass plate on the floor connects bodily activity to concept formation, thus leading to learning (Kirkeby et al. 2009:14,52).

Fig. 6. Photo of the Vidensbrønden (Eng. "knowledge well") interactive floor[8]

Thus, in order to increase the accessibility of, and learning from the content of a digital learning material, one can benefit from connecting the learning material to physical activity.

Elements from here can be usefully incorporated in digital learning materials, where one could, for example, imagine the learning material encouraging users to move their bodies in a figure eight, in order to learn how to tie a reef knot; or otherwise connecting sensors to the subject and content of the learning material. Thus the context (also) of what is traditionally understood as a book is broken down.

Co-creative Dimension. The physical form of learning is used by getting pupils to produce videos with content relevant to their education[9], which provide them with

---

8 The picture is from Kirkeby et al. 2009:52.

9 You can see one example of such a video here `http://www.youtube.com/watch?v=Zu5SmcZuepw`, retrieved 02.02.2014.

"the opportunity to anchor their understanding in a bodily sensation. One could say that pupils are offered a wider repertoire of possibilities for learning" (Carlsen and Krog 2012:62). As Carlsen and Krog say, "The students should have access to knowledge through various channels" (ibid.:52). In this case the pupil becomes a manufacturer (ibid. 2012), in the same way that a digital book can have an interactive design, for which the reader can personally create content.

Hansen and Bundsgaard talk about the interactivity principle in their recommendations for the design of digital learning materials (Hansen and Bundsgaard 2013:32). The options generated by interactivity, such as giving response to tasks, can thus be described as means of anchoring the understanding of content.

3 Conclusion

This article has presented research perspectives on accessibility to provide an insight into a new and broader concept of accessibility, related to multimodal digital learning materials. It could lead to some general principles for accessibility applicable to everyone, regardless of age and stage of education. These principles are summarised below.

- The architectural structure must be included in the digital book's content.
- There should be the option of adapting form to suit the needs of the reader.
- The interaction between modalities should be considered in relation to the purpose and the reader's skills and socio-cultural framework for understanding.
- Software should be open and independent.
- It should be possible to anchor assimilation and understanding of content in a kinaesthetic way, with the benefit of involving the pupil as a manufacturer.

Thus in many ways there is a difference between the concept of accessibility in the printed learning material and that in the multimodal learning material. Options to customise the content and structure to the reader's context and capacity in crucial ways can lead to more people gaining access to the content and relevance of the learning material. But it is crucial constantly to explore, debate, and examine for evidence the principles of accessibility in multimodal digital learning materials.

References

1. Andersen, D.: Kan unge med dårlige læsefærdigheder gennemføre en ungdomsuddannelse? The Danish National Institute of Social Research (2005)
2. Apple Accessibility, `https://www.apple.com/accessibility/` (retrieved February 01, 2014)
3. Arnbak, E.: Faglig læsning – fra læseproces til læreproces, 1. ed., 2. imp. Gyldendal, København (2005)
4. Carlsen, D., Gissel, S.T., Kabel, K.: Læsbare læremidler EUD. EMU.dk (2009)

5. Carlsen, D., Krog, A.B.: Kurt og Kubik-knægtene. Om brug af QR-koder i udviklingen af et didaktisk design for undervisningen i arbejdsmiljø på en erhvervsskole. Knowledge Lab, Odense (2012)
6. Dyslexie Font for Dyslexics, http://www.studiostudio.nl/en/the-designer/ (retrieved February 01, 2014)
7. Egelund, N.: PISA 2012. Undersøgelsen – En sammenfatning. KORA (2013)
8. Hansen, T.I.: Læremiddelanalyse – multimodalitet som analysekategori. Viden om læsning 7, 1–5 (2010)
9. Hansen, T.I.: Evaluering af digitale læremidler. Læremiddel.dk (2012)
10. Hansen, T.I., Bundsgaard, J.: Kvaliteter ved digitale læremidler og ved pædagogiske praksisser med digitale læremidler. Ministry of Education (2013)
11. Kress, G.: Literacy in the New Media Age. Routledge, London (2003)
12. Læremiddeltjek, http://www.laeremiddeltjek.dk (retrieved February 01, 2014)
13. Løvland, A.: Multimodalitet og multimodale tekster. Viden om læsning 7, 1–5 (2010)
14. Mikkelsen, J.D., From-Poulsen, L.: Dum, dummere, internet? Chronicle. Berlingske (2011)
15. Rainger, P.: A Dyslextic Perspective on e-Content Accessibility. TechDis. (2003)
16. UN. Convention on the Rights of Persons with Disabilities http://www.un.org/disabilities/convention/conventionfull.shtml (retrieved January 22 2014)
17. Video. Ind- og udstigning, http://www.youtube.com/watch?v=Zu5SmcZuepw (retrieved February 2, 2014)
18. Woller, H.: Vejledning i politisk perspektiv. Ministry of Education (2013)
19. World Wide Web Consortium (W3C). Web Content Accessibility Guidelines (WCAG) 2.0, http://www.w3.org/Translations/WCAG20-da/ (retrieved February 3, 2014)

Accessible Open Educational Resources for Students with Disabilities in Greece: They are Open to the Deaf

Vassilis Kourbetis and Konstantinos Boukouras

Institute of Educational Policy, Athens, Greece
{Vk,kboukouras}@iep.edu.gr

Abstract. The development Open Educational Resources is the main outcome of the project "Design and Development of Accessible Educational & Instructional Material for Students with Disabilities". A portion of the deliverables of the project that mainly concerns Deaf students, a population that is usually under presented, is presented in this article. The Collection of Educational Resources, the Bilingual Hybrid books and the online videos with interactive text navigation cover mainly elementary school needs of Deaf students. Making textbooks accessible, as Open Educational Resources, by all students including the Deaf, on a national level meets the needs of all the students in the country by creating equal opportunities for learning, participating and accessing the curriculum.

Keywords: deaf children, Greek Sign Language, open educational resources.

1 Introduction

The development, availability and use of Open Educational Resources (OERs) offers numerous opportunities to reshape special and general education.

OERs is an umbrella term used to define any type of educational material that is in the public domain or uses an open license. The main characteristic of these open materials is that anyone can legally and freely copy, use, adapt and re-share them. OERs vary from textbooks to curricula, syllabi, lecture notes, assignments, tests, projects, audio, video and animation [1].

OERs are usually made available under licenses that allow free use, re-use and sharing in order to improve accessibility and foster equity of education for all children. OERs are developed principally for children with disabilities in special educational situations. The rapid expansion of OERs initiatives and the millions of learners they attract is interpreted as an indicator of a forthcoming revolution in education and learning [2].

This paper describes a project that adapts OERs, for specific learning needs. The project is entitled: *"Design and Development of Accessible Educational & Instructional Material for Students with Disabilities"*. The main goals of the project are to efficiently increase access to lectures, textbooks, video, etc. for students in both special and general education.

C. Stephanidis and M. Antona (Eds.): UAHCI/HCII 2014, Part II, LNCS 8514, pp. 349–357, 2014.

The project follows the principles and strategies of differentiation support, part of the principles of Universal Design for Learning (UDL). UDL promotes information and knowledge representation in a variety of ways, especially curricula design and development, as well as methods, material and evaluation procedures [3-5].

In this paper focus has been mainly placed on the development of accessible educational & instructional material for deaf students. Similar projects for the Deaf have been developed recently and made available free of charge via the web [6] or are web-based video lectures on demand [7].

The deliverables of the above project have been developed through peer-based learning, collaboration and individual creativity using rapidly changing information and communication technologies (ICT). The deliverables include production of publicly funded educational resources incorporating universal design to ensure accessibility for all users with special educational needs. Designing for accessibility includes the inclusion of subtitles, interactive transcripts, Easy Read text, Greek Sign Language, symbols, pictograms and audio description using human voiceover. The material available on the web is not merely uploaded as a form of digital library; it includes the capability of educators to choose and adapt these resources so as to be fully accessible for all students.

In what follows, we will present a portion of the deliverables of this project that mainly concerns Deaf students, a population that is usually under represented. Specifically, the focus of this paper will be:

- Collection of educational resources
- Hybrid books
- Online videos with text navigation.

2 Collection of Educational Resources

Comprehensive, up-to-date information on more than 350 educational resources has been collected for the project. Each educational resource has been examined and described according to the following content structure: general information about the resource (e.g., author, publication date, copyright, availability etc.), brief descriptions and educational information (e.g., subject area, topic, target group, educational usage).

Digital educational resources for special educational needs are widely distributed through the web within the framework of this project. All resources can be downloaded, used in their original version or modified through the structure of OERs in order to meet a wide range of special educational needs. The project is also designed for students who are visually impaired, are in the Autism Spectrum Disorders, have motor or mental disabilities, or have attention deficit disorders in addition to the Deaf and hard of hearing.

The educational resources for the Deaf fulfill a number of requirements regarding content, use and accessibility of educational materials by Deaf and hard of hearing students.

With reference to the use and the accessibility of educational materials, there is a generalized trend of using videotext in multimedia format which is narrated and expressed by native signers, focusing mainly on videotext analysis of Greek Sign Language (GSL) stories, narratives, and general educational context.

The resources comprises of 23 distinct support materials; 12 of these educational materials were developed for the learning of Greek sign language and 9 for bilingual (Greek - GSL) education. All educational materials were developed from 1999 to 2013 and are available for reproduction, or use.

Initially, the first products (two out of the 12) were developed to be recorded and reproduced using analogue and digital video tapes. Subsequently, the remaining materials were produced in a CD-ROM format. It is important to note that the first DVD-ROM created in Greece was the bilingual (GSL - Greek) dictionary of Greek Sign Language, containing more than 3.000 signs and also lexicographic and linguistic information about GSL. All video productions have been digitalized and are becoming gradually available on the web, for example see [8].

These resources cover mainly elementary school needs but also include high school needs. All materials are available in a multimedia format in CD-ROM that can be used by individuals or groups for learning and instructional purposes. The content is presented in sign language by native signers, professional interpreters or the collaboration of both.

Most of the titles can be used for learning GSL both as a first and second language [9]. Specifically, five titles have been developed in GSL and three of them have also been interpreted into spoken Greek. Some of the materials are trilingual (with written English as the third language) for their potential use in other countries. Therefore, they can be used for comparative analysis in documenting various signed languages. The materials cover different content vocabulary; namely, specialized terminology (math & science) and vocabulary about nature (e.g. Biology), ICT and political content.

The main purpose of making the collection available as an OER of all existing educational materials is for the teaching and learning of GSL as a first language, using GSL to learn Greek as a second language and using GSL to teach academic content.

3 Hybrid Books

A recent study [10] of dyslexic children in Denmark showed that "The positive correlation between use of audiobooks, well-being in school, reading frequency and time spent on homework combined with the high amount of hybrid reading, suggest that hybrid audio books are in many ways an obvious candidate for a standard format for accessible schoolbooks for people with reading difficulties" (p.211). Still, questions regarding the appropriate formats for different end users or contexts, the use of speech synthesis, typography and structure remain unanswered.

A similar technology used by the Masaryk University known as "Hybrid Book" [11] was used as a model for the creation of study materials aimed at users with different disabilities; that is, visual, hearing, motor, mental and others

Our initial focus group consists of students with disabilities attending the first two grades of primary school. As a consequence, the format that has been developed in order to cover the educational needs of this age group follows the original text format of the national curriculum books.

3.1 Development of Hybrid Books as Bilingual Applications for Deaf Students

The multimedia electronic form of the ***Hybrid books*** (either in the form of a single copy or a web application) combines the presentation of the original printed book in a video using GSL, the meaning in subtitles overlaying the screen presentation of the GSL video, ***videos with text navigation (see Online videos with text navigation)*** as well as the voicing of the text by a native speaker. The data in multimedia PDF, video and audio files will be available as independent files for multiple uses.

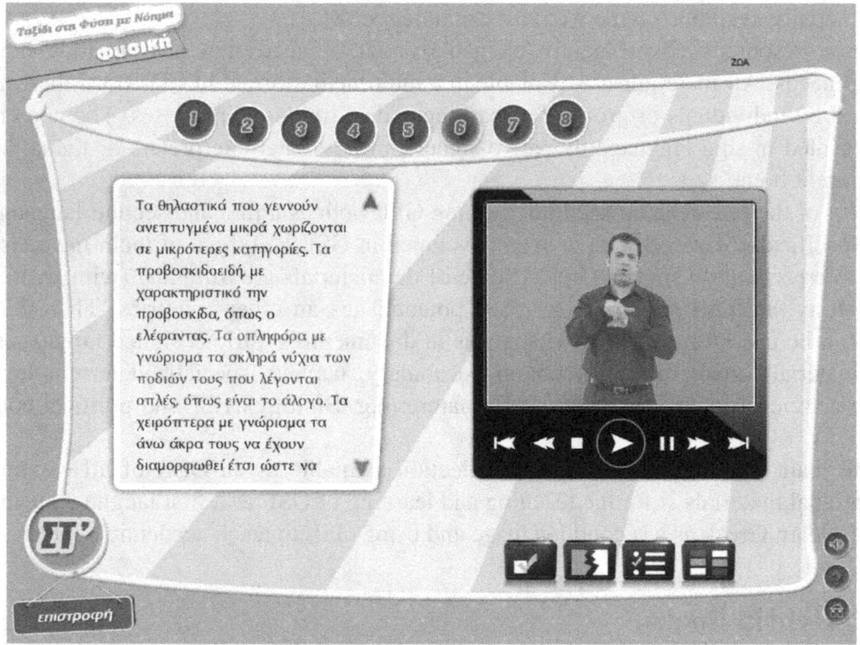

Fig. 1. A bilingual science hybrid book

Major attention has been paid to the relationship between written and sign language text, so that the end-product will be used effectively in bilingual educational practices (Fig. 1).

The signed text is in accordance with the Greek text at a word, phrase or sentence level. The quality of the text in GSL is the most important aspect of accessibility and will play a key role in the evaluation of the end-product. The translation of a text in GSL can be either very close to the original structure, interpreting the meaning, or a free translation. Within the same textbooks, the authors sometimes either look for content comprehension or emphasize learning vocabulary, Modern Greek grammar or the acquisition of phonological awareness. If the objective is to understand the text, then the signers - interpreters may follow a more liberal approach. If the objective is grammatical, syntactic or phonological awareness, then interpretation mostly follows the original source.

It is made evident from all the previous productions that signing Greek texts is an extremely demanding and difficult task. The signing of the texts is done in cooperation with experienced native signers, deaf tutors or consultants (all fluent in Greek) on the one hand and professional interpreters of GSL on the other. These two categories of professionals work collaboratively in order to achieve an accurate bilingual translation. When choosing consultants and interpreters, the subject knowledge, knowledge of the target group and experience in educational interpreting are also important factors and are taken into account.

As far as the process of translating Greek texts to GSL is concerned, the following methodology is proposed. First, the text is divided into smaller sections, so that it can be easily memorized and explained in front of the camera. Second, the GSL interpreter who is a native speaker of Greek will translate the text into GSL. Finally, the native signer and the interpreter will watch the signed text twice or three times and compare the signed text with the Greek text. It is emphasized that, during the conversion of textbooks in accessible educational materials, signed text is crucial because the efficiency of GSL is the core of the project.

4 Online Videos with Text Navigation

In the past decade publishing sign language videos has been a widely accepted and effective practice. However, searching the video content is very difficult and has proven to have questionable effectiveness.

Various technologies have been combined for the development of interactive text for video including the use of CaptionBox Interactive transcripts [12], the EdX open source platform created by Harvard and MIT [13], the YouTube video capabilities and numerous other plugins.

In our attempt to design an easy to navigate and search sign language video for educational uses, a true interactive educational tool for interactive video transcripts has resulted. Specifically, through interactive video transcripts viewers can refer to the transcript as the video plays. Viewers are able to navigate to different parts of the video by clicking on the text. Namely, viewers are offered the choice of selecting parts of interest, moving backwards and forwards, searching for signed quotes within the video and modifying its quality.

In order to implement the International Convention on the Rights of Persons with Disabilities (Public Law 4074/11-4-2012) for developing integration policies and practices in the Greek educational system and the use of Information and Communications Technology (ICT), and in particular interactive applications, within our project, a supportive interactive open source application customized to the needs of Greek deaf students was developed. The development process consisted of using and adjusting an existing open source media archive platform, which incorporates interactive video transcripts, with concomitant use of the Greek Sign Language. Such applications are necessary to access the material of the project and specifically to maximize the efficient use of customized textbooks in the first two elementary grades for deaf students.

4.1 Design Approach

For deaf students it is extremely important to introduce the use of information and communications technology on all levels of education [7]. It has been suggested that signed language videos added to text hyperlinks improve Web search efficiency for Deaf Signers [14]. Viewers' perceived understanding significantly improves when using transcripts over captions, even if they were less easy to track [15]. The "SignOn" project [6] encapsulates interactive video transcript in an application to enable sign language users to use written English for international communication via the Internet.

The application has to fulfill some basic criteria, it has to be: licensed as open source, quick and easy to navigate, easily adapted to the needs of deaf students and able to use the content of the educational material in Greek Sign Language (GSL) with the interactive subtitles. Flexible customization and database search and support of the uploaded material are also necessary.

Bearing the above guidelines in mind the *pan.do/ra* platform [16], was chosen for the development of the application, which is an open source media archive platform that allows management of large decentralized collections of video, creation of metadata and of time-based annotations collaboratively and serving an archive as a desktop-class web application. The platform is based on OxJS [17], a javascript library is used to build pan.do/ra's frontend and it is consisted of both javascript and python files.

4.2 Development of the System

The pan.do/ra platform was installed at an Ubuntu 12.04.3 LTS 64 bit system and configured to run on nginx webserver. The whole platform content was translated into Greek, by editing the javascript and configuration files and the new language was added to the platform's language options. Also the layout of the platform was edited by enlarging and customizing the menus and fonts in order to meet deaf student's needs. Additionally the initial categories were changed to reflect the educational material. The platform offers the possibility for the viewers to sign up but since this wasn't desired or needed, it was disabled.

The application is free and accessible to all interested or involved in the educational and learning process of deaf children and other students. Access to the platform will be available from the website [18]. The application provides easy navigation to the videotaped content by choosing timed subtitles. The educational content is attributed both to natural voice of the speaker, the natural speed of sign language and the associated built-in video captions which can be read by the user.

The interactive application concerns a) the use of interactive subtitles and b) promoting the creation and enrichment of an online library archive- depository.

Videos with Interactive Subtitles. The *pan.do/ra* platform can accept videos in .webm or .mp4 format, which are uploaded and then automatically converted to .webm format (in case the uploaded file is in .mp4 format) at the server. The uploaded videos are stored on the local server and the reproduction is made from the same server without using a central video service like YouTube. This offers more autonomy and is not limiting our bandwidth as well as the quality and the size of downloaded files. Furthermore, the upload time of the added material is much less since it's done through the local network. The uploaded video then can be freely downloaded within the video player in .webm format.

The platform's embedded video player offers various features, such as automatic resizing, full screen play and automatic replay of a scene. The video view quality ranges from 240p to 1080p. Also the video timeline can be shown beneath the video in four different formats (Anti-Alias, Slit-Scan, Keyframes and Waveform). The video subtitles can be uploaded in .srt format and the interactive transcripts are synchronized and shown along the video automatically. The user can navigate through the video by clicking on the corresponding transcript. Along with the transcript the uploader can also insert other information like keywords and notes. Moreover, the transcripts are searchable and the matching information is highlighted. The subtitles can be seen along with the video (Fig. 2). Another feature is the ability to copy the video URL at a specific time and use this address for video playback from the time it was copied. Finally, the entire application with the material can be easily transported and installed in schools or locations that do not have network access, operating on a local basis. This feature is of great importance to rural or island schools in Greece.

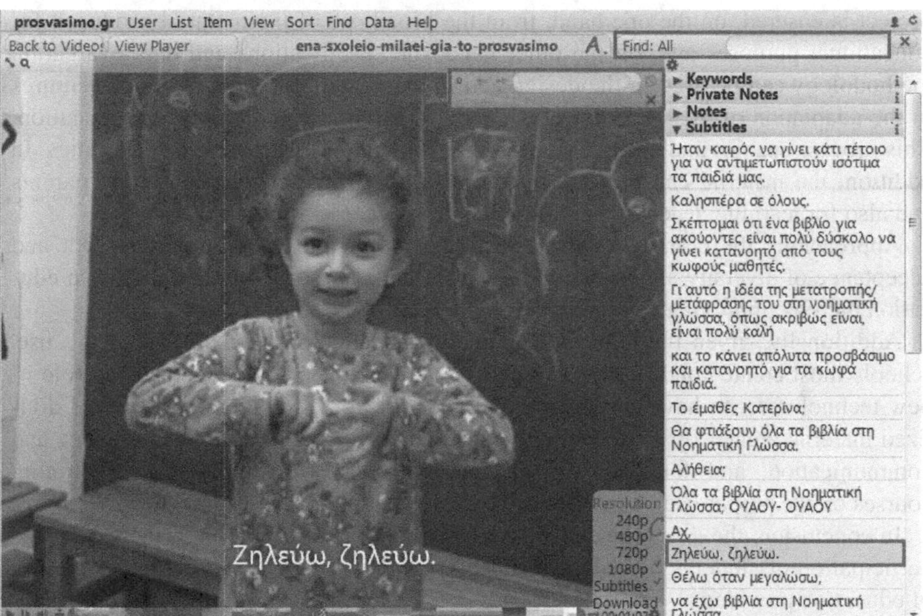

Fig. 2. Interactive video transcript. A: search database, B: search transcript text, C: the text reflects the current position of the video. Clicking on the other subtitles moves the video to another position. The above interface has been translated to Greek as well.

Online Media Archive. The videos uploaded to pan.do/ra create a digital database that it is easily searchable and customizable. It consists of a repository of audiovisual material that can accept also documents (pdf, word) which can be combined and connected to specific videos, creating thus a comprehensive database. The system is using the postgres database system. The interactive application as a digital library provides the ability to archive and search the deposited material by several criteria: thematically and geographically (showing them on a map) or by calendar, with the option to view a histogram of the deposited files. All accessible text material has printing capabilities and data (documents, audio and video) are distributed automatically during upload to independent files and directories on the server.

5 Conclusions

This innovative action of making textbooks accessible, such as the Open Educational Resources, by all students including the Deaf, on a national level meets the needs of all students by creating equal opportunities for learning, participating and accessing the curriculum.

Deaf students gain access to knowledge and information and sign language learning is promoted, increasing their involvement and supporting their ability to understand and process the incoming information.

The viability and functionality of the educational material developed within the project is ensured, on the one hand, from the broad use of the material produced for educational purposes and, on the other hand, the specifications and data evaluation methodology can be used in the design and implementation of other similar ventures in the adaptation of textbooks for all subjects in all grades of compulsory education. This process enables and ensures accessibility for students with various disabilities. In addition, the material can be used by students, teachers, school counselors, parents and also for learning, teaching and training purposes.

Approaching the curriculum through accessible textbooks, promotes respect and acceptance of diversity and, more widely, differentiated pedagogy and inclusive education thereby improving the quality of education in Greece.

Additionally, given the rapid development of technology and its increasing use, schools must create conditions that will allow each student to understand the role of new technologies, to have access to them, and to learn using them. The use of digitized material creates opportunities for expanded use of information technologies and communication, and familiarizing students with these or implementing training courses on the proper use of the material by teachers in the classroom.

In conclusion, the development of accessible material contributes to increasing the participation of students in inclusive education and moreover, improving the quality of education provided.

Acknowledgments. This project has been co-financed by the European Union (European Social Fund – ESF) and Greek national funds through the Operational Program "Education and Lifelong Learning" of the National Strategic Reference Framework (NSRF) under the project: "Design and Development of Accessible Educational & Instructional Material for Students with Disabilities".

References

1. UNESCO: Guidelines for Open Educational Resources (OER) in Higher Education. UNESCO Archives (2012)
2. Tuomi, I.: Open educational resources and the transformation of education. European Journal of Education 48(1), 58–78 (2013)
3. Blamires, M.: Universal design for learning: Re-establishing differentiations as part of the inclusion agenda? Support for Learning, 14(4), 158-163 (1999)
4. CAST: Universal Design for Learning Guidelines version 2.0. Wakefield, MA: Author (2011)
5. Hockings, C., Brett, P., Terentjevs, M.: Making a difference-inclusive learning and teaching in higher education through open educational resources. Distance Education 33(2), 237–252 (2012)
6. Hilzensauer, M., Dotter, F.: SignOn, a model for teaching written language to deaf people. In: 2011 IST-Africa Conference Proceedings (2011)
7. Debevc, M., Peljhan, Ž.: The role of video technology in on-line lectures for the deaf. Disability and Rehabilitation 26(17), 1048–1059 (2004)
8. The Deaf Tree story, `http://www.youtube.com/watch?v=vOVW59O6MBQ`
9. Kourbetis, V.: Documenting Greek Sign Language. In: The 2nd Symposium in Applied Sign Linguistics, Centre for Deaf Studies, University of Bristol, Bristol (2011), `http://www.bris.ac.uk/deaf/english/news/2011/97.html`
10. Moe, S., Wright, M.: Can Accessible Digital Formats Improve Reading Skills, Habits and Educational Level for Dyslectic Youngsters? In: Stephanidis, C., Antona, M. (eds.) UAHCI 2013, Part III. LNCS, vol. 8011, pp. 203–212. Springer, Heidelberg (2013)
11. Hladík, P., Gůra, T.: The hybrid book – one document for all in the latest development. In: Miesenberger, K., Karshmer, A., Penaz, P., Zagler, W. (eds.) ICCHP 2012, Part I. LNCS, vol. 7382, pp. 18–24. Springer, Heidelberg (2012)
12. CaptionBox Interactive transcripts, `http://speakertext.com`
13. EdX, `http://www.edx.org`
14. Fajardo, I., Parra, E., Cañas, J.J.: Do sign language videos improve web navigation for deaf signer users? Journal of Deaf Studies and Deaf Education 15(3), 242–262 (2010)
15. Kushalnagar, R.S., Lasecki, W.S., Bigham, J.P.: Captions versus transcripts for online video content. Paper presented at the W4A 2013 - International Cross-Disciplinary Conference on Web Accessibility (2013)
16. pan.do/ra open source media archive platform, `http://pan.do/ra`
17. OxJS javascript library for web applications, `https://oxjs.org/`
18. Project "Design and Development of Accessible Educational & Instructional Material for Students with Disabilities", `http://www.prosvasimo.gr`

Measuring the Effect of First Encounter with Source Code Entry for Instruction Set Architectures Using Touchscreen Devices: Evaluation of Usability Components

Mihael Kukec[1], Vlado Glavinic[2], and Sandi Ljubic[3]

[1] Medimurje University of Applied Sciences in Cakovec,
Bana Josipa Jelacica 22a, 40000 Cakovec, Croatia
mihael.kukec@mev.hr

[2] Faculty of Electrical Engineering and Computing, University of Zagreb,
Unska 3, 10000 Zagreb, Croatia
vlado.glavinic@fer.hr

[3] Faculty of Engineering, University of Rijeka,
Vukovarska 58, 51000 Rijeka, Croatia
sandi.ljubic@riteh.hr

Abstract. In this paper we address the possibility of writing program code for instruction set architectures using the touchscreen as the input device. Instruction set architecture is the common name for a collection of resources computer engineers use when developing code at the hardware level. One of the most important subsets among these resources are instructions which programmers use to create algorithms. Students enrolled in computer engineering curricula are trained to develop such solutions, using standard personal computers equipped with keyboard and mouse, thus providing them with a high level usability working environment. As technology progress has enabled the introduction of mobile platforms in the educational process, touchscreen based m-learning becomes a viable tool. To that end, in our previous research we developed a specific keyboard VMK that supports entry of assembly language code, which is based on mnemonic keys, with the aim to achieve a better efficiency of assembly coding. In the present paper we present the outcome of an improved empirical research targeting the comparison of VMK and the standard QWERTY keyboard. The results thus obtained show improved results of key usability attributes of efficiency and subjective satisfaction.

Keywords: Technology enhanced learning, usability, mobile devices, touchscreen keyboards.

1 Introduction

Though not lacking the computing power to leverage mobile learning principles [1–3] to execute complex learning systems [4, 5], mobile devices are restrained by inherent usability issues [6, 7] which are especially manifest when inputting text [8].

C. Stephanidis and M. Antona (Eds.): UAHCI/HCII 2014, Part II, LNCS 8514, pp. 358–369, 2014.

As already noted elsewhere, virtual on-screen keyboards are "slow, uncomfortable, and inaccurate" [9] and "even expert typists have to look down at their fingers instead of feeling for the home row keys to situate their hands" [9]. Writing a small message can easily turn to a rather daunting mission hence writing computer software code on a touchscreen may seem like a rather impossible task.

Still, programming languages have considerably simpler grammar rules and a much smaller vocabulary than natural languages. Furthermore, assembly programming languages, which are the ones used at the Instruction Set Architecture (ISA) level, consist of simple commands (instructions) represented by appropriate mnemonics. Instructions are executed sequentially, in the order specified by the program, and the responsibility of the programmer is to create this logical sequence of instructions. Typically, creating an assembly language program involves the use of a text editor for inputting instruction names (operators) and related operands, each in a separate line. To reduce the amount of effort the user has to apply when writing assembly language programs on touchscreen devices, we have devised a rather simple approach [10], which is based on the reduction of the number of taps needed to input the instruction mnemonic using a virtual mnemonic keyboard (VMK), where each key represents one mnemonic (Fig. 1.). As assembly programs usually abound with mnemonic-only instructions, writing such program code usually reduces on tapping mnemonic (soft) keys mostly, eventually providing both efficiency and correctness of code entry.

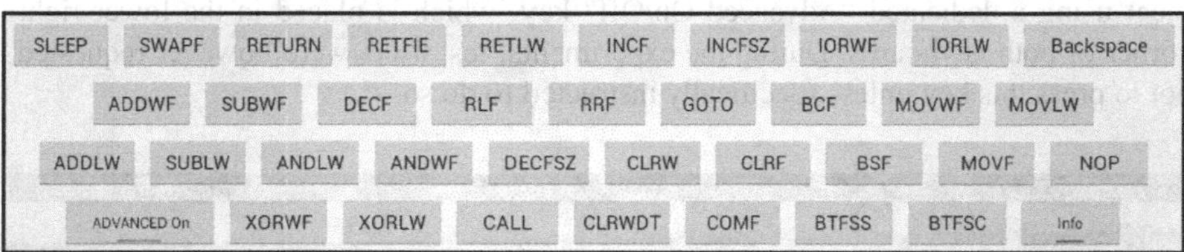

Fig. 1. Mnemonic keyboard consisting of 35 keys ("soft" buttons), with each key representing an assembly language instruction

2 Related Work

Many authors have contributed to the design of virtual keyboards and accompanying interaction styles for touchscreen devices. Virtual keyboards displayed on device screens are software generated, hence they have the ability to be transformed, modified and redesigned in many ways. The primary interaction technique for classic QWERTY virtual keyboards is direct touch. Zhai introduced a major advancement for faster writing, called *Shape Writing*, by using a sliding gesture technique [11]. Other researchers and companies developed similar techniques (e.g. *Swype* [12] and *SlideIT* [13]). The traditional concept of keyboard has also been abandoned in the Dasher project [14], which selects "flying letters" in a 2D space using a zoom-and-point interaction. To the best of our knowledge, however, no research on ISA code entry has tackled the issues we address in this paper, as all of the known solutions utilize algorithms and prediction techniques suitable for general text entry such as writing e-mails or SMSs, which makes them not exactly the most suitable for ISA code entry.

3 Design of Virtual Mnemonic Keyboard and Testing Tool

When creating a VMK (see Fig. 1.), we have based on the Microchip reduced instruction set computer architecture for PIC10, PIC12, and PIC16 microcontroller family [15], see Fig. 1. The instruction set consists of 35 mnemonics, their lengths being between 3 and 6 characters (letters) with an average of 4.6, while most of them are 5 letters long. Therefore, we could hypothesize that a VMK will decrease the time needed for assembly language program entry approximately up to a factor of 5 (i.e. replacing five taps with just one). However, there are additional aspects of human perceptual, cognitive and motoric subsystem [16] which influence the effects of using a VMK.

To evaluate our assumption, we have created a testing tool, which is an Android mobile device application, as shown in Fig. 2. and Fig. 3. The application divides the screen into two parts. The testing tool displays instructions randomly selected from a previously generated list, which the user has to type, in the upper part of the screen (approx. half of the screen real estate), while the keyboard resides in its lower half. Users entering the ISA code can switch between these keyboard layouts at every moment using a dedicated "Advanced On/Off" key, which is placed in the lower right corner of both keyboards. During the experiments, test users were however requested not to press this key unless specifically instructed to do so.

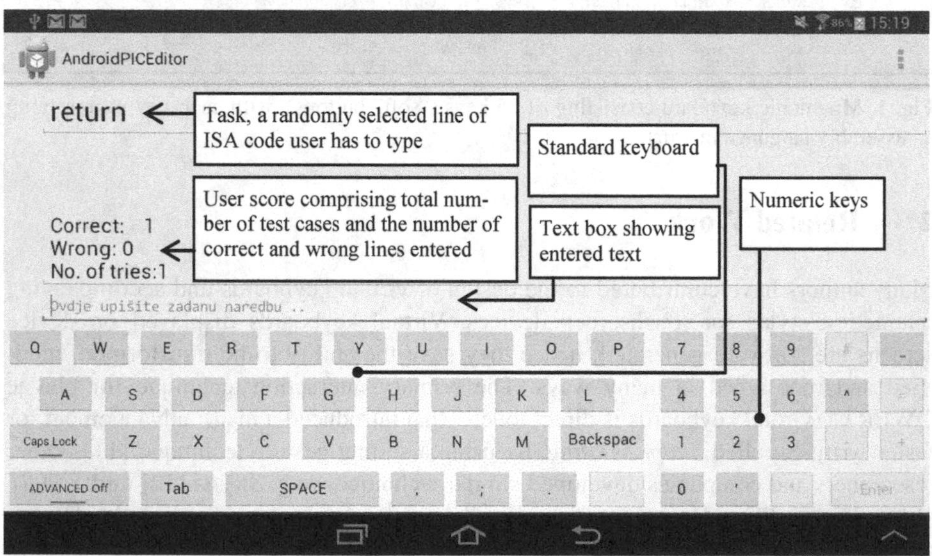

Fig. 2. Mobile device application for measuring ISA instructions reaction time and typing speed when using a standard keyboard layout. The classic QUERTY keyboard is on the left using approx. 2/3 of the available space, while its numeric part is on the right.

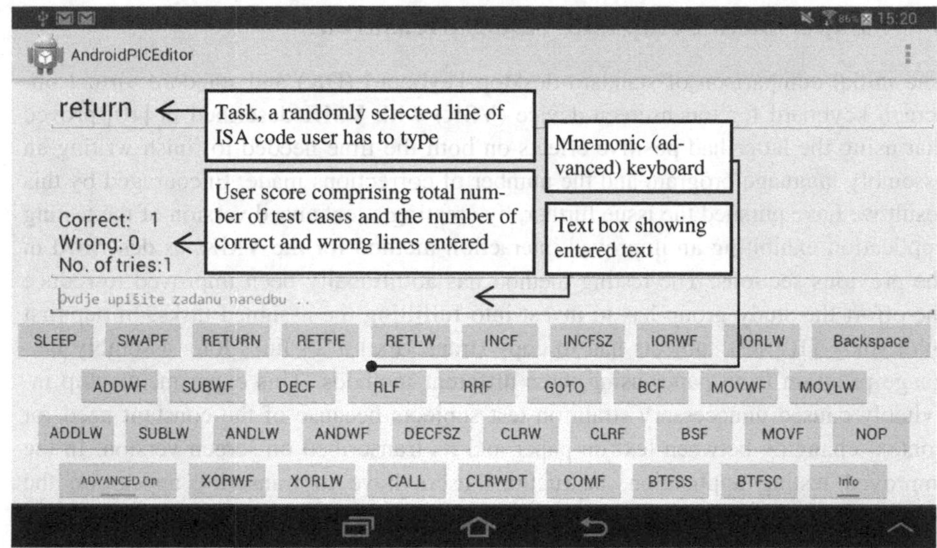

Fig. 3. Mobile device application for testing reaction time and speed of typing ISA instructions when using a mnemonic (advanced) keyboard layout. Each ISA instruction is on the keyboard represented by one key (soft button).

In the advanced mode ISA program code entry (activated with the "Advanced On/Off" key), the testing tool automatically switches between standard virtual keyboard (VSK) and VMK: the user starts typing an ISA code line using VMK, while the keyboard change from VMK to VSK is automatically performed after keying in the instruction mnemonic, as it can be seen in Fig. 4. Such behavior is necessary as each ISA code line comprises of the instruction mnemonic and (possibly) the accompanying operands which can be e.g. (binary, hexadecimal, octal or decimal) numbers, register names, labels etc.

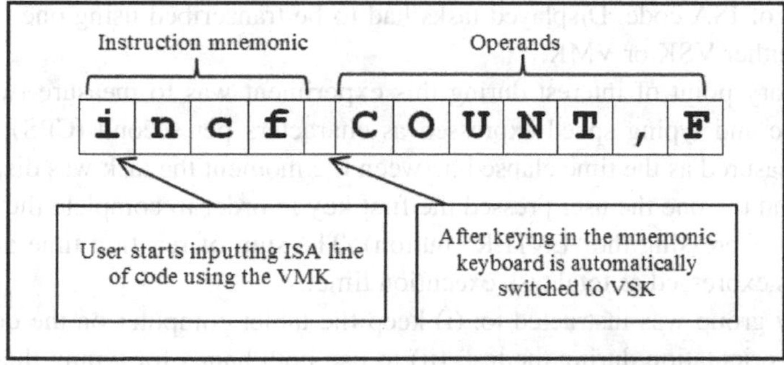

Fig. 4. Automatic switching between VSK and VMK

4 Experiment Setup and Values Measured

The initial comparison of standard desktop keyboard (DK) and standard virtual on-screen keyboard for touchscreen device (VSK) with VMK described in [10] proved that using the latter had positive effects on both the time needed to finish writing an assembly language program and the number of corrections made. Encouraged by this result we have pursued the issue further, by creating a, enhanced version of the testing application exhibiting an improved interaction method for the VMK, as described in the previous sections. The testing method has additionally been improved to reduce the effort the study group has to invest into fulfilling the assigned tasks. In our first pilot study [10] test subjects had to copy (transcribe) a 24 lines long assembly language program from paper using three different methods. This experiment setup inevitably caused unnecessary strain on test subjects because of the constant need for context changing between text on paper and its transcribed on-screen version. In the improved testing application, instructions users have to transcribe appear on the screen above the virtual keyboard she/he is using (as shown in Figs. 2 and 3), thus enabling her/him to remain focused on the task. Testing of the desktop keyboard has been dropped from this experiment.

Our study group comprised out of eight students, all male, averaging 20 years of age, that have fulfilled all the requirements for the *Computer Architecture* course at the BSc level; this allowed us to regard them as being acquainted with both the assembly language for the Microchip 14 bit instruction microcontroller family and the associated tools. The mobile device used for testing was an Android tablet computer with a 10" screen and resolution of 1280x800 pixels (Toshiba AT100-100). The study group was briefly introduced to the testing application by demonstration, while none of the participants was allowed to use it before testing actually took place. This ensured that this was their first encounter with testing application.

During the experiment, the testing application presented test subjects a continuous sequence of tasks, with each individual task consisting of one line of ISA code displayed on the screen. Tasks were randomly selected from a list of previously prepared typical lines of ISA code. Displayed tasks had to be transcribed using one of the two keyboards, either VSK or VMK.

Our primary point of interest during this experiment was to measure two values, reaction time and typing speed expressed as characters per second (CPS). Reaction time was measured as the time elapsed between the moment the task was displayed on the screen and the one the user pressed the first key in order to complete the task (i.e. the moment of pressing the "ENTER" button). The sum of reaction time and typing duration was expressed as total task execution time.

The study group was instructed to: (i) keep the tablet computer on the desk in the "landscape" orientation during the test, (ii) to use both hands for typing the ISA program code as test users would do using the classic hardware keyboard, (iii) be fast and accurate while performing the test tasks, (iv) not to rest between test tasks in order to complete as much tasks as possible. The latter request is of most importance for measuring reaction time. As a new task is displayed immediately after completing the previous one, it is very important that the members of the study group do not take a rest between tasks.

5 Results and Discussion

The study group did not have any previous experience with VMK, hence we could consider this to be the worst case scenario evaluation where learnability, satisfaction and efficiency component of usability have to be tested [17].

The testing application uses the system clock (class *android.os.SystemClock*) to retrieve time data, by executing the related system call *System.nanoTime()*. The retrieved values were converted to milliseconds and logged into a comma separated values (CSV) formatted file. After collecting data files from all of the devices used in the experiment, the CPS value was calculated for each task using ordinary spreadsheet software. Data was analyzed using IBM's Statistical Product and Service Solutions Software (IBM SPSS).

5.1 Correlation of Reaction Time and Typing Speed

The primary goal of the study is to assess the impact of users' first encounter with the VMK. Due to the lack of tactile feedback, virtual keyboards displayed on touchscreen devices create a number of difficulties to their users [8, 9], hence the reduction of the number of keystrokes per character [18] (KSPC) should help users to enter the program code in a more efficient way. Still, the effects of learnability and memorability for a new keyboard and its layout cannot be neglected. To investigate this issue further, we have examined the correlation of CPS and task reaction times for both VSK and VMK.

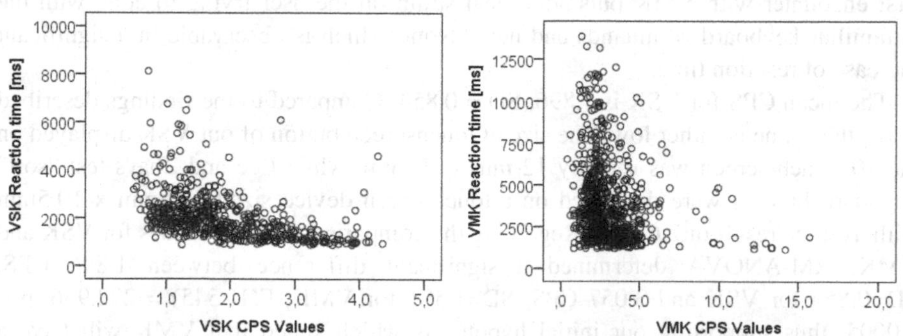

Fig. 5. Scatter plots of CPS values and reaction times for VSK and VMK

We found a moderate negative correlation between CPS and reaction time for the standard keyboard (VSK): r(544) = –0.461, p<0.0005 (see the left scatter plot on Fig. 5.). As for the mnemonic keyboard (VMK), we have found a small correlation between CPS and reaction time, r(544) = –0.219, p<0.0005 (see the right scatter plot on Fig. 5.). The coefficient of determination in the first case is 21.2%, while in the second case it is 4.8%. Both correlations are negative, which was expected, as more proficient users will have higher CPS and lower reaction time. Undoubtedly, users are more proficient in the case of VSK, hence this proficiency is observable as a higher correlation determination of VSK. On the other hand, correlation determination between CPS values and reaction times is considerably lower for VMK, since users have used the mnemonic keyboard for first time, and consequently had to apply am additional amount of effort in finding the mnemonic keys.

5.2 Comparison of Reaction Times and Speed of Typing

Data gathered from the experiment was examined before proceeding to statistical analysis. Lines of ISA code which were not typed correctly where removed from the data set submitted to analysis. It must be noted that extreme values which were outside the three interquartile (3xIQR) range were also removed. Although not directly observable from histograms (see Fig. 6.) gathered data across all combinations of factor levels violates assumption of normality, as assessed by Shapiro-Wilk's test, p < 0.005. However, given the robustness of the F test [19, 20] we consider the results of RM-ANOVA to be valid.

Concerning task reaction time, test subjects while using VSK reacted in 2003.92 ms, SD = 991.802 ms, on the other hand while using VMK the reaction to the task was slower: 3686.77ms, SD = 2323.744 ms. These values are depicted on Fig. 6. showing boxplots with whiskers for both reaction time and CPS values for both types of keyboards, VSK and VMK.

Repeated Measures ANOVA determined a significant difference between reaction time for VSK and VMK, F(1, 545) = 258.164, p < 0.0005. The test showed that the first encounter with VMK puts additional strain on the user trying to cope with the unfamiliar keyboard commands and new layout, which is observable in a significant increase of reaction time.

The mean CPS for VSK is 1.896, SD = 0.854. Compared to the findings described in [8] this value is rather low. The size of touchscreen button of our VSK displayed on the 10.1 inch screen was roughly 12 mm x 10 mm, while Lee and Zhai's test "soft" keyboard buttons were displayed on a touchscreen device sized 16.5mm x 10.5mm with average result of 2.6 CPS. Regarding the comparison of CPS values for VSK and VMK, RM-ANOVA determined a significant difference between 1.896 CPS, SD=0.854 for VSK and 3.057 CPS, SD=1.581 for VMK, F(1, 545) = 223.936, p < 0.0005, thus supporting our initial hypothesis which stated that VMK will have a positive effect on the efficiency of ISA code typing on touchscreen devices.

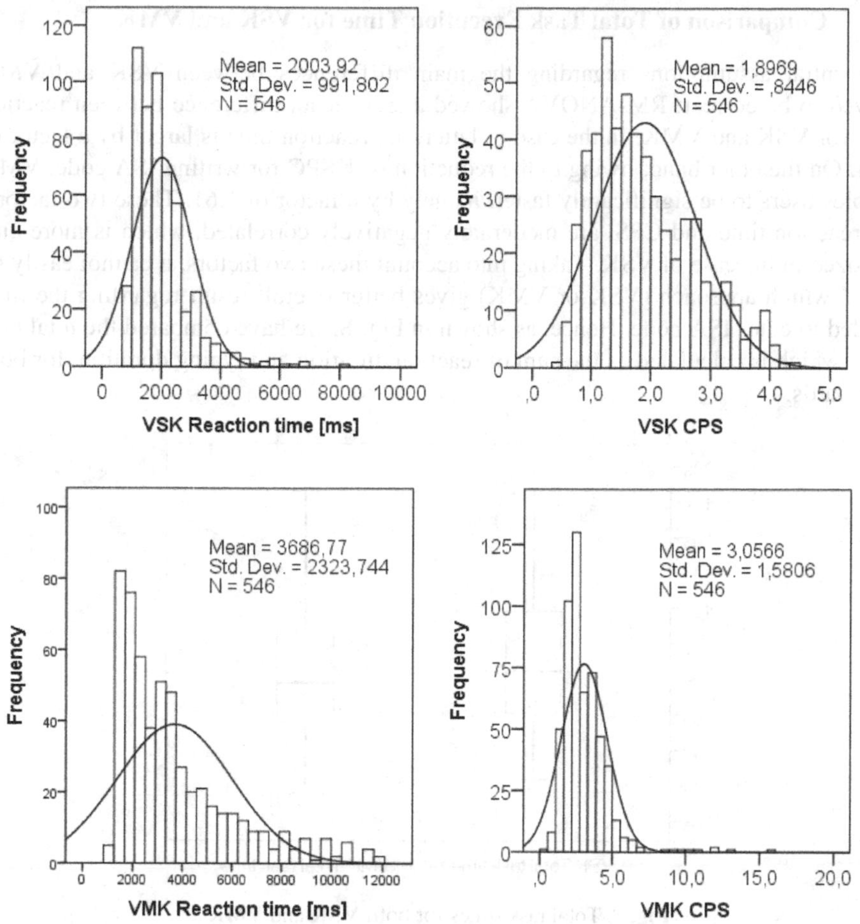

Fig. 6. Histograms of data gathered for all combinations of factor levels

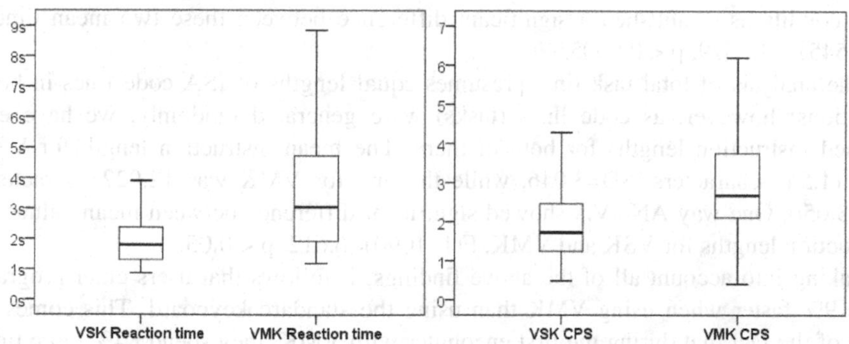

Fig. 7. Boxplot of reaction time and CPS values for VSK and VMK

5.3 Comparison of Total Task Execution Time for VSK and VMK

The initial assumptions regarding the main differences between VSK and VMK proved to be correct: RM-ANOVA showed a significant difference between reaction time for VSK and VMK. In the case of latter, the reaction time is larger by a factor of 1.84. On the other hand, owing to the reduction of KSPC for writing ISA code, VMK enables users to be significantly faster, namely by a factor of 1.61. These two factors, i.e. reaction time and CPS, are moderately negatively correlated, which is more emphasized in the case of VSK. Taking into account these two factors, it cannot easily be stated which approach (VSK or VMK) gives better overall result regarding the time needed to enter ISA code. Hence, as shown in Fig. 8, we have compared the total task time, which is calculated as the sum of reaction duration and typing duration, for both keyboards.

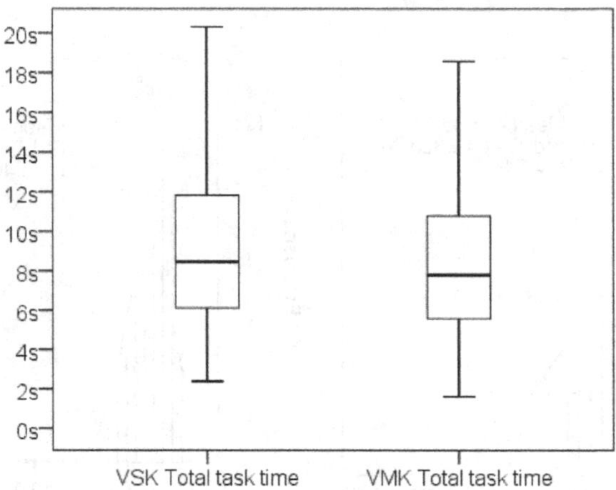

Fig. 8. Total task times for both VSK and VMK

The mean of total task times for VSK is 9.430s, SD=4.4s. For VMK, the mean of total task times is 8.575s, SD=3.8s. RM-ANOVA conducted for total task times of both conditions established a significant difference between these two mean times, $F(1, 545) = 12.579$, $p < 0.0005$.

The analysis of total task time presumes equal lengths of ISA code lines in both situations; however, as code lines (tasks) were generated randomly, we have examined instruction lengths for both of them. The mean instruction length for VSK was 11.547 characters, SD=3.046, while the one for VMK was 12.022 characters, SD=3.056. One way ANOVA showed significant difference between mean values of instruction lengths for VSK and VMK, $F(1, 1090)=6.612$, $p < 0.05$.

Taking into account all of the above findings, it follows that users enter program code 9% faster when using VMK than using the standard keyboard. This comes in spite of the fact that during the first encounter with VMK, they spend 84% more time on the average to look for the first key to type the instruction mnemonic, once they have located it, however, the reduction of KSPC will eliminate this deficiency.

Additionally, we must also note the statistically significant difference between task lengths, as in the case of VMK the respective tasks were approximately 4% longer.

5.4 Qualitative Validation of VMK

The subjective attitude towards VMK was validated through short interviews with study group members, after which students were asked to answer a questionnaire based on a seven point Likert scale. The questionnaire builds upon the theory of planned behavior (TPB) containing questions regarding: perceived ease of use, perceived usefulness, attitude towards using VMK during study projects, instructor and student readiness, subjective norm, perceived self-efficacy, learning autonomy, behavioral control, and intention [21], an contains altogether thirty items (questions). In the following we will describe student attitudes thus obtained through a short outline of questionnaire results instead of a comprehensive analysis of each item.

Two facts became evident during the short interview with the study group. Firstly, students claimed that testing was somewhat demanding: the requirement of being fast and accurate while typing on an unfamiliar keyboard put additional strain on them, thus they felt as losing pace towards the end of the test. However, the general conclusion of the study group was that they would be much faster after spending some time using VMK.

Secondly, the questionnaire results showed positive attitude towards perceived ease of use and perceived usefulness of the VMK. The prevalent grading of items in this category was within the upper part of the Likert scale (5, 6, or 7). Regarding students' opinion about the instructor's readiness to embrace m-learning, values were equally distributed around 5 which was the most used grade in this category, reflecting the students' opinion about a positive instructors' attitude towards m-learning, but with less confidence. Student readiness to embrace m-learning and subjective norm (an individual's attitude toward behavior) was mostly graded with 6 or even 7, thus emphasizing a very positive attitude towards use of mobile devices in learning. Self-confidence in using such systems is very high among the participants of the study group, and items in this category were rated mostly with grade 6 or 7, with no grade lower than 5. Furthermore, readiness to use such a system was also very high among students; again, most of the items were graded with a 6 or 7, and even fewer with grade 5. There was no grade lower that 5 in this category.

6 Conclusion

Usability is one of the main four measures of software quality, along with correctness, maintainability, and integrity [22, 23]. Inclusion of usability principles in the software engineering process in general is of utmost importance. In this respect, software systems used in learning should provide users with usable interface and effective interaction styles [24], while their subset – m-learning systems – suffer from even a greater number of additional usability problems [6, 7] inherited from mobile devices [25], that are their primary platform. The necessity of decreasing the cognitive overload

[26] for m-learning systems becomes thus increasingly prominent. The design of both the system interface and interaction methods must allow the user to focus her/his energy solely to accomplish the requested learning outcomes and create new mental structures regarding the knowledge she/he is trying to comprehend.

In this paper, we present results of quantitative and qualitative validation of a specially designed virtual mnemonic keyboard in the case of a user's first encounter with it. Using our testing system, users that had never before used such a keyboard were even more proficient than in the case of using the classic QWERTY layout, thus giving us enough confidence to state that such keyboard layout can help in the reduction of cognitive overload Indeed, test subjects involved in our experiment made similar claims, stating a positive attitude towards our keyboard design for support ISA code entry.

Acknowledgments. This paper describes the results of research being carried out within the project 036-0361994-1995 *Universal Middleware Platform for e-Learning Systems*, as well as within the program 036-1994 *Intelligent Support to Omnipresence of e-Learning Systems*, both funded by the Ministry of Science, Education and Sports of the Republic of Croatia.

References

1. Sharples, M.: The design of personal mobile technologies for lifelong learning. Comput. Educ. 34, 177–193 (2000)
2. Corlett, D., Sharples, M., Bull, S., Chan, T.: Evaluation of a mobile learning organiser for university students. J. Comput. Assist. Learn. 162–170 (2005)
3. Hwang, G.-J., Chang, H.-F.: A formative assessment-based mobile learning approach to improving the learning attitudes and achievements of students. Comput. Educ. 56, 1023–1031 (2011)
4. Holzinger, A., Kickmeier-Rust, M.D., Wassertheurer, S., Hessinger, M.: Learning performance with interactive simulations in medical education: Lessons learned from results of learning complex physiological models with the HAEMOdynamics SIMulator. Comput. Educ. 52, 292–301 (2009)
5. Hinckley, K., Zhao, S., Sarin, R., Baudisch, P., Cutrell, E., Shilman, M., Tan, D.: InkSeine: In Situ search for active note taking. In: Proceedings of the SIGCHI Conference on Human Factors in Computing Systems, pp. 251–260. ACM, New York (2007)
6. Holzinger, A., Nischelwitzer, A., Meisenberger, M.: Mobile Phones as a Challenge for m-Learning: Examples for Mobile Interactive Learning Objects (MILOs). In: Third IEEE International Conference on Pervasive Computing and Communications Workshops. pp. 307–311. IEEE (2005)
7. Arnedillo Sánchez, I., Sharples, M., Milrad, M., Vavoula, G.: Mobile Learning: Small Devices, Big Issues. In: Barnes, S., Montandon, L., Balacheff, N., Ludvigsen, S., de Jong, T., Lazonder, A. (eds.) Technologu-Enhanced Learning - Principles and Products, pp. 233–251. Springer, Berlin (2009)
8. Lee, S.C., Zhai, S.: The Performance of Touch Screen Soft Buttons. In: Proceedings of the 27th International Conference on Human Factors in Computing Systems CHI 2009, pp. 309–318 (2009)

9. Findlater, L., Wobbrock, J.O.: From plastic to pixels: in search of touch-typing touch-screen keyboards. Interactions 19, 44–49 (2012)
10. Kukec, M., Ljubic, S., Glavinic, V.: Improving Students' Technical Skills Using Mobile Virtual Laboratory: Pilot Study of Assembly Language Input Methods for Touchscreen Devices. In: Holzinger, A., Ziefle, M., Hitz, M., Debevc, M. (eds.) SouthCHI 2013. LNCS, vol. 7946, pp. 514–533. Springer, Heidelberg (2013)
11. Zhai, S., Kristensson, P.O.: Introduction to shape writing (2006)
12. Swype, `http://www.swype.com/`
13. SlideIT, `http://www.mobiletextinput.com/`
14. The Dasher project, `http://www.inference.phy.cam.ac.uk/dasher/`
15. Microchip 14-bit instruction set, `http://ww1.microchip.com/downloads/en/devicedoc/31029a.pdf`
16. Card, S.K., Newell, A., Moran, T.P.: The Psychology of Human-Computer Interaction. L. Erlbaum Associates Inc., Hillsdale (1983)
17. Nielsen, J.: Usability Engineering. Morgan Kaufmann (1993)
18. MacKenzie, I.S.: KSPC (Keystrokes per Character) as a Characteristic of Text Entry Techniques. In: Paternó, F. (ed.) Mobile HCI 2002. LNCS, vol. 2411, pp. 195–210. Springer, Heidelberg (2002)
19. Garson, D.: General Linear Models: Univariate GLM, Anova/Ancova, Repeated Measures (Statistical Associates Blue Book Series). Statistical Associates Publishers (2012)
20. Theodore, D.S.: Power of the F-Test for Nonnormal Distributions and Unequal Error Variances (1966)
21. Cheon, J., Lee, S., Crooks, S.M., Song, J.: An investigation of mobile learning readiness in higher education based on the theory of planned behavior. Comput. Educ. 59, 1054–1064 (2012)
22. Pressman, R.: Software Engineering: A Practitioner's Approach. McGraw-Hill, Inc., New York (2010)
23. Holzinger, A.: Usability engineering methods for software developers. Commun. ACM 48, 71–74 (2005)
24. Glavinić, V., Granić, A.: HCI Research for E-Learning: Adaptability and Adaptivity to Support Better User Interaction. In: Holzinger, A. (ed.) USAB 2008. LNCS, vol. 5298, pp. 359–376. Springer, Heidelberg (2008)
25. Shudong, W.S.W., Higgins, M.: Limitations of mobile phone learning. In: IEEE Int. Work. Wirel. Mob. Technol. Educ. WMTE 2005. pp. 179–181 (2005)
26. Harrison, R., Flood, D., Duce, D.: Usability of mobile applications: literature review and rationale for a new usability model. J. Interact. Sci. 1, 1 (2013)

Framework for Adaptive Knowledge Transmission Supported by HCI and Interoperability Concepts

Fernando Luís-Ferreira[1,2], João Sarraipa[1,2], and Ricardo Jardim-Goncalves[1,2]

[1] Departamento de Engenharia Electrotécnica, Faculdade de Ciências e Tecnologia, FCT, Universidade Nova de Lisboa, 2829-516 Caparica, Portugal
[2] Centre of Technology and Systems, CTS, UNINOVA, 2829-516 Caparica, Portugal
{flf,rg}@uninova.pt

Abstract. Teachers and educators have the mission of transmitting the best of their knowledge using the most from available resources and following established programmatic guidelines. The continuous evolution of technology, proposing new tools and apparatus for knowledge representation and transmission, has offered innumerous options for the mission of teaching. However, more then providing a wide set of experimental setups, or multimedia contents, would be important to determine the best content for each student. Hypothetically, the best content would be defined as the most suited to promote a seamless transmission of knowledge, according to the student status and his readiness to receive those concepts. Human Computer Interfaces can promote a better interoperability between those who teach and those who learn and can better adapt contents and transmission methods to the needs and abilities of each student in class. The present paper proposes a framework for adapting knowledge transmission, either local or remotely, to the needs and circumstances of each teaching act.

Keywords: HCI, Interoperability, Emotions, Knowledge Management, Neurosciences.

1 Introduction

The ages of paper and pencil, board and chalk or overhead projectors are overpast. With the diversity of online contents and multimedia options, it is plausible to question at what point paper books will remain confined to libraries as objects of the past. Whatever the option each educator takes, the need to adjust contents to students was in the past a choice for the right books, and is today the choice for selected links. Nevertheless this is a reductionist question as with the growth of Internet contents, doubling every 18 months [1], it is necessary to address, not the existence of contents but, the right contents for each student under specific teaching circumstance. Next, we can assume that, if contents are diverse and adequate, attention should be provided to the process of transferring information and knowledge to learners. Since Internet information is accessed from a computer device, being a laptop or a portable device with computational capabilities, it is important to turn attention to Human-Computer

C. Stephanidis and M. Antona (Eds.): UAHCI/HCII 2014, Part II, LNCS 8514, pp. 370–377, 2014.

Interaction (HCI). The relationships between people (e.g. students and teachers) can have better moments and can be easier between some duplets of persons interacting. Nevertheless, people have the ability to sense how others are receiving the message and identifying the peaks of interaction. If other persons are bored or restless, it is within teacher's perceptional capacities to identify those states and react accordingly in order to reestablish the learning process (e.g. change attitude, change message or even pause interaction). The authors propose a framework to adapt knowledge transmission by adjusting HCI using lessons learned in Interoperability research area. The next section describes some aspects that support the hypothesis that emotional assessment can intervene and contribute to improve the learning process. Then it is presented a framework to support the development of this hypothesis by exploring the implementation of such concepts. Finally, the last section provides some discussion and conclusions.

2 Research Background

From hundreds of years most of the great classical philosophers like Plato, Aristotle, Spinoza, Descartes, Hobbes and Hume, had recognizable theories of emotion [2] and tried to develop cognitive models and understand how the mind works. Since then no theory could be assumed as definite answer to what are emotions and how can they be represented. Plutchic's wheel [3] represent one of the interesting possibilities by depicting some of the most consensual emotions that we experiment in life. Emotions play such an important role in our lives that raises the question of its importance in the cognitive process [4]. Different authors present theories on how visual cortex influences our perception and cognition. A growing number of neuroscientists accept the existence of two streams at human brain; one ventral that identifies what we are observing and another dorsal that determines the spatial context of what we are seeing [5]. The process of identifying what is seen is based on a comparison between observed objects and what are previously stored objects, belonging to our memories, from past experiences. Furthermore, when we compare what we see with our memories, we bring to our mind objects, persons or scenes from the past and all that is attached to them. That includes whatever has established affective bonds, related existences and, most probably, the feelings attained will emerge promptly. These days we use computers and the Internet as extensions of our brains capabilities either for calculations or to store what we want to save and recall later. At the Internet we store and share pictures sound and movies, people and objects from our lives are digitized with cameras or scanners as sound is captured and converted to digital. In our research work some tools where developed in order to support representations of sensorial and emotional information at the Internet [6]. The result from those exploratory actions consists in collections of selected sampling of real world objects and events. In the best chances, later when we view and listen those samples we can invoke what is in our brains, from that episode or person and revive the whole experience attained. Instead of adapting ourselves to that restricted internet sampling of human sensorial experiences, (e.g. images and sound) a new model could be defined where those two streams are considered along with wider sensorial and emotional information added to images and scenes [7].

Learning is about to acquire new knowledge, behaviors, skills, values or preferences, and it may involve the processing of different types of information. Learning functions can be performed by different brain learning processes, which depend on the mental capacities of the learning subject/agent, the type of knowledge, which has to be acquitted, as well as on the socio-cognitive and environmental circumstances [8].

Instructional methodologies are founded on models for Instructional Design (ID). Such models provide procedural frameworks for the systematic production of instruction, and incorporate fundamental elements of the ID process including analysis of the intended audience or determining goals and objectives [9][10].

It could be stated that instructional models are guidelines or sets of strategies on which the approaches to teaching by instructors are based. Effective instructional models are based on learning theories. Learning Theories describe the ways that theorists believe people learn new ideas and concepts [10]. Theories about human learning can be grouped into four broad "perspectives": 1) Behaviorism - focus on observable behavior; 2) Cognitive - learning as purely a mental/ neurological process; 3) Humanistic - emotions and affect play a role in learning; and 4) Social - humans learn best in-group activities [11]. In our research, a highlight is made on a human centric learning environment. That is underlined by Damasio when he states that we feel therefore we learn [12] reinforcing that tendency to take emotion and affect with central role in Humanistic theories. This emotional enrolment is clearly identified in the traditional classroom, but that may not be the case for eLearning or for the classes supported by computational interfaces.

The proliferation of technical information at the Internet with its complex insides to very specific subjects could lessen, in a simplistic assessment, the role of the teacher, as he can no longer be considered the supreme knower of some matter. However, this would be a fundamental mistake as we are neglecting both his experience as educator and his abilities interpret and react to other human beings. Thus, we cannot forget that once in a classical classroom, teachers are able to regulate the teaching process by delivering less knowledge to a less attentive class or finding some funny examples to illustrate some tedious content. A teacher could also emphasize how important those subjects are for future studies and for that he would request special attention from the class. In this case, the teacher acts as a living sensor of students emotional states. Then, how can we have that same emotional assessment when we remove the teacher from the equation, as in eLearning or blended learning, or if the teacher is in class but students are interacting with a computational device?

Rosalind Picard has been studying aspects of affective computing and the emotional relation that humans have with computers [13]. Affective Computing is computing that relates to, arises from, or deliberately influences emotion or other affective phenomena [14]. Emerging areas are addressing human aspects, like affectivity and emotions to the human computer interactions, as in affective computing or Affective HCI [15]. This emotional assessment, which can be applied, either to eLearning with a student remotely displaced or in local setups where student use computational equipment, can be achieved by different measurements. Text assessment [16] or reading facial expressions [17], as most laptops have cameras, can be used locally or remotely to give emotional information to professors and trainers. Using those emotional clues, teachers can introduce new topics or relate matters to aspects of students life's and later verify how that is affecting their attention and their motivation.

Despite the intention of understanding emotional signals from students, that can become a complex task, teaching process involves sometimes a degree of misunderstanding between both parties. This has some similarities to the interoperability problems already identified between technological systems. Usually interoperability is mentioned in relation to enterprise systems and software applications as they struggle to manage and progress in collaborative business [18][19]. Interoperability is the capacity of performing any kind of operation (could be through communication) across over certain boundaries [20]. One of the classical definitions describes interoperability around three main aspects: organizational, technical, and semantic [21].

Organizational is related to business processes and internal organization structures appliance for better exchange of data. Technical is focused in how systems are linked up, which could be with agreed standards for presenting, collecting, exchanging, processing, transporting data. Semantic aspects are related to the ensuring that transported data shares the same meaning between the linked systems or actors.

The proposed framework mainly relates to semantic and technical aspects of the interoperability concept. In accordance to existent semantic interoperability developed solutions it is needed to have a system with knowledge management capabilities. To reach this purpose it is needed to understand how to organize, in this case, learning contents and transform it in appropriate and appellative eLearning objects. In additional, such related knowledge should be organized to assure such eLearning objects handling. Thus, the build of an ontology to represent the learning theme and its metadata is an appropriate goal [22]. All this to notice that, as already known, computers accomplished with these approaches can bring added value to the teaching process but they can also add new concepts, tools and artifacts, to the dynamics of teaching environment. It is also known that, unlike people, computers and multimedia contents are highly configurable and adapted to specific needs.

In align with this, Sarraipa et Al. In [23] proposed a methodology focused in the creation of training materials in a structured and formal way, supported by ontologies, which enables specific reasoning over the developed training materials facilitating the creation of web services able to provide adaptable training programs from the developed materials for specific purposes or profiles. That could address part of the problem when dealing with remote classes but still needs the contribution from emotional assessment either local or remotely accessed.

In this case, we propose a framework with the goal to answer the research question, which asks if the transmission of knowledge can be adapted by HCI adjustment based on interoperability concepts.

3 Framework for Adapting Knowledge Transmission Based on Emotional Assessment

The integration of such concepts results in a framework that has the ultimate objective of supporting contents adjustment to students' emotional status. In remote environments, those contents can be tailored for each student and selected according to feedback received at teaching institution. In a classroom, they can be shifted for better results of the group dynamics or to overcome identified problems with students motivation. With different levels of maturity and degrees of depth, the pursue of a better HCI is a permanent goal that is now stepping to a new level, the evaluation and adaptation to emotional status on the human side of the equation. This research drives two directions, on one side to promote the representation of objects on the Internet with emotional information and wider sensorial information, supported by specific ontologies [6]. The other direction is to monitor emotion as part of the learning process, using that information to establish a personalized class contents.

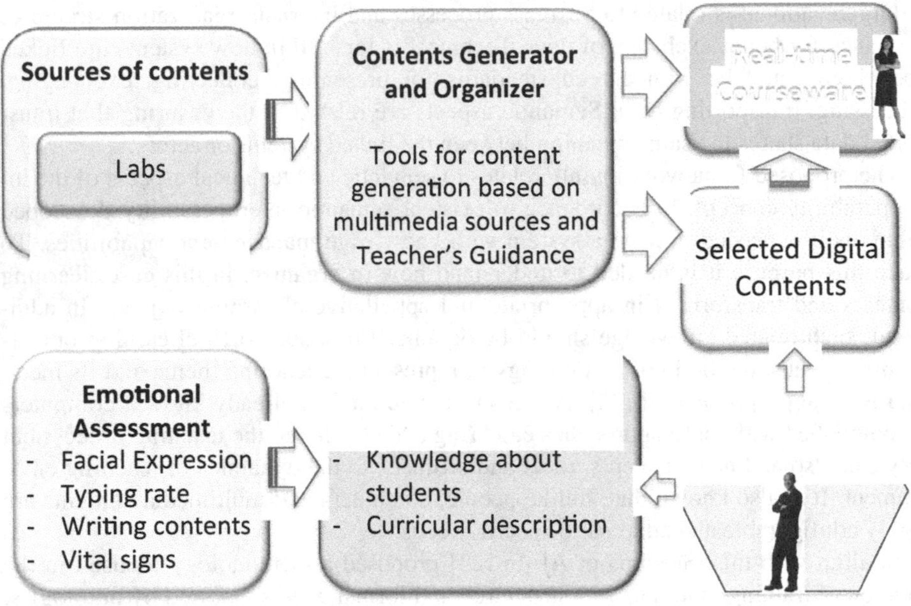

Fig. 1. Architecture of the framework for content generation, based on Emotional Assessment

The source courseware material includes all different types of available contents for that course. It can range from traditional class contents to more elaborated multimedia setups, and include labs or remote lab installations [24]. The innovation in the present work relies in the possibility of making an assessment in real-time of emotion related readings from students. In Fig. 1 an emotional assessment is organized using several options as available for a given course. Some of those are more likely to be measured in classroom others can be captured remotely with a recommended set of devices. If the student is using a computer with camera, either locally or remotely, facial expression can be used to assess his emotional state [17]. If he student is typing, it can be used to give clues about emotional state, either by speed rates or by the nature of contents if available for assessment. In regard to physiological readings, including heartbeat, they are becoming more accessible to get by the usage of mobile phone specific applications[1], even if they remain less practical than would be desirable. Teachers become able to guide lessons based on what is the established curriculum but also taking in account emotional information from devices, weighted with their knowledge about each student. As an example a History teacher can evoke some travel he made to an historic place when he feels like he is loosing attention, and present some slides or some recorded video. The core of the proposed framework is the contents generator and organizer that can assume diverse technological aspects depending on remote or local setup and a previous selection of adequate contents. It can work as a planning tool for the teacher allowing an organization of the teaching materials and preparing several options to react to students' feedback in real-time. The course is adjusted in real-time providing multimedia content as needed by activation from the contents generator and organizer, serving teacher's options for the class deployment. This framework can be created in a sophisticated environment with real-time multimedia orchestration with multimodal assessment of student's emotions but can also be downsized to the available technological means available. The best solution would be an elaborated assessment of emotions but that is not possible unless using sophisticated equipment like MRI of fMRI [25]. Those are pieces of equipment not suitable to have in a classroom; an elaborated measurement as described above or a simple face-reading algorithm would mean an opportunity of obtaining emotional and attention clues. Whatever the human computer interaction is being established, the current research aims to increase the interoperability between students and teachers using emotional assessment to facilitate the learning process.

4 Discussion

Today's immense availability of technological means and multimedia contents can make us suppose that capturing students' attention is an infallible accomplishment. However, without a proper utilization of all those vehicles of knowledge transmission, it can become poorly efficient and give a false impression of success. The research work developed and presented in this paper relies on the premise that knowledge transmission can be adapted based on monitoring of students' feedback and, in particular, evaluating emotional evidence from students' assessment. That evaluation could be made by text mining, morphologic analysis of the face and by physiological measurements, like the heartbeat monitoring or face reading assessment.

Another perspective for the presented work puts an emphasis in the real-time evaluation and the possibility of immediately reacting and adjusting contents. There are many options for evaluating course effectiveness and the quality and substance of knowledge transmitted in teaching environments but an identifiable omission on real-time assessment is explored in our current work.

On the other hand, the concepts of interoperability are mostly applied to systems. IEEE defines Interoperability as the ability of two or more systems or components to exchange information and to use the information that has been exchanged[26]. In our

[1] https://itunes.apple.com/us/app/iheart-pulse-reader/id300289653

approach, lessons learned from interoperability of systems can be adapted to HCI in particular regarding the learning process. The proposed framework has diverse types of possible usage, depending on the channels used and the users addressed. In response to that diversity, some deployments where made for establishing learning environments either in Industrial context [27] or in scholar environment [24]. This ongoing work has a main direction in the possibility of adapting contents for universal usage independently of cultural or linguistic differences. This perspective has been developed in the scope of our participation in Alter-Nativa[2] project with different types of learners from diverse cultures. Our contribution is the development of a framework that is growing from the ontological scope to the emotional assessment.

5 Concluding Remarks and Future Work

The different between mood and emotion is that mood is a state with low intensity but lasting longer while emotions are limited in time and related with what an individual is experiencing [28]. A student can be in a good mood but the subject of study make him stressed or anxious about some topic. If a teacher is able to detect such problems, he can react in real-time. The growing interest in wearable devices will contribute to the simplicity of measurements making available diverse parameters on human physiology and from that to infer emotional states. This is the challenge proposed by our work that is growing and suggesting new insights in the learning process. The main conclusion is that new media is available, resulting from permanently emerging technologies, but those disperse pieces need to be united for a new technology-driven learning environment. Technology is providing means that can be exploited for the benefit of parties in the learning process and would be a waste not using them to promote better interaction between teachers and students and, in summary, promote an emotionally balanced learning environment for the future.

Acknowledgments. The research leading to these results has received funding from the EC 7th Framework Programme under grant agreement FITMAN nr 604674 (http://www.fitman-fi.eu) and also from the European Union 7th Framework Programme (FP7/2007-2013) under grant agreement: IMAGINE nr 285132, (www.imagine-futurefactory.eu/).

References

1. John, G., David, R.: As the Economy Contracts, the Digital Universe Expands (2009)
2. De Sousa, R.: Emotion, `http://plato.stanford.edu/archives/spr2012/entries/emotion/`
3. Plutchik, R.: The Emotions. University Press of America (1991)
4. Zadra, J.R., Clore, G.L.: Emotion and Perception: The Role of Affective Information. Wiley Interdiscip. Rev. Cogn. Sci. 2, 676–685 (2011)
5. Goodale, M., Milner, A.D.: One brain – two visual systems. Psychologist 19, 660–663 (2006)

[2] ALTER- NATIVA Project (DCI-ALA/19.09.01/10/21526/245-575/ALFA III(2010)88).

6. Luis-Ferreira, F., Sarraipa, J., Marques-Lucena, C., Jardim-Goncalves, R.: Framework for Management of Internet Objects in Their Relation with Human Sensations and Emotions. IMECE, San Diego (2013)
7. Luis-Ferreira, F., Jardim-Gonçalves, R.: Modelling of Things on the Internet for the Search by the Human Brain. In: Camarinha-Matos, L.M., Tomic, S., Graça, P. (eds.) DoCEIS 2013. IFIP AICT, vol. 394, pp. 71–79. Springer, Heidelberg (2013)
8. Gadomski, A.M.: Application of System-Process-Goal Approach for description of TRIGA RC1 System. In: 9th European TRIGA Nuclear Reactor Users Conference (1986)
9. Braxton, S., Bronico, K., Looms, T.: Instructional design methodologies and techniques
10. Edutech Wiki: Instructional design model, `http://edutechwiki.unige.ch/en/Instructional_design_model`
11. Cooper, S.: Theories of Learning in Educational Psychology
12. Immordino-Yang, M.H., Damasio, A.: We Feel, Therefore We Learn: The Relevance of Affective and Social Neuroscience to Education. Mind, Brain, Educ. 1, 3–10 (2007)
13. Picard, R.W.: Toward Machines with Emotional Intelligence, 1–22
14. Picard, R.W.: Affective Computing (1997)
15. Hudlicka, E.: To feel or not to feel: The role of affect in human–computer interaction. Int. J. Hum. Comput. Stud. 59, 1–32 (2003)
16. Shivhare, S.N., Khethawat, S.: Emotion Detection from Text 7 (2012)
17. Adolphs, R.: Recognizing Emotion from Facial Expressions: Psychological and Neurological Mechanisms. Behav. Cogn. Neurosci. Rev. 1, 21–62 (2002)
18. Jardim-Goncalves, R., Grilo, A., Steiger, A.: Challenging the interoperability between computers in industry with MDA and SOA. Comput. Ind. 57(8-9), 679–689 (2006)
19. Panetto, H., Jardim-Gonçalves, R., Pereira, C.: EManufacturing and web-based technology for intelligent manufacturing and networked enterprise. J. Intell. Manuf. 639–640 (2006)
20. Sarraipa, J., Jardim-Goncalves, R.: Semantics Adaptability for Systems Interoperability. In: Proceedings of the 1st UNITE Doctoral Symposium, Bucharest, Romania
21. Communities, E.: European Interoperability Framework for Pan-European eGovernment Services., IDA working document - Version 4.2 (2004)
22. Sarraipa, J.: Semantic Adaptability for the Systems Interoperability (2013)
23. Sarraipa, J., Gomes-de-Oliveira, P., Marques-Lucena, C.R., J.-G., Silva, J.M.: E-Training Development Approach for Enterprise Knowledge Evolution. In: ASME International Mechanical Engineering Congress and Exposition, IMECE 2013, San Diego, California, USA (2013)
24. Leao, C.P., Luis-Ferreira, F., Jardim-Goncalves, R.: Learning challenges: Remote labs powered by the five senses. In: 2013 International Conference on Interactive Collaborative Learning (ICL). pp. 696–699. IEEE (2013)
25. Baumgartner, T., Esslen, M., Jäncke, L.: From emotion perception to emotion experience: emotions evoked by pictures and classical music. Int. J. Psychophysiol. 60, 34–43 (2006)
26. IEEE Standard Computer Dictionary: A Compilation of IEEE Standard Computer Glossaries, 610 (1990)
27. Hadjileontiadis, L., Martins, P., Todd, R., Paredes, H., Rodrigues, J., Barroso, J., Sarraipa, J., Baldiris, S., Fabregat, R., Jardim-Goncalves, R.: Knowledge Representation in Support of Adaptable eLearning Services for All. Procedia Comput. Sci. 14, 391–402 (2012)
28. Scherer, K.R.: What are emotions? And how can they be measured? Soc. Sci. Inf. 44, 695–729 (2005)

HCI-Based Guidelines for Electronic and Mobile Learning for Arabic Speaking Users: Do They Effectively Exist?

Muhanna Muhanna and Edward Jaser

King Hussein School for Computing Sciences, Princess Sumaya University for Technology, Amman, Jordan
{m.muhanna,ejaser}@psut.edu.jo

Abstract. Electronic and mobile learning in recent years has been considered as an invaluable tool to support the learning process. Several tools and comprehensive platforms have been developed in the paradigms of e-learning and m-learning. One issue is the usability of these tools. It is essential to define metrics to measure efficiency, learnability, satisfaction and other usability properties. Another equally important issue is the presence of guidelines compiled based on accumulated scientific reasoning behind design decisions. In this paper, we discuss the issue of HCI-based guideline specific to designing e- and m-learning platforms and tools intended for Arabic users. We present our analysis on the availability of such guidelines, their deployment and to whether they adequately address the challenges characteristic to Arabic language.

Keywords: HCI, Arabic, E-Learning, M-Learning, Guidelines.

1 Introduction

The teaching methods at universities and educational institutions in the Arab world are still dominated by delivering education using the traditional knowledge delivery model. However, there are strong evidences that this is about to change especially with (i) the convenience and affordability of the Internet; and (ii) the popularity of recent advancement and development in distance learning (e.g. MOOCs) which has been attracting attentions in the Arab region. We believe the next few years will witness a rapid growth in interest in technologies to compliment, and maybe is some cases replace, traditional knowledge delivery systems. As a result, Arabic electronic and mobile learning (e- and m-learning) tools and platforms have been increasingly researched. There have been surging interests in Arabic digital content, an important component in learning systems. This is inferred from the number of initiatives, dedicated fund and research work concerning enriching and enhancing this content. Another equally important component is the interaction with these content. In the traditional setting, it is instructors and the educational tools they are using. In technology based learning, it is the user interface layer. The satisfaction in using the e- and m-learning tools and platforms is certainly dependent on, and influenced by,

C. Stephanidis and M. Antona (Eds.): UAHCI/HCII 2014, Part II, LNCS 8514, pp. 378–387, 2014.

this interaction layer. Certainly, there is a common agreement that "The learning effectiveness and interface design are substantially intertwined" [1].

The paper explores and presents the challenges of interacting with e- and m-learning platforms. Such interaction can take place during the process of either authoring Arabic content or using the platform's interface by the students. In addition, we identify and report on other challenges that might be faced in terms of developing an e- or m-learning software application. The challenges identified should be carefully considered by software engineers as well as interaction designers in the early stages of the software life cycle. As a result, unpredictable software risks could be minimized. Moreover, interested researchers and practitioners could benefit from the identification of these challenges in opening the directions for future research studies and investigations that could address each of the challenges. Understanding these challenges can help in compiling user interface guidelines, important HCI tools drafted to help in improving user experience, designing high quality user interface and making application interfaces more intuitive. Some research questions can be identified with this regards including: (i) do current and widely used e- and m-learning tools and platforms targeting Arabic users employ guidelines; (ii) how effective are these guidelines if this is the case; and (iii) do these guideline adequately address the challenges characteristic to Arabic language.

In this paper, we attempt to address these research questions. We provide discussion of the main challenges presented by cultural issues as well as language issues specific to the Arab region when designing interfaces. We survey existing guidelines and study the logic behind them and map these guidelines to the identified challenges to evaluate adequacy and applicability. To validate our study we use the survey of Arabic e- and m-learning platforms and explore examples that demonstrate and evaluate some aspects of them against the guidelines/challenges analysis.

The paper, in its remaining part, is organized as follows. In Section 2, we discuss Arabic support in the e- and m-learning platform based on four metrics. In Section 3, we identify challenges of developing user interfaces specific to Arabic users. A survey of existing work related to guidelines and recommendations to address the identified challenges is presented in Section 4. Moreover, in Section 4 we discuss the mapping of the identified challenges against the explored guidelines. The paper is concluded in Section 5.

2 Arabic Support in E- and M-Learning Platforms

Several tools and comprehensive platforms have been developed in the paradigms of e- and m-learning. Only few, however, are targeted to support the Arabic language. In this section, we present a detailed view of some of the widely used e- and m-learning proprietary as well as open-source platforms, including Aplia, Articulate, Atutor, Blackboard, Captivate, Claroline, Desire2Learn, E-College, HotChalk, LearnMate, Moodle, OUCampus, Sakai, and SlideWiki. Our focus has been to survey these platforms in terms of supporting the Arabic language. In particular, we have based our survey on four metrics, namely: (i) interface, (ii) content authoring, (iii) language processing, and (iv) cost. The objective of this detailed survey is to allow interested stakeholders to be aware of the current status and trends of the most popular e- and m-learning platforms in supporting the Arabic language. We believe that this survey, in turn, should provide decision makers of institutions in Arab countries with useful insights that support their decisions in considering e- and m-learning platforms.

2.1 Metrics of the Survey

In our survey, we have focused on four metrics that can be clearly identified in e- and m-learning platforms in terms of the Arabic language support. The first metric is the interfaces, in which we report on whether the surveyed platform supports Arabic in its interface or not. A platform that does not support Arabic in its interface layout and widgets would not be considered by educators looking for a completely Arabic platform or those looking to deliver education to Arabic speakers. In fact, in his book [2], Nielsen has stated that the ideal international user interface should be available in the user's preferred language. Translating words to Arabic is not the only concern here, right-to-left design, for example, should be considered as well.

The second metric studied in the survey is the content authoring. This is also an important metric as it provides instructors with an overview of the platform's ability to create Arabic content. Content authoring could be in the form of textbooks, discussion forums, comments, presentations, assignments, or questions.

For the third metric, language processing, we aimed at studying the platform's support of natural language processing for Arabic. Over the last few years, several investigations have been conducted to study the challenges of Arabic natural language processing [3]. Natural language processing has been identified as an important element of e- and m-learning platforms [4], [5], as it provides the platform with the capabilities of word and phrase searching, indexing, voice recognition, text recognition, text-to-speech, and auto-grading.

The cost is the last, but not least, metric that has been considered in the survey. We believe that cost is a challenge to many institutions in general and the Arab world in particular. Countries in the Arab region vary in terms of the budgets dedicated to e-learning systems and infrastructures from millions of dollars in the Arab Gulf to almost only in concepts in Sudan and Yemen [6]. Therefore, the cost of the platform is still an issue for many Arab institutions. The focus in the survey has not been on the exact cost of the platform. Rather, the cost has been categorized into: open-source (no cost), cost on students, and cost on educators (instructor or institution).

2.2 Survey Results and Discussion

Table 1 shows a summary of the results of the survey. It is important to mention here that the findings of this survey are the results of deep searching through the official websites of the platforms and up to the date in which this paper has been written. The table shows each platform along with the four metrics discussed in the previous subsection. As Table 1 depicts, Arabic support in the current e- and m-learning platforms is still challenging and immature. In terms of the user interface, several platforms have supported, or recently started to support, Arabic language. However, most of the support comes in the form of only translating words and dictionaries. Much more have to be done here, such as supporting right-to-left interfaces, layout mirroring, using Arabic dates, time, first day of the week, etc. Section 3 of this paper introduces an in-deep discussion of the HCI challenges and guidelines of building the e- and m-learning platforms. Although most of the surveyed platforms support authoring Arabic content, the same challenge is found here in terms of the need to not only translate or write in Arabic, but also to change many of the content elements stated earlier and explained later. Furthermore, Arabic natural language processing was not found in any of the surveyed platforms except for very basic searching for words, which might be done using third-party engines. This, however, was not considered a clear natural language processing that can be further used in auto-grading or voice recognition for example. Moreover, Table 1 shows how the costs of the platforms vary from cost on educators and institutions, through cost per course on students, to open-source. Open-source solutions provide an opportunity for institution with low-budgets assigned for e- and m-learning to consider such platforms.

Table 1. Arabic Support in E- and M-Learning Platforms

Platform	Interfaces	Authoring	Processing	Cost
Aplia	No	No	No	Students
Articulate	No	No	No	Educators
Atutor	Translation	Yes	No	Open-Source
Blackboard	Translation	Yes	No	Educators
Captivate	No	Yes	No	Educators
Claroline	Translation	Yes	No	Open-Source
Desire2Learn	Locales	Yes	No	Educators
E-College	No	No	No	Educators
HotChalk	Translation	Yes	No	Educators
LearnMate	Translation	Yes	No	Educators
Moodle	Locales	Yes	No	Open-Source
OUCampus	Locales	Yes	No	Educators
Sakai	Locales	Yes	No	Open-Source
SlideWiki	Translation	Yes	No	Open-Source

3 HCI-Based Challenges of Developing and Using E-Learning and M-Learning Platforms for Arabic Speaking Users

This section explores and presents the challenges of interacting with e-learning and m-learning platforms. Such interaction can take place during the process of either authoring Arabic content or using the platform's interface by the instructors and students. In addition, we identify and report on other challenges that might be faced in terms of developing an e- or m-learning software application.

3.1 Language Translation and Cultural Identities

The first and foremost challenge is the identity and localization of the language and culture. The solution here would not be through only translating words. Rather, a complete study of the Arabic culture should be considered and further explored. Digital calendars, for example, should be customized to allow for changing the start of the week as most of the Arabic countries start their weeks on Sunday. In fact, Lebanon, Morocco, and Tunisia are the only Arab countries to start their week on Monday. In addition, Saudi Arabia officially uses Umm-al-Qura calendar, which is based on the Hijri calendar instead of the Gregorian calendar [7]. Moreover, many Arab countries use the Hijri calendar as well in calculating religious holidays.

Translation of words is not a straight forward approach either. Some commonly used words in English user interfaces, for example, are not simply translated into Arabic, such as the word ‘Home’. Furthermore, some Arabic words can be confusing when translated; the word "تقويم", for example, could mean either a ‘Calendar’ or a ‘Correction’, it could be also confused to mean “Assessment”. Another example is in the words ‘design’ and ‘layout’, which are translated to mean one word: ‘design’. Also, ‘Wi-Fi’ is not translated in Apple iOS 7 nor in Android Jellybeans, as seen in Fig. 1 and Fig. 2.

Fig. 1. Part of the Settings Menu of the Apple iOS 7 (in Arabic)

Fig. 2. Part of the Settings Menu of the Android Jellybean 4.1.2 (in Arabic)

In addition, “Bluetooth” is not translated in Apple iOS, and only its transliteration is used in Android Jellybean. The figures also show how the ‘Settings’ menu title is translated inconsistently in the two operating systems.

3.2 Arabic Numerals vs. Eastern Arabic Numerals

Although Arabic sentences are read from right to left, its numbers are read from left to right. This would raise the challenge of voice recognition of Arabic sentences that include numbers as well as text-to-speech features. In fact, the Hindu numerals, also called the Eastern Arabic numerals, are used in most of the Arab countries as opposed to the Arabic numerals used in Europe and America; Glyphs are different, and thus, finger gestures should be updated accordingly in case a touch screen system is being used.

3.3 Arabic Natural Language Processing

The nature of the Arabic language has imposed many challenges in terms of the language processing. For example, prefixes, suffixes, and pronouns in Arabic are attached to the same word making a new word, which would be challenging to process. The authors in [3] have identified and described several challenges and suggested some solutions to guide interested researchers and practitioners working on Arabic natural language processing. Several other research studies have been conducted to further explore the challenges of the Arabic natural language processing and suggest usable solutions, such as in [8] and [9].

3.4 Inconsistent Keyboard Layouts

It is essential to have consistency words, situations, or actions in any one user interface. In fact, Nelsen has indicated that consistency is one of the ten usability heuristics for user interface design [10]. However, current versions of Arabic keypad layouts are not consistent. For example, the IBM Desktop Arabic keyboard layout, shown in Fig. 2, is not consistent with the layout of the Mac Desktop Arabic keyboard layout, shown in Fig. 3. This is clearly a challenge to consider in e-learning platforms where students, for example, have inconsistent layouts.

3.5 Arabic Support in Mobile Operating Systems

Although Arabic has been well supported in desktop operating systems, several mobile operating systems have only recently started supporting Arabic. Table 2 shows a summary of the Arabic support in the currently most used operating systems of smart phones [11], [12], and [13]. Furthermore, Arabic support in these operating systems is still limited to right-to-left designs, auto-layouts, or layout mirroring. Apple Siri and Samsung S-Voice, for example, do not support Arabic yet.

Fig. 3. IBM Desktop Arabic Keyboard Layout (*Courtesy of Wikimedia Commons*)

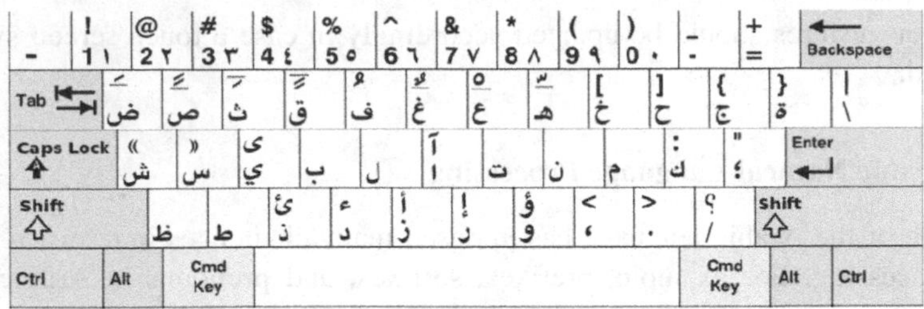

Fig. 4. Mac Desktop Arabic Keyboard Layout (*Courtesy of Wikimedia Commons*)

Table 2. Arabic Support in Mobile Operating Systems

Operating System	Version Suporting Arabic	Date of Release
Windows Phone	Windows Phone 8	October 2012
iOS	iOS 6.0	September 2012
Android	Android 4.2	October 2012

3.6 User Interface Design: Typography

An important element of user interface design in general, and in e- and m-learning platforms in particular is the typography. Although some operating system vendors, such as Microsoft [14] and Google [15], have identified a specific font to be used for Arabic content, many other typography guidelines for Arabic have to be explored as well. This includes the typeface itself, its size, its weight, leading, kerning, tracking, and other guidelines that could be specific to the Arabic language.

3.7 User Interface Design: Color

Color is another issue of the user interface design that could effectively affect the usability of an e- and m-learning platform designed for Arabic users. Color should be further explored in its application to the Arab culture in terms of color interpretation, color accessibility, color themes, and color meanings. In fact, color interpretation is usually dependent on the cultural background of the user [16].

3.8 User Interface Design: Other Visual Design

Another challenge that can be identified is the lack of recent investigations and guidelines that are specifically studied for Arabic user interfaces. Such as dialog boxes, icons, menus, cursors, buttons, error messages, etc. An exploration of Arabic graphical user interfaces has been published in [17], which is old in comparison with the current graphical user interface guidelines and it lacks a study of the visual design elements specific to Arabic interfaces.

4 HCI-Based Guidelines for Arabic Speaking Users: Analysis

Guidelines are generally considered as some rules and recommendations that need to be followed in order to satisfy some usability properties. They usually address issues such as platform characteristics, main user interface principles, design strategies, user interface element usage, and the design of user interface assets among other things. We made a survey of research efforts that have addressed or discussed the challenges we presented in Section 3. Table 3 maps these challenges to the related research, and in some cases technical, work found in the literature.

Table 3. Identified Challenges vs. Available Guidelines

Challenge	Availabe Guidelines
1. Language Translation and Cultural Identities	[17], [18], [19], [20], [21]
2. Arabic Numerals vs. Eastern Arabic Numerals	[17], [19]
3. Arabic Natural Language Processing	[3], [8], [9]
4. Inconsistent Keyboard Layouts	[17], [20]
5. Arabic Support in Mobile Operating Systems	[11], [12], [13]
6. User Interface Design: Typography	[17], [18], [21]
7. User Interface Design: Color	[19]
8. User Interface Design: Other Visual Design	[19], [20], [21]

As stated earlier, the author in [17] explored the Arabization of graphical user interfaces in terms of localization, culture, characters fonts, numerals, etc. The publication, however, is relatively old in comparison with the current graphical user interface guidelines. Another example of a relatively old publication that explored the basic requirements for a UNIX Arabic graphical user interfaces is [20]. In this paper, the authors presented the requirements in terms of the Arabic characteristics, graphical components, graphical tools, and dictionaries. In [19], the authors presented their insights and strategies of a case study in which a team, mostly of non-Arabic speakers, worked on designing an Arabic user experience. The focus was on translation, information architecture, and visual design. Although the authors listed the results of end users of the developed application in the form of bulleted points, details about the usability study were not presented.

We stress the fact that related work listed in Table 3 may not qualify as a comprehensive and evidence based guidelines. Some of the work (e.g., [19], [20], and [21]) can be considered as a technical document compiled by programming languages experts. They are mainly intended for those developers who need to do customization and localization specific programming language products. On the other hand, we found that some work (e.g., [18], [22], and [23]) has included a sound usability testing to justify through experiments their proposed guidelines. Though, their analysis was targeting certain age group and cannot be generalized.

There are some reported work that addressed challenges and issue when developing user interfaces for e- and m-learning tools. As a result, guidelines and recommendations have been proposed. However, the mapped guidelines partially, and often do not, cover all the aspects needed to adequately address identified challenge. We believe that for those guidelines and recommendations to be effective, they need to be based on a thorough evidence-based analysis and well-planned usability evaluation. This is not the case in most reviewed work as it mainly relies on expert reviews.

Another aspect is that Arabic users are spread across a wide region and across many countries. Naturally, this means there are many dialects spoken. We estimate that there approximately 13-15 Arabic dialects that vary, to some extent, from one another. Currently, majority of interfaces are in formal modern standard Arabic. Little research have been addressing and scientifically justifying whether the use of standard Arabic is satisfying the entire Arabic users. Similar issue can be found in Wikipedia with content in both standard Arabic and dialects are available. We believe more research is needed with this regards. The issue of bilingualism among Arab users is a major issue. Many terms that are being used are not Arabic. For example, many French terms are used in countries like Morocco and Algeria while English words are used in countries like Jordan and Egypt. No properly compiled recommendations exist on how to handle this issue.

We can therefor argue that most available Arabic specific guidelines to ensure usable and effective interface layers do not exist and are not sufficient to address most language specific challenges. Many design decisions are made based on recommendations from experts and users that are rather subjective and cannot be considered as generalizations. There is a pressing need for research efforts to scientifically validate existing guidelines and compile challenge-based guidelines to enhance and maximize user experience.

5 Conclusion

In this paper, we discussed the topic of usability issues for e- and m-learning tools and platforms for Arabic speaking users. Currently, this topic is gaining momentum with the increasing demands for such tools to support the educational process in schools and universities. We surveyed popular tools in terms of Arabic support and we presented main challenges that need to be addressed in such tools. Based on the challenges we discussed, we provided a preliminary survey of related research and technical works and provided some sort of recommendations to address these challenges. We concluded based on our analysis that existing guidelines do not adequately address the pressing challenges designers and developers are facing when dealing with usability issues in the user interface layers of e- and m-learning tools and packages.

References

1. Guralnick, D.: User Interface Design for Effective, Engaging E-Learning, `http://goo.gl/mmo2Ko` (retrieved on February 03, 2014)
2. Nielsen, J.: Designing Web Usability: The Practice of Simplicity, New Riders (2000)
3. Farghaly, A., Shaalan, K.: Arabic Natural Language Processing: Challeges and Solutions, ACM Transactions on Asian Language Information Processing. ACM Transactions on Asian Language Information Processing 8(4), Article 14, 1–22 (2009)

4. Wahl, H., Winiwarter, W., Quirchmayr, G.: Natural Language Processing Technologies for Developing a Language Learning Environment. In: Proceedings of the 12th International Conference on Information Integration and Web-based Applications & Services, pp. 381–388. ACM, New York (2010)
5. Smrz, P.: Integrating Natural Language Processing into e-learning: a Case of Czech. In: Proceedings of eLearning for Computational Linguistics and Computational Linguistics, pp. 1–10. Association for Computational Linguistics, Stroudsburg (2004)
6. Guessoum, N.: Online Learning in the Arab World. In: ACM E-Learn.: Education and Technology in Perspective, vol. 2006 (10), ACM (2006)
7. Glasse, C.: New Encyclopedia of Islam, 3rd edn. Rowman & Littlefield Publishers (2008)
8. Alansary, S., Nagi, M., Adly, N.: A Suite of Tools for Arabic Natural Language Processing: A UNL Approach. In: Proceedings of the 1st IEEE International Conference on Communications, Signal Processing, and their Applications, pp. 1–6. IEEE Press (2013)
9. Osman, Z., Hamandi, L., Zantout, R., Sibai, F.N.: Automatic Processing of Arabic Text. In: IEEE International Conference on Innovations in Information Technology, pp. 140–144. IEEE Press (1999)
10. Nelsen, J.: Ten Usability Heuristics for User Interface Design (1995), `http://goo.gl/hy0HA9` (retrieved on February 6, 2014)
11. Meglio, F.D., Native, R.T.L.: Support in Android 4.2, Android Developers Blog, `http://goo.gl/V0Ond8` (retrieved on February 6, 2014)
12. iOS Developer Library, What's New in iOS 6.0, `http://goo.gl/wDuPLK` (retrieved on February 6, 2014)
13. MSDN, Culture and Language Support for Windows Phone, `http://goo.gl/KEuviO` (retrieved on February 6, 2014)
14. Guidelines for Typography, Windows Dev. Center, `http://goo.gl/7UvkSX` (retrieved on February 3, 2014)
15. Google Fonts, Early Access!, `http://goo.gl/JzKFgQ` (retrieved on February 3, 2014)
16. Bortoli, M.D., Maroto, J.: Colours Across Cultures: Translating Colours in Interactive Marketing Communications. In: Proceeding of the European Languages and the Implementation of Communcation and Information Technologies Conference, UK (2001)
17. Amara, F., Portaneri, F.: Arabization of Graphical User Interfaces. In: Galdo, E., Nielsen, J. (eds.) International User Interfaces, pp. 127–150. Wiley and Sons (1996)
18. Al-Osaimi, A., Alsumait, A.: Design Guidelines of Child e-Learning Applications with an Arabic Interface. Kuwait J. Sci. Eng. 39(1B), 149–173 (2012)
19. Hemayssi, H., Sanchez, E., Moll, R., Field, C.: Designing an Arabic User Experience: Methods and Techniques to Bridge Cultures. In: Proceedings of the 2005 Conference on Designing for User eXperience, American Institute of Graphic Arts, Article 34 (2005)
20. Al-Muhtaseb, H., AlAbdulhadi, A.: Basic Requirements for a UNIX Arabic Graphical User Interface. In: Proceedings of the 5th International Conference and Exhibition on Multilingual Computing, London, UK, pp. 1–14 (1996)
21. Arabic Style Guide, Mircorosft Language Portal, `http://goo.gl/OsEp3k` (retrieved on February 3, 2014)
22. Alsumait, A., Al-Osaimi, A.: Usability heuristics evaluation for child e-learning applications. In: iiWAS pp. 425–430 (2009)
23. Alsumait, A., Al-Osaimi, A., AlFedaghi, H.: Arab Children's Reading Preference for Different Online Fonts. HCI (4), 3–11 (2009)

Accessible Online Education: Audiovisual Translation and Assistive Technology at the Crossroads

Emmanouela Patiniotaki

Imperial College London, Translation Studies Unit, South Kensington Campus, London SW7 2AZ, UK
emmanouela.patiniotaki08@imperial.ac.uk

Abstract. The purpose of this paper is to give prominence to the potential of the combination of access services emerging within Translation, and more specifically Audiovisual Translation and what is also known as Accessible Media or Media Accessibility, with Assistive Technology tools, which have been more widely realised as the media for accessibility. Through a thorough investigation of access provision practices within the two fields, the research aims to combine the best applications within the two fields to suggest potential implementation of AVT and AST elements towards accessible online educational environments while catering for the needs of students with sensory impairments.

Keywords: online education, assistive technology, audiovisual translation, accessibility, access services, subtitling, audio description, deaf, hard-of-hearing, sensory impairments, blind, partially sighted.

1 Introduction

In the age of e-Inclusion (European Commission, 2010) and equality in opportunities, it is crucial to define research by the skopos[1] it serves and combine knowledge in order to make it more effective and useful to society. In the case of accessibility and access services, it is particularly difficult to conduct fruitful research that would be of factual value for people with sensory impairments due to the complexity of its nature. Two completely heterogeneous and relatively new fields of research, Assistive Technology (AST) and Audiovisual Translation (AVT), have given signs of prosperity with regard to access services, particularly with the aim to provide accessible educational material on the Web. However, their combination is not an easy task, especially with the absence of a common theoretical background applying to educational purposes. The multiple risks of the 'uncontrolled' use and provision of access services regarding their source, manner of provision and coverage, make such an attempt an extremely challenging one, especially considering the purpose of such provision in

---

[1] Term used in Translation to indicate the 'purpose' satisfied through a translation task, as introduced by Vermeer [1]. It is expressed as IA(Trl) = f(Sk) (ibid: 100), indicating that translation is a function of its purpose. Adopted in this research in a wider context, to indicate the purpose of an attempt to provide content through the use of assistive practices.

C. Stephanidis and M. Antona (Eds.): UAHCI/HCII 2014, Part II, LNCS 8514, pp. 388–399, 2014.

education, meaning accurate and informative-educational transmission of input. The lack of visibility in the potential of AVT towards that end, as well as the lack of training and information about AST and its use might hold this attempt back. Still, the plentiful points of join and the usefulness of such a combination for the provision of a more holistic and inclusive approach in online education could overcome those barriers.

2 AVT, Access Services and AST

2.1 Access Services within Translation and AVT

AVT is widely considered as a field that is limited to screen translation, i.e. translation for cinemas, DVDs and TV programs, and thus that the skills required for the translation of AV material by AVT practitioners are limited to the translation of its content and their ability to use software for its preparation, taking into consideration mainly linguistic and technical restrictions, such as synchronization between text and sound, syntax, etc. The value of AVT services as means of access to entertainment for people with sensory impairments has led to a recent research trend towards the use of specific AVT types with the aim of accessibility, meaning the availability of content to people with sensory impairments, which they would otherwise not be able to access. These AVT types have evolved according to the purpose they serve and have led to the gradual establishment of access services within AVT.

The two main types of AVT put under the microscope for the needs of the current research are Subtitling for the deaf and hard-of-hearing (SDH) and Audio Description (AD). SDH is subtitling produced for deaf and hard-of-hearing viewers, featuring audiovisual material which is either broadcast or watched in any form of distribution of audiovisual material. It might also be used to advance interaction through the Internet and in technology applications in general (e.g. video games), often with an educational aim addressing a wide audience, too. SDH can be both intralingual and interlingual, two terms introduced by Jakobson [2]. Intralingual SDH is performed within the same language, i.e. from Greek into Greek for deaf and hard-of-hearing, while interlingual SDH is the same process albeit between one or more different languages, i.e. English into Greek for deaf and hard-of-hearing. SDH differs from typical interlingual subtitles mainly because it adheres to slightly different norms as far as the reading speed and the syntax of the subtitle content is concerned, and it includes additional information (e.g. indication of speakers through the use of standard colouring of the subtitles associated to them) [3]. AD is a process that "provides a narration of the visual elements – action, costumes, settings, and the like – of theatre, television/film, museums exhibitions, and other events" and it "allows patrons who are blind or have low-vision the opportunity to experience arts events more completely – the visual made verbal" [4]. AD falls under the intersemiotic category of translation as he describes this practice as "the conversion of nonverbal signs into words" [5].

The matter of succession between conventional AVT and AVT in the form of access services is very complex considering that the first form of subtitles, intertiles, was not actually used to translate context between different languages, but rather to transmit a message for purposes of comprehension. This fact alone is a proof for the rightful study of access services within the branch of AVT, which is also reinforced by the notion that "Accessibility is a form of translation and translation is a form of accessibility, uniting all population groups and ensuring that cultural events, in the broader sense of the word, can be enjoyed by all" [6]. Orero and Neves trace two mainstream access services, audio description (AD) and subtitling for the deaf and hard-of-hearing (SDH), back in the 1940s (for AD) and the 1970s (for SDH) in Spain and the UK respectively [7-8]. However, it was not until the last decade that AVT researchers took the plunge to call attention to access services within the academia, following their advent and use on a rather steady base on public and private TV channels around Europe. Media Accessibility is defined as "a new research line which has been perfectly accommodated under the umbrella of AVT studies" [9].

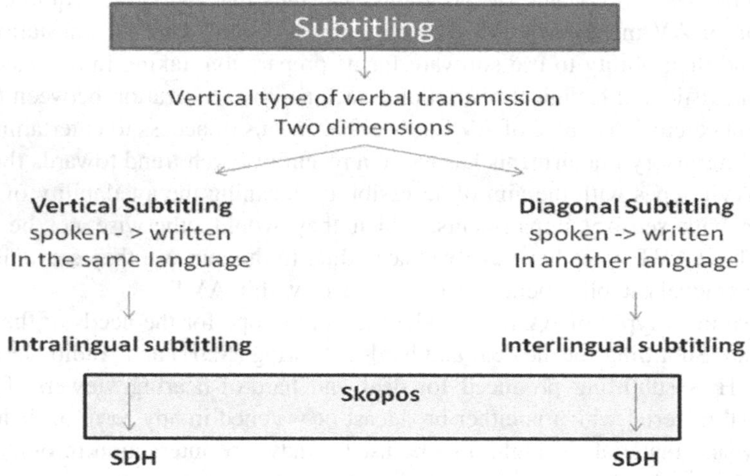

Fig. 1. Gottlieb and Jakobson's theories combined with skopos in SDH [2, 10-11]

The challenge of the transmission channel in Translation and AVT, along with the skopos served each time, forms a very solid basis for the explanation of the main differences between conventional and access AVT. While in Translation and Interpreting, the two main types of Translation, the verbal transmission is one-dimensional, i.e. transferring/translating spoken material to spoken material of text material to text material between two languages, Gottlieb identifies subtitling as a two-dimensional translation practice, since it can be both vertical and diagonal, terms relevant to what Jakobson describes as intralingual and interlingual [10]. In subtitling the media of transmission changes completely, making SDH a different task to that of conventional subtitling. On top of the common challenges of subtitling, with SDH there is the need to transfer sound, style, tone, etc. into image through 'translation' and there is a whole different skopos, i.e. to allow people to access the input of the screen and based on the type of input, meaning access-education or access-entertainment (Fig. 1). The task is also challenging with AD, and it is claimed within the AVT industry that audio describers need to be extremely skilled professionals, since they need to do the opposite, often with more restrictions (time, length, resources, etc.). The audio describer needs to turn any visual elements into sound, changing the skopos of a conventional documentary commentary or voice-over, while this description of theirs does not always carry a meaning expressed with words, but rather faces, behaviors, etc.

2.2 Assistive Technology on the Web for Sensory Impairments

During the last decades, Assistive Technology has been gaining ground within Information and Communications Technology (ICT), Human-Computer Interaction (HCI) and the Web, providing various ways to make the use of computers possible, easier and more flexible for people with disabilities. The first instance of modern AST[2] in the broader term of "any item, piece of equipment, or system, whether acquired commercially, modified, or customized, that is commonly used to increase, maintain, or improve functional capabilities of individuals with disabilities" (section 508 ADA) [12], dates as early as in 1874 with the invention of the audiophone bone conduction amplifier. Assistive Technology no longer limits itself to assistive and adaptive hardware as introduced by the Individuals with Disabilities Education Act of 1990 in the United States. More recent definitions of AST, for example "any item, piece of equipment, or product system… that is used to increase, maintain, or improve functional capacities of individuals with disabilities" [13], are much more inclusive and more relevant to the current research context. Software developments, such as screen readers, are gradually substituting hardware since they have proved to be affordable, more practical and rather multifunctional, and in many cases accompany them in their use for more effective results. With the development of the field, assistive technology can be categorized even further according to the disabilities it caters for, e.g. mobility, visual and assistive listening, since it encompasses multiple resources.

However, another two important parameters need to be considered within the context of assistive technology used in education by people with sensory impairments, – which is the scope of the Accessible Online Education research– although those parameters could facilitate the choice of AST in different contexts and for different purposes too. The mere provision of AST, no matter how well it has been matched to the needs of the intended user, will probably not suffice without the right interventions that will enable the proper use of a given technology [14]. Within this context, such interventions need to be provided and communicated by educational and social institutions to trainees and their families/support mechanisms. Interventions in a more wide sense could vary from training to use of supplementary aids and their aim is for users to handle technologies effectively. Another important parameter is the nature of assistive technologies: hardware or software, online and offline, by the user or by the provider (e.g. website host), as well as features of assistive technology that rank them in the continuum of low and high-tech assistive tools for young children with disabilities, including factors like cost, training requirements and transportability [15].

---

2 As opposed to assistive tools that have accompanied human nature since its existence, e.g. wooden splints.

People with sensory impairments use assistive technologies in their everyday life through commonly used devices, in order to satisfy the basic needs of communication, information and entertainment. In education, these also include from expanded keyboards to on-screen tools. At the same time, several applications are implemented 'internally', by specific hosts/providers of applications and services, making life even easier for users who visit their websites. The Web is an area that has massively affected the growth in use of assistive technologies and set the ground for the development of online and user-interface-based solutions, like screen readers. The new, more democratic 'Web for all' opens new possibilities in education. With regulations and directives demanding it, like the eGovernment Action Plan of the European Union and the European Accessibility Act of the EU Disability Strategy for the decade 2010-2020, as well as guidelines that instruct developers and content providers in order to achieve this goal, like the Web Content Accessibility Guidelines of the World Wide Web Consortium (W3C), AST on the Web has been gaining ground and spreading very fast. Even if "improvements in Web accessibility have arisen, in part, as side effects of changes in Web technology and associated shifts in the way Web pages are designed and coded" [16], they have played a crucial role in the inclusion of users with sensory disabilities on the Web.

3 SDH and AD: Assisting Users on the Web

According to version 2.0 of the W3C guidelines [17], developers need to provide alternatives for time-based media when they offer such material on their websites. These alternatives include equivalents for pre-recorded audio-only and video-only media, captions, conventional or extended/descriptive audio description for pre-recorded media, as well as live captions for live audio content in synchronised media. With this step, SDH and AD establish their role as access services in online contexts. Before that, SDH and AD were mostly present on the Web either in the form of amateur services provided by AVT enthusiasts (e.g. in the form of fansubbing[3]) or as parts of pre-recorded material whenever providers decided to publish this material on the Web. The HTML5 development made the inclusion of forms of SDH and AD easier for developers. HTML5 is the outcome of the collaboration between the Web Hypertext Application Technology Working Group and W3C. It natively supports video without the need for third party plugins. Its <video> and <audio> elements can be inserted in a website's code for media playback while the <track> element allows authors to specify alternatives, or more correctly, support content to multi-media content.

These developments might seemingly favour SDH, AD and AST, still they have brought about big changes to the nature and preparatory process of the services. The first major change with regard to AST was the emergence of the "open source

[3] Fansubs or amateur subtitles are subtitles created by fans who want to watch movies or television broadcasts by downloading them from the Internet. Their quality is widely questioned as they do not adhere to specific guidelines or rules and thus they can be very creative or sometimes too unconventional.

movement" [18], which is based on the general idea that software product distribution should go hand in hand with source code distribution for successful implementation. This kind of software includes infrastructure technologies, server and desktop operating systems, Web browsers, desktop application software and Web applications, but its implementation lacks long-term support or comprehensive user documentation and causes issues with regard to data sensitivity [18]. It is also significant that once they are applied on the Web, access services and tools are nowadays implemented to several devices very fast, including smartphones and iPads, as well as new Web products, like "the cloud" and Web/hybrid TV, making the task even more complex.

These developments, in turn, require more labour and time, which has led to the rise of crowd-sourcing, as well as mechanic and synthesized "on demand" or real-time captioning and AD, two trends that are widely accused of threatening the quality of access services, especially in terms of accuracy and precision. Synthesized AD, speech-to-text narration, video description and annotation, are some of the latest developments in the field of synthesized speech and voice recognition that attempt to substitute audience-targeted and humanly produced SDH and AD. The possibilities they offer, especially with regard to AD, are many and they include text-to-speech narration for AD that has been initially produced by the script editor and annotation for the enrichment of videos with the use of speech synthesis and earcons (i.e. non-verbal audio messages) by enrichment producers [19]. In an attempt to evaluate synthesized video descriptions, Kobayashi et al. [20] conducted research in Japan and the USA and reached the conclusion that they are generally accepted regardless of the quality of language, but that they should be used where the aim is to inform rather than to entertain. This conclusion supports access services as seen within AVT, i.e. services provided for people with sensory impairments, in order to satisfy their particular needs.

With regard to subtitling, crowdsourcing has become available through both simple and more sophisticated means. Open source software and platforms hosting audiovisual material offer users a simple working environment in order to create captions for their videos or to acquire captions that have been produced through machine translation and speech recognition. The open availability of subtitles for editing purposes, the lack of conventions that make them address deaf and hard-of-hearing audiences, as well as the lack of identification of their editors can often contribute to questioning their quality and usefulness. At the same time, networks of crowdsourcing subtitling are being built in an attempt to produce fast real-time captioning with minimum latency and maximum precision with hybrid contributors, rather than solely humans. One indicative example of crowd-sourced subtitling is Legion:Scribe, a system that "captions speech on-demand and with less than 3 seconds latency", as the company claims, "by automatically merging the simultaneous input of multiple crowd workers" [21].

Although these developments seem to undermine the importance of the human factor in the process of SDH and AD preparation —and automatic captioning is nowhere near proper SDH with regard to the skopos it serves since it does not include the conventions that make SDH subtitling for deaf people through the provision of acoustic information or conventions used for identification of speakers, etc.—, they have led to a number of positive developments and realizations. AD is now also treated as a tool for navigation for blind and illiterate people, while new types of AD have made their appearance, adding value to the access service and attracting more researchers. A new kind of "enhanced AD" has been proposed with the aim to attract a wider audience, including visually impaired viewers, and to turn AD into a "revenue generation product widely adopted by production companies" [22]. Another suggestion in the field is "Dynamic Captioning approach" with the implementation of a number of technologies, including visual saliency analysis and face detection, for the enhancement of AD with scripts that aid comprehension of the video material [23]. A similar approach is that applied by the Smith-Kettlewell Video Description Research and Development Center, which advanced video annotation methods for use in various educational settings. Within this technological bloom, the existence and importance of SDH and AD are spread to countries where the provision of access services is at a very low level. However, it is crucial to differentiate between conventional captioning and SDH and in the case of synthesised or crowd-sourced captioning, the realisation of the need of the human mediator in order for captions to serve SDH purposes plays an important role when these methods are suggested for the provision of online educational material.

4 Accessible Online Education

The value of AV material in education was recognized long before computers existed in class. With the use of video recorders and TV sets, students could watch video tapes with educational content. And although technology would seem to promote the use of AV material in education, the paradox of different perceptions can be summarized in the following quotes [24-25]:

"We know the importance of pedagogy in the use of audio-visual aids. […] …we must look at audio-visual aids and the various questions which they raise." (Lestage in UNESCO)

"Given the speed constraints of networks today and the lack of necessary hardware and software available to learners, we advise instructors to use multimedia resources sparingly." (Haughey and Anderson)

The paradox is not limited to the fact that technology should enhance the use of other than the traditional teaching models. It is the time when these quotes were made that could intrigue education specialists as it would be expected that technology would be seen as an aid rather than a hurdle in class in the 1990s. However, different provisions and contexts within educational institutions might have led to people being discouraged to use AV material, as well as advanced technologies in class. Nowadays, AV material has a dominant position in education. A major factor that has contributed to that is their availability on the Web, as well as new technologies that have made their use and reproduction much easier for educators. With the advent of podcasts, webinars and video file hosting services online (e.g. TeacherTube), education has found an enormous resource both for students and teachers, whether this is indeed used in class or not.

AVT has often been studied in terms of its potential in education and has mostly been related to second language learning. However, and especially during the last decade, SDH and AD have been examined as tools for education and have both been associated with Special Education in particular. While SDH and AD gain their position in entertainment, they are gradually being discovered from the angle of education for people with sensory impairments, as well as in second language acquisition. Since 2008, research has indicated that AD is a very useful tool for children's education, yet it is necessary to adjust it to the particular age and general needs of the intended audience. Described and captioned media have proved to be important in learning environments with the aim to raise literacy levels, while SDH proves to be functional for deaf children. SDH is greatly valued as a service that advances learners' reading and writing skills in the same way that AD enhances their speaking and listening skills. At the same time, and from a more sociological point of view, SDH bridges the gap between pre-lingual and post-lingual deafness, since it provides a solution for those who use sign language as well as people who lost their hearing at a later stage in their lives and in many cases prefer not to learn another language, but rather use written texts as a means for communication. Finally, just as SDH and AD have been designed for particular audiences and they end up being used by wider groups of people (e.g. elderly or illiterate), they can cater for more disabilities and learning difficulty-related problems, such as dyslexia and color blindness.

Online Education, e-Learning or Online Learning are three terms generally used to refer to education provided on the Web with the use of ICT technology. The material provided in the context of Online Education can be distinguished between those used in class or as supplementary class content/resources and those provided on the Web alone as individual online courses. Computers were used in education since the 1960s, when the first virtual classroom was formed in the University of Illinois. Computer-assisted training in class was introduced in the 1970s, while the first online courses appeared as early as in the 1980s. Web-based learning is generally differentiated among three models [26]: Web-support for information storage, dissemination and retrieval, Web-support for two-way interaction and Web-based teaching, all of which are currently performed with the use of AV material through virtual libraries, video-calls, live lectures, etc. Today, many universities around the world offer online courses where students can attend and participate in a virtual class using their computer. With the e-Inclusion policy of the European Commission, the elevation of the idea of the 'accessible Web' with standards and guidelines that make it inclusive, as well as the prominence of AST and access services, e-Learning gains more potential by addressing wider audiences and provides opportunities for development in online accessibility. Two trends can be observed in the use online contexts for higher education with or without the support of assistive technology. Universities might offer online courses or resources but avoid the use of AV material (live or pre-recorded), while they might also use online platforms for educational purposes without making the material accessible to users. Many universities include non-accessible AV material on their general websites and others make attempts to provide access services, for selected material in most cases, but do not do so collectively, i.e. by providing these services in an overall accessible context and at a regular pace. In a multi-method analysis conducted by Kane et al. for home pages of 100 top international universities, results showed that there are still many accessibility problems that are in essence obstacles to accessible Online Education [27].

Using a Functional Accessibility Evaluator, they measured the functionality of home pages. Although this sample is partial as the research does not examine the provision of online AV material or even whole websites, since the status of the home page of each university indicates that on average accessibility guidelines are only partially implemented, then it could be argued that these universities did not seem to offer a friendly environment to people with disabilities. However, based on the Europe 2020 Initiative, it is expected that educational institutions will have to provide accessible Online Education within the idea of "accessibility as a right for all" (European Commission, 2010) [28] with focus on digital technologies and assistive tools. As distance learning is becoming more popular within and outside Europe, educational institutes could benefit from the provision of accessible educational material, both AV and other (e.g. editable texts allowing magnification, selection, screen-reading, etc.), as such a provision would attract more students, as well as set the grounds for more in-depth and pioneer research in education from several angles (including Special Education and Sociology).

A number of products, most of which result from research projects in the field of AST, have emerged as an attempt to provide more inclusive solutions with regard to Online Education and AV material, still offering various levels of accessibility, rather than holistic solutions. Most of them seem to focus on assisting either deaf and hard-of-hearing or blind and partially sighted students. Some interesting recent research projects include ClassInFocus, DELE, SSTAT, MVP and the Photonote system.

Table 1. Functional accessibility of top 100 university sites (Kane et al.: 153).

Functional category	Average error (%)	Accessibility status
Navigation & Orientation	36.07	Not Implemented
Text Equivalents	51.24	Partially Implemented
Scripting	54.00	Partially Implemented
Styling	50.95	Partially Implemented
HTML Standards	69.74	Partially Implemented

SSTAT (Semantic and Syntactic Transcription Analysing Tool) provides accurate lecture transcriptions through analyzing and editing Automatic Speech Recognition-generated transcripts, while ClassInFocus offers in-class information in one screen, allowing deaf and hard-of-hearing students to engage in group work, capture the class to review any missing information and observe sign language interpreters along with the instructor. The Photonote system combines visual information in the same way to provide pre-recorded lectures to deaf and hard-of-hearing students. DELE (Deaf-centered E-Learning Environment) is a fully-iconic e-learning environment through which tutors can "define, generate and test e-learning courses for deaf people, which are automatically managed, published and served by the system itself." [29]. Finally, MVP (Multiple-View Platform) can be used by students in class to edit lecture visuals through their own devices, as well as cooperate in groups.

Most of the research conducted in the field focuses on the provision of captioning for deaf students and it seems that this is also the trend in commercial solutions obtained by universities around the world. Among the most prominent commercial solutions that are in use are Panopto, Tegrity, MediaSite and Echo306. All of them are systems which form learning environments that capture video, audio and screen activity. They support captions, whether these are produced by people or machines (speech-to-text technologies) and offer users the opportunity to edit videos, make notes annotated to the video, as well as have access to further material provided by the instructor, e.g. PowerPoint presentations. Individual open-source solutions that allow providers to create accessible AV material through AD and captioning include Amara, YouTube, MAGpie, CapScribe and LiveDescribe. These are tools rather than learning solutions, which however satisfy the needs of both blind and deaf students when combined accordingly by teachers. Finally, large-scale projects funded by the EU are gradually aiming towards educational solutions for students with sensory impairments with the use of AVT and other related practices, with the example of ClipFlair (2011) which aims to develop an online social network for the provision of material for learning languages purposes through a series of access services (including captioning and re-voicing) and lesson plans that allow learners to practise their speaking, listening, reading and writing skills.

5 Concluding Remarks

Based on the above, it is important to provide holistic solutions that will encompass the needs of all students with sensory impairments. AST and access services have proved to be the catalysts towards that direction, but what is missing is a functional approach that will allow students to enter learning environments as self-serviced individuals, an idea introduced by Cornford and Pollock [30], illustrating the meaningfulness of Web-based learning for the students who use it avoiding the need for guardians in education. Towards that end, and based on the specificity of the skopos for the provision of access services, the latter should be respected in terms of their nature too. Where synthetic and machine-oriented solutions are not appropriate in education, solutions that provide this kind of accessibility should be critically viewed and carefully chosen. It is also important to re-evaluate the existing standards and guidelines for the provision of accessible content on the Web. These guidelines may often make demands for accessible AV material, still they do not specify the process of their production and provision. Finally, AST tools and access services should be combined in order to achieve that aim and maybe the best place to start is by bridging the gap between these disciplines at a research level. The Accessible Online Education research aims to (a) set the theoretical background for the collaboration of the two fields, (b) provide an overview of attempts towards the design and effective use of accessible educational environments and (c) data for the level of accessibility offered by selected universities through an online survey, and (d) make a coherent and practical suggestion for the design of a new universal educational platform that will cater for the needs of the intended users in higher education as it is provided online. The research considers all the limitations explained in this paper, giving emphasis to the quality of educational material which is considered crucial.

References

1. Vermeer, H.J.: Skopos and commission in translational action. Chesterman A (trans.). In: Venuti, L. (ed.) The Translation Studies Reader, pp. 221–233. Routledge, London (2000)
2. Jakobson, R.: On Linguistic Aspects of Translation. Harvard University Press, New York (1959)
3. Ivarsson, J., Carrol, M.: Subtitling. TransEdit, Simrishamn (1998)
4. Snyder, J.: Fundamentals of Audio Description. Teaching Audio Description: An On-Line Approach. In: 4th International Conference Media for All 4, June 28-July 1. Imperial College, London (2011)
5. Díaz Cintas, J.: Audiovisual Translation Today – A Question of Accessibility for All. Translating Today 4, 3–5 (2005)
6. Díaz Cintas, J., Orero, P., Remael, A. (eds.): Media for All: Subtitling for the Deaf, Audio Description, and Sign Language. Rodopi, Amsterdam (2007)
7. Orero, P.: Sampling Audio Description in Europe. In: Díaz Cintas, J., Orero, P., Remael, A. (eds.) Media for All: Subtitling for the Deaf, Audio Description, and Sign Language, pp. 111–125. Rodopi, Amsterdam (2007)
8. Neves, J.: Audiovisual Translation: Subtitling for the Deaf and Hard of Hearing. Roehampton University, London. PhD Thesis (2005)
9. Díaz Cintas, J., Matamala, A., Neves, J. (eds.): Media for All 2: New Insights into Audiovisual Translation and Media Accessibility. Rodopi, Amsterdam (2010)
10. Gottlieb, H.: Teaching Translation and Interpreting 2: Insights, aims and visions. In: Dollerup, C., Lindegaard, A. (eds.) Papers from the Second Language International Conference Elsinore 1993, pp. 262–274 (1994)
11. Patiniotaki, E.: An approach to subtitling for deaf and hard of hearing audience in Greece. Dissertation. Imperial College, London, pp. 41–43 (2009)
12. Information and Technological Assistance of the Americans with Disabilities Act (ADA): SECTION 508 SURVEYS and REPORTS, `http://www.ada.gov/508/`
13. SEDL: Empowering Rural Students with Disabilities Through Assistive Technology, `http://www.sedl.org/rural/seeds/assistivetech/atdefine.html`
14. Lancioni, G.E., Sigafoof, J., O'Reilly, M.F., Singh, N.N.: Assistive Technology: Inteventions for Individuals with Severe/Profound Multiple Disabilities. Springer Science and Business Media, New York (2013)
15. Parette, H.P., Parette Jr., H.P., Murdick, N.L.: Assistive Technology and lEPs for Young Children with Disabilities. Early Childhood Education Journal 25, 3 (1998)
16. Richards, J.T., Montague, K., Hanson, V.L.: Web Accessibility as a Side Effect. In: ASSETS 2012, Colorado, October 22-24, pp. 79–86 (2012)
17. World Wide Web Consortium (W3C). Web Content Accessibility Guidelines (WCAG) 2.0 (2008), `http://www.w3.org/TR/WCAG/`
18. Heron, M., Hanson, V.L., Ricketts, I.: Open source and accessibility: advantages and limitations. Journal of Interaction Science 1 (2013)

19. Encelle, B., Ollagnier-Beldame, M., Pouchot, S., Yannick, P.: Annotation-based Video Enrichment for Blind People: A Pilot Study on the use of Earcons and Speech Synthesis. In: ASSETS 2011, Dundee, October 24-26, pp. 123–130 (2011)
20. Kobayashi, M., O'Connell, T., Gould, B., Takagi, H., Chieko, A.: Are Synthesized Video Descriptions Acceptable? In: ASSETS 2010, Florida, October 25-27, pp. 163–170 (2010)
21. Rochester Human Computer Interaction (ROC HCI): Legion:Scribe (2012), http://hci.cs.rochester.edu/currentprojects.php?proj=scb
22. Sade, J., Naz, K., Plaza, M.: Enhancing Audio Description: A Value Added Approach. In: Miesenberger, K., Karshmer, A., Penaz, P., Zagler, W. (eds.) ICCHP 2012, Part I. LNCS, vol. 7382, pp. 270–277. Springer, Heidelberg (2012)
23. Hong, R., Meng, W., Mengdi, X., Shuicheng, Y., Tat-Seng, C.: Dynamic Captioning: Video Accessibility Enhancement for Hearing Impairment. In: MM 2010, Firenze, October 25-29, pp. 421–430 (2010)
24. UNESCO. UNESCO Chronicle: The use of audiovisual aids in education (1959), http://www.unesco.org/education/nfsunesco/pdf/LESTAG_E.PDF
25. Haughey, M., Anderson, T.: Network Learning: The Pedagogy of the Internet. Chenelière/McGraw-Hill, Montreal (1998)
26. Aggarwal, A.: Web-based Education. In: Aggarwal, A. (ed.) Web-Based Learning and Teaching Technologies: Opportunities and Challenges, Idea Group Publishing, Hersley (2000)
27. Kane, S.K., Shulman, J.A., Shokley, T.J., Ladner, R.E.: A Web Accessibility Report Card for Top International University Web Sites. In: W4A 2007 Communications Paper, Banff, May 7-8, pp. 148–156 (2007)
28. European Commission: Digital Agenda for Europe: A Europe, Initiative – Action 63: Evaluate accessibility in legislation (2020), http://ec.europa.eu/digital-agenda/en/pillar-vi-enhancing-digital-literacy-skills-and-inclusion/action-63-evaluate-accessibility
29. Bottoni, P., Capuano, D., De Marsico, M., Labella, A., Velialdi, S.: Experimenting DELE: a Deaf-centered e-Learning Visual Environment. In: AVI 2012, Capri Island, May 21-25, pp. 780–781 (2012)
30. Cornford, J., Pollock, N.: Putting the University Online: Information, Technology and Organizational Change. SRHE and Open University Press, Buckingham (2003)

Skill Development Framework for Micro-Tasking

Shin Saito[1], Toshihiro Watanabe[2], Masatomo Kobayashi[1], and Hironobu Takagi[1]

[1] IBM Research – Tokyo, 5-6-52 Toyosu, Koto, Tokyo 135-8511, Japan
{shinsa,mstm,takagih}@jp.ibm.com
[2] The University of Tokyo, 7-3-1 Hongo, Bunkyo, Tokyo 113-8656, Japan
toshihiro_watanabe@mist.i.u-tokyo.ac.jp

Abstract. We propose a framework of micro-tasking that intrinsically supports the development of workers' skills. It aims to help developers of micro-tasking systems add skill development capabilities to their systems with minimal development costs. This will allow micro-tasking of skill-intensive work and improve the sustainability of micro-tasking systems. Based on the results of the micro-tasking projects we have carried out, our framework has three core modules: tutorial producer, task dispatcher, and feedback visualizer, which are supported by a back-end skill assessment engine. In closing, we discuss ways to apply the proposed framework to realistic micro-tasking situations.

Keywords: Crowdsourcing, Micro-Tasks, Skill Assessment, Skill Development, Gamification, Senior Workforce.

1 Introduction

Crowdsourcing provides an emerging type of labor market. There are two major types: macro-tasking and micro-tasking. Macro-tasks involve freelancers who work on complex tasks in projects or contests. Micro-tasks split a job into small pieces of work distributed to a number of workers via the Internet. Although both types of crowdsourcing call for skillful workers who can produce high-quality outcomes, particularly for micro-tasking there has been little attention to developing the skills of the workers, so the scope has generally been limited to lightweight tasks that need relatively less skill. The quality of the outcomes is controlled by filtering for workers who have higher skills, without considering the development of the individual workers' skills. However, if micro-tasking systems support skill development, they can produce outcomes of higher-quality and make their use more sustainable. This could expand the new labor market in two ways. First, it can provide younger workers with vocational training to learn job skills. Second, it can allow senior workers, who have advanced vocational knowledge but limited skills in information-communication technologies (ICT), to learn ICT skills so that they can do online work. The skill development support will make micro-tasking more suitable for more advanced tasks that call for expert skills.

This paper proposes a micro-tasking framework that develops the skills of the workers. First we review the literature as well as two of our own micro-tasking

C. Stephanidis and M. Antona (Eds.): UAHCI/HCII 2014, Part II, LNCS 8514, pp. 400–409, 2014.

projects, leading us to three capabilities the framework needs to have: tutorial producer, task dispatcher, and feedback visualizer. The tutorial producer generates learning materials based on task examples. The task dispatcher assigns a series of tasks to each worker based on the worker's learning curve. The feedback visualizer provides each worker with feedback about their efforts, their contributions, and the results of their skill development. The three functions require a back-end analytics module to analyze the results produced by each worker to assess the profiles of each worker, e.g., work accuracy, and the characteristics of each task, e.g., difficulty. Since the modules are encapsulated and connected with abstract interfaces, implementations of each module can be reused among different types of micro-tasking. This allows the developers to build micro-tasking systems that support skill development, by simply implementing task-specific operations.

This paper is organized as follows. In the next section, we review related work. Section 3 reviews our micro-tasking projects and discusses some implications. Section 4 describes the proposed framework. Then we discuss the applications of our framework in Section 5 and conclude the paper.

2 Related Work

Regarding worker education, macro-tasking services such as oDesk [29] and CrowdFlower [30] provide various training material and the learning history of each worker is used by requesters to choose workers. In contrast, skill development in micro-tasking receives a weaker focus. Amazon Mechanical Turk [31] and other micro-tasking platforms are interested in how to use inexpensive workers to produce more accurate results in less time. Although some studies have proposed frameworks to solve complex tasks via micro-tasking [1, 2], they paid little attention to skill development. One of the few exceptions is the work of Satzger et al. [3], which used the "tandem task assignment" approach to improve the skills of low-confidence workers. Kittur et al. [4] pointed out the potential of "crowd work-based education". Weld et al. [5] discussed personalized online education in crowdsourcing. They suggested maximizing learners' skills, whereas the typical goal in crowdsourcing is minimizing the costs to obtain high quality results. RABJ [6] tried to educate workers by selecting managers from the workers. These managers are responsible for creating task-specific guidelines and validating workers' output. Duolingo [32] allows users to learn foreign languages while contributing to crowdsourced translation work.

The assessment of workers' skills is essential for skill development. Several methods have been proposed with probabilistic models to simultaneously estimate both the skill of the workers and the difficulty of tasks [7-9]. There are also some studies that addressed task assignment based on the estimated skills [10, 11]. Tracking skill improvement over time is also essential. Donmez et al. [12] worked on the modeling of skills that are changing over time. However their system only handled short-term changes caused by fatigue. The changes were related to the time spent working, and were not affected by the properties of the tasks.

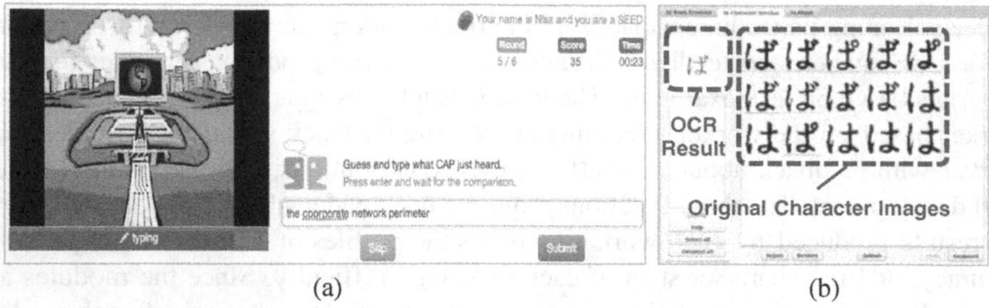

Fig. 1. Screenshots of (a) video captioning and (b) proofreading interfaces

3 Implications of Micro-Tasking Projects

We now describe two micro-tasking projects conducted by the authors and analyze them to clarify the requirements for our framework. In both cases the workers were unpaid volunteers and certain skills were required to complete the tasks. The two projects have similar implications for the skill development of the workers. These implications span many of the issues discussed in existing crowdsourcing research.

3.1 Crowdsourced Video Captioning

CapCap [13] provides video captions while also developing the linguistic skills of non-native workers (Fig. 1(a)). It is a gamified version of Collaborative Caption Editing System (CCES) [14], where each micro-task transcribes a short video segment (typically less than 10 seconds). A CapCap task is a game based on a similar concept to the ESP game [15], where workers iteratively caption the same segment, earning points in proportion to the degree of similarity between the outputs. CapCap has additional motivating features: levels, ranks, and teams. The level goes up as the worker's accumulated points increase. The system shows the team ranking and the level distribution within the worker's team. We introduced teams to motivate novices who could not earn high scores by themselves. CapCap was tested for three weeks in the authors' institution. See [13] for details of this experiment.

Findings. In the pilot period, 713 video segments with English narrations were distributed to 105 volunteer workers. A total of 60 segments were completed, with an average word error rate (WER) of 4.0%. The workers consisted of 15 native English speakers and 81 native Japanese speakers. The skill of each worker, which we defined as the average WER of the captions created by the worker, varied widely from 13.2% to 67.2% (among those who played more than 5 rounds). Due to the short pilot period, we could not verify its actual educational effect, though we will study this in the future. The workers generally rated the game design positively. However a novice who does not use English on a daily basis found "the content was too difficult for me", which suggests that the skill gaps could demotivate workers. Some novice workers criticized the motivational system, saying that it was too hard to get to higher levels. Such comments indicate that slightly different incentives are needed for skill-focused workers versus task-oriented workers versus the most skilled workers who produced the highest quality results. We want to maximize overall participation by recognizing and responding to the motivational differences among these three groups of workers. Other comments included "I did not know how to play the game" and "I wanted to know the scoring rules", even though CapCap included instructions. Since it was a real-time game, the simple static instructions were inadequate.

3.2 Crowdsourced Proofreading

EBIS (E-Book Improvement System) [16, 17] crowdsources proofreading, with the workers correcting OCR (Optical Character Recognition) errors (Fig. 1(b)). The system has multiple types of proofreading tasks and an online forum where workers can communicate with each other and ask questions about the tasks. The system allows workers to work on their preferred types of tasks. Each worker received visual feedback about their task history, such as the number of contributed books and the worker ranking based on the amount of completed work. Prior to the project launch, we held a full-day introductory session for the initial workers. We also provided them with printed manuals. The project started in October 2013, with an open participation policy. We analyzed the data for approximately the first three months of operations. See [18] for details of the experiment.

Findings. As of January 2014, 178 workers had registered, with 112 who did at least one task. They contributed more than 1,200 hours of work and completed 182 books. The attendees of the introductory session liked the session and the manuals, confirming the findings in [19, 20]. Those instructions were designed mainly for older workers who had no prior experience with crowdsourcing. However they should also be useful for other workers, since the micro-tasks in EBIS involve a number of editorial rules that workers had to learn. A total of 60 questions about the editorial rules and other topics were posted in the forum. Some of them had been addressed in manuals, but others were undocumented. The already addressed questions were asked mostly due to difficulties in understanding the rules, while the new topics were mostly related to the difficulty of the tasks. The preferences for task types varied among the workers. With regard to the visual feedback, Itoko et al. [18] reported that the visualization of their contributions was preferred by the workers of all ages, while the younger workers liked the ranking scores more than the seniors did. A worker commented that she strongly wanted feedback on the accuracy of her work rather than rankings, which indicates the potential for personalized feedback.

3.3 Implications

Here are three similarities among the two projects: *importance of instructions*, *need for appropriate task assignment*, and *effectiveness of feedback to workers*. These findings lead to the following requirements for a skill development framework that allows gamified learning: (1) support for tutorial generation, (2) task assignment for gradual learning, (3) motivating feedback by visualization, and (4) back-end skill assessment engine that provides these three components with estimated skill information by analytics.

Support for Tutorial Generation. Although interactive lectures and printed instructions are effective, it is expensive to prepare them. While automatic manual generation techniques like GraphScript [21] may reduce the costs, human work is still needed. One alternative approach is RABJ [6], which selects *managers* from the workers, and these managers create guidelines for the tasks. As an alternative to interactive lectures, online interactive tutorials [22] may work well. Many modern computer games have interactive tutorials using the same user interface as the game itself. Such tutorials are provided in chunks of gradually increasing complexity and users naturally learn how to play the game [23]. Since authoring such tutorials is costly work, systems to help create tutorials from example tasks and from workers' behaviors are needed to reduce the costs.

Task Assignment for Gradual Learning. In our experiment with CapCap, the range of skills among workers varied widely, ranging from native English speakers to non-native beginners. The task difficulty also varied from studio-recorded content to a conversation among four people in a noisy environment. As pointed out by the novice worker in the experiment, the difficulty of the tasks assigned to a worker should be suitable for the worker's skills. After a task is completed, the worker may try a slightly more difficult task. This idea matches the evolving-skill model discussed in [3] as well as the *gamenics* theory [23]. Gamenics is a design principle for video games, which has two objectives: intuitive operability and gradual learning.

Motivating Feedback by Visualization. The visual feedback is effective motivation for workers (e.g., [24]). Motivation is divided into *intrinsic* and *extrinsic* motivation [25]. For example, progress visualization and content personalization improve intrinsic motivation, while social mechanisms such as competition work for extrinsic motivation. In the EBIS project, which aimed to benefit from both types of motivation, the young workers tended to prefer feedback for extrinsic motivation while the seniors had the opposite preference. Since there are a number of design choices for visualization, it is desirable that the administrator of the system be able to easily choose and change those settings.

Skill Assessment. Accurate assessment of workers' skills plays a crucial role in all of these three requirements. The estimated skills can be used to select appropriate tutorial content and micro-tasks for each worker as well as to present feedback for their progress in skill development. Various skill models can be used. For example, if we use the multi-dimensional skill model of Welinder et al. [8] for CapCap, the skills will

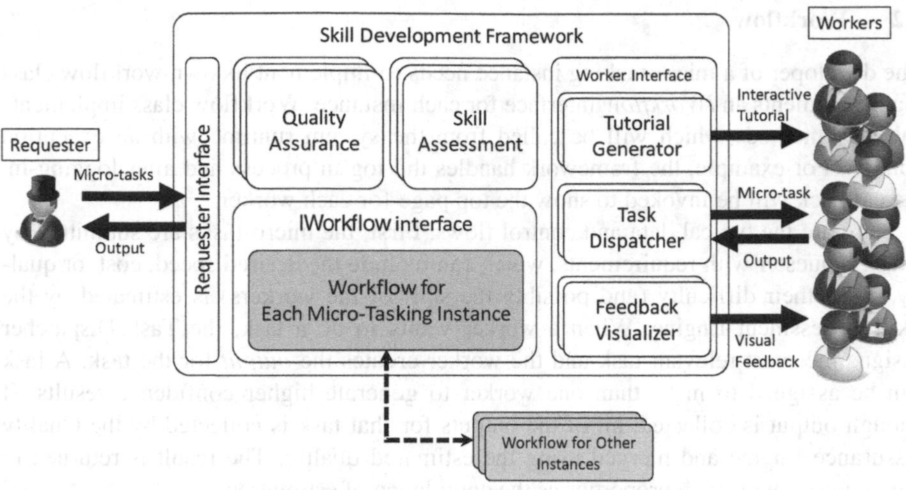

Fig. 2. Component diagram of the proposed framework

be represented as a combination of listening, writing, and keyboard typing skills. In EBIS, the skills consist of a sub-skill for each task type and each sub-skill is further divided into latent skills (ICT skills, visual acuity, etc.). Since a number of skill models have been proposed (see Related Work) and it is difficult to determine the best model in advance, the framework should allow easily switching skill models to find the most appropriate model through a tailoring approach.

4 Framework

Based on the discussion in the Section 3, we propose a micro-tasking framework that takes into account the development of each worker's skill, which is greatly different from the earlier micro-tasking frameworks.

4.1 Overall Architecture

The architecture of the proposed framework (Fig. 2) is inspired by OSGi [33], a Java modularity framework based on a plug-in architecture, where loosely-coupled components communicate with each other via standard or instance-specific APIs. It consists of core components including Tutorial Producer, Task Dispatcher, Feedback Visualizer, and Skill Assessment Engine, which correspond to the four functions discussed. It also has a Quality Assurance Engine, which tries to produce the best aggregate result for each requester considering the assessed skills, as well as shared libraries that help developers reuse frequently used functions among each instance. For example, the skill estimation algorithms used in the Skill Assessment Engine, the output merging algorithms used in the Quality Assurance Engine, and some user interface components, including the logging-in/out features, are shared. The workflow defines the instance-specific data and control flows, as described in Section 4.2.

4.2 Workflow

The developer of a micro-tasking instance needs to implement its own workflow class that implements an *IWorkflow* interface for each instance. Workflow class implements callback methods which will be called from the system runtime with an execution context. For example, the framework handles the log-in process and after logging-in, the callback will be invoked to show the top page for each worker.

Here are the typical data and control flows. First, the micro-tasks are submitted by a task requester with requirements, which can include the desired speed, cost, or quality. Then their difficulty (and possibly the skill of the workers) is estimated by the Skill Assessment Engine. When a worker wants to do a task, the Task Dispatcher assigns the most relevant task and the worker creates the *output* for the task. A task can be assigned to more than one worker to generate higher confidence results. If enough output is collected, all of the outputs for that task is collected by the Quality Assurance Engine and merged using the estimated quality. The result is returned to the requester with such properties as the confidence of estimation.

4.3 Core Components

Here we consider CapCap and skill assessment by Welinder et al. [8] as examples, where the workers are denoted by $u_i \in U$ and each CapCap task, i.e., a video segment, is denoted by $t_j \in T$, whose skill is expressed as a *d*-dimensional vector, $\boldsymbol{w}_i \in [0,1]^d$.

Skill Assessment Engine. Skill Assessment Engine plays a crucial role in the framework. We define a *work* element as a triplet of a user, a task, and its output, denoted by $(u_i, t_j, l_{ij}) \in U \times T \times L = W$, where l_{ij} is an output for task t_j by a worker u_i. This engine maintains a work history, which stores all of the work information, using $H = \mathfrak{P}(W)$. Then the engine computes or estimates the current skill of each worker, based on the history. It can also estimate the skill improvements by dividing H into time segments. These estimates are used by the other core components to make decisions on the workflow.

Tutorial Producer. This component provides helper functions for generating the graded-difficulty learning tutorial. For example, it provides sample task lists ordered by estimated difficulties, or it can identify the difficult tasks for which many workers produced wrong answers with the support of the Skill Assessment Engine. The developer needs to provide a tutorial user interface. Typically this is almost the same as the actual task UI, but runs when the *tutorial* flag is set to true.

Task Dispatcher. This component dispatches the most relevant micro-task to a specified worker with the help of the Skill Assessment Engine. Based on how the skills of each worker improve over time, it assigns the appropriate task to the worker. For example, if a worker is a novice, then easier tasks are assigned, while if the system (or the requester) wants a worker with intermediate skills to improve, then it dispatches challenging tasks to that worker.

Feedback Visualizer. This component provides visual feedback to motivate workers. Visualization includes showing the worker's skill set that changes over time, a work history including accuracy, and recommended tasks, as well as social-network-related visualizations such as competitive or collaborative features, with the help of the Skill Assessment Engine.

5 Discussion

5.1 Implementation Patterns Using the Framework

We describe several implementation patterns with this framework using EBIS and CapCap as examples. First, implementing EBIS from scratch using this framework would be straightforward. The developers would only need to implement EBIS-specific features such as task decomposition, which breaks down a single book into micro-tasks, output merging, and the user interface. They can benefit from the shared libraries including the worker account management, task assignment, and skill management. Starting from an EBIS implementation, CapCap could be easily implemented using this same framework. The developers would need to implement the CapCap task decomposition, the other components including the output merging and user interface can be reused from shared library or from EBIS. As a third case, if EBIS has already been implemented without using the framework, then the framework could be used to enhance EBIS to support skill development, but additional work would be needed. The current implementation would need to be refactored to match the framework APIs. In the first and second cases, the developments cost would be greatly reduced by using the framework. In the third case, though the costs would be higher than in the first and second cases, the code would be better and future modifications of the system would be much easier.

5.2 Applicability of the Framework

We believe the proposed framework will be applicable to a wide variety of micro-tasking applications. Our framework easily incorporates micro-tasking frameworks that focus on the quality of the output. For example, Dai et al. [26] and Lin et al. [9] use decision theoretic algorithms to assign tasks, where they compute a utility U to decide whether to dispatch a task to one of the workers or to generate final result. We can define and add new utility by considering the skill development of the workers, for example, by defining a utility based on improvement of skill when a task t_j would be assigned to a worker u_i.

We introduced the visualization as a motivational mechanism. What about other motivating mechanisms or incentives? It has been reported that extrinsically motivating factors like monetary incentives work for improved speed, but do not improve the quality, while intrinsic motivations improve accuracy [27, 28]. From the perspective of social learning, the framework could incorporate techniques that Weld et al. introduced [5] for more effective learning by the workers.

6 Conclusion

This paper proposed a micro-tasking framework that supports skill development of individual workers. We designed the framework based on the review of two micro-tasking projects we have conducted. It consists of four key components, a tutorial generator, a task dispatcher, a feedback visualizer, and a skill assessment engine. The framework will help developers create sustainable micro-tasking systems. Also, it will expand the scope of micro-tasking, by supporting new types of tasks, such as skill-intensive work, and new types of workers, such as senior citizens. Our future work will includes more investigations of practical problems that must be addressed when using the proposed framework in realistic systems. We hope this will leads to the development of a reference implementation.

Acknowledgements. We appreciate the help of Kaoru Shinkawa in analyzing the data from CapCap. This research was partially supported by the Japan Science and Technology Agency (JST) under the Strategic Promotion of Innovative Research and Development Program.

References

1. Kittur, A., Smus, B., Khamkar, S., Kraut, R.E.: Crowdforge: Crowdsourcing complex work. In: Proc. UIST 2011, pp. 43–52. ACM (2011)
2. Kulkarni, A., Can, M., Hartmann, B.: Collaboratively crowdsourcing workflows with turkomatic. In: Proc. CSCW 2012, pp. 1003–1012. ACM (2012)
3. Satzger, B., Psaier, H., Schall, D., Dustdar, S.: Auction-based crowdsourcing supporting skill management. Information Systems 38(4), 547–560 (2013)
4. Kittur, A., Nickerson, J.V., Bernstein, M., Gerber, E., Shaw, A., Zimmerman, J., Lease, M., Horton, J.: The future of crowd work. In: Proc. CSCW 2013, pp. 1301–1318. ACM (2013)
5. Weld, D.S., Adar, E., Chilton, L., Hoffmann, R., Horvitz, E., Koch, M., Landay, J., Lin, C.H., Mausam, M.: Personalized online educationa crowdsourcing challenge. In: Proc. HCOMP 2012 (2012)
6. Kochhar, S., Mazzocchi, S., Paritosh, P.: The anatomy of a large-scale human computation engine. In: Proc. HCOMP 2010, pp. 10–17. ACM (2010)
7. Whitehill, J., Ruvolo, P., Wu, T., Bergsma, J., Movellan, J.R.: Whose vote should count more: Optimal integration of labels from labelers of unknown expertise. In: Proc. NIPS 2009, pp. 2035–2043 (2009)
8. Welinder, P., Branson, S., Belongie, S., Perona, P.: The multidimensional wisdom of crowds. In: Proc. NIPS 2010, pp. 2424–2432 (2010)
9. Lin, C.H., Mausam, M., Weld, D.S.: Crowdsourcing control: Moving beyond multiple choice. In; Workshops at the Twenty-Sixth AAAI Conference on Artificial Intelligence (2012)
10. Yan, Y., Fung, G.M., Rosales, R., Dy, J.G.: Active learning from crowds. In: Proc. ICML 2011, pp. 1161–1168 (2011)
11. Wauthier, F.L., Jordan, M.I.: Bayesian bias mitigation for crowdsourcing. In: Proc. NIPS 2011, pp. 1800–1808 (2011)

12. Donmez, P., Carbonell, J., Schneider, J.: A probabilistic framework to learn from multiple annotators with time-varying accuracy. In: Proc. SD 2010, pp. 826–837 (2010)
13. Kacorri, H., Shinkawa, K., Saito, S.: Introducing game elements in crowdsourced video captioning by non-experts. In: Proc. W4A 20114. ACM (2014) (in press)
14. Sobhi, A., Nagatsuma, R., Saitoh, T.: Collaborative caption editing system—enhancing the quality of caption editing system. In: CSUN 2012 (2012)
15. von Ahn, L., Dabbish, L.: Labeling images with a computer game. In: Proc. CHI 2004, pp. 319–326. ACM (2004)
16. Ishihara, T., Itoko, T., Sato, D., Tzadok, A., Takagi, H.: Transforming Japanese archives into accessible digital books. In: Proc. JCDL 2012, pp. 91–100. ACM (2012)
17. Kobayashi, M., Ishihara, T., Itoko, T., Takagi, H., Asakawa, C.: Age-based Task Specialization for Crowdsourced Proofreading. In: Stephanidis, C., Antona, M. (eds.) UAHCI 2013, Part II. LNCS, vol. 8010, pp. 104–112. Springer, Heidelberg (2013)
18. Itoko, T., Arita, S., Kobayashi, M., Takagi, H.: Involving senior workers in crowdsourced proofreading. In: Stephanidis, C., Antona, M. (eds.) UAHCI/HCII 2014, Part III. LNCS, vol. 8515, pp. 106–117. Springer, Heidelberg (2014)
19. Leung, R., Tang, C., Haddad, S., McGrenere, J., Graf, P., Ingriany, V.: How Older Adults Learn to Use Mobile Devices: Survey and Field Investigations. ACM Trans. Access. Comput. 4(3), Article 11 (2012)
20. Kobayashi, M., Ishihara, T., Kosugi, A., Takagi, H., Asakawa, C.: Question-Answer Cards for an Inclusive Micro-Tasking Framework for the Elderly. In: Kotzé, P., Marsden, G., Lindgaard, G., Wesson, J., Winckler, M. (eds.) INTERACT 2013, Part III. LNCS, vol. 8119, pp. 590–607. Springer, Heidelberg (2013)
21. Huang, J., Twidale, M.B.: Graphstract: Minimal graphical help for computers. In: Proc. UIST 200707, pp. 203–212. ACM (2007)
22. Rowe, S.C., Cohen, C.J., Tang, K.K.: Applying computer game tutorial design techniques to simulation-based training. In: Proc. 2004 Fall SIW (2004)
23. Isbister, K., Schaffer, N.: "gamenics" and its potential. In: Game Usability: Advancing the Player Experience. CRC Press (2008)
24. DiMicco, J., Millen, D.R., Geyer, W., Dugan, C., Brownholtz, B., Muller, M.: Motivations for social networking at work. In: Proc. CSCW 2008, pp. 711–720. ACM (2008)
25. Kaufmann, N., Schulze, T., Veit, D.: More than fun and money. worker motivation in crowdsourcing-a study on mechanical turk. In: Proc. AMCIS 2011 (2011)
26. Dai, P., Mausam, W.D.S.: Decision-theoretic control of crowd-sourced workflows. In: Twenty-Fourth AAAI Conference on Artificial Intelligence (2010)
27. Mason, W., Watts, D.J.: Financial incentives and the "performance of crowds". SIGKDD Explor. Newsl. 11(2), 100–108 (2010)
28. Rogstadius, J., Kostakos, V., Kittur, A., Smus, B., Laredo, J., Vukovic, M.: An assessment of intrinsic and extrinsic motivation on task performance in crowdsourcing markets. In: Proc. ICWSM 2011 (2011)
29. oDesk, `http://www.odesk.com`
30. CrowdFlower, `http://crowdflower.com`
31. Amazon Mechanical Turk, `http://www.mturk.com`
32. Duolingo, `http://www.duolingo.com`
33. OSGi, `http://www.osgi.org/Specifications`

Utilizing Eye Tracking to Improve Learning from Examples

Amir Shareghi Najar, Antonija Mitrovic, and Kourosh Neshatian

Department of Computer Science and Software Engineering
University of Canterbury, Christchurch, New Zealand
amir.shareghinajar@pg.canterbury.ac.nz
{tanja.mitrovic,kourosh.neshatian}@canterbury.ac.nz

Abstract. In recent year, eye tracking has been used in many areas such as usability studies of interfaces, marketing, and psychology. Learning with computer-based educational systems relies heavily on students' interactions, and therefore eye tracking has been used to study and improve learning. We have recently conducted several studies on using worked examples in addition to tutored problem solving. In this paper we discuss how we used eye-tracking data to compare behaviors of novices and advanced students while studying examples. We propose a new technique to analyze eye-gaze patterns named EGPA. In order to comprehend SQL examples, students require information available in the database schema. We analyzed students' eye movement data from different perspectives, and found that advanced students paid more attention to database schema than novices. In future work, we will use the outcomes of this study to provide proactive feedback.

Keywords: eye tracking, learning from examples, intelligent tutoring.

1 Introduction

Eye tracking involves determining the point of gaze of a person's eyes on a visual scene [9]. In recent years, eye tracking has been employed in many areas, ranging from usability studies of interfaces, to marketing and psychology [4, 13, 18]. Many Human Computer Interaction (HCI) projects utilize eye tracking data to investigate which interface design enables users to complete tasks and find the necessary information. Similarly, research on computer-based educational systems also relies heavily on students' interactions with systems. In order to have a more comprehensive and accurate picture of a user's interactions with a learning environment, we need to know which interface features he/she visually inspected, what strategies they used and what cognitive efforts they made to complete tasks [1, 21].

A category of educational systems we are interested in is Intelligent Tutoring Systems (ITS), which provide individualized instruction by observing the student's behaviour, modelling his/her knowledge and adapting to the student by providing adaptive guidance [24]. ITSs have been shown to increase learning by one standard deviation in comparison to traditional classroom learning [22]. Research on eye tracking in ITSs

C. Stephanidis and M. Antona (Eds.): UAHCI/HCII 2014, Part II, LNCS 8514, pp. 410–418, 2014.

ranges from predicting student errors and determining whether students read system feedback [8], over its use as a form of input [23], to the analysis of how students interpret open learning models [3, 14]. Eye tracking data can be used to improve student modelling by providing low-level information about the student's attention [5, 7, 11]. Results from such investigations can be used to further improve ITSs by providing adaptive hints to draw the student's attention to the important elements of the screen or to inform the student about suboptimal behaviour [6].

Although ITSs have proven their effectiveness in improving learning, they are still not close to the effectiveness of expert human tutors working with students one-on-one [2, 22]. A crucial difference between human tutoring and ITSs is in human tutors' versatility. Human tutors use multiple instructional strategies and switch between them seamlessly, while ITSs typically just support problem solving. One of the goals of our research is to expand the set of instructional strategies supported by ITSs. We have recently conducted a study on using worked examples in addition to supported problem solving [19, 20]. The study was conducted in the context of SQL-Tutor, a mature ITS that teaches SQL [16, 17]. SQL-Tutor complements traditional lectures; it assumes that the student has already acquired some knowledge via lectures and labs, and therefore provides numerous problem-solving opportunities to the student. We extended the system by adding the worked-example mode, which presents a problem, the solution, and the explanation to the student. The study had three conditions: learning from examples only, alternating examples and tutored problems, and tutored problems only. The results showed that students benefitted the most from alternating examples and problems.

Prior research, to the best of our knowledge, has never investigated productive and unproductive behavior in learning from examples. Knowing such information could improve ITSs by prompting students to avoid unproductive behavior and guide them towards successful behavior. Therefore, we conducted a study to find productive and unproductive behavior while students study SQL examples. Section 2 presents the experiment design, while the results are presented in Section 3. Section 4 concludes the paper.

2 The Study

Similar to our previous work, this study was conducted in the context of SQL-Tutor, but only using the worked-example condition, as we wanted to investigate how students learn from examples. We chose the Book database from the thirteen databases available in SQL-Tutor. The system presented a fixed sequence of six worked examples specified on the same database. A screenshot presenting one of these examples is presented in Figure 1. The schema of the database is shown at the bottom of the screen; primary keys are underlined, and foreign keys are in italics. The student can request additional information by clicking on the table or attribute names.

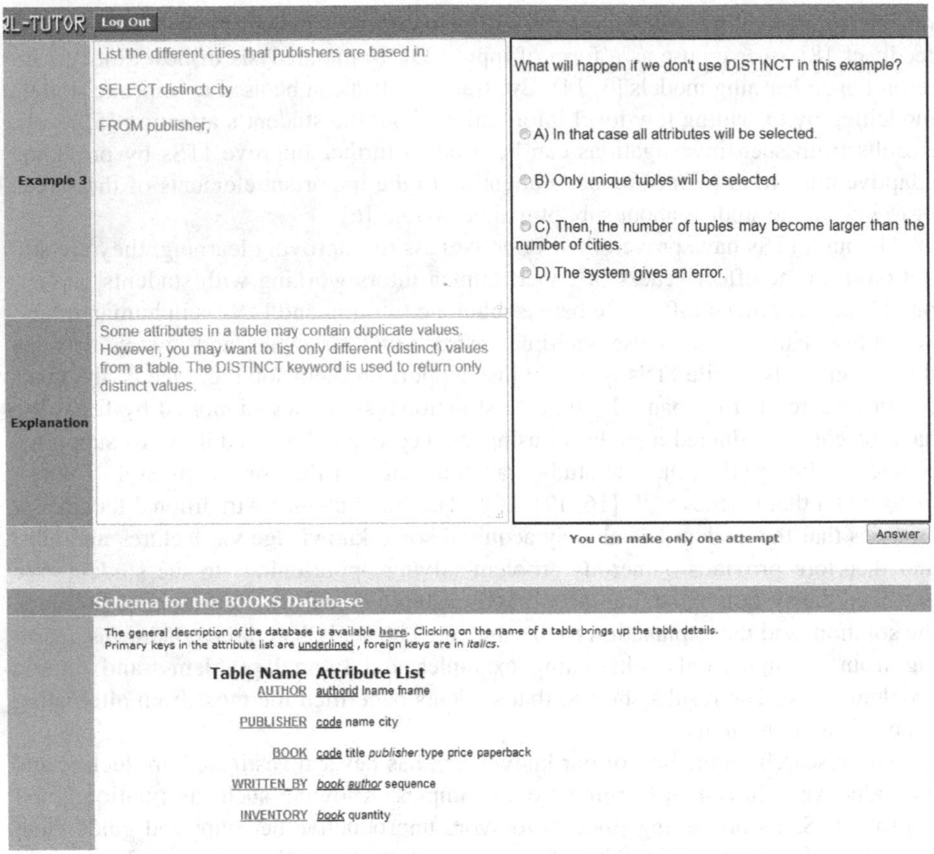

Fig. 1. Screenshot of SQL-Tutor

For each example, the system presents the problem text, the solution and an explanation (see Figure 1). Once a student confirms that s/he has finished studying the example (by clicking the *Continue* button), the system presents a self-explanation question. The goal of this question is to reinforce the knowledge presented in the example by making the student think about a particular construct used in the solution. The student has only one attempt at the question, after which the system informs him/her whether the answer is correct, and if it is not, reveals the correct answer.

For this study, we made minor changes to the interface used in the previous study [19]. We added fixed gaps (> 30 pixels for the 1920*1200 resolution) between the prompt text and each of the options, in order to make identification of eye gaze easier. Moreover, we disabled scrolling to fix the position of page elements on the screen.

3 Results

We collected data from 22 students recruited from an undergraduate course on relational databases. The participants had previously used SQL-Tutor in scheduled labs, but they had not seen the examples from the Book database before. The students participated in individual sessions which were one hour long. All the actions that the students performed through the user interface were recorded in the system log, and we used the Tobii TX300 eye tracker to capture students' eye movements.

Since the sessions were short, we have not used pre/post-tests in this study. However, we had pre-test scores for the same group of students from our previous study, held a week earlier [19]. Using those scores alone to classify students is not justified, since the students have learnt more about SQL in between the two studies. For that reason, we used the K-Medoids clustering algorithm [12] with the following data: pre- and post-test scores from the previous study, session length, and scores on self-explanation questions. The algorithm produced two clusters. The students in one cluster happen to have low scores on the pre-test scores, while the student in the other cluster have high scores, and therefore we refer to the clusters as novices and advanced students in the rest of the paper. There were 12 novices and 10 advanced students. The two groups differ significantly on the pre/post-test scores and the scores on self-explanation questions, while there is no significant difference on the time spent with SQL-Tutor (Table 1).

Table 1. Comparisons between the two clusters (standard deviations in brackets)

	Total (22)	**Novices (12)**	**Advanced (10)**	**p**
Pre-test (%)	40 (13)	33 (11)	48 (11)	<.01*
Post-test (%)	70 (16)	63 (16)	79 (12)	.02*
P-SE (%)	83 (13)	76 (11)	92 (9)	<.01*
Time (s)	129 (54)	120 (59)	139 (52)	.43

We then analyzed the quality of the eye tracking samples, and had to eliminate data from four participants as there were too few valid data samples recorded. That left 10 students in the advanced group and 8 novices.

In order to be able to explore how students studied examples, we defined important Areas Of Interest (AOIs) for the system's interface, such as worked example (W), explanation (E) and database schema (D), and analyzed the data in terms of fixations on these AOIs and transitions between them. In order to analyze the differences in student behaviors, we defined a coding scheme EGPA (Eye Gaze Pattern Analysis) which categorizes eye movements into patterns and combine patterns into behaviors. Patterns are the smallest elements that describe eye gaze movements over a short time interval (1.5 seconds). We define four types of patterns: pure reading, mixed reading, transferring, and scanning. A pure reading pattern indicates that a student is solely paying attention to one AOI. For example, if the student keeps reading the explanation, such pattern is labelled *E*. If the student has a quick look at an AOI while reading another area, then we call it a mixed pattern. An example pattern of this type is *EdE*, showing that the student started reading the explanation, quickly glanced at the database schema and then continued with the explanation. A transferring pattern shows that the student's eye gaze moved from one area of interest to another AOI. An example is *WE*, in which the student's eye gaze moved from the example to the explanation. Finally, the scanning pattern (*S*) describes the situation when the student scans the screen. Behaviours are sequences of patterns. An example is (*W WE EdE EW WdW*), in which the students started by reading the example, then moved to read the explanation, during which he/she had a quick glance at the schema. Then, the student's eye gaze moved from the explanation to the worked example, and had another quick look at the database schema.

Table 2. Average pattern frequencies

	Percentages of students using the pattern		Average pattern frequency		
	Advanced	Novices	Advanced	Novices	p
All patterns			18.60 (5.19)	18.75 (5.26)	0.97
W	100%	100%	4.8 (2.2)	5.25 (1.39)	0.83
E	90%	100%	2.2 (1.32)	2.37 (1.19)	0.83
D	90%	25%	1.1 (0.57)	0.37 (0.74)	0.03*
WeW	40%	63%	1.2 (1.81)	0.62 (0.52)	0.90
WdW	50%	25%	1.4 (1.84)	0.25 (0.46)	0.24
EwE	60%	75%	1.2 (1.32)	2.12 (2.1)	0.41
EdE	20%	38%	0.3 (0.67)	0.5 (0.76)	0.57
WE	90%	100%	3.5 (2.01)	4.62 (1.69)	0.24
WD	40%	25%	0.4 (0.52)	0.25 (0.46)	0.63
EW	50%	50%	0.7 (0.82)	0.87 (1.13)	0.90
ED	50%	0%	0.5 (0.53)	0	0.08*
DW	30%	0%	0.3 (0.48)	0	0.32
DE	0%	25%	0	0.25 (0.46)	0.41
S	70%	100%	1 (0.94)	1.25 (0.46)	0.41

We classified all the eye gaze data using EGPA, and analyzed the data in terms of frequencies of patterns and behaviors for novices and advanced students (Table 2). There was no significant difference between the total number of patters used by novices and advanced students. The advanced students used the D and ED patterns significantly and marginally significantly more often than the novices (p = .03 and p = .08 respectively). The D pattern was used by 90% of advanced students compared to only 25% of novices. The ED pattern was not used by novices at all, while 50% of advanced students have used it.

We identified 42 distinct behaviors, of which 10 were used by more than one student. Table 3 presents those behaviors and their average frequencies. One behavior was used only by advanced students: (W WE E ED D). As the advanced students had prior knowledge about the concepts covered in the examples, they looked at the explanation and database schema to find new information which they have not learnt before. Advanced students used B8, B9 and B10 more often than novices. These three behaviours contain only one pattern; therefore, advanced students used less complex behaviour than novices. Such simple behaviours may be explained by advanced students having more knowledge. On the other hand, novices used B2, B4 and B6 more than advanced students. In B2, students first studied the worked example followed by reading explanation, and finally they restudied the worked example. B4 is similar to B2, but instead of restudying worked example, students had a quick look at the worked example while reading the explanation. B6 represents that students first studied the worked example followed by reviewing explanation, but they did not pay attention to the database schema.

Table 3. Average behaviour frequencies

Name	Behaviour	Advanced	Novices
B1	W WE EwE EW W	0.1	0.1
B2	W WE E EW W	0.2	0.4
B3	W WE E ED D	0.2	0.0
B4	W WE EwE	0.4	1.3
B5	W WE EdE	0.1	0.4
B6	W WE E	1.5	1.8
B7	W WD D	0.2	0.1
B8	WeW	1.1	0.6
B9	WdW	1.0	0.3
B10	W	1.7	1.0

The eye tracking data was also used as input for several Machine Learning algorithms available in RapidMiner [15] with the Weka plug-in [10]. We were interested in classifiers that predict the class of the student (novice or advanced) based on patterns and behaviors exhibited while studying examples (over the whole session). The input vectors were specified in terms of 26 features (16 patterns and 10 behaviors), the values of which are frequencies of use of a particular pattern/behavior. Leave-one-out cross-validation was carried out on the normalized data. We generated classifiers using the following algorithms: W-J48, W-Ladtree, W-BFTree, Rule Induction, W-JRip, and Naiive Bayes. A 'W' prefix indicates that the Weka implementation of the algorithm has been used. Table 4 reports the accuracies of the generated classifiers.

Table 4. Accuracy of classifiers

Classifiers	Accuracy
W-J48	61.1%
Rule Induction	66.6%
W-BFTree	72.2%
W-JRip	77.8%
Naive Bayes	77.8%
W-Ladtree	94.4%

The best classifier was produced by the W-Ladtree algorithm (Figure 2), with 94.4% accuracy. The classifier predicted the advanced students with 100% accuracy, while novices were predicted with 90% accuracy. The W-Ladtree classifier indicates that advanced students study database schema more than novices.

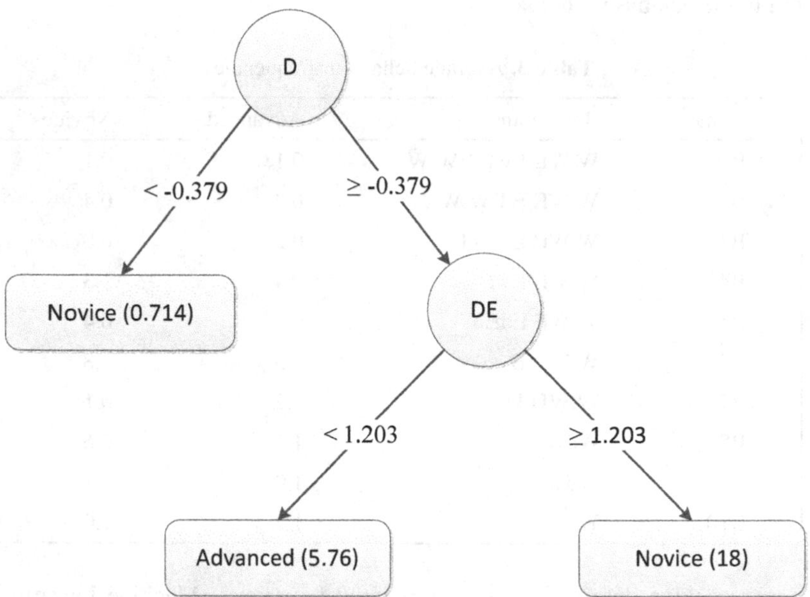

Fig. 2. The W-Ladtree classifier

4 Conclusions

Previous work has shown that learning from examples is beneficial but there has been no deep investigation of how students study examples. We conducted a study of the behaviors that novices and advanced students exhibit while studying examples in SQL-Tutor. Such information enables us to identify productive and unproductive approaches that students take to study examples. We collected information about all actions the participants took as well as the eye gaze data.

We found no significant difference in the time students spent studying the examples. The analyses of the students' eye gaze patterns show that advanced students studied the database schema significantly more than novices. Machine learning classifiers also corroborate this finding. Overall, the results emphasise the importance of the database schema for advanced students. Students need database information, such as names and semantics of tables and attributes, to understand examples. Therefore, looking at the database schema is a sign of learning from SQL examples. Now the question is why novices did not pay attention to this crucial area? Perhaps novices do not know how to study SQL examples. For instance, they may not know the basic concepts of primary keys and foreign keys in a database. Therefore, it is interesting to investigate whether or not prompting novices to study database schema while they study examples would improve students learning. All the analyses performed were based on data captured over the whole session; therefore, the results may change for longer or shorter sessions. It will be interesting to observe how patterns and behaviours change as students become more knowledgeable.

References

1. Bednarik, R.: Potentials of eye-movement tracking in adaptive systems. In: Proc. 4th Workshop on the Evaluation of Adaptive Systems, pp. 1–8 (2005)
2. Bloom, B.S.: The 2-sigma problem: the search for methods of group instruction as effective as one-to-one tutoring. Educational Researcher 13, 4–16 (1984)
3. Bull, S., Cooke, N., Mabbott, A.: Visual attention in open learner model presentations: An eye-tracking investigation. In: Conati, C., McCoy, K., Paliouras, G. (eds.) UM 2007. LNCS (LNAI), vol. 4511, pp. 177–186. Springer, Heidelberg (2007)
4. Charness, N., Reingold, E.M., Pomplun, M., Stampe, D.M.: The perceptual aspect of skilled performance in chess: evidence from eye movements. Memory & Cognition 29(8), 1146–1152 (2001)
5. Conati, C., Merten, C.: Eye-tracking for user modeling in exploratory learning environments: An empirical evaluation. Knowledge-Based Systems 20(6), 557–574 (2007)
6. D'Mello, S., Olney, A., Williams, C., Hays, P.: Gaze tutor: A gaze-reactive intelligent tutoring system. Int. Journal Human-Computer Studies 70(5), 370–389 (2012)
7. Elmadani, M., Mitrovic, A., Weerasinghe, A.: Understanding Student Interactions with Tutorial Dialogues in EER-Tutor. In: Proc. 21st Int. Conf. Computers in Education, pp. 30–40 (2013)
8. Gluck, K.A., Anderson, J.R., Douglass, S.A.: Broader bandwidth in student modeling: What if ITS were "Eye"TS? In: Gauthier, G., VanLehn, K., Frasson, C. (eds.) ITS 2000. LNCS, vol. 1839, pp. 504–513. Springer, Heidelberg (2000)
9. Goldberg, J.H., Helfman, J.I.: Comparing information graphics: a critical look at eye tracking. In: Proc. 3rd BELIV 2010 Workshop: Beyond Time and Errors: Novel Evaluation Methods for Information Visualization, pp. 71–78 (2010)
10. Hall, M., Frank, E., Holmes, G., Pfahringer, B., Reutemann, P., Witten, I.H.: The WEKA data mining software: an update. ACM SIGKDD Explorations Newsletter 11(1), 10–18 (2009)
11. Kardan, S., Conati, C.: Exploring gaze data for determining user learning with an interactive simulation. In: Masthoff, J., Mobasher, B., Desmarais, M.C., Nkambou, R. (eds.) UMAP 2012. LNCS, vol. 7379, pp. 126–138. Springer, Heidelberg (2012)

12. Kaufman, L., Rousseeuw, P.J.: Clustering by means of Medoids. In: Dodge, Y. (ed.) Statistical Data Analysis Based on the L_1–Norm and Related Methods, pp. 405–416. North-Holland (1987)
13. Liu, Y., Hsueh, P.Y., Lai, J., Sangin, M., Nussli, M.A., Dillenbourg, P.: Who is the expert? analyzing gaze data to predict expertise level in collaborative applications. In: IEEE Int. Conf. on Multimedia and Expo, pp. 898–901 (2009)
14. Mathews, M., Mitrovic, A., Lin, B., Holland, J., Churcher, N.: Do Your Eyes Give It Away? Using Eye Tracking Data to Understand Students' Attitudes towards Open Student Model Representations. In: Cerri, S.A., Clancey, W.J., Papadourakis, G., Panourgia, K. (eds.) ITS 2012. LNCS, vol. 7315, pp. 422–427. Springer, Heidelberg (2012)
15. Mierswa, I., Wurst, M., Klinkenberg, R., Scholz, M., Euler, T.: YALE: Rapid Prototyping for Complex Data Mining Tasks. In: Ungar, L., Craven, M., Gunopulos, D., Eliassi-Rad, T. (eds.) KDD 2006: Proc.12th ACM SIGKDD Int. Conf. Knowledge Discovery and Data Mining, pp. 935–940 (2006)
16. Mitrović, A.: Experiences in Implementing Constraint-Based Modeling in SQL-Tutor. In: Goettl, B.P., Halff, H.M., Redfield, C.L., Shute, V.J. (eds.) ITS 1998. LNCS, vol. 1452, pp. 414–423. Springer, Heidelberg (1998)
17. Mitrovic, A.: An Intelligent SQL Tutor on the Web. Artificial Intelligence in Education 13(2-4), 173–197 (2003)
18. Rayner, K.: Eye movements in reading and information processing: 20 years of research. Psychological bulletin 124(3), 372 (1998)
19. Shareghi Najar, A., Mitrovic, A.: Examples and Tutored Problems: How can Self-Explanation Make a Difference to Learning? In: Lane, H.C., Yacef, K., Mostow, J., Pavlik, P. (eds.) Proc. 16th Int. Conf. Artificial Intelligence in Education, pp. 339–348 (2013a)
20. Shareghi Najar, A., Mitrovic, A.: Do novices and advanced students benefit differently from worked examples and ITS? In: Wong, L.H., Liu, C.-C., Hirashima, T., Sumedi, P., Lukman, M. (eds.) Int. Conf. Computers in Education, pp. 20–29 (2013b)
21. Sibert, J.L., Gokturk, M., Lavine, R.A.: The reading assistant: eye gaze triggered auditory prompting for reading remediation. In: Proc.13th Annual ACM Symposium on User Interface Software and Technology, pp. 101–107 (2000)
22. VanLehn, K.: The relative effectiveness of human tutoring, intelligent tutoring systems and other tutoring systems. Educational Psychologist 46(4), 197–221 (2011)
23. Wang, H., Chignell, M., Ishizuka, M.: Empathic tutoring software agents using real-time eye tracking. In: Symposium on Eye Tracking Research & Applications, pp. 73–78 (2006)
24. Woolf, B.: Building intelligent interactive tutors: student-centered strategies for revolutionizing e-learning. Morgan Kaufmann (2008)

Engaging Students with Profound and Multiple Disabilities Using Humanoid Robots

Penny Standen[1], David Brown[2], Jess Roscoe[1], Joseph Hedgecock[1], David Stewart[3], Maria Jose Galvez Trigo[2], and Elmunir Elgajiji[2]

[1] University of Nottingham, Nottingham, UK
{p.standen,mzyjr,mzyjh1}@nottingham.ac.uk
[2] Nottingham Trent University, Nottingham, UK
david.brown@ntu.ac.uk,
{maria.trigo2013,elmunir.elgajiji2012}@my.ntu.ac.uk
[3] Oak Field School and Sports College, Nottingham, UK
d.stewart@oakfield.nottingham.sch.uk

Abstract. Engagement is the single best predictor of successful learning for children with intellectual disabilities yet achieving engagement with pupils who have profound or multiple disabilities (PMD) presents a challenge to educators. Robots have been used to engage children with autism but are they effective with pupils whose disabilities limit their ability to control other technology? Learning objectives were identified for eleven pupils with PMD and a humanoid robot was programmed to enable teachers to use it to help pupils achieve these objectives. These changes were evaluated with a series of eleven case studies where teacher-pupil dyads were observed during four planned video recorded sessions. Engagement was rated in a classroom setting and during the last session with the robot. Video recordings were analysed for duration of engagement and teacher assistance and number of goals achieved. Rated engagement was significantly higher with the robot than in the classroom. Observations of engagement, assistance and goal achievement remained at the same level throughout the sessions suggesting no reduction in the novelty factor.

Keywords: Robots, education, engagement, profound and multiple intellectual disabilities, case studies, video analysis.

1 Introduction

Intellectual disabilities are estimated to affect between 1 and 2% of the population in most western countries and currently 20% of the population with intellectual disabilities will be of school age. Although the number who are of school age is remaining stable [1] there has been a large rise in the number of children with profound and multiple disabilities (PMLD). This has been attributed to an increase in the survival of premature babies due to medical advances made in recent years [2]. These children often have the most complex needs, due to a combination of extremely delayed intellectual and social functioning, no verbal communication and the presence of

C. Stephanidis and M. Antona (Eds.): UAHCI/HCII 2014, Part II, LNCS 8514, pp. 419–430, 2014.

associated medical conditions usually neurological, sensory or physical impairments [3]. This makes it almost impossible for them to benefit from available educational provision and new ways are needed to foster their learning. According to Iovannone et al. [4] engagement is "the single best predictor" of learning for children with intellectual disabilities. Discussing children with complex needs, Carpenter [5] writes that "Sustainable learning can occur only when there is meaningful engagement. The process of engagement is a journey which connects a child and their environment (including people, ideas, materials and concepts) to enable learning and achievement" (p35). Can computer technology help to foster engagement in these learners?

Most educational interventions using computer technology have been designed for the more able. A recent systematic review [6] on the use of iPods, iPod Touch and iPads in teaching programs for people with developmental disabilities noted an absence of studies on individuals with profound and multiple disabilities. They concluded that this group presents unique challenges with respect to the design of technology-based interventions, a major one being their lack of sufficient motor control to activate the device and software.

There have been some attempts to circumvent this problem of motor control. Work by Lancioni [7] has demonstrated there is a way for almost anyone to activate a microswitch, the most common being a push switch, which is activated by applying pressure to a large button. However they can also be triggered by pressure sensors on the armrest of a wheelchair, by chin or eyelid movement [8] or by vocalisation [9]. This then allows the user to exert environmental control, activate a piece of equipment which may produce speech on their behalf, or begin a pleasurable stimulus for the user.

There have also been attempts to capture gesture or body movements using infrared sensor-based systems to enable those with multiple disabilities to control multimedia [10]. A more recent development that can allow a profoundly disabled person to interact with their environment has been enabled by the appearance of low cost headsets that enable gamers to interact with games using their own brain activity [11].

Work with typically developing children has shown that robots can help attainment in a wide range of areas, particularly by motivating children [12,13]. A wide range of robots has already been used with children with disabilities [14], although the majority of these have focussed on children with autism [15]. Studies involving children with intellectual disabilities are promising but focus on those who are more able. Klein et al. [16] showed that working with a robot increased "playfulness" and therefore engagement in two out of the three young children with developmental disabilities in their study. Introducing a mobile robotic platform to eight children with either autism, Downs syndrome or severe learning disabilities showed high levels of motivation and engagement in all the children [17].

As a preliminary step to investigate the suitability of robots for profound and multiply disabled school aged children, Hedgecock [18] interviewed teachers of children with intellectual disabilities to discover their opinions of using a NAO humanoid robot as an educational tool, which children they believed would benefit, what learning aims they would target, and what methods they would suggest to achieve them. Information derived from the interviews was then used to design a series of five case studies to evaluate potential teaching methods and outcome measures. For example, in one case study a nine year old boy with severe intellectual disabilities and reduced vision learnt that by clapping his hands he could get the robot to perform a dance.

However, he had problems with perseveration so the aim of the sessions was to help him learn to perform the action only once and to stop when the robot did what he wanted. The case studies were video recorded and recordings analysed to measure engagement, teacher assistance and goal achievement. A questionnaire completed by the pupils' teachers was also used to compare engagement in class to engagement within the final session. Analysis of the interviews highlighted the importance of having an appropriate input device to make the robot accessible, for example by making it sensitive to vocalisations, gestures or switch operations: whatever was favoured by the child. Teachers also emphasised the importance of "productive learning" ie that leads to being able to achieve something important for the pupil rather than being seen as just play and of designing sessions tailored to individuals' needs and interests. In the case studies, pupils showed significantly higher engagement when working with a robot when compared to not working with a robot.

The teachers in this study came up with many more possible uses for the robot than it could perform. This indicated a need for the robot to be able to perform a greater range of actions as a reward or cue that could be personalised for individual students. What the study also showed was that the robot needed a greater range of ways to be controlled to enable a wider range of pupils to use it. The aims of the present study were:

1. To produce adjustments to the robot's programming in order to
   a. make it controllable by other input devices (eg switches, joystick)
   b. enable it to emit a greater range of behaviours (eg different dances, tunes etc)
2. To evaluate the new repertoire with a series of case studies.

2 Methods

2.1 Design

Changes to the robot's programming were informed by results from the previous study [18] and from discussions with teachers. Changes were evaluated using a series of single case studies where teacher-pupil dyads were observed during four planned video recorded sessions with a robot. Engagement was rated in a classroom setting and during the last session with the robot.

2.2 Participants

Eight members of teaching staff (six teachers and two teaching assistants) from a school in Nottingham with around 150 pupils with severe, profound or complex learning and/or physical disabilities nominated one or two pupils to work with. Four teachers nominated two pupils. There were no exclusion criteria for the pupils other than parents not consenting. The characteristics of the pupils are shown in Table 1.

Table 1. Characteristics of participants

Pupil	Gender age (years)	Details of disability	Attainment levels
S1	Male, 17	S1 has complex intellectual disabilities, epilepsy and global developmental delay. He has fine and gross motor development difficulties, limited speech and no awareness of danger.	NC1, NC1, C1.
S2	Female 12	S2 has dyskinetic cerebral palsy resulting in mobility difficulties, varying muscle strength and involuntary movements. S2 also struggles substantially with language and communication.	P7, P7, P8
S3	Male 7	S3 suffers from Duchene Muscular Dystrophy and an Autistic Spectrum Disorder. He struggles to understand spoken language, is wary of unfamiliar environments and has difficulties with learning, communication and social interaction.	P1, P1, P1
S4	Male 5	S4 suffers from Down's syndrome. He has learning, language, social interaction and behavioural difficulties. S4 also has violent tendencies and a preference for solitary play.	P3, P3, P3
S5	Male 18	S5 has cerebral palsy due to oxygen deprivation at birth. He suffers from severe physical and medical difficulties including learning and communication challenges. With low muscle tone and poor control of his trunk and limbs, S5 is either wheelchair or walker bound at all times.	NC2,NC2, P8
S6	Female 20	S6 has cerebral palsy and severe intellectual disabilities. Wheelchair bound with impaired cognitive and communication skills due to brain damage at birth. Home languages are Romani and Polish	P6, P6, P4
S7	Male 18	S7 has severe and multiple intellectual difficulties with no known cause. S7 is non-verbal and wheelchair or walker bound, showing minimal communication abilities.	P4, P4, P4
S8	Male 12	S8 suffers from cerebral palsy resulting in spastic quadriparesis. As a result he suffers from a mild delay in cognitive development and speech and language deficits. S8 is wheelchair bound, showing no evidence of difficulties with attention or concentration.	NC3, NC1, P8

Table 1. *(continued)*

S10	Male 11	S10 suffers from ATRX syndrome, resulting in limited mobility, delayed learning and minimal communication skills. S10 is tube fed and suffers from recurrent chest infections and urinary tract infections.	P3, P3, P3
S11	Male 11	S11 has an Autistic Spectrum Disorder with severe intellectual disabilities and significant hearing loss. He has microcephaly and hypermetropia. S11 suffers from a short attention span and has little understanding of words relying instead upon verbal cues.	P2, P3, P2
S12	Male 7	S 12 has bilateral sensori-neural hearing loss, congenital hypothyroidism, language and communication difficulties and epilepsy. As a result he has delayed self-help and independent skills.	P6, P6, P5

Attainment levels are given in the form of either National Curriculum levels (NC) or Performance Scales (P levels). P levels are a performance measure for children with Special Educational Needs, who do not meet the criteria for the lowest national curriculum level 1 [19]. P levels range from 1 to 8 with 1 being the lowest level of attainment. Pupils in the study are described in terms of their attainment levels for English, Maths and ICT.

2.3 Intervention

The robot used in this project was a NAO NextGen (Model H25, Version 4) humanoid robot, which is commercially available from robotics manufacturer Aldebaran Robotics. NAO is manufactured with a wide range of behaviours, including walking, standing up and sitting down, dancing, and recognising speech, sounds and objects as well as producing speech from text and playing sound files. These behaviours can all be programmed into the robot using Choregraphe [20], a user-friendly graphical interface that allows users to control the robot and create sequences of complex behaviours. Following the interviews with teaching staff in the previous study [18] and the collection of feedback from other staff at the school, changes were made to allow the control of the robot by Jellybean switches (see Figure 1) and a joystick thus allowing pupils to interact with the robot using a method suitable to their needs.

In order to allow a switch or joystick to control the robot, Pygame, a cross platform set of Python modules designed for writing video games was used. Pygame is built over a library that allows the use of a high-level programming language like Python in order to structure a program that could be used with several input devices. Next, a piece of Python code was written to produce a virtual server that could act as a bridge between the robot and any input device the pupil required such as Jellybean switches

Fig. 1. Four Jellybean switches labelled with the symbols representing the micro-switches' action

or a joystick. In this way, executing the program corresponding to the server and running the appropriate behaviour in Choregraphe it was possible to tele-operate the robot with different input devices.

There were three ways to increase the range of behaviours from those already offered by Choregraphe. First of all, there were some routines freely available for download from the internet. Secondly, favourite pieces of music could be transformed into .wav files and then included as a complete instruction in Choregraphe. Finally, more complex behaviours such as kicking a football, were first of all broken down into components for which script was written in Python and then included as a complete instruction in Choregraphe.

2.4 Outcome Measures

As in the previous study [18] engagement was rated using the scale developed by the Special Schools and Academies Trust [21] as part of a classroom tool for teachers of children with complex disabilities. The pupil is given a rating between 0 (no focus) and 4 (fully sustained) for each factor, giving a total score out of 28, with a higher score indicating greater engagement. Video recordings of sessions were analysed to measure three variables: duration of pupil engagement, duration of assistance from staff, and the frequency of goals attained. These were converted to a percentage of the session to take account of the variation in session length.

2.5 Procedure

Teachers were recruited from those that attended a demonstration of the robot at the school given by the research team. In individual meetings with one of the authors (JR) they identified a pupil whom they thought would benefit from working with the robot. Once parental consent had been obtained, discussions were held with the teachers to devise an appropriate learning objective for the pupil to achieve in the sessions and

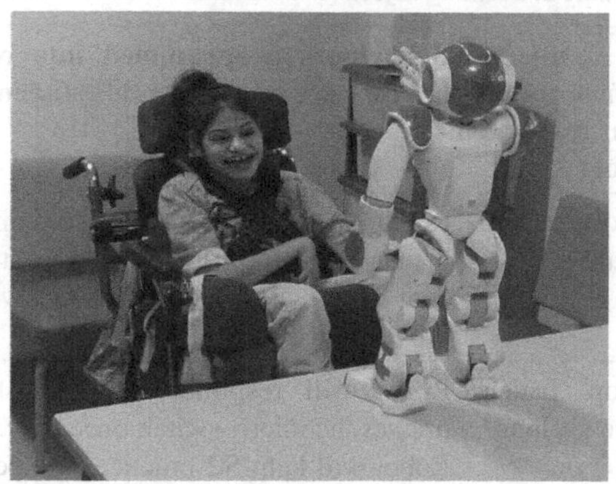

Fig. 2. A pupil working with the robot

discuss how this may be achieved. Information from these discussions was then used to individually design the sessions for each pupil, focussing on their interests and learning style, to help them achieve their learning objective. Figure 2 shows an example of how a pupil might be positioned to interact with the robot. Initial plans for the sessions were finalised with the teachers. However, depending on how sessions proceeded, plans could be refined. The main objective to be achieved over the four sessions could be broken down into smaller goals for each session.

Five sessions were conducted with each teacher-pupil dyad, all of which were digitally video recorded although the first session was intended to familiarise the pupil with the arrangements and to judge whether any adjustments to plans were required. Session length depended upon each child's ability to maintain focus, varying from seven to fifty minutes with a mean duration of twenty-two minutes. Sessions were scheduled at regular intervals over three weeks at times convenient to the teachers. Sessions were carried out in a room with just the pupil, researcher and a member of staff present.

The engagement scale [21] was completed by one of the authors (JR) in each pupil's normal classroom setting and again during each pupil's final session with the robot. Teachers attempted to follow similar learning objectives in the classroom as the ones they were planning for the session with the robot. Video recordings of each session were analysed by one of the authors (JR) using OBSWIN (http://www.antam.co.uk/obswin.htm) for the duration of engagement, duration of assistance provided and the frequency of achieving a goal. Due to the inherent variability of the pupils, each pupil had individual criteria for the presence/absence of each variable. In order to determine what constitutes the presence/absence of a variable, videos of the sessions were watched before the analysis began, and exact criteria defined for each.

Table 2. Learning objectives of sessions and robot actions

	Learning Objective derived from interview with associated staff member	**Behaviours programmed into robot that are specific to this student**	**Input device(s) used**
S1	To improve verbal communication.	Robot will respond to voice commands from the student, if the student is not clear enough NAO will provide encouragement.	Micro-switches, voice input
S2	To develop patience and practice spelling	Robot will respond to S2 if she presses the micro-switch once only. Robot will help S2 practice her spelling using her hand-held computer to vocalise words. If correct NAO will reward S2 with a song or dance and will encourage if incorrect.	Micro-switches, voice input
S3	To learn cause and effect	Robot will perform songs that S3 has shown interest in if S3 correctly selects the active switch. For additional engagement, NAO will perform in the dark lit up with many different lights	Micro-switches
S4	To practice switch activation	Robot will verbally encourage S4 to mimic him and warn him not to be violent (as is his tendency)	Micro-switches
S5	To improve verbal communication	Robot will demonstrate one of S5's physiotherapy exercises encouraging her to touch her ear with her hand prior to pressing the micro-switches	Micro-switches, voice input
S6	To learn to obey commands	Robot will give verbal commands to S6 asking him to pick up/throw/pass a ball with encouragement	Voice input
S7	To practice switch control with only one hand	Robot will verbally encourage S7 to use only one hand to trigger micro-switches	Micro-switches
S8	To develop confidence in using a joystick similar to that of his electric wheelchair	Robot will move forwards, backwards, left and right if S8 uses the joystick effectively	Joystick

Table 2. *(continued)*

S10	To learn cause and effect	For S10, Robot has been programmed with a wider range of songs. One of NAOs switches will be inactive for S10 to learn cause and effect and not simply press random switches	Micro-switches
S11	To practice holding objects for a long period of time	Robot will walk towards S11 once the switch is pressed and hand him an object (initially food) to hold	A single micro-switch
S12	To improve verbal communication	Robot will respond to voice commands from the student, if the student is not clear enough NAO will provide encouragement as with S1	Voice input

3 Results

Figure 3 summarises the group results for all outcome measures. Engagement scale results indicated that engagement with the robot (mean = 18.18, SD = 7.60) was

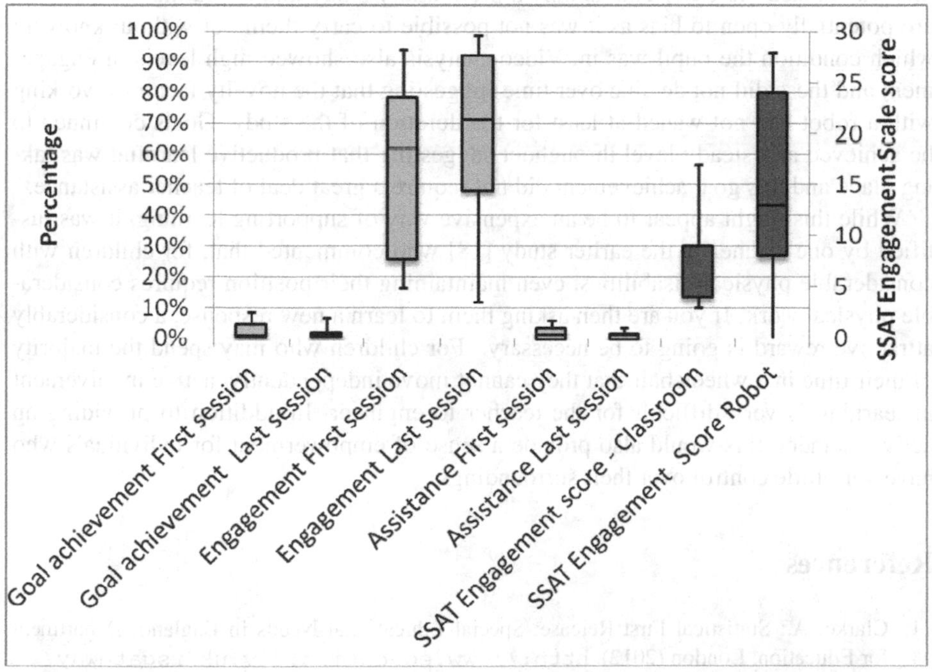

Fig. 3. Medians, quartiles and ranges for ratings of engagement and behaviours from video analysis

significantly (t = 4.9, df 10, p<0.001) higher than when in the classroom (mean = 8.64, SD = 4.11). All but one of the pupils showed higher engagement when working with the robot: one received 28 points, the maximum score possible indicating full engagement throughout the entire session with the robot, compared with minimal engagement (9 points) in the classroom setting. Video analysis indicated that pupils were spending a high percentage of the time scored as showing engagement and although comparing scores from the first recorded session with those from the last session indicated an increase with time, this did not reach significance. Similarly, there was no significant change in either teacher assistance or goal attainment from first to last sessions

4 Discussion

The first aim of the study was to enable the robot to be controlled remotely by microswitches and a joystick and to enlarge its range of behaviours to allow it to support the learning of a wider range of pupils. This was successful to the extent that eleven pupils who varied considerably in ability, needs and interests had sessions with the robot tailored to their learning objectives. In evaluating these interventions, one of the hopes in using the robot was to improve pupil engagement given the importance of this quality in learning in pupils with intellectual disabilities. The higher ratings of engagement during the final session with the robot than in the classroom suggest that this was indeed the case. This is only a preliminary study and the rating scale results are potentially open to bias as it was not possible to carry them out without knowing which condition the pupil was in. Video analysis also showed high levels of engagement and these did not decline over time suggesting that the novelty factor of working with a robot had not waned at least for the duration of the study. Goals continued to be achieved at a steady level throughout suggesting that productive learning was taking place and this goal achievement did not require a great deal of teacher assistance.

While this might appear to be an expensive way of supporting learning, it was justified by one teacher in the earlier study [18] who commented that, for children with considerable physical disabilities, even maintaining their position requires considerable physical work. If you are then asking them to learn a new response, a considerably attractive reward is going to be necessary. For children who may spend the majority of their time in a wheelchair that they cannot move independently, active involvement in learning is very difficult for the teacher to engineer. In addition to providing an active element, this would also provide a sense of empowerment for individuals who have very little control over their surroundings.

References

1. Clarke, A.: Statistical First Release: Special Educational Needs in England, Department for Education, London (2012), http://www.education.gov.uk/rsgateway/DB/SFR/s001075/sfr14-2012v2.pdf

2. Salt, T.: Salt Review: Independent Review of Teacher Supply for Pupils with Severe, Profound and Multiple Learning Difficulties (SLD and PMLD) Ruddington (2010), http://www.thedyslexia-spldtrust.org.uk/media/downloads/inline/the-salt-review.1298547606.pdf
3. Bellamy, G., Croot, L., Bush, A., Berry, H., Smith, A.: A study to define: profound and multiple learning disabilities (PMLD). Journal of Intellectual Disabilities 14(3), 221–235 (2010)
4. Iovannone, R., Dunlap, G., Huber, H., Kincaid, D.: Effective Educational Practices for Students With Autism Spectrum Disorders. Focus on Autism and Other Developmental Disabilities 18(3), 150–165 (2003)
5. Carpenter, B.: Overview of the research project: steps and impact. Paper to the Complex Learning Difficulties and Disabilities Dissemination Conference. London (March 24, 2011), http://complexld.ssatrust.org.uk/uploads/SEN54%20complex%20needs.pdf
6. Kagohara, D., van der Meer, M., Ramdoss, L., O'Reilly, S., Lancioni, M.F., Davis, G.E., Rispoli, T.N., Lang, M., Marschik, R., Sutherland, P.B., Green, D., Sigafoos, V.A., Using, J.: iPods and iPads in teaching programs for individuals with developmental disabilities: A systematic review. Research in Developmental Disabilities 34, 147–156 (2013)
7. Lancioni, G.E., O'Reilly, M.F., Singh, N.N., Sigafoos, J., Oliva, D., Antonucci, M., Tota, A., Basili, G.: Microswitch-based programs for persons with multiple disabilities: an overview of some recent developments. Perceptual and Motor Skills 106, 355–370 (2008)
8. Lancioni, G.E., O'Reilly, M.F., Singh, N.N., Oliva, D., Coppa, M.M., Montironi, G.: A new microswitch to enable a boy with minimal motor behaviour to control environmental stimulation with eye blinks. Behavioral Interventions 20, 147–153 (2005)
9. Lancioni, G.E., O'Reilly, M.F., Oliva, D., Coppa, M.M.: A microswitch for vocalization responses to foster environmental control in children with multiple disabilities. Journal of Intellectual Disability Research 45(3), 271–275 (2001)
10. Brooks, A.L.: Soundscapes: the evolution of a concept, apparatus and method where ludic engagement in virtual interactive space is a supplemental tool for therapeutic motivation. PhD thesis (2011), http://vbn.aau.dk/files/55871718/PhD.pdf
11. Welton. T., Brown, D.J., Evett, L., Sherkat, N. A Brain-Computer Interface for the Dasher Alternative Text Entry System. Special Issue of Journal of Universal Access in the Information Society: 3rd generation accessibility: Information and Communication Technologies towards universal access (In press)
12. Barker, B.S., Ansorge, J.: Robotics as means to increase achievement scores in an informal learning environment. Journal of Research on Technology in Education 39(3), 229 (2007)
13. Johnson, J.: Children, robotics, and education. Artificial Life and Robotics 7(1-2), 16–21 (2003)
14. Salter, T., Werry, I., Michaud, F.: Going into the wild in child–robot interaction studies: issues in social robotic development. Intelligent Service Robotics 1(2), 93–108 (2008)
15. Robins, B., Dautenhahn, K., te Boekhorst, R., Billard, A.: Robotic Assistants in Therapy and Education of Children with Autism: Can a Small Humanoid Robot Help Encourage Social Interaction Skills? Universal Access in the Information Society 4(2),105–120 (2005)
16. Klein, T., Gelderblom, G.J., de Witte, L., Vanstipelen, S.: Evaluation of short term effects of the IROMEC robotic toy for children with developmental disabilities. Paper presented at the IEEE International Conference on Rehabilitation Robotics, ICORR (2011), http://ieeexplore.ieee.org/xpls/abs_all.jsp?arnumber=5975406&tag=1 (retrieved February 5, 2014)

17. Ibrani, L., Allen, T., Brown, D., Sherkat, N., Stewart, D.: Supporting Students with Learning and Physical Disabilities using a Mobile Robot Platform. Paper presented at the Interactive Technologies and Games (ITAG), Nottingham, UK (2011), http://itag.gamecity.org/proceedings/2011-2/
18. Hedgecock, J.: Can working with a robot enhance learning in pupils with intellectual disabilities? B Med. Sci. Dissertation submitted to the University of Nottingham (2013)
19. Department for Education (2012), http://www.education.gov.uk/schools/teachingandlearning/assessment/a00203453/about-the-p-scales (accessed January 29, 2014)
20. Aldebaran Robotics. Solutions for Autism, Paris, France: Aldebaran Robotics (2006), http://www.aldebaran-robotics.com/en/Solutions/For-Autism/NAO.html (accessed January 11, 2013)
21. The Special Schools and Academies Trust. The Complex Learning Difficulties and Disabilities Research Project: Developing Meaningful Pathways to Personalised Learning. Executive Summary. London: Schools Network (2011), http://www.ssatrust.org.uk (retrieved February 6, 2014)

Transfer of Learnings between Disciplines: What S-BPM Facilitators Could Ask Progressive Educators (and might not dare to do)

Chris Stary

University of Linz
Department of Business Information Systems –Communications Engineering
Knowledge Management Competence Center
Altenbergerstraße 69, 4040 Linz, Austria
Christian.Stary@JKU.AT

Abstract. Subject-oriented Business Process Management (S-BPM) is a novel paradigm in Business Process Management (BPM). Educating students and business stakeholders in S-BPM requires facilitating a substantial mind shift from function- towards communication-oriented (re-)construction of processes. Reformist pedagogy, as driven by Maria Montessori, allows learners grasping and applying novel concepts in self-contained settings and in an individualistic while reflected way. So why not learn from her experiences for introducing S-BPM? In this contribution her analysis of human cultural factors enabling literacy has been transcribed to S-BPM education. When informing S-BPM capacity development according to progressive education, understanding the actual situation and readiness of learners seems to play a crucial role, as it influences their engagement in learning environments. These factors need to be differentiated when conveying S-BPM concepts and activities.

Keywords: Subject-oriented Business Process Management, learning, literacy, progressive education, prepared environment, BPM capacity building.

1 Introduction

Besides structural deficiencies in curricula development relevant to Business Process Management (BPM) [16], the demand for informed education in this field is steadily increasing. The latter could be demonstrated with the advent and use of complex modeling languages, such as BPMN [12], and paradigm shifts, such as Subject-oriented BPM (S-BPM) [5]. Recent studies analyzing BPM education programs, such as by Bandara et al. [1], tend focusing on content and domain structures rather than learning issues. Besides these core elements essential for understanding BPM, the quality of education should become focus of investigations [14]. It might also influence the acceptance of dedicated learning communities, such as established by Schmidt et al. for S-BPM [15], by facilitating access to the capabilities of the novel paradigm.

C. Stephanidis and M. Antona (Eds.): UAHCI/HCII 2014, Part II, LNCS 8514, pp. 431–442, 2014.

In the following we briefly introduce S-BPM from the content and didactic requirements' perspective in section 2, before discussing fundamentals of capacity building as conceptualized by Maria Montessori in section 3. In section 2 we also discuss S-BPM as BPM-for-All approach due to its structural similarity to natural language sentences and possibility for direct execution enabling immediate user experience of process models. In section 3 the suggested proposals redesigning current BPM education recognize cultural factors relevant for learning. Section 4 concludes the paper summarizing the findings and upcoming research.

2 Challenges of S-BPM Facilitators

Subject-oriented Business Process Management (S-BPM) [5,6] provides means for both, early and continuous stakeholder involvement in organizational development, and seamless (automated) execution of validated business processes. The activity bundles of the open S-BPM development cycle enable continuous organizational change under direct control of stakeholders. These aspects have not been implemented in this way and are novel in BPM. With respect to education they are likely to require shifting mind sets due to the prevalent functional perspective on organizations - for a comparison of modeling techniques see ([5], ch. 14).

2.1 Function Follows Communication

Organizational development is increasingly driven by business complexity and dynamics, as the term dynaxity [20] reveals. Business Process Management is one of the major methodological frames for operating businesses in dynamic and complex situations, with business process models at disposition [21]. While traditional approaches to modeling are mainly driven by functional decomposition of value chains, S-BPM considers behavior primarily emerging from the interaction between active system elements termed subjects, based on behaviors encapsulated within the individual subjects.

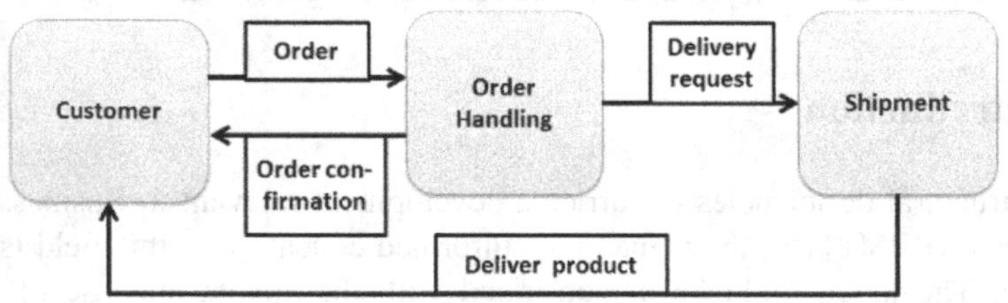

Fig. 1. A Subject Interaction Diagram for order handling

Figure 1 shows 3 subjects (Customer, Order Handling, Shipment) and their interactions (order, order conformation, delivery request, deliver product) identified for handling customer orders to finally ship a product to a customer. The representation is termed Subject Interaction Diagram, allowing to overview business operations in terms of subjects and their interactions for processing customer orders, while abstracting from their behavior as active organizational elements. Customer, Order Handling, and Shipment are not further in detailed in Subject Interactions Diagrams.

As in actual business operation, subjects as active elements operate in parallel and can exchange messages asynchronously or synchronously – processes are autonomous, concurrent behaviors of distributed entities. A subject is an abstraction of behavior referring to a role an active entity is able to play through performing actions. The entity can be a human, a piece of software, a machine (e.g., a robot), a device (e.g., a sensor), or a combination of these, depending on the purpose of modeling. Most important for parallel operation, subjects can execute local actions that do not involve interactions with other subjects, e.g., calculating costs (subject Order Handling). Besides performing actions, each subject exchanges messages with other subjects using the operations send and receive message.

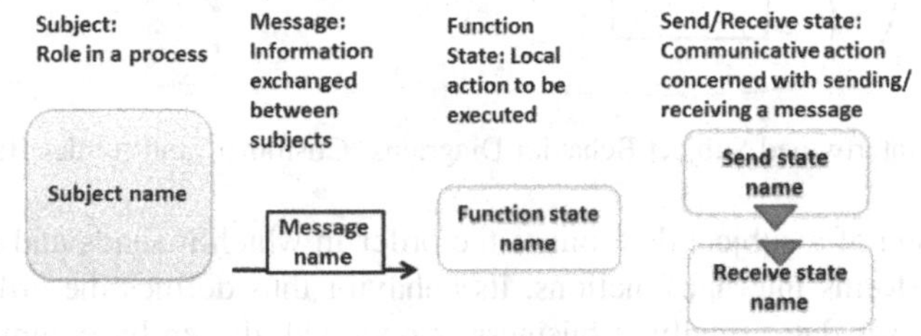

Fig. 2. Set of diagrammatic elements capturing subject behavior in S-BPM

The interaction capability of subjects completes the set of core diagrammatic elements in S-BPM (see Figure 2), as used in two types of diagrams representing a business process completely: Subject Interaction Diagrams (SIDs) like the one in Figure 1 and Subject Behavior Diagrams, as given for Customer and Order Handling in Figure 3. SIDs provide the global view of a process, including the subjects involved and the messages they exchange. The SID of an ordering process is shown in Figure 1. Subject Behavior Diagrams (SBDs) provide the internals of individual subjects. They include sequences of states representing local actions and communicative actions including sending messages and receiving messages. State transitions are represented as arrows, with labels indicating the outcome of the preceding state. In Figure 3 the local view is provided partially for Customer and Order Handling (SBDs), comprising the interactions required for overall task accomplishment.

From a procedural perspective, in S-BPM business operations are constructed along defining relevant

- Subjects involved in a business process, e.g., Customer, Shipment in Figure 1,
- Interactions occurring between the identified subjects, e.g., order in Figure 1,
- Messages the specified subjects send or receive in the course of each interaction, e.g., To: Order Handling order in Figure 3 for the subject Customer,
- Internal behavior of the individual subjects, as shown for Customer and Order Handling in Figure 3, and the
- Business objects (data) exchanged, e.g., order confirmation in Figure 1, that need to be detailed in terms of their structure for processing and implementation purposes.

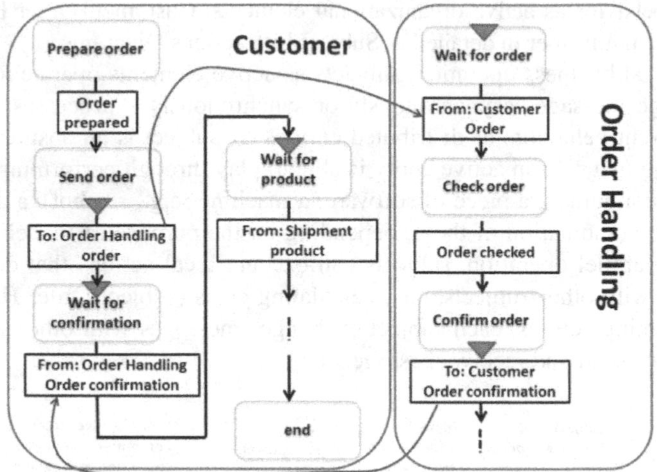

Fig. 3. Intertwined Subject Behavior Diagrams 'Customer' and 'Order Handling'

The description of a subject determines the order in which it sends and receives messages and performs internal functions. Its behavior thus defines the order in which a subject processes data, finally, a business is operated, driven by communication and followed by subject-internal functional task accomplishment.

2.2 S-BPM = BPM-for-All?

The S-BPM notation can be utilized to actively involve business stakeholders in organizational developments, as already demanded for effectively handling increased complexity and dynamics in business when using BPM models [7]. However, their active participation and degree of involvement heavily depend on their capability to provide relevant inputs for modeling or model by themselves processes. As shown above, the design of the S-BPM notation aims reducing complexity. In fact, the diagrammatic elements correspond to elements used by humans in natural language (see also [5,6]). The structure of sentences in natural language corresponds to S-BPM's notational convention. We can specify handling of orders along the fundamental sequence *subject – predicate - object*, both, on the abstract process layer addressed by SIDs, and the behavior layer represented through SBDs:

- Global view (SID): A Customer (*subject*) sends (*predicate*) an order (*object*) to Order Handling. Order Handling (*subject*) sends (*predicate*) an order confirmation (*object*) to the Customer (i.e. another S-BPM subject).
- Local view (Customer SBD): A Customer (*subject*) prepares (*predicate*) an order (*object*). The Customer (*subject*) sends (*predicate*) an order (*object*). The Customer (*subject*) waits (*predicate*) for the order confirmation (*object*), and so forth.

'Subject' is not only used to denote the constituent of natural language sentences, but also as a term encapsulating behavior specifications including activities (predicates).

Predicates either represent dedicated problem solving functions, or denote sending/receiving messages. The latter are constituent for S-BPM, function following communication: A subject, e.g., Customer, needs to communicate to get a process done, specified in SIDs (see Figure 1). Hence, before functions can be detailed, the communication pattern needs to be set up and clarified. The focus on interacting roles and systems leads to a complete control and data flow specification of a process. Consequently, each model can be validated and executed reflecting interactive behavior (lower part of the screen in Figure 4).

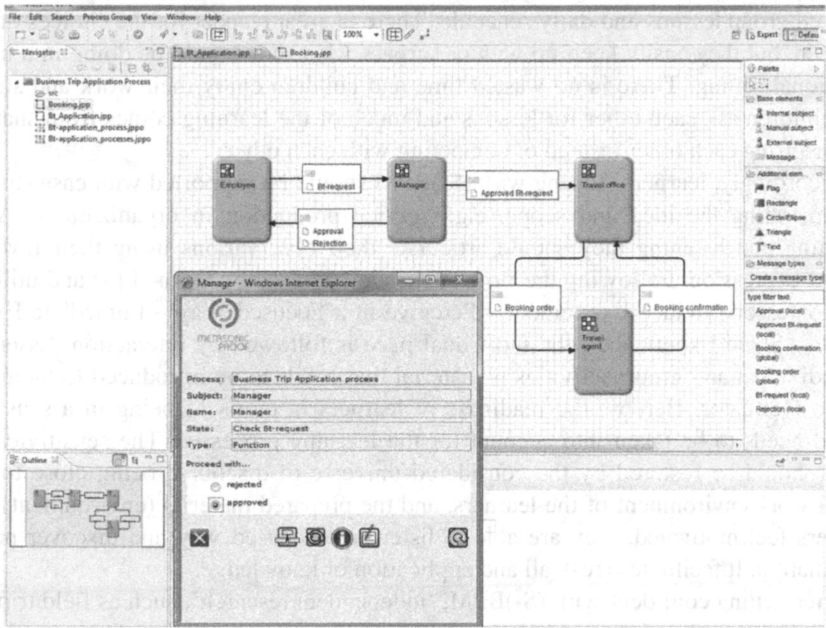

Fig. 4. Creating immediate User Experience

3 Facilitating S-BPM Education

In this section we follow frequently discussed issues in progressive education (http://mariamontessori.com/mm/?page_id=551) abbreviated MM-FDI in the following. The relevance to S-BPM education is evident in the respective heading of each subsection. After providing Montessori-specific inputs to each item we apply Montessori's method of analysis [9] for contextualizing S-BPM issues. Inputs have also been taken from language learning [17] and creating meaningful representations [18].

What Should be the Difference in S-BPM Education and Current BPM Education? To this respect we could learn from the difference between Montessori and traditional education – MM-FDI: 'For children six and under, Montessori emphasizes learning through all five senses, not just through listening, watching, or reading. Children in Montessori classes learn at their own, individual pace and according to their own choice of activities from hundreds of possibilities. They are not required to sit and listen to a teacher talk to them as a group, but are engaged in individual or group activities of their own, with materials that have been introduced to them 1:1 by the teacher who knows what each child is ready to do. Learning is an exciting process of discovery, leading to concentration, motivation, self-discipline, and a love of learning.

Above age 6 children learn to do independent research, arrange field trips to gather information, interview specialists, create group presentation, dramas, art exhibits, musical productions, science projects, and so forth. There is no limit to what they can create in this kind of intelligently guided freedom. There are no text books or adult-directed group lessons and daily schedule. There is great respect for the choices of the children, but they easily keep up with or surpass what they would be doing in a more traditional setting. There is no wasted time and children enjoy their work and study. The children ask each other for lessons and much of the learning comes from sharing and inspiring each other instead of competing with each other.'

Accordingly, learners starting with (S-)BPM should be supported with case studies demonstrating the idea and scope, e.g., service production in organizations. After watching and listening they should articulate their observations using their favorite way of expression. Following the flow of learning advised by Cornell [4] and utilized by Montessori 'Induce Excitement – Perceive in a Focused Way – Immediate Experience – Share Experience', the individual pace is followed by interaction. Essential for individual and group activities is material that needs to be introduced to them 1:1 by the facilitator. Hereby, the readiness of learners in terms of being in a sensitive period needs to be taken into account for the learning processes. The sensitivity for BPM should be fostered by the considered universe of discourse being close to the actual work environment of the learners, and the prepared material (environment). As learners feel motivated, they are able to listen in a focused way and discover novel information. It facilitates (re-)call and application of knowledge.

After getting confident with (S-)BPM, 'independent research', such as field trips or interviews to collect information, group presentations and collaborative experience design help to deepen knowledge. Hereby, facilitators need to respect the choices of the learners, as this freedom pays back in terms of knowing. S-BPM, in contrast to function-oriented BPM, has the focus on actors as active systems, their role-specific behavior and communication. Consequently, S-BPM allows getting into the flow of learning through role playing, sharing perceived behavior, and triggering reflection based on feedback of the peer group (rather than the facilitator).

For BPM Bandara et al. [1] have identified not only a lack of educational materials and facilitators. They have recognized mostly high-level overviews of BPM topics rather than in-depth learning resources. Such a finding induces further work to generate awareness for different types of BPM. It could become part of open initiatives, such as the Foundry for learning and teaching [11]. While still evolving as a collaborative virtual space for students to learn the concepts of BPM in combination with Service-Oriented Architectures (SOA), practicing skills using real-world examples is a core concept. Learners interact with their peers across classes, institutions or even disciplines, hereby generating BPM material.

Further inputs could stem from experiences with motivation labs (cf. Caporale et al. [3]) to excite potential learners, or from gamification with respect to simulation (cf. Vuksic et al. [20]) conveying possible impact when executing BPM models. S-BPM could then either be perceived through multimodal access facilities, or Social Media sharing inputs and reflections. The latter could also trigger communication skill development, as recently demanded by Bergener et al. [2].

Do We Need All Stakeholders Involved In A Process? Montessori had multi-age classrooms which have been argued for – MM-FDI: 'Multi-age classrooms afford us the luxury of adapting the curriculum to the individual child. Each child can work at his or her own pace, while remaining in community with his or her peers. In addition, the multi-age format allows all older children to be the leaders of the classroom community – even those children who may be shy or quiet.' This finding helps educating in S-BPM in progressive environments, both, from an organizational and individual perspective:

- S-BPM is oriented towards business stakeholders and active systems relevant for an organization. Hence, a process description is not complete unless all subjects have been identified.
- Even for each stakeholder role there should be more than one person involved. It allows capturing the variety of behavior specifications within the scope addressed by each subject.
- Experienced business stakeholders might model behavior in a differentiated way, e.g., distinguishing routine versus non-routine behavior, strict rules versus non-regulated behavior, in contrast to non-experienced business stakeholders.
- From the perspective of organizing learning processes the facilitator could profit from different levels of competences and experiences, as they might trigger corresponding learning designs, expressed through material and navigation paths of the learning environment.

The latter issue indicates the generation of meta-data that could be used for navigating resources, as shown by Neubauer et al. [10] who related content tags for structuring navigation to (S-)BPM content elements. Latest developments in web navigations go even a step further, as WebML's enriched navigation model explicitly addresses the flow of interaction in IFML (Interaction Flow ML - www.ifml.org). Such structures support the development of agile communication skills [2].

Is S-BPM Good For Stakeholders Without Any Modeling Or Process Experience? Montessori has been questioned with respect to children's learning (dis)abilities - MM-FDI: 'What about gifted children? Montessori is designed to help all children reach their fullest potential at their own unique pace. A classroom whose children have varying abilities is a community in which everyone learns from one another and everyone contributes. Moreover, multi-age grouping allows each child to find his or her own pace without feeling "ahead" or "behind" in relation to peers.'

Looking to organizations, their main asset is the set of stakeholders contributing to its wealth [12]. Since S-BPM considers stakeholders and their interaction to be the key for modeling and organizational development, each stakeholder needs to be aware of individual and organizational behavior. In particular,

- The barrier to modeling is low, as it only requires natural language capabilities for stakeholders to contribute to modeling,
- Sticking to the structure of simple sentences (subject-predicate-object) an entire business process can be described from a stakeholder perspective, thus enabling complete task descriptions.
- Memory load in the course of modeling has been minimized – once a subject can be named, each level of competence can be expressed in terms of doing, sending and receiving messages.
- Models can easily be shared, as the behavior abstraction is intelligible in the given universe of discourse.
- Various competence levels can be mapped to subject behavior description and supported dynamically.

Competence using adequate means of expression could become crucial in education, referring to Montessori's observation of the different skill levels for diagrammatic and text expression [9]. For getting acquainted to learning environments, such as the Foundry [11], these systems need to be enriched with articulation tools facilitating interaction and meaningful (re)presentation [18].

Are S-BPM Stakeholders Successful Later In Organizations? MM-FDI: 'Are Montessori children successful later in life? Research studies show that Montessori children are well prepared for later life academically, socially, and emotionally. In addition to scoring well on standardized tests, Montessori children are ranked above average on such criteria as following directions, turning in work on time, listening attentively, using basic skills, showing responsibility, asking provocative questions, showing enthusiasm for learning, and adapting to new situations.'

Although no long-term studies are available so far, the (BPM) education towards behavior encapsulation combined with communication skills to articulate and share qualify operational stakeholder for participating in S-BPM model reflection and adaptation. In case educational environments contain context-sensitive content, such as proposed by Mircea [8] intertwining (S-)BPM with SOA (Service-Oriented Architecture), the implementation of organizational developments could be facilitated.

Is S-BPM a Dogma? This question comes close to the MM-FDI: 'Are Montessori schools religious? No. Montessori educates children without reference to religious denomination. As a result, our classrooms are extremely diverse, with representation from all peoples, cultures and religions.' Analogously, organizations comprise a variety of stakeholders that need to be understood in their diversity, from their background and attitude towards (S-) BPM. Hence, S-BPM, both in operation and education, is considered a paradigm, enforcing to look from a certain perspective on operating a business. In order to facilitate understanding support on a meta(-data) level, such as enabled by IFML (www.ifml.org) or ontology-based content navigation [10] can be provided.

Is S-BPM Education A Franchise? Who Can Educate S-BPM? MM-FDI: 'Is Montessori a franchise? Who can open a Montessori school? The term Montessori is not trademarked and anyone, regardless of training, experience or affiliation can open a "Montessori" school. It is essential that parents researching Montessori act as good consumers to ensure the authenticity of their chosen program.' Since a reliable baseline needs to be provided for organizations and educators, reference material to S-BPM and its education has been provided by Fleischmann et al. [5]. It is available as open text in a learning platform at www.i2pm.net. Although S-BPM has been integrated into BPM study programs at several university (KIT Karlsruhe, FH Fulda, JKU Linz, FH Joanneum Graz etc.), so far no comparative studies with respect to curriculum embodiment similar to Bandara et al. [1] or teacher qualification are available.

Who accredits S-BPM entrepreneurs? MM-FDI: 'Who accredits Montessori schools? Dr. Montessori founded the Association Montessori Internationale in 1929 to preserve her legacy. AMI ensures that Montessori schools and teachers are both well-grounded in the basic principles of the method and ready to carry those principles forward in the modern educational world. AMI offers teacher training and conferences, approves the production of Montessori materials and books, and, through their AMI-USA branch office, accredits schools.'

So far, S-BPM educational and development activities have been bundled in the Institute for Innovative Process Management (www.i2pm.net) under the umbrella of the S-BPM Open Initiative. This learning community not only facilitates exchanging S-BPM knowledge but also is intended to attract entrepreneurs, aligning with standardization bodies, such as OMG moving towards IFML (www.ifml.org).

Isn't S-BPM Just A Modeling Instrument? MM-FDI: 'Isn't Montessori just a preschool? Montessori schools may be best known for their programs with young children, but the underlying educational method describes programs for students up through high school.'

More than in other BPM approaches modeling is the core activity in S-BPM, thus models forming the baseline for articulation, refinement, and sharing business process knowledge. Since validated models can be executed automatically, allowing direct user experience, stakeholders need to be guided by means such as the motivation lab [3], tabletop modelling (www.metasonic.de/touch), or socially networked content (cf. Paik et al. [11]). Domain-specific teasers can be ontological navigation structures [10], agile communication skill trainings [2], and organizational simulation games [20].

If Stakeholders Are Free To Choose Their Own Style Of Work, How Can Be Ensured That An Organization As A Whole Works? MM-FDI: 'If children are free to choose their own work, how do you ensure that they receive a well-rounded education? Montessori children are free to choose within limits, and have only as much freedom as they can handle with appropriate responsibility. The classroom teacher and assistant ensure that children do not interfere with each other, and that each child is progressing at her appropriate pace in all subjects.'

It is the nature and origin of S-BPM that each participating stakeholder is likely to represent at least one subject in the course of modeling. Scoping a business process is achieved by role-specific stakeholder or active systems behaviors, respectively. Once business stakeholders use standard sentence semantics processes can be elicited and represented. For the latter besides tasks the interaction perspective using send and receive for data exchange need to be recognized. Running a business process operation beyond validation and automated execution of models might require organizational simulation games [20], targeting to avoid side effects when organizational structures become operational. Additionally, they could trigger readiness for change.

S-BPM Education And Applications Do Not Look Like Regular BPM Education And Applications. Where Are The Functions? Who Is In Control? MM-FDI: 'Montessori classrooms don't look like regular classrooms. Where are the rows of desks? Where does the teacher stand? The different arrangement of a Montessori classroom mirrors the Montessori methods differences from traditional education. Rather than putting the teacher at the focal point of the class, with children dependent on her for information and activity, the classroom shows a literally child-centered approach. Children work at tables or on floor mats where they can spread out their materials, and the teacher circulates about the room, giving lessons or resolving issues as they arise.' In S-BPM, there is no need for central control, rather sensitivity to model individual behavior in terms of communication and function. Each stakeholder is in charge of his/her individual task including the flow of interaction (cf. IFWL). In order to complete a learning cycle, specifications need to be put into an S-BPM execution engine, regardless which way the S-BPM models have been constructed.

Is S-BPM as Academically Rigorous as Traditional BPM? MM-FDI: 'Are Montessori schools as academically rigorous as traditional schools? Yes; Montessori classrooms encourage deep learning of the concepts behind academic skills rather than rote practice of abstract techniques. The success of our students appears in the experiences of our alumni, who compete successfully with traditionally educated students in a variety of high schools and universities.'

S-BPM has been integrated into curricula and become a topic of peer-reviewed research activities – see www.S-BPM-ONE.org. In this way, not only study but also development and research programs contribute to rigorous academic education. Momentum will be gained when these programs are aligned with the latest OMG developments towards standardizing IFML (www.ifml.org).

Since S-BPM Models Emphasize Non-Centralized Control, How Are Stakeholders Adequately Prepared For Real-Work Work Later on? MM-FDI: 'Since Montessori classrooms emphasize non-competitiveness, how are students adequately prepared for real-life competition later on? Montessori classrooms emphasize competition with oneself: self-monitoring, self-correction, and a variety of other executive skills aimed at continuous improvement. Students typically become comfortable with their strengths and learn how to address their weaknesses. In older classes, students commonly participate in competitive activities with clear "winners" (auditions for limited opera roles, the annual spelling bee, etc.) in which students give their best performances while simultaneously encouraging peers to do the same. It is a healthy competition in which all contenders are content that they did their best in an environment with clear and consistent rules.'

It is the set of interfaces (send, receive) that enables connecting business operation to stakeholder behavior (SBDs). Moreover, using SOA on the level of functional activities in S-SBDs ensures compatibility with organizational implementation architectures (cf. [8]). With respect to self-organized change management S-BPM models can be constructed or updated at run time, thus allowing stakeholders to learn and share on the fly. Each stakeholder is responsible for encoding his/her competence in terms of individual behaviour that could become effective on the organizational layer. This process can be started anytime, structuring organizational change according to the progressive learning cycle of Cornell [4].

4 Conclusions

When introducing a novel paradigm in Business Process Management, in particular Subject-oriented Business Process Management, educators should be aware of the required mind shift for learners. Instead of focusing on function flows the interaction among business stakeholders is at the center in S-BPM. Inputs from progressive educators should help facilitating the acquisition of novel concepts while establishing stakeholder-driven organizational development. Once business stakeholders have learnt to articulate ideas and proposals effecting business processes, they influence the operational agility of their organization directly. By that time, S-BPM has advanced from a guided to a mentally anchored concept.

References

1. Bandara, W., Chand, D.R., Chircu, A.M., Hintringer, S., Karagiannis, D., Recker, J.C., van Resnburg, A., Usoff, C., Welke, R.J.: Business process management education in academia: Status, challenges, and recommendations. Communications of the Association for Information Systems 27, 743–776 (2010)
2. Bergener, K., vom Brocke, J., Hofmann, S., Stein, A., vom Brocke, C.: On the importance of agile communication skills in BPM education: Design principles for international seminars. Knowledge Management & E-Learning: An International Journal (KM&EL) 4(4), 415–434 (2013)
3. Caporale, T., Citak, M., Lehner, J., Oberweis, A., Schoknecht, A., Ullrich, M.: Motivating course concept: Using Active Labs for BPM education. ECIS, Research in Progress. Paper 12 (2013), http://aisel.aisnet.org/ecis2013_rip/12
4. Cornell, J.: Sharing the Joy of Nature. DAWN Publications, Nevada City (1989)
5. Fleischmann, A., Stary, C.: Whom to talk to? A stakeholder perspective on business process development. Universal Access in the Information Society 11(2), 125–150 (2012)
6. Fleischmann, A., Schmidt, W., Stary, C., Obermeier, S., Börger, E.: Subject-orientied Business Process Management. Springer, Heidelberg (2012)
7. Jeston, J., Nelis, J.: Business Process Management. Practical Guidelines to Successful Implementations, 2nd edn. Elsevier, Oxford (2008)
8. Mircea, M.: SOA, BPM and cloud computing: connected for innovation in higher education. In: International Conference on Education and Management Technology, pp. 456–460. IEEE (2010)

9. Montessori, M.: Analysis. Die Neue Erziehung. VIII. Jhg., 243 (1926) (in German)
10. Neubauer, M.: E-learning support for business process modeling: Linking modeling language concepts to general modeling concepts and vice versa. In: Stary, C. (ed.) S-BPM ONE 2012. LNBIP, vol. 104, pp. 62–76. Springer, Heidelberg (2012)
11. Paik, H.-Y., Rabhi, F.A., Benatallah, B., Davis, J.: Service learning and teaching foundry: A virtual SOA/BPM learning and teaching community. In: Muehlen, M.z., Su, J. (eds.) BPM 2010 Workshops. LNBIP, vol. 66, pp. 790–805. Springer, Heidelberg (2011)
12. Post, J.E., Preston, L.E., Sauter-Sachs, S.: Redefining the corporation: Stakeholder management and organizational wealth. Stanford University Press, Stanford (2002)
13. Recker, J.: Opportunities and constraints: the current struggle with BPMN. Business Process Management Journal 16(1), 181–201 (2010)
14. Schmidt, W.: Relationship between BPM education and business process solutions: Results of a student contest. In: Stephanidis, C. (ed.) Universal Access in HCI, Part IV, HCII 2011. LNCS, vol. 6768, pp. 622–631. Springer, Heidelberg (2011)
15. Schmidt, W., Stary, C.: Establishing an Informed S-BPM Community. In: Buchwald, H., Fleischmann, A., Seese, D., Stary, C. (eds.) S-BPM ONE 2009. CCIS, vol. 85, pp. 34–47. Springer, Heidelberg (2010)
16. Seethamraju, R.: Business process management: a missing link in business education. Business Process Management Journal 18(3), 532–547 (2012)
17. Stary, E.: How to Learn to "Speak S-BPM" - Lessons from Language Learning. In: Oppl, S., Fleischmann, A. (eds.) S-BPM ONE 2012. CCIS, vol. 284, pp. 57–76. Springer, Heidelberg (2012)
18. Stary, C., Stary, E.: Creating Meaningful Representations. Journal of Information & Knowledge Management 12(4), 1350041, 13 pages (2013)
19. Tiltmann, T., Rick, U., Henning, K.: Concurrent Engineering and the Dynaxity Approach. How to Benefit from Multidisciplinarity. In: Ghodous, P., Dieng-Kuntz, R., Loureiro, G. (eds.) Leading the Web in Concurrent Engineering – Next Generation Concurrent Engineering. Frontiers in Artificial Intelligence and Applications, pp. 488–495. IOS, Amsterdam (2006)
20. Vuksic, V.B., Bach, M.P.: Simulation Games in Business Process Management Education. In: Proceedings of World Academy of Science, Engineering and Technology, vol. (69), World Academy of Science, Engineering and Technology (2012)
21. Weske, M.: Business process management. Concepts, languages, architectures, 2nd edn. Springer, Berlin (2012)

DayByDay: Interactive and Customizable Use of Mobile Technology in the Cognitive Development Process of Children with Autistic Spectrum Disorder

Vanessa Tavares de Oliveira Barros, Cristiane Affonso de Almeida Zerbetto, Kátia Tavares Meserlian, Rodolfo Barros, Murilo Crivellari Camargo, and Táthia Cristina Passos de Carvalho

Universidade Estadual de Londrina, Londrina, Brazil
{vanessa,cra,rodolfo}@uel.br, katia.meserlian@hotmail.com, {murilocrivellaric,tathiacarvalho}@gmail.com

Abstract. Autistic Spectrum Disorder (ASD) was firstly described as a disturbance of affective contact, including language deficiency, social interaction limitation, and repetitive/restrictive behaviors. ASD individuals are to be motivated and encouraged to seek for independence and cognitive development, in order to overcome the restrictions imposed by the disturbance. This paper presents the development of an application aimed specifically at helping ASD children aged 8-12 years improve, by establishing a sequential and highly-customizable routine. Developed with the help of professionals that work with autistic children and their caregivers, the application proves to be a support tool for the ASD individuals' reality.

Keywords: Autistic Spectrum Disorder (ASD), Assistive Technology (AT), Accessibility.

1 Introduction

Technology has been used in several health fields to assist illnesses treatment, to improve medical assistance quality and as a tool that comes in aid of people with different kinds of impairment. In this context, this research took into consideration the difficulties faced by children with Autistic Spectrum Disorder (ASD) in order to try to ease or supplement their needs. Although each child faces unique difficulties and potential, some problems are common to the vast majority of them, namely: difficulty or disinterest in socializing, problems in significant language usage, repetitive movements and behaviors, among others. To do so, it was defined to create an application, since smartphones and tablets have becoming increasingly affordable.

An application was opted also because of its high degree of customization, in order to develop a system with functions and interactions designed to reach every user as a unique individual. Furthermore, mobile devices support touchscreen technology, which allows direct contact from the user, providing more precision and motor control during interaction. Therefore, especially for ASD individuals, direct control provides

C. Stephanidis and M. Antona (Eds.): UAHCI/HCII 2014, Part II, LNCS 8514, pp. 443–453, 2014.

the application to be better controllable and more interesting, in addition to increase their learning capacities, instead of a desktop, for example, which would require intermediaries (the mouse and the keyboard, in this case).

Thus, a research was conducted on how to conceive an application designed to reach each subject as a unique individual, with the purpose that this application would draw ASD children's attention.

2 Theoretical Background

Austrian psychiatrist Leo Kanner wrote the pioneer publication on autism in 1943, which he initially called "autistic disturbances of affective contact". After conducting a research, Kanner concluded that the autism comes from an innate incapacity of establishing usual and biological affective contact with people, given, however, the proper importance of environmental aspects in development [Bagarollo & Panhoca, 2010, Mattos & Nuerberg, 2011].

Nevertheless, autism early concept has been altered based on scientific research, which verified different etiologies, degrees of severity and specific or non-usual features, as it appears on the International Classification of Diseases Revision 10 (ICD-10), including autism in Global Developmental Disorder. Well known as ICD F84, this Code on autistic disorder settles diagnosis criteria to identify autism, such as: qualitative loss in social interaction; qualitative loss in oral and non-oral communication, imaginative play; and repetitive/restrictive behaviors and interests.

Since May 2013, there has been a new edition of the Diagnostic and Statistical Manual of Mental Disorders (DSM-V) discoursing on communication and social deficits. An individual is diagnosed with Autistic Spectrum Disorder (ASD) if he holds the three following deficits: alternative emotional or social interaction problems; serious problems in maintaining relationships; and non-oral communication problems. Besides, he must hold at least two repetitive/restrictive behaviors, such as: utter addiction to patterns and routine, and consequent resistance to routine changing; repetitive speech or movements; intense and restrictive interest; and difficulty in integrating sensory information or a strong need to avoid behavioral sensory stimuli.

Furthermore, Schwartzman [2003] adds that this addiction to the routine may cause a catastrophic crisis, resulting even in aggression, simply by changing the itinerary back home, or attempting to change clothes, or placing an object out of its usual field of sight.

2.1 Cognitive Development of ASD Children

This work relates some approaches of ASD study, such as: theory of mind; neuropsychological theory; information processing.

Theory of Mind. The theory of mind, according to Cohen, Leslie and Frith [1985], refers to the ability of inferring what other people think, in relation to their beliefs, wishes and intentions, aiming to explain or predict their behavior.

Neuropsychological Theory: Executive Function. The Executive Function, according to Fuster [2002], is understood as a group of functions responsible for the initiation and development of an activity, with a settled final objective. This is also known as the frontal lobes function, since it appears to be metacognitive rather than merely cognitive. It does not refer to any specific mental ability, but instead embraces all of them. It is important to mention, also, the prefrontal cortex, responsible for the evaluation of success or failure of actions directed to previously set objectives.

Information Processing: Central Coherence. The Central Coherence, according to Hill and Frith [2003], refers to information processing style, specifically the proclivity of processing information inside its context.

However, ASD individuals experience the absence of natural inclination for joining chunks of information to form a total provided with meaning, expressing a poor performance in tasks that demand an unabridged and global acknowledgement of context. In fact, this opposes the idea of a superior performance, which requires attention to sectional information [Bosa & Callias, 2000]. The interesting part of this theory is that ASD individuals' abilities are valued, rather than analyzing only their deficits.

2.2 Digital Universe for Accessibility: Assistive Technology

Assistive Technology (AT) can be defined as every resource and/or service that is able to truly offer functional abilities to impaired people and, consequently, provide higher and better quality of life to these individuals. Accordingly to the Comitê de Ajudas Técnicas (CAT), which is a Brazilian committee to help promote the rights of people with disabilities, the main goal of AT can be described as promoting functionality (activity, interaction) to disabled people, to people with restricted mobility, or elderly people, aiming at their autonomy, independence, quality of life and social inclusion growth, through products, resources, strategies, practices, processes, methods, and services, including the principles of Universal Design and Social Technology [CAT, 2007.a]. CAT approved by unanimity, in December 2007, VII Reunion, the adoption of the following formulation for the concept: Assistive technology is a field of knowledge, of interdisciplinary disposition, that encompasses products, resources, methodologies, strategies, practices, and services aiming at promoting functionality, related to activity and participation of people with disabilities, incapacities or restricted mobility, in order to improve their autonomy, independence, quality of life and social inclusion [CAT, 2007.c].

Regarding the organization or classification of Assistive Technology resources, it occurs according to the functional objectives they are aimed at. The following classification has a didactic purpose, and was proposed by Bersch [2008]. It lists eleven AT areas, based on other classifications, especially on the Assistive Technology Applications Certification Program (ATACP), provided by the College of Extended Learning and Center on Disabilities, from California State University of Northridge: (1) Daily life and practical life aid; (2) Augmentative and Alternative Communication (AAC);

(3) accessibility resources on the computer; (4) environmental control systems; (5) architectural projects for accessibility; (6) orthotics and prosthetics; (7) postural adequacy; (8) mobility aid; (9) support for blind or vision impaired individuals; (10) support for deaf or auditory impaired individuals; (11) vehicles adaptations. Finally, it is noteworthy to mention that this research takes into consideration the accessibility resources on the computer.

3 Methodological Procedures

In order to reach further understanding on the universe of ASD children and technological devices, an analysis was conducted over four similar applications. All of the applications analyzed have the intention to help children with some kind of impairment. The result of this analysis showed that the vast majority of the applications available are not aimed at children with behavioral disturbances and, if they are, they still show graphically or interactively inadequacy.

The first similar analyzed was PROLOQUO2GO, an application developed for people with speech impairment, in other words, it was not developed exclusively for ASD individuals, but for anyone with language disturbances. Its function is to teach the user to build up statements through symbols and pictures. It utilizes text-to-speech technology (text to voice conversion), words prediction and customizable vocabulary. The interface itself keeps unaltered, while the functions can be customized. Illustrations are rather simplified and iconic.

The second similar, FIRST THEN VISUAL SCHEDULE HD (FTVS-HD), aims to assist subjects in need of a clear routine, therefore it comprises disturbances such as dyslexia, autism and attention deficit. This application holds an interface similar to a blackboard that allows the conception of a customized schedule based on pictograms and on the tasks' timetable to help users mark the completed tasks. Pictograms can be replaced with photos, videos and/or sounds.

AUSTISMATE was the third application analyzed. It combines functionality of various applications and was developed specifically for ASD individuals, aiming to embrace the entire spectrum. Parents can set dynamic scenes, like the kitchen of the house, in which the child is able to touch the image of a tap and watch a video of how to wash the hands correctly. The application focuses especially on photographs and videos to help the user fulfill daily tasks, although the highly pictorial interface proves to be complex and, furthermore, there is no evident linearity in the tasks description. These textual descriptions, moreover, are extensive and can be meaningless for ASD individuals. The application also incorporates extra functions to create a visual schedule and a section for statements building.

The fourth and last similar analyzed was MY PAL, also developed specifically for ASD individuals that resorts on Aesop fables jointly with sounds and smooth-colored illustrations to teach children at home or in school. The objective is to teach them basic concepts, such as help identify emotions and teach social interaction behaviors. Through a fable, and a friendly and interactive interface so that the child finds it funny, the application works like a game, in which every completed task is rewarded with an accessory for the character. Photographs and videos are not included in this application and its image and sound library is preset and limited, becoming impossible to add new files.

Finally, a table was generated to synthesize the main features and functions of the applications analyzed. Table 1 joins information on the applications analyzed and the new application: on the one hand, it shows the features provided by the applications mentioned above, and on the other hand, it summarizes the features to be expected from the new one.

After that, it was carried out talks with two professionals (from the psychology and education fields) that work directly with ASD children. Such interviews helped delimitate the range of target audience the application intended to reach, as well as other important features.

In a talk carried with a psychologist, it was found the ASD children's reality is rather particular and individualized, so the idea of developing an application to support a wide range of common needs to ASD individuals was put away, once it certainly would require a very complex system to be developed and programmed, as well as the possibility of error and inefficiency of the application be much greater. The professional also reported that many institutions make use of technology while working with ASD children, but the majority of tested softwares and applications is not specifically developed for them. Indeed, they are developed, commonly, for a specific problem, such as speech disabilities, which is common not only for ASD individuals, but also to other types of impairment.

Table 1. Similar applications' features/functions

Feature/function	Does the application have the feature/function?				
	Proloquo2go	FTVS-HD	Autismate	My Pal	DayByDay
Graphic interface aimed at ASD	No	No	Yes	Yes	Yes
Parental control	No	No	Yes	Yes	Yes
Customizable interface	Yes	Yes	Yes	No	Yes
Sound support	Yes	Yes	No	Yes	Yes
Stimulus through rewards	No	No	No	Yes	Yes
Sharing network	No	No	No	No	Yes

Another talk, with a pedagogue, shed light on the most common problems in the routine between ASD children and parents/educators and, starting from this point, the approach of the research began in seeking a way to help establish a pleasurable routine for the children and that could be customizable by their parents. The professional also reported it would be extremely important that the application was not restricted to technological reality, but that its activities and outcomes provided real interaction among the participants.

Having those topics in mind, the application was conceived and given the name DAYBYDAY, aimed exclusively at ASD children aged 8 to 12 years as a tool to establish a routine and the tasks they perform. The application main goal is to organize scheduled and sequenced routine, through creation and management of tasks in day shifts.

Regarding the application development, DAYBYDAY was conceived to assist both ASD individuals and parents/educators. Although giving autonomy to ASD individuals is important to help improve their self-reliance, supervision is still required, especially in performing tasks that demand abilities not fully mastered by them. Thus, the application offers two particular kinds of profile, selected while running the application for the first time: the ASD individual profile and the parent/educator profile.

By choosing the ASD individual profile, the user will be given access, basically, to the tasks platform. Such tasks are neither standardized nor preconceived or, to clarify, they can be created and customized accordingly to ASD individuals' particular needs. Assuming that ASD individuals often face difficulties with fixed routines, it is possible to generate tasks such as "have breakfast", "brush the teeth", "take a shower" and "change clothes". But, if the child is unable to have his meals by his own, for example, the task "have breakfast" can be customized and divided in several chunks of a task, such as "fix the sandwich" and "have coffee milk" so that the application proves to be as much relevant as possible for that individual reality.

Tasks are displayed in chronological order and divided in day shifts. Completed tasks display an icon to mark them, while posterior tasks display a padlock icon to indicate they are "locked". Just the current task keeps active and "unlocked". This mechanism prevents the child from, for example, accessing the task "change clothes" before completing the task "have a shower", providing a logical sequence that helps ASD individuals follow the routine. Enriching the idea of day sequence, screen background alters its colors and elements to indicate the day shifts: morning, afternoon and evening. In the morning, there are clouds and the blue color indicates the shift, whilst in the afternoon the blue is replaced with orange; in the evening, stars replace the clouds (Figure 1). Every single color or element was applied to suit the target age selected, and in order to be enticing for ASD children.

By accessing a specific task, the user is taken to a step-by-step screen, pictorially represented, to complete the task. For example, accessing the task "change clothes" will lead to a screen where the child sees pieces of clothes arranged in the righteous order they must be put on (underwear, t-shirt, pants, socks and shoes) to complete the task. By completing the task, the child receives a motivational message from his parent/educator, leading to the understanding of reaching success and therefore being encouraged to complete more tasks. Successfully completed tasks will accumulate points that appear as stars. When the child collects five stars, he can choose a reward.

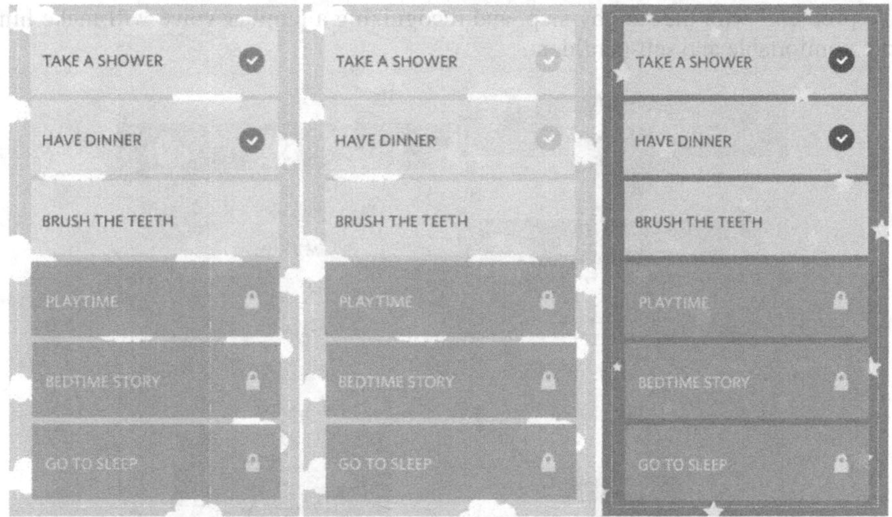

Fig. 1. Tasks' list screen, in three day shifts: morning, afternoon and evening. Note that the original version of DAYBYDAY is in Portuguese.

Such rewards are determined by the caregiver, and must be customized to meet the child's particular interests. After choosing a reward, another message from the parent/educator shows up, setting when it will be handed in. For example, if the child chose a park stroll as reward, parents/educators can set it will take place on the weekend. The rewarding system was developed so that the child could be motivated and encouraged to complete more tasks, and consequently improving his cognitive development. This action is the last of ASD individuals profile cycle so that, from this point, the application returns to the tasks' list screen. The system's linearity simplifies the path to be followed and decreases error possibility.

But by choosing the parent/educator profile, the platform will be completely different. This profile grants access to the control and the creation of tasks and rewards, and also to the system customization settings. In the first screen, there is a calendar giving access to the tasks scheduled for each day, divided in day shifts. Parents/educators can easily verify the programmed tasks for each day, make changes and include new tasks to be completed (Figure 2). It also gives the possibility to observe, in real time, ASD individuals performance, as well as which tasks have been completed.

Accessing the option "add new task" will grant the parent/educator the possibility to create specific tasks according to the ASD individual reality. Settings include adding a name for the new task and a short description, besides pictures and/or sounds. Pictures or photos inclusion leads to the emergence of a familiarity bond to facilitate ASD individuals' performance. For example, by including on the task "change clothes" photos of the child's own clothes, the parent/educator allows the child to recognize the pieces, preventing the ASD child from having to decide which pieces of clothing to wear, since this decision-making might not be simple for him. Similarly, by recording sounds describing the tasks, the speech impaired ASD child will not have problems with the step-by-step, and recognizing a familiar voice will make him more comfortable and self-confident.

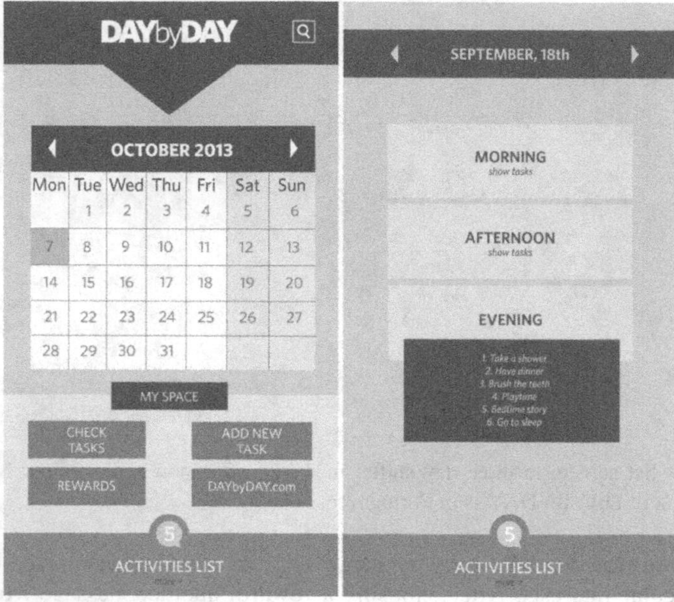

Fig. 2. Parent/educator first screen (to the left) and tasks control screen (to the right). Note that the original version of DAYBYDAY is in Portuguese.

A similar system was applied for the rewards, which can be customized like the tasks. Besides, it is possible to create a picture/sound library, and store the tasks and rewards created to insert them at will, according to the child's needs and schedule. The possibility of customization at high-level provides a safe and useful environment, since the interface enables the user to determinate more relevant aspects for the ASD child.

Furthermore, it is the parent/educator's responsibility to write the motivational messages that will be sent to the child after completing a task or choosing a reward. Thus, the communication between them flows more naturally and veridically, considering that the parent/educator knows exactly what to say to the child. Finally, the parent/educator receives relevant notifications in his own mobile, for example whether the child completed or not a task, which grants him utter control over the ASD individual's development.

In order to integrate and share ideas and experiences, a site for the application was also developed. In the site, information on the application is available, so that any non-registered person could gather more data about it. On the other hand, for DAYBYDAY users there are more possibilities. The site was conceived to work as a large repository of integrated ideas and experiences available for the users. After creating a new task or reward, the parent/educator can upload it to the site, and add tags to it. While exploring the site, other users can find the uploaded task or reward, through the search system, and download it, whether to have ideas or even to use the ready resource with his own child.

The same applies to pictures, which remain available in the site for the users to download it. Submitted material is subjected to analysis and would pass the sieve of a team of specialists before being incorporated to the site library. This settles an indirect network of communication that keeps in track with ASD individuals' needs, filled with good ideas and experiences to be shared with other parents/educators. Finally, there is a "specialists' recommended activities" section, in which psychologists, doctors, pedagogues, and other professionals provide ideas of games and activities to stimulate ASD child's cognitive development, and to be used as rewards. By doing that, the child can be rewarded with an activity from which he can benefit motor and cognitively.

After the conception and development of DAYBYDAY application, the following step comprised its consistency verification, through a qualitative research using the deductive method. Also, it was carried out the application of a questionnaire with open questions related to the topics mentioned hitherto. The research was conducted with the support from AMA (Associação de Amigos do Autista), an autism-friendly association in the city of Londrina. Seven ASD individuals' caregivers participated in a session of DAYBYDAY presentation at Universidade Estadual de Londrina, and afterwards, responded to the questionnaire.

3.1 Results

The first question asked the caregivers if they think the application would be able to help the ASD child complete daily tasks, and why. The responses obtained were: Yes, to help the routine; Yes, it helps the routine; Yes, it improves the routine; Maybe, my son is hyperactive, so I think it will be a little hard for him to concentrate and benefit from it; Yes, in planning and organizing the routine and to contextualize situations.

In the second question, it was asked if they would include any topic/feature to facilitate the daily tasks with child. The responses were: Yes, something about food. Something that motivates him to eat other kinds of food; Do not know the application completely; I need to know more about the application first; I don't think so, as the child gets accustomed to the program, it gets easier for him; I believe it will improve his autonomy, according to my son's individual potential.

The third question encouraged them to cite more activities they perform which are not on the application. The caregivers answered: Swimming; I don't know; Comb the hair; Specify the game at playtime. In question four, it was asked whether the caregivers would make use of the application or not, as they responded: Yes; Not yet, I need to get to know the application better; Yes; Yes, I believe everything is worth doing to help the child development; Yes.

The fifth question found out if the caregivers enjoyed the graphic interface and why. Obtained responses were: Yes; It is really beautiful; No, it needs more color, although the use of soft colors was explained; I liked it, I think it is simple; Yes, it appears to be relevant for the autistic children. The sixth question asked if DAYBYDAY graphic interface would possibly draw ASD children's attention, and the responses were: I think it can be more colorful and have pleasurable noises; Yes;

Yes; I have to show it for my son to know, because there are some things I think he won't like, but he does; Yes.

Finally, in question seven, it was asked if the caregiver found the application easy to use and why. It was obtained the following responses: Yes, my son even has a tablet; Yes, for the parents; It is easy for the parents, but we have to see if it will work with the kids; Yes; Yes, I caught a glimpse of this application in the daily routine of my son. Since this research was addressed to the caregivers view in relation to DAYBYDAY, it can be concluded that the application satisfactorily met this sampling, in the view of the fact that they were receptive to use it in their children's routine.

4 Conclusion

This work intended to develop an application of interdisciplinary disposition in order to reach a satisfactory result and to ensure its efficiency. The integration of several fields, such as design, psychology, pedagogy and data processing proved to be essential in the preliminary stage of development, which was supported by a theoretical background. The conducted study had the intention to show all of the evolution stages of a product designed to outdo expectations in terms of market and social contribution.

Testing stage, conducted with the caregivers, was also crucial to confirm the application strengths, given the positive feedback in relation to its efficiency. The application of the questionnaire was also important to expose possible flaws as well as improvements to be done both on the interface and on its features, from the viewpoint of those who truly face ASD difficulties. Future stages include improving the final product through usability tests conducted with ASD children to gather further data on whether they adapt to it or not. Finally, it will include the participation of neuropediatricians in order to reach a clinical understanding on the positive effects of the application for the ASD children.

References

1. Abbas, P.: Material de apoio para o curso de coolhunting e pesquisa de tendências. Animatrends, Curitiba (2013)
2. Brasil. Ministério da Saúde. Secretaria de Atenção à Saúde. Departamento de Ações Programáticas Estratégicas. Diretrizes de Atenção à Reabilitação da Pessoa com Transtornos do Espectro do Autismo. Ministério da Saúde, Brasília (2013)
3. Bagarollo, M.F., Panhoca, I.: A constituição da subjetividade de adolescentes autistas: um olhar para as histórias de vida. Revista Brasileira de Educação Especial 16(2), 231–250 (2010)
4. Bosa, C., Callias, M.: Autismo: breve revisão de diferentes abordagens. Psicologia: Reflexão e Crítica, Porto Alegre vol.13(1) (2000)
5. Baron-cohen, S., Lesliel, A.M., Frith, U.: Does the autistic child have a 'theory of mind'. In: Cognition, pp. 37–46 (1985)

6. Comitê de Ajudas Técnicas, Ata da Reunião III, de abril de 2007, Comitê de Ajudas Técnicas, Secretaria Especial dos Direitos Humanos da Presidência da República, CORDE/SEDH/PR (2007a), http://www.mj.gov.br/corde/arquivos/doc/Ata%20III%2019%20e%2020%20abril2007.doc
7. Comitê de Ajudas Técnicas, Ata da Reunião VII, de dezembro de 2007, Comitê de Ajudas Técnicas, Secretaria Especial dos Direitos Humanos da Presidência da República (CORDE/SEDH/PR) (2007c), http://www.mj.gov.br/corde/arquivos/doc/Ata_VII_Reunião_do_Comite_de_Ajudas_Técnicas.doc
8. Fuster, J.M.: Frontal lobe and cognitive development. J. Neurocytol. 31(3-5), 373–385 (2002)
9. Goldberg, E.O.: cérebro executivo: lobos frontais e a mente civilizada. Imago, Rio de Janeiro (2002)
10. Hill, E.L., Frith, U.: Understanding autism: insights from mind and brain. Philosophical Transactions of the Royal Society Series B: Biological Sciences 358(1430), 281–289 (2003)
11. Kanner, L.: Autistic disturbances of affective contact. Nervous Child 2, 217–250 (1943)
12. Mattos, L.K., Nuenberg, A.H.: Reflexões sobre a inclusão escolar de uma criança com diagnóstico de autismo na educação infantil. Revista de Educação Especial, Santa Maria 24(39), 129–142 (2011)
13. Schwartzman, J.S.: Autismo Infantil. Editora Memon, São Paulo (2003)

An Introduction to the FLOE Project

Jutta Treviranus, Jess Mitchell, Colin Clark, and Vera Roberts

Inclusive Design Research Centre, OCAD University,
100 McCaul St. Toronto, Ontario Canada, M5T 1W1
{jtreviranus,jmitchell,cclark,vroberts}@ocadu.ca

Abstract. Learners learn differently. Research shows that learners learn best when the learning experience is personalized to individual needs. Open Education Resource (OER) platforms potentially provide an ideal learning environment to meet the diverse needs of learners, including learners with disabilities. Unfortunately accessibility was not a consideration when OER were initially designed or developed. When the FLOE (Flexible Learning for Open Education) Project was asked to address the accessibility of OER, rather than a traditional approach to accessibility with a single set of fixed criteria, FLOE set out to support the OER community in providing a personalized and fully integrated approach to accessible learning. This approach advances the strengths and values of open education and also encourages pedagogical and technical innovation. While ensuring the resources are accessible to diverse learners, including learners with disabilities, the approach also supports content portability, ease of updating, internationalization and localization, content reuse and repurposing, and more efficient and effective content discovery.

Keywords: Accessibility, inclusive design, open education, personalization, open education resources.

1 Introduction

Learning breakdown, school "drop out" and lack of engagement in education occurs when students face barriers to learning, feel marginalized by the learning experience offered or feel that their personal learning needs are ignored[1, 2]. Although it is recognized that personalized learning is the ideal, most educational institutions do not have the resources to address the diverse needs of each learner. This significantly compromises learners at the margins, such as learners with disabilities. Digital content and digital delivery mechanisms can be harnessed to assist in addressing the diversity of learning needs – due to the potential mutability or plasticity of digital systems and content but more importantly due to the opportunity for collaboration, cumulative production and support for networked communities[3]. A prime example of such a networked open community that supports cumulative and collective production of resources is the Open Education Resource (OER) community. Collectively pooling and sharing resources reduces redundancy and can result in a greater diversity of learning resources to address the broad range of learning needs. The open licenses

C. Stephanidis and M. Antona (Eds.): UAHCI/HCII 2014, Part II, LNCS 8514, pp. 454–465, 2014.

associated with OER also permit the modification and repurposing of resources to suit unique needs.

1.1 Legal and Policy Imperative

Most countries, states and educational institutions have committed to provide equal access to education for students classified as being disabled[4]. All educational institutions in the US, for example, are governed by policies that require that curriculum be accessible to learners recognized as having a disability. Many of these policies are currently based upon a somewhat restrictive definition of disability and accessibility. Accessibility in formal education in the US has become a large and complex framework focused on policy compliance and specialized service delivery. Students must qualify and resources must comply with a fixed binary notion of disability and accessibility – to constrain special service expenditures and to enable compliance monitoring and enforcement.

1.2 The OER Community Meets the Accessibility Community

In 2010 when the FLOE Project was initiated, the OER "movement" was quickly gaining popularity. Thousands of OER had been developed in part with support from organizations such as the William and Flora Hewlett Foundation, the Gates Foundation and the MacArthur Foundation. However, most Open Education Resources (OERs) were not designed to be accessible for learners with disabilities[5], most OER producers or developers were not aware of how to create accessible OERs, and most OER delivery mechanisms (e.g., OER portals) presented significant barriers to learners using alternative access systems. Consequently OERs did not meet legislative requirements in many countries and the OER initiative fell short of the commitment to inclusive education.

This scenario could be in part attributed to early encounters between the accessibility and OER communities. The formal accessibility framework received a less than welcoming reaction from the OER community for a variety of reasons including:

- Conceptions of accessibility based on a single set of fixed legislated technical criteria were seen to constrain creativity and innovation in both technological and pedagogical approaches, they were seen to be counter to interactivity or more engaging learning experiences,
- OER creators were not aware of learners with the constrained set of qualifying disabilities among their user group,
- the OER movement was dependent on voluntary participation which tends to be less responsive to enforced standards, and
- the guidelines for complying were seen to be too complex and confusing and in some cases impossible to achieve.

The pervasive and well-entrenched accessibility framework and the reaction it had engendered in the OER community had acted as an impediment to adoption of OER as a curriculum alternative in many formal education systems which feared litigation or other consequences of non-compliance with accessibility policy. This situation was unfortunate as the fundamental principles and motivations of OER and Accessibility are well aligned (inclusion, respect for diversity, equal access, open access, freedom to share and refine). More importantly the reforms required to achieve the OER community's vision of learning and education were the same reforms required to achieve the ultimate goals of accessibility (reforms to digital rights management (DRM) and intellectual property (IP), move to digital content and delivery, recognition of the diversity of learners, learner choice, recognition of alternative learning delivery models, focus on deep learning, inclusive education). The two communities should have been strong allies but found themselves relegated to opposite sides of a number of policy and advocacy debates.

The traditional approach to addressing the challenge of OER accessibility would have been to modify all OERs and OER sites to meet a fixed set of accessibility criteria such as the Web Content Accessibility Guidelines, (WCAG) 2.0. However there were and continue to be several problems with this approach:

- There are a vast number of OERs, many of which are not amenable to modifying to meet WCAG 2.0. The time and resources required to modify all of the resources would be prohibitive.
- This approach provides a one-size-fits-all solution and does not recognize the full diversity of learners. The retrofit may compromise the learning experience for certain learners (e.g., learners requiring an image intensive learning experience).
- The approach would restrict the types of technologies, technical advances and range of interactive experiences that can be used in creating OERs for fear of contravening the accessibility criteria.

More significantly this traditional digital resource accessibility approach and the underlying policies and services that are based on fixed, binary notions of disability and accessibility do not serve the needs of learners with disabilities. This approach and framing:

- Excludes learners that do not fit the categories (notably, learners with disabilities have less degrees of freedom or flexibility to fit assigned classifications and are therefore more likely to "fall between the cracks"; in addition there are many learners who do not qualify as having a disability but would benefit from or need alternative learning experiences),
- Treats learners with disabilities as a homogeneous group when they are in fact the most heterogeneous group of learners,
- Classifies learners based on a single parameter, ignoring the multiplicity of needs and skills that affect learning,
- Constrains the design of learning resources thereby giving less leeway to address minority needs and non-normative learning styles or approaches faced by people with disabilities, and
- Compromises the learning experience for many of the learners the services are intended to serve (e.g., learners with learning disabilities who rely on visual learning).

The fixed binary definitions also encourage specialized, segregated services for people with disabilities (i.e., they serve to "ghettoize" education for students with disabilities). This makes these services less sustainable (more vulnerable to funding cuts, open to the whims of shifting funding priorities, peripheral to mainstream efforts and investments, etc.) and more costly (duplicating services found in the mainstream)[6].

1.3 Reframing the Problem

The FLOE project proposed a relative framing of disability and accessibility recognizing the range of human diversity. All learners potentially face barriers to learning. Like barriers faced by people with disabilities these can be seen as a product of a mismatch between the needs of the learner and the learning experience and environment. Learning needs that affect learning can include:

- Sensory, motor, cognitive, emotional and social constraints,
- Individual learning styles and approaches,
- Linguistic or cultural preferences,
- Technical, financial or environmental constraints.

Using this framing an accessible learning experience is a learning experience that matches the needs of the individual learner or the learners within a group. Thus a resource cannot be labeled as accessible or inaccessible until we know the context and the learner/s. This aligns well with OER best practices, learning outcomes research and evidence regarding good pedagogy in OER-based education[7]. This framing merely adds an additional critical impetus to the broader goals and values of the OER community. The added push recognizes that some learners are more constrained than others and are therefore less able to adapt to the learning experience or environment offered, with the result that the learning environment or experience must be more flexible.

With this framing, to achieve an accessible or inclusively designed OER system required the capacity to match the learning needs of individual learners [8]. This required OER resources amenable to reuse and a large, diverse pool of OERs. If the default OER is inaccessible to a specific learner the inclusively designed system would either:

1. Transform the resource (e.g., through styling mechanisms),
2. Augment the resource (e.g., by adding captioning to video), or
3. Replace the resource with another resource that addresses the same learning goals but matches the learner's specific access needs.

To achieve this required:

1. Information about each learner's access needs
2. Information about the learner needs addressed by each resource
3. Resources that are amenable to transformation, a pool of alternative equivalent resources, and
4. A method of matching learner needs with the appropriate learning experience

Programmatically deriving or soliciting this information and performing these functions must be embedded into the current and future OER infrastructure. Fortuitously these steps are not foreign to the OER effort but could be seen as nudges to advance the OER agenda as a whole.

However this approach was helped by conceptual and practical adjustments in both the OER and Accessibility communities. The approach required that the OER community:

- Fully adopt and support the principles of cumulative authoring, derivative works, reuse and repurposing that was already a part of the OER mantra,
- Improve learner-focused resource discovery and the prerequisite labeling,
- Promote an authoring attitude that lets go of the tight control on a fixed presentation or rendering,
- Invest further in a learner-centric approach to resource design,
- Commit to support open interoperability standards for both file formats and programming/scripting environments,
- Support open source tools with open APIs to enable interoperability with assistive technologies, and
- Improve portability or device independence of resources.

The Accessibility community needed to:

- Adjust the interpretation and implementation of accessibility legislation and policy to a learner-centric approach; notably this did not require that the letter or spirit of existing legislation be changed only the interpretation and implementation,
- Recognize that OER is a viable alternative to the complex, confounding and deeply entrenched DRM conundrum that is consuming so much accessibility effort and passion,
- Let go of the focus on equivalent content and focus on equivalent learning, and
- Recognize that in the digital realm it is possible and effective to shift from a one-size-fits-all to a one-size-fits-one approach to providing accessible learning.

The FLOE project supported this shift in both communities.

1.4 Addressing the Needs of Doubly Marginalized Learners

One problem with the implementation and interpretation of accessibility legislation intended to support inclusion is that it has become exclusive and narrowly defined. This is in part due to the pressure to contain costs and create a testable legislative compliance mechanism. Unfortunately this creates a large group of doubly marginalized learners. These learners are not served by mainstream education nor by service enhancements and programs intended to serve learners with disabilities. This includes children whose families or support mechanisms do not have the financial resources, administrative savvy or advocacy skills to enable the child to qualify for special services. It includes learners who do not fit the narrow classifications of disability, especially as it relates to learning or cognitive disabilities. It includes students who only receive attention once it is too late, once they have become a “disciplinary” or "behavior problem." OER and the inclusive design approach of the FLOE project are designed to help address this dilemma by supporting a relative framing of accessibility that recognizes the unique needs of all learners and by providing a system to match those needs.

1.5 Obviating the Need to "Catch Up"

One real risk faced by the accessibility community is that the community has been fighting so hard to catch up with where the rest of the education system is at presently that it will get there just as everyone else has moved on. The accessibility community is spending a great deal of passion and energy to achieve equal access to:

- printed textbooks as textbooks are moving to digital, interactive formats,
- traditional learning management systems as online learning is moving to social-network-based mash-ups,
- didactic pedagogical practices such as lectures as these are being called into question, and
- traditional tests and standardized assessments as alternative assessment and certification processes are being sought.

The irony is that learners with disabilities are best served by the advances being advocated by educational innovators. FLOE aims to redirect the focus of the accessibility effort to the options and opportunities offered by OER efforts and the associated innovative educational practices. FLOE offers a more integrated alternative for providing learners with disabilities inclusive access to education. If the accessible approach is used and demanded by all learners it will be much more sustainable and will be updated with mainstream approaches. This will significantly reduce the need to "catch up."

1.6 Collateral Benefits

The FLOE approach to accessibility is based on the notion of designing for diversity and as such brings with it a host of associated benefits related to diversity, flexibility and adaptability in several realms. In many cases these are powerful motivators for adopting inclusive design principles that may be invoked if and when accessibility is not seen as a critical priority. Even when accessibility is seen as a requirement, these associated benefits can be added motivators for applying inclusive design principles. These associated benefits include:

- ease of internationalization and translation,
- OER portability across operating systems and browsers,
- ease of reuse, repurposing, and updating,
- improved discovery and selection of appropriate OER, and
- ease of delivery through a variety of mobile devices whether phones, smart phones, tablets or laptops.

1.7 Integration into OER Workflow

The FLOE project design recognizes the very distributed, unregulated, largely voluntary nature of the OER community. It has been argued that the most effective means of achieving accessibility goals is through the use of "the stick" in the form of legislation and the threat of litigation. However the "stick" is too blunt an instrument to properly address the complexities of learning and like its use in child rearing usually has unintended side effects (e.g., scarce time and energy devoted to developing creative means to bypass legislation or seek exemptions to legislation; rigidity in adhering to the letter of the law, suppressing innovation; legalistic application of the regulations that do not recognize the diversity or nuanced nature of learning needs) and does not in itself lead to systemic, long-term cultural change. The "stick" is also less effective in a voluntary community such as the OER community. The FLOE project seeks to embed inclusive design in the day to day OER workflow making inclusive design largely automatic and unconscious wherever possible and providing the supports and decision making tools to enable efficient and effective inclusive design where human judgment and effort are required.

The FLOE project design also recognizes the complex, sometimes emotionally charged and highly political nature of the accessibility policy and compliance framework and was in tune with conceptual trends in the political, technical and advocacy efforts of this community. The approach has the support of the majority of thought leaders in the accessibility field but had not yet had impact on the policy framework.

2 Background and Prior Work

The FLOE project leverages many years of work in Canada and internationally. The Connecting Canadians Initiative and the eLearning program of Canarie Inc. supported a large body of research into learning object repositories (which can be said to be the precursors of Open Education Resources) [9]. Canada pioneered curriculum pooling, sharing and reuse in the late 90s and early 2000s (e.g., http://edusource.netera.ca/english/home_eng.html, www.sfu.ca/~mhatala/pubs/CATE2002-hatala-richards.pdf). Unfortunately this program was abandoned with the new federal administration in 2005. This research effort was in part continued through networks such as LORNET, Quality4Reuse and other efforts (http://lornet.ca, http://www.q4r.org). The European Commission through IST projects, JISC research and CEN workshops has advanced this research agenda more recently.

2.1 AccessForAll Metadata and Implementations

The eLearning research in Canada led to the creation of a number of foundational technologies and practices to support inclusive online learning such as Web4All and AccessForAll. AccessForAll is a learning delivery approach and the associated interoperability standards and specifications needed to support learner-centric optimization of the learning resources and delivery environment. AccessForAll was developed in part to address access to learning for people with disabilities in a more sustainable, integrated way. Spearheaded by Treviranus and the ATRC with support and participation from NCAMs Specifications for Accessible Learning Technologies, the IMS Global Learning Consortium, the Open University in the UK, IBM, ISO/IEC JTC1 SC36 and many others AccessForAll is now an IMS specification, ISO standard. AccessForAll has been implemented in projects and services such as TILE (The Inclusive Learning Exchange), TransformAble, ATutor, the Angel Learning Management System, EU4All, Teacher's Domain and the K12 Library [10]. These implementations have yielded a considerable body of evidence and research that have been used to refine both the standard and subsequent implementations.

The AccessForAll specification and standard consists of two main parts: a) a common language for expressing the learning needs of a learner with respect to presentation of material, method of controlling the learning experience, organization, supports or scaffolds and learning style or approach (embedded in LIP and other preference systems) as well as b) a common language for describing resources and user interfaces so that they can be matched to learner needs and preferences (with bindings to Dublin Core and IEEE LOM metadata).

FLOE both exploits the lessons learned from prior AccessForAll implementations and provides feedback to the ISO and IMS standards process to update the standard to address changes in the learning and online delivery domains.

2.2 Fluid Components and Architecture

Fluid is an international open source community that works on infusing inclusive design into other software projects (http://fluidproject.org). Fluid addresses the dilemma of providing a consistent interface while meeting the diversity of user needs including needs associated with language, culture, ability, age and other forms of human diversity. Fluid includes a living library of inclusively designed user experience components, a supporting software architecture, supports for user experience design, and community processes for open source communities to address usability, accessibility, effective documentation, quality assurance, security and other precarious values. Fluid components are part of the most popular Web application toolkits including JQuery and Dojo. This implies that when developers develop Web applications using standard software development processes using these popular toolkits, they will automatically address accessibility requirements. Fluid components are embedded into applications such as FireFox, academic applications such as Sakai, ATutor, uPortal, CollectionSpace, and OpenCast as well as over 100 IBM applications. FLOE uses Fluid as a base to create useful components to embed in existing and future OER initiatives.

2.3 Open Source Authoring Utilities and Toolkits

One of the lessons learned in monitoring compliance to accessibility requirements is that compliance is not achieved by providing a set of rules, guidelines or regulations to be followed. A far more successful means of achieving broad compliance is by embedding the creation or production of accessible resources or content into the tools used for authoring the content. This has the effect of achieving compliance even when the author has neither the knowledge nor the motivation to comply with accessibility requirements. Even when there is motivation and knowledge, authors require supportive authoring tools to enable efficient production of accessible resources. FLOE integrates and enhances a number of authoring utilities and toolkits to support the creation of inclusively designed learning resources. These include metadata wizards, captioning and description tools, styling and "skinning" systems, accessible activity templates and checking tools.

2.4 Participatory Design Practices

FLOE employs a participatory design approach, refined through the Fluid project, to create outreach materials, embeddable components, mobile learning systems, and inclusive authoring supports. The OER community is as diverse as the learners it hopes to serve. The project engages participatory design approaches to tailor the deliverables to the diverse contexts and perspectives represented by this community and the Accessibility community. The participants include individuals in the full range of roles.

3 Outcomes

The overarching goal of FLOE is to achieve a cultural shift in three interlinked broad communities: the accessibility community, the OER community and the wider education community. The key message is that all learners learn differently and that connected sources of OER make it possible to deliver education that meets the unique needs of each learner. FLOE creates the necessary infrastructure to enable learners to discover the qualities of learning experiences that work best for them, then FLOE provides the tools and services needed to deliver OER-based learning experiences that match those individual requirements drawing upon the pool of federated OERs globally and providing supports for OER producers to design for learner diversity. This promotes an integrated approach to special education through OER. It frees OER developers from designing to a restrictive standard to achieve accessibility and from retrofitting the large pool of existing resources. It also highlights the opportunity for greater accessibility afforded by OER, to the accessibility community.

Floe's tools are increasingly being adopted and integrated into OER initiatives such as OER Commons (http://oercommons.org), PHeT (http://phet.colorado.edu), and OERPub, as well as popular content management systems such as WordPress.

The next phase of FLOE will enable learners and their support team to review how well the resources actually matched their needs. This will be used to refine the understanding of the learner's personal needs as well as learner needs in aggregate It will also be used to refine the matching process and to provide feedback to suppliers and producers on the efficacy of the resource produced (see Fig. 1).

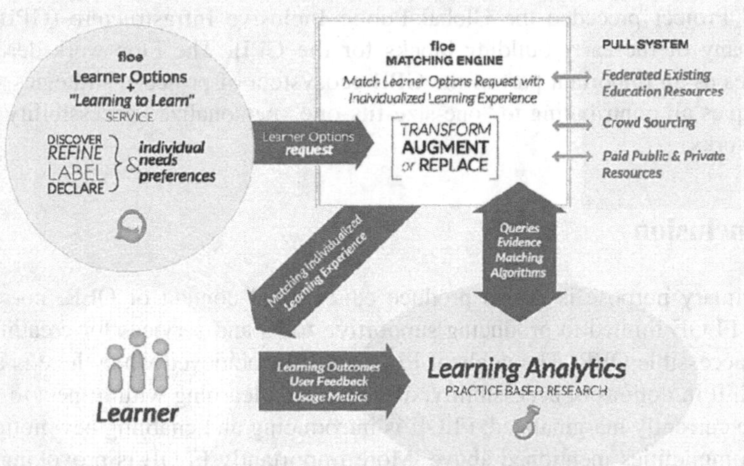

Fig. 1. The FLOE workflow, finding matching learning experiences for individual learner needs

FLOE has implemented a number of social media data mining, text analysis and discourse analysis tools to measure and refine the impact of FLOE. Discourse analysis of the online forums and social media within the OER community shows continued increase in the discussion of inclusion and accessibility and this discussion continues to change in its nature. In analyzing the utterances it is clear that discourse has become more positive, mention of accessibility or inclusive design is more frequently related to planned action and assumed responsibility. In the last year the discussions have become increasingly associated with practical and operational challenges and less related to cost and efficacy. A similar shift has occurred in the accessibility community. Analyzing the discourse data in popular accessibility discussion forums shows that OER are now seen as an opportunity and a positive trend rather than an accessibility threat. The mention of OER in a number of accessibility forums has increased and is predominantly associated with positive statements or practical queries.

Large educational authorities such as the US Dept. of Education have initiated and funded feasibility studies to determine the viability of a FLOE approach to delivering accessible education in the US. The same has happened in the European Commission, which has funded a large scale European partnership to further the FLOE approach (ALTER-NATIVA E-ACCESS Project, http://inclusive-learning.eu/node/18). FLOE has both supported these high-level feasibility studies built upon FLOE innovations, and further enabled bottom-up changes through educator, learner and producer supports and tools. FLOE has also worked to integrate the approach into complementary educational efforts that focus on personalized learning.

3.1 The FLOE Project within the Global Public Inclusive Infrastructure

The FLOE Project preceded the Global Public Inclusive Infrastructure (GPII) and provides many of the early building blocks for the GPII. The Floe work described above serves as an important part of the GPII ecosystem of projects, strategies, tools, and techniques all contributing to "one-size-fits-one" personalized accessibility using global networks.

4 Conclusion

FLOE's primary purpose is not to produce educational content or OER, nor is the purpose of FLOE limited to producing supportive tools and services for creating and delivering accessible OER. The goals of FLOE will be achieved when there is a fundamental shift in notions of accessibility, disability and learning with respect to learners who are currently marginalized. FLOE is introducing and enabling new notions in the three communities mentioned above. More importantly FLOE is provoking a reframing of the perceived problem, rather than providing a solution for an old or currently dominant conception of the problem. Many thought leaders, in all three communities, who viewed the FLOE ideas dubiously and skeptically, now concede that of course this is the only way to go. Others now claim that this was their idea of how to proceed in this problem space from the start, a true sign of successful cultural change [11]. More importantly, as with all efforts to address the needs of people with disabilities, the personalization and self-awareness supported by FLOE are benefitting all learners.

References

1. Pearson Personalized Learning: The Nexus of 21st Century Learning and Educational Technologies Pearson Issue Papers, pp. 1–12 (2009)
2. Rose, D.H., Meyer, A.E.D.: Teaching every student in the Digital Age: universal design for learning 2002. Association for Supervision and Curriculum Development, Alexandria (2002)
3. Solomon, G., Allen, N., Resta, P.E.: Toward digital equity: bridging the divide in education. Allyn and Bacon, Boston (2003)
4. United Nations. The Universal Declaration of Human Rights, http://www.un.org/en/documents/udhr/index.shtml (cited February 18, 2014)
5. Rush, S.: Unpublished Report commissioned by the William and flora Hewlett Foundation, Knowbility (2010)
6. President's Commisssion in Special Education. Final report to the President (May 23, 2011), http://www.dys-add.com/resources/SpecialEd/PresidentialCommission.pdf (cited February 18, 2014)
7. Atkins, D.E., Brown, J.S., Hammond, A.L.: A Review of the Open Educational Resources (OER) Movement: Achievements, Challenges, and New Opportunities, p. 84 (February 2007)

8. Treviranus, J., Roberts, V.: Inclusive E-learning. In: Weiss, J., Nolan, J., Trifonas, P. (eds.) The International Handbook of Virtual Learning Environments, pp. 469–497. Kluwer Academic, Dordrecht (2006)
9. Anderson, T.: A Response and Commentary to: A Review of e-Learning in Canada. Canadian Journal of Learning and Technology / La revue canadienne de l'apprentissage et de la technologie 32(3), 1499–6685 (2006)
10. Treviranus, J., Roberts, V.: Disability, Special Education and IT. In: Voogt, J.M., Knezek, G. (eds.) International Handbook of Information Technology in Primary and Secondary Education, Springer, Hamburg (2007)
11. Hewlett Grantees Meeting (April 2013)

Design of a Virtual Reality Driving Environment to Assess Performance of Teenagers with ASD

Joshua Wade[1], Dayi Bian[1], Lian Zhang[1], Amy Swanson[2], Medha Sarkar[5], Zachary Warren[2,3], and Nilanjan Sarkar[4,1]

[1] Electrical Engineering and Computer Science
Vanderbilt University, Nashville, TN 37212, USA
[2] Treatment and Research Institute for Autism Spectrum Disorders (TRIAD)
Vanderbilt University, Nashville, TN 37212, USA
[3] Pediatrics, Psychiatry and Special Education
Vanderbilt University, Nashville, TN 37212, USA
[4] Mechanical Engineering
Vanderbilt University, Nashville, TN 37212, USA
[5] Computer Science
Middle Tennessee State University, Murfreesboro, TN 37132, USA
{joshua.w.wade,nilanjan.sarkar}@vanderbilt.edu

Abstract. Autism Spectrum Disorder (ASD) is an extremely common and costly neurodevelopmental disorder. While significant research has been devoted to addressing social communication skill deficits of people with ASD, relatively less attention has been paid to improving their deficits in daily activities such as driving. Only two empirical studies have investigated driving performance in individuals with ASD—both employing proprietary driving simulation software. We designed a novel Virtual Reality (VR) driving simulator so that we could integrate various sensory modules directly into our system as well as to define task-oriented protocols that would not be otherwise possible using commercial software. We conducted a small user study with a group of individuals with ASD and a group of typically developing community controls. We found that our system was capable of distinguishing behavioral patterns between both groups indicating that it is suitable for use in designing a protocol aimed at improving driving performance.

Keywords: Virtual Reality, Autism intervention, Adaptive task, Physiological signals, Eye gaze.

1 Introduction

Autism Spectrum Disorders (ASD) is an extremely common (i.e., 1 in 88 children in the U.S.) and costly neurodevelopmental disorder [1]. While significant research has been devoted to addressing social communication skill deficits of people with ASD [2], relatively less attention has been paid to improving their deficits in daily activities such as driving. Driving is a particularly important skill for individuals with ASD to

C. Stephanidis and M. Antona (Eds.): UAHCI/HCII 2014, Part II, LNCS 8514, pp. 466–474, 2014.

develop because it is often a very important component of optimal adaptive independence and quality of life. Further, it has also been shown in several studies that people with ASD tend to exhibit challenges with driving and in fact may demonstrate behaviors that may lead to unsafe driving practices [3-5]. Sheppard et al. [4] found that when teenagers with ASD were shown video clips of driving scenarios, they were less likely to recognize driving hazards that were social in nature (i.e., involving a person not operating a motor vehicle) than a group of typically developing (TD) controls. In the same study, both groups were found to be equally capable of identifying non-social hazards. Reimer's group [5] conducted a study comparing young adults diagnosed with higher-function autism spectrum disorder (HF-ASD) and a group of TD controls using a driving simulator paradigm where the research team collected performance, eye gaze and physiological signal data from participants. Reimer's study found that the HF-ASD group's gaze tended to be higher in the vertical dimension and further to the right in the horizontal dimension. Although there were no group differences in terms of performance in the simulated driving task, the gaze behavior could indicate dangerous driving behavior in an actual driving scenario. Classen and colleagues [6] also conducted a comparison study using a driving simulator paradigm in which they compared a group of pre-driving teenagers diagnosed with both ASD and attention deficit hyperactivity disorder (ADHD) against a group of TD controls. They found that the ASD-ADHD group demonstrated a higher number of driving errors than the TD group including errors related to lane-maintenance and speed-regulation.

Both of the previously mentioned driving simulation studies utilized proprietary simulation software. One of the major drawbacks of designing a protocol around a commercial driving simulator is that it may not provide access to the source code necessary to embed rules to customize for specific interventions. In addition, a novel simulator allows the creation of a network of sensory modules that can seamlessly interact with the simulator. As a result, we presented the preliminary design of a novel virtual reality (VR) driving environment for autism intervention [7]. In this paper, we build upon our previous work by designing a paradigm capable of assessing and eventually improving the driving skills of teenagers with ASD. We also present the results of a small comparison study between a group of teenagers with ASD and a group of TD controls. The following sections are organized in this way: Section 2 gives an in-depth description of the design of the system that we developed, Section 3 outlines the structure of the experiment, Section 4 highlights our findings and Section 5 concludes the paper with a discussion of our contribution and future work.

2 System Design

Our system is composed of four primary modules that interact over a local area network (LAN): the VR module (the driving simulator), an eye gaze data acquisition module, a physiological signal acquisition module to measure attentive and affective states and a therapist report module. A detailed description of each of these follow. Figure 1 diagrams the system architecture.

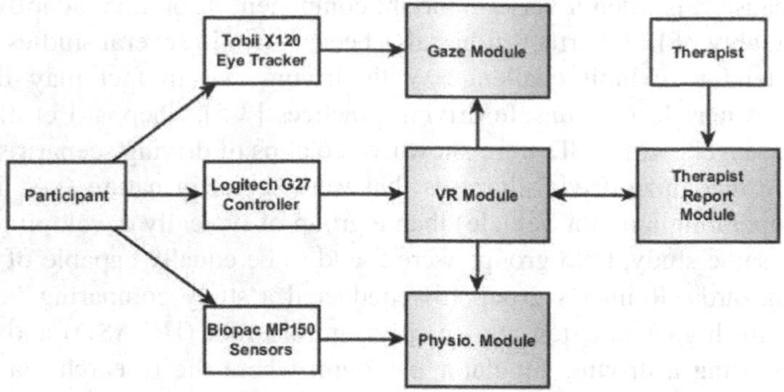

Fig. 1. Driving simulator system architecture

2.1 VR Module

The VR module was modeled as a hierarchical state machine (HSM). Each HSM and low-level finite state machine (FSM) is dedicated to a particular behavior such as monitoring driving errors or establishing network connections with the various sensory modules. Transitions on the top level are preemptive while low-level FSM transitions are either reset-transitions or maintain history.

This study utilized the virtual environment we developed in previous work [7] that was created using the modeling software tools Autodesk Maya and ESRI CityEngine and the game engine Unity. The interactive component of the VR module is modeled as a game with a set of levels with increasing difficulty. Each level contains three assignments (or missions) in which the user must complete a set of eight discretely measureable objectives which we refer to as trials. Trials include scenarios such as decreasing speed in a construction zone, pulling over to the side of the road while emergency vehicles pass and turning left at an intersection when there is oncoming traffic. Trials occurred in a variety of environments including busy city streets and crowded highways.

Users operate the virtual vehicle using a Logitech G27 steering wheel controller and pedal board. The G27 was mounted to a specially designed playseat as seen in Figure 2. Control of the graphical user interface (GUI) was mapped to the device so that users can navigate the menu without using another input device such as a mouse or keyboard. Vehicle controls were logically mapped to the device and a few additional features were added to allow better control of the vehicle. For example, the user can "look around" while stopped at an intersection by simultaneously pressing the brake pedal and rotating the steering wheel in the direction of interest. Additional functionalities included a radio operated by buttons on the steering wheel and turn signals mapped to switches behind the wheel.

Fig. 2. Driving interface (left) and Logitech G27 and playseat (right)

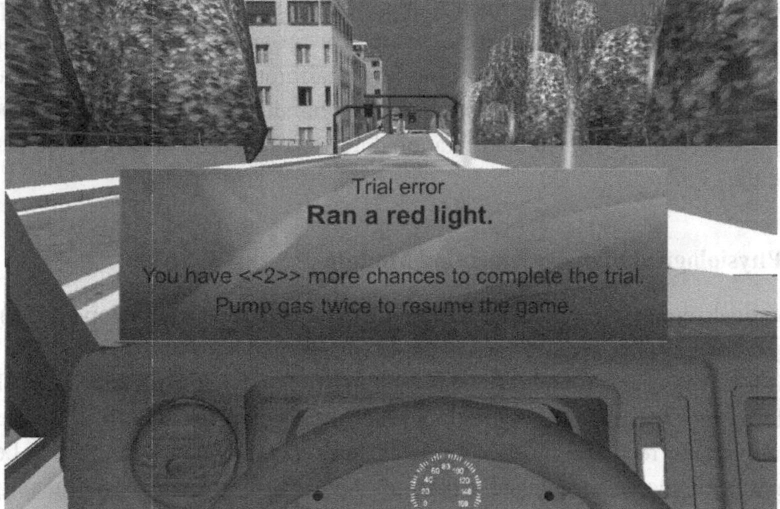

Fig. 3. Feedback generated from running a red light

The VR module can detect a variety of driving errors and signal a trial failure event whenever a failure is detected. Examples of driving errors that the system can detect include speed-regulation, collision detection, running red lights and stop signs, taking an incorrect turn, driving in the wrong lane, driving on the sidewalk and more. When a failure event is triggered, the system generates feedback based on the circumstances of the failure and this feedback is presented to the user in both text and audio format. For example, Figure 3 shows feedback generated when a user travels through an intersection when it is unsafe to do so. Failure events, as well as other types of events that the system generates, trigger messages to be sent to the various sensory modules in the LAN so that time-synchronized event markers can be logged with the data collected. The VR module logs a large amount of performance data such as vehicle speed, input signals from the G27, position of the vehicle in the environment, trial duration time and details about trial failures.

2.2 Gaze-Acquisition Module

We acquired eye gaze information using a Tobii X120 (www.tobii.com) remote eye tracking device which has a high degree of accuracy and precision [8] and has been effectively used in other studies [9]. We sampled data from the device at a rate of 120 Hz. This data included independent gaze positions of both eyes, composite gaze position, blink rate, and fixation duration for various regions of interest (ROI) in the virtual environment. Examples of ROI that we measured were traffic lights, speedometers, pedestrians and stop signs. This information was logged for offline analysis.

The eye tracker was re-calibrated for each participant according to the specifications of the device manual [8] which required that users be at a distance of approximately 70 cm from the device. We developed a program using the Tobii software development kit (SDK) to perform a nine-point calibration task on a 24 inch monitor (1920 × 1080 px resolution). This program also handled the TCP socket connection with the VR module and calculated fixation durations based on data received from the VR module.

2.3 Physiological Signal-Acquisition Module

Physiological signals were collected using a Biopac MP150 (www.biopac.com) wireless physiological data acquisition system at a sampling rate of 1000 Hz. We measured the following physiological signals from participants: electrocardiogram (ECG), photoplethysmogram (PPG), respiration, electromyogram (EMG), skin temperature and galvanic skin response (GSR). These physiological signals were chosen because they have been shown to indicate a person's levels of engagement and anxiety [10-15]. A program was developed in MATLAB to accumulate and record the signals for offline analysis. This module also handled socket communication to the VR module and recorded event markers received from the VR module when some event occurred.

2.4 Therapist Report Module

The therapist report module was operated by a trained therapist and was not operated by the participant in the driving simulator. The purpose of this module was to record subjective assessment information from a therapist about the affective state of the participant. This module received an event message every two minutes while an assignment was in progress and at that time, the therapist was prompted to input their assessment. At the end of each assignment, whether successfully completed or failed, the therapist was prompted to give an assessment of the appropriateness of the ended assignment's difficulty level. This information was recorded on a nine point Likert scale and logged for offline analysis.

3 Experimental Design

3.1 Participants

We recruited four participants that were diagnosed with an ASD between 13 and 17 years of age (all males) and four TD controls (three males and one female). The mean age of the ASD group participants was 16.87 years (standard deviation: 0.42) and the mean age of participants in the TD group was 15.34 years (standard deviation: 0.94). Each participant completed a driving task that was approximately 90 minutes in length. Participants were reimbursed for their travel and time. The experiment protocol was approved by Vanderbilt University's Institutional Review Board.

3.2 Session Structure

At the start of a session, participants were seated in the driving playseat which was then adjusted for each individual's comfort. Physiological sensors were then placed on the participants' bodies followed by a calibration of the eye tracker. Each participant was shown a short tutorial that explained the vehicle's controls as well as the objectives of the game. Participants then began a three minute practice session in order to become accustomed to the vehicle operation and G27 interface. The main part of the session consisted of two assignments from level four, two from level five and two from level six. Each assignment was required to be attempted in order to progress to the next assignment, but we did not require successful completion of each assignment before moving on to other assignments. Assignments were completed if no more than three trials were failed during an assignment. If more than three trials were failed during an assignment, the assignment was failed and could not be reattempted. A short survey followed each assignment and participants responded to survey questions using the G27 to manipulate the GUI.

4 Results and Discussion

For group comparisons, we utilized two-tailed t-tests. The number of trial failures accumulated during a level was found to be significantly different ($p < 0.05$) between the two groups (Table 1) with the ASD group experiencing a higher number of failures. There was no difference in the time that it took for groups to complete assignments. Table 2 shows that there was an inverse relationship between the number of trial failures per level and level difficulty. This could indicate that the assignments' difficulty levels were not perceived as significantly different and/or the practice with the system from proceeding through the easier levels strongly affected performance.

Table 1. Individual Trial Failures Per Level

ASD Mean	SD	TD Mean	SD	p-value
4.583	2.178	2.833	1.572	0.042

Table 2. Total Group Trial Failures Per Level

Level	ASD	TD
4	22	13
5	19	12
6	14	9

Analysis of the gaze data shows the average vertical and horizontal gaze positions differ between each group. Among the ASD group, the gaze is significantly higher ($p < 0.001$) in the vertical direction (0.92 cm) and towards the right ($p < 0.001$) in the horizontal direction (1.02 cm). These results seem to support results found by Reimer's group [5]. As can be seen in Table 3, the ASD group had a significantly higher skin conductance level (SCL) and skin conductance response rate (SCR) than the TD group. From our previous work [12-13, 15], this may indicate that the participants in the ASD group experienced higher levels of anxiety during the session.

Table 3. Extracted feature means from both groups

Signal features	ASD	TD	p-value
Sympathetic power of ECG (Unit/s^2)	2948.29	2210.83	0.15
Skin conductance level of GSR (μS)	9.59	8.59	< 0.05
Skin conductance response rate of GSR (Response peaks/s)	6.46	2.09	< 0.05

5 Conclusion

We designed a novel driving simulator that can effectively measure driving performance as well as input from several sensory modules. From our user study, we found that the system is sensitive enough to detect significant group differences between individuals with ASD and TD controls. Such differences were present not simply in performance, but the system was able to detect gaze differences in how individuals were processing information within the paradigm. This is the first step towards development of a task aimed at improving the driving performance of teenagers with ASD while making use of online gaze and physiological signals. Our hierarchical state machine model allows for relatively easy modification of the system and addition of new sensory modules which we can utilize in future work to add, for example, an electroencephalography (EEG) sensory module.

Acknowledgement. This work was supported in part by the National Institute of Health Grant 1R01MH091102-01A1, National Science Foundation Grant 0967170 and Hobbs Society Grant from the Vanderbilt Kennedy Center.

References

1. Center for Disease Control (CDC): Prevalence of autism spectrum disorders—autism and developmental disabilities monitoring network, 14 sites, United States, MMWR. 61(3), 1–19 (2012)
2. Palmen, A., Didden, R., Lang, R.: A systematic review of behavioral intervention research on adaptive skill building in high-functioning young adults with autism spectrum disorder. Research in Autism Spectrum Disorders 6, 602–617 (2012)
3. Reimer, B., Fried, F., Mehler, B., Joshi, G., Bolfek, A., Godfrey, K., Zhao, N., Goldin, R., Biederman, J.: Brief report: examining driving behavior in young adults with high functioning autism spectrum disorders: a pilot study using a driving simulation paradigm. Journal of Autism and Developmental Disorders 43(9), 2211–2217 (2013)
4. Sheppard, E., Ropar, D., Underwood, G., van Loon, E.: Brief report: driving hazard perception in autism. Journal of Autism and Developmental Disorders 40(4), 504–508 (2010)
5. Cox, N., Reeve, R., Cox, S., Cox, D.: Brief report: driving and young adults with ASD: parents' experiences. Journal of Autism and Developmental Disorders 42(10), 2257–2262 (2012)
6. Classen, S., Monahan, M.: Evidence-based review on interventions and determinants of driving performance in teens with attention deficit hyperactivity disorder or autism spectrum disorder. Traffic Injury Prevention 14(2), 188–193 (2013)
7. Bian, D., Wade, J.W., Zhang, L., Bekele, E., Swanson, A., Crittendon, J.A., Sarkar, M., Warren, Z., Sarkar, N.: A Novel Virtual Reality Driving Environment for Autism Intervention. In: Stephanidis, C., Antona, M. (eds.) UAHCI 2013, Part II. LNCS, vol. 8010, pp. 474–483. Springer, Heidelberg (2013)
8. Tobii Technology. Accuracy and precision test method for remote eye trackers. Tobii Technology AB 2.1.1, 1–28 (2011)
9. Lahiri, U., Warren, Z., Sarkar, N.: Design of a gaze-sensitive virtual social interactive system for children with autism. IEEE Transactions on Neural Systems and Rehabilitation Engineering 19(4), 443–452 (2011)
10. Rani, P., Sarkar, N., Smith, C., Adams, J.: Affective communication for implicit human-machine interaction. In: IEEE International Conference on System, Man and Cybernetics, vol. 5, pp. 4896–4903. IEEE (2003)
11. Liu, C., Rani, P., Sarkar, N.: Human-robot interaction using affective cues. In: The 15th IEEE International Symposium on Robot and Human Interactive Communication - ROMAN 2006, United Kingdom, pp. 285–290. IEEE (2006)

12. Liu, C., Rani, P., Sarkar, N.: An empirical study of machine learning techniques for affect recognition in human-robot interaction. In: Intelligent Robots and Systems, pp. 2451–2456 (2005)
13. Liu, C., Rani, P., Sarkar, N.: Affective state recognition and adaptation in human-robot interaction: a design approach. In: EEE/RSJ International Conference on Intelligent Robots and Systems, pp. 3099–3106 (2006)
14. Rani, P., Sarkar, N., Smith, C., Kirby, L.: Anxiety detecting robotic system-towards implicit human-robot collaboration. Robotica 22(1), 85–95 (2004)
15. Zhai, J., Barreto, A.: Concurrent analysis of physiologic variables for the assessment of the affective state of a computer user. In: HCI (2005)

Learning from Each Other: An Agent Based Approach

Goran Zaharija, Saša Mladenović, and Andrina Granić

Faculty of Science, University of Split, Nikole Tesle 12, 21000 Split, Croatia
{goran.zaharija,sasa.mladenovic,andrina.granic}@pmfst.hr

Abstract. This paper presents an agent based approach to knowledge representation and learning methods. Agent architecture is described and discussed, together with its advantages and limitations. Main purpose of the proposed approach is to gain further insight in current teaching methods with a foremost aspiration for their improvement. Two different experimental studies were conducted; the first one addressing knowledge representation and the second one regarding knowledge transfer between agents. Obtained results are presented and analysed.

Keywords: learning, artificial intelligence, machine learning, agent based systems.

1 Introduction

There are many different approaches in agent based learning like distributive [1], cooperative [2], [3], reinforced [4] and collaborative [5] learning, but most of these approaches make strict differentiation between teacher and learner agents. We intend to present an agent based approach in which, depending on different circumstances, agents possess the ability to act both as a teacher and as a learner. Although agents will not be differentiated by their role, each of them could possess individual characteristics (dimensions, mobility, number and type of sensors) making them unique or at least different from each other. As a result a system that is more flexible than those aforementioned should be designed. It should also enable much simpler and efficient transfer of knowledge among all agents acting within the system.

This paper aims to present a type of agent that can act both as a teacher and a learner, while using robots as physical representation of those agents. Primary reason for developing such kind of agents is to discover new or improve existing teaching methods. Accordingly, we are proposing a framework that could be used for those purposes. To successfully act as a teacher, it is desirable that agents are able to switch their role from the teacher to the student. Desired effect of such change of roles is an embracement of a same student mental model, thus allowing successful knowledge transfer between subjects and avoiding traps in form of potential misconceptions.

Every single individual has its own perspective of the surrounding world (egocentric view) that differs from the collective or global representation of that same world (allocentric view) [6], [7]. This should be taken into consideration when talking about teaching; anyone taking the role of the teacher should be aware that not everybody shares his/hers view of the world.

C. Stephanidis and M. Antona (Eds.): UAHCI/HCII 2014, Part II, LNCS 8514, pp. 475–486, 2014.

When talking about knowledge transfer and teaching methods, regardless of a human or a robot actors, there are some different approaches considering the interaction between involved subjects [8], [9]:

- Individualistic – interactions between learners are not affecting the results of the learning. Each learner works on his own in order to complete her/his goal, without paying attention to other learners and their progress.
- Competitive – learners are competing between themselves in order to achieve their goals. They may not obstruct other learners on purpose, but they will certainly interact in a way to avoid helping others. Competition is unavoidable aspect of life and this type of learning is present in majority fields of education [10].
- Cooperative – learners are working together in order to achieve their goals. They can have one common goal or more individual goals, but all interactions among students are aimed to help each other to achieve those goals.
- Collaborative – similar to the cooperative learning, learners are also working together aiming to achieve their goal (to learn something), but with slightly different roles then in cooperative learning.

However, there are some differences between cooperative and collaborative learning [11]. In cooperative learning an instructor is the centre of authority in the class, with group tasks usually more closed-ended and often having specific answers. In contrast, with collaborative learning the instructor abdicates his or her authority and empowers the small groups who are often given more open-ended, complex tasks.

When discussing different types of learning methods and processes, emphasis is usually put on interaction between teacher and one or more students, while relations among students themselves are relatively often ignored. Nevertheless, interactions among students should also be considered as an important part of the whole learning process because they undoubtedly affect learning outcomes.

All the above mentioned approaches share one common characteristic – the roles of the subjects involved in an interaction are predetermined. Namely, it is clearly defined who the teacher is and who the learner is. In this paper we would like to expand current work in the field and introduce an approach to interaction between humans and robots which can be used as a two-way communication channel. By developing such type of interaction, we would not be using predetermined roles anymore. This implies that the knowledge could be exchanged in any direction between different subjects regardless of their initial role. Without strictly defined roles, such approach could reflect a universal interaction and could be applied to any human/robot combination and variation, regardless of their characteristics.

2 Proposed Approach

In this paper we consider the former teaching method (collaborative learning) in which the learning goals may be structured since the relevant literature provides recommendation for teachers to structure learning situations collaboratively majority of time, i.e. [8]. To further examine collaborative learning and interactions among students, we present an agent based approach to collaborative learning. In such approach agents are aiming to exchange knowledge between each other and therefore techniques from machine learning, agent based systems and distributed artificial intelligence should be employed.

2.1 Model of the World

In previous section, we have briefly discussed the difference between egocentric and allocentric view of the world. Now we will present a model of the world in which our agents are located. For the purposes of an experimental study, the model of the world is intentionally reasonably simple: (i) agents are located in a finite, discrete environment and (ii) there are two types of obstacles ("wall" and "hole") along with two types of paths ("empty field" and "goal") see Figure1.

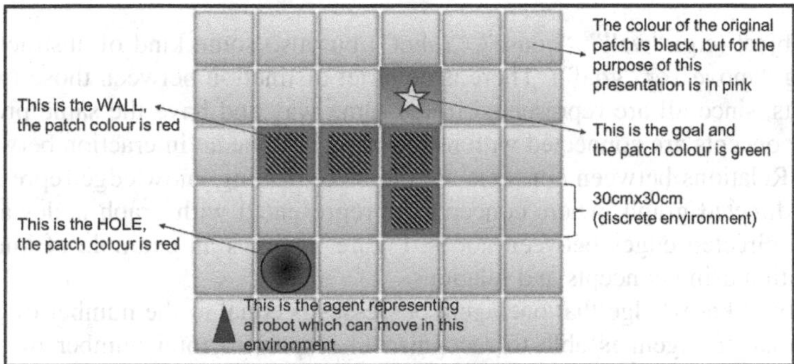

Fig. 1. Model of the World along with descriptions of concepts

2.2 Model of the Agent

There are many different ways to describe and define an intelligent agent [12]. Our agent is based on definition describing the agent as a computer system that is situated in some environment and that is capable of autonomous action in this environment to meet its design objectives [13]. In order to adhere to this definition, we are considering three main aspects of our agent model – abilities, knowledge representation and knowledge mapping. Each of these aspects is briefly described in following sections.

Abilities. Each agent possesses a different set of characteristics and abilities, depending on a construction of its physical representation. Common capabilities of all agents are their ability to navigate through their environment (i.e. they are all mobile) and their possession of a kind of perception (one or more sensors), allowing them to receive some kind of information from their surroundings. They also have perfect and unlimited memory, allowing them to store and use obtained knowledge.

Knowledge Representation. Agent's knowledge is represented through different concepts and relations between those concepts. Single concept can describe particular

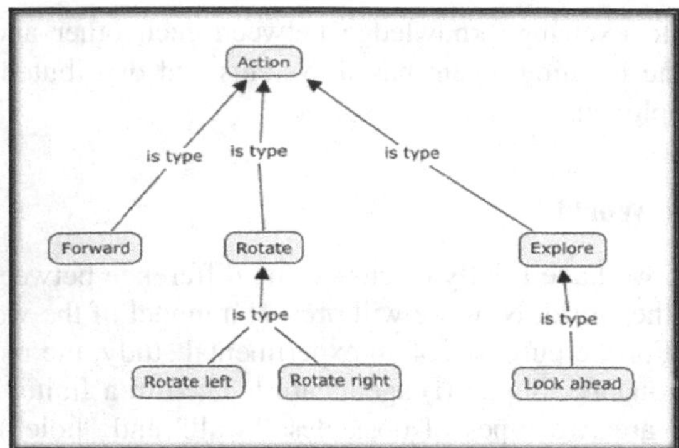

Fig. 2. Knowledge representation using concepts and relations

existing object (e.g. "wall", "house", "robot") but also some kind of abstract idea or action (e.g. "move" or "goal"). There is no strict distinction between those two types of concepts, since all are represented in the same way and have the same properties. Different concepts are connected with relations that define an interaction between two concepts. Relations between concepts are directed, making knowledge representation a type of directed graph, where concepts are represented with graph nodes and relations with directed edges between nodes. Figure 2 shows an example of knowledge representation using concepts and relations.

Quantity of knowledge that one agent possesses is equal to the number of different concepts that the agent is able to recognize in respect to total number of concepts existing in agent's world. Quality of that knowledge depends on how successful the agent is in recognizing each individual concept that has been learned and how well it can use that concept. Each agent should be capable to expand its knowledge, i.e. to be precise to learn new concepts. In order to acquire new concept, the agent must undergo the learning phase in which it makes connection between sensor input values and one particular concept. Consequently, each time when the agent receives that same input values, it should recognize the corresponding concept.

Our goal is to secure successful exchange of information between different systems (in this case different agents) without affecting the original ones. An achievable way to accomplish this goal is by mapping different types of knowledge.

Knowledge Mapping. Suppose we have two different types of knowledge K_1 and K_2. Knowledge mapping is an act of trying for every concept in K_1 to find a matching concept in K_2 that has same or similar meaning. This mapping can be injective (one-way) or bijective (two-way) [14]. There is a difference between partial and full mapping. Full mapping pairs every element from the source knowledge K_1 to the destination knowledge K_2, while partial mapping pairs only a sub-set of the knowledge K_1 to the destination knowledge K_2. In that way we are creating reference knowledge K_0, a common knowledge that contains concepts and relations that both sides wishing to exchange information agreed upon, see Figure 3.

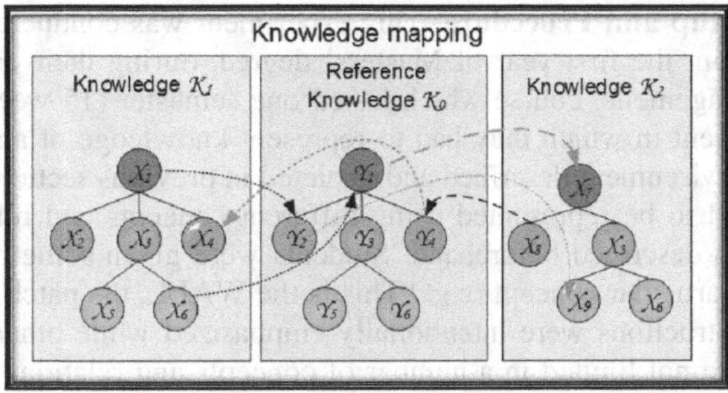

Fig. 3. Knowledge mapping

Therefore, to learn from each other agents must satisfy one main requirement for successful knowledge transfer. Namely, agents attempting to interact must have at least one common characteristic that will be used as foundation for knowledge exchange. It has been already mentioned that knowledge is represented through different concepts and that every single agent uses its sensors to recognize them. To successfully transfer knowledge regarding particular concept, the agent that is trying to learn a concept must possess the ability to receive same type of sensor input as the teacher agent. It is not crucial to have all common characteristics, just some of them (i.e. at least one sensor of the same type). Advantage of this approach is that one single agent can acquire knowledge from many different agents with different characteristics.

From a technical standpoint, process of teaching along with underlying interactions between teacher and student can be presented using a concept of interoperability. There are different definitions of interoperability [15-18], but generally speaking it represents an ability of two or more systems to successfully exchange some kind of information and also to effectively use it. There are also various standards for classifying different types and levels of interoperability. For the purposes of this research, we are considering European Interoperability Framework (EIF) [19], which recognizes three different levels of interoperability – technical, semantic and organizational. Our proposed approach corresponds to semantic level of interoperability, which defines local exchange of information using shared maps, key data and ontologies.

3 Experimental Study

For the purposes of this paper, we have conducted two different experimental studies aiming to address two questions: is there any difference in knowledge representation between two agents and is it possible to exchange that knowledge between agents.

3.1 Knowledge Representation Experiment

First experimental study was conducted in order to prove our claim that every agent has an egocentric view of the surrounding world and also a distinct representation of its knowledge.

Experimental Setup and Procedure. This experiment was conducted with a group of 10 students from the first year of Masters' degree, during their engagement in a "Knowledge management" course which lasted one semester (15 weeks). They were given the assignment in which they had to represent knowledge of a single agent located in simple environment described and depicted in previous section of this paper.

Knowledge had to be represented using different concepts and relations between those concepts, as described beforehand. Students were given some basic guidelines how to describe particular concept (e.g. "This is the WALL, the patch colour is red"). Some parts of instructions were intentionally emphasized while others were left vague. Students were not limited in a number of concepts and relations that they could use and there were no strict rules to be followed. Their task was to build a conceptual map of given environment using those descriptions. As the final result, ten individual conceptual maps were acquired, each one depicting the knowledge of a single agent in a simple, discreet space. The main goal of this experiment was to see if there will be any differences in obtained conceptual maps, considering simplicity of both the world and the agent. Figure 4 represents several conceptual maps used in the experiment.

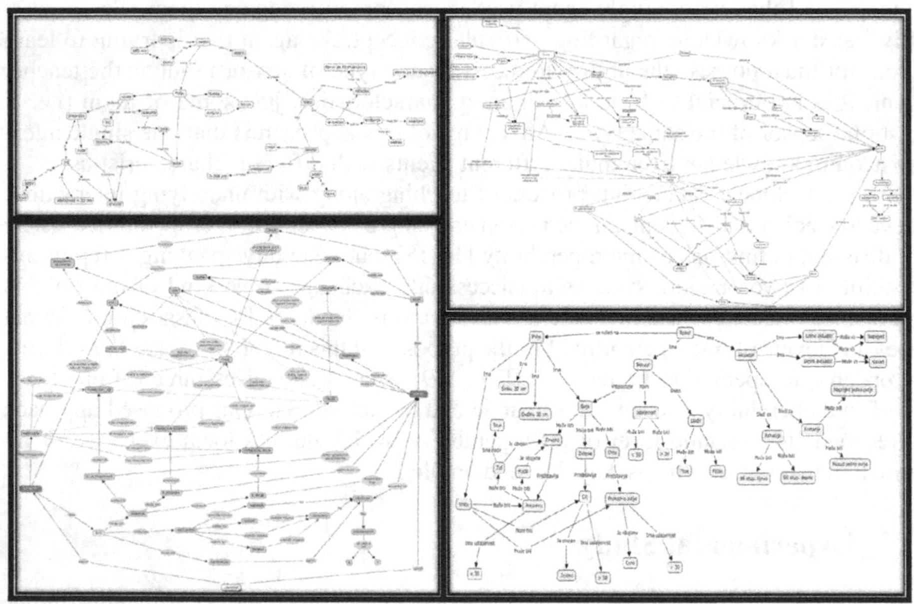

Fig. 4. Several conceptual maps obtained in the first experimental study

Results. At the end of the semester, we have analysed and compared all obtained conceptual maps. The maps were not associated with particular student, just numbered from 1 to 10. In order to compare obtained results, we first have conducted search for two basic concepts, "wall" and "red", in addition to any relation between them. These two concepts correspond to the first provided description of the world and should be part of every map attempting to represent the given environment. For every single map, information regarding the presence of the two concepts in the map along with the related relation (if applicable) is offered in Table 1.

Table 1. Analysis of concepts and their relations

Map	*Concept "red"*	*Relation (direction)*	*Concept "wall"*
1.	No	n/a	Yes
2.	Yes	Is coloured (←)	Yes
3.	Yes	Is (←)	Yes
4.	No	n/a	Yes
5.	Yes	n/a	Yes
6.	Yes	Is (←)	Yes
7.	Yes	Indicates (→)	Yes
8.	No	n/a	Yes
9.	Yes	Is coloured (←)	Yes
10.	Yes	n/a	Yes

Table 2. Concepts associated with the basic "wall" concept and their frequency

Concept	*Times used*
patches	3
ultrasound sensor	6
touch sensor	5
obstacle	7
red	4
memory	1
object	1
move	1

It was interesting to observe that three different maps didn't even include the concept "red", despite being the key concept for defining obstacles in the given environment. It can also be noted that some maps, although having both concepts, did not have a direct relation between them. Only half of them had defined both concepts and relation between those concepts, but those relations were differently named or directed. Only two pairs of conceptual maps could be considered to have the same representation of the two simple concepts, but only if they are analysed excluding the rest of the map. If we take into account other relations linked with those concepts, then even those two pairs of maps have different knowledge representations.

Additionally, we have also selected one basic concept that is present in all maps (concept "wall") and analysed how many different relations and concepts were associated with that one particular concept in the obtained maps. Throughout 10 maps, there were 8 unique concepts, some of which were used only once ("memory", "object") while others appeared in the majority of maps ("obstacle" and "red"). Another interesting remark is related to the fact that there was not a single concept that was used in all maps in relation to the "wall" concept. Table 2 shows those 8 concepts and frequency of their appearance in ten conceptual maps.

Table 3. Used relations and their frequency

Relation	*Times used*
Type of	1
Locates	2
Is	4
Has	2
Is coloured	2
Can be	7
Contains	2
Recognizes	2
Memorizes	1
Means	2

Regarding relations between concept "wall" and those other mentioned concepts, there were 10 different relations used. Yet again, some of them appeared only once, while others were used multiple times even in the same map. Table 3 shows used relations and frequency of their usage.

3.2 Knowledge Transfer Experiment

With the intention to test the proposed approach to knowledge exchange, another experiment was conducted in both physical and simulated environment. Two different software frameworks were used, Netlogo and Microsoft .NET.

The goal of the experiment was twofold: (i) to successfully train two different robots to effectively recognize different concepts in their environment and (ii) to try afterwards to exchange acquired knowledge between them. The physical representation of agents was achieved using Lego Mindstorms robots where different types of agents have been represented with differently constructed robots. Figure 5 shows few different robots that were used in the experimental study.

Experimental Setup and Procedure. A specific .NET application was developed for storing knowledge in a form of a database (MS SQL) containing a list of concepts and relations. That same application also handles the task of executing the learning phase, in which sensor values gained from the robot are used for training the agent to recognize a particular concept. Training was carried out by using artificial neural networks, also incorporated within the application. Single agent possesses a single artificial neural network for every concept that he/she can recognize.

In order to visually present those steps in the learning process, special simulated environment was developed. It was implemented using NetLogo, a multi-agent programmable modelling environment [20]. For the purpose of this experiment, several different simulations were developed, each representing a part of the agent architecture (learning phase, knowledge representation, knowledge exchange etc.).

One developed simulation used for training single artificial neural network (ANN) is presented in Figure 6.

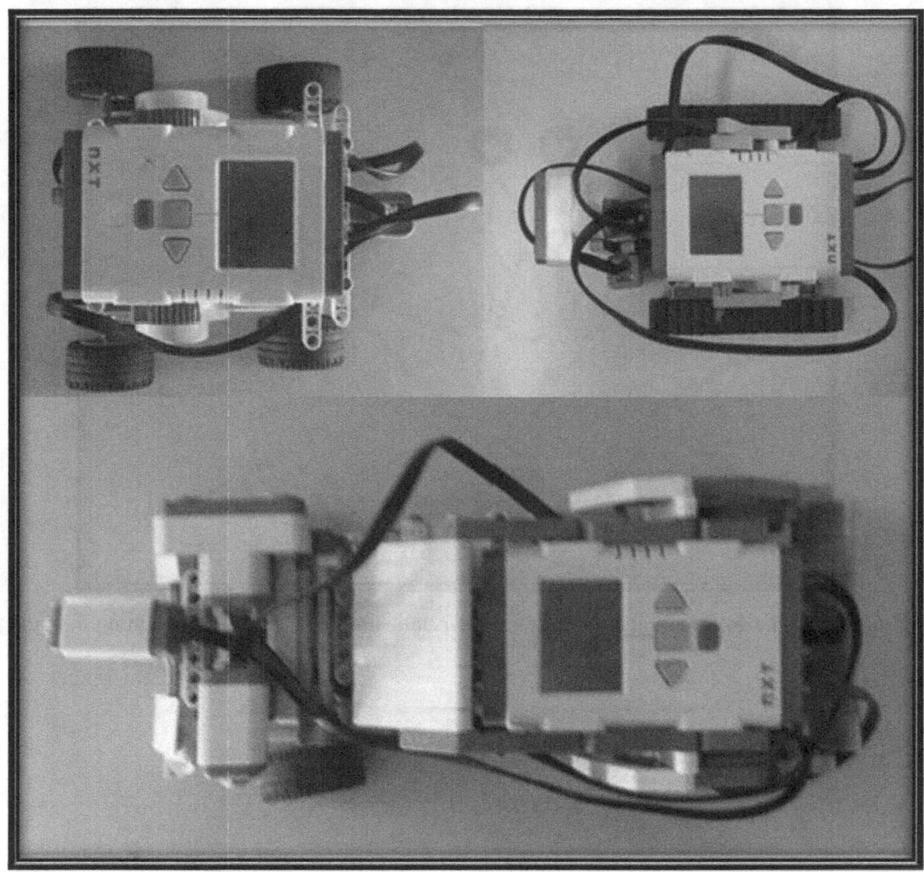

Fig. 5. Lego Mindstorms robots used in the second experimental study

During the experiment, two differently constructed robots were used, one equipped with both ultrasound and colour sensor (agent A) and other with only colour sensor (agent B). Real sensor values were obtained from those robots and used within.NET and Netlogo applications. First, one robot (agent A) was trained to recognize three different concepts ("wall", "obstacle" and "hole") as they were described in model of the world. Detailed description of the learning phase can be found in our previous work [21]. Afterwards, agent A took the role of teacher and we have used his trained ANNs in order to teach other agent those same three concepts. For the both agents (robots), learned concepts were not organized hierarchically, as they were represented in mental maps. This would require more complex procedure and is behind the scope of this paper.

Results. At the end of experiment, we have analyzed how successful were both agents in recognizing given concepts. We also considered the outcome of knowledge exchange between the two agents. After finishing the learning phase, the agent A had

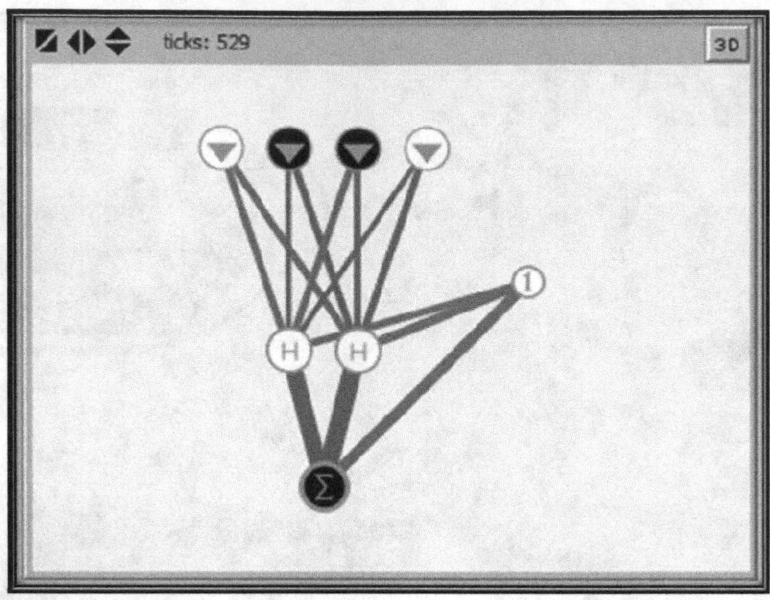

Fig. 6. Part of the Netlogo simulation used for visualization of a process of training a single ANN

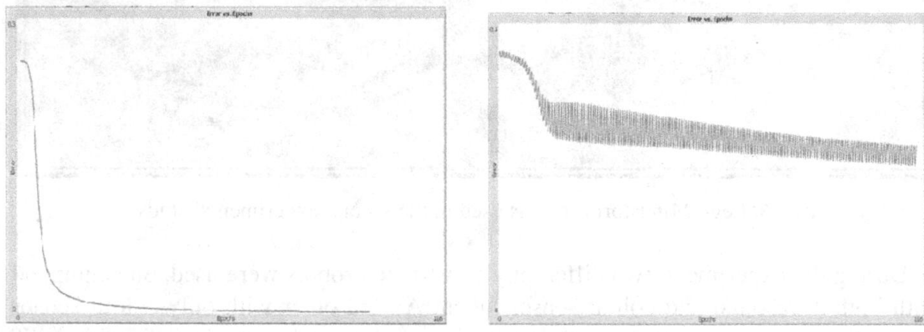

Fig. 7. Examples of successfully (left) and unsuccessfully (right) trained ANNs

nearly 100% success rate in recognizing all three different concepts and was used as a teacher for the agent B. The agent A was able to successfully train the agent B to recognize one concept ("obstacle") but was unable to teach him how to differentiate other two concepts ("wall" and "hole"). Process of training the ANN for one of those concepts could not be completed because error ratio could not be reduced to near zero value (indicator of a well-trained neural network), regardless of number of examples given to the particular ANN. Figure 7 shows difference between error ratios per epoch for successfully and unsuccessfully trained ANNs.

This was caused by the agent B's reduced abilities compared to the ones of the agent A, as it was not equipped with ultrasound sensor. There could possibly be some other ways for the agent B to differentiate those two concepts (e.g. adding a touch sensor), but the agent A would not be able to teach that. These results further support our statement regarding egocentric view of the world as well as different knowledge representations.

4 Conclusion

According to the acquired results, there were numerous differences in knowledge representation in conceptual maps obtained in the experimental study. Additionally, when taking into account simplicity of the world and relative similarities between test subjects (students with similar level of knowledge), these differences are even greater. This leads to a conclusion that given a more complex agent (with more sensors, abilities and the like) and a more complex world (different types of obstacles, other agents, movable objects etc.) differences between conceptual maps would be even bigger. Such conclusion coincides with our attitude in two aspects: (i) when discussing different teaching methods it is essential to consider particular characteristics of every individual and (ii) teaching must be regarded as something more than just a simple transfer of information from one subject to another.

Acknowledgments. This work has been carried out within project 177-0361994-1998 *Usability and Adaptivity of Interfaces for Intelligent Authoring Shells* funded by the Ministry of Science and Technology of the Republic of Croatia.

References

1. Choi, J., Oh, S., Horowitz, R.: Distributed learning and cooperative control for multi-agent systems. Automatica 45(12), 2802–2814 (2009)
2. Díez, F., Cobos, R.: A case study of a cooperative learning experiment in artificial intelligence. Computer Applications in Engineering Education 15(4), 308–316 (2007)
3. Soh, L.K., Jiang, H., Ansorge, C.: Agent-based cooperative learning: a proof-of-concept experiment. ACM SIGCSE Bulletin 36(1), 368–372 (2004)
4. Busoniu, L., Babuska, R., De Schutter, B.: A comprehensive survey of multiagent reinforcement learning. IEEE Transactions on Systems, Man, and Cybernetics, Part C: Applications and Reviews 38(2), 156–172 (2008)
5. Allen, J., Chambers, N., Ferguson, G., Galescu, L., Jung, H., Swift, M., Taysom, W.: PLOW: A collaborative task learning agent. In: Proceedings of the National Conference on Artificial Intelligence, vol. 22(2), p. 1514. AAAI Press, Menlo Park (2007)
6. Pederson, T., Janlert, L.E., Surie, D.: Towards a model for egocentric interaction with physical and virtual objects. In: Proceedings of the 6th Nordic Conference on Human-Computer Interaction: Extending Boundaries, pp. 755–758. ACM (2010)
7. Wagner, T., Visser, U., Herzog, O.: Egocentric qualitative spatial knowledge representation for physical robots. Robotics and Autonomous Systems 49(1), 25–42 (2004)
8. Johnson, D.W., Johnson, R.T.: Cooperative, Competitive, and Individualistic Learning Environments. In: Hattie, J., Anderman, E.M. (eds.) International Guide to Student Achievement, pp. 372–375. Taylor & Francis (2013)

9. Roschelle, J., Rosas, R., Nussbaum, M.: Towards a design framework for mobile computer-supported collaborative learning. In: Proceedings of the 2005 Conference on Computer Support for Collaborative Learning, pp. 520–524. International Society of the Learning Sciences (2005)
10. Stutts, M.A., West, V.: Competitive Learning: Beyond project based classes. Journal for the Advancement of Marketing Education 7, 55–62 (2005)
11. Rockwood, H.S., Rockwood III., H.S.: Cooperative and collaborative learning. The National Teaching & Learning Forum 4(6), 8–9 (1995a)
12. Franklin, S., Graesser, A.: Is it an Agent, or just a Program?: A Taxonomy for Autonomous Agents. In: Jennings, N.R., Wooldridge, M.J., Müller, J.P. (eds.) ECAI-WS 1996 and ATAL 1996. LNCS, vol. 1193, pp. 21–35. Springer, Heidelberg (1997)
13. Padgham, L., Winikoff, M.: Developing intelligent agent systems: A practical guide, vol. 13. John Wiley & Sons (2005)
14. de Bruijn, J., Ehrig, M., Feier, C., Martín-Recuerda, F., Scharffe, F., Weiten, M.: Ontology mediation, merging and aligning. In: Davies, J., Studer, R., Warren, P. (eds.) Semantic Web Tenologies: Trends and Research in Ontology-Based System, John Wiley, West Sussex (2006)
15. IEEE and I. O. E. &. E. Engineers, In: IEEE Standard Computer Dictionary: A Compilation of IEEE Standard Computer Glossaries: 610. Inst. of Elect & Electronic (1991)
16. E. IDABC, European Interoperability Framework for Pan-European E-Government Services. Office for Official Publications of the European Communities, Luxembourg (2004)
17. F. Standard, "Department of Defense Dictionary of Military and Associated Terms in support of MIL-STD-188," 1037C
18. The Open group, TOGAF Version 9. Van Haren Publishing, (2009)
19. Kubicek, H., Cimander, R.: Three dimensions of organizational interoperability. European Journal of ePractice 6 (2009)
20. Wilensky, U.: NetLogo. Center for Connected Learning and Computer-Based Modeling, Northwestern University, Evanston, IL (1999), `http://ccl.northwestern.edu/netlogo/`
21. Mladenović, S., Granić, A., Zaharija, G.: An approach to universal interaction on the case of knowledge transfer. In: Stephanidis, C., Antona, M. (eds.) UAHCI 2013, Part II. LNCS, vol. 8010, pp. 604–613. Springer, Heidelberg (2013)

Access to Games and Ludic Engagement

SMART VIEW: A Serious Game Supporting Spatial Orientation of Subjects with Cognitive Impairments

Rosa Maria Bottino, Andrea Canessa, Michela Ott, and Mauro Tavella

Institute for Educational Technologies, CNR, Genoa, Italy
{canessa,bottino,tavella,ott}@itd.cnr.it

Abstract. The paper presents SMART VIEW a serious game developed with the aim of helping young people with moderate cognitive disabilities acquire those spatial abilities that are key prerequisites to autonomous mobility. The game was conceived for cognitively impaired teenagers; it proposes exercises supporting the acquisition and consolidation of competences related to space awareness and self-perception in the space; such skills are necessary to develop the sense of spatial orientation, which is critical for the target population. SMART VIEW makes use of Touch Screen tables so to allow easier access to the game content and augmented interaction. Particular attention has been devoted to the game interface design, so to make it free from cognitive barriers and fully accessible to the target population. Contents are as close as possible to reality and the educational strategy entails slow and gradual increase of the game complexity, so to properly sustain the users' cognitive effort.

Keywords: Serious Games, Spatial Orientation, Cognitive Disabilities, Perspective Taking, E-inclusion, Technology Enhanced Learning.

1 Introduction

The sensation of being sure of our own position in the environment is an element that combine both cognitive and emotional aspects, and its importance appears when this skill is impaired. This is the case of individuals with intellectual disabilities, as for example people with Down syndrome.

Unfortunately, few individuals with intellectual disability practice independent travel, and sometimes they feel lost, even when walking routes that they are familiar with [1].

This is due to a conceptual deficit in spatial representational abilities, which reflect a poor generation of a cognitive map. The term "cognitive map" [2] has been coined by Tolman in the 40's during his research on learning, and successively retrieved in the 70's in studies on orientation and space representation. Cognitive map represents the form by which the spatial knowledge and awareness is acquired, and it can of two type: route and survey maps ([3-6]).

Route maps constitute egocentric representations where a one-dimensional sequential understanding of landmarks leads to learn a route. The information, learned in a progressive manner from a route and its landmarks, is used to effectively reach a

C. Stephanidis and M. Antona (Eds.): UAHCI/HCII 2014, Part II, LNCS 8514, pp. 489–500, 2014.

given target. In this case, the way through which the subject experiences the environment and he creates his own spatial knowledge strictly depends on his actual point of view.

Survey maps are based on an allocentric perspective and they can be seen as a higher-level two-dimensional representation analogous to human-made maps. The direct dependence on the point of view lets the place to multiple perspectives, taken by different orientation, among which there is also a bird's eye view. This ability allows an individual to perceive the spatial relations among different points in the environment, judging their closeness or distance on a two dimensional Cartesian reference frame.

The intellectual disabled individuals rely on an egocentric navigation ability strategy, with great difficulties to adopt an allocentric strategy. Indeed, individuals with intellectual disabilities generate a one-dimensional sequential understanding of landmarks that leads to learn a route, but they have a random two-dimensional configuration of them, which indicates an inability to integrate routes information into a coordinated reference frame [1],[2].

Obviously, this is a real issue since the gaining of independent travel skills and of the confidence to learn and travel new routes are essential for independent living and community participation. These abilities allow the individuals to access a wide range of vocational, educational and recreational opportunities.

The author has been involved in developing educational software for people with intellectual disabilities. This work originates from the fruitful collaboration of the researchers of the Institute of Educational Technology of the Italian CNR and the psychologists and tutors of a socially useful non-profit organisation (NPO) both interested in intellectual disabilities. The starting motivation is the desire to develop new methodologies for the learning and the training of those requirements necessary to gain spatial representational abilities.

The paper presents SMART VIEW, an educational game conceived for training, in cognitively impaired teenagers, some skills that can be useful for correctly mastering the sense of spatial orientation, which is critical for the target population and preparatory for higher level spatial cognitive skills.

2 Related Work

Looking at what has been done till now to find ways of teaching skills necessary for independent living, in particular for mobility and orientation, to people with intellectual disabilities we find that great effort has been spent in the last decades to develop solution based on virtual environments (VE).

The VE is increasingly being recognized as a potential tool for the assessment and rehabilitation of human cognitive and functional processes. Different researches show, in fact, that VE, applied to the treatment of motor and cognitive problems, are more effective than other standard approaches since the brain perceives the simulated activities as real and the knowledge built in the virtual world is transferred as concrete competences in the real world [7]. The educational games based on VE provide an environment which resembles everyday life; they therefore may serve as learning "gym" and can be used as a safe test-bed to be freely explored, at one's own pace, attempting hypothesis and obtaining immediate feedback [8].

VEs are increasingly used in experimental research to address questions about spatial processes in typical or atypical populations. Several researchers have used virtual technology for training skills necessary for independent living, and these learnt skills were found to be transferable to real-world environments [5-17].

Notwithstanding there exist different examples of programs oriented to train spatial abilities in cognitive impaired subjects, they mainly focus on environment learning.

Though environment knowledge can be acquired directly through navigation or indirectly with symbolic tools such as navigation systems or maps, with respect to cognitive abilities involved in spatial awareness, visuo-spatial abilities have been shown to have a crucial role in explaining the accuracy of spatial mental representation formed [18].

From one side, it should be noted that in most cases environment learning was tested and trained through navigation in Virtual Environments, but from the other hand we observe a lack of educational software exploring and training the relation between environment learning, spatial awareness and visuo-spatial abilities in cognitive impaired people.

The sense of spatial orientation is deeply grounded on the subjects' cognitive ability to carry out abstract cognitive processes. For instance, for subjects with the Down syndrome the cognitive process of "abstraction" represents a great issue; in adults we often observe a total inability to "abstract" so that they are almost unable to put themselves in someone else's shoes. They are not able to imagine what the view of the world around them could be if taken from another point of view. Thus, they have relevant difficulties in understanding that the same scene, for example, a square or a street cross generates different images if it is seen from different positions.

Hence, we got the idea to create an educational game facilitating the emergence of the ability to change the point of view and supporting its enhancement, by visualizing how the observed world would be from another perspective.

3 The Game SMART VIEW

The game SMART VIEW was created in the framework of the project SMART ANGEL, supported by the Liguria Region Administration; this project is aimed at supporting the autonomous mobility of mentally disabled young people. The growth will be supported in a first rehabilitative phase by means of innovative models based on latest generation ICT devices (tablet, touchscreen devices) and in a successive prosthetic action toward the independence with mobile devices, GPS and cloud services. The game was thus conceived having in mind the target population of teenagers with mild mental retardation and the key issue of supporting the development of the prerequisites for them to be able to move around with limited external help; in this respect, spatial orientation was found to be one of the key aspects to be trained.

3.1 Objectives and Specific Abilities Addressed

SMART VIEW is a serious game ([19]) which aims to train the mastering and consolidation of competences related to space awareness and self-perception in the space.

In particular, the proposed exercises train those visuo-spatial abilities that allow an individual to execute an embodied self-rotation, through which s/he can actively imagine her/himself assuming different positions in the environment. This ability subserves not only reasoning about where objects are in relation to someone else but also how the objects in their environment appear to them. In particular, the following skills are trained: the perspective-taking and the mental rotation.

The ability to put ourselves into the shoes of another is called perspective-taking: the ability to non ego-centrically represent the aspects of the world around. The key concept is the perspective: a relationship between the subject and the objects and other people in the environment.

The perspective-taking ability is related to the visual-spatial experiences of an individual, and involves a relationship based on if and how other people see an object or a relationship based on the relative spatial locations of the other people and the object. In both cases, the ability to identify the position and the orientation of someone else and the ability to understand that their perspective may be different from our own [20-21] is required.

Visual-spatial perspective-taking (VPT) is the ability to appreciate how the world looks to another person and to predict his visual experience. In particular, one can predict: (1) if another person can see an object and (2) how objects are located in relation to another person's egocentric reference frame.

Studies of VPT distinguish two levels of ability, which develop sequentially. Level 1 visual perspective taking (VPT1) refers to knowledge about which objects in one's reference frame of view another observer can or cannot see. It is related to what lies within someone else's line-of-sight, i.e., which objects are visible and which occluded; the ability to judge that someone else might not see what you see (Figure 1). Level 2 visual perspective taking (VPT2) refers to the knowledge that different people experience seeing an object differently. VPT2 tasks require to realize that an object which both individuals can see at the same time may nevertheless appear different to each of them, for example, if one can see the face of a toy sheep, the other on the opposite side of the table may see only the tail. It is related to how someone sees the world: the ability to judge that two different people with different points of view can experience an object differently [20;22] (Figure 1).

Both levels are not acquired simultaneously. Typically, 2 year olds children pass tests of VPT1. The emergence of VPT2, instead, occurs at the age of 4 and seems to require more sophisticated cognitive abilities.

Michelon and Zacks [23] provided conclusive evidence for a qualitative difference between VPT-1 and VPT-2, concluding that VPT-1 is based on imagining the other person's line-of-sight that determines the relevant inter-object spatial relations, while VPT-2 requires some sort of mental self-rotation, imagining one's own bodily motion [20;22].

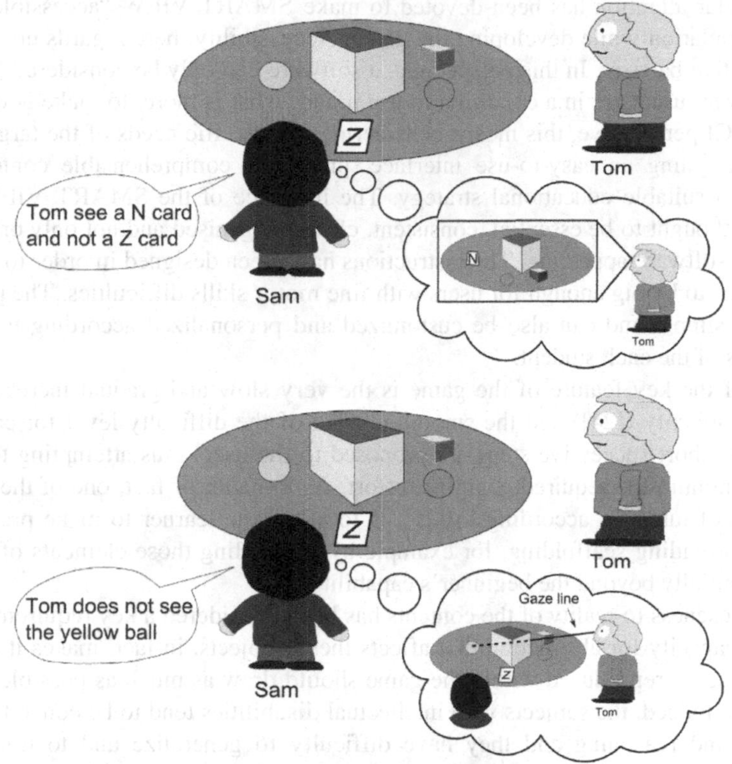

Fig. 1. Examples of perspective taking issues

The mental rotation is one particular aspect of a more complex cognitive skill: the visual mental imagery, the ability to see with the mind's eye. It is defined as the ability to mental rotate two or three-dimensional figure rapidly and accurately and to imagine the aspect of the figure after it was rotated around an axes with a certain number of degrees. Mental rotation is the process of transforming the mental image of a three-dimensional object to represent the same object as if seen from a different point of view. The mental rotations as well as the underpinning perspective taking ability have a fundamental importance in orientation tasks: they allow, for example, to recognise a place even when we perceive it from a perspective different from a previous one, or to align our perspective with the one showed on a map in order to be able to read it.

3.2 Design Principles Followed

The initial phase of the work was spent trying to understand the problems, to collect information and to define the user needs of the target group through meetings with the carers and the trainers of the NPO.

Particular attention has been devoted to make SMART VIEW "accessible" to the target population while developing the game. Accessibility, here regards not physical but cognitive barriers. In this perspective, a software can only be considered "accessible" if target users are in a condition to use it and, what is more, to make good use of it. In a HCI perspective, this means considering the specific needs of the target population, designing an easy-to-use interface, providing comprehensible contents and adopting a suitable educational strategy. The interface of the SMART VIEW game has been thought to be essential, consistent, clearly organised and not only oriented to make the software appealing. The instructions have been designed in order to be clear, the buttons to be big enough for users with fine motor skills difficulties. The proposed tasks are simple and can also be customized and personalized according to the real capacities of the each student.

One of the key feature of the game is the very slow and gradual increase of the game complexity ([24]) and the smooth change of the difficulty level for each task. Very little/short successive steps are proposed to the users thus attempting to reduce to the minimum the required cognitive effort. As a matter of fact, one of the primary functions of tutoring, according to [25], is to allow the learner to make progress by initially providing scaffolding, for example by controlling those elements of the task that are initially beyond the beginner's capability.

The closeness to reality of the contents has been considered a key requirement. The reduced capacity for abstraction that affects these subjects, in fact, makes it essential that the scenes reproduced within the game should draw as much as possible real life situations. Indeed, the subjects with intellectual disabilities tend to be concrete in their thinking and reasoning and they have difficulty to generalize and to transfer the knowledge or the behavior learned for doing one task to another task across different settings or environments.

For these reasons, it was decided to develop the game scenes as a non-immersive virtual environment, in order to reduce to the minimum the level of "abstraction" and make it closer to the actual reality.

In order to monitor the learning trend and to evaluate the educational efficacy of the software in the context of training the aforementioned spatial skills we decided to introduce some learning analytics inside the game development. These allows the trainers to measure, collect, analyse and report data about learners and their contexts, for purposes of understanding and optimising learning.

3.3 Technological Aspects

Besides influencing choices related to interface and educational strategy, the specific needs of the target population also influenced the type of computer device to be adopted. Because of the overall decisions taken in the SMART ANGEL project and in consideration of the specific requirements for the target population touch technology was adopted. SMART VIEW, then, makes use of TouchScreen (i.e Microsoft Surface or MultiTouch Philips) tables, which allow easier access to the game contents and augmented interaction for disabled users.

To orient ourselves toward a suitable development environment, we considered different Game Engines having in mind these base features:

- Quality of 3D rendering;
- Graphical User Interfaces (GUI);
- Sound reproduction
- Support of common programming languages.

The game engine we chose is Unity3D, a powerful rendering engine fully integrated with a complete set of intuitive tools. It allows the creation of 3D interactive environment, with high performance in term of execution time, frame rate and rendering. In fact, it presents, among other features, an integrated and expandable graphic interface (Editor) that allows visual 3D objects placement. Here the developer can compose realistic virtual scene, adding terrains and managing the lights, the sounds, the physics, the collisions and the animations of the objects, with the possibility to create code in C#, JavaScript or Boo. Finally, it also provides a simple project deployment environment for multiple platforms, with no need for additional configuration, including the web (which makes it possible to run any game on a web browser).

Currently, our framework contains a single exemplar scenario. It takes place in a kitchen, precisely in front of a table. The kitchen model together with a library of common use objects present in the game were created using Blender so as to recreate them as realistically as possible in terms of dimensions, scale and proportions. An example is depicted in Figure 2, which gives a fairly good idea of how realistic such an environment is.

Fig. 2. Using Blender to realistically represent object in an environment

3.4 SMART VIEW: Exercises Under the Lens

The exercises proposed in SMART VIEW draw on the experimental setups presented in [22] and [26], which were used to test the development of perspective taking abilities in children with autistic spectrum disorder and William Syndrome, with the purpose of training VPT2 and mental rotation abilities.

In the SMART VIEW game, the subject is in front of a touchscreen table, free to move around it, and observes a virtual scene of a table, as if they are sitting on a chair. Different objects are represented on the table, and their number varies, from a minimum of 1 to a maximum of 3, according to the difficulty level reached or selected by the tutor.

In the following, a general view of the available exercises and their actual difficulty progression is illustrated.

Familiarization Exercises. Three introductory exercises are foreseen. In the former, at the centre of the display the subject sees the main scene view. He can freely move around the touchscreen table and, by pressing some buttons depicted on the four sides of the monitor, he can change the view of the scene observing how it looks like from different perspectives (see Figure 3). In the second, the subject is presented, together with the main scene view, four images representing four views of the same scene taken from different positions around the table. The user is then asked: "Which scene are you looking at?". The participant is instructed to click the image that matches the perspective of the objects as they appear on the virtual table. If the subject makes errors, the game corrects him by showing the right answer (see Figure 4). In the latter, the subject is presented one image representing a scene view taken from his actual position around the table, while the main scene presents the virtual table rotated by a random angle. The participant is then asked and instructed to rotate the virtual table in the main scene, until the perspective of the objects, as they appear, does not match the image view (see Figure 5).

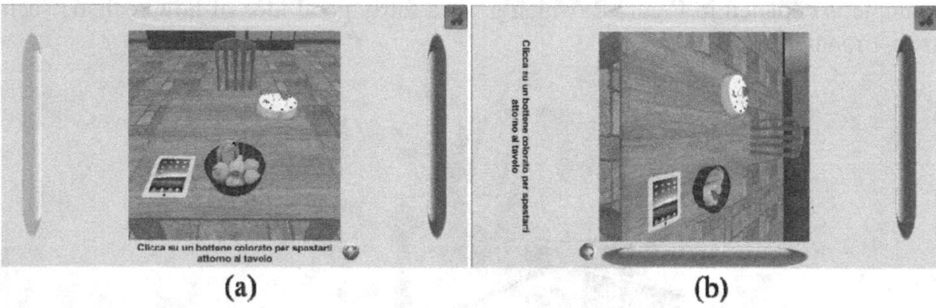

Fig. 3. Aspects of familiarization exercises. (a) Imagine observing the table and the objects over it from your actual position. Now suppose you to move on your left, placing yourself on the green side of the table. Clicking the green button (b), the main view changes accordingly to your new position.

Game Exercise 1: VPT2 Ability. The game exercise 1 trains the VPT2 ability, putting the accent on the judgement about the other one's perspective. Once the objects appear on the virtual table, the participant has to watch carefully the scene and choose the image that matched it. Then the tutor changes his location to the left, to the right or opposite side of the touchscreen table with respect to the subject's actual position. The participant is then asked: "Which scene will the tutor see from his new position?". The participant is instructed to click the image that matched the objects view that he thinks the tutor would see from his new location (see Figure 4).

Game Exercise 2: Self-Motion Imagery. The game exercise 2 trains the VPT2 ability, but in this case the accent is on the one's own bodily motion imagery. Once the

Fig. 4. An instance of game exercise 2. At the center of the display the subject sees the main scene view. At the right there are four images representing the view of the main scene taken from the four sides of the table. The colored button allow the subject to change his actual point of view around the table. Below the main scene there is the instruction to follow. In this example, the subject has to click the image he thinks representing what scene s/he will see if s/he moves to the blue (i.e. the right) side of the table. Exercise 1 is similar except for the fact that the tutor moves on the table side indicated in the instructions.

objects appear on the virtual table, the participant has to watch carefully the scene and choose the matching image. Then the tutor makes the subject pay attention to a location to the left, to the right or opposite side of the touchscreen table with respect to his actual position. The participant is then asked: "Which scene will you see, if you move to this position?". The participant is instructed to click the image that matches the objects view that he think he would see from his new imagined location (see Figure 4).

Game Exercise 3: VPT2 + Mental Rotation. The game exercises 3 and 4 are similar to exercises 1 and 2, respectively. In this case, however, there is also a training component regarding the mental rotation skill. In exercise 3 the tutor changes his location to the left, to the right or opposite side of the touchscreen table with respect to the subject's actual position. The subject is presented one image representing the scene view taken from the tutor position, while the main scene presents the virtual table rotated by a random angle. Given the tutor's view, the participant is then asked to rotate the virtual table in the main scene until the perspective of the objects, as they appear, does not match what he thinks he should see from his actual position (see Figure 5).

Game Exercise 4: Self-Motion Imagery + Mental Rotation. Exercise 4 is equal to the exercise 3 but in this case, as in exercise 2, the subject has to imagine himself in a

Fig. 5. An instance of game exercise 3 and 4. At the center of the display the subject sees the main scene view. At the right there is one image representing the view of the main scene taken from one among the four sides of the table. The colored button allow the subject to change her/his actual point of view around the table. Below the main scene there is the instruction to follow. In this example, the subject has to look at the image on the right, which represents what s/he would see from the yellow (i.e. the opposite) side of the table. Hence, given the subject's view taken from her/his imagined position, the subject has to rotate the table, following the arrows, until the scene represented in the main view does not match what s/he thinks he should see from her/his actual position.

particular position. Given the subject's view taken from his imagined position, the participant is then asked to rotate the virtual table in the main scene (originally rotated by a random angle) until the perspective of the objects, as they appear, does not match what he thinks he should see from his actual position (see Figure 5).

4 Conclusion

We have briefly presented SMART VIEW a Serious Game aimed at paving the way to further interventions supporting and enhancing the autonomous mobility of young persons with cognitive disabilities.

Actually, the game is intended to help teenagers with mild mental retardation developing a variety of prerequisites for individual mobility such as space awareness, self-perception in the space and basic spatial orientation. All these abilities are critical for the target population and call for specific training activities, which, if proposed in the form of digital games and virtual environments, can effectively contribute to sustain motivation ([27]) and, consequently, to enhance learning. After briefly explaining the context and the basic inspiring principles and concepts, we have focused on the key ideas that have in-formed the game design and development with regard to two aspects that are particularly important for the target population: interface and educational strategy. Accessibility and ease of use were the key pillars underpinning the interface design while the educational strategy was basically grounded on the idea of reducing the users' cognitive effort by acting on the smooth gradual increase of the exercises difficulty.

Field experiments involving the use of the SMART VIEW game are presently being performed, which will provide concrete data about the game appropriateness, suitability and effectiveness. They will, hopefully, also provide further food for thoughts and an in-depth perspective on how the game interfaces and other HCI related aspects of virtual environments can better suit the needs of cognitively impaired subjects.

References

1. Mengue-Topio, H., Courbois, Y., Farran, E.K., Sockeel, P.: Route learning and shortcut performance in adults with intellectual disability: A study with virtual environments. Research in Developmental Disabilities 32, 345–352 (2011)
2. Tolman, E.C.: Cognitive Maps in Rats and Men. Psychol. Rev. 55, 189–208 (1948)
3. Golledge, R.: Cognition of physical and built environments. In: Garling, T., Evans, G. (eds.) Environment, Cognition and Action; a Multidisciplinary Integrative Approach, Oxford University Press, New York (1990)
4. Golledge, R.: Wayfinding behavior: cognitive mapping and other spatial processes. John Hopkins University Press, Baltimore (1999)
5. Kitchin, R., Freundschuh, S.: Cognitive mapping: Past, Present and Future. Routledge, London (2000)
6. Taylor, H.A., Tversky, B.: Perspective in spatial descriptions. Journal of Memory and Language 35, 371–391 (1996)
7. Rose, F.D., Attree, E.A., Brooks, B.M., Parslow, D.M., Penn, P.R., Ambihipahan, N.: Training in virtual environments: transfer to real world tasks and equivalence to real task training. Ergonomics 43(4), 494–511 (2000)
8. Torrente, J., del Blanco, Á., Moreno-Ger, P., Fernández-Manjón, B.: Designing Serious Games for Adult Students with Cognitive Disabilities. In: Huang, T., Zeng, Z., Li, C., Leung, C.S. (eds.) ICONIP 2012, Part IV. LNCS, vol. 7666, pp. 603–610. Springer, Heidelberg (2012)
9. Brown, D.J., Shopland, N., Lewis, J.: Flexible and virtual travel training environments. In: Proc. 4th Intl. Conf. Disability, Virtual Reality & Assoc. Tech., Veszprém, Hungary (2002)
10. Brown, D.J., Battersby, S., Shopland, N.: Design and evaluation of a flexible travel training environment for use in a supported employment setting. International Journal of Disability and Human Development 4(3), 251–258 (2005)
11. Lloyd, J., Powell, T.E., Smith, J., Persaud, N.V.: Use of a virtual-reality town for examining route-memory, and techniques for its rehabilitation in people with acquired brain in-

jury. In: Proc. 6th Intl Conf. Disability, Virtual Reality & Assoc. Tech., Esbjerg, Denmark, pp. 167–174 (2006) ISBN 07 049 98 65 3
12. Sánchez, J.H., Sáenz, M.A.: Assisting the mobilization through subway networks by users with visual disabilities. In: Proc. 6th Intl Conf. Disability, Virtual Reality & Assoc. Tech., Esbjerg, Denmark, pp. 183–190 (2006) ISBN 07 049 98 65 3
13. da Costa, R., de Carvalho, L., de Aragon, D.F.: Virtual reality in cognitive training. In: Proc. 3rd International Conference on Disability, Virtual Reality & Associated Technology, Alghero, Italy, pp. 221–224 (2000)
14. Tam, S.F., Man, D.W.K., Chan, Y.P., Sze, P.C., Wong, C.M.: Evaluation of a computer-assisted, 2-D virtual reality system for training people with intellectual disabilities on how to shop. Rehabilitation Psychology 50(3), 285–291 (2005)
15. Yip, B.C.B., Man, D.W.K.: Virtual reality (VR)-based community living skills training for people with acquired brain injury: a pilot study. Brain Injury 23(13-14), 1017–1026 (2009)
16. Rose, F.D., Brooks, B.M., Attree, E.A.: An exploratory investigation into the usability and usefulness of training people with learning disabilities in a virtual environment. Disability and Rehabilitation 24, 627–633 (2002)
17. Brooks, B.M., Rose, F.D., Attree, E.A., Elliot-Square, A.: An evaluation of the efficacy of training people with learning disabilities in a virtual environment. Disability and Rehabilitation 24, 622–626 (2002)
18. Meneghetti, C., Fiore, F., Borella, E., De Beni, R.: Learning a map environment: the role of visuo-spatial abilities in young ond older adults. Appl. Cognit. Psychol. 25(6), 952–959 (2011)
19. Michael, D.R., Chen, S.L.: Serious Games: Games that Educate, Train, and Inform. Muska & Lipman/Premier-Trade (2005)
20. Surtees, A., Apperly, I., Samson, D.: Similarities and differences in visual and spatial perspective-taking processes. Cognition 129, 426–438 (2013)
21. Surtees, A., Apperly, I., Samson, D.: The use of embodied self-rotation for visual and spatial perspective-taking. Front. Hum. Neurosci. 7, 698 (2013), doi:10.3389/fnhum.2013.00698
22. Hirai, M., Muramatsu, Y., Mizuno, S., Kurahashi, N., Kurahashi, H., Nakamura, M.: Developmental changes in mental rotation ability and visual perspective-taking in children and adults with Williams syndrome. Front. Hum. Neurosci. 7, 856 (2013), doi:10.3389/fnhum.2013.00856
23. Michelon, P., Zacks, J.M.: Two kinds of visual perspective taking. Percept. Psychophys. 68, 327–337 (2006)
24. Bottino, R.M., Ott, M., Benigno, V.: Digital Mind Games: Experience-Based Reflections on Design and Interface Features Supporting the Devlopment of Reasoning Skills. In: Proc. 3rd European Conference on Game Based Learning, pp. 53–61 (2009)
25. Wood, D., Bruner, J.S., Ross, G.: The role of tutoring in problem solving. Journal of Child Psychology and Psychiatry 17, 89–100 (1976)
26. Hamilton, A.F., de, C., Brindley, R., Frith, U.: Visual perspective taking impairment in children with autistic spectrum disorder. Cognition 113, 37–44 (2009)
27. Ott, M., Tavella, M.: A contribution to the understanding of what makes young students genuinely engaged in computer-based learning tasks. Procedia Social and Behavioral Sciences 1, 184–188 (2009)

Tabletop Computer Game Mechanics for Group Rehabilitation of Individuals with Brain Injury

Jonathan Duckworth[1], Jessica D. Bayliss[2], Patrick R. Thomas[3], David Shum[4], Nick Mumford[5], and Peter H. Wilson[5]

[1] School of Media and Communication, RMIT University, Melbourne, Australia
jonathan.duckworth@rmit.edu.au

[2] School of Interactive Games and Media, Rochester Institute of Technology, Rochester, USA
jdbics@rit.edu

[3] School of Education and Professional Studies, Griffith University, Brisbane, Australia
p.thomas@griffith.edu.au

[4] Behavioural Basis of Health, Griffith Health Institute and School of Applied Psychology, Griffith University, Brisbane, Australia
d.shum@griffith.edu.au

[5] School of Psychology, Faculty of Arts and Sciences, Australian Catholic University, Melbourne, Australia
{nimumford,peterh.wilson}@acu.edu.au

Abstract. In this paper we provide a rationale for using tabletop displays for the upper-limb movement rehabilitation of individuals with brain injury. We consider how computer game mechanics may leverage this technology to increase patient engagement and social interaction, and subsequently enhance prescribed training. In recent years there has been a growing interest among health professionals in the use of computer games and interactive technology for rehabilitation. Research indicates that games have the potential to stimulate a high level of interest and enjoyment in patients; enhance learning; provide safe task conditions; complement conventional therapy; and become intrinsically motivating. We explore how game mechanics that include reward structures, game challenges and augmented audiovisual feedback may enhance a goal-orientated rehabilitation learning space for individuals with brain injury. We pay particular attention to game design elements that support multiple players and show how these might be designed for interactive tabletop display systems in group rehabilitation.

Keywords: Computer Game Mechanics, Game Design, Group Interaction, Tabletop Display, Movement Rehabilitation, Acquired Brain Injury.

1 Introduction

Acquired brain injury, particularly from stroke and traumatic brain injury, causes a broad range of cognitive and physical problems for patients. One of the major impediments to recovery is a patient's reduced ability to engage in therapy and to persist with it [1]. For example, movement performance in brain injured patients is

C. Stephanidis and M. Antona (Eds.): UAHCI/HCII 2014, Part II, LNCS 8514, pp. 501–512, 2014.

constrained by a number of physiological and biomechanical factors including the increase in muscle tone that occurs as a result of spasticity, reduced muscle strength, and limited coordination of body movement [2]. Physical and cognitive impairments often lead to a significant incidence of depression and low self-esteem among people with physical and intellectual disabilities, which presents a psychological barrier to engaging in rehabilitation and daily living [3]. Designing therapeutic tasks and environments that can be presented in a meaningful and stimulating way is one of the key challenges facing therapists. Rehabilitation orientated games may offer a viable adjunct to traditional therapy, offering patients highly engaging environments and playful activities.

A number of rehabilitation systems using computer games to present activity to a diverse range of users have emerged in recent years. One example, which shows the flexibility needed for rehabilitation, is the Makoto Arena [4]. The concept of the Makoto Arena is simple and requires the player to listen for a tone, watch for a light, and then hit the column and area that lit up quickly. This type of game is commonly called a *toy* in academic literature due to the open-ended and flexible nature of how the physical device may be used.

Another example of a game used for rehabilitation is the game Lazy Eye Shooter [5]. This game is a first-person shooter used for the treatment of Amblyopia and has a traditional game structure (see Figure 1). Lazy Eye Shooter is a bit different from the Makoto Arena as the former only lasts for 40 hours but the latter could be considered a long-term exercising game. In addition the Lazy Eye Shooter uses an adaptive training regime so that people with different types of amblyopia may still use the same training.

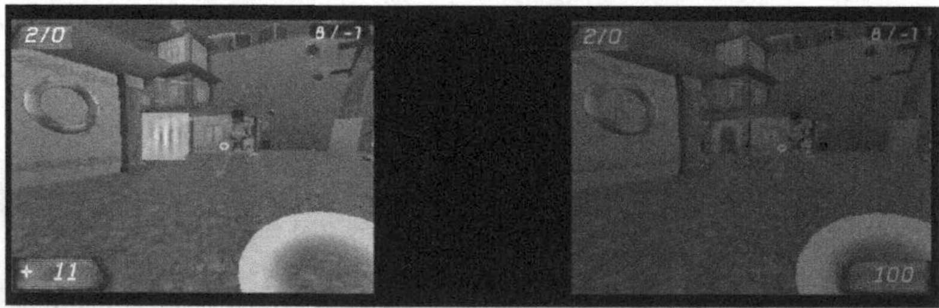

Fig. 1. Lazy Eye Shooter, an example of a traditional first-person shooter game that has been reworked into a successful game treatment for amblyopia.

Our previous rehabilitation application called Elements shows how tabletop displays support upper-limb interaction as the main form of user input and enable an embodied, first-person view of performance [6] [7]. The Elements system provides goal directed and exploratory game-like tasks of varying complexity geared toward reaching, grasping, lifting, moving and placing tangible user interfaces on a tabletop display (Figure 2). We also discussed the key advantage of tabletop displays that support co-located face-to-face social interactions and facilitate multimodal forms of communication between co-located users in the context of rehabilitation [8]. This has important implications for rehabilitation game design that supports social play as studies indicate co-located play evokes stronger social engagement and increased levels of enjoyment [9]. Co-located game orientated rehabilitation may provide patients with a more comprehensive social experience that is visual, tactile, auditory and enriched.

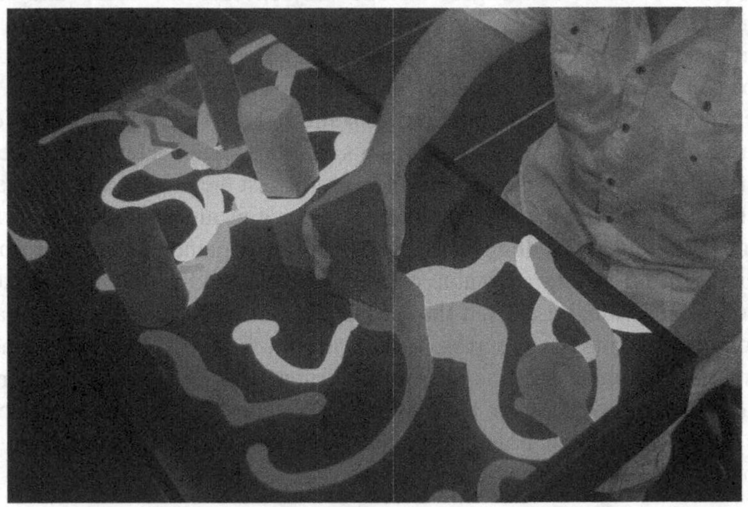

Fig. 2. An individual using the Elements system explores the functions of several soft graspable tangible user interfaces to draw and paint digitally

When considering game design for rehabilitation, it is important to consider the time needed for treatment. It is likely that short treatments such as Lazy Eye Shooter may be more successful using traditional game techniques, but longer-term treatments such as Elements may need to be more 'toy-like', embodied and tangible in their approach to sustain patient motivation beyond the initial 'novelty' of the technology [7].

In general, existing commercial game systems often lack appropriate game mechanics, design, and user interfaces for movement rehabilitation, which presents a barrier for patients engaging in therapy [10] [11]. Within the game design field, more research is needed to inform developers who are designing games for health about the circumstances under which specific game mechanics might be most effective [12]. However motor and cognitive impairments can present a broad range of significant problems for patients using existing commercial game systems and adapted solutions for movement rehabilitation [13]. The developers of rehabilitation systems could significantly benefit from analysing the principles of game design to engage and motivate patients [14].

2 Game Design for Brain Injury Rehabilitation

A wide variety of mechanics are used in game media to deliver game play experiences that motivate and engage players. According to Johan Huizinga [15], the first rule of play is that play must be voluntary and with this the central element of all design must be the player(s). The other elements of game design include objectives, procedures, rules, resources, conflict, boundaries, and outcome [16]. Feedback is inherent and necessary in these elements and game mechanics are commonly a combination of procedures and rules. Reward structures map to objectives and the game outcome. Game challenges include objectives, resources, and conflict. Boundaries may be the edge of a game map or emotional as in social play.

The integration of game design, social play and rehabilitation does not have a strong presence in current therapy. To develop rehabilitation tabletop games, developers and designers need to be aware of the patient's particular needs, deficits, the characteristics of group social interactions and how these relate game mechanics particular to tabletop interfaces. Recent findings suggest the principles of game design relevant to acquired brain injury rehabilitation include meaningful play that translates into learning outcomes; handling the level of failure in game play so as to maintain patient engagement; setting adaptable challenges, rules and goals appropriate to the abilities of the individual user; and the setting of game reward structures to assist in motivation and tracking the progress of the patient over time [17]. Furthermore, the social aspects of gaming such as shared user interfaces may provide patients with additional important avenues for learning [18]. We consider how these game design elements might be used for brain injury rehabilitation in a co-located group context using tabletop display interfaces.

2.1 Feedback

Audiovisual feedback is a central mechanic of most games that is provided to the player in response to some action. Typically, this involves the player performing an action that in turn causes some effect within the game. The player receives feedback on their action that informs how they perform the next action to progress in the game. In movement rehabilitation contexts, audiovisual feedback provides the patient with additional functions that revolve around understanding the nature of their movement. Feedback provides patients with additional knowledge of the outcomes of their actions to aid in future movement planning. The audiovisual feedback can also direct the patient to focus their attention on the external effects of their movement, rather than the internal biomechanics of the movement itself.

Intrinsic feedback (i.e., sensory information from the body) is often compromised as a result of brain injury. Extrinsic feedback, an external focus of attention to the effects of action, has been shown to be more effective in enhancing motor learning as opposed to internally focused attention [19] [20]. In motor learning theory feedback is provided to the learner about their movement patterns or knowledge of performance (KP), as well as feedback about the outcome of the movement or knowledge of results (KR). For example, a therapist's corrective feedback provided to a learner during an improper movement pattern is a form of KP.

The use of KP and KR in game design can provide task related information about the skill being learned. However, there is limited evidence to support the amount and frequency schedule of feedback for optimal results in rehabilitation [21]. While modern digital games give consistent and frequent feedback, this may be detrimental for rehabilitation games.

Frequent presentation of feedback may have several detrimental impacts on learning a task. For example, a learner may become too reliant on feedback to detect errors, thus unable to perform independently when the feedback is withdrawn. In addition, frequent feedback may result in the learner making too many corrections that interfere with the stability of their overall performance. Several researchers have indicated that feedback 'faded' over time compared with a continuous schedule may be more beneficial to longer-term retention and learning [22] [23]. However, more research is required to establish how the frequency and intensity of feedback in games can best be utilised to enhance real-world outcomes.

Our initial discussion with therapists suggests that complete therapist control over the presentation of KP, KR and augmented audiovisual feedback variables is desirable. As such, in Elements all forms of feedback are switched off by default with control options that enable the augmented feedback, performance and results to be selected and presented at the discretion of the therapist (Figure 3). In this way, the therapist can adapt the frequency of the feedback and task variables to the appropriate level to suit the client and their progress. As the game Lazy Eye Shooter shows [5], it is also possible to use dynamic difficulty adjustment with the therapist setting the initial difficulty and feedback structure.

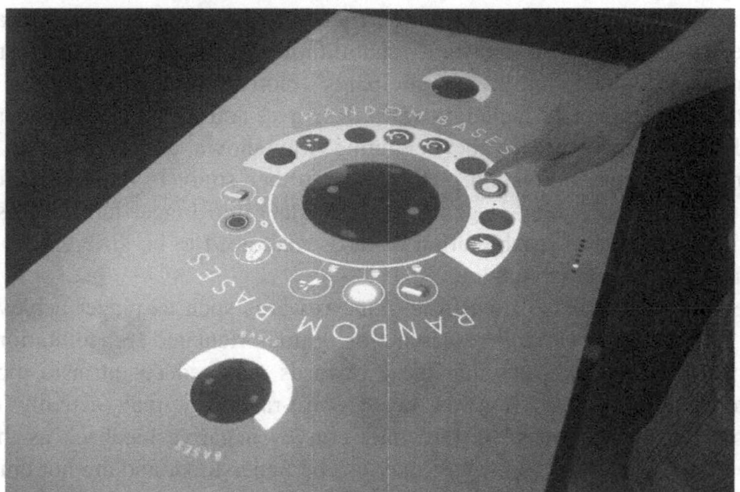

Fig. 3. A therapist manually touch-selects a range of augmented feedback options using the Elements rehabilitation system

2.2 Reward Structures

Reward structures in games are designed to intrinsically motivate engagement in game challenges and increase expenditure of effort [24]. Intrinsic motivation is defined as a person's free will of doing an activity for its inherent satisfaction rather than for some separable consequence [25]. Game rewards can take many different forms depending on the game, including score systems, experience points, resources, item unlocks, achievements, and feedback messages [24]. These incentives might lead to increased enjoyment that in turn motivates the player to complete a particular task and reach certain goals.

In movement rehabilitation contexts reward structures may be linked to performance accomplishments, for example, a range of movements or time engaged in play may be rewarded using a scoring mechanism. Rewards might occur on multiple levels, from moment to moment during task performance to cumulative rewards based on overall performance. The purpose of rewards may allow the players to experience challenge as well as demonstrate mastery and are understood to be extrinsically motivating. Games rewards such as scoring may assist the individual assess his or her capability to perform a certain task, and be used to foster individual feelings of autonomy and self-efficacy [17]. Extrinsic rewards provide tools for self-assessment and comparison that satisfy the innate needs for competence and self-determination.

Strategies that focus primarily on extrinsic rewards to control behavior may undermine rather than promote intrinsic motivation [26]. Findings indicate that the primary negative effect of rewards (particularly tangible rewards such as money) tend to forestall self-regulation, or in other words people taking responsibility for motivating or regulating themselves [26].

In a recent study, operant conditioning (a schedule of reinforcements, rewards and punishments to change behavior) in a rehabilitation game targeting hand and wrist movement was found to increase participants' motivation to play longer [27]. A combination of parameters including reward scores, activity bonuses, and aversive stimuli that reset the game to the beginning was shown to increase the level of enjoyment and player motivation. However, further study is required to evaluate whether operant conditioning in games can translate into longer-term acquisition of motor skills. Short-term rehabilitation rewards may need to be different from those meant for longer-term rehabilitation.

Furthermore, the effects of extrinsic game rewards such as player achievements, trophies and badges warrant research for game-orientated rehabilitation. Prior motivational research indicates that these rewards may reduce intrinsic motivation [26]. Interestingly enough, rewards given semi-randomly may actually enhance motivation. Extrinsic forms of reward may convey negative feedback as they may impose values on behavior and status, may not be understood, and are not universally appreciated [28].

Other than operant conditioning rewards, verbal persuasion that provides encouragement or information about performance may be of benefit. For example, in Elements we provide short positive messages as a form of reward at the end of each task. These messages are generally encouraging, humorous in tone and we are careful not to introduce value judgments. In the case of severe brain injury it may be desirable to reward all engagement with success in the initial stages of game play. By doing so, failure is dealt with in a positive way rather than highlighting the player's impaired capabilities.

2.3 Game Challenges

The level of challenge in games is a primary mechanism to increase player engagement with the game. In general, the level of difficulty in a game is designed to gradually increase as the game progresses to maintain a level of challenge for the player. In motor rehabilitation it is unlikely that designers will know the skills and capabilities of players in advance. A range of movement tasks may seem trivial for some patients whilst challenging (and often painful) for many others. For optimal player engagement, games should present an ideal level of challenge for each individual player that is neither too difficult that it becomes frustrating, nor too easy that the player loses interest [29]. Dynamic difficulty adjustments are of particular importance in games for rehabilitation.

Games for rehabilitation should be designed so that the therapist can always set the level of difficulty according to their assessment of the patient's capabilities. Typically, video games use levels to structure difficulty. For example, new game levels are made available to the player on completion of the previous ones. As the game progresses each successive level builds upon the skills and knowledge acquired by the player, requiring the acquisition of new skills or fine-tuning of existing skills as the difficulty increases with each new level. Challenges used in this example allow the player to progress only after once they understand enough of the game play.

There are many different types of challenges in games. Chris Crawford provides a list including cerebellar, sensorimotor, spatial reasoning, pattern recognition, sequential reasoning, numerical reasoning, resource management, and social reasoning [30]. Within rehabilitation game design the preferred challenges are based on sensorimotor skills, which are the skills used to throw a balled up piece of paper into a waste paper basket. The Makoto Arena discussed earlier is a good example of this type of challenge. These skills may be mixed with other types of challenges such as spatial reasoning and pattern recognition.

Spatial reasoning is commonly used in puzzles such as Tetris and when combined with sensorimotor learning can create a variety of potential rehabilitation games. It is possible to create puzzles that can enhance sensorimotor learning. Pattern recognition is useful for boss fights, an enemy-based challenge usually at the end of a video game level. In order to overcome the boss, game players may need to learn its attack patterns in terms of both attack frequency as well as movement. This may be useful in rehabilitation contexts where a specific movement may need to be learned repeatedly.

2.4 Social Play

Social play can be categorized into collaborative, cooperative, and competitive play [31]. In rehabilitation games, competitive play is a poor design choice as the existence of competition means that there are winners and losers. Losers may experience reduced motivation to continue with therapy, which is undesirable.

In contrast, in both collaborative and cooperative game play individuals play a game together to achieve a desired outcome. In collaborative game play, individuals form a team that obtains the game's objective. In cooperative game play, individuals may choose to form a team, but each will receive their own benefits from their cooperation. Group play in general is seen as beneficial and may facilitate vicarious learning when individuals can observe and imitate each other's behavior. Observing others' success in accomplishing certain tasks provides a sense of self-efficacy to the observer that they might also have the ability to accomplish the task.

One of the guiding factors in encouraging true collaborative play is to encourage selfless decisions by bestowing different abilities or responsibilities upon the players [31]. In rehabilitation games this is beneficial since different individuals will likely have different strengths and weaknesses. This also reduces the tension involved in a group setting where individuals may see each other's abilities and compare themselves to the other participants.

Tabletop media offer unique instances of how feedback can be presented to the patient, particularly in a group setting. Feedback may be targeted to an individual, the group or both. For example, private feedback in a shared environment context can be provided in a user's local space directly in front them. Depending on the size of the tabletop display a local space may not be easy for other users to see or reach. Morris et al. report that in a shared learning environment private feedback assisted in reducing potential embarrassment over incorrect actions by not highlighting them to the entire group [32]. This can be used to highlight the different roles for users in a shared game environment.

Activities on tabletop displays are generally designed for shared activities. Individual feedback that others can see as well as feedback on the group performance on a shared task could be made to facilitate awareness of others' actions [33] [34]. In this way, participants might learn by observing and imitating others' performance and feedback in manipulating objects and environments, consequently directing higher levels of attention and focus in users.

Rewards in a group setting add social dimensions that may motivate game play, foster social relationships and encourage social interactions between players. Many games require players to work together cooperatively to complete a goal such as collecting resources. Rewards that show group achievement can enhance feeling of belonging and team building. In the case of rehabilitation, team rewards may add a social component that enables the player to feel strongly committed to remain in the game and work together with other players to develop strategies to maximise the reward. The social aspects of game rewards may enable players with severe impairments to find new ways to increase communication and social support related to their health issues. Indeed, recent surveys with stroke patients indicate that the opportunity for social interaction as part of rehabilitation is a key motivation to participate in therapy [35].

Most co-located video games direct players to focus attention on a common wall-mounted screen but not on other players. This configuration hinders social interaction and reduces opportunity for more complex interpersonal communication. Tabletop display interfaces offer several advantages in this regard by offering a shared workspace where users can clearly observe the actions of others face-to-face, communicate in a collaborative setting, and coordinate activities between each other. Furthermore, studies indicate that co-located face-to-face play provides additional fun, challenge, and perceived competence in games [36]. Studies indicate that co-located play increases player enjoyment through shared attention, increased motivation, higher arousal and performance contingent on the social context of the game setting [37].

The ability to give players different roles in a shared game environment also enhances the ability for players to play the game many times. By changing roles players can experience the same game but from a different perspective incorporating unique challenges and rewards specific to the character. This is partially what makes role-playing fantasy games playable over long periods of time.

3 Summary and Future Work

We have discussed four key game design parameters that can be used in the development of multi-user rehabilitation games for tabletop displays. We maintain that tabletop rehabilitation activities that incorporate game design challenges, judicious rewards, meaningful feedback, and co-located social play afford a powerful therapeutic tool to engage individuals with brain injury socially in rehabilitation and motivate them to persist in therapy. A critical predictor of success in therapy is time on task, together with high levels of user engagement and investment in the activity [39]. For designers, the critical task is to find a balance between these key ingredients.

This paper has discussed some of the design principles developers may consider and how they might be applied to create cooperative and collaborative games in a group therapeutic setting. With respect to feedback (both real time and summary), the challenge for the designer is to consider carefully how, when, and in what form feedback is supplied to the performer, and reduce potential cognitive overload. Indeed, the take-home message is "more is not always better". A good example of this is the use of Nintendo Wii Fit games in rehabilitation where the effects of repeated failure are made apparent in the game avatar combined with discouraging comments [39]. Related to this point is embedding appropriate reward structures into the game environment. It is important that both extrinsic and intrinsic forms of reward be considered, and how these are integrated over different time scales—short-term and longer term. Short-term rewards may promote persistence in the game and enable users to learn basic game rules. But this does not necessarily translate to persistence over extended time, from session to session and month to month. Research shows that users must be fully engaged in the activity, which presupposes some discretion or independence in selecting game attributes and the level of challenge.

To facilitate user engagement, designers and therapists should consult clients during the research and development phase to ensure that game elements, rewards and challenges are presented in an appropriate format or in a way that is motivationally significant. Bridging all the above is the social element of the game environment, specifically the use of co-located systems. For example, rewards that are shared in a group context, even vicariously, can enhance levels of participation (i.e., on task behavior plus engagement), which predicts longer-term persistence and therapeutic gains [40]. Added to this are (i) the positive effects of social engagement in a therapeutic context and its flow on effect for psychosocial adjustment and well-being, and (ii) the opportunities social activity affords for observational learning. The game design principles discussed in this paper are a starting point toward understanding how to build co-located games for movement rehabilitation that are social, motivating, engaging and are effective.

Acknowledgements. This work is supported by an Australian Research Council (ARC) Linkage Grant LP110200802, and Synapse Grant awarded by the Australia Council for the Arts.

References

1. Murphy, T.H., Corbett, D.: Plasticity during stroke recovery. Nature Rev. Neurosci. 10, 861–872 (2009)
2. McCrea, P.H., Eng, J.J., Hodgson, A.J.: Biomechanics of reaching: clinical implications for individuals with acquired brain injury. Disability and Rehabilitation 24(5), 780–791 (2002)
3. Esbensen, A.J., Rojahn, J., Aman, M.G., Ruedich, S.: The reliability and validity of an assessment instrument for anxiety, depression and mood among individuals with mental retardation. J. Autism and Devel Disorders 33, 617–629 (2003)
4. Hilton, C.L., Cumpata, K., Klohr, C., Gaetke, S., Artner, A., Johnson, H.: Dobbs, Effects of Exergaming on Executive Function and Motor Skills in Children with Autism Spectrum Disorder: a Pilot Study. American Journal of Occupational Therapy 68(1), 57–65 (2014)
5. Bayliss, J.D., Vedamurthy, I., Nahum, M., Levi, D., Bavelier, D.: Lazy eye shooter: making a game therapy for visual recovery in adult amblyopia usable. In: Marcus, A. (ed.) DUXU 2013, Part II. LNCS, vol. 8013, pp. 352–360. Springer, Heidelberg (2013)
6. Duckworth, J., Wilson, P.H.: Embodiment and play in designing an interactive art system for movement rehabilitation. Second Nature 2(1), 120–137 (2010)
7. Mumford, N., Duckworth, J., Thomas, P.R., Shum, P., Williams, G., Wilson, P.H.: Upper-limb virtual rehabilitation for traumatic brain injury: A preliminary within-group evaluation of the elements system. Brain Injury 26(2), 166–176 (2012)
8. Duckworth, J., Thomas, P.R., Shum, D., Wilson, P.H.: Designing Co-located Tabletop Interaction for Rehabilitation of Brain Injury. In: Marcus, A. (ed.) DUXU 2013, Part II. LNCS, vol. 8013, pp. 391–400. Springer, Heidelberg (2013)
9. Gajadhar, B., de Kort, Y.A.W., Ijsselsteijn, W.A.: Rules of Engagement: Influence of Co-player Presence on Player Involvement in Digital Games. International Journal of Gaming and Computer-Mediated Simulations 1(3), 14–27 (2009)
10. Flynn, S.M., Lange, B.S.: Games for rehabilitation: the voice of the players. In: Proc. 8th Intl. Conf. on Disability, Virtual Reality and Assoc. Technologies, Viña del Mar/Valparaíso, Chile, pp. 185–194 (2010)
11. Rand, D., Kizony, R., Weiss, P.L.: Virtual reality rehabilitation for all: Vivid GX versus Sony PlayStation II EyeToy. In: Fifth International Conference on Disability, Virtual Reality and Associated Technologies, Oxford, UK, September 20 -22, pp. 87–94 (2004)
12. Baranowski, T., Lieberman, D., Buday, R., Peng, W., Zimmerli, L., Widerhold, B., Kato, P.M.: Videogame Mechanics in Games for Health. Games for Health Journal 2(4), 194–204 (2013)

13. Flores, E., Tobon, G., Cavallaro, E., Cavallaro, F.L., Perry, J.C., Keller, T.: Improving Patient Motivation in Game Development for Motor Deficit Rehabilitation. ACM Advances in Computer Entertainment Technology 352, 381–384 (2008)
14. Rizzo, A.A.: A SWOT Analysis of the Field of VR Rehabilitation and Therapy. Presence 14, 119–146 (2005)
15. Huizinga, J.: Homo Ludens: a Study of the Play Element in Culture. Beacon Press, Boston (1955)
16. Fullerton, T.: Game Design Workshop: a Playcentric Approach to Creating Innovative Games, pp. 28–33. Morgan Kaufmann, Boston (2008)
17. Burke, J.W., McNeill, M.D.J., Charles, D.K., Morrow, P.J., Crosbie, J.H., McDonough, S.M.: Optimising engagement for stroke rehabilitation using serious games. The Visual Computer 25(12), 1085–1099 (2009)
18. Xu, Y., Barba, E., Radu, L., Gandy, M., Macintyre, B.: Chores Are Fun: Understanding Social Play in Board Games for Digital Tabletop Game Design. In: Proc. of Think Design Play: The Fifth International Conference of DiGRA (2011)
19. Wulf, G., Prinz, W.: Directing attention to movement effects enhances learning: A review. Psychonomic Bulletin & Review 8(4), 648–660 (2001)
20. van Vliet, P.M., Wulf, G.: Extrinsic feedback for motor learning after stroke: what is the evidence? Disability and Rehabilitation 28(13-14), 831–840 (2006)
21. Subramanian, S., Massie, K., Malcolm, C.L., Levin, M.P., Does, M.F.: the provision of Extrinsic Feedback Result in Improved Motor Learning in the Upper Limb Poststroke? A systematic review of the evidence. Neurorahbilitation and Neural Repair 24(2), 113–124 (2010)
22. Winstein, C.J., Schmidt, R.A.: Reduced Frequency of Knowledge of Results Enhances Motor Skills Learning. Journal of Experimental Psychology: Learning, Memory, and Cognition 16(4), 677–691 (1990)
23. Hemayattablab, R., Rostami, L.R.: The effects of feedback on the learning of motor skills in individuals with cerebral palsy. Research in Developmental Disabilities 31(2010), 212–217 (2010)
24. Wang, H., Sun, C.: Game Reward Systems: Gaming Experiences and Social Meaning. Proceedings of DiGRA 2011 Conference: Think Design Play (2011)
25. Przybylski, A.K., Scott Rigby, C., Ryan, R.M.: A motivational Model of Video Game Engagement. Review of General Psychology 14(2), 154–166 (2010)
26. Deci, E.L., Koestner, R., Ryan, R.M.: A Meta-Analytic Review of Experiments Examining the Effects of Extrinsic Rewards on Intrinsic Motivation. Psychological Bulletin 125(6), 627–668 (1999)
27. Shah, N., Basteris, A., Amirabdollahian, F.: Design Parameters in Multimodal Game for Rehabilitation. Games for Health Journal 3(1) (2014)
28. Antin, J., Churchill, E.F.: Badges in Social Media: A Social Psychological Perspective. In: ACM CHI 2011, Vancouver, BC, Canada, May 7-12 (2011)
29. Salen, K., Zimmerman, E.: Rules of Play: Game Design Fundamentals. MIT Press, Cambridge (2003)
30. Crawford, C.: Chris Crawford on Game Design, pp. 35–53. New Riders, Indianapolis (2003)
31. Zagal, J., Rick, J., Hsi, I.: Collabortive Games: Lessons Learned from Board Games. Simulation & Gaming 37(1), 24–40 (2006)
32. Morris, M.R., Cassanego, A., Paepcke, A., Winograd, T., Piper, A.M., Huang, A.: Mediating Group Dynamics through Tabletop Interface Design. IEEE Computer Graphics and Applications 26(5), 65–73 (2006)

33. Rick, J., Marshall, P., Yuill, N.: Beyond one-size-fits-all: How interactive tabletops support collaborative learning. In: IDC 2011, Ann Arbor, USA, June 20-23 (2011)
34. Nacenta, M.A., Pinelle, D., Gutwin, C., Mandryk, R.: Individual and group support in tabletop interaction techniques. In: Müller-Tomfelde, C. (ed.) Tabletops – Horizontal Interactive Displays, pp. 303–333. Springer, London (2010)
35. Lewis, G., Rosie, J.A.: Virtual reality games for movement rehabilitation in neurological conditions: how do we meet the needs and expectations of the users? Disability and Rehabilitation 34(22), 1880–1886 (2012)
36. Kruger, R., Carpendale, S., Scott, S.D., Greenberg, S.: How People Use Orientation on Tables: Comprehension, Coordination and Communication. In: Proceedings of GROUP 2003, pp. 369–378. ACM Press (2003)
37. Gajadhar, B.J., de Kort, Y.A.W., IJsselsteijn, W.A.: Shared Fun Is Doubled Fun: Player Enjoyment as a Function of Social Setting. In: Markopoulos, P., de Ruyter, B., IJsselsteijn, W.A., Rowland, D. (eds.) Fun and Games 2008. LNCS, vol. 5294, pp. 106–117. Springer, Heidelberg (2008)
38. Almqvist, L., Hellnas, P., Stefansson, M., Granlund, M.: 'I can play!' Young children's perception of health. Pediatric Rehabilitation 9(3), 275–284 (2006)
39. de Kort, Y.A.W., IJsselstein, W.A., Gajadhar, B.J.: People, Places, and Play: A research framework for digital game experience in a socio-spatial context. In: DiGRA 2007 Proceedings "Situated Play", pp. 823–830 (2007)
40. Lange, B., Koenig, S., Chang, C., McConnell, E., Suma, E., Bolas, M., Rizzo, A.: Designing informed game-based rehabilitation tasks leveraging advances in virtual reality. Disability and Rehabilitation 34(22), 1863–1870 (2012)

Learning through Game Making: An HCI Perspective

Jeffrey Earp, Francesca Maria Dagnino, and Michela Ott

Istituto per le Tecnologie Didattiche – Consiglio Nazionale della Ricerche, Italy
{jeffrey.earp,dagnino,ott}@itd.cnr.it

Abstract. One of the areas of Game-Based Learning (GBL) that has been attracting considerable interest in recent years is digital game making, whereby learners play games but also design, construct and share them as active participants in a learning community. Human Computer Interaction (HCI) is a critical aspect of processes and tools within game making, and plays a key role in ensuring that learning experiences are both engaging and educationally fruitful. In this light, this paper examines two different game authoring environments from an HCI perspective, taking account of certain interface characteristics can affect and shape the authoring process and thus have a potential bearing on educational effectiveness. The investigation draws on findings from an EU co-funded project called MAGICAL (MAking Games In CollaborAtion for Learning), which is exploring the potential that game making offers for activating key transversal skills such as problem-solving, creativity and ICT competency, particularly at primary school level.

Keywords: Game Making, Game-Based Learning, Technology Enhanced Learning, Human Computer Interaction, Usability, Accessibility.

1 Introduction

In recent years, interest and enthusiasm for Game Based Learning (GBL) has strengthened considerably within the educational research community and GBL is now gaining wider acceptance among educational policy makers, administrators, practitioners and the public at large [1]. Some see GBL in practical terms as a way to kindle – or rekindle – learner interest, and to get students in formal learning to engage deeply with subject-related contents. From a more theoretical perspective, many GBL advocates see interaction with digital games as a process of active, learner-centered meaning making [2]. In this sense GBL is considered an alternative (or antidote) to instructionist-style "talk & chalk" lecturing, aligning more closely to modern, constructivist visions of education and with the educational principles underpinning the Knowledge Society [3]. It is held to motivate and engage players, immersing them in a learning experience that combines playfulness, challenge and fun [4-5]

While enthusiasm for GBL is spreading, many educational researchers warn that these hallmark characteristics do not *per se* generate effective learning outcomes, and simply having learners play one or other digital game will not necessarily yield the expected educational benefits [6]. Effectiveness depends on a range of factors that includes the nature and suitability of the core digital GBL environment itself. To start

C. Stephanidis and M. Antona (Eds.): UAHCI/HCII 2014, Part II, LNCS 8514, pp. 513–524, 2014.

with, this needs to blend educational and fun dimensions in a manner that is complimentary, suitably balanced, and an integral part of gameplay. This critical factor is summed up thus by a group of eminent UK educational researchers reporting for Nesta [7]: "*games that integrate the knowledge and skills to be learnt directly into the structure of the game activity are both more fun … to play and more effective than those where the game is used as motivation but without connection to the learning content.*" GBL environments proposing unconnected play and learning activities are often dismissed as "chocolate-coated broccoli"; they provide little opportunity for active meaning making and, as Luckin and colleagues [7] point out, are unlikely to foster the sustained engagement needed to enhance learning processes.

Against this background, a growing number of researchers (and practitioners) are taking GBL beyond the confines of game playing and encouraging learners to design and make their own digital games, which they can subsequently share with peers in a learning community. Indeed there is a steadily growing body of academic literature advocating game making as a way to empower learners, letting them take the driving seat in active, hands-on activities [8]. These activities are held to offer opportunities for building a range of knowledge and skills, not just within specific subject areas, such as language and math, but across them too. This covers skills like creativity, problem solving and collaboration, which are commonly characterized as Twenty-First Century Skills (21CS) and, as such, central pillars of modern education [9], [1].

A number of initiatives are currently emerging to investigate the adoption of game making for learning. One of these efforts is an EU co-funded project called MAGICAL (Making Games in Collaboration for Learning)[1], which is conducting school experiments to explore the potential that game making offers for activating key transversal skills such as problem-solving, creativity and ICT competency, particularly at primary school level [10].

Among the various activities undertaken in MAGICAL is investigation of different digital environments that have been (or might be) used fruitfully to support learning processes and educational objectives in game-making contexts. This effort has resulted in the establishment of a community library of game making environments[2], which currently catalogues over fifty game authoring tools. These vary widely and in different ways. For example, the games they can produce range from simple 2D arcade-style platform games to quite elaborate 3D game worlds. The nature of user-system interaction in the editing process also varies quite markedly. Some environments feature a limited set of elementary game elements and properties, making them particularly suitable for younger learners, for game makers with special learning needs (whether specific or non-specific), and also for use in restricted educational time frames. Other authoring tools have an extensive authoring palette that, amongst other things, offers game makers the chance to create fairly sophisticated relations and interactions in games, opening the way to the design of rich and complex gameplay experiences.

When it comes to selecting a game-making environment for educational purposes, HCI aspects are particularly critical, especially where younger students are concerned. Accordingly, adoption of a digital authoring tool calls for careful consideration of usability and ease-of-use factors [11-12]. Furthermore, all-important efforts to

[1] www. magical-project.net

[2] http://amc.pori.tut.fi/game-building-tools/

guarantee Universal Access to education demand that due attention also be devoted to accessibility issues.

In the following, we examine two game authoring environments that have featured in MAGICAL activities and that in certain respects exemplify different approaches to game making. After providing an overview of their main features, we identify some of the differences that these tools present from the viewpoint of adoption within digitally-enhanced learning activities. The ultimate purpose of the comparison is not to "evaluate" the tools or quantify their respective educational potential; doing so is a very complex and contentious matter. Rather, the aim is to provide food for thought on the aspects of HCI that are pivotal for the deployment of digital game making in educational contexts, aspects which may have a decisive bearing on the success of game making for enhancing learning outcomes.

2 Two Game Making Environments Under the Lens

The following section gives a general description of two popular game making environments: Kodu[3], a downloadable application for PC and console, and Sploder[4], an online browser-based tool. For details about these, readers should refer to the respective websites. In this contribution we concentrate on key differences in the authoring interfaces, which exemplify different approaches to game making.

2.1 Kodu: A Code-Based Game Authoring Tool

Kodu presents a visual programming language specially designed to allow non-programmers, and especially young children, to engage in code-based game authoring. As a tool for learning through computer programming, it builds on the constructionist philosophy and legacy of Seymour Papert and others, who developed the Logo visual programming language for children in the 1960s. In the words of Microsoft, "*the Kodu language is designed specifically for game development and provides specialized primitives derived from gaming scenarios.*" To render programming concepts more readily comprehensible to young game makers, the language is largely anthropomorphic: behaviors are expressed metaphorically in the graphic interface in terms of real-world physics and human senses like vision, hearing and touch.

Kodu presents a 3D world in which you can build games using its special visual coding language. You can start from scratch with a near-empty 3D space or edit an existing game(world) to make a new, personalized version. Either way, you can opt to set your game in a minimalist-style 3D space with few embellishments or construct a graphically richer fantasy world for the player to explore and interact in. The authoring mode (**Error! Reference source not found.** and Fig. 2 below) offers a palette of easy-to-use graphics tools designed to support rapid generation of stylized 3D environments, which can be enriched with stylized characters and props, as well as sound

[3] `http://www.kodugamelab.com/`

[4] `http://www.sploder.com/`

and animation. The range of game making elements to choose from is reasonably varied but, at the same time, is not so extensive as to overwhelm the game author with myriad variations and endless choice.

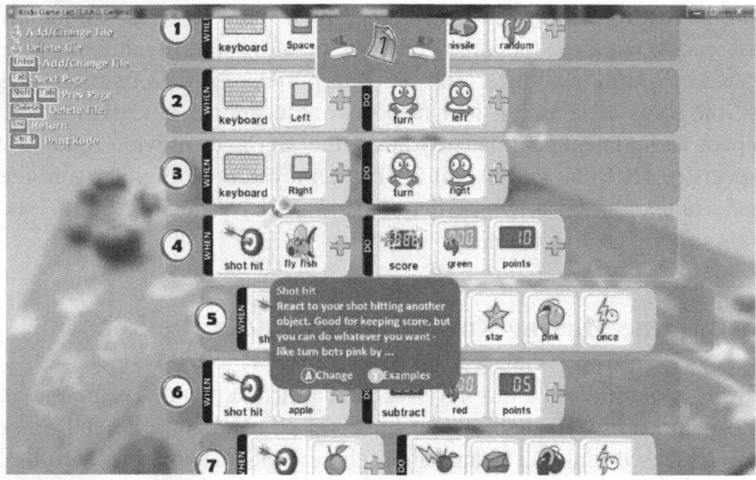

Fig. 1. Lines of WHEN/DO visual code generated by a Kodu author (with contextual help)

Programming with Kodu is based on constructing WHEN>DO conceptual couplets, each of which generates a condition>response instance in the Kodu world. These building blocks of visual code can be strung together in a sequence to form a complete program (**Error! Reference source not found.** above), which runs as an interactive 3D game in Kodu's play mode. You start programming by selecting an element that you've included in the 3D game-space and associating a WHEN>DO unit to it. To make the unit, you choose two "atoms" (primitives) from the graphic library of ready-to-use objects, behaviors and actions (Fig. 2 below). Coupling these atoms together forms a WHEN condition, e.g. <player-clicks mouse>, <Kodu sees-target>. This WHEN condition then needs to be paired with a corresponding DO response, made by coupling two more atoms, e.g. <missile-fires>, <Kodu moves - to target>. The resulting WHEN-DO molecule forms a logical condition-response instance: e.g. <when player clicks mouse, missile is fired>, <when Kodu sees target, Kodu moves to target>. The programming syntax also includes the possibility to attach a condition to the WHEN-DO molecule, e.g. <when missile hits target, Kodu jumps once>, <when missile hits target, score increases by 50>. These conditions allow you to generate the specific behaviors needed to create a functioning game. Much of the programming logic involved in Kodu revolves around the application of these conditions, which are selected from the same graphical object library containing all the other atomic game elements.

So making a game in Kodu entails stringing together a sequence of these molecules to form the complete code. This can be very basic, e.g., a single programmed mechanic triggered, say, by the player's mouse clicks, or a complex multi-level scenario with gameplay that involves multiform interaction.

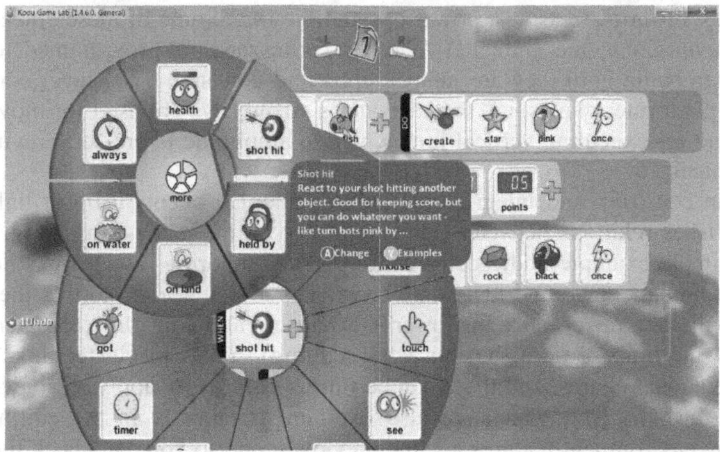

Fig. 2. Selecting elements from Kodu's visual programming library to generate lines of WHEN/DO visual code: contextual help displayed

Very experienced users may attempt to string code lines together in a single sweep, making a whole game "sight unseen" as it were; indeed Kodu allows cut-and-paste editing of whole lines of code to facilitate the process. However, most users will find themselves adding a molecule in Editing mode, then switching to Play mode to see how it runs, and then switching back again to tweak code or add a further molecule. Such progressive Edit-Play iterations allow you to check the result of coding on-the-fly and also to monitor how the game you're designing/making is unfolding.

2.2 Sploder: Creating Games through an Online Platform

Sploder in an online platform targeted largely at digital gaming enthusiasts. Along with a set of game making tools, it features social networking functions designed not just to promote game sharing but to support the formation and consolidation of a game-oriented community. Sploder offers five different game making formats: Retro Arcade, Platformer, Physics Puzzle, Classic Shooter and Algorithm Crew. These are largely similar but provide some variation in theme, style of game play, authoring palette and complexity of use. This overview concentrates on the Retro Arcade environment (Fig. 3 below), which is fairly representative of Sploder's game making approach. In Retro Arcade, you can generate tile-based, 2D scrolling platform games of the type that rose to popularity with the advent - and ubiquity - of the first generation game consoles. Like all the other Sploder formats, Retro Arcade allows you to build multi-level game structures, with levels made up of different stages or scenarios. The scenarios are built by selecting from the three ready-to-use game-world templates on offer: Forest, Cave and Tech World. These worlds can be personalized and extended using Retro Arcade's graphic drawing tools, which have been designed expressly to make game-world construction quick and simple. This allows the author's efforts to be channeled into the selection and integration of key game elements like characters, interactions and mechanics. Each game-world template is complimented by more or less the same palette of game-making elements and properties. In keeping with the retro arcade theme, the palette offers a set of player avatars, enemy sprites, hazards, collectables, rewards, treasures, power-ups and the like. Some of these embed default game behaviors, e.g. the animated "baddie" sprites are pre-programmed to engage the player in battle until they are jumped upon and defeated. The player controls are typical of platformer games, i.e. the keyboard's arrow keys are used for moving horizontally and for executing vertical jumps, whose amplitude is pre-set; gravity is also preset and is fixed.

You can construct and integrate particular gameplay events using a linking tool that establishes relations between elements placed in the game-world. Fig. 3 below shows a simple example under construction in the authoring mode: links have been set between a pair of ground-level on/off switches and a barrier, so that the player's passage will first raise and then lower the barrier, allowing the character to pass (obviously the links are only visible while editing). You can cluster links together to build relational chains, and these can be further refined by applying logical operators like And, Or, Not, which are also overlain graphically in the editing phase. The editing environment features a game preview mode so you can check the game's development on-the-fly before publishing it.

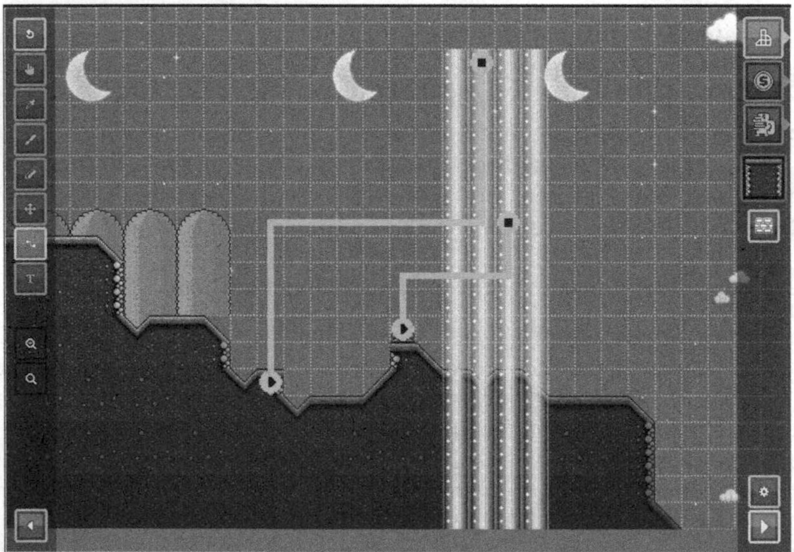

Fig. 3. Sploder Retro Arcade authoring mode: construction of mechanics using links

A distinguishing feature of the Sploder platform is its social networking capabilities. These support a community of game makers and players numbering over 25,000 members, allowing them to share games, graphics, ratings, reviews and comments.

2.3 The Two Game Authoring Environments: Comparison of Main Features

From the examination of the two game making environments presented above, we can draw the following picture (Table 1 below), which provides a synoptic view of how they differ in terms of specific HCI characteristics.

Table 1. Main differences between the two game authoring environments considered

Kodu	Sploder
Downloadable	Online, browser-based
Code-based game authoring	Object-based authoring
Visual programming language	Logical linking in situ for building game mechanics (drag & drop)
All behaviors user programmed	Some object behaviors preprogrammed
3D world	2D platform
User controls camera point-of-view (via mouse only)	Fixed point-of-view
Free movement of game characters in game-world (to be programmed)	Automatic side scrolling
Step-by-step construction of detailed 3D landscape, possibly from scratch	System-facilitated drag & drop construction of highly simplified landscape templates
Point & click navigation of palette menu	Drag-and-drop scrolling of palette menu
Single, open game type	Choice of five preset game types
Possible to structure game by level (<10)	Possible to structure game by level and sub-level
Create game levels from scratch	Create new (sub)levels using preset game-world templates
Switch between authoring and play modes	Switch between authoring and preview modes
Palette of game-world graphics, objects & behaviors	Palette of game-world graphics and objects (some preprogrammed)
Closed set of graphics	Editor for creating personalized graphics and textures
Soft, "toy-like" GUI style: soft tones, contours & shading; fluid/elastic motion; "cute" objects and sounds	Hard, high-contrast gaming-style GUI: pixel-style graphics, sharp motion and sounds, objects inspired by classic console games (nasties etc.)
Game-oriented behaviors: shooting, collecting etc.	Game-oriented behaviors: shooting, collecting, battles etc.
All animation to be programmed	Animated sprites (some preprogrammed)
Games can be saved to 2 external websites for sharing.	Integrated in native social networking platform with high activity levels
No advertising	Advertising present on website

Some of the above are determining factors for these environments' levels of accessibility, usability and ease of use, key areas of HCI. One obvious example that illustrates this point is the employment of drag-and-drop control in both environments, which poses a significant challenge for students with sensory disabilities of various kinds [13]. Without an alternative control method, these environments' accessibility is compromised and, as a result, game-making activities performed with them are less inclusive than they otherwise might be. Factors such as these not only impact on the ultimate effectiveness of game-making as an innovative learning method deployed in educational settings, they can have serious repercussions on practitioners' (and administrators') inclination to approach and adopt game-making in the first place. So, mindful of these considerations and their importance for MAGICAL's mission to support wider uptake of game-making for learning, we have carefully examined accessibility, usability and user experience issues.

2.4 The Two Game Authoring Environments: Accessibility and Usability

To begin with, the two environments were tested for *accessibility* according to the specifications laid out in Italy's law governing software applications destined for or used by public institutions[5] [14]; this law is largely based on Section 508 of the US Rehabilitation Act [15];. Neither application proved to be fully compliant with key accessibility requirements, as illustrated by the above-mentioned absence of any alternative where drag-and-drop control is required. Another obvious accessibility issue regards navigation of palette menus. In Kodu, the menus and items are quite clearly shown on large, graphically bold wheels that pop up automatically and are point-and-click controlled (Fig. 2). The nesting of menu levels is clearly apparent and readily comprehensible through transition from the large main menu wheel to the smaller sub-menu wheel at the point of juncture. While contrast and color differentiation between active/non-active menu items is far from optimal, the items themselves are clearly represented both textually and graphically. In addition, contextual help is presented automatically via high-contrast roll-over text (this function can be disabled). Sploder's palette menu is accessed via the three small icons in the top right-hand corner of the screen (Fig. 3). These open the next level, presented as a vertical toolbar that pops up to the right with much larger labeled icons (not shown in Fig. 3). Although this needs to be scrolled vertically there is no scroll bar, only a text hint displayed in a small help bar at the bottom of the editing window. If a toolbar item contains other sub-items to navigate to, this is indicated by tiny, almost imperceptible dots displayed under the icon. Navigating through these sub-items calls for a mouse-controlled point-click-hold-swipe motion left or right. Graphically, the distinction between active and non-active items is barely discernable. The browser's zoom function and the F11 keyboard shortcut for displaying the browser window full screen are often disabled; the authoring window does not rescale. The native zoom only zooms

---

5 Italian Law 4-2004, also called *Legge Stanca* `http://www.pubbliaccesso.gov.it/biblioteca/quaderni/rif_tecnici/Quaderno_4.pdf`

the game world canvas, not the editing dashboard. By contrast, Kodu can be displayed full screen and at various resolutions. To investigate the applications' *usability*, we refer to the eight Golden Rules proposed by [16]. Compliance with these varies considerably in the two environments, as shown in Table 2 below.

Table 2. Usability Golden Rules and application in two Game Making Environments

Golden Rule	Kodu	Sploder
1. **consistency** Employ uniform actions, terminology, color, layout, and text style. Limit exceptions like confirmation of delete command.	Generally compliant	Some noncompliance: color codes of control panel buttons confusing and sometimes inconsistent. Palette menu organized inconsistently.
2. universal usability Design for plasticity and facilitate content transformation. Cater for differences in expertise, age, (dis)abilities and technology.	Some compliance: display options for GUI buttons; advanced options available for experts; main keyboard/mouse controls displayed by default (text & icon); menu items clearly indicated, contextual help displayed; Windows keyboard controls & shortcuts; guided tutorials embedded in editable games and scaled in complexity	Very little compliance: some limited contextual help for toolset and dashboard controls
3. informative feedback Provide system feedback for all user actions - modest response for frequent / minor actions, more substantial for infrequent / major actions. Visual presentation of objects of interest	See note below	See note below
4. yielding closure group action sequences into beginning, middle, and end. Give accomplishment feedback at completion of a roup	See note below	See note below
5. (user) errors Where possible block or filter inappropriate user actions or input; these should leave system state unaltered (no response). Provide simple, constructive, specific recovery instructions.	Generally compliant: invalid editing selections & actions trigger no system state change. Undo/redo function available for recovery after user errors.	Generally compliant: invalid editing selections & actions trigger no system state change.

Table 2. (*continued*)

Golden Rule	Kodu	Sploder
6. easy action reversal fosters sense of user control and encourages exploration of unfamiliar options	Compliant: Undo/Redo button for back and forward tracking. Access to complete change history. Manual Save/Save- As for versioning. Auto Save prompt when closing editing sessions. Sessions automatically assigned a default version number to foster versioning.	Editor has a toggling eraser to remove objects that are unwanted but no Undo function. Each edit is automatically saved. No versioning function.
7. internal locus of control controllable, responsive interface requiring little menial effort or repetition. No obstacles to desired result.	Compliant: visual programming designed with features to reduce effort and repetition.	Compliant: production of game landscape and textures specifically designed to reduce effort and repetition.
8. short term memory load no memorization required between screens. Allow sufficient training time.	Generally compliant: step-by-step tutorials provided in the form of real, editable games	Non compliant: no tutorials or online guide.

With regard to Shneiderman's Golden Rule 3 on feedback and Rule 4 on closure, authoring environments present some specificities, especially those devoted to the production of more complex, interactive multimedia artefacts such as games. Firstly, game authoring is generally performed iteratively in a sequence of user-driven alternations between design/editing and preview/run phases. In a sense, core "system feedback" and closure can only come when the author triggers a preview/run to check the outcome of executed editing steps. So feedback and closure loops are actually very long and loose, and their amplitude and frequency is user governed (although it could be argued that allowing multiple-level game structuring, as Sploder does, encourages tighter looping to some degree). Furthermore, while the WYSIWYG principle of editing does apply to some (static) graphic elements included in the editing space, it cannot apply to the "programmed" interactions that are the hallmark of digital games.

Following the considerations in [17] related to the fact that "*users approach new software with diverse skills and multiple intelligence*", we acknowledge that the considerations reported above need to be integrated with data from user experience.. Findings on these aspects are expected to emerge from the conclusive stages of the MAGICAL project.

3 Conclusions and Further Work

In this paper we have examined some different aspects of HCI in game authoring environments that emerge from an investigation of two different game authoring environments currently being used with and by young students. The general objective has been to provide useful indications to support the implementation of game making for learning, which is steadily gaining support in formal education, especially for transversal skills development. The examination was carried out in the framework of MAGICAL, an EU project on game making that incorporates teacher training actions as well as school experiments. One of the main results expected of MAGICAL is the production of MAGOS, an authoring environment specifically intended for collaborative game making [18]. The design and development of MAGOS is grounded on a thorough analysis of existing authoring environments, some aspects of which are reported in this paper.

Issues of Human Computer Interaction are of particular significance in this sector, as indeed they are in Games-Based Learning and Technology Enhanced Learning, the wider fields to which digital game making belongs. Here, it is imperative that HCI poses no hindrances to the cognitive processes underpinning learning, but rather supports these in the global effort to achieve efficacy. It is with these concerns in mind that the work reported here was initiated and directed towards fulfilling two immediate aims: informing the game-making experiments performed in schools in MAGICAL's partner countries (Italy, Finland, Belgium and UK); and providing input for the development of the MAGOS environment. In both these areas valuable user-experience data is currently being generating that will serve to validate and enhance the initial findings reported in the paper. The authors intend to integrate that data so as to form a clearer, more detailed picture of HCI within the design and making of digital games for learning. The ultimate aim is to generate HCI-related indications for enhancing interface capabilities and affordances of authoring environments, and thus contribute to the appeal, efficacy and, eventually, wider uptake of game making as an educational practice.

References

1. Lizzy, B., All, A., Ilse, M., Dana, S., Van Looy, J., An, J., Koen, W., et al.: State of Play of Digital Games for Empowerment and Inclusion: a Review of the Literature and Empirical Cases. Publications Office of the European Union, Spain (2012)
2. Frossard, F., Barajas, M., Trifonova, A.: A Learner-Centred Game-Design Approach: Impacts on Teachers' Creativity. Digital Education Review (21), 13–22 (2012)
3. Lytras, M.D., Sicilia, M.A.: The Knowledge Society: a manifesto for knowledge and learning. International Journal of Knowledge and Learning 1(1/2), 1–11 (2005)
4. de Freitas, S., Neumann, T.: The use of 'exploratory learning' for supporting immersive learning in virtual environments. Computers & Education 52(2), 343–352 (2009)
5. de Freitas, S.: *Serious virtual worlds*. A scoping guide. JISC e-Learning Programme, The Joint Information Systems Committee (JISC), UK (2008)

6. Arnab, S., Berta, R., Earp, J., de Freitas, S., Popescu, M., Romero, M., Usart, M.: Framing the Adoption of Serious Games in Formal Education. Electronic Journal of e-Learning 10(2), 159–171 (2012)
7. Luckin, R., Bligh, B., Manches, A., Ainsworth, S., Crook, C., Noss, R.: Decoding Learning: The Proof, Promise & Potential of Digital Education. NESTA, London (2013)
8. de Freitas, S., Ott, M., Popescu, M.M., Stanescu, I.: Game-Enhanced- Learning: Preliminary Thoughts on curriculum integration. In: New Pedagogical Approaches in Game Enhanced Learning: Curriculum Integration. IGI Global (2013)
9. Dagnino, F., Earp, J., Ott, M.: Investigating the "Magical" effects of game building on the development of 21st Century Skills. In: ICERI 2012 Proceedings, pp. 5778–5785 (2012)
10. Bottino, R.M., Earp, J., Ott, M.: MAGICAL: Collaborative Game Building as a Means to Foster Reasoning Abilities and Creativity. In: 2012 IEEE 12th International Conference on Advanced Learning Technologies, pp. 744–745. IEEE (2012)
11. Holzinger, A.: Usability engineering methods for software developers. Communications of the ACM 48(1), 71–74 (2005)
12. Davis, F.D.: Perceived usefulness, perceived ease of use, and user acceptance of information technology. MIS Quarterly, 319–340 (1989)
13. Benigno, V., Bocconi, S., Ott, M.: Inclusive education: helping teachers to choose ICT resources and to use them effectively. eLearning Papers (6), 4 (2007)
14. CNIPA, Italian Law 4/2004 Provisions to support the access to Information Technologies for the disabled (2004), http://www.pubbliaccesso.gov.it/normative/law_20040109_n4.htm (retrieved February 1, 2014)
15. USA Access Board, Section 508 of the US Rehabilitation Act (2011), http://www.section508.gov (retrieved February 1, 2014)
16. Shneiderman, B., Plaisant, C.: Designing the User Interface: Strategies for Effective Human-Computer Interaction, 5th edn., 606 pages. Addison-Wesley Publ. Co., Reading (2010), http://www.pearsonhighered.com/dtui5einfo/
17. Shneiderman, B.: Universal usability. Communications of the ACM 43(5), 84–91 (2000)
18. Earp, J., Ott, M., Romero, M., Usart, M.: Learning through playing for or against each other? Promoting collaborative learning in digital game based learning. In: Proceedings of the ECIS 2012. AIS Electronic Library, Paper 93 (2012), http://aisel.aisnet.org/ecis2012/03

Videogaming Interaction for Mental Model Construction in Learners Who Are Blind

Matías Espinoza[1], Jaime Sánchez[1], and Márcia de Borba Campos[2]

[1] Department of Computer Science and Center for Advanced Research in Education (CARE), University of Chile, Santiago, Chile
{maespino,jsanchez}@dcc.uchile.cl

[2] Faculty of Informatics – FACIN, Pontifical Catholic University of Rio Grande do Sul – PUCRS, Brazil
marcia.campos@pucrs.br

Abstract. The purpose of this work is to present the design, development and evaluation of a videogame that allows users who are blind to gradually build up a mental model based on references between different points on a Cartesian plane, in a way that is both didactic and entertaining. Two prototypes were iteratively created, and were subjected to usability evaluations by the end users, who used the videogame in the context of a set of defined tasks. This allowed researchers to adjust, improve and validate various aspects of the interfaces that had been designed and implemented. In addition, the cognitive impact of the game on blind learners was evaluated, based on the use of the final version of the videogame, and leading to revealing results regarding the proposed objectives.

Keywords: People who are blind, Videogame, Reference system, Mental model, Audio and haptic based interfaces, Wiimote.

1 Introduction

For people who are blind, the adoption of a mental model that allows them to orient themselves through the use of reference points does not occur naturally as it does with sighted people. This is because the latter have associated and familiarized themselves visually with the environment since the day they were born. In this way, it is interesting to research the mechanisms that are able to foment the construction of a mental model in people who are blind, through a structure of reference points that allows them to develop an improved approach to problems, such as orientation and mobility when navigating [8][14][15][16], or interpreting graphics and relationships between points on a Cartesian plane [1][5].

One method for the reproduction of haptic and audio trajectories in order to teach and transfer information on shapes, gestures and trajectories to people who are blind (and those with visually impairment) has been reviewed [3]. The combination of audio and haptic-based information significantly improved the performance of blind and visually impaired users, for tasks based on recreating shapes [3].

C. Stephanidis and M. Antona (Eds.): UAHCI/HCII 2014, Part II, LNCS 8514, pp. 525–536, 2014.

Sonic Grid is a system of audio representation in two-dimensional space that provides visually impaired users with a spatial context while navigating graphic user interfaces (GUIs) [6]. A multimodal, interactive system based on audio, haptics and visualization was designed, in order for users to create, edit and explore graphic structures through direct manipulation operations [2]. The MaskGen system was developed in order to transfer the illustrations from schoolbooks into tactile graphics in an interactive manner [11]. The results showed that the tactile graphics allowed visually impaired users to explore the illustrations and to answer questions regarding their content [11].

The various problems for visually impaired users regarding different kinds of graphics supported by Excel (lines, bars, circles, scatter plots) were studied [1]. In order to approach this problem, a system was proposed with the objective of supporting a multimodal presentation of two-dimensional graphics through haptic (using the Novint Falcon device) and audio (both spoken and iconic) feedback [1].

A tangible interface called Tangible Graph Builder was designed, which allows visually impaired users to access the information displayed in graphs [10]. Through the use of this tool, visually impaired users were able to adequately create graphs and perform navigation-based tasks [10].

The use of audio feedback techniques in order to recognize shapes and gestures based on spatial sound relations was reviewed [13]. The interaction is based on the use of common pointers such as the mouse, pen or finger on touch screens. When navigating a curve, the intensity of the sound reproduced is inversely proportional to the distance between the pointer controlled by the user and the curve itself [13].

GraVVITAS is an audio and haptic-based tool that serves to provide accessibility to graphs, allowing users who are blind to understand a series of graphs, tables and planes that model a particular place [5]. The transfer of information from statistical graphs to visually impaired people was also studied [7]. TeslaTouch is a technology that provides tactile sensation when moving one's fingers over a touch screen surface, through which the device represents the information in 2D [17]. TeslaTouch helps to show people with visual impairment certain kinds of complex information, such as mathematical expressions, illustrations, diagrams and maps [17].

A multimodal system of interactive cubes for the orientation of objects that can be manipulated by people with visual impairment was developed [9]. Through this system, users can create, modify and interact naturally with diagrams and graphs on a Cartesian plane, using a multi-touch screen [9].

Finally, the use of audio graphics for blind high school learners was also studied [4]. The proposal considers audio graphics to be an acceptable alternative to visual and tactile graphics, in terms of curriculum compatibility, learner performance and teacher satisfaction [4].

In this context, the purpose of this work is to present the design, development and evaluation of a videogame that allows users who are blind to gradually build up a mental model based on references between different points on a Cartesian plane, in a way that is both didactic and entertaining. The research considered the use of a Wiimote as an entry device in order to record the user's interactions. In addition, a cognitive analysis was made of the adoption of this structure of coordinates as a theoretical basis for moving through real environments.

2 Videogame

The Tower Defense game metaphor was adopted, as this implicitly allows learners to be able to interpret and associate points on a Cartesian plane. The videogame was designed, redesigned and adapted in order to fulfill the requirements proposed for the project. To achieve this, the trajectories of the game's enemy units were controlled, in order for the user to gradually generate a mental model of their paths, directionalities, and the association of their coordinates in order to attack them.

The videogame is presented on a limited two-dimensional plane, in which the unit values for the X and Y-axes are in the range of [-10, 10]. In this way, it is important to point out that the solution can be scaled to more extensive planes. The different trajectories of enemy movement determine the various levels that the game offers. These trajectories are determined by points on the Cartesian plane. The enemies start off at point (0,0), which is referred to as the starting point, and they eventually arrive at an ending point. In order to pass a level, the player must arrive to the ending point of the enemy's trajectory first, and install the tower that will be used to attack them.

In order to develop the videogame, C# language was utilized, as well as the videogame development framework Microsoft XNA Framework 4.0. This was used together with the Visual Studio 2010 Ultimate and Microsoft XNA Game Studio 4.0 tools.

2.1 Design

The videogame contains the following main elements: map, player pointer, enemies, towers and levels. The videogame map is displayed on a Cartesian plane made up of whole numbers, along which the enemies travel. The player moves and can locate the towers that will attack the enemies. This map identifies the points on the Cartesian plane that the player can navigate and those that he cannot, in addition to the points where the towers are located. The map also identifies the start and end points of the enemies' trajectories. In addition, the characteristics named on the map vary according to the different levels of the game. The map uses a graphic representation in order to identify the areas that can be navigated and those that cannot.

The enemies, the player pointer and the towers all have specific positions on the Cartesian plane, and are represented graphically and also have corresponding sound effects in order to provide feedback regarding their location and actions. The enemies also have an associated direction and speed regarding their movement through the map, as well as an energy value (which must be higher than zero for them to be alive). On the other hand, the towers have a damage value (corresponding to the diminished value of the enemies' energy when they are shot), a reach value (which is the maximum distance to which a tower can attack the enemies), and shot direction towards the closest enemy.

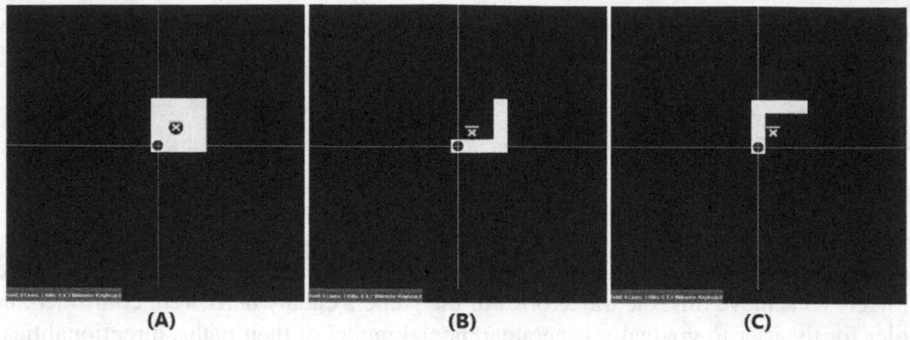

Fig. 1. Modes of navigation (A) Free Navigation, (B) X Axis Priority Navigation, (C) Y Axis Priority Navigation

The levels of the game are determined based on the points on the Cartesian plane, excluding the (0, 0) point. Based on these points, various significant aspects of the level are determined, such as: the characteristics of the map, the points of the enemies' trajectories, the points that can be navigated and those that cannot be navigated by the player, and the points where the player can install towers. This point (where the player installs the tower) determines the end point of the enemies' trajectory, as well as the end point for the player's navigation. The end point is defined as (Xf, Yf). It is important to point out that both the enemies and the player begin their navigation at the starting point (0, 0). In addition, a further characteristic was added, establishing a mode of navigation for the player through the map, restricting his or her navigation through space. The following options are available to the player (Figure 1):

- Free Navigation. Here the player can move freely through the area determined by (0, 0) and (Xf, Yf).
- X Axis Priority Navigation. The player can move down a restricted path. Initially, the player can navigate the path determined by the (0, 0) and (Xf, 0) points. Later, the navigation can continue down the path determined by the (Xf, 0) and (Xf, Yf) points.
- Y Axis Priority Navigation. The player can move down a restricted path. Initially, the player can navigate the path determined by the (0, 0) and (Yf, 0) points. Later, the navigation can continue down the path determined by the (Yf, 0) and (Xf, Yf) points.

An additional characteristic was added, which can be configured in both the X and Y Axis Priority Navigation modes. This characteristic consists of blocking the return to the previous point, once the player has advanced. This makes the path uni-directional.

2.2 Interfaces

In order to play, the learner uses a Wiimote control, which allows him to execute actions such as: move about, obtain clues, and install towers within the game. The videogame includes 3 interfaces: (i) an audio interface, which provides all of the information related to carrying out actions and the status of the game; (ii) a haptic interface, which provides feedback associated with movements that are blocked within the game through the vibration of the Wiimote; and (iii) a graphic interface, which is presented in high contrast (black and white) on the screen, so that users with low levels of vision can visualize the map and the various elements of the game.

The videogame provides the user with feedback related to the various actions that are taken as a result of the interaction. This feedback is provided through audio cues that can be either spoken, stereo iconic sound, or spatialized iconic sounds. Haptic feedback is also provided through the vibration of the Wiimote. In sum, feedback related to the following events in the videogame was incorporated:

- When the player moves from cell to cell along a navigable path (stereo iconic sound).
- When the videogame blocks a player's movement towards a non-navigable area (stereo iconic sound and Wiimote vibration).
- When the player installs a tower (stereo iconic sound).
- When the towers shoot at the enemies (spatial iconic sound).
- When the enemies move (spatial iconic sound).
- When the videogame automatically provides instructions or relevant information, or when the player requests information (sound with spoken texts).

3 Usability Evaluation

Two prototypes (initial and final prototype) were iteratively created, and were subjected to usability evaluations by the end users, who used the videogame in the context of a set of defined tasks. The objective of the usability evaluation was to adjust, improve and validate the interfaces proposed for the videogame. The methodology utilized is presented in the following.

3.1 Sample

The sample of end users consisted of 7 learners who are blind (3 female and 4 male) between 9 and 13 years of age, from the Hellen Keller School in Santiago, Chile. The sample was divided up into two groups, in which group 1 consisted of an 11-year-old girl and a 9-year-old boy, and group 2 included two girls and three boys, between 9 and 13 years of age. Having had prior experience using similar products was not a prerequisite to make up part of the sample.

The learners included in the sample correspond to videogame end users. For this reason their participation in the usability evaluation represents a direct contribution for improving the design of the application, further adjusting its needs, and validating the videogame interfaces.

3.2 Instruments

An adaptation of the end-user and facilitator questionnaire for software usability [12] was used. The original questionnaire consisted of 18 statements that the user has to evaluate on a scale between 1 and 10, in which 1 is 'a little' and 10 is 'a lot'. The adaptations were made by changing the word "software" to "videogame" in the statements included in the questionnaire. The statements were classified into the following dimensions, according to the user's perception regarding the interface: "Satisfaction", "Learning", "Control and Use", and "Sounds". In addition, the questionnaire included a section with 5 open questions (just as in the original questionnaire), and as in the case of the sentences, the only change was to include the word 'videogame' instead of the word 'software'. However, 5 additional questions were added. The first added question was: "Did you like the joystick? Why or why not?". This question sought to obtain the level of the user's satisfaction with the use of the Wiimote. The following 4 added questions were: "Did you understand the videogame's instructions?", "Did the videogame help you to move around?", "How did you use the instructions in order to move around?", and "Did the joystick's vibration help you to move around?". These questions aimed to measure the learner's perception and satisfaction regarding the mechanisms of interaction, and the transfer of information needed to be able to play the game.

3.3 Tasks

Two sets of tasks were established. The first set of tasks consisted of three different levels [(5, 5), (5, 6), and (5, -6)], all of which included the ability to return to the previous cell, and with an X-axis Priority over the Y-axis. This is a minimal set of tasks that allowed researchers to observe the learner's behavior when playing the videogame. The second set of tasks consisted of 3 sets with 4 levels: (5, 4), (5, -4), (-5, 4), and (-5, -4). The first subset of tasks included navigation without being able to go backwards, and with priority of the X-axis over the Y-axis. The second subset included navigation without being able to go backwards, and with priority given to the Y-axis over the X-axis. The third subset included free navigation.

3.4 Procedure

First, researchers worked individually with each learner in Group 1 of the sample, explaining the basic premise of the game. The various devices that were to be utilized were presented: headphones, the Wiimote control and the Nunchuk. The actions that can be taken in the game were summarized, as well as the buttons that can be used on the Wiimote control. It is worth highlighting that the learners were asked to explore the entry interface, and not every single button was explained to them. They were instructed to discover the various actions that they could take with the buttons themselves. The first set of tasks was configured on the initial videogame prototype, and the players began to play the videogame. Once the tasks had been completed, the end user usability questionnaire was applied.

During a second stage, researchers worked individually with all of the learners from group 2 of the sample. First, the game was explained to them. The devices that would be used were also presented: headphones and the Wiimote control. The various actions that could be taken in the game were explained, but the corresponding buttons were not explained. The second set of tasks was configured sequentially for the final prototype of the game. In this way, the learners were able to start up and play the videogame. Once the tasks had been completed, the end user questionnaire was applied.

3.5 Results

In quantitative terms, increments between the initial prototype and the final prototype were observed regarding the means of all of the dimensions of the end user evaluation: Satisfaction (Initial prototype mean = 7.42; Final prototype mean = 9.77), Learning (Initial prototype mean = 5.00; Final prototype mean = 6.90), Control and Use (Initial prototype mean = 4.38; Final prototype mean = 9.00), and Sounds (Initial prototype mean = 5.50; Final prototype mean = 8.67).

Researchers went into more depth regarding the statistical significance of the differences observed between the two means. First, a T-test for independent samples was run with the values obtained for the different dimensions, based on the users' evaluations of the second prototype and the final prototype. From this test, it was observed that the increase in the mean scores for the "Sounds" dimension ($t = -2.942$, $p < 0.05$) was statistically significant. The increases in the means for the other dimensions were not observed to be statistically significant.

Qualitatively, the users' appreciation improved notoriously for the final prototype. The learners expressed a clear level of acceptance regarding how fun the game is, its elements, the use of the controls, and the mechanisms for providing information. All of these were aspects that were criticized for the initial prototype, and were then improved and validated for the final prototype. One aspect worth pointing out regarding the results obtained from the open-ended questions is the unanimous acceptance of the Wiimote control. All of the users liked this control, as it is easy to use and helped them to move around in the game.

4 Cognitive Impact Evaluation

Once the final videogame prototype had been created, following the redesigns based on the results of the previous usability evaluations, a cognitive impact evaluation of the videogame was performed. The methodology utilized and the results obtained from this process are described below.

4.1 Sample

The sample was made up of 4 visually impaired learners from the Hellen Keller School of Ñuñoa, in Santiago de Chile (2 boys and 2 girls), between 9 and 13 years of age. The learners from this sample had previously participated in the final prototype usability evaluation.

Fig. 2. Learners playing the game

4.2 Instruments

The instrument of evaluation was integrated as part of the videogame, through the log files that recorded the actions performed by the users. In processing the videogame log files for each level that the player had completed, records were obtained regarding the number of steps taken (*Ne*), and the number of optimal steps needed to pass the level (*No*). From these records, the efficiency indicator (*E*) was defined as:

$$E = No / Ne$$

With this indicator, a quantitative mean for the progressive construction of the learners' mental maps was obtained. The paths in the game lead to a final destination, and the learner was free to choose the best strategy for reaching that destination. These decisions are reflected in the efficiency indicator.

4.3 Tasks

Twenty levels were considered for the tasks: (3, 3), (3, -3), (-3, 3), (-3, -3), (4, 4), (4, -4), (-4, 4), (-4, -4), (5, 3), (5, -3), (-5, 3), (-5, -3), (5, 4), (5, -4), (-5, 4), (-5, -4), (5, 5), (5, -5), (-5, 5), y (-5, -5). Afterwards, 3 sets of tasks were determined. First, for the pretest tasks, the free navigation modality was configured for all the levels considered. Following the development tasks, the X-Axis Priority navigation mode without being able to go backwards was configured for all of the levels considered. Finally, for the post-test tasks, the free navigation mode was configured for all of the levels considered.

4.4 Procedure

Researchers worked individually with all of the learners in the sample. The main premise of the game was explained, and they were given instructions on how to use the devices for interacting with the game (headphones and Wiimote). The actions available within the game and the associated buttons were also explained. The sets of tasks for the videogame were configured sequentially, as each learner completed the tasks required by the videogame.

Each learner completed each of the 3 sets of tasks in successive work sessions. Each of these sessions lasted for approximately 15 minutes. For each set of tasks, the learner played individually with the videogame, until he was able to pass the levels involved in each game. Once the sets of tasks had been completed by all of the users, the records obtained in the log files were analyzed.

4.5 Results

The total efficiency was determined for each user, considering the total numbers of steps taken. The total efficiency indicator increased between the pretest and post-test for all learners in the sample (pretest mean = 75.74%, post-test mean = 85.75%). In order to further research these results, a T test for related samples was performed. The results showed that the difference in the total efficiency means (meaning the increase in the total efficiency mean between the pretest and the post-test) was statistically significant ($t = -3.198$, $p < 0.05$).

5 Discussion

As a result of this study a videogame was designed and developed for visually impaired learners, allowing them to learn as well as interpret points on a two-dimensional plane, and to apply their knowledge directly within a system of references. The final videogame operates within a limited 2D plane, with X and Y values ranging in whole numbers between [-10, 10]. In this way, it is important to point out that the solution can be scaled up to more extensive planes.

The iterative cycle of design, implementation and usability evaluation led to the generation of the final videogame prototype, for which all of the designed and implemented characteristics were validated by the end users. The final prototype was clearly well-accepted by the end users, which is reflected in the quantitative data corresponding to the "Satisfaction", "Control and Use" and "Sounds" dimensions, as well as from the answers to the open-ended questions, which were generally very positive.

One interesting result obtained regarding usability pertains to the modest level of satisfaction obtained for the "Learning" dimension, which can be interpreted as the user not perceiving that he or she is actually learning anything. This result is complemented by the opinions of the learners that they had fun playing the videogame. Taken together, these two aspects are quite positive when it comes to motivating the learners to work with the game.

Regarding the cognitive impact evaluation, the increase in the total efficiency of blind learners when performing the cognitive tasks, points to the fact that the videogame allows users to gradually construct a mental map. This occurs through the interpretation and use of the information that the game provides, which is used at first to locate oneself on the Cartesian plane, after which users were able to utilize their own strategies to complete the levels by reaching the destination points. Although the number of users in the sample was low, and the extension of the two-dimensional planes was limited, the results showed that using the established working modality, positive changes were produced regarding the desired skills.

6 Conclusions

The purpose of this work was to present the design, development and evaluation of a videogame that allows users who are blind to gradually build up a mental model based on references between different points on a Cartesian plane, in a way that is both didactic and entertaining. The objective of the research was fulfilled. A tool was designed and developed for blind users, allowing them to gradually construct a mental reference model based on an association between points on a two-dimensional plane. The videogame implicitly integrated the interpretation of points on a Cartesian plane. In addition, as part of the tasks, learners applied their knowledge towards orientation within the integrated system of references built into the videogame.

The usability evaluations allowed researchers to detect problems and generate new requirements for redesigning the videogame. This allowed researchers to adjust and improve the interfaces in the following prototype, in addition to validating aspects of the interfaces that had been designed and implemented. All of these changes were made by taking the perspective of the end user into account.

Regarding the cognitive impact evaluation, the desired skills to be developed by the learners were those related to the interpretation of points on a Cartesian plane, and to knowledge applied within the system of references established by the videogame.

For future work, it is proposed to work with a larger sample and to apply further and more complete cognitive impact evaluations. It is also proposed to increase the scope of the tasks that users perform, and to explore other ways of evaluating cognition. Such measurements could be through the application of the knowledge gained in a real life context, or through their application to daily activities performed by the blind users.

Acknowledgments. This report was funded by the Chilean National Fund of Science and Technology, Fondecyt #1120330, and Project CIE-05 Program Center Education PBCT-Conicyt. It was also supported by the Program STIC-AmSud-CAPES/CONICYT/MAEE, Project KIGB-Knowing and Interacting while Gaming for the Blind, 2014.

References

1. Abu Doush, I., Pontelli, E., Son, T., Simon, D., Ma, O.: Multimodal Presentation of Two-Dimensional Charts: An Investigation Using Open Office XML and Microsoft Excel. ACM Trans. Access. Comput. 3(2), Article 8, 50 pages (2010)
2. Bernareggi, C., Comaschi, C., Marcante, A., Mussio, P., Provenza, L., Vanzi, S.: A multi-modal interactive system to create and explore graph structures. In: CHI 2008 Extended Abstracts on Human Factors in Computing Systems (CHI EA 2008), pp. 2697–2702. ACM, New York (2008)
3. Crossan, A., Brewster, S.: Multimodal Trajectory Playback for Teaching Shape Information and Trajectories to Visually Impaired Computer Users. ACM Trans. Access. Comput. 1(2), Article 12, 34 pages (2008)
4. Davison, B.: Evaluating auditory graphs with blind students in a classroom. SIGACCESS Access. Comput. 102, 4–7 (2012)
5. Goncu, C., Marriott, K.: GraVVITAS: Generic multi-touch presentation of accessible graphics. In: Campos, P., Graham, N., Jorge, J., Nunes, N., Palanque, P., Winckler, M. (eds.) INTERACT 2011, Part I. LNCS, vol. 6946, pp. 30–48. Springer, Heidelberg (2011)
6. Jagdish, D., Sawhney, R., Gupta, M., Nangia, S.: Sonic Grid: an auditory interface for the visually impaired to navigate GUI-based environments. In: Proceedings of the 13th International Conference on Intelligent User Interfaces (IUI 2008), pp. 337–340. ACM, New York (2008)
7. Kim, D., Lim, Y.: Handscope: enabling blind people to experience statistical graphics on websites through haptics. In: Proceedings of the 2011 Annual Conference on Human Factors in Computing Systems (CHI 2011), pp. 2039–2042. ACM, New York (2011)
8. Lahav, O., Mioduser, D.: Haptic-feedback support for cognitive mapping of unknown spaces by people who are blind. International Journal Human-Computer Studies 66(1), 23–35 (2008)
9. Manshad, M., Pontelli, E., Manshad, S.: MICOO (multimodal interactive cubes for object orientation): a tangible user interface for the blind and visually impaired. In: Proc. of the 13th International ACM SIGACCESS Conference on Computers and Accessibility (ASSETS 2011), pp. 261–262. ACM, New York (2011)
10. McGookin, D., Robertson, E., Brewster, S.: Clutching at straws: using tangible interaction to provide non-visual access to graphs. In: Proc. of the 28th International Conference on Human Factors in Computing Systems (CHI 2010), pp. 1715–1724. ACM, New York (2010)
11. Petit, G., Dufresne, A., Levesque, V., Hayward, V., Trudeau, N.: Refreshable tactile graphics applied to schoolbook illustrations for students with visual impairment. In: Proc. of the 10th International ACM SIGACCESS Conference on Computers and Accessibility (Assets 2008), pp. 89–96. ACM, New York (2008)
12. Sánchez, J.: End-user and facilitator questionnaire for Software Usability. Usability evaluation test. University of Chile, Santiago, Chile (2003)
13. Sanchez, J.: Recognizing shapes and gestures using sound as feedback. In: Proceedings of the 28th of the International Conference Extended Abstracts on Human Factors in Computing Systems (CHI EA 2010), pp. 3063–3068. ACM, New York (2010)
14. Sánchez, J.: Development of navigation skills through audio haptic videogaming in learners who are blind. In: Proc. 4th Intl. Conf. on Software Development for Enhancing Accessibility and Fighting Info-Exclusion (DSAI 2012). Procedia Computer Science, vol. 14, pp. 102–110 (2012)

15. Sánchez, J., Mascaró, J.: Audiopolis, navigation through a virtual city using audio and haptic interfaces for people who are blind. In: Stephanidis, C. (ed.) Universal Access in HCI, Part II, HCII 2011. LNCS, vol. 6766, pp. 362–371. Springer, Heidelberg (2011)
16. Sánchez, J., Espinoza, M., Garrido, J.: Videogaming for wayfinding skills in children who are blind. In: Sharkey, P.M., Klinger, E. (eds.) Proc. 9th Intl Conf. on Disability, Virtual Reality and Assoc. Technologies, Laval, France, September 10-12, pp. 131–140 (2012)
17. Xu, C., Israr, A., Poupyrev, I., Bau, O., Harrison, C.: Tactile display for the visually impaired using TeslaTouch. In: Proc. of the 2011 Annual Conference Extended Abstracts on Human Factors in Computing Systems (CHI EA 2011), pp. 317–322. ACM, New York (2011)

A Data-Driven Entity-Component Approach to Develop Universally Accessible Games

Franco Eusébio Garcia and Vânia Paula de Almeida Neris

Federal University of Sao Carlos (UFSCar), Sao Carlos, Brazil
{franco.garcia,vania}@dc.ufscar.br

Abstract. Design and implementing accessible games can be challenging, particularly when the designers wish to address different interaction capabilities. Universally-Accessible Games (UA-Games), for instance, follow the principles of the Design for All, aiming to enable the broadest audience as possible to play. Although there are papers regarding the design of UA-Games, the implementation can still be challenging. This paper presents a flexible and extensible approach to implement an UA-Game. The approach relies in a data-driven and component based architecture to allow game entities to be created, managed and customized during run-time. Doing so, it is possible to change the behavior and presentation of the game whilst it is running, allowing the game to adapt itself to better address the interaction needs of the user. Furthermore, being data-driven, it is possible to create and customize user profiles to address specific interaction requirements.

Keywords: Universal Design, Game Accessibility, Universally-Accessible Game, Game Design, Game Development.

1 Introduction

Digital games importance increases every day, with their usage ranging from leisure and entertainment to learning and even healthcare. Gaming is becoming more social – users are sharing experiences, playing together and even creating new content for their favorite games. However, despite the growing importance, many people are still unable to play – for instance, due to a disability.

Playing a game requires many different users' sensory, cognitive and motor abilities [1–4]. Most of the required abilities to play are common to average users – users which belong to the standard deviation of a normal distribution of users [5, 6]. If, however, a user lacks a required ability, playing the game becomes harder or even impossible. This is often the case for users with disabilities: if a user cannot receive the game's stimuli or is unable to determine or provide a response, his/her overall playing experience is hindered.

There are different approaches to improve game accessibility. Some approaches try to address specific interaction requirements for a particular user group or disability – such as audio games for visually impaired users [4]. Other approaches aim to be accessible to as many users as possible. Universally-Accessible Games (UA-Games)

C. Stephanidis and M. Antona (Eds.): UAHCI/HCII 2014, Part II, LNCS 8514, pp. 537–548, 2014.

[1, 7] are an example of the latter: UA-Games follow the principles of the Design for All [8], aiming to enable as many users as possible, regardless of their (dis)abilities, to play.

In order to support the range of requirements and users abilities, accessible games must be flexible from its design to its implementation. For UA-Games, some of the design strategies include abstract design, polymorphic physical specialization and user profiles [1]. These strategies allow the designers to tailor the game interactions in order to address the interaction abilities and capabilities of a group of users. This way, it is possible to enable – or, at least, to improve – the game experience for users encompassed by the available interaction profiles.

As the tailored interactions may range from audio subtitles to completely different game presentations, the game architecture should be flexible enough from the start. Otherwise, implementing a new profile might require changes to core modules, potentially increasing the required development efforts and costs. It is, therefore, necessary to decouple all the logic (such as the game's rules and mechanics) from the presentation of the game without compromising the ease of creating new tailored interactions.

This paper presents a flexible and extensible approach to implement accessible games – in special, focused in the tailoring of UA-Games. It relies in an entity-component and data-driven architecture to allow the customization of game entities during run-time. This allows the game to adapt itself to better address the interaction needs of the user and, being data-driven, eases the creation and improvements of user profiles.

This paper is organized as follows: Section 2 briefly discusses game accessibility strategies and design. Section 3 discusses limitations of traditional game entities definition in games. Section 4 presents a more flexible approach to defining games entities and its application to UA-Games. Section 5 discusses how to enhance the approach using a data-driven architecture and how to apply it to UA-Games profiles. Section 6 discusses some limitations of the approach. Finally, Section 7 presents the conclusions and possibilities of future work.

2 Game Accessibility Overview

In 2004, the International Game Developers Association (IDGA) published the white-paper "Accessibility in Games: Motivation and Approaches" [2]. More recently, Yuan *et al.* [4], the "AbleGames Foundation" [9] and Barrie *et al.* [10] further discussed the theme. These works debate the importance of accessibility, describes common types of disabilities and discusses how some games approached them. According to them, there are two main strategies to creating accessibility games: supporting one specific disability or supporting many disabilities. Most of the studied games do the former: they focus on a specific disability and try to create the most accessible, compelling and interesting gaming experience for users with that disability. [2] and [4] discusses strategies employed by various games to achieve the best results for their target users.

The second approach tries to address multiple disabilities. As interaction needs may vary, designing games for everyone can be challenging or, depending on the desired gameplay, even impossible. Thus, the goal of this approach is to enable a game to have the broadest audience as possible [9].

As indicated in Section 1, UA-Games are an example of the second approach. These games combine many of the strategies of accessible games to support as many users as possible. Some interesting UA-Games include Universal Tic-Tac-Toe, UA-Chess, Access Invaders and Terrestrial Invaders [1]. These games offer different polymorphic specializations, tailoring the game to suit the abilities of visually, hearing and motor impaired users.

2.1 Game Stimuli

In [4], Yuan *et al.* describe an interaction model for games. The model describes the required sequential steps a user performs to play a game: (1) receiving stimuli, (2) determining the response and (3) providing input to the game. The model is cyclic, going from (1) to (3) and restarting at (1). The authors state that the subsequent steps rely on each other, *i.e.*, if a user cannot receive the stimuli, he/she will be unable to perform the other step and, therefore, to play.

Yuan *et al.* categorize the stimuli in two groups: primary stimuli and secondary stimuli. Primary stimuli is essential to the game comprehension – the case of graphics in most games. Therefore, if a user is unable to perceive or understand a primary stimulus, he/she will be unable to play. Secondary stimuli are usually complementary to a primary stimulus, such as sound effects in most game, and, therefore, not essential to the comprehension. Thus, if a user is unable to perceive it, he/she might be able to play, albeit with a minor loss in the experience.

2.2 UA-Games Design Framework: The Unified Design

The UA-Games mentioned in Section 2 were design using the Unified Design [1, 7]. According to Grammenos *et al.* [1], the Unified Design is a framework which offers a "step-by-step, top-down approach, starting with a high-level abstract task definition process, leading eventually to the creation of a complex, but well-structured, design space, populated by numerous interweaved physical designs".

The framework describes how to design a game in an abstract level, eliminating references to physical-level interactions (such as interactions with input and output devices). The designers tailor the physical-level interactions for each disability they want to support in a posterior step – the polymorphic physical specialization. In this step, the designers choose and tailor the primary and secondary stimuli of the game to suit the interaction needs of a disability.

The tailored interaction can be grouped in a user profile. When a user plays the game, he/she chooses the best profile for his/her needs. The chosen profile determines how the game is presented to the user and how he/she interacts with the game.

Although guiding the design, the Unified Design leaves the implementation to the designer. Thus, hoping to contribute with the implementation of UA-Games, the next sections describe a flexible and extensible approach to the implementation[1].

3 Object-Oriented Entity Hierarchies

The Object-Oriented Programming (OOP) is one of the most used paradigm in software [11]. In the game industry, it is not different: C++, C# and Java are among the most used programming language [12] – and all of them favor OOP. As the implementation of games usually employs the OOP paradigm, game entity implementations are often class hierarchical. They define a base class containing the common data for all entities (such as the object's world position and orientation) and derived classes extending the base class functionality.

Human perception is mostly visual [13]. As such, the primary stimuli of most digital games are also visual – hence the word videogame. Thus, it is usual consider the visual representation as part of a game entity and, for convenience, near the root of the hierarchy, as most entities shall have one (*e.g.* Fig. 1).

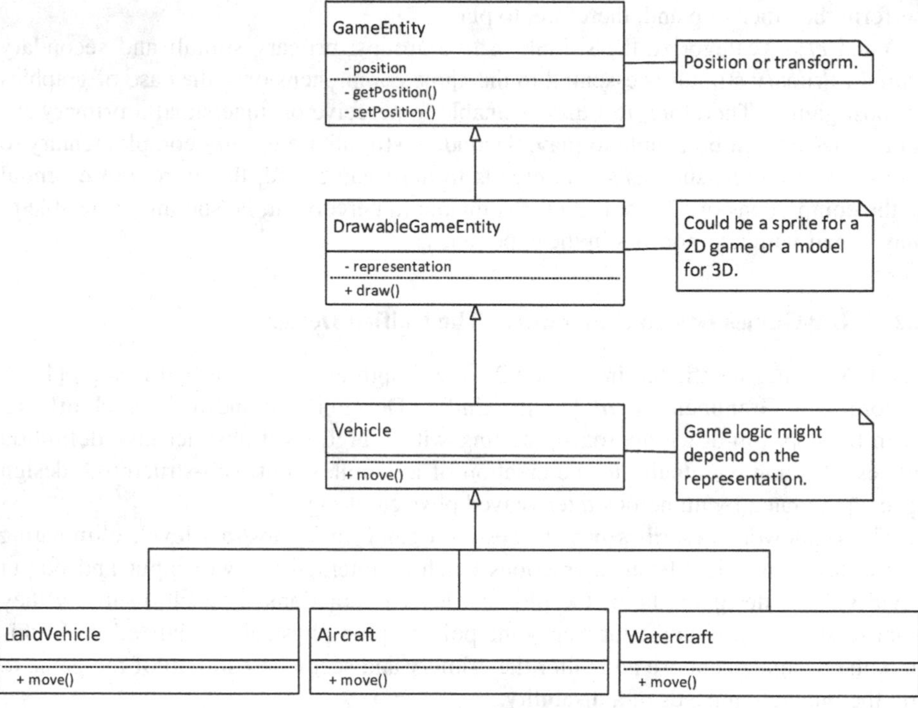

Fig. 1. A hierarchical approach for game entities. Creating a hybrid vehicle class (such as a land and air vehicle) would require multiple inheritance or code duplication.

[1] A reference implementation of the approach is available at <http://lifes.dc.ufscar.br/>.

For a UA-Game, however, the entity representation can greatly. For a certain disability, the best representation might be an image; for another, a sound or a haptic stimulus. The best form to convey the representation varies as well; therefore, it is difficult to create a general enough abstraction.

It could be argued to implement the representation at the bottom of the hierarchy. However, this would compromise reusing existing specializations when they are appropriate for multiple cases. Where would a multisensory representation fit? The new class either would inherit from multiple classes (causing the diamond problem – refer to Fig. 1 caption for an analogy) or would require duplicating existing code.

Whilst some languages have constructs to deal with the issue (*e.g.*, virtual inheritance in C++), there is a more flexible way of solving the problem: using an entity-component approach.

4 An Entity-Component Approach to UA-Games

An entity-component[2] approach aims to decouple the characteristics and functionality of a game entity into smaller, self-constricted components[3] [14–20]. It has been used in various games, promoting faster prototyping, iteration times and content creation [17, 19]. In addition, as discussed in this section, it can contribute to developing accessible games.

The approach can be seen as an extreme case of favoring "composition over class inheritance" [21] – has-a is preferred to is-a relationship. The entity can be very simple – as simple as an identifier in some implementations. This way, an entity definition is not rigid nor static: its data and behavior only depends on (and are defined by) the components attached to it.

It is possible to attach to or detach components from an entity during run-time – thus, it is even possible to customize an entity while the game running. In a UA-Game context, this means it is possible to switch from one polymorphic physical specialization to another by switching physical-level interaction components whenever it is appropriate.

Depending on the implementation, components can be data-only or have data and logic. Data-only components are processed by appropriate game subsystems. For instance, a Transformable Component can store the position, scale and orientation of an entity. A Physics or Movement system may process and manipulate these data.

Components with data and logic can also perform data processing themselves, *i.e.*, the component can update its own logic or state. Although this can appear flexible, it may cause problems when a component depends on other components. Besides, for the purposes of this paper, it may be more appropriate to have a very specialized subsystem than a component – keeping the component simple helps it being agnostic.

---

[2] The name and implementation of the approach may vary according to the author. Some variations include entity systems, component based systems, actors model and properties. Their goal, however, is similar.

[3] The components, therefore, should not be confused with Commercial of the Shelf components (COTS).

The data structure utilized in an entity-component implementation also varies – it depends on the chosen language and its available paradigms or on how often the game attach or detaches components from entities. Common choices include the use of collections or in-memory databases. The former, usually implemented in OOP languages, define a component interface. It acts as a handler to all the components – new components inherit and implement the interface, adding their data members[4]. The latter uses database facilities to store the data-only components.

We have chosen the actor's model defined by McShaffry and Graham's for this paper [17]. Their model uses a (mostly) data-only component implemented with a collection. **Fig. 2** illustrates a contextualized adaptation of their model, using data-only components and changing the focus to game accessibility.

In Fig. 2, all components implement the Component interface directly. If the designers create non-physical-level components to handle the game logic by themselves, then the game logic shall not depend on output data. For instance, a Transformable, a Collidable and a Kinematic component can hold the data for the game physics. The Physics subsystem process and manipulate these components and updates the game logic accordingly.

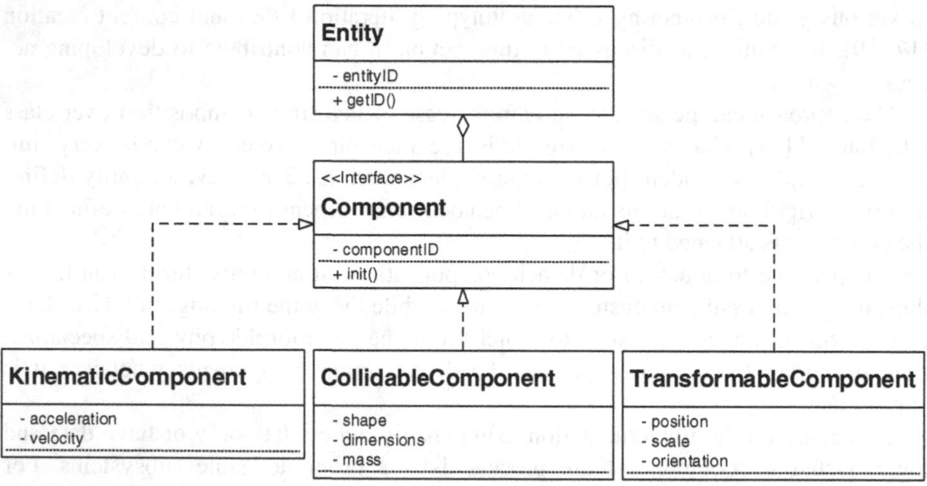

Fig. 2. An entity-component approach using data-only components

With this approach, implementing a new physical-level specialization consists of creating and specializing physical-level components, such as stimuli components. Thus, if the designers want graphical, auditory and haptic output for different polymorphic physical specialization, they create a Graphics, Audio and Haptic subsystem and their respective components. It is also possible to create components or subsystems considering the primary and secondary stimuli for each polymorphic physical specialization – as illustrated in Fig. 3.

[4] This is necessary in strong-typed languages to offer a common handle to the components.

When the game is running, the modal presentation will depend on the components attached to an entity. The game subsystems will read the data from the components and convey the information to the user as defined by the designers – resulting in an accessible gaming experience. If the input is also abstracted (for instance, into game commands), then it is possible to create a fully non-physical-level game logic using only components.

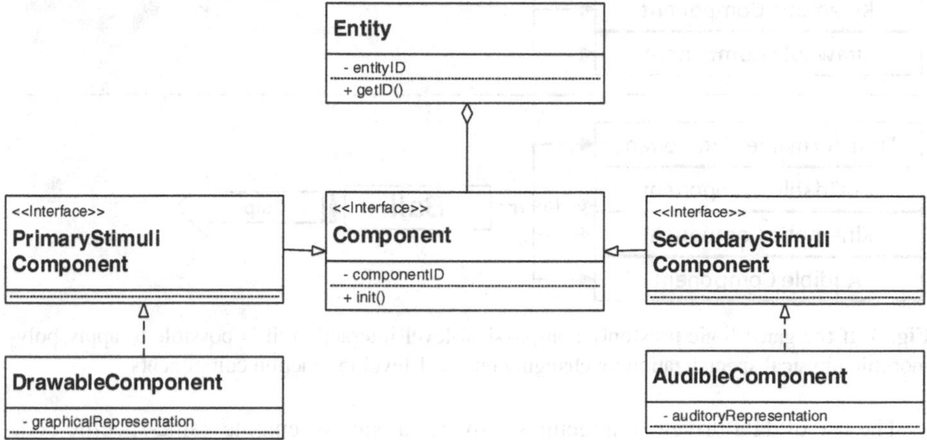

Fig. 3. Defining a stimuli component

To illustrate the approach, one can design an entity-component game - for simplicity, let us consider a Ping-Pong game. The ball of a Ping-Pong must move, collide with a table and paddles and be displayed to the user. Using the components of Fig. 2, the movement data could be stored in a Transformable component; the material, shape, inertia and mass of the ball in a Collidable component; and the velocity and acceleration of the ball in a Kinematic component. The Movement and Physics subsystem manipulates these components and update the ball's position and velocity.

Up to this point, there is no mention of a physical-level interaction: it can define to suit the user's abilities. For instance, for sighted users the primary stimuli component could be a Drawable component (such as the one from Fig. 3). The Graphics system would use its data along the Transformable component position, orientation and scale to draw the ball into the screen. For a visually impaired user, instead, the primary component could be an Audible one. This time, the Audio system would gather the required data from the components and play the sounds to the user. As one can see, the differences in the presentation are only due the chosen components – nothing else changes. Fig. 4 illustrates the example.

5 Improving the Approach with a Data-Driven Architecture

Section 4 discussed how entities and components contribute to make a game more flexible. However, using an entity-component approach alone either requires the developers to hardcode the profiles or the user to choose the desired components when the game is running. It would be more interesting to allow the creation and customization of user profile from an outer data source – using a configuration file, for instance.

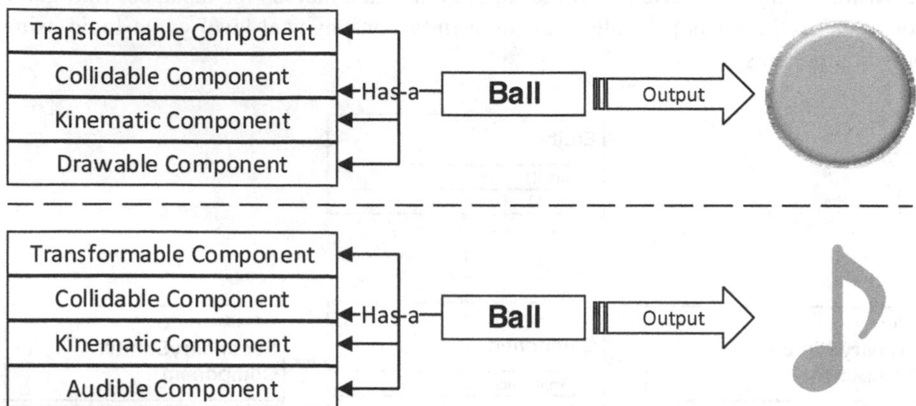

Fig. 4. If the game logic uses only non-physical-level interaction, it is possible to apply polymorphic physical specialization by changing physical-level interaction components

The use of data-driven architectures provides a way to separate game-specific code from application or engine code. Instead of hardcoding all possibilities into the game, the game-specific settings are defined in an outer data source. This contributes to increasing the flexibility and decreasing time for adjusting and tweaking settings for the entity – especially in case of a compiled programming language. Data-driven architectures share many of the advantages of entity-component approaches; they are also useful alongside game tools, such as editors, and for user generated content creation.

Combining an entity-component approach with a Factory pattern [21], it possible to load and create the components according to their definition from a data file [17, 19, 22]. For this paper, we once again choose McShaffry and Graham's implementation [17]. For each game entity, the designers define an Extensible Markup Language (XML) file containing all the entity's components and their initial data. **Listing 1** shows an example of the ball from the Ping-Pong game of Section 4. The game implementation parses the file and create the desired entity, with its respective behaviors and presentation data defined by the components, during run-time.

In the given example, the XML file contain both physical-level and non-physical level interaction. From a reuse perspective, it would be more interesting to split the file in two: one file for the physical-level components and another for the non-physical. From an accessibility perspective, however, the authors found it useful to replicate the data for some components. This way, it is possible to override the default values, allowing allows the designers to tweak the game's parameters to suit different interaction requirements.

For instance, as sound is perceived by time, it could make sense to raise the speed of the paddle for a non-visual profile in a Ping-Pong game. Likewise, in a low-vision profile, it could be useful to scale and increase the size of graphical components.

Listing 1. The components which will be used by the entity

```
<?xml version="1.0" encoding="UTF-8"?>
<Actor type="Ball" resource="entity/ball.xml">

  <TransformableComponent>
    <Position x="-85.0f" y="0.0f" z="0.0f"/>
    <Rotation yaw="0.0f" pitch="0.0f" roll="0.0f"/>
    <Scale x="1.0f" y ="1.0f" z="1.0"/>
  </TransformableComponent>

  <KinematicComponent>
    <Velocity vx="1.0f" vy="-1.0f" vz="0.0f"/>
    <Acceleration ax="0.0f" ay="0.0f" az="0.0f"/>
  </KinematicComponent>

  <CollidableComponent shape="sphere"/>
    <Density d="glass"/>
    <Material m="normal"/>
    <Mass m="1.0f"/>
    <Radius r="1.0f"/>
  </CollidableComponent>

  <PrimaryStimuliComponent>
    <DrawableComponent>
      <MeshFileName file="graphics/sphere.mesh"/>
      <MaterialFileName file="graphics/ball.material"/>
    </DrawableComponent>
  </PrimaryStimuliComponent>

  <SecondaryStimuliComponent>
    <AudibleComponent>
      <SoundFileName m="sounds/ball.wav"/>
      <SoundSettings volume="1.0f" loop="true"/>
    </AudibleComponent>
  </SecondaryStimuliComponent>

</Actor>
```

Using a data-driven architecture allows the creation of new profiles by mixing and matching the available physical-level interaction components and tweaking the attributes values (Listing 2). This way, it is easier to create presets or default configurations for different polymorphic physical specialization.

Listing 2. As components can be attached to entities during run-time, each player can create his/her own custom profile

```
<?xml version="1.0" encoding="UTF-8"?>
<PlayerProfiles type="Profiles" re-
source="config/player_profile.xml">

  <PlayerProfile name="Average User: Default">
    <PrimaryStimuliComponent type="graphical"/>
    <SecondaryStimuliComponent type="aural"/>
    <Settings re-
source="config/average_user_default.xml"/>
  </PlayerProfile>

  <PlayerProfile name="Visually Impaired: Blind">
    <PrimaryStimuliComponent type="aural"/>
    <SecondaryStimuliComponent type="none"/>
    <Settings resource="config/blind_default.xml"/>
  </PlayerProfile>

  <PlayerProfile name="Visually Impaired: Low Vision">
    <PrimaryStimuliComponent type="aural"/>
    <SecondaryStimuliComponent type="graphical"/>
    <Settings resource="config/low_vision_default.xml"/>
  </PlayerProfile>

  <PlayerProfile name="Mary">
    <PrimaryStimuliComponent type="aural"/>
    <SecondaryStimuliComponent type="graphical"/>
    <Settings resource="save/mary_profile.xml"/>
  </PlayerProfile>

</PlayerProfiles>
```

6 Limitations of the Approach

The XML listings of Section 5 use only one resource for the stimuli component. The use of more resources is encouraged – and, many times, even required.

As the perception of stimulus varies depending on the human sense, only one representation may not be enough to fully convey the game information to the user. For instance, vision and hearing are very different senses. One model might be enough to represent graphically a game character; a single sound, however, is often not enough.

A possible solution to this problem is using the approach with an event based architecture – for instance, as described by the authors in [23]. This way, it is possible to use stimuli components alongside with events to convey more information to the user – which is even more interesting with scriptable events.

7 Conclusions and Future Work

While creating an accessible game, especially when considering very different interaction requirements for a UA-Game, both the design and implementation must be flexible. This paper presented the combination of a data-driven architecture with an entity-component to decouple game logic from game presentation.

With the approach, it is possible to create new presentations for the game without changing the game logic. Due to the nature of components, it is possible to choose and modify the presentation of the game during run-time. In addition, with a data driven-architecture, it is easier to create new profiles to suit different interaction abilities – which is essential for UA-Games.

As suggested in Section 5, by using a data-driven architecture with components, users can customize the game and create their own profile based on existing specializations provided by the designers (*c.f.* Listing 2). Potentially, this could allow designers to create accessible game editors, allowing users themselves to modify or create new content to the game – thus, turning people originally excluded from playing game into aspiring game designers.

Towards this goal and hoping to enable more people to enjoy digital games, the authors are currently working on an open-source game engine to aid and ease the development of UA-Games. More information is available at <http://lifes.dc.ufscar.br/>.

Acknowledgment. We acknowledge the financial aid from FAPESP (2012/22539-6) for the realization of this work.

References

1. Grammenos, D., Savidis, A., Stephanidis, C.: Designing universally accessible games. Mag. Comput. Entertain. CIE - Spec. ISSUE Media Arts Games 7, 29 (2009)
2. International Game Developers Association: Accessibility in Games: Motivations and Approaches (2004)
3. McCrindle, R.J., Symons, D.: Audio space invaders. In: International Conference on Disability, Virtual Reality and Associated Technologies, Alghero, pp. 59–65 (2000)
4. Yuan, B., Folmer, E., Harris, F.: Game accessibility: a survey. Univers. Access Inf. Soc. 10, 81–100 (2011)
5. Fischer, G.: Meta-design: Expanding boundaries and redistributing control in design. In: Baranauskas, C., Abascal, J., Barbosa, S.D.J. (eds.) INTERACT 2007. LNCS, vol. 4662, pp. 193–206. Springer, Heidelberg (2007)
6. de Almeida Neris, V.P., Baranauskas, M.C.C.: Interfaces for All: A Tailoring-Based Approach. In: Filipe, J., Cordeiro, J. (eds.) ICEIS 2009. LNBIP, vol. 24, pp. 928–939. Springer, Heidelberg (2009)

7. Grammenos, D., Savidis, A., Stephanidis, C.: Unified Design of Universally Accessible Games. In: Stephanidis, C. (ed.) HCI 2007. LNCS, vol. 4556, pp. 607–616. Springer, Heidelberg (2007)
8. Story, M.F., Mueller, J.L., Mace, R.L.: The Universal Design File: Designing for People of All Ages and Abilities. Revised Edition (1998)
9. AbleGamers Foundation: Includification - Actionable Game Accessibility, `http://includification.com/`
10. Ellis, B., Ford-Williams, G., Graham, L., Grammenos, D., Hamilton, I., Lee, E., Manion, J., Westin, T.: Game Accessibility Guidelines: A straightforward reference for inclusive game design, `http://www.gameaccessibilityguidelines.com/`
11. TIOBE Software: Tiobe Index, `http://www.tiobe.com/index.php/tiobe_index`
12. Sweeney, T.: The Next Mainstream Programming Language: A Game Developer's Perspective. In: Conference Record of the 33rd ACM SIGPLAN-SIGACT Symposium on Principles of Programming Languages, pp. 269–269. ACM, New York (2006)
13. Parker, J.R., Heerema, J.: Audio Interaction in Computer Mediated Games. Int. J. Comput. Games Technol. 2008, 1–8 (2008)
14. Gregory, J.: Game Engine Architecture. A K Peters (2009)
15. Gamadu.com: Artemis Entity System Framework, `http://gamadu.com/artemis/`
16. Fox, M.: Game Engines 101: The Entity/Component Model, `http://www.gamasutra.com/blogs/MeganFox/20101208/6590/Game_Engines_101_The_EntityComponent_Model.php`
17. McShaffry, M., Graham, D.: Game Coding Complete, 4th edn. Course Technology PTR (2012)
18. Nystrom, R.: Component, `http://gameprogrammingpatterns.com/component.html`
19. Bilas, S.: A Data-Driven Game Object System. In: Game Developers Conference (2002)
20. Pallister, K.: Game Programming Gems 5. Charles River Media, Hingham (2005)
21. Gamma, E., Helm, R., Johnson, R., Vlissides, J.: Design Patterns: Elements of Reusable Object-Oriented Software. Addison-Wesley Professional (1994)
22. Laramee, F.D.: A Game Entity Factory. In: DeLoura, M.A. (ed.) Game Programming Gems 2, pp. 51–61. Cengage Learning, Hingham (2001)
23. Garcia, F.E., de Almeida Neris, V.P.: Design de Jogos Universais: Apoiando a Prototipação de Alta Fidelidade com Classes Abstrata. In: Anais do XII Simpósio Brasileiro sobre Fatores Humanos em Sistemas Computacionais, Manaus (2013)

Players' Opinions on Control and Playability of a BCI Game

Hayrettin Gürkök, Bram van de Laar, Danny Plass-Oude Bos, Mannes Poel, and Anton Nijholt

University of Twente, Human Media Interaction Group,
P.O. Box 217, 7500 AE Enschede, The Netherlands
m.poel@utwente.nl

Abstract. Brain-computer interface (BCI) games can satisfy our need for competence by providing us with challenges that we should enjoy tackling. However, many BCI games that claim to provide enjoyable challenges fail to do so. Some common fallacies and pitfalls about BCI games play a role in this failure and in this paper we report on a study that we carried out to empirically investigate them. More specifically, we explored (1) active and passive interaction with BCI games, (2) BCI gaming as a skill and (3) playability of a BCI game. We conducted an experiment with 42 participants who played a popular computer game called World of Warcraft using a commercial BCI headset called EPOC. We conducted interviews about the participants' experiences of the game and ran a phenomenological analysis on their responses. The analysis results showed that (1) the players would like to play a BCI game actively if the BCI controls critical game elements, (2) the technical challenges of BCI cannot motivate the players to play a BCI game and (3) the players' enjoyment of one-time playing of a BCI game does not imply playability of the game.

1 Introduction

Brain-computer interfaces (BCIs) are physiological computing systems that satisfy or support the needs of their users by interpreting the user's brain activity [1,2]. There are different groups of BCI users and each of them has different needs. Besides paralysed individuals who use BCIs to satisfy their basic physiological needs for survival, there is a larger user group including not only paralysed but also healthy individuals who use BCIs to satisfy their psychological needs. BCI games are prominent applications for this group of users thanks to their capability to satisfy some psychological needs such as competence, pleasure and relatedness [3]. For example, by overcoming the challenges posed by a BCI game, people can satisfy their need for competence [4].

Many BCI games have been developed with the claim of satisfying psychological needs but without succeeding to do so. Common fallacies and taken-for-granted assumptions about BCI games (or BCIs) play a role in this. Our goal in the paper is to test some of these issues empirically so that we have a better

C. Stephanidis and M. Antona (Eds.): UAHCI/HCII 2014, Part II, LNCS 8514, pp. 549–560, 2014.

understanding of them and that we can consider them while developing BCI games. The first issue is about active and passive BCI games. Active BCI games are those in which the players generate brain signals intentionally, in order to control the game. In passive BCI games, players do not generate brain signals for controlling the game but their naturally occurring brain signals influence the game play. The fallacy with active and passive BCI games is that they are thought of as distinct applications, as we have just introduced above as well. However, this is not necessarily the case. We conjecture that active or passive is a property not of a BCI game alone but rather of the interaction between the BCI game and its player. More specifically, while some players interact with a particular BCI game actively, others may do so passively. Furthermore, a player can interact with a BCI game in a dynamic manner, switching between active and passive interaction modes. This is the basis of the first research question (RQ) in the paper:

RQ1: When and why do players opt for active or passive interaction while playing a BCI game.

The second issue is about the challenges that BCI games pose and the player skills required to overcome them. We have mentioned that BCI games can satisfy people's need for competence by offering some challenges to them. Many BCI games claim to be challenging simply because the technical shortcomings of BCIs (e.g. noise in acquired brain signals) pose a fundamental challenge to players [5]. However, such technical challenges cannot satisfy people's need for competence because they cannot be overcome (merely) by the player's effort. The real challenge a BCI game should offer is to find out how to generate the desired brain patterns to control the game. This is the second research questions which is addressed in the paper:

RQ2: Do BCI game players consider BCI control as a skill?

The third issue concerns long-term interaction with BCI games. The majority of the user studies on BCI games have asked participants to evaluate their experience of a particular experiment that they took part in (e.g. [6,7,8]). The potential pitfall with such an evaluation is that participant responses may reflect their experience of, rather than the BCI game as a product, the whole experiment which includes visiting a new place, interacting with new people and trying novel technology. Participants may find *the experiment* to be *fun* but may not ever want to play the BCI game again. People's view of BCI games as products and their willingness to bring them to their homes and play as they do with other computer games is therefore as yet unclear. This is partly because the BCI games evaluated so far were simple toy games and/or they required expensive hardware (e.g. electroencephalographs or near-infrared spectrographs). Under these conditions, it would not be realistic to imagine playing BCI games as playing, for example, a casual game on a personal computer. However, the situation is changing with the emerging consumer grade hardware [9]. We envision people playing computer games in their homes using such hardware. This brings us to the third research question:

RQ3: Are people willing to play a non-toy computer game using consumer grade BCI hardware?

We opted for phenomenology to investigate our RQs due to its power in extracting lived human experience [10]. We let people play a popular computer game called World of Warcraft [1] (WoW) once using its default controllers (i.e. the mouse and the keyboard) and once using a consumer grade BCI hardware called EPOC[2]. This way, we could evaluate their experience of BCI control independent of their experience of the game. They could interact both actively and passively with the BCI version of the game. After they had played the games, we conducted interviews to collect people's experiences of the BCI game. In this paper, we present our findings of the analyses that we ran on the interview responses.

2 Methodology

2.1 Participants

To support generalisability of our findings, we tried to obtain a participant space that is as diverse as possible with respect to participants' age, gender, nationality and experience with computer games and the game WoW. We recruited the participants through the posters we hung around our institution, word-of-mouth, social media and our mailing lists from previous studies. Forty-two people (12 female, 30 male) participated in the experiment. Their ages ranged from 17 to 49 years (mean = 24.86). Three participants were Spanish, 2 were Chinese, 2 were German, 1 was Ecuadorian and the rest were Dutch. Thirty-six participants indicated playing or having played computer games. Fourteen participants were experienced WoW players (reached level 35 or above with their game character). The participants were paid according to the regulations of our institution.

2.2 Game

WoW is a massively multiplayer online role-playing game (MMORPG). At the time of writing, it was the world's most-subscribed MMORPG with more than 10 million subscribers[3]. It has frequently been used in human behaviour and experience [11,12,13] and also BCI research [14,15]. In WoW, people play the role of a fantasy hero. They control a character to fight other players' characters or non-player characters and complete quests. The more quests they complete, the higher the level they reach. Although there is a maximum level that players can

[1] From Blizzard Entertainment, Inc., CA, USA
[2] From Emotiv Systems, CA, USA
[3] http://www.ign.com/articles/2012/10/04/mists-of-pandaria-pushes-warcraft-subs-over-10-million

reach, the game does not end when this level is reached. Players can still keep on playing to finish awaiting quests, enjoy regular content updates or socialise with other players. By default, they use the mouse and the keyboard to interact with the game. The characters the players control belong to a class that determines the type of weapons and armor the character can use, as well as the abilities it can gain. For example, a character belonging to the class of Druids has the unique ability to transform into different forms (also called shapeshifting). For this, the players with a Druid character can click on the icon representing the form they want to transform into (e.g. an elf or a bear). Each form has its strengths. For example, an elf can cast attacking and healing spells, and attack from a distance while a bear can resist attacks for a long time and cause high damage in close combat. We created a BCI game based on WoW, called alpha WoW (aWoW), which infers the player's state of relaxation and transforms the player's character into an elf or a bear form [14]. We tried to achieve an intuitive match between the character forms and the player's relaxation state. If the player is relaxed, then their character transforms into the elf form. If they are not relaxed (but, for example, stressed or occupied with executing mental processes) then their character transforms into the bear form. A bar on the top left of the screen indicates the player's level of relaxation (see Figure 1). Relaxation is estimated by analysing the player's brain activity over the posterior region (see §2.3 for details). Players can also transform their character by clicking on the designated icons, as in the original WoW game. We consider aWoW as a BCI game that offers both active and passive interaction modes. In active interaction players might voluntarily regulate their relaxation to benefit from the advantages of a specific form while in passive interaction they might simply enjoy seeing the game reflect their natural state and improve their sense of presence.

2.3 Relaxation Estimation

In aWoW, the player's relaxation is inferred by analysing their alpha rhythm. The alpha rhythm oscillates between 8-13 Hz over the posterior region. It is blocked or attenuated by attention and mental effort. Therefore it has been associated with physical relaxation and relative mental inactivity [16]. The feedback of alpha rhythm has frequently been used in treatment of stress-related anxiety disorders [17].

To evaluate the estimation accuracy in aWoW, we conducted a pilot study with 10 participants (2 female). Instead of aWoW, we used a simpler game (see Figure 2) that used the same relaxation estimation method as aWoW. In this game, a ball fell from the top centre to the bottom of the screen in 7 seconds and the participants steered the ball to the left or right so that it hit the bottom at the target half of the screen. The target half was indicated by a green bar and the other half with a red one. The target half was randomly chosen for every falling ball. The ball moved to the left with increasing relaxation and otherwise to the right. If the ball hit the target half of the screen, the player score was increased by one. Participants first played 3 training sessions each of which contained 20 trials (i.e. 20 falling balls). We did not keep track of their training game scores.

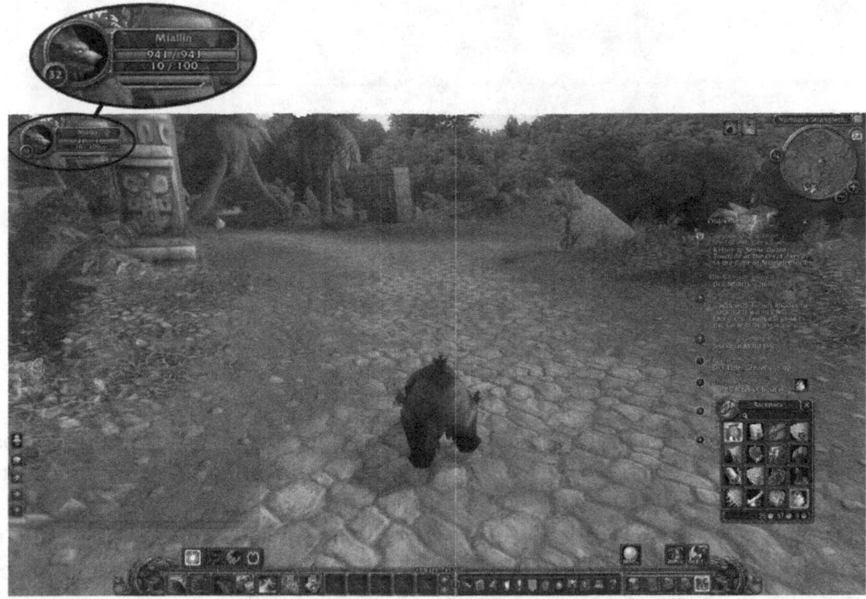

Fig. 1. A screenshot from aWoW. The orange bar located to the top left corner of the screen, under the health and mana bars, indicates player's relaxation state.

Then, they played 5 sessions (i.e. 100 trials per participant) and we recorded their scores. For each participant we computed the relaxation estimation accuracy by averaging their game scores. The mean estimation accuracy over all participants was 74.1% (SD = 13.9). Although such an accuracy cannot compete with the reliability of traditional controllers (e.g. the keyboard), it meets the de facto threshold accuracy for BCIs[4]. According to this threshold assumption, half of the participants could not control the game since 5 people remained under the mean (as well as the threshold).

2.4 Experiment Protocol

Each experiment was carried out by one of three experimenters. To prevent biases, all three experimenters followed a written, itemised protocol strictly. The participants also received instructions written down in English so the experimenters refrained from giving oral instructions unless the participants asked for specific information. The basic instruction sheet introduced WoW and contained information on moving, quests, transformations, armors, areas, chatting with other players and how to re-start playing the game if the game character died. This sheet and an informed consent form were available to the participants online so that they could read them before coming to the experiment. They also

[4] An accuracy of 70% is widely assumed in the BCI community as the threshold to operate a BCI for communication [18,19].

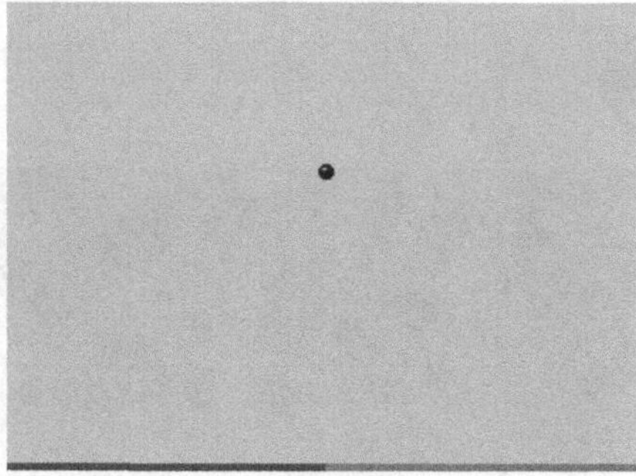

Fig. 2. A screenshot from the game used in the pilot study

filled out in advance an online demographic questionnaire. In addition to the basic instruction sheet, the participants received two additional instruction sheets; one before playing WoW with the default controllers and one before playing it with BCI. These sheets gave specific instructions on shapeshifting (e.g. not to use the icons to transform while playing with BCI). Participants could access the instruction sheets at any time during the experiment.

The experiment protocol was executed as follows. The participants signed the informed consent form while the experimenter mounted the EPOC electrode headset on them. The experimenter tilted the headset forward at an angle of approximately 25° (see Figure 3) so that the electrodes touched the scalp on the desired locations (see §2.3). After (re-)reading the basic instructions, the participants played the official tutorial of WoW with a level 1 character until they felt that they were comfortable with playing the game. Afterwards, they played the game with a level 28 character in two sessions. We chose a level 28 character because we wanted the game character to be sufficiently high level so that the participants could (1) transform into the bear shape, and (2) investigate an area that would remain interesting enough for some levels. In one of the sessions they used the default controllers and in the other the BCI. The order of these games were counterbalanced across the participants. In each session, the participants first received and read the additional instruction sheet. Then, the experimenter left the room. According to the instructions they had read, the participants rang a bell when they did not want to play anymore. If they did not ring the bell within 30 minutes the experimenter interrupted them, but this was not written in the instructions. After that, they filled out a user experience questionnaire[5] and took a break for as long as they wished. Finally, after completing both sessions, they took part in an interview.

The experiments were carried out in two separate rooms, using two separate laptops. Each laptop was associated with a different WoW account. This allowed two experiments to be carried out simultaneously. To ensure that the participants began playing the game under the same conditions, we created characters

[5] The questionnaire responses were analysed in the context of another study and the results are reported elsewhere [20].

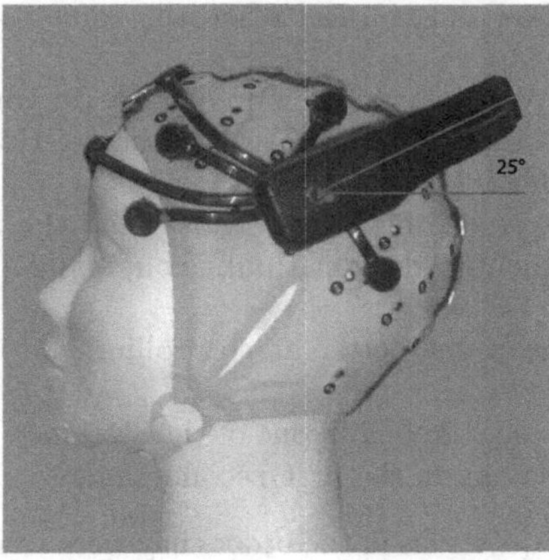

Fig. 3. Illustration of the mounted electrode headset

that were equally levelled on both accounts. Moreover, we placed the game character at the same location in the game world after each experiment with its armor repaired. The starting location of the game character was a safe area so that the participants would not need to start fighting as soon as they started playing. The layout of the experimental setup was consistent in both rooms. The experimenters were not in the same room with the participants during the play sessions but could monitor the participants through the cameras located to the top corners of the rooms.

2.5 Data Collection and Analysis

We recorded the play sessions and interviews using cameras with a microphone. Using Emotiv TestBench we recorded the electrical brain activity as electroencephalograms. We logged key presses along with corresponding screenshots. For the purpose of this paper, we only analysed the interview recordings.

Interview. We conducted semi-structured interviews with the participants to investigate their experience. The questions asked are:

1. You played the first/second game with BCI. In this game, you could have used BCI in two ways. The first way was to actively try to manipulate your state when you wanted to transform. The second way was to let BCI passively monitor and reflect your natural mental state. So in the first case, *you* would take the initiative to transform while in the second case you would let the *game* take the initiative. Which of these ways did you take?
2. In the BCI game, did things ever go wrong when you actively tried to transform?

3. In the BCI game, how did you feel when the game took the initiative and transformed you?
4. (If an experienced WoW player) How frequently do you play WoW?
   (Else) Let's assume that you have WoW at home. How frequently, do you think, you would play it?
5. Let's assume that you also have this headset and the BCI version of WoW at home. How frequently, do you think, you would play WoW using the headset?
6. Do you think you can get better at controlling the transformations with BCI?
7. (If the participant rang the bell in one of the sessions) What was the reason that you stopped playing in the first/second game?

We asked the interview questions in the order they were written on the interview sheet. When necessary, we encouraged the participants to elaborate on their responses by telling us about specific events that happened during the experiment and the consequent experience they had. The interviews took place in English unless the experimenter spoke the native language of the participant. As a result 21 interviews were conducted in English and 21 in Dutch.

Adhering to the goal of phenomenology, the interview questions aimed at unfolding the participants' experiences, rather than collecting their abstract interpretations or opinions [21]. So, instead of questions that referred directly to our RQs, we asked questions that encouraged the participants to talk about their experiences during the game. The first question of the interview addressed our first RQ on active and passive BCI games. If the participants did not motivate their choice for an interaction mode then the experimenter asked explicitly for it. The second, third and sixth questions addressed our RQ on BCI control as a skill. More specifically, the second and third questions explored participants' opinions on who was responsible for the errors in active and passive shapeshifting respectively. The sixth question investigated whether the participants required the technology to improve or they thought that they could improve just by practising. The fourth, fifth and seventh questions explored participants' experience of playability; our third RQ.

We transcribed all the interviews except for two, which did not contain audio due to a software error. For each question, we performed decontextualisation and recontextualisation procedures as proposed by [22] and we took an immersion/crystallisation analysis style [23]. More specifically, from participant responses we extracted texts that were potentially significant to our hypotheses. Then, we assigned codes to units of meaning by looking at the relationships between the texts. Finally, we examined the codes to identify patterns and reduced the data into central categories and category relationships.

3 Most Important Findings

In this section we summarize the important findings concerning the most relevant questions in the structured interview.

Question 1: Did you play the game actively or passively? Only a small number of participants played the game actively. They came up with different strategies to generate the necessary brain signals to play the game and claimed that they succeeded in transformations. Some participants had control over transformation into an elf but not into a bear. Many other participants played the game passively but their responses implied that passive play was not a free-will choice but a consequence of failure with active play. In short, all participants did want and try to play the game actively but only some succeeded.

Question 2: Did things go wrong during active play? None of the participants indicated that they could control the transformations perfectly. Some participants explained that they could trigger transformations but they were transformed back quickly by the BCI. Others could not trigger transformations at all. One of the reasons stated was simply their failure in figuring out how to trigger transformations. Another reason was the competition between the attention required to transform and that required to play the game. The detrimental influence of competing attentional demands on play experience while playing BCI games has been reported before as well [24].

Question 3: How did you feel during passive play? Participants appreciated functional passive play mainly for pragmatic reasons. They liked it when the game transformed them at the 'right' time and saved the effort of issuing explicit commands for transforming. When the transformations did not comply with the mental state that they believed to be in, the participants trusted their self-assessment rather than the assessment of the BCI. One of the factors that damaged the credibility of the BCI was the seemingly randomness of transformations. Another prominent factor was the instability of transformations.

We will not elaborate on the responses to Question 4 as this question served as a baseline for Question 5.

Question 5: How frequently would you play aWoW? Participant responses to Question 5 were divided into two. One group indicated that they would never play the game using the headset and stated three main reasons for that: controllability, equal opponents and comfort of the headset.

The other group indicated that they would like to play the game using the headset. However, their responses implied that rather than playing the game, they would actually like to interact with the headset itself because the BCI was not accurate enough to steer the game.

Question 6: Can you get better in transformations? Participants had two distinct views. One group hypothesised that they could get better in time with practising. On the one hand, some had theoretical reasoning. On the other hand, some had empirical reasoning. They expressed that their control over transformations already improved during the experiment.

The other group was more skeptical. Some indicated that they would not be able to improve without the help of, for example, pointers or tricks. Some participants indicated that their ability of control was conditioned on personalisation of the BCI.

Question 7: Why did you stop playing the game? There were three main reasons for the participants to stop playing aWoW. The first one was the frustration caused by lack of control. The second reason was the discomfort with the headset. The last reason was not related to BCI. At particular moments during play (e.g. upon completion of quests), some participants remembered that they were in an experiment and decided to stop.

4 Limitations of the Study

Although we were able to answer our RQs through the study we conducted, there are limitations to adopting our findings. Firstly, the phenomenology approach we took in this study is inherently subjective as the human is the instrument for analysis. To minimise the possibility of a biased analysis, we abided by the principles of bracketing.

Secondly, given the imperfect recognition accuracy of the BCI running behind aWoW and the prominent influence of lack of control on user experience as revealed by our study, it is possible that a more accurate BCI could have provided a different user experience and yielded different results.

Thirdly, we drew our findings from a single experiment in which we used a particular game and hardware. This means that the findings might not be generalisable to BCI games in general.

5 Conclusions for BCI Game Development

As we mentioned in §1, our RQs served as a means to inform our readers about the common fallacies and assumptions about BCI games. In this section, we will provide some guidelines for BCI development, drawn from the answers to our RQs.

- Not all BCI games are suitable to be played actively and passively. If the BCI is used in controlling critical game dynamics (e.g. movements of a player avatar, which needs timely action and the consequences of errors are intolerable) and if the control is imperfect (which is the case with current BCIs), then the players are expected to interact actively. They would hand the control over to the BCI only if they fail at active interaction.
- When interacting actively, players should predict (to some extent) the outcome of their mental activity. They should feel that they play a role in both successful and unsuccessful driving of the game. Thus, they should be able to overcome the challenges the BCI game poses. Because BCI is a faulty technology, an extra burden is put on game designers in order to make a BCI game both challenging and enjoyable.

– While interacting passively, players should be able to figure out the mapping between their mental state and game events. They should perceive that the actions the BCI game takes are reasonable (e.g. consistent) and stable.
– The attention required to control the BCI should not exhaust the overall attention devoted to the game. Players should be able to use other controllers, monitor the progression of the game and simply enjoy the game visuals.
– The experience of fun resulting from playing a BCI game once does not reliably represent the experience of pleasure that unfolds by playing the game. Thus, BCI games should be developed and evaluated for the pleasure rather than the fun they provide.
– The pragmatic quality (or usability) of a BCI game (e.g. the comfort of the headset, the amount of control a player has) is important for long-term user experience. Pragmatic quality of a BCI game should not be so low that it worsens or otherwise masks the game's hedonic quality.

Acknowledgments. The authors gratefully acknowledge the support of the BrainGain Smart Mix Programme of the Netherlands Ministry of Economic Affairs and the Netherlands Ministry of Education, Culture and Science and of the the European FP7 Project BNCI Horizon 2020 (The Future of Brain/Neural Computer Interaction: Horizon 2020), Grant agreement no: 609593. They would also like to extend their thanks to Lynn Packwood for her precious help in transcribing the interviews and improving the language of this paper.
This paper only reflects the authors' views and funding agencies are not liable for any use that may be made of the information contained herein.

References

1. Gürkök, H., Nijholt, A.: Brain-computer interfaces for multimodal interaction: A survey and principles. International Journal of Human-Computer Interaction 28(5), 292–307 (2012)
2. Tan, D., Nijholt, A.: Brain-computer interfaces and human-computer interaction. In: Brain-Computer Interfaces, pp. 3–19. Springer, London (2010)
3. Gürkök, H., Nijholt, A., Poel, M.: Brain-computer interface games: Towards a framework. In: Herrlich, M., Malaka, R., Masuch, M. (eds.) ICEC 2012. LNCS, vol. 7522, pp. 373–380. Springer, Heidelberg (2012)
4. Nijholt, A., Reuderink, B., Oude Bos, D.: Turning shortcomings into challenges: Brain-computer interfaces for games. Entertainment Computing 1(2), 85–94 (2009)
5. Tatum, W.O., Dworetzky, B.A., Schomer, D.L.: Artifact and recording concepts in EEG. Journal of Clinical Neurophysiology 28(3), 252–263 (2011)
6. Mühl, C., Gürkök, H., Plass-Oude Bos, D., Thurlings, M.E., Scherffig, L., Duvinage, M., Elbakyan, A.A., Kang, S., Poel, M., Heylen, D.: Bacteria Hunt: Evaluating multi-paradigm BCI interaction. Journal on Multimodal User Interfaces 4(1), 11–25 (2010)
7. George, L., Lotte, F., Abad, R., Lecuyer, A.: Using scalp electrical biosignals to control an object by concentration and relaxation tasks: Design and evaluation. In: 2011 Annual International Conference of the IEEE EMBS, pp. 6299–6302. IEEE, Piscataway (2011)

8. Gürkök, H.: Mind the Sheep! User Experience Evaluation & Brain-Computer Interface Games. PhD thesis, University of Twente, Enschede, The Netherlands (2012)
9. Liao, L.D., Lin, C.T., McDowell, K., Wickenden, A.E., Gramann, K., Jung, T.P., Ko, L.W., Chang, J.Y.: Biosensor technologies for augmented brain-computer interfaces in the next decades. Proceedings of the IEEE 100, 1553–1566 (2012)
10. Sokolowski, R.: Introduction to Phenomenology. Cambridge University Press, Cambridge (2000)
11. Nardi, B., Harris, J.: Strangers and friends: Collaborative play in World of Warcraft. In: Proceedings of the 2006 Conference on Computer Supported Cooperative Work, pp. 149–158. ACM, New York (2006)
12. Yee, N., Ducheneaut, N., Nelson, L., Likarish, P.: Introverted elves & conscientious gnomes: The expression of personality in World of Warcraft. In: Proceedings of the SIGCHI Conference on Human Factors in Computing Systems, pp. 753–762. ACM, New York (2011)
13. Billieux, J., van der Linden, M., Achab, S., Khazaal, Y., Paraskevopoulos, L., Zullino, D., Thorens, G.: Why do you play World of Warcraft? An in-depth exploration of self-reported motivations to play online and in-game behaviours in the virtual world of Azeroth. Computers in Human Behavior 29(1), 103–109 (2013)
14. Nijholt, A., Plass-Oude Bos, D., Reuderink, B.: Turning shortcomings into challenges: Brain–computer interfaces for games. Entertainment Computing 1(2), 85–94 (2009)
15. Scherer, R., Friedrich, E.C.V., Allison, B., Pröll, M., Chung, M., Cheung, W., Rao, R.P.N., Neuper, C.: Non-invasive brain-computer interfaces: Enhanced gaming and robotic control. In: Cabestany, J., Rojas, I., Joya, G. (eds.) IWANN 2011, Part I. LNCS, vol. 6691, pp. 362–369. Springer, Heidelberg (2011)
16. Deuschl, G., Eisen, A. (eds.): Recommendations for the Practice of Clinical Neurophysiology, 2nd edn. Elsevier, Amsterdam (1999)
17. Moore, N.C.: The neurotherapy of anxiety disorders. Journal of Adult Development 12, 147–154 (2005)
18. Quek, M., Höhne, J., Murray-Smith, R., Tangermann, M.: Designing future BCIs: Beyond the bit rate. In: Towards Practical Brain-Computer Interfaces, pp. 173–196. Springer, Heidelberg (2012)
19. Vaughan, T.M., Sellers, E.W., Wolpaw, J.R.: Clinical evaluation of BCIs. In: Brain-Computer Interfaces: Principles and Practice, pp. 325–336. Oxford University Press, New York (2012)
20. Van de Laar, B., Gürkök, H., Plass-Oude Bos, D., Poel, M., Nijholt, A.: Experiencing BCI control in a popular computer game. IEEE Transactions on Computational Intelligence and AI in Games 5(2), 176–184 (2013)
21. Starks, H., Brown Trinidad, S.: Choose your method: A comparison of phenomenology, discourse analysis, and grounded theory. Qualitative Health Research 17(10), 1372–1380 (2007)
22. Tesch, R.: Qualitative Research: Analysis Types and Software Tools. RoutledgeFalmer, London (1990)
23. Malterud, K.: Qualitative research: standards, challenges, and guidelines. Lancet 358(9280), 483–487 (2001)
24. Gürkök, H., Nijholt, A., Poel, M., Obbink, M.: Evaluating a multi-player brain-computer interface game: Challenge versus co-experience. Entertainment Computing 4(3), 195–203 (2013)

Designing Playful Games and Applications to Support Science Centers Learning Activities

Michail N. Giannakos[1,2], David Jones[1], Helen Crompton[1], and Nikos Chrisochoides[1]

[1] Old Dominion University
Norfolk, VA, USA
[2] Norwegian University of Science and Technology, Trondheim, Norway
{mgiannak,nikos}@cs.odu.edu, {djone564,crompton}@odu.edu

Abstract. In recent years there has been a renewed interest on science, technology, engineering, and mathematics (STEM) education. Following this interest, science centers' staff started providing technology enhanced informal STEM education experiences. The use of well-designed mobile and ubiquitous forms of technology to enrich informal STEM education activities is an essential success factor. The goal of our research is to investigate how technology applications can be better used and developed for taking full advantage of the opportunities and challenges they provide for students learning about STEM concepts. In our approach, we have conducted a series of interviews with experts from science center curating and outdoor learning activities development, with the final goal of exploring and improving current learning environments and practices. This paper presents the development of set of design considerations for the development of STEM games and applications of young students. An initial set of best practices was first developed through semi-structures interviews with experts; and afterwards, by employing content analysis, a revised set of considerations was obtained. These results are useful for STEM education teachers, curriculum designers, curators and developers for K-12 education environments.

Keywords: Design Guidelines, Considerations, STEM Education, Informal Learning, Technology Enhanced Learning, Design for All, Best Practice, Field Trips, Science Centers.

1 Introduction

In recent years there has been a renewed focus on science, technology, engineering, and mathematics (STEM) education [19]. According to the Association of Science-Technology Centers (ASTC), which represents 353 U.S. science centers and museums, science centers and museums see nearly 63 million visits each year. In addition, young generations are growing up in a digital age and are often familiar with various forms of technology, especially mobile and ubiquitous technology. Using these forms of technology via playful applications can promote and enhance students' mental exercise, fantasy, creativity, and communication [2], [7]; however,

C. Stephanidis and M. Antona (Eds.): UAHCI/HCII 2014, Part II, LNCS 8514, pp. 561–570, 2014.

the introduction of technology applications in informal learning activities and science centers is often complex, and students do not always use them as expected [9], [27]. Additionally, students do not perform as expected when they are using them [11].

Based on these conditions, the opportunity to improve technology enhanced learning within the context of science centers is to learn how to design games and application in order to engage students and optimize informal outdoor learning. In our efforts to investigate how interactive games and applications could be better designed in order to motivate students during a museum visit, we conducted a series of semi-structures interviews with experts in order to capture their ideas and experiences with regard to the development of informal STEM activity. Next, we employed a content analysis technique [15] in order to organize the data. As the final step of the process we used the structured data and derived guidelines for improving the design of STEM games and applications focusing on young students.

2 Related Work

Dale [6] indicated that rather than learning through abstract thinking, students should learn from concrete experience, such as direct experiences (real-life experiences), contrived experiences (interactive models), and dramatic participation (role plays). Outdoor education often provides learners with first-hand and concrete experience, which connects the learner with real people and real issues [10]. Woodhouse & Knapp [26] postulated that outdoor education aims to provide learners with meaningful contextual experiences by using both natural and constructed environments. This method further gives teachers and students an opportunity to complement and expand classroom instruction with print and electronic media. The outdoor environment, although extremely beneficial, is often neglected by teachers, curriculum developers, and researchers [17]. Moreover, when carrying out outdoor education, teachers must consider using limited teaching materials, which often impede effective instruction [28].

Informal learning is becoming increasingly popular, and mobile technology in particular has opened up a vast range of possibilities concerning learner feedback [16], context awareness opportunities, and reinforcement [16] [4]. Prior research on interactivity in learning has shown that the interactivity of the devices can improve students' learning [14]. The success of handhelds as museum guidebooks and learning systems [24] [25] is apparent from the growing interest in the use of interactive devises as learning tools in informal learning contexts. Previous research [12] has revealed the benefits of certain properties of mobile technologies (i.e., portability, environment, sensitivity) in informal learning. Although there has been much research on how mobile devices can support and enhanced learning [23] [5], limited empirical work currently exists focusing on students' needs and how the current design and development can reinforce and enhance learning. In this study, we focus on design practices for the successful development and use of technology devices to support learning within informal settings (with particular focus on STEM disciplines).

Gaming activities provide structure for collaboration and promote students engagement through rewards. It also provides a context to these activities (e.g., with materials in the aquarium). As such, students are motivated to interact and be engaged throughout the learning process in a way that is meaningful for them [21]. Learning by playing encourages interactions and stimulates collaboration [22]. Collaborative playing requires different skills to be deployed simultaneously [12]. Evidence of students' performance of learning by playing has been shown to leverage their experience with the learning context and increase the educational effectiveness [18]. In addition, learning by playing has been successfully applied in history [1], arts [12], cultural heritage [3], and mathematics [25]. In all cases, gaming elements (e.g., co-operation, competition, score, time limits) can motivate and attract students [16]. In this study, by extracting knowledge from experts, we identify effective design patterns to support the development of technology applications to support STEM learning.

In particular, our research is intended to shed light in the area of how games and applications could be designed to motivate students for informal learning activities, especially in STEM disciplines. We conducted field studies, collected empirical data and provide insights that enable scholars and educators to efficiently design and develop applications to support STEM field trips. Our research follows a three-step process (Figure 1). In the three consecutive steps, we proceed with the data collection, data analysis and ending up with the design considerations.

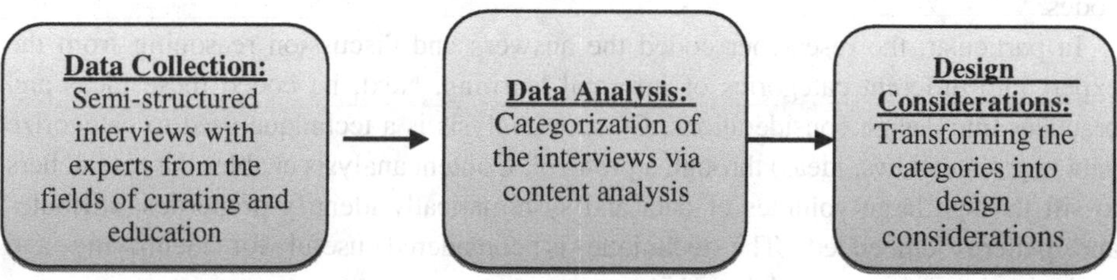

Fig. 1. Overview of the research process

3 Methodology

3.1 Procedures and Participants

During the initial research phase we contacted experts from the area of science center curating and informal learning activities development. In particular we arranged and implemented semi-structured interviews with the Director of Education and the Instructional Technology and Outreach Specialist of the Virginia Aquarium & Marine Science Center, as well as corresponded via email with a science education consultant for the aquarium.

We chose to conduct semi-structured interviews to gain insight in preconditions, practical implications, and success factors of K-12 informal learning activity in science centers. We started the interview by asking the interviewees to identify some of the challenges of teaching high school students in informal learning settings, such as the Virginia Aquarium. Following we discussed best practices and recommendations for teaching high school students in informal learning settings. The interviews continued by addressing the main challenges of teaching high school students STEM curricula through an informal technology enhanced learning environment. The interviews lasted approximately 1 hour with the Director of Education and 45 minutes with the Outreach Specialist. The researcher recorded the interviews and kept notes.

3.2 Data Collection and Analysis

As aforementioned, these data collected were from interviews with experts. A semi-structured interview guide was used in the personal in-depth interviews. Interview questions were designed to probe for different aspects and difficulties of informal learning and designing materials to support field trips.

Following the interviews the material was transcribed and evaluated, then it became clear that the point of saturation was reached and interviewing more experts was not expected to provide radically different or more in depth material. After the interviews collection, we proceed with a content analysis. The researcher read all responses first, and coded important keywords until categories emerged from similar codes.

In particular, the researcher coded the answers and discussion reasoning from the expert into different categories of informal learning. Next, he coded these ideas and practices into design considerations. Content analysis is a technique used to categorize data (e.g., interviews, ideas) through a protocol. Content analysis enables the researchers to sift through large volumes of data and systematically identify properties, attributes and patterns embedded. The technique is considered useful for identifying and analyzing issues in gathered data [15].

4 Research Findings

Next, we present the extracted design guidelines by giving a brief description with some sample coded phrases and some illustrative examples.

1. The structure must be easy and understandable

Description: The gaming application should avoid overly complex operations and tasks, which can produce user frustration and disappointment. The user should be able to immediately understand any on-screen instructions, and promptly begin assigned tasks. As the experts noted, "The application must be user-friendly. Usually, the easiest systems are the best." They suggested that game creators should "start small" and build from that point.

Example: The game's control panel and format should be simple to understand, so the user can focus on game content while enjoying smooth operation.

2. Use Visual and Interactive Elements

Description: The majority of game material should be conveyed through visual and interactive means instead of written. According to the Instructional Technology and Outreach Specialist, *"75% of people are visual learners and would thus benefit more from visual elements*". The user very quickly will be overwhelmed from too much written material *"There is some data that shows only 13% of your guests really ever read written material that's there for interpretive purposes,"* noted the Director of Education in regards to the aquarium's exhibits. *"There is plenty of information around, but they [students] don't take the time to read that because they are busy looking at things."* Written material should be kept to a minimum, with only the most important information being put in print or better the screen of a mobile device.

Example: Having an animated narrator provide gaming instructions would be one possible method. Using diagrams instead of writing to explain different parts of a system (e.g. the water cycle) is another possible way to convey information. For instance, when the game's key character is floating down a mountain stream, the game could visually show his vessel rocking in the current and the water rippling across rocks. The sounds of chirping birds and bubbling brooks could resonate in the background. This would create a realistic sensation for the user and promote engagement.

3. Incorporate Entertaining Responses for On-Screen Actions

Description: Game users enjoy receiving "cool" or surprising responses when they complete an action. The more they anticipate responses, the more they will experiment with different actions. "*Students find it engaging when they get an answer right and something 'cool' happens on-screen*" the Director of Education explained. "*Particularly when they can play around on their own cell phone – that is the type of thing that is appealing to that audience*" Both the experts emphasized about the importance of animation.

Example: When users complete the correct action, a pop-up congratulatory message could appear, perhaps with some cash or other reward. Conversely, when they commit an error, they receive a negative response. Their character could fall, be bitten by an animal, or loose valuable resources whenever mistakes are made. Surprising or humorous responses, when accompanied by special sound effects, can be especially entertaining.

4. Enhance Interaction with Large Touch-Screen

Description: Large touch-screens provide enhanced viewing and interaction. According to the science education consultant, improving interaction in games is critical. *"Teachers are looking for interesting ways to engage their students with [STEM material], so the more interactive the app can be, the better it will be received."* Incorporating a large touch-screen is one way to promote more engaging interaction. The Instructional Technology and Outreach Specialist explained that in her experience, the most engaging and well-received applications are those performed on large touch screens. During the interview, she pulled out a tablet with a touch-screen and demonstrated how students can move through the on-screen environment by "scrolling" with their finger, select objects by touching the surface, and even use the camera function to take pictures. This encourages additional exploration. *"They are great for visual learners,"* she said.

Example: Being able to physically touch objects of interest, as opposed to clicking them with a mouse or keyboard, also delights the game user. The large size of the touch-screen will be able to convey more realistic, entertaining images.

5. Apply Short-Term Scalable Design (Include Multiple, Short Stages)

Description: The game should consist of a series of stages, each of which can be completed within a minute or two. Spending too much time on a level may cause users to become restless. As stated earlier by one of the experts, user-friendliness is critical to a gaming applications success. Thus, anything that would frustrate users (such as game levels that take too much time to complete) should be avoided. In addition, the game should be in accordance with the field trip time limits; during the field trip (e.g., Virginia Aquarium) visitors usually spend a limited amount of time in any one area. After a few minutes or less, guests move on to other exhibits. The Director of Education explained that when educators try to teach guests in informal learning settings, "*we've got a 'one-shot-deal.' That interaction could last 5 seconds, it could be 5 minutes… We have to make people, in a very short period of time, feel like it's worth their time to give us 30 seconds or a couple minutes… to show them something, to show that it's worth doing this rather than going around the corner to see*" other exhibits. Thus, it is important that the game be divided into different segments that convey interesting material in short periods of time.

Example: Each stage of the game should correspond to a different exhibit area of the science center, progressing in the same order as the exhibits (e.g., see figure 2). The game could have short stages and allow users to track their progress with an animated map. The map would show the different parts of the river (representing stages) and identify the users' current location along the river (representing current status).

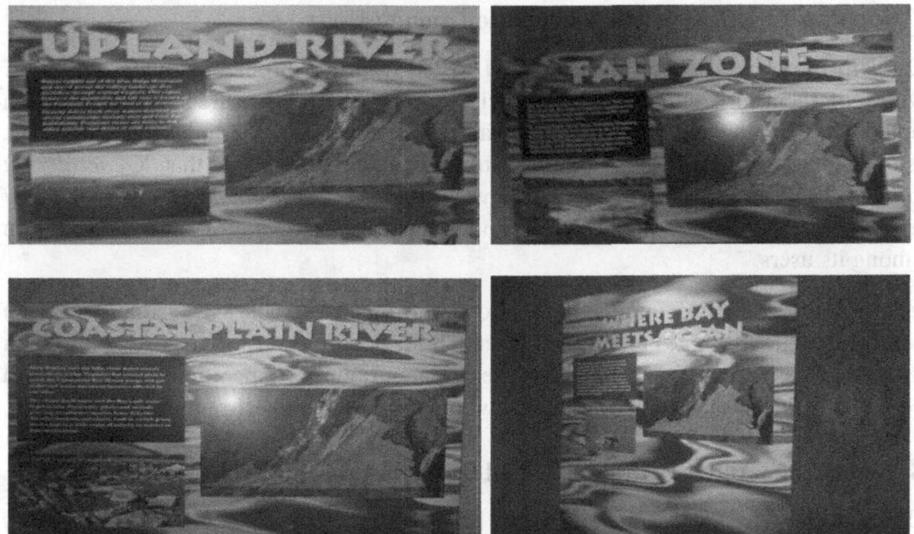

Fig. 2. The VAQ's "Journey of Water" exhibit series follows the course of water from a mountain stream to the ocean. The different exhibits represent different stages in the journey.

6. Direct Users' Attention to Specific Topics

Description: Student visitors often miss valuable material presented in informal learning settings unless someone or something directs their attention. "*With your average high school group, unless someone is directing their activities, they are going to be less apt to spend time in an exhibit where they need to look a little more closely or do a little more reading or spend a little more energy to see what is going on,*" the Director of Education explained. The game should direct the attention of its users to particular topics. Especially for institutions where tours are self-guided (such as the Virginia Aquarium), a mobile game can and should act as a guide or docent. According to the Director of Education, this consists of "*pushing somebody to get interested in something by giving them a tid-bit of information. This gets the guests to say 'Oh, that is kind of interesting,' and then they'll go read the material because they decide it's worth their time*".

Example: Each stage of the game should focus on a specific skill or concept, which users must master in order to complete that stage. If desired, the game could direct users to actual exhibits within the center that cover topics associated with that stage. As an illustrated example, the game could refer the user to the "Getting to the Bottom" station in the Chesapeake Bay Interactive Gallery in order to address how different types of sediment settle in water to form layers. This station shows how coarse-grain and fine-grain sediments settle at different speeds.

7. Support Cooperation and Competition among Users

Description: High school students tend to enjoy group problem-solving activities. Many of them also enjoy competing with one another. The Director of Education noted that planning and executing group activities, especially for high school students, is difficult due to logistics and time constraints. However, she said that "*Generally, in education, they [students] like to have group-based, problem-solving types of activities*". The game should allow and encourage cooperation and competition among its users.

Example: The gaming application could be arranged in such a way that users can send electronic messages to another. Users could be allowed to share resources (such as virtual cash or tools) with other users, encouraging cooperation. A scoreboard could be included on each user's device with a list of the highest-ranking players.

8. Connect the Activity with the School Curriculum Emphasize

Description: The game's material must be based on curriculum standards. "*The key thing right now is to identify what teachers need help with in terms of standards and STEM content. Then you can focus your game on that,*" explained the Director of Education. Hence it is important to actually contact teachers and science supervisors to hear what topics and needs must be addressed. She mentioned also that these topics will often depend on mandated academic standards such as the standards of learning (SOLs). "*We can guess and say, 'This would be a great thing to do,' but unless we meet their [teachers' and students'] needs, they're probably not going to use the game.*" The science education consultant also expressed the importance of basing the game's content on relevant SOLs. The game should prompt students to rigorously investigate these topics and develop a thorough understanding of them.

Example: Assuming that the game is directed to Virginia students, the game needs to address the Virginia Standards of Learning (SOL). As such, important earth science content, like ocean tides and currents can be addressed in conjunction with Virginia Beach the aquarium's "Ocean Gallery". Geometry and earth science material can be integrated in creative ways, like; locating points on a coordinate plane (Geometry SOL) and apply them to interpret latitude and longitude on a map (Earth Science SOL).

5 Discussion and Conclusions

This paper presents an initial attempt to exploit knowledge from experts in informal science learning and model this knowledge into useful guidelines for designers and developers who aim to address students as potential users of STEM games and applications. Our research is characterized by a close collaboration between designers, STEM educators, developers, HCI practitioners/researchers and Museum and Aquarium experts.

The study described in this paper has led to a set of research-derived guidelines for designing games and applications for Science museums. The guidelines were backed by addressed experts' best practices and has been exposed to several stages of validation and organization (semi-structured interviews, content analysis), which should provide some assurance of their validity. Based on this, eight design guidelines have been proposed to take advantage of STEM learning in contextualized environments outside the school context.

We want to emphasize that our findings are clearly preliminary with inevitably limitations. Probably the main limitation is the absence of students' in this work. Our future research will concentrate on further refinement of the proposed guidelines by applying and evaluating them on real conditions. In the next step of this ongoing project we will continue our research with evaluating these guidelines with a mixed methods approach, and aim to improve and optimize them. Furthermore, educators, practitioners and researchers in the area of technology-enhanced STEM learning can also evaluate the proposed guidelines in order to ensure their understanding and seek suggestions and extensions.

Acknowledgements. The authors wish to thank Virginia Aquarium & Marine Science Center staff, and in particular Lynn Clements, Stephanie Hathcock, Katie Vaughan and Chris Witherspoon for sharing their time and expertise. This work is supported by CCF-1139864 NSF grant and the Richard T. Cheng Endowment.

References

1. Ardito, C., Lanzilotti, R.: Isn't this archaeological site exciting!: a mobile system enhancing school trips. In: Proc. of AVI 2008, pp. 488–489. ACM, New York (2008)
2. Cassell, J., Ryokai, K.: Making Space for Voice: Technologies to Support Children's Fantasy and Storytelling. Personal and Ubiquitous Computing 5(3), 169–190 (2001)
3. Costabile, M.F., Ardito, C., Lanzilotti, R.: Enjoying cultural heritage thanks to mobile technology. Interactions 17(3) (2010)
4. Crompton, H.: A historical overview of mobile learning: Toward learner-centered education. In: Berge, Z.L., Muilenburg, L.Y. (eds.) Handbook of Mobile Learning, pp. 3–14. Routledge, Florence (2013)
5. Crompton, H.: Mobile learning: New approach, new theory. In: Berge, Z.L., Muilenburg, L.Y. (eds.) Handbook of Mobile Learning, pp. 47–57. Routledge, Florence (2013)
6. Dale, E.: Audio–visual methods in teaching, 3rd edn. Holt, Rinehart & Winsto, New York (1969)
7. Defazio, J., Rand, K.: Emergent Design: Bringing the Learner Close to the Experience. In: Stephanidis, C. (ed.) Universal Access in HCI, Part I, HCII 2011. LNCS, vol. 6765, pp. 36–41. Springer, Heidelberg (2011)
8. Gerber, S., Scott, L.: Gamers and gaming context: Relationships to critical thinking. British Journal of Educational Technology 42(5), 842–849 (2011)
9. Giannakos, M.N., Jaccheri, L.: What motivates children to become creators of digital enriched artifacts? In: Proc. of the 9th ACM Conference on Creativity & Cognition (C&C 2013), pp. 104–113. ACM, New York (2013)
10. Higgins, P., Nicol, R.: Outdoor education: Authentic learning in the context of landscapes, vol. 2. Kisa, Sweden (2002)

11. Ketelhut, D.J., Schifter, C.C.: Teachers and game-based learning: improving understanding of how to increase efficacy of adoption. Computers & Education 56, 539–546 (2011)
12. Klopfer, E., et al.: Mystery at the museum: a collaborative game for museum education. In: Proc. CSCL 2005, pp. 316–320. ACM Press (2005)
13. Knapp, C.E.: Just beyond the classroom: community adventures for interdisciplinary learning. ERIC Clearinghouse on Rural Education and Small Schools, Charleston West Virginia, Charleston (1996)
14. Looi, C.-K., Seow, P., Zhang, B., So, H.-J., Chen, W., Wong, L.-H.: Leveraging mobile technology for sustainable seamless learning: a research agenda. British Journal of Educational Technology 42(1), 154–169 (2010)
15. Maguire, M., Bevan, N.: User requirements analysis: A review of supporting methods. In: Proc. IFIP 17th World Computer Congress, pp. 133–148. Kluwer Academic Publishers (2002)
16. Mikalef, K., Giannakos, M.N., Chorianopoulos, K., Jaccheri, L.: Does informal learning benefit from interactivity? The effect of trial and error on knowledge acquisition during a museum visit. International Journal of Mobile Learning and Organisation 7(2), 158–175 (2013)
17. Orion, N., Hofstein, A.: Factors that influence learning during a scientific field trip in a natural environment. Journal of Research in Science Teaching 31(10), 1097–1119 (1994)
18. Papastergiou, M.: Exploring the potential of computer and video games for health and physical education: A literature review. Computers & Education 53(3), 603–622 (2009)
19. PCAST-2010. Prepare and Inspire: K-12 Education in Science, Technology (2010), https://www.nsf.gov/attachments/117803/public/2a-Prepare_and_Inspire-PCAST.pdf
20. Pia, S., Eila, J., Sirpa, K., Marka, L.V.: Rural camp school eco learn: Outdoor education in rural settings. International Journal of Environmental & Science Education 6(3), 267–291 (2011)
21. Rogers, Y.: Introduction to distributed cognition. In: Brown, K. (ed.) The Encyclopedia of Language and Linguistics, pp. 181–202. Elsevier, Oxford (2006)
22. Schrier, K.: Using augmented reality games to teach 21st century skills. In: ACM SIGGRAPH Educators Program, Article 15 (2006), doi:10.1145/1179295.1179311
23. Sharples, M., Roschelle, J. (eds.): Special Issue on Mobile and Ubiquitous Technologies for Learning. IEEE Transactions on Learning Technologies 3(1) (2010)
24. Sung, Y.T., Chang, K.E., Hou, H.T., Chen, P.F.: Designing an electronic guidebook for learning engagement in a museum of history. Computers in Human Behavior 26, 74–83 (2010)
25. Tatar, D., Roschelle, J., Knudsen, J., Shechtman, N., Kaput, J., Hopkins, B.: Scaling up innovative technology-based mathematics. Journal of the Learning Sciences 17(2), 248–286 (2008)
26. Woodhouse, J.L., Knapp, C.E.: Place-based curriculum and instruction: outdoor and environmental education approaches (Publication no. ERIC digest – EDO-RC-00-6). From ERIC Clearinghouse on Rural Education and Small Schools (2000)
27. Yi, M.Y., Hwang, Y.: Predicting the use of web-based information systems: self-efficacy, enjoyment, learning goal orientation, and the technology acceptance model. International Journal of Human-Computer Studies 59(4), 431–449 (2003)
28. Yi-Ju, P.: Effect of web-based learning on six-grade students' 3Rs education. National Hsinchu University of Education, Hsinchu (2000)

Designing Sociable CULOT as a Playground Character

Nihan Karatas, Nozomi Kina, Daiki Tanaka, Naoki Ohshima, P. Ravindra S. De Silva, and Michio Okada

Interactions and Communication Design Lab, Toyohashi University of Technology
Toyohashi 441-8580, Japan
{karatas,kina,tanaka,ohshima}@icd.cs.tut.ac.jp, {ravi,okada}@tut.jp
http://www.icd.cs.tut.ac.jp/en/profile.html

Abstract. CULOT is designed as a playground character with the aim of grounding the playground language (verbal, non-verbal, playing-rules, etc) between children through play-routing while experiencing the pleasure of play. A robot establishes "persuasiveness" activities inside the playground, through the process of generating play rules/contexts and executive social interactions and engagement toward the intention of "attachment" of the children to the robot through interaction and activities. The behavior of the robot plays a significant role in executing the above playground activities (or interaction). As a primary study, our focus is to explore how robot behaviors (cues) are capable of generating the playground rules, social interaction and engagement in order to convey its intention to children and extract the potential dimensions in order to design CULOT behaviors as a playground character by considering the above factors.

Keywords: Playground language, persuasiveness, attachment.

1 Introduction

Playground is a space that enables child to expand their imagination, social intelligence, and language for their initial growth and development [5]. Through play routing, children can learn social and cultural rules, experience expressions of affective behaviors, language experiences, and utilize their own language

Fig. 1. Sketch of the playground activities with CULOT robots

C. Stephanidis and M. Antona (Eds.): UAHCI/HCII 2014, Part II, LNCS 8514, pp. 571–580, 2014.

through symbolic communication [8]. There is substantial research showing the clear connection between play and brain development, motor-skills, and social capabilities [2][1]. All learning, whether it be emotional, social, motor, or cognitive, is accelerated, facilitated, and fueled by the pleasure of play [14].

We can comprise a variety of playground environments to facilitate different patterns of playing structures, including free-play contexts and structured-play contexts. Structured-play (e.g., football, baseball, etc.) already includes established rules, number of players, and who the winner or loser will be; however, a free-play structure does not have any rules, restriction of players, etc., which therefore provides more opportunities for children to build up their own rules and procedures. In the context of a free-play structure, children are provided a greater environment to develop their social interaction, communication capabilities, leadership, etc., because they have to communicate interactively to establish the activities while playing harmoniously with other members in the playground [10].

A caregiver (parent, teacher, etc.) also plays a vital role on the playground in establishing interaction between children and also assisting their activities [9]. In this phase, the caregiver pretends to be a teacher, parent, or colleague to support the pleasure of play and also to enhance the social interaction and social intelligence of the children. Through considering the above role of the caregiver, researchers in field of social robotic have been motivated to develop a robotic platform for children in playing contexts [6][7]. These project motivations are directed toward a variety of goals; recently, Cynthia [12] developed a playground character which can be connected to a blended reality (connecting the physical world and virtual world) while establishing a variety of interactive scenarios. Muu [11] was designed to explore the effectiveness of the minimal design and meanwhile establish interaction between children as a social mediator. Aurora [15], IROMEC [4], and ROBOSKIN [13] all explore the usability of a robotic platform for children with autism to enhance their social interaction through game-playing scenarios.

Particular studies have contributed either to exploring a robot's cognitive development model or have attempted to explore how children respond to the robotics platform toward the aim of building social robots. Our attempt is to build up a spatiotemporal foundation toward constructing a playground language based on our social robot, CULOT. As such, the primary motivation of our study was to understand the essential dimensions when designing the CULOT as a playground character - especially in designing the robotic behaviors inside the playground for conducting the rules of play, social interaction, as well as to convey a robot's intention, including determining the characteristics (attributes of the communication channel) of the powerful cues (behaviors). In addition, we attempt to extract the potential dimensions as a roadmap in designing the robot's behaviors as a playground character.

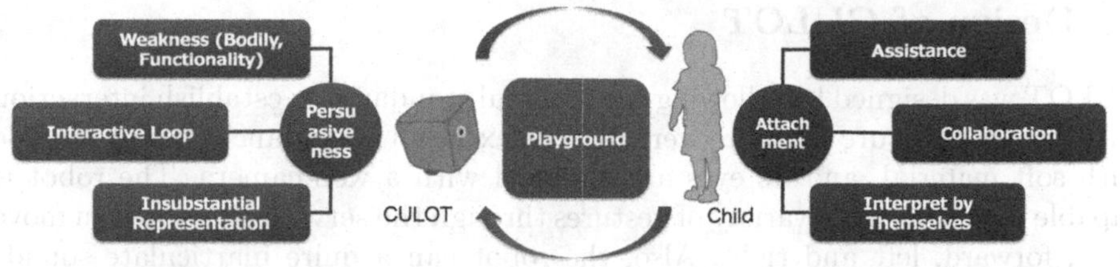

Fig. 2. Interactive process of the implementation

2 Sociable CULOT as a Playground Character

CULOT executes the "persuasiveness" interactions toward "attachment" children into the playground activities (Figure 2). Robot mainly grounds the persuasive interactions through its weakness and insubstantial representations [16]. A weakness of CULOT can be defined based on its body and functionality; CULOT does not have hands and legs, and it cannot grasp any other object. However, CULOT can execute minimal behaviors (e.g., move, push, and express non-verbal behaviors), and through these interactive behaviors the robot can express its intention. Due to the weakness of CULOT's behaviors, it is necessary to evoke children's assistance and collaboration via the insubstantial representation of the playground activities through the interactive loop. Children might anticipate (interpret by themselves) CULOT's interaction and playground activities through the process of insubstantial representation. With this proposed concept, a variety of activities and playground language (symbolic communication, vocal communication, etc.) might be grounded through the child-CULOT interactions.

3 Playground Activities

The robot has to be involved various activities on the playground in order to generate the play rules/contexts, to execute social interactions and engagement, and to convey its intention to the children. Accordingly, it can demonstrate the play rules/contexts while tracking the children's interests and motivation, social interaction, and engagement to establish interactive communication toward enhancing the pleasure of play, and CULOT can also determine how to convey its intention through the behaviors. CULOT can execute the above activities/ interaction through "direct asking (straightly convey robot intention (explicit behaviors))," "indirect asking (insubstantial representation about the intention (implicit behaviors))," "collaboration (working together)," and "encouragement (cheering to activities)." These behaviors can be generated through its inarticulate sounds and pushing/moving behaviors (non-verbal behaviors).

4 Design of CULOT

CULOT was designed by following the minimal standards to establish interaction with the user (Figure 3). Moreover, all of its external appearance (body) is made with soft material, and its eyes are designed with a web-camera. The robot is capable of generating a variety of gestures through the servo-motors - it can move back, forward, left and right. Also, the robot can acquire inarticulate sounds which vary according to the interactions. Several image processing algorithms were embedded to obtain the environmental conditions and changes.

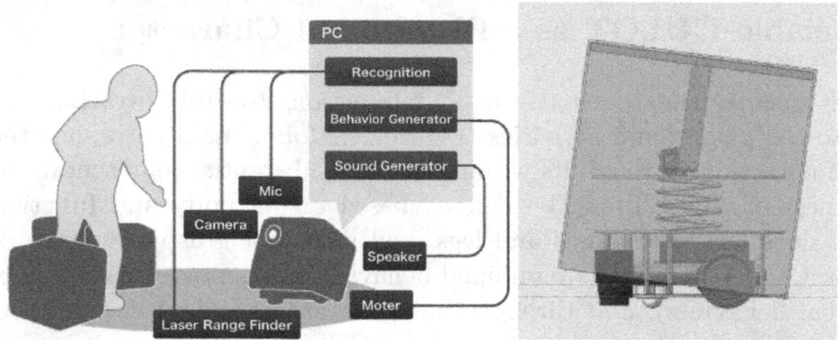

Fig. 3. Designing the architecture of the robot

5 Experimental Protocol

The primary objective of the study was to explore potential social cues for a robot to generate the playground rules, social interaction and engagement in order to convey its intention to the children. Several combinations of communication channels (inarticulate sound, moving behaviors, gestural interactions,

Table 1. Twelve videos created by representing "direct asking (explicit)," "indirect (implicit)," "encouragement," and "collaborative ."

Category	Code of the Videos	Descriptions of the Behaviors	Number of robots/Communication Channels
Direct	A1	One robot is pushing a block into outside	Body gestures
	A2	Two robots are conveying to push a block	Multi-robots, Eye-gaze, Vocal, and Nodding
	A3	One robot is conveying to push a block	Nodding, and Body Orientation
Indirect	B1	One robot is requesting to push a block	Body Movement, Eye-gaze, and Vocal
	B2	One robot is moving around a block	Body Movement
	B3	Multi-robots are establishing the inarticulate sound while looking at a block	Multi-robots, Eye-gaze, and Vocal
Encourage	C1	One robot is doing body interactions and vocalizing while an another robot is pushing a block	Multi-robots, Body Movement, and Vocal
	C2	One robot is moving between two blocks while another robot is nodding by synchronizing inarticulate sound	Multi-robots, Body Movement, and Vocal
	C3	One robot is nodding toward a block while another robot also turns toward a same-block	Multi-robots, Body Orientation, and Nodding
Collaborative	D1	Two robots are pushing two different blocks	Multi-robots, Body Movement
	D2	Two robots are pushing a block	Number of Robots, Body Movement
	D3	One robot is nodding toward two blocks (green and orange), and another robot is pushing an orange block	Multi-robots, Body Movement, and Nodding

etc.) have been considered in generating a robot's social cues, and to finally educe the optimum design dimensions (road-map) in order to design the CULOT behaviors as a playground character. As shown in Table 1, the study developed the "direct (straightly convey robot intention (explicit behaviors))," "indirect (insubstantial representation of the intention (implicit behaviors))," "encourage (cheering activities)," and "collaboration (working together)" behaviors by considering the inarticulate sounds, moving behaviors, gestural interactions, etc. (Figure 4). Twelve total numbers of behaviors were designed by preparing twelve videos with a real playground setup (Table 1) (context of block arrangement as shown in (Figure 1). To explore the above goals, the following two experiments were conducted.

Experiment 1: An initial experiment was conducted to explore what are the most powerful cues (behaviors) to generate the playground rules, social interaction and engagement, and to convey its intention by using the subjective rating of the participants. We used the above twelve videos to obtain the subjective ratings through the interface of LimeSurvey; we included a single video with nine questions (the questioner being depicted in Table 2) on a single page and each participant had to access twelve pages, with a total 108 (12 pages * 9 questions) ratings being obtained from each user. The questions were designed as follows: questions ($Q1, Q2, Q3$) represents the evaluation of the behavioral capability to establish the playground rules; consequently ($Q4, Q5, Q6$) evaluates the potentiality to establish social interaction & engagement, and to evaluate the capability to convey its intention from questions ($Q7, Q8, Q9$) with the rating scale of $(1-5)$. The participants indicated their ratings through a website, with 32 people (19-27 years of age, 9 males and 23 females) participating in the experiment.

Experiment 2: The second experiment was directed to extract the optimum dimensions to design the robot's behaviors. We selected eight videos (direct (A1, A2), indirect (B2, B3), encouragement (C1, C3), and collaboration (D1, D2) according the higher subjective ratings of Experiment 1. Moreover, the highest mean value of the subjective rating for each behavior was considered for all of the

Fig. 4. Figures show a screen shot of the robot's behaviors of $A3$ and $D1$

questions in selecting the above eight behaviors. Our experimental procedure was as follows. We randomly arranged the two videos (suppose video1 and video2) with the following three questions on a single page using LimeSurvey: (1) video1 and video2 had a similar power to build "play ground rules," (2) video1 and video2 had a similar power to establish "social interaction and engagement," and (3) video1 and video2 had a similar power to convey "its intention to the participants." The participants rated the 28 comparisons, and the experiment was conducted with 28 participants between 19-27 years of age (8 male, 20 female).

6 Results

6.1 Results for Experiment 1

Figure 5 depicts the subjective ratings for the each of the videos with relevant questions ($Q1 - Q9$) from the questionnaire. In addition, we applied an ANOVA to expose the significant differences of the subjective ratings of the twelve videos within the each question. The left-hand figure shows the subjective ratings for "capable to establish playground rules," with "capable to establish the social interaction & engagement" in the middle of the figure, and "potential to convey its intention" being also depicted on the right-hand figure. As shown in Table 2, we found significant differences within the all of the questions, which suggests that participants closely evaluated how each of the behaviors could potentially generate playground rules, social interaction & engagement, and convey the robot's intention, since all of the rated ($Q1 - Q9$) questions were represented from the above categories.

Another motivation of this study was to extract the characteristics (or attributes) of higher rated behaviors in each category: playground rules, social interaction & engagement, and convey the robot's intention. We selected the highest and lowest mean values of behaviors in each question (represented in the above categories), as shown in Table 2. We applied independent t-tests to

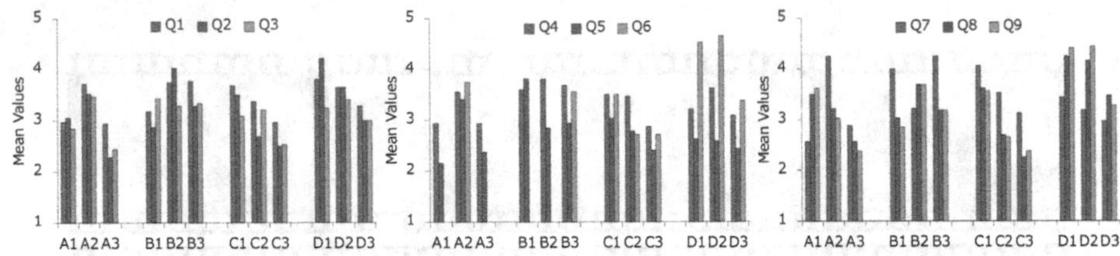

Fig. 5. The figures show the subjective rating for each video (behaviors) by considering each of the questions of the questioner. According to the questionnaire category, the left-hand figure shows the subjective ratings for "playground rules," with the middle of the figure showing the "social interaction & engagement," and "convey its intention" also being depicted in the right-hand figure. All Codes (e.g $A2$, $B2$. etc) were described in Table 1

determine the significant differences of the rating between the highest and lowest behavior ratings in each question. The significant difference between each question suggests that the subjective ratings had clear rating differences, which is important in examining the behaviors and understanding the attributes (characteristics) by synchronizing the robot activities.

If we consider the category of "playground rules," which represents questions $Q1$ to $Q3$, we obtained higher ratings for $D1, D2, A2$, and lower ratings for $A3, A3, A3$. When we look at the higher rated videos of $D1, D2, A2$, all of these behaviors have a common characteristic in that multiple robots were involved in the activities. However, only a single robot was involved in the lower-rated video. These results might suggest that the swarming behaviors of robots with explicit behaviors (directly indicating the activities) are more powerful in making the playground rules. We had higher ratings for $B2, B1, D2$ and lower ratings for $C3, A1, C2$ questions of $Q4$ to $Q6$, which represents the "social interaction & engagement." If we carefully look at these higher rated behaviors, all are defined as implicit (did not directly indicate the task) behaviors. Implicit behavior always evokes the curiosity of humans which intensifies their social interaction and engagement. This might indicate that the implicit behaviors are more positional in establishing the social interaction and engagement in a playground context. Inarticulate sounds and the robot's swarm behaviors were powerful in conveying the robot's intention when we look at the higher rated videos in $Q7$ to $Q9$.

6.2 Results for Experiment 2

In applying multidimensional scaling (MDS) [3], we separately considered the ratings for (1) video1 and video2 had a similar power in building the "play ground rules," (2) video1 and video2 have a similar power in establishing "social interaction and engagement," and (3) video1 and video2 had a similar power in conveying "its intention to the participants." MDS is useful to extract the structure or patterns of the rating (similarity and dissimilarity) through the distance of the visualizations. We can also derive new dimensions to represent the plotted variables by the underlying dissimilarity, since we can explore what are the patterns of the participants rating for each category and how we can acquire the road-map (dimensions) in order to design the robot's behaviors as a playground character.

Figure 6 depicts the results of the multidimensional scaling (MDS) for the subjective ratings of "playground rules", "social interaction and engagement", and "convey its intention to the participants." According to the distance of each plotted points (A1, A2, B2, B3, C3, D1, and D2), we created three boundaries by considering the distances between the points for each figure. Three clusters were extracted as follows: $(C3, B3)$, $(C1, D2, D1, A1)$, and $(A2, B2)$, which are common for the above three categories. The extracted clusters were clearly separated on the visualization, which indicates that a type of road-map appears in the design of the robot's behaviors on the playground. Through MDS, we could extract the optimum dimensions from the visualization, which can defined as follows: The $(C3, B3)$ cluster mainly represents the robot's eye gaze

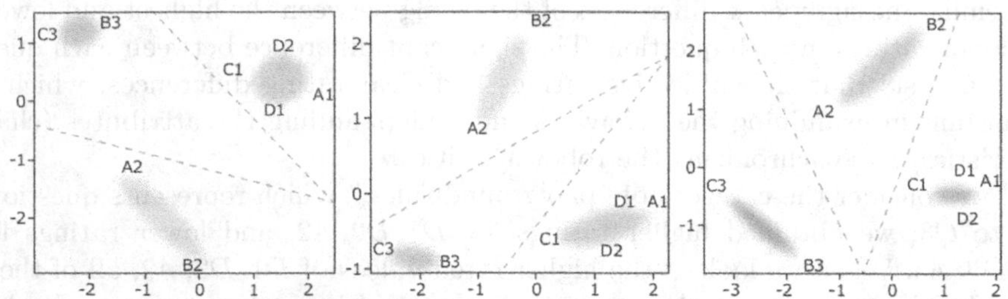

Fig. 6. Results of the MDS for the subjective ratings of "playground rules (left-hand side)," "social interaction and engagement (center)," and "convey its intention to participants (right-hand side)." All Codes (e.g *A*2, *B*2. etc) were described in Table 1.

Table 2. There were significant differences when we consider each question, and the higher and lower rated videos (behaviors) and the information of these significant differences were placed at the end of the table

Questions \ Behaviors	A1	A2	A3	B1	B2	B3	C1	C2	C3	D1	D2	D3	Significance	High & Low Mean Values
Q1: Robot can merged into playground.	2.97	3.72	2.94	3.19	3.75	3.78	3.69	3.38	2.97	3.81	3.66	3.28	F(31,341)= 9.87, p<0.001	high - D1 low - A3 t(31)=5.602 p<0.05
Q2: Robot can built the play rules.	3.06	3.53	2.28	2.88	4.03	3.28	3.50	2.69	2.50	4.22	3.66	3.00	F(31,341)= 18.47, p<0.001	high - D1 low - A3 t(31)=9.887 p<0.05
Q3: I wanted to play with robot(s).	2.84	3.47	2.44	3.44	3.28	3.34	3.09	3.22	2.53	3.25	3.41	3.00	F(31,341)= 8.40, p<0.001	high - A2 low - A3 t(31)=6.126 p<0.05
Q4: Robot(s) look like child.	2.94	3.56	2.94	3.59	3.81	3.69	3.50	3.47	2.88	3.22	3.63	3.09	F(31,341)= 7.08, p<0.001	high - B2 low - C3 t(31)=5.356 p<0.05
Q5: Robot(s) tried to interact with human.	2.16	3.41	2.38	3.81	2.84	2.94	3.03	2.78	2.41	2.63	2.59	2.44	F(31,341)= 11.11, p<0.001	high - B1 low - A1 t(31)=8.324 p<0.05
Q6: Robot can establish a collaboration.	-	3.75	-	-	-	3.56	3.50	2.72	2.72	4.53	4.66	3.38	F(7,217)= 18.91, p<0.001	high - D2 low - C2 t(31)=8.285 p<0.05
Q7: Robot(s) tried to tell something.	2.56	4.25	2.88	4.00	3.22	4.25	4.06	3.53	3.13	3.44	3.19	2.97	F(31,341)= 12.90, p<0.001	high - B3 low - A1 t(31)=7.552 p<0.05
Q8: I can understand robot's behavior.	3.50	3.22	2.56	3.03	3.69	3.19	3.63	2.69	2.25	4.25	4.16	3.47	F(31,341)= 13.64, p<0.001	high - D1 low - C3 t(31)=8.584 p<0.05
Q9: I can understand robot's intention.	3.63	3.03	2.38	2.84	3.69	3.19	3.56	2.66	2.38	4.41	4.44	3.28	F(31,341)= 15.71, p<0.001	high - D2 low - A3 t(31)=8.360 p<0.05

behaviors and bodily interactions, the explicit behaviors were extracted in the $(C1, D2, D1, A1)$ cluster, and the implicit behaviors were found in $(A2, B2)$. The above finding indicate that when we designed the robot's behaviors as playground characters, it was necessary to pay attention to three types of dimensions of behavioral design: (1) the category can be designed by considering the gaze and body interactions, (2) the category can be designed by considering the explicit behaviors (directly indicating the activities/goal), and

(3) the category can be designed by considering the implicit behaviors (do not directly indicate the activities/goal). It is important to consider the above categories in designing the robot's behaviors as a playground character, which are important in executing the variant behaviors by closely tracing the children's behaviors and feedback, for example, initially the robot can execute the implicit behaviors, and then if it does not succeed it can execute the explicit behaviors to fulfill its goal.

7 Discussion and Conclusion

The results of Experiment 1 revealed that an explicit behavior (directly indicating the activities) was more powerful in making playground rules, while implicit behavior was more powerful in establishing the social interaction & engagement (do not directly indicate the task); and for conveying a robot's intention, inarticulate sounds and bodily interactions were powerful. The second experiment of the study that depicted a roadmap and dimensions in designing the robot's behaviors were as follows: The behaviors of CULOT might be designed using three category types: (1) considering the gaze and body interactions, (2) explicit behaviors (directly indicating the activities/goal), and (3) implicit behaviors (do not directly indicate the activities/goal).

As a conclusion, we can combine the experimental results as follows. When we design the CULOT behaviors as playground characters, we should consider the above three dimensions (gaze and bodily interaction, implicit behaviors, and explicit behaviors). According to the activities (make playground rules, social interaction & engagement, and convey robot's intentions) on the playground, the robot could select the suitable behaviors to be executed according to the results of Experiment1, e.g., if the robot needs to establish social rules, then it can use explicit behavior (directly indicating the activities). In our future work, we will focus on utilizing the above higher-rating behaviors. Additionally, the extracted road-map will utilized to design playground activities toward the goal of exploring playground language through child-CULOT interactions.

Acknowledgement. This research has been supported by both Grant-in-Aid for scientific research of KIBAN-B (21300083) and Grant-in-Aid for scientific research for HOUGA (24650053) from the Japan Society for the Promotion of Science (JSPS).

References

1. Brown, J.G., Burger, C.: Playground design and preschool children's behaviors. Environments and Behavior 16, 599–626 (1984)
2. Copple, C., Bredekamp, S.: Developmentally Appropriate Practice in Early Childhood Programs Serving Children from Birth through Age 8. National Association for the Education of Young Children, Washington, DC (2009)
3. Cox, T.F., Cox, M.A.A.: Multidimensional Scaling. Chapman and Hall (1994)

4. Ferari, E., Robins, B., Dautenhahn, K.: Robot as a social mediator - a play scenario implementation with children with autism. In: 8th International Conference on Interaction Design and Children, IDC 2009 (2009)
5. Frost, J.: Children's Play and Playgrounds. Allyn and Bacon, Boston (1979)
6. Ho, W.C., Dautenhahn, K.: Designing an educational game facilitating children's understanding of the development of social relationships using iVAs with social group dynamics. In: Ruttkay, Z., Kipp, M., Nijholt, A., Vilhjálmsson, H.H. (eds.) IVA 2009. LNCS, vol. 5773, pp. 502–503. Springer, Heidelberg (2009)
7. Ito, M., Tani, J.: Joint attention between a humanoid robot and users in imitation game (2004)
8. Johnson, J.E., Christie, J.F., Wardle, F.: Play, Development and Early Education. Pearson (2004)
9. Kwon, K.-A., Bingham, G., Lewsader, J., Jeon, H.-J., Elicker, J.: Structured task versus free play: The influence of social context on parenting quality, toddlers' engagement with parents and play behaviors, and parent? toddler language use. Child & Youth Care Forum 42(3), 207–224 (2013)
10. Nelson, S.: Play: Structured or Unstructured? Otago Polytechnic (2012)
11. Okada, M., Sakamoto, S., Suzuki, N.: Muu: Artificial creatures as an embodied interface. In: ACM SIGGRAPH Conference Abstracts and Applications, p. 91 (2000)
12. Robert, D., Breazeal, C.: Blended reality characters. In: HRI, pp. 359–366 (2012)
13. Robins, B., Dautenhahn, K.: Developing play scenarios for tactile interaction with a humanoid robot: A case study exploration with children with autism. In: Ge, S.S., Li, H., Cabibihan, J.-J., Tan, Y.K. (eds.) ICSR 2010. LNCS, vol. 6414, pp. 243–252. Springer, Heidelberg (2010)
14. Sawyers, J.: The preschool playground: Developing skills through outdoor play. The Journal of Physical Education, Recreation & Dance 65 (1994)
15. Werry, I., Dautenhahn, K.: Applying mobile robot technology to the rehabilitation of autistic children proceedings. In: 7th International Symposium on Intelligent Robotic Systems, pp. 265–272 (1999)
16. Yamaji, Y., Miyake, T., Yoshiike, Y., Silva, P.R.S.D., Okada, M.: Stb: Child-dependent sociable trash box. I. J. Social Robotics 3(4), 359–370 (2011)

KidSmart© in Early Childhood Learning Practices: Playful Learning Potentials?

Eva Petersson Brooks and Nanna Borum

Centre for Design. Learning and Innovation, Department of Architecture and Media Technology, Aalborg University, Niels Bohrs Vej 8, 6700 Esbjerg, Denmark
{ep,nb}@create.aau.dk

Abstract. This paper reports on a study exploring the outcomes from children's play with technology in early childhood learning practices. The study is grounded in a sociocultural perspective on play and learning and consists of an analysis of children's interaction with the KidSmart furniture, particularly focusing on playful learning potentials and values suggested by the technology. The study applied a qualitative approach and included125 children (aged three to five), 10 pedagogues, and two librarians. The results suggests that educators should sensitively consider intervening when children are interacting with technology, and rather put emphasize into the integration of the technology into the environment and to the curriculum in order to shape playful structures for children's individual and collective interaction with technology.

Keywords: Early childhood learning, playful learning, interaction, technology, affordances.

1 Introduction

This paper addresses questions related to how technology can enrich early childhood learning environments. Traditional environments for children's play and learning have undergone major changes in recent years. With the rapid development of technology, these environments have expanded their resources for play and learning. While technologies are used for a variety of activities in early childhood years, the use of computers for playing games is the most common activity [1]. It is only recently that technologies have been introduced in a more widely sense to younger children's education. Research shows that the technology has been considered as a supplement, rather than a resource with qualities that can enhance and renew a pedagogical practice [2]. Jernes et al. [3] state that this can have several reasons, e.g. limited access to equipment and lack of digital competence, which might have resulted in a limited critical discussion regarding how digital technologies can be implemented as a resource contributing to the pedagogical content and form.

The term play has many different definitions and is used differently across different disciplines, field and contexts. In this paper we take on a sociocultural approach to

C. Stephanidis and M. Antona (Eds.): UAHCI/HCII 2014, Part II, LNCS 8514, pp. 581–592, 2014.

play where it is considered as a leading activity in a child's development. Vygotsky [4] has argued, "Play is the source of development and creates the zone of proximal development" (p. 16). Furthermore the author emphasizes that play is not solely an intellectual activity, but embedded in a social situation determined by the social and cultural context in which the child is surrounded. In this sense, motives interests and incentives of the child shape the play and this will be different across cultures, thus influencing the nature and pattern of play [5].

Technology in the context of this paper refers to a computer housed in specially designed furniture equipped with educational software. Such a design can be considered as a resource for play, and should thereby be a useful resource by affording various forms of play and learning potentials appropriate to different social situations. Thus, children can explore the technology in playful ways, where a progression in use moves from exploration to mastery of the technology. Price et al. [6] have defined a range of elements that are essential for playful forms of learning, e.g. exploration through interaction, engagement, reflection, imagination, creativity and thinking at different levels of abstraction, and collaboration. These elements can be related to how children in their everyday life naturally, and often playfully, explore the world [7], [8]. It is envisioned that such playful explorations, based on children's own motives, interests and incentives, elicit learning opportunities through their involvement with the world.

The focus of this study, how technology can enrich early childhood learning environments, is based on the assumption that play and playfulness need to be deliberately cultivated to support effective use of technology in learning environments for young children. The study is part of a bigger project being conducted by Varde Library, Denmark, 13 kindergartens in Varde municipality, Aalborg University, Denmark. IBM KidSmart Early Learning Program, Denmark and the Danish Agency of Culture, Denmark.

2 Theory

This study applies a playful approach to learning and play in order to investigate how technology can enrich early childhood learning environments. Technologies are defined as including both hardware and software. In this study, this refers to a computer housed in specially designed furniture equipped with educational software.

Furthermore, the playful approach outlined in this study, builds on a sociocultural notion of learning, play and interaction as developed by Vygotsky [4], [5] and Rogoff [9]. This offers an understanding of children's play and learning with technology as an emergent, situated and reciprocal process comprising interactions as well as an interplay between the subject(s) and the environment (cf. [10], [11], [12], [13], [14]).

Technology and play(fullness) are important aspects of learning, yet they are not used to their fullest potential in educational practices. Building on recent work in the fields of learning theories (e.g. [15], [14]), the study starts from a notion of play(fullness) as socially and materially mediated processes. In line with this perspective, the focus is on particular play potentials of such processes.

2.1 Play and Learning Potentials and Values

This study focuses on play potentials offered by the technology in order to explore how technology can enrich play and learning in early childhood by offering a playful approach to such situations. Play potentials refer to a thinking of the technology in terms of how it affords different ways of playing; emergent play patterns. In this regard, the concept of affordance provides a way to investigate the play potentials of the technology. The term was introduced by Gibson [16] and describes how we perceive a tool's potential uses. Norman [17] appropriated the term in the context of human-computer interaction referring to the action potentials that are perceivable by the user of the technology. From a common sense point of view, of course technology developed for play and learning should also afford play and learning. However, as stated before, play is a complex situated phenomenon including that there is not only one single way of designing play potentials in technology. The appropriation of the technology implies that the child is the master, and the technology is subordinate and offering play potentials to the child. Leading on from the theories of affordance, we suggest that play and learning scenarios emerging from interaction with technology, are suggestions. This is in line with [18]. In other words, this study targets to identify suggestions for how technology can enrich early childhood learning environments.

Considering that technology suggests certain ways of playful explorations leading to certain learning potentials - but what about the value of these suggestions? This question can be reflected upon from at least two perspectives. Technology as such offers extrinsic and intrinsic values pondering the questions of whether and how it can be interacted with in a playful way (cf. [19]). So, to analyze the play value, we should consider the different types of play and learning experiences the technology suggests.

3 Method

The study had a qualitative approach and was inspired by a human-centred design methodology in order to investigate how technology can enrich early childhood learning environments, particularly focusing on the aspects of play and learning potentials and values suggested by the technology. Gill, in [20], defines human-centeredness as "a new technological tradition, which places human need, skill, creativity and potentiality at the centre of the activities of technological systems." The way we apply this is by questioning how and why the technology enrich learning environments and thereby promoting human interests rather than technical. We consider design as expression of intentions leading to suggestions and, thereby, not only related to the materials, forms or design processes, which is in line with [21] (2012).

3.1 Participants and Procedure

The study is grounded in an analysis of children's interaction with the KidSmart furniture, particularly focusing on play and learning potentials and values suggested by the technology. In line with this, we considered whether and how the technology invites to playful learning situations. Interviews and observations (including video and note writing) were conducted with in total 125 children (aged three to five), 10 pedagogues, and two librarians. The participants were representatives from eight different kindergartens and a public children's library department in Varde municipality, Denmark. The investigation at the library included four different groups of children (aged three to five) from nearby located kindergartens visiting the library together with their pedagogues. The children were observed when interacting with the KidSmart. During this time they were also interviewed in an informal and unstructured way. The pedagogues and the libraries were interviewed using semi-structured questions.

The study was carried out during free play sessions in the kindergartens and in the library as an offered activity to the visiting children. In the library the pedagogues were present in the room, but not the librarians who took care of children not participating in the study. The latter was also the case in the kindergartens, where the pedagogues were not present due to that they were occupied with the children that were not participating in the study. The sessions were exploratory with duration of 30 minutes each. All groups had the same introduction to the KidSmart session. They were instructed that they should explore the computer software and that they could choose and play the games they preferred. There were few restrictions and the children could leave whenever they wanted to. The sessions were video recorded with 2 cameras in total.

The data was analyzed using [22] approach to analyzing qualitative data. The video recordings were transcribed, coded and categorized using the critical incident technique [23]. The analysis focused on how the children mastered the KidSmart furniture unit and, hence, how the technology contributed to playful learning situations for children.

3.2 Apparatus

The technology used in the study was the IBM KidSmart computer furniture. KidSmart is part of IBM's social responsibility program and they have from 1999, in collaboration with early childhood education practices and public institutions (e.g. libraries and hospitals), developed the KidSmart Early Learning Program. Recently IBM has initiated projects together with libraries and kindergartens in Danish municipalities (including the kindergartens and children's library department from Varde municipality participating in this study). The intention from IBM's side is to establish bridges between libraries and kindergartens in local areas.

KidSmart is specifically designed for children aged three to six and consists of the Young Explorer, which is a computer housed in colored Little Tikes™ furniture (see Fig. 3).

Fig. 1. KidSmart is a computer housed in colored Little Tikes™ furniture.

The design of the furniture is supposed to encourage the children to collaborate with each other. It is equipped with the educational software Riverdeep to support children's learning through exploration and play [24]. In particular, the software should strengthen children's language, speech understanding and concept development. In Varde municipality there is a specific focus on: strengthening of bilingual children's language competencies, children's information competencies, children's individual abilities to appropriate language and mathematical skills, and of children's social relations.

The educational software included in the study consisted of games such as Baileys Book House, Millies Math House, Millie's Mouse Skills, Sammy's Science House and Trudy's Time and Place House. A web site is available, which provides advice for early education teachers and the parents of young children on the appropriate use of information and communication technology to support child development [25].

4 Results

This study investigated how technology can enrich early childhood learning environments, particularly focusing on the aspects of play and learning potentials and values suggested by the technology. The context of the study included kindergartens and a children's library department in a Danish municipality and involved children between three to five years of age, pedagogues and librarians. The unit of analysis was the children's actions and interactions with the KidSmart furniture unit and the related educational software. The individual findings are discussed in the next sessions; children in control; physical and practical concerns; and need for transparent and pedagogically integrated applications.

4.1 Children in Control

The findings from the study revealed that KidSmart suggests social play and encourage children to create relations between each other. In many examples it was clear that the children helped each other to make meaning of the system. The more technology-skilled children spontaneously guided other children and when children were seated around the furniture, they seemed to all consider the task at the screen as a shared one. On one occasion when the children did not know how to understand a task and at another instance when they could not navigate the system, they asked their peers for help. These children then joined the game play activity, took control of the task for a short while explaining their actions. When this was done, they handed over the mouse to the child who initially did not understand the task and, again from the side, took part in the interaction around the screen. One pedagogue stated:

> The computer often has a reputation for being an asocial experience, but we do not see that at all. The children gather around it, play together and help each other through the games. There is a lot collaboration happening while they are playing.

The children practiced to use a mouse and regular computer screen, where the mouse ensured that only one child at the time was in control. This, on the other hand, facilitated a range of social learning, such as turn taking. In one instance, four girls were playing together. Three of them were sitting on the KidSmart furniture bench and one girl was standing behind them. Without adult guidance the girls practiced their social skills by allowing all to take turns and controlling the mouse. When it was another of the girls turn to control the mouse, they all changed their seats so that she could sit where the mouse is most conveniently manoeuvred (in contrast to moving the mouse). The non-verbalised agreement seems to be that every girl could try a game once and then they shifted to the next girl. Independent on who was in control, they all participated in a game where they should dress a doll. They were very keen on that the clothes should be placed properly on the doll and also communicated a lot about the imagined needs of the doll.

> She should have a rain jacket on. It's raining!

After a short while one of the girls began to push the boundaries of the agreement the girls had on taking turns. When a game was over, she quickly changed to another game so that she would be first in line to play that, and repeated this action when also this game was over. The other girls started to become frustrated, asking for their turns but she ignored the request. The girl standing behind the bench quickly lost interest and left, but the two girls sitting on the KidSmart furniture bench tried more explicitly to suggest what she should do in the game. They pointed on the screen where she should click, but they were again ignored. This continued for a couple of minutes until they also left the game play situation. Another girl sits down next to the playing girl and asked if she could try. Without hesitation she was allowed to take over the mouse and they shifted their seating places. Similar instances occurred in many of the observed play sessions where one child would get immersed in the game to a degree where they briefly would forget the social conduct, but it never led to a real conflict. The children in all instances communicated their way out of the situation.

4.2 Physical and Practical Concerns

One of the major limitations of the KidSmart furniture unit is the mouse. It is a reoccurring incident that children do not know how to control the mouse or that the mouse was simply too big for the children. A pedagogue put it like this:

> The mouse is just very difficult for the children. By now they are used to using an Ipad, and they expect a regular computer to be navigated in the same way.

In a few instances the difficulty with controlling the mouse, instead of causing frustration, it opened up for peer learning. The children would try to help one another by explaining and showing how to navigate the mouse.

Fig. 2. A child tries to stand up in an effort to get control of the mouse.

In the instances where the mouse was too big the children would most often quickly let others take over. The pedagogues reported that the size of the mouse led to a lot of frustrations in the children because in contrast to the difficulty in learning how to navigate the mouse, this was not something that the children could learn.

Another report from the pedagogues was of a more practical state. Repeated periods of time the KidSmart was not functioning due to the children accidentally having accessed operation system settings leading to malfunction. The observations showed that when the children sitting next to the child in control of the mouse got frustrated with the actions in the game, they would at numerous occasions obstruct the game by either pushing the "windows"-button and hence leave the game or by frantically pounding the keyboard. In addition to this, there were also instances where children accidentally cut the chord to the speakers, mouse, and/or keyboard. The pedagogues reported that the reoccurring instances made them feel a bit helpless and demotivated towards the system.

In more than half of the participating kindergartens the pedagogues had decided on a time-based use of the KidSmart. This meant that they had, for example, placed an egg timer by the side of the furniture unit, which the children naturally used without involvement of the pedagogues. They put the timer on (10 minutes) and when the bell of the egg timer rang, they left their place on the KidSmart bench in front of the screen as well as the mouse over to the next child. Another example was that even if there was no timer at hand during the study, most children handed over their place and the mouse to another child after a few minutes as a natural action. From the pedagogues side, the use of a timer was explained both in terms of safety, i.e. that the children should not sit in front of the screen too long time, and in terms of fostering turn taking.

Another practical report was that the pedagogues considered the KidSmart being too big in size. They found it difficult to fit into the kindergarten environment. One kindergarten had to reorganize a shared space to fit it in. Another kindergarten had originally planned to let the KidSmart relocate between the group rooms, but had to rethink this, as they needed to take out the doors of the room every time the KidSmart unit should be moved.

The library had a bigger room disposal, which meant that they conveniently could integrate the system into the space. Two KidSmart furniture units were placed next to each other, which enabled the children to communicate and collaborate crossover the units and talk about the two games being played at the same time.

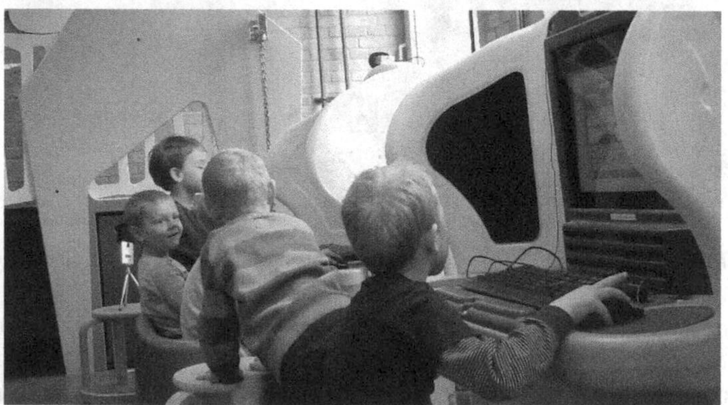

Fig. 3. Children communicating across the computer furnitures

4.3 Need for Transparent and Pedagogically Integrated Applications

The games were merely concerned with problem solving and achieving clear goals. They were structured with defined tasks, rather than being open-ended and ambiguous. Furthermore, the games included too little or no narrative, which resulted in that the children quickly found the games meaningless. According to the pedagogues some games need adult guidance to support the children's collaboration skills. From the observations it was also clear that there were games where the children needed adult assistance. In one game the children should click at objects in no particular order and then gradually a figure behind the objects would reveal. The game does not promote collaboration and thus the children sitting next to the child in control of the mouse quickly became bored. In an effort to keep the children engaged the adult created small playful tasks and tales about the figure that revealed.

In some of the kindergartens the pedagogues were concerned about what kind of applications they offered for the children's play and they described how they shifted the games to be aligned with the current curriculum activities, for example when they focused on a certain season, such as autumn, they integrated programs that included tasks developing concept development in this regard. In the library there was a concern about introducing KidSmart so that it could support early literacy and bilingual children's language competencies. On one occasion a group of children from a multicultural kindergarten were invited to the library premises to take part in a variety of activities, including KidSmart. The children had linguistically diverse backgrounds. The KidSmart was, as mentioned before, well integrated in the library surrounded by other material for children, such as books, costumes, vehicles and toys (see Fig. 4).

Fig. 4. KidSmart units naturally integrated in the library environment.

The children from the visiting group explored the environment and the different tools altering between the KidSmart and other material. In particular two children, a boy and a girl, spent more time than the other children by the computers. They used different kinds of software, addressing math, language and science learning, and the different words and numbers that were embedded in the program prompted them to repeat and to talk about them in the Danish language.

5 Conclusions and Implications

We have investigated in what way technology can enrich early childhood play and learning. In this regard we have looked at emerging play and learning potentials and values when children have interacted with technology. In particular, we have been interested in how this interaction provided different ways of playing encouraging a sense of playfulness. However, we have emphasized that it is important to also understand the influence of the context in such situations.

In the library the design of the space encouraged integration of the KidSmart as well as social learning, which also was a specific focus for the implementation. In the kindergartens, the KidSmart was often considered too big to fit into the design of the kindergarten environment, which isolated rather than integrated the unit. This means that in some of the kindergartens the KidSmart was not really used, but rather put aside in a corner or in an inaccessible place. In some kindergartens, where the KidSmart was part of the environment, the unit was more of a social hub, which was promoting both social and cognitive learning. The rule of turn taking and that the children should help each other encouraged social usage, sharing and a peer-interaction when the children used the technology. [26] emphasize that careful planning is required in order to establish such collaborative opportunities for children when playing with a computer. *This suggests that when technology is well integrated in the learning environment, it has the potential to foster social interaction and collaboration.*

The pedagogues was aware of establishing as safe conditions as possible for the children's use of the technology, which is seen in the example of using an egg timer to avoid that they sit in front of the KidSmart screen too long. This procedure resulted in that the children themselves became responsible for taking turns and, thereby, they did not expose themselves too long in front of the screen. KidSmart is designed as child-sized when it comes to how the computer is embedded in a furniture adjusted to children's size. However, the mouse did not have the right size for children's bodies, which in many instances also caused frustration as well as ergonomically restricted performance by the children. This is a concern, not only for the usability issues exemplified in section 4.2, but also from a health awareness point of view (cf. [27]). The authors furthermore emphasize that even though newer technologies with alternative interfaces that seem to be more child-sized in their design, for example touch-screens and handheld computers, are not necessarily automatically ergonomic suitable for children's use. *This suggests that when the physical and practical conditions of the technology are not completely in place, the child cannot become the master of the technology; rather it is the technology that is superordinate and, thereby, limiting play and learning potentials to the child.*

In most of the situations when the children interacted with the technology, they were without adult support. The intervention from the adults, mostly concerned practical concerns. According to [28] these are situations where children learn to develop and apply rules to their play. In our study, such interaction situations when the children were without or had limited support from the educators, they developed individual as well as peer engaged social situations. For example, the boy and the girl with bi-lingual backgrounds and how they were prompted by the software to in Danish repeat and talk about different words and numbers, and how the girls collectively practiced their social skills by allowing all to take turns and controlling the mouse as well as collective interests to the clothing needs of the doll. *This suggests that the children benefitted in their own way from the collective and collaborative aspects of the interaction, which as such created playful experiences.*

We have addressed the potentialities and values of interaction with technology within a framework of what these situations suggest relative to playful learning opportunities, where the affordances were interpreted as kinds of action possibilities [18]. The most outstanding patterns of play and learning when the children interacted with the technology were based on the values of socialized play in the form of collaboration. We also identified patterns of individual engagements, primarily related to the programs' affordance of tasks that are inquiry-based with different levels of abstraction. However, some of the KidSmart programs had limited transparency, which limited the children's opportunities to explore the games and tasks in playful ways. Overall it seems like the children when possible enjoyed mastering the interaction themselves. *This suggests that educators should sensitively consider intervening when children are interacting with technology, while rather put emphasize into the integration of the technology into the environment and to the curriculum in order to shape playful structures for children's individual and collective interaction with technology.*

References

1. Plowman, L., Stephen, C.: Children, Play, and Computers in Pre-school Education. British Journal of Educational Technology 36(2), 145–157 (2005)
2. Cuban, L.: Oversold and Underused: Reforming Schools Through Technology, 1980-2000. Harvard University, Cambridge (2001)
3. Jernes, M., Alvestad, M., Sinnerud, M.: "Er det bra eller?" Pedagogiske Spenningsfelt i Møte med Digitale Verktøy i Norske Barnehager. Nordisk Barnehageforsking 3(3), 115–131 (2010)
4. Vygotsky, L.: Play and Its Role in the Mental Development of the Child. Voprosy Psihologii 12(6), 62–76 (1966)
5. Vygotsky, L.S.: The Collected Works of L.S. Vygotsky. Child Psychology, vol. 5. Plenum Press, New York (1998) (Editor: Rieber, R.W.)
6. Price, J., Rogers, Y., Scaife, M., Stanton, D., Neale, H.: Using 'Tangibles' to Promote Novel Forms of Playful Learning. Interacting with Computers 15(2), 169–185 (2003)
7. Howard, J.: Eliciting Young Children's Perceptions of Play, Work and Learning Using the Activity Apperception Story Procedure. Early Child Development and Care 172, 489–502 (2002)
8. Howard, J., Bellin, W., Rees, V.: Eliciting Children's Perception of Play and Exploiting Playfulness to Maximise Learning in the Early Years Classroom. In: Proceedings from BERA (British Educational Research Association) Annual Conference, University of Exeter, September 11-12, pp. 1–15 (2002)
9. Rogoff, B.: Apprenticeship in Thinking. Cognitive Development in Social Context. Oxford University Press, New York (1990)

10. Biskjaer, M.M., Dalsgaard, P.: Toward a Constrating Oriented Pragmatism Understanding of Design Creativity. In: Proceedings of the 2nd International Conference on Design Creativity (ICDC 2012), Glasgow, UK, September 18-20, pp. 65–74 (2012)
11. Petersson, E.: Non-formal Learning through Ludic Engagement with in Interactive Environments. Doctoral dissertation, Malmoe University, School of Teacher Education, Studies in Educational Sciences (2006)
12. Petersson, E.: Editorial: Ludic Engagement Designs for All. Digital Creativity 19(3), 141–144 (2008)
13. Petersson, E., Brooks, A.: Virtual and Physical Toys – Open-ended Features towards Non-formal Learning. CyberPsychology and Behavior 9(2), 196–199 (2006)
14. Petersson Brooks, E.: Ludic Engagement Designs: Creating Spaces for Playful Learning. In: Stephanidis, C., Antona, M. (eds.) UAHCI 2013, Part III. LNCS, vol. 8011, pp. 241–249. Springer, Heidelberg (2013)
15. Shneiderman, B.: Creativity Support Tools – Accelerating Discovery and Innovation. Communication of the ACM 50(12), 20–32 (2007)
16. Gibson, J.: The Theory of Affordances. In: Shaw, R., Bransford, J. (eds.) Perceiving, Acting and Knowing: Toward an Ecological Psychology, Lawrence Erlbaum, Hillsdale (1977)
17. Norman, D.A.: The Design of Everyday Things. Basic Books, New York (1988)
18. Kudrowitz, B.M., Wallace, D.R.: The Play Pyramid: A Play Classification and Ideation Tool for Toy Design. International Journal of Arts and Technology 3(1), 36–56 (2008)
19. Jacobs, D.: The Cultural Side of Innovation. Adding Values. Routledge, London (2007)
20. Gasson, S.: Human-Centered vs. User-Centered Approaches to Information System Design. Journal of Information Technology Theory and Application 5(2), 29–46 (2003)
21. Giacomin, J.: What is Human Centred Design? In: 10th Congresso Brasileiro de Oesquisa e Desenvolvimento em Design, P&D Design 2012, Sao Luis (MA) (2012), http://hcdi.brunel.ac.uk/files/What%20is%20Human%20Centred%20Design.pdf (retrieved February 18, 2014)
22. Dey, I.: Qualitative Data Analysis: A User-Friendly Guide for Social Scientists. Routledge Taylor & Francis Group, London (1993)
23. Flanagan, J.: The Critical Incident Technique. Psychological Bulletin 51(4), 327–358 (1954)
24. Berry, C.: IBM KidSmart Early Learning Programme: Case Studies from 15 Countries which Demonstrate the Impact of KidSmart for Children with Special Educational Needs. Unpublished Manuscript (2009), http://blog.eun.org/insightblog/upload/brochure_Kidsmart_148x210_ANG_1.pdf (retrieved February 18, 2014)
25. Siraj-Blatchford, J., Siraj-Blatchford, I.: Developmentally Appropriate Technology in Early Childhood: 'Video Conferencing'. Contemporary Issues in Early Childhood: Technology Special Issue 3(2), 216–225 (2004)
26. Labbo, L.D., Sprague, L., Montero, M.K., Font, G.: Connecting a Computer to Themes, Literature and Kindergarteners' Literacy Needs. Reading Online 4(1) (2000), http://readingonline.org/electronic/labbo/index.html (retrieved March 12, 2014)
27. Siraj-Blatchford, J., Whitebread, D.: Supporting Information and Communications Technology in the Early Years. Open University Press, Berkshire (2003)
28. Bodrova, E., Leong, D.J.: Tools of the Mind: The Vygotskian Approach to Early Childhood Education, 2nd edn. Pearson Education/Merrill, Upper Saddle River (2007)

Interactive Multimodal Molecular Set – Designing Ludic Engaging Science Learning Content

Tine Pinholt Thorsen[1], Kasper Holm Christiansen[1], Kristian Jakobsen Sillesen[1], Torben Rosenørn[2], and Eva Petersson Brooks[1]

[1] Centre for Design. Learning and Innovation, Department of Architecture and Media Technology, Aalborg University, Niels Bohrs Vej 8, 6700 Esbjerg, Denmark

[2] Centre for Design. Learning and Innovation, Department of Learning and Philosophy, Aalborg University, Niels Bohrs Vej 8, 6700 Esbjerg, Denmark

tthors10@student.aau.dk

Abstract. This paper reports on an exploratory study investigating 10 primary school students' interaction with an interactive multimodal molecular set fostering ludic engaging science learning content in primary schools (8th and 9th grade). The concept of the prototype design was to bridge the physical and virtual worlds with electronic tags and, through this, blend the familiarity of the computer and toys, to create a tool that provided a ludic approach to learning about atoms and molecules. The study was inspired by the participatory design and informant design methodologies and included design collaboratorium sessions, interviews and observations. The results indicated that bridging the physical and digital worlds can support learning where the affordances of the technologies can be described in terms of meaningful activity: exploration, reasoning, reflection, and ludic engagement. Here, the electronic tags facilitate the application and provide the students to articulate knowledge through different modes; images, gestures, and 3D objects

Keywords: Human-computer interaction, multimodality, ludic engagement, learning, abstract concepts, pedagogy.

1 Introduction

This paper describes the design process of an interactive multimodal molecular set for fostering ludic engaging science learning content in primary schools (8th and 9th grade), and encouraging the students to explore and reflect upon science learning content. Currently Danish schools increasingly emphasis teaching and learning of science, which has resulted in that a range of new initiatives have been implemented to enhance children's interest in science [1]. How is it possible to realize the potentials of interactive multimodal systems to motivate students' interest and mastery of abstract science concepts?

C. Stephanidis and M. Antona (Eds.): UAHCI/HCII 2014, Part II, LNCS 8514, pp. 593–604, 2014.

In recent years digital technologies have become increasingly essential resources in teaching and learning activities. In parallel, new games using the RFID (radio frequency identification) tags have become increasingly popular among children [2], for example games like Skylanders and Disney's Infinity. According to [3] the genius of these games is that they blend the fun of video games and toys. This study investigates how designing a resource combining the familiarity of the computer and the blend between a game and tangible physical artifacts, might create conditions for a multimodal and more ludic engaging science learning scenario. The multimodality is considered as semiotic resources [4], [5], which are organized as choices providing different affordances [6] enabling interactions concerned with the emergence of new and improved forms of thought [7]. Hence, the system (molecular set) intends to foster ludic engagement through visual, tangible, spatial and textual modes of interaction. Since science is a broad concept, the focus is in particular on atoms and molecules.

In order to create explorative and reflective experiences when interacting with a multimodal system, in this case a molecular set, our claim is that students through the alteration between different modalities might elicit qualities in interaction through ludic engagement. The term "ludic" originates from the latin "ludus", which means "game" (http://www.latinwordlist.com/latin-words/ludus-17816915.htm). However, related work (c.f. [8]) has shown ludicity to be about far more than simply playing a game. It relates to the engagement of the body and mind, where a ludic activity is something that can create a good feeling for a person. In terms of [6] and [9], this constitutes a crucial foundation for learning. Rather than being useful, systems designed to support ludic values are rich, ambiguous and open-ended [10]. Thus, systems that promote ludic engagement should not be concerned with achieving clear goals, or be overly structured with defined tasks [11], [12], [13]. In this paper, this captivation of ludicity and fun is related to having playful experiences.

2 Background

Technology-enhanced learning was introduced in educational contexts already in the 1960s and has since then been debated by a wide range of stakeholders. From teachers, politicians and researchers to parents, and producers of software, information technology is discussed in terms of potentials and limitations in relation to teaching and learning, e.g. [14], [15], [16]. Seymour Papert was one of the pioneers within this field, primarily through his design of LOGO, a programming language, targeting students to learn about programming. Papert argues that when working with LOGO, students create their own resources for learning. The role of the teacher, then, is to take a step back and interfere as little as possible and, in doing so, allowing the students to learn by themselves [17]. This is inspired by Piaget's instructional notion emphasizing that students should not be instructed, but rather develop their own understanding through engaging in exploratory work.

In the 1980s, the core issue of pedagogical attention concerned how information and communication technology could be designed and implemented to become more accessible. Learning activities were predicted to change from the traditional teacher-centered teaching to more student-initiated approaches. While the implementation of digital technology in schools did not proceed as fast as promoters had predicted, technology was to some extent implemented in teaching and learning activities. However, it was primarily used in traditional ways, meaning that learning situations were still teacher-centered and information and communication technology was used as a complement to a traditional way of teaching [14]. As a response to the individualistic approach to including information and communication technology in schools, computer-supported collaborative learning (CSCL) as a pedagogical approach, was developed in the 1990s. CSCL implied a design of learning activities where students work together in groups using information and communication technology as resources for joint learning. This implies that students take an active part in the learning activities and work together in the exploration of problems [18]. Recently the discussion of theories of technology-enhanced learning has developed to include the relationship between technology and the context. For example, questions of how augmented physical spaces can be supported by digital technologies are developments currently on the research agenda (cf. [19], [20]).

Yet, while constituting a resource for teaching and learning, the interactive multimodal system described in this paper, should entail the ability to evoke the user to release their ludic potential. In other words, it should create engaging experiences through actualization of affordances. This might be described as a process where the student, when approaching the system, potentially become inspired and start to explore perceived affordances. The learning potentials offered by the system, then, is actualized by the student's ludic engagement with the system and its content. What optimally happens next is that the student, through this exploration and ludic engagement, adds his or her own values, needs, and desires to the interaction. This, then, might lead to that the student finds new and different pathways of learning and, potentially, inspires peers to (inter)act towards ludicity in learning. From this perspective, technology-enhanced learning is more than mere information processing but a direct involvement with the world aimed at its transformation; a perspective that has substantial implications for the classroom habitus [21].

In the next section, we will elaborate in more detail the potentials of interactive multimodal systems providing a framework from which to consider how to design an interactive system that can foster ludic learning experiences through exploration and reflection.

3 A Framework for Interactive Multimodal Systems

A way to deal with the potentials of artifacts that is used to foster ludic learning experiences is to aim at optimizing their affordances. In doing so, we create user experiences targeting agency and ludic engagement as design goals (cf. [22]).

> "When the behavior of the computer is coherent and the application is designed so that a human interactor knows what to do and receives clear and immediate feedback on the results of their actions, the interactor experiences

the pleasure of agency, of making something happen in a dynamically responsive world." ([22], p. 100).

How is it possible to achieve ludic engagement? To explore the possibilities to realize the potentials of an interactive multimodal system to evoke students' ludic engagement, we have identified two specific design guidelines. These provide us with a framework from which we can consider meaningful activities that might captivate and hold the students' interest and mastery of abstract concepts. There are, of course, many ways to create meaningful learning activities and interactions by means of interactive technologies, and it is not our intention to provide extensive design guidelines, but rather to put forward two main recommendations, namely: designing for multimodal interfaces and designing for ludic interaction.

3.1 Designing for Multimodal Interfaces

Providing more than one modality for user interaction can benefit a wider range of users as the technology in this way become more ubiquitous, flexible, and capable [23]. Tangible interfaces using electronic tags that seamlessly link to a computer-based application responding to the information by displaying the corresponding information on the screen, is a way to bridge physical and virtual worlds offering multimode interfaces. This kind of human-computer interaction stipulates user activity considered in respect of real-world input to computers. This is where the electronic tags facilitate the application, which in turn is triggered by the user handling tagged physical objects (cf. [24]). Such a flexible interactive learning set provides the students to perceive and articulate knowledge through different modes, e.g. images, gestures, and 3D objects.

3.2 Designing for Ludic Interaction

Currently, research focuses on how interactive technologies offer new forms of compositional and representational affordances, e.g. [22]. [25] (p. 194) states that interactive technologies and multimodal forms of communication offer flexibility of sensory engagement with the environment and, furthermore, that they enable real-time selection of 'how to processes' rather than the 'what of content accumulation'. Accordingly, multimodal interfaces embody learning opportunities through transformation, e.g. re-ordering of elements, and through transduction where the students can move meaning from one mode to another, by re-articulating meaning in the entities of the new mode, leading to instances of learning.

[26] have suggested support for exploration as a design principle for creativity supporting tools. [27] stress the positive features of explorative searches and state that systems that support it "help users engaged in browsing maximise their rate of information, make decisions about which navigational path to follow, and understand the information they encounter" (p. 7).

4 Design Implementation

The concept of the prototype design was to bridge the physical and virtual worlds with electronic tags and, through this, blend the familiarity of the computer and toys, to create a tool that provided a ludic approach to learning about atoms and molecules; an interactive multimodal molecular set. The molecular set should motivate students' interest and mastery of abstract science concepts, in particular by encouraging exploration and reflection.

The study was inspired by the participatory design [28] and informant design [29] methodologies and included interviews and observations. 10 students were involved in the design process as primary users [30] and in line with [29] they participated as informants. The teacher was part of the design process as an equal participatory designer and based on his expert competence, he took active part in the iterative design cycle of the prototype. The study included two iterations of the life cycle model, where the concept of the idea and the first prototypes were evaluated. The study took place at a primary school in southwest Jutland, Denmark. In total, three visits at the primary school were conducted. In addition to this, the science teacher participated in five design collaboratorium [31] sessions outside the school environment. These were combined with unstructured interviews focusing on how attributes and affordances of the prototype could be aligned with curriculum learning goals.

Initially, naturalistic observation was conducted in order to gain insight and understanding of the everyday life in the school, in particular during science lectures. The observation was combined with unstructured interview with the teacher and the students. Our interest was directed towards the question of how to foster ludic engagement in learning situations.

Next, we will describe the initial physical design and the technical specifications of the interactive multimodal molecular set, which represents the outcome from the design colloboratorium sessions, unstructured interviews with the teacher and the students, and naturalistic classroom observation. Finally, we explain the methods that were used for the evaluation of the prototype.

4.1 Physical Design

The physical design included multiple phases. Initially the physical representation should be able to build molecules to emulate already existing molecule sets. However, RFID (radio-frequency identification), which was used for the implementation, limited the degree to which physical structures could be recognized by the computer. In order to adapt to this limitation, the prototype was redesigned to only have physical representations of the atoms but not illustrating how they can interact – make a chemical reaction – with each other in the physical world, which, in the real world, would be possible for some of the selected atoms.

Alternative solutions would make the structures readable, but as this is a tool that should be used by children in an educational practice, the wireless system was prioritized over implementing features of building molecules in the physical world.

The atom-tags were designed to look like a poker-chip, similar to atoms already used in physical molecule set by students. The poker-chip protects the RFID tags and provides a tangible physical representation. Initially, the poker-chip was sketched on paper and afterward modeled in Autodesk Inventor (see Fig. 1).

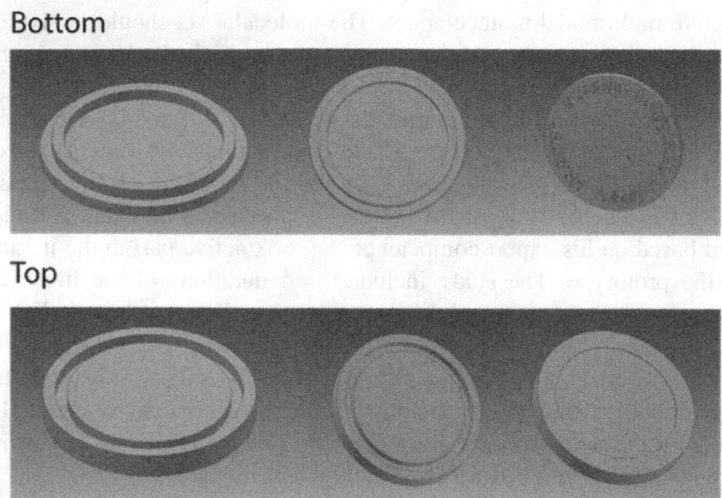

Fig. 1. 3D model of the physical representation of the atoms made in Inventor

After the modeling, the design was printed using 3D printing and the labels were laminated and glued on top (see Fig. 2). For this study, seven atoms were made; these were hydrogen (H), helium (He), carbon (C), oxygen (O), fluorine (F), sulfur (S), and chlorine (Cl). These atoms were chosen based on the curriculum and in collaboration with the chemistry teacher.

Fig. 2. 3D-printed physical representation of the atom Sulphur

4.2 Technical Specification

The hardware for the prototype comprised of an Arduino, an open-source electronics prototyping platform, and an Arduino shield for RFID/NFC; radio frequency identification and near field communication. The Arduino is a microcontroller allowing sensor connections. In relation to this study, the Arduino served as interface between the computer running the application and the RFID shield and MiFare classic clear tags (13.56 MHz FRID/NFC) for making the physical part of the prototype. Once a RFID tag is read by the Adafruit RFID shield, the Arduino receives the identification of the tag, which then is translated into an atom symbol. Next, the symbol is communicated via serial communication to the computer. The information is captured by the application running on a computer. Unity was used to design and develop the application to be used on the computer. The information from the tags is received by the Arduino Uno, which translates it into the atoms symbol and sends it to the Unity program. The application responds to the information by displaying the corresponding atom on the screen (see Fig. 3).

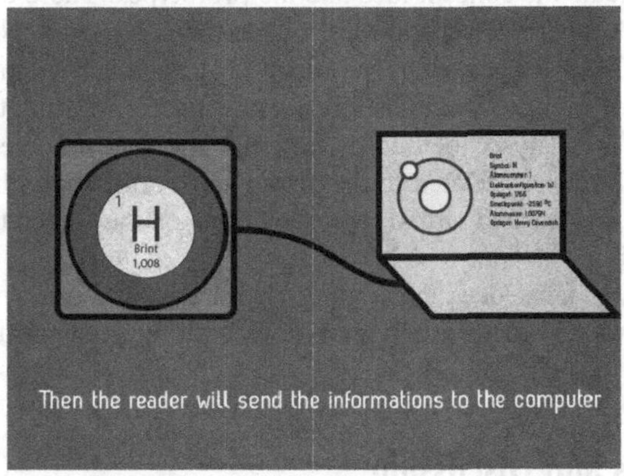

Fig. 3. The atom-tag symbol communicated to the computer

4.3 Learning Specification

The molecular set should support the students' understanding of how electrons move around atomic cores. Existing 2D models give the impression of that electrons are locked in some thin shells around atomic cores. Other existing models soften this perception by showing probability fields of small black dots instead of a circle whereas a third form try to demonstrate this 3-dimensionally [32]. The product (molecular set) should illustrate how the electron probability field looks like in the real world, when the electrons randomly move around the core. Then, after moving around the core for a while, a 'shell' should appear, where it is likely to hit the electron.

For substances with electrons in a number of shells, it should be possible to identify the single shell. Based on this, the students should optimally learn that:

- electrons move in a probability space;
- different chemical elements have different nuclei and electron configurations;
- chemical reactions occur through the exchange/sharing of electrons; and
- assess how the various chemical elements from the chemical main groups can be expected to react with each other.

However, as mentioned above (section 4.1), the physical design was limited to only have physical representations of the atoms but not illustrating how they can interact.

The challenge included in these requirements, which are related to abstract processes and illustrations, is to design the product so that its affordances evoke ludic engagement inviting the students to explore and reflect upon atoms and electrons.

4.4 Prototype Evaluation

The prototype was evaluated iteratively using sketching, low-fi and high-fi prototyping. Semi-structured interviews [33], focus group interviews, and video observations were used to evaluate the concept idea and the prototypes. These evaluation activities were conducted during three separate sessions at the school and included the students (as informants). The data was analyzed using [34] approach to analyzing qualitative data. The video recordings were transcribed and categorized using the critical incident technique [35]. The analysis focused on how the students mastered the visual representations and affordances related to the prototype. Furthermore, how the navigation between physical objects and virtual representations on the screen trigged their exploration and reflection.

The next section introduces the findings from the prototype evaluation evolving from the interviews and focus group interviews with the students and observations in the classroom.

5 Findings and Discussion

The interactive multimodal molecular set was developed to represent a way to bridge physical and virtual worlds using tagged objects to enable students in primary school (8th and 9th grades) to explore and reflect upon abstract science concepts, in particular atoms and molecules. The electronic tags were linked to a computer-based application responding to the information by displaying the corresponding information on a screen. The intention was that, in line with [22], focusing on multimodal (tagged objects and computer assisted) and user-directed affordances of the molecular set, should optimally evoke a sense of interest and a satisfying experience of mastery.

Manipulating the poker-chips was, for the students, a familiar physical activity. To physically turn the poker-chips resulting in 3D displayed molecule representations appearing on the computer screen, is a different experience compared to reading a 2D image in a textbook. A crucial difference is the movement of the molecules afforded by the poker-chip, which is not possible with a 2D image in a textbook. This physical-digital connection, where the physical action had a virtual effect that resulted in interactions, which ignited peer discussions about the electrons, in particular related to how the electrons moved around the atomic cores and came up with thoughts about chemical reactions. Furthermore, the colors of the electrons were discussed. The ways of manipulating the moving of the electrons was clearly afforded by the prototype. The students appreciated the immediate feedback provided by the physical and virtual connection. However, the students commented on that the amount of different substances was too few and they missed a function where they actually could experiment with chemical reactions. This meant that when using the tags to explore and reflect upon, for example, chemical reaction, the interest, after a while, was dependent on a facilitator promoting the discussions. The students, then, were less exploratory in their actions not using the tags as much as was possible and they were also less engaged with the task as such. Thus, the physical modality seemed to foster more engaged interaction in the sense that the students were more spontaneous, explorative, and curious with some, though limited, reflections about how the chemical processes worked. This suggests that the poker-chips, through physically manipulating them, afforded potentials for ludic engagement in learning, for example in the form of more opportunities for self-driven sharing and negotiation of knowledge between the students.

The molecular set combines artifacts providing the students with opportunities to explore electrons, atomic cores, shells, and more through abstract visual 3D representations. The computer was found to be an appropriate well-known tool to master by the students, for example, the students easily navigated the application. The intention of providing this kind of digital visual representations was to provide a familiar link between the abstract data and the toy-like physical tags, which optimally should facilitate an alteration between different modalities igniting questioning, negotiation of data, and peer interaction to evoke the students' to release their ludic potential. However, the findings show that the visual representation were not always understandable, which influenced the students' relationship to the visuals as such. In this way, the 3D visual representations seemed to afford an interest-based relationship with the (moving) visuals presented on the screen. This suggests that the physically created digital visual representations can enhance the reasoning about abstract and complex chemical processes. Furthermore, the students missed text-based (written) information sheet complementing the visuals and the physical tags explaining, for example, a specific atom. Accordingly, the molecular set should provide representations that are multimodal and in that way facilitating complex learning activities and reasoning about chemical processes such as chemical reactions and how electrons move in a probability space. Hence, this would create conditions for the students to be in control of the interaction and reflect upon underlying chemical processes. We assume that in this way, the connection between the physical handling of the tags creating digital representations of the atoms, could afford another bridging, namely between the physical exploration and the reflection upon abstract processes. However, in order for the students to be increasingly encouraged to gain interest in using and learn from the molecular set, it needs more visualizations, challenges, and multimodal designs. For example, it should be possible to create molecules and molecular processes in order to create engaging experiences through the actualization of affordances optimally leading to the mastery of abstract concepts.

6 Conclusions

This paper described the design process of an interactive multimodal molecular set for fostering ludic engaging science learning content in primary schools (8th and 9th grade), and encouraging the students to explore and reflect upon molecules and atoms. The guiding question was addressing how it was possible to realize the potentials of interactive multimodal systems to motivate students' interest and mastery of abstract science concepts? The concept of the prototype design was to bridge the physical and virtual worlds with electronic tags and, through this, blend the familiarity of the computer and toys, to create a tool that provided a ludic approach to learning about atoms and molecules.

The study was inspired by the participatory design [28] and informant design [29] methodologies and included design collaboratorium sessions, interviews and observations. 10 students were involved in the design process as primary users [30] and informants. The teacher was part of the design process as an equal participatory designer and based on his expert competence, he took active part in the iterative design cycle of the prototype.

The results indicated that bridging the physical and digital worlds can support learning where the affordances of the technologies can be described in terms of meaningful activity: exploration, reasoning, reflection, and ludic engagement. It is in such activities that the electronic tags facilitate the application and provide the students to perceive and articulate knowledge through different modes; images, gestures, and 3D objects. The prototype enabled reasoning about 'how to processes', but should more explicitly afford multimodality, mastery and the evoking of students' interest. Furthermore, the molecular set provided learning through transformation, whereas transductional processes including re-articulation of meaning in the entities of the new modes were not so apparent.

The next design iteration would be to establish more precise requirements and guidelines, including an expansion of the initial conceptual models and an inclusive process of 'getting concrete', i.e. to put the findings presented in this paper in to action. For example, to concretize and explore in more detail which technologies that can be used for what actions, which functions the different technologies should perform and which the students and teachers would perform, how the functions are related to each other and what information needs to be available in order to resonate with the pedagogical practice and the curriculum. Thus, the focus would be on different kinds of requirements; technical and pedagogical, which might include requirements such as learning goals (for a specific subject), design of learning environments/situations, functional, data, context of use, student (and teacher) characteristics, and usability goals.

References

1. Undervisningsministeriet. Aftale af 28. Maj 2013 mellem Regeringen (Venstre of Det Konservative Folkeparti) og Socialdemokraterne, Dansk Folkeparti, Socialistisk Folkesparti, Det Radikale Venstre of Kristeligt Folkeparti om reform af de gymnasielle uddannelser (2013), http://uvm.dk/Uddannelser/Gymnasiale-uddannelser/Styring-og-politik/Politiske-oplaeg-og-aftaler-for-de-gymnasiale-uddannelser/Gymnasiereformen

2. Reiche, P.: The Skylanders Story Successfully Combining Toys and Video Games. In: Proceedings of the Games Innovation Conference. IGIC IEEE International, Rochester (2012)
3. Kain, E.: Skylanders Giants-Review: Basically Diablo for the Kids, but with Toys. Forbes (2012)
4. Halliday, M.A.K.: An introduction to functional grammar. Arnold, London (1994)
5. Kress, G., van Leeuwen, T.: Reading Images. The Grammar of Visual Design. Routledge, London (1996)
6. Petersson, E., Brooks, A.: Virtual and Physical Toys – Open-ended Features towards Non-formal Learning. CyberPsychology and Behavior 9(2), 196–199 (2006)
7. Wertsch, J.V.: Mind as Action. Oxford University Press, New York (1998)
8. Cook, G.: Language Play, Language Learning. Oxford University Press, Oxford (2000)
9. Petersson Brooks, E.: Ludic Engagement Designs: Creating Spaces for Playful Learning. In: Stephanidis, C., Antona, M. (eds.) UAHCI 2013, Part III. LNCS, vol. 8011, pp. 241–249. Springer, Heidelberg (2013)
10. Petersson, E.: Non-formal Learning through Ludic Engagement with in Interactive Environments. Doctoral dissertation, Malmoe University, School of Teacher Education, Studies in Educational Sciences (2006)
11. Gaver, W., Bowers, J., Boucher, A., Gellerson, H., Pennington, S., Schmidt, A., et al.: The rift Table: Designing for Ludic Engagement. In: CHI EA 2004 - CHI 2004 Extended Abstracts on Human Factors in Computing Systems, pp. 885–900. ACM, New York (2004)
12. Petersson, E.: Editorial: Ludic Engagement Designs for All. Digital Creativity 19(3), 141–144 (2008)
13. Gao, Y., Petersson Brooks, E.: Designing Ludic Engagement in an Interactive Virtual Dressing Room System – A Comparative Study. In: Marcus, A. (ed.) DUXU 2013, Part III. LNCS, vol. 8014, pp. 504–512. Springer, Heidelberg (2013)
14. Cuban, L.: Oversold and Underused. Computers in the Classroom. Harvards University Press, Cambridge (2001)
15. John, P., Sutherland, R.: Affordance, Opportunity and the Pedagogical Implications of ICT. Educational Review 57(4), 405–413 (2005)
16. Selwyn, N.: Realising the Potential of New Technology? Assessing the Legacy of New Labour's ICT agenda 1997–2007. Oxford Review of Education 34(6), 701–712 (2008)
17. Papert, S.: The Children's Machine: Rethinking School in the Age of the Computer. Basic Books, New York (1993)
18. Stahl, G., Koschman, T., Suthers, D.: Computer-supported Collaborative Learning: A Historical Perspective. In: Sawyer, R.K. (ed.) Cambridge Handbook of the Learning Sciences, pp. 409–426. Cambridge University Press, Cambridge (2006)
19. Loveless, A.M.: Creativity, Technology and Learning – a Review of Recent Literature, Futurelab Series, No. 4 Update (2007)
20. Petersson Brooks, E., Borum, N., Rosenørn, T.: Designing Creative Pedagogies through the Use of ICT in Secondary Education. Procedia – Social and Behavioural Sciences 112, 35–46 (2013)
21. Bordieu, P.: The Forms of Capital. In: Richardson, J. (ed.) Handbook of Theory and Research for the Sociology of Education, Greenwood, New York, pp. 241–258 (1986)
22. Murray, J.H.: Inventing the Medium. Principles of Interaction Design as a Cultural Practice. The MIT Press, Cambridge (2012)

23. Bangor, A.W., Miller, J.T.: Multimode Interfaces: Two or More Interfaces to Accomplish the Same Task. In: Kortum, P. (ed.) HCI Beyond the GUI. Design for Haptic, Speech, Olfactory, and Other Nontraditional Interfaces, pp. 359–389. Elsevier, Morgan Kaufmann Publishers, New York (2008)
24. Want, R., Fishkin, K.P., Gujar, A., Harrison, B.L.: Bridging Physical and Virtual Worlds with Electronic Tags. In: Proceedings from CHI 1999, pp. 370–377 (1999)
25. Kress, G.: Multimodality. A Social Semiotic Approach to Contemporary Communication. Routledge, London (2010)
26. Resnick, M., Myers, B., Nakakoji, K., Shneiderman, B., Pausch, R., Selker, T., Eisenberg, M.: Design Principles for Tools to Support Creative Thinking. In: NSF Workshop Report on Creativity Support Tools, Washington, DC, pp. 25–36 (2005)
27. White, R.W., Roth, R.A.: Exploratory Search. Beyond the Query–Response Paradigm. Synthesis Lectures on Information Concepts, Retrieval, and Services Series 1(1), 1–98 (2009)
28. Spinuzzi, C.: The Methodology of Participatory Design. Technical Communication 52(2), 163–174 (2005)
29. Scaife, M., Rogers, Y., Aldrich, F., Davies, M.: Designing For or Designing With? Informant Design For Interactive Learning Environments. In: Proceedings CHI 1997, Proceedings of the ACM SIGGCHI Conference on Human Factors in Computing Systems, pp. 343–350. ACM, New York (1997)
30. Eason, K.D.: Information Technology and Organizational Change. Taylor and Francis Group, London (1987)
31. Bødker, S., Buur, J.: The Design Collaboratorium: A Place for Usability Design. ACM Transactions on Computer-Human Interaction (TOCHI) 9(2), 152–169 (2002)
32. Mygind, H., Vesterlund Nielsen, O., Exelsen, V.: Basiskemi C, 1st edn. Haase & Søns Forlag, Copenhagen (2010)
33. Fontana, A., Frey, J.: The Interview: From Neutral Stance to Political Involvement. In: Denzin, N.K., Lincoln, Y.S. (eds.) The SAGE Handbook of Qualitative Reseach, 3rd edn. SAGE Publications, Inc., New York (2005)
34. Dey, I.: Qualitative Data Analysis: A User-Friendly Guide for Social Scientists. Routledge Taylor & Francis Group, London (1993)
35. Flanagan, J.: The Critical Incident Technique. Psychological Bulletin 51(4), 327–358 (1954)

Modeling Videogames for Mental Mapping in People Who Are Blind

Jaime Sánchez[1], Matías Espinoza[1],
Márcia de Borba Campos[2], and Letícia Lopes Leite[3]

[1] Department of Computer Science and Center for Advanced Research in Education (CARE), University of Chile, Santiago, Chile
{maespino,jsanchez}@dcc.uchile.cl

[2] Faculty of Informatics – FACIN, Pontifical Catholic University of Rio Grande do Sul (PUCRS), Porto Alegre, Brazil
marcia.campos@pucrs.br

[3] Faculty of Education – FACED, Pontifical Catholic University of Rio Grande do Sul (PUCRS), Porto Alegre, Brazil
leticia.leite@pucrs.br

Abstract. Mental maps allow users to acquire, codify and manipulate spatial information, as they are schematics that guide behavior and help to deal with spatial problems by providing solutions. This is to say that mental or cognitive maps involve processes of spatial reasoning. The purpose of this work was to design a videogame development model to serve as a framework for designing videogames to help learners who are blind to construct mental maps for the development of geometric-mathematical abilities and orientation and mobility (O&M) skills.

Keywords: Development model, videogames, mental map, geometry, orientation and mobility.

1 Introduction

Mental maps allow users to acquire, codify and manipulate spatial information, as they are schematics that guide behavior and help to deal with spatial problems by providing solutions [10]. This is to say that mental or cognitive maps involve processes of spatial reasoning [12]. To represent space, both sighted and visually impaired learners take part in what is known as cognitive mapping [12], which in general terms can be understood as an internal model of the world [4]. The result is a construct based on the perceptions and experiences of the individual, put together based on his interaction with the environment, and providing a particular point of view.

A mental map is memorized intellectual knowledge of the form and components of a certain trajectory or area [7]. As the notion of a map refers to an internalized representation of space, it mixes objective knowledge and subjective perception [12]. Regarding the focus of our research, the following research questions have been posed:

C. Stephanidis and M. Antona (Eds.): UAHCI/HCII 2014, Part II, LNCS 8514, pp. 605–616, 2014.

what degree of abstraction is it possible to achieve when representing space, if one does not have the sense of sight? How complex can mental maps are in the case of blind individuals?

In this context, the purpose of this work was to design a videogame development model to serve as a framework for designing videogames to help learners who are blind to construct mental maps for the development of geometric-mathematical abilities and orientation and mobility (O&M) skills. This work presents a literature review regarding the construction of mental maps, geometry learning, and the learning and use of O&M techniques by people who are blind. Then it presents and discusses a model for the design, implementation and evaluation of videogames, in order to create videogames that help learners who are blind to construct mental maps. Finally, it discusses the desired results of future work related to the use of this model.

2 Literature Review

2.1 Construction of Mental Maps

Some authors propose that children create mental maps sequentially by using landmarks, routes and configurations, or spatial relations. This sequence begins with the representation of isolated elements, these elements are then connected, and finally relations between different points are established according to a system of references and coordinates, which is to say that each one contains the other. On the one hand, a route is defined as the way from one landmark to another, for which reason it is necessary to recognize such points before beginning to construct a mental map. The configurations, on the other hand, correspond to a set of mini-maps that integrate the various routes. Configurations are not simply the memorization of all of the routes in an environment, but are rather the structure of the set of routes [16].

Other researchers explain that the creation of a cognitive map can be achieved based on direct contact with the environment (the individual's movements), verbal descriptions, and supporting material. The internal representation of the space through direct contact with the environment is always achieved gradually, through the integration of information from various sources [1]. For visually impaired individuals, the use of supporting material can represent the only way of acquiring structured knowledge in order to organize spaces and places [12].

Cognitive maps in human beings cannot be reduced to knowledge of the relative disposition of places and routes, as they also include conceptual information and procedural knowledge regarding the use of such information. These three aspects represent the spatial reasoning needed to plan and make decisions when faced with spatial problems [1].

2.2 Learning Geometry

The use of digital technology for learning geometry has acquired an essential value, as it provides for the representation, construction and reproduction of geometric shapes, which favors the development of deductive and inductive processes of interpretive reasoning [1]. This is directly related to mathematical modeling, which as a skill allows for the construction of a simplified and abstract version of more complex systems. Such a skill allows students to learn to use different representations of data, and to select and apply methods and tools for problem solving. One basic example is providing an equation in order to express a real-life, problematic situation.

Although mathematics can be performed through verbal, graphic, formal, symbolic and other expressions, the basis is rooted in physical reality [3]. In most cases, learning geometry in the classroom is supported by graphs, diagrams, drawings and pictures, all of which are commonly utilized as ways of communicating visual information in order to solve a mathematical exercise or problem. It thus worth posing the question: how simple, complex or pertinent would it be to communicate visually referenced information to learners with visual disabilities during a geometry class? Teaching geometry to learners who are blind has traditionally been based on the creation of material that allows for the tactile and concrete exploration of shapes and representations, which in turn allows for an approximation to geometrical notions of volume, area and perimeter [11]. Some studies on such methods show that together with didactic material, the use of mathematical language and gesturing based on the activities performed by the student who is blind and the teacher are both relevant aspects for learning [2].

2.3 Learning O&M

A person with visual impairment must be skilled at O&M in order to achieve a solid level of navigation, including moving about safely, efficiently and with agility, as well as independently in both familiar and unfamiliar environments [6]. The learning of O&M skills includes a set of defined techniques that children, young people and adults who are blind (or those with visual impairment) must practice stage by stage. However, learning such skills also involves other aspects such as training and refining systems of perception, and both conceptual and motor skill development [6]. Such skills are essential precedents for learning formal O&M techniques [6]. The primary objective of O&M is to achieve independence and to improve the quality of life for people who are blind or who have visual impairments. Instruction in such skills occurs in stages, in which the level of difficulty of the training involved varies according the learner's particular characteristics [6]. For example, mobility along a given route supposes not only moving from point A to point B, but doing so in an efficient manner, knowing where one is located, where one wants to go, and how to get there [1].

It is worth pointing out that movement refers to the act and practice of moving, but also the act of evaluating known facts and places within the environment, in order to facilitate effective mobility and exercise one's capacity for independent movement [7]. This means that people with visual impairment, when relating to their environment, have "spatial problems", for which reason they must continuously make pertinent "spatial decisions" in order to achieve effective movement.

Regarding O&M, ideally the capacity for orientation progresses from a concrete understanding of the principles of mobility on a functional level, and finally arrives at an abstract level through which the learner is able to function effectively within an unfamiliar environment [6]. While navigating, it can be deduced that psycho-motor, senso-perceptive and conceptual training, as well as practice in the use of O&M materials and techniques, are important tools for producing a representation of space. This is because these elements allow the user to practice and test contextualized movement actions several times, use memory, as well as understand and interpret the environment.

A cognitive map, as a process of spatial reasoning, provides useful spatial information to achieve mobility [12]. The function of cognitive maps in an individual is to coordinate adaptive spatial behaviors, or to generate action plans prior to or during movement, and to execute such plans within the environment [1].

3 Videogame Development Model

Software engineering includes several different development models, among which are the waterfall and spiral models, the latter of which has been the most used and accepted in recent years [8]. These models are generic and only provide one way to monitor the development process, without taking the particularities that one kind of development or another might have into account [13]. Currently, teams are multidisciplinary and it is important to consider all the areas involved in software design and development. It is especially important to consider the end user that will use the applications developed, and this must be reflected in the design and development model that supports the work [15].

The proposed design model for the human-computer interaction in videogames was created based on the adjustment, improvement and extension of a previous model [14]. Following the analysis, restructuring and generation of new components, a complete videogame development model was generated that integrates aspects of learning, software engineering and cognition, in order to improve the cognitive abilities related to geometry and O&M skills in people with visual impairment.

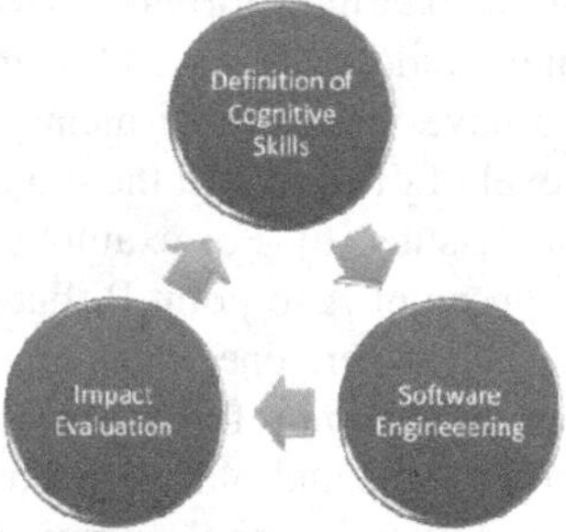

Fig. 1. Iterative cycle of videogame development

In accordance with the model, in order to develop such videogames it is necessary to execute the following three processes in a cyclical and iterative manner (Figure 1): (i) Definition of the cognitive skills that will be dealt with, whether related to geometry and/or O&M, (ii) The software engineering process for the design and development of the applications, based on the 5 traditional phases of systems development: Preparation, Analysis, Design, Implementation and Evaluation (See Figure 2), and (iii) An end user impact evaluation process to measure the effects that the tools developed have on the user. In this way, the technological tool being developed is adjusted incrementally in order to provide appropriate solutions to the cognitive objectives related to navigation by users who are blind. These three processes are described in the following.

3.1 Cognitive Abilities

This stage is fundamental for being able to initiate the process for development of the technological tools. Here the most significant problems that are to be dealt with in the posterior process of software engineering are identified. As such, the totality of the cognitive skills that must be supported are determined.

Some authors have pointed out that the O&M skills that can be supported are: (i) On a cognitive level, spatial relations (perceptions, distinguishing between different objects and the individual), spatial organization (organization of elements), and reference points (objects with a certain, permanent location); (ii) On a sensory level, the determination of the sources of sounds, classification of textures; (iii) On a psychomotor level, directionality and laterality (capacity to recognize a direction, maintaining alignment with the body), action time and reaction times, and route efficiency and efficacy [5].

On the other hand, from the perspective of a geometry student, it is necessary to construct a certain understanding of the world and access knowledge in a progressively autonomous fashion. This demands that students use mathematical language, concepts, procedures and reasoning as tools to be able to understand the world and act on day-to-day problems. This influences learning of the natural, social and technological world as well.

Both in primary school and during the first years of high school, the focus is on being able to recognize, visualize and draw shapes, describe their characteristics and properties both in 2D and 3D and in both static and dynamic situations, understand the structure of space and describe it through certain concepts, and to study the movement of objects, in order to develop spatial thinking. Skills such as spatial visualization, analytical thinking, calculations, modeling and skills related to solving problems, analyzing the problem solving procedures and strategies utilized, arguing and communicating, forming opinions and making decisions, and verifying and demonstrating properties, all must be achieved by attending to a great degree of diversity. This implies the promotion of learning by understanding that the need for education in a differentiated manner implies recognizing the personal, didactic requirements that some students require.

3.2 Impact Evaluation

Given the nature of users with visual impairment, it is difficult to work with very large samples of end users, especially when these users are completely blind. For this reason, the methodology generally follows a case study logic, involving a transversal and in-depth analysis of each case and context [15]. In performing a case study analysis, there is no need to work with random samples or to include a minimum number of subjects [9].

Even with a case study, researchers have been interested in understanding the learning gains in terms of pre-test/post-test scores, as a result of using the application (videogame). In this way, the dependent variable corresponds to mental map creation skills to aid in the comprehension of shapes, bodies and the geometry skills under review. Basically, this design responds to three steps: (i) Application of a pretest, to measure the behavior of the dependent variable before the intervention; (ii) Application of the intervention, through the use of the videogame software; and (iii) Application of a post-test, to measure the behavior of the dependent variable after the intervention.

Depending on the focus of the videogame, there are several different cognitive skills that can be studied through the application of the impact evaluation [5]. In order to identify spatial orientation, indicators such as "recognizes spatial relations between rooms", "recognizes the cardinal orientation of the rooms", "identifies the spatial orientation of objects in the room", and "describes the cardinal orientation of objects in the room" were utilized. For spatial representation, the indicators used are those such as "represents the space that was navigated", "represents the room correctly", "represents the cardinal points correctly", and "represents the presence/absence of objects in the rooms". Finally, spatial knowledge can be obtained by using indicators such as "identifies spatial relations between different objects", "recognizes the walls", "recognizes the doors to the rooms", and "gets back on the path after taking a detour to avoid an obstacle".

In order to identify the generation of mental images of shapes and the spatial representation of objects, indicators were utilized such as "adequate representation with concrete material", "draws and explains which shapes were envisioned in the proposed problematic situation", "recognizes changes in the spatial orientation of the shape", "explores geometric shapes and bodies through haptic and audio feedback, both internally and externally, identifying their component elements", "explores the movement possibilities of geometric objects, creating a mental map of the new positions", "represents the space navigated and associates it to a shape", "correctly represents changes to the spatial position of shapes and geometric bodies", "solves geometric problems by communicating problem solving strategies", and "constructs and breaks down geometric bodies into parts". Finally, geometric, mathematical knowledge can be obtained by utilizing indicators such as "identifies spatial relations between different objects", "recognizes the number of surfaces and associates them to a particular volume", and "understands basic geometrical concepts (lines, sides, vertices, edges, angles, volume, perimeter, area)".

Drawing on a plane or using concrete models can be strategies for studying mental maps, although the latter is more suitable to younger children [10]. Other strategies include making a list of the places that were navigated, recognizing slides and estimating distances. However, these resources include some methodological limitations [1]. A map of a city provides symbolisms for a large amount of information, and usually humans learn to get to know their city through direct experience, and not necessarily by memorizing a map. It is worth mentioning that knowledge of the environment is not only a visual record of places, buildings, routes, etc., but also one of events, concepts, and personal meanings. For this reason, the internal representation of space is not an accurate copy of reality.

Several authors have made reference to how the creation of a mental map by visually impaired or blind learners should be evaluated [1,12,16]. This is because the cognitive map of a person with visual impairment differs from that of a sighted person, due to the differentiated sensory inputs that make up their mental images, which makes it difficult for visually impaired people to generate fixed and precise images [12]. The positions of the objects must be maintained in memory, and in the case of a blind person, visual signals from the environment will not be available for use at any given moment, or to constantly influence the directions that he or she chooses to take. As such, what is important is not what is represented on the map, but how it is represented and what are used as references in order to organize spatial information [10]. Utility must be considered as the primary evaluation criteria, rather than establishing how complete or precise the map that has been recreated by a visually impaired person is.

3.3 Software Engineering

A model is proposed based on the 5 traditional phases of systems development: Preparation Phase, Analysis Phase, Design Phase, Implementation Phase and Evaluation Phase (Figure 2). The objective of this model is to guide researchers and developers in the software engineering process for the design and development of videogames oriented towards improving specific cognitive skills in visually impaired children and young people. In particular, in this process a previous model is modified [14] by adjusting, improving and extending it in terms of the cognitive abilities implied by O&M, and geometric thinking. In addition, it points directly to the design of videogames as a tool for the development of these skills in people with visual impairment.

In the following, the process is explained (in the form of guidelines) according to its different phases and main components, providing the objective of each phase, as well as the activities involved and the expected results.

Preparation Phase. During this phase, the feasibility for the development of the application is determined. This phase requires the relevant information taken from the definition of the particular cognitive skills that are to be developed (Figure 2). The corresponding stages are:

Cognitive skills. Determine what effective cognitive skills will be supported by the videogame to be developed:

- Activities. List the skills to develop based on the available technology.
- Result. The skills that are to be developed and positively influenced through the use of the videogame are determined a priori.

Technological Context. Determine the technology available in the market that would be considered for the development of the videogame:

- Activities. Generate a list and analysis of available technologies, and identify the cost/benefit of these technologies.
- Result. Information on which technological devices and development tools will be used for the development of the videogame is obtained.

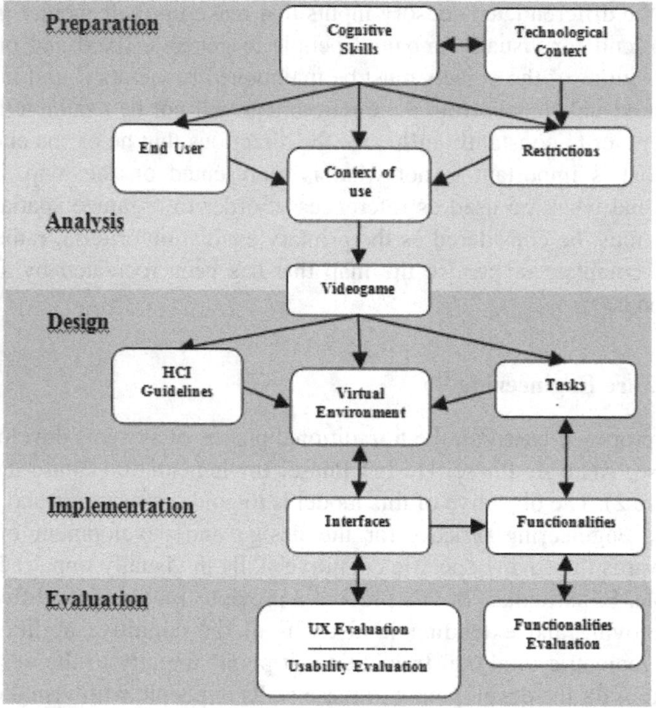

Fig. 2. Software engineering model

Analysis Phase. The objective of this phase is to comprehend the problem that is being solved, analyzing the end users of the videogame, internal and external limitations, and the context of its use. The stages are:

End-User. Analyze the end user of the videogame:

- Activities. Specify the characteristics of the end users on a cognitive level, regarding their mental models, degrees of vision, and the most significant descriptive variables.
- Result. The end user of videogame is specifically defined.

Restrictions. Analyze the limitations involved in the use of the videogame by the end users:

- Activities. Identify the behavioral characteristics of the end user when using the available technologies, as well as the social behaviors involved.
- Result. The rules of behavior or limitations of the end user regarding use of the videogame are obtained, to be able to adequately develop the desired cognitive skills.

Context of Use. Analyze the real contexts in which the users would be able to carry out their activities, given the specific skills that are to be supported:

- Activities. Identify the problems that are presented to the users in different real contexts, considering a complete profile of the end user and the corresponding limitations to using the videogame.
- Result. The specific kinds of problems that the end users may have in using the videogame in real contexts are identified.

Design Phase. In this phase, the best possible solution is designed, considering that the problem has been clearly defined in the preparation and analysis phases. The stages are:

Videogame. Define how the creation of mental maps for the comprehension of specific elements and for the development of skills related to the cognitive abilities that are to be studied will be supported through the use of a videogame:

- Activities. Define the user's didactic and recreational elements of interaction with the videogame (playability), as a support mechanism for the development of the proposed skills.
- Result. A videogame profile is obtained in order to support the specific cognitive skills to be developed.

Human-Computer Interaction Guidelines. Determine specific Human-Computer Interaction (HCI) guidelines regarding how the interfaces and interaction between the users and the videogame should be designed, in order to support the development of the cognitive skills involved in the study:

- Activities. Create or reutilize guidelines for the design of software interfaces and those for the interaction between the end users and the videogame.
- Result. How the user who is blind will interact with the technology is defined, based on specific guidelines from the field of HCI. This assures that the technology will facilitate the correct development of the abilities that are to be improved through use of the videogame.

Tasks. Define the tasks that the end user will perform with the videogame, in order to support the creation of mental maps for the comprehension of specific elements and the development of abilities related to the cognitive skills that are to be studied:

- Activities. Define objectives and activities for each task to be carried out, and the objectives, procedures and time limits for each task.

- Result. The tasks that the videogame will support for the development of the cognitive skills to be studied are obtained.

Virtual Environment. Define the representation of the virtual environment and its relation to reality, in order to achieve the development of the desired skills through the tasks that the end users will perform within the videogame, while also considering the HCI guidelines:

- Activities. Design the virtual elements of the videogame, determining their relation to reality and the support they are to provide for the development of the skills under review, applying usability evaluation methods for the software design.
- Result. The elements included in the interfaces that will facilitate the development of the desired cognitive skills are defined, also establishing a relation between reality and the virtual representation.

Implementation Phase. The objective of this phase is to implement the videogame, based on the previous stages during which the problem was clearly defined and a way to solve this problem was designed. The corresponding stages are:

Interfaces. Produce the different interfaces that the blind user will use to develop the previously defined tasks:

- Activities. Iteratively design and implement the interfaces, considering the application of usability evaluation methods with end users or pertinent experts.
- Result. Correctly designed interfaces will facilitate the interaction between the users and the videogame developed. This will also facilitate the process for the development of the desired skills.

Functionalities. Produce the specific functionalities of the videogame:

- Activities. Define and implement the necessary functionalities, designing the kinds and structures of associated data, and relating the different interfaces.
- Result. The correct and efficient implementation of the videogame's functionalities will lead to the satisfactory development of the user's skills through the activities performed within the videogame.

Evaluation Phase. During this phase, usability evaluation and functionality tests are applied, in order to solve any possible errors or defects, as well as to modify and improve the videogame in general. The stages are:

Usability Evaluation. Validate the videogame interfaces through specific usability evaluations, in order to assure that the interaction between the users and the videogame are adequate and pertinent:

- Activities. Evaluate the usability before, during and after the development of the interfaces, following the logic of a user-centered design methodology. To achieve this, evaluations of use both in context and in a laboratory setting must be considered.

- Result. The videogame developed will consider the users' mental models, interests and ways of interacting, based on the usability evaluations applied. These evaluations will allow researchers and designers to understand and validate the prior stages of the model, during which the modes of user interaction, as well as any problems and the ways in which the users confront such problems were identified.

Functionalities (Evaluation). Validate that the functionalities of the videogame that has been developed fulfill the criteria established in the design phase:

- Activities. Perform functionality stress tests in the laboratory regarding the behavior of the videogame under different conditions of simulated use.
- Result. It is determined if the functions implemented really allow for the user to perform the tasks for the development of cognitive skills through use of the videogame that has been designed and implemented.

4 Conclusions

The purpose of this work was to design a videogame development model to serve as a framework for designing videogames to help learners who are blind to construct mental maps for the development of geometric-mathematical abilities, as well as orientation and mobility (O&M) skills.

This model for the design of Human-Computer Interaction in videogames is geared towards guiding researchers and developers in the process of software engineering for the design, development and usability evaluation of these applications. It also includes the implications regarding the cognitive impact of using the videogames, oriented towards improving geometric-mathematical skills and mental representations in children and young people with visual impairment.

The present model represents a significant contribution to the production of thought-supporting videogames. This is because the model sustains the generation of audio and haptic-based mental images and representations, through innovative mechanisms for improving the user's comprehension of space. The end user plays a leading role in the design of the videogame, which is based on the user's mental model and adjusted to the user's form of interaction, improving the overall user acceptance of the game. This methodology definitely translates into a usable tool that can aid in the improvement of skills that are generally acquired through visual channels. As a result, the construction of the model has the objective of supporting the design and development of such tools, considerably improving the pertinence, acceptance and use of these systems by end users.

For actual and future work, this model is been used for diverse videogame applications and will be used as the basis for the development of videogames that strengthen O&M skills and/or geometric-mathematical abilities in users that are blind and those with visual loss, by stimulating the construction of mental maps.

Acknowledgments. This report was funded by the Chilean National Fund of Science and Technology, Fondecyt #1120330, and Project CIE-05 Program Center Education

PBCT-Conicyt. It was also supported by the Program STIC-AmSud-CAPES/CONICYT/MAEE, Project KIGB-Knowing and Interacting while Gaming for the Blind, 2014.

References

1. Carreiras, M., Codina, B.: Cognición espacial, Orientación y Movilidad: consideraciones sobre la ceguera (1993)
2. Fernández, S., Healy, L.: Inclusion of bild student in the mathematics classroom: tactile exploration of area, perimeter and volume. Mathematics Education Bulletin 23(37), 1111–1135 (2010)
3. Fernández, J.: La enseñanza de las Matemáticas a los ciegos. Juma, Madrid (1986)
4. Golledge, R., Stimpson, R.: Spatial behaviour: a geographic perspective. The Guilford Press, Nueva York (1997)
5. González, F., Millán, L., Rodríguez, C.: Orientación y Movilidad. Apuntes del curso "Psicomotricidad y Orientación y Movilidad para la persona con discapacidad visual", VII semestre Trastornos de la visión, Universidad Metropolitana de Ciencias de la Educación (2003)
6. Hill, E., Ponder, P.: Orientación y técnicas de Movilidad: Una guía para el practicante (1981)
7. ONCE, Organización Nacional de Ciegos Españoles: Glosario de Términos de Rehabilitación Básica de las Personas Ciegas y Deficientes Visuales. Entre Dos Mundos. Revista de traducción sobre discapacidad visual (1998)
8. Pressman, R.: Software engineering: A practitioner's approach. McGraw-Hill, S.l. (2009)
9. Robert, Y.: Case Study Research: Design and Methods, 3rd edn. Applied Social Research Methods Series, vol. 5. Sage Publications (2003)
10. Rodríguez, P., Díaz, C., Santamaría, M., Lago, B., Rodríguez, G., Mahtani, V.: Bases teóricas de la representación espacial en la infancia (2009)
11. Rovira, K., Gapenne, O., Ammar, A.: Learning to recognize shapes with a sensory substitution system: A longitudinal study with 4 non-sighted adolescents. In: 2010 IEEE 9th International Conference on Development and Learning, ICDL 2010 Conference Program, pp. 1–6 (2010)
12. Sanabria, L.: Mapeo cognitivo y exploración háptica para comprender la disposición del espacio de videntes e invidentes. Tecné, Episteme y Didaxis: Revista de la Facultad de Ciencia y Tecnología 21, 45–65 (2007)
13. Sánchez, J., Flores, H., Baloian, N.: Modeling mobile problem solving applications for the blind from the context of use. In: International Workshop on Improved Mobile User Experience, IMUX 2007, Toronto, Canada, May 13 (2007)
14. Sánchez, J., Guerrero, L., Sáenz, M., Flores, H.: A model to develop videogames for orientation and mobility. In: Miesenberger, K., Klaus, J., Zagler, W., Karshmer, A. (eds.) ICCHP 2010, Part II. LNCS, vol. 6180, pp. 296–303. Springer, Heidelberg (2010)
15. Shneiderman, B.: Designing the user interface: Strategies for effective human-computer interaction. Pearson Education, Upper Saddle River (2009)
16. Siegel, A., Kirasic, K., Kail, R.: Stalking the elusive cognitive map. In: Human Behavior and Environment, Advances in Theory and Research. Plenum Press, New York (1978)

Most Important in the Design: Focus on the Users' Needs, a Case Study

Cecilia Sik Lanyi, Agnes Nyeki, and Veronika Szücs

University of Pannonia, Veszprem, Hungary
lanyi@almos.uni-pannon.hu, nyekiagnes92@gmail.com, szucs@virt.uni-pannon.hu

Abstract. This paper presents the design process of the rehabilitation game "Gardener" that was carried out within the StrokeBack project as a case study. The game was developed for the purpose that stroke patients with upper limb injuries should carry out flexion and extension movements with their fingers several times in a row constantly. During the development, the developers did not only perform the alpha testing with stroke patients, but they were in connection with the therapists and were seeking for their views at the creation of each new version. As a result, the "Gardener" game is not only useful, but also a delightful rehabilitation game for patients.

Keywords: stroke, rehabilitation, game, user needs.

1 Introduction

The goal of the 'StrokeBack' project is to improve the speed and quality of stroke recovery [1] by the development of a telemedicine system which supports ambulant rehabilitation at home settings for stroke patients with minimal human intervention. The part task in the 'StrokeBack' project is to create games [2] (Break the Bricks, Birdie and Gardener) which can be used during the home rehabilitation process by the patients or replacing clinical rehabilitation and speeding up the process of recovery. These games are single player games, which the patient can play by himself/herself. It is expected that the patients will play more with the games, than they would do exercises.

During the developing process we had to take into account not only the reviews of the therapists but the patients' opinions and needs too. In this article the development process of the "Gardener" game is showed. Playing with the "Gardener" game the user has to make repetitive movement: fingers extension.

After the first version of the games the alpha test was made. The alpha testing took place in May 2013. For the test 10 questions were used. Based on patients' and therapists' opinion the games have been changed this way the new versions of the games have been developed. In this publication the redesign of Gardener game will be presented. The first part of this paper gives an overview of the state of the art. The developing method is written in the 3rd section. The alpha test and results are written in the 4th section. The 5th one shows the re-design process and the 6th section concludes the article.

C. Stephanidis and M. Antona (Eds.): UAHCI/HCII 2014, Part II, LNCS 8514, pp. 617–625, 2014.

2 State of the Art

2.1 Multimedia and Virtual Reality in the Stroke Rehabilitation

Many applications have been developed all over the world for stroke rehabilitation[3], [4]. One of the most interesting of these researches is the VividGroup's Gesture Xtreme System [5], [6]. It is a unique approach to Virtual Reality (VR), which might have important applications for the rehabilitation of children and adults with physical and/or cognitive impairment. Another way to develop VR applications is to start from existing occupational treatment methods and to develop plat-forms for home rehabilitation. Such telemedically controlled systems using low-cost web-based video/audio telemedicine units have high much potential [7].

The project called "Virtual Reality for Brain Injury Rehabilitation" developed at Lund University in Sweden produced many interesting results. They investigated usability issues of VR technology for people with brain injury, examined the issue of transfer and training, developed different applications of VR for training in daily tasks, such as kitchen work, using an automatic teller machine, finding one's way in a complex environment, using virtual vending and automatic service machines [8], [9].

At the University of Ulster rehabilitation videogames have been developed for such patients, who have, as a result of stroke, upper limb paralysis [10]. In one of such games, for example, bubbles appear around the user, which they should prick with their arms before they disappear. To detect hand movements a low-cost camera is used. Burke, one of the associates of University of Ulster, also examined, how well can the videogames used in stroke rehabilitation, and came to the conclusion that there is a good potential in this kind of virtual reality applications.

Standen et al. also developed games for home rehabilitation of stroke patients [11]. They, however, use virtual gloves for recognition of gestures. The software that they produced serves research purposes, because it is able to collect data about the frequency and duration of the games; and also data about which games, with what kind of results do the participants in the tests play with. From these data further conclusions can be drawn for more efficient software development.

2.2 Usability and Utility

Critical issue in the case of software is usability. The question of usability often fails, because during the life cycle of the software it is not enough time for testing, and because the developers – due to financial, temporal or other problems during the timing of a project – do not accordingly know the future users of the software. Usability and utility are equally important and together determine whether something is useful as it is defined by Nielsen [12]:

- Definition: Utility = whether it provides the features you need.
- Definition: Usability = how easy and pleasant these features are to use.
- Definition: Useful = usability + utility.

According to Nielsen, 5 users are adequate for testing usability [13]. Most arguments for using more test participants are wrong, but some tests should be bigger and some smaller. 5 users find almost as many usability problems as the test supervisor would find using many more test participants.

As with any human factors issue, however, there are exceptions [13]:

- Quantitative studies (aiming at statistics, not insights): Test at least 20 users to get statistically significant numbers; tight confidence intervals require even more users.
- Card sorting: Test at least 15 users.
- Eyetracking: Test 39 users if you want stable heatmaps.

In the alpha testing of StrokeBack project 9 patients took part.

3 Developing Method

In this part the development process of the game is being presented. First, the specification of requirements, than the technology used and the structure of "Gardener" game are presented.

3.1 Specification of Requirements

Functional requirements:

- on the screen flowers are standing near to each other, in more rows
- these can be watered by the opening and closing of patients' fingers
- in some kind of form the user will receive the results of the watering
- on the screen, watering is completed by a person (character), e.g. gardener, girl
- the game should provide opportunity for using more themes, where
- there are different plants
- in different environments
- stimulating elements should appear :
- if the user is not sprinkling, the flower starts to wither, for what some kind of warning should be given
- scoring system: cannot be negative, it should stimulate the patient
- background events and supporting characters should appear
- for the customization a level editor is needed, which can set :
    - the theme being played
    - the number of plants that should be watered
    - time till the withering
    - number of movements required for sprinkling of a plant

Non-functional requirements:

Under StrokeBack project [1], several rehabilitation games have been completed [2]. To this a framework has also been developed, where these games and the associated level editors can be integrated, thus can be launched from the same surface [2].

Therefore, important non-functional requirements are as follows:

- the Gardener game should be fitting this framework
- in its structure and style should be similar to the already completed games
- uses the already written code sections of the framework to avoid redundancy

3.2 Technology Used: the Qt Framework

At the start of the project the platform, where the rehabilitation system runs, was not defined, therefore a platform independent developer environment was the most suitable choice for the development. The Qt is a multi-platform framework, which uses the C++ language. Its main advantage is the multi-platformity and the free usability. The multi-platformity means, that the developer implements the program, which can further be used on PC, mobile device, or embedded systems. The most popular platforms supported by Qt are [14]: Windows, Linux, Mac OS, Android, iOS etc.

Qt provides a unified development environment (IDE) for the different platforms, and that is the Qt Creator.

The development also can be performed on multiple platforms, but some operating systems may need different compilers. The StrokeBack system will probably run on the Windows platform, so the game was also developed on Windows. To do so, Microsoft Visual Studio 2010 C++ compiler has been used.

3.3 Folder Hierarchy

In the "Gardener" game most of the items will be displayed as an image, such as the sprinkling character, plants, background and the characters that appear in the background. Appearance of these elements in the game depends on which theme does the user play with, on a particular level. This information is of course located in external files that must be loaded into the program at the beginning of each level.

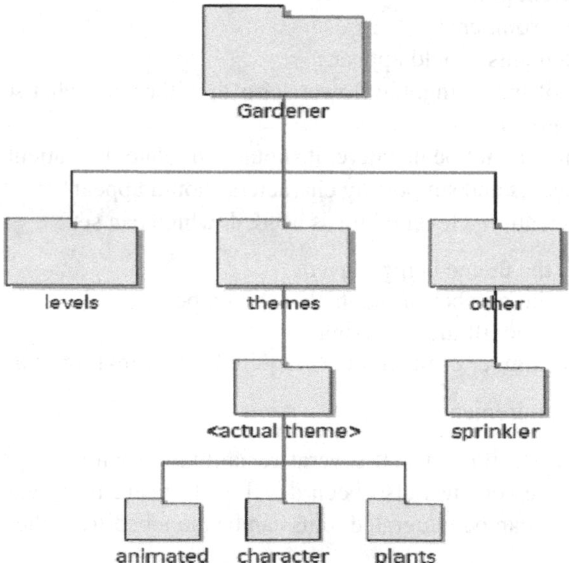

Fig. 1. Folder hierarchy of Gardener

As shown in Fig. 1., the subject-specific images and other information are located in the 'themes' folder. The certain themes are as follows: bluebell, carrot, currant, geranium, grapes, pepper, rose, strawberry, tomato, tulip. They each have a separate folder. Inside the specific theme's folder, in the 'animated' folder the background events, in the 'character' folder the gardener and the 'plants' folder the plants' images can be found. In the 'other' folder such images can be found which do not change in every theme, like the sprinkler which is located in the 'sprinkler' folder. Each of the fields are described by the level files included in the levels folder.

4 Alpha Test and Results

The clinical test was made by 9 stroke patients in the Brandenburg Clinic in Bernau (Berlin) early May 2013 [15].

The questionnaire contained 10 questions, and 5 points could be given at maximum. (1: I do not agree absolutely, 5: I absolutely agree). The average points are in parenthesis.

Q1: The loading of the games were not problematic. (5.0)
Q2: I could easily acquire the usage of the game. (5.0)
Q3: The game is understandable, easily usable. (5.0)
Q4: The game was impulsive, amusing, I would like to play with it more. (2.44)
Q5: The audio effects used during the game were disturbing for me. (0.22)
Q6: At the start and when I got stuck, I got enough help from the Users' Guide of the game. (1.00)
Q7: The intermission of the game (pause, quit) was not problematic. (3.33)
Q8: The appearance of the game is pleasing/ I like it. (4.44)
Q9: The game, according to the feedback (game scores, time-check), is easily traceable. (4.44)
Q10: Open questions for remarks and suggestions

From the average of the answers given for the questions, it can be seen that the patients – except for three questions – gave a higher score than 4.4. Although for the 4th question the average score was only 2.4, because only the basic theme was only ready by that time and the patients found it a little bit boring. The score of 0.22 for the 5th question counts as a good rate, because it is a "negative" question, whether the sound was confusing. This is the reason of the low rate, since it was not disturbing (i.e. the low rate means that I do not agree with the question that the sound was confusing). The answer for the 6th question was irrelevant, since the testing of the game was performed with the help of a therapist, thus the patients did not use the 'help' function. In the case of the 7th question there have not been any motivating animations between the games at that time. The introduction of the motivating animations was the result of alpha testing.

5 Re-Design the Game

From the answers given for the open questions we also found out that the users did not consider the Gardener to be an entertaining game, they would not like to play with it again. The reasons for this may be the monotone character and the lack of motivating elements in the previous version of the game, for the correction of which we had developed the following solutions:

- The certain fields to appear in different environment with different plants
- The plants to be watered by different characters
- Interesting events to be in the background, animals to appear in order to maintain the interest
- After completing a level, motivating, reward animations to appear
- Levels with increasing difficulty to be introduced

Therefore the "Gardener" game in this article will be presented as a case study, because the patients found it "boring".

The Gardener game has undergone several versions during the development.

On Fig. 2, the first plan of "Gardener" can be seen. According to this plan, a first version of has been created, where the plants and the sprinkler have already appeared (Fig. 3).

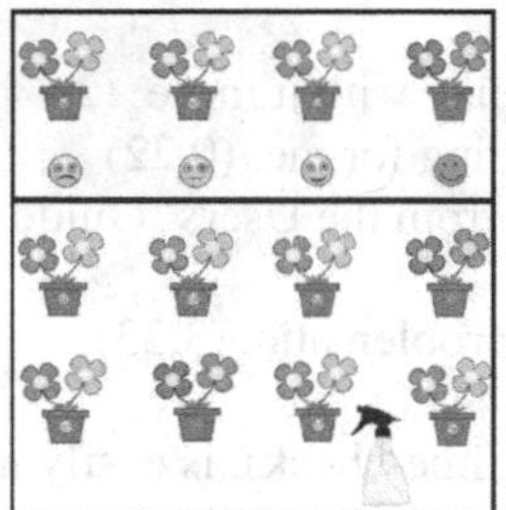

Fig. 2. First Plan of Gardener

Fig. 3. First version of Gardener

However, several functions have still been missing, like the fading of the plants, the alert, and a character that does the watering. According to these demands a new version has been created, where various themes and plants (bluebell, carrot, currant, geranium, grape, pepper, rose, strawberry, tomato, tulip) were introduced, and a girl appeared with a sprinkling-can and passed along the plants (Fig. 4).

For this version, however, we got the negative feedback (from the therapists) that the game does not correspond to the rehabilitation process, because the girl moving along the plants can be misleading, and can make the patients think that they should do the same movement. Such a visualization was needed which is realistic and inclines the user for the imitation of the movement. The movement in the case of this game is the repetitive movement of closing and opening the fingers fifty times or for five minutes.

According to these demands had the current version been made, where the gardener as avatar is standing in the left side of the screen and controls the watering with the pressing of the hose (Fig. 5).

Fig. 4. Girl watering with a sprinkling-can

Fig. 5. The new arrangement of Gardener

Another opinion was that animations should appear during the game, such as some animals peeping out from behind the plants (Fig. 6).

These requests of the therapists were also actualized in a newer version, moreover not only a boy and a girl "avatar" are sprinkling, but an older man has also been introduced, he sprinkles e.g. the grapery/vineyard. After all of the 10 themes of the current version a motivating animation is running – after the patient successfully accomplishes the level – which fits the level's theme; e.g. after the successful sprinkling of the fruits, the girl harvests them and uses them for the preparation of a cake (Fig. 7).

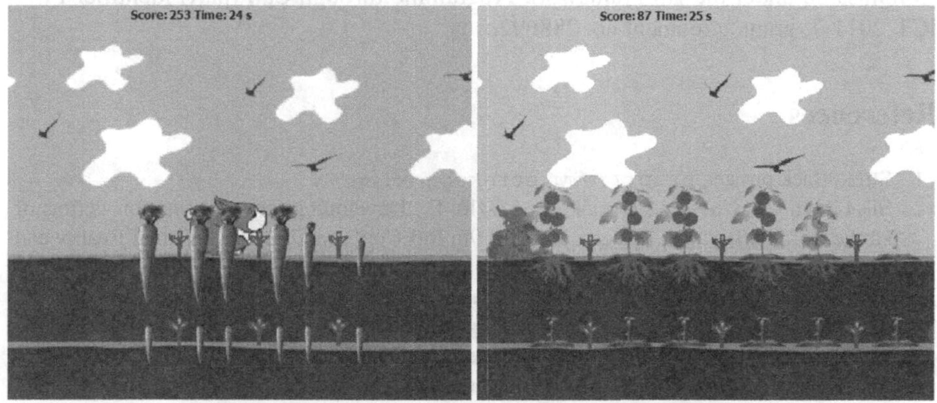

Fig. 6. Some examples: bunny running through the screen, or a mole appearing near plants

Fig. 7. Screenshot from the animation

To the game a level editor module has also been created with which the therapists can edit the level of difficulty (this level editor in this article is not presented).

The clinical testing of this new version of „Gardener" game is going to be in February –March in 2014. The results of this testing will be presented at the conference.

6 Conclusion

This paper showed the new version of "Gardener" game, based on it's alpha test by stroke patients' and therapists' opinion. During the development of the game both the advices of the therapists and the needs of the future users were taken into consideration. This is how the actual version of the "Gardener" game was created. The "Gardener" game will be a good and interesting motivating game for stroke patients, which was created in such a co-production, that the developers took maximally into consideration the needs, requests and comments of the patients and therapists.

The future plans include the testing of the game with the Kinect sensor according to the original plans in the project.

Acknowledgements. The StrokeBack research project is supported by the European Commission under the 7th Framework Programme through Call (part) identifier FP7-ICT-2011-7, grant agreement no: 288692.

References

1. StrokeBack project, `http://www.strokeback.eu/`
2. Sik Lányi, C., Szűcs, V., Dömők, T., László, E.: Developing serious game for victims of stroke. In: Sharkey, M., Klinger, E. (eds.) 9th Intl Conf. on Disability, Virtual Reality and Assoc. Technologies, pp. 503–506. University of Reading, UK (2012)
3. Sik Lányi, C.: Multimedia Medical Informatics System in Healthcare. In: Ichalkaranje, N., Ichalkaranje, A., Jain, L.C. (eds.) Intelligent Paradigms for Assistive and Preventive Healthcare. SCI, vol. 19, pp. 39–91. Springer, Heidelberg (2006)
4. Sik Lányi, C.: Virtual Reality in Healthcare. In: Ichalkaranje, N., Ichalkaranje, A., Jain, L.C. (eds.) Intelligent Paradigms for Assistive and Preventive Healthcare. SCI, vol. 19, pp. 92–121. Springer, Heidelberg (2006)
5. Kizony, R., Katz, N., Weingarden, H., Weiss, P.L.: Immersion without encumbrance: adapting a virtual reality system for the rehabilitation of individuals with stroke and spinal cord injury. In: Sharkey, Sik Lányi, Standen (eds.) 4th Intl Conf. on Disability, Virtual Reality and Assoc. Technologies, pp. 55–62. University of Reading, UK (2002)
6. Kizony, R., Katz, N., Weiss, P.L.: Virtual reality based intervention in rehabilitation: relationship between motor and cognitive abilities and performance within virtual environments for patients with stroke. In: Sharkey, McRindle, Brown (eds.) 5th Intl Conf. on Disability, Virtual Reality and Assoc. Technologies, pp. 19–26. University of Reading, UK (2004)
7. Broeren, J., Georgsson, M., Rydmark, M., Stibrant Sunnerhagen, K.: Virtual reality in stroke rehabilitation with the assistance of haptics and telemedicine. In: Sharkey, Sik Lányi, Standen (eds.) 4th Intl Conf. on Disability, Virtual Reality and Assoc. Technologies, pp. 71–76. University of Reading, UK (2002)

8. Davies, R.C., Davies, R.C., Löfgren, E., Wallergård, M., Lindén, A., Boschian, K., Minör, U., Sonesson, B., Johansson, G.: Three applications of virtual reality for brain injury rehabilitation of daily tasks. In: Sharkey, Sik Lányi, Standen (eds.) Proc. 4th Intl Conf. on Disability, Virtual Reality and Assoc. Technologies, pp. 93–100. University of Reading, UK (2002)
9. Wallegård, M., Cepciansky, M., Lindén, A., Davies, R.C., Boschian, K., Minör, U., Sonesson, B., Johansson, G.: Developing virtual vending and automatic service machines for brain injury rehabilitation. In: Sharkey, Sik Lányi, Standen (eds.) 4th Intl Conf. on Disability, Virtual Reality and Assoc. Technologies, pp. 109–114. University of Reading, UK (2002)
10. Burke, J.W., McNeill, M.D.J., Charles, D.K., Morrow, P.J., Crosbie, J.H., McDonough, S.M.: Designing engaging, playable games for rehabilitation. In: Sharkey, P.M., Sánchez, J. (eds.) 8th Intl Conf. on Disability, Virtual Reality and Assoc. Technologies, pp. 195–201. University of Reading, UK (2002)
11. Standen, P.J., Threapleton, K., Connell, L., Richardson, A., Brown, D.J., Battersby, S., Platts, F.: Can a home based virtual reality system improve the opportunity for rehabilitation of the upper limb following stroke? In: Sharkey, P.M., Klinger, E. (eds.) 9th Intl Conf. on Disability, Virtual Reality and Assoc. Technologies, pp. 25–32. University of Reading, UK (2012)
12. Nielsen, J.: Usability 101: Introduction to Usability (2012), http://www.nngroup.com/articles/usability-101-introduction-to-usability/
13. Nielsen, J.: How many Test Users in a Usability Study? (2012), http://www.nngroup.com/articles/how-many-test-users/
14. Qt platforms, http://qt-project.org/doc/qt-5.0/qtdoc/platform-details.html
15. Szücs, V., Antal, P., Dömök, T., Laszlo, E., Sik Lanyi, C.: Developing the "Birdie" game for stroke patients' rehabilitation. In: Encarnação, P., et al. (eds.) 12th Europen AAATE Conference, pp. 1006–1012. IOS Press, Vilamoura (2013)

Combining Ludology and Narratology in an Open Authorable Framework for Educational Games for Children: the Scenario of Teaching Preschoolers with Autism Diagnosis

Nikolas Vidakis[1], Eirini Christinaki[1], Iosif Serafimidis[1], and Georgios Triantafyllidis[2]

[1] Technological Educational Institute of Crete,
Dept. Informatics Engineering, Heraklion, Crete, Greece
nv@ie.teicrete.gr, echrist@ics.forth.gr, sjosef23@gmail.com

[2] Aalborg University, Medialogy Section, AD:MT,
Copenhagen, A.C.Meyers Vænge 15, Denmark
gt@create.aau.dk

Abstract. This paper presents the initial findings and the on-going work of IOLAOS[1] project, a general open authorable framework for educational games for children. This framework features an editor, where the game narrative can be created or edited, according to specific needs. A ludic approach is also used both for the interface as well as for the game design. More specifically, by employing physical and natural user interface (NUI), we aim to achieve ludic interfaces. Moreover, by designing the educational game with playful elements, we follow a ludic design. This framework is then applied for the scenario of teaching preschoolers with autism diagnosis. Children with autism have been reported to exhibit deficits in the recognition of affective expressions and the perception of emotions. With the appropriate intervention, elimination of those deficits can be achieved. Interventions are proposed to start as early as possible. Computer-based programs have been widely used with success to teach people with autism to recognize emotions. However, those computer interventions require considerable skills for interaction. Such abilities are beyond very young children with autism as most probably they don't have the skills to interact with computers. In this context, our approach with the suggested framework employs a ludic interface based on NUI, a ludic game design and takes account of the specific characteristics of preschoolers with autism diagnosis and their physical abilities for customizing accordingly the narrative of the game.

1 Introduction

Increasingly, experts, teachers, parents and students look to technology as a complimentary support for their educations. Educational gaming is a great platform that helps in motivating students to learn and is designed to teach students about a specific subject and/or skills. Prensky in [1] argues that children are naturally motivated to

[1] IOLAOS in ancient Greece was a divine hero famed for helping with some of Heracles's labors.

C. Stephanidis and M. Antona (Eds.): UAHCI/HCII 2014, Part II, LNCS 8514, pp. 626–636, 2014.

play games. Educational games are interactions that teach students goals, rules, adaptation, problem solving, interaction, all represented as a narrative. Such games give them the fundamental needs of learning by providing enjoyment, passionate involvement, structure, motivation, ego gratification, adrenaline, creativity, interaction and emotion. "Play has a deep biological, evolutionarily, important function, which has to do specifically with learning" [1].

In general, computer games and other digital technologies such as mobile phones and the Internet seem to stimulate playful goals and to facilitate the construction of playful identities. This transformation advances the ludification of today's culture in the spirit of Johan Huizinga's homo ludens [2]. In this context, this ludification of today's culture can be also used in educational activities to strengthen the motivation and the engagement of the students.

Moreover, the narrative of an educational game plays an important role in its success. The story is the root of the whole gaming experience. Up to now, educational games are usually created with a closed architecture and a single narrative, resulting to fail in providing a more personalized or customized learning procedure.

In this paper, we introduce the IOLAOS project, which is an open authorable framework for educational games for children. IOLAOS aims to combine ludology and narratology improvements to provide efficient educational gaming for children.

Regarding the game narrative, IOLAOS suggests a fully authorable editor (implemented in Unity game engine [3]), with which, experts can create templates and teachers can shape and customize the template-based games according to specific needs for a more personalized education. It's important that such customizations can be performed easily and without the reliance on software developers. The editor is also open. This means that new templates can be added easily for creating new games serving new educational goals.

Regarding the ludic approach, IOLAOS features the use of natural user interface. A natural user interface (NUI) is a human-computer interface that allows humans to communicate with the computer using standard modes of human communication such as speech or gestures, and to manipulate virtual objects in a fashion similar to the way humans manipulate physical objects. During the last few years, technology has been improved rapidly and allowed the creation of efficient and low-cost applications featuring natural user interfaces.

One of the characteristics of a successful natural user interface is thus the reduction of cognitive load on people interacting with it. This is an important feature that makes NUI a suitable interface in developing successful learning applications for children. In our design, NUI (instead of a restricted human-computer interface) is used to enhance playfulness and thus establish a ludic interface. NUI features and focuses also on the kinesthetic factor (gestures, movements, etc), which is an important element in achieving this playfulness of a ludic interface. For example, it is much more "fun" in a game to drive a car with your hands naturally, compared to pressing some key-board keys. And this is even more important and critical when the target group is children.

Besides the NUI-based interface, ludic design for the game has been also employed in order to improve playfulness, make the educational games more attractive for the children and aim to improve the learning procedure.

Briefly, IOLAOS project:

- Introduces an open authorable narrative editor for creating templates and customizing educational games, without the reliance on software developers.
- Employs a twofold ludic approach for both the interface (NUI) and the game design.
- Aims to a creation of more personalized educational games that support the educational activities better.

As a proof of concept for the IOLAOS project, a work scenario is presented in this paper, for creating an education game for teaching preschoolers with autism spectrum conditions (ASC) to improve their skills in recognizing facial expressions. Facial expressions give important clues about emotions and provide a key mechanism for understanding, identifying and conveying them. Children with ASC often fail to recognize the qualitative differences and associations between various expressions of emotions [4]. Due to limited social and emotional understanding they do not know how to adequately interact with other people; a problem which sometimes leads to inappropriate behaviors. Studies have reported that individuals with ASC experience difficulties in recognizing expressions while in youth and experience problems recognizing emotions as adults [5].

Treatment approaches aim to improve social interaction, conquest communication and control inappropriate behavior. Children with ASC are more likely to initiate positive interaction after treatment [6]. Education is also considered as a solution for the socio-emotional deficits and training is claimed to improve face processing abilities and strategies in autism [7]. A variety of educational interventions have been proposed for children with autism and many proponents have claimed developmental improvement and other benefits [8].

In this context, this paper also presents how IOLAOS platform can be used in order to create an educational game featuring playfulness both in playing (NUI) and in designing the game, along with a customized narrative of the game, which can be edited according to the needs. Our aim is twofold, (a) to teach facial emotion recognition to preschoolers with ASC, and (b) to enhance their social interaction.

The rest of the paper is organized as follows. In section 2, a brief presentation of similar existing work in creating educational games is presented. Section 3 focuses on the proposed open architecture of the IOLAOS project. To illustrate the concepts of the proposed architecture, Section 4 presents the scenario for teaching preschoolers with ASC about expression recognition and how is this possible by using the IOLAOS framework. Finally, Section 5 describes conclusions and discusses future work.

2 Background

Educational games for children have been widely used in supporting learning in-side and out of school and as a result a growing interest has appeared for the potential of digital games to deliver effective and engaging learning experiences [9]. There is a variety of computer games and software that intend to assist users to achieve various educational goals. Well-known educational software is the project Scratch from MIT Media Lab [10], a programming language for learning to code. With Scratch users can program their own interactive stories, games and animations by putting together images, music and sounds with programming command blocks. Monterrat et al [11] in their study claimed that game moding as an educational activity could be interesting not only to learn programming but for any kind of learning. Their pedagogical tool allows people without game design skills to modify and share digital games. It allows a learner to become a teacher by designing an educational game that others can use to learn. Their main idea is that if learning a game helps students to acquire knowledge, then being able to change the game can provide students with the ability to deeply learn the content.

Narrative architecture and ludic design are two major approaches in contemporary video game theory. They both play important roles in teaching and learning as parts of educational gaming. Lester et al. [12] described the design issues and the empirical findings about motivation in narrative-centered learning environments. They found a strong connection between narrative and educational games and they claimed that narrative-centered learning environment is a promising approach for fostering positive learning gains, as well for promoting student motivation. On the other hand, Padilla-Zea et al. [13] included digital storytelling in an educational video game and introduced narrative elements to foster the students' motivation in learning processes by integrating specific educational models and ludic aspects. They claimed that ludic tasks in educational games are important elements to maintain students' interest, motivation and immersion.

During the last decade, researchers have begun to explore the use of computer technologies dedicated to ASC as intervention tools for improving and eliminating different deficits. In a recent review, Wainer and Ingersoll [14] examined innovation computer programs as educational interventions for people with ASC. They focused on studies describing programs to teach language, emotions or social skills. Their analysis showed that those tools are promising strategies for delivering direct intervention to individuals with ASC. Bernardini et al. [15] proposed a serious game for children with ASC to practice social communication skills; they used an intelligent virtual character that acts both as a peer and as a tutor on a number of different learning activities. These activities can be selected manually by a human operator (practitioner, parent or other carer) through a graphical interface. Their experimental results showed encouraging tendencies by relating the effectiveness of the children's interaction with the virtual character acting as a social partner to them. Porayska-Pomsta et al. [16] suggest an intelligent and authorable environment to assist children with ASC in gaining social interaction skills. Their tool contains an intelligent agent and a play environment that allows teachers and parents to become co-creators and tailor the game according to the needs of the individual children in their care. Although the design and creation of personalized games is crucial for children with ASC, as reported by the authors, limitations in the agent's intelligence (agent inability to deal with inappropriate or unexpected behavior from the user) contradicts the structured, stable and predictable learning environment that is also crucial.

Ludology and narratology can also be considered as two important elements when creating educational games for children with ASC. Game narrative can provide context that assists children to apply the skills learned within the game. Ludology in both the interface and the game design also can engage children with autism in playful interactions and strengthen their motivation. Foster et al. [17] have suggested embedding interactive narrative in multimodal learning environments for social skill improvement of children with ASC. Castelhano et al. [18] studied therapeutic activities for children with developmental disabilities with the use of multisensory stimulation environments and documented its perception concerning ludic content, play and the computer-mediated ludic activity. The main theme that emerged from their study regarding playfulness was that the computer-mediated ludic experience is perceived as useful for intervention.

In general, educational computer games for children that combine ludology and narratology can provide an effective and engaging learning experience. Hence, developing learning environments that are both story-telling and play-based by combining narrative and ludicity may empower children to achieve great impact, improve deficits and gain new skills.

3 The IOLAOS Platform

The design of IOLAOS exhibits several novel characteristics, which differentiate an IOLAOS-based game from other forms of educational computer games and platforms. First of all, IOLAOS is not only concerned with educational computer games, but instead, it seeks to provide a guided learning environment for both educators and children, that is story-telling and play-based by combining narrative and ludic for harnessing knowledge. Consequently, its primary focus is to enable educators and children with the use of ludology and naratology to perform learning tasks and provide an effective and engaging learning experience. To achieve this, IOLAOS builds on a range of technologies, including semantic web, game engines and advanced human-computer interaction. Secondly, IOLAOS adopts a knowledge-based, reuse-oriented and natural user interaction model to attain high quality during the performance of learning tasks.

3.1 The Architecture

The system architecture (figure1) consists of four distinct components that collaborate together to: (a) codify all different elements of educational theories and learning styles available and to create templates which are then offered to game developers, (b) compile games through a three step process, namely *template customization*, *game creation* and *utilization definition*, (c) manage learning session and play room attributes and (d) administer all necessary elements, users and their roles, game engine parameters etc. Peripheral to the system architecture are knowledge derived from educational theories, learning styles and classroom practices. The components of our architecture are the "*Template Codifier*", the "*Game Compiler*", the "*Play Room*" and the "*System Administration*".

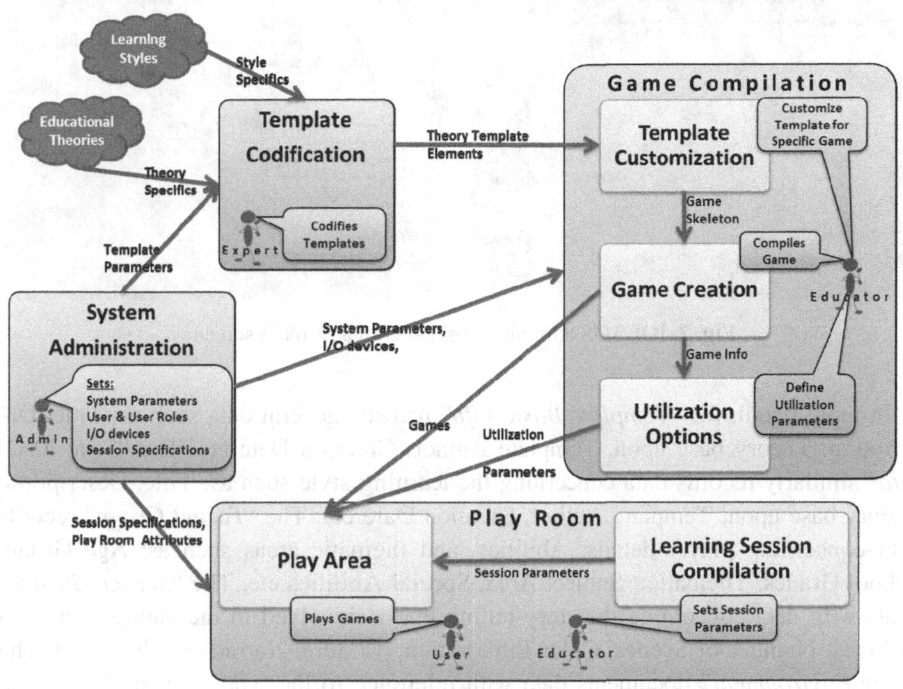

Fig. 1. System architecture

The "*System Administration*" component (see Figures 1 & 2) of the system is responsible for managing system attributes, template parameters, game elements, artifacts and behaviors, session attributes, input / output modalities, and user accounts and roles.

The "*Template Codifier*" component (see Figures 1 & 3) of the system is accountable for systemize / codify the various elements of the educational theories and learning styles. This is achieved by imprinting the theory's elements using a tabbed stepwise process by the expert. Apart from the first steps, that imprint basic information about the theories, the process has no strict order of step execution. The template codification process that has been developed in IOLAS in different tabs (see Figure 3) gives the user the capability to define the theory elements in an organized and clear manner. The educational theories and learning styles imprinting is performed by the role "Expert". The different groups of data that have been developed in IOLAOS for imprinting the theory's elements are: Template Basic Info, Style Basic Info, Target Group, Scenery Basics, Play Environment, Audio / Motion, Rewarding, Feedback, Evaluation (see Figure 3).

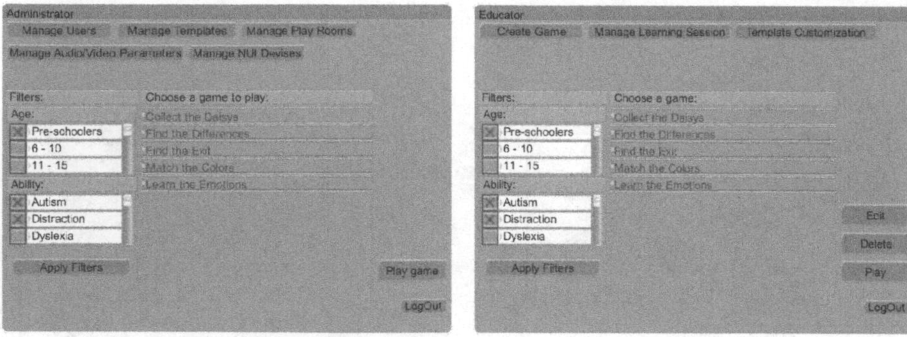

Fig. 2. IOLAOS administrator and educator main screens

In more detail, the "*Template Basic Info*" records general data such as: Title, Description, Theory base upon, Template Author, Creation Date etc. The "*Style Basic Info*" similarly records data concerning the learning style such as: Title, Description, Theory base upon, Template Author, Creation Date etc. The "*Target Group*" records data concerning player details, Abilities, and thematic areas such as: Age Group, School Grades, Thematic / Subject Area, Special Abilities etc. The "*Scenery Basics*" deals with data concerning the story telling that is involved in the game. Such data includes: Number of Scenes, Color Information, Texture, Narrative Criteria etc. The "*Play_Environment*" documents data with reference to the type of game (i.e. single player, small group, etc.), the environment played (i.e. supervised or not supervised) and the peripherals used (i.e. classic I/O devises, NUI devices, etc). The "*Audio/Motion*" records data concerning the use of sound and image input/output modalities such as Audio (yes, no, scalable), Motion (yes, no, number and frequency of moving artifacts) etc. The "*Rewarding*" deals with data concerning the rewarding of the player such as type of rewarding (i.e. textual, sound, movie, puzzle, etc.). The "*Feedback*" records all necessary information about feedback before, during and after the game flow (i.e. text, sound, movie, score, etc.). Finally the "*Evaluation*" deals with data concerning the evaluation of the player (i.e. evaluate per level or per game, or per game section etc.) as well as the evaluation type.

The "*Game Compiler*" component (see Figure 1) of the system consists of the "*Template Customization*" the "*Game Creation*" and the "*Utilization Management*". It is responsible for providing the "Educator" with the necessary tools to set up a ludic educational game. In other words, it gives the "Educator" the possibility to (a) customize the generic template set up by the "Expert" at the "*Template Codification*" component in such a way that suits the specific game requirements (see Figure 3) needed according to target user group abilities and educational goals to be achieved, (b) create a ludic game with the use of the tools provided by IOLAOS platform (c) to define game utilization parameters such as: Free Use, Registered User Only, etc.

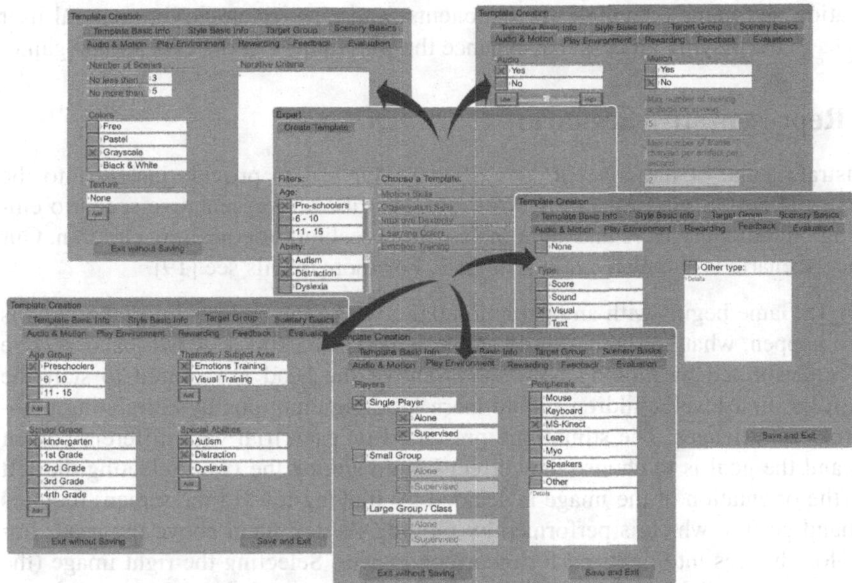

Fig. 3. The IOLAOS template codification and customization

Figures 3 exhibit selected elements of the individualized template for our representative scenario. In more detail we show that our game used a generic template for children with autism diagnosis and individualized it to fit the specified group abilities and educational goals, namely emotions recognition, set by the "Educator". The outcome is a Ludic Educational Game for preschoolers with special abilities and specific educational goals and is presented in detail in the next section.

The "*Play Room*" component (see Figure 1) of the system is responsible for setting up the appropriate space for playing games and consists of "Learning Session Compilation" and "Play Area".

The "*Learning Session Compilation*" gives "Educator" the ability to fully manage learning sessions according to individual, group or class requirements every time she/he needs to run an educational game. In specific "Educator" can determine: Players and/or Group, Marking / Evaluation Specifics / Procedure, Session Statistics, and Session parameters. She/he can also save incomplete learning sessions in order to be completed in the future.

The "*Play Area*" deals with game runtime specifics such as save, load, single player or multi player parameters etc.

The proposed architecture has been designed in order to support a game platform that fulfils the requirements of customized narratives, ludic interfaces and ludic game designing. The narrative is created by the expert and edited by the teacher according to learning needs and goals by using the template codification and template customization modules of the suggested architecture. The ludology is supported in two ways, first by creating and customizing ludic-based designed games through the template codification and game compilation components, and also by employing natural user interfaces to the playing process that enhance the playfulness of the educational game.

4 Representative Scenario

To illustrate some of the concepts described so far and to provide insight into the features of IOLAOS platform, we will briefly describe a representative scenario emphasizing on ludic, narrative and authorable game creation for educating children. Our reference scenario is summarized in Exhibit 1. For more details see [19].

Exhibit 1: Game begins with an instruction page where the child is informed what is going to happen, what he/she has to do and how he/she can do it. A two-hand gesture which is performed by moving both hands above the head is required to start the game. In the first level, children should learn labeling emotions by correlating emotion terms with images. The stimuli are presented on each trial with different pair of photos and the goal is to choose the correct image among the two. Selecting the left image (the orientation of the image is decided by looking toward the screen) requires a one-hand gesture which is performed by moving the left hand above the head. Image's color changes into light red for incorrect answer. Selecting the right image (the orientation again of the image is decided by looking toward the screen) requires a one-hand gesture which is performed by moving the right hand above the head. Image's color changes into light green for the correct answer. Moving to the next play area requires a two-hand gesture which is performed by moving both hands above the head. In the second level they should learn to recognize emotions from their description and their association with facial features. In the third level they should learn to identify the causes of various feelings in different situations, obtained through the use of social stories. At the end of the game, there is a congratulation message.

According to our reference scenario the "Educator" creates the game by performing the following steps in IOLAOS platform: (a) Select appropriate template, (b) Customize template according to scenario requirements, (c) Generate game framework upon which, the "Educator", will construct/fabricate the game, by defining artifacts and behaviors. The outcome of the above process is an educational game for children with autism diagnosis for emotion recognition.

In more detail, the "Educator" selects "Create Game" and at the "Select appropriate template" step he/she selects the appropriate template provided by IOLAOS, in our case the "Emotion Training" template. At step 2 ("Customize template according to scenario requirements") the "Educator" applies the scenario requirements which in our case are: 1) number of game levels are limited to 3 excluding welcome screen and final screen, 2) feedback is passed to player through light coloring of his choices (light red for wrong answer, light green for correct answer) during game execution and as concluding feedback at the end with the form of a congratulation message, and 3) Game navigation is performed via hand gestures with the use of MS-Kinect NUI device (raise left hand, right hand or both hands). At step 3 "Generate Game Framework" the platform allows the "Educator" to construct the game (see Figure 4) by using the artifacts and behaviors provided by IOLAOS according to his desires and the boundaries set up at step 2.

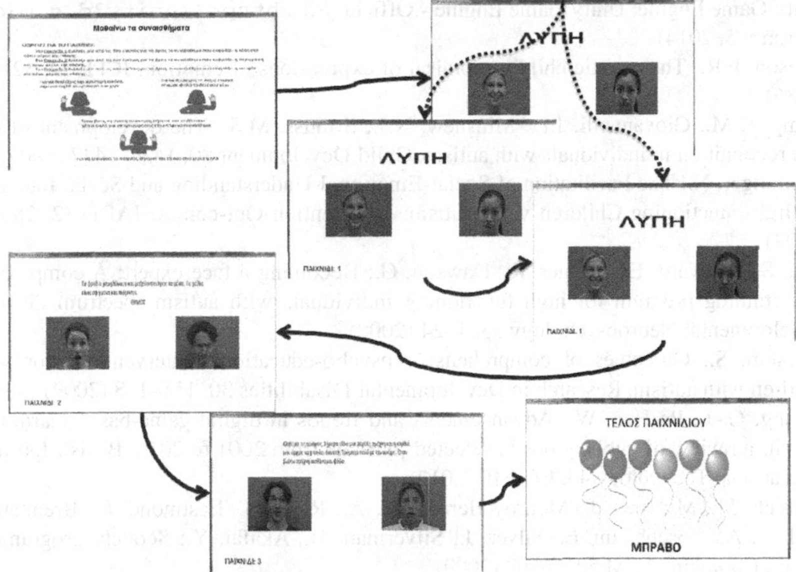

Fig. 4. Representative scenario [19]

5 Conclusion and Future Work

In this paper we have attempted to sketch the organizational underpinnings of the IOLAOS– a pilot effort aiming to build an open authorable framework for educational games for children by combining ludology and narratology. Our primary design target is to set up an operational model for carrying out the codification of educational theories and learning styles as well as the generation of ludic, narrative, and educational games according to needs, abilities and educational goals and to support this model with appropriate software platform and tools.

Ongoing work covers a variety of issues of both technological and educational engineering character. Some of the issues to be addressed in the immediate future include: (a) Elaborate on the Learning session compiler, (b) Further exploration of learning styles and educational theories in collaboration with expert and educator professional associations, (c) Run various use cases in vivo with the guidance and involvement of expert and educator professional associations (d) Enhance ludology aiming not only to children experience, but also to experts and teachers, and (e) Introduce further involvement of multimodal NUI devices so that the roles between game player and machine are reversed and the player performs gestures, sounds, grimaces etc. and the machine responds.

References

1. Prensky, M.: Fun, play and games: What makes games engaging. In: Digital Game-Based Learning, pp. 1–31. McGraw-Hill, New York (2001)
2. Huizinga, J.: Homo ludens: A study of the play-elements in culture. Routledge & K. Paul, London (1949)

3. Unity Game Engine. Unity Game Engine - Official Site, `http://unity3d.com` (cited: February 5, 2014)
4. Hobson, P.R.: The autistic child's appraisal of expressions of emotion. JCPP 27, 321–342 (1986)
5. Rump, K.M., Giovannelli, J.L., Minshew, N.J., Strauss, M.S.: The development of emotion recognition in individuals with autism. Child Development 80, 1434–1447 (2009)
6. Bauminger, N.: The Facilitation of Social-Emotional Understanding and Social Interaction in High-Functioning Children with Autism: Intervention Out-comes. JADD 32, 283–298 (2002)
7. Faja, S., Aylward, E., Bernier, R., Dawson, G.: Becoming a face expert: A computerized face training program for high functioning individuals with autism spectrum disorders. Developmental Neuropsychology 33, 1–24 (2008)
8. Eikeseth, S.: Outcomes of comprehensive psycho-educational interventions for young children with autism. Research in Developmental Disabilities 30, 158–178 (2009)
9. Hwang, G.-J., Po-Han, W.: Advancements and trends in digital game-based learning research: a review of publications in selected journals from 2001 to 2010. British Journal of Educational Technology 43, E6–E10 (2012)
10. Resnick, M., Maloney, J., Monroy-Hernández, A., Rusk, N., Eastmond, E., Brennan, K., Millner, A., Rosenbaum, E., Silver, J., Silverman, B., Akafai, Y.: Scratch: programming for all. Commun. ACM 52, 60–67 (2009)
11. Monterrat, B., Lavoué, E., George, S.: Learning Game 2.0: Support for Game Modding as a Learning Activity. In: Proceedings of the 6th European Conference on Games Based Learning, pp. 340–347 (2012)
12. Lester, J.C., Jonathan, R.P., Bradford, M.W.: Narrative-Centered Learning Environments: A Story-Centric Approach to Educational Games. In: Emerging Technologies for the Classroom, pp. 223–237. Springer, New York (2013)
13. Padilla-Zea, N., Gutiérrez, F.L., López-Arcos, J.R., Abad-Arranz, A., Paderewski, P.: Mod-eling storytelling to be used in educational video games. Computers in Human Behavior (2013)
14. Wainer, A.L., Ingersoll, B.R.: The use of innovative computer technology for teaching social communication to individuals with autism spectrum disorders. Research in Autism Spectrum Disorders 5, 96–107 (2011)
15. Bernardini, S., Porayska-Pomsta, K., Smith, T.J.: ECHOES: An intelligent serious game for fostering social communication in children with autism. Information Sciences (2013) (in press)
16. Porayska-Pomsta, K., Anderson, K., Bernardini, S., Guldberg, K., Smith, T., Kossivaki, L., Hodgins, S., Lowe, I.: Building an Intelligent, Authorable Serious Game for Autistic Children and Their Carers. In: Reidsma, D., Katayose, H., Nijholt, A., et al. (eds.) ACE 2013. LNCS, vol. 8253, pp. 456–475. Springer, Heidelberg (2013)
17. Foster, M.E., et al.: Supporting children's social communication skills through interactive narratives with virtual characters. In: Proceedings of the International Conference on Multimedia. ACM (2010)
18. Castelhano, N., Silva, F., Rezende, M., Roque, L., Magalhães, L.: Ludic Content in Multisensory Stimulation Environments: An Exploratory Study about Practice in Portugal. Occupational therapy international (2013)
19. Christinaki, E., Vidakis, N., Triantafyllidis, G.: Facial expression recognition teaching to preschoolers with autism: a natural user interface approach. In: Proceedings of the 6th Balkan Conference in Informatics, pp. 141–148. ACM (2013)

Access to Culture

Engaging People with Cultural Heritage: Users' Perspective

Maria Eugenia Beltrán[1], Yolanda Ursa[1], Silvia de los Rios[2], María Fernanda Cabrera-Umpiérrez[2], María Teresa Arredondo[2], Miguel Páramo[2], Belén Prados[3], and Lucía María Pérez[3]

[1] INMARK Estudios y Estrategias, Spain
{xenia.beltran,yolanda.ursa}@grupoinmark.com
[2] Life Supporting Technologies, Universidad Politécnica de Madrid, Spain
{srios,chiqui,mta,mparamo}@lst.tfo.upm.es
[3] Patronato de la Alhambra y Generalife, Spain
belenprados@wonderbrand.es, luciam.perez@juntadeandalucia.es

Abstract. Although Culture is a very important asset of population and a driver for personal and economic development, the engagement of citizens with their cultural heritage environment remains low. The European project TAG CLOUD explores the use of cloud-based technologies that lead to adaptability and personalisation to promote lifelong engagement with Culture. Within the context of this project, early-stage evaluations with users have been carried out for designing the scenarios and use cases that will be developed, and will act as a general framework, for the project. This paper presents the results of two evaluations: the user-driven evaluation conducted in the Monumental Complex of Alhambra and Generalife, which assessed the main users` needs and expectations; and the Cultural Heritage managers' focus group, which assessed technologies and approaches for alignment with users' expectations.

Keywords: engagement, cultural heritage, UCD, ICT, TAG CLOUD.

1 Introduction

Despite cultural heritage is a very important asset of citizens, it is the fact that there is a huge part of the general public who does not include culture as part of their lifestyle. Currently, about the 50% of the population does not visit any museum, and only 38% of the population participates in other cultural activities regularly [1]. There is a need to involve people in Culture and make them to be in contact with their cultural heritage environment. With this purpose, the European Commission co-funded project TAG CLOUD [2] is investigating on how to enable cultural engagement by using cloud-based technologies that leverage adaptability and personalisation, in order to support deeper engagement and learning over time.

Having the challenge of building engaging technological solutions for the visitors of cultural places, requires a very good understanding of the likes, needs, preferences and trends of the users. For this purposes, TAG CLOUD has focused during its first

C. Stephanidis and M. Antona (Eds.): UAHCI/HCII 2014, Part II, LNCS 8514, pp. 639–649, 2014.

stage, in developing a framework of scenarios, supported by use cases, that captures the insights and expectations of visitors in three different sites through Europe: The Monumental Complex of Alhambra and Generalife (Spain), the Barber Institute of Fine Arts (United Kingdom) and the County of Sør Trøndelag (Norway). Avoiding gathering this information would probably lead into ICT systems that are based on the developers' team self-intuition and ideas and the result might not what the users expect at all.

Following a User-Centered Design (UCD) methodology [3], the TAG CLOUD project places the user at the centre of developments and follows an iterative design cycle which serves to feedback the design, development, improvement and optimisation of TAG CLOUD solutions. In particular, UCD links the ideation process and the action; consequently a set of user interaction scenarios and use cases put users at the heart of the design process ensuring that the systems or applications are easy to use; as they are designed upon an explicit understanding of users' needs [4]. In order to master a behavioural, cultural and emotional context, TAG CLOUD team has also gathered the needs and challenges of the different cultural sites involved in the project, aiming at creating "empathy" and sound user models that enable compelling approaches and diffusion of cultural digital content produced by cultural sites.

This paper presents the results of two empirical and qualitative evaluations performed during early stage of TAG CLOUD project in Spain, presented on the following sections, namely: "Getting on the Alhambra visitors shoes" and "Reviewing the needs and challenges of Spanish cultural and natural heritage sites." These evaluations aimed at capturing and collecting insights and needed information to support next steps of ideation, prototyping and testing of TAG CLOUD user-centered applications and developments.

The paper is organised as follows: section 2 presents the TAG CLOUD contextual framework for early stage evaluations; section 3-4 present the results of performed evaluations; section 5 presents the Conclusions.

2 Framework for Early-Stage TAG CLOUD Evaluations

Convergence of personalization, augmented reality, storytelling tools are opening new opportunities to Cultural Heritage sites for improving the exploration, adaptation and presentation of cultural-driven content, the adaptation of such content for specific users/groups, the collaboration and sharing of content among users having similar interests, as well as its adaptation to heterogeneous user contexts and devices.

Through evaluations and pilot sites scenarios developments, TAG CLOUD supports a realistic UCD approach taking in account users (as individuals and groups) in daily or sporadic interactions with cultural heritage. Thus TAG CLOUD places users/visitors' at the centre of the design and developments; from the inception of the project through all the ideation, prototyping, development and launching processes.

The iterative evaluation approach, ensures that users' perspectives feedbacks the all project lifecycle. Hence, the TAG CLOUD general framework gathers scenarios and use cases from: a) different contexts of use in three pilot sites in Europe with different multicultural environments, sizes and cultural natures; b) different interaction locations (i.e., off-site or on-site) and visiting relationship cycles (i.e., before, during or after a visit); c) different cultural heritage management perspectives (e.g. user and group management, on-site vs virtual interaction, user profile management, cultural artefact management, itinerary management, etc.); and d) through different interactive technologies (i.e. augmented reality, storytelling and sharing through social networks, etc.).

In addition, this framework has four interaction perspectives that will support the personalization and adaptation of content to users in order to facilitate the exploration of content and an enjoyable cultural driven experience, which are: 1) interaction with curators, who as cultural experts can provide and adapt cultural driven content for different users' segments; 2) interaction with individual users, which comprise those that are interested in discovering and exploring cultural sites further than walls and main collections, and experts which look for grained and highly specialized information and content that relates with their professional profile, hobbies or expertise (e.g. architects, archaeologist, teachers, etc.); 3) interaction with small heterogeneous groups, such as families with elderly members and children families, and different skills, backgrounds or knowledge; and 4) interaction with homogeneous groups such as groups of school classmates or tourists, which in addition have a teacher, guide or facilitator which might have special requirements (i.e. teaching-learning driven content).

In order to align scenarios with potential technological solutions [5], and explore opportunities for the application contexts, the TAG CLOUD is performing an ideation process; in which the team is exploring the following dimensions to focus on the generation of UCD driven solutions:

- Environment settings and issues: indoor (problems with limited space, internet connection while extremely rich in content); outdoor (high connectivity, high availability of mobile guides, large areas – a city or part of it – with connection to integrated services and points of interest); remote from site itself (use of galleries, motivation, virtual travellers, long lasting interactions, etc.); and "on the go" (no defined itinerary; dynamic user models and adaptation based on interest, preferences, knowledge, context, higher interaction with spaces, etc.).
- Ways of adaptation of content for users: based on context-aware features (physical oriented: opening times, proximity, events, etc.); based on individuals (personal and socio-cultural interests and context); and based on groups (identity-related features like heterogeneity in age or similar interests or objectives).
- Interaction models: through domains (similar interests e.g. school, experts), content (images, audios, videos, 3D representations…), and technologies (augmented reality, storytelling, social media).
- Relation of the user with the cultural heritage place: first-time users, eventual users, loyal users (users that go frequently to the cultural place), etc.
- Scope of the visit: individual (as part of a trip, local individuals, summers holidays vs. weekend holidays, etc.), and group (as part of a guided tour, a school visit, group of experts, etc.).
- Devices: taking into account different devices for different types of interactions (tablets, smartphones, PC/laptops, etc.).

3 Getting on the Alhambra Visitors' Shoes

For this empirical and qualitative approach two people from the TAG CLOUD team spent two days with 35 randomly chosen visitors (as potential TAG CLOUD users) at the Monumental Complex of Alhambra and Generalife (Granada, Spain). The selected participants were of different ages, nationalities and gender. The Monumental Complex of Alhambra and Generalife is a major European cultural, declared as World Heritage site by the UNESCO in 1984 and that receives more than 3 Millions of visitors from all over the world.

For this purpose TAG CLOUD developed an interview guideline that comprised questions and points to discuss on the behavioural and motivational drivers for having an enjoyable visit; this process included letting participants to speak freely on their preferences, technology, interests, use of social media etc. In addition, some mock ups that use augmented reality and storytelling were shown, in order to perform observations on reactions and discuss on how these technologies could better support their visiting experience.

People visiting a cultural place, are people who often enjoy visiting cultural heritage places, such as the Monumental Complex of Alhambra and Generalife, museums, art galleries, cities or natural landscapes. 40% of the people that participated commented that they regularly visit cultural places, 34% stated that they do so frequently, while 25% of them said that they were just casual visitors and rarely visit cultural places (or would do it during a touristic trip). Hence, during the evaluation experience we found two types of potential users: those who are actually engaged by the culture and may be looking for improved and better experiences, and those who are not yet engaged and are just looking for random cultural experiences. Despite the different interests and likes of these two groups of people, the fact is that both of them were actually visiting a cultural site. So both groups` segments could be potential users of app solutions that can support their cultural-driven experience. This is the starting point to address for TAG CLOUD services and products in development. Also, this evidence opens the opportunity for personalized support, based not only in socio-cultural profile information but also with cultural identity-related aspects.

Most notable is high number of visitors (72%) that did not plan their visit beforehand. Those who did, gathered the Alhambra's information across internet and other non-specific ways. Additionally, most of the visitors expected to find guiding routes and on-site information; but they were usually given a map and an audio-guide so they could follow the route on their own way. The most common behavioural response was to improvise the Monument Complex routes. The main problem was that there are no estimations on the overall time for visiting the Monument Complex; the Alhambra is a Palace City where the rhythm of the visit is your own rhythm, and the people can take different time spaces for nurturing themselves with this marvellous heritage jewel. But, not having a time perspective produces many cases in which the visit cannot be completed. In addition, the Alhambra has some spots that are scheduled to be opened during specific time windows due to the UNESCO requirements; thus some people was not able to estimate the time for the routes and missed a couple of site's visits.

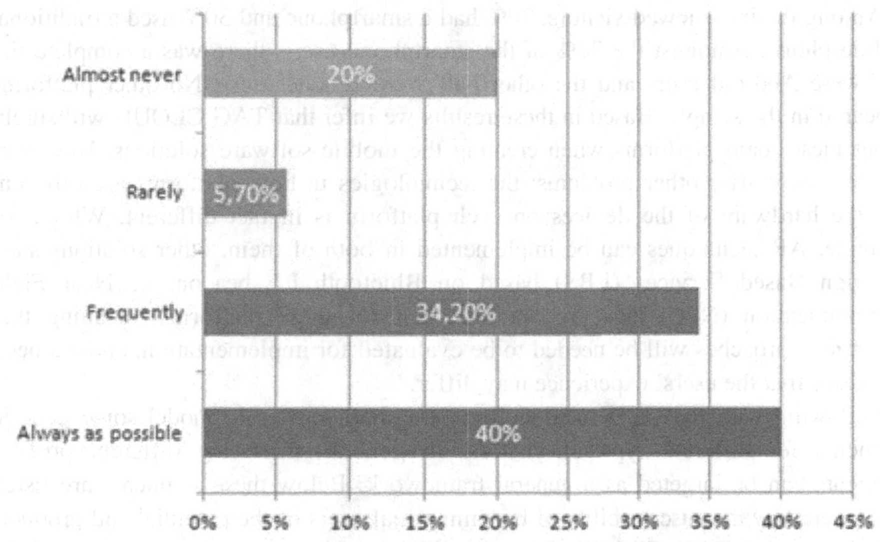

Fig. 1. Classification of visitors by frequency of cultural consumption

Also, some visitors expected to receive on-site, information related to their curiosities; while other visitors perceived that the given information was dense and provided in spoken or textual format, which often distracted from the experience. In any case, none of the participants used a mobile application for being guided inside the Monument Complex or getting additional information about it; even despite there was an official app for the cultural place.

When people were asked for the motives for not downloading the app, the answers were very different. Among main reasons commented we have that: people were not aware of the existence of the app; the app did not matched their devices operative system; they did not know the app's benefits; people didn't know how to download it as they were not familiar with QR codes; others did not differenced at all between different platforms such Symbian, WM, iOS, Android, etc. and some others just thought that the app would consume their bandwidth or would cost them an unknown amount of money.

Apart of the software engineering process, for the TAG CLOUD team is very clear that visitors shall benefit from individualized support services, that takes into account contextual and personal attributes; evidence shows that visitors` behaviour usually not remain consistent during the visits and their itinerary may require ongoing adaptation, as well as support. In addition, solutions and e-services to be provided need to respond to trendy devices with big market quota. Currently, the Alhambra is increasing efforts to raise awareness of the solutions in a more clear, concise, attractive and intense manner, especially on-site. The promoting campaign has been recommended to include accurate descriptions of the benefits of using the system and the downloading instructions.

Among the interviewed visitors, 70% had a smartphone and 30% used a traditional mobile phone. Amongst the 70% of the smartphone users, there was a complete tie: half were Android users and the other half were iPhone users. No other platforms appeared in the sample. Based in these results we infer that TAG CLOUD will surely target these main platforms when creating the mobile software solutions. However, this fact may arise other problems; the technologies in both platforms are different and the hardware of the devices on each platform is in fact different. While, for example, AR techniques can be implemented in both of them, other solutions such Location Based Services (LBS) based on Bluetooth LE beacons or Near Field Communication (NFC) tags are not universal for these platforms; meaning that different approaches will be needed to be evaluated for implementation, and we need to foresee that the users' experience may differ.

Following with the UCD methodology, we shall foresee to model some generic segments for different type of visitors. In general, three big different profiles segments can be targeted as a general framework. Below these segments are listed and ordered by the susceptibility of becoming real users of the potential end products and services of TAG CLOUD. This classification does not take into account the country, sex or age of the potential users. Although there are some correlations between different "persona" parameters, the most relevant for the cultural engagement purpose are the technological skills and the degree of interest in cultural places. Thus, the following are the user segments identified:

1. Familiar with the technology. Frequently visits cultural places.
2. Familiar with the technology. Rarely visits cultural places.
3. Not familiar with the technology. Frequently visits cultural places.

During the evaluation experience, there was also a chance to gather information regarding the preferences about Social Networks (SN) platforms and their usage; especially it was important to detect the type of content that is usually shared and the main social networks, more commonly used by participants. This gathered information will feedback the potential opportunity of integration of social networks' features in TAG CLOUD, as collected information comprises the kind of features that users demand, i.e. image sharing, microblogging, etc.

54% of people used SN platforms while and the remaining 46% didn't use any of them. Of those that use SN, 95% used Facebook, 25% used Google+ and 15% used Twitter. No SN with geo-localized points of Interest such Foursquare were mentioned.

The next step of the conversation went over the type of content that the SN users shared on the Internet. It was relevant that 53% of the participants shared images in their SN, and doing so, it was very meaningful for them. Although, 47% did not share any content, these users were "spectators" and watched the content generated and uploaded by others, as well as took in account the recommendations posted in the SN.

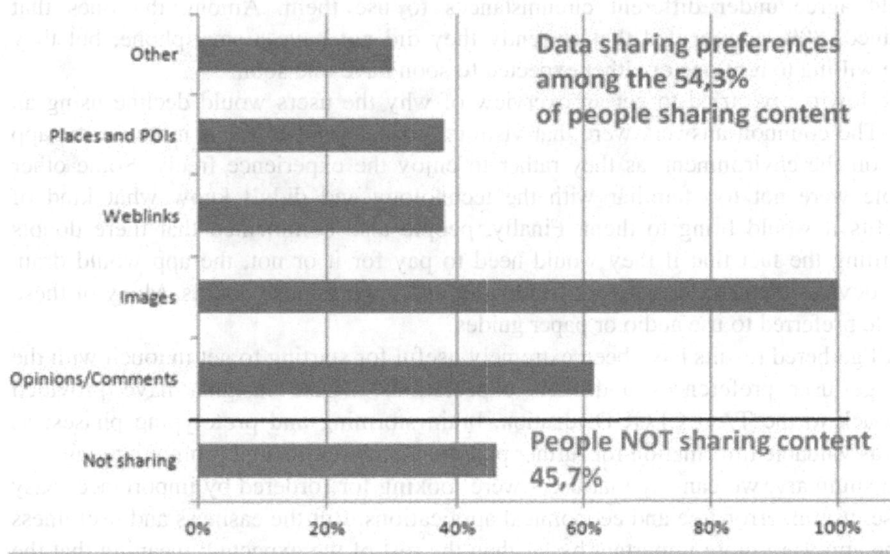

Fig. 2. Content shared by Social Network users in their preferred platforms

When talking about engaging users through relatively newer technologies there was a big correlation between the knowledge of the technology mentioned and this technology's maturity; as it is stated by Garter in the hyper-cycle maturity adoption methodology and charts [6]. Thus, the more mainstream and useful technologies are, the more likely to be used and comprehended by the users.

The evaluation identified that the knowledge of a technology for the general public seems to be independent from the "hype" that technology has raised. When we asked for some of the technologies TAG CLOUD might be considering to embed in the app, the results were: 63% of people know what the QR codes were. The Augmented reality is a familiar concept for just 14% of the interviewed people and 8,5% of the people ever heard about NFC. Only 5,7% of the people knew about gamification (one of the philosophies behind the engaging techniques), albeit the name of this technology is unveiling. However, when mock ups and examples where shared and explained to participants; in general people were receptive and commented that will be great to use them, as long as they will receive interesting content and services of interest. Hence, although people might not know the technology that underlies a use case, it does not mean that the users will not be willing to use/enjoy it. If fact, when pitching some of the ideal benefits and use cases of exposed technology to people under the idea of personalized services, all technologies received higher signals of interest by the participants.

The results show that the visitors expect valuable solutions, but usually they do not care about the underlying technologies. The level of awareness and benefits of offered solutions it is also important.

Alhambra's visitors were also asked whether they would use or not a mobile app for enhancing their cultural experience during a cultural visit. 60% of people agreed while a 20% of the interviewed declined. The remaining 20% were just sceptic and would agree under different circumstances to use them. Among the ones that declined, 80% commented that currently they did not have a smartphone, but they were willing to rent one or either expected to soon have one soon.

Following, we tried to get an overview of why the users would decline using an app. The common answers were that visitors did not want to focus more on the app than on the environment, as they rather to enjoy the experience freely. Some other people were not too familiar with the technology and didn't know what kind of benefits it would bring to them. Finally, people also commented that there doubts regarding the fact that if they would need to pay for it or not, the app would drain their devices batteries or network bandwidth and having those doubts. Many of these people preferred to use audio or paper guides.

All gathered results have been extremely useful for starting to get in touch with the average user preferences and their expectations. These insights have provided feedback to the TAG CLOUD ideation, brain storming and prototyping phases; as well as valuable information for further potential exploitation and promoting plans.

In summary, we can say that users were looking for (ordered by importance) easy to use, useful, error free and economical applications. But the easiness and usefulness of the app were more important by far than the rest of the expected; meaning that the potentials users would even pay for the app and tolerate minor bugs if the overall experience provided is good enough. Users/visitors are looking for an app that works easily with almost no user intervention offering interesting and light information that complements the existing one but without distracting from it and engaging through technological benefits. The application should not disturb the experience and potentially could even substitute the audio and paper guides; but also without consuming a lot of network bandwidth.

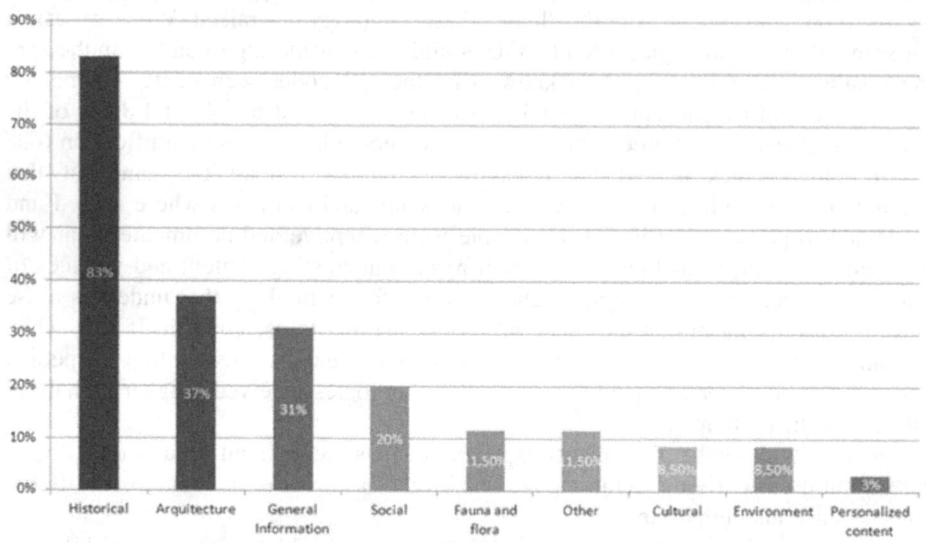

Fig. 3. Cultural heritage categories preferred by users

At this point, the only remaining question was to understand what the users consider useful information and which topics they needed to be covered in order to provide an attractive and interesting content. The following chart represents the different categories. The categories would change depending on the cultural place the users are in but it is relevant to have at least defined the top informative categories the users shall demand in order to fully enjoy a cultural experience.

4 Reviewing the Needs and Challenges from Spanish Cultural and Natural Heritage Managers

In parallel to users' evaluations, that allowed us to put ourselves in the "visitors' shoes" we have performed a focus group with 20 managers from different cultural and natural heritage sites with different sizes and needs (i.e. improving visiting experiences, increase visitation, new research, shrinking resources and new ways of sustainability). For this purpose an interview guideline and brainstorming session was developed in order to evaluate the different approaches they have to connect with visitors, as well as their future plans.

All participants agreed that there is a need towards a visitor and human-centered strategy in order to increase engagement with cultural sites. As commented by Gail Anderson in his book "Reinventing the museum: historical and contemporary perspectives on the paradigm shift", there is a need for a "paradigm shift from collection-driven institutions to visitor-centered museums has really taken hold" [7]. In this regard experts agreed that, even their institutions had a different nature, all their represented cultural sites have a story to tell: how it was made, how it originally appeared, how it has changed over time, etc., and engaging to a wide variety of individuals of all ages in a personalized way is needed. They feel that young people desires more information and contemporary presentations. Also, to engage with local people/visitors are important, as they can be linked to them in the full context of their rich heritage, rather than in cultural isolation. Thus, currently their mind-set is going towards providing experiences and services that increase active participants and not to visitors as passive spectators. Among main results, regarding needs and expectations, we have:

- Approaching different visitors with different preferences with a customized offering is recognized as very important need. It is expected that personalization could support an enjoyable cultural-driven experience that will empower visitors' motivation and engagement for culture, when incorporating personalization in the process of communicating the wealth of cultural heritage sites.
- There is an increasing importance of reaching and connecting with young people; they are the adults of tomorrow. Young people are seen as visitors, which are the most avid users of emerging technologies and social media. They need to be reached where they are and they want; and like to maintain their independence and power to engage the way they wish, not the way the mangers or city governors would do it.

- Technologies such storytelling and social media tools can be used for creation of a shared understanding, participatory dialogue as well as access, learn, share, experience and create your personalized views of an enjoyable cultural experience.
- There is a need for efficient solutions to manage all created digital content to be used in a user-centric and targeted manner; but the challenge is to guarantee high-quality information standards at low costs.
- TAG CLOUD scenarios could take effectively place and in a mainstream way, in 5-8 years. Thus there is a need to be fully prepared and integrate the understanding of the visitors' interests, likes and preferences.

5 Conclusions

TAG CLOUD puts users / visitors at the centre of the project, from its inception. All evaluations experiences insights feed not only the TAG CLOUD application and project but also Cultural Heritage pilot sites.

From visitors/users point of view we can say that the novelty of technology is not the main driver to get engaged in ICT-based participative experiences. Users' adoption of mobile technologies is increasing and foresees to increase. In this regard, the following opportunities for increasing engagement can take place as long as the users perceive their value, awareness will be channelled and visitors experiences will be untapped driving differentiated activities and participation.

Use of technologies as augmented reality and social media are envisaged as a driven for increasing engagement of people with cultural heritage sites. They can be used for providing personalised experiences and thus, have a great potential to improve the user experience and enjoyment of culture.

Moreover, institutions and cultural heritage sites are willing and ready to adopt emerging technologies related with personalisation and customized services. There is a need to build and converge into a set of integrated services to be used before, during and after the visit for lifelong engagement.

Insights and results from evaluations, coupled with above conclusions, are seen as very valuable information for the TAG CLOUD project. This information really provides useful feedback for working toward a platform that supports sustaining the users/visitors' interests, build new cultural sites' audiences, increase shared heritage, identity and citizenship, as well as provide new cultural-driven learning environments.

TAG CLOUD team believes that through personalisation and keeping users in the centre of all cultural-driven processes, the Cultural Heritage sites can make visitors' preferences, interests, prior cultural-driven knowledge and hobbies/skills, a valuable asset to enable cultural engagement.

Acknowledgements. This work has been partially funded by the EC FP7 project TAG CLOUD (Technologies lead to Adaptability & lifelong enGagement with culture throughout the CLOUD); http://www.tagcloudproject.eu/, Grant Agreement No. 600924.

References

1. Eurobarometer 67.1 (2007), http://ec.europa.eu/culture/pdf/doc958_en.pdf (accessed October 14, 2013)
2. TAG CLOUD project, CN. 600924, 7th Framework Programme, ICT for access to cultural resources (February 2013), http://www.tagcloudproject.eu/
3. Abras, C., Maloney-Krichmar, D., Preece, J.: User-Centered Design. In: Bainbridge, W. (ed.) Encyclopedia of Human-Computer Interaction. Sage Publications, Thousand Oaks (2004)
4. Carroll, J.M.: Five reasons for scenario-based design. In: Interacting with Computers, vol. 13. Elsevier (2000)
5. Isaac, A., Matthezing, H., van der Meij, L.: The value of usage scenarios for thesaurus alignment in Cultural Heritage context. In: Proceedings of the First International Workshop on Cultural Heritage on the Semantic Web, 6th International Semantic Web Conference (ISWC 2007), Busan, Corea (2007)
6. Gartner, Inc., Gartner's 2013 Hype Cycle for Emerging Technologies Maps Out Evolving Relationship Between Humans and Machines (2013); Online Published (August 19, 2013), http://www.gartner.com/newsroom/id/2575515 (accessed December 11, 2014)
7. Anderson, G.: Reinventing the museum: historical and contemporary perspectives on the paradigm shift. AltaMira Press, Walnut Creek (2004)

The Practice of Showing 'Who I am': A Multimodal Analysis of Encounters between Science Communicator and Visitors at Science Museum

Mayumi Bono[1,2], Hiroaki Ogata[3], Katsuya Takanashi[4], and Ayami Joh[1]

[1] Digital Content and Media Sciences Research Division, National Institute of Informatics
[2] Department of Informatics, School of Multidisciplinary Sciences,
The Graduate University for Advanced Studies (SOKENDAI)
2-1-2 Hitotsubashi, Chiyoda-ku, Tokyo 101-8430, Japan
{bono,joh}@nii.ac.jp
[3] Graduate School of Information Science and Electrical Engineering, Kyushu University
744, Motooa, Shishi-ku, Fukuoka 819-0395, Japan
hiroaki.ogata@gmail.com
[4] Academic Center for Computing and Media Studies, Kyoto University
Yoshida-Honmachi, Sakyo-ku, Kyoto 606-8501, Japan
takanasi@ar.media.kyoto-u.ac.jp

Abstract. In this paper, we try to contribute to the design of future technologies used in science museums where there is no explicit, pre-determined relationship regarding knowledge between Science Communicators (SCs) and visitors. We illustrate the practice of interaction between them, especially focusing on social encounter. Starting in October 2012, we conducted a field study at the National Museum of Emerging Science and Innovation (Miraikan) in Japan. Based on multimodal analysis, we examine various activities, focusing on how expert SCs communicate about science: how they begin interactions with visitors, how they maintain them, and how they conclude them.

Keywords: Multimodal Interaction Analysis, Social encounter, Science Communicators (SCs), Science Museum.

1 Introduction: Visiting the Science Museum

When we visit a medical clinic, we typically have a clear reason to go there, for example, we have a fever or stomachache, and so forth. The doctor has specific knowledge, skills, and techniques to cure those diseases for the patient. According to the concept of a membership categorization device proposed by Sacks (1974), the relationship between doctor and patient is explicit, i.e., the doctor is a *plus K* person, a professional, and the patient is a *minus K* person, a nonprofessional. Furthermore, people do not visit a medical clinic unless they have some kind of health question or issue. Thus, the clinic is an institutional setting in which the purposes of the activities, the roles of the participants, and the direction of the provision of specific knowledge are almost pre-determined (Drew & Heritage, 1992).

C. Stephanidis and M. Antona (Eds.): UAHCI/HCII 2014, Part II, LNCS 8514, pp. 650–661, 2014.

On the other hand, science museums are sometimes ambiguous spaces. Some visitors have a concrete motivation or intention when they visit museums, such as learning about current trends in science and technology, learning about Newton's theory of universal gravitation, and so on. However, many people visit museums on school trips, which means that the individuals do not have the clear intention to visit them. They do not necessarily understand in advance what kinds of scientific things they will learn at the museums.

Some science museums in Japan, for instance the National Museum of Emerging Science and Innovation (hereafter Miraikan) and the National Museum of Nature and Science in Japan, have established Science Communicators (hereafter SCs) to share their knowledge of science with people visiting the museum. However, people who visit the museum as a part of school trip usually do not know about the existence or even the concept of SCs. Thus, we assume that there is no explicit relationship between SCs and museum visitors who are interested in scientific knowledge.

In this paper, we try to contribute to the design of future technologies used in science museums where there is no explicit, pre-determined relationship regarding knowledge between SCs and visitors and we illustrate the practice of interaction between them, especially focusing on social encounter.

2 Background: What 'SC' Is

Starting in October 2012, we conducted a field study at Miraikan in Japan. In April 2012, before we started our fieldwork, one of the science communicators, who had 3 years' experience as a SC at that time, gave us the opportunity to observe and examine their daily activities at Miraikan. He had been trying to establish criteria by which to evaluate the skills of science communicators and to build an education system for better communication between SCs and visitors before his projected departure from Miraikan in March 2014.

Almost all of the SCs at Miraikan have 5-year employment contracts. They were selected from various academic fields, and some SCs hold masters or doctoral degrees. The SC who explained this position to us also works under this contract, and he had a long academic career before coming to Miraikan. During these 5 years, SCs learn communication skills intended to interest the public in science and to entertain them. They meet visitors directly on the exhibition floor.

When SCs describe their activities at Miraikan to outsiders, they always say that there is a clear boundary between science communicators and interpreters or curators in a museum. Even if they start to explain an exhibition to visitors, they explain that expert SCs are able to change the exchange from a straightforward explanation to a dialogue.

SCs at Miraikan mainly have three kinds of activities inside the museum: (1) they have a booth where they sit to explain specific research themes using model kits of objects such as the brain; (2) they sometimes present mini-lectures in a lecture hall, explaining specific knowledge regarding science based on their own experience; and

(3) each of them has time in which to interact with visitors on the exhibition floor for a pre-determined 1-hour shift.

In this paper, we examine the third of these activities practiced by SCs, focusing on how expert SCs communicate about science: how they begin interactions with visitors, how they maintain them, and how they conclude them, based on multimodal analysis.

2.1 Repository of Skills in the Oral Tradition

This research project is a collaborative work with the practitioners, namely SCs. One of the aims of this project is to detect the features of these interactions that SCs believe contribute most significantly to effective science communication based on multimodal interaction studies and conversation analysis (CA) of SCs' work in the field. When we asked expert SCs what kind of interactions are suitable and ideal as science communication, showing video clips that we filmed, their answers, amazingly, coincided. It seems that some of the expert SCs have already established common ways and standards by which to evaluate SC skills. Based on these shared standards among the expert SCs, criteria to evaluate trainee SCs and manuals for teaching science communication methods were developed at this museum.

However, from the perspective of observers, we suspect that it is impossible to create definitive criteria and write a standard manual for this field. This is related to the issue of the ambiguity of visitors' intentions and the amount of knowledge transferred between SCs and visitors, mentioned in the previous section. If visitors have clear intentions and if an epistemic difference (Heritage, 2012) between those involved in the interaction is apparent, it is easy for SCs to understand what kinds of actions they need to take in terms of specific interactions, which makes it easier to develop a manual about how to better interact with visitors.

Through observing their daily activities for a year, we realized that, in fact, aspects of science communication are rooted in the oral tradition. The oral tradition is a Japanese-specific way in which professionals hand their special skills on to the next generation, e.g., traditional arts, crafts, and performances. We assume that SCs at Miraikan have unintentionally chosen this Japanese-specific way in which to share their special skills and knowledge for better science communication. This is in spite of the fact that the SC position was part of a top-down program developed and implemented by the ministry of Science and Technology in Japan as a modern and scientific system by which to share knowledge with the public. During this transitional period, as they work to complete the task of creating criteria and preparing a manual that identifies scientific ways to share their skills and knowledge, we attempt to illuminate how the repository of skills of expert SCs is shared within the SC community.

2.2 Video Recording and Reflexive Anthropology

Using recording technology, we established an environment that enabled us to observe a targeted phenomenon over and over again (Heath, Hindmarsh, Luff, 2010).

As we mentioned before, because SCs have their own views and opinions regarding the practice of science communication, we prepared a place where SCs and interaction analysts could discuss the concrete purposes of their actions and their alignment with the traditional understandings of conversation analysis (CA) related to the following: how SCs initiate conversational sequences in semi-open spaces such as museums; how SCs invite visitors to participate in a scientific dialogue; and how SCs manage their time during interactions with visitors and explain their choices during conversations with other SCs, which we refer to as 'reflection meetings' in this paper. We assumed that we could use the practitioners' voices at these meetings, selecting crucial segments from their practices to illuminate how expert SCs evaluate the communication skills of other SCs.

To this end, we decided to film the embodied actions of SCs not only with visitors but also at a reflection meeting held after closing to discuss the events that occurred on the day. We expected to obtain input from the SCs about their own skills (e.g., how they evaluate their skills and share experiences about similar cases) during this meeting. This paper adopts the perspective of CA to discuss how we can use the knowledge of SCs to analyze their interactions with visitors. The reflection meeting provided information about the current SCs' impressions of events and visitors, such as why they chose to engage in a particular action with visitors at a given time. Additionally, we also obtained advice from senior SCs regarding what can be done to include visitors in science communication. It is impossible to obtain this type of information about the behaviors of SCs using only a traditional transcription system. In other words, the current CA system is unable to elicit information about the impressions of the interacting individuals and to solicit advice from key individuals. These shortcomings preclude our understanding the personal observations that lead to particular organizations of sequences and potential next steps. We discuss the boundary between the resources that can and cannot be involved in CA.

3 The Data

The data collection was divisible into three phases according to the recording devices used and the purpose of filming. For the first phase, we mainly conducted research using a professional high-definition camera and a professional microphone (see Fig.1) for filming the practices of two expert SCs (7 and 3 years' experience, respectively), one medium-level SC (1 year's experience), and two novice SCs (1 month's experience) from October to November 2012. After each filming session, we convened a reflection meeting, held within 1 or 2 hours after SCs finished their interactions with visitors on the floor (see Fig.2). We filmed the meeting at which SCs and conversation analysts discussed current SCs' impressions of events and visitors, such as why they chose to engage in a particular action with visitors at a given time. Additionally, we also obtained advice from senior SCs regarding what could be done to include visitors in science communication. This filming was conducted under the supervision of the ethics board of National Institute of Informatics, Japan.

Before the filming, we determined the permanent exhibition at which we would collect data, deciding on an exhibition on the third floor of the Miraikan that focused on future technologies. This exhibit, called 'The Driving Force of Innovation' consists of three elements (see Fig.3). The first element, 'The Spring of Wishes,' was designed so that past visitors' written wishes concerning technology come up from the central hall spinning in a circle triggered by current visitors when they put a ball into a slot outside. The second element, 'The River of Creativity,' was designed so that each of five rivers has one scientific question written Japanese and one interactive model for learning about scientific innovations. These rivers reach 'The Sea of Fertility' at the end, which is just a blackboard on which visitors can write down their ideas about society in 2020 in relation to science and technology. It is titled 'Let's think about our society in 2020,' which is written at the top of the blackboard, and it has magnets representing 'seeds of technology.' This is where visitors come at the end of the exhibition, a place where they can write or draw their ideas for the future using magnets.

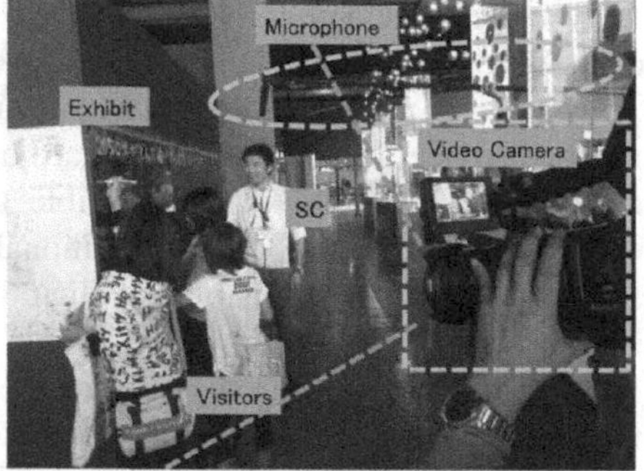

Fig. 1. Filming during the first phase

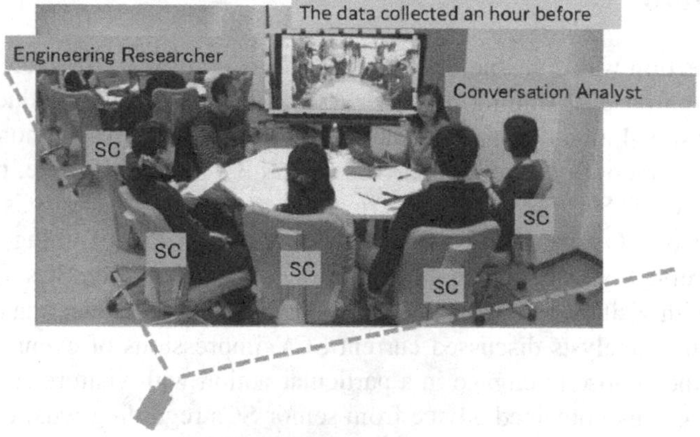

Fig. 2. Reflection meeting

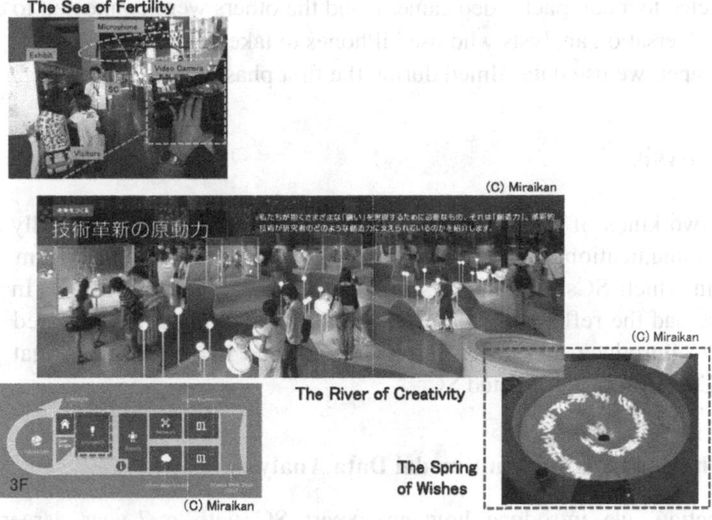

Fig. 3. Targeted Exhibition: 'The Driving Force of Innovation'

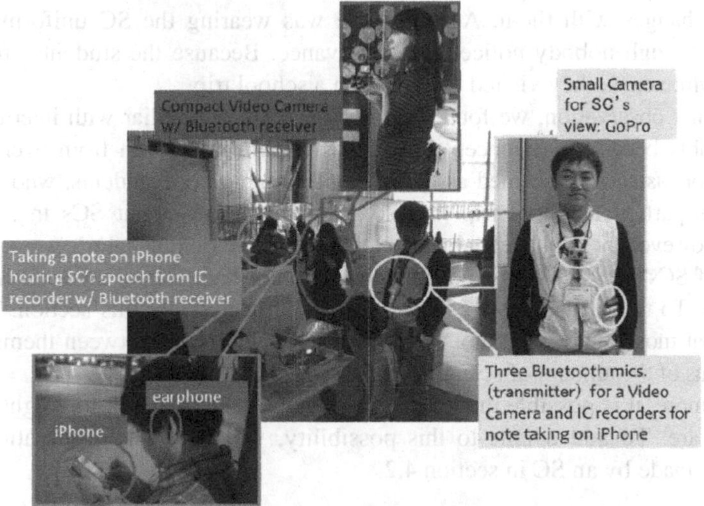

Fig. 4. Filming during the second phase

In the second phase, referring to our filming method, expert SCs filmed novice SCs' behaviors on the floor and reflection meetings between senior SCs and novice SCs for the purpose of training from February to September 2013. The devices used were basic home video cameras with a Bluetooth microphone for recording the SCs' speech. Three Bluetooth microphones were put on each SC's jacket, as shown in Figure 4; one was connected to a compact video camera, and the others were connected to earphones worn by conversation analysts who used iPhones to take notes.

In this paper, we use data filmed during the first phase.

4 Analysis

We show two kinds of data analysis: (1) multimodal analysis of naturally occurring science communication on the exhibition floor; and (2) findings from reflection meetings in which SCs and analysts observe the data analyzed in (1). In this case, because we had the reflection meeting a month after filming, we prepared a detailed transcript to introduce the basic concept of CA and the phenomena that happened there to SCs, including a targeted SC.

4.1 'Who She Is' from Multimodal Data Analysis

In this section, we introduce how an expert SC with a 7-year career initiated conversational sequences with junior high school students around the exhibition 'The Spring of Wishes' (see Fig. 3) and how she let them know who she was through several exchanges with them. Although she was wearing the SC uniform jacket, it seemed as though nobody noticed her in advance. Because the students are wearing identical white caps, they visited Miraikan on a school trip.

In our first observation, we found that visitors were unfamiliar with interacting with SCs, probably because the concept of SC was imported to Japan from overseas fairly recently. For instance, it seemed as though junior high school students, who visited the museum as part of a school trip to Tokyo, did not know about SCs in advance. In addition, however the alphabetical characters, 'science communicator', were printed on the back of SCs' jacket, it was too difficult for junior high school students to read and understand. To reveal details, we show multimodal analyses in this section. Thus, it is possible that most Japanese visitors do not notice a difference between themselves and SCs in terms of the amount of scientific knowledge they have.

Furthermore, it is possible that even SCs do not notice that visitors might not know what SCs are. To add details to this possibility, we show our observations of the impression made by an SC in section 4.2.

Focus Point 1: How The Sc Initiates Conversational Sequences With Visitors. Unfortunately, we observed that SCs and visitors tended to talk about the purpose of filming and the camera operator at the beginning part of the first phase of filming. Because of this, we replaced the devices with simpler and smaller ones for the second phase of filming. However, we hoped that we would be able to observe a practical phenomenon: SCs employing the unusual atmosphere in which they are filmed by a high-definition camera as an environmental resource to initiate contact with visitors.

```
Excerpt 1
01    DOT:  hayaku ichirinsha ni noremasu youni (.) nori- noritai desu
            soon   monocycle   P  ride-could wish     ride- ride-want FP
            'I wish I could ride a monocycle soon. I would like to ride (it).'
02          (1.0)
03    DOT:  °*nani yo [kore°
              what F   this
              'What's this?'
      red   *comes close (frame in)
04    ?:              [(      )
05          (1.*0)#@
      red      *turns around and looks up camera
      sc        @looks *at RED--->
      red              *looks back to exhibition
               #drawing 1
06    SC:   a, ushiro kita:? +(.) kyou ha↑↓(.)~
            oh, behind came        today P
            'Oh, (the camera) came up from behind (you)? Today is'
      red                    +Looks at SC---->
      blue                                      ~turns around camera
                                                #drawing 2
```

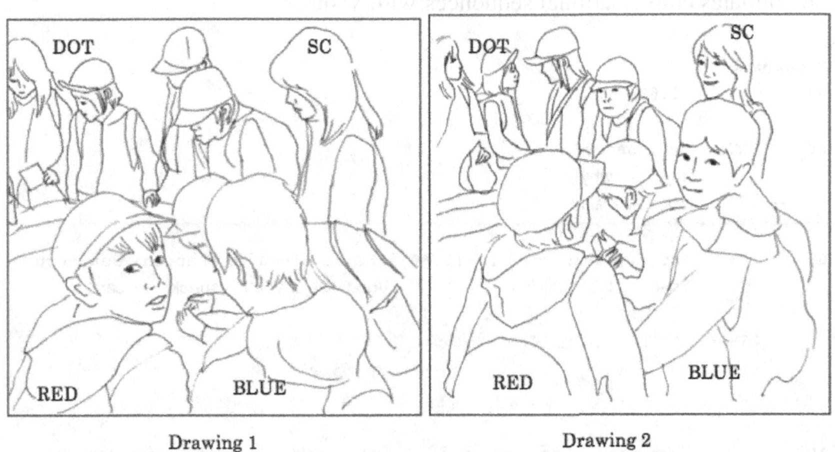

Drawing 1 Drawing 2

Line 01 of Excerpt 1 is the beginning point of filming. The person labeled as DOT reads the letters that come up from the hall with a flat intonation. At this point, the SC has already taken a position in the frame touching the edge of the exhibition without getting the museum visitors' attention. She looks like she is listening to DOT's voice as well as those of the other visitors. In line 06, SC starts to talk with visitors, addressing to RED an 'a (oh)'-prefaced utterance indicating that she is changing her interactive state (Heritage, 1984); 'a, ushiro kita:?' 'Oh, (the camera) came up from behind (you)?' This utterance is a casual form of speech in Japanese, similar to talking with friends.

RED comes closer to this gathering from outside the video frame at the beginning of line 03. Before that, he had already noticed that the cinematographer was filming them using a high-definition camera (see Drawing 1). Needless to say, the SC knew why the camera operator was filming them. We consider that SC tried to show the other participants that she had noticed RED's observing the camera operator by using an ‘a (oh)’-prefaced utterance. As a result, SC got the attention of BLUE and that of the boy standing to the left of SC, and they changed the direction of their gaze toward the camera (see Drawing 2). In other words, she succeeded in inviting them into the participation framework between RED and SC.

It is striking that even though SC formulated her utterance as a question in line 06, SC continued her explanation about the filming activities of the cinematographer, ‘kyou ha↑↓(rising and falling intonations)’ ‘Today is,’ without waiting for RED’s reaction. So, despite the fact that ‘a, ushiro kita:?’ took the form of a question with rising intonation, it was not sequentially positioned as a first-pair-part (FPP) in this context (Schegloff & Sacks, 1973). It seems that it worked as a device for getting the attention of other participants to let them hear her explanation.

We consider that her continuing to produce a next-turn constructional unit (TCU; Sacks, Schegloff, & Jefferson, 1974) by rushing through the possible completion point and a transition relevance place (TRP) is an approach to forming a participation framework (Goffman, 1981), which is conducted at SC’s initiative.
Thus, she initiates conversational sequences with visitors.

Excerpt 2

```
07            (0.@2)
      sc         @looks up
08    BLUE:   o+u, nande?
              oh,      why
              'Oh, why's that?'
      red      +Looks up camera
09    SC:     @sou(.)atashi ga↑↓ ~(1.*0)@chanto minna to ohanashi dekiteru
              Yeah    I        P                good  all-of-you P speak    can
              @looks at BLUE
      blue:                        ~looks back to SC
      red                             *Looks back to SC
      sc                                 @Looks up--->

10            kana tte    iu   no  o:↑ (1.@0) kiroku shi ni kiterun desu yo.
              P   quoted-P Thing What P        film  to-do P coming  FP   FP
              'Yeah, they are filming me to know whether I can successfully interact with you.'
      SC                                @Looks back to BLUE--->
11            (1.4)
```

Focus Point 2: How She Let Them Know Who She Is. Excerpt 2 is a continuation of Excerpt 1. At the end of line 06, ‘kyou ha↑↓’, BLUE turns around to look for the camera, as shown in Drawing 2. Then, in line 08, BLUE says ‘ou, nande?’ ‘Oh, why’s that?’ After SC answers BLUE saying ‘sou’ ‘yeah’ at the beginning of line 09, she restarts her explanation, which is formed by connecting it to her previous speech in line 06.

Here, we would like to focus on why she did not say anything about 'who she is' using her job title, SC, at this moment. Instead, she just says, 'chanto minna to ohanashi dekiteru kana tte iu no o,' meaning 'whether I could successfully interact with you' in line 09 to line 10. In these lines, she represents the content of SCs' work, which is successfully interacting with visitors, in this case, to explain the reason that the camera operator was filming.

Excerpt 3

13 SC: datte miraikan tte kouiu hito ippai iru jan tatteru hito
because miraikan Q like-these people many be FP standing people
'You know, there are many people like me, who are standing (in front of exhibitions).'

14 (1.0)

15 SC: sore o [shirabe ni kiterun desu
it P to-investigate P coming FP
'and they come here to investigate them.'

16 DOT: [naroranai byouki ga nakunari masu [youni
incurable disease P eliminate FP wish
'I wish incurable diseases would be eliminated (in near future).'

17 STRIPE: [(anaun)saa?
announcer
'(Are you) an announcer?'

18 SC: terebi janai ¥terebi janai¥
television not television not
'(This is) not TV (station, this is) not TV (station).'

We omitted one line between Excerpt 2 and Excerpt 3, in which DOT was reading the letters coming up from the hall. Like line 01 in Excerpt 1 and line 16 in Excerpt 3, this activity is not sequentially related to interactions between the SC and visitors. We would like to focus on why she, once again, did not say anything about 'who she is' using her job title directly. In line 13, she just said, 'datte miraikan tte kouiu hito ippai iru jan tatter hito,' 'You know, there are many people like me, who are standing (in front of exhibitions).' Especially, 'kouiu hito' 'LIKE-THESE PEOPLE,' 'people like me' and 'tatteru hito' 'STANDING PEOPLE,' 'people who are standing' are striking here. She mentioned two things, (1) the fact that there are a lot of people like her here, and (2) that they are standing near the exhibitions. (1) was designed as a confirmation question, i.e., 'jan' is a final particle used in Japanese to get confirmation from an interlocutor and (2) was incremental to the previous TCU. These examples make it seem as though she is trying to avoid saying her job title directly to visitors for some reason.

Finally in line 17, another visitor, STRIPE, asks her 'anaunsaa?' '(Are you) an announcer?' while coming close to the right side of the SC. Then, SC immediately answers his question in line 18, 'terebi janai \terebi janai' '(This is) not TV (station, this is) not TV (station).'

Thus, she had never said who she is or what her position is called during the explanation of the reason for filming with high-definition camera. Because of that, visitors did not get crucial information about who she is at this moment.

Summury of Analyses and Discussions. In our analysis of Excerpt 1, we considered how the SC opens conversational sequences with visitors. We found that the SC utilized visitors' observations of the environmental resources surrounding them; a cameraman directed his camera to them. In our analysis of Excerpts 2 and 3, we investigated how she let them know who she is. We found that the SC never said her job title during the explanation of the reason for the camera operator's filming them. Instead, she mentioned the content of SC work, 'successfully interacting with you' (Excerpt 2) and the fact that there are a lot of people like her here, with brief mention of their characteristics (Excerpt 3). It seems that she tried to avoid saying her job title directly to visitors for some reason. We could not confirm why she did not say her job title at that moment or whether she intentionally formulated her explanation as we have suggested. However, we consider that if the SC used a job title to explain the situation, it is possible that nobody would understand the purpose of filming, i.e., visitors would not have the opportunity to learn any details concerning SCs' purpose, as in this case. In addition, their job title,'science communicator', was imported into Japanese as a loan word using katakana, 'saiensu comyunikeetaa'. This Japanese convention of importing English words makes the practice of showing 'who I am' a complex matter in interaction.

4.2 'Who I Am' from Practitioners' Voices in the Reflection Meeting

In the reflection meeting, we showed some crucial points of our observations based on our analysis from the perspective of CA, as discussed in section 4.1, which involved watching the video clip repeatedly over the period of an hour. As a result, we obtained SCs' impressions of the issue of initiating conversational sequences and of whether the SC should always reveal who s/he is. One of the striking narratives by an SC in the reflection meeting was as follows:

> *I have never paid attention to whether visitors already knew who I was. On the other hand, it is possible for us to get visitors' information before interacting with them. Because the table on the working shift includes this information when we are going to have a group tour like a school trip. We always got it before interacting with them. Until now, we have been paying attention not to showing who we are but to knowing who they are, which means what are their interests, how much science knowledge they have, what they want to be in the future, and so on. However, I was very surprised there was the possibility that visitors did not know about the existence of SCs at Miraikan. This fact perhaps will be related to the planning of encounters with visitors in our future activities.*

5 General Discussions and Conclusions

As we mentioned in section 1, visiting a museum is an ambiguous event for not only visitors but also SCs from the perspective of territories of knowledge. In cases in which there is no common understanding between people about the amount of knowledge the other possesses, it might be difficult to understand who would provide new information for their knowledge to progress and to invite them to the activities at the museum. Of course, visitors may learn what an SC is through interacting with them directly. However, we suppose that if SCs know that most visitors do not know about the position or concept of SCs in advance, they could plan their interactions based on this condition.

This paper presents a preliminary result of our ongoing research project, focusing on the case of social encounters between SCs and visitors at a museum. When we design a museum guide robot, we tend to make it introduce itself at the beginning of interaction, such as 'Hi, my name is Nancy. I am a guide robot of this museum. Please ask me if you have any questions.' However, we found that this is not real in the case of museum where there is no explicit, pre-determined relationship regarding knowledge between SCs and visitors. The expert SC presented her role at the museum and the nature of her job through the interaction with the visitors. We consider that future technology should be designed integrating the insights gained from the analysis of our daily interactions.

Acknowledgments. This research was partially supported by The Center for Promotion of Integrated Sciences (CPIS), The Graduate University of Advanced Studies (SOKENDAI), Grant-in-Aid for Challenging Exploratory Research, Japan Society for the Promotion of Science, and Interaction Science Project: IDO-ROBO, Grand Challenge 2012-2013, National Institute of Informatics (NII).

References

1. Drew, P., Heritage, J.: Talk at Work: Interaction in Institutional Settings. Cambridge University Press, Cambridge (1992)
2. Goffman, E.: Forms of Talk. University of Pennsylvania Press, Philadelphia (1981)
3. Heath, C., Hindmarsh, J., Luff, P.: Video in Qualitative Research. Sage, London (2010)
4. Heritage, J.: A change-of-state token and aspects of its sequential placement. In: Atkinson, J.M., Heritage, J. (eds.) Structures of Social Action, pp. 299–345. Cambridge University Press, Cambridge (1984)
5. Heritage, J.: Epistemics in Action: Action Formation and Territories of Knowledge. Research on Language and Social Interaction 45, 1–29 (2012)
6. Sacks, H.: On the Analyzability of Stories by Children. In: Turner, R. (ed.) Ethnomethodology, pp. 216–232. Penguin, Harmondsworth (1974)
7. Sacks, H., Schegloff, E.A., Jefferson, G.: A simplest systematics for the organization of turn-taking for conversation. Language 50, 696–735 (1974)
8. Schegloff, E.A., Sacks, H.: Opening Up Closings. Semiotica VIII(4), 289–327 (1973)

Using Augmented Reality and Social Media in Mobile Applications to Engage People on Cultural Sites

Silvia de los Ríos[1], María Fernanda Cabrera-Umpiérrez[1], María Teresa Arredondo[1], Miguel Páramo[1], Bastian Baranski[2], Jochen Meis[2], Michael Gerhard[2], Belén Prados[3], Lucía Pérez[3], and María del Mar Villafranca[3]

[1] Life Supporting Technologies, Universidad Politécnica de Madrid, Spain
{srios,chiqui,mta,mparamo}@lst.tfo.upm.es

[2] GeoMobile GmbH, Dortmund, Germany
{b.baranski,j.meis,m.gerhard}@geomobile.de

[3] Patronato de la Alhambra y Generalife, Granada, Spain
belenprados@wonderbrand.es,
{luciam.perez,mariamar.villafranca}@juntadeandalucia.es

Abstract. One of the toughest challenges that curators and professionals in the heritage sector face is how to attract, engage and retain visitors of heritage institutions. The current approaches have only limited success since they still follow the same centralized strategy of producing and delivering cultural content to the general public. This paper provides an overview of current trends in information technology that are most relevant to cultural institutions, and investigates how augmented reality, gamification, storytelling and social media can improve visitors' experience by providing new means of participation, proposing a radically new approach in defining cultural content and creating personalised experiences with cultural heritage objects. The paper considers actual use cases provided by the European research project TAG CLOUD to define the functional range of suitable applications and proposes a set of system components that are being implemented in TAG CLOUD.

Keywords: Augmented reality, social media, gamification, storytelling, mobile applications, cultural heritage, TAG CLOUD.

1 Introduction

Many Europeans consider cultural heritage a highly valuable social asset. However, reality shows that actual engagement with cultural heritage by the general public is low [1]. In an attempt to meet the main challenge of curators and professionals in the cultural sector, that is to attract, engage and retain visitors of heritage sites, institutions have already been applying and deploying a wide range of digital technologies, ranging from static kiosk systems and multimedia websites to on-site location-based systems. More recent trends in mainstream information technology such as augmented reality, mobile geo-social networks, big data and cloud computing have not yet a big impact in the area of cultural heritage, but they have a great potential.

C. Stephanidis and M. Antona (Eds.): UAHCI/HCII 2014, Part II, LNCS 8514, pp. 662–672, 2014.

Augmented reality allows users to see the real world through the smartphone camera, with virtual objects overlaid upon or composed with the real world image. Social network platforms such as Facebook and Twitter have already attracted hundred millions of users and are still growing [2]. They help sharing stories and connecting people based on common interests or common activities. From a technological perspective, augmented reality and social media are promising ways to attract, engage and retain visitors of heritage places [3-7]. Through augmented reality, visitors are able to interact with cultural artefacts in a more natural way. They can explore, touch and manipulate virtual representations of artefacts what otherwise might not be possible. Extending the real-world environment with historical photos and pictures allows immersing visitors in past times. Social media can help to realize the vision of the participatory museum [8] by attaching user-generated impressions to curated content. Additional techniques such as 'Gamification' and 'Serious Games' can help cultural heritage institutions to educate as well as to entertain, which is important for dedicated target audiences.

The use of these technologies applied to the cultural heritage sector through mobile applications is being explored within TAG CLOUD (Technologies lead to Adaptability & lifelong enGagement with culture throughout the CLOUD) [9], a European research project co-funded by the Seventh Framework Programme of the European Commission addressing the issue of lifelong engagement with cultural heritage through social media, augmented reality and storytelling applications based on the cloud.

Within this project, some studies carried out during the first months show that people that tend to visit cultural sites frequently, in most cases, do not prepare their tours in advance. Instead, visitors often prefer a spontaneous experience. They enjoy discovering new environments for themselves. Studies also show that most visitors carry personal smartphones and that people would benefit from mobile applications providing additional information about the cultural site.

As a first proof of concept, TAG CLOUD has implemented augmented reality modules and proposed new concepts for integrating social media within a mobile application that guides and attracts visitors of the Monumental Complex of Alhambra and Generalife, a famous historical palace and fortress complex located in Granada, Spain.

2 Current Technologies in Cultural Heritage

2.1 Augmented Reality in Cultural Heritage

Thomas Caudell and David Mizell [10] point the term "Augmented reality (AR)" in 1992. This term is defined as a "combination of real and computer-generated digital information into the user's view of the real world in a way that they appear as one environment [11]".

Cultural heritage sector has done an increasing digitization effort during the last decade. That makes AR applications perfect showcases of any kind of cultural artefact (objects, building, etc., but also, ceremonies, music or stories). Augmented reality improves the visitors' enjoyment during the visit, enhancing the sense of being present in the place and obtaining additional information about any object of his interest, offering an efficient communication with the user through multimedia presentations, natural and intuitive techniques and low maintenance and acquisition costs for the museum. It also improves the experience in the in site environment as the information is shown in real time according to the user's physical location, mitigating confusion in large spaces and improving the sensation of having the information controlled and under demand.

The necessary technologies for augmented reality (mobile processing, image recognition, object tracking, display technology and location) have already been available several years ago in mobile devices: a camera, a relatively fast internet connection, accelerometers, gyroscope, digital compass and GPS. The main mobile platforms, Android and iOS have recently started to gain third party AR-like applications. Thanks to the smartphone popularity, and the increasing maturity of AR technology, the number of potential users is increasing and, consequently, the number of available AR applications.

Currently, there are two main approaches of commercial AR applications: AR browsers based on geo referenced positioning and image-recognition-based AR. The technologies below are different but support the same principle, both of them follow a magic lens configuration [12] that means the user sees the augmented space directly behind the display.

AR browsers are able to delivery points of interests (POI), notations or graphics based on GPS locations superimposing the captured image by a mobile camera view (Geo-Tagging) [13]. This type of applications usually shows information resources from several data storages and webs. They use a combination of the digital compass, accelerometers and GPS to identify the user's location and field of vision, to retrieve data based on the geographical coordinates and overlay that data over the camera view. One successful commercial example of a good AR browser is Layar [14]. It is available for Android and iOS, the developers can contribute by an application programming interface that sets up "layers" in the browser. Other very used AR browser is Aurasma [15]. There are also a lot of AR applications able to use these browsers. Wikitude Me [16] is an Android, iPhone and Symbian compatible application that pulls the information from Wikipedia [17] and Qype and in which the user can also create his own POIs and location-based, hyper-linked digital content that is show through the Wikitude browser application, and Junaio [18] information about POIs and supports 3D animations and share images via the social networking sites. Each user generated geo-tagged POI is then visible by all the other users. Tagwhat4 also allows the sharing of information.

An interesting use of AR browsers for cultural heritage initiatives is made by the Museum of the City of London [19] that allows superposing old photographs of London over real images. Other examples can be Lights of St Etienne [20] a commercial application that uses the AR-browser Argon in order to create an embodied, location-based experience, St Etienne Cathedral in Metz, MoviAr a research project that assists users who need touristic information about a city, Historypin [21] that allows sharing of images of the past between other members of the community. However, most of the applications and research projects related with culture heritage are tourism focused applications that do not take care of the engagement of the people living in those places. On the other hand, new apps basically overly information onto a screen with no relationship to the real world, or personalization of content or interaction.

The other type of AR, image recognition-based AR applications, establishes connections between surrounding physical targets and digital information through image recognition. The mobile identifies QR codes, barcodes or other graphical markers that trigger the desired action (e.g. information search). There is a huge amount of this type of applications, some of the most popular are ShopSavvy [22], pic2shop [23], StickyBits [24], Google Goggles [25] that after gaining maturity will show relevant results about any object in the user's vicinity, GoodGuide [26] based in scanning barcodes, and Vuforia [27] that is an SDK for augmented reality image recognition that support iOS, Android and Unity 3D.

Most of the AR applications for cultural proposes use AR browsers and rarely explore the image recognition-based AR like Google Goggles as engagement mechanism.

2.2 Social Media in Cultural Heritage

The first personal systems for cultural heritage were desktop applications which automatically generated hypertext pages with text and images from different cultural items repositories, according, somehow, to information of the user (interest, knowledge, age, physical abilities, etc.). With the extensive use of the web, the online web sites were extended to the majority of the cultural places. The evolution of these groups of technologies offers very attractive solutions to present information to the users in a more attractive fashion and it is one of the preferred technologies to engage new visitors. In parallel, the reduction in the cost of devices and internet access has provided users with information off the cultural site as well as the access to multimedia resources, personalization of the routes, bookmark interesting content or the creation of a personal collection of cultural items. The creation of social virtual spaces (for instance Second Life [28]) and 3D virtual cultural sites have revolutionized the interaction ways and have provided new personalized content. The web 2.0 approach added some new services, such as blogs, wikis, social networks, and they turn visitor into an active part in the creation, management and conservation of cultural heritage and allow the active sharing of information between users. Some museums are pioneers in the use of Web 2.0 applications, for instance:

- Brooklyn Museum [29] was one of the first museums actively participating in Facebook and Twitter.
- TATE Museum [30] was pioneer in the use of user generated content as source for creating new cultural experiences.
- OMEKA.NET [31]. Omeka is an open-source platform and it was created for the storage and display of library, cultural space, archives, and scholarly collections and exhibitions. It was thought to bring to the cloud museum's collections and exhibitions. The system is similar to the micro-blogging structure of Wordpress

(wordpress.org) helping to publish online cultural web-site or texts. The Omeka team decided to contribute to a movement that is helping to standardize data about digital objects. While there are different standards available, the Dublin Core Metadata Initiative is the most widely adopted and offers users more flexibility.

- ARTBABBLE.com [32]: The Indianapolis Museum of art created ArtBabble in late 2008 an on-line video website dedicated to art related content that runs entirely in the cloud and allows streaming of high definition video content in a scalable and cost-effective manner.
- STEVE Project [33]: STEVE is a collaboration of museum professionals and others who use the social tagging to describe and access cultural heritage collections and encourage visitor engagement with collection objects. This activity includes researching social tagging and museum collections; developing open source software tools for tagging collections and managing tags; and engaging in discussion and outreach with members of the community who are interested in implementing social tagging for their own collections.

In addition, nowadays, there is a wide variety of content that is shared using social networks or application based on social networks, for example Twitter, Instagram, Flickr, YouTube, Facebook, etc. and the most important museums, cultural events and archaeological sites have an account in Facebook, Twitter and other social virtual networks, but despite this virtual presence, the involvement of the general public and consequently the engagement of the population with their cultural heritage are low.

3 Engaging People with Culture through Mobile Technologies

With the aim to promote engagement of people with cultural heritage TAG CLOUD takes advantage current technologies to promote cultural adaptive experiences ubiquitously using low cost personal devices and technology for the general public and cultural institutions.

TAG CLOUD aims to engage both visitors and people living in their home cities, in order to introduce cultural heritage in their life style, so the developed system will not only show information with tourism purposes, but also information to include cultural events in daily life of the people.

Within TAG CLOUD, the type of content delivered to the user is also adaptable based on the user choices, past and social networking content. By integrating with social networking sites, such as Flick, Facebook, Twitter or Foursquare, the information about the user likes, dislikes and areas they visit can be found.

TAG CLOUD explores augmented reality for creating personalized AR based experiences according to the context (community and cultural site) and the dynamic user profile (from the social web and current wishes and needs) that combine both, AR browsers and image recognition-based AR, to offer adaptive experiences to each user. In that way, TAG CLOUD uses AR browsers to offer personalized information, content and interaction mechanisms (voice, text, video, user's opinions, friends previous experiences, games, intelligent itineraries, etc.) according to the user profile and the preferences at that time, in combination with image-recognition AR that allows the users to interact physically with the cultural digital artefacts, during the experience in a personalized fashion.

Social web modelling is a new discipline that is not highly explored in cultural heritage engagement projects because cultural heritage experiences are usually social. It has revolutionised the participation of the users on Web providing their users with the means to generate and share content. TAG CLOUD takes advantage of social web modelling in order to predict user interests and preferences and thus, engage users with their cultural heritage environment.

These social networks have the goal of linking people with common interest and needs. The active role of the users provides rich information about their preferences and needs, they choose their friends and colleges in the network, publish and share their content, rate and tag content from other users and participate in online activities and events. This rich interaction with the system requires a wild need of personalization, because it will affect what the user will generate, participate, consume, create, and, consequently, all this activity will affect the structure of the community and the interaction with other communities.

Collaborative filtering and recommendation (User-based Collaborative Filtering) have been the most widely adopted type of personalization in traditional social communities. According to this, the personalization is based on the interest shown by other similar users, they assume, in fact, that similar users are interested in similar items. In the case of social networks, this approach is frequently used in behavioural profiling recommendations filtering [34] that monitors and collects data about user's activities and tailors user experience based on those activities. In social web, the profiles are based on sites visited; product pages viewed, emails sent, keywords in comments published, etc.

This approach is effective in large e-commerce applications, but in social web, the users provide much more information about their needs, preferences, wishes and relationships than logs in a traditional web server, and User-based Collaborative Filtering become ineffective because data is sparse with few co-rated items and being purely statistical does not make use of the structure of the data. That is knowing someone has an interest in Napoleon would now allow us to say they would be interested that his troops used Sphinx's Nose for target practice, unless a statistical relationship is established by the users.

The following general characteristics of Augmented Reality technologies and applications are also important benefits over the digital technologies that are already established in cultural heritage.

- *Uniqueness* – Both AR browsers and image recognition-based AR applications are bounded to a specific location and are unique for an actual cultural heritage site/object. Compared to classic mobile tourist guides, it offers not only valuable curated information about places and artefacts but also gains new experiences of the surrounding. In TAG CLOD the possibilities of AR are explored for cultural heritage only, any new IT developments are expected to achieve further exposure.
- *Interactivity* – AR applications allow to virtually interact with historical places and artefacts (e.g. touch and rotate the environment). Studies have shown that receiving and interpreting visual inputs, coordinating motors skills even in virtual environments

and involvement with symbols, stories and experiences foster emotions, which is potentially highly entertaining and stimulating for users [35].

- *Personalization* – Depending on the use case and the actual implementation, the utilization of AR technologies allows to integrate self-generated content from users (e.g. self-portraits or paintings) as an overlay into the virtual representation of the environment. That helps to create highly personalized media while being at the heritage, which is more engaging to visitors than presenting plain text, image or video.
- *Virality* – Such self-generated and personalized media can be shared perfectly within social networks, which helps other people to receive a more personalized impression of the possibilities on-site what most likely attract them to visit the cultural heritage themselves. The element of surprise that is achieved by sharing individual content about cultural heritage can also result in a so-called viral loop.
- *Content* – By creating their own content in AR applications, such as making pictures on-site or telling their own personal stories about places and artefacts, users are able to create a quality piece of content that wouldn't otherwise exist. Thus, integrating such user-generated content into the curated exhibition at the cultural heritage (even if only through social media channels) would mean a substantial step towards a more engaging cultural experience.

Although AR and social media have not yet a big impact in the area of cultural heritage, it seems to have a great potential to foster the engagement of people by means of innovative interaction possibilities to bring history alive.

4 An Example in the Monumental Complex of Alhambra and Generalife, in Spain

"Experiencing culture in Alhambra Gardens in a group" is a scenario that has been developed for the Monumental Complex of Alhambra and Generalife. In this scenario, TAG CLOUD offers Maria (teenager tourist) and her family several sightseeing tours for the heritage institution. Maria is a teenager, who is in Granada for two days. When Maria arrives at the Alhambra, she logs into TAG CLOUD from her mobile phone in order to receive up-to-date information about what she and her family can do on-site, because the ticket "Alhambra General" is not available today (Thursday).

As mentioned earlier, the TAG CLOUD system shows several opportunities to visit the Alhambra: Alhambra Other Look (includes areas generally closed to the public in the Monumental Complex and other selected places in Granada city), Alhambra Experiences (evening visit to the Nasrid Palaces and a morning visit to the Alcazaba and Generalife Palace and Gardens on the following day), Alhambra Gardens (visit all areas of the Monumental Complex open to the public, except the Nasrid Palaces) and Alhambra Night (the night visit around the palaces) .

Maria explores the possibilities that TAG CLOUD is offering them to visit the Alhambra.

She explores about the interactive routes of "Alhambra Other Look", by checking images, photographs extracted from Flickr, comments from other visitors (social media), videos from YouTube, etc. This is a type of visit focused on special subjects. Maria deeps in a special route: the Alhambra and Charles' Granada: The Emperor´s dream. She likes it so much, because in this case it is possible to visit the Palace of Charles the Fifth. TAG CLOUD App shows her this information. But this activity will be offered: Mondays and Sundays between 9:30 and 14:00, with a duration of four hours.

So, they decide to buy Alhambra Experiences, because they can visit the gardens in the morning and the Nasrid Palaces at night.

Maria's Twitter account is associated with TAG CLOUD, so she can publish on Twitter a comment about her decisions directly from TAG CLOUD system.

Once TAG CLOUD learns that Maria has decided to take the Nasrih Palaces night visit, the system shows her the itineraries that she will be able to experience, and other digital resources available, such as: the basic guide from iTunes Play Store and Augmented Reality application of the Monumental Complex of Alhambra and Generalife.

Maria and her family are at the entrance of the Alhambra ready for their visit. They decide to join the "Gardens guided tour" at 12:00 because they are very interested in the complex and do not want to miss any detail. Alhambra offers devices for rent with TAG CLOUD system installed. Guides create specific "group visits" in the system so that the whole group can enjoy the same experience along the route. Maria uses her smartphone to introduce in TAG CLOUD the code that identifies the tour. She logs into TAG CLOUD as "guest".

At 12:00, the guide join together all the tour participants and ask them to select the option to "join a tour" in the system, and to enter the respective code to start the visit.

During the guided tour, TAG CLOUD App combines augmented reality and the basic guide with its functionalities in order to offer an adaptive experience to Maria and the rest of the group: the interesting places nearby, information of the Point of Interest (POIs), and the way to go there by GPS. When she is near the Palace of Charles the Fifth, she remembered the beautiful rooms in this palace that she saw before, so she decides go to the Court of the Palace of Charles the Fifth; when she is inside, she discovers with the AR application a "virtual guardian" near a pillar, which gives her more information about this actual place.

Fig. 1. TAG CLOUD App using AR in the Palace of Charles V, Monumental Complex of Alhambra and Generalife, Spain

After the Palace of Charles the Fifth, Maria and the rest of the group go to the Palace of the Lions. Once there, at the Court of the Lions, a place that she had seen lots of times in books and TV series, she is amazed by its beauty. So, she decides to point out with her smartphone using the TAG CLOUD App, and clicking on the Twitter icon that appears when TAG CLOUD detects her location, she decides to let her friends know that she is there by sharing her location on a Tweet.

Fig. 2. TAG CLOUD App using AR combined with social media in the Court of the Lions, Monumental Complex of Alhambra and Generalife, Spain

5 Conclusions

As explained within this manuscript, there exist several approaches of cultural heritage institutions that attempt to attract their visitors using new technologies, such as augmented reality and social media. Although these technologies have not yet a big impact in the area of cultural heritage, they provide a huge range of possibilities to offer new ways to interact with cultural artefacts, personalise the cultural experience, share content and experiences and interact with the social environment. Thus, they have a great potential to foster the engagement of people on cultural heritage sites, not only tourists but also residents.

TAG CLOUD is advancing the methodology of developing adaptive systems that will form the basis for personalised interactions between users and cultural resources, before, during and after the visit to a cultural site. For this purpose, the system provides both virtual and real experiences which engage users to take part and be involved with cultural heritage, at home, during the course of their daily life activities and, of course, when visiting a heritage institution. TAG CLOUD is taking advantage of social communities where users and experts create, share, change and add content and personal experiences, building together a huge culture framework which allow the generation of personalised and unique culture experiences for each user. This will promote users to actively participate in their own cultural environment, and integrate culture in their lifestyle.

Acknowledgements. This work has been partially funded by the EC FP7 project TAG CLOUD (Technologies lead to Adaptability & lifelong enGagement with culture throughout the CLOUD); http://www.tagcloudproject.eu/, Grant Agreement No. 600924.

References

1. Eurobarometer 67.1 (2007), http://ec.europa.eu/culture/pdf/doc958_en.pdf (accessed October 14, 2013)
2. Digital Insights, http://blog.digitalinsights.in/social-media-facts-and-statistics-2013/0560387.html (accessed October 14, 2013)
3. Ardissono, L., Kuflik, T., Petrelli, D.: Personalization in cultural heritage: the road travelled and the one ahead. User Modeling and User-Adapted Interaction 22(1-2), 73–99 (2012)
4. Giaccardi, E. (ed.): Heritage and Social Media. Understanding Heritage in a Participatory Culture. Routledge, London (2012)
5. Gartner, Inc., Gartner's 2013 Hype Cycle for Emerging Technologies Maps Out Evolving Relationship Between Humans and Machines (2013); Online Published (August 19, 2013), http://www.gartner.com/newsroom/id/2575515
6. Azuma, R.T.: A Survey of Augmented Reality. Presence 6(4), 355–385 (1997)
7. Ellison, N.: Social Network Sites: Definition, History, and Scholarship. Journal of Computer-Mediated Communication (2007)
8. Simon, N.: The Participatory Museum. Museum 2.0 (2010) ISBN-13: 978-0615346502
9. TAG CLOUD project, CN. 600924, 7th Framework Programme, ICT for access to cultural resources (February 2013), http://www.tagcloudproject.eu/
10. Caudell, T.P., Mizell, D.W.: Augmented reality: an application of heads-up display technology to manual manufacturing proceses. In: IEEE Hawaii International Conference on Systems Sciences (1992)
11. Höllerer, T., Feiner, S.: Mobile Augmented Reality. In: Karimi, H., Hammad, A. (eds.) Telegeoinformatics: Location-Based Computing and Services. Taylor & Francis Books Ltd. (2004)
12. Kruijff, E., Swan, E., Feiner, S.: Perceptual isssues in augmented reality revisited. In: ISMAR 2010, Seoul, Korea (2010)
13. Höllerer, T., Feiner, S.: Mobile Augmented Reality. In: Telegeoinformatics: Location-Based Computing and Services. Taylor & Francis Books Ltd. (2004)
14. Layar, http://www.layar.org (accessed February 7, 2014)
15. Aurasma, http://www.aurasma.com/ (accessed February 7, 2014)
16. Wikitude, http://www.wikitude.org (accessed February 7, 2014)
17. Wikipedia, http://www.wikipedia.com (accessed February 7, 2014)
18. Junaio, http://www.junaio.com (accessed February 7, 2014)
19. Museum of London, http://www.museumoflondon.org.uk/Resources/app/you-are-here-app/home.html (accessed February 7, 2014)
20. Argon, http://argon.gatech.edu/ (accessed February 7, 2014)
21. Historypin, http://www.historypin.com (accessed February 7, 2014)
22. Shopsavvy, http://shopsavvy.com/ (accessed February 7, 2014)
23. pic2shop, http://www.pic2shop.com (accessed February 7, 2014)
24. Stickybits, http://www.crunchbase.com/company/stickybits (accessed February 7, 2014)
25. Google Goggles, http://www.google.com/mobile/goggles (accessed February 7, 2014)
26. Goodguide, http://www.goodguide.com/about/mobile (accessed February 7, 2014)

27. Vuforia, https://developer.qualcomm.com/mobile-development/add-advanced-features/augmented-reality-vuforia (accessed February 7, 2014)
28. Second Life, http://secondlife.com/ (accessed February 7, 2014)
29. Brooklyn Museum, http://www.brooklynmuseum.org/ (accessed February 7, 2014)
30. Tate Museum, http://www.tate.org.uk/ (accessed February 7, 2014)
31. OMEKA Project, http://omeka.org (accessed February 7, 2014)
32. ARTBABBLE, http://www.artbabble.org/ (accessed February 7, 2014)
33. Steve museum, http://www.steve.museu (accessed February 7, 2014)
34. Ben Schafer, J., Frankowski, D., Herlocker, J., Sen, S.: Collaborative filtering recommender systems. In: Brusilovsky, P., Kobsa, A., Nejdl, W. (eds.) Adaptive Web 2007. LNCS, vol. 4321, pp. 291–324. Springer, Heidelberg (2007)
35. Radoff, J.: Game On: Energize Your Business with Social Media Games. John Wiley & Sons (2011)

Using Cloud Technologies for Engaging People with Cultural Heritage

Silvia de los Ríos[1], María Fernanda Cabrera-Umpiérrez[1], María Teresa Arredondo[1], Patricia Abril[1], Viveca Jiménez[1], and Christos Giachritsis[2]

[1] Life Supporting Technologies, Universidad Politecnica de Madrid, Spain
{srios,chiqui,mta,pabril,vjimenez}@lst.tfo.upm.es
[2] BMT Group Limited, UK
cgiachritsis@bmtmail.com

Abstract. Cultural heritage is an important asset of Europe which is largely underexplored. One of the main reasons is that the general public do not really incorporate cultural activities in their life style. Currently, curators and professionals in the heritage sector face the toughest challenges on how to attract, engage and retain visitors of heritage institutions (libraries, museums, archives and historical societies). TAG CLOUD FP7 European project seeks to overcome this situation and promote lifelong engagement with culture by personalising the visitors' cultural experiences through cloud technologies.

Keywords: cultural heritage, cloud technologies, TAG CLOUD, engagement, personalisation.

1 Introduction

Nowadays, in Europe, although cultural heritage is an important value for the population, it is not sufficiently explored. People do not really incorporate cultural activities in their lifestyle, and thus, the engagement with culture is low. About 50% of the population does not visit any museum, has not been to a public library or has not visited any historical monument, and the participation in other cultural activities regularly is minor (about 38%) [1]. Meanwhile, the current curators and professionals in the heritage sector are continually trying to capture and retain visitors.

Generally, they try to monitor how visitors interact with artefacts and sites during their visits and engage them on the basis of general information about their social and cultural background. For this purpose, a range of digital technologies from relatively cheap interactive websites to expensive on-site 3D visualisations are being used. However, these approaches have only limited success since they still follow the same "centralised" strategy of producing and delivering cultural content to the general public; that is, the content of the artefact and the characteristics of the visitors, which are used for "personalising" experiences, are still defined by the "experts". This means that, despite the employment of these technologies, the success of significantly increasing their visitors' base has been limited.

C. Stephanidis and M. Antona (Eds.): UAHCI/HCII 2014, Part II, LNCS 8514, pp. 673–680, 2014.

Especially nowadays, with the framework of the economic crisis, culture promotion is at the hearts of the European policies. According to the European Commission President Jose Manuel Barroso “Culture and creativity touch the daily life of citizens. They are important drivers for personal development, social cohesion and economic growth. [...] Today's strategy promoting intercultural understanding confirms culture's place at the heart of our policies” [2]. Moreover, culture is an important economical resource. As it states the European Commission's Communication on "An integrated industrial policy for the globalisation era", "the cultural and creative industries are important drivers of economic and social innovation in other sectors" [3]. The Communication is accompanied by the annual European Competitiveness Report, which highlights that "creative industries are increasingly a source of growth in the EU", accounting for "3.3% of total EU GDP and 3% of employment" [4].

Taking into account this socioeconomic framework, promoting engagement with cultural heritage and active participation of the people with their cultural environment entails a great opportunity for social and economic development, at European and global level.

With this aim, and framed in the Call 8 “ICT for access to cultural resources” of the 7th Framework Programme of the EU, the European project TAG CLOUD [5] started on February 2013. TAG CLOUD, that means “Technologies lead to Adaptability & lifelong enGagement with culture throughout the CLOUD”, seeks to personalise cultural experiences for promoting lifelong engagement with culture through cloud technologies.

2 Background

In the last decade, the rapid growth on the Internet has benefited the initiatives for the transmission of cultural heritage [6]. About the 42% of all leisure-time users say that they use the Internet to obtain information on cultural events and products, and 73% of them use social networks [1]; their own experience and the experience of their community influence them on how and where to spend their leisure time. On the other hand, cultural institutions are gradually adopting new technologies for promoting culture, (some examples in Spain, augmented reality in some cities like Segovia [7] and Salamanca [8], Street Museum of London [9]...). However, still the number of museums and cultural institutions that use the Internet and social media for information purposes are low [6], and they do not incorporate innovative personalized uses of ICT or take into account the trends of the population to engage their visitors.

Technology has a big potential to fulfil the needs of cultural institutions and their visitors. From the desktop computers to smartphones, the cultural heritage institutions have gradually introduced technologies as tools to engage visitors. However, it offers a lot of opportunities that still do not have a high impact in culture:

- It provides new ways of interaction with the cultural environment.
- It allows personalisation of content according to the profile of the user.

- It enables active participation in Culture.
- It allows collaboration between curators and professionals of the cultural sector with experts and end users.

In an attempt to incorporate technology into Culture several on-going and recently finalised projects from different European research areas have explored the field of adaptive cultural experiences, such as DECIPHER [10], CULTURA [11], CHESS [12], ARtSENSE [13] and PATHS [14]. Solutions proposed by these projects offer adaptive systems to assist the user during a cultural experience, online (CULTURA, PATHS) or in situ (DECIPHER, CHESS and ARtSENSE).

However there is still the need to achieve the cultural engagement thought a life-long experience. A new approach is necessary that can facilitate private and public cultural institutions efforts to engage visitors, help them to reduce costs and increase the number of new visitors while ensuring that those that previously had visited them, continue their lifelong experience with the cultural institution. This approach should be based on collaboration between professionals in the heritage sector and ICT developers. It should address adaptive interaction and personalised content of existing artefacts and cultural heritage institutions through the involvement of the general public and professional users. In addition, this collaboration should take advantage of existing and widely available technologies in order reduce cost, access more people and increase profitability.

3 The Concept

TAG CLOUD aims to develop a new paradigm in adaptive cultural heritage engagement systems that enable the active involvement of the individuals in the creation of cultural content as a mechanism for truly personalized interaction between user and cultural objects through social media and mobile technologies.

The project has a consortium of ten partners, from five European countries: Spain, Germany, United Kingdom, Italy and Norway. Within the partners, three of them are the pilot sites where TAG CLOUD is being implemented and assessed. These are three cultural sites with different needs and represent three different cultural environments: a large building complex, The Monumental Complex of Alhambra of Granada and Generalife, in Granada (Spain); a museum, the Barber Institute of Fine Arts, in Birmingham (United Kingdom); and an open landscape, the County of Sør Trøndelag, in Norway.

TAG CLOUD offers a radically new approach in defining cultural content and creating personalised experiences with cultural heritage objects. TAG CLOUD uses cloud technologies to create context-aware artefacts where the context is being defined on the basis of information about the cultural background, habits and motives of individuals. TAG CLOUD harvests personal (non-sensitive) information from social media about individuals and fuse it with "expert" information about artefacts and sites in order to produce instances of cultural heritage objects that will appeal to and captivate individuals. Then, affordable cloud based technologies are used to attract and engage individuals with "their" cultural heritage objects.

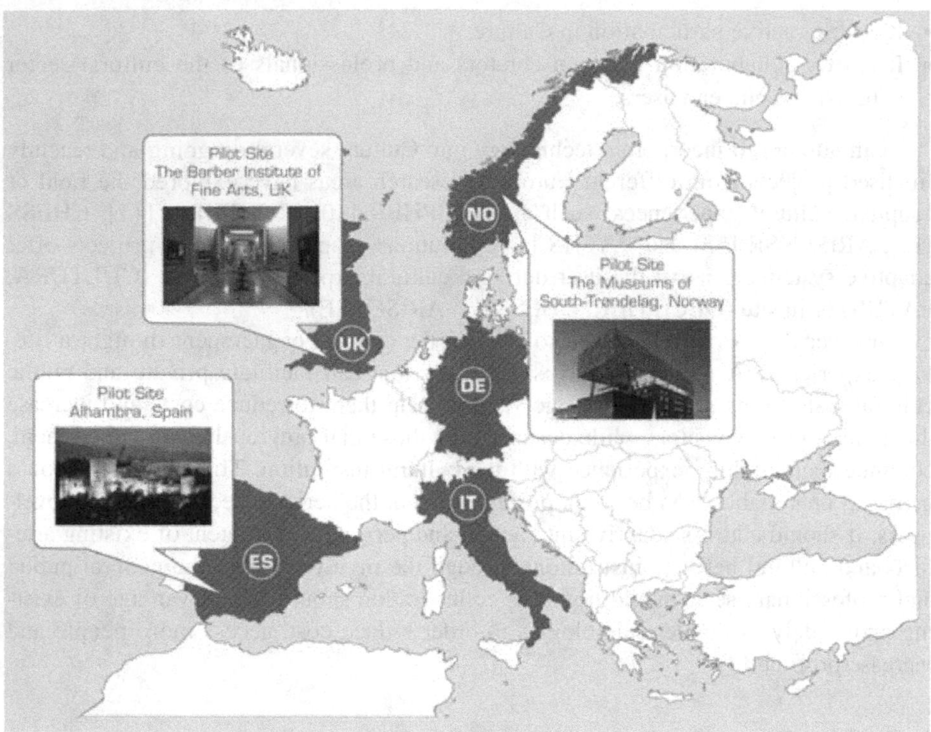

Fig. 1. TAG CLOUD consortium and pilots

The proposed TAG CLOUD system aims at increasing the active participation of general public in cultural events and experiences, by inviting to contribute with new content, opinions, as well as sharing their own experience with other people and heritage institutions, curators and researchers in the cultural area, before, during and after the visit. It is being designed to be dynamically personalized and adaptive to the needs, preferences and interests of the individuals and the community and is placed in the cloud, thus tapping the wide range of capabilities that cloud usage provides, allowing the availability of access from different locations in a secure fashion, as well as cost effective for both, individuals and cultural heritage institutions.

4 The Methodology

The TAG CLOUD system is based on a hybrid cloud, based on Software as a Service (SaaS) approach [15], composed by a public cloud which contains applications, tools and algorithms necessary to personalize the interaction between users and digital cultural artefacts, and several private clouds in which each heritage institution keeps its private digital cultural content, only available when the user is living a real cultural experience in such institution. In order to achieve this, TAG CLOUD adopts a multi-disciplinary and multi-sector approach that includes cultural experts, curators, engineers and industrial partners with expertise in exploitation of cultural heritage and market research.

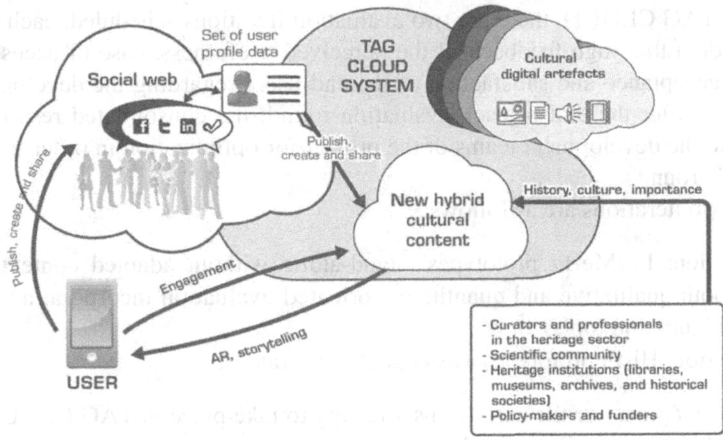

Fig. 2. TAG CLOUD system blocks diagram

TAG CLOUD (see Fig. 2) uses information from the public profile and contributions of the user in different social virtual networks and webs to acquire dynamic information about them (non-sensitive information) which is used to automatically update the static profile of the user (age, socio-cultural status, academic level, etc.) through the application of matching algorithms, and fuse it with information from experts about artefacts and cultural heritage places. The result of this fusion generates unique content for each user that is delivered through augmented reality or storytelling techniques creating new user's content that is used to dynamically adapt the experience.

TAG CLOUD explores the use of these technologies, like augmented reality, storytelling and social media, for a dynamic adaptation of cultural contents according to the visitors' profile, based on their preferences, likes and interests, providing a personalised interaction with culture. Through these technologies, the project encourages active participation in the creation of experiences and cultural content. The fusion of individuals' and experts' contents adds value and new meaning to the existing cultural artefacts, for promoting an effective communication between cultural institutions and final users towards the lifelong user engagement. Thus, TAG CLOUD offers a personalised cultural experience.

Based on this approach, TAG CLOUD aims to create a new relationship between individuals and cultural heritage, which will become part of the individual's life-style and will contribute to a lifelong cultural experience.

TAG CLOUD system design follows an iterative user centred approach that enables the users to be involved in all the phases of the project development. This iterative evaluation process enables on the one hand, the participation of the different stakeholders in the definition and design of TAG CLOUD system and on the other to test and validate the intermediate and final TAG CLOUD system prototype in different situations and domains.

Within TAG CLOUD, there are two evaluation iterations scheduled, each of which will provide a thorough feedback of the perceived usefulness, ease of access and interaction, acceptance and satisfaction of the end users regarding the developments of the project. After the end of each evaluation round, the consolidated results will be provided to the development teams of the project for optimization in order to continue with the 2nd round.

These two iterations are as follows:

- 1st iteration: Lo/Me-Fi prototypes (stand-alone without adapted content) assessment (both qualitative and quantitative oriented evaluation incorporating a variety of techniques and tools).
- 2nd iteration: Hi-Fi prototypes assessment (integrated).

The current plans for the iterative user testing to take place in TAG CLOUD are reflected in short in the following table:

Table 1. Pilots plans of TAG CLOUD

Iteration cycle	Prototype to be tested	Pilot site/ number of users		
		Spain	Norway	United Kingdom
1st iteration	- First version of social media communities - First version of augmented reality module - First version of storytelling module - First prototype of Data Management Module - Matchmaking algorithms	- 15 beneficiaries of various groups - 3 professionals in cultural heritage	- 15 beneficiaries of various groups - 3 professionals in cultural heritage	- 15 beneficiaries of various groups - 3 professionals in cultural heritage
2nd iteration	- All WP2 and 3 applications	- 30 beneficiaries of various groups - 5 professionals in cultural heritage	- 30 beneficiaries of various groups - 5 professionals in cultural heritage	- 30 beneficiaries of various groups - 5 professionals in cultural heritage

End users and experts will be selected and recruited to represent the range of stakeholders in a balanced way. For end users who are not adult, the process will be performed in close co-operation with families as well as with schools, etc. that we will be depending on to perform user evaluation and testing. The ethical issues will be assessed and taken into account throughout the whole recruitment and evaluation process.

The selection criteria for the end users include, among others:

- willingness to participate in the TAG CLOUD requirements' selection and testing activities,
- sex - if possible, 50 % man and 50 % women in each group,
- age - different age groups to ensure a spread across the population,
- previous experience of participation in similar activities of past or ongoing projects. This last criterion will be a huge benefit in terms of reducing the steepness of the user learning curve and bringing previous end user experiences (both good and bad) to the table and up to speed. It will also have the effect of avoiding some of the potential pitfalls that sometimes occur during iterative, heuristic evaluation processes.

5 Conclusions

TAG CLOUD offers a radically new approach in developing truly personalised cultural experiences to engage people with cultural heritage. The project seamlessly incorporates cloud-based (non-sensitive) information about the habits, preferences and motives of individuals into the digital content of a cultural object (e.g. artefacts, buildings, sites, etc.) and allows personalising the cultural experience. It will increase the users' interest for cultural heritage by making them active participants in the assignment of the 'importance' of a cultural artefact; thus they become actors in the creation of their own cultural experiences, creating, sharing, and adding information within social media. TAG CLOUD plans to add new meaning to cultural digital content by producing adaptive cultural contents based on fusion of expert and visitor information.

The methodology and interactive technologies that are being developed in TAG CLOUD will result in introducing more people into cultural heritage activities, improving the quality of their engagement and increasing the frequency of their visits to cultural sites.

At this point, after assessing the user needs and expectations through interviews and focus groups, the main scenarios and use cases that define the whole functionality of the system have been developed. First demonstration prototypes have been implemented and tested in the pilot sites at the early-stage evaluations of the project.

Acknowledgements. This work has been partially funded by the EC FP7 project TAG CLOUD (Technologies lead to Adaptability & lifelong enGagement with culture throughout the CLOUD); http://www.tagcloudproject.eu/, Grant Agreement No. 600924.

References

1. “Eurobarometer 67.1” (2007), http://ec.europa.eu/culture/pdf/doc958_en.pdf (accessed October 14, 2013)
2. European Commission, Press Releases of the European Commission (2007), http://europa.eu/rapid/press-release_IP-07-646_en.htm (accessed October 14, 2013)
3. European Commission, An integrated industrial policy for the globalisation era (2010), http://ec.europa.eu/enterprise/policies/industrial-competitiveness/industrial-policy/files/communication_on_industrial_policy_en.pdf (accessed October 14, 2013)
4. European Commission, European Competitiveness Report (2010), http://ec.europa.eu/enterprise/policies/industrial-competitiveness/competitiveness-analysis/european-competitiveness-report/index_en.htm (accessed October 14, 2013)
5. TAG CLOUD project, CN. 600924, 7th Framework Programme, ICT for access to cultural resources (February 2013), http://www.tagcloudproject.eu/
6. EGMUS “European Group on Museum Statistics”, http://www.egmus.eu/index.php?id=88&L=&STIL= (accessed October 14, 2013)
7. Augmented Reality App for Segovia, Spain, http://www.turismodesegovia.com/es/noticias/noticias-actuales/232-varios/481-descargate-la-guia-de-realidad-aumentada-de-segovia (accessed February7, 2013)
8. Augmented Reality App for Salamanca, Spain, http://www.salamanca.es/es/node/701 (accessed February7, 2013)
9. Street Museum of London App, http://www.museumoflondon.org.uk/Resources/app/you-are-here-app/home.html (accessed February7, 2013)
10. DECIPHER project, CN. 270001, 7th Framework Programme, ICT-2009.4.1 Digital Libraries and Digital Preservation (January 2011), http://decipher-research.eu/
11. CULTURA project, CN. 269973, 7th Framework Programme, ICT-2009.4.1 Digital Libraries and Digital Preservation (February 2011), http://www.cultura-strep.eu/
12. CHESS project, CN. 270198, 7th Framework Programme, ICT-2009.4.1 Digital Libraries and Digital Preservation (February 2011), http://www.chessexperience.eu/
13. ARtSENSE project, CN. 270318, 7th Framework Programme, ICT-2009.4.1 Digital Libraries and Digital Preservation (February 2011), http://www.artsense.eu/
14. PATHS project, CN. 270082, 7th Framework Programme, ICT-2009.4.1 Digital Libraries and Digital Preservation (January 2011), http://paths-project.eu/
15. Verma, G.: Software as a Service. Pragyaan: Journal of Information Technology 9(1), 32–37 (2011)

Tailoring Lifelong Cultural Experiences

Jacqueline Floch[1], Shanshan Jiang[1], Maria Eugenia Beltrán[2], Eurydice Georganteli[3], Ioanna N. Koukouni[3], Belén Prados[4], Lucia María Pérez[4], María del Mar Villafranca[4], Silvia de los Ríos[5], María F. Cabrera-Umpiérrez[5], and María T. Arredondo[5]

[1] SINTEF ICT, N-7465 Trondheim, Norway
{jacqueline.floch,shanshan.jiang}@sintef.no
[2] INMARK Estudios y Estrategias, Spain
xenia.beltran@grupoinmark.com
[3] University of Birmingham, United Kingdom
{e.georganteli,i.koukounis}@bham.ac.uk
[4] Patronato de la Alhambra y Generalife, Spain
belenprados@wonderbrand.es,
{luciam.perez,mariamar.villafranca}@juntadeandalucia.es
[5] Life Supporting Technologies, Universidad Politécnica de Madrid, Spain
{srios,chiqui,mta}@lst.tfo.upm.es

Abstract. ICT-based personalization in cultural heritage has been an important topic of research during the last twenty years. Personalization is used as a means to enhance the visitors' experience of a cultural site. Little consideration has however been set on lifelong cultural experiences, i.e. engaging the public in culture beyond the visit of a single site and bridging multiple sites. Cultural sites differ leading to a diversity of needs that should be taken into account through a personalization approach. This paper presents a set of scenarios tailored to suit the needs of three different Cultural Heritage sites in different EU countries. These scenarios have been developed within the EU funded project TAG CLOUD that aims at leveraging existing technologies to support realistic lifelong engagement experiences with cultural heritage through personalized content and interaction.

1 Introduction

Despite a rich European cultural heritage and the deployment of novel exhibition approaches and tools in museums and cultural institutions, the public engagement in cultural heritage remains low. According to recent statistics, 55% of the European population did not visit any cultural site in 2010 [1]. The EU funded project TAG CLOUD addresses the challenge of engaging a global audience with cultural heritage. To that aim, the project devises a set of applications built upon a personalization framework. The approach will enable the support of multiple forms of interaction with culture in multiple cultural sites. Personalization is thus envisaged at two levels: both contents and interactions can be adapted to individual user profiles. We use the term "interaction" in a broad sense to depict different dissemination goals, e.g. storytelling and gamification,

C. Stephanidis and M. Antona (Eds.): UAHCI/HCII 2014, Part II, LNCS 8514, pp. 681–692, 2014.

different augmented modules, e.g. information layers and avatars, and different social interactions, e.g. commenting and sharing.

Personalization in cultural heritage is not new. Much research has been conducted in the field during the last twenty years, but no satisfactory solution has yet been achieved. According to Ardissono et al., a major issue is the lack of realistic scenarios and experiments that put research works into practice [2]. This is the strategy adopted by TAG CLOUD. Rather than developing new advanced technologies, we wish to leverage existing technologies and cultural databases, and to combine them in order to create an experimental platform.

Beyond the variety of visitors, the diversity of needs of the cultural sites should also be taken into account by a personalization approach. This is illustrated in this paper through the presentation of a set of selected scenarios tailored to suit the needs of the three cultural pilot sites involved in TAG CLOUD. Interestingly, the result of the scenario design work is that the needs expressed by the pilot sites through the scenarios acknowledge the new opportunities for personalization identified in the survey presented in [2], i.e. adaptive cultural experience, social experience and user generated content, as well as benefits from individualized support that takes into account contextual and personal attributes.

TAG CLOUD scenarios illustrate different contexts of use, such as location (i.e., off-site or on-site) and time (i.e., before, during or after a visit), and different users (i.e. cultural users, non-cultural users and professionals). The scenarios also illustrate different use cases: user and group management, user profile management, cultural artefact management, itinerary management, interaction though virtual environments, storytelling, social behavior, content search and recommendation, and content adaptation. Due to space limitations, the paper concentrates on one selected scenario per pilot site. The selected scenarios relate to the new opportunities depicted in [2]: The Monumental Complex of Alhambra and Generalife focuses on adaptive cultural experience, the Barber Institute of Fine Arts on group experience and the County of Sør Trøndelag on user-generated content.

The rest of the paper is organized as follows: Section 2 shows the different settings and needs of the pilot sites, Section 3 describes the methodology for scenario design, Sections 4-6 present the selected scenarios from the three pilot sites and finally Section 7 gives the evaluation results obtained so far and outlines the road ahead.

2 The Pilot Sites

TAG CLOUD involves three cultural pilot sites: the Monumental Complex of Alhambra and Generalife in Spain, the Barber Institute of Fine Arts at the University of Birmingham in United Kingdom, and the County of Sør Trøndelag in Norway. The reason for including three sites is twofold: On one hand, the pilot sites present different characteristics and raise different requirements to the project. On another hand, we wish to provide solutions for lifelong experiences rather than focusing on experiences in a single site.

The Monumental Complex of Alhambra and Generalife is a major European cultural site that attracts more than 3 Millions of visitors each year. In this case, the main goal is not to increase the number of visitors but rather to explore different interaction modes in order to provide an enhanced adapted experience to different users and to offer a varied repertory of theme-based itineraries. Such itineraries will include internal and external routes that support new ways of enjoying the urban and country environment of the Alhambra. Another concern is also that of engaging users in other cultural activities after their visit in Alhambra, thus facilitating a diversification of the tourism and cultural offer. A technical challenge in the pilot site is the combination of an indoor and outdoor visit.

The Barber Institute of Fine Arts, the "mini National Gallery of Britain" in the West Midlands, United Kingdom, is an art collection and gallery at the University of Birmingham. It houses a superb collection of works of art, among which the finest collection of Byzantine coins worldwide. Seals, Roman, and medieval Islamic and western coins supplement the collection. Only a fraction of the Barber Institute's 16,000 coins and seals are on permanent display (20-30), whilst another 100-200 are showcased on a rolling base in a state-of-the-art Coin Gallery. Through its participation in the TAG CLOUD project the Barber Institute aims to converse more effectively with its core audience, and to reach out to a global audience, furthering social engagement and alerting its diverse audience of the endless possibilities cultural heritage provides for the exploration of interfaith and intercultural dialogue.

The third pilot site relates to the development of digital cultural heritage in the landscape, more specifically in the County of Sør Trøndelag. In that case, the cultural artefacts are places, e.g., buildings, heritage sites or art in the landscape. They do not always lie under the responsibility of a cultural institution and thus may not yet be registered and catalogued in databases. In addition, as there are a large number of artefacts, it is not always possible to rely on the curators or other professionals for registration and storytelling due to personnel resource limitations. A main goal is to increase participatory approach and engage the community in discovering and telling stories about places they live in and are fond of.

3 A User-Centered Approach

In addition to the diversity of sites, the project fosters a user-centered design approach. At an early stage of the project, the pilots have contributed to the definition of realistic scenarios that fit their environments and needs. These scenarios were evaluated by potential users and by professionals in the cultural sector.

Scenario building is a widely accepted way to generate design ideas for new systems and products and to identify the possible users and contexts of use for these systems and products. Scenarios describe individual users in individual usage situations and are not meant to describe the whole system functionality. The value of scenarios is that they concretize something for the purpose of analysis and communication [3-4]. In particular, user-oriented design emphasizes representing the use of a system or application with a set of user interaction scenarios as these make the use of the system (or application) explicit, and make it easy to evaluate and document a given design decision in terms of the specific consequences within defined scenarios [4]. Use cases describe interactions with the system at a more detailed level than scenarios. When a scenario-based approach is used, the use cases are normally extracted from the scenarios. Use cases then serve as functional requirements to the system from the stakeholder viewpoint.

The TAG CLOUD approach to scenario and use case specification has been derived after reviewing state-of-the-art methodologies on scenario design [5-7]. We define an overall methodology consisting of the following main steps and each pilot site has refined the process according to the special needs of the sites.

1) *Scenario brainstorming*: Stories and scenes were produced illustrating the system features. The partners were organized in three clusters built around the three trial sites in United Kingdom, Spain and Norway. In this stage the user needs and pilot site expectations had been identified through user surveys carried out either by pilot sites, e.g. visitor surveys in United Kingdom and Alhambra, or by others, e.g., available surveys about cultural participation in Norway [8-10] and Denmark [11]. These served as an input for brainstorming. Thus, TAG CLOUD could be used in multiple sites through Europe.

2) *Internal feedback and scenario revision:* The scenarios were reviewed by partners from other trial sites and revised. To give better understanding of the features a set of generic scenarios were defined, which cover the scenarios proposed for each trial site, but are not dependent on the cultural contents specific to the trial sites.

3) *Use cases identification and description:* Use cases were identified for describing the interaction of the users with the system at a more detailed level than the scenarios. The same use cases were often extracted from multiple scenarios, e.g. system logging and sharing on Facebook. Therefore the use cases were first extracted and classified, before being described in more details.

4) *User evaluation:* The scenarios were evaluated by potential users (the public and professionals in the cultural domain). This step can be performed before or in parallel with the previous step. The evaluation was conducted at different points of time and using different approaches at the different trial sites depending on the needs of the sites. For instance, in Norway where the target user groups for the evaluation of TAG CLOUD solutions are secondary school students, the scenarios were evaluated in the spring before the school holidays, and before the identification of use cases. In addition, different evaluation methods were used, including user surveys, workshops and focus group with both end users and professionals. For instance, exploratory focus groups [12-13] with school students and professionals from the culture, tourism and IT sectors were organized to evaluate scenarios in Norway. Protocols for focus group including question routes were designed following the methodology and guide-lines from literature [14]. Storyboards [15] were prepared for presenting the scenarios in focus groups, also allowing us to identify unclear points in the scenarios.

5) *Scenarios and use cases finalization:* The scenarios were refined based on the feedback from the user evaluation.

4 Scenario 1: Adaptive Cultural Experience

"Tour at the Palace of the Lions: Enjoying an adaptive cultural experience in a heritage institution" is a scenario that has been developed and adapted to the specificities of the Monumental Complex of Alhambra and Generalife. This scenario presents how the Alhambra aims at enhancing the visitors' cultural experience by integrating augmented reality and storytelling techniques, as well as supporting a better understanding of this Monumental Complex and its cultural value to different type of visitors, by using personalization and adaptation embedded capabilities.

Hence, this scenario emphasizes, among others things, on how the TAG CLOUD App will provide personalized multimedia content and information to small heterogeneous groups (e.g., families), through different ways of interaction and using augmented reality to enrich the architectural remains and cultural value of the Alhambra Monument Complex and its Palace City context, with information that would be otherwise not perceivable. The scenario also illustrates the adaptation and personalization approach by displaying information in different formats and with significant differences depending on the user's profile.

The scenario's main character, Martin, is an architect who visits the Monumental Complex of Alhambra and Generalife with his two children. Martin is especially interested in how the Fountain Court of the Lions, placed within the Monumental Complex, has been restored, its complexity, and the large number of studies that have been done around it; as the restoration of the Fountain Court of the Lions won the prize of conservation Europa Nostra in 2013. But also, Martin wants that his children John (8Y) and Mary (6Y) also enjoy the visit.

Therefore, the visit will be done using the TAG CLOUD App. Martin and his children already have an account in TAG CLOUD, and can log into the TAG CLOUD App through different devices. When they arrive to the Monumental Complex of Alhambra and Generalife, Martin rents a mobile device (tablet), John uses his iPad and Mary her smartphone.

At the entrance, the App shows each member of the family a list places in Alhambra that relate to their interests. Martin is shown a list about architectural conservation and restoration. Along the route, the TAG CLOUD App guides him through the points of interest and hints him that he can use Augmented Reality (AR) when pointing different buildings and places with the mobile device camera. The AR mode superposes information on the image scanned by the mobile device, such as the direction to follow, the suggested interesting points of interest and information related to them. In the AR mode, the TAG CLOUD App shows an icon related to each point of interest on the tablet screen. Martin only has to touch an icon to access information about a point of his interest, and then can receive personalized information. In addition, the App provides access to stories about the sites through the storytelling tool.

When Martin arrives to the Court of the Lions the App displays various kinds of information related to the Court of the Lions, e.g., about the heritage landmark and about the restoration, and in different information modes, e.g., text, photo and video. TAG CLOUD allows a deeper understanding to restoration process with the combination of documentation and audiovisual exhibitions through the storytelling tool, such as the documentation associated with the exhibition about the restoration process of the first lion. Also, TAG CLOUD gives access to videos from visitors on the Court of the Lions and from the media that match with Martin's interests.

Fig. 1. Augmented Reality in the Court of the Lions

While Martin enhances his knowledge of the Court of the Lions and enjoys his visit, his children get the suggestion to use the game of the Court of the Lions. They start the game and have fun painting directly on their iPad and smartphone, choosing a lion to paint and colour.

After the visit, when Martin and his children return home, Martin starts participating in one of the group of interest of the Monumental Complex of Alhambra and Generalife. One of the members of this group recommends him some publications. The children continue playing at home with the different games offered by the web of the Alhambra through TAG CLOUD and they can also share pictures from their visit with their Facebook friends, as well as details of the places that they have discovered through the games. In this way, the family continues enjoying culture after visiting the Monumental Complex of the Alhambra.

Through the enriched cultural experience like the one illustrated in this scenario, the Monumental Complex of Alhambra and Generalife expects to foster engagement and boost the spreading of word of mouth. In the future, John and Mary will ask their father to visit the Alhambra again, go on their own and with their own families.

5 Scenario 2: Group Experience

In the context of TAG CLOUD the University of Birmingham chose to develop the theme "Along Europe's Cultural Routes", as it provides an excellent platform for visitors to explore important themes such as shared heritage, identity and citizenship. The theme can greatly impact on a very large audience in Europe and beyond.

Use of mobile devices is very popular nowadays among all age groups [16]. We find it intriguing to imagine how a group of visitors with similar interests or objectives (e.g., students, mature visitors doing a guided tour or school children) will respond to a novel system applied on a cultural site.

In the context of their course on Medieval Archaeology – Creating Europe: Complex Societies 1000 BC – AD 1000, students will be visiting the Barber Institute Coin Collection to handle and discuss medieval coins and compare them with other contemporary works of art from the Barber Institute Collections.

Prior to their visit to the Barber Institute, their academic tutor Lydia, has prepared the visit in the seminar room by alerting students to the TAG CLOUD App downloadable from the Barber website. She discusses with them a virtual itinerary for the visit and makes quizzes related to the visit. The students register to TAG CLOUD via the museum's web page and the App leads them to the virtual itinerary entitled "Along Europe's Cultural Routes" customized by Lydia.

One of the journeys begins with a splendid Byzantine gold solidus from the Coin Collection of the Barber Institute of Fine Arts. A virtual historical character (in this case the Byzantine emperor depicted on the obverse of the coin) narrates the story of the coin from Constantinople/Istanbul, where it was minted, all the way to Durrachium/Durrazo/Durrës on the Adriatic Sea and along the Via Egnatia, one of Europe's major and oldest cultural routes. The students follow the coin's journey, exploring medieval cities, major landmarks and related artefacts along that route, and deepening their understanding of urban life in the Middle Ages.

Other carefully selected coins from the Barber Institute Collection allow them to follow other important European cultural routes, namely the ones linking Byzantium with Anglo-Saxon Britain, Byzantium with Norway (Scandinavia), and Byzantium with medieval Spain.

Fig. 2. Up close and personal with life in medieval Europe: Byzantine gold solidus of Emperor Justinian I (527-565) from the Barber Institute Coin Collection

For the visit, tablets are provided by the University of Birmingham Digital Humanities Hub. The tablets have the same group code so that students embark on the same itinerary. On-site visits offer students the experience of handling coins and understanding them in the context of the medieval and early Renaissance section of the Barber Institute Collections. TAG CLOUD provides handy information with links and images for handling coins and carrying out the task of comparison. Through enquiry-based learning, quizzes, online games, puzzles, and close-up viewing and handling of select Barber Institute artefacts students are at the centre of learning process, understanding the Middle Ages as a highly interconnected world.

After their visit the students discuss their experience and write their stories and impressions using TAG CLOUD collaborative storytelling tool, where they can find the participation of fellow students and experts in the field that enrich their story. They also share their stories via social networks.

This scenario emphasizes the creation of group experience adapted to groups with similar needs through customised group itineraries, and the social interactions within the group through quizzes and games.

Visitors follow groups' personalized itineraries through time and space; the historical characters-guides, who are being developed for the needs of the four itineraries, can bring history to life and engage visitors with aspects of European cultural heritage, tangible and intangible. The interaction design of the Apps is easy to use (www; digital images; geo-references; graphics), making the information components appealing to visitors of different age groups.

Along each route visitors see real-life images of monumental architecture, paired with appropriate coins and select 3D and AR visualizations of historical topography and artefacts. Geo-spatial information and selected historical sources enhance significantly the Barber Institute experience and aim to put visitors at the centre of learning process through storytelling and attractive virtual journeys, and to alert them of Europe's shared heritage, superbly showcased in the messages and iconography displayed on medieval coins.

6 Scenario 3: User-Generated Content

This scenario is inspired by the initiative Væggen by the Museum of Copenhagen[1]. Væggen is a large multitouch screen allowing people to tell, share and experience stories. This scenario explores the concept of wall as means to discover and share cultural stories related to buildings and heritage places in city open spaces. It is however not practical to install and maintain physical walls such as Væggen all around. Instead we propose a digital representation of walls, that we call Virtual Wall.

The storyline of the scenario is as follows. Kjersti, a research librarian, decides to create and share virtual walls for her home city Trondheim. When she launches the Virtual Wall through the TAG CLOUD App, a map of the city marked with available walls is shown. Since no one has created a wall for the cathedral, she positions the mouse pointer to the front of the cathedral and selects the creation button. Then she uploads a picture of the West Front. The wall is automatically tagged with the location selected by her and the creator name. She annotates the wall by selecting among

---

1 http://vaeggen.copenhagen.dk/en/. Væggen is the Danish word for Wall.

tags suggested by the system or creating new tags. She then opens the project allowing others to add annotations.

Kjersti has selected some of the 57 west front sculptures for annotation. She zooms in/out the wall picture and adds annotations by clicking on the sculpture in the picture and adding information. She can provide a name and a description consisting of text and multimedia links. She can also add predefined or new tags to her annotations.

She shares the wall with her friends through Facebook and gets a lot of responses. Her Facebook friends have added "likes" to her annotations and commented. Her friend Kjell-Jørgen has added a timeline to the wall and annotated dates with references to some old pictures he found on websites. Øystein, an archaeologist working at the restoration workshop, also reviews the work and adds overall information to the wall.

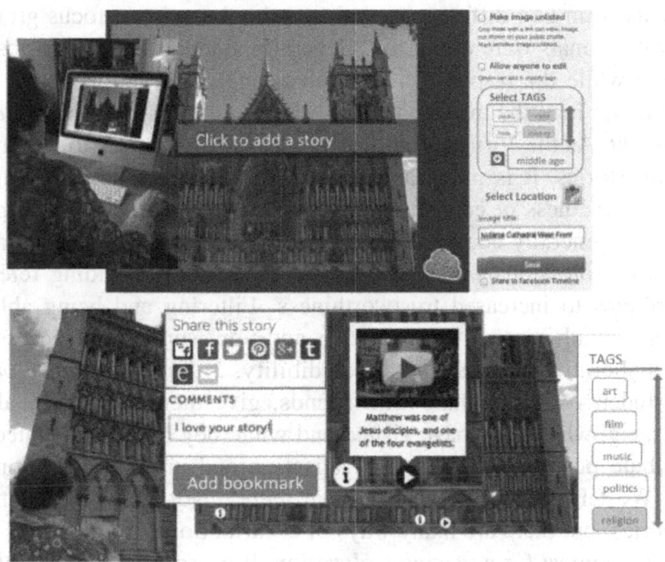

Fig. 3. Virtual Wall and storytelling: creating stories at home and experiencing on site

On his first visit to the cathedral, Paul can easily retrieve the wall and the stories using the Virtual Wall on TAG CLOUD App on his smart phones. Both location- and tag- based search is available. The "personalize" feature highlights his personal tags. He selects "music" and finds that no story is under this tag. He remembers that his grandfather told him that a sculptor of statue of the Archangel Michael was inspired by musician Bob Dylan, so he adds the story and shares with Facebook.

The Virtual Wall demonstrates important features of adaptive and social storytelling, e.g., retrieval of wall and filtering stories according to location, popularity, topics and other metadata (e.g. author, duration), sharing walls and stories for editing and commenting, as well as sharing walls and stories through social networks. Its novelty lies in allowing users to generate contents, share with others for commenting and collaborative editing, as well as the presentation on map and timeline. Moreover, the

Virtual Wall aims at having an active participation of the Trondheim community and visitors, supporting sustainable use and knowledge of the city`s cultural heritage and provide knowledge through several interpretations of cultural heritage, identity, and voices for the different city spaces by their community and visitors.

7 Status and Further Work

Two initial evaluations were conducted. Both potential users and cultural heritage managers were involved. The first evaluation organized in Norway had focus on adaptive and social storytelling. The second organized in Spain had focus on adaptive content and interaction.

In Norway, evaluation was conducted through focus groups. Four focus groups involving students from two different secondary schools and two focus groups involving culture professionals were organized. Generally students were very positive to the ideas presented while the response from professionals was more mixed. Among all feedback, we retain here the three most important points: 1) *Trustworthiness of user-generated content*. As the Virtual Wall was presented as a means to let any person to contribute with stories, it is important to maintain a high quality of contents. This applies to the correctness of content and tags associated to them. Descriptions from professionals are generally considered to be trustworthy. A mixed approach of contents created by professionals and amateurs is suggested. Providing references and sources contributes to increased trustworthiness. Filtering and being able to report spam is essential with respect to quality. In addition, support for access control is needed for collaborative editing to retain credibility. 2) *The importance of social behavior*. The students wish to share with friends, give them hint. They also wish to follow friends, e.g. where they have visited and what they have commented. The public can contribute positively to the personalisation and promotion of contents: "not only that the West Front exists, but *I've* been there". Not all would contribute with creation of stories, but there are many ways of contributions, for example, review and commenting. 3) *Support for personal exploration*. It is essential to have quality-based search, filtering and personalized recommendation: "Not only what others do, but what *I* may like". User history and different needs in different contexts should be considered for recommendation.

During the evaluation in Spain, participants recognized that nowadays there are more and more technological initiatives towards personalization of Cultural Heritage sites experiences, however these are scattered. Participants also agreed that these experiences depend on the physical, personal, and socio-cultural context, and identity-related aspects. Hence participants acknowledged that they can benefit from individualized support that takes into account contextual and personal attributes, ongoing adaptation offsite and “on the go” as visitors’ behavior may not remain consistent during a visit and new opportunities to capture and share the “whole story” (e.g. history, stories and culture) in a meaningful way. Participants affirmed that when the users’ background and preferences are recognized and incorporated into the process of communicating the wealth of cultural heritage sites, the cultural experience will empower visitors' motivation and engagement for culture; specially young people. Cultural heritage sites' managers commented that they have the need of efficient solutions to manage all created digital content to be used in a user-centric and targeted way; this process is seen as a labor intensive and costly activity. Thus the challenge that needs to be overcome by large and small cultural heritage sites derives from the growing interest in supporting socialization and collaboration in small (e.g., archaeologists) and large-size communities (e.g., schools) and the interest in user-generated content, coupled with a need to guarantee high-quality information standards at low costs. Participants saw the scenarios provided in TAG CLOUD could take place in 5-8 years.

After the evaluations, a set of initial prototypes that concretize some important features of the scenarios were created. Based on these prototypes, that allowed us to identify practical implementation concerns, an initial selection of the features of the TAG CLOUD system, including cloud services and applications, was made. A set of final use cases was extracted from both the scenarios and initial prototypes. These prototypes will be further extended to realize these use cases.

As a next step in our work, a preliminary laboratory testing of Low/Medium Fidelity prototypes will be performed before the pilot trials that will be organized at each site. The aim is to collect feedback about TAG CLOUD solutions from both visitors and cultural institutions.

Acknowledgement. This work is partially funded by the EC FP7 project TAG CLOUD (Technologies lead to Adaptability & lifelong enGagement with culture throughout the CLOUD), G.A. No. 600924. http://www.tagcloudproject.eu/

References

1. Eurostat: Cultural statistic. Publications Office of the European Union (2011)
2. Ardissono, L., Kuflik, T., Petrelli, D.: Personalization in cultural heritage: the road travelled and the one ahead. User Modeling and User-Adapted Interaction 22(1-2), 73–99 (2012)
3. Carroll, J.M.: Scenario-based design: envisioning work and technology in system development. John Wiley & Sons (1995)
4. Carroll, J.M.: Five reasons for scenario-based design. In: Interacting with Computers, vol 13, pp. 43–60. Elsevier (2000)
5. Di Nitto, E., et al.: S-Cube Deliverable CD-IA 2.2.2: Collection of Industrial Best Practices, Scenario and Business Cases. S-Cube consortium (2009)
6. Frank, K., et al.: PERSIST Deliverable 2.1: Scenario description and Requirements Specification. PERSIST consortium (2008)
7. Roussaki, I., et al.: SOCIETIES Deliverable 2.2: Scenario Description, Use Cases and Technical Requirements specification. PERSIST consortium (2011)
8. Bjørnsen, E., Lind, E., Hauge, E.S.: Kunstkonsum i storbyene – en studie av brukere og ikke-brukere av det offentlig finansierte kunsttilbudet i byene Oslo, Bergen, Trondheim, Stavanger og Kristiansand. FoU-rapport nr. 7/2012. Agderforskning (July 2012). Report available, `http://norskpublikumsutvikling.no/2012/10/kunstkonsum-i-storbyene` (in Norwegian)

9. Gran, A.-B., Wedde, E.: Publikum: Hvem, hva, hvorfor? Perduco Kultur. Report available at http://norskpublikumsutvikling.no/2012/05/for-lite-synlig-museum (in Norwegian)
10. Gran, A.-B., Figenschou, A., Gaustad, T., Molde, A.: Digitalt kulturkonsum- En norsk studie. Forskningsrapport (2012), Handelshøyskolen BI (2012). Report available at http://norskpublikumsutvikling.no/2012/12/digitalt-kulturkonsum (in Norwegian)
11. Danish Agency for Culture: About the National User survey: http://www.kulturstyrelsen.dk/english/institutions/museums/museum-surveys (last access February 1, 2014)
12. Stewart, D.W., Shamdasani, P.N., Rook, D.W.: Focus Groups: Theory and Practice, 2nd edn., vol. 20. Sage Publications, Newbury Park (2007)
13. Tremblay, M.C., Hevner, A.R., Berndt, D.J.: The Use of Focus Groups in Design Science Research. In: Integrated Series in Information Systems, vol. 22, pp. 121–143. Springer, US (2010)
14. Krueger, R.A., Casey, M.A.: Focus Groups: A Practical Guide for Applied Research, 4th edn. Sage Publications, Thousand Oaks (2000)
15. Truong, K.N., Hayes, G.R., Abowd, G.D.: Storyboarding: an empirical determination of best practices and effective guidelines. In: Proceedings of the 6th Conference on Designing Interactive systems (DIS 2006). ACM, New York (2006)
16. Love, S.: Understanding mobile human computer interaction. Elsevier (2005)

Designing Personalised Itineraries for Europe's Cultural Routes

Eurydice S. Georganteli and Ioanna N. Koukouni

School of History and Cultures, University of Birmingham, Edgbaston, Birmingham B15 2TS, UK
{e.georganteli,i.koukounis}@bham.ac.uk

Abstract. Throughout history it has been necessary for mankind to travel: for a better life, for pilgrimage, for religious or political freedom, for trade, for communication between nations or for conquest. Each culture as it developed found in coinage the most powerful means to facilitate and control economic activities within and outside its territories. And as peoples from different cultures travelled and mixed with others, so did their coins. Byzantine, Islamic, and western medieval European coins circulated and changed hands along routes of migration, trade, war, pilgrimage and diplomacy; the routes set out from Constantinople/Istanbul to the Adriatic in the western Balkans; from the Black Sea to the eastern and western Mediterranean; from Britain, Scandinavia to Russia. The Barber Institute of Fine Arts at the University of Birmingham houses one of the finest collections of medieval Christian and Islamic coins worldwide. This paper presents select case studies based on the numismatic resources of the Barber Institute to show the role of coins as a means to track and discuss inter-cultural dialogue that took place along Europe's cultural routes. The combination of storylines based on coins, related artefacts and sites, and the implementation of modern technologies can further social engagement and alert existing and new audiences of the potential of cultural heritage as a major connecting thread of Europe's diverse cultural communities.

Keywords: cultural routes, coins, lifelong learning, Byzantium, medieval Europe, medieval Islam, cross-cultural encounters, global audience, museum, exhibition, heritage, cultural routes.

1 Background: The Collection and Its Audience

Founded in 1967, the Barber Institute Coin Collection became since 2000 and following the creation of its New Coin Gallery, research facilities, and the digitization of its 15,000 numismatic holdings, the focus of academic teaching, research and public enjoyment. Award-winning exhibitions, accompanying publications, activity leaflets for younger visitors, public lectures, gallery tours, seminar series and conferences have been exploring themes of cross-cultural encounters in Europe and beyond, from 5th-century BC Athens to 19th-century Britain. Visitors are both local and international travellers, and there are rising numbers of children on school visits

C. Stephanidis and M. Antona (Eds.): UAHCI/HCII 2014, Part II, LNCS 8514, pp. 693–704, 2014.

and family days thanks to a close collaboration between the Coin Collection and the Barber Institute's educational department. Since the opening of the Coin Study Room, research visits by students in Higher Education to the Coin Collection have exceeded 200 per year.

2 Aims and Scope of the University of Birmingham as One of TAG CLOUD's Pilot Sites

Through its contribution to the TAG CLOUD project the Barber Institute of Fine Arts at the University of Birmingham wishes to converse more effectively with its existing and very diverse audience, offering visitors a personalized and more fulfilling educational experience, based on their cultural background, preferences and educational needs. A recurrent observation, not limited to the Barber Institute, is the under-representation of audiences of the age groups 18-25 (typically students and young professionals) and 40-55 (mid career). Other groups, such as school children and people over 60 are better represented. Visitor surveys conducted in the course of the last Barber Institute numismatic exhibition *CITYSCAPES: PANORAMIC VIEWS ON EUROPEAN COINS AND MEDALS* (April 2012-October 2013) showed that visitors enjoy themed exhibitions, even though many of them know little of the Barber Institute Coin Collection; during their visit they prefer to enhance their knowledge through workshops, public lectures, gallery talks and handling sessions. Visitors commented on the clear and attractive layout of the New Coin Gallery with visitor friendly graphs, maps and select enlarged images of coins complementing the numismatic display and interpretation texts developed for the exhibition. Searching the Barber Institute's online resources, including numismatic ones, has been less popular either because people are not aware of these resources, or because they are reluctant to navigate the University of Birmingham's museum database (http://www.birmingham.ac.uk/culture/collections/online-collections.aspx). The largest percentage of the interviewees came mainly from continental Europe (50% European, 40% British, 10% other), a finding that hints at the regular associations the Barber Institute's visitors make between coins and art (ancient Greek, Roman, medieval).

Reaching out to new audiences remains an equally important part of the Barber Institute's vision. Links between major themes, discussed in temporary exhibitions and permanent displays in the Barber Galleries, and Europe's cultural routes could provide precisely an excellent new platform for audience engagement. As the strongest points of the Barber Coin Collection are Byzantine and medieval Islamic coins, the personalised itineraries the TAG CLOUD project proposes allow visitors to use coins as their personal compasses for their navigation along routes of faith, culture and trade in Europe and beyond. Byzantine, western medieval and medieval Islamic coins from the Barber Institute collections are linked to major European and little illustrated cultural routes (the *Via Egnatia*; the route connecting Constantinople/Istanbul to Scandinavia through the story of fur trade via the Varangians; the sea route connecting Western to Eastern Mediterranean, the Black Sea and Trebizond/Trabzon as the western terminus of the Silk Route; the route connecting Britain with Byzantium) through select data on architectural remains, art and topography, geo data on medieval sites available on the public domain (see, for instance, the Harvard University-hosted DARMC Atlas of Roman and Medieval Civilization). Appropriate coin data available on the web sites of partner museums and societies (American Numismatic Society; British Museum; Fitzwilliam Museum, Cambridge; Dumbarton Oaks Research Library and Collection, Trustees for Harvard University) supplements data provided by the University of Birmingham collections online.

The third goal challenge that artefacts behind the Barber Institute's participation in TAG CLOUD is the attractive challenge artefacts and cultural sites from TAG CLOUD's two other pilot sites in Spain (the Patronato de la Alhambra y Generalife in Spain) and Norway (the County of Sør Trøndelag) present for meaningful links with the Byzantine and Islamic coins from the Barber collections in the context of European cultural routes. This is particularly timely, as Birmingham and other European places are increasingly becoming meeting places of faith and culture. Coins as both agents of cultural definition and facilitators of fluidity of ethnic and cultural identities can be used to engage diverse communities in a constructive dialogue. The use, for instance, of Christian imagery on medieval Islamic coins and of Arabic script on Crusader coins from the Holy Land[1] can be discussed in conjunction with the architectural splendour of al-Andalus, best illustrated in Alhambra's cityscape.

3 Cultural Routes: Storytelling

Cultural routes are an important part of our heritage, both tangible (monuments, cities, artefacts) and intangible (contacts, influences, values, ideas, traditions, etc).[2] ICOM defines the cultural route as "a land, water, mixed or other type of route, which is physically determined and characterised by having its own specific and historic dynamics and functionality; showing interactive movements of people as well as multi-dimensional, continuous and reciprocal exchanges of goods, ideas, knowledge and values within or between countries and regions over significant periods of time; and thereby generating a cross-fertilization of the cultures in space and time, which is reflected both in its tangible and intangible heritage".[3] In acknowledgement of the importance of cultural routes the Council of Europe established in 1987 the cultural, educational, heritage and tourism co-operation project Cultural Routes, which is been managed by the European Institute of Cultural Routes in Luxemburg.[4] Among some

[1] See for instance, Georganteli, E., Cook, B. 2006; Georganteli, E. 2012A.

[2] Martorell Carreno, A. 2003.

[3] www.icomos-ciic.org.

[4] www.coe.int/routes; www.culture-routes.lu/php/fo_index.php; the aim of the CR programme is "to demonstrate, by means of a journey through space and time, how the heritage of the different countries and cultures of Europe contributes to a shared cultural heritage". An Enlarged Partial Agreement on Cultural Routes (EPA) was stipulated "to enable closer co-operation between states particularly interested on the development of Cultural Routes". (www.coe.int/t/dg4/cultureheritage/culture/routes/default_en.asp, conventions.coe.int/Treaty/EN/PartialAgr/Html/CulturalRoutesStatute.htm).

twenty-four historical cultural routes currently recorded by CoECR (Council of Europe/Cultural Routes) none of the four ones we are developing for the needs of TAG CLOUD is present.[5] Showcasing, therefore, four of the longest, significant and little illustrated European cultural routes allows us to use medieval coins from the Barber Institute Coin Collection and its partner institutions as important but underrated tools to explore intercultural and interfaith dialogue. In the context of TAG CLOUD we have been developing datasets for the following four cultural routes:

1. The Via Egnatia: One of Europe's oldest, longest, most travelled, and culturally influential land routes it linked Constantinople/Istanbul in the eastern Balkans to Dyrrachium/Dürres on the Adriatic Sea, covering a distance of 1120km (696 miles). Part of the road, identified by the ancient Greek historian Polybius as the *Candavia odos*, was created by King Philip II of Macedon in the fourth century BC as a conduit for his expansionary policies in Asia and the Western Balkans. In 146-120 BC a superbly engineered road was constructed under the supervision of the Roman Proconsul Gnaeus Egnatius following the old *Candavia*. Named after him, the *Via Egnatia* initially linked the cities of Dyrrachium (modern Durrës in Albania) and Apollonia (near the village of Pojani, also in Albania) on the Adriatic coast to the city of Thessaloniki (Greece). Roman emperors, from Trajan (52-117 AD) to Constantine the Great (272-337), invested on repair works and the extension of the road to Kypsela (modern Ipsala, Turkey) on the Hebros/Maritsa/Meriç River and eventually to the new imperial capital, Constantinople (modern Istanbul, Turkey). Initially conceived as a continuation of Via Appia, to serve Rome's military campaigns and administrative needs in the East, the *Via Egnatia* became over time the most travelled and enduring European route of trade, cultural exchange, warfare, diplomacy and pilgrimage, connecting western to southeastern Europe, and Europe to Asia and beyond. In the first century AD the *Via Egnatia* became intertwined with Saint Paul's travels and the spread of Christianity in Europe, and from 330 AD with the political and cultural trajectory of Byzantium and its western and eastern neighbours. Ancient and medieval sites, castles and villages, temples, churches, mosques and synagogues, bridges and inns, dotted along the route speak of Europe's shared culture. The study of this route can significantly enhance our understanding of the archaeology and history of southeastern Europe, and can further develop fundamental European principles such as cultural diversity and citizenship.

---

[5] Other aspects are the orientation of the programme towards the tourism industry, and the development of Small Medium Enterprises, as is extracted by the criteria of selection and their objectives. On the impact of European Cultural Routes on SME's Innovation and Competitiveness' see `http://www.coe.int/t/dg4/cultureheritage/culture/routes/StudyCR_en.pdf`; `http://www.em-a.eu/en/home/newsdetail-ema-members-report/crossroads-of-europe-toulouse-2013-cultural-routes-between-local-development-and-european-ident.html`. See also Richards, G. 2011.

2. The maritime trade route that connected the Black Sea to Constantinople, the Aegean, and the Western Mediterranean and Spain. The Mediterranean has always been a major conduit for cross-cultural interaction and fertilization.[6] The route extended along two axes: a. the North-South axis led from the Black Sea to the Aegean through the Dardanelles and thence to Crete, and down to Alexandria; b. the East-West axis connected Crete, Cyprus and the Near Eastern coast to Sicily and southern Italy and thence to the western part of the Mediterranean and the straits of Gibraltar. Byzantine, Genoese, Venetian, Jewish, Arabs and Norman merchants, to mention a few, mercenaries, pirates, travellers, pilgrims and explorers met and interacted at various points, making the Mediterranean coastal cities and islands a palimpsest of cultures. Cultural interaction impacted on architecture, religious identity and dialogue, and on the transmission and exchange of knowledge, traditions and languages.
3. The route connecting Constantinople to Britain: Direct and indirect relations between Byzantium and medieval England, in the context of trade, pilgrimage, diplomacy and Byzantine administration, are evidenced by significant number of Byzantine pottery, glass, coins, seals and luxury products found on British soil. [7] Discussing coins and related works of art, pottery, sites and monuments related to the story of this route allows us to create a more organic connection between the Barber Institute's Byzantine holdings and the eastern Mediterranean and the Balkans, from where they originate.
4. The route linking northern Europe to the Baltic Sea, the Black Sea and the Eastern Mediterranean traces the connection between Scandinavia and the Mediterranean. In their search for profit and plunder in the 8th and 9th centuries Vikings sailed the Dnieper Rivers reaching the Black Sea, and came into contact with the Byzantine and Islamic worlds. They sold furs, amber and slaves in Constantinople, carrying silver, silk, and wine on the trip back home. Norse people formed the famed and feared Varangian imperial guard in Constantinople, and played a major role in disseminating Byzantine coinage and culture in northern Europe.[8]

4 Travelling Coins: Straddling Physical and Virtual Reality

Coins because of their small size and great numbers in which they were minted remained the most widely circulated economic and art medium in the medieval world. Those same qualities often become challenging for museums which host coin collections, and the Barber Institute is no exception. The great number of the Barber

---

[6] On the multifaceted contacts in the medieval Mediterranean see, for instance, Spufford, P. 2002; McCormick, M. 2001; Abulafia, D. 2011; Jacoby, D. 2009; Jacoby, D. 1979; Museum of Byzantine Culture, 2013.

[7] Harris, A. 2003; Georganteli, E., Cook, B. 2006: 14-18; Georganteli, E. 2012B.

[8] Georganteli, E., Cook, B. 2006; Kazanski, M., Nercessian, A., Zuckerman, C. (eds), 2000; Morrisson, C. 1981; Malmer, B., 1981; Ellis Davidson, H.R. 1976.

Institute numismatic holdings, coupled by the small space of the Coin Gallery, which at the moment accommodates both permanent and temporary displays, limits the number of coins we can physically present as part of the TAG CLOUD scenario on European Cultural Routes. To remedy this we are using the superb digital images of the Barber Institute coins, commissioned by the Barber Institute Trustees and created and developed by Jan Starnes of Oxford Imaging Ltd since 2000. By combining them with appropriate digital resources from partner institutions, augmented reality and 3D applications we are aiming to offer visitors a more versatile interaction with coins onsite and off-site, ultimately enriching their experience. Interaction will be enhanced with visualizations of real and 3D images of select architectural landmarks, historical maps, and geo-referenced archaeological sites along each cultural route (Figs. 1-3). This method allows visitors/users a less piece-meal approach of medieval coins, and better appreciation of their role in the context of medieval routes and communications.[9] Short and simple stories, told by fictional characters, will guide visitors/users of the TAG CLOUD app to the various stops along a cultural route.

Fig. 1. The *Via Egnatia*: coins, sites, and memory. (from left to right): The Barber Institute of Fine Arts, Birmingham, UK: gold solidus of Emperor Anastasios I (491-518); Didymoteichon, Greece: Mosque built under Sultans Bayezid (1389-1402) and Mehmed I, (1413-1421); Philippi, Greece: 6th-c. Basilica B; Greece, Thessaloniki: the commercial hub of the Byzantine city; Ohrid, Former Yugoslav Republic of Macedonia: baptismal fond and mosaic floor, polyconchal church at Plaoshnik, 4th-5th c.; Dyrrachium, Albania: wall mosaics in the Byzantine chapel in the city's amphitheatre

Our approach is based on the principle that learning is a lifelong journey, which should be enjoyable and adequately supported by cultural and educational practitioners. The interface we are therefore proposing is simple: when used in the secure and visitor-friendly environment of the Barber Institute New Coin Gallery it will make the experience attractive and engaging; when used off-site it will enable visitors/users to connect with artefacts and monuments through a range of fun activities (storylines, quizzes, serious games). Our affiliation with major European and North American institutions further supports the off-site experience by presenting an impressive pool of online resources available to visitors/users.[10] The linked open data approach offers free access to content (and metadata), and remains the aspect in collections management that can truly "bridge the gap between online and offline collections".[11]

---

[9] Gabellone, F. et al, 2013.

[10] Haslhofer, B., Isaac, A. 2011; Baltussen, L.B. et al. 2013.

[11] Edelstein, L., et al, 2013.

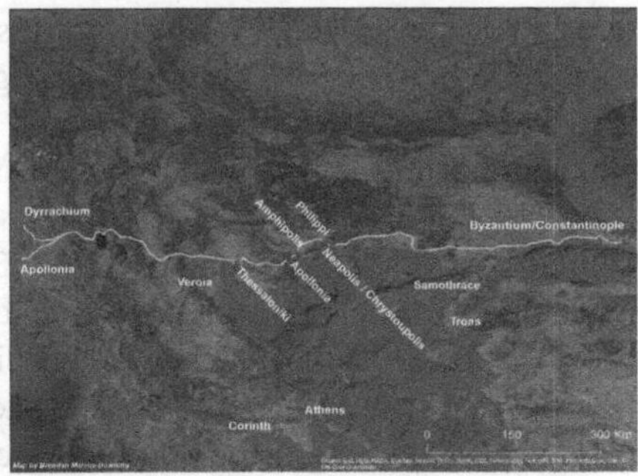

Fig. 2. The Via Egnatia and the Balkan stops of Saint Paul's journeys

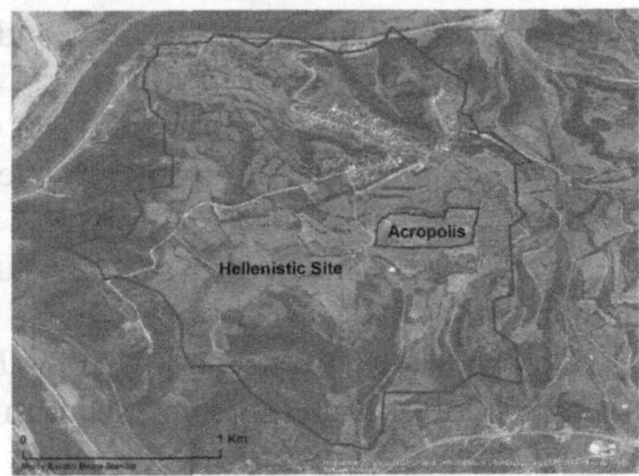

Fig. 3. The fortified ancient and early Byzantine city of Amphipolis, important stop on the *Via Egnatia*, half way between Philippi and Thessaloniki

5 Methodology

The scope of TAG CLOUD is to generate lifelong engagement with cultural heritage through social media, augmented reality and storytelling applications based on cloud technologies.[12] It takes into account different user profiles in order to deliver information and to design personalised cultural itineraries for the Barber Institute's visitors, before, during, and after their visit. To do that, the scenario "Along Europe's Cultural Routes" combines easy-to-use wireless mobile technologies to enhance understanding of cultural heritage assets.

- The Internet is nowadays an effective platform for museums to showcase select works of art, communicate their exhibition programmes, related family, educational and outreach activities, and attract sponsorship. Digital content and the way it becomes available rank among the new interfaces towards a better user approach to cultural heritage. Fast and easy delivery of online digital resources can be particularly useful to audiences, especially to vulnerable and hard-to-reach people.[13] The presence of the Barber Institute Coin Collection and its partner institutions on the web makes available in the public domain an array of web resources, including – among others – coins, medals and related artefacts, sites, monuments and architectural remains, and maps.
- A more important aspect deriving from the web availability of digital content and museum partnerships is the linked open data.[14] Data sharing between museums is more and more a *desideratum*, as it ensures reliability and up-to-date content and metadata; in the 21st century these are becoming prerequisites for the sustainability

12 www.tagclouproject.eu
13 Dunmore, C. 2006; Hawkey, R. 2006; Samuels, J. 2006.
14 Baltussen, L.B. et al. 2013; Edelstein, J. et al. 2013; Haslhofer, B., Isaac, A. 2011.

and growth of museum collections and cultural organizations.[15] The Barber Institute has already joined the open data model through MIMSY (Museum Management System). In the context of TAG CLOUD the Barber Institute will expand its participation by making available over 600 numismatic entries in the public domain.

- Cutting-edge technologies such as augmented reality, serious games, select 3D digitisations and visualizations, social media, interactive maps and geo-references are being used in the scenario "Along Europe's Cultural Routes".[16] Nowadays digital technologies are implemented on mobile devices (smartphones, tablets, i-pads, netbooks and computers) facilitating visitors' needs. Gaming technology has redefined human-computer interaction as it provides solutions for online and mobile gaming for millions of users. More and more people have been incorporating games in their daily life for challenge (goals), fantasy (emotions), curiosity (novelty and surprise) and fun.[17] Virtual reality games in particular are increasingly becoming a very popular entertainment.[18] Although ongoing research confirms that prolonged use of video and other games can have a negative effect on peoples' – particularly youths' – behaviour and health,[19] it is also a fact that the new generations of children are brought up from an early age with a very clear understanding and dexterity of virtual environments. Considering this reality the user interfaces in serious gaming that are being developed in the context of TAG CLOUD can stimulate interaction and active participation of the users. Visitors/users can become empowered and motivated to improve their personalised journey. We are aiming at quality entertainment, which motivates and promotes learning. Other human-computer interaction technologies such as select 3D modelling (with the aid of relevant online data), augmented reality (AR) visualisations and Geographic Information Systems (GIS) are added to digital images of real-life monumental architecture and artefacts. The scope is to deliver accurate information on artefacts, monuments and sites by linking data to specific locations and enhance the users' cultural experience.[20] Digital models of artefacts or entire contexts are increasingly used by museums and cultural and educational organizations as a means to communicate their collections to a wider audience.[21] 3D digitisation is increasingly applied in cultural heritage and is considered a very effective tool for digital archiving, conservation, reconstruction and the study of artefacts and monuments.[22]

---

15 Lang, C. 2006; http://www.digitalmeetsculture.net/article/the-participatory-museum.

16 http://www.interchopen.com/books/human_computer_interaction/user_experience_in_digital_games (2008); Remondino, F. et al. 2013; Emmanouilidis, C. et al. 2013.

17 Takatalo, J. et al. 2008.

18 www.bbc.co.uk/news/technology-25661997

19 Fujiki, Y. et al. 2008.

20 Emmanouilidis, C. et al. 2013.

21 Some examples are the New Acropolis Museum in Athens, the British Museum, the Victoria and Albert Museum, the Metropolitan Museum of Arts (NY) to mention a few.

22 Remondino, F. et al. 2013; Bandiera, A. et al. 2013.

It also offers visitors/users a truly immersive experience. For example, the project byzantium1200.com, which we wish to incorporate in the *Cultural Routes* scenario, offers computer reconstructions of the major landmarks of Constantinople/Istanbul of the year AD 1200, and is widely being used by academics in delivering archaeology and history courses.[23] Use of augmented reality provides interactive experiences to both on-site and virtual visitors of the Barber Institute Coin Collection.[24] In the course of this project we will use visitor surveys, interviews and questionnaires to evaluate the users' experience.

- Online services are combined with onsite services to allow users to navigate along their selected cultural route and explore its components before, during and after their visit. Interactive digital heritage applications change the dynamics of learning and entertainment: supporting structures combine things to do at home with things to do at the museum. For instance, visitors will be able to scan coins and use images to navigate along a selected cultural route. Onsite visits will also offer visitors the unique experience to handle and view coins close up (Fig. 4), discussing them with curators and educational practitioners. Stunning examples of Byzantine, western medieval and Islamic coins in the Barber Institute Coin Collection make this experience all the more engaging and memorable.

Fig. 4. Handling and viewing medieval coins at the Barber Institute of Fine Arts, University of Birmingham

- Storage base with the chosen information and datasets related to each of the cultural routes will allow visitors/users to have access to the digital content both online and offsite. Users will be contributing with their own-generated content (comments, thoughts, etc) and file sharing through social media, platforms that offer space for personalisation.[25]
- Fictional fictional characters, appropriate to the story of particular routes, will accompany visitors of the Coin Collection on their virtual journeys. For instance, a retired Varangian from Winchester will lead visitors from the Barber Institute Coin Gallery to Constantinople, where he served in the imperial guard, and back to Anglo-Saxon and Norman England, providing meaningful links to the story of

---

23 www.byzantium1200.com; Emmanouilides, C. et al. 2013.

24 http://hitl.washington.edu/artoolkit; Lu, Y. et al. 2008. (http://www.intechopen.com/books/Human_computer_interaction/ augmented_reality_e-commerce_how_the_technology_benefits_people_s_lives).

25 Emmanouilidis, C. et al. 2013; Suh. Y. et al. 2008.

Byzantium and medieval Britain; likewise, a Norse king and former member of the Byzantine imperial guard will be traveling with visitors along the routes that brought together Scandinavia and Byzantine Constantinople; an Italian merchant will take visitors aboard his ship to show them the maritime route from Constantinople to Spain, whereas his Greek colleague will take the land route from Constantinople to Dyrrachium/Dürres on the Adriatic Sea; finally, a Byzantine emperor will show visitors Byzantium's imperial capital Constantinople (modern Istanbul). The interface is designed as simple as possible, to enable users with minimal mobile technology experience to use it. Such an immersive approach offers visitors/users the chance to navigate along historical routes of faith, warfare and trade, to see how peoples and nations of diverse cultural, social and religious backgrounds met and interacted, and how reciprocal influences impacted on each other. The chosen routes are an essential part of Europe's cultural fabric, and virtual journeys along these routes can encourage users of the TAG CLOUD application to reflect on issues of shared heritage, identity and citizenship, all particularly timely in the increasingly multi-cultural landscape of Birmingham, Britain, and Europe.

6 Conclusion

The combination of storylines and implementation of modern technologies can further social engagement and alert existing and new audiences of the potential of cultural heritage (medieval Christian and Islamic coins housed by the University of Birmingham) as a major connecting thread of Europe's diverse communities. This kind of public engagement is undoubtedly far more effective than physical museum displays. The endless possibilities for audiences to respond to the proposed scenarios by creating their own digital storytelling [micro-blogs (e.g. twitter), social networks (e.g FaceBook, GoodReads), social sharing (e.g. YouTube, Flickr)], can contribute to the much-anticipated open access scholarship, a desideratum for Higher Education and Cultural Institutions.

Acknowledgements. This work has been partially funded by the EC FP7 project TAG CLOUD (Technologies lead to Adaptability & lifelong enGagement with culture throughout the CLOUD); http://www.tagcloudproject.eu/, Grant Agreement No. 600924.

References

1. Abulafia, D.: The Great Sea: A Human History of the Mediterranean, Oxford (2011)
2. Abulafia, D.: Commerce and Conquest in the Mediterranean, 1100-1500, London (1993)
3. Arbel, B. (ed.): Intercultural Contacts in the Medieval Mediterranean, London (1996)
4. Baltussen, L.B., Brinkerink, M., Timmermans, N., Zeinstra, M.: Open Culture Data Position Paper: Open Data on the Web (2013), http://www.w3.org/2013/04/odw/odw13_submission_24.pdf
5. Bandiera, A., et al.: Replicating Degradable Artefacts. A Project for Analysis and Exhibition of Early Medieval Objects from the Byzantine Village at Scorpo (Supersano, Italy). In: Addison, A., Guidi, G., De Luca, L., Pescarin, S. (eds.) Proceedings of the Digital Heritage International Congress 2013 (DHIC 2013), Marseille, vol. 1, pp. 161–168 (2013)

6. Dunmore, C.: Museums and the Web. In: Lang, C., et al. (eds.) The Responsive Museum, pp. 95–114 (2006)
7. Edelstein, J., Galla, L., Li-Madeo, C., Marden, J., Rhonemus, A., Whysel, N.: Linked Open Data for Cultural Heritage: Evolution of an Information Technology. In: Simplifying Complexity Conference Proceedings, SIGDOG, Greenville, NC, pp. 1–66 (2013)
8. Ellis Davidson, H.R.: The Viking Road to Byzantium, London (1976)
9. Emmanouilidis, C., Koutsiamanis, R.-A., Tasidou, A., Leontiadis, S.: Supporting Cultural Route Sustainability via innovative digital heritage applications and services. Manual of Wise Management, Preservation, Reuse and Economic Valorisation of Architecture, of Totalitarian Regimes, of the 20th Century. Forli and Ljubljana. 1-7 (2013)
10. European Institute of Cultural Routes: documents/presentations, `http://www.culture-routes.lu/php/fo_index.php?lng=en&dest=bd_do_lst`
11. Fujiki, Y., Kazakos, K., Puri, C., Buddharaju, P., Pavlidis, I., Levine, J.: NEAT-o-Games: Blending Physical Activity and Fun in the Daily Routine. Computers in Entertainment 6(2), 1–22 (2008)
12. Gabellone, F., Ferrari, I., Giannotta, M.T.: From Museum to Original Site: A 3D Environment for Virtual Visits to Finds re-contextualised in their Original Setting. In: Addison, A., Guidi, G., De Luca, L., Pescarin, S. (eds.) Proceedings of the Digital Heritage International Congress 2013 (DHIC 2013), Marseille, vol. 2, pp. 215–222 (2013)
13. Georganteli, E., Cook, B.: Encounters. Travel and Money in the Byzantine World, London (2006)
14. Georganteli, E.: Trapezuntine Money in the Balkans, Anatolia and the Black Sea, 13th-15th Centuries. In: Kyriakides, T. (ed.) Trebizond and the Black Sea, Thessaloniki, pp. 93–112 (2010)
15. Georganteli, E.: Transposed Images. Currencies and Legitimacy in the Eastern Mediterranean. In: Harris, J., Holmes, C., Russell, E. (eds.) Byzantines, Latins, and Turks in the Eastern Mediterranean World after 1150, Oxford, pp. 141–179 (2012a)
16. Georganteli, E.: The Coins. In: Biddle, M. (ed.) The Winchester Mint and Coins and Related Finds from the Excavations of 1961-1971, Oxford, pp. 669–679 (2012b)
17. Harris, A.: Byzantium, Britain and the West: The Archaeology of Cultural Identity, AD 400-650. Stroud (2003)
18. Haslhofer, B., Isaac, A.: data.europeana.eu: The Europeana Linked Open Data Pilot. In: Proceedings of International Conference on Dublin Core and Metadata Applications, Hague (2011), `http://dcpapers.dublincore.org/pubs/article/viewFile/3625/1851`
19. Hawkey, R.: Digital Technologies and Museum Learning. In: Lang, C., et al. (eds.) The Responsive Museum, London, pp. 115–116 (2006)
20. Hooper-Greenhill, E.: Museums and their Visitors, London, New York (1994)
21. ICOMOS-CIIC, `http://www.icomos-ciic.org/INDEX_ingl.htm`
22. Lang, C.: The Public Access Debate. In: Lang, C., et al. (eds.) The Responsive Museum, London (2006)
23. Lang, C., Reeve, J., Woollard, V. (eds.): The Responsive Museum, London (2006)
24. Jacoby, D.: Latins, Greeks and Muslims: Encounters in the Eastern Mediterranean, 10th-15th Centuries London (2009)
25. Jacoby, D.: Recherches sur la Méditerranée orientale du XIIe au XVe siècle: peuple, sociétés, économies, London (1979)
26. Kazanski, M., Nercessian, A., Zuckerman, C. (eds.): Les centres proto-urbains russes entre Scandinavie, Byzance et Orient, Paris (2000)

27. Kelly, L.: The Interrelationships between Adult Museum Visitors' Learning Identities and their Museum Experiences, Sydney (2007)
28. Lu, Y., Smith, S.: Augmented Reality E-Commerce: How the Technology Benefits People's Lives. In: Pavlidis, I. (ed.) Human Computer Interaction, pp. 215–238 (2008), http://www.intechopen.com/books/Human_computer_interaction/augmented_reality_e-commerce_how_the_technology_benefits_people_s_lives
29. Malmer, B.: The Byzantine Empire and the Monetary History of Scandinavia during the 10th and 11th century A.D. In: Zeitler, R. (ed.) Les Pays du Nord et Byzance, Uppsala, pp. 125–129 (1981)
30. Martorell-Carreño, A.: Cultural Routes: Tangible and Intangible Dimensions of Cultural Heritage. In: 14th ICOMOS General Assembly and International Symposium: 'Place, Memory, Meaning: Preserving Intangible Values in Monuments and Sites', Victoria Falls, October 27-31 (2003)
31. McCormick, M., Turnator, E., Maione-Dowing, B., Zambotti, G., et al.: Digital Atlas of Roman and Medieval Civilization, Harvard University, http://darmc.harvard.edu/icb/icb.do
32. McCormick, M.: The Origins of the European Economy: Communications and Commerce 300-900, Cambridge (2001)
33. Morrisson, C.: Le rôle des Varanges dans la transmission de la monnaie byzantine en Scandinavie. In: Zeitler, R. (ed.) Les Pays du Nord et Byzance, Uppsala, pp. 131–140 (1981)
34. Museum of Byzantine Culture, Η Τιμή του Αγίου Μάμαντος στήν Μεσόγειο: Ένας Ακρίτας Άγιος ταξιδεύει, Thessaloniki (2013)
35. Pavlidis, I. (ed.): Human Computer Interaction (2008)
36. http://www.intechopen.com/books/human_computer_interaction
37. Remondino, F., Menna, F., Koutsoudis, A., Chamzas, C., El-Hakim, S.: Design and Implement a Reality-based 3D Digitisation and Modelling Project. In: Proceedings of the Digital Heritage International Congress 2013 (DHIC 2013), Marseille, vol. 1, pp. 137–144 (2013)
38. Richards, G.: Cultural Tourism Trends in Europe: A Context for the Development of Cultural Routes. In: Khovanova-Rubicondo, K. (ed.) Impact of European Cultural Routes on SMEs' Innovation and Competitiveness, pp. 21–39. Council of Europe Publishing, Strasbourg
39. Samuels, J.: A Collective Responsibility: Making Museums Accessible for Deaf and Disabled People. In: Lang, C., et al. (eds.) The Responsive Museum, London, pp. 195–196 (2006)
40. Spufford, P.: Power and Profit: The Merchant in Medieval Europe, London (2002)
41. Suh, Y., Park, Y., Yoon, H., Woo, W.: Context-aware Mobile AR System for Personalisation, Selective Sharing, and Interaction of Contents in Ubiquitous Computing Environments. In: Pavlidis, I. (ed.) Human Computer Interaction, pp. 295–314 (2008)
42. Takatalo, J., Hakkinen, J., Kaistinen, J., Nyman, G.: User Experience in Digital Games. In: Pavlidis, I. (ed.) Human Computer Interaction (2008)
43. http://hitl.washington.edu/artoolkit
44. http://www.digitalmeetsculture.net/article/the-participatory-museum

Widening Access to Intangible Cultural Heritage: towards the Development of an Innovative Platform

Michela Ott, Francesca Maria Dagnino, Francesca Pozzi, and Mauro Tavella

Istituto per le Tecnologie Didattiche – Consiglio Nazionale della Ricerche, Italy
{ott,dagnino,pozzi,tavella}@itd.cnr.it

Abstract. The paper discusses around Human Computer Interaction aspects of advanced learning systems. It underlines the added value (in terms of widening the learning possibilities and enhancing the learning experience) of designing the system itself only after having carefully taken into account the users' requirements regulating the interactions between the learners and the technological environments. In doing so, it offers the view of what has been done in the EU project i-Treasures, which focuses on Intangible Cultural Heritage (ICHs) and investigates whether and to what extent new technology can play a role in widening the access to the underpinning rare know-how, and possibly sustaining its transmission / passing down to next generations. The project can be regarded as exemplar since it instantiates a very peculiar situation where HCI aspects are deeply affected by the fact that the i-Treasures technological system foresees the massive use of cutting edge sensors.

Keywords: Cultural Heritage Education, Intangible Cultural Heritage, Human Computer Interaction, Learning Management Systems, Educational platforms, Accessibility, Usability.

1 Introduction

In recent times, cultural heritage education has encountered digital technology [1-2-3] and ICT technologies are increasingly becoming one of the pillars of teaching and learning interventions in the field of cultural heritage [4].

Actually, a variety of digital tools exist that can support Cultural Heritage Education. In a very rough categorization, we can distinguish among:

- Virtual Museums (VMs) i.e. those ICT-based environments that support the virtual visit (via the Internet, on-site, through standalone applications) of past and present cultural heritage artifacts and expressions (e.g. the Scrovegni Chapel[1], Giza 3D[2]),
- Domain specific Serious Games i.e. those gaming environments aimed at supporting the learning of cultural heritage related issues (e.g. APA game[3]) and

[1] http://www.padovanet.it/salamultimediale/index_english.htm
[2] http://giza3d.3ds.com/index.html#discover
[3] http://www.youtube.com/watch?v=yDZe_r3QQug

C. Stephanidis and M. Antona (Eds.): UAHCI/HCII 2014, Part II, LNCS 8514, pp. 705–713, 2014.

- More complex digital systems that are not only oriented to information delivery (so to merely support the acquisition of knowledge), but are also aimed at supporting the passing down/transmission of specific know how (so to also support the acquisition of specific competences and abilities).

In the following, we will mainly focus on this last category of tools. It is particularly specific of the field of Intangible Cultural Heritage (ICH) which, according to UNESCO [5] encompasses all those "*practices, representations, expressions, as well as the knowledge and skills (including instruments, objects, artefacts, cultural spaces), that communities, groups and, in some cases, individuals recognize as part of their cultural heritage*".

The above mentioned three different types of ICT tools potentially supporting Cultural Heritage Education also instantiate different types and/or levels of interaction between the software and the user [6]. Virtual Museums (VMs)[4] use cutting edge technologies and allow an in-depth view of cultural heritage artifacts but, from the HCI viewpoint, often they only offer limited possibilities, mainly oriented to having an exhaustive view of the objects themselves: choosing the item to focus on, zooming in and out, watching them from multiple perspectives etc… Fig.1 shows two screenshots from the Virtual Museum on the Giza pyramids where the users are allowed to make a virtual visit to the Giza archaeological territory [5]

Fig. 1. 3D views from the GIZA 3D Virtual Museum

Some more sophisticated and educationally oriented VMs [7] also allow conducting immersive experiences (e.g. Etruscanning[6]) by also offering the possibility to carry out personalized paths and to customize the view of CH objects. The possibility of customizing the learning paths is also shared by most Serious Games specific of the domain of Cultural Heritage; such tools, by relying on basic game mechanics offer educational experiences where the interaction between humans and the software is

---

[4] A specific network of excellence about Virtual Museums has been co-funded by EU in 20010. In the network web site `http://www.v-must.net/` relevant examples can be found and specific features of VMs are detailed

[5] GIZA 3D by Dassault Systemes `http://archeomatica.it/ultime/visita-virtuale-delle-piramidi-di-giza` and `http://giza3d.3ds.com/index.html#discover`

[6] `http://v-must.net/virtual-museums/vm/etruscanning-3d-2011-2012`

larger and more advanced. Fig 2 shows a screen shot from the APA game[7], a Serious Game, set in the13th century and oriented to inform about the life in the Roman Bologna.

Fig. 2. Screenshot from the APA game

In this paper we focus on the third category of tools mentioned above, namely those aimed at supporting the passing down/transmission of specific know how and we discuss how some issues related to Human Computer Interaction in this specific area can be tackled. This is done by referring to the i-Treasures project which is aimed at designing and delivering an integrated platform supporting the transmission of some expressions of intangible cultural heritage.

2 The i-Treasure Project: An Overview

I- Treasures is an Integrated Project co-financed by EU under the ICT theme (Information and Communication Technologies) of the FP7 (7th Framework Program) which has just started in 2013 and will conclude its activities in four years. It makes an in-depth use of cutting- edge ICT and sensor technologies to sustain the passing down and transmission of ICH in the fields of dancing, singing, music composition and craftsmanship.

The ultimate and main outcome of i-Treasures will be "*an open and extendable platform providing access to ICH resources, enabling knowledge exchange between researchers and contributing to the transmission of rare know-how from Living Human Treasures to apprentices*". This means that the project aims at going far beyond the simple ICT-enhanced dissemination and the mere digitization of cultural contents;

[7] The game is developed by CINECA, CNR-ITABC and Fraunhofer Institute see `http://www.v-must.net/vm-blog/apa-game-short-presentation`

it, rather, aims at analyzing and modeling the different ICHs thus supporting the learning of the rare know how behind them and its passing down to new generations.

In particular, in I-Treasures relevant and detailed information on the different artistic expressions recognized as ICHs are obtained from expert performers and researchers in the field and, based on this information, key aspects and features of this ICH are "captured" by using advanced ICT and sensor technologies.

As examples: 1) as to singing the specific vocal emissions are analyzed by tracking the vocal tract of the singers during performance; 2) as to dance, body motion, posture and movements are detected, coded and registered by means of advanced motion capture techniques; 3) as to pottery hand gestures are tracked and coded. A thorough process of modeling the available data is then carried out by relying on advanced Semantic Multimedia Analysis techniques.

This process allows shaping and directing the learning process of apprentices (also through avatars assuming the role of virtual exemplar performers). Learners are exposed to multi-modal and multi-sensory learning experiences, carrying out individual trials and receiving appropriate feedback, so to reach increased levels of competence in an easier, more direct, quicker and effective way [8-9].

The envisaged learning process is, thus, expected to take the learners beyond the concept of "learning by imitation" and will allow them to:

- acquire relevant conceptual information in different formats (audio, video, narrative, etc...),
- view in details the performances of expert artist (and this can be done by each student at his own pace following personalized paths)
- put oneself to the test, carrying out individual trials, receive appropriate feedback (in different formats e.g. audio or video as well) and hints so as to be able to adjust individual performance and reach increased levels of competence in an easier, quicker and more direct way.

The entailed innovative learning/teaching process is strongly based on innovative technologies and tools. Of course, it is not meant to substitute but rather to complement the traditional learning/teaching methods and actions; the traditional role of teachers is not diminished or set aside but rather safeguarded and valued thanks to the provision of new educational tools and related innovative teaching methodologies.

3 HCI Issues in i-Treasures

In the i-Treasures platform users are supposed to interact with the system in order to:

- Learn basic (and, eventually, detailed) information about the specific ICH, (understanding cultural background, viewing/listening to performances, etc…)
- Acquire the ability to perform in the specific ICH so to be enabled to act themselves as performers (thus gaining both theoretical and practical competences)

While the first objective can be easily pursued using traditional online learning methodologies (be they individual, collaborative, based on guided searches or self-regulated approaches…) the reaching of the second objective is strongly dependent on the use of cutting edge combined ICT and sensor technologies.

If we look at the i-Treasures project from an HCI perspective we must, then, acknowledge that it instantiates a very peculiar situation where the innovative use of multiple sensors plays a major role and, thus, also affects relevant aspects of Human-Computer Interaction. Actually two different types of sensor-based learning processes take place in the different phases of the project:

- One that "goes" from humans to the computer (the capturing via sensors and the modeling of relevant aspects of entailed know how so that the computer is able to master and reproduce it, where the computer learns from humans)
- One that "goes" from the computer to humans (the passing down of the know how acquired by the computer to the actual apprentices/learners, where humans learn from the computers and sensors help the computer interpreting and assessing human performance)

In both cases, the use of sensors is key to the reaching of the intended results: from the one hand, (by tracking experts' performance) they enable the computer to acquire the information needed to model correct behavior and, from the other, they intervene in the learning process (by tracking the students' performance) so to allow the computer to assess the apprentices' performance, in order to fine tune feedbacks and exercises.

In both cases, again, the sensors mediation/interference highly affects relevant aspects of the interaction between humans and the system.

Summarizing we can say that the i-Treasures platform supports both traditional and sensors-based learning actions: it makes an extensive use of sensor technology to support learning but also foresees a variety of more "traditional" learning actions (i.e. typically those related to the acquisition of general and specific information /knowledge on the topic). In an HCI perspective, the interaction between humans and the computer is both mediated or not by sensors.

The basic possible different learning paths (and therefore different types/levels of interactions between the users and the system) can, then, be represented as follows:

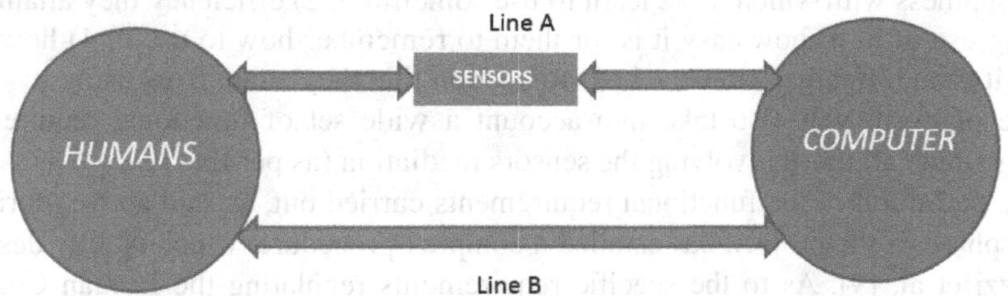

Fig. 3. I-Treasures learning paths in an HCI perspective

Line A represents the sensor mediated path from humans to the computer and vice versa while Line B represents the traditional interaction between the computer and humans and vice versa.

4 HCI Requirements/Solutions in i-Treasures

The i-Treasures project has the main goal of widening as much as possible the access to intangible cultural heritage and of fostering its knowledge, learning and transmission. In this light, while designing the i-Treasures platform, a User Centered Design (UCD) approach [10-11] is being adopted and specific attention is devoted to properly managing all the HCI issues involving the actual relationships between human-users and the system, with the final aim to make the i-Treasures platform easily accessible, comprehensible and useful to the largest possible audience.

Based on these considerations and taking into account the peculiarities of the i-Treasures project (mainly related to the massive use of sensor-mediated learning techniques), during the initial phase of requirements elicitation, a set of detailed requirements for the HCI aspects of the i-Treasures system and platform has been defined.

Ease of use, Multilingual, Personalized and Universal Access are established as pillar-requirements for the system and the platform [9].

Within the consortium it is, in fact, felt as mandatory that the platform could offer equal access opportunities to all users, including those with disabilities, provide relevant interaction facilities to any kind of learner and that different paths could be followed according to the users' specific needs.

Among the non functional requirements, (i.e. among the properties of the system architecture or, rather, the standard "built in" features instantiating how the system is supposed to be), we particularly focused on both "Accessibility" (i.e. features guaranteeing the actual possibility to access and use the system to a variety of users with different abilities) and "Usability" (i.e. general aspects involving the effectiveness, efficiency and satisfaction of use of the system).

As to Accessibility attention has been particularly devoted to "the degree to which the platform and related tools are actually available/can be used by as many people as possible", including people with functional/sensory disabilities such as vision, hearing impairments etc... Requirements in this area should mainly comply with existing accessibility legislations [12].

As to Usability [13], attention will be devoted to the general clarity of the system and in particular, following Nielsen & Loranger 14], to its overall quality in terms of: 1) promptness with which users learn to use something, 2) efficiency they attain while making use of it, 3) how easy it is for them to remember how to use it, 4) how error-prone it is and, finally 5) the level of satisfaction that they attain from using it

The platform will also take into account a wide set of functional requirements, among which all those involving the sensors mediation (as per line A).

The definition of the functional requirements carried out, as said above, during the initial phase of the project, has entailed a complex procedure, which is fully described in Pozzi et al. [9]. As to the specific requirements regulating the Human Computer Interaction issues, they can be basically distinguished into the following categories:

- Sensors-specific requirements, regulating the interaction among human-users and sensors and vice-versa (e.g. Requirement n° 8: *Sensors should not affect or hinder performance and vice versa*)

- Learning-specific requirements, regulating interactions with the LMS Learning Management System (e.g. Requirement n° 18: *The educational platform shall adjust lessons/difficulty levels according to students' characteristics and abilities*)
- Environmental requirements, regulating interactions of the human users with the environment, including both physical objects and places (e.g.: Requirement n° 5: *The system shall adapt to the place where the performance happens*)
- Inter-human actors requirements, including partner-performers in the case of group activities, (e.g. Requirement n° 4: *The system should detect physical interactions among performers in a group*)
- Content-dependent interaction requirements, regulating the interactions of the users with the system but strongly dependent upon the relationship with the specific contents of the learning activities (e.g. for the specific content area of dance related learning processes. Requirement n° 34B: *The platform shall visually highlight the student's mistakes*). In this line, the system design will particularly focus on feedback provision issues; actually, feedback represents a key HCI aspect in all learning systems but in the i-Treasures case, it is vital, being at the very core of the overall educational approach adopted.

In the light of the the requirements defined above, we can acknowledge that the i-Treasures platform will be designed and developed by taking into account the seven basic principles of Universal Design set by the Center for Universal Design at North Carolina State University[8], namely:

- Equitable use -The design makes the system useful and marketable to people with diverse abilities.
- Flexibility in use -The design accommodates a wide range of individual preferences and abilities.
- Simple and intuitive -The design is oriented to make the system easy to understand, regardless of the user's experience, knowledge, language skills, or current concentration level.
- Perceptible information -The design allows the system communicating necessary information effectively to the user, regardless of ambient conditions or the user's sensory abilities.
- Tolerance for error - The design minimizes hazards and the adverse consequences of accidental or unintended actions.
- Low physical effort -The design entails that the system can be used efficiently and comfortably and with a minimum of fatigue; this principle was partially extended to include due limitation to cognitive efforts.
- Size and space for approach and use -The design of the system foresees that appropriate size and space is provided for approach, reach, manipulation, and use regardless of user's body size, posture, or mobility.

[8] http://www.ncsu.edu/ncsu/design/cud/about_ud/udprinciplestext.htm

5 Conclusions and Future Work

The paper has briefly discussed around the issue of widening access to Cultural Heritage Education by means of innovative ICT tools. In doing so, it has first casted a glance to the different types of digital resources available for the scope. It has, then, focused on Intangible Cultural Heritage expressions and, drawing on the i-Treasures project, it has also outlined some ideas about the relevant HCI aspects that can contribute to ease access to dedicated resources, increase usability and make more effective the entailed learning processes. The main peculiarity of the i-Treasures project is an in-depth and massive use of cutting edge sensors for supporting learning and transmission of the rare know how behind Intangible Cultural Heritage expressions. The paper has looked in-depth at these aspects, by outlining some Human Computer Interaction related issues and challenges, which take into account the mediation/interference of sensor in the dialogue between the users and the computer systems. In the light of the requirements defined in the first phases of the project (which still is in its initial stages), an attempt has been made to produce a categorization of HCI related requirements for innovative learning systems encompassing the use of multiple-modal sensors. During the following phases of the project, field experiences and demonstrations will be conducted and HCI aspects will be explored in practice so to possibly allow revising and updating the existing list of requirements.

References

1. Gaitatzes, A., Christopoulos, D., Roussou, M.: Reviving the past: cultural heritage meets virtual reality. In: Proceedings of the 2001 Conference on Virtual Reality, Archeology, and Cultural Heritage, pp. 103–110. ACM (2001)
2. Veltman, K.H.: Challenges for ICT/UCT Applications in Cultural Heritage. In: Carreras, C. (ed.) ICT and Heritage (2005), http://www.uoc.edu/digithum/7/dt/eng/dossier.pdf
3. Branchesi, L.: La pedagogia del patrimonio e la sua valutazione: ambiti di ricerca, metodologie, risultati e prospettive. In: Branchesi, L. (ed.) Il patrimonio Culturale e la sua pedagogia per l'Europa. Armando Editore (2006)
4. Ott, M., Pozzi, F.: Towards a new era for Cultural Heritage Education: Discussing the role of ICT. Computers in Human Behavior 27(4), 1365–1371 (2011)
5. UNESCO, Convention for the Safeguarding of the Intangible Cultural Heritage 2003 Paris (October 17, 2003), http://portal.unesco.org/en/ev.php-URL_ID=17716&URL_DO=DO_TOPIC&URL_SECTION=201.html
6. Ott, M., Pozzi, F.: ICT and Cultural Heritage Education: Which Added Value? In: Lytras, M.D., Damiani, E., Tennyson, R.D. (eds.) WSKS 2008. LNCS (LNAI), vol. 5288, pp. 131–138. Springer, Heidelberg (2008)
7. Antonaci, A., Ott, M., Pozzi, F.: Virtual Museums, Cultural Heritage Education and 21st Century skills. In: Davide, P., Valentina, P., Andrea, T. (eds.) ATEE-SIREM Winter Conference Proceedings "Learning & Teaching with Media & Technology", Genoa, Italy, March 7-9, pp. 185–195. ATEE Association for Teacher Education in Europe, Brussels (2013)

8. Dias, B.D., Diniz, J.A., Hadjileontiadis, L.J.: Towards and intelligent Learning Management System under blended learning. Trends, Profiles and Modelling Perspectives. ISRL, vol. 59. Springer, Heidelberg (2014)
9. Pozzi, F., Antonaci, A., Dagnino, F.M., Ott, M., Tavella, M.: A Participatory Approach to Define User Requirements of a Platform for Intangible Cultural Heritage Education. In: Battiato, S., Braz, J. (eds.) VISAPP 2014: 9th International Conference on Computer Vision Theory and Applications, Lisbon, Portugal, January 5-8, vol. 2, pp. 782–788. SCITEPRESS - Science and Technology Publications (2014)
10. Bødker, S.: Scenarios in user-centred design—setting the stage for reflection and action. Interacting with Computers 13(1), 61–75 (2000)
11. Abras, C., Maloney-Krichmar, D., Preece, J.: User-centered design. In: Bainbridge, W. (ed.) Encyclopedia of Human-Computer Interaction, vol. 37(4), pp. 445–456. Sage Publications, Thousand Oaks (2004)
12. Bocconi, S., Dini, S., Ferlino, L., Ott, M.: Accessibility of educational multimedia: in search of specific standards. International Journal of Emerging Technologies in Learning, iJET 3, 1–6 (2006)
13. Holzinger, A.: Usability engineering methods for software developers. Communications of the ACM 48(1), 71–74 (2005)
14. Nielsen, J., Loranger, H.: Prioritizing web usability. New Riders Press, Berkeley (2006)

Adaptive User Experiences in the Cultural Heritage Information Space

Luke Speller, Philip Stephens, and Daniel Roythorne

BMT Group Ltd, Research Directorate, UK
{lspeller,pstephens,droythorne}@bmtmail.com

Abstract. Given the thematic diversity, richness and variance in exposition of published cultural heritage information and artefacts, accessing pertinent information can be a cumbersome task. The TAGCLOUD project aims to create an adaptive cultural heritage experience for individuals based on their personal preferences, allowing users to navigate with ease around both cultural artefacts and the related information space. Users will establish a narrative between themselves and their cultural heritage experience.

We propose metrics and methods for making the transition from a pull-based dynamic to a successful push-based methodology. Users are inevitably overwhelmed by the volume and specificity of cultural data, so traditional query-based interaction (e.g. filtering and sorting) is insufficient to guarantee a relevancy to the user of the retrieved information. Further, the small form factor of mobile devices poses strict limitations on the complexity of the interface and interaction methods available.

The TAGCLOUD system applies content personalisation and context aware techniques from web search and marketing, to the realm of cultural heritage. We incorporate the geographical, chronological, historical and narrative relationships between cultural items, and span levels ranging from entire cities to individual artefacts. For each of these levels it is important to broadly define the possible ways the experience can be tailored. Information may be presented via different modalities, including audio, text, and augmented reality; and can vary according to an individuals interests and level of understanding. The context of the user can affect how and what is delivered, and may depend on their location, familiarity with their surroundings, or who they are with. Information and media should be presented so as to complement the experience and not detract from it.

We investigate how we can retrieve information about the user both passively and actively. Information from the users device allows us to investigate their interaction with artefacts, and enables the system to form assumptions of their respective interest levels. Additional information is procured from social networking information, such as local graph traversal, and interactions related to the cultural heritage experience. We investigate how preference is extracted from the user model, how the system mitigates against destructive feedback that would show inappropriate suggestions. We propose the use of non-normative expressions of preference, to circumvent the tendency towards the populist mean, a generic weakness of ratings-based recommender systems.

C. Stephanidis and M. Antona (Eds.): UAHCI/HCII 2014, Part II, LNCS 8514, pp. 714–725, 2014.

1 Summary of TAGCLOUD

TAGCLOUD is a European Commission funded project focussed on enhancing cultural experiences. The aim of the TAGCLOUD project is to introduce more people to cultural heritage activities across Europe, while improving the quality of engagement and increasing the frequency of visits to cultural heritage sites. TAGCLOUD will facilitate life-long engagement with cultural heritage starting before a physical cultural visit and extending long after the conclusion of the visit.

TAGCLOUD will use information about the habits, preferences and motives of individuals to provide a personalised experience of cultural objects (e.g. artefacts, buildings, sites, etc). TAGCLOUD will allow users to actively participate in the evaluation of content through social media, and by harvesting this information about individual interests, the system can enhance a user's experience through effective selection of content, recommendation of exhibits, and the provision of a digital space for self-expression and discussion.

We foresee the TAGCLOUD recommendation engine as being equivalent to a bag of algorithms in constant competition with each other. In effect there will be a recommender system deciding which algorithms to use in making recommenders. This is the approach that is used by, for example, Netflix. Adding a new algorithm costs little or nothing, and it gets trained on historical data, and if it scores well enough it replaces an active algorithm.

2 Statement of the Problem

Visitors to cultural heritage sites are currently expected to "pull" information about their surroundings, i.e. they are expected to manually find information about an exhibit or artefact that interests them, be it through using an audio guide, selecting the exhibit number then waiting for further instructions or manually browsing through information. We propose to move to a "push" modality through the use of active and passive tracking of the user to create a high performance recommender engine. The system will present information to the user based on what they were looking at, what they were interested in and their interactions both in the physical and digital spaces. As an example, instead of typing a number into an audio guide, as a visitor approached an artefact the system will display personalised information about the artefact, the system would know that the visitor is a child and will present the user with a game or quiz related to the item.

The cultural heritage information space is incredibly large. To get some sense of the scale of data that we will be dealing with, let us consider a current open platform for cultural data that will be utilised by TAGCLOUD: Europeana, a cultural heritage internet portal bringing data from over 1,000 institutions in Europe. Europeana launched with over 4.5 million digital artefacts and now has over 30 million digital objects in its catalogue[1]. Compare this to the often cited

[1] `http://www.europeana.eu/portal/search.html`

Netflix recommender system which has a catalogue of less that 50,000 digital objects. Such a large quantity of information is difficult to browse without overloading the user with information, simple techniques like searching and filtering do not limit the data sufficiently and are a detriment to the user experience.

A recommender system such as that of Netflix or Amazon only has to make one suggestion: which films or which products to show the user. TAGCLOUD on the other hand must suggest the artefacts to visit, the information to show about the artefact, and how to present that information to the user. Multiple digital cultural artefacts, including textual information, photos, videos, social comments etc are related to an instance of a physical cultural artefact. There is a complex relationship between cultural artefacts and users based on physical, historical, social and cultural context, this provides a complicated structure to navigate and infer from.

To make suggestions to the user we must first identify a user model, to represent the preferences of the user. We must then identify the method for seeding the user model and then the inference techniques that are utilised to update the user model.

The practice and application of recommender systems are now widely studied, but we can break down the approaches into three main types[2]:

1. User Similarity - where one attempts to classify users, and select those items rated highly by similar users.
2. Content Similarity - where one attempts to classify items, and selects those items most like those the user has rated highly.
3. Knowledge based - where one stores information about the items, and then asks users for specific requirements which can be used to find matches.

Hybrid approaches combine some or all of these elements, either by providing the user with alternate lists of matches based on different methods, or by combining scores on these different methodologies to provide a single hybrid recommendation list.

There exist a large number of strategies for building recommendation engines. However, they are usually posed as solutions to the problem *given a particular data set*. Indeed, for most recommender systems in real world application, the Achilles' heel is that the dataset is not sufficiently rich so as to allow a definition of "similarity" which is robust enough to find good matches. Within TAGCLOUD we are in the unusual position of being able to build our classification data set from scratch, and we plan to use this advantage to build the kind of rich classification set that will allow an effective matching. Therefore the problem considered in this paper is how to extract the right information for categorisation and classification of users and artefacts from the users themselves. Insight can be gleaned from the study of categorisation theory in Psychology[3].

We will also define a graph based notion of similarity, and describe a class of fast graph based algorithms for calculating similarity scores by transforming the problem into a network flow problem.

3 Classification Strategies

3.1 Content Classification

Since the times of Aristotle, it has been known that categorisation is central to human perception[5]. The modern view differs somewhat, but is adequately summarised by the following quotation:

> Growing up in any society involves, in large measure, discovering what categories are relevant in the particular culture in which we find ourselves. Within a few years after birth, we have established mental 'control' over many, if not most, of the 'objects' within our experience. 'Things' are classified as the same, similar or different, and we construct mental 'boxes' in which to put objects which 'match' in some way.[6]

When a human is asked a question about their interests, the first thing that one must do is to choose an appropriate categorisation for ones answers. Within the domain of recommender systems, we should think of the machine learning aspect as one of devising proxies for an appropriate categorisation. The more that the data corresponds to an appropriate categorisation, the better the results of this machine learning process will be. If the data is already optimally categorised, then no further classification is needed. The goal is to categorise your data with this in mind.

The heart of any classification system is a notion of 'similarity'[2], such that two similar objects have a high probability of getting similar responses. From the point of view of TAGCLOUD, we are primarily considering cultural exhibits and events. The difficulty is that cultural exhibits can be popular for many different reasons. Exhibits which seem superficially similar according to some ontological categorisation can garner widely different responses based on as little as the quality and quantity of information displayed, or merely the aesthetics of the exhibit. Conversely, two paintings of different subjects in different styles from different periods may nevertheless evoke similar emotional responses.

Thus, while there exists a lot of latent data about cultural exhibits and artefacts, it mostly represents classifications that were created to aid academic study, and are of limited use in predicting user perceptions. For example, is it likely that our target TAGCLOUD user really knows the difference between a Yuan Dynasty Vase and a Ming Dynasty Vase? Or is it the case that the user thinks that all Chinese ceramics are conceptually similar, and that these distinctions are irrelevant? In the real world we would find that there are some users who like both because they like Chinese culture generally, and others whose opinions differ because they are basing their opinions purely on the aesthetics of the vases, and still others because one of the exhibits was better laid out and more informative. These distinctions rapidly become too much for the current generation of learning algorithms, partly because the signals are too noisy, and partly because the more parameters you have the more computationally expensive it becomes - the curse of dimensionality[4].

[2] Sometimes referred to as a kernel is Machine Learning.

The intuitive solution to this type of categorisation problem *is to ask humans to categorise*. If we can get a large group of humans to categorise the exhibits in a museum we can expect that the categorisation is intuitive, stable, widely shared, and appropriate[3]. This approach has been studied under the name 'folksonomy'[8] and was found to be a significant improvement over content only machine learning approaches[7].

Recently, an approach to improving Netflix recommendations using a tag cloud was attempted in [9], and found to be a useful technique. To summarise: IMDB maintains a tag cloud of user annotations that are user created. There are no controls on what tags could be completed, they are simply user entered strings. These can be used to create a weighted tag cloud, and a notion of similarity based on TF-IDF techniques was used to create similarity scores. The resulting recommendations were a significant improvement over basic techniques, predicting the correct rating in around 44% of cases, and with a similar RMSE to the best contenders for the Netflix Prize. In conclusion, a user generated tag cloud is comparable to the very best neighbour based machine learning algorithms for the case where the average user only views a small fraction of the content.

3.2 User Classification

User classification is a much more difficult problem than that of content classification. This is because although there are many users, each user will typically visit only a few cultural sites, and hence will have a relatively limited set of data for classification. Nevertheless, if we can infer ratings for exhibits with known tag clouds, then we can infer from these a tag cloud for the user. This can be used either as part of a hybrid recommendation system that compares both users and exhibits to say what a user would like, or to provide similarity between different users as part of a categorisation of users to use with nearest neighbour techniques.

4 Information Gathering

We divide up our information gathering into two different sections, active, and passive. An active strategy is one that directly solicits specific feedback from a user,e.g. a rating mechanism, or a survey. A passive strategy is one in which the user interacts normally with the artefact, but by monitoring these interactions one can infer some relevant information, such as the level of interest in an artefact. These distinctions can become somewhat blurred, in the sense that decisions about the information that might be included in a TAGCLOUD public user profile are reflected in the design of the web interfaces, which encourages people to enter certain information. E.g. Having an 'interests' box on one's Facebook page encourages one to enter some interests, which can be useful information for user profiling.

4.1 Initialisation

Initialisation of the User Model. There are three basic ways to seed an initial profile: Stereotyping is where a default model is created based on a handful of pieces of information such as gender, age and location; Actively asking users to state a preference as in a knowledge based recommender system; Or by harvesting information passively from a social network. Note that this discussion occasionally assumes that the system is already up and running with at least some active users, the problems of a cold start (when all users are new) is separately considered later in this section.

In keeping with the general philosophy of the TAGCLOUD recommender as a bag of algorithms, we will not simply choose one technique, but will use all three as inputs to different algorithms and compare the results. For example, if a user has friends who are on TAGCLOUD we might create a new tag cloud by averaging over the interests of their friends. As the user interacts with the TAGCLOUD ecosystem we will rapidly learn whether this technique gives better or worse recommendations than stereotyping, or directly asking the user.

Using the location data provided by their mobile device, alongside the context of their portal, we can discover if the user is building a profile while in an exhibit or at home. Consequently we can infer that it is appropriate to ask more questions in the desktop setting, which will not inhibit the users prime focus on the cultural exhibit at hand. This type of context awareness will be a feature of TAGCLOUD. Suppose that the user is building their profile through the desktop portal, in order to reduce the cognitive load to the user in determining their initial preference we propose to split the choices into a number of categories. It has been shown that well defined categories improve the choice of the user[11] and will thus improve the seed data of the system.

Rather than rating a number of terms, which would be a long and tedious exercise, we will solicit information from the user via PRanking [14]. That is, we will ask the user to select in order their preferred topics in the cultural heritage domain. As an initial user profile is augmented by passively gathered data, the recommender engine will naturally switch from using the seed profile to using a the dynamically generated profile.

Initialisation of the Content Model. If a new artefact is added to an existing exhibit, the initialisation procedure is not likely to be crucial, as the exhibit's foot traffic will likely result in a fairly robust flow of user interactions. On the other hand, when an entire new site is initialised simultaneously into TAGCLOUD there is a danger of a self fulfilling cycle where a lack of information prevents the site being recommended which prevents it getting the information needed for a robust rating. This means that we must carefully consider how to treat the opening of a new site. We propose that if there is a large quantity of a material available about the artefacts (almost always the case) then we can create a tool which scans the material to create a tag cloud. While this is likely, for the reasons discussed above, to be far inferior to a user generated tag cloud, it may be sufficient to get a site started. Note that we can provide a crude correction to the quality of matches to ameliorate the fact that these automatically generated tag clouds are likely to be systematically under-ranked. We could also 'promote' new exhibits for a period of time, so as to attract sufficient traffic for ranking.

4.2 Active Information Gathering

Active information gathering has the advantage that one can quickly build a dataset of exactly the information that you require, but it also has the disadvantage that it can impinge on the user experience if it is excessive. Worse, an overly long survey may have low rates of participation. Since the overall objective of TAGCLOUD is to enhance the cultural experience, it is counterproductive to constantly ask users to fill out tedious surveys.

Ideally we would like the users to build up the tag clouds through their normal interaction with the TAGCLOUD ecosystem similar to the way that users do on the IMDB database. However, particularly early on when the system is just starting up, or when new artefacts are exhibits, active information gathering is a vital part of quickly creating a usable tag cloud.

Therefore we propose that through the mobile TAGCLOUD interface, which is providing information to the user, we occasionally ask users to provide a maximum of three tags for a user from a suggested list of around ten tags. These ten tags will be intelligently drawn from a larger list of tags which has tags that fall into one of the following three classifications:

1. Artefact Type: Is it a painting, a panorama, a video, is it interactive, etc.
2. Period/Culture: Is it Renaissance European, or Roman? Is it Celtic, or ancient Egyptian?
3. Content Descriptors: This is a collection of semantic descriptors, is it uplifting? awe-inspiring? Violent? Militaristic? Experimentation will be needed to determine the right descriptors for a particular attraction.

This is a slight refinement of the folksonomy idea, which in effect creates a (very) lightweight ontology of tags. The question structure of choosing three words from a suggested list of ten takes into account the fact that too much choice demotivates participants[1].

However, these ten will be chosen from a long list of semantic descriptors, and some thought must go into picking word which give the most information. In this it is useful to consider Feynman's restaurant problem. This problem is usually posed in the following way:

> Given N (dishes on the menu) and $M \leq N$ (meals to be eaten at the restaurant), how many new dishes D should you try before switching to ordering the best of them for all the remaining (MD) meals, in order to maximise the average total ratings of the dishes consumed?[3]
>
> Soln:

$$D = \sqrt{2(M+1)} - 1 \tag{1}$$

[3] Further details, including a full solution can be found at: `http://www.feynmanlectures.info/exercises/Feynmans_restaurant_problem.html`

The relevance of this problem is clear - for a given menu of semantic descriptors, the number that we should introduce in order to find an optimal categorisation from a given number of visits depends only on the number of visits, not on the size of the semantic database. For attractions that have little foot traffic therefore, we need a smaller and more general set of descriptors. This can be optimised through the use of an ontology, where there are more specific terms which are used as sub-categories of more general terms. For those visits with lots of traffic we can use the more specific terms, for those with less traffic we can make do with the less specific categorisations.

Another advantage of this approach is that in the standard tag cloud approach there are often more than one tag with functionally equivalent meanings. This can mean that tag clouds appear more different than they really are because in one location they prefer 'cool' to 'awesome' as a semantic descriptor. Of course, the advantages of the free form tagging can be combined with an ontology if in the TAGCLOUD ecosystem freeform tags are allowed, and an expert monitor places these new tags into an ontology which links them conceptually. The similarity measure is made from the semantic concepts, rather than the descriptors actually used. This hybrid measure should offer some protection from issues of noise due to regional spelling differences and choices of diction.

Over time we hope that these flexible questions will represent a stable and useful categorisation. This is based primarily on the assumption that humans will be able to categorise attractions in terms of a few principal features, and that these impressions of the most important features will be widely shared, and that these categorisations will usefully reflect an appropriate notion of similarity.

4.3 Passive Information Gathering

TAGCLOUD will have a number of features which allow the passive gathering of data about user interactions. These can be split to those in the physical space, information relating to the user's location and motion, and the digital space, how the user is interacting with the digital artefacts. As a mobile application, TAGCLOUD is in a position to be able to use passive information gathering based on users location and position. In the cultural domain, one of the first systems to utilise the idea of gathering location information was HyperAudio [12] [13], which used a user's location to adapt the information presented to them. Advancements in technology such as the introduction of BLE (Bluetooth Low Energy) beacons for precise positioning, allows much more detailed information to be gathered. As such, TAGCLOUD will employ a physical 'checking-in' method to display information about an artefact, and minimise the need for user interactions with the mobile device. In order for the system to be available to many different users working on different devices, a number of methods will be utilised, these will include QR-codes, NFC and iBeacons. Apples iBeacons will provide the richest data on the user for use in recommendations. Based on the BLE standard, iBeacons adds a layer for allowing micro-location and the ability to trigger functions in iPhone or android applications. The hardware beacons give the distance from them that the user is situated, thus allowing us to determine if a user is engaging in the physical domain with an artefact, we can collect information about the amount of time they physically interacted with an artefact and draw comparisons with the amount of time they interacted with the associated digital artefacts.

While we expect that the direct interaction of a user and their closest beacon will provide the most pertinent data on a user's activity, we will also use trilateration across multiple beacons to determine the users exact location in the cultural site. Some further data that can be extracted via trilateration is whether the user is moving around an artefact, whether the user has line of sight with the exhibit, the speed at which the user is navigating around the site and the general path the visitor took through the exhibit. By monitoring the time spent at various artefacts, as well as the preferred types of content, we can build up an accurate picture of what a user likes and dislikes. By combining the actively gathered data on user preferences with the passively gathered data about time spent at particular attractions, we will infer rankings for many artefacts without having to resort to further active strategies, which impinge on the user experience.

Within the TAGCLOUD ecosystem, there is also a host of further information that can be gleaned from a users interaction with TAGCLOUD systems. Did they post a comment? Did they recommend this exhibit to their friends? As the TAGCLOUD ecosystem takes shape the type of data that can be harvested will be better known. The level of interaction with the system is a good indicator of the importance that should be attributed to a users interest in an artefact. While a user doing a query or search for a topic can give us an idea of their interest in that topic, the user making a comment on an artefact or exploring many digital cultural artefacts related to an artefact give a much stronger indicator of the users interest in that object.

4.4 The Cold Start

In every machine learning and classification problem, the initial categorisation provides a profound problem. There are various possibilities:

1. Stereotyping - Every artefact starts with one of a handful of generic profiles.
2. Survey - Get some population to fill out a detailed survey about the artefacts, for example, we could get museum employees to answer questions on their surveys.
3. Exploit some existing database, using some technique like TD-IDF to create a tag cloud out of existing information.
4. Employ at least some content based algorithms which are capable of functioning on already existing information, and replace them with the folksonomy based algorithms only as the continuous evaluation shows them to be outperforming the content based algorithms.

Given the fact that there is a virtually limitless amount of information existing about cultural artefacts, we suggest that the last two of these approaches are likely best. In keeping with the idea of TAGCLOUD as a bag of algorithms in competition, we can simultaneously use both of the last two and have the content recommendation system choose at run time which technique is making better recommendations.

5 Notions of Similarity

Intuitively, we can think of the weighted tag-cloud as creating a radar plot which describes the 'shape' of the attraction. Let us consider the notion of 'similarity' for these two tag clouds. Suppose that we have generated two appropriately normalised radar plots, such that

$$\sum_{i} \mathrm{S}_{\mathrm{i}}^{\mathrm{P}} = 1, \tag{2}$$

where S is the relative popularity of each descriptor. We can transform this into a network flow problem like in Figure 1, where we can see that the total 'flow' across the diagram in this simple case is

$$\sum_{i} \min(\mathrm{S}_{\mathrm{i}}^{\mathrm{PATTERN1}}, \mathrm{S}_{\mathrm{i}}^{\mathrm{PATTERN2}}) \leq 1 \tag{3}$$

from which it follows that two identical patterns have a flow (similarity) of 1. The advantage of defining similarity in terms of a network flow problem, is that they are extremely fast, typically being close to linear in the number of edges, and are thus scalable. Ideally we want to provide a web service which is capable of comparing a user's preferences with all of the thousand or so artefacts that might be found in a typical large museum.

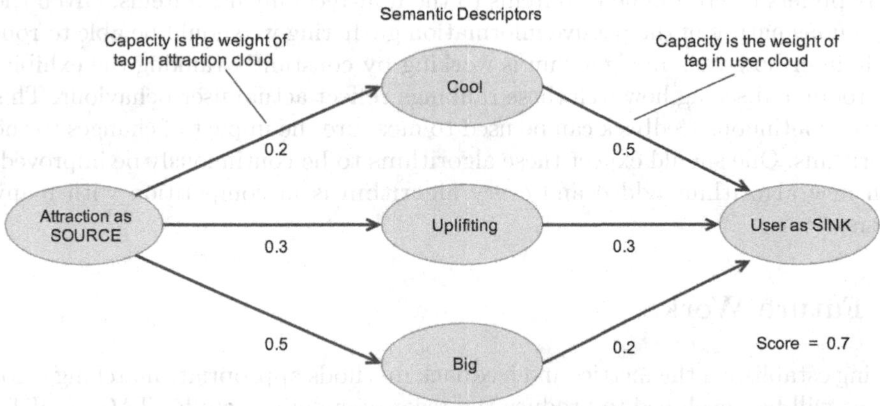

Fig. 1. This shows the similarity measure portrayed as a network flow problem. The similarity is the maximum flow from the attraction to the user, constrained by the capacity of the pipes which flow through the semantic descriptors.

The question of whether this type of comparison works better than a typical 'bag of words' comparison kernel like the weighted TF-IDF used in [7] is an open one. However, it does have several other advantages. Firstly, this type of graph based structure lends itself to building more complex structures with little reduction in speed. Suppose that a user routinely rates highly small renaissance galleries, and large museums of medieval weaponry. To the simple notion of similarity described above, it would appear that a user might like a large renaissance gallery, or small museum of medieval weaponry. However, graphs are easily extended into more complex structures. Suppose that we decide to treat the three concepts of 'attraction type', 'physical descriptors' and 'content descriptors' differently, we can simply redraw the graph with three levels of semantic descriptors and again compute the maximum flow. A good learning algorithm should be able to learn these categorisations, and how to draw a multi-levelled graph which is more effective than a single layered graph at capturing these contextual distinctions. Since the number of nodes is constant, and the number of edges has only increased from E to $(E/L)^L$ where L is the number of levels, we get sub-polynomial increases in complexity for typical network flow algorithms.

6 Evaluation Methodology

An important part of any machine learning situation is that of continuous improvement. In this case, we will be applying a number of different approaches on different segments of the data, and we wish to have a concrete way to evaluate which algorithms are working best, or even if different approaches work better for different users. A novel approach of Netflix was that a recommendation engine is used to rank the recommendation engines which should be used for each user.

In the case of TAGCLOUD, an algorithm is successful if a user quantitatively prefers the recommended items to the non-recommended items. Given the continuous nature of the passive information gathering we should be able to routinely infer how well an algorithm is working by constantly ranking the exhibits in a room and seeing how well these rankings reflect actual user behaviour. This type of continuous feedback can be used to measure the impact of changes to the algorithms. One should expect these algorithms to be continuously be improved, with new algorithms added and every algorithm is in competition with many others.

7 Future Work

Having established the metrics and feedback methods appropriate matching algorithms will be developed to produce the recommender system for TAGCLOUD. We will also need to identify the relative weightings of the different active or passive feedback and matching algorithms, so as to provide a best fit to the typical data that is encountered in the cultural heritage domain.

The concepts introduced in this paper will be implemented in the TAG-CLOUD system, which will be trialled in a number of cultural heritage sites including: the Barber Institute in the UK, Alhambra in Spain and in the city of Trondheim in Norway. These will provide a diverse test-bed for the system given the different types of cultural heritage sites they represent. We will use the trials to test the ideas proposed in this paper, such as comparing the accuracy of folksonomies versus expert taxonomies or for determining the optimal amount of information that can be solicited from a user. This will allow us not only to produce a system that provides a personalised cultural experience, but to do so with minimal disruption to the user experience.

References

1. Iyengar, S.S., Lepper, M.R.: When choice is demotivating: Can one desire too much of a good thing? Journal of Personality and Social Psychology 79(6), 995 (2000)
2. Jannach, D., Zanker, M., Felfernig, A., Friedrich, G.: Recommender Systems - An Introduction. Cambridge University Press (2010) ISBN: 978-0-521-49336-9
3. Loken, B., Barsalou, L.W., Joiner, C.: Categorization theory and research in consumer psychology. In: Handbook of Consumer Psychology, pp. 133–165 (2008)
4. Hastie, T., Tibshirani, R., Freidman, J.: The Elements of Statistical Learning, 2nd edn. Springer (2009)
5. Aristotle (40BC): The Organon - Categories
6. Dienhart, J.M.: A linguistic look at riddles. Journal of Pragmatics 31, 95–125 (1999)
7. Lops, P., de Gemmis, M., Semeraro, G., Musto, C., Narducci, F., Bux, M.: A Semantic Content-Based Recommender System Integrating Folksonomies for Personalized Access. In: Castellano, G., Jain, L.C., Fanelli, A.M. (eds.) Web Person. in Intel. Environ. SCI, vol. 229, pp. 27–47. Springer, Heidelberg (2009)
8. `http://vanderwal.net/folksonomy.html`
9. Szomszor, M., Cattuto, C., Alani, H., O'Hara, K., Baldassarri, A., Loreto, V., Servedio, V.D.P.: Folksonomies, the Semantic Web, and Movie Recommendation. In: 4th European Semantic Web Conference, Bridging the Gap between Semantic Web and Web 2.0, Innsbruck, Austria, June 3-7 (2007)
10. Mogilner, C., Rudnick, T.: Iyengar: The Mere Categorization Effect: How the Presence of Categories Increases Choosers' Perceptions of Assortment Variety and Outcome Satisfaction. S.S. Journal of Consumer Research 35(2), 202–215 (2008)
11. Ziegler, C.N., et al.: Improving Recommendation Lists Through Topic Diversification. In: Proc. 14th International Conference on World Wide Web, pp. 22–32 (2005)
12. Giaccardi, E.: Heritage and Social Media: Understanding heritage in a participatory culture. Routledge (2012) ISBN: 978-0415616676
13. Petrelli, D., Not, E.: User-Centred Design of Flexible Hypermedia for a Mobile Guide: Reflections on the HyperAudio Experience. User Modelling and User-Adapted Interaction 15(3-4), 303–338 (2005)
14. Crammer, K., Singer, Y.: Pranking with Ranking. In: Advances in Neural Information Processing Systems, vol. 14, pp. 641–647 (2001)

The concepts introduced in this paper will be implemented in the TAG-CLOUD system, which will be trialled in a number of cultural heritage sites including the [illegible] in the Alhambra in Spain and in the city of Trondheim in Norway. These will provide a diverse test bed for the system [illegible] of cultural heritage [illegible] we will use the [illegible] to test the [illegible] proposed [illegible] such as computing the [illegible] or [illegible] taxonomies [illegible] for interpreting [illegible] information [illegible]. This will allow [illegible] the system that provides a personalised cultural experience, but [illegible] information [illegible].

References

1. [illegible]
2. [illegible]
3. [illegible] (2008)
4. [illegible] Springer (2000)
5. [illegible]
6. [illegible] (2004)
7. [illegible]
8. [illegible]
9. [illegible]
10. [illegible] How the Best [illegible] Argument [illegible] Journal of Consumer Research [illegible]
11. [illegible] World Wide Web [illegible]
12. [illegible]
13. [illegible] Mobile [illegible]
14. [illegible] Natural Language Processing [illegible] vol. 14, pp. [illegible]

Author Index